I0798522

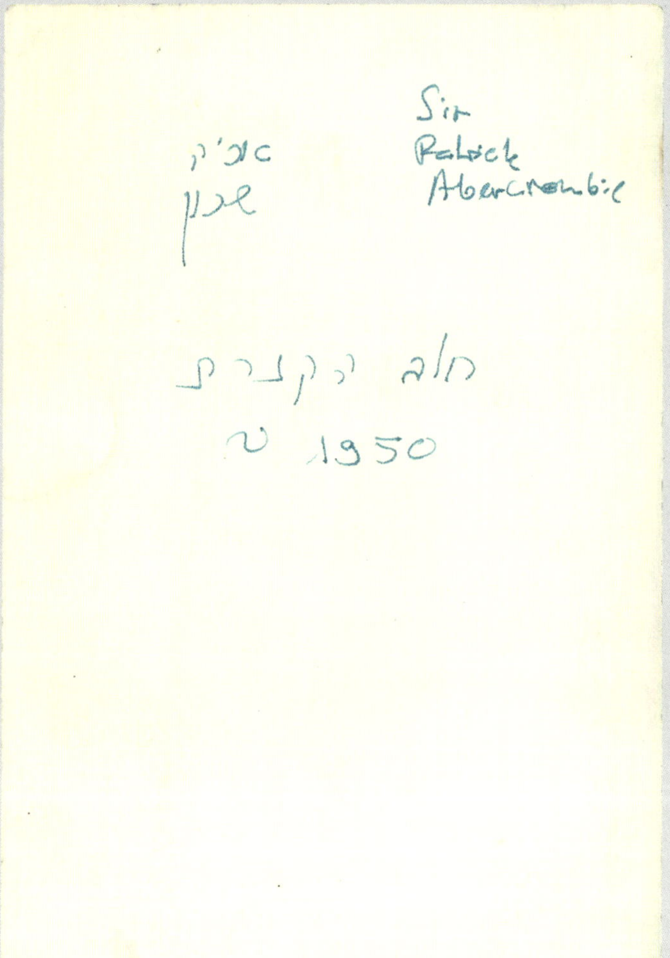


(Previous page) Patrick Abercrombie (left) and Arieh Sharon, Sea of Galilee, 1950. Yael Aloni Photo Collection. Courtesy of the Azrieli Architectural Archive, Arieh Sharon Collection.

To Meira Kowalsky, my companion all along

# The Object of Zionism
# The Architecture of Israel

## Acknowledgements

This book would never have materialized without the support and inspiration of Beatriz Colomina and Eyal Weizman. It owes just as much to Georges Teyssot, who first encouraged me to study the architecture of Statehood in Israel, and to Kenneth Frampton, who carefully read my dissertation.

I am thankful to all the extraordinary people who labored and speculated with me on Zionist space-planning and object-making during a twenty-year lead-up of archival research, exhibitions, publications, academic courses, and public debates. First to be acknowledged among them are the young architects and scholars who have direct gains and losses in *The Object of Zionism*: Gili Merin, the most prolific research coordinator and assistant editor one could hope for; Michael Cidor, Keren Kinberg, and Alon Sarig, who proved remarkably resourceful in harvesting valuable archival material; Sharbel Halloun, Nagham Copty, and Fouad Habash, who at last deciphered the enigma of Ein Rafa; and Avinoam Sharon, who shared with me not only vital documents from Arieh Sharon's private domain, but also his own reflections on the social and professional milieux of Israel's foremost master planner.

The superb production team has earned my admiration and deepest gratitude: Jan Wenzel of Spector Books, who had no hesitation about the book and chose for it the finest editors and designers; Rebekka Kiesewetter, who coordinated the entire production process with authority and ease; Rita Forbes, who insightfully transformed the manuscript into a published work; Michael Pilewski and Elias F. Quijada Link, who assisted with the final proofreading; Jan Caspers, who translated Julius Posener's article from the German; Tamar Cohen, who not only translated from the Hebrew but also edited early versions of several essays; and Michal Sapir, who translated David Avidan's vision of vertical territoriality from the Hebrew.

Matthias Görlich, with whom I hope to collaborate again, is not only the book's designer, but also its ingenious structural engineer. Together with Anna Kraus, Pawel Wolowitsch and Charalampos Lazos, his skillful associates, he managed to condense a work initially conceptualized as three separate volumes into a single compound with visible splinters and shifting moods.

A memorable group of scholars, curators, artists, and architects shared with me the making of *The Israeli Project*, a lexical display presented at the Tel Aviv Museum of Art in 2000 and a reader in Hebrew that followed in 2004. These include Daniel Bauer, Eran Ben-Dov, Zvi Elhyani, Michael Gordon, Nadav Harel, Meira Kowalsky, Roy Kozlovsky, Nathan Marom, Moshe Ninio, Mordechai Omer, Daphna Raz, and Meira Yagid-Haimovici. More agitators joined the team of *Borderline Disorder*—a masquerade show covering the Israeli pavilion at the 2002 International Architecture Biennale in Venice—including Keren Avni, Yotam Bezalel, Yehoshua Gutman, Yossi Mar-Haim, Avi Mograbi, Shira Szabo, and Eyal Weizman. My collaborators on *The Object of Zionism* exhibition, a pseudo-didactic display that opened in 2011 at the Swiss Architecture Museum in Basel, were Hubertus Adam, Manuel Herz, Elena Markus, and Joshua Simon. Moshe Flor and Daphna Levin worked on the project as research assistants. *Communal by Commune*, an installation of amateur architecture at the 2015 *Wohnungsfrage* exhibition at Haus der Kulturen der Welt, Berlin, was realized with Galia Bar Or and included contributions by Gili Merin and Neil Cohen.

I am profoundly indebted not only to these partners and stakeholders, but also to my persistent interlocutors, who readily provided their critical perspective: Senan Abdelqader,

Shlomo (Solly) Angel, Ariella Azoulay, Sigal Bar-Nir, Tamar Berger, Regina Bittner, Etan Bloom, Matthijs Bouw, Yonatan Cohen, Joseph Dadoune, Stav Efrat, Oren Eldar, Natanel Elfassy, Erez Ella, Liat Etgar-Brix, Yona Fischer, Mario Gandelsonas, Iddo Ginat, Amos Gitai, Sharon Golan-Yaron, Shmuel Groag, Dor Guez, Drorit Gur Arie, Dan Handel, Dan Hasson, Tim Heide, Sarah Hinsky, Ariel Hirschfeld, Elad Horn, Uriel Kon, Miki Kratzman, Anke Kühnel, Asaf Lerman, Nurit Lissovsky, Haim Lusky, Philipp Misselwitz, Hanna Nave, Gilad Ophir, Philipp Oswalt, Guy Raz, Oren Sagiv, Eran Schaerf, Ori Scialom, Malkit Shoshan, Ines Sonder, Ran Tal, Oren Tatcher, Joachim Trezib, Yaron Turel, Wouter Vanstiphout, Els Verbakel, Verena von Beckerath, Marion von Osten, Ines Weizman, Pavel Wolberg, and Esther Zandberg.

I have also benefited from the work of many more colleagues who have left their mark on the architectural discourse in Israel and offered an intellectual context that has been central in developing the ideas of this book. Most pertinent to my work are Or Aleksandrowicz, Meron Benvenisti, Daniel Boyarin, Erik Cohen, Sigal Davidi, Diana Dolev, Zvi Elhyani, Ita Heinze-Greenberg, Gilbert Herbert, Jeremy Hoffman, Freddy Kahana, Rachel Kallus, Adriana Kemp, Yossi Klein, Roy Kozlovsky, Michael Levin, Hubert Lu-Yon, Talia Margalit, Nathan Marom, Nitza Metzger-Szmuk, Daniel B. Monk, Daniel Monterescu, Eran Neuman, Alona Nitzan-Shiftan, Robert Oxman, Dan Rabinowitz, Sharon Rotbard, Rafi Segal, Rona Sela, Hadas Shadar, Smadar Sharon, S. Ilan Troen, Haim Yacobi, and Oren Yiftachel.

My research and writing were supported by generous grants and fellowships from the Graham Foundation, Princeton University's Barr Ferree Publication Fund, the Bauhaus Foundation Research Fellowship, the Israeli Foundation for the Advancement of Man, the Rabinowitz Foundation's Endowment for the Arts and Humanities, the Bezalel Academy's Advanced Study Fund. My special thanks to the donation of Rüdiger Lugert, Keimfarben GmbH.

The following archives and libraries in Israel provided special assistance: Azrieli Architecture Archive; Bezalel Academy Library; B'Tselem Archive; Central Zionist Archives; Hebrew University Central Archive; Information Centre for Israeli Art, Israel Museum; Israel State Archives; Lavon Institute for Labor Movement Research; National Library of Israel; Shikun & Binui historical archive and Solel Boneh archive; Technion Architecture and Town Planning Library; Yad Tabenkin Archives.

Foreign collections and archives assisting with the research for the book include: Austrian Frederick and Lillian Kiesler Private Foundation, Vienna; Bakema and Van den Broek collection, State Archive for Dutch Architecture and Urban Planning, Rotterdam; Constantinos A. Doxiadis Archives, Benaki Museum, Athens; Judaica Collection, Harvard Library, Harvard University; Isamu Noguchi Foundation and Garden Museum, New York; Louis I. Kahn Collection, Architectural Archives, University of Pennsylvania; Matson (G. Eric and Edith) Photograph Collection, Library of Congress; New York Public Library digital collections; Philip Johnson collection, Avery Drawings & Archives, Avery Architectural and Fine Arts Library, Columbia University, New York.

I appreciate the kindness of dozens of Israeli architects of the so-called "1948 generation" and their families who shared their private collections with me over the past twenty years and allowed me to publish their work. Among them, I am especially thankful to Amnon Alexandroni, Yael and Ariel Aloni (Arieh Sharon archive), Ziva Armoni, Maya Bar (Michael Bar collection), Shmaya Ben Avraham, Mordechai Ben Horin, Varda Bennett (Robert Bennett collection), David Best, Micha Burt, Menachem Cohen, Nahum Cohen, Ze'ev Drukman, Avital Efrat (Shmuel Bickels

Archive), Zalman Einav, Aba Elhanani, Yigal Elhanani and Michal Golan (Arieh Elhanani collection), Dan Eytan, Leora Federman (Heinz Fenchel collection), Yona Friedman, Giora Gamerman, Leopold Gerstel, Tsibi Geva (Kuba Gever collection), Shlomo Gilad, Amos Gitai and Michael Gordon (Munio Gitai Weinraub collection), Israel Goodovitch, Amiram Harlap, Achsa Havkin (Daniel Havkin collection), Zvi Hecker, Shimshon Heller and Daphna Levin (Heller brothers' archive), Hanan Havron, Ada Karmi and Rivka Karmi (Ram Karmi collection), Leora and Thea Kisselov (Theodor Kisselov collection), Thomas Leitersdorf, Edna and Rafi Lerman, Rami Lotan (Israel Lotan collection), Moshe Lufenfeld, Michael Mansfeld (Al Mansfeld collection), Shmuel Mestechkin, Zvi Miller, Shulamit Nadler, Yaakov Perlstein (Yitzhak Perlstein collection), Gideon Powsner (Shimon Powsner collection), Micha Ratner (Yohanan Ratner collection), Amnon Rechter (Zeev and Yaacov Rechter collection), David Resnick, Arie Rosov (Shmuel Rosov collection), Harold Rubin, Yael Rubin (Gad Asher collection), Moshe Safdie, Morris Segal, Shimon Shapiro, Arad Sharon, Ran Shchori (Dora Gad collection), Orna Verberne (Paul Verberne collection), Lipa Yahalom, Yaacov Yaar, David Yannay, Yitzhak Yashar, Yuval Yasky (Avraham Yasky collection), Shmuel Yavin, Daniel Zarhi (Moshe Zarhi collection), Barak Zippor (Gershon Zippor and Benjamin Idelson collection), Tova and Gideon Ziv, and Nahum Zolotov.

The look of Israeli architecture during its formative decades is produced by the exquisite work of photographers. If these photographers are not consistently credited in this book, it is because we were not always successful in tracing the creators of images found in public archives and private collections. Among the prominent architectural photographers of the period are Yakov Agor, Naftali Avnon, Benni Badarshi, Artur Berger, Alfred Bernheim, Werner Braun, Hille Burger, Boris Carmi, Fred Chesnik, Fritz Cohen, Yehuda Eisenstark, David Eldan, Efraim Erde, Ran Erde, Amiram Erev, Yaakov Farkash, Sam Frank, Kalman Givon, Erich Glas, Moshe Gross, Paul Gross, David Hadar, David Harris, Avraham Hauser, Yitzhak Kalter, Zoltan Kluger, Rolf Kneller, Avraham Malevsky, Theodor Marmorstein, Hugo Mendelsohn, Moshe Milner, the Photo Orient and Photo Pri-Or agencies, Moshe Pridan, Zeev Radovan, Beno Rothenberg, David Rubinger, Fritz Schlesinger, Ricarda Schwerin, Julius Shulman, Rudi Weissenstein, and Israel Zafrir. I also wish to thank the following contemporary photographers, whose work remains autonomous in this book: Daniel Bauer, Josef Koudelka, Miki Kratsman, Gili Merin, Gilad Ophir, and Eli Singalovski.

Earlier versions of several texts in this book were previously published elsewhere:

— A version of "The Epos of Jewish Autochthony" was published as "The Haunt of the Rural: Zionist Colonization and Space Planning" in *Collectivize! Essays on the Political Economy of Urban Form*, ed. Marc Angélil and Rainer Hehl (Berlin: Ruby Press, 2013).
— Early versions of "The Master Plan" were published as "The Plan" in *A Civilian Occupation: The Politics of Israeli Architecture*, ed. Rafi Segal and Eyal Weizman (Tel Aviv and London: Babel and Verso, 2003); "Mold" in *Constructing a Sense of Place: Architecture and the Zionist Discourse*, ed. Haim Yacobi (Burlington: Ashgate, 2004); and "The Jewish State" in *Homeless Home*, ed. Ariella Azoulay (Jerusalem: Museum on the Seam, 2010).
— A short version of "The Missing Letter" was published in *Bauhaus – The Bauhaus Dessau Foundation's Magazine* 2 (November 2011).
— A version of "The Garden Cities of Yesterday" was published as "City-State" in *The Israeli City*, ed. Michael Levin and Oded Heilbronner [in Hebrew] (Tel Aviv: Resling, 2007).
— A version of "The Iconic Architecture of the Israel Museum and the Shrine of the Book" was published as "L'Architecture Emblematique de la 'National Museum Hill'" in *Pré/Occupations d'Espace: Jérusalem au Pluriel*, ed. Corinne Diserens (Marseille: Carta blanca, 2000).
— A version of "Proxy Colonialism: The Export of the Israeli Project to Africa" was published in *African Modernism*, ed. Manuel Herz (Zurich: Park Books, 2015).

[Every reasonable attempt has been made to identify owners of copyright. Omissions and errors brought to the author's attention will be corrected in subsequent reprints.]

Finally, this book is a tribute to my parents, Shulamit and Ilan, first generation of native Israelis, and a gift to my daughters, Tamara and Nour, first generation of native cosmopolites.

Zvi Efrat
Tel Aviv, August 2017

# Introduction

> There is no document of civilization which is
> not at the same time a document of barbarism.
> *Walter Benjamin*[1]

In 1950, just two years after the declaration ceremony of the State of Israel, the Tel Aviv Museum once again found itself hosting the national mouthpiece.[2] Within the confines of its domestic layout and salon curatorship, the museum held an extensive planning exhibition—the first and last of its kind—made up of photomontaged posters and data panels projecting the Israel of the immediate future, as engineered on the drafting tables of the Planning Department professionals, headed by architect Arieh Sharon.

Regardless of the exhibition's seductive demagogy ("Planning is a Requisite for an Organic Society") and its pastoral aptitude (in accord with the government's "From the City to the Village" campaign), the visitors to the exhibition—"sooner or later everyone came to see [it]," recalled Arieh Sharon in his autobiography, "civil servants, the 'intelligentsia,' technicians, workers, soldiers, and, of course, the politicians from the different parties"[3]—were not at all stirred by it to actively migrate, settle the countryside, and animate the national project.

This utter failure to mobilize the veteran urban population in no way diminishes the incredible ambition of the exhibition: to sear the newly fabricated State onto the consciousness of its citizens, allegorically as a primal leap (*Ursprung*), perceptually as a colossal project, aesthetically as an integral design (*Gestaltung*), and instrumentally as a territorial machine clearing space, regulating geographic and demographic equilibrium, and molding a national common ground.

Graphic and textual traces of the 1950 National Planning Exhibition, found in 1994 in the attic of Sharon's office, triggered my own chronic research into the architectural making of Israel, informed my initial counterintuitive hypotheses regarding over-planning and compulsive design during the formative decades of Israel, and eventually resurfaced in a "follow-up" exhibition that opened in 2000 at the relocated Tel Aviv Museum of Art under an emphatic title: *The Israeli Project: Building and Architecture, 1948–1973.*

①

① Tel Aviv Museum, 1930s. David B. Keidan Collection, Central Zionist Archives.
② National Planning Exhibition, Tel Aviv Museum, 1950. Matityahu Shilon Collection, Israel Architecture Archive.

②

Rather than imposing a solid account, *The Israeli Project* exhibition, and the book which was published later in Hebrew with the same title, presented an extensive primary archive of Israeli architecture, juxtaposed with a secondary lexicon of thematic constructs, symptomatic performances, critical readings, and all-too-often uncritical iconographies. As such, it was destined to oscillate between an intentionalist historiography (deciphering the workings of a single predetermined master plan) and its functionalist shattering into parallel studies, divergent methodologies, makeshift collections, and conflicting narratives. The designed porosity and open-endedness of *The Israeli Project* invited the return of the architecturally repressed to the local cultural sphere and nurtured a surge of research, academic courses, exhibitions, and publications on the topic.

The present volume, *The Object of Zionism: The Architecture of Israel*, pushes the intentionalist theorem to its rhetorical limits and embeds the Israeli architecture of Statehood within the larger historical, ideological, and strategic process of Zionizing Palestine. It argues, somewhat tautologically, that Zionism is primarily an operative mode of space-planning, place-making, terrain-marking, land-grabbing, landscaping, facts-grounding, settlement-setting, rural-prototyping and urban-reforming. Indeed, it interprets Zionism, in its proper context of late nineteenth- and early twentieth-century national projects and settler-colonialisms, as a peculiarly deviceful architectural movement.

Regarding the formative decades of Israeli Statehood (1950s and 1960s), *The Object of Zionism* reiterates the general premise of *The Israeli Project* that practically all works of architecture produced in that period—from the public housing blocks in the peripheral new towns to the mannerist workers' retreats of the Labor Federation; from the monumental communal structures in the rural settlements to the austere culture-palaces in the big cities; from institutional Brutalist monoliths to experimental Structuralist polygons—are manifestations of a single political hegemony, efficient enough, for a time, to dictate a social-realist regime of taste, envision a fully designed model state, and administer an elaborate building project. This project entailed—as groundwork—the destruction of hundreds of Palestinian villages and neighborhoods, the mass expulsion and expatriation of native communities, the installation of comprehensive infrastructural systems, the refashioning of the countryside, and, ultimately, the erection of about thirty new towns and over four hundred new rural settlements.

Yet again, the book's title and dominant thrust are constantly defeated by the articles, documents, and visual records occupying its chapters. The major narrative disintegrates into minor plotlines, patchy storyboards, historical lacunae, dissimilar formats, parallel locations, multiple protagonists, conflicting testimonies, adversarial architectures, and suspended ethical predicaments. Moreover, most chapters contain autonomous subchapters—monographic files about singular projects, built or not, or about a distinct body of architectural work—which may function as either the climax or the counterpoint of the chapter.

The sequence of chapters offers a certain chronological itinerary, from early twentieth-century Jewish colonization to early twenty-first-century Israeli occupation, while at the same time presenting enough digressions, crosscuts, blockages, and dead ends to discourage a linear reading. The opening chapters of "Object" (ground) and "Project" (figure) set up a bipolar condition that recurs in different modes throughout the book. "Theory" (referring to Walter Christaller's central-place theory) advances an argument, admittedly controversial among scholars, about the odious origin of Israel's master plan. "Jewish Style", under cover of a fake letter from Arieh Sharon to Hannes Meyer, probes into the overly stigmatized correlation between Zionism and architectural modernism. "Fair Levant" exacerbates skepticism by positing the white wall as a trope of simultaneous erasure and *Bildung*. "Camps" documents the concurrent exodus and influx of refugees during and after the War of 1948 and the *Nakba*, as well as the attempt by Louis Kahn to work out the design of emergency shelters in Israel as a viable strategy of housing prefabrication. The two "Ruins" chapters unfold the State-administered confiscation and the bohemian fetishization of war-ravaged estates and archaeological vestiges during the "*Sturm und Drang* period" (as Arieh Sharon referred to the years 1948 to 1953) and beyond. Soon after the 1967 takeover of the Old City of Jerusalem, historicized Orientalism overwhelmed the Israeli sense of place and triggered a premature, yet highly resilient, local dialect of postmodernist architecture. "Appropriation" follows the successive visits to Jerusalem of an international committee of illustrious figures (including Buckminster Fuller, Nikolaus Pevsner, Lewis Mumford, and Christopher Alexander) who were expected to ratify Israel's custody of the holy sites. Louis Kahn was invited to Israel once again, now to transform a ruined synagogue ("The Ruin") into a (prefab?) monument.

"Forests" and "Desert" are scenic constructs depicting a forsaken terrain Zionized. "Rural" and "Communal" detail the idiosyncrasies of an engineered grassrootedness. "Pasolini's Travelogue," tracing Pier Paolo Pasolini's 1965 *Sopralluoghi in Palestina*, is a melancholic commentary on a land condemned to undercut its own epic representations.

The dual, yet often rival, designations of "State Architecture" and "Union Architecture" comprise the institutional core of the Israel project. "New Towns" accounts for the master-planned garden cities of the 1950s and 1960s, dedicating a separate subchapter to the ephemeral 1970s city of Yamit. "Public Housing" and "Serial Blocks" amass generic building types toward a graphic taxonomy of standardized housing. "Hyper-Urbanism", in contrast, highlights the *folie de grandeur* of 1965 by reviewing the international urban competitions conducted in Israel that year, focusing in particular on the awesome megastructures proposed by Bakema and Van den Broek for Ashdod, Jerusalem, and Tel Aviv.

"The National Museum and the Shrine of the Book" studies at some length a compound of three exquisite architectural icons that left their imprints on the Israeli surface: the museum itself, designed by Al Mansfeld and Dora Gad;

the sculpture garden, designed by Isamu Noguchi; and the Shrine of the Book, designed by Frederick Kiesler and Armand Bartos. The following episode of "Ein Rafa," a new village for Palestinian refugees commissioned by the State and designed by the avant-garde group of Neuman-Hecker-Sharon, is the only case of (partial) architectural reparations during Israel's formative decades; as such, it remains enigmatic.



The rather crude classifications of "Brutalism" and "Structuralism" encompass Israel's swift naturalization of postwar trends, prolific production of buildings of heightened tangibility, and conspicuous predilection for morphological complexity. A monolith temple encasing a nuclear reactor, designed by Philip Johnson in 1956, is annexed here to the local canon of original imitations. The order of simulacra is further complicated in "Tropics," which goes out of the country to track the flow of exported Israeli architecture and urban planning, driven by entrepreneurship and regulated by diplomacy, to developing countries (mainly in Africa and Asia). "Speculation" depicts the early projects of commercial bigness produced in Israel under the aegis of the welfare state in the mid-1960s, when international architects were invited to raise local expectations upward and release gainful air rights. Oscar Niemeyer, in exile from Brazil, spent half a year in Israel and designed numerous large-scale projects, including a vertical city in the Negev Desert. The closing brief of "Occupation" resuscitates the longings of "Object" and intensifies the machinations of "Project."

Below the book's variegated surface are buried two reciprocal principles, or histrionic conditions, simultaneously catalyzing and paralyzing the Zionist course of action: urgency and peripherality.

Urgency, or the Tower and Stockade syndrome, is more than a canny tactic to prevail over imminent danger; it is the constant flare-up of a pioneering ethos, the ritual exorcism of horror vacui (see David Ben-Gurion's statement in the chapter "Desert": "If you look at the map you will see that the South contains many empty places, and nothing causes me so great a horror as this emptiness"[4]), a broken alarm system allowing the perpetuation of emergency regulations (to this day) and the preparation of passive-aggressive contingency plans on every possible scale.

③

An agitated sense of urgency, then, is one short explanation for the astounding success of the project of Israel—its sweeping territorial takeover, unprecedented rate of growth, and remarkable efficiency in providing temporary and permanent housing for a population of Jewish refugees and immigrants that doubled and tripled over the course of just a few years after 1948. But the phantom of urgency is also the mark of Cain of Israel's formative years, a lingering trauma associated with the welfare state's blitz-architecture, which replicated itself all over the country, deliberately obliterating the cultural diversity and fragile habitus of a young émigré society. This trauma is believed to be the trigger of the 1977 political turnabout in Israel, which ended the longstanding hegemony of Labor parties and brought about the ascendancy of various Likud right-wing coalitions. The notion of urgency was further expedited under Likud regimes, but it took a curious architectural turn—away from the minimum standards and housing blocks of the workers' new towns, toward the wellness ambience and semidetached red-roofed houses of new dormitory communities disseminated within and beyond the Green Line.

Zionism's "borderline disorder," as the principle of peripherality is labeled in the last chapter of this book, is nothing less than a constitutive ideology (and founding myth) with profound implications for the structure, texture, and shifting contours of Israel. The radical core of this ideology is made up of various land and social-reform pseudo-theories, distinctly utopian, which began to imagine not just a story of Jewish emigration out of Europe and colonization in Palestine, but an actual fiction of Jewish autochthony, a vision of a modern Jewish physiocracy, a picture of an agrarian proletariat ingrained in the landscape, an exotic counter-staging to the Jewish diasporic mise-en-scène.

The principle of peripherality has different modes and scopes. Architecturally, it adopts a marginal status by rejecting canonical styles and traditional typologies, trading these for proxy "minor architecture." In relation to the "center" (which is always elsewhere), it prescribes a liminal zone, never sufficiently developed, but always developing, always susceptible to change. In this zone, there are essentially no masters or masterpieces, no rigid routines, no aesthetic theories, no native arts and crafts. It is frivolously derivative and feeds on procedures of appropriation, simulation, aberration, and hybridization. Manifestly, when the liminal zone overlapped the entire state apparatus and became a trademark of the local culture industry, it produced a surplus of "experimental" projects which, premature as they may have been, were instantly built, venerated for their youthful audacity, and circulated internationally through professional magazines. Liminality, then, was the liberating factor that boosted both Mandatory Palestine's and Israel's reputations as hyperactive laboratories of prewar and postwar architectural trends.

In relation to town planning and urban culture, the principle of peripherality assumes a totally different meaning. It signifies Zionism's pronounced resentment of the big city, a sentiment shared with and propelled by the various contemporaneous garden-city movements. Ipso facto, Zionism was itself a garden-city movement, recruiting in the 1920s such reformer-planners as Patrick Geddes and Richard Kauffmann (who became the official planner of the Zionist movement and designed the first collective and communal settlements), and from the 1930s through the 1950s Patrick Abercrombie, whose work with the British new-town movement had a formative impact on the program, structure, and shape of the Israeli new town.

Resolute to posit the city as a menace to the national back-to-the-land project, Zionist political and spiritual leaders issued apocalyptic warnings, such as the following 1935 historiographic tale by Ben-Gurion:

> Read about the internal situation of Carthage in the days of Hannibal and you will find the image of Tel Aviv: the same disconnected culture, the same rootlessness, the same dependence on an alien, antagonist, rural environment, the same ostensible independence—does the same end await us?[5]

The actual implementation of anti-urban or soft-urban doctrines is fairly consistent throughout the history of Zionism. It is manifested most noticeably in the astounding record that up to the moment of Statehood, the Zionist movement invented numerous rural typologies and carefully shaped countless settlements, probably more than any other national movement in history, but never designed a city (except for Kauffmann's unbuilt *Emek Stadt*, which was called an "urban village" in Hebrew anyway). After Statehood, the propagation of rural settlements accelerated, but this was now an official policy based on an imported and already implemented *Raumplanung* theory. The settlements were distributed according to a national master plan and organized systematically around regional centers; intimate slow towns were promoted as the antidote to the alienation, degeneration, and hardships of the big city.

On a territorial scale, the Zionist principle of peripherality was always tantamount to a boundless fluidity of military and civilian occupation, to the degree that the whole country was perceived as frontier (Heb. *sfar*), an ever-volatile space inducing apprehension and vigilance throughout both public and domestic realms. The pathology of frontier emptied the geometry of borders of its political content and portrayed so-called "practical Zionism" as an open-ended process of inner colonization whose imperatives were to ensure constant cartographic mutability, to generate an impetus of proactive patriotism, and to suspend the Israeli State as an eternally negotiable space. It could be speculated, therefore, that the dialectics of territorialization and deterritorialization in itself, rather than the biblical blessing of "the rest and the inheritance" (Deuteronomy 12:9), constitutes the Zionist apotheosis. Nothing illustrates this abysmal condition better than the "separation fence," the ever-temporary architectural wonder gradually closing on Israel to the north, east, and south, pushing the dictates of population dispersal, territorial expandability, and "enlightened occupation" to the wall of self-imposed ghettoization. ■

④

③ Chanan Frenkel building a model of Tower and Stockade settlement (model of a model) for the Jewish Palestine pavilion, New York World's Fair, 1939. Photographer: Zoltan Kluger, Israel State Archive.
④ "Cooperation Conquers Wilderness," Histadrut pavilion, *Conquest of the Wilderness Exhibition,* Binyenei Ha'Uma, 1953. Photographer: Yehuda Eisenstark. Israel State Archives.

1 Walter Benjamin, "Theses on the Philosophy of History" [1940], in *Illuminations*, ed. Hannah Arendt (New York: Knopf Doubleday Publishing Group, 1968), p. 256.

2 The declaration of the State of Israel ceremony on May 14, 1948, and the first reading of the Declaration of Independence, the founding text of the State of Israel, occurred, curiously enough, at the Tel Aviv Museum, formerly Mayor Meir Dizengoff's residence, on Rothschild Boulevard.

3 Arieh Sharon, *Kibbutz + Bauhaus: An Architect's Way in a New Land* (Stuttgart and Tel Aviv: Karl Kramer Verlag and Massada, 1976), p. 79.

4 Minutes of Israeli Government Session #12, May 3, 1949 (Israel State Archives).

5 David Ben-Gurion, "Zionist Players and Their Role at This Time," in *On Settlement: Collected Writings, 1915–1965*, ed. Menachem Dorman [in Hebrew] (Tel Aviv: Hakibbutz Hameuhad, 1986), pp. 63–64.

⑤ Wall. This Place, Tel Aviv Museum of Art, 2011. Josef Koudelka.

# Object

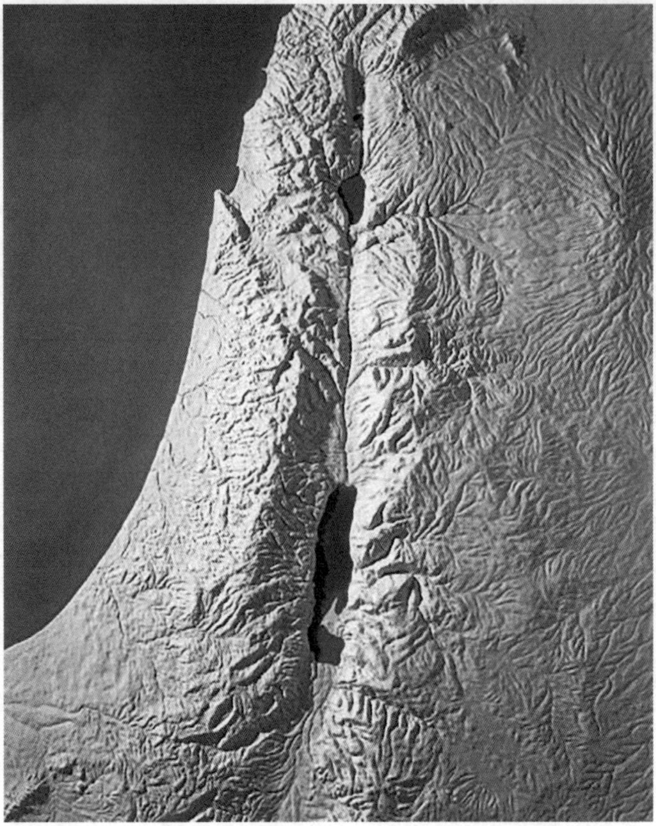

①

## The Epos of Jewish Autochthony

### 1. Utopia

The haunt of the rural and the specter of the peasant occupy the Zionist scene of origin. Their perplexing emergence is satirically enunciated in the following citation from Theodor Herzl's 1896 *The Jewish State*:

> Whoever would attempt to convert the Jew into a husbandman would be making an extraordinary mistake. For a peasant is in a historical category, as proved by his costume which in some countries he has worn for centuries; and by his tools, which are identical with those used by his earliest forefathers. [...] The agrarian question is only a question of machinery. America must conquer Europe, in the same way as large landed possessions absorb small ones. The peasant is consequently a type which is in course towards extinction. Whenever he is artificially preserved, it is done on account of the political interests which he is intended to serve. It is absurd, and indeed impossible, to make modern peasants on the old pattern. No one

is wealthy or powerful enough to make civilization take a single retrograde step. [...]

Are we, therefore, to credit Jews who are intelligent with a desire to become peasants of the old type? [...] Under these circumstances the Jews are perfectly justified in refusing to stir when people try to make peasants of them.[1]

In this foundational text, Herzl, a journalist/novelist-cum-author of political Zionism, responded to the contentious situation that had been developing since the 1880s in Palestine. Jewish leaders, planners, philanthropists, agronomists, and adherents of various back-to-the-land movements—some holding an archaic ideal of a rural economy based on communities of peasants, and others emulating various modern models of colonization[2]—were calling upon Jews, mainly Russian Jews escaping pogroms, to forgo urban areas for rural life on Palestine's moshavot (sing. moshava; a traditional type of agrarian colony whose members farmed their land independently). This undermined both the technical positivism of Herzl's building manual *The Jewish State* and the bucolic scenery of his later novel *Old-New Land* (originally published in 1902 as *Altneuland*).

②

But perhaps more than sparring with his contemporaries, Herzl's dismay seems directed anachronistically at his socialist successors in the Zionist organizations (those belligerent prophets of the hinterland whom he would never meet). Indeed, his derisive portrayal of the peasant Jew would be superseded, for decades to come, by accounts and tales ranging from pastoral utopias and agrarian manifestos to redemptive petitions and apocalyptic sermons. These reached their climax with the following text from 1935 by David Ben-Gurion, leader of the Zionist Labor Movement:

There is a warning to be heeded from world history. Anyone who has studied the history of Rome will remember the dramatic chapter known as the Phoenician War. In Hebrew it is referred to as the "Canaanite War." There once was a great military leader who was close in race to the ancient Hebrews; he had a Hebrew name and a Hebrew title: Hannibal, the Judge of Keret Hadeshet [New City] or Carthage. [...] Roman mediocrity defeated Canaanite genius. Carthage was a city-state, and Rome was a rural state, and in the desperate struggle between an urban nation and a rural nation, it was the rural nation that won. All of the commercial wealth

① "Map of Israel" [sic], 1979. Relief by Yaacov Fleming. Reuven Milon collection, Harvard College Library. This naked image of carnal terrain epitomizes the territorial syndrome described in "Borderline Disorder" at the end of this volume.
② Cover of Altneuland by Theodor Herzl, 1902.

> of Carthage, and all of the genius of its great military leaders, came to nothing. Hannibal's heroism was broken in the face of the persistent combat of the farmers of Rome. These farmers were not discouraged by one defeat after another—because they were rooted in the soil and connected to their land. They overcame Carthage and wiped it off the face of the earth, without leaving a trace. And here we have come to build a city-state and to establish an urban nation—while we are surrounded by a people that is connected to the land, not only in this country but in all the neighboring countries. We have the opportunity to establish a large urban state in Tel Aviv and in Haifa, with a million inhabitants or more—but its end will be like that of Carthage. Read about the internal situation of Carthage in the days of Hannibal and you will find the image of Tel Aviv: the same disconnected culture, the same rootlessness, the same dependence on an alien, antagonist, rural environment, the same ostensible independence—does the same end await us?[3]

Ben-Gurion's doomsday interpretation of the Phoenician War set the official tone from the 1920s and well into the 1950s. The more immigrants flooded the "Hebrew Carthage" and the more "ostensible independence" the city of Tel Aviv assumed, the bolder and broader the propaganda and concrete action toward colonizing the countryside became. Indeed, beyond rhetoric, the physical manifestation of Zionism's romance with the rural is astounding: between the 1880s and the 1980s, some 700 new villages, rural towns, and garden cities were designed and built in Palestine by and for Jewish citizens, mostly new immigrants (about 250 settlements before Israeli Statehood and 450 after).

But before we look into actual territorial operations and planning procedures—those demanding an architect-protagonist in the Zionist script—let us linger a moment longer on the return of the object of desire, the rural-of-plenty, in modern Jewish writing. The earliest and perhaps the most inspiring fictional depiction of Arcadian Zion appears in a forgotten text, the first utopic novel written in Modern Hebrew: "Voyage to the Land of Israel in the Year 2040" by the journalist Elḥanan Leib Lewinsky, first published in 1892 in Odessa.

> We had hardly begun our journey; we were just two or three hours from Jaffa, when before us lay a new land, with a new people and new ways of life.
>
> The country is like one great garden, like a single field sown with vegetables and all sorts of grains. From the window of the coach we can see groves and orchards. [...] Fields of grain, wheat, barley, and spelt, and herds grazing in the plentiful pasture. Villages and plantations wherever one treads. Twenty, thirty houses—and behold, a village. The children of Israel pass through the fields, plowing, hoeing, sowing, and reaping, and man and beast are healthy and satiated, bountiful and fresh.

> The houses are built with pride, clean and beautiful [...]. Anyone who beholds this sight will understand that these are masters of their own land who live here [...] and the whole village, by its modernity and cleanliness and by the good order that reigns, is like a modern estate, like beautiful toys. Such villages are on every road, and every road is like a single village [...].
>
> Throughout the days of their exile, in particular during the seventh century, the Jews came to understand the "secret of the earth." They saw and understood that a king, the king of the world, is he who works the fields [...]. They learned this great lesson in that University of Exile. Working the land —man's only natural work—has become the legacy of an entire nation, not just one part of the nation, but, simply put, the entire nation. Israel now returns to its ancient ways, as it was in the days of the forefathers—an agrarian nation.[4]

In the spirit of quasi-Marxist utopian literature and reformist social manifestos of the time, Lewinsky sketched an economic accord underlying his landscape of bliss, based on a crude collectivist bypass of the common market economy (and of commonplace Jewish Diasporic habitus):

> I did not see many merchants, sellers, or brokers in and around the [village], because merchants whose whole being is trading merchandise for money and money for merchandise are not to be found here. [...] Here one central village houses the granaries, where all the harvests for sale are collected. The granaries are administered by the village delegates, and merchants come from the large cities and buy the harvest. [...] And there will be a large cooperative store with all sorts of merchandise and goods, under the administration of the delegates, where it will be possible to attain any merchandise at its original price.[5]

More delirious Jewish travelogues and odysseys were to follow around the turn of the century—most illustrious of which was Herzl's *Old-New Land*. Herzl, who had acrimoniously dismissed the very attempt to reinvent the Jew as a peasant in his book *The Jewish State*, written only six years before *Old-New Land*, now meticulously built an exhaustive and seductive mise-en-scène of sumptuous landscapes inhabited by well-informed, happy farmers and creative urbanites; a dialectical image of Jewish futuristic autochthony (as the title of the novel indicates); an allegorical model society of radical colonizers under constant intellectual scrutiny.

## 2. Neudorf

In the preface to his report titled *Merchavia: A Jewish Co-operative Settlement in Palestine*, published in 1914, Franz Oppenheimer, a German-Jewish economist, sociologist, and leading theorist of agrarian settlement, recounted his initial encounter with the Zionist Organization:

> As early as 1902 [Herzl] honored me with an invitation to co-operate in his great movement, as I was then, I believe, the only economist who had occupied himself ex officio with problems of settlement. [...] I frankly declared to Dr. Herzl that his views about the possibility of colonization of Palestine in the way he proposed were impracticable. [...]
> At that time I had no relations with the Zionist movement, but I soon became a convinced adherent, and at the Basel Congress in 1903 I read a paper in which I outlined the process of colonization. During the next few years various negotiations took place between Herzl and me. Shortly before his death we met in Vienna and it was almost half agreed that an Experiment Station should be founded in Europe, if possible in Galicia, a country farm conducted upon a co-operative basis, where experiences could be gathered and where the laborers should be trained who would then go out as pioneers to Palestine.[6]

Oppenheimer was already in search of a field experiment in 1902. His intellectual background was rooted in a liberal-socialist tradition, and his planning experience was accumulated in the context of the colonization of Prussia.[7] The main objective of this colonization project was the Germanification of the Prussian regions, which were populated mostly by Poles, but it was also a planning endeavor that addressed the larger problem of the exodus from the countryside to the cities. The Prussian settlement plan included two main forms: villages (*Dorfsystem*) and individual farms (*Hofsystem*); between 1886 and 1906 the Prussian settlement committee erected 315 villages and 278 farms. These were based on three operative principles: self-help or self-labor; public or national(ized) land; and mutuality or cooperation. These principles—adopted to varying degrees and in different constellations by nineteenth-century social reformers such as Robert Owen, Pierre-Joseph Proudhon, Charles Fourier, Herbert Spencer, and Ferdinand Lassalle, as well as by utopian writers such as Edward Bellamy, Theodor Hertzka, and Theodor Herzl—crystallized during the 1890s in Franz Oppenheimer's plans for training farms that would gradually transform themselves into self-sustaining cooperative settlements.

③

Herzl himself was well-versed in utopian practices, as he readily demonstrated in *Old-New Land*. While the account of the social contract and the economic superstructure seem somewhat offhand and superfluous in Lewinsky's

"Voyage," they form the didactic mold of the narrative in *Old-New Land*. Herzl took special scholarly care to demonstrate his profound familiarity with the history of reformist and utopian practices and to spell out his analysis and critique. A speech delivered by his protagonist, David, at the farmers' assembly reads like an indoctrination lecture (and in fact sets the tone for the oratorical tradition that would characterize comrades' assemblies in Jewish collective settlements):

> "Don't imagine I am jesting when I say that *Neudorf* [New Village] was built not in Palestine, but elsewhere. It was built in England, in America, in France and in Germany. It was evolved out of experiments, books, and dreams. The unsuccessful experiments of both practical men and dreamers were to serve you as object lessons, though you did not know it. [...] The 19th century was a curiously backward era. [...] Muddle-headed visionaries were taken seriously, while sober, practical men were branded as lunatics. Napoleon the Great did not believe that Fulton's steamboat was practical. On the other hand, the absurd Fourier easily won adherents for his *phalansteries*, which were intended to provide homes and workshops for several hundred families. Stephenson, the inventor of the railway, and Cabet, the dreamer of Icaria, were contemporaries. [...] Edward Bellamy outlined a noble communistic society in his *Looking Backward* [in which] all may eat as much as they please from the common platter. [...] After Bellamy's book came *Freiland*, a utopian romance by the publicist Hertzka. [...] Beautiful dreams. The scholars among you—and I know that in *Neudorf* today there are educated peasants—will understand me when I say that they were guilty of a *petitio principii*. [...] It is among the English that we find the first traces of the cooperative social order, which we have taken over and adapted. German science, too, has added its profound word here. [...] The honest pioneers of Rochdale, as they are called, did much for you. [...] When you go to your consumers' cooperative societies and buy goods of the best quality and at the lowest prices, you have the pioneers of Rochdale to thank for it. And if your *Neudorf* is a prosperous producers' cooperative, you owe it to the poor martyrs of Rahaline in Ireland. [...] There is nothing here in *Neudorf* that was not implied in Rahaline. The one difference is, that instead of Mr. Vandaleur [the landlord], we have a large association to which everyone belongs; that is, the New Society."[8]

*Neudorf*, then, a village of the new, appears to be the main figure of *Old-New Land*. In the above passage it is constructed teleologically and contextualized within the immediate history of the social avant-garde, but as the novel progresses, it assumes its poetic autonomy to become the emblem of fresh authenticity and graceful domesticity, an optimal habitat for social creativity, economic equity, and technological ingenuity. Indeed, *Neudorf* would henceforth be both the ultimate metaphor and the prevailing metonymy of the emergent Zionist civilization: the "building block" of the colonization enterprise and the marker of its transformative force. *Neudorf's* prototype had to be built, and it was to be structured according to scientific theories and empirical methodologies.

By virtue of its careful balance between notions of mutuality and privacy, Oppenheimer's theoretical "scientific planning" model mediated gracefully between the various liberal and socialist factions within the Zionist movement. His scheme, which laid out in great breadth and detail matters of economy, agronomy, psychology, and sociology, was applied verbatim in the built prototype of Merchavia. For my purposes here, I shall simplify Oppenheimer's scheme into three evolutionary stages: in the first stage, a training farm is established and managed by an appointed agronomist; in the second stage, the training farm is transformed into a self-administered farm, run by the workers themselves, now jointly operating as an "agrarian-productivist-collaborative workers' union"; and in the third and final stage, a permanent cooperative agrarian settlement is formed on a nearby property leased from the communal farm.[9]

Merchavia struggled for several years until it was finally dismantled in 1918 due to tensions between the settlers and the Zionist institutions. According to several accounts, the born-again émigré farmers found it difficult to accept the system of an authoritative administration led by an appointed agronomist, which Oppenheimer considered to be indispensable in the initial stage. Neither did they agree with the principle of payment according to productive achievements.

But Merchavia's failure proved to be a seminal moment; it was destined to become the big bang from which a galaxy of Zionist agricultural settlements would expand for decades to come. One could argue that practically all new rural settlements that developed in the Jewish community in Palestine, and subsequently in the State of Israel, stemmed directly from or referred polemically to the Merchavia prototype. These new settlements can be classified boldly into three main groups, ranging from radical communality to limited cooperation: the kibbutz, a commune of individuals; the cooperative moshav, a commune of families; and the workers' moshav, a cooperative of families. Unlike their prototype, which simply transported the layout of a Prussian training farm, each of these typologies developed an architectural morphology and a territorial practice of its own.

As for Oppenheimer, he apparently regarded the collective agrarian settlement as a springboard to a much broader vision of a new civilization. His plans for Merchavia were intended as a blueprint for a new social order, beginning with trained immigrants generating a sustainable farming economy and increasingly building up an industrial and professional superstructure. "The Cooperative Settlement Association [...] represents the highest conceivable form of cooperative settlement," he declared, expounding:

> It can be developed best and most easily from the agricultural settlement, but under favorable conditions it could be established immediately as an urban settlement, as a garden city of a higher grade. [...] The Cooperative Settlement Association is a mixed community, composed of farmers, artisans, dealers and members of liberal professions, even of persons of independent means, which is not distinguished from any other community in the world except by the fact that the land belongs not to individuals but to the community.[10]

So it was not top-down rural planning but rather bottom-up social restructuring that truly interested Oppenheimer. Once out of the laboratory, his model settlement proliferated mutatis mutandis according to the ideological and territorial convictions of the various Zionist parties. Given his personal disagreement with the all-too-literal identification of Zionism with Jewish nationalism and the exclusion of the Arabs from his cooperative scheme, by 1920 Oppenheimer found himself alienated from the Zionist establishment, and in the 1930s, when forced to leave Germany, he immigrated to the United States.

## 3. The Archetype

In the opening scene of the Zionist rural epic, a social planner stood at center stage. With the fade-out of this scene emerged another figure, this time that of an architect—the first architect formally invited by the Zionist movement to give structure and form to the new settlements.

In 1920, Richard Kauffmann, who had studied at the Technische Hochschule in Munich (with Erich Mendelsohn) and was greatly influenced by the garden-city concepts of Theodor Fischer, was nominated by Arthur Ruppin to be head planner of the Palestine Land Development Company (PLDC), a company formed by the World Zionist Organization (WZO) to function as the main land-acquisition agent in Palestine. Ruppin, the so-called "father of Zionist settlement," was the founder and director of the WZO's local office in Palestine.

Kauffmann's early pre-Zionist professional experience included work for Georg Metzendorf in Munich, where he was involved in the design of a group of houses for the Krupp estate near Essen. In 1914 he received a prize for a small housing project in Bickendorf, near Cologne. He had just started his own office in Frankfurt when he was drafted into the Prussian army in 1915. In 1919 he won first prize in a competition for an urban plan of the garden city of Raigorod, near Kharkov. In that same year he moved to Norway, where he worked for Paul Oscar Hoff and won several urban competitions. In Palestine, Kauffmann had a prolific career. Throughout the 1920s and 1930s, he designed over one hundred rural settlements and numerous garden neighborhoods, garden cities, and urban villas, many of which are considered architectural landmarks today. But it is his

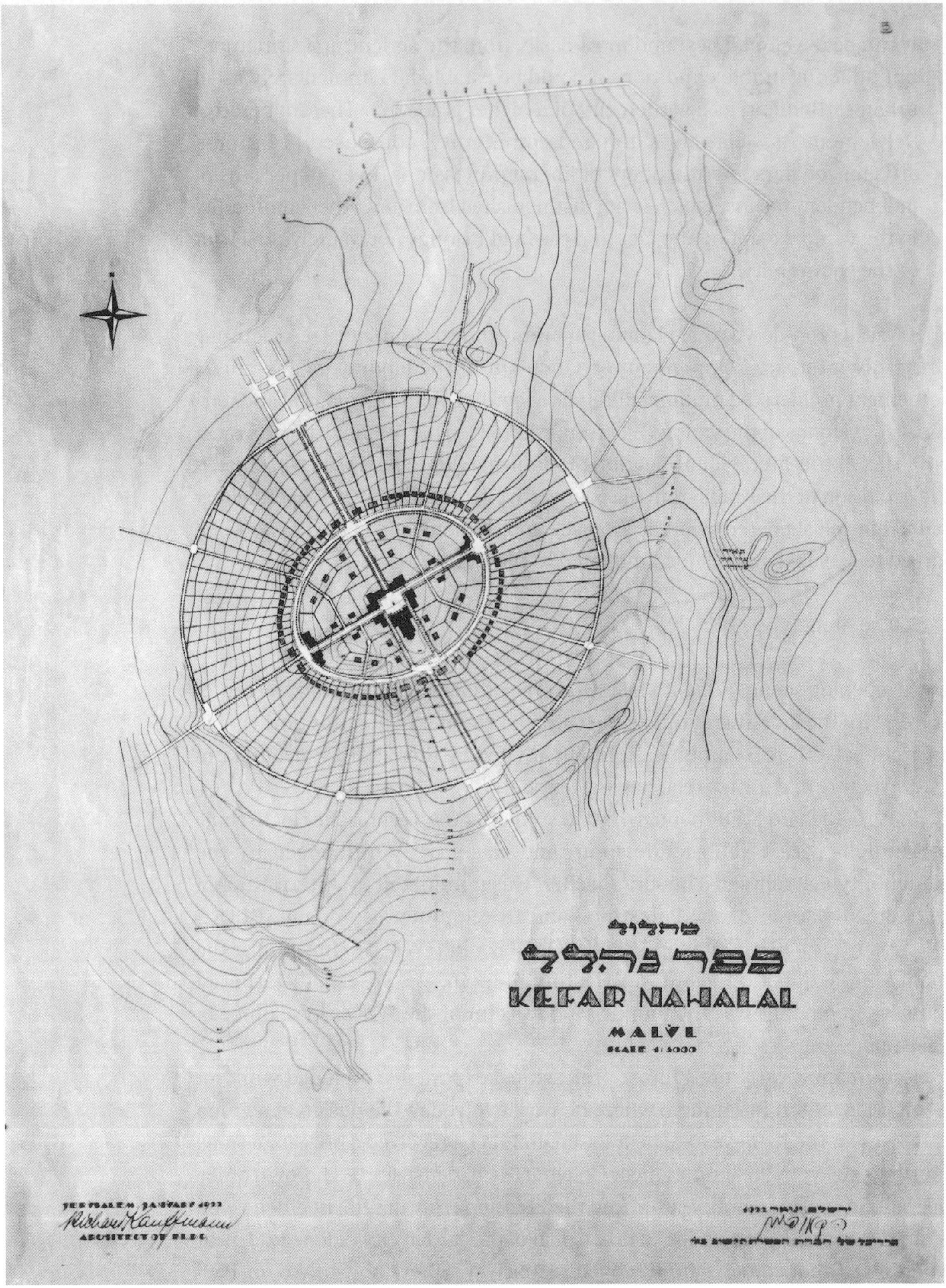


④

very first assignment, his first architectural project in Palestine—the design of the workers' moshav of Nahalal—which remains his most iconic work, both in its perfect paper version and in its extant physical form.

The program for the typology of the workers' moshav was developed by Eliezer Yaffe, founder of the Jewish-American Young Farmer Movement. His program was based on similar principles of commonality, mutuality, equality, self-labor, and national land as set out in Merchavia, but in comparison to Oppenheimer's model, it placed a greater emphasis on notions of individuality, privacy, personal initiative, and the "natural" evolution of the nuclear family. After the failure of Merchavia, an open debate regarding the social structure of future settlements erupted within both administrative and workers' circles. While the devout socialists believed that the principle of collectivism should be doubly reinforced, the pragmatists concluded that collectivism was too contrived and repressive and should function only as a transitional construct, effective for purposes of land occupation and agrarian training. In 1919 Yaffe published a manual, directed at this latter group, for a model workers' moshav, detailing recommended rules and regulations, quantifying the optimal number of families and size of plots, and circumscribing the layout and scope of public spaces.

Once the location of Nahalal, the first workers' moshav, was decided—on a hilltop in the heart of Jezreel Valley—it seems that young Richard Kauffmann was called upon to simply transliterate Yaffe's prescription into a spatial diagram. And so he did. His perfectly oval scheme imprints the terrain with a powerful emblem: an image at once hermetic, panoptic, and defensive, while radiating outward and drawing in the landscape; a totalizing structure that consecrates the cohesive community and its communal center; but also an effective system of land parcelization and demarcation of private property. Technically speaking, the design of Nahalal is based on the following principles: eight radial roads extending from the central public space to the village perimeter, thereby subdividing it into eight equal sections; two round belts surrounding the central area, which is designated for public buildings and communal facilities; a subdivision of the external belt into equally sized farmers' lots, with dwellings in front and private farms in the back; and transversal axes intersecting the circles and shortcutting the circulation.

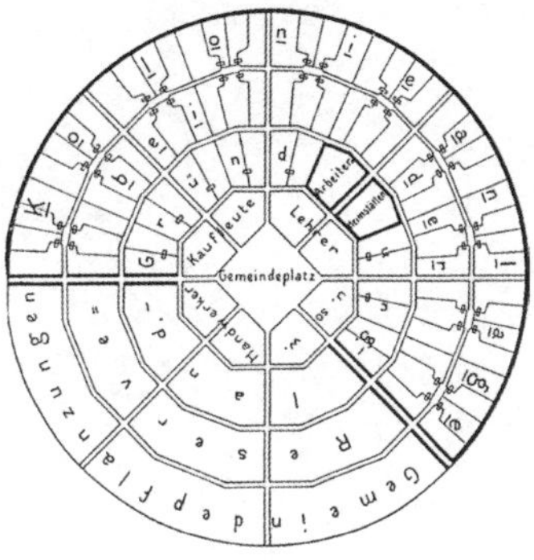


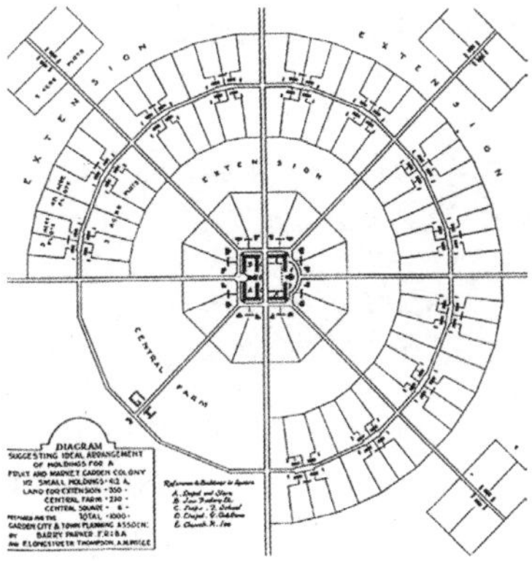


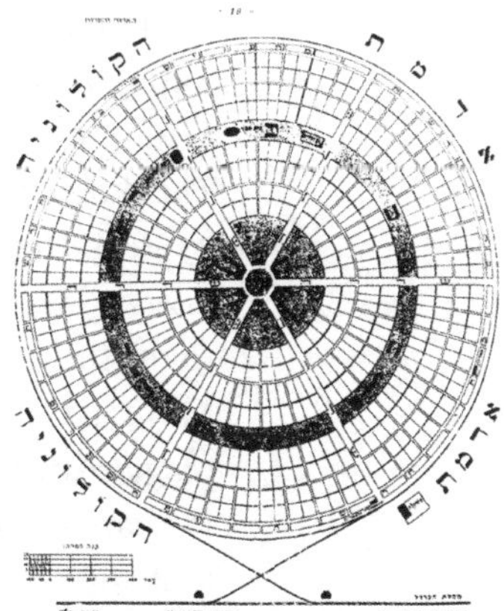

⑤ ⑥ ⑦

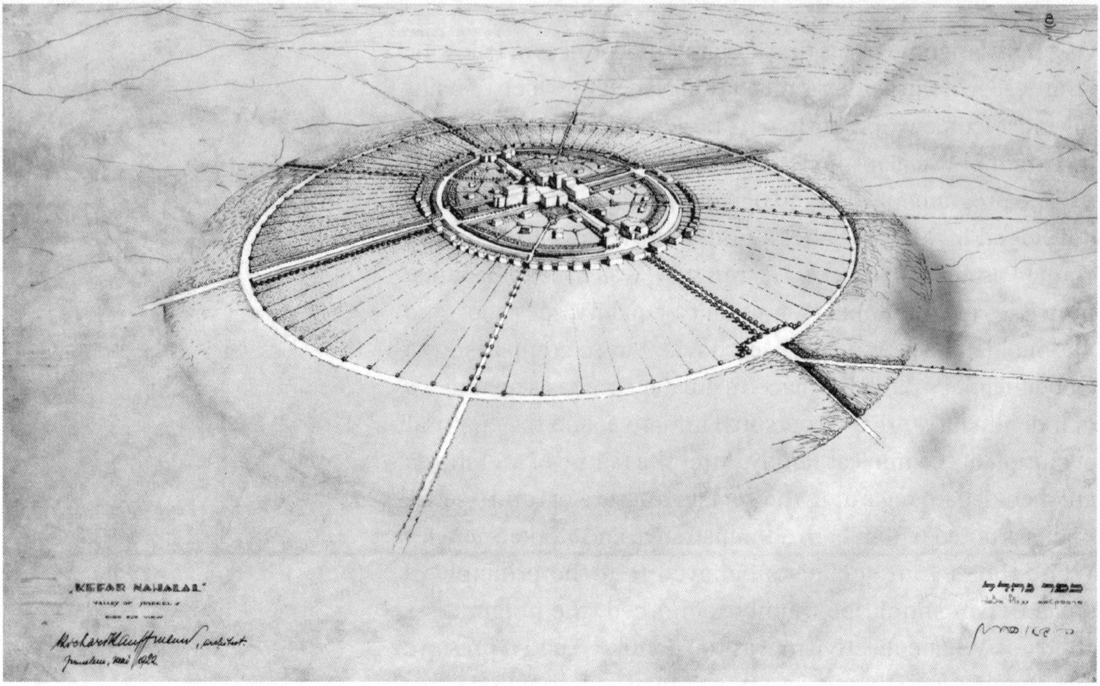


(8)

Nahalal was built precisely as drawn by Kauffmann, and it maintains its initial shape to this very day. Documents reveal, however, that Kauffmann's scheme was not at all original. It was in fact borrowed from a prior circular settlement plan, drawn up by the agronomist Jacob Oettinger—head of the Agrarian Settlement Department of the WZO between 1914 and 1924—in his 1916 pamphlet *Methoden und Kapitalbedarf jüdischer Kolonisation in Palästina*. The direct affinity between Kauffmann's and Oettinger's schemes is illustrated by Ruth Hanin-Rabinowitz in her book *Cooperative Settlements as Models for the Zionist Garden Colony and a School Farm* (in Hebrew). She attributes this affinity to the full control of the Zionist institutions over the entire planning apparatus. More astounding is her revelation that Oettinger's scheme itself was pure plagiarism. According to her, his scheme leads directly not only to Ebenezer Howard's generic garden-city diagram, but specifically to the garden colony that appeared in a report by the Committee on Land Settlement for Discharged Sailors and Soldiers in the April 1916 issue of *Garden Cities and Town Planning Magazine*. The article, entitled "Land Settlement after the War," contains a circular diagram of a "Fruit and Market Garden Colony," which, according to Hanin-Rabinowitz, is identical to Oettinger's scheme.

And so it happens that Zionism's most graphic emblem, the ultimate visual synthesis of utopian morphology and rustic domesticity, is in fact a plagiarized version of an English garden colony. Needless to say, such a predicament regarding matters of authenticity, originality, or the order of aberrational types is not at all foreign to our discussion. In fact, it is precisely the subject of inquiry here. We shall return later to the garden colony and its vicissitudes, and to the whereabouts of four hundred new workers' villages, successors of Nahalal (see chapter "Rural"), but we cannot postpone any longer a discussion of the emergence of the most deviceful habitat of the Zionist vanguard—the kibbutz.

### 4. The Exemplary Non-Failure

At long last, the Jews had struck roots, or at least so it seemed from Zionist utopian projections and early experimental projects. Their staged return to history was construed above all as a vigorous and corporeal return to geography. Idiomatically, this return was at once authenticated and mystified by a pioneering vernacular infused with such messianic dicta as "redeeming the land," "conquering the soil," and "making the desert bloom," suggesting an epic salvation of a *terra nullius*.

A new culture of transformation and reform gradually led up to a momentous migration and settlement movement. This movement constituted one of the latest, and possibly the most sustainable, of European colonialist projects. Its singularity should not be overlooked: unlike the other colonialisms, Zionism was colonialism without a motherland, a *metropole*; it was a colonialism of the missing motherland, or of the longed-for "land of the Fathers." It therefore never conceived of Palestine, or the Land of Israel, as an exterritorial outpost, a protectorate, or a mere natural resource to be exploited, but rather as a site of an enduring auto-colonization, the proper locus for a future ethnocracy, a platform to perpetually enact and reenact the imperative negation of the Diaspora (Heb. *shlilat hagalut*) and the transmutation of the figure of the Diasporic Jew. The formative notion and praxis of ongoing occupation and transformation of the land identify Zionism as an exemplary settler colonialism seeking to replace (or "integrate") the indigenous society and establish its own authenticity by laboring and domesticating the land. Thus the rural was Zionism's ultimate haunt—the constructed bareness that must be dominated.

Unlike other New World rural colonization movements (in North America, South America, South Africa, Australia, etc.), Zionist colonization was based not on family farms and individual pioneering, but rather on an array of newly invented rural communities (mostly without direct historical precedents)

③ Albert Einstein looks at a display of new forms of rural settlements. Jewish Palestine pavilion, New York World's Fair, 1939. New York Public Library digital collections.
④ Nahalal, 1922. Plan. Richard Kauffmann. Central Zionist Archives.
⑤ Colony plan in ring form. *Methoden und Kapitalbedarf jüdischer Kolonisation in Palästina* by Jacob Oettinger, 1916.
⑥ Diagram of a fruit and market garden colony. "Land Settlement after the War," *Garden Cities and Town Planning Magazine*, April 1916.
⑦ Provisional plan of a garden city for Hama'agal (The Circle) Cooperative.
⑧ Nahalal, 1922. Drawing of a bird's-eye view. Richard Kauffmann. Central Zionist Archives.

operating as communes or cooperative associations—something akin to the "miniature commonwealths" minted by the Puritans of the seventeenth and eighteenth centuries in America. As these forms evolved, they generated a profusion of efficient spatial strategies and innovative architectural typologies.

Unlike the Puritan settlements—or indeed almost any known utopian endeavor—the Zionist rural communities never operated as isolated, sectarian, ideologically radical, or hyper-spiritual cults, nor were they perceived as such. Quite the contrary: they were conceived and designed as a grounding and burgeoning network of productivist nodes, spread across the countryside and controlling most (over 90 percent) of the centralized agricultural product. Although these rural communities constituted no more than 8 percent of the local Jewish population at their peak, they were backed by powerful political, economic, and cultural organizations, including industrial and financial institutions, distribution networks, educational and cultural organisms, media and newspapers, sports and recreation groups, youth movements, and paramilitary forces.

In spite of the idiosyncrasy of their social contract, they never posed a contentious paradigm of difference to the normative social, cultural, and political structure. Paradoxically, these settlements—especially the manifestly collectivist, communist, or Marxist among them—embodied the ethno-national avant-garde and provided a patriotic model of pioneering Zionism. In this sense, they functioned not only as exemplary mini-commonwealths, but also as "imagined communities"[11] par excellence: the pastoral collectivist settlement, with its premise of acquired nativism, inner egalitarianism, mutual accountability, and self-sufficiency, reflected Zionism's emerging spectacle of the ingathering of the exiles in the Arcadian Land of Promise. Such metonymic affiliation between the idealized social cell and the allegorized national body is certainly one of the most profound—and perplexing—of Israel's founding myths.[12]

In his seminal study of the Israeli Labor Movement, with which practically all Jewish rural settlements of the twentieth century were affiliated (until the post-1967 religious settler movement, that is), the historian and political scientist Zeev Sternhell deconstructs this movement's epic synthesis of socialism and nationalism and questions its fundamental pledge: "Was equality a genuine goal, however long-term, or was it only a mobilizing myth, perhaps a convenient alibi that sometimes permitted the movement to avoid grappling with the contradiction between socialism and nationalism?"[13]

Sternhell unequivocally rejects the redemptive Zionist narrative and describes its reformist agenda as a masquerade:

> The pioneering ideology, with its central principles—the conquest of the land, the reformation of the individual, and self-realization—was not an ideology of social change; it was not an ideology that could establish a secular, liberal state and put an end to the war with the Arabs. [...] The labor movement was not equipped with a conceptual framework that permitted

> it to move beyond the national revolution it had led and presided over with such conspicuous success.[14]

The inherent incongruity of a nationalist-socialist hegemony would confuse and rip apart Israeli society in decades to come, but during the formative pre-State period and in the early years of the State, it was precisely this ambiguity that was the secret formula of the "conspicuous success"—or, as philosopher Martin Buber put it in 1949, "the exemplary non-failure"—of the Zionist rural settlements.[15] Buber considered these settlements to be non-failures in relation to the history of failed utopian experiments, and he offered two main explanations for their proliferation and sustainability. First, they were established in a sparsely populated country that lacked a social class infrastructure, and hence they faced no resistance from an existing, already stratified, society. Second, as the spearhead of a national territorial project, they assumed disproportionate symbolic power and expediently embodied a national ethos.

Sternhell offers a more skeptical account of the origin and potency of these settlements, claiming that "collective settlement was a pragmatic rather than an ideological choice." Hollowing out their revolutionary impetus, he describes the settlements as mere facts on the ground, "which were set up on a national land with the aid of national funds, and constituted a pragmatic Zionist solution to the problems of conquering the land, lack of work, and the need to absorb the immigrants."[16]

Sternhell's critique of pragmatic Zionism does not fail to notice the genuine Vitalist sentiment feeding its romance with the rural, as is illustrated in his quote from Chaim Arlosoroff's 1919 essay "The Popular Socialism of the Jews":

> The European-American civilization has made the life of humanity mechanical. Everything has become technical. The whole life of humanity has become one great machine: not an organism, but an organization. Urban civilization and the division of labor—these are the two pillars of the modern temple of idolatry.[17]

But Romanticism and socialism present an intolerable impasse to Sternhell:

> The condemnation of the city and the cult of a return to nature, to the simplicity, authenticity, and rootedness of the village, was always one of the myths of radical nationalism, not of socialism. Socialism was oriented toward the modern world, industrialized and urban.[18]

Physiocracy, or rurality, is a well-thought-out Zionist plot, going deliberately against the grain of the actual pattern of urban migration, as Sternhell clarifies:

> The myth of a return to nature was nurtured by the labor movement even in the 1920s and 1930s, when Jewish society was already an urban society. In fact, Jewish Palestine under the British mandate was one of the most urbanized countries in the world: eight out of ten Jews lived in cities.[19]

Sternhell's depiction of the actual Jewish community in Palestine as exceedingly urban is historically accurate, as is his insinuation regarding institutional efforts to avert spontaneous urbanization through the settlement project. Indeed, the utilization of "Zionism's corps of planning experts"[20] to implement the doctrine of centralized decentralization was—and remains—a common practice, which will be discussed in the next chapter, with regard to Israel's 1950 master plan.

Sternhell's critical analysis is supported and expanded by several historians, sociologists, and political scientists,[21] but in the context of our spatial account it seems to have two considerable shortcomings: First, his strict dissociation of the Zionist Labor Movement's anti-urban tendency from its socialist ideology is questionable. At the very least, he disregards the urban/rural and industrial/agrarian dialectics that are so fundamental to Marxist discourse and, indeed, so formative to the architecture of the Jewish collective settlements. Second, his focused examination of the Labor Movement overlooks the fact that the Zionist pastoral scene of origin was drawn well before the 1920s and the ascent of the Labor Movement and its political apparatus.

As to the first issue, it should be emphasized that anti-urban sentiments have historically spanned the entire ideological spectrum—from Thomas Jefferson's *Notes on the State of Virginia* of 1785, a vision of an agrarian liberal democracy devoid of cities (and, subsequently, the writings of Thoreau, Emerson, Melville, Poe, and Wright); through Karl Marx and Friedrich Engels's *Communist Manifesto* of 1848, with its critique of the way "the bourgeoisie has subjected the country to the rule of the towns" and Engels's call for the abolition of cities in his 1872 essay "The Housing Question"; up to Mao Zedong's mobilization of millions of Chinese youth "up to the mountains and down to the villages" in the framework of the Rustication Movement of the 1950s and the Cultural Revolution of the 1960s. Urban studies scholar Shlomo Angel, in his analysis of urban expansion in developing countries, claims that communist countries consistently translated the anti-urban attitudes of Marx and Engels into policies that sought to limit the size of large cities, to prevent rural-urban migration, and to force urban populations into the countryside.[22] In this context, the Zionist colonization project, with its direct intellectual roots in Bolshevism, could be regarded as a pioneering pseudoscientific Soviet-style de-urbanization project.

As for the itinerary of the Zionist pastoral, in the following chapters we will begin reconstructing the early pre-socialist scene of visionary texts, imported planning theories, and adopted colonization practices. ■

1 Theodor Herzl, *The Jewish State: An Attempt at a Modern Solution of the Jewish Question*, trans. Jacob M. Alkow (New York: American Zionist Emergency Council, 1946), pp. 88–89. Originally published as *Der Judenstaat* (Leipzig and Vienna: M. Breitenstein's Verlags-Buchhandlung, 1896).

2 According to sociologist Gershon Shafir, "Between 1882 and 1900 Baron Edmund de Rothschild followed the model of French agricultural colonization in Algeria and Tunisia, which was based on the development of privately owned monoculture agriculture. When this French model floundered, three others were suggested in its place in the first decade of the [twentieth] century. First, Aharon Eisenberg [...], who directed Agudat Netaim (The Planters' Society), the largest capitalist company in Palestine before the First World War, recommended a Californian design for enabling urban people to move to the countryside. Secondly, members of Hashomer (The Guard) organization [...] longed to emulate the Cossack's military colonization of parts of south-eastern Russia. [...] Thirdly, Otto Warburg and Arthur Ruppin, the heads of the World Zionist Organization's Land Development Company, highly consciously tried to reproduce the 'internal colonization' model developed by the Prussian government to create a German majority in some of its eastern, ethnically Polish territories." Gershon Shafir, *Land, Labor and the Origins of the Israeli-Palestinian Conflict, 1882–1914* (Berkeley: University of California Press, 1996), pp. 10–11.

3 David Ben-Gurion, "Zionist Players and Their Role at This Time," in *On Settlement: Collected Writings, 1915–1965*, ed. Menachem Dorman [in Hebrew] (Tel Aviv: Hakibbutz Hameuhad, 1986), pp. 63–64.

4 Elḥanan Leib Lewinsky, "Voyage to the Land of Israel in the Year 2040," in *Yesterday's Tomorrow: The Zionist Utopia*, vol. 2, ed. Rachel Elboim-Dror [in Hebrew] (Jerusalem: Yad Izhak Ben-Zvi, 1993), pp. 77–78. Translated for this article by Tamar Cohen.

5 Ibid.

6 Franz Oppenheimer, *Merchavia: A Jewish Co-operative Settlement in Palestine* (Cologne and New York: Co-operative Society for Erez-Israel and Jewish National Fund, 1914).

7 On Oppenheimer and his roots in German sociology and Prussian settlement plans, see Ruth Hanin-Rabinowitz, *Cooperative Settlements as Models for the Zionist Garden Colony and a School Farm* [in Hebrew] (Haifa: Pardes Publishers, 2006).

8 Theodor Herzl, *Old-New Land*, trans. Lotta Levensohn (New York: Bloch Publishing, 1960), p. 165. Originally published as *Altneuland* (Leipzig: Seemann, 1902).

9 Franz Oppenheimer, *Die Siedlungsgenossenschaft* (Cologne and New York: Duncker and Humblot, 1914). Cited in Hanin-Rabinowitz, *Cooperative Settlements as Models*, p. 32.

10 Oppenheimer, *Merchavia*, p. 8.

11 See Benedict Anderson, *Imagined Communities: Reflections on the Origin and Spread of Nationalism* (London: Verso, 2006).

12 See Zeev Sternhell, *The Founding Myths of Israel: Nationalism, Socialism and the Making of the Jewish State*, trans. David Maisel (Princeton: Princeton University Press, 1998), p. 3.

13 Ibid.

14 Ibid.

15 Martin Buber, *Paths in Utopia*, trans. R. F. C. Hull (Albany: Syracuse University Press, 1996), p. 142.

16 Sternhell, *Founding Myths*, pp. 32–33.

17 Chaim Arlosoroff, "The Popular Socialism of the Jews," in *Writings of Chaim Arlosoroff*, vol. 3 [in Hebrew] (Tel Aviv: Schtibel, 1933), p. 52. Originally published as *Der Jüdische Volkssozialismus* (Berlin: Hapoel Hazair, 1919). Cited (in English) in Sternhell, *Founding Myths*, p. 25.

18 Sternhell, *Founding Myths*, p. 25.

19 Ibid.

20 A phrase used by S. Ilan Troen in *Imagining Zion: Dreams, Designs, and Realities in a Century of Jewish Settlement* (New Haven: Yale University Press, 2003), p. 44.

21 See, e.g., Shafir, *Land, Labor*; Yoav Peled, *Class and Ethnicity in the Pale: The Political Economy of Jewish Workers' Nationalism in Late Imperial Russia* (London: St. Martin's Press, 1989); Baruch Kimmerling, *Immigrants, Settlers, Natives: Israel Between Plurality of Cultures and Cultural Wars* [in Hebrew] (Tel Aviv: Am Oved, 2004); Baruch Kimmerling, ed., *The Israeli State and Society: Boundaries and Frontiers* (Albany: State University of New York Press, 1989).

22 Shlomo Angel writes in "Preparing for the Coming Urban Expansion in Developing Countries" (unpublished paper, 2008):
"Anti-urban attitudes have sometimes driven radical anti-urban policies—policies that aim at sending people away from cities. [...] In the Soviet Union, for example, internal migration was no longer to be seen as subject to the whim of the individual or the market. It was to be scientific, predictable, and planned. The regime implemented a series of explicit controls on internal migration: incentives to move to certain areas, restrictions on industrial investment in certain cities, and the *propiska* (resident permit) system. [...]
"From the 1950s to the 1970s, China went further than simply requiring permits to reside in cities and sought to move urban youths in great numbers to rural areas. China's *rustification* movement—officially known as 'Up to the Mountains and Down to the Villages'—was launched in the early 1950s and gained real momentum during the Cultural Revolution in 1967. Between 1967 and 1976, some 16 million urban youths were forced into the countryside."

# DOSSIER:
# JULIUS POSENER'S TABLEAU

Julius Posener fled Berlin in 1933 and immigrated to Palestine in 1935. Erich Mendelsohn, for whom Posener had briefly worked in Berlin, invited him to join the team in his Jerusalem office. Ultimately, the position at Mendelsohn's office did not work out for Posener, nor did any other long-term collaboration with local architects. He invested himself in writing for local and international periodicals and became the most eloquent critic of the "Jewish style" in Palestine during the second half of the 1930s.[1]

In letters to his mother written en route from Alexandria to Haifa and upon his arrival in Palestine, Posener described the overwhelming sensorial intensity of the Oriental bazaar of Alexandria and the unexpected serenity he encountered upon his arrival in Palestine:

> This, dear mother, was my first acquaintance with the Orient. Therefore I was relieved when I saw beautiful Haifa, [...] and the bazaar in Jerusalem, which [Aunt] Lotte found so repulsive, to me seemed very elegant, almost European. There seems to be a difference between Africa and Asia, but I am very happy to have seen Alexandria first, because after it Palestine almost seems familiar.[2]

Like so many travelers who reported from the Holy Land before and after him (see chapter "Pasolini's Travelogue"), Posener was bewildered by the disparity between the layers of textual and visual representations of the land and his own unmediated experience of it:

> In all the books and movies about Palestine, and in a vast amount of description, it appears as a blinding deadly-yellow desert. [But] Palestine is beautiful in its soft forms and curves, which could be observed also in the Judean Mountains which are similar in their fluidity to the mountains of Provence.[3]

About a month later, in a letter to Le Corbusier, Posener was still captivated by the soft Mediterranean landscape, but he could not resist an early categorical judgment—many more would follow—of the modern building culture he was encountering:

> The Jews can neither build cities nor houses. They had an exceptional chance but they failed.[4]

Posener seemed to be settled and buoyant by early 1937. He had become *L'Architecture d'Aujourd'hui*'s correspondent in Palestine and was probably already working on the September issue, which was dedicated to architecture in Palestine and which he guest-edited with Sam Barkai. He would soon also become one of the editors and writers of *Habinyan*, the local magazine of architecture and town planning associated with the circle (Heb. *Chug*) of diehard modernists. He wrote to Mendelsohn:

> I am in Tel Aviv working vigorously and with success for *L'Architecture d'Aujourd'hui* [...] and I begin to consider establishing an archive and research for publishing on architecture in Palestine. Maybe the Chug Adrihalei Israel will give me the opportunity to do so.[5]

During World War II, Posener's writing opportunities dwindled. He remained in Tel Aviv until 1941, when he registered with the British army and departed for Egypt, where he stayed until the end of the war. After the war he moved to England and taught at the Brickstone School of Building. Between 1956 and 1961 he established a school of architecture and taught in Kuala Lumpur, Malaysia. In 1961 he returned to Berlin, where he taught building history at the Hochschule für bildende Künste (today the University of the Arts) until 1971 and served as chairman of the Deutscher Werkbund from 1973 to 1976. ■

1 On Posener's hypothesis of "Jewish architecture" and its mimetic relation to the modern movement, see chapter "Jewish Style."

2 Letter from Julius Posener to Gertrud Posener, October 15, 1935, in Matthias Schirren and Sylvia Claus, eds., *Julius Posener: Ein Leben in Briefen* (Basel: Birkhäuser, 1999), p. 58.

3 Letter from Julius Posener to Gertrud Posener, October 9, 1935, in ibid., p. 60.

4 Letter from Julius Posener to Le Corbusier, November 3, 1935, in ibid., p. 65.

5 Letter from Julius Posener to Erich Mendelsohn, January 1, 1937, in ibid., p. 95.

(9)

Landschaft jenseits Jerusalem, letzte Dörfer und Steinwüste

Landscape beyond Jerusalem: last villages and rocky desert

## Traditionelles und modernes Bauen in Palästina

Der Aufsatz von Julius Posener, dem früheren Herausgeber der Zeitschrift «L'Architecture d'aujourd'hui», berührt grundsätzliche Probleme des Verhältnisses von moderner Architektur zur alteinheimischen Architektur eines Landes. Es geht hier nicht nur um einen vergleichsweise exotischen, speziellen Fall, sondern um das zentrale Problem der Beziehung zwischen Landschaft und Architektur überhaupt, und es dürfte von Interesse sein, dieses «Heimatschutz»-Problem einmal an einem fremden Beispiel vorgeführt zu sehen, an das wir nicht gefühlsmässig gebunden sind. Red.

Palästina gehört zu den Ländern des Mittelmeeres, denen der Beginn unseres Jahrhunderts zu einer unerwarteten Entwicklung verholfen hat. Bis zu diesem Augenblick sind die Formen des Lebens und der Wirtschaft, vor allem auf dem Lande, archaisch gewesen. Die Art, wie der Bauer pflügt, gräbt, kocht, sich kleidet, unterscheiden sich nicht von den Beschreibungen der Bibel. Der jähe Einfall intensiver Kolonisation, ausgestattet mit allen Apparaten und Ansprüchen unseres Jahrhunderts, schafft ein Nebeneinander, Durcheinander, welches zunächst nur verwirrt. Schärfste Kritik reagiert selbstverständlich auf die Lebensäusserungen der Neueingewanderten, welche sich so viel weniger harmonisch und beschaulich darstellen, als die ihrer Vorgänger und Nachbarn im Lande, und die Schwärmerei für Arabisches ist auch, und gerade in der Zeit seit den Unruhen, viel stärker in den Reihen der Neuangesiedelten, als man draussen glauben möchte.

Wo es sich aber darum handelt, die Kritik zu begründen und womöglich in die Richtung zu deuten, in die ein Weg zum Besseren sich wenden sollte, darf man sich mit solcher Gefühlsreaktion nicht begnügen. Um einen Standpunkt zu gewinnen, scheint das beste, zunächst das Land selbst anzuschauen, und zwar so, wie der Architekt ein Land sieht.

Landschaft, um damit zu beginnen, wird dem Architekten nicht als etwas Gegebenes erscheinen, als ein Hintergrund für Bauten. Er ist sich bewusst, dass Landschaft

DAS WERK HEFT 9 SEPTEMBER 1938

257

(9) Traditional and Modern Construction in Palestine

This article by Julius Posener, the former editor of the magazine *L'Architecture d'Aujourd'hui*, deals with fundamental problems in the relationship between modern architecture and the long-established indigenous architecture of a country. This is not about a comparatively exotic particular case, but rather about the central problem of the relationship between landscape and architecture in general, and it should be of interest to look at this "homeland preservation problem" through the prism of a foreign example in which we are not emotionally invested. Eds.

Palestine is one of the countries around the Mediterranean for which the dawn of our century has brought about unforeseen progress. Up to this moment in time, the modes of life and economy had been archaic, especially in the countryside. The farmer's way of plowing, digging, cooking, dressing was no different to biblical accounts. The sudden onslaught of intensive colonization, equipped with all the apparatus and expectations of our century, creates a juxtaposition and confusion that must initially perplex the observer. Of course the new immigrants' manners of living are subject to severe criticism, since they appear so much less harmonious and pleasant than those of their predecessors and neighbors in the country, and the enthusiasm for all things Arab is much stronger among the ranks of the newly-settled than it may appear from the outside—especially in the time since the disturbances.

But if the goal is to justify criticism and perhaps point to a way things may be improved, one must not make do with such an emotional response. In order to arrive at a point of view, it is probably best to start by observing the country itself, specifically in the manner an architect sees a country.

Landscape, to begin with, does not appear to the architect as a given, as a backdrop for buildings. He is aware that landscape is created by nature as well as by man. In Palestine, a multitude of distinct formations, each with its own climate, is condensed into the smallest of areas. The coastal plain: Light, red soil, undulating up-

Landschaft bei Bethlehem

Landscape near Bethlehem

unten:
Beduinen in Galiläa beim Flechten von Rohrmatten, wie in alttestamentlicher Zeit, aber der Petroleumkanister rechts zeigt die Nähe der westlichen Zivilisation

Bottom: Bedouins in the Galilee weaving mats from rushes as in Old Testament times; only the petroleum canister on the right indicates the proximity of Western civilization.

von der Natur und vom Menschen geschaffen wird. In Palästina ist eine Fülle verschiedenster Formationen, jede mit ihrem eigenen Klima, auf engstem Raum zusammengerückt. Die Küstenebene: leichter, roter Boden, in Wellen von der Küste ansteigend und dann wieder zum Rand des Hügellandes sich abflachend; herrlich belebt von den ausgedehnten Pflanzungen von Orangen, Bananen, Mandeln. Schwere Luft, im Sommer sehr feucht in den Nächten. Am Fuss des Hügellandes dunkler Boden, in grossen Flächen bestanden mit Mais, Durra, Gerste, auch Weideflächen. Haben die Dörfer in dem Pflanzungsgebiet Mauern aus dem weichen tertiären Stein, der an Hügeln zutage tritt, und Dächer aus Holz, so sind sie hier aus Lehmwänden aufgebaut und ducken sich grau auf den Rücken der niedrigen Vorberge.

Die Hügel selbst, kaum bewachsen, bis auf Terrassen von Wein- und Olivenkulturen, durch die Einwirkung starker Regengüsse und eines dauernden Windes abgerundet, ohne jeden steilen Abfall. Sehr grosses Relief, kupplige Höhen, gestufte Täler. Die Dörfer, steinerne Häuser, gewölbt (kein Holz zum Dachbau), beherrschen mit Vorliebe die höchsten Kuppen und geben dem in grossen Wellen bewegten Land eine bauliche Steigerung, wie es in Europa seltener alte Schlösser tun. Die Luft ist dünn, alpin, in der Sonne sehr warm, im Schatten auffallend kühl. Die Winter sind empfindlich kalt mit Hagel, nassem Schnee und Sturm. Der Himmel durchscheinend, sehr hell am Rand, entsetzlich blau im Zenith. In dieser weiten Landschaft nun hält jedes Zeichen menschlichen Lebens den Blick fest: niedrige Mauern aus Feldsteinen, Wegen folgend, Gehege abgrenzend; stämmige Oliven und kriechender Wein, eine Sykomore bei grauen Häusern, ein Blumengarten am Wege. Die mageren Aecker, an den Flanken der Hügel in dünnen Serpentinen sich hochwindend: ein jedes erhält Bedeutung, wird mit Liebe angeschaut, lebt in dem herrlichen Licht ein gesteigertes Leben. Es wäre pedantisch, die kurze Reise in ein weiteres Land fortzusetzen, die Steinwüste jenseits Jerusalem; oder im einzelnen die grössere Mannigfaltigkeit zu beschreiben, welche der Weg durch das Land von Norden nach Süden bietet.

Eines ist allen diesen Landschaften gemeinsam: der Teil, den der Mensch an ihrer Formation genommen hat, wird sichtbarer als in Europa. Die Möglichkeiten der Bepflanzung sprechen stärker, da sie begrenzter und

258

ward from the coast and then leveling out toward the edge of the hill country; delightfully vitalized by the extensive plantations of oranges, bananas, almonds. Heavy air, during the summer very humid at night. At the foot of the hill country dark soil, with large fields of corn, millet, barley, even pastureland. While the villages in the plantation region have walls made from the soft Tertiary stone that can be seen on the hills, and roofs made from timber, here they are built with mud walls, forming gray clusters on the ridges of the low foothills.

The hills themselves, sparsely covered with vegetation, with the exception of terraced vineyards and olive orchards, rounded by the effects of heavy rainfall and constant wind, without any steep drops. Rolling terrain, vaulted peaks, tiered valleys. The villages—stone houses, domed (no timber for roofs)—prefer to command the highest summits and lend the generously undulating land a structural magnification, as old castles do, more rarely, in Europe. The air is thin, alpine, very hot in the sun, remarkably cool in the shade. The winters are bitterly cold, with hail, wet snow, and gales. The skies are translucent, very light at the edges, shockingly blue at their zenith. In this sweeping landscape every sign of human life draws the eye: low walls of fieldstone, tracing paths, enclosing paddocks, hefty olive trees and creeping vines, a sycamore next to gray houses, a flower garden by the road. The meager fields, winding up the hillside in thin serpentines: each of them assumes a significance, is regarded with love, lives in the glorious light of intensified life. It would be pedantic to continue the short journey into another country, the rocky desert beyond Jerusalem, or to describe the even greater diversity on offer when traversing the country from north to south.

There is one thing all of these landscapes have in common: The part man played in their formation is more obvious than it is in Europe. The opportunities for cultivation are more outspoken, because they are limited and monotonous, and orchards, fields, and dwellings are more intimately inscribed into the land. They magnify the landscape, using its limited resources—which are only thus made visible in the first place.

One cannot say that nature dictates the style of landscape. In Palestine in particular, very different landscapes evolved under

Jüdische Kulturlandschaft. Das Tal Jesreel

Jewish cultivated landscapes: the Jezreel Valley

einseitiger sind, und Gärten, Felder und Wohnungen sind dem Lande enger eingeschrieben. Sie steigern die Landschaft, deren begrenzte Möglichkeiten sie ausnutzen und dadurch erst sichtbar machen.

Man kann nicht sagen, die Natur schreibe den Stil der Landschaft vor. Gerade in Palästina sind unter gleichen Bedingungen sehr verschiedene Landschaften entstanden, da, wo verschiedene Völker siedeln. Diese Bemerkung gilt in gesteigertem Masse von der Architektur.

Der Architekt sieht, neben Landschaft und Klima, Sitten einwohnender Völker. Hier muss man sich vorsehen, «Naturgegebenheiten» und «Gebräuche» als zwei fremde Einheiten einander entgegenzusetzen. Wo der Mensch eine Furche zieht, einen Garten einhegt — oder gar ein Haus baut — folgt er nicht blindlings zwingenden Gesetzen der Umwelt, sondern gibt Eigenes hinzu. Anderseits ist durchaus nicht erforscht und — glaube ich — nicht erforschbar, wieviel in diesem «Eigenen» wieder an Reaktionen auf äussere Gegebenheiten steckt. In Palästina verwandelt die überlieferte Art fremder Völker die Landschaft. Zugleich wird diese Ueberlieferung bei allen Völkern vom Lande Palästina beeinflusst, und es entsteht etwas wie eine gemeinsame Sprache, an der die Bauten der Araber, Griechen, Russen, Deutschen und auch der ersten jüdischen Siedler teilhaben.

Eine Kreuzfahrerkirche unterscheidet sich von einem saladinischen Bau. Sie unterscheidet sich ebenso von einer französischen Kirche des zwölften Jahrhunderts. Sie hat deren Wölbungssystem, ihre Fensterschlüsse und Kapitelle. Aber der ruhige Körper, die grossen Flächen,

oben: Deutsches Templerdorf Wilhelma in der Küstenebene
unten: Alte jüdische Kolonie Rosh Pinah in Galiläa

Top: The German Templer village of Wilhelmina on the coastal plain

Bottom: The old Jewish colony of Rosh Pina in the Galilee

259

similar conditions where different nationalities settled. This observation is even more true with regard to architecture.

Besides landscape and climate, the architect takes account of the customs of indigenous peoples. One must be careful not to pit "natural phenomena" and "customs" against each other as two alien categories. Wherever man plows a furrow, fences off a garden —or perhaps even builds a house—he doesn't blindly follow mandatory laws of the environment, but adds something of his own. On the other hand, it is not yet confirmed—and, in my opinion, may indeed never be confirmed—how much "of his own" is in turn determined by reactions to external conditions. In Palestine, the traditional ways of life of foreign nationalities transform the landscape. At the same time, the traditions of all these nationalities are influenced by the country of Palestine, and something like a common language emerges in which the edifices of the Arabs, Greeks, Russians, Germans, and also the first Jewish settlers all have a part.

A Crusader church differs from a Saladinian structure. It also differs from a French church of the twelfth century. It shares the same system of vaults, the same window arches and capitals. But the serene volume, the expansive surfaces, the small openings, and finally the way sculptural ornaments are concentrated in a few places, the way the masonry bond itself and the inlaid borders of differently colored stone create a vibrant, lucent surface: all of this qualifies it as an Oriental building.

Palestine is essentially the country of foreign nationalities, each of which builds its own "vernacular" architecture into the land. We are not aware of any original Palestinian construction style. We hear of Egyptian and Assyrian elements and Phoenician variations. Later of Greek and Byzantine architectures. The sight of the Machpelah Cave in Hebron—huge, smooth bossage, a large cube, divided by flat pilasters—is so convincing in the Judaean landscape, and the solid walls of Greek monasteries seem so evidently to

kleinen Oeffnungen, endlich die Art, wie plastischer Schmuck an wenige Stellen konzentriert ist, wie der Mauerverband selbst und eingelegte Bänder andersfarbiger Steine eine lebende, schillernde Fläche herstellen, ordnet sie orientalischen Bauten zu.

Palästina ist schlechthin das Land der fremden Völker, deren jedes seine eigene, «bodenständige» Architektur in das Land baut. Wir wissen nichts von irgendeiner ursprünglich palästinensischen Bauart. Wir hören von ägyptischen und assyrischen Elementen und phönikischen Abwandlungen. Später von griechischen und byzantinischen Architekturen. Der Anblick der Höhle Machpela in Hebron: riesige, glatte Bossenquadern, grosser Kubus, durch flache Lisenen gegliedert, wirkt so überzeugend in der judäischen Landschaft, die geschlossenen Mauern griechischer Klöster scheinen so durchaus von diesem Baugeist abgeleitet, dass man glauben möchte, es habe zu Herodes Zeit und vorher eine palästinensische Architektur gegeben.

Wir kennen von dieser Architektur nur Substrukturen, Mauern, Ingenieurbauten grossen Maßstabes (Salomons Talsperren), und es ist bezeichnend, dass ein Platz, ein hochgehobenes, abgestütztes Plateau auf einem der höchsten Hügel — gerade vor dem letzten Kamm, der sich zur Steinwüste abdacht — das grösste Bauwerk Palästinas geblieben ist. Die Schönheit der Moscheen und Brunnen, die sich heute auf diesem Raum befinden, zählt erst in zweiter Linie. Für jeden Besucher ist der Platz selbst, die schimmernde Fläche am Ende einer dunklen Stadt, der überzeugende Eindruck vom «Haram es Sherif».

Diese Monumente sind einzig auch deshalb, weil sie so gar nicht einen Tatbestand ornamental überhöhen. Sie sind die Sache selbst und in dieser Eigenschaft Väter

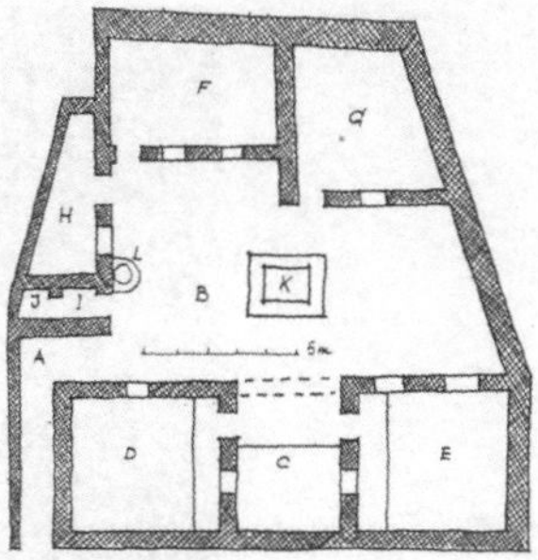


Grundriss eines wohlhabenden Hauses in Damaskus, 1:300

Floor plan of an affluent home in Damascus, 1:300

der palästinensischen Bauart, von der wir sprachen. Diese tritt um so reiner hervor, wenn alle Ueberlieferungen von draussen sich in ihr fast ausgelöscht haben. Wir werden sie im Wohnhaus am ersten finden.

Um diese Bauart im Wohnhaus besser zu erkennen, tut man vielleicht gut, sich die Frage zu stellen: Welches sind die Bedingungen, denen jedes Wohnhaus in Palästina entsprechen muss. Abgesehen vom Material und, folglich, von der Konstruktion, die in den verschiedenen Landschaften sehr verschieden sind, kommen wir da auf eine Reihe von Forderungen, etwa: Das Haus muss vor Regengüssen schützen. Es muss vor Sonnenstrahlen schützen. Es muss den Wind einlassen. Es muss schattige Plätze zum Leben im Freien bieten. Solche Forderungen erklären schon einiges: die starken Mauern, die Art der Fenster, die tiefen Oeffnungen im Baukörper, durch die Wind hereingesaugt wird, die Vorliebe für Lauben, Per-

**Jerusalem**, links Stützmauer des Tempelplatzes; Mitte Soukbasar. Aus einer dieser dunklen, gewölbten Gassen betritt man den Tempelplatz. Rechts Stadttor aus dem XVI. Jahrh., mit starken hölzernen Flügeln geschlossen; es führt ins Dunkle gegen eine Wand

Jerusalem: on the left, retaining walls of the Temple Mount; in the center, a souk bazaar. From one of these dark, arched alleys the Temple Mount is entered. On the right, a city gate from the 16th century, closed with strong wooden doors; it leads into the dark against a wall.

260

be derived from this spirit of construction, that one wants to believe that during the time of Herod and before there must have been a Palestinian architecture.

Of this architecture we know only substructures, walls, large-scale civil engineering projects (Solomon's Pools), and it is telling that a plaza, an elevated, buttressed plateau atop one of the highest hills—just before the final crest that slopes toward the rocky desert—has remained the biggest edifice of Palestine. The beauty of the mosques and fountains situated in this space today counts only secondarily. To every visitor, it is the plaza itself, the gleaming expanse at the end of a gloomy city, that forms the conclusive image of the "Haram es Sherif."

These monuments are unique also because they are by no means mere ornamental elaborations of some other fact. They are the fact itself, and in this function are the progenitors of the Palestinian construction style we mentioned earlier. This style is all the purer where every external influence has been erased. We will first discover it in the dwelling house.

In order to recognize this construction style in the dwelling house, it may be of benefit to ask oneself the following question: What are the conditions that every dwelling house in Palestine must meet? Apart from the material and consequently the construction, which is very different in different landscapes, we arrive at a number of requirements, for example: The house has to offer shelter from heavy rain. It must protect against the sun's rays. It must let in the wind. It must provide shaded spaces for life outdoors. Such requirements already explain a number of things: the thick walls; the type of windows; the deep vents in the structural shell that draw in the wind; the fondness for alcoves, vaults, courtyards, and drafts that are to be found in all Palestinian architectures.

On the other hand are the expectations that different nationalities have of their dwellings. Examples of these include the Arab's

Jerusalem: Temple Mount

Bottom: Near Jerusalem. Walls 60–100 cm thick, in two layers, between them infill of earth and stone chipping. First the barrel vaults are built up; on top of them is a dome finished with exterior clay plaster.

Jerusalem
Tempelplatz

unten:
Bei Jerusalem.
Mauern 60—100 cm dick, in zwei Schichten, dazwischen Füllung aus Erde und Steinschlag; zuerst werden die Schildbögen aufgemauert, darauf die aussen nur mit Erdmörtel eingeebnete Wölbung

golen, Gewölbe, Höfe, Züge, die sich in allen palästinensischen Architekturen finden.

Auf der anderen Seite stehen die Forderungen, welche verschiedene Völker an ihr Wohnhaus stellen. Dahin gehört zum Beispiel das abgekehrte Wohnen des Arabers, seine Geselligkeit, die einen grossen Raum fordert (Halle oder Hof), das Festhalten des schwäbischen Bauers an seinem heimischen Grundriss (Mittelflur, rechts Wohnräume, links Küche) und dergleichen mehr.

Ich komme noch auf eine «ausgleichende» Bedingung zu sprechen, welche in diesem Lande gegenwärtig so wichtig ist, wie sie es in jedem Land in der Vergangenheit war: die Sicherheit. Es mag mit der Diskretion ebenso wie mit der Sicherheit zusammenhängen, dass der Eingang in einen arabischen Hof nie in der Achse geschieht, sondern immer an der Seite und immer in einem gebrochenen Eingangsweg. Dass das gleiche bei allen orientalischen Stadttoren der Fall ist, so dass man niemals das mittelalterlich europäische Bild der Strasse sieht, die sich hinter dem Torbogen entwickelt, sondern stets gegen eine Wand läuft, ist sicher eine reine Verteidigungsmassnahme. Ebenso, dass Dorfeingänge in Schikane verlaufen, und ausserdem möglichst unscheinbar sind. Die Klöster sind starke Festungen. Die ältesten jüdischen Kolonien waren durchaus mit Mauern umgeben; und wenn sie heute offener daliegen, so hat das seinen Grund an einer geänderten Waffentechnik. Immerhin stehen die öffentlichen Gebäude in den Siedlungen auch aus Sicherheitsgründen stets an der beherrschenden Stelle oder am Eingang des Zugangsweges, und die neuesten, vorgeschobenen Siedlergruppen im Jordantal sind befestigte Blockhäuser: eine doppelte Holzwand, mit Erde ausgefüllt und mit reichlichen Schießscharten versehen, umzieht sie; an Diagonalecken sind Bastionen angeordnet; ein Wachtturm steht in der Mitte.

Man kann also folgendes sagen:

Verschiedene Gemeinschaften bauen in Palästina nach der Art, welche sie aus ihren Ursprungsländern mitbringen. Ihre Häuser und Ortschaften, auch die umgebenden Gelände werden nach auswärtigen Urbildern gestaltet. Sie sind aber genötigt, ihre Bauten, mehr oder weniger bewusst, nach der palästinensischen Umwelt zu richten. Es sei nicht verschwiegen, dass an dem glücklichen Ergebnis dieses Vorganges die gleichmässige Verwendung heimischer Handwerker im Dienst verschiedenster Völker beteiligt ist.

261

secluded way of living and his gregariousness, which calls for a large room (hall or courtyard); the Swabian farmer's stubborn adherence to his native floor plan (central hallway, living area on the right, kitchen on the left); and other such phenomena.

I must also mention an "equalizing" condition that is as important in this country at present as it was in every country in the past: security. It may relate to discretion as much as to security that the entrance to an Arab courtyard never runs along the axis but always opens from the side, the passage always taking a sharp turn. That this is the case with all Oriental city gates, and that one never finds the medieval European vista of the street that opens behind the archway, but rather always walks against a wall, must surely be a purely defensive measure. That access roads to villages follow a meandering course and are as inconspicuous as possible will have the same reason. The monasteries are strong fortresses. The oldest Jewish colonies were in fact also surrounded by walls; if they are more exposed today it is because of changed weapons technology. But public buildings in the settlements are still built in a dominant location or at the entrance to the approach road, and the newest settler outposts in the Jordan Valley are fortified blockhouses: they are surrounded by a double wall, filled with earth, and equipped with plenty of embrasures; turrets are placed on diagonal corners; a watchtower stands at the center.

We can ascertain the following:

In Palestine, different communities build according to the customs they have brought with them from their countries of origin. Their houses and their villages or towns, as well as the surrounding terrain, are shaped according to foreign archetypes. They are, however, compelled to make their buildings, more or less consciously, correspond to the Palestinian environment. The positive result of this process is in part due to the prevalent employment of local craftsmen in the service of the most diverse nationalities.

«Nationale Baukunst»

links oben: «Alt-Tel-Aviv», Ecke Allenbystrasse Bld. Rothschild. Transformatorenhäuschen von Architekt A. Bärwald (die Wohnhäuser bestehen nicht mehr, sie waren nicht schlecht)

darunter: Technion in Haifa
Architekt A. Bärwald

rechts: Anglo-Palästinabank, Haifa
Architekt A. Bärwald, ca. 1925

"National architecture"
Top left: "Old Tel Aviv," corner of Allenby Street and Rothschild Boulevard. Electricity substation by architect A. Bärwald (the dwelling houses don't exist anymore; they weren't bad).
Bottom: Technion in Haifa
Architect A. Bärwald
Right: Anglo-Palestine Bank, Haifa
Architect A. Bärwald, ca. 1925

Wie steht nun in diesem Zusammenhang das jüdische Bauen?

Tatbestände:

1. Die Juden kommen von den verschiedensten Ländern. Fällt schon der Unterschied zwischen den Wohngewohnheiten im polnischen «Städtel» und in der Grunewaldvilla ins Auge, um wieviel mehr der zwischen beiden und Ymen oder Buchara. Sie zusammen anzusiedeln ist nicht möglich, und in der Tat bleiben die Landsmannschaften im grossen ganzen geschieden. Auf jeden Fall orientalische und europäische Juden. Es könnte also sein, dass die jüdischen Völker ein jedes seine eigenen Wohnsitten mitbringt. Aber, wie in allen Dingen, ist auch hier die jüdische Situation ein Unikum. Seine eigenen Ueberlieferungen bringt der Jude nicht mit; eher schon die seines Wirtslandes. Und doch gibt es etwas wie eine jüdische Wohnweise, aber man kann sie fast nur definieren, indem man die Eigenschaften zeigt, die sie nicht besitzt. Keine engere Beziehung zur Umwelt und keine soziale oder berufliche Prägung. Es ist eine städtische Wohnweise — auch, wo auf dem Lande gewohnt wird.

Es gibt freilich jüdische Gewohnheiten, welche sehr wohl sich im Plan der Wohnung niederschlagen dürften: der starke Familienzusammenhang, die ebenso starke Familiengeselligkeit. Aber unter den traurigen Verhältnissen des Judentums in der Welt ist es zu keiner Gestaltung gekommen. Und diejenigen, welche in bessere Lebenssphären kamen, haben sich diesen Kreisen leidenschaftlich assimiliert, wobei ihnen überall eine städtische Oberschicht Vorbild war, welche selbst nur noch über sehr wenig geformte Art von Wohnen besass. Die Juden kommen ohne Bautradition ins Land.

2. Sie leisten bald Verzicht auf die einheimische Bauarbeit. Sie übernehmen dies Geschäft selbst. Dies geschah nicht sofort. Während der Jahre von 1885 bis nach dem Kriege, den Jahren der Alliance Israélite, der Rothschild-Kolonisation und der ersten russischen Siedler wurden die Häuser fast durchweg von arabischen Handwerkern ausgeführt. — Selbstverständlich war das der Fall bei den noch älteren Vorstädten von Jerusalem, welche von ausländischen Spendern für fromme Juden gebaut wurden (Mea Shearim, Montefiore, Warschau). — Erst nach dem Kriege beginnt sich die «Eroberung der Arbeit» fühlbar zu machen. Von da an verdrängt die Betonfachwerkwand die Steinwand, und nun tauchen sofort Fragen auf, und keineswegs nur ästhetische Fragen.

Schutz vor Hitze und Bestrahlung, welche die ara-



In this context, what is the situation of Jewish construction?

The facts of the case are:

1. The Jews come from a great range of different countries. If the difference between living habits in the Polish shtetl and the Grunewald mansion is already striking, how much greater it must be between these two and Yemen or Bukhara. To settle the inhabitants of both in the same place is impossible, and the different national groups remain largely segregated. Or the Oriental and European Jews do, at any rate. It is possible, then, that the various Jewish ethnicities bring their own customs of dwelling with them. But in this matter, as in all others, the Jewish situation is unique. The Jew does not bring with him his own traditions, but rather those of his host country. And yet there is something that can be called a Jewish mode of living, but this can really only be defined by pointing out the attributes it lacks. No close connection to the environment and no social or vocational heritage. It is an urban mode of living—even where the living takes place in the countryside.

There are of course Jewish habits that may indeed find expression in the layout of a dwelling house: the strong family cohesion, the equally strong familial sociability. But under the woeful conditions faced by Jewry around the world, this has not resulted in design. And those who ascended into better spheres of life have been eager to assimilate into these circles, always modeling themselves on an urban upper class which had in itself preserved little in the way of an established mode of dwelling. The Jews come into the country without an architectural tradition.

2. They soon renounce local construction labor. They take on this trade themselves. This did not happen outright. In the years from 1885 until the end of the Great War, the years of the Alliance Israélite, the Rothschild colonization, and the first Russian settlers, houses were almost exclusively erected by Arab craftsmen.—This was also the case, of course, with the older suburbs of Jerusalem (Mea Shearim, Montefiore, Warsaw) which were built by foreign benefactors for devout Jews.—Only after the war does the "conquest of labor"

"National architecture"

«Nationale Baukunst»

Top two photographs: Archaeological Museum of Palestine. Architect Harrison, Jerusalem

Right: Headquarters of the Zionist Executive Concrete construction, clad in ashlar Architect Eugen Ratner

die beiden oberen:
Das Archäologische Museum von Palästina. Architekt Harrison, Jerusalem

rechts:
Sitz der zionistischen Exekutive
Betonbau, mit Haustein verkleidet
Architekt Eugen Ratner

bische Wand aus zwei Steinschichten mit dazwischen gegebenem Lehmbeton gewährt, musste nun ausserhalb der reinen Konstruktion gesucht werden. Diese Schwierigkeit ist ja allgemein mit dem Fortschritt der Konstruktion verbunden, ja, macht wohl das Wesen dieses Fortschrittes aus: dass die tragenden und die schützenden Funktionen, welche die dicke Mauer zugleich ausübt, von verschiedenen Baugliedern übernommen werden. Das Betonfachwerk trägt; Ausfachung, Luftraum und poröse Schicht isolieren. Für den Sonnenschutz müssen besondere Gesimse oder Ausbauten sorgen.

Dass der jüdische Handwerker anfangs keine sehr gute berufliche Bildung besass — ein Mangel, der erstaunlich schnell behoben wurde — scheint neben dieser Schwierigkeit weniger wesentlich.

Noch einen Punkt müssen wir berühren: Wir haben gesagt, was die Juden nicht mitbrachten. Sie brachten aber auch etwas mit, wenigstens die letzte Welle der Einwanderung. Man hat in Deutschland die Architektur der flachen Dächer, Fensterbänder, Kragplatten, Eckfenster, Treppenschlitze und «dynamischen» Gesimse «Laubhüttenarchitektur» genannt und sie aus unserem orientalischen Blut herleiten wollen. Wahr ist, dass sie hier fremd und europäisch wirkt. Aber wahr ist ebenfalls, dass die jüdischen Baumeister und das jüdische Publikum dieser Architektur nachhängen, vielleicht als einem Erbe aus den zehn Jahren verhältnismässiger Unangefochtenheit, die sie in Mitteleuropa genossen. Wie manche politischen Theorien der gleichen Zeit erscheint sie ihnen noch «fortschrittlich», da sie doch nachgerade historisch wird. Der «moderne Stil» überwand das östliche «Städtel» und auch die Versuche einer nationalen Architektur, die vor dem Kriege unternommen wurden, und so kommt es, dass unsere Strassen neueren Vierteln von Steglitz im grossen ganzen recht ähnlich sehen, mit dem Unterschied nur, dass in Tel-Aviv die Miethäuser einzeln stehen, nicht aneinandergebaut, und einander eine lange Reihe von Küchenbalkons, Bädern, Rohrleitungen — leider auch Zimmern — auf nächste Sicht zukehren. Dass unsere Strassenprofile, Plätze, Ladenstrassen anders aussehen dürften als die einer fortschrittlichen europäischen Stadt, ist unseren Städtebauern nicht deutlicher zum Bewusstsein gekommen, als denen irgendeines kolonialen Landes, und ein Entwurf, wie der von Mendelsohn für einen modernen Bazar mit überdeckten Ladengassen (Business-Centre Haifa, 1923), wird wohl noch heute nicht recht goutiert.

Die Aufgabe der Juden war also eine andere, als die

263

become palpable. From then on the concrete shear wall replaces the stone wall, and immediately questions arise, by no means only of an aesthetic nature.

Protection from heat, as provided by the Arab wall of two layers of stone with mud concrete as infill, now had to be sought outside the construction itself. This challenge is generally connected to progress in construction and, yes, it probably represents the very essence of this progress: that the load-bearing and the protective functions carried out simultaneously by a thick wall are taken on by different structural elements. The concrete framework bears the load; infill, cavities, and a porous layer contribute to insulation. Protection against the sun must be provided by special cornices or bays.

The Jewish tradesman's initial lack of solid vocational training —a deficiency that was overcome with remarkable speed—seems less crucial in comparison to this challenge.

We must touch upon another point: We have stated what the Jews did not bring with them. They did, however, bring something, or at least the last wave of immigration did. In Germany the architecture of flat roofs, ribbon windows, cantilever plates, corner windows, stairwells, and "dynamic cornices" has been called "Succoth architecture," and an attempt was made to seek its origin in our Oriental bloodline. The truth is that out here it appears foreign and European. But it is also true that the Jewish architects and the Jewish public are very fond of this architecture, maybe as a result of the relatively uncontested status they enjoyed during the past decade in central Europe. Like some of the political theories of that same period, these things still appeal as "progressive" to them when really they are on the verge of becoming essentially historical. The "modern style" overcame the Eastern shtetl as well as the attempts at a national architecture that were made before the war, and it is for this reason that our streets are by and large fairly similar to the newer parts of Steglitz, the only difference being that in Tel Aviv the blocks of flats are self-contained rather than contiguous and have long rows of kitchen balconies, baths, exposed plumbing—as well as living rooms, unfortunately—facing each other. That our street profiles, plazas, shopping streets might look different than those in a progressive

der anderen Völker, die nach Palästina gekommen sind. Sie kamen ohne Tradition. Was sie mitbrachten und, ungenau genug, modernes Baudenken nannten, war eine Mode. Hatten andere Völker ihre eigene Art dem Lande anzupassen — wobei die Beschäftigung einheimischer Bauleute ihnen eine Erleichterung bot — so hatten die Juden in diesem Lande ganz neu zu beginnen. Die Aufgaben, die sie vor sich sahen, waren übrigens nicht nur für sie selbst neu. Genossenschaftliche und kollektive Siedlungen, Planung landwirtschaftlicher Distrikte sind an sich neue Gegenstände der Planung. Um sie mit dem Lande in Beziehung zu bringen, tat man wohl gut daran, früheres palästinensisches Bauen zu betrachten und zu versuchen, das herauszufinden, was daran, wie wir sahen, «allgemein palästinensisch» ist. Bewusste Beobachtung musste bei uns an die Stelle dessen treten, was bei anderen Völkern eine unwillkürliche Umformung gewesen war.

Aber diese Beobachtung wurde in den Jahren des hastigen Aufbaues kaum gemacht. Der jüdische Architekt kennt nur ganz obenhin die Bauarten des Landes. Bücher und Dokumente darüber sind so gut wie nicht vorhanden. Universität, «Technion», oder auch die Zionistische Organisation, welche sich wohl damit beschäftigen dürfte, war von Aktualität, Politik, Propaganda absorbiert. In der nationalen Kolonisation war für solche Unternehmungen kein Widerhall; und heute, wo er sehr stark ist, macht die Gefahr jede Annäherung an die Häuser unserer feindlichen Mitbürger unmöglich.

So wurde nicht betrachtet und gesichtet, sondern es wurde nur das Auffällige, eben das Exotische bemerkt und auch nachgeahmt. Das kam dem Bestreben entgegen, einen nationalen Stil zu finden, ein Bestreben, so alt wie der politische Zionismus selbst. Herzl spielt oft darauf an, und in seinen Tagebüchern findet sich die Zeichnung zu einem Regierungsbau mit Hufeisenbögen und Zinnen. Wenn Alexander Bärwald (wichtige Bauten zwischen 1912 und 1930) mehr gesehen hatte, so sind doch in seinem Werk wesentliche und unwesentliche Beobachtungen gemischt, und die Zinnen und Kuppeltürme

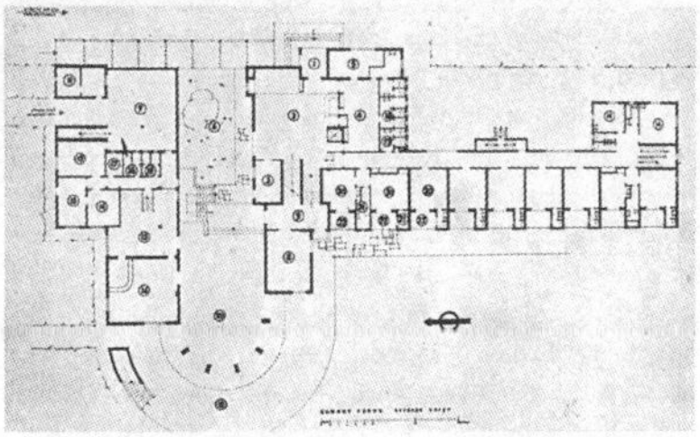

oben (mit Grundriss): Hotel Teltsch auf dem Westrücken des Berges Karmel, mit Blick über den Forst westwärts zum Meer. Die Badezimmer sind zwischen den Gastzimmern vorgezogen; so entstehen abgeschlossene Loggien vor den Zimmern. Unter dem Speisesaal ein luftiger Tanzsaal im Freien. Architekt Leopold Krakauer.

Top (with floor plan): Hotel Teltsch on the western ridge of Mount Carmel, with a view westward over a forest toward the sea. The bathrooms protrude between the guest rooms, creating enclosed loggias in front of the rooms. Below the dining room an airy alfresco ballroom. Architect Leopold Krakauer.

Neue Aufgaben:

Speisehäuser für Kollektivsiedlungen im Tal Jesreel, beide von Arch. Leopold Krakauer (mit techn. Bureau der Jewish Agency)
oben: Beth Alpha, unten: Tel Yossef
(Gründungen des Keren Hayesod, auf N. F.-Boden)

New objectives:
Canteens for collective settlements in the Jezreel Valley, both by architect Leopold Krakauer (with the Jewish Agency's Technical Bureau)
Top: Beth Alpha; bottom: Tel Yosef (established by Keren Hayesod, on National Fund land)

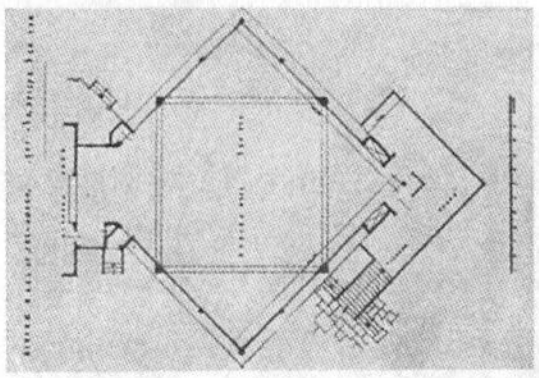

264

European city did not enter the consciousness of our planners any more than it would those of any colonial country, and a design like that of Mendelsohn for a modern bazaar with covered shopping alleys (business center in Haifa, 1923) is still not really appreciated, even today.

The role of the Jews was, therefore, different from that of other nations who came to Palestine. They came without tradition. What they brought with them and somehow inaccurately referred to as modern architectural thought was just a fashion. While other nationalities had to adapt their traditions to the country—the employment of local builders made this much easier for them—the Jews had to start from scratch in this country. It must be added that the objectives they saw in front of them were not new to them alone. Cooperative and collective settlements and the planning of agricultural districts are in themselves novel objects of planning. In order to relate them to the country, one was well advised to examine earlier Palestinian construction and to try to establish what could be described as Palestinian, as we saw earlier. In our case, conscious observation had to take the place that instinctive adaptation took for the other peoples.

But this observation was scarcely made during the years of rushed development. The Jewish architect has only a superficial knowledge of the country's building styles. There are hardly any books or documents on this subject. University, "Technion," and the Zionist Organization, which doubtless should have been concerned with this matter, were absorbed by the current situation, by politics, and by propaganda. Within the national colonization effort there was no interest in such endeavors; and today, when interest is immense, the inherent danger makes any approach to the houses of our hostile fellow citizens impossible.

Thus we did not look and survey, but really only noticed—and indeed imitated—that which seemed exotic. This suited the effort of establishing a national style, an effort that is as old as political Zionism itself. Herzl often alluded to it, and his diaries contain the drawing of a government building with horseshoe arches and battlements. While Alexander Bärwald (important buildings between 1912 and 1930) understood more, in his work essential and nonessential observations are conflated and the battlements and

haben späteren Beobachtern den Zugang zu dem verwehrt, was aus diesen Bauten zu lernen war.

Bärwald baute Vollbetonwände, mit Stein verkleidet. Etwa 15 cm Beton, 12 cm Bruchstein. Man baut allgemein so in Jerusalem. Die dünne Aussenwand sucht er dadurch zu vertiefen, dass er in grössere Räume gern eine Pfeilerstellung mit wenig Abstand von der Wand hineinstellt. Das Licht wird so, wie durch Kulissen, vom Rauminnern entfernt. Oder er umrahmt Baukörper mit weit vorstehenden Pfeilern und Bögen, deren tiefe Nische eine massive Wand vortäuscht. Am Technion hat er dies beim Mittelbau und den beiden Eckkörpern getan. Freilich wirken dann die Klassentrakte mit ihren gereihten Fenstern in flacher Wand doppelt zerbrechlich zwischen festen Türmen. Die Hofseite mit offenen Arkadengängen vor den Klassen ist überzeugender. Hier braucht der Baumeister nichts vorzutäuschen. Bärwald war verliebt in das Zufällige freistehender arabischer Häuser: stark gestaffelte Baukörper mit herausgezogenem, kleinem Erker, einer dünnen Aussentreppe, die womöglich bis zur obersten Etage führt, unregelmässig über die Flächen gestreute Oeffnungen, wo dann oft in der Mitte, oder ganz oben, der grosse Bogen einer Loggia sich öffnet. Er ergriff diese Bauart mit grösstem Geschick und übertrieb sie. In seinen Villen fehlt auch nie die grosse, tief eingeschnittene Loggia hinter Arkaden. Aber ihr Grundriss bleibt gut muthesianisch und es fällt ihm nicht ein, etwa den grossen, freien Raum im Innern des Hauses nachzuahmen, an welchem die Treppe aufsteigt, in den ein Teil der Zimmer sich öffnet, um Gegenluft zu erhalten, in dessen unterem Teil man auf kühlen Bänken Stunden des Tages sitzt; und dieser Raum ist ja wohl der grösste Reiz solcher halb städtischen arabischen Häuser.

So blieb dies Werk zwitterhaft, zwischen Auswertung gewusster Tatsachen und Bauen nach dem Reiseskizzenbuch. Es kam viel darauf an, nach welcher Seite man es entwickeln würde.

Sieht man das Haus der zionistischen Institutionen in Jerusalem an, so meint man, es sei hier die Bärwaldsche

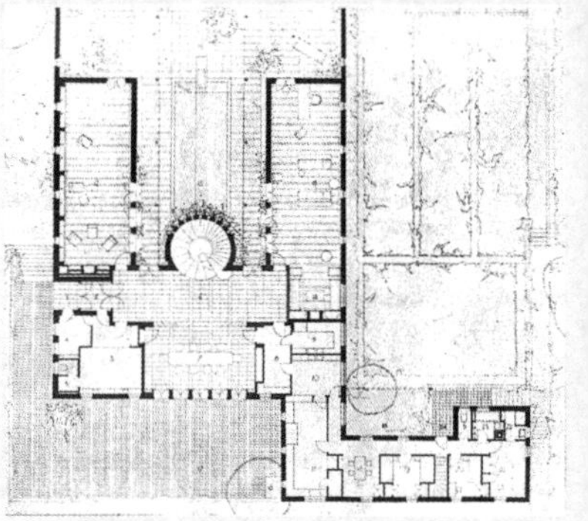

Neue Aufgaben:
Haus Chajim Weizmann, Rehovoth
Architekt Erich Mendelsohn, ehemals Berlin
Im Grundriss: Eingang von links, in der Ecke links unten Garderobe, Portier usw.; im Flügel links vom offenen Hof Bibliothek, rechts grosser Wohnraum, axial unter dem Treppenturm Halle und Esszimmer, im Anbau rechts unten Küche, Dienerschaft usw.

New objectives:
Chaim Weizmann residence, Rehovot
Architect Erich Mendelsohn, formerly of Berlin
In the floor plan: Entrance on the left, downstairs in the left corner the cloakroom, concierge, etc.; in the wing left of the open courtyard the library, on the right a large living room, axially below the stairwell tower lobby and dining room, in the extension on the right kitchen, domestic staff, etc.

links: Bld. Rothschild in Tel-Aviv

Left: Rothschild Boulevard in Tel Aviv

265

cupolas have denied later observers access to the lessons that could have been learned from these structures.

Bärwald built solid concrete walls, clad with stone. Approximately 15 cm of concrete, 12 cm crushed stone. This is the universal way of building in Jerusalem. He tries to deepen the thin outer shell by adding columns close to the walls of larger rooms. Thus the light is deflected from the interior space, as if through stage wings. Or he frames volumes with prominent columns and arches, their deep recesses feigning a solid wall. In the case of the Technion, he has done this with the central block and both corner volumes. Of course, this causes the classroom wings, with their lines of windows in a flat wall, to appear even more fragile between sturdy towers. The courtyard side with open arcades in front of the classrooms is more convincing. Here the architect does not have to feign anything. Bärwald was in love with the randomness of detached Arab houses: densely staggered volumes with a small, prominent bay window, narrow external stairs that may even lead all the way to the top floor, apertures spread randomly across the surfaces, often with the grand arch of a recessed balcony opening up in the center or at the very top. He adopted this design with great skill and exaggerated it. Nor do his villas ever lack the generous, deeply recessed balcony behind arcades. But their floor plan remains faithfully Methusian, and he never considers imitating the large, open space inside the building which is accessed by the stairs, which opens to some of the rooms so that they may receive ventilation, which in its lower parts provides a place to sit on cool benches for many hours of the day; although it really is this space that represents the main appeal of such semi-urban Arab houses.

Thus this body of work remains a hybrid of an analysis of known facts and building after a traveler's sketchbook. Much depended on the direction in which it would be developed.

Looking at the Zionist Institutions House in Jerusalem, one gets the impression that here the Bärwaldian style has been refined and rid of tedious adornments. It is a delicate building, the stone cladding expertly executed to appear quite "stonelike," punctuated by narrow windows. The building blocks have elegant volume and

Genossenschaftliches Dorf Nahalal (Keren Hayesod) im Tal Jesreel. Stadtplan und Haustypus von Architekt Richard Kaufmann (und Jewish Agency)

Kleinere Anwesen: Familienarbeit, keine Knechte, gemeinschaftliche Einkaufs- und Verkaufsorganisation, gemeinsam benutzte Maschinen. Dorfkern: Volkshaus, Schule, Lager, Krankenkasse. Am Eingang des Zufahrtsweges (links unten) Mädchenfarm der Women Internationel Zionist Organisation (W.I.Z.O.). Im Ring kleine Anwesen: Hilfswirtschaften für Lehrer, Kaufleute, Handwerker. Aussen Siedlerhäuser. Intensive Kulturen beim Haus: Obst, Gemüse, bewässertes Futter. Weiter aussen Orangen, dann Getreide.

unten:
Genossenschaftliche Siedlung Kfar Jeheskel im Tal Jesreel (Keren Hayesod, Boden: Nationalfonds)
Architekt Richard Kaufmann, Jerusalem (u. Jewish Agency) Organisation wie vorhin, «Forum» an beherrschender Stelle, grössere Bauten in der Strassengabelung

Art weiterentwickelt, von störendem Beiwerk befreit. Es ist ein taktvoller Bau, seine Steinverkleidung mit grossem Wissen recht «steinern» ausgeführt, von schmalen Fenstern unterbrochen. Die Körper haben schöne Volumen und sind gut gegeneinandergestellt. Aber einmal hineingetreten, vergisst man das Aeussere ganz. Man befindet sich in einem nicht organisierten Verwaltungsbau mit vielen Winkeln und ohne bedeutende Mitte und man merkt, dass der Ehrenhof ohne Inhalt und die «gemässigt orientalische» Haltung ohne inneren Sinn ist. Mit den malerischen Einzelheiten sind zugleich alle wesentlichen Züge fortgefallen, welche Glanz und Wärme Palästinas so oft denen eingegeben hat, die hier bauten.

Ganz erfüllt von diesen Anregungen sind dagegen die Bauten des Engländers Harrison, Architekten des Public Works' Department. Sein zerrissener, weisser Museumsbau ist eine wahre Schule der Möglichkeiten hiesiger Architektur. Man betrachte den Hof, die Arbeitshöfe, die Lichtführung in den Ausstellungssälen. Man muss freilich sagen, dass dieser Bau in der landesüblichen Bauart ausgeführt ist. Wo er in Beton gebaut ist — in den beiden langen Ausstellungssälen an den Längsseiten des Hofes — wird durch tiefe innere Strebepfeiler ein Mittel gefunden, die breiten, der Konstruktion angemessenen Fenster in genügendem Abstande vom Raum zu halten.

In der gleichen Richtung, eine heutige, palästinensische Architektur zu finden, bewegen sich die Arbeiten von Erich Mendelsohn. Ein Körper, wie der des Hauses Weizmann in Rechovoth, erscheint echt, nicht ungenau beobachtet, wie die von Ratner, oder angelsächsisch getrübt, wie die von Harrison. Mir scheint, dass der orientalische Baumeister, wo er es vermeiden kann, nicht zwei Baukörper hart, Quader neben Quader, zusammenstellt, sondern den einen aus dem anderen entwickelt. Mendelsohn hat diese Art zu komponieren immer geliebt. Er fühlt sich beim Anblick der arabischen Dörfer aufs schönste bestätigt. Freilich hat dieser Aufbau bei ihm einen anderen Sinn als beim orientalischen Hause. Bei diesem sucht man die grosse Fläche, die sich aus einem Baukörper in den nächsten hinein fortsetzt, weil alles Abgesetzte, das unter nördlichem Himmel frei und lebhaft wirken würde, unter dem weissen Licht Palästinas zerklüftet erscheint. So ruht das Haus, in sich selbst zurückgebogen, Bauteil an Bauteil flächig angeschlossen. Mendelsohn reisst Fläche aus Fläche, umfährt die wachsenden Körper mit einer ungebrochenen Kontur, einem Bewegungszug, der stets in einer Bewegungsspitze gipfelt. Das Haus Weizmann wäre ein Baukörper dieses Landes, ohne den Treppenturm. Diese Dominante bringt einen fremden Klang in den Akkord. Das Treppenhaus wäre gut denkbar seitlich, im Hintergrund der langen Halle, welche dadurch erst eine Verbindung mit dem Patio erhalten hätte. Die Raumgruppe: gesammeltes Esszimmer hinter Ostterrasse, breite Halle, an den westlichen Hof gelagert, hätte sich so frei wie möglich ausleben dürfen. Das Haus liegt auf einem Hügel, inmitten des Fruchtlandes von Judäa. Man sieht Gebirge im Osten über die Terrasse, Meer im Westen durch den Hof. Aber ein Treppenhaus mit dünnen Schlitzfenstern fährt vor der Halle nieder und verstellt den Hof, der Mittelraum

266

New objectives:
Cooperative village Nahalal (Keren Hayesod) in the Jezreel Valley. Urban layout and house type by architect Richard Kaufmann [*sic*] (and the Jewish Agency).
Smaller properties: Family labor, no servants, shared purchase and sale organization, shared use of machinery. Village core: community center, school, stores, health-insurance company. At the entrance of the approach road (bottom left): girls' farm of the Women['s] International Zionist Organization (W.I.Z.O.). Inside the ring, small properties: allotments for teachers, merchants, artisans. Outside the ring: settler houses. Intensive cultivation around the houses: fruit, vegetables, irrigated crops for animal feed. Further out: oranges, then cereal crops.

Bottom:
Cooperative settlement Kfar Jeheskel in the Jezreel Valley (Keren Hayesod, land: National Fund)
Architect Richard Kaufmann [*sic*], Jerusalem (and the Jewish Agency)
Organization as above, "forum" in commanding position, larger buildings on the road junction.

are well arranged. But as soon as one enters the building, the exterior is instantly forgotten. One is now inside a disorganized administrative building full of nooks and crannies and void of any significant center, and one realizes that the forecourt is void of substance and the "moderate Oriental" approach lacks inner purpose. The picturesque details have fallen by the wayside, and with them all those essential characteristics that the brilliance and warmth of Palestine have so often inspired in those who built here.

The buildings of the Englishman Harrison, an architect in the Public Works Department, are in contrast deeply suffused with these inspirations. His serrated, white museum building is a veritable school of the potential of local architecture: observe the main courtyard, the work yards, the lighting design in the exhibition halls. Of course, we must add that this building is constructed in the customary local way. Where it is constructed from concrete—in both of the long exhibition halls on the long sides of the courtyard—deeply recessed buttresses are employed to keep the wide windows, suitably proportioned to match the overall structure, at a sufficient distance to the room.

A similar route toward the formation of a contemporary Palestinian architecture is pursued by Erich Mendelsohn. A structure like that of the Weizmann House in Rehovot appears genuine, neither imprecisely observed like those by Ratner nor marred by an Anglo-Saxon hue like those of Harrison. It seems to me that the Oriental architect will at all costs avoid pairing two volumes hastily, cuboid to cuboid, but rather derive one from the other. Mendelsohn always loved this way of composing. To him, looking at Arab villages is the sweetest vindication. Of course, in his case, the composition serves a different purpose than it does in the Oriental home. There one strives for the expansive surface that continues from one edifice to the next, because all that is contrastive and may appear lively under a northern sky seems jagged under the white light of Palestine. This way the building is settled, curved back into itself, with all the building's components joined on a single plane. Mendelsohn draws one surface from another, framing the growing volume with an uninterrupted contour, a kinetic stroke that always culminates in a kinetic climax. The Weizmann House would be a building of this

New objectives:
The beginnings of the collective settlement Mishmar Haemek.

Tents, prefabs, as soon as possible a solid stone building for defense and the accommodation of the children.

Bottom:
New settlement spot in the Jordan Valley, Beth Joseph. The standardized walls are prepared the settlement where the new one is established. Location and time are kept secret, and the settlement is erected in a single day.

Settlements of Keren Hayesod. Land: National Fund
Bottom: Settler house with bay windows near Pardes Hanna
Architect Harry Rosenthal

Neue Aufgaben

Die Anfänge einer Kollektivsiedlung Mishmar Haemek.

Zelte, Baracken, möglichst bald ein festes Steinhaus zur Verteidigung und zur Unterbringung der Kinder

unten:
Neuer Siedlungspunkt im Jordantal Beth Joseph. Die Standardwände werden in der Siedlung vorbereitet, von wo aus die Gründung erfolgt. Ort und Zeit wird geheim gehalten, und die Siedlung an einem Tag aufgestellt

des Hauses hätte sein können. Was der Treppenturm übriglässt, belegt ein Schwimmbecken, und man muss schon ins Wasser springen, um sich an der Schönheit des Hofraumes zu erfreuen. Selten ist ein Bau der Wahrheit so nahe gewesen — um dann vom Architekten selbst in Frage gestellt zu werden. Die Sache verdient darum, dass man näher darauf eingeht, weil nicht Schmuckwerk kopiert wurde, sondern wesentliche Elemente: Aufbau des Hauses, Patio, wurden lebhaft gefühlt und im letzten missverstanden, wie wir meinen.

Solche Missverständnisse begegnen auch im einzelnen, wo der moderne Architekt glaubt, in weitem Sinne traditionell zu bauen. Ein Fenster ist, hierzulande, von aussen gesehen, ein Auge im ruhigen Gesicht des Hauses; von innen ein tiefer Schacht aus Kühle und Gewölbeschatten ins gleissend Helle. Die Fensterform: ob hoch und schmal, oder quadratisch, oder auch breit, spielt keine grosse Rolle. Im arabischen Haus ist sie nicht allzu hoch, oft quadratisch durch das Zusammenkoppeln zweier Fenster unter einem Bogen. Macht man nun hohe, schmale Fenster und reiht sie zu langem Band, so ist das, um mich eines Beispiels aus der Syntax zu bedienen, als ob man den Akzent auf den Nebensatz legt. Man hat die Fenster*form* sehr ernst genommen, und dann das schmale Fenster, das man südlich nennt, in einer hanseatischen Weise angewandt: Reihung mit schmalen Pfeilern. Man hat endlich die Oeffnungen in eine «Steinwand» geschnitten, die in Wahrheit eine Betonwand ist, und nicht die Steinverkleidung gibt einer ausgestanzten Tafel Schwere und Tiefe.[1]

Siedlungen des Keren Hayesod, Boden: Nationalfonds
unten: Siedlerhaus mit Fenstererkern bei Pardess Hanna
Architekt Harry Rosenthal

Diese Art der Kritik lässt den Verdacht aufkommen, als verlangten wir, dass diese modernen Villen genauer nach orientalischen Vorbildern kopiert würden. Keineswegs. Was wir meinen, ist, dass alle Versuche, aus Orient und unserer Art zu leben, eine Synthese zu finden, bisher in sich selbst widerspruchsvoll geblieben sind. Ich fände nichts einzuwenden gegen ein Haus, welches aus dünnem, sichtbarem Betonskelett ein langes Fensterband weit hervorzieht und auf neue Art mit dem beissenden Licht fertig wird. Im Lesesaal der Bibliothek Schocken (Mendelsohn) tritt das Licht durch ein schmales Fensterband, unter der Decke einer Längswand ein. Diese Wand erscheint verstärkt durch die vorgebauten Bücherschränke. Die gegenüberliegende Wand, ebenso ausgebildet, ist bis zur Decke geschlossen. Aber eine Oeffnung, in der Mitte, die vom Boden bis zur Decke reicht, lässt ein starkes, belebendes Licht einstrahlen. Das sind gewiss keine traditionellen Mittel der Lichtführung;

[1] Es ist interessant, zu bemerken, dass auf der Strassenseite die gleichen, gereihten Fenster hinter einer tiefen Pergola sehr überzeugend wirken.

267

country were it not for the stairwell tower. This dominant feature adds an alien sound to the chord. The staircase would be conceivable at the side, behind the long hall which would only thus have acquired a connection to the patio. The ensemble of rooms—gathered dining room behind the eastern terrace, wide hall attached to the western courtyard—could thus have unfolded as freely as possible. The house is situated on a hill amid the fertile country of Judea. On the eastern side, you can see the mountains over the terrace, on the western side the sea through the courtyard. But a stairwell with narrow slit windows runs down right in front of the hall, blocking the courtyard, which could have been the central room of the building. What little is spared by the staircase tower is occupied by a swimming pool, and one really must dive into the water to enjoy the courtyard's beauty. Rarely has a structure been so close to the truth—only to be called into question by the architect himself. The matter thus merits closer attention, since it wasn't ornamentation that was copied, but essential elements: the structure's makeup and the patio were vividly perceived but finally misunderstood, in our opinion.

Such misunderstandings are also encountered wherever the modern architect believes himself to be building in a broadly traditional manner. In this country, a window seen from the outside represents an eye in the calm face of the house; seen from the inside, it is a deep duct of coolness and shade leading into blinding brightness. The window shape—whether tall and narrow, or square, or wide—is of no great importance. In the Arab house, it is not all-too-tall, often forming a square when two windows are paired under one arch. If one now makes tall, narrow windows and strings them together in a long row, it is the same as if one were to put the accent on the subordinate clause, to use an analogy from the realm of syntax. One would have given due attention to the shape of the window, only to then employ the same narrow window commonly referred to as southern in a Hanseatic fashion: strung together with thin mullions. In the end, one has cut the openings into a "stone wall" that is really a concrete wall, and a perforated panel does not gain weight and depth from stone cladding.[1]

This type of criticism may feed the assumption that we think all these modern villas ought to be more faithful copies of Oriental

Privatkrankenhaus «Assutah» in Tel-Aviv. Arch. Joseph Neufeld. Ansicht von Westen

Links Behandlungsräume, vor den Patientenzimmern 3 m tiefe Terrassen. In der Mitte Einzelzimmer mit eingeschnittenen Loggien. Die Krankensäle liegen gegen Westen, erhalten aber über die niederen Gänge hinweg auch Lüftung von Osten.

Private hospital "Assuta" in Tel Aviv. Architect Joseph Neufeld. View from the west.

On the left are consulting rooms, in front of the ward rooms terraces, 3 m deep. At the center single private rooms with recessed loggias. The wards face west but are also ventilated from the east by way of the low hallways.

aber dieser Raum lebt vom palästinensischen Licht und lässt die Möglichkeiten erkennen, die es dem Architekten in die Hand gibt. Wir sagten ja, was beobachtet werden sollte: nicht die einzelne Form, sondern das «Gemeinsame» palästinensischer Architektur. Und um uns über dieses Gemeinsame und den Grund, warum man es beobachtet, besser verständlich zu machen, möchte ich sagen: Das Ziel einer solchen Beobachtung ist, aus den Lösungen die Aufgabe zurückzugewinnen, die man sodann mit unseren Mitteln zu lösen versucht. Wer einwenden möchte, dass so intellektuellem Vorgehen die Beobachtung unnötig würde, da man ja die Aufgabe unmittelbar postulieren könne, dem möchte ich erwidern, dass, in einem fremden Lande, immer erst die Lösung, die man vorfindet, die Aufgabe sichtbar macht.

Es erscheinen für das palästinensische Haus folgende Forderungen:

Plan: Schaffung wenigstens eines grossen Raumes, wenn möglich von zwei gegenüberliegenden Seiten durchlüftet. Möglichst Fortsetzung dieses Raumes ins Freie, sei es durch eine tiefe Loggia (im Etagenhaus), sei es durch einen Gartenhof. (Der Gartensaal «Liwan», welcher eigentlich mehr dem Hof angehört als dem Haus, ist im arabischen Palais des siebzehnten Jahrhunderts der wichtigste Raum.) Anderseits Schaffung einer Anzahl vom grossen Raum genügend abgetrennter Einzelzellen. Anordnung aller Räume so, dass Zugluft sie durchstreicht. (Der Tagwind kommt in Palästina von Westen, der Nachtwind von Osten, grob gesprochen.)

Uebergang innen-aussen: Das Fenster in der Mauer: wie stellt man in unserer Konstruktion den Sonnenschutz der tiefen Leibung wieder her? Uebergangsräume: im Etagenhaus: Terrassen, Loggien. Im Einzelhaus: Lauben, Höfe. Der Idealfall ist, dass sich vor jede breite Lichtöffnung ein Uebergangsraum schiebt, und dass nur schmale Lufteinlässe unmittelbar ins Freie gehen. Enge Beziehung zwischen dem Haus und einem geschlossenen, räumlichen Garten, der wohl Ausblicke, aber nicht Einblick gestatten darf.

Isolierung gegen Wärme: Für Wände kein Problem, es sei denn eine Geldfrage. Für das Dach schwieriger. Das flache Dach gewöhnlicher Ausführung ist nicht die ideale Decke über Wohnräumen. (Der Dachgarten, sollte man meinen, müsste hier sehr en vogue sein. In Jerusalem ladet die Bauordnung, welche kleinere Wohnungen auf dem Dach erlaubt, geradezu dazu ein, Dachgärten anzulegen. Merkwürdigerweise sieht man sie nicht. Dagegen sieht man häufig den Garten unter dem auf Pfeiler gestellten Hause, und diese schattigen Gärten bei Eingängen von Miethäusern haben hier vollen Sinn.) Isolierung gegen Regen. Sie ist sehr nötig, da hier der Winterregen fast waagrecht gegen die Wände getrieben wird Die dünne Betonfachwerkwand ist dagegen ein

268

models. This is by no means the case. What we are trying to say is that all attempts to live by Oriental as well as our own traditions, to find a synthesis, have in themselves remained contradictory. I would have no objections to a house that draws a long window ribbon across a thin, visible concrete skeleton and masters the searing light in a novel fashion. In the reading room of the Schocken Library (Mendelsohn) the light enters through a narrow window ribbon at the very top of a longitudinal wall. This wall appears visually reinforced by the protruding bookcases. The facing wall, built in the same way, is windowless right up to the ceiling. But an opening in the center, reaching from the floor to the ceiling, lets in a strong, invigorating light. This is certainly not a traditional means of directing light, but this room is brought to life by the Palestinian light and hints at the possibilities it bestows upon the architect. We have already said what should be examined: not the individual form, but the "common denominator" of Palestinian architecture. And in order to better explain this common denominator and the reason why it should be examined, I would like to add the following: the goal of such examination is to draw a line from the solutions back to the objective at hand so that we can try to solve it with the means we have at our disposal. To those who may argue that this kind of intellectual approach would make the investigation redundant, because the objective itself could be postulated outright, I would like to say that in a foreign country the real objective at hand is only ever made visible by the situation one finds in place.

The following requirements emerge for the Palestinian house:

Layout: Provision of at least one large room, ideally ventilated from two opposite sides. If possible a continuation of this room to the outside, either by way of a deeply recessed loggia (in a multistorey building) or by way of a courtyard garden. (The garden hall "liwan," which really belongs to the courtyard more than the house, is the most important room in the Arab palais of the 17th century). On the other hand, provision of a number of individual chambers sufficiently separated from the large room. The arrangement of rooms in such a way that a draft will pass through them (in Palestine the wind blows from the west during the day and from the east during the night, generally speaking).

Interior-exterior transition: The window in the wall: in our construction, how do we restore the protection against the sun offered

Mishmar Haemek boarding school in the Jezreel Valley.
Architect Joseph Neufeld
Established and built by the Hashomer Hatzair youth movement, which aims to achieve agricultural development in Palestine on a broad social platform. The school is meant to advance the children's education, in close contact with agricultural life.
When completed, the school is meant to contain a boarding school for 160 to 180 children between 6 and 16 years of age, who shall receive the education of a traditional middle school as well as agricultural training; also a canteen with a training kitchen for girls; classrooms for instruction purposes; and housing for the teachers. The living quarters face west and north, and the hallways face east and south; one terrace playground faces east, for the afternoon, and another west, for the morning. Each dorm room is 3.1 m wide and contains four folding beds; a large window faces west, set 80 cm deep into the wall, with the space below used for bookshelves and the square above for piping. In the daytime, the dorm room is opened up by way of a door measuring 1.60 m in width onto a hallway that is 2.2 m wide. Loadbearing structure of reinforced concrete, internal walls of lightweight bricks, ceiling slabs of soft, smooth lime plaster.
The collective settlement Mishmar Haemek where the school is situated was built by the Foundation Fund (Keren Hayesod) on land owned by the National Fund.

Private hospital "Assuta" in Tel Aviv
Architect Joseph Neufeld
View of the yard, facing the service wing with main kitchen and laundry; staff accommodation on the upper floor
Left: Hospital (note the vents for cross-ventilation)
Right: Quarantine station

Internat Mishmar-Haemek im Tal Jesreel. Arch. Joseph Neufeld

Gegründet und erbaut von der Jugendbewegung Hashomer Hazair, die auf breiter sozialer Basis den landwirtschaftlichen Aufbau in Palästina zu verwirklichen sucht. Die Schule soll der Erziehung der Kinder dienen, in engem Kontakt mit dem landwirtschaftlichen Leben.

Die Schule soll nach dem endgültigen Ausbau enthalten: Ein Internat für 160—180 Kinder von 6—16 Jahren, die die Ausbildung einer klassischen Mittelschule plus Landwirtschaft erhalten, ferner Esshalle mit Schulküche für Mädchen, Klassenräume für Unterrichtszwecke, Lehrerhäuser. Die Wohnräume liegen gegen Westen und Norden, die Gänge gegen Osten und Süden; eine Spielterrasse liegt gegen Osten für den Nachmittag und eine gegen Westen für den Morgen. Jede Schlafzelle ist 3,1 m breit und enthält vier Klappbetten; grosses Fenster gegen Westen in 80 cm tiefer Nische, der Raum darunter ist als Bücherschrank, darüber für die Leitungen ausgenützt. Tagsüber ist die Zelle durch eine 1,6 m breite Tür nach dem 2,2 m breiten Gang geöffnet. Tragkonstruktion in Eisenbeton, Zwischenwände aus Leichtziegeln, Rippendecken, weicher glatter Kalkputz.

Die kollektive Siedlung Mishmar-Haemek, in der die Schule liegt, wurde durch den Aufbaufonds (Keren Hayesod) auf Boden des Nationalfonds aufgebaut.

unzureichender Schutz, wird aber aus wirtschaftlichen Gründen in Tel-Aviv stets gebaut. Die volle Betonwand ist ohne Zweifel besser.

Anblick. Nur grosse Flächen, rein geschnittene Körper sind hier möglich. Vor allem sollten vorgeschobene Bauglieder: Aussentreppen, Balkons, sehr leicht vor dem geschlossenen Hauptkörper stehen. Wenn man Fenster, um ihnen Leibung zu geben, als einzelne Fenstererker vor die Wand vorzieht, so ist dagegen nichts zu sagen. Die gesamte orientalische Architektur tut es. Das weit vorgezogene Fensterband ist mit mehr Vorsicht zu behandeln. Ein Vorschlag von Le Corbusier für Alger bringt eine einleuchtende Lösung.

Maßstab: Aus allem Gesagten wird man verstehen, dass nichts gefährlicher ist als turmartige, ungelagerte Körper, spitze Dächer, Turmhauben: alles Bröcklige, Spitzige. Da in der Landschaft alle Einzelheiten klein sind: niedrige Oelbäume, schmale Feldstücke, kleine Mauern, so sind am schönsten auch kleine Bauten. Grosse Körper aber sollten sehr gross und fest sein, um mit dem Kleinen rundum dann lieber gar nichts gemeinsam zu haben.

Privatkrankenhaus «Assutah» in Tel-Aviv
Architekt Joseph Neufeld
Blick in den Hof gegen das Wirtschaftsgebäude mit Hauptküche, Wäscherei, im Obergeschoss Personalwohnräume
links: Krankenhaus (zu beachten die Schlitze für die Querlüftung)
rechts: Absonderungshaus

269

by the deep window arch? Transition spaces: In the multistorey building: terraces, loggias. In the detached building: arcades, courtyards. In an ideal scenario, every wider light aperture is preceded by a transitional space and only narrow air vents lead directly outside. Close connection between the house and an enclosed, spatial garden that may facilitate looking out but not looking in.

Insulation from heat: For walls, this does not present a problem, unless it is a question of money. For the roof, it is a greater challenge. The flat roof in its most common form is not the ideal ceiling above living rooms. (One would think the roof garden would be en vogue here. In Jerusalem, the building regulations which allow smaller apartments on the roof are an open invitation to create roof gardens. It is surprising that they are nowhere to be seen. Very common, on the other hand, are gardens underneath the elevated house, and these shaded gardens by the entrances of apartment blocks make perfect sense here.)

Insulation from rain: This is very much needed, since the winter rain in these parts is driven nearly horizontally against the walls. The thin concrete frame-wall offers insufficient protection, but is still consistently favored in Tel Aviv, on economic grounds. Without a doubt, the solid concrete wall is superior.

Appearance: Only large surfaces, well-proportioned structures, are possible here. It is important that protuberant elements like external staircases or balconies stand effortlessly before the main structure. If windows are pulled out from the wall as individual bays, there is nothing wrong with that. All Oriental architecture does the same. A prominently protruding window ribbon should be treated with greater caution. Le Corbusier made a suggestion for Algiers which offers a convincing solution.

Scale: From all that was said above, one will understand that nothing is more dangerous than towerlike, unsettled structures, pitched roofs, cupolas. All that is brittle and pointy. Since everything in the landscape is small—low-growing fruit trees, narrow strips of fields, low walls—the most beautiful buildings are also small in size. Large structures, however, should be very tall and solid so they

Ich setze diese magere Liste her, um nicht ganz im Vagen zu bleiben. Ich sagte ja schon, dass die Beobachtungen, aus denen Forderungen abzuleiten sein möchten, noch durchaus Programm bleiben. Jede neue Tatsache, die man sieht, präzisiert die Aufgaben. Die Möglichkeiten sind ungeheuer. Immerhin besitzen wir schon eine Reihe von Bauten, die sich erfolgreich mit solchen Aufgaben auseinandersetzen.

*Julius Posener*

Alle hier abgebildeten Siedlungen wurden von dem Aufbaufonds (Keren Hayesod) gegründet und finanziert. Der Boden, auf dem sie stehen, ist unveräusserliches nationales Eigentum, vom Nationalfonds (Keren Kayemet Jesreel) den Siedlern verpachtet. Die Planung geschah von Privatarchitekten, in enger Zusammenarbeit mit dem technischen Bureau der Jewish Agency. Die Siedlungen sind genossenschaftlich oder kollektiv aufgebaut. In der kollektiven Siedlung (Kvouzah) herrscht Gütergemeinschaft.

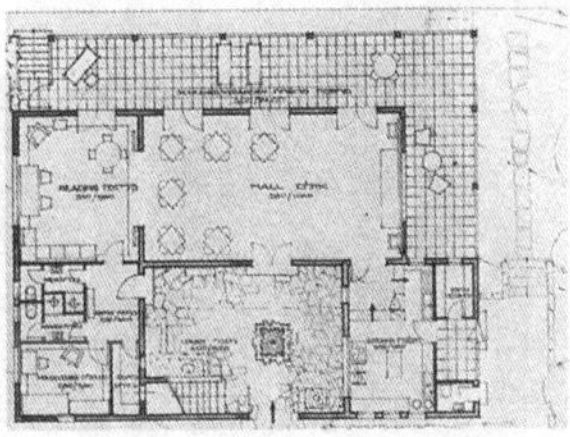

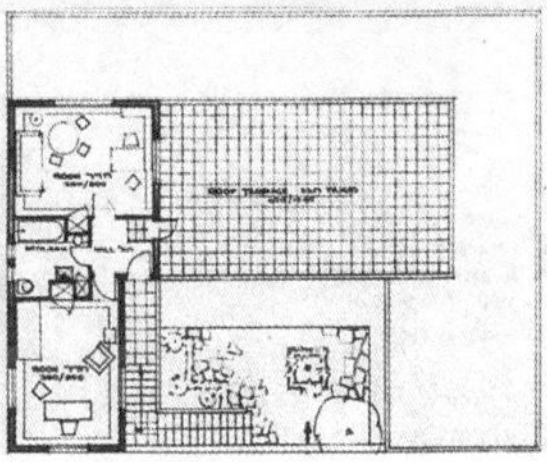

Klubhaus der Landwirtschaftlichen Versuchsstation der Jewish Agency in Rehovoth
Architekt Arieh Sharon
Grundrisse 1:400. Norden ist oben rechts, vorherrschender Wind von oben links. Eine Veranda als Uebergangsraum umzieht auf zwei Seiten die Gesellschaftsräume, die dritte öffnet sich auf einen engen, hoch ummauerten Hof

270

All settlements depicted here were established and financed by the Foundation Fund (Keren Hayesod). The land on which they are built is inalienable national property leased to the settlers by the National Fund (Keren Kayemet Jezreel [*sic*]). Planning was carried out by private architects, in close cooperation with the Jewish Agency's Technical Bureau. The settlements are cooperative or collective in their constitution. Collective settlements (*kvouzah*) practice a community of goods.

Clubhouse of the Agricultural Experiment Station of the Jewish Agency in Rehovot
Architect Arieh Sharon
Floor plans 1:400. North is top right, prevailing winds from top left.
A veranda as transition room surrounds the common rooms on two sides; the third opens to a narrow, high-walled courtyard

become something completely different from all the small things surrounding them.

I put forward this modest list so as not to remain completely vague. As I said before, observations from which further requirements can be deduced remain very much on the agenda. Every new detail one discovers serves to make the objectives more focused. The possibilities are immense. And we do already possess a number of buildings that deal with these objectives.

Julius Posener

1 It is interesting to note that, when facing the street, these same stringed windows are very convincing behind a wide pergola.

School in the Kvouzah Deganyah (Keren Hayesod, land: National Fund) by Lake Tiberias (200 m below sea level) Architect Richard Kaufmann [sic] (and Jewish Agency)

Subtropical climate. A wide overhanging roof protects the classroom ceiling from direct sunlight. Ventilation windows to the west and east inside the classrooms. In the picture, the eastern windows can be seen above the open corridor running in front of them. The space under the roof is protected with mosquito netting and is popular as an outdoor resting area. This building forgoes the search for a modernist-Oriental synthesis. It stands easily in a well-tended garden area by the lake, and nowhere more than here does one get a sense that the Jewish arrivals have built "something of their own" into the country.

Canteen in Deganyah
Architect Leopold Krakauer
(and the Jewish Agency)

Photo credits:
The America Colony [sic]
Photo Department, Jerusalem
Keren Hayesod, Jerusalem
Hirschin
J. Kalter, Tel Aviv
Z. Kluger, Tel Aviv
W. Loewenheim, Haifa
Palphot, Tel Aviv
Schleissner
Schweig
Sebba
Soskin
Spanjer-Herford

Neue Aufgaben

Schule in der Kvouzah Deganyah
(Keren Hayesod, Boden: Nationalfonds)
am Tiberiassee (200 m unter Meer)
Architekt Richard Kaufmann (und Jewish Agency)

Subtropisches Klima. Ein weit überstehendes Dach schützt die Klassendecke vor unmittelbarer Bestrahlung. Lüftungsfenster nach Westen und Osten in den Klassen. Die Ostfenster werden im Bild über dem offenen Gang sichtbar, der vor den Klassen liegt. Der Raum unterm Dach ist durch Fliegennetze geschützt und wird als Ruheraum im Freien gern benutzt. Dieser Bau leistet auf das Suchen nach modern-orientalischer Synthese Verzicht. Er steht ungezwungen in dem gepflegten Gartenland am See, und nirgends empfindet man stärker als hier, dass auch die jüdischen Neueinwohner «Eigenes» ins Land gebaut haben.

Speisehaus in Deganyah
Architekt Leopold Krakauer (und Jewish Agency)

Herkunft der Fotografien:
The America Colony photo Dept., Jerusalem
Keren Hayesod, Jerusalem
Hirschin
J. Kalter, Tel-Aviv
Z. Kluger, Tel-Aviv
W. Loewenheim, Haifa
Palphot, Tel-Aviv
Schleissner
Schweig
Sebba
Soskin
Spanjer-Herford

271

# Project

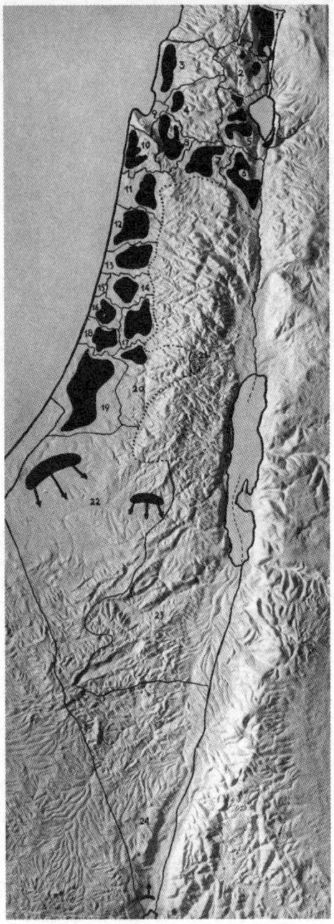

①

## The Master Plan

Everything will be systematically worked out in advance. In the elaboration of this plan, which I am capable only of suggesting, our keenest minds will participate. Every achievement in the fields of social science and technology of our own age and of the even more advanced age, which will dawn over the protracted execution of the plan, must be utilized for the cause. Every happy invention that is already available or will become available must be used. Thus the land can be occupied and the State founded in a manner as yet unknown to history, with unprecedented chances of success.
Theodor Herzl, *The Jewish State* (*Der Judenstaat*), 1896[1]

The great revolution is not over yet, and its essential functions have barely begun. In the near future we must lay foundations that will stand for decades and possibly centuries to come. We must shape the character of the State of Israel and prepare it to fulfill its historical mission.
David Ben-Gurion, *The War Diary*, January 1949[2]

① The division of the country into regions, drawn on a photo of a relief map, 1950. Planning Department.
② Members of the Planning Department, ca. 1950. Arieh Sharon digital archive.

Swarming, cluttered, frantic at the center; scattered, dissociated, monotonous at the margins—the fabricated space of Israel is a "manner as yet unknown to history" whereby "land can be occupied and the State founded" in a brief moment of history. Contrary to common belief and to visual impression, Israel was born not of haphazard improvisation, emergency routine, or speculative ventures, and certainly not of gradual spontaneous buildup, but rather of the unprecedented objective to put into practice one of the most comprehensive, controlled, and efficient architectural projects in the modern era.

Indeed, this is Israel's singularity among nation-states; it was "systematically worked out in advance," formulated a priori by means of arithmetic, planimetry, and demographic blueprints; drafted and modeled by planning professionals from various disciplines who were called upon to actualize Ben-Gurion's prescript "to transform the country, the nation, our entire modes of life"—or, to put it in a more technical language, to engineer and redesign the country's geographic, ecological, and agronomic mold; its patterns of urbanization, socialization, and employment; the overall framework of production and service; the character of public life as well as the patterns of domestication in the new Jewish State.

Such an all-encompassing planning ambition is exceptional, even in the context of its own period—one that revered the "planning sciences" and perceived mega-architects, infra-engineers, macro-economists, and master sociologists to be the omnipotent agents of progress itself.

Direct precedents for the "Israeli project" can be found in Stalin's Five-Year Plan for the Soviet Union, in the American New Deal infrastructural projects

②

③

④

⑤

⑥

and public works of the 1930s, in the German National Socialist regional plans for the occupied territories of Poland, and in the post–World War II British schemes of new towns. But its sweeping vision, exceeding all instrumental models and circumstantial explanations, is rooted in the utopian imagination and redemptive territorialism of the Zionist movement itself. These roots call for some elaboration, in order to recall the bedding upon which the master plan of Israel was drafted immediately upon the "outbreak" of the State.

The very notion of the "Zionist enterprise," or the "Zionist project," encompasses the highly institutionalized, explicitly synthetic, and vigorously transformative character of the process of land appropriation and nation-building by the Zionist movement throughout the twentieth century. Any attempt to "normalize" Zionism by over-emphasizing aspects such as spontaneous immigration or forced exile, inner colonization or organic settlement, underestimates Zionism's self-portrayal as an inversive, corrective, and redemptive intervention in historical time and geographic space.
In this context, centralized planning is the ultimate trope that binds words and things; it is the Zionist spirit itself, emanating from layers of fictional prose, ideological manifestos, and programmatic protocols, printed on the landscape over and over again with every new spatial move or architectural object.

The most conspicuous use of centralized planning—not merely for territorial organization, but as an apparatus for molding a new ethos—is manifested in the consistent efforts to shift the political, cultural, and economic weight from the city to the countryside and from the center to the periphery. As a rule, it may be said that in its first fifty years, the Zionist movement devised and developed a

range of pioneering models for rural settlements—supported by a sophisticated manufacturing, organizational, and marketing apparatus—but never imagined, planned, or actually built a city (except for Afula, or *Emek Stadt*, the paper "urban settlement" designed by Richard Kauffmann in 1925). In fact, the big city was consistently portrayed in both literary utopias and ideological propaganda as anathema to the Zionist notion of *Am Ha'aretz* (people of the land), as a parasitic growth threatening to undermine the project of settler colonization and the Arcadian vision of the reemerging Hebrew civilization.[3]

Revolutionary objectives, fully controlled centralized planning, and a well-coordinated course of action had thus characterized the Zionist enterprise from its very outset. However, the country's crucial "conversion" occurred only with the founding of a sovereign state.

A number of factors came together to provide an opportunity and ostensible legitimization for a project of demolition and construction more daring than any of its paper precedents, a project that turned the entire country into a frenzied building, landscaping, and refurbishing site for over two decades. These included the end of the British Mandate in 1948 and the ensuing regulatory vacuum; the detrimental War of 1948 and the ruinous landscape it created; the "turnover" of refugee populations during the war and immediately following it (with 700,000 Palestinian refugees expelled or fleeing the territory of the new State and an equal number of Jewish immigrants and exiles arriving or being brought over in the years following); the immediate confiscation and nationalization of over 90 percent of the country's land, as well as the Palestinian "abandoned property," by the State; the temporary emergency legislation (most of which is technically still valid today) and austerity decrees put in place in the early 1950s; the virtual monopoly of the Israeli Labor Party (*Mapay*) over all political, juridical, military, economic, and cultural grids; the moral and material support provided by the world's superpowers for the new State (including a supplemental budget for infrastructural projects which was separate and equal in size to the overall national budget).

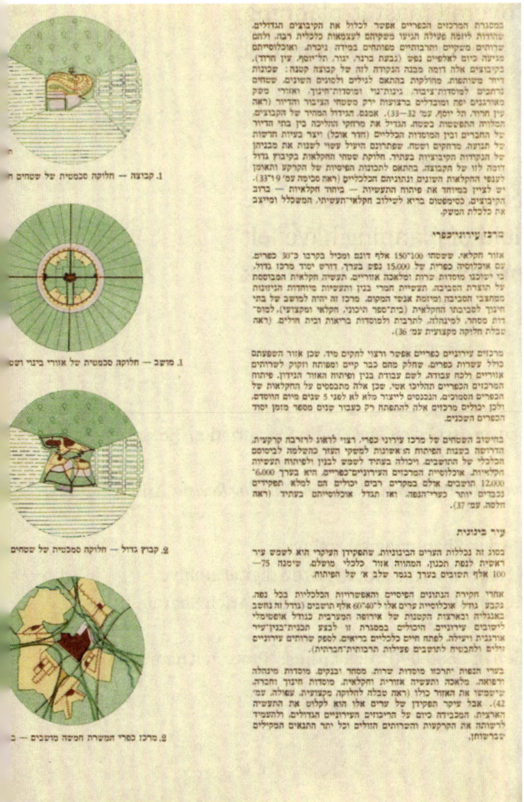

Only a few weeks after the Israeli Declaration of Independence, during the war and long before its ground results could be determined, Arieh Sharon, a Bauhaus graduate, an avid disciple of Hannes Meyer's "Marxist architecture," and already a prominent architect of the Jewish Labor Movement, was commissioned to establish the governmental Planning Department.[4]

Sharon recruited a "planning brigade," a team of 170 experts, including sociologists, economists, agronomists, engineers, architects, and town planners. Some had previously been members of the Planning Committee set up by Ben-Gurion as early as 1942 to examine the practical aspects of the mass settlement of two million Jews in Palestine; others had participated in an independent Settlement Reform Forum in early 1948.

By 1951, the outcome of the Planning Department's work was published in a didactically written and illustrated format under the title *Physical Planning in Israel* (or, in some versions, *The Planning of Israel*), often referred to as "the Sharon Plan." This publication is by no means a statutory document, but it should all the same be considered as the initial master plan of Israel, the protocol according to which the State was set up almost verbatim.

Was it a radical and farsighted blueprint, based on genuinely situated research, responsive to actual geographic or ethnographic idiosyncrasies, tolerant to divergent political and civilian scenarios, questioning indeed the very ethical predicament of centralized planning, or rather an indoctrinated and uniform guidebook, reflecting a long-standing Zionist agenda and an emerging State apparatus with an inborn predisposition for a fully contrived and "scientifically balanced" nation-state?

As we can learn from Arieh Sharon's presentation at the opening session of the Governmental Districts and Zone Planning Committee (December 6, 1948), the master plan was already a closed dogma when the team of planners had barely begun their work. In this presentation, a general rejection of past and present living conditions and a blunt critique of "Old World" unruly urbanization patterns demonstrate, as it were, the inevitability of overall master-planning, and by implication centralized decentralization, for the survival of the frail, newborn State of Israel:

> I am glad to have been granted the opportunity to present to you some of our work and discuss with you the problems and difficulties that we encounter. For many years those engaged in the field of planning have felt the lack of central and national planning—a factor that hinders our work and restricts our capacity to build the country. [...]

③ *The Planning of Israel* by Arieh Sharon, 1951. Front cover. Issued by The Zionist Organization, Keren Hayesod Division, Jerusalem. Arieh Sharon digital archive.

④ *Planning in Israel* by Arieh Sharon, 1952. Front cover. Reprint from *The Town Planning Review*. Arieh Sharon digital archive.

⑤ *Physical Planning in Israel* by Arieh Sharon, 1951. Arieh Sharon digital archive.

⑥ *Physical Planning in Israel* by Arieh Sharon, 1951. Hebrew cover. Arieh Sharon digital archive.

⑦ Double spread from *Physical Planning in Israel* describing settlement typologies. Arieh Sharon, 1951. Arieh Sharon digital archive.

⑧ Left panel: "Distribution of the country's population of 2,500,000." Right panel: "Protected nature reserves and heritage sites." 1950. Planning Department.

We are told that various, wealthy countries have existed and thrived for many years without central planning institutions. To this argument one should reply by stressing that affluent nations can perhaps afford experimentation and lack of planning. At the same time, one must also note the incurable chronic ills in the big cities of these countries.

We know that we are incapable of withstanding such maladies. If we were to spawn such entities as those big cities, with their grave conditions, we wouldn't have the means at our disposal to rectify the situation. The health and welfare of the people dwelling in these entities would deteriorate, until entrepreneurs would have no power left for creation and construction.

We can see that after one or two generations, at the most, of the country's construction, the results of unguided construction would be highly burdensome. We live in apartments overlooking our neighbors, or at best over hot and narrow streets. Our homes do not have a view of rolling green lands that may pacify us. The new ownership of the land thus makes it possible to formalize and re-arrange the space and to ensure the people's physical and mental well-being through central planning. The "Old World" (which, for the purpose of this argument, comprises not only Europe, but also the migration countries of the "New World") is already degenerate, sick, spawning urban monsters. Here there exists an opportunity for a fresh start on a *tabula rasa*, as it were. Here, as opposed to there, there is not enough space, there is no leeway for uncontrolled developments, and there is no room for degeneration.[5]

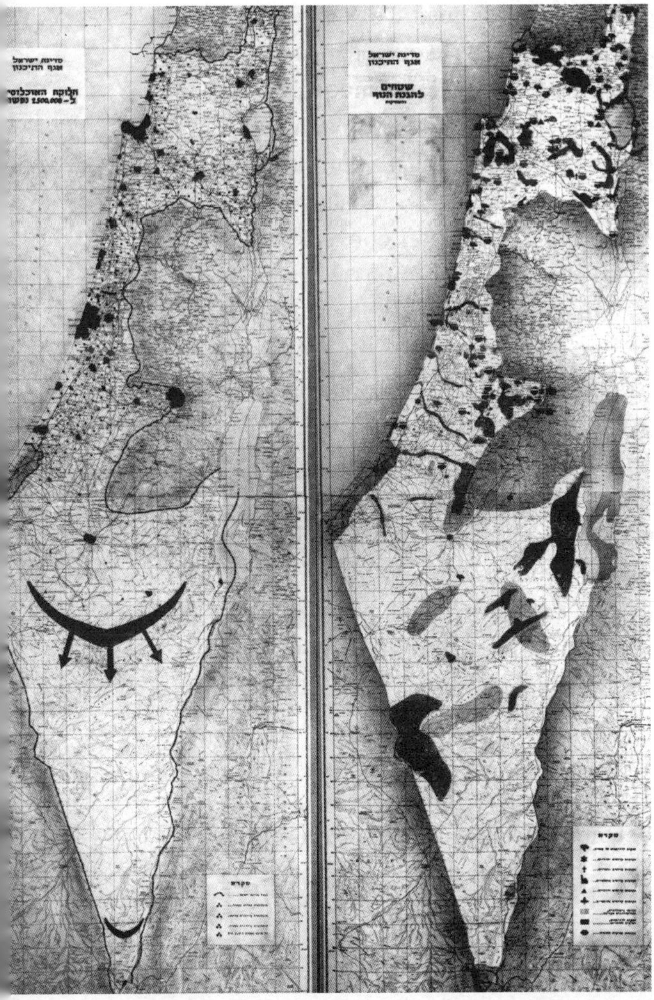

⑧

Attentive reading of this text brings up not merely the chronic and disturbing use of hygiene and medical metaphors, but also the slippage of the social-realist parlance—"a fresh start on a *tabula rasa*"—into the nationalist haunt of "a land without people for a people without a land."

Suspended rhetorically between Abaddon and Arcadia, the actual assignment of Sharon and his team at the Planning Department was initially rather ordinary and dictated a swift campaign to establish the architectural vocabulary of perennial temporality. The pressing tangible task was to provide provisional shelters for the masses of incoming immigrants and to settle the country's frontiers in order to stabilize the 1949 cease-fire lines, preclude territorial concessions, and inhibit the return of Palestinian refugees displaced during and after the war. This interim project materialized by delineating a network of civil frontiers composed of transit camps and settlement outposts, as well as by resettling deserted Arab villages with new Jewish immigrants and refugees (coming mainly from Arab countries).

Concurrently, a long-term project was outlined, preparing a national plan for a population of 2,650,000 inhabitants[6] who would be dispersed as evenly as possible throughout the country, thus adjusting the "anomaly" or the "colonialist pattern," as the planners dubbed the distribution of the Jewish community in the country during the British Mandate.[7]

The master plan was divided into five categories: agriculture, industry, transportation, forestry and parks, and new towns. Rural settlement was perceived as the major factor for developing and ensuring economic autonomy. The village, new and (several decades) old, was narrated as the national "building block," and agronomy was to be the deus ex machina resolving the plot. Accordingly, the plan portrayed a vision of 600,000 farmers living on 120,000 farms, in units of 20 to 25 dunam (5 to 6.25 acres) per family. They were to provide 75 percent of the population's food. Industry (and its social and environmental discontents) was a main subject of critique and reform. It was therefore zoned off and modeled after various circulating "soft" paradigms of the garden city, the cite industrielle, or the company town. Although there was actually no local history of industrialization (and unruly urbanization), the modern environmentalist reformation was routinely adapted and reiterated in the texts of the master plan to illustrate the social sensibility of the welfare state: "The medium-sized, more conveniently organized town will facilitate the lives of industry workers, furnishing them with comfortable and inexpensive public housing, convenient transportation to their workplaces and to parklands for recreation."[8]

Profoundly physiocratic as it was, the plan nevertheless identified the ideological and logistic breach between the rural and the urban as the major obstruction in creating a quasi-organic national space that functions like a unified body. It therefore sketched hierarchical diagrams progressing from the village to the rural center to the medium-sized town and then to the big city, and substantiated these incredibly synthetic spatial constructs in ostentatious planning theories of the time. Architect and planner Artur Glikson, one of the leading and most articulate members of Sharon's team at the Planning Department, recounted the "missing links" thesis in 1956:

> There were at least "two Israels" in the country; the one represented by over-centralization in three big towns and their environs, the other represented by extreme trends of social, institutional, and even economic

> decentralization in small villages striving for self-sufficiency.[9] The collective and cooperative villages, being self-sufficient, and ideologically disapproving of city life, did not provide the necessary rural hinterland for the establishment and consolidation of small urban centers, the intermediaries between the large urban concentration and the villages. [...] The planners thus decided to forge the missing links of the hierarchy. [...] The national plan divided the settlements by size into five main groups: (a) The village [...] (b) Rural centers [...] (c) Urban-rural centers [...] (d) Medium-sized towns [...] (e) Big towns [...]. The "missing links" were of course types b–d.[10]

As a footnote to this concise and rather typical text, I should state the unspoken: the organic, clustered, rhizomatic, balanced, and symbiotic hinterland sought for by the national master plan reconstitutes, mutatis mutandis, the indigenous rural and urban fabric it has just obliterated.

The double quest for spatial consolidation and demographic distribution was manifested in comprehensive infrastructure works designed for long-term physical development. These would double and triple the country's capacity to receive the massive immigration and enable instantaneous implementation of the policy of population dispersal.[11] A nationwide transportation network was designed to include a new port, two airports, and railroads (mainly for freight trains), as well as a highly intricate road network to provide access to the dispersed villages and small towns (as opposed to an axial railroad system that would directly connect population centers and accelerate the growth of big cities).

A national irrigation network was laid out to conduct water from northern Israel through the lowlands to the northern Negev desert and the Judean Mountains, thus enabling the Negev de-desertification and inhabitation project and providing the essentials to deal with Prime Minister Ben-Gurion's greatest anxiety—his illustrious horror vacui. A Government Session protocol of May 3, 1949, records his momentous words:

> If you look at the map you will see that the South contains many empty places, and nothing causes me so great a horror as this emptiness—not because nature cannot withstand emptiness, but because people cannot stand it and politics cannot withstand emptiness.[12]

The distribution of new towns was presumably based on "location factors," which were described in the appendices to the master plan: "A location characterized by a high quality of life, soil suitable for easy cultivation, proximity to employment centers, to quarries, and to a national transportation network." In reality, as will be later discussed, these "location factors" proved to be either misguided by false assumptions regarding natural resources and rates of migra-

⑨

⑩

⑪

⑫

tion influx, or subordinated to larger, "scientific," regional schemes. One of the senior planners on Sharon's team later recalled the often surreal in-situ situation created soon after the master plan was launched:

> In one of the meetings at the Planning Department, during the peak period of mass immigration from Iraq in 1951, the director of the Absorption Department, G. Yoseftal, expressed the situation figuratively: "In the past we have accommodated immigrants where there was already a town and sources of employment; or even where there was a settlement without a source of employment; with the increase of immigration waves we were forced to erect transit camps on sites having plans for future towns; now we are ready to emplace transit camps even on sites indicating dreams of future towns. Tell us where you have dreams of future towns and we shall instantly build there a camp."[13]

Professionally speaking, the national master plan, the Sharon Plan, was by no means an innovative document. It presents an assemblage of derivative models, amalgamated theories, and inflated experiments. Some of these had been developed locally during the pre-State era, mainly by members of the Planning Committee or the Settlement Reform Forum,[14] and others were imported, ready-made, primarily from England and Germany, and swiftly "naturalized." Arguably, the Sharon Plan is unique only in its scope—in its ambition to set forth in one go a single layout, a single vision, a single stately concept, on a scale of 1:20,000. Such ambition could have remained anecdotal—too rational, instrumental, and progressive; or alternatively, too phantasmagoric, gestural, and reactionary—had it not been implemented verbatim, almost in its entirety, often while bypassing standard planning procedures; always through the systematic reproduction of zoning doctrines, building typologies, and construction methods. While it had no statutory status (or perhaps precisely because it did not have to face legislation procedures), the Sharon Plan almost instantaneously, within less than a decade, transformed from a statement of principles into a mega-project encompassing about thirty new towns and over four hundred rural settlements (approximately the number of destroyed Palestinian towns and villages), *ex machina*; extensive woodlands, national parks, and nature resorts, *ex fabrica*; and networks of roads, electricity, water, ports, and factories, *ex nihilo*.

⑨ Arieh Sharon with Prime Minister David Ben-Gurion and the planning delegation in Eilat, early 1950s. Arieh Sharon digital archive.
⑩ Detail.
⑪ Golda Meir, minister of labor, with members of the Planning Department, ca. 1950. Arieh Sharon digital archive.
⑫ The first planning survey in the Negev Desert, with Prime Minister David Ben-Gurion and his deputies, 1950. Arieh Sharon digital archive.

Soon after the official publication of the plan in 1951, Sharon and his team of planners realized that they had provided the government with an all-too-readable building manual. Despite their enduring commitment to overall centralized planning and their loyalty to the welfare-state apparatus, they made efforts to slow down the literal application of their plan on the ground. However, the genetic code that had been devised on paper in their architectural laboratory had already been cloned and disseminated throughout the country, proving its durability in vivo, even under the most adverse conditions.[15]

The momentous proliferation of the Sharon Plan may be attributed to two guiding principles of spatial distribution: deterritorialization (which was effectively imposed upon the local Palestinian population but was by and large futile vis-à-vis the veteran Jewish population) and decentralization (according to the strategic precept, developed in the early pre-State days and in effect to this day, of using civilian settlements as military outposts). These principles formed a hallowed cause that dictated all moves and procedures of the national master plan, even if at times they were inconsistent with professional scrutiny, even if they entirely failed the test of economic viability, even if they actually worked against the grain of rhetorical patriotism (the "ingathering of the exiles," the "melting pot," etc.) and in effect created severe geographic and social segregation between veteran residents at the center and new immigrants at the outer periphery.

Mass immigration was the solution, however, since were it not for this yielding body of citizens-in-the-making, the historical opportunity to reinvent the Israeli space would not have emerged. Indeed, in spite of the government's considerable propaganda efforts to induce mass migration to the periphery, it was clear to leaders and planners alike that the Sharon Plan would not be implementable on a voluntary basis. Eliezer Brutzkus described its achievements in hindsight, comparing it with the project of new workers' towns in Stalin's Soviet Union:

> Truth be told, these results were obtained, here too, against the free will of the settled subjects, namely the immigrants, through a method whose underlying principle was "straight off the boat to development regions." We must not forget the basic fact that the creation of the new towns, and the settlement of the peripheral regions, was done primarily through directing the new immigrants, and only marginally by attracting the "veteran" population.[16]

The forced marginalization of the new immigrants was justified "scientifically" by the planners, who were routinely engaged with the idea of "optimum population" which had circulated widely in German planning discourse —and simultaneously in Zionist professional and political forums—since the 1920s. In fact, the sociologist Arthur Ruppin, head of the Palestine Office of the World Zionist Organization from 1908 to 1943, was sent to Palestine by the Zionist Organization as early as 1907 to draw on his training in demography, statistics, law, and business to scientifically research the land's capacity to absorb immigrants. Ruppin argued for moderate immigration, and in his 1919 essay "The Selection of the Fittest," he wrote that the Zionist Organization should carefully screen candidates for immigration and give preference to those fit and willing to work the land.[17]

The abovementioned Soviet project, efficient as it was in constructing and inhabiting dozens of new provincial towns and peripheral cities, was not the primary model from which the Israeli planners drew their inspiration. The rehabilitation projects of Western Europe after World War II, especially the new satellite towns around London founded by the British Labour government, provided a closer model and were thoroughly analyzed by Sharon and his team. Patrick Abercrombie, the "father of the new towns" and perhaps the most important British town planner in the postwar period, visited Israel several times, met with Ben-Gurion, and wrote a professional report about the Israeli project.[18] Arieh Sharon traveled to England to meet with him and get his approval before submitting his national master plan. The seemingly rapid urbanization of Israel through the propagation of regional new towns led some scholars to describe a paradigm shift within the Zionist colonization project. S. Ilan Troen, for example, observes the end of the "physiocratic utopia":

> In 1950, the newly established State of Israel radically departed from its established ideology and practice of investing in agricultural and communitarian settlements. Israel's first master plan [...] assumed that the majority of Israel's population, approximately 80 percent, would live in towns and cities. Its adoption signified that the initial Zionist dream of a renaissance in a physiocratic utopia of Jewish peasants had been supplanted by a vision of a modern, urban, technologically advanced society modeled on Western Europe and Japan.[19]

Yet others argue that although the pressure to speed up the absorption of immigrants and refugees indeed technically increased the housing capacity of the new settlements, it never called into question the moral primacy of the rural. Erik Cohen, for one, rejects the crude rural/urban dichotomy and argues for a conceptual assimilation or hybridization of the two:

> But the shift to planned urban absorption of immigrants was not accompanied by a change in outlook from a rural to an urban colonizing or pioneering ideology. The cherished ideals of pioneering Zionism were not abandoned—on the contrary, they were actually introduced into urban planning.[20]

Following Cohen's hypothesis, we may articulate the following question: What were the formative planning theories and concrete architectural mechanisms that introduced the rural ideals of early Zionism into the 1950s national master plan and determined Israel's frontier culture for decades to come? ■

1 Theodor Herzl, *The Jewish State*, trans. Harry Zohn (New York: Herzl Press, 1970). Available online (accessed April 1, 2017): http://library.gayhomeland.org/0001/EN/content_index.htm. Originally published as *Der Judenstaat* (Leipzig and Vienna: Breitenstein, 1896).

2 David Ben-Gurion, *The War Diary: The War of Independence, 1948–1949*, vol. 3, ed. Gershon Rivlin and Elhanan Oren [in Hebrew] (Tel Aviv: Ministry of Defense Publishing House, 1982), p. 937.

3 On this, see the exemplary text by Ben-Gurion comparing Rome and Tel Aviv quoted in chapter "Object."

4 The Planning Department was first set up within the Labor and Construction Ministry, but Ben-Gurion transferred it to the Prime Minister's Office so that he could work directly with the planners. The department was later moved to the Ministry of the Interior, and eventually evolved into the Ministry for Housing and Construction.

5 Transcript of presentation by Arieh Sharon at the Governmental Districts and Zone Planning Committee on December 6, 1948 (Israel State Archives).

6 A target already achieved in 1966, much faster than anticipated.

7 Upon the establishment of the State of Israel, two-thirds of the Jewish population was concentrated in the three large cities of Tel Aviv, Jerusalem, and Haifa. Eighty-two percent lived along the coastal plain. The aim of the Sharon Plan was for only 45 percent of the urban population to dwell in the big cities, with 55 percent settling in the new rural medium- and small-sized towns and in agrarian settlements.

8 Arieh Sharon, *Physical Planning in Israel* [in Hebrew] (Jerusalem: Government Printing Press and Survey of Israel Press, 1951).

9 Indigenous Palestinian villages are not even mentioned by Glikson, and were rarely mentioned by any other planner at the time.

10 Cited in Erik Cohen, "The City in the Zionist Ideology," *Jerusalem Urban Studies* 1 (1970), p. 132.

11 "We have two important things at our command: a million and a half Jews, and all the territory in Israel. Most of the Jews dwell in a few towns; most of the land is empty and untilled. The resultant danger is great, both for Jews and land. There are means of destruction today no one could have dreamt of a generation ago, and crowding the bulk of our population into the cramped area of Tel Aviv and its environs constitutes a deadly peril to our future: it would be easy to blot out the whole complex at a stroke—and then Israel is lost! Dispersal of population over a wide area is the only safeguard; the smaller and more widely spread the settlements, the less the risk. And the land in our possession is in danger, so long as it is underpeopled. The Arabs have held, they still hold, vast wildernesses, and no one is likely to take them away, but we, who have returned to our Homeland to settle and till it, dare not leave any part a desert." David Ben-Gurion, "Achievements and Tasks," in *Like Stars and Dust: Essays from Israel's Government Year Book* (Sde-Boker Campus: Ben-Gurion University of the Negev, Ben-Gurion Heritage Institute, 1997), p. 354.

12 Minutes of Israeli Government Session #12, May 3, 1949 (Israel State Archives).

13 Eliezer Brutzkus, "The Rural Settlement and the Urban Settlement in the State of Israel: Which is Preferable?," *Journal of Environmental Planning* 33 [in Hebrew] (September 1985), p. 57.

14 The Settlement Reform Forum was formed in January 1948, immediately following the UN Partition Plan; it was comprised of physical planners, economists, and legal experts, including Eliezer Brutzkus, Josef Tischler, Heintz Rau, Zvi Berenson, and Eliezer Livne. Many members of the Reform Forum eventually joined the government's Planning Department, headed by Arieh Sharon, and had a noticeable impact on the national master plan. Brutzkus writes in retrospect: "On the eve of Statehood, at the initiative of physical planners, a Settlement Reform Forum was born. It was a forum with a distinctively regionalist ideology, propagating the ideas of population dispersal, building of new towns, and regional organization based on tight interrelations between the rural region and the regional town located within it." Brutzkus, "Rural Settlement," p. 57.

15 An interesting example of the critical second thoughts expressed by one of these establishment planners can be found in the writings of Alfred Neumann: "We lost our innocent belief in the automatic regulation of economic and social processes long ago. It seems that the belief in a single planning theory that can provide happiness for everyone is also naïve [...]. We now know that there is always a component of restriction in planning which tends to oppress the individual." Alfred Neumann, "About Planning," *Journal of the Union of Engineers and Architects in Israel* [in Hebrew] (January 1953), p. 17.

16 Eliezer Brutzkus, "Transformations in the Network of Urban Centers in Israel," *Engineering and Architecture: The Union of Engineers and Architects in Israel* 3 [in Hebrew] (1964), p. 43.

17 Arthur Ruppin, "The Selection of the Fittest," in *Three Decades of Palestine* (Jerusalem: Schocken, 1936), pp. 66–80. Cited in S. Ilan Troen, *Imagining Zion: Dreams, Designs, and Realities in a Century of Jewish Settlement* (New Haven: Yale University Press, 2003), p. 179. Ruppin believed that a gradual approach was required to develop the resource-poor country, and even in 1933, in the face of the threat of Nazism, he claimed that only some tens of thousands of German Jews could be absorbed in Palestine. His analysis was based on a "scientific" formula that for every Jew settled on the land, only another two or three could be settled in towns.

18 See dossier "Patrick Abercrombie's Synopsis" in chapter "Theory."

19 Troen, *Imagining Zion*, p. 167.

20 Cohen, "City in the Zionist Ideology," p. 130.

# Outline of the National Plan

The physical planning of a country must be based on economic, social, and defence considerations. A *conditio sine qua non* of its success will be the organisation, coordination, and synthesis of these factors within a planning frame that is followed by development proper. The physical characteristics of the land, i.e., its vegetation, climate, soil, water resources, and mineral deposits, constitute a basis for the National Plan, which aims effectively to serve the interests of the individual and the community.

The objectives of a national plan include: siting of agricultural settlements and location of agricultural areas; determination of a rational and sound distribution of urban centres; effective disposition of industry in the various regions of the country; indication of the road network and centres of communication, and provision of forests and national parks.

To attempt the development of a small state like Israel, without some such national master plan would simply mean court failure. In vast and rich territories such as Australia and the Americas, to be sure, enormous tracts of virgin soil have been opened up and developed without any plan at all. This development, however, was usually superficial and led to a sometimes ruthless exploitation of the land, frequently resulting in rapid impoverishment of the soil, erosion, floods, etc. The extensive exploitation of the undeveloped areas in some of those countries was accompanied by a concentration of the majority of the urban population in the large coastal towns, which were transformed into vast and congested conurbations, while immense tracts of the hinterland remained undeveloped. Israel, however, is far too poor in land and natural resources, to permit any repetition of the mistakes made in vaster and richer countries, which are capable of rectifying errors in due course. The intensive and all-embracing development of this country calls for effective and comprehensive planning.

## THREE-FOLD BASIS FOR PLANNING LAND, PEOPLE, TIME

Three factors impose a unique character of planning in Israel. They are: land, people, time.

*Land.* Israel, a bridge between three continents, is bordered by the Mediterranean on the west, Lake Tiberias and the Dead Sea on the east, the Mountains of Lebanon to the north, and the Sinai Penninsula, the Gulf of Elath and the Arabian Desert to the south. Its limited area of 20,800,000 dunams includes regions varying widely in their natural characteristics. They range from the level and fertile coastal plains of the Shfelah and the Sharon to the at present desolate Hills of Galilee in the north, and the Judean Hills near Jerusalem; from the wastes of the Southern Negev, rich in mineral deposits, to the sloping plain of the Jordan Valley; from Lake Tiberias 200 metres below sea-level to the Dead Sea 400 metres below sea-level, and the deepest depression on the surface of the earth. Climate may also vary from region to region within distances of a few kilometres. From the mild Mediterranean climate of the Coastal Plain or the dry, cool climate of the Hills of Galilee and Judea, to the sub-tropical heat of the Jordan Valley, or the aridity of Elath and the Red Sea. The variations in climate are accompanied by changes in the properties of the soil. The vegetal and topographical conditions produce a rich and colourful mosaic offering ample planning opportunities.

*People.* The second factor involves the social structure, character and composition of the population in this country. The Jewish population of Israel, numbering 655,000 before the establishment of the State, had succeeded in integrating and achieving a measure of homogeneity in the course of a single generation, although it stemmed from widely varying cultural and social groups. With the completion of the first three years of the State, the number of inhabitants has been doubled. These new residents, and all those who will eventually join them, offer exceedingly diverse cultural and vital patterns.

This Ingathering of Exiles will consolidate and achieve unity only if afforded a background of physical, social and economic conditions that are both adequate and encouraging. It is therefore essential that this second, social factor, should play a basic part in our planning policy. With the founding of new and the enlargement of existing settlements, with the establishment of new towns, and an objective of balanced distribution of the population, attention must be paid to social composition; and a planning framework prepared that will promote the acclimatisation of the diverse groups of the population, old and new, and expedite their integration into one organic and productive entity.

*Time.* The third factor, that of time, makes it urgently necessary for the State to treble its population within a few years. This urgency, translated into concrete fact, means the trebling of agricultural and urban settlements, the erection of sufficient dwellings, schools, public buldings and industrial structures, as well as the expansion of communications. The quickened tempo of development, and the resultant pressure, combine to exert a great and sometimes negative influence on planning proper. Planning is by its very nature a slow process, demanding the basic survey of economic causes and careful research into physical and social conditions as a prerequisite condition. Yet the introduction of the time element, i.e., the

*NOTE*:
***Population figures, areas in dunams, and classifications refer to the completion of Stage One of the Master Plan for Israel, at which point the population of the country is envisaged as 2,650,000. In the course of development, changes will doubtless ensue in the areas and data quoted, leading to certain alterations in the general range and specific details of the Master Plan. These, however, will not affect the basic principles or general framework of the latter.***



⑬ "Outline of the National Plan," *Physical Planning in Israel*, Arieh Sharon, 1951. Arieh Sharon digital archive.

need to ensure that immediate requirements be satisfied first, is in itself detrimental to the quality of planning. Immigrant and transit camps, housing estates and settlements, all planned and built in haste will remain as social and economic blots on the landscape and may be succeeded by even worse blemishes later on. Since the primary task of planning is to shape the future pattern of the land, its settlements, towns, and country-wide services, the time factor calling for compromise may prove to be detrimental to planning and country alike. These three factors, land, people and time, determine planning in Israel and dictate its objectives.

## AIMS OF THE NATIONAL MASTER PLAN

When the State was founded the overwhelming majority of the population, totalling 82%, was concentrated in a narrow coastal strip extending from Haifa to Tel Aviv. Jerusalem contained 11%, and only an insignificant part, 7%, lived in Galilee and in the south of the country. Following the establishment of the State and the extension of its sovereignity to the whole present area of the country, there arose the problem of the development of abandoned regions, and the direction of population thither. The rural population is distributed naturally throughout the country, its density determined by the qualities of the soil and the quantities of water available for irrigation. The urban population, however, is expected to constitute almost 80% of the total population and its distribution depends to a great extent on planning policy. The latter should be the means of guiding it in the directions desirable from the national and economic standpoint, and may determine its character.

When considering urbanisation, we distinguish between large urban concentrations of 100,000 inhabitants and over, and those of lesser size. The large towns of the world are sustained by special economic, industrial and commercial conditions, such as mineral deposits, harbours, and transport junctions. Medium-sized and small towns are natural centres for their agricultural environs, and offer central market-town facilities to their regions. Such towns are now beginning to attract those types of industry which endeavour to escape from the congestion of large cities. The ratio between large and medium-sized towns varies according to the structure and character of the different states. In rich overseas colonial countries (e.g., Australia and South America) two thirds of the urban population is concentrated in the big port towns and live at the expense of the vast hinterlands, rich in soil and mineral deposits. In small Central and West European countries, which are economically, physically and sociologically similar to Israel, the urban population is well balanced and distributed, and a large proportion of them (55%-75%) can be found in medium-sized and small towns.

It is worth noting that under the mandate the character of settlement in this country, excluding the organised agricultural communities, resembled that of colonial territories. The Jewish urban population was concentrated in the three large cities (82% of the total). No more than 18% lived in the small towns, and of them two thirds lived in such satellites of Tel Aviv as Rehovot, Rishon Lezion, Petah Tikva, Herzlia and Kfar Saba. Greater Tel Aviv comprised more than 43% of the Jewish population at that time, thus creating a world record.( Vienna numbered 33% of the population of Austria, and Greater London 22% of the population of England). It is of interest that during the great economic crisis which Germany and America experienced in the Twenties, the large cities and the purely agricultural areas were the main victims, whereas the small and medium towns with their relatively well-balanced economy stood firm. Many examples can be cited of other evils that have grown into malignant diseases gnawing at the giant bodies of the world's largest cities. The first symptoms of these diseases, i.e. costly services, disrupted communications, high cost of living and overcrowding in home and street, all reducing the standard of public health and hygiene, are already apparent in the large towns of Israel.

The restrictive political conditions under the mandatory government served to promote the growth of exaggerated urban concentrations in this country. An example of these conditions may be found in the White Paper of 1939, which confined Jewish settlement to a small fraction of the country, thereby promoting speculative development and congestion on the perimeter of the large towns. Since the establishment of the State of Israel a great proportion of land is in governmental and public ownership. This facilitates the possibilities of urban expansion and agricultural settlement, and of harmonious and well-balanced population distribution throughout the country. In Israel, however, with its mass immigration, the process entailed in the "distribution of population" does not involve a transfer of the existing population resulting in economic and social loss, as it would in other countries. The directing of the incessant and ever-growing stream of immigration to undeveloped agricultural areas, and to new urban centres, is a relatively simple task.

With the purpose of guiding this development, plans for a well-balanced disposition of the population have been prepared. A division of the country into planning regions has been proposed as a planning measure for accomplishing this decentralisation of the population and its economy. Each planning region is a distinct geographical entity delimited by physical and topographical factors, such as water-catchment areas or river basins; due consideration being given to present urban and rural concentrations, land-ownership and existing services. Twenty-four of these planning regions, each to contain between 75,000-120,000 inhabitants, have been provided for in the initial stage of the country's development, not including the principal large towns. It should be possible to reduce this number to sixteen by uniting neighbouring regions during the transition stage, prior to the completion of development. One or two urban centres have been assigned to each region, to serve the rural hinterland as *foci* of trade, industry, social and educational activity, and seats of administration. The regions mapped out as geographical and economic units may be expected to evolve into complete and well-balanced social and economic entities, deriving benefit from the mutual relations between the urban centres and their hinterland.

## THE SCOPE OF PLANNING

Investigation and research into physical and economic conditions and the absorptive capacity of the country show that the first stage of development will be complete when the population numbers 2,650,000, including the minorities. At this stage the number of persons engaged in agriculture will be 600,000, comprising 22.6% of the total population. They will be able to supply the greater part of the demand for agricultural produce on the part of the urban population, which draws its livelihood from services, industry, trade and commerce.

The urban population, consisting of 2,050,000 souls, will be divided into two categories. Some 930,000 persons, constituting 45% of the urban population, will reside in the three main cities Haifa, Tel Aviv and Jerusalem, which enjoy the advantages of national as well as international factors of development. The remaining 55% of the urban population (1,120,000), will be found in the medium-sized and small towns which are to be distributed throughout the country. The first stage of national development is based on the assumption that the national economy can ensure a fair standard of living, while maintaining a balance between agriculture, industry, the trades and services. The second stage in development will be reached with the exploitation of the wealth and mineral deposits of the Negev, the linking of the country's ports to the commerce of the Near East, and the further expansion of industry.

The proposed distribution of the population, accompanied by a comprehensive plan determining the location of settlements, towns, industries and services, is imperative from the national and defence standpoints, and can be fulfilled only by a daring and consistent planning and development policy. In the absence of such a policy the masses of the population will apathetically follow the line of least resistance, drifting towards the existing conurbations, so that large stretches of the country will be left void of population and of human enterprise.

## FIVE BRANCHES OF PLANNING

The National Master Plan is a synthesis of the following five branches of planning: A directed agriculture, the location of industry, a communications system, a national scheme for parks and forests, and new towns.

### 1. DIRECTED AGRICULTURE

The plan for agriculture is based on a countrywide irrigation scheme (see Fig. 12) which envisages the exploitation of abundant water resources drawn from the Jordan, and the rivers in the northern zone; the Yarkon, and the subterranean waters of the Shfela; and the creation of reservoirs in the arid sections of the Hills of Judah and the northern Negev. The execution of the national irrigation scheme will permit the setting-up of about 120,000 farms, most of them under intensive cultivation, in units of 20-25 dunams per family. The remainder will be divided between extensive dry-farming units in poorly watered areas, and hill-farming in Judea and Galilee. The rural population should then number about 600,000 persons, 22.6% of the total population. At this stage of development, local agricultural production will meet about 75% of the population's food requirements, and in addition will allow the export of citrus fruit, vegetables, seeds, and flowers.

The agricultural plan constitutes the main factor of development by providing the population with essential products. It ensures economic self-sufficiency and serves as a key factor to a healthy, well-balanced economy. The agricultural overall plan including afforestation, extended to all parts of the country, makes a natural green background for the location of the various types of towns, industrial areas, and communication centres. Land devoted to agriculture also needs well-knit and detailed planning; for our agriculture is intensive, our farming economy mixed and many-sided, and the social structure of our agricultural settlements diverse in types, ranging from the communal settlement to the cooperative and work village.

An agricultural development plan prepared for the south of the country determines the division of land among various types of agricultural settlements according to farming needs, economy, and social structure. This plan has served as a background for the coordinated planning of other elements including the siting of local and regional centres, and the lay-out of local roads, benefiting agricultural settlements, and feeding the national highways.

### 2. LOCATION OF INDUSTRY

A balanced distribution of the population requires a planned geographical distribution of industry. Economic considerations and the needs of town-planning proper, which are opposed to exaggerated concentrations of industry in only a few places, are strengthened in Israel by political and security factors. The general tendency nowadays is to withdraw industry from congested centres and disperse it in country towns, which involves considerable financial expenditure and social difficulty. Israel's course is simpler as our industry is still in its infancy. We therefore have to direct most of the new industries to the various parts of the country in which they can best serve the requirements of economics, security and planning.

As a result of chance factors, Israel's industry has found its seat in the large towns. The survey of industry showed that more than 50% of the country's industry is at present concentrated in and around Tel Aviv (see Fig. 15). Our study of the possibilities of developing industry has shown us that only part of our industry requires the immediate vicinity of ports and large communication and population centres. Ours is largely light industry which may be easily located elsewhere if the necessary transport, water, drainage, electrical and man-power facilities are available. These industries will find greater amenities and more encouraging conditions in the small and medium centres, which have at their disposal cheaper land and more effective municipal services. The medium-sized town will make the life of industrial workers more easy, providing them with cheap and comfortable residential quarters, convenient transport to their places of employment and with green areas for recreation. Direct contact with agriculture also increases economic stability and cheapens the cost of living. All these factors together bring about lower wages in middle-sized and small towns.

A constructive and effective means of guidance towards new areas is the establishment of industrial zones near the new towns. These planned zones are located in areas suitable for industrial development and provided with transport, drainage, power and water supply. Their detailed planning requires a consideration of the various kinds of industry, the isolation of dangerous or noxious industries, and provision of car-parks and public and service buildings at suitable spots. All these allow manufactures to establish their enterprises in effective fashion. The first industrial zones are now being developed near the new towns of Beersheba, Migdal Gad, Ludd anr Ramleh, Acre, and Tiberias (see Fig. 17).

## 3. COMMUNICATIONS NETWORK

An effective system and well-organised transport system is, under modern economic conditions, a prerequisite for successful industrial development, for reducing the transport distance of agricultural produce to markets, and for general development. A dense and intensive settlement in a comparatively small country like Israel will impose a particular burden on the various traffic-routes. It is therefore necessary to carefully weigh the purpose and scope of each means of communication (road, railway, air and water-routes) and its integration within the comprehensive communication plan.

The general communication plan has laid down vital new routes for the development of empty and desolate areas: roads which are non-existent in the present network, but are needed to reduce the distance between the various districts, and roads by-passing the large centres, thus preventing congestion and bottle-necks. National routes linking the various parts of the country must avoid the large and medium-sized towns, with which they should be linked by subsidiary connections distributing the burden of traffic and leading to the various parts of the town, by the shortest possible routes. The section of the National route which has been marked in a straight line from Rishon Lezion through Bnei Brak to the Raanana—Kfar Saba crossroads may serve as an example. This new section will reduce distances and by-pass all such towns as: Rehovot, Rishon Lezion, Tel Aviv, Ramat Gan, Bnei Brak, Petah Tikva, which are now passed through by all traffic, leading to delay, economic loss, and road fatalities.

The communications plan for the country is determined by the latter's shape, and the narrow waist in the middle. This shape makes it necessary to establish two communication centres, northern and southern, respectively. The northern centre is to be near the Bay of Haifa, the principal port of the country which is linked with other sections by train and road. The development of the country requires the expansion of the port, the improvement and widening of roads and the establishment of an airfield near Haifa, making the town the natural centre of communications for Galilee, the Zvulun, Jezreel, Beth Shean and Jordan valleys, and for the Shomron. The second centre in the south does not at present exist, as this part of the country was not developed in the past. The railway junction at Ludd is unsuitable for this purpose, and its proper place should be in the vicinity of Ashdot-Yavneh. The latter is the natural focal point for the north-south and east-west (Jerusalem) railway lines and for parallel national roads. Together with a deep-water port to be established near the mouth of the Sukreir it will be the second centre of communications, naturally and efficiently serving the three principal areas of the south: the Tel Aviv region, Jerusalem and the Corridor, the south of the country and the Negev (see Fig. 8).

## 4. PARKS, AFFORESTATION AND LANDSCAPE PRESERVATION

The National Plan provides for afforestation areas on the mountain and hill slopes which are at present desolate on account of neglect and soil erosion for many generations. Within these afforestation areas, at spots whose agricultural value is non-existent or negligible, special areas have been earmarked because of their characteristic flora and fauna, beautiful landscape or other special natural qualities. All these constitute protected areas, including botanical and zoological reservations and special sites of outstanding historic, archaeological or architectural importance. They are included within the system of national parks, which will serve as the lungs of the entire country. A specially appointed public body has ascribed priority for immediate execution to four parks. These are: The Jarmak Park east of Safed, covering an area of 95,000 dunams as a national recreation centre (see Fig. 21); the Carmel Park near Haifa over an area of 105,000 dunams; the Falik-Shfaim-Yarkon Park along the sands of the seashore for weekend recreation of the densely populated Tel Aviv region (see Fig. 20); The Nahal Sorek Park over an area of 96,000 dunams on the slopes of the mountains of Judea west of Jerusalem (see Fig. 22).

The planning of the Galilee park shows our approach to park-planning. The starting point is the shore of the Sea of Galilee near Tiberias, in the reconstruction area of the Old City, containing the latters future public buildings. The park will spread north along the shore of the Sea of Galilee in a protected area containing such important historical sites as Kfar Nahum and Tabgha, and embrace the northern shore of the sea. This protected area will be linked by strips of forest and greenery along the steep Wadi Hamam to the Horns of Hattin, and will continue along Wadi Amud to the hills of Safed and the Jarmak park. From there footpaths will lead to the beautiful landscapes in the vicinity of Wadi Keren and will continue to the Mediterranean coast at Nahariya. This plan provides convenient approaches to spots earmarked for hotels, convalescent homes and rest-camps, and footpaths leading into the inner parts of the park intented for youth-rambles and tourists.

## 5. THE NEW TOWNS

It should be noted that the term "new towns" also includes existent centres (such as Safed, Tiberias, Nahariya, Acre, Afula, Migdal Gad, Beersheba, Ludd and Ramleh) of limited population which are not in themselves capable of effective development without a basic programme and comprehensive government aid. In each case the size, character and functions of the town are determined by the economic and physical data of the region. The more important of these towns are planned for an average size of fourty to sixty thousand inhabitants, and will serve as administrative, commercial and industrial centres for the planning regions.

The following considerations led to the selection of the areas on which the new towns will be built: the function of the city as a geographical centre in its area of influence; elevated ground, a rich landscape and pleasant climate, which favour productivity and the social stability of the population; land suitable for building and cheap development, drainage and road network; the accessibility of employment factors, mineral deposits and the national communications system. The structure of the new cities is determined by their division into neighbourhood units. This differs from the more conservative town-planning methods still followed in the older cities of Europe and also in this country, which are built in endless monotonous gridirons of buildings, streets and residential quarters. The basic idea of the new method is that the city should be divided into a number of neighbourhood units each of which will constitute an independent entity satisfying the requirements of its residents in the most effective fashion. Each unit containing residential buildings of various types according to the family and social structure; public and commercial buildings at central points; educational institutions with public gardens nearby; and sports and recreation grounds. The size of these units varies in accordance with a number of factors, the most important of which are: the capacity of the school, optimum size of a commercial centre, and length of streets and paths within the neighbourhood. The aim is to prevent any unnecessary dangerous traffic within the limits of these neighbourhoods, to permit access by foot to vital services on the part of the residents (at distances not exceeding 750 metres) and to provide footpaths for school children. The size of a neighbourhood unit, varying from 6,000 to 10,000 persons, changes with the topographical situation, structure, character and area of the town.

In the new towns a number of neighbourhood units will be located round the urban centre, which should be of a distinctive architectural and urban character. The centre will contain the central institutions of the town, the business buildings, banks, shops and store-houses, social and public buildings, central educational and cultural institutions with parks and gardens nearby. The industrial zone will be linked with the national communications system (road and rail), and will be situated at the spot most suitable for the town in respect of prevailing winds and separated from it by a broad green strip (see plans for new towns, Fig. 29-48). National communication routes will be linked with the new towns by short approach roads and an internal road network linking the centre with the trade and industrial areas and the functionally organised neighbourhood units.

# FORMS OF SETTLEMENT IN THE NATIONAL PLAN

A survey of existing settlement and the consideration of future planning-needs led to a classification of five main settlement types in the country. These differ in size, social and economic characteristics and purposes, as follows:

1. Village unit constituting a basic agricultural cell with a population of about 500;
2. Rural centre composed of several agricultural units linked to a common service centre, with about 2,000 inhabitants;
3. Rural-urban centre providing economic, cultural, commercial and industrial services for dozens of villages in the vicinity, with a population of 6,000-12,000;
4. Medium town to serve as the centre of its region, with a population between 40,000 and 60,000;
5. Large town containing regional and national development factors with a population exceeding 100,000.

Only the first and fifth of these types, i.e. village and the large town, are at present to be found in Israel.

There is a gap between them, in which can be seen the first faint indications of the remaining types. This phenomenon of isolated agricultural units on the one hand, and two congested and crowded conurbations on the other, does not contribute to the social and economic stability of the country. The second, third and fourth basic types will fill the gap existing between the villages and large towns as cultural and economic centres, and will provide a graded social and economic continuity.

## VILLAGE UNIT

A village unit contains up to 100 agricultural families who till an irrigated area of some 2,000-3,000 dunams or larger areas of extensive agriculture. In this type we differentiate between two basic social structures: the *kvutza* (or small *kibbutz*) and the *moshav*.

In the *moshav* cooperation is restricted to joint purchases and sales, and common use of agricultural machinery. The area is divided into equal-sized plots, one of which belongs to each member and lies wholly or partially beside his house; hence the dwelling-houses are at a distance from one another across extensive area. Close together in the centre of the village are found public buildings like the school, kindergarten, community halls, and such economic services as the consumers' cooperative store, the smithy, garage and store-houses (see diagrams, Fig. 2 and Fig. 25). In the *moshav shitufi* (cooperative moshav) land is tilled and farm work performed jointly. Family houses and small hold-are concentrated in a central spot (see Fig. 26).

In the *kvutza* the partnership covers all aspects of the economy and everyday life which find expression in the planning scheme. Here cooperation leads to the separation of various building areas: dwelling areas for adults, youth and children; a central area for public buildings such as dining and community halls and library; and the farm buildings area for poultry runs, cowshed, workshop, and store-houses. The agricultural land is divided according to soil qualities and scientific methods of cultivation in the varied farm branches such as: grain-farming, vegetables, fruit trees, etc. (see schematic diagram, Fig. 1).

## RURAL CENTRE

The cultural and economic rural centre will be common to groups of three to five *moshavim* resembling parts of a large village numbering 400 to 500 families. This centre will contain the cooperative consumer stores, bakery and restaurant, store-houses and refrigeration plants, packing houses and garages, areas for handicrafts and light industries; schools with sport grounds, community-hall and synagogue. The centre will also contain the secretariat, dispensary, police station, and residential quarters for persons engaged in the economic and cultural institutions. The natural spot for a rural centre will be in the midst of the cultivated areas between the villages, on an elevated site with suitable physical characteristics (see Beer Tuvia scheme, Fig. 4). Within the framework of the rural centres may be included the large *kibbutzim* which have achieved a high degree of economic maturity thanks to their own initiative, and have well-developed economic and cultural services, while their populations now amount to about 2,000 persons each (Givat Brenner, Yagur, Tel Joseph, En Harod). In these *kibbutzim* the scheme resembles that of a small *kvutza.* There are several types of common living quarters for different age groups, extensive areas for public and educational buildings with spacious gardens, and well-organised farm sections separated by green strips from public and residential areas (see En Harod and Tel Joseph, Fig. 27). However, the rapid growth of the *kibbutzim,* which is accompanied by an expansion in area, has increased the walking distances between the living quarters and the communal buildings (dining halls), creating new problems of circulation, distance and space, whose adequate solution may change the structure of future *kibbutz* settlements. The division of the agricultural areas in a large *kibbutz* resembles that of the *kvutza,* and depends on the physical qualities of the soil and its suitability to the various branches of agriculture and other economic data (see scheme, Fig. 3). Industries, particularly of an agricultural character, have developed in most *kibbutzim* as a healthy sign of an agricultural-industrial combination that maintains a balance in the local economy.

## RURAL-URBAN CENTRE

An agricultural area of a 100,000 dunams containing about 30 villages with a rural population of some 15,000 requires a large centre containing regional services and handicrafts, agricultural industry using the produce of the vicinity, a building materials industry and special industries based on local mineral resources, and the initiative of the population. This centre will contain regional secondary, agricultural and vocational schools; administration, commercial, cultural and health institutions. Rural-urban centres should be established at once, as there are areas comprising dozens of villages, some of them well-developed, requiring regional services and man-power for building and development. The population of the rural-urban centres is between 6,000 and 12,000. In some cases they can serve as regional towns, with a subsequent growth in the population (see Khalsa, Fig. 29).

## MEDIUM TOWN

This type includes the medium-sized towns, whose purpose is to serve as the central city for a planning region constituting an economic entity with a population of 75,000-120,000 at the end of the First Stage of Development. Consideration of the topographical and physical data and the economic possibilities of a region suggest a town population of 40,000-60,000. (This size of urban centre, regarded in England and the smaller countries of Western Europe as an optimum, permits the carrying out of an organic and effective town-planning scheme, the development of a healthy economy, the provision of cheap municipal services and the promotion of cultural and social activities). The regional town will contain regional banking, administrative and medical institutions, agricultural craft and industries, and educational and communal buildings (see table of population distribution in Afula on page 20 below). However, the chief purpose of these towns is to absorb the national industries which now burden the major urban centres, and to place cheap land and services and other encouraging factors at their disposal.

## THE LARGE TOWNS

Jerusalem, Tel Aviv and Haifa, the three large towns of Israel, have special functions and their development is influenced by various national and international factors.

Jerusalem, the capital, is the seat of government, higher educational and cultural institutions (the university) and leading public and social bodies. There are obvious factors favouring the development of tourism, a cool summer climate suitable for a national recreation centre, and quarries on which a building materials industry can be based. Tel Aviv is the large centre of industry and finance, and has a rich hinterland of citrus groves in the Shfela, as well as an enterprising population possessed of much initiative.

Haifa with its large port is a natural centre for heavy industry, international commerce, oil pipeline terminals and oil refineries. Its situation on the spacious bay and on the slopes of the Carmel favours the development of healthy living conditions even in summer, and provides the basis for a stable economy, together with convenient and pleasant living conditions for the inhabitants.

In preparing our plan for the distribution of the population it has been assumed that, as compared with the 15th of May 1948, the urban population in Haifa and Jerusalem will be trebled, while there will be a growth of 60%-75% in the population of Tel Aviv—the most densely inhabited place in the country. The surplus of the growing population of Tel Aviv can be easily directed to its surrounding sattelites.

The present town-planning schemes of the large towns do not respond to their function and growth. The main reason for this is their rapid development, which has already gone beyond the initial targets set without foresight. There were supplementary factors of land speculation, leading to excessive exploitation of the building area, and narrow streets, depriving the cities of open spaces and public gardens. The plans prepared also adhered to the conservative methods of continuous and gridiron development. Following the establishment of the State of Israel, crowded conditions have changed radically. Much land, partly public and state, has been added to the building areas of the large towns. The targets of development have been decided on, and opportunities have been afforded for preparing master-plans for the large cities.

Planning efforts in the latter must endeavour to ensure the improvement of the build-up areas, to solve traffic problems and rehabilitate slum quarters. In particular efforts must be made to secure an effective and basic planning of the new parts of the towns by the development of residential units or specifically planned quarters, separated from one another by broad green wedges.

Fig. 1. Kvutza — schematic distribution of agricultural areas.

Fig. 2. Moshav — schematic distribution of building zones and agricultural areas.

Fig. 3. Large Kibbutz — schematic distribution of agricultural areas.

Fig. 4. Beer Tuvia — a rural centre serving five moshavim.

Fig. 5. Khalsa — a rural-urban centre which will serve some thirty rural settlements.

Fig. 6. Afula — a medium-sized town as a regional centre.

Fig. 7. Haifa — a large town with its hinterland.

Fig. 8. Principal zones of influence in the national plan. Zone of influence — circumscribed by brown line. Population on 15.5.48 — black segment. Population upon completing first stage of development — red segment. Industry — violet symbol, in ring. Port — anchor within blue ring. Traffic junction — black symbol. Park — tree within green ring.

## THE MASTER PLAN AND ITS PRINCIPAL ZONES

The Master Plan (see Fig. 8 and map on page 26) indicates four principal zones: Northern, Central, Jerusalem Corridor and Southern.

A. THE NORTHERN ZONE extends over the mountainous areas of Galilee and Shomron, embracing the fruitful valleys of the Huleh, the Jordan and Jezreel, and contains eleven planning regions. On 15th May 1948 its Jewish population was 177,500. Upon completion of Stage One of Development the population of this zone should consist of more than 1,000,000 inhabitants. It contains well-watered and fruitful agricultural areas in the valleys, and mountain and hill tracts suited for orchards and mountain farming. The rich agricultural hinterland will provide a basis for the establishment of many medium and small towns enjoying physical and climatic conditions conductive to the development of light industries and skilled crafts. The capital of the zone is Haifa, the city with the second largest natural harbour in the Middle East, an international centre of trade and heavy industry, and a communications centre for the north and its hinterland. This Northern zone has many climatic advantages favouring the development of large recreation areas, and in it are also located the two large National Parks of the Jarmak and the Carmel.

B. THE CENTRAL ZONE extends from Natanya to Rehovot, comprising the fruitful Shfela along the shores of the Mediterranean as far as the range of the foothills of Judah to the East. It includes seven planning regions, and its population, which numbered 396,000 on 15th May 1948, should amount to 1,000,000 inhabitants upon completion of Stage One of Development. The agricultural land within this zone is fertile and has adequate water for irrigation. It contains the citrus belt and provides the sites for its ancillary industry. Within this agricultural area are the colonies which, thanks to the development of the citrus trade, have absorbed a large population and been transformed into well-established country towns. Following the completion of the Master Plan, these country towns (Herzlia, Kfar Saba, Petah Tikva, Rishon Lezion, Rehovot) may be expected to expand into firmly established medium towns absorbing the surplus of the population of Tel Aviv. They will constitute a strong ring of satellite cities around Tel Aviv, attracting industries which tend to concentrate in that already overcrowded centre. The principal city of this zone is Tel Aviv, the trade, financial and light industry centre, with the largest concentration of productive and enterprising population in the country. The wandering sand dunes along the seashore between Nathania and Yavneh, which will be transformed into national park areas following their impending afforestation, will serve as the recreation area and maritime sports region for the zone and the country as a whole.

C. THE THIRD ZONE, which is limited in area but rich in past and present values, consists of Jerusalem and the Corridor leading thereto. This zone contains two regions: The Jerusalem City region, and the Judea region extending over the mountains of Judea and the chains of foothills that descend to the valleys on the West and the South. On 15th May 1938 this zone contained 78,150 Jews, but at the completion of Development Stage One its population should have grown to 300,000. The Jerusalem Corridor contains mountain areas which

# DOSSIER:
# ARIEH SHARON'S MISE-EN-SCÈNE

⑭

In his autobiography, *Kibbutz + Bauhaus: An Architect's Way in a New Land*, Arieh Sharon describes the "information drive" that led to the 1950 planning exhibition at the Tel Aviv Museum:

> We tried very hard to gain the support of public opinion for our national planning, using various channels, such as press conferences, articles and lectures. The high point of this information drive was a town-planning exhibition in the Tel Aviv Museum—the first exhibition ever held there which was not devoted to the arts. We presented panels showing the principles of the National Plan, some regional plans, including communication networks, agricultural and industrial areas, distribution of population, National Parks and open spaces, and the general layout of new towns spread all over the country. In addition, a few instructive, partly humorous panels presented the most burning subjects and problems of planning, such as traffic jams, noise, pollution, and over-crowding. We indicated ways of solving such problems by clever and architecturally comprehensive planning. Sooner or later everyone came to see the exhibition—civil servants, the "intelligentsia," technicians, workers, soldiers, and, of course, the politicians from the different parties.
>
> Ben-Gurion, when asked how he liked the exhibition, said: "Those are the most beautiful colors I have seen in my life," referring to the English watercolors of the new town plans. [...] The Minister of Finance, Eliezer Kaplan, a very able economist, was our most severe critic. He said bluntly: "Even if you were the world's best architects, it is not your job but the Government's to decide on the location, size and ultimate goals of the new towns." I replied: "These are only proposals—it is up to you, the Government, to study them, to consider them and then to make the decisions." He laughed, and said: "You know very well that the Government will never have the time and patience, especially with the war going on, to concentrate on these matters. Once the plans are drawn, the development, if any, will follow your suggestions." He was right.[1] ■

1 Arieh Sharon, *Kibbutz + Bauhaus: An Architect's Way in a New Land* (Stuttgart and Tel Aviv: Karl Kramer Verlag and Massada, 1976), p. 79.

⑭ "Planning or Laissez-Faire." Map A: "80% of the country's population today lives on Israel's narrow coastline." Map B: "The population is equally distributed across the entire country." Bottom: "National planning—the way toward equal population distribution." Poster, National Planning Exhibition, Tel Aviv Museum, 1950. Arieh Sharon, Planning Department.
⑮ Preparation work, National Planning Exhibition, Tel Aviv Museum, 1950. Detail. Benjamin Idelson collection (Gershon Zippor), Israel Architecture Archive.
⑯ Preparation work, National Planning Exhibition, Tel Aviv Museum, 1950. Detail. Benjamin Idelson collection (Gershon Zippor), Israel Architecture Archive.

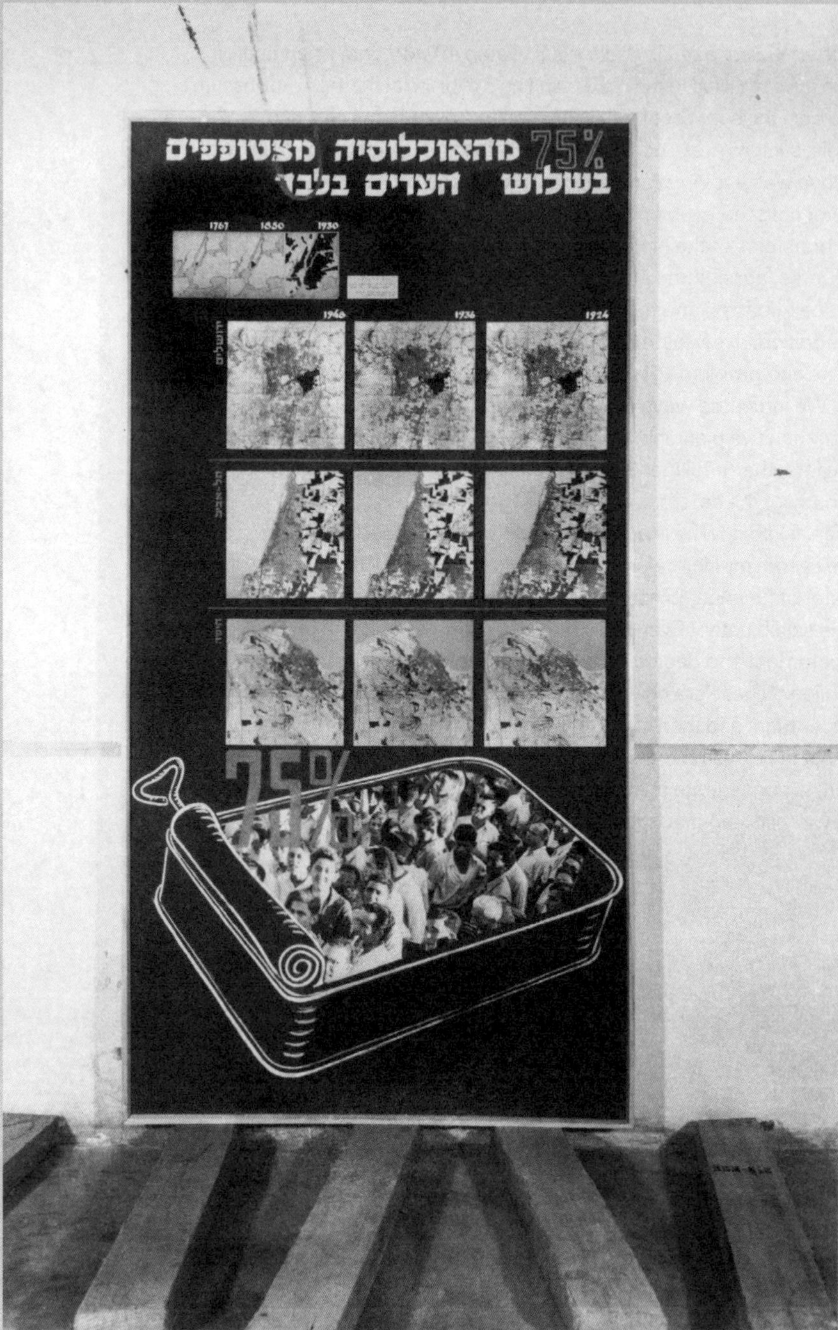

75% מהאוכלוסיה מצטופפים
בשלוש הערים בלבד
1767 1850 1930
1946 1936 1924
75%


⑮

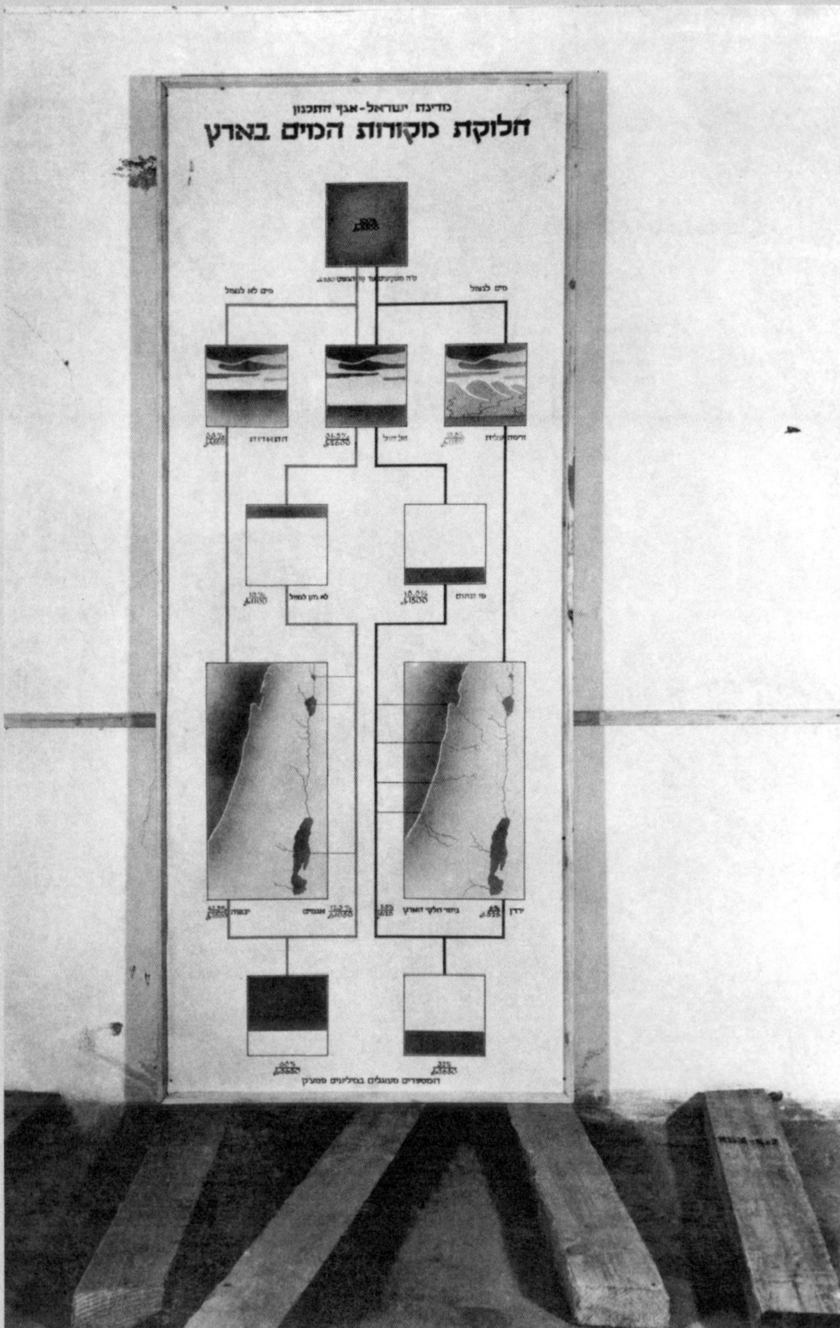


⑯

⑰

⑱

⑰ “The Problem—Where Will We Settle the New Immigrants? Not in Crowded Cities, But All Over the Country.” “With 1000 immigrants arriving every day, it is necessary to raise a roof above a new family every 2 minutes.” “Mass housing will be developed all over the country.” Poster, National Planning Exhibition, Tel Aviv Museum, 1950. Arieh Sharon, Planning Department..
⑱ “The Beach—A Source of Rest and Recreation.” Poster, National Planning Exhibition, Tel Aviv Museum, 1950. Arieh Sharon, Planning Department.

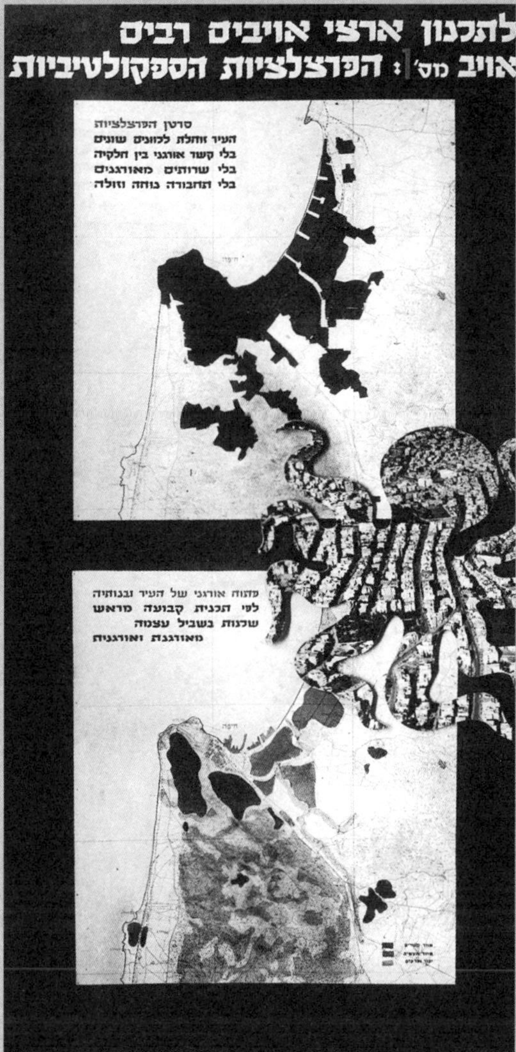


⑲

⑳

⑲ “The National Planning Scheme Has Many Enemies. Enemy No. 1: Speculative Parcellations.” Top: “The cancer of parcellations: The city creeps in different directions. With no organic connection between its parts. With no adequate social services. With no affordable public transportation.” Bottom: “An organic development of the city and its satellite towns, according to a well-organized plan, exhibiting virtues of neighborliness, well organized and organic.” Poster, National Planning Exhibition, Tel Aviv Museum, 1950. Arieh Sharon, Planning Department.
⑳ “How would a person in Israel make a living?” “Planning is fundamental to a stable economic structure”. Poster, National Planning Exhibition, Tel Aviv Museum, 1950. Arieh Sharon, Planning Department.

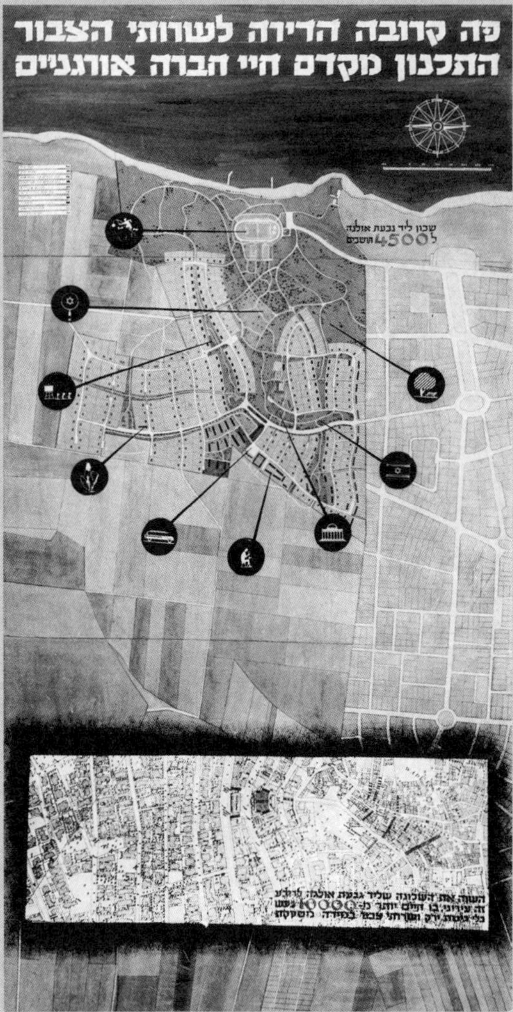


㉑

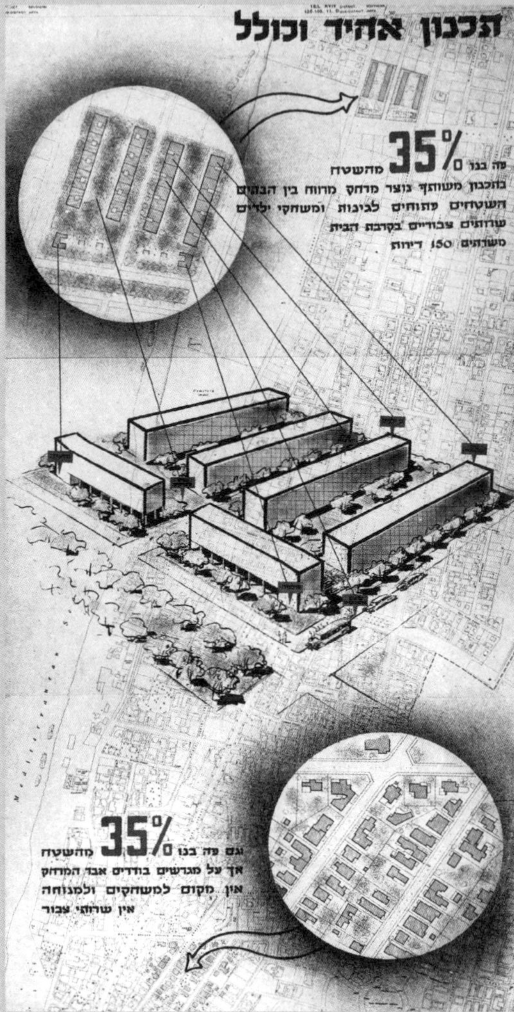


㉒

㉑ “Here the Apartment Is Close to Public Services. Planning Promotes Organic Social Life.” Poster, National Planning Exhibition, Tel Aviv Museum, 1950. Arieh Sharon, Planning Department.

㉒ “Uniform and Comprehensive Planning.” Top: “Here we made use of 35% of the lot. Uniform planning enables balanced distances between buildings. Areas are then vacant for developing parks and for children’s activities. Public services are in reach—and can serve up to 150 households.” Bottom: “In this case, 35% of the area was also developed. But on private lots, the advantages of the distance between buildings are lost. No space left for children’s play or recreation—none for public amenities.” Poster, National Planning Exhibition, Tel Aviv Museum, 1950. Arieh Sharon, Planning Department.

㉓

㉔

㉓ "The Spread of Speculation Attacks the Village As Well. Following Land Parcellation, Agriculture Turns to Wasteland." Poster, National Planning Exhibition, Tel Aviv Museum, 1950. Arieh Sharon, Planning Department.

㉔ "Town Planners Preserve the Natural Values of the Landscape." Poster, National Planning Exhibition, Tel Aviv Museum, 1950. Arieh Sharon, Planning Department.

# Theory

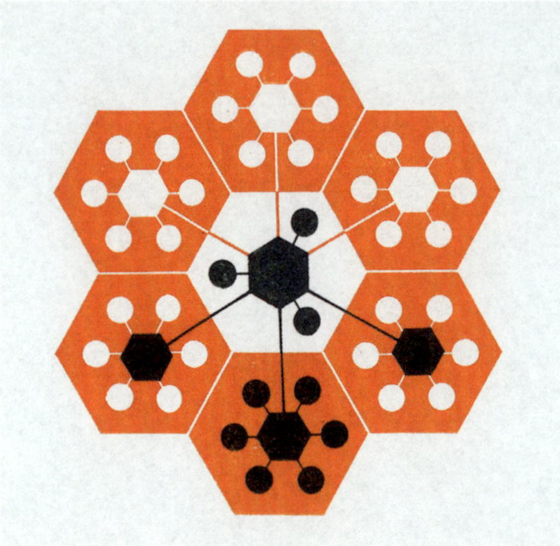

①

## The Specter of *Raumplanung*

The Israeli master plan rests on the inexplicable proposition of a systemic, pseudoscientific, and abrupt fabrication of an "organic," "regionalist," "historical" landscape. The most rudimentary device for achieving this unusual construct was the division of the country into twenty-four districts, designed mathematically to contain an equal number of residents. The districts were determined according to geographic characteristics and were planned as arrays of agricultural settlements clustered around central villages and served by a regional town. Size and quantity (of population, area, distance, or employment) were perceived as reliable criteria for obtaining the optimal interactions between center and periphery, city and country, industry and agriculture. The pattern overruled singularities, as could be traced in the planners' discourse of the time:

> From the perspective of national and regional planning, we are not interested in the town per se, but rather in its position and its status within the general law of *Siedlungsstruktur* (pattern of settlement) of the region or the entire country.[1]

While the primary effort was indeed to mold the State as a whole into a general law of *Siedlungsstruktur*, the "town per se," or the district town, was in fact the focal point of concerted professional efforts, and the question of its optimal shape and size was the subject of lengthy discussions among urban planners. A setup of an intimate town, housing between 20,000 and 50,000 residents, was idealized and advertised as a perfected urban prototype designed for a model community. The idealized image of the new town was contrasted verbally and graphically with the image of the "congested" city in caricature warfare, which aimed to prevent or divert the development of spontaneous colonization and socialization patterns that were typical of New World countries.

The regional restructuring of the country and the patterned setup of district towns supposedly emulated the historical European layout, wherein the majority of the population dwells in small- and medium-sized towns integrated into the agricultural hinterland and only a minority lives in the big cities. Needless to say, this hierarchical matrix originated in

②

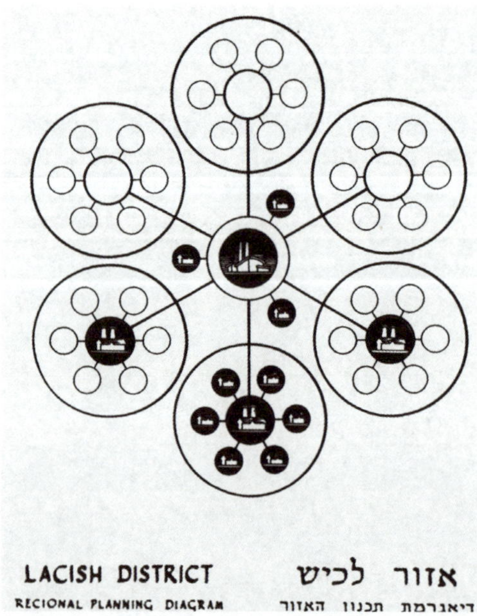

③

pre-industrial agrarian culture and reflected centuries of adaptation, modification, and homeostasis. Israel's planners tried to squeeze this course into a single heroic decade, buttressing their ambitions with a wealth of architectural and spatial theories that projected urban and rural diagrams and analyzed the correlation between settlement patterns and perseverance during times of crisis. In contrast to the "balanced" European environment, the Israeli planners described the "New World" countries as structurally "bipolar" and colonially juvenile:

> We find a different character of settlement pattern in new countries colonized "from the outside" by immigrants at the end of the nineteenth century (Australia, Argentina, West United States, and Canada). [...] Population, industry, and services concentrated there in a few cities and created a "polar" structure without the formation of a web of small and medium centers. This structure indicates the settlement immaturity of a country or a region.[2]

By contrast, Israel's alleged instant maturity is self-promoted as simultaneously revolutionary and restorative:

> The essence of the "geographic revolution" initiated with the establishment of the State and still in operation is not only "population dispersal," but more so the dismantling of the "polar" structure and the creation of a foundational and hierarchical network of centers. [...] The goal is to introduce between the "poles" of the big city and the primary rural cell another three degrees of centers and to divert the service functions gradually [...] to the new network.[3]

The Israeli "dismantling of the 'polar' structure" relied on the two grand spatial theories of the time and their various dialects:

①–② Regional planning diagram, Lachish district, mid-1950s.
③ *The County of London Plan: Social and Functional Analysis*, 1943. Patrick Abercrombie.

Ebenezer Howard's garden city, as formulated in his 1898 treatises, *Tomorrow: A Peaceful Path to Reform* and *Garden Cities of To-Morrow*, and illustrated in his universally applicable cartwheel-shaped hexagonal diagram of "Communities in the Green"; and Walter Christaller's central-place theory, as proposed in his 1933 doctoral thesis, *Die zentralen Orte in Süddeutschland*, and demonstrated in a regional grid pattern of hierarchical rural and urban settlements, also arranged hexagonally. Indeed, the hexagon is a common leitmotif in these two expansion theories, but their vectors point in opposite directions: the garden city evolves in radiating rings from the urban to the countryside, while the central places extend rhizomatically from the village to the town.

The history of the garden-city movement ran in parallel to that of the Zionist movement. These two movements were born simultaneously; they evolved within the same zeitgeist and shared similar reformist values. Zionism interpreted the garden city as a "back to the land" mentality with explicit anti-capitalist and anti-bourgeois principles of land ownership and a preference for agricultural occupations. Garden-city planners found in Zionist Palestine a fertile ground for some of the earliest and most insightful applications of garden-city ideals. According to historian S. Ilan Troen, British architect and town planner Clifford Holliday, in his 1933 article "Town and Country Planning in Palestine," claimed that "Zionism's preference for garden cities even predated Howard, and that the basis for welcoming his ideas was inherent in Zionist colonization."[4] Patrick Geddes, perhaps the most illustrious adherent of the garden-city movement, had by 1919 become the first official town planner for the World Zionist Organization as well as an adviser to the Mandatory government in Palestine.

Conceptually, then, Zionism was a Jewish-Levantine dialect of the garden-city movement all along, and this affiliation was kept after the establishment of the State by emulating the template of the British postwar new towns. Practically, however, it was the central-place theory that provided the Israeli planners a gestalt, an imposing structural scheme and an effective organizational tool with which to boost the scale of their spatial precepts and territorial operations. It would be far-reaching, but not at all inaccurate, to suggest that Christaller's central-place theory presents the conceptual template into which the State of Israel was engraved. Let us, then, look closely at this theory and its deplorable applications before returning to the Israeli garden city.

In his dissertation on central-place theory, published in 1933 as *Die zentralen Orte in Süddeutschland*, Walter Christaller constructed a mathematical model to calculate population dispersal in Europe, meticulously analyzing the distances between centers. According to his theory, the Great Depression, which affected both Europe and the United States from 1929 through the 1930s, was proof that big cities and distinctly agricultural areas suffered economic destruction and unemployment, while medium-sized and small towns located in rural areas, which sustained a mixed economy of agriculture, industry, and craft, maintained relative social and economic stability due to mobility of employment. According to architectural historian Joachim Trezib:

> [Christaller's theory] portrayed the model of a spatially balanced population optimum as a hexagonal geometric structure. It was setting a precedent in that it appeared to impose a mathematical predictability on a system of settlements which were perfectly in balance with one another in respect of their population size,

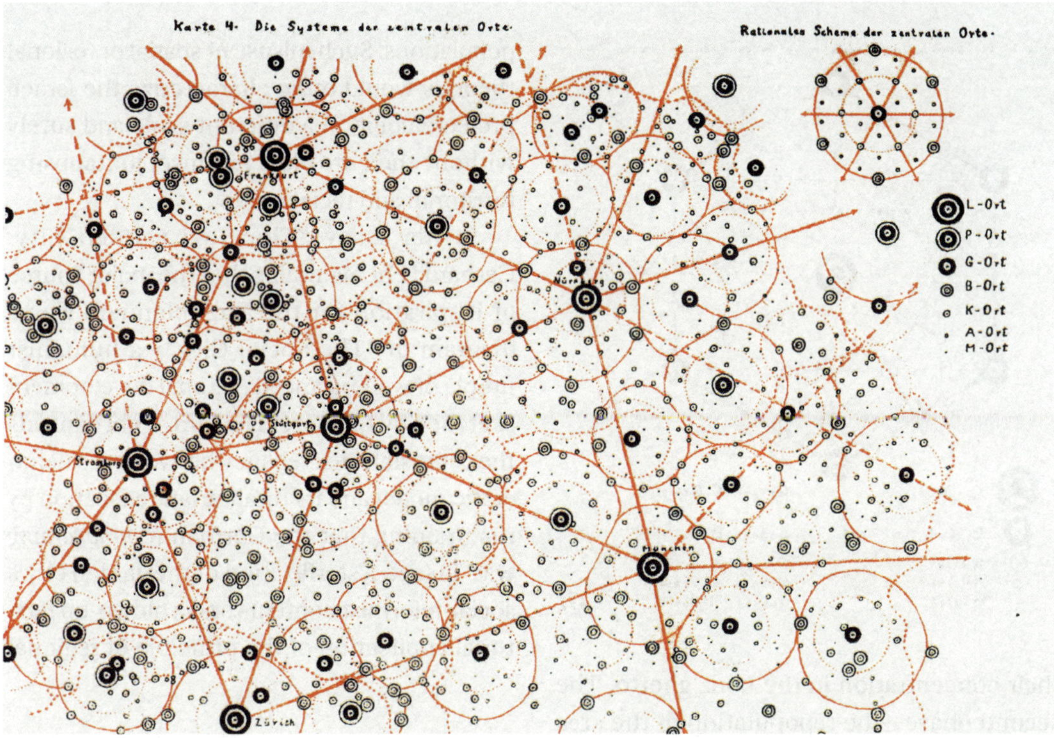

4

> their economic and social function and their spatial distribution.[5]

The first to capitalize on Christaller's academic work were Nazi officials, specifically Heinrich Himmler, who was appointed Reich Commissar for the Strengthening of German Ethnic Stock in 1939. Himmler appointed Christaller as master planner of the "Eastern Provinces," namely, the Polish regions of Wartheland and Danzig (Gdańsk), which had been invaded and annexed by the Nazis. This appointment resulted in a number of plans known collectively as the *Generalplan Ost* (Master Plan East), "one of the biggest planning exercises ever."[6]

Between 1940 and 1942, Christaller developed an overall plan for Germanification and spatial reorganization, proposing administrative subdivisions into districts, the building of new towns, and the construction of a hierarchical system of settlement units. "The basic structure was a grid pattern of hexagons, with a village at every point, and in the middle a market village (*Marktflecken*), then a hexagon with six rural towns in the corners and a regional city (*Kreisstadt*) in the middle, and so on."[7]

The Eastern Provinces were not only the site of the "ethnographic reorganization" demanded by Hitler in his 1939 speech in the Reichstag, but also the prime testing ground for the development of comprehensive territorial plans, generically entitled *Raumplanung* (spatial planning) and based on idealist perceptions of *Raumordnung* (spatial order).

These plans, first implemented in Nazi-occupied Poland, were designed for eventual realization in Germany itself, but thanks to the outcome of the war, they never assumed their full scale. The first stage of spatial reorganization—the transfer of indigenous Polish populations, ethnic "cleansing" of Jews and Gypsies, confiscation of property and land, annulment of existing land parcelization, and planning regulations to free up territories for replanning—culminated in the deportation of more than half a million inhabitants and

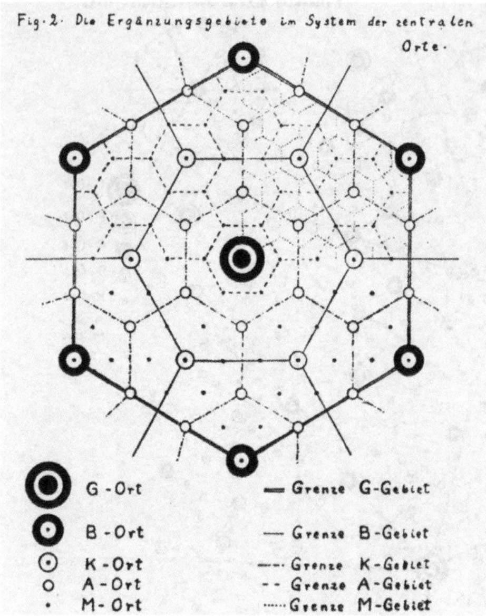


⑤

their concentration in the Lodz ghetto. The second phase—the repopulation of the area with German farmers—was slow to proceed and was only partially realized.

According to Trezib, the scale and potential impact of Christaller's applied theory went beyond the occupied Polish provinces:

> The "Central Place" system ensured the demographic penetration of densely populated regions as well as the calming of other spaces. In particular a variation of the plan, settlement corridors with defensive cores in Christaller's hexagonal forms, extended as far as the Baltic States, the Crimea and the Urals. However, these projections were just an image made visible against the negative foil of the devastated landscape: their realization necessitated gigantic resettlement and expulsion measures for the native populations, the dimensions of which affected up to 30 million people.[8]

Planning here is literally a weapon of mass destruction and an effective mechanism of ethnic cleansing and "exchange" of entire populations. Such misuse of spatial or regional theories would often characterize the Israeli project, albeit on a different scale and surely without the core Nazi premise, juxtaposing territorial and racial order.

In his essay "The Nazi Garden City," Gerhard Fehl maintains that the major source of inspiration for the Nazi planners was a diagram of "The Social City"—a humanist utopia of well-balanced regional development sketched by Ebenezer Howard.[9] Fehl explains the ostensible discrepancy between the democratic model and its totalitarian realization by maintaining that the German *Raumordnung* was, in fact, a sterilization of the garden city's social-reformist contents and a blown-up territorial application of the principle of regional

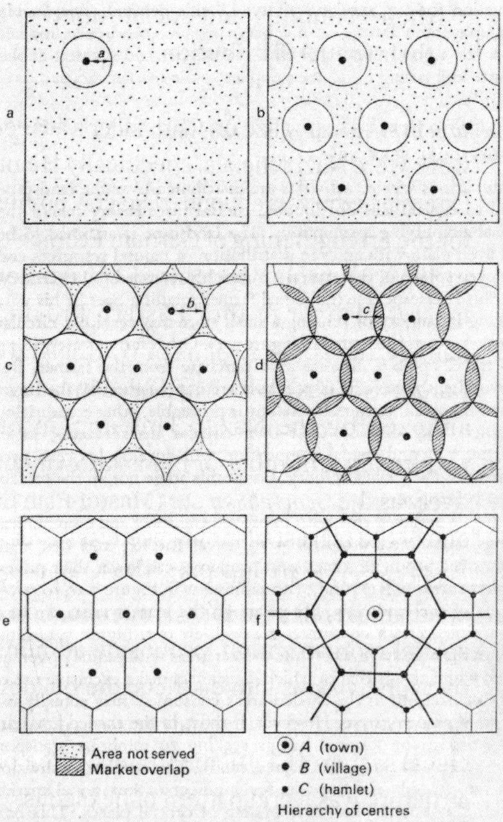


*Fig. 7.2 Evolution of hierarchy of central places*

130

⑥

hierarchy. The justification for such a misuse of localist concepts was the supposed shortage of *Lebensraum* ("living space"), a result of the fact that Germany, unlike the colonial empires that dominated a "world of empty spaces," was a "space-less country."

Fehl's account of modern German planning is particularly relevant to the Zionist case. According to him, by the turn of the nineteenth century, two strategies to curb urban and suburban growth had evolved. The first of these was decentralization: the export of surplus, mainly working-class, populations from the inner parts of the overpopulated city to the outer suburban periphery. The second strategy was that of inner colonization, which was manifested by several approaches:

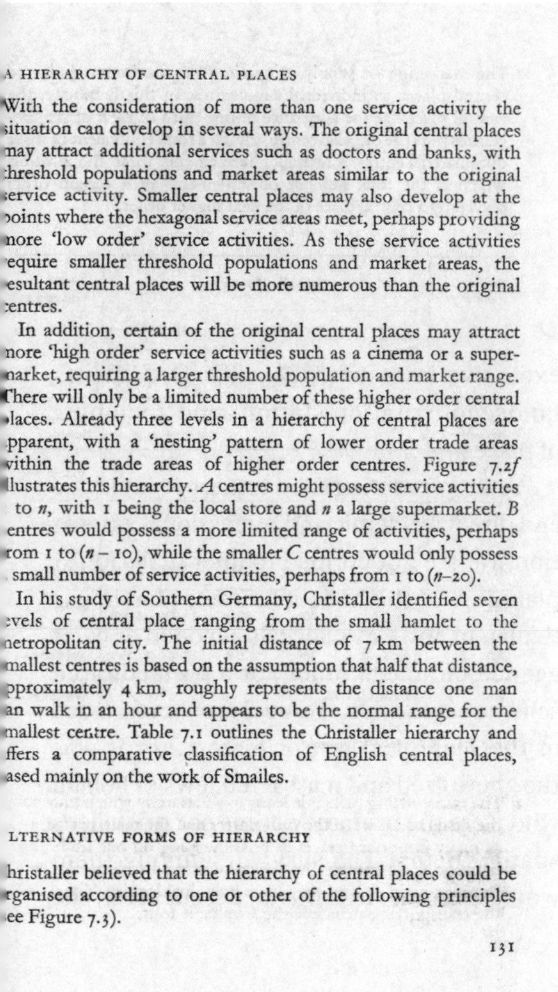

A HIERARCHY OF CENTRAL PLACES

With the consideration of more than one service activity the situation can develop in several ways. The original central places may attract additional services such as doctors and banks, with threshold populations and market areas similar to the original service activity. Smaller central places may also develop at the points where the hexagonal service areas meet, perhaps providing more 'low order' service activities. As these service activities require smaller threshold populations and market areas, the resultant central places will be more numerous than the original centres.

In addition, certain of the original central places may attract more 'high order' service activities such as a cinema or a supermarket, requiring a larger threshold population and market range. There will only be a limited number of these higher order central places. Already three levels in a hierarchy of central places are apparent, with a 'nesting' pattern of lower order trade areas within the trade areas of higher order centres. Figure 7.2f illustrates this hierarchy. *A* centres might possess service activities 1 to *n*, with 1 being the local store and *n* a large supermarket. *B* centres would possess a more limited range of activities, perhaps from 1 to (*n* – 10), while the smaller *C* centres would only possess a small number of service activities, perhaps from 1 to (*n*–20).

In his study of Southern Germany, Christaller identified seven levels of central place ranging from the small hamlet to the metropolitan city. The initial distance of 7 km between the smallest centres is based on the assumption that half that distance, approximately 4 km, roughly represents the distance one man can walk in an hour and appears to be the normal range for the smallest centre. Table 7.1 outlines the Christaller hierarchy and offers a comparative classification of English central places, based mainly on the work of Smailes.

ALTERNATIVE FORMS OF HIERARCHY

Christaller believed that the hierarchy of central places could be organised according to one or other of the following principles (see Figure 7.3).

131

improving rural living standards in order to maintain the population; diverting outward migration from the rural areas to the smaller country towns; and founding new garden cities away from larger towns.[10] (Note that Zionism, too, employs decentralization and inner colonization as its main strategies, but it tends to ignore indigenous rural settlements in favor of devising and proliferating new garden colonies and garden cities).

Fehl maintains that Howard's diagram was stripped of its social-reformist message as early as 1911 so that it could become part of a more conservative project of territorial reorganization. Herein lies an essential disparity between the German and the Zionist adaptation of the garden city. While the *Deutsche Gartenstadt* was the foundation for a protomodern romanticism—including such architectural tendencies as Camillo Sitte's and Hermann Muthesius's "enlightened eclecticism," or Heinrich Tessenow's and Theodor Fischer's "*Heimat* style"—the Zionist garden city, as well as the rural garden colony in Palestine, was a framework for social and architectural experimentation, often radicalizing the original British and German models, stripping them of their Arts and Crafts context and presenting them anew within a culture of *Neue Sachlichkeit*.

The Germans' decisive break with the Anglo-Saxon garden-city model of decentralization came in 1937, with the rise of the Nazi concept of *Lebensraum*. This concept entailed the inversion of the garden-city paradigm and a rethinking of spatial development—not as a radially expanding city, but as rhizomatically spreading countryside.[11] The inversion of the garden-city paradigm, whereby spatial planning supersedes urban reform, is precisely the intersection of the German and the Zionist projects, and it is my assertion that this affinity is the backdrop for the abrupt and all-too-literal appropriation of Christaller's central-place theory by the team drafting the Israeli national master plan.

References to Christaller's work recur in various documents that relate to the master plan or were written by members of Sharon's team at the Planning Department. They reveal themselves graphically in the "plagiarized" hexagonal diagrams rationalizing the spatial premise and territorial agenda of the plan. Trezib perceptively writes that "the 'Central Place' model served [the Israeli planners] as an econometric heuristic for the spatial distribution of the immigration waves and therefore for the siting of new towns and their subcenters—a planning model that was described, not without irony, as 'planning by numbers.'"[12]

The apparent parallelisms between German National Socialist *Raumplanung* and Israeli Zionist-socialist regional planning should be cautiously studied and openly discussed. We can hardly overlook their common rhetorical and empirical tendencies to decentralize and expand, to mobilize and expel, to dictate itineraries of inner colonization and curb urban growth, to invent new rural typologies and monitor their social makeup—all in the name of national interests and nationalist values. It should be further specified that, to these ends, both the Germans and the Israelis denounced the city as a source of spiritual degeneration; propagated the village as the "building block" of the new spatial order; performed acts of massive deportation and systematic destruction; claimed rights over military gains by means of civilian occupation; and nationalized the terrain by means of

④ "Central-Place Theory in Southern Germany," dissertation, 1933. Walter Christaller.

⑤ "Central-Place Theory in Southern Germany," dissertation, 1933. Diagram. Walter Christaller.

⑥ *An Introduction to Regional Planning,* 1974. John Glasson.

⑦ *Regional Planning and Development,* 1953. Artur Glikson.

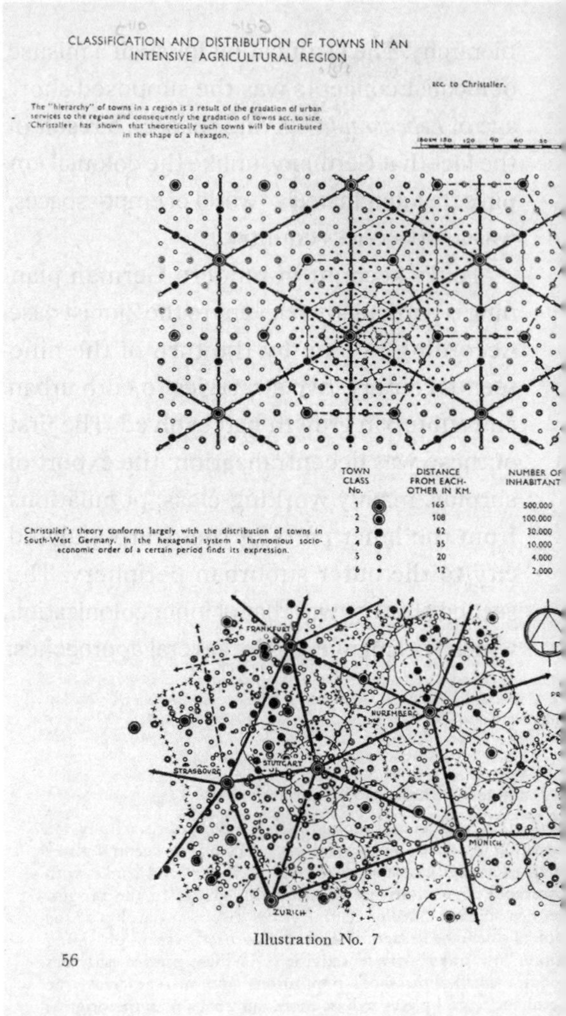


⑦

extensive infrastructure, new settlements, landscaping, afforestation, and renaming of places.

Yet in presenting such uncanny similitude and direct academic and professional association, we are not entitled to infer that Zionist planning, or the national master plan in particular, in any way conceals a hidden or overt agenda of "racial order" or a premeditated scheme of genocide. We are also to be reminded of the diabolical jest of history, for it was the ghettoized and massacred Jews of Poland who were the primary victims of Christaller's spatial theory. The survivors among them would become, less than a decade later, the causes a reduction in the size of the town's direct influence area. The communications' factor in urban location processes, therefore, may cause a certain distortion of their regional efficiency.

The Netherlands present another interesting socio-economic factor in urban location: Differences in soil quality. A number of important towns have been located on the borderline between areas differing in soil quality, as these places were suitable as exchange centres for the different agricultural products of these areas. Similar marginal locations of towns we find all over the world. The topographical factor is of special importance too. The location of towns along narrow river valleys is necessarily made in accordance with the principles of "linear" location, i.e. distribution according to communication lines instead of areas of influence. Conditions of water and power supply too constituted a most important factor in settlement location. When we add geographical, soil, economic, hydraulic, climatic, religious, political and other factors, we understand the diversity of causes influencing urban location. It is important to realize that theories like Christaller's explain only the effect of one of these factors and that each region and town have their specific combination of factors of location.

The Medieval system of urban distribution has generally withstood the test of time to an extraordinary degree. It crystallized a complex regional structure, embodying characteristic occupations and functions and characteristic numbers of the component population, thus creating a social ecology whose definition is in principle the same as A. Leopold's definition of biotic ecology. In this sense we have good reasons to call it an organic regional structure. But the growth of cities and their homogeneous distribution by size was affected in a revolutionary way by the development of industry in the 19th century. The impact of industrial development introduced radically new factors in urban location in the structure of occupations and urban functions and the concept of regional structure.

It is not easy to give an exact description of the industrial location factors, which changed the traditional regional structure. We will summarize here briefly the conclusions relating to this subject which have been arrived at in Western Europe: First of all a distinction has to be made between basic (motivating) industries and service (secondary) industries. Service industries develop on a basis of socio-economic surpluses consequent upon a rich agriculture, the presence of raw materials or a basic industry. They are characterized by the fact that they sell their products within a limited area. Based on regional surplus, they, in their turn, strengthen the independence and way of life of the region.

The influence of the establishment of service industries on a region, therefore, is evolutionary rather than revolutionary. Basic industries on the other hand, sell their manufactures in wider areas, that exceed the limits of local markets, and create an income surplus in the region where they are located. They, therefore, constitute a fundamental factor in economic activity, and create a new primary basis for the existence of a certain proportion of the population. The establishment of new basic industries in a region means mostly a revolutionary change in its demographic and occupational structure, its society, culture and way of life generally.

57

subjects of this theory's epiphenomenon in the Jewish State of Israel.

In all probability, the Israeli planners who ardently embraced central-place theory were not aware of its Nazi appropriation and of Walter Christaller's own war crimes in Poland—possibly the most disastrous instrumentalization of planning theory in modern history. Since Christaller was not tried at the Nuremberg trials and since the *Generalplan Ost* was discussed mainly as a paramilitary operation and not as an intellectual construct, postwar planners and geographers could be conveniently ignorant not only of Christaller's shameful past, but also of the ethical premise and the cataclysmic effect of large-scale spatial theories. Soon after the war, Ludwig Hilberseimer, once Arieh Sharon's teacher at the Bauhaus, based his ideas of decentralization in North America and his book *New Regional Pattern* (1949) on Christaller's hypothesis of rural hierarchical equilibrium. A decade later, in the 1960s, central-place theory would be considered foundational in the "planning sciences," especially, but not only, in the Anglo-Saxon academy. Christaller's participation in the illustrious Delos Symposia organized by Doxiadis in the 1960s, alongside such figures as Buckminster Fuller, Margaret Mead, Marshall McLuhan, and indeed Arieh Sharon, certifies his intellectual status at the time. Today, central-place theory is still on the curriculum and in the bibliography of geography, urban design, and landscape departments, and Christaller's hexagons keep resurfacing as proto-parametric "radical planning" in Israel as well. ■

1 Eliezer Brutzkus, "The New Towns in the Framework of the National and Regional Plan," *Journal of the Union of Engineers and Architects in Israel* 14, no. 2 [in Hebrew] (1956), p. 7.

2 Ibid.

3 Ibid.

4 S. Ilan Troen, *Imagining Zion: Dreams, Designs, and Realities in a Century of Jewish Settlement* (New Haven: Yale University Press, 2003), p. 90.

5 Joachim Trezib, "The Great Dream," *Bauhaus—The Bauhaus Dessau Foundation's Magazine* 2 (November 2011), pp. 12–21.

6 See Wouter Vanstiphout, "The Source Code: Modes for a Perfect Society," in *Common Ground: A Critical Reader*, ed. David Chipperfield, Kieran Long, and Shumi Bose, catalogue of the 13th International Architecture Biennale in Venice (Venice: Marsilio, 2012), p. 263.

7 Ibid., p. 271.

8 Trezib, "Great Dream," pp. 18–19.

9 Gerhard Fehl, "The Nazi Garden City," in *The Garden City: Past, Present and Future*, ed. Stephan Ward (London: E & FN Spon, 1992), pp. 88–103.

10 Ibid., p. 94.

11 Ibid.

12 Trezib, "Great Dream," p. 18.

⑧

⑨

(10)

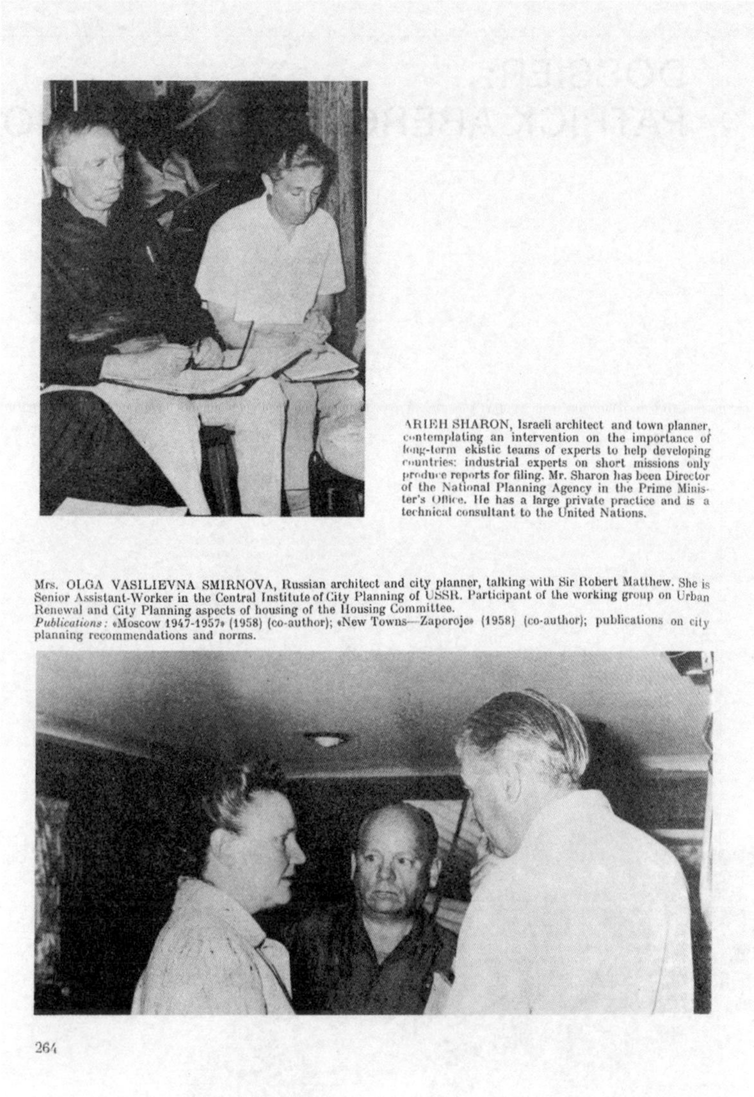
ARIEH SHARON, Israeli architect and town planner, contemplating an intervention on the importance of long-term ekistic teams of experts to help developing countries: industrial experts on short missions only produce reports for filing. Mr. Sharon has been Director of the National Planning Agency in the Prime Minister's Office. He has a large private practice and is a technical consultant to the United Nations.

Mrs. OLGA VASILIEVNA SMIRNOVA, Russian architect and city planner, talking with Sir Robert Matthew. She is Senior Assistant-Worker in the Central Institute of City Planning of USSR. Participant of the working group on Urban Renewal and City Planning aspects of housing of the Housing Committee.
*Publications:* «Moscow 1947-1957» (1958) (co-author); «New Towns—Zaporoje» (1958) (co-author); publications on city planning recommendations and norms.

264

(11)

(8) Delos Symposium, session on board, 1964. Constantinos A. Doxiadis Archives, Athens.
(9) Arieh Sharon presents the master plan of Israel at the Delos Symposium, 1965. Constantinos A. Doxiadis Archives, Athens.
(10) EKISTICS, vol. 18, no. 107, October 1964, p. 264.
(11) Arieh Sharon and Walter Christaller, Delos Symposium, 1965. Constantinos A. Doxiadis Archives, Athens.

# DOSSIER: PATRICK ABERCROMBIE'S SYNOPSIS

⑫ Arieh Sharon (center) and Patrick Abercrombie (right), ca. 1950. Arieh Sharon digital archive.

Architect and town planner Patrick Abercrombie, "the man who created London" and the acclaimed "father" of the British postwar new towns, left his distinctive imprint on the (counter-)urban character of the newly fabricated State of Israel. Abercrombie had been involved with Zionist and British planning in Palestine as early as the 1920s and 1930s. He corresponded and met with prominent local planners such as Richard Kauffmann, the head planner of the Palestine Land Development Company; Clifford Holliday, a former student of Abercrombie's, who was consulting on the planning of Jerusalem and Haifa; and Yaakov (Shiffman) Ben-Sira, the city engineer of Tel Aviv.

In 1951 Abercrombie was officially invited by the government's Planning Department—indeed, by his admirer Arieh Sharon—to review the newly published national master plan with its central feature of peripheral new towns. It seems that Sharon and his team of planners wanted more than to recruit an international authority to promote their plan locally and convince the politicians, as stated below: they yearned for the affirmation of the rather literal and swift implementation of Abercrombie's doctrine in Israel (see chapter "New Towns"). In his autobiography, *Kibbutz + Bauhaus: An Architect's Way in a New Land*, Sharon recounted the circumstances of Abercrombie's visit to Israel:

> To promote our ideas about planning, we invited Sir Patrick Abercrombie, the father of contemporary town-planning, to study and to criticize our proposals. An informal meeting was arranged with Ben Gurion, and Abercrombie warmly praised our approach, and mentioned the similarity of our planning policy to that of the Greater London Plan, which aimed at taking one million inhabitants out of London and settling them in 20 new towns, on the periphery of the metropolitan area. Ben Gurion remarked that it was easier to do this in Israel, where we had only to direct the immigrants into the development areas and new towns. Actually, we studied and learnt from the planners of the English new towns; we even made the same mistakes as they did, of setting our population marks and density targets too low. These mistakes were corrected later on.
>
> We also took Sir Patrick Abercrombie to talk to the Mayor of Tel Aviv, Israel Rokah. The intention was to persuade the Mayor to slow down Tel Aviv's growth and to cancel some municipal plans for markets and retail business centers in the heart of the city. Naturally, we failed to overcome his local patriotism.[1]

Before submitting his report on his visit to Israel, Abercrombie sent a draft and a handwritten letter to Arieh Sharon (plainly titled 15 June 51), in which he invited Sharon to read his review and make changes if needed. The letter indicates that he was particularly critical of the urban planning of Haifa and Tel Aviv, and it suggests that he would not reject a commission to prepare a new master plan for these cities.

The letter ends with an enigmatic cautionary tale: Abercrombie quotes his colleague and friend (Pierre) Vago, who says that "there is frequently a tendency for a small group, what the French call 'une Chapelle,' to get things into their exclusive hands and then do very little but light candles before their altar & clos[e] the gates to the main cathedral!"[2]

Is Abercrombie here warning Sharon of an insurgent group about to demote him from his position as head of the Planning Department, or is he alluding to the drawbacks of an exclusive and indoctrinated clique taking over the planning of the country at large? ■

1 Arieh Sharon, *Kibbutz + Bauhaus: An Architect's Way in a New Land* (Stuttgart and Tel Aviv: Karl Kramer Verlag and Massada, 1976), p. 79.

2 Letter from Patrick Abercrombie to Arieh Sharon, 15 June 1951. Available online (accessed July 19, 2017): http://www.ariehsharon.org/Archive/Physical-Planning-in-Israel/Appendix-B-Letters-and/i-RJ4xT2h.

⑬ *Report on Visit to Israel*, Patrick Abercrombie, 1951. Yael Aloni Photo Collection. Courtesy of the Azrieli Architectural Archive, Arieh Sharon Collection.

R E P O R T

o n

VISIT TO ISRAEL

I.

The Background: tendencies in the Mandatory Period

The distinctively Jewish developments during the Mandatory period took two marked forms: the creation of a great new central city at Tel-Aviv and the establishment of a number of Agricultural settlements. The additions to Jerusalem and Haifa, as well as to other towns, were of a more cosmopolitan character.

Whereas the legacy of Tel-Aviv is an embarrassing one to the new State of Israel, the Agricultural settlements are a continuing source of inspiration.

Tel-Aviv represents the normal tendency of people to concentrate in the capital city; for it was in effect the capital of Jewish Palestine: it also perpetuated the Jewish characteristic, the result of the Dispersion, to live together in urban communities. Many criticisms have been levelled against Tel-Aviv - most of them applicable to all rapidly overgrown capitals:- a failure at a given moment to realise the inevitability of growth and to provide any sort of main structure: the small Geddes Plan was an attempt for a limited area, but it had, even for that great prophet, far too limited a vision. Perhaps the chief defect in Tel-Aviv has been the absence of any adequate system of open spaces and the neglect of the great opportunities of the seafront. But in detailed development - in street lay-out and house-plotting - through densities are much too high, there is a general urban effect which compares favourably with that of other towns built at the same time: this is noticeable where the first quasi-temporary and feebly-eclectic buildings have been replaced by good modern urban architecture (due to the leadership of a number of good designers), and where the tree planting has had time to assert itself. But of course the grave defect was, as already mentioned, the concentration of some 33% of the population in Tel-Aviv and 80% in the coastal strip from Tel-Aviv to Haifa. There is little doubt that this process of concentration will continue, not only if a policy of laissez-faire is adopted but unless most powerful efforts at active disposition of the population are undertaken. In this connection it may be remarked that the loose expression Tel-Aviv covers three areas (as indeed does the expression London): there is the Town or Municipality proper: there is a closely related group or Conurbation: and there is a Tel-Aviv Region which may be said to stretch from Natanya in the north to Richon and Rehovot in the south: for this distance it occupies the full width of the coastal strip of the territory of Israel.

Again, similarly to the great urban spread of Greater London there is the other side of the population picture: the building over of some of the best agricultural land in the country: this is both a physical absorption & damage and a financial drawback, land having acquired throughout the region a building value.

It is attractive to turn from Tel-Aviv, which represents an exaggeration of old-world city defects, to the Agricultural settlements in which the Jewish race has made a real contribution to living conditions, with their varied social and financial experiments. It is fortunate that these were carried out by first-rate planners and architects and can now (after some years of maturing) be studied as examples of development upon the "limited unit" principle, similar to that adopted by Ebenezer Howard for the First Garden City. They represent therefore the exact antithesis of the continuous growth or sprawl of Tel-Aviv. It is true that it may be found, as in the case of Letchworth, that the original size of the unit was too small: in certain examples in Israel, these units, designed for a finite size, have been successfully enlarged (proving the flexibility of good planning). But this does not by any means mean that these settlements can be taken as the nucleus of large New Towns. For these, new sites must be found or expansions (not necessarily concentric spread) of older towns can be made, again fixing an upper limit, beyond which continuous growth is not desirable.

Israel in fact is faced by the same problem that is posed in other countries of high industrial population and limited areas of land, especially of a fertile character. A balance must be struck, and the determining factor must not be the mere financial one - who can give the highest price for the land - nor one of prestige - what town can boast the greatest population or rate of increase. It is the most efficient use of the limited amount of land of Israel which should be the aim.

Whether upon these premises (of most effective use of land) Israel is capable of absorbing a 2 1/2 million population today, (without waiting for the development of the southern arid zone) the writer of this report does not feel that he personally has given sufficient time to study on the spot to give an authoritative opinion: but from a general acquaintance with the country and a detailed knowledge of part of it, and after a full exposition of the proposals of the joint Government Planning Departments, he believes that Israel is in no worse case than a country like Belgium. The particular problem of Israel, is the rapidity with which the growth is taking place owing to immigration: this is strictly speaking a question of temporary economics and of rapidity of construction.

## II.

### The immediate task of Population Distribution

The present task, therefore, which the writer was asked to study was the disposition of a population of 2 1/2 million as a first stage in the development of the country, the present population being estimated at somewhat over a million (this estimate should be dated Dec: 1950). It is assumed that this population could be accommodated without embarking on any gigantic preliminary works of reclamation, water supply, etc.: though of course the normal services required for 2 population increase of something slightly under 1 1/2 million are sufficiently formidable. (It is a curious coincidence that this figure closely compares with the decentralisation figure of the overcrowded parts of Greater London, to be re-located in the New Towns and enlarged existing Centres in the surrounding Region of the Home Countries).

The proposed subdivision of this 2 1/2 million population (or 2,600,000 to be more precise) is:

| | |
|---|---|
| Agriculture | 600,000 |
| The tree Cities | 1,000,000 |
| The New or Quasi-New Towns | 1,000,000 |
| | 2,600,000 |

For the purposes of administrative planning the country has been divided into 6 major Regions.

1. Jerusalem
2. Tel-Aviv
3. Haifa
4. Galilee
5. Beersheba
6. The Southern areas (Negev, S'dom, etc.)

These in turn are subdivided into 24 Planning Regions of which (reading from North to South)

11 are in Haifa and Galilee Regions
7 " " Tel-Aviv Region
2 " " Jerusalem Region
2 " " Beersheba Region
2 " " Southern Region.

Agricultural. In estimating the agricultural population for these planning regions, no allowance is made for the three urban Planning Regions, Haifa, Tel-Aviv and Jerusalem, nor for the desert south. Otherwise a careful allocation of agricultural population has been made, based upon an intensive study of fertility conditions in co-operation with the Agricultural Research Institute of Rehovot. These population possibilities in relation to areas show the wide variation due to the nature of the ground, e.g. the Nazareth planning region, considerably larger than the Tiberias, but estimated to carry an agricultural population of 6,800 as compared with 41,800.

The agricultural population is thus expected to represent about 20% of the total and with a high degree of agricultural skill and intensity, it is intended that the country will become self-supporting in vegetables, milk, eggs, fruit, cereals, oil and meat.

The new agricultural communities will follow the lead of the early ones, only rather larger in size; and it will probably be found convenient for groups of 5 or 6 normal communities to focus on one, rather larger, where the secondary school and other features of a larger community will be placed.

There will also be a number of small country or market towns serving 20 or 30 of these Agricultural settlements. Here there will be a larger shopping centre, some local industry and possibly an agricultural college.

It is very much to be regretted that a large number of "strung-out" agricultural holdings have been recently set up: these are impractical and anti-social in their arrangement. It is surprising that with so many admirable examples of rural settlement planning, these retrograde developments should have been allowed. They do not fit into any system, and may be described as "panic planning".

Medium sized New or quasi-New Towns. Normally each of the Planning Regions will have its local capital corresponding to the "County Town". If there is to be a population of 1,000,000 in such medium sized towns and they are to have an average population of 50,000, twenty would be required. It has been suggested, however, that there would probably be 12 towns of about this population and 12 somewhat smaller.

The twelve Medium Towns would be:

| | | |
|---|---|---|
| 1. Naharia | 5. Affuleh | 9. Lydda-Ramleh |
| 2. Acre | 6. Hedera | 10. Ascalon |
| 3. Safad | 7. Natanya | 11. Beersheba |
| 4. Tiberius | 8. Petah Ticva | 12. New Port. |

The new Port situated between Tel-Aviv and Ascalon might well have a population of 60,000 or more. It will be found that, with the exception of this new Port, there is an existing nucleus to the other towns, though in several cases the New town is physically distinct from the old.

The Tree Cities. The million inhabitants of the three Cities are to be disposed as follows:-

| | |
|---|---|
| Tel-Aviv (Conurbation) | 450,000 |
| Haifa | 300,000 |
| Jerusalem | 250,000 |
| | 1,000,000 |

It will be seen therefore that there is a schematic arrangement of communities, in an ascending scale of size, which may be summarised as follows:-

| | | Approximate population |
|---|---|---|
| (A. | The agricultural Unit (Kvuzah or Mochav) | 500 |
| (B. | The Kibbuz, serving 5 or 6 of the units | 2,500 |
| (C. | The County or Market Town serving 30 agricultural units | 6-10,000 |
| (D. | The smaller sized Regional Planning Centres | 26-30,000 |
| (E. | The normal "Medium Towns" also Regional Planning Centres | 50-60,000 |
| F. | The three Cities | 250-450,000 |

These are considered as target figures, both of minimum and maximum size: they will be subject to variation, but no great departure should be allowed if a healthy social and economic development of the country is to be aimed at.

## III.

### Notes on the Plans: the three Cities

**Jerusalem**. It is of course the greatest misfortune that, owing to continuing political difficulties the plan of Jerusalem has to be confined to the area in the state of Israel and that thus even the Hebrew University and the great Hospital as well as the ancient City are outside its scope. In spite of these difficulties, a Master Plan for the administrative Capital of the country has been prepared. It consists, roughly, of the modern Mandatory extension as the Commercial, Shopping, Hotel and partially residential area: of the new Seat of Government on the plateau due west of this existing town, and a series of new Neighbourhood Units located on the high grounds, further west again. It is in fact, as is inevitable, a great westwards extension, most of it south of the old Jaffa Road. The intention is broadly, while building on the high ground, to keep the numerous valleys open: in early days for cultivation and later for parks, school playgrounds, reservoirs, etc. These open spaces will link up with each other and with the Herzl Memorial and National Sanctuary and eventually with the open Judean Hills and Forest. A road system, linked up with the new approaches from the plain, and largely dictated by the extremely marked topography, has been planned.

The Government Centre is well chosen on its splendid site which is shared also with an international Convention Centre.

The plan is a fine conception which will require first-rate skill in supervision. The Government Buildings are to be the subject of an

For an area comprising the following communities and loosely called the conurbation, a population target of 450,000 has been proposed:

1. Tel-Aviv, proper, as existing.
2. Jaffa.
3. New Neighbourhood north of the Yarkon River.
4. " " east of the proposed Railway.
5. Benei Berak.
6. Ramat Gan.
7. Givatayim.
8. Holon.
9. Bat Yam.

The Region includes the following towns. with their target populations:

| | | |
|---|---|---|
| 1. | Natanya | 50,000 |
| 2. | Herzleia and Ra'anana | 20,000 |
| 3. | Peta Ticva | 50.000 |
| 4. | Rishon | 25,000 |
| 5. | Lydda and Ramleh | 50,000 |
| 6. | Rehovoth | 30,000 |
| | | 225,000 |

To these must be added the figures for the agricultural communities in the "planning regions":

| | | |
|---|---|---|
| 1. | Natanya Region | 34,300 |
| 2. | Kfar Saba | 20,900 |
| 3. | Dan | 20,800 |
| 4. | Rishon le Zion | 20,800 |
| 5. | Yavneh | 20.800 |
| | | 146,400 |

The three groups:

| | |
|---|---|
| Conurbation | 450,000 |
| Urban Region | 225,000 |
| Agricultural Region | 146,400 |
| | 821,400 |

It will thus be seen that, as in the case of Greater London, it is a loosening up over a Region rather than the dispersal over the whole country that is contemplated. But this spreading of the huge population over the Region from Natanya to Rehovot would constitute a much healthier condition than the compact urban growth of Tel-Aviv itself.

A sketch Master Plan has been prepared for this Region which should be implemented at the earliest possible moment, as the forces behind uncontrolled sprawl are very powerful and will require to be restrained by a firm hand in the interests of community planning on one hand and agriculture (in the widest sense) on the other.

Equally urgent is a more detailed master plan for the Conurbation. There was not apparently in February of this year anything in hand for the municipal area of Tel-Aviv or for co-operative action for the Conurbation on the lines that is happening, for example, at Melbourne, where there is a statutory metropolian Planning Board. In Tel-Aviv itself there are many urgent problems: the rebuilding of the damaged area between Tel-Aviv and Jaffa: the site of the railway station: the possibility of a local harbour: the use of the small area of neglected Arab land which has come into public possession within the town: the projected civic centre (now possibly to be modified): the ultimate use of the delightful Hakirya area: the treatment of the coast (where possibilities still exist): the final plan of the large unit north of the Yarkon River and the coastal strip between it and the western extension of Herzleia. Nearly every one of these separate items are not the concern of Tel-Aviv alone but also of the surrounding Conurbation. Fortunately the three urban Parks approved by the Government have done something to provide recreation space and the Regional plan proposes further green wedges to break up the continuous spread and to preserve the Yarkon and Musrara rivers.

The whole Conurbation is alive with possibilities, opportunities and, it must be added, dangers; if no positive steps are taken, growth will continue unabated, piling up problems of traffic congestion, over-crowding, expensive public services and industrial confusion.

A master plan for Greater Tel-Aviv (the Conurbation) is required at once, prepared by a joint planning Board consisting of all the municipalities in this area. This plan must be closely integrated with the Regional plan prepared by the Government Planning Department for this part of Israel.

## IV

### Notes on the Plans: the New or Quasi-new Towns

During the short period of the visit, it was impossible to give any serious study to twenty-four towns, twelve Medium and twelve Small, every one of which presented problems of topography, history, agriculture, land ownership, social structure, economics and public services. It was clear, however, that each of these is receiving detailed thorough study based upon preliminary surveys of existing conditions and prospects of future development. The method of working and the regional subdivision of staff has ensured full local consideration and there were no signs of any sort of stereotyped solution being applied.

An outlet to the Far East is already assured (subject to the use of the Gulf of Akaba) through Elath.

The advocates of Tel-Aviv as the universal commercial centre, have pointed to an enlarged Jaffa and a further increase of 50-60,000 inhabitants - if nor more. But although a good case can be made out for a town of this size and manufacturing importance having its own domestic outlet to the sea, this is a very different question from becoming the chief port for southern Israel. Although the topographic parallel does not hold good - there was a strong case for Manchester creating its own domestic docks and passage to the sea - but no case for acting as a Liverpool.

There appears, however, to be a good reason for establishing a minor Liverpool somewhere between Holon and Ascalon. Its direct connection with Jerusalem which appears attractive on paper is not perhaps so important as its nearness to Beersheba as the focal point of the South. It would also serve the whole coastal plain south of Hedera, and so relieve pressure on Haifa.

It would be an artificial port, created on this flat and almost featureless coast; but the wadi at Ir Hadarem appears to be a possible site, with a residential area to the South.

Though in the first instance planned for a population of 50,000, this port might well grow to double that size, depending of course upon the development of the Negeb.

VI.

## Some General & National Planning Considerations

Although formal approval is not given to the planning proposals described, it must be understood that the writer is in agreement with what he saw in the planning office and on the ground: this agreement was of course of a general character and was arrived at after searching questioning discussion and argument. Such questions as sizes of neighbourhood units, detailed site planning, densities, road design, areas of playground, cut-off and green belt space, location of special buildings, etc. etc. were discussed in addition to broader principles of general lay-out and disposition of community activities. Owing to the long period, since the earliest days of the mandate, during which experimental work in all directions has been tried and a generation has been able to watch the results (many admirable - some to be avoided) there is not much danger of the rapid realisation which is now necessary, following lines which might be theoretically sound, but in practice unworkable. The development of Palestine and Israel has had focussed upon it some of the best brains of the world. Examples of maturity of growth - architectural, engineering and landscape, can be pointed to, which completely answer gloomy prognostics, which were heard, of barren rocky hills, sandy wastes, malarious marshes and other examples of four centuries of neglect. Thus the 'open-planning' of neighbourhoods, shown at Beersheba and Affuleh, has not caused amy misgiving: one case in the past where a pessimistic outlook caused a bold conception to be reduced (the Haifa-Acre Road) has proved that the original scheme of a park-way was the right treatment.

There are,of course, a number of National Planning considerations which are beyond the scope of the present Report to comment upon. Some of them are of immediate concern, other look ahead to a long term programme of works.

These aspects include, in addition to the over-riding one of population distribution already dealt with:-

(i) Communications, road, rail and air.

(ii) Industrial Location, particularly through trading or "Industrial Estates" laid out and even built, in advance.

(iii) A central Irrigation Scheme.

(iv) Agriculture and Afforestation.

(v) National Parks, Landscape Preservation, Green Belts, Footpaths and long distance Trails.

(vi) Antiquities and Archaeological sites.

## VII.

## Methods of Planning

A thorough commentary on the legal and administrative aspects of Planning for the country of Israel would require an investigation and report to itself. Nevertheless, there are certain points which emerge from a brief visit of inspection and discussion with government and municipal officials. These will be briefly touched on.

Whether there should be a Ministry of Planning is perhaps a question outside the scope of a mere technician. The evolution in England has been somewhat cyclical: into the great Ministry of Local Government (later known as Health) was inserted a small department of Town Planning which was more or less subservient to Housing. Towards the close of the last war a separate Ministry of Town and Country Planninh was created: the Health aspects of that eponymous Ministry have now been segregated and the Ministry of Town and Country Planning has finally absorbed the residue of Local Government under the new title of Ministry of Local Government and Planning. Logically there is a great advantage in the location of housing, roads, industry, etc. being handled in one originating and co-ordinating Ministry: but it is also an advantage for the supervision of carrying out (though not necessarily of constructional works) being in the same hands.

The best agency for the production of both general and detailed plans of development, depends to a great extent upon the status of Local Government in a country and on the question of speed of production. In England the recent Act (1947) effected a drastic reduction in the number of Local Authorities which were competent to prepare plans: the large cities retained their powers, but the smaller towns and urban and rural districts have been joined or amalgamated into "County" planning Authorities (corresponding to the Planning Regions of Israel). These <u>new</u> authorities have taken some time to get their organisations complete and they had the advantage over the Israeli Planning Regions that they (the Counties) were already well established Authorities for other Local Government purposes.

With the absolute essential of speed, it would seem inevitable that in Israel the Development Schemes (both of Town and Country) of the Planning Regions should be prepared at Ministerial Headquarters. The same argument holds for the Israel capital of Jerusalem, and (as already remarked) a Master Plan has been prepared.

But Haifa and Tel-Aviv have been accustomed to deal with their own various problems; and it would seem reasonable that they should prepare Master Plans for their own area which should be combined into a joint Planning Board with the surrounding district. In the case of Tel-Aviv the Conurbation would probably make the most convenient unit: (it is a mistake to attempt detailed planning and supervision of Development for too large an area). It was rather surprising to find that neither in Haifa nor Tel-Aviv did there appear any evidences of the active preparation of a comprehensive plan, though in both cities there were many features that were receiving detailed consideration. The author of this report suggests that such joint planning Boards should be set up at once, for both these cities.

It will be necessary to determine the exact scope and status of these master plans. There are three English types of Town Plan, none of which is precisely applicable.

(i) There was the statutory Planning Scheme under the 1932 Act: this was a rigid legal Document, every detail of which had to be approved and 'sealed' by the Government Department: it then had the validity and permanence of an Act of Parliament. Every owner of property had a right to object and the Minister was the sole arbiter of reasonableness.

(ii) In the other extreme have been the post-war Master Plans (e.g. London County, Greater London, Plymouth, Manchester, Oxford, Edinburgh, rtc.) in many cases produced as a result of war damage. These Plans and published Reports were prepared, at the instigation of the Minister,

Lord Reith, by a single individual (or a group) who was given free hand to propose what he thought best and to consult whom he thought necessary. Until endorsed (by Local Authority and Ministry, in whole or part) they have no legal validity, but they have had an influence which can only be described as astonishing. Such a feature as a figure for population Density or Decentralisation or a Green Belt has been accepted by the Public and given a stronger force than mere legal sanction.

(iii) The 1947 Act has aimed at a sort of continuous flexible control, based upon an "interim" Development Plan which does not look ahead more than 20 years and is subject to revision every five years. There are many advantages in this method but it is not very successful in dealing with an existing city where definite improvements must be initiated, but where long term policies must be looked to.

It is possible that an adaptation of the 1947 Development Plan may be the most suitable for Israel - but it is strongly advised that it should be accompanied by some form of publication (which policy has been adopted by some of the Planning Authorities under the 1947 Act). In Israel an 'imposed' plan would not, for these two cities, have the same support as that which was endorsed by and familiar to the public.

The most pressing of the detailed economic problems of planning in Israel concerns the large areas of parcellated lands. This problem is somewhat similar to that of compensation and betterment which stultified the working of the English 1932 Act. In one way the problem is not so grave in Israel as there is a much greater proportion of land in public or quasi-public ownership (although the latter bodies sometimes take too narrow a view of their economic obligations): the large amount of abandoned property, much of which is ripe for development which will enhance its value, is in full Government ownership. In another direction, however, the Israel position is worse than the English one was, as not only is it a question of high land values (generally artificially stimulated) but the land is saddled with a mechanical, dull and uneconomic lay-out whose revision is rendered much more difficult as many of the standard plots have been sold off (a large number of small owners being always more difficult to deal with than a few large ones), and in certain cases the owners are absentees, in other cases the owners cannot be traced. Again, there was a misplaced patriotic feeling of owning a plot in Israel, which was often translated into a desire to hold on to it while its value increased, through the activities of others. Examples of these drawbacks have already been mentioned in the case of Haifa.

As is well known, the English "Uthwatt Report" recommended the assumption by the state of all this potential value in undeveloped land and the granting of a lump sum to be distributed by way of compensation. It was recognised that this lump sum would by no means represent the sum of the values placed by the owners (or even by a local valuer) on the individual holdings, which were considered to have forced up the real value of the land. The English 1947 Act departed from the Uthwatt recommendation by making the system applicable to all land, whether built upon or not. This has led to the imposition of a "Development charge" when any improvement is made to land or building: it has the effect of a Government tax on initiative, which is not satisfactory.

It would be necessary to institute a special Inquiry into the conditions in Israel, if, as the writer believes, this is an abuse which requires remedying. To sum up, it might be said that there are three distinct but inter-related factors which require dealing with:

1. The revision of parcellation lay-out.
2. The prevention of the hold-up of land, required for development by the community.
3. The obtaining of freedom for the community to plan in the best interests without being faced by artificial high cost of land.

In general, attention is drawn to the high price of land in Israel which far exceeds any (except perhaps in the heart of the City) land in London, particularly undeveloped land immediately adjoining built-up areas.

No word has been said in connection with Methods of Planning about the preliminary Survey work which has been done. This has been thorough, scientific and comprehensive: moreover, it has been translated into a series of admirable diagrams for popular appreciation. The exhibition of these will enable the public, not only to realise the extent of the need for planning but to form some judgement as to how the plans are fulfilling that need.

# Jewish Style

# Hannes Meyer's Inquiry Regarding Jewish National Style

to architect a. sharon, pinsker street 14, TEL AVIV

dear a. sharon,

bella ullmann and your wife told me a lot about construction activity when they were passing through zurich a short while ago, and about yours in particular.
I would like to be able to get a grasp of what is achieved over there and wanted to ask if there are any dedicated periodicals on the subject. Since I've been involved in the urban planning effort in Birobidzhan in 1933/34 I would also be interested in the character of the Jewish construction enterprise in your country.[1] are there any attempts to establish a distinctive jewish-national style?? even if it were just exquisite kitsch of the highest order I would still be interested. is there any comprehensive publication on the jewish settlement and the projects of the past year that also accounts for the economic conditions? have you got printed material on any of your own buildings? bella ullmann told me of a hospital project.
if there are other bauhausians in your vicinity I send my regards to all of them.
I could send you USSR material on building and construction now and again if you expect something in return.
I should be at this geneva address until the spring of 1938.
are there also experiments from the fields of painting and sculpture?

with best regards from lena & me.
hannes meyer

GENEVA, SUISSE
4, rue St. Laurent
26.9.1937

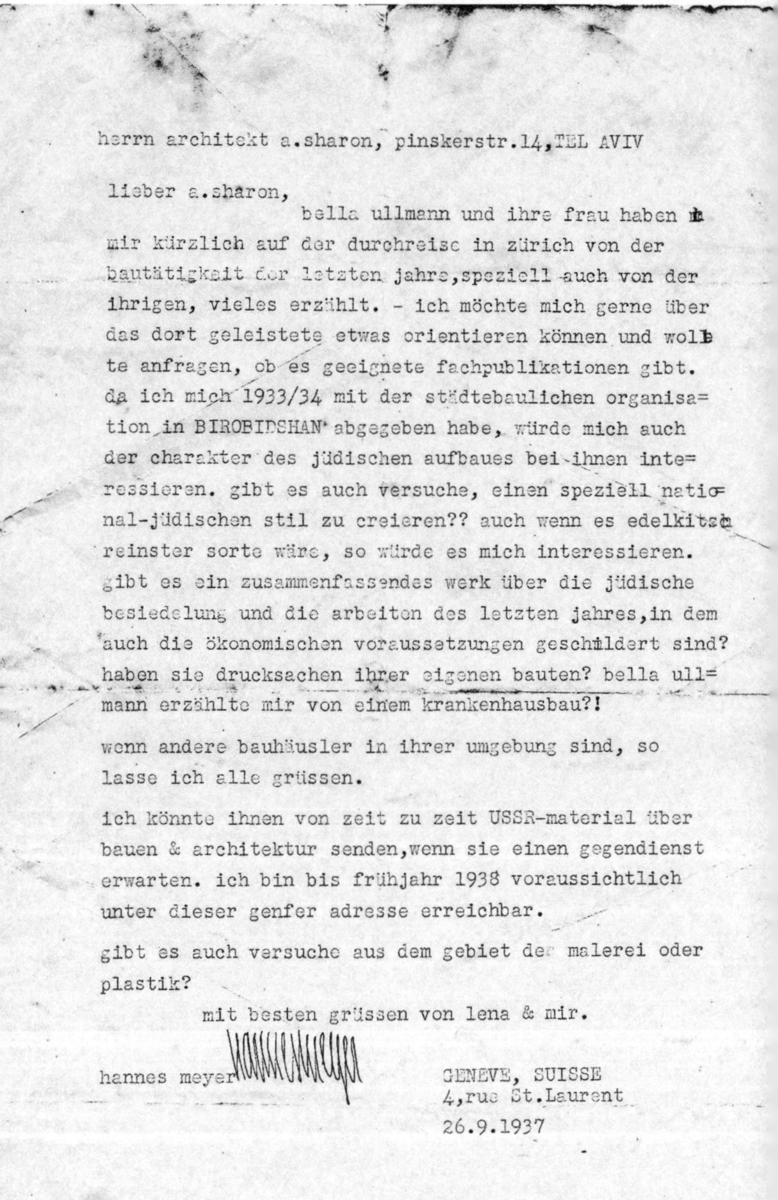

herrn architekt a.sharon, pinskerstr.14,TEL AVIV

lieber a.sharon,
bella ullmann und ihre frau haben mir kürzlich auf der durchreise in zürich von der bautätigkeit der letzten jahre,speziell auch von der ihrigen, vieles erzählt. - ich möchte mich gerne über das dort geleistete etwas orientieren können und wollte anfragen, ob es geeignete fachpublikationen gibt. da ich mich 1933/34 mit der städtebaulichen organisation in BIROBIDSHAN abgegeben habe, würde mich auch der charakter des jüdischen aufbaues bei ihnen interessieren. gibt es auch versuche, einen speziell national-jüdischen stil zu creieren?? auch wenn es edelkitsch reinster sorte wäre, so würde es mich interessieren. gibt es ein zusammenfassendes werk über die jüdische besiedelung und die arbeiten des letzten jahres,in dem auch die ökonomischen voraussetzungen geschildert sind? haben sie drucksachen ihrer eigenen bauten? bella ullmann erzählte mir von einem krankenhausbau?!

wenn andere bauhäusler in ihrer umgebung sind, so lasse ich alle grüssen.

ich könnte ihnen von zeit zu zeit USSR-material über bauen & architektur senden,wenn sie einen gegendienst erwarten. ich bin bis frühjahr 1938 voraussichtlich unter dieser genfer adresse erreichbar.

gibt es auch versuche aus dem gebiet der malerei oder plastik?

mit besten grüssen von lena & mir.

hannes meyer

GENEVE, SUISSE
4,rue St.Laurent
26.9.1937

① Letter from Hannes Meyer to Arieh Sharon, September 1937, Bauhaus Dessau Foundation.

(In Lieu of) Sharon's Reply

*Arieh Sharon's letter of response to his former and much-admired teacher and employer was never found. Perhaps it was never sent. In its stead, I present the following belated counterfeit in order to prolong and complicate Meyer's inquiry regarding attempts to establish a Jewish national style.*[2]

Tel Aviv, 15 December 1937

To: Herrn Architekt H. Meyer
4, Rue St. Laurent, Geneva, Switzerland

Dear Professor Meyer,

Your letter finds me in a moment of ecstatic fatigue. Tel Aviv, as Bella and Haya probably described to you in much detail, feels like a boundless construction site and architectural labor seems to be self-perpetuating. We barely have the time to properly complete our working-drawings before we are called on site to instruct the builders.
For the time being, the menacing angst reported by our comrades who remained in Germany, and as much by those still absorbed by the Soviet project, dissolves here into a delirium of white walls and flat roofs. Clearly, an erratic exile culture is escalating in the Levant. The "planning brigades" should be called up right away, before your manifesto of *Marxistische Architektur* is completely forgotten and wiped out by a tasteful and rather contagious modernist decorum.
In my own practice, I remain your devout emissary and study with great care new organizational schemes and rational building techniques for cooperative workers' housing. I have won already several architectural competitions conducted by the General Federation of Jewish Labor, and my first housing project, comprising 144 apartments, is by now built and inhabited. I'm pleased with the result and believe that the project demonstrates quite well the idea of *Genossenschaftswohnung* as an urban organism in which the various domestic and public components, including a host of communal facilities

and open spaces, are neatly integrated. The compact three-room cross-ventilated flats with projecting balconies are reminiscent of your *Volkswohnungen* in Törten, Dessau, though—and I beg your understanding—they are all covered with white plaster, de rigueur.

In order to clarify the premise of my work and differentiate it from the commonplace petty-bourgeois and bohemian architecture of Tel Aviv, I published a belligerent article in a local magazine. Under the insipid title of “Minimum Apartment in Cooperative Housing,” I launched a direct attack on pretentious mannerism, and reasoned for design economy in the spirit of your memorable preaching that a building should be merely the “plastic translation of its socio-pedagogic functions.”[3]

Professor Meyer, you may remember a letter I sent you some years ago, upon my return from Berlin to Tel Aviv in 1931. I was quite depressed then by the trivial architectural miscellanea and conformist urban design I found here. For a while, I regretted discarding the invitation to join you and Mart Stam in Magnitogorsk.

But since then so much has changed and by now Palestine appears to be the radical architectural frontier of our time and a most vulnerable territory to colonize with the “norms, types and standards,” as you would often say, of the *Neue Sachlichkeit.*

Dozens of new rural settlements are being built here every year, all by design, and the Jewish cities are thriving, especially since the 1933 Transfer Agreement (*Haavara*) between the Nazi authorities and the Zionist organizations. This “trade deal,” diabolical as it may be, triggered a flow of exiles and exports from Germany, considerably improved our local industry, and transformed irrevocably our juvenile culture industry.[4] Modern architecture, indeed, has swiftly become a localized mass culture, a vernacular dialect, a fashion system, and incredibly, spontaneously as it were, the ubiquitous marker of the Zionist project in cities and countryside alike.

There is even an active intellectual milieu to contextualize the various formal and ideological affiliations of modern architecture. It was initially conceived by Joseph Neufeld, who just came back from Mendelsohn’s Berlin office, Zeev Rechter, who returned from Paris and was under the spell of Le Corbusier, and myself, still

②

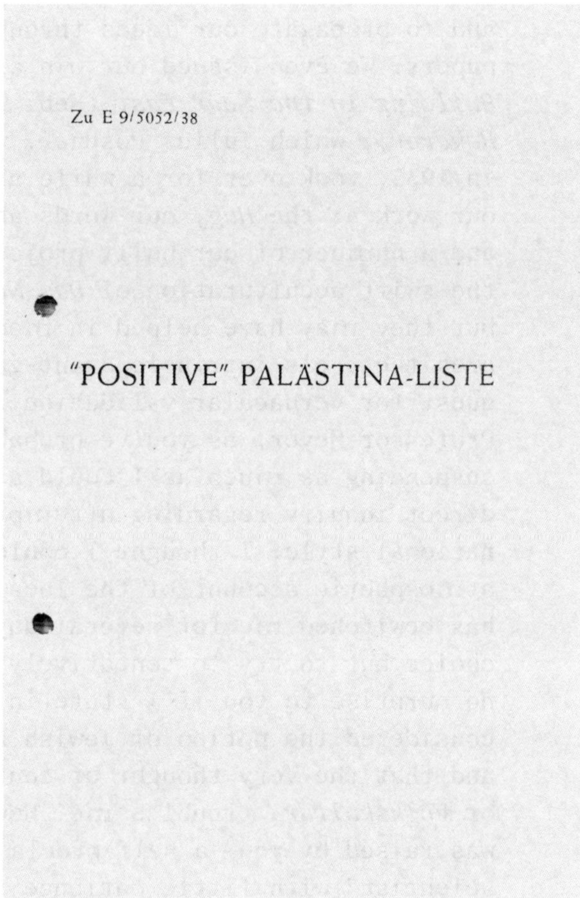
Zu E 9/5052/38

"POSITIVE" PALÄSTINA-LISTE

③

② Transfer Agreement folders, 1938. Central Zionist Archives. Courtesy of White City Center's research team.
③ *"Positive" Palästina-Liste*, Transfer Agreement folders, 1938. Central Zionist Archives. Courtesy of White City Center's research team.

trying to ward off my Bauhaus agitation. We came up with the idea to establish an "Architecture Circle" (*Hug* in Hebrew), much like the Expressionists' *Der Ring*. Soon, the Circle was joined by Carl Rubin, also from Mendelsohn's office, Dov Karmi, who returned from studies in Ghent, Sam Barkai, who briefly worked at Corbu's office, and several other enthusiasts. Overworked in our studios in the daytime, we would meet at night to argue our differences and to discuss effective ways to infiltrate the Union of Engineers and Architects in Israel and the official town-planning committees, and to propagate our ideas through daily and weekly newspapers. We even issued our own architectural magazine, *Building in the Near East* (Heb. *Habinyan Bamisrah Hakarov*), which Julius Posener, who arrived here via Paris in 1935, took over for a while as the editor. Surely, our work at the *Hug*, our words and images at *Habinyan*, and a number of our built projects cannot at all explain the swift acculturation of *Das Neue Bauen* in Palestine, but they may have helped in mediating between modern architecture's intrinsic avant-gardism and its genuine quest for vernacular validation and popular affection. Professor Meyer, as you've probably noticed, I was suspending as much as I could a proper answer to your direct inquiry regarding attempts to establish a Jewish national style. I thought I could get by with an atmospheric account of the local scene, but your question has bewitched me for several days now and I have no choice but to try to tentatively unravel it. It will be no surprise to you if I state in advance that I've never considered the notion of Jewish architecture as such and that the very thought of contemporary *Heimatstil*, or *Volkskultur*, troubles me. However, since the issue was raised by you—a self-proclaimed "architectural scientist" with little patience for any chauvinist folklore or aesthetic taxonomy; a "fanatical functionalist," as Alfred Barr called you (and only you) in his preface to Hitchcock's and Johnson's triumphant book *The International Style*—I was compelled to delve into the nebulous notions of Jewish character, Jewish physiognomy and Jewish predispositions, as they manifest themselves in the Zionist project, often under the alias of Hebrew style.

(4) *Habinyan: A Magazine of Architecture & Town Planning,* no. 3, 1938. Cover, "Village Buildings."
(5) *Habinyan: A Magazine of Architecture & Town Planning,* no. 2, 1937. Cover, "Villas and Gardens."
(6) *Habinyan Bamisrah Hakarov: A Palestine Periodical for Architecture in the Near East*, no. 4, 1935.
(7) *Habinyan Bamisrah Hakarov: A Palestine Periodical for Architecture in the Near East*, no. 1, 1934.

(5)

(7)

I will share with you my cryptic conclusion that the figure of speech *Jewish Style* is above all a dialectical image of anti-Semitic attributes. As such, it appears at times as a dismal reflection of ethnographic caricatures and at other times as a vigilant iconoclastic force aiming to displace all preconceptions and self-afflictions regarding the cultural debility and the aesthetic deficiency of the Jews.

But, before I go down in my own muddy argument, let me finally provide you with a literal answer by reporting that indeed there was in Palestine a lively discussion of *Jüdischer Aufbau*, mainly during the 1910s and 1920s. This discussion was bound to a larger discourse of Jewish cultural revival and entailed a search for Semitic *Ur*-forms. In fact, most of the architectural production during these decades, especially in the cities, is expressive of a quest for a Jewish national style. Practically every public edifice of the time had a revivalist allegory written on its walls and each residential building was dressed to the occasion of the birth of a nation-state. Yes, precisely as you guessed, it was architecture of exquisite kitsch; a pastiche of *Jugendstil* biblical fantasies; Eastern European casual neo-classicisms; and an assortment of Oriental motifs, geometrical figures and patterned surfaces.

You may be familiar with some of the central protagonists of that *Jüdischer Aufbau* of the 1920s (which strangely enough was sometimes referred to as the "German Style"), like the Berliner Alexander Bärwald, who designed the illustrious Technion building in Haifa and was the first professor of architecture in Palestine; or the artist and utopian writer Boris Schatz, who founded Bezalel, the first arts and crafts school in Palestine, and designed the first Hebrew Gymnasium, together with the architect Joseph Barsky, as a reconstruction of the old Jewish Temple; or yet another Berliner, Alexander Levi, who established in the '20s the *Palästina-Baugesellschaft* in order to promote ideas of Jewish architects for building in Palestine, published the booklet *Vom Bauen und Wohnen im neuen Palästina*, and was obsessed with the idea of building 1000 *Kleinhäuser* in Palestine each year.

The impromptu character and eclectic taste of the early *Jüdischer Aufbau* reflects a profound confusion regarding

⑧

⑨

⑩

⑧ Eclectic buildings in Tel Aviv, 1920s. Matson Collection, Library of Congress.
⑨ Allenby Street, Tel Aviv, 1920s. Matson Collection, Library of Congress.
⑩ Galei Aviv Casino, Tel Aviv, 1922. Yehuda Magidovitch. David B. Keidan Collection, Central Zionist Archives.

the proper iconography of the Jewish enterprise in Palestine and attests to a semantic dispute over the designations and affiliations of this migrant culture. Architects and chroniclers were speaking in tongues, referring to "biblical reconstruction," "Land of Israel Style" (Heb. *signon Eretz Israeli*), "Zionist building," "Jewish *Heimat* art" (Heb. *Omanut hamoledet*), or "Hebrew Style."[5]

The designation "Hebrew," or "Modern Hebrew," seemed to prevail over all others. It offered the most effective bypass of the Jewish diasporic history and the fastest shortcut to the biblical scene of origin.[6] But what is Hebrew architecture? And what should the "first Hebrew city" look like?

In contrast to the actual revival of the written and spoken Hebrew language, architecture had neither source material nor any valid image whatsoever to reconstruct. It had to invent its own allusions and composites in order to forge a "Hebrew Architectural Order" (an incredible blend of "ancient Hebrew," Greek, neoclassical, *Jugendstil*, Oriental and Moorish motifs).[7]

Oriental architecture and Palestinian vernacular certainly provide the most plausible image bank for Jewish time travel, but they are also the tangible artifacts of the present, the seductive-repulsive agents of cultural assimilation. They are familiar symptoms of the Jewish style of the '20s, but they always appear revised and revamped and mixed up with antiquarian figures, religious tokens and national symbols—turning the city into a stage set for an ongoing reenactment of Jewish avowal/disavowal of Semitism.

So made up is this architectural Hebrewism, that one may even suspect that it has no local sentiment at all, but rather is fueled by the migrant community's nostalgia for symbols of Jewish buoyancy in Europe.

After all, during the nineteenth century, synagogues across Europe—like that outlandish *Neue Synagoge* in Berlin we once visited together—were often built in free Moorish style and applied a surfeit of Islamic silhouettes and arabesques in order to evoke the Jewish Semite origin and enunciate ethnic difference and cultural autonomy.[8] This Diasporic Orientalism may have traveled to Palestine[9] and been reincarnated in buildings like the Herzliya

⑪

⑫

⑬

⑪ Technion, Haifa, 1912. Alexander Bärwald.
⑫ Herzliya Gymnasium, Tel Aviv, 1909. Joseph Barsky. David B. Keidan Collection. Central Zionist Archives.
⑬ Rothschild Boulevard, Tel Aviv, 1920s. Matson Collection, Library of Congress.

Gymnasium in Tel Aviv—a pseudo-artistic-scientific reconstruction of the presumed plan of the Old Temple, which was praised by Bärwald, in his *Bauliche Probleme in Palästina* of 1910, as a good example, curiously enough, of a Zionist building well adapted to the Oriental context of Palestine.

Well, Professor Meyer, the '10s and '20s have long faded away and the Zionist gymnasium-ex-Temple already looks preposterous. The quest for *Jüdischer Aufbau* and the debate on Hebrew Style have lost their impetus as well and you can hardly hear a solid word on national architecture nowadays. Contemporary architecture has clearly elevated the rhetorical over the symbolic and at least partially averted the traditional predisposition for local patriotism. But does it render your inquiry regarding a Jewish national style irrelevant? Not at all! In fact, as far as I can grasp, the longer it hovers above, the easier the conundrum of vernacular modernism in Palestine seems to decipher itself. Why, indeed, has modern architecture spread here so swiftly? How did it overwhelm the entire local Jewish community, without any political agenda to speak of, or a proper manifesto, or a formal theory, or an urban crisis, or a technological paradigm shift, or a radical school, or authoritative masters? The answer, I argue, is set in the question. Modern architecture is currently being appropriated and misappropriated by the Jews as their own precisely because it is utterly displaced here, hollowed out, seemingly spontaneous, indistinctly eclectic, unambiguously popular.

In the latest issue of *Habinyan*, Julius Posener, the sharpest observer we could hope for, sums up the local situation in a few lines: "One is not keen on the Oriental appearance anymore. In any case, we renounced giving an Oriental image by domes and arcades. This rejection was necessary and also suited the real demands of the Jewish taste."[10] Posener's "Jewish taste" may have sarcastic undertones. He sometimes takes pleasure in exacerbating anti-Semitic profanity. But he is right ipso facto. Almost simultaneously with the American proclamation of the International Style, the reframing of modernism as an exterritorial order, it was naturalized here en bloc and was endorsed as an ordinary marker

⑭

⑮

⑯

⑭ House in Ramat Gan, 1936. Photographer: Zoltan Kluger. Israel State Archives.
⑮ House on the Carmel, 1934. Photographer: Zoltan Kluger. Israel State Archives.
⑯ House in Bnei Brak, 1940s. Heintz Rau. Photographer: Yitzhak Kalter.

# בית פרטי של ה' ג. בתל־בנימין
## על־יד תל־אביב
יוסף נויפלד

# RESIDENCE OF MR G.
TEL-BENJAMIN NEAR TEL-AVIV|

JOSEPH NEUFELD

1936

פוטו:
י. קלטר

View from Garden — מראה מהגן

הבית שמש נושא לוכוחים רבים. מה שנראה בעינינו למוצלח: גוף הבנין חצוב יפה בעל ארכיטקטורה אלגנטית וברורה. הפרגולה, החלון הגדול, סדור חדרי הקבלה — משפיעים בעוז רוחם. קומת חדרי השינה מסודרת יפה ומוגנה ע"י מרפסת רחבה.

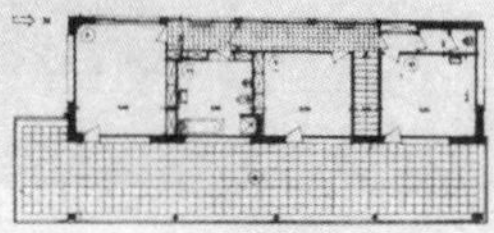

Upper Floor — קומה עליונה

Terrace — מרפסת

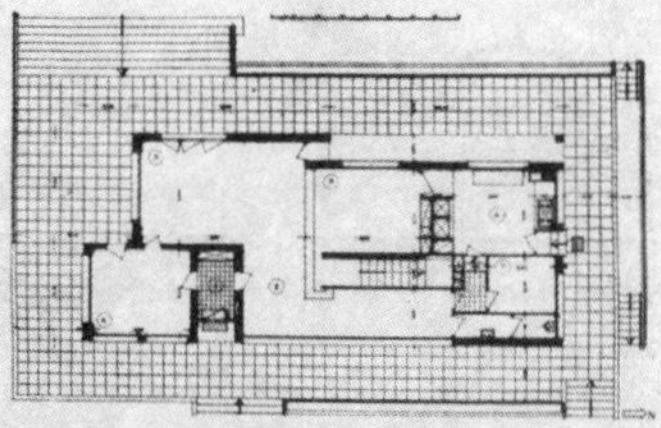

Ground Floor — קומת הקרקע

View from the Road — מראה מצד הרחוב

Hall — פרט



⑰

across the Zionist ideological, sectorial, territorial and cultural divide. Civil servants, ideologues, developers, poets, Beaux-Arts architects: all acquired an instant modernist savoir faire. In Tel Aviv at the moment, *Sachlichkeit* is *Yiddishkeit*. Cosmopolitan whiteness provides a common ground for the various groups of settlers, émigrés and exiles; infuses an ambience of acculturation and aesthetic *Bildung*; and above all, instills a sense of elsewhereness.

Apparently, the local politicians and planning administrators are quick to embrace, indeed often to boost by legislation, the modernist fashion. Our municipal engineer Jacob Shiffman, for instance, brags in *Palestine & Middle East Economic Magazine*: "An outstanding feature of the recent developments has been the very definite improvement in building methods and style. The architecture of the new houses in Tel Aviv sets a very credible standard and modern tendencies are strongly in evidence. The new architecture, with its essential features of simplicity and functional appropriateness effects a closer harmony between buildings and their settings than was previously the case. There is now in Tel Aviv no lack of buildings to which one can point as good examples of modern architecture and these have contributed to the general improvement in the standard of taste in Building."[11]

I find the overall delight and consensual pride associated with the new standard of taste truly encouraging. For the first time I realize that modern architecture could actually work on a large scale and be accepted both publicly and officially. The only nagging second thoughts I have are due to my frequent evening walks with Julius Posener. After two years here, he remains a skeptic, a bystander ready to submit his report and leave. During one of our walks, he pulled out a draft of a letter he wrote to Le Corbusier shortly after his arrival in Palestine, while he was provisionally working for Mendelsohn in his Jerusalem office. His letter opens with a delicate portrait of the local countryside, which only amplifies his subsequent malicious account of modern Tel Aviv. "In Tel Aviv," he wrote, "apartment buildings are crowded on plots of 15 × 50 square meters, facing towards narrow, dusty streets, but with a

General View — פוטו: י. קלטר — מראה כללי

## RESIDENCE OF DR. W., REHOVOTH

ERICH MENDELSON

## בית פרטי של ד"ר ו. ברחובות

אריך מנדלסון

**באורים לקומת הקרקע**

1. כניסה ראשית
2. מסדרון
3. חדר הלבשה
4. חדר פרחים
5. חדר טואלט, ב"כ
6. הול וחדר מדרגות
7. חדר אוכל
8. הכנה
9. חדר המזון
10. שטיפת כלים
11. מטבח
12. ספריה
13. חדר דיור
14. „גישה" ע"י האח
15. ברכת שחיה
16. חלק מכוסה של ה„פטיו"
17. מרפסת מזרחית
18. חדר העוזרות
19. חדר שינה של העוזרות
20. מבשל
21—22. משרת
23. חדר רחצה של העוזרות
24. חצר השרות וכניסה

**באורים לקומה ראשונה**

1. חדר שינה של הגברת
2. חדר הלבשה של האדון
3. חדר שינה של האדון
4. חדר אמבטיה של האדון
5—6. חדרי אורחים
7. חדר־אמבטיה לאורחים
8. הול של חדר המדרגות
9. חדר תפירה
10. חדר אמבטיה של הגברת
11. חדר הגברת
12. גגת הגג
13. פתח מעל ל„פטיו"
14. אמבטיות שמש

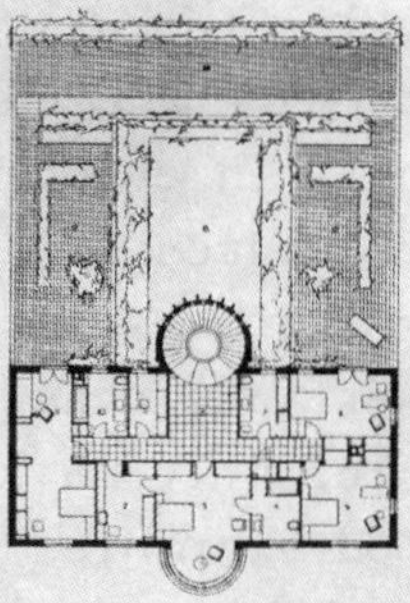

Upper Floor — קומה עליונה

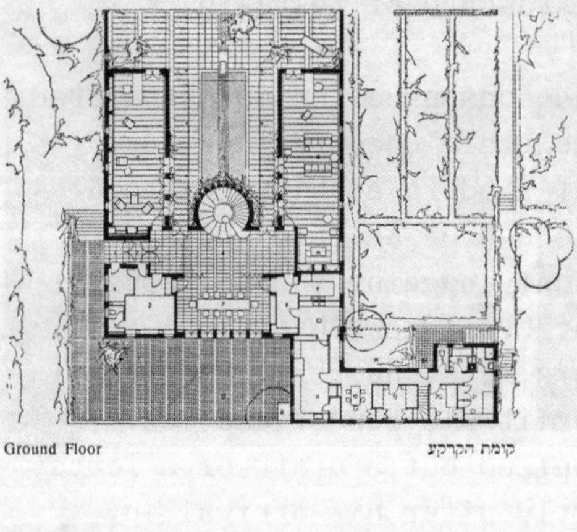

Ground Floor — קומת הקרקע

Stair Hall — אולם המדרגות

22

⑱

⑰ Pages from *Habinyan: A Magazine of Architecture & Town Planning*, no. 2, 1937.
⑱ Pages from *Habinyan: A Magazine of Architecture & Town Planning*, no. 2, 1937.

modern pretension; corner windows, … too wide, too low windows, brutal openings, through which light falls abruptly into sleeping rooms … Looking at these houses one would like to say: Your architect left Stuttgart (or Breslau) in 1926. He stopped at the latest trend of the day before yesterday. He never understood that Palestine is not Silesia, and that architecture has progressed since 1926."[12]

Posener in this letter deplores Tel Aviv as a collection of awkward misappropriations and ludicrous anachronisms. For him, the sheer quantity and variety of modernist adaptations is a categorical symptom of a provincial émigré society that never really processed the ideals of modern architecture in the countries of origin, nor genuinely grasped the native conditions in the country of arrival.

I must confess that even though I did not spare my own critique regarding excessive design and careless planning in Tel Aviv, I was surprised by the brutality of Posener's initial reading of the city. He is appalled by mediocrity and plagiarism, but fails to see that modern architecture may have finally fulfilled itself as mass culture here. Yes, of course, it is merely proverbial and plainly habitable and by no means rhetorical, quintessential, or experimental. But isn't that the best possible destiny for the European avant-garde—to die out and fade away on the eastern shores of the Mediterranean as "the trend of the day before yesterday"? After all, can't we already suspect that the rise of reactionary politics and *Heimatschutz* movements all over Europe signals not simply the forced exodus and exotic relocation of the avant-garde, but possibly its epistemological demise? At least based on my own itinerary of the last years, I may determine that once dislocated, the avant-garde becomes something else, anything else: it may be diluted as an "international style," or solidified as a "national style"; it may offer a phantasmal refuge for refugees, or a colonial masquerade for colonizers.

Posener mentions Stuttgart of 1926 in his letter. He's probably alluding to the date Mies presented the initial model for the Werkbund exposition in Weissenhof which opened a year later. What a climax it was for modern architecture when sixteen international participants were assigned housing projects with the single directive of a flat roof! I remember it so vividly. 1926 was the most exhilarating year of my life. I had just arrived in Dessau and enrolled in the Bauhaus *Vorkurse*. A year later, you established the *Bauabteilung* and we all traveled together to Stuttgart to see the marvel of a built modernist showcase neighborhood.

But as I related to Posener on one of our evening walks, inspiring as the *Weissenhofsiedlung* was for us, it was also the accelerator of a *Blut-und-Boden* demagogy in architectural debates and the prime target of *Heimatschutzers* and Nazi aficionados like Paul Schultze-Naumburg, Paul Bonatz, and Walther Darré, who began to apply nationalist and racial theories to architectural historiography and building analysis. To them, *Neue Sachlichkeit* is as rootless as the flat roof is roofless.[13] Schultze-Naumburg, for instance, wrote that the modernist house is in effect a "stationary sleeping car" which could be moved according to the whims of the "nomads of the metropolis, who have long lost the idea of the native land, and are not at all acquainted with the idea of the parental, let alone the ancestral, home."[14] And if the identity and origin of those "urban nomads" was not explicit enough, he went on to explain that these people offer models "which no longer keep us under German skies and on German soil, but displace us to the edge of the desert or into an Oriental setting. Instead of taking the Northern conditions of rain, snow, and ice as the basis for the Northern house, the roofless house is demanded."[15]

The "roofless house," then, was construed as an Oriental Trojan horse on German soil, and Mies's entire project, according to Paul Bonatz, who hoped to replace him as artistic director of Weissenhof, looked like a "Suburb of Jerusalem."[16] Evidently, this was just the prelude for architectural bigotry which, with the onset of the Third Reich, de-sublimated and reached one of its notorious releases with the Stuttgarter *Bund für Heimatschutz* publishing in 1934 the surreal photomontage of Weissenhofsiedlung with an Oriental, or African, bazaar and the inscription *Araberdorf*.

⑲

⑳

⑲ “Stuttgart Weissenhofsiedlung, Araberdorf,” Nazi propaganda photomontage, 1940.
⑳ View of Tel Aviv, early 1930s. Arieh Sharon, *Kibbutz + Bauhaus*, p. 44.

Professor Meyer, these hateful protocols are all too familiar to you. I was briefly referring to them only to speculate that perhaps the doctrine that drove those "nomads of the metropolis" out of their homeland may have something to do with their "instinctual" embrace of allegedly Oriental, Semitic, Arab or Mediterranean architecture in their land of exile. They, we, decisively took a side in the "war of the roofs." We've built a modernist front on "the edge of the desert," disregarding for the time being inner differences or even adversarial dispositions. My own *Sachlich* workers' housing project, a Corbusian apartment building on pilotis, a Cubist urban villa, and a quasi-expressionist office building, stand side by side with ease and add up to a city of makeshift modernism.

Aesthetes like Mendelsohn and Posener have no mercy for such whitewashed bric-a-brac. Mendelsohn, understandably, has a special aversion to phony replications of his own trademark motifs. He describes Tel Aviv as more or less the slaughterhouse of modernist ideas:

"Engineers of European contemporary architecture, who were trying to find adequate architectural expression for their new materials—steel, reinforced concrete, and glass—found that their experiments had come through with hundreds of bastard buildings in Palestine. Experiments were to become a perennial model of the visible rebuilding of the National home: broken corners, stripes of wall-openings and the exuberance of glass, designed originally for close contact between indoor and outdoor life, but wholly unsuitable to the subtropical climate of Palestine. That transition stage which almost degenerated into a pestilence is not yet entirely overcome."[17]

Mendelsohn's choice of words here is unfortunate. His account of "hundreds of bastards" which almost "degenerated into pestilence" reverberates racist attacks on modern architecture as essentially inferior, whereas he actually tries to make a contrary argument and present his notion of Oriental modernism. His critical stance is aimed at the Zionist double renunciation of indigenous Palestine and of its own Semitic origins. Since his arrival here over two years ago, he is keen on developing what he calls "Semitic architecture," a new modernist dialect, based on a material and stereometric interpretation of native Arab structures. He has already designed

㉑ Bat Galim Casino, Haifa, 1934. Alfred Goldberger.
㉒ May Cinema, Haifa, 1947. Yehuda Lilienfeld. Photographer: Yitzhak Kalter.
㉓ Okava Factory, Rishon LeZion, 1934. Matson Collection, Library of Congress.
㉔ Zion Square, Netanya, 1939. Photographer: Zoltan Kluger. Government Press Office.

㉑

㉒

㉓

㉔

several buildings here, which are far more serene than his gestural buildings in Germany, but the finest and broadest exemplar of this Semitic architecture is the Hadassah University Hospital on Mount Scopus, in Jerusalem, now under construction.[18]

Professor Meyer, you asked if there is any comprehensive publication on recent Jewish architecture in Palestine. Coincidentally, the September ’37 issue of *L’Architecture d’Aujourd’hui*, guest-edited by Julius Posener (*qui d’autre*) and Sam Barkai, is dedicated mostly to modern architecture and urban planning in Palestine. In German, an extensive and thought-provoking article by Posener will be published in the September 1938 issue of *Das Werk*. Its title is “Traditionelles und modernes Bauen in Palästina.” Posener just asked me to read the manuscript and give him my comments. I find it both inclusive and incisive. Wait for it. It will give you a most credible depiction of the Zionist project.

Evidently, Posener’s initial contempt for the derivative culture he found here is somewhat pacified and replaced by more introspective commentary. He is now striving to interpret why indeed “modern architecture seems progressive to the Jews at the point where it has in fact become historical.” He seems to be the only one around haunted by the occurrence of belated modernism, after he himself, and only he as far as I am aware, defined it as such and diagnosed it as a distinctively Jewish “pathology.” In the dense pages of the manuscript of “Traditionelles und modernes Bauen in Palästina,” I found out that Posener generated such a quandary only to propose an uncanny resolution, which, if I may suggest, you could also consider as a certain answer to your own inquiry regarding *Jüdischer Aufbau*. We should wait for the full printed version in *Das Werk*, but for now I can’t resist sharing with you the following polemics:

“We have stated what the Jews did not bring with them. They did, however, bring something, or at least the last wave of immigration did. In Germany the architecture of flat roofs, ribbon windows, cantilever plates, corner windows, stairwells, and ‘dynamic cornices’ has been called ‘Succoth architecture’, and an attempt was made to seek its origin in our Oriental bloodline. The truth is that out here it appears foreign and European. But it is also true that the Jewish architects and the Jewish public are

very fond of this architecture, maybe as a result of the relatively uncontested status they enjoyed during the past decade in central Europe. Like some of the political theories of that same period, these things still appeal as 'progressive' to them when really they are on the verge of becoming essentially historical. The 'modern style' overcame the Eastern shtetl as well as the attempts at a national architecture that were made before the war."[19]
Professor Meyer, would you agree that Posener throws us here into a Freudian abyss with his astounding analysis that the Jews took the blame, as it were, for modern architecture's "shameful origin" and, in a sudden leap of faith, appropriated the aesthetic of efficiency as their collective mark of Cain?[20] After all, such a mirroring effect between Jewish and anti-Semitic hermeneutics is not at all uncommon and feeds on the Jews' own racial polysemy.[21] If we follow Posener's logic, we can see that the act of self-stereotyping, of embracing "Succoth architecture" as our own "pestilence," transgressive as it may be, is also highly functional and operates on several registers: First, it provides the Jews with an architectural myth of origin. Their alleged traceless nomadism finally has a proper object, a building culture, even if it is merely the makeshift *Existenzminimum* of the *Sukkah*. Second, the "Modern Style," as Posener sardonically indicates, is an elegant way out of the visual ghetto of the Eastern European *shtetl* and its reincarnation in the eclectic search for a Jewish national style in Palestine. In other words, the expulsion from *Heimat* is also the exodus from Diaspora; the opportune obliteration of centuries of "minor" Jewish culture, and the eventual prospect of universal assimilation.
And finally, while the indigene trope "Succoth architecture" authenticates the Jews as *Ur*-Orientals, as epic returnees, the pedant image of white architecture safeguards their estrangement in the Orient. "It seems alien and European here," Posener tautologically comments on the specter of the "Modern Style" in Palestine, only to overturn the Nazi allegation that the "Modern Style" "seems alien and Oriental here," in Germany. And so the postcard *Araberdorf*, by being incarnated *ad nauseam* in the first Hebrew city, becomes a prophecy of the Jews' eternal exile in the Levant, their colonial remoteness. Against the grain of history, modern architecture be-

comes Jewish by guilt, by negation, by masquerade, and by conformity: "the Jewish architects and the Jewish public are very fond of this architecture."

Posener's psycho-historical analysis has become ever more convoluted in our recent walks and in his latest writing. He's drifted away both from his early Mendelsohnian romanticism and from the zeitgeist discussions at the *Hug*. For him, once modern architecture is widely accepted as both formal and informal language, it inexorably develops local dialects, hybrid forms and double-talk. Previous loyalties and affinities to certain genres, agendas, or old masters are broken in favor of a new vitality.

A few days ago he showed me for the first time Le Corbusier's brief letter of response to him, in which the master dictated from afar: "no formula for Palestine. [...] create an architecture that is not merely functionalist."[22] Posener never really explained what could possibly be modern architecture "that is not merely functionalist," but in his latest article for *Habinyan*, entitled "One-Family Houses in Palestine,"[23] his writing becomes emphatically pedagogical and prescribes a primer of a sort for the interior adaptation of modernist houses to the local conditions.

For Posener, the modernist house in Palestine, "reminiscent of the German modern villas of the years 1925–1930," is already an imperative, an instant relic of German-Jewish bonding. But as such, it is an empty shell, a disembodied figure awaiting a fitting body. "Many architects are talking about the Oriental body of their houses," he writes, "but they are not explaining how exactly to create such an Oriental body without imitating the plan of the Arab house. [...] Our wide open houses with their sharp angles stand under our sky as if they were cut out of a white cardboard."[24]

Two years ago, Posener would have left his readers at this point, stunned by the cutting metaphor of "white cardboard." But today he is generous enough to share his erudition and illustrate a process of cultural appropriation: "Undoubtedly, we'll be right to familiarize ourselves with the way people used to build and dwell in this country before us. [...] Such a research should not be limited to the Land of Israel, to the buildings of the Arabs in the present time." He goes on to lay out floor plans of various Mediterranean and Islamic typologies, all based on the portico, the atrium, or the patio—the shadowed inner spaces of the region. It becomes clear that his plot for the domestication of modern architecture in Palestine is based on domesticity itself, on the gradual submission to the Oriental interior.[25] In contrast to the decorative biblical Orientalism of earlier Hebrew nationalists; to Mendelsohn's compositional and tectonic Semitic architecture; to Le Corbusier's primitivist poiesis of the white wall; or indeed to the Nazi contempt of the "roofless"—Posener audaciously suggests an "Arab plan" with a modernist elevation; an "Oriental body" encased within a German artifact "of the years 1925–1930."

His implicit argument is quite compelling and nullifies any claim, by protagonists and antagonists alike, for modern architecture's intrinsic authenticity, purity and rigor. His Jewish-Palestinian modernism is non-autochthonous and non-authoritative. It has no profound origin, nor a Bauhaus climax. It is by second nature migrant, displaced, Diasporic and eclectic. Precisely because it is patently derivative and out-of-date here, as Posener insists all along, these attributes are amplified, turning it into the open signifier and accumulator of ambiguous meanings it ought to be. As such, it suits very well the taste of the Zionist Jews, their progressive self-image, their reformist aspirations, their colonial violence, and their blinding overexposure to native Palestine. After all, what is modern about modern architecture, if I properly remember your announcement almost ten years ago in the "bauen" manifesto, "is not the flat roof and vertical-horizontal division of the façade, but its direct relationship with human existence."[26]

Professor Meyer, I got carried away with speculations on the dubious notion of *Jüdischer Aufbau* which you laid on my doorstep. I hope I did not at all satisfy your curiosity, so that you will find it necessary to visit us in Tel Aviv and see it with your own eyes.

Best regards to Lena.

Yours truly,

Arieh Sharon

4 Pinsker Street, Tel Aviv

(written by Zvi Efrat)

1 Translator's note: Hannes Meyer is using the term *Jüdischer Aufbau*. *Aufbau* is a concept that has no straightforward equivalent in the English language. It implies a purposeful creation of something that has not been there before, beyond the mere physical erection of edifices. It is therefore popular in utopian contexts such as socialism, where prolific use was made of this term. "Reconstruction" is often used because it implies a similar sense of mission. One of the main German-language Jewish newspapers is called *Der Aufbau; it* temporarily used "Reconstruction" as an English title in its masthead. Strictly speaking, this is incorrect, since "reconstruction" should be *Wiederaufbau* (though it is of course a perfect fit in the Zionist context).

2 The letter from Hannes Meyer to Arieh Sharon was introduced to me by Philipp Oswalt, the director of the Bauhaus Foundation from 2009 to 2014. It was Oswalt's proposal to write a retrospective letter of response in Sharon's name. The "letter" was published as "lieber hannes meyer" in *Bauhaus—The Bauhaus Dessau Foundation's Magazine* 2 (November 2011), pp. 22–23. The letter presented here is an extended version of that one.

3 Arieh Sharon describing the work on the Bundesschule des ADGB project and quoting Hannes Meyer, in Sharon, *Kibbutz + Bauhaus: An Architect's Way in a New Land* (Stuttgart and Tel Aviv: Karl Kramer Verlag and Massada, 1976), p. 31.

4 Historian Yf'aat Weiss writes: "In the summer of 1933, the Jewish Agency for Palestine, the German Zionist Federation, and the German Economics Ministry drafted a plan meant to allow German Jews emigrating to Palestine to retain some of the value of their property in Germany by purchasing German goods for the Yishuv, which would redeem them in Palestine local currency. This scheme, known as the Transfer Agreement or *Ha'avarah*, met the needs of all interested parties: German Jews, the German economy, and the Mandatory government and the Yishuv in Palestine." Yf'aat Weiss, "The Transfer Agreement and the Boycott Movement: A Jewish Dilemma on the Eve of the Holocaust," Shoah Resource Center, The International School for Holocaust Studies, accessed June 5, 2017, https://www.yadvashem.org/odot_pdf/Microsoft%20Word%20-%203231.pdf, p. 1.

5 For an extensive discussion of the Hebrew Style of the 1910s and 1920s, see Yossi Klein, *The Beginning of Tel Aviv's Americanization* [in Hebrew] (Jerusalem: Carmel, 2011), pp. 15–72.

6 On the distinction between Jews and Hebrews, see Etan Bloom, *Arthur Ruppin and the Production of Pre-Israeli Culture* (Leiden and Boston: Brill, 2011), pp. 11–12: "It must be remembered, then, that the new social field in Zionist Palestine was built not by *Jews* but by *Hebrews*: The workers' organization was called the *General Federation of Hebrew Workers* and, similarly, the first teachers were organized under the title of the *Hebrew Teachers' Association*. The first units that joined the British army in World War II were called the *Hebrew Regiment*, the banners in the Zionist demonstrations called for 'Hebrew work' and a 'Hebrew state,' the slogan of the Hebrew language revivalists was 'Ivri daber Ivrit' (Hebrews, speak Hebrew), the university in Jerusalem was the first 'Hebrew University,' Tel Aviv was 'the first Hebrew city' and so on. The dichotomy of *Jew* and *Hebrew* was at the core of identity formation in the Zionist community in Palestine, and, to a large extent, shaped pre-Israel cultural identity."

7 Klein, *Beginning of Tel Aviv's Americanization*.

8 The anthropologist Ivan Kalmar terms this tendency "complimentary Orientalism." See Ivan Kalmar, "Moorish Style: Orientalism, the Jews, and Synagogue Architecture," *Jewish Social Studies: History, Culture, and Society* 7.3 (2001), pp. 68–100.

9 The intriguing argument that Jewish Orientalism in Palestine begins when it ends in Europe is made by Jacobé Huet in an unpublished paper: "Nazism, Zionism, and Orientalism: Modern Architecture in 1930s Tel Aviv."

10 Julius Posener, "One-Family Houses in Palestine," *Habinyan: A Magazine of Architecture & Town Planning* 2 (November 1937), p. 1.

11 Jacob Shiffman, "Building and Town Planning in Tel Aviv," *Palestine & Middle East Economic Magazine* (March 1933), p. 110.

12 Letter from Julius Posener to Le Corbusier, November 1935, Jerusalem. Cited in Ita Heinze-Greenberg, "This Once Gold-Diggingly Created City: Eric Mendelsohn and Tel Aviv," *Docomomo Journal* 40 (March 2009), p. 96.

13 See Richard Pommer, "The Flat Roof: A Modernist Controversy in Germany," *Art Journal* 43, no. 2 (1983), p. 165.

14 Paul Schultze-Naumburg, *Kulturarbeiten*, vol. 4, *Das Gesicht des deutschen Hauses* (Munich, 1920), pp. 7–10. Cited in "Flat Roof" by Richard Pommer, who notes that the "stationary sleeping car" is a reference to Le Corbusier's double house at Weissenhof, which was presented by the architect as an architectural wagon-lit.

15 Ibid.

16 Ibid.

17 Erich Mendelsohn, "Twenty Years of Building: An Exposition and a Publication," *Palestine Post*, December 29, 1940, p. 5. Cited in Heinze-Greenberg, "This Once Gold-Diggingly Created City," p. 96.

18 See dossier "Erich Mendelsohn's Semitic Architecture" in this chapter.

19 Julius Posener, "Traditionelles und modernes Bauen in Palästina," *Das Werk* 9 (September 1938), pp. 257–271. See full English translation by Jan Caspers in dossier "Julius Posener's Tableau" in chapter "Object."

20 The allegorical figure of Cain represents the eternal fugitive and wanderer (Heb. *na vanad*) who was cursed from the earth, banned from farming, and therefore doomed to become a city builder.

21 On occasional mirroring and various symmetrical relations between Zionism and modern anti-Semitism, see Itamar Even-Zohar, "The Emergence of a Native Hebrew Culture in Palestine: 1882–1948," *Studies in Zionism*, no. 4

(1981), p. 178; and Etan Boom, "Arthur Ruppin and the Production of Pre-Israeli Culture," *Studies in Jewish History and Culture,* vol. 31 (Leiden: Koninklijke Brill NV, 2011), p. 85.

22 Letter from Le Corbusier to Julius Posener, October 21, 1937. The letter was first published and translated into Hebrew in Avi Mayer, *Sam Barkai: The Architect of Right Dimensions* [in Hebrew] (Tel Aviv: Stoa, 2015), pp. 176–177.

23 Posener, "One-Family Houses," p. 1.

24 Ibid., p. 2.

25 Ibid., p. 3. Leo Adler, also a member of the *Hug*, elaborated the notion of Mediterranean architecture; see Yossi Klein, "Leo Adler and the Definition of Tel Aviv as a Mediterranean City" (unpublished paper) and David Tal, "Israeli Identity: Between Orient and Occident," *Routledge Studies in Middle Eastern Society* (New York: Routledge, 2013), p. 126.

26 From the manifesto "bauen," published in the *Bauhaus* magazine in 1928.

# DOSSIER: ERICH MENDELSOHN'S SEMITIC ARCHITECTURE

㉕ Erich Mendelsohn and Richard Kauffmann, Mount Scopus, Jerusalem, 1936. Hebrew University Photography Archive.

"What compels us to live in the north?" asked Erich Mendelsohn in a letter written on December 10, 1934, to his wife, Luise. "Isn't our place here—is not Palestine the only island for 18 million, their origin and historical destination?"[1] Just a few months after his arrival in Palestine, Mendelsohn delineated the meta-historical narrative that temporarily transformed him from a resentful exile to an affectionate émigré:

> Internally I've resolved to stay here. I see the people of the field, even city dwellers, even the European Jews inhabiting the hotel, more as my brothers with each passing day. Their faces, behind them our own history, good or bad, happy or disastrous, always knowing, always damaged. What the land needs the most is creative people. Only they will earn our name respect and honor again. [. . .]
>
> I am fulfilled by the work as in the good days—England was just an interlude. We will live quietly for ourselves, for the task—for our people. There is no other, no greater duty. Only here will what I believe in come to pass—the monumental is not tied to scale. [. . .] We have to achieve something on a par: as you put it, "Build the Bible!"[2]

Mendelsohn's first architectural commission in Palestine was the Weizmann House (for Chaim Weizmann, the president of the Zionist Organization); other projects followed. He established his office in Jerusalem and designed the Schocken House and

(26) View of Temple Mount from Mount Scopus, Jerusalem, 1930s. Hebrew University Photography Archive.

(27) Erich Mendelsohn, Richard Kauffmann, and university professors on Mount Scopus, Jerusalem, 1936. Hebrew University Photography Archive.

(26)

(27)

Library and the Anglo-Palestine Bank in Jerusalem; laboratories at the Weizmann Institute of Science in Rehovot; and a vocational school in Kibbutz Yagur. He was also employed by the British Public Works Department to design the Rambam Hospital in Haifa. His most extensive and significant architectural engagement in Palestine was related to the Hebrew University campus on Mount Scopus in Jerusalem, for which he prepared a master plan and designed several buildings which were constructed: the Students' Club, the Hadassah University Hospital, and the Nurses' Training School. After his first tour on the campus site, he despondently wrote to Luise:

> The university matter has become even worse through the resistance of Mr. Green and the unmanliness of [university president] Dr. Magnes. [...] I've inspected all the buildings on Mount Scopus. A God-given piece of land —between Dead Sea and Mediterranée— has been tainted by devils' hands. A woeful muddle of incompetence and self-complacency. I feel like Jeremiah of old—deeply despondent and inwardly scarred. This continues and makes me truculent, hard, and insecure. What is it with the Jews?[3]

Nevertheless, according to the architectural historian Diana Dolev, "Mendelsohn included the existing buildings in his master-plan, integrating them into his own concept of a unified complex."[4] The overall scheme of the campus presents "a standard scale, a quite uniform pattern of buildings closing on three sides of each courtyard, and a few curved forms that soften the uniform effect. [...] Connected by different sized open spaces, the L or U shaped buildings create patios, thus presenting a constantly changing environment, from open to closed spaces, and a range of options in between."[5]

Mendelsohn's master plan for the Hebrew University campus was not realized due to disagreements with the university's administration. His plans for the Hadassah medical complex, however, materialized: the building still functions as a hospital today, after undergoing substantial alterations and extensions. Dolev explicates the building's scenic layout: "On the whole, to adjust to the topography Mendelsohn did not imitate the curved lines of the mountain terraces; quite the contrary. The curved shapes of the terrain and the strictly angular lines of the buildings emphasize each other's formal qualities. Thus the landscape and the buildings, bulging out of the mountain ridge and adding floors as they stretch out onto the slope, create a dialogue between autonomous entities."[6]

During his years in Palestine, Mendelsohn consistently expressed his aversion to Tel Aviv's "bastardized" modernism, objected to the misguided effort to establish a Jewish-European cultural enclave in the Levant, and tried to articulate the idiosyncrasies of a "Semitic architecture" (see chapter "Jewish Style"). His Zionist-Orientalist digression, alas, had run its course by 1941. According to the architectural historian Ita Heinze-Greenberg, Mendelsohn "recorded his political credo in a publication titled *Palestine and the World of Tomorrow*" before leaving Palestine for America:

> Palestine is not an uninhabited land. On the contrary it forms a part of the Arabian world. The problem that confronts the Jew in Palestine is how to reach equal rank among its neighbors; how to become a cell of the future Semitic commonwealth, to which they in fact belong by their race, tongue, and character ... Palestine of today is symbolizing the union between the most modern civilization and the most antique culture. It is the place where intellect and vision, matter and spirit meet. In the arrangement commanded by this union both Arabs and Jews, both members of the Semitic family, should be equally interested. On this solution depends the fate of Palestine.[7] ■

1 Letter from Erich Mendelsohn to Luise Mendelsohn [in German], December 10, 1934, Erich Mendelsohn Archive, Staatliche Museen zu Berlin. Available online (accessed July 14, 2017): http://ema.smb.museum/1101.

2 Ibid.

3 Letter from Erich Mendelsohn to Luise Mendelsohn [in German], December 27, 1934, Erich Mendelsohn Archive, Staatliche Museen zu Berlin. Available online (accessed July 14, 2017): http://ema.smb.museum/1109.

4 Diana Dolev, *The Planning and Building of the Hebrew University, 1919–1948: Facing the Temple Mount* (Lanham, MD: Lexington Books, 2016), p. 99. Dolev's book includes a thorough and captivating description of Mendelsohn's involvement with the design of the Hebrew University campus, as well as insightful observations about his views on Zionism, Semitism, the Orient, and the Mediterranean.

5 Ibid., p. 106.

6 Ibid., p. 111.

7 Erich Mendelsohn, *Palestine and the World of Tomorrow*, pamphlet (Jerusalem: 1940), pp. 11 and 19. Cited in Ita Heinze-Greenberg, "This Once Gold-Diggingly Created City: Eric Mendelsohn and Tel Aviv," *Docomomo Journal* (March 2009), p. 96. For further reading about Mendelsohn's work in Palestine, see Ita Heinze-Mühleib, *Erich Mendelsohn: Bauten und Projekte in Palästina (1934–1941)* (Munich: Scaneg, 1986); Alona Nitzan-Shiftan, "Contested Zionism – Alternative Modernism: Erich Mendelsohn and the Tel Aviv Chug in Mandate Palestine," in *Constructing a Sense of Place: Architecture and the Zionist Discourse*, ed. Haim Yacobi (Burlington: Ashgate, 2004).

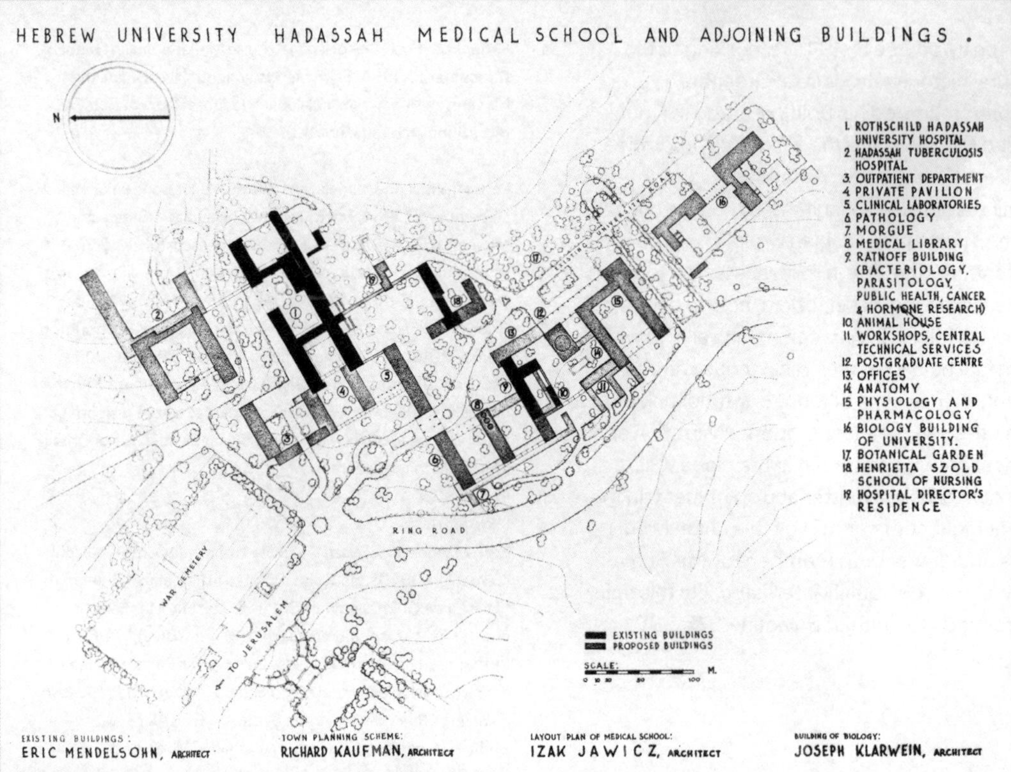
HEBREW UNIVERSITY HADASSAH MEDICAL SCHOOL AND ADJOINING BUILDINGS.
N
1. ROTHSCHILD HADASSAH UNIVERSITY HOSPITAL
2. HADASSAH TUBERCULOSIS HOSPITAL
3. OUTPATIENT DEPARTMENT
4. PRIVATE PAVILION
5. CLINICAL LABORATORIES
6. PATHOLOGY
7. MORGUE
8. MEDICAL LIBRARY
9. RATNOFF BUILDING (BACTERIOLOGY, PARASITOLOGY, PUBLIC HEALTH, CANCER & HORMONE RESEARCH)
10. ANIMAL HOUSE
11. WORKSHOPS, CENTRAL TECHNICAL SERVICES
12. POSTGRADUATE CENTRE
13. OFFICES
14. ANATOMY
15. PHYSIOLOGY AND PHARMACOLOGY
16. BIOLOGY BUILDING OF UNIVERSITY.
17. BOTANICAL GARDEN
18. HENRIETTA SZOLD SCHOOL OF NURSING
19. HOSPITAL DIRECTOR'S RESIDENCE
EXISTING UNIVERSITY ROAD
RING ROAD
WAR CEMETERY
TO JERUSALEM
EXISTING BUILDINGS
PROPOSED BUILDINGS
SCALE:
0 10 20 50 100 M.
EXISTING BUILDINGS:
ERIC MENDELSOHN, ARCHITECT
TOWN PLANNING SCHEME:
RICHARD KAUFMAN, ARCHITECT
LAYOUT PLAN OF MEDICAL SCHOOL:
IZAK JAWICZ, ARCHITECT
BUILDING OF BIOLOGY:
JOSEPH KLARWEIN, ARCHITECT

(28)

(29)

בנייני המרכז הרפואי
הסתדרות מדיצינית הדסה
MEDICAL CENTRE BUILDINGS
HADASSAH MEDICAL ORGANIZATION
קבלנים כלליים: משרד קבלני
יוסף פפרמן
GENERAL CONTRACTORS: MISRAD KABLANI
J. FEFERMAN
אדריכל אריך מנדלסון לונדון-ירושלים
ARCHITECT ERICH MENDELSOHN LONDON JERUSALEM
מהנדס יועץ ד"ר אריך קמפינסקי ירושלים
CONSULTING ENG: DR. ERICH KEMPINSKI JERUSALEM

(30)

(31)

(32)

(28) Hadassah University Hospital, Mount Scopus, Jerusalem, 1930s. Erich Mendelsohn. Hebrew University Photography Archive.
(29) Hadassah University Hospital, Mount Scopus, Jerusalem, 1930s. Model. Erich Mendelsohn. Hebrew University Photography Archive.
(30) Hadassah University Hospital, Mount Scopus, Jerusalem, 1930s. Sign on construction site. Hebrew University Photography Archive.
(31) Hadassah University Hospital, Mount Scopus, Jerusalem, 1930s. Erich Mendelsohn. Hebrew University Photography Archive.
(32) Hadassah University Hospital, Mount Scopus, Jerusalem, 1930s. Erich Mendelsohn. Hebrew University Photography Archive.

(33)

(34)

㉟

㊱

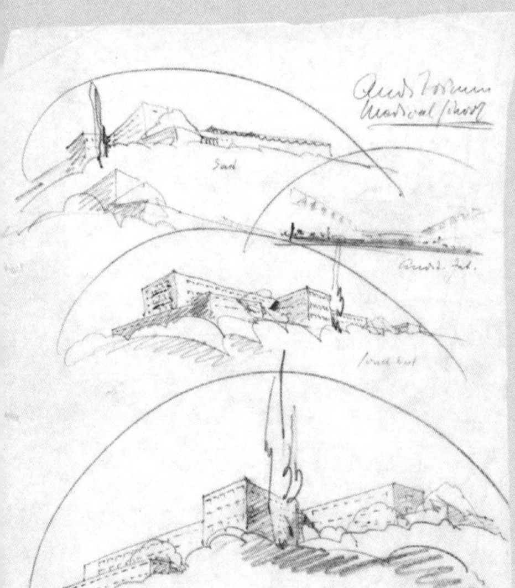

㊲

㉝ Hadassah University Hospital main entrance and courtyard, Mount Scopus, Jerusalem, 1930s. Erich Mendelsohn. Hebrew University Photography Archive.
㉞ Erich Mendelsohn at the Hadassah University Hospital, Mount Scopus, Jerusalem, 1939. Photographer: Zoltan Kluger. Israel State Archives.
㉟ Hadassah University Hospital main entrance, Mount Scopus, Jerusalem, 1930s. Erich Mendelsohn. Hebrew University Photography Archive.
㊱ Hadassah University Hospital, Mount Scopus, Jerusalem, inauguration ceremony, 1939. Photographer: Zoltan Kluger. Israel State Archives.
㊲ Sketches of the Hadassah University Hospital, Mount Scopus, Jerusalem, Erich Mendelsohn,1936.

# Fair Levant

① Balcony, Tel Aviv, 1930s.

## Tel Aviv

> Whitewash is extremely moral. Suppose there were a decree requiring all rooms in Paris to be given a coat of whitewash. I maintain that that would be a police task of real stature and a manifestation of high morality, the sign of a great people.
> Le Corbusier, *A Coat of Whitewash: The Law of Ripolin*, 1925[1]

Suppose there were a decree requiring that all new buildings in Tel Aviv be given a coat of whitewash, inside and out, or at least be plastered white. Would this be the "manifestation of high morality, the sign of a great people"? Or would it rather be a nebulous sign of a displaced people, a symptom of "something that can be called a Jewish mode of living," to borrow Julius Posener's words from 1938? Something that "can really only be defined by pointing out the attributes it lacks"; something with "no close connection to the environment and no social or professional heritage"?[2]

Now suppose that by a sudden twist of fate, Le Corbusier's rhetorical decree becomes literal, actual and instantaneous, but that it presents itself in a slight deferral, a moment too late: around 1932, precisely when the white wall has run its discursive course and dissipated into the International Style. As Mark Wigley wrote in his seminal study *White Walls, Designer Dresses*:

> If, as so many commentators argue, the Weissenhofsiedlung became the first international manifestation of the white, prismatic, flat-roofed mode of building which was to be identified in 1932 as the "International Style," that moment of canonization in 1932 is the moment that white itself slips into

the background, the moment that white can become the default condition of the discourse that never needs to be addressed as such.[3]

This, in effect, is the brief of the story of Tel Aviv—a city burgeoning in the "moment that white can become the default condition"—or at least the story of Tel Aviv as told by Julius Posener, an iconoclast who chronicled in real time the rise and fall of the *Neues Bauen* in Germany in the late 1920s and early 1930s, and found himself by 1935 an exile in Palestine, bewildered by the "white city" frenzy and its peculiar anachronism.

Nearly all veteran and incoming expat architects and critics operating in Tel Aviv in the 1930s either celebrated the belated modernist party (like the members of the renowned "Hug") or acrimoniously condemned it (like Erich Mendelsohn; see chapter "Jewish Style"). Posener, however, remained an inquisitive observer, watching the time-lapse parody of the city and reporting on the somewhat ludicrous modernist spell bewitching the Jews in Palestine. "Like some of the political theories of that same period," he wrote, "these things [i.e., modern architecture] still appeal as 'progressive' to them when really they are on the verge of becoming essentially historical."[4] Posener never properly unraveled the workings of the Jewish "progressive" imaginary, but if we read between the lines of his several articles and letters from Palestine, we can extract a psycho-historical hypothesis that modernism had become the generic signifier of imposed or self-inflicted lack: lack of tradition, lack of vocational training, lack of taste, lack of status, lack of both urban and rural habitus, eternal lack of *Heimat*, and a newly acquired lack of orientation in the Orient.

In this mental context, both the impulsive Jewish and the official Zionist canonization of the white wall seemed to Posener to be a misconstrued monolithic affirmation of Western identity, an unprocessed disavowal of the Jewish Diasporic history (with the cluttered shtetl as its haunting image), a long-anesthetized sense of genius loci, an attempt to project a surrogate folklore of the plainly new.

Posener's account is frequently ambiguous, but against the grain of black-and-white polemics, which tend to focus on bipolar architectural attributes of political hegemony and brutal violence, it opens up a tentative reading of Tel Aviv's vernacular modernism as a rather dirty and erratic practice: at once a double agent of familiarization and alienation; a binary modus of *Bildung* and cultural erasure; a transitional object and a permanent masquerade; a discreet charm of the bourgeoisie and a proletarian common denominator; a decolonizing reflex (in the context of British institutional architecture) and the ultimate colonial style in service of a national project.

In this last respect, Zionist modernism is an intense and highly instructive instance of the International Style. After all, this American title, which cannibalized the various early-twentieth-century avant-gardes, was primarily

②

③

② Zina Dizengoff Square, Tel Aviv, 1935. Genia Averbuch. Photographer: Yitzhak Kalter. Matson Collection, Library of Congress.
③ Beit Hadar, Tel Aviv, 1935. Carl Rubin. Photographer: Yitzhak Kalter.
④ Aginsky House, Tel Aviv, 1934. Sam Barkai. Photographer: Yitzhak Kalter.
⑤ Angle House, Tel Aviv, 1934. Zeev Rechter. Photographer: Yitzhak Kalter.

④

⑤

⑥

⑧

⑨

⑦

⑩

⑥ Dizengoff Street, looking north, Tel Aviv, 1934. Matson Collection, Library of Congress.
⑦ Reisfeld House, Tel Aviv, 1930s. Pinhas Bizonsky. Photographer: Yitzhak Kalter.
⑧ Zlotopolsky House, Tel Aviv, 1930s. Dov Karmi. Photographer: Yitzhak Kalter.
⑨ Bialik School, Tel Aviv, 1930s. Yaakov Shiffman. Photographer: Yitzhak Kalter. Matson Collection, Library of Congress.
⑩ Migdalor Cinema, Tel Aviv, 1934. Harry Luria, Arieh Sharon. Photographer: Yitzhak Kalter.

(11)

(12)

(13)

(11) Heller House, Tel Aviv, 1936. Benjamin Anekstein. Photographer: Yitzhak Kalter.
(12) Nemtsov House, Tel Aviv, 1935. Y. Zarinsky. Photographer: Yitzhak Kalter.
(13) Max Liebling House, Tel Aviv, 1936. Dov Karmi. Photographer: Yitzhak Kalter.
(14) Assuta Medical Center, Tel Aviv, 1934. Joseph Neufeld. Photographer: Yitzhak Kalter.
(15) Apartment building, Tel Aviv, 1935. Pinchas Hütt. Photographer: Yitzhak Kalter.
(16) Rabinovicz House, Tel Aviv, 1930s. Ben Ami Shulman. Photographer: Yitzhak Kalter.

⑭

⑮

⑯

intended to nullify the previous native and colonial mimetic economy and to trade the exoticism of the "styles" for the authority of an overstyle. The universalist gesture of all-overness and free flow revealed itself as the most conspicuous form of cultural colonialism.

## Bauhaus Colonial

In the last decades of the twentieth century, thanks to the rather casual moniker "Bauhaus," Tel Aviv's architecture of the 1930s and 1940s underwent a process of canonization and was sentenced—through academic, curatorial, journalistic, municipal, and, most effectively, real-estate trends—to eternal, Faustian youth. Hundreds of buildings were listed for preservation, and the residential core of the city was designated by UNESCO as a World Heritage Site. Politically awkward and architecturally confusing as this hype might be, it is not entirely baseless. After all, the swift dissemination and comfortable domestication of various architectural modernisms in Tel Aviv was indeed phenomenal and did in fact result in an incredible stock of stylized buildings. Practically all the residential and public buildings built in Tel Aviv during the 1930s and most of the 1940s wear a modernist look (virtually none of those built in the 1910s and 1920s do). In Europe, early modern architecture presented and represented itself primarily as an intellectual work; as critical pedagogy and discourse; as a marginal practice producing some showcase buildings, prototype housing, or exemplary neighborhoods. In Tel Aviv, however, modern architecture became both compulsory and compulsive. It was a mode dictated by the municipal authorities, who simply would not issue building permits to the newly outmoded Orientalist, biblical, or Jugendstil schemes. And it was also a mood transmitted by the print media, desired by the residents and commodified by the developers. In 1933, Yaakov Shiffman, Tel Aviv's city engineer, was already promoting modernism as the city's vernacular:

> Although it is too early to speak of a Palestinian architecture, it is clear that the new builder is freeing himself from the fetters of a hampering and alien tradition [...]. A pioneer population has no time for architectural niceties or for the excessive decoration of a more leisured generation. A rationalism, at times admittedly harsh, is evident in the planning of buildings and in their architectural treatment devoid of surcharged ornament. The architectural effect is obtained chiefly through the relation of masses, spacing and color.[5]

Was the architecture of mass, space, and whiteness indeed an index of the harsh rationalism and frugal functionalism of a pioneer population, as suggested by Shiffman, or was it a reflection of the optical imaginary of a dislocated community of émigrés, exiles, settlers, and colonizers who were inexorably preoccupied by the overwhelming condition of "elsewhere"?

The local culture industry has long flooded the architectural discourse with hollow terms and common truths based on elliptical scholarly research, creating a coded plane of intentions and actions and constructing a profound homology between Zionism (i.e., a mystified pioneer mentality) and modernity-modernization-modernism (the negation of "architectural niceties") in general. The equation is bilateral but has a single message: the Zionist movement is supposedly the laboratory, or the frontier, of modern architecture. Modern architecture is demonstrably the progressive expression and cosmopolitan look of the Zionist body. In this context, white is either the marker or the eraser, either the complacent tale of utopianism or the critical discourse of colonialism.

However, closer scrutiny of Tel Aviv's "Zionist Bauhaus" exposes the lingering "Diasporic" habits and the exuberant mannerism of the city's formative eclectic decades. In fact, the so-called "white city" of the 1930s and 1940s is a rather random pastiche of architectural derivatives and deviants, clutters and lapses, fakes and slip-ups borrowed from assorted sources, only a few of which can be traced directly back to one of the Bauhaus's own divergent doctrines. At best, and as an homage to earlier cultural imports, the city's free style could be called "Bauhaus colonial." Erich Mendelsohn was appalled by the "hundreds of bastard buildings" he saw in Tel Aviv in the mid-1930s: he denigrated the "broken corners, strips of wall openings and the exuberance of glass, designed originally for close contact between indoor and outdoor life, but wholly unsuitable to the subtropical climate of Palestine" and concluded that Tel Aviv's plagiarized modernism was a "transition stage which almost degenerated into a pestilence."[6]

Mendelsohn's misgivings reverberate, years later, in the seminal book *Houses of the Sand: The Architecture of the International Style in Tel Aviv, 1931–1948* by Nitza Metzger-Szmuk, architect, scholar, and the former head of the Preservation Department at the Tel Aviv municipality. According to this book, "A group of structures with 'theatrical scenery elevations' was the most common [in the 1930s]. The local public often referred to these structures with derision and mocked their façadism, claiming they were by all means traditional architecture camouflaged with motifs, materials, and references of the modern movement."[7] Recent scholarship has further demonstrated that beneath the overall ambience of cultural masquerade there coexisted a genuine multiplicity of modernist sources, notions, and personae negotiating their positions in the city's brief climax.[8]

Yet as conflicting, colloquial, base, or "dirty" as Tel Aviv's modernism may have been for people of taste and for scholars of rigor, we should still not assume a simple continuity between the exotic eclecticism of the 1920s and the exiled modernisms of the 1930s. Standards of building and living were abruptly changing; the scope of construction was significantly widened and buildings' volumes were greatly increased; structural skeletons of columns and beams gradually replaced the old system of retaining walls, releasing the ground floor, the building envelope, and the interior partitions and presenting for the first time "free plans" and "free façades"; family houses became family estates and investment opportunities (i.e., apartment buildings for rent); the typical apartment changed entirely from the former cluster of equally sized rooms (typically 4 by 4 meters) to an organic layout of designated spaces organized according to daily (living room, kitchen, terraces) and nightly (bedrooms) functions; special adjustments to local climatic conditions, especially those concerning suitable shading and ventilation, became habitual in any design scheme. These adjustments, which endowed the local buildings with conspicuous plasticity, must have been truly original, since they could not possibly have relied on literal replication of European models. The flat modernist envelopes evolved in Tel Aviv into protruding or recessed volumes; the ribbon windows into ribbon balconies; and the hinged doors into sliding doors which could open wide and allow for cross-ventilation of the entire apartment. Le Corbusier's *Five Points of a New Architecture*, which in effect referred to rural or suburban domesticity, became the guidelines for urban regulations, producing a city on pilotis and a datum of roof gardens.

The pervasiveness of such adaptations and misappropriations exposes the highly pragmatic and palpably conformist nature of Tel Aviv's architecture of the 1930s and 1940s. It was modernism without a revolutionary platform, without a political manifest, without a social context, with no industry to mechanically propel it, and with no urban vision to sustain it. Le Corbusier's rhetorical models of the Maison Dom-Ino or the Maison Citrohan, for instance, or his radical urban visions of the 1920s, never seemed to have any relevance to Tel Aviv. Serial reproduction of buildings or building parts was marginal, and the architectural object remained essentially as it had been: freestanding, particular (one of a kind), crafted, and self-integral (Gesamtkunstwerk).

Tel Aviv expanded rapidly and gained municipal autonomy (until 1925 it had been a suburb of Jaffa; only in 1934 was it officially designated a city). Its urban mold remained provincial, however, still parceled into small single-building lots of 400 to 500 square meters. The "Geddes master plan" for Tel Aviv, and its various annexes and revisions (1925–1929), could not accommodate the influx of workers,[9] mainly immigrants arriving in the second and third aliyot (the Hebrew term for waves of immigration). Of these, 75 percent settled in the cities, mostly in Tel Aviv, under harsh living conditions and with high rent. They were also excluded from the civic apparatus: only homeowners could vote in municipal elections.

Indeed, the reformist disposition of the Geddes master plan, recasting British garden-city patterns in the Levant, only amplified the original ex-urban founding narrative of Tel Aviv and determined its neighborhood character. The porous garden-city layouts and bylaws called for detached buildings retracted from the edges of the plots, elevated on pilotis, and surrounded by gardens, thus avoiding commercial ground floors, continuous street elevations, and urban blocks. To a certain extent, this complemented the a-formal and anti-monumental taste of the 1930s, but at the same time it hindered the development of mixed-use streets and weakened the routine operation and symbolic attributes of the public space.

All in all, then, the "white city" of Tel Aviv was patently modernist in style and gesture, possibly even in the articulation of new domesticity. But it was hardly modern in structural and ethical terms. European architectural modernisms of the 1910s and 1920s were actual manifestations, literal or figural, of rapidly changing dimensions of time and space; of the accelerating transformation of means of production and habits of consumption; and of growing social disparity and deteriorating living conditions in the big industrial cities. In contrast, Tel Aviv's "Bauhaus" was an epiphenomenon; an aftereffect; yesterday's trend, as the eyewitness Julius Posener pointed out; a readymade repertoire of professional conventions and aesthetic compositions stripped of their polemical stance. Indeed, this eccentric "flying camel" appeared "of the sand," shifting like sand in a preindustrial environment, a precapitalist society, and a pre-metropolitan culture—without apparent cause, relevant technologies, or powerful protagonists. It was a modernist syndrome that came about not in a place of modernity and modernization, but in their place; an architecture that was to devise the missing context, to stage a revolution that never was, to recall processes of modulation and serialization that occurred elsewhere, and to fabricate not the city itself, but the cosmopolitan mise-en-scène and petit bourgeois decorum longed for by the incoming central European Jewish immigrants and the exiles of the fourth and fifth aliyot.

At the very moment modern architecture appeared belated, dislodged, disarmed of ideology, emptied of genius loci, freed of national revivalist obligations—just when it was reincarnated as the International Style, the meta-colonial style—it crashed onto the eastern shores of the Mediterranean as the "white city" of Tel Aviv, providing an instantaneous folklore that effectively suspended both the expulsion from *Heimat* and the coming to the Orient.

Should a certain polemical attitude nonetheless be read into the "white city," it would be a residual civic resistance to institutional Zionism's increasing hegemony, acquired social-realist taste, and anti-urban party line.

## Workers' Housing

"Below" the distinctive middle-class stratum of Tel Aviv, the federation of labor unions (Histadrut) began to claim a foothold in the city through the Center for Workers' Neighborhoods. Founded at the end of the 1920s, "the Center" was a cooperative designed to provide affordable dwellings to urban workers and gradually build up leftist strongholds—"red fortresses," as they were called—in the heart of the bourgeoisie. The "housing question," as defined by Friedrich Engels, was indispensable to the contract between the Histadrut and its members. Converting the worker from tenant to homeowner and from day

⑰

laborer to permanent unionized worker meant securing his long-term stability and commitment to the union. The Center, therefore, was responsible for organizing workers in cooperatives; for finding and purchasing relatively large plots of land for new neighborhoods; for financing mortgages and construction costs; for supervising architectural design and the building process, for purchasing building materials wholesale; for setting up the entire ensemble of commercial, cultural, and educational services in the neighborhood; and, finally, for writing the cooperative protocol that ensured the proper maintenance of public facilities and the ideological homogeneity of the community (it was forbidden, for instance, to rent out an apartment or a portion of one without the authorization of the cooperative's board).

Between 1931 and 1936, twenty cooperative workers' housing estates were built in Tel Aviv. The architects of these projects were chosen through open competitions, and the design process was carried out in collaboration with the boards of residents under the close supervision of the Center's representatives, who had previously traveled to Sweden, Germany, and Austria to learn about different typologies of cooperative housing. Although these cooperative housing projects made up an almost negligible portion (393 housing units in all) of the new residential architecture in 1930s Tel Aviv, they occupy their own chapter in the city's historiography, representing a potential paradigm shift in the distribution of public goods, the organization of communal facilities, and the configuration of domestic space—a path not taken that seems ever more intriguing as the neoliberal system takes over the city.

Architecturally speaking, the cooperative workers' housing estates primarily meant a change of scale in the city's urban fabric. The organizational apparatus of the Center enabled the formation of an alternative mode of operation which did not obey the existing system of parcellation and plot-line regulation in Tel Aviv. Instead of small private plots intended for freestanding buildings of four to eight apartments, surrounded on all sides by unusable strips of open space, the cooperative housing estates proposed the consolidation of adjoining plots and the construction of continuous perimeter blocks or elongated parallel blocks around a large communal inner courtyard. In their journey of appropriation and recontextualization in Tel Aviv, these fairly common European prototypes were rhetorically radicalized, presented as harbingers of progressive urban futures and arsenals of simple, affordable apartments.

Arieh Sharon, who was the architect for thirteen cooperative housing projects, published an article entitled "The Minimal Apartment in Cooperative Housing" in the August 1935 issue of *Habinyan Bamisrah Hakarov* (*Building in the Near East*). For Sharon, these projects epitomized the rational core of the modernist project and the ethical obligation of the modernist architect. Following his teacher Hannes Meyer, who used to ridicule tendencies of over-design and self-expression in the early Bauhaus under Walter Gropius, Sharon denounced the eccentricities of "redundant angles," "exclusive modernism," and "individualistic spatiality" performed by his fellow Tel Aviv architects: "Walls broken by redundant angles and dents only burden the apartment and create, as proclaimed by many, uncomfortable living conditions that go against reality's demands. One must therefore compose a restricted number of rooms according to their functions and not create an exclusive modernist structure of individualistic spatiality."[10] Sharon's text is by no means a compelling manifesto, but it is as close to Hannes Meyer's article "On Marxist Architecture" as any document written in Hebrew has ever come. It can be read as prescriptive not only of 1930s cooperative housing in Tel Aviv, but even more so of 1950s national standardized housing campaigns across the country (see chapters "Public Housing" and "Serial Blocks"):

> A. A simple and evident construction of the building volumes, befitting the clarity and simplicity of the organizing plan. Continuous bearing walls, a continual interior construction, and avoidance of internal and external corners, as is common in Tel Aviv.
>
> B. A design of uniform apartment types with doors, windows, and other details according to equal modules—enables a progressive execution, a repetitive process and thus fast work, though this is possible only with the

⑱

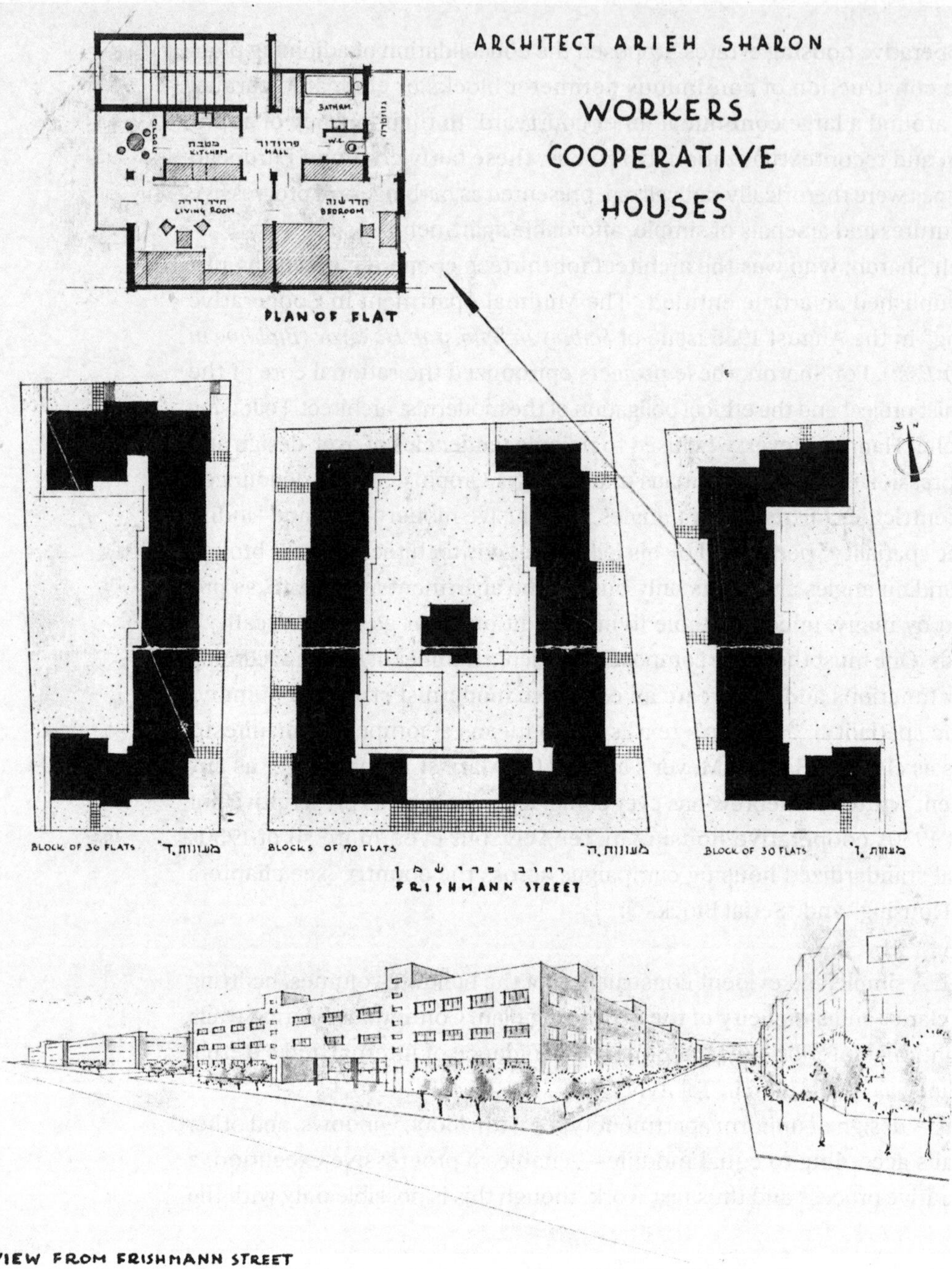
ARCHITECT ARIEH SHARON
WORKERS
COOPERATIVE
HOUSES
BATHR.
KITCHEN
HALL
W.C.
LIVING ROOM
BEDROOM
PLAN OF FLAT
BLOCK OF 36 FLATS
BLOCKS OF 70 FLATS
BLOCK OF 30 FLATS
FRISHMANN STREET
VIEW FROM FRISHMANN STREET

⑲

מראה כללי מרחוב שפינוזא
ק. רובין

General View, Spinoza St.
K. Rubin

הגן הפנימי

Garden court

מראה כללי מרחוב ריינס
י. נייפלד

Reines St. facade
J. Neufeld

הגן הפנימי

Reines St., block from court
פוטו: י. קלטר

13

⑳

distancing of the apartment owners, whose intervention in the adaptation of the plan has until now been common in cooperative buildings in Israel.

C. A good and orderly organization of the building site and the work process is based upon preceding experiments in serial buildings abroad [...].

D. On the other hand, I do not place too much importance on the new building materials that have been flooding the building market in Israel lately, especially from the point of view of lowering building costs. [...]

Although the problem of the minimal apartment seems simple and easy for amateurs and experts alike, it is due to this simplicity that it proves difficult in reality. Therefore, the problem cannot be solved at once, by a more or less ingenious idea, but through systematic and analytical work with research on all the relevant conditions, and through the creation of experimental buildings to better the minimal apartment typologies each time.[11]

Sharon elegantly avoids socialist pathos, strips the argument down to a catalogue of architectural essentials versus redundancies, and wastes no words on the urban layout and communal vision of the cooperative workers' housing, possibly because this was already common knowledge to the readers of *Habinyan*.

The architectural *parti*, programmatic distribution, cultural attributes, and urban impact of the workers' housing projects are retrospectively summarized in *Houses of the Sand*:

The buildings were built like walls around a wide interior garden which symbolized the cooperative social life. On the ground floor were the social functions, all of them turned toward the garden: the grocery, the launderette, the medical clinic, the reading room, the kindergarten, etc. The interior courtyard also symbolized the importance of working the garden and the bond with the soil.

From both physical and social perspectives, the internalized structure was a declaration of segregation from bourgeois city life. The cooperative workers' housing projects were later nicknamed the "laborer's fortresses": the large building block, prominent in the urban fabric, demonstrated the power of a homogeneous society possessing self-organizational capacity [...].

⑰ Interior courtyard, cooperative workers' housing IV, Tel Aviv, 1934. Perspective. Arieh Sharon. Arieh Sharon digital archive.

⑱ Cornerstone-laying ceremony, cooperative workers' housing IV, Tel Aviv, 1934. Arieh Sharon digital archive.

⑲ Cooperative workers' housing, Tel Aviv, 1934. Plans and perspective. Arieh Sharon. Arieh Sharon digital archive.

⑳–㉑ Spreads from Habinyan: *A Magazine of Architecture & Town Planning*, documenting workers' housing projects. August 1937.

שכונת „קרית מאיר" י. סגל

„Kiryat Meier" Quarter J. Segal

צלומים ע"י שטולצר

19

> Construction around a courtyard enabled the maximization of the distance between the buildings: in this way, similar light and aeration conditions were provided for all of the residents.[12]

Conceptually and practically, then, the architectural novelty of the cooperative workers' housing estate is reducible to a new articulation of the inner courtyard of the imported perimeter block. Rather than serving as a backyard, it was reconfigured as a social stage, the epicenter of daily life, a panoptic space enveloped not by back service elevations of the surrounding apartments, but by the main elevations of family rooms, as they were called, which were perceived as prosthetic extensions of the open shared living space. The communal facilities on the ground-floor levels, "the grocery, the launderette, the medical clinic, the reading room, the kindergarten, etc.," which replaced the commercial and public functions of these levels in the typical European block, were also flipped outside-in to create a self-sustained compound. Indeed, the overall sentiment of the workers' housing projects in Tel Aviv is anti-urban: the design scheme always turns its back (or blind side, in the case of the parallel blocks) to the street, and the opportunist ploy consists in residing in the city, where work is provided, and living away from it, in a gated commune, shielded, as it were, from the speculative economy outside.

This proletarian model of exclusive inclusivity and "rural urbanism" is an architectural allegory of utopia: the more literal and tangible (and designed) the specter of a perfectly egalitarian cooperative society becomes, the more it is bound to produce protocols of segregation, homogenization, social control, and urban phobias.

In Tel Aviv, the cooperative workers' housing projects, with their large surrounding walls and augmented public spaces, seemed for a brief moment to offer a vigorous alternative to the Geddesian garden-suburb pattern of small lots with hardly any continuous street façades and much leftover space. But in reality, they did not. In fact, they never intended to propose a new system of urban blocks, or a new street section, or a different performance of urban life. In order to retain their ideological integrity, they had to remain urban enclaves, to act out their structural difference and pose as artificial transplants in the body of the city.

In retrospect, we may detect in the workers' housing prototypes of the 1930s the formative paradoxes of the national housing project of the 1950s: both are cases of architecture-against-urbanism; both are setups of minimum standards embedded in spatial abundance; both present a benevolent agenda of social equity and solidarity which turned out to be the fastest track to segregated neighboring units. On expansive city lots, these fragmented urban units produced exclusive gated communities. In peripheral new towns, they propelled ever-increasing isolation and deprivation.

However, this grim destiny should not prevent us from speculating on the relevance of updated and modified layouts of cooperative housing projects, whether based on the peculiar hybridization of the industrial-city-type phalanstery and the Arcadian-village-type kibbutz, like those built in Tel Aviv in the 1930s, or on new and far more intricate models of common housing, communal spaces, and shared domesticity. ■

1 Le Corbusier, "A Coat of Whitewash: The Law of Ripolin," in *The Decorative Art of Today* (Cambridge, MA: MIT, 1987), p. 192. Originally published as *L'art décoratif d'aujourd'hui* (Paris: Éditions G. Crès, 1925).

2 Julius Posener, "Traditional and Modern Construction in Palestine," trans. Jan Caspers, p. 47 in this volume. Originally published as "Traditionelles und modernes Bauen in Palästina," *Das Werk* 9 (September 1938).

3 Mark Wigley, *White Walls, Designer Dresses: The Fashioning of Modern Architecture* (Cambridge, MA: MIT, 1995), p. 330.

4 Posener, "Traditional and Modern Construction," p. 48 in this volume.

5 Yaakov Shiffman, "The Building Industry in Palestine," *Palestine & Middle East Economic Magazine*, no. 7–8 (1933), p. 287.

6 Erich Mendelsohn, "Twenty Years of Building: An Exposition and a Publication," *Palestine Post*, December 29, 1940, p. 5. Quoted in Ita Heinze-Greenberg, "This Once Gold-Diggingly Created City: Eric Mendelsohn and Tel Aviv," *Docomomo Journal* 40 (March 2009), p. 96.

7 Nitza Metzger-Szmuk, *Houses of the Sand: The Architecture of the International Style in Tel Aviv, 1931–1948* [in Hebrew] (Tel Aviv: Ministry of Defense Publishing House, 1994), p. 36.

8 Research in progress on the work of various modernist architects operating in Tel Aviv was presented at the conference "Modernisms: A Rashomon Effect of 1930s–40s Architecture in Tel Aviv" at the White City Center (March 2017; moderator: Zvi Efrat). Sigal Davidi presented the work of Elsa Gideoni and Genia Averbuch; Sharon Golan Yaron presented Oscar Kaufmann, Anke Kuehnel presented Richard Kauffmann; Avi Mayer presented Sam Barkai; Yossi Klein presented Leo Adler and Yaakov Shiffman (Ben Sira); Baruch Ravid presented Yosef Berlin.

9 In his autobiography, *Kibbutz + Bauhaus: An Architect's Way in a New Land* (Stuttgart and Tel Aviv: Karl Kramer Verlag and Massada, 1976), Arieh Sharon described the Geddes plan as follows: "A town planning scheme was prepared by the famous planner scientist Sir Patrick Geddes, along the ideological guidelines of the first Tel Aviv settlers, as reinterpreted by an Englishman." Sharon regarded the vision of a serene garden city for 40,000 citizens as a misconception that would constrain the development of the city.

10 Arieh Sharon, "The Minimal Apartment in Cooperative Housing," *Habinyan Bamisrah Hakarov [in Hebrew]*, August 1935.

11 Ibid.

12 Metzger-Szmuk, *Houses of the Sand*, p. 247.

# DOSSIER: LEVANT FAIR

(22)

Sir Arthur Wauchope, the British High Commissioner for Palestine, wrote in the opening pages of the catalogue of the 1934 Levant Fair:

> The Levant Fair performs services of the highest value to Palestine, as a medium for the display and advertisement of local produce to foreign buyers, and for the display to Palestinian buyers of foreign commodities [. . .]. In this way the Fair helps to make Palestine produce more widely known: it draws visitors, it awakens in many countries an interest which should conduce to mutual profit, it strengthens existing commercial relations. Not the least of its uses is that it enables the public to see, in miniature, the work that is being carried out by those Departments of Government which have most to do directly with the inhabitants.[1]

The Levant Fair—like all colonial exhibitions, world fairs, and expos—was indeed a miniature, a model city, a pedagogical paragon, an episodic spectacle of good governance, abundant wellness, regional equilibrium, and free trade between East and West, Old and New Worlds, mother country and colonies. The objective of "enabling the public to see" ultimately meant cultivating a looking public, promoting techniques of observation, and managing the visual character of the public sphere. In retrospect, it seems that the successive Levant Fairs of 1932, 1934, and 1936 had only a marginal role in invigorating the local economy, and no consequence whatsoever on a Levantine alliance—but they had a transformative impact, a bleaching effect, on the complexion of Tel Aviv's public sphere.

Meir Dizengoff, the mayor of Tel Aviv, was the first to recognize and play out the metonymic relationships between the fair and the city. In "Tel Aviv and the Levant Fairs," also published in the 1934 catalogue, he described Tel Aviv as a pop-up urban show turned into a showcase of accelerated urbanism:

> Tel Aviv is, after all, an Exhibition City in itself, in the best sense of the word, for it demonstrates the power of the human will and the victory of creative endeavor. The development of the Levant Fair is very similar in outline to that of Tel Aviv. Beginning as a small local display, the Levant Fair has advanced to the status of an international fair and is a member of the Union of International Fairs.[2]

The international status of the fair—and hence of the city at large—was inflated rhetorically by the official speakers and the various producers of the fair, who figuratively paraphrased "international status" in the optical attributes of the "International Style," a timely curatorial slogan just arriving from America. While the trade shows in Tel Aviv in the late 1920s, as well as the 1932 Levant Fair, were makeshift exhibitions, the 1934 and 1936 fairs were total works of art, design, and architecture, displaying not only an assortment of local and foreign products, but, more ambitiously, the fair itself as an artifact—an international object of local desire.

The photo albums of the fairs document an almost surreal incongruity between the crafted and industrial bric-a-brac amassed in the interiors and the glaring whiteness of their casings. So much so that the Levant Fair appears above all as a modernist *Bauausstellung* transplanted in the Mediterranean and is described time and again, in scholarly writing and preservation endeavors, as the city's architectural *Ursprung*. In their essay "The Flight of the Camel: The Levant Fair of 1934 and the Creation of a Situated Modernism," architectural scholars Sigal Davidi Kunda and Robert Oxman embed the Levant Fair within an ancestry of modernist exhibitions and situate it in the Zionist national project:

> A series of international fairs and exhibitions served to reinforce the rhetoric of "new form for new social order." Among these were "Exposition des arts decoratifs" in Paris, 1925; Barcelona, 1929; [and] Stockholm, 1930[;] and The International Style exhibition in New York, 1932. By 1932–33, [. . .] the international fair had become the medium of choice for the manifestation of the semantics of being progressive. The promotion of modernism in a situated, or localized, form began to be the preferred strategy for the creation of an emerging impetus for national identity.[3]

Situated or uprooted, the fair's architecture operated simultaneously on different cultural and ideological registers and in parallel economies of representation and signification. In the context of international exhibitions, it should be pointed out that although the Levant Fair indeed looked like a modernist design exhibition, it was not. Its true forerunners were the various fin-de-siècle world fairs and expos which staged the fascination with the exotic (using both vernacular authenticity and machine reproducibility) and built up their spectacle by larger-than-life folly architecture. Compared to these ostentatious

23

1 Arthur Wauchope, foreword to *The Levant Fair Catalogue* (Tel Aviv, 1934)

2 Meir Dizengoff, "Tel Aviv and the Levant Fairs," in *The Levant Fair Catalogue (Tel Aviv,* 1934), p. 69.

3 Sigal Davidi Kunda and Robert Oxman, "The Flight of the Camel: The Levant Fair of 1934 and the Creation of a Situated Modernism," in *Constructing a Sense of Place: Architecture and the Zionist Discourse*, ed. Haim Yacobi (Abingdon: Routledge, 2004), p. 52.

4 As a counterimage to the overall posh dogmatism of the 1934 Levant Fair, I would like to suggest the Jewish Labor Federation (Histadrut) pavilion of 1932, designed by Arieh Sharon at the fairgrounds in the Neve Sha'anan area of Tel Aviv. This pavilion consisted of four parallel, repetitive structures, designed as trapezoids varying in length and height and made of wooden planks and jute sheets. The first—and possibly the last—modernist structure built in Tel Aviv worthy of the title "avant-gardist" or "Constructivist," it was certainly the most eloquent attempt to formulate a local "fair architecture": open; light; cheap; modular; provisional; perishable; easy to dismantle and reassemble; and, above all, eliminating the disparity between exterior and interior design, between building and display. Form does not follow function, program, or ideology here; it is the function itself, the program itself, the ideology in its bare manifestation. The jute surfaces in the pavilions were dyed in colors symbolic of the subjects presented: red for the professional union, blue for the urban cooperatives, green for the workers' settlements, and orange for the citrus industry.
If the architecture of the 1932 Histadrut pavilion was boldly exposed and candidly political, the architecture of the 1934 Histadrut pavilion, now located in the new fairground among the modernist pavilions, was a hybrid structure, a composite of a white box and a dynamic Constructivist installation, with slanted walls, exposed wooden frame, dynamic graphics, and a slender tower (which was not built).

events—and even compared to the refined decorative arts exhibitions of the 1920s, with their iconic architectural highlights—the Levant Fair was a rather artless display of boxy pavilions with no eccentricities to speak of, except for its striking emblem of a flying camel and the monument to the Hebrew worker at the fairground entrance (both designed by Arieh Elhanani, the fairground architect).

In the context of British patronage of the Levant Fair and British colonial architecture in Palestine, the fair's *sachlich* architecture—including the austere British pavilion itself—seems almost subversive in its outright rejection of masonry techniques, arts and crafts surfaces, and Orientalist motifs. Clearly, the image of architecture de rigueur was also played against the romantic notion of the Levant and the regionalist vision of a Middle Eastern bazaar. The Egyptian and Lebanese pavilions, therefore, had the very same streamlined design as the Belgian and Polish pavilions. The fair's visionary Levant had no tolerance for traditional habits, distinct identities, or folklorist idiosyncrasies. It was to be—for a moment—the newest cultural theme park.

The Levant Fair project is widely recognized as the emblem of Zionism's progressive modernism (some would even say avant-gardism), but it is precisely such demagogy that exposes the mild temperament and utterly conformist stance of the white architecture of the fair, and by extension of the white fair city. Fresh and elegant as it may have been, it was fully prescribed and manipulated by the national institutions and municipal administrations. Unlike the *Weissenhofsiedlung* project—its oft-imitated precursor—it was merely demonstrative and not at all contested; promotional but not polemical; complacent rather than anxious; magnificent yet rarely experimental. It was, if I may turn Le Corbusier's purist dictum against itself, a coat of whitewash.[4]

The peculiar list of Zionist pavilions in the fair's catalogue includes the Jewish Agency pavilion, the PICA (Palestine Jewish Colonization Association) pavilion, the Jewish Labor Federation pavilion, the pavilion of Palestine Industry (which in Hebrew was called Totzeret Ha'aretz, lit. "produce of the land"), the Agricultural pavilion, and the Tel Aviv pavilion. Such confusing multiplicity certainly attests to the fact that beyond good business, the Levant Fair was a prime podium for Zionist propaganda. But even more so, it is a record of the inner ideological conflicts, political rivalries, and antagonistic systems of organization and representation that proliferated in the Zionist public sphere and its Jewish stratosphere. The agreeable family of pristine volumes effectively kept domestic feuds inside, as is evident from the pavilions' interiors, which were overburdened with didactic agitprops, boastful manifestos, and Bolshevik graphics. In this regard, the coat of whitewash presents itself as the slight yet definitive veneer over the Zionist divide; the medium mediating between municipal, national, and Jewish-international interests and tastes; the flattening effect of exceptionally diverse coinciding practices of rural colonization and settler colonialism, urban culture and liberal economy, proletarian *Gesellschaft* and collectivist *Gemeinschaft*.

The Levant Fair was brief. It appeared in full modernist regalia only twice, in 1934 and 1936. Growing national tensions in Palestine rendered the fair's fanciful flying camel ever more preposterous. Its architectural phantasmagoria, however, intoxicated Dizengoff's "exhibition city" for almost two decades. ■

(22) Levant Fair's emblem, designed by Arieh Elhanani, 1932.
(23) Monument to the Hebrew worker, Levant Fair, Tel Aviv, 1934. Arieh Elhanani. Matson Collection, Library of Congress.

㉔

㉕

㉖

(24) Woman and Home pavilion, Levant Fair, Tel Aviv, 1934. Arieh Elhanani. Matson Collection, Library of Congress.

(25) Levant Fair, Tel Aviv, 1934. Matson Collection, Library of Congress.

(26) Entrance area and Great Britain pavilion, Levant Fair, Tel Aviv, 1934. Joseph Neufeld. Matson Collection, Library of Congress.

(27) Lebanon pavilion, Levant Fair, Tel Aviv, 1936. Photographer: Zoltan Kluger. Government Press Office.

(28) Sketch for unidentified pavilion, Levant Fair, Tel Aviv, 1933. Richard Kauffmann. Central Zionist Archives.

(29) Palestine Industries pavilion, Levant Fair, Tel Aviv, 1933. Perspective drawing. Richard Kauffmann. Central Zionist Archives.

(27)

(28)

(29)

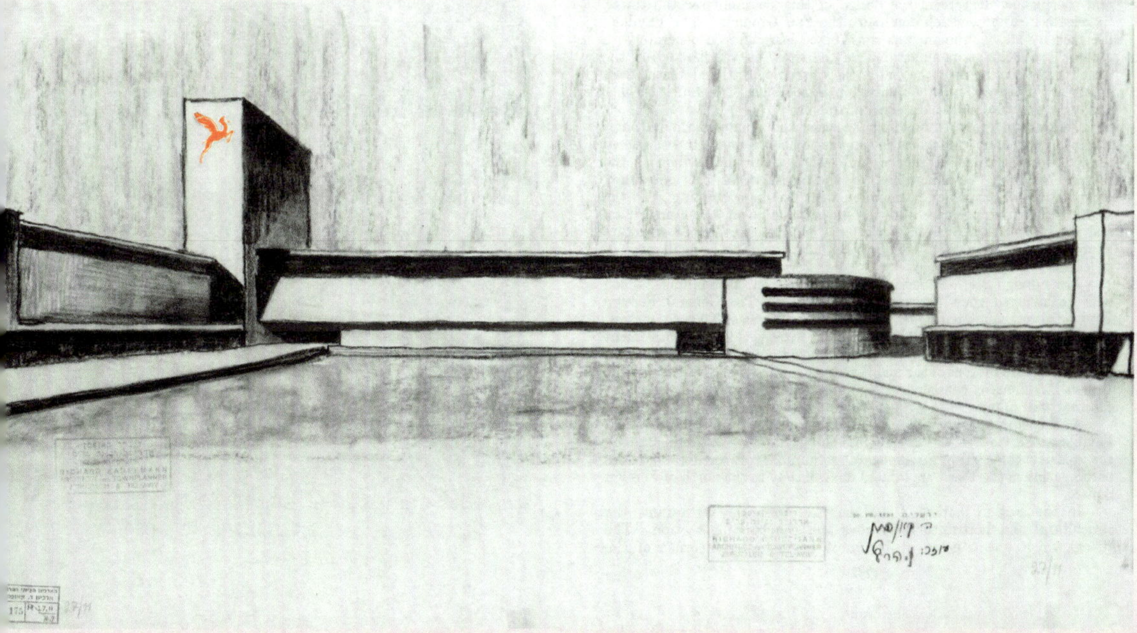

# PALESTINE

## THE LEVANT FAIR, TEL AVIV

The Levant Fair, which was held at Tel Aviv last year, was the third International Trade Fair to be arranged in Palestine since 1929. The 1934 Exhibition was of particular interest, not only on account of its increased commercial scope and the extended area of its grounds, which were 100,000 sq. metres as compared with the 25,000 sq. metres of 1929, but chiefly because of the permanent nature of the buildings which housed the exhibits. The Fair was sponsored by a committee of prominent citizens who received the wholehearted support of the Government of Palestine and the Municipality of Tel Aviv, as well as of many public bodies and private individuals. These joined forces in order to make it truly representative of the development of Palestine. The site was purchased and placed at the disposal of the promoters on a long-term lease by the Tel Aviv Development Company, a semi-public body actuated by civic rather than commercial motives, and generously supported by the public-spirited citizens of Tel Aviv. This assistance enabled the Management to plan the Fair on a permanent basis.

The site is situated to the north-west of Tel Aviv and south of the Stadium, and stretches from the Mediterranean on the west to the River Yarkon on the east. The natural beauty of the site is emphasised by the proximity of the sea and the green, fertile plain north of the river. The Fair Grounds, in the most north-westerly corner of the layout, were designed as a stimulus to the development of better class building in their vicinity and marked a welcome phase in the northward expansion of Tel Aviv. In view of the heavy traffic which was expected to occur in connection with the Exhibition, it was found necessary to replan the approaches to the site. Plans were also drawn up for a bridge over the Yarkon, thus providing for future expansion to the other side of the river.

The land on which the Fair was built consists of low-lying sand dunes three and a quarter metres above mean sea-level at the entrance, sloping gently down to two metres above sea-level at the furthest corner. Difficulties were encountered in the planning, through the limited area available. After much consideration, it was decided to choose between two methods of planning. The first plan was to develop the site on a road net system. The alternative, which was eventually adopted, was to group the buildings around public squares or open spaces. It was felt

FIG. 2. *The Machinery Hall.*

FIG. 3. *The main Restaurant.*

*TEL AVIV FAIR.*



that the site was not sufficiently spacious to allow of it being fully exploited by the first method, whereas grouped development round squares presented great architectural opportunities and pleasing varieties of view.

A plan was finally drawn up by Mr. Richard Kauffman, assisted by the Levant Fair Technical Advisory Committee. The most prominent position in the grounds was allotted to the building to house local industries. The Palestine Industries Pavilion (see Fig. 4) was situated at the end of the 30 metre wide main approach avenue and formed the background to the square marked *A* on the plan. The most noteworthy and conspicuous feature of the design of this Pavilion was the tower, 24 metres in height, which dominates the Fair Grounds. The Pavilion, designed by Mr. Kauffman, was constructed of reinforced concrete with external wall fillings manufactured on the site. It was flanked on the west by the pavilions of the Tel Aviv Township, National Institutions and the Palestine Jewish Colonisation Association, the four together making a group of essentially local character.

The second group of buildings enclosed the square marked *B*, and was intimately connected with the main approach avenue. It was named the British and Imperial Square, and had the British Pavilion as the central building. Flanking this to the north were the one-storey Dominion Pavilions which harmonised with the main building. To the south of the British Square were the Automobile Salon, the Fair Offices, and the Information Bureau, the latter a one-storey U-shaped structure approached on the north through gates and enclosing a small pool in a central lawn.

The Foreign Section constituted the third group of buildings, which were constructed round square *C* on the plan. The General Foreign Pavilion was the dominating feature and, with an area of 3,000 sq. metres, was the largest of the Fair buildings. It was so designed as to complement the Fair Offices to the south-west, and thus symmetrically enclosed the approach square in front of the main entrance. Like the Palestine and the British Pavilions, it consisted of a reinforced concrete frame with light external wall filling.

At the sides of Foreign Square were the Belgian and Czechoslovakian Pavilions, the view to the river across this square being terminated by the apsidal café. The Pavilions of a number of foreign countries participating in the Fair were located immediately to the north of Foreign Square.

In the section marked *D* on the plan were the restaurant, the agricultural and horticultural sections and the building section. The latter, which was situated at the most north-westerly corner of the

FIG. 4. *Palestine Industries Pavilion.*

FIG. 5. *The Home Pavilion.*

*TEL AVIV FAIR*

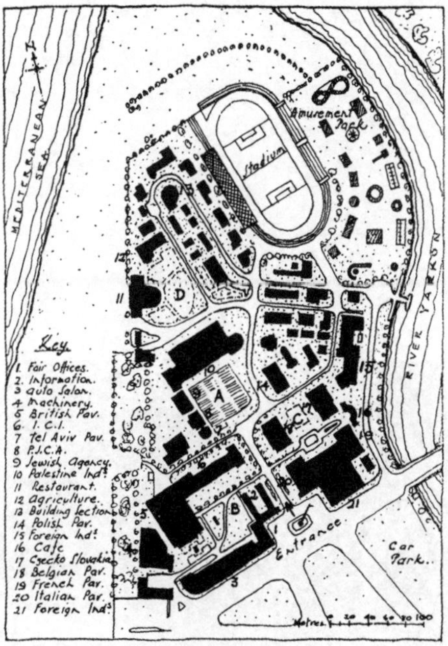


*Fig. 1. General Plan of the Fair.*

Fig. 9. *Another view of Tel Aviv Pavilion.*

Fig. 8. *Model of the lay-out.*

TEL AVIV FAIR.

Fig. 6. *Aerial view of the Fair and its neighbourhood.*

Fig. 7. *The Tel Aviv Pavilion.*

*TEL AVIV FAIR.*



grounds, formed the nucleus of a permanent building exhibition. Here model houses were constructed of various types of materials, forming an exhibit of great value, since the provision of well-planned but inexpensive housing is a primary consideration in an immigrant country like Palestine.

Of the other buildings, the most noteworthy are marked on the plan. Except for the four buildings mentioned specifically, they were all designed under the leadership of Mr. Sapoznikov, who was also personally responsible for the design of the main approach square. This square, in its well-proportioned design, emphasised the functional aspect of the entrance. An interesting feature was the white metal column 16 metres high, surmounted by the Flying Camel, the emblem of the Fair.

The lighting of the grounds at night was designed with a view to stressing the architectural features of the main buildings, but it was intended at the same time to create a traditional oriental night atmosphere, which it was thought would be admirably suited to the purposes of an Exhibition.

The colour scheme of the Exhibition Buildings in general was quiet, in spite of the colour demands imposed by a layout of this character. The large surfaces of the main buildings were unbroken by openings, and were painted in very light colours, with darker shades at the bases. In the case of the British Pavilion, for example, the upper surfaces were broken white, the window recesses red, and the base dark blue. The only decoration was the 16 metre high column bearing the Lion Rampant and the traditional heraldic coat of arms over the entrance. Similar schemes were adopted for other buildings.

A tribute must be paid to the many technicians, architects, engineers, and draughtsmen who worked together in a spirit of harmony, accepting guidance from the Advisory Committee, the Chief Engineer and the Head of the drawing office. Notwithstanding marked individualistic tendencies, a generous effort was made on all sides to create a satisfactory whole. This spirit of co-operative enterprise can surely be regarded as a symbol of the creative endeavour which characterises the new Palestine.

J. Shiffman.

31

32

33

㉞

㉟

㉚ Yaakov Shiffman, "Palestine: The Levant Fair, Tel Aviv," *Town Planning Review* 16, no. 3 (June 1935).
㉛ – ㉝ Pavilion interior, Levant Fair, Tel Aviv, 1934. Matson Collection, Library of Congress.
㉞ Palestine Industry pavilion, interior, Levant Fair, Tel Aviv, 1934. Matson Collection, Library of Congress.
㉟ Pavilion interior, Levant Fair, Tel Aviv, 1934. Matson Collection, Library of Congress.

(36)

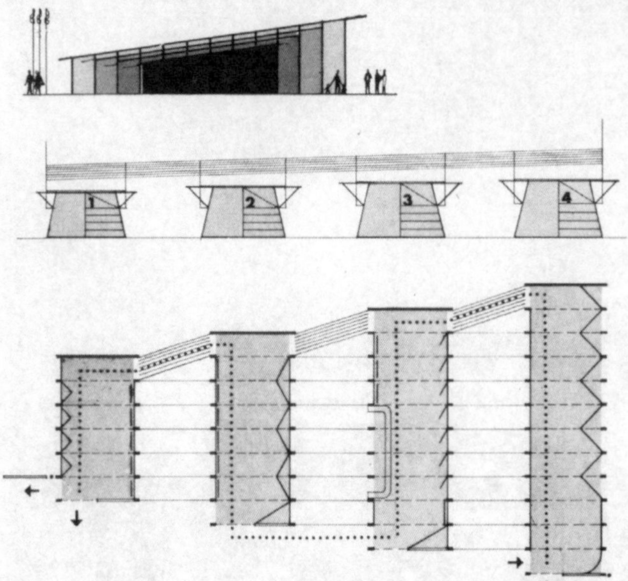

1
YAKHIN

(37)

YAKHIN

(38)

(39)

AGRICULTURAL CONTRACTING CO-OPERATIVE ASSOCIATION LTD.
YAKHIN

(40)

(41)

(36) Jewish Labor Federation (Histadrut) pavilion, Levant Fair, Tel Aviv, 1932. Plans and sections. Arieh Sharon digital archive.
(37) – (38) Jewish Labor Federation (Histadrut) pavilion, Levant Fair, Tel Aviv, 1932. Arieh Sharon digital archive.
(39) Jewish Labor Federation (Histadrut) pavilion, Levant Fair, Tel Aviv, 1934. Interior display. Arieh Sharon. Arieh Sharon digital archive.
(40) Aerial view of the Levant Fair, with the Jewish Labor Federation (Histadrut) pavilion, Tel Aviv, 1934. Arieh Sharon. Arieh Sharon digital archive.
(41) Jewish Labor Federation (Histadrut) pavilion, interior, Levant Fair, Tel Aviv, 1934. Arieh Sharon. Interior design: Moshe Raviv-Vorobeichic, photographer: Yitzhak Kalter. Arieh Sharon digital archive.

# Ruins of War

① "Planned Demolition" in Manshiya, 1948. Ledder Collection, "Israel Revealed to the Eye" project, Yad Izhak Ben-Zvi Archives.
For the depiction and analysis of the "planned demolition" actions in Manshiya, see "Civilian Demolition: The Premeditated Destruction of Jaffa's Manshiya Neighborhood, 1948–1949" [in Hebrew] by architectural scholar Or Aleksandrowicz.

## "Abandoned Property"

On the eve of the establishment of the State of Israel, the population of Mandatory Palestine numbered approximately 650,000 Jews and 1.4 million Palestinian Arabs. The November 29, 1947, announcement of the United Nations Partition Plan to divide Palestine into two states, one Jewish and one Arab, sparked a massive wave of Jewish immigration, which in three and a half years would double the Jewish population in the land. From that moment until the official declaration of the State on May 15, 1948, some 120,000 Jews immigrated to Israel. During the War of 1948, the pace of immigration quickened, and by the end of 1951, just three years into Israeli Statehood, the number of newcomers reached some 700,000. For the sake of comparison, the entire thirty years of the British Mandate (1917–1948) saw the arrival of 483,000 Jewish immigrants.

As early as December 1947, following the UN decision and with the outbreak of disturbances in the cities and the beginning of the violent clash between armed Jewish and Arab militias, came the first reports of the flight of Arabs—from the cities of Jaffa and Haifa, from the western neighborhoods of Jerusalem, and from the villages. The Jewish leadership, predicting that the cities would be emptied of their Arab inhabitants as a result of "lack of food," proposed tightening a ring of economic strangulation around the urban Arab population by blocking the ports, cutting off supply routes, and destroying vehicles. In February to March 1948, the clashes became more frequent and the situation began to escalate toward outright war. By March 1948, about 75,000 Arabs had fled—primarily from among the wealthy and middle classes in Jaffa, Haifa, and Jerusalem, and from the villages outside of Jerusalem and on the coastal plain—toward Arab population centers further to the east, such as Nazareth and Nablus, or beyond the borders of Palestine.[1]

During that period—from late 1947 into the first months of 1948—the Palestinian community virtually ceased to exist as a social and political entity. Of the 450 Arab villages that existed before 1948 in the territory that would become the State of Israel, some 370 villages and urban neighborhoods were completely or partially abandoned—primarily those around Jaffa, Lydda, Ramle, Bet She'an, and Tiberias—and Arab urban life in the coastal cities was almost entirely wiped out. In Jaffa, for example, where 70,000 to 80,000 Palestinians had lived before the war, only 3,000 to 4,000 remained in the wake of the war and the exodus. Nearly half of the Palestinian population was displaced, and by September 1949, approximately 700,000 Palestinians had become refugees, effectively making room for the similar number of Jewish refugees and immigrants that was flowing into Israel in those same years.[2]

By mid-1949, most of the abandoned Arab villages and towns had been physically demolished. Arab agricultural lands stood uncultivated or were taken over by Jews; new Jewish settlements were built on the abandoned lands and populated by new immigrants.[3] The "abandoned properties"—whose total area is estimated at 3.5 million square meters—were confiscated by the Israeli government and transferred to Israel's General Custodian of Absentee Property, which in turn transferred them, after a certain period of suspension, to the hands of the Jewish settlement organizations. The question of the right of return of the refugees was postponed de jure through the emergency regulations and blocked de facto through the demolition of the villages and the construction of Jewish settlements in their place. A process of radical change thus

②

③

④

② Destroyed village, location unknown, 1948. Government Press Office.
③ Tents and huts of new Jewish immigrants in the abandoned Palestinian village of Suhmata, 1949. Photographer: Zoltan Kluger. Government Press Office.
④ Establishment of Moshav Beit Meir, 1950. In the background are the ruins of the village of Bayt Mahsir in the Jerusalem Hills. Photographer: Werner Braun.

⑤

⑥

⑤ City of Lydda (Lod), early 1950s.
⑥ Palestinian refugees, Manshiya, 1948. Photographer: Beno Rothenberg. Israel State Archives.

occurred not only in the population of the land but in the structure of land ownership.

One of the earliest documentations of the official policy of seizing Arab property can be found in David Ben-Gurion's instructions from late January 1948 to the Hagana's commander in Jerusalem, David Shaltiel, to "move Jews into every house in the abandoned half-Arab neighborhoods, such as Romema."[4] In the government meeting of June 1948, the decision was made to prevent the return of the Palestinian refugees to their houses, to pick up the pace of Jewish immigration, and to hasten settlement in areas abandoned by the Arabs (an emergency regulation on the matter of "abandoned properties" transfers the property of the "absentees" to the General Custodian). An initial proposal to settle immigrants in the abandoned villages—mainly in the Arab houses that remained intact—was presented to the commission of the interim government on September 23, 1948. The military governor, Major General Avner, submitted a list of villages that were suited to this purpose—all in the Tel Aviv–Rehovot–Ramle triangle. Once the conquests of the Galilee, the Jerusalem corridor, and the northern Negev were completed, the government discussed the proposal to establish forthwith ninety-six settlements in the disputed areas and to populate the Arab settlements that had been abandoned. Thus, no less pressing than the need to find housing for the new immigrants was the need to appropriate and settle the conquered territories. In his memoirs, then head of the Land Settlement Department of the Jewish Agency Levi Eshkol tells how the idea of housing Jewish immigrants in "absentee property" arose:

> It was the end of the War of Independence, [...] and the great immigration had begun to stream in. Immigrants began to arrive, and we had not yet prepared the proper conditions for their absorption and settlement. This wave of immigrants came pushing, squeezing, frothing the human dust and remains of the camps. [...] We passed by the village of Birya—a small village at the top of a rocky hill that towers over the road toward Latrun, surrounded by wide fields. [...] We stopped the car and headed out by foot to tour the village and its environs. The houses were solid stone houses, which had been abandoned in the sudden flight [...]. After we toured the whole village, we found a few dozen houses that, with some repair, could provide refuge for families. Here, in an Arab village, within the expanses of fields. We returned to the car, I took the wheel once again, and from there to Jerusalem we continued to spin and weave this new idea that had arisen. After all, there were hundreds of abandoned villages in the country, and even if we don't include the villages that are built from clay, which are certainly not suitable to house Jews, there would remain dozens, maybe hundreds, of villages built from stone [...]. We must rush upon them and prepare them for the approaching winter, and house in each one of them dozens of families and with them counselors from the veteran moshavim and kibbutzim. Every such group will be given tools and will start cultivating the fields. What do we have to lose? As it is, the immigrants are sitting in camps; as it is, their existence is costing the Jewish Agency much money; the fields must not be left idle.[5]

In the months leading up to the declaration of the State in May 1948, those responsible for immigration absorption predicted that the first wave of immigration would consist of about 150,000 immigrants and would necessitate the building of more than 60,000 housing units. At the time, the discussion still

⑦

⑧

⑨

⑩

⑪

revolved around the prospects of new construction and did not consider taking over Arab settlements and houses. In September 1948, the Housing Department of the Planning Authority of the Labor Ministry was established, its role being to prepare a sound planning infrastructure for housing across the country. Thus the committee for the "1948–1950 Plan" was established, with the goal of putting together a two-year construction plan.

According to a calculation from 1948, an estimated 55 million Israeli lira would be needed in order to create housing for 250,000 immigrants. The national budget for that year, excluding defense expenses, came to a mere 7.8 million Israeli lira.[6] Then Treasury Minister Eliezer Kaplan said that "to a great extent, the war helped us. [...] As a result of it, we have received possession of thousands of apartments. In Haifa alone, since the day of liberation of the city, 12,000 people have moved in, and there are those who say 13,000. [...] Haifa is claiming another 20,000. [...] We tried to send hundreds to Tiberias and Safed."[7]

The forecasts underestimated the situation: by autumn of 1949, some 200,000 immigrants had arrived. Of these, 110,000 were settled in "absentee property," mostly in the Arab neighborhoods of Jaffa and in the mixed cities of Jerusalem, Haifa, and Safed. Some 16,000 were settled in the Arab cities of Ramle, Lydda, and Acre, and about 18,000 in the "abandoned villages." Within a few months, the number of new immigrants living in those villages had risen to 25,000, in a total of twenty-one villages. On September 1, 1949, the writer Moshe Smilanski described in the newspaper *Haaretz* the snatching gluttony that had seized those who wished to take over abandoned property. He criticized the State for not restraining the public or protecting the property from looting and theft.[8] ■

1 See Benny Morris, *The Birth of the Palestinian Refugee Problem, 1947–1949* [in Hebrew] (Tel Aviv: Am Oved, Sifriyat Ofakim, 1991), p. 51.

2 See Baruch Kimmerling and Yoel Shmuel Migdal, *Palestinians: The Making o...eople* [in Hebrew] (Jerusalem: Keter, 1999), p. 117. (English edition published in 1993 by Free Press, New York.)

3 Morris, *Birth of the Palestinian Refugee Problem*, p. 213.

4 Ibid., p. 257.

5 Cited in Alex Bein, *Immigration and Settlement in the State of Israel* [in Hebrew] (Tel Aviv: Am Oved, Hasifriya HaZiyonit, 1982), pp. 80–81.

6 Dvora Hacohen, *Immigrants i...torm* [in Hebrew] (Jerusalem: Yad Ben-Tzvi, 1994), pp. 178–179.

7 Morris, *Birth of the Palestinian Refugee Problem*, p. 506, n. 138.

8 Cited in Adi Ophir, ed., *50 to 48: Critical Moments in the History of the State of Israel—Essays and Chronicle* [in Hebrew] (Jerusalem and Tel Aviv: Van Leer Jerusalem Institute and Hakibbutz Hameuhad, 1999), p. 30.

⑦ A street in Safed after the 1948 War, 1949. Photographer: Zoltan Kluger. Government Press Office.
⑧ The conquering of Ramle, 1948. Photographer: Beno Rothenberg. Israel State Archives.
⑨ Demilitarized zone, Jaffa, December, 1948. Photographer: Beno Rothenberg. Israel State Archives.
⑩ Manshiya, 1948. Photographer: Beno Rothenberg. Israel State Archives.
⑪ "Planned Demolition" in Manshiya, 1948. Ledder Collection, "Israel Revealed to the Eye" project, Yad Izhak Ben-Zvi Archives.
⑫ Stills from a film entitled *The Destruction of Jaffa as Part of Its Renewal: Residents Moving to Temporary or New Housing*, 1951. Israel State Archives.

⑫

# DOSSIER: MARCEL JANCO'S BOHEMIAN COLONY

⑬

⑬ "The Discovery of Ein Hod by Marcel Janco and Friends, 1953," from the book Marcel Janco (Tel Aviv, Masada, 1982).

The presentation boards submitted to the 1959 national museum competition by architects Al Mansfeld and Dora Gad left no room for misinterpretation regarding their scenic inspiration. At the top of the first board appeared an analogical sketch depicting an Arab village, specified in writing as the village of Malha near Jerusalem. Below it was a perspective of the proposed museum, portraying an irresistible stereoscopic image of a hilly cubic cluster endowed with the borrowed authenticity and spontaneity of vernacular architecture. We learn from the competition proceedings that it was this sketch, this enchanting analogy, that caught the jury's attention and was the prime reason for their choice of this project. The village of Malha was thus consecrated as the mythical origin of the National Museum of Israel.

Etiological tales aside, the hallowed image of Malha (which reappeared time and again in later presentations of the museum, including as an emblem printed on cafeteria napkins) cannot be left in peace as a picturesque allusion and should rather be contemplated as a haunting memento mori, a lingering trace of the massive ruination, confiscation, and cultural appropriation that followed the War of 1948, Israeli independence, and the Palestinian *Nakba* (catastrophe).

The actual village of Malha was not demolished during the war, only irrevocably emptied of its inhabitants. Many of its sturdy stone houses were spared: confiscated, suspended under the legal definition of Deserted Property, and reused as temporary accommodations for new Jewish immigrants, most of them of North African origin. Later on, during the 1960s, the immigrants were funneled into prefab housing projects while Malha underwent a process of gentrification by resourceful squatters—bohemians, dilettantes, and opportunists—who could appreciate its beauty, afford to purchase the houses from the Custodian of Absentee Property, and revamp the village as an "artists' colony."

Against such a tangible backdrop of expropriation and transfiguration, it is hardly surprising to find an illustration of an indigenous village emerging as the poetic-truth factor in modish architectural drawings. In fact, many Israeli architects at the time were obsessed with the effigy of the native village, willfully confusing the Arab with the Mediterranean, but the National Museum may be the first—and is certainly the most significant—instance of its embodiment in actual built form: a "village" for a village.

Mansfeld and Gad's noticeable references in their competition drawings to modernist icons (Mies's Brick House of 1923) and structuralist open-ended accumulative systems (Team 10 mats), and the immediate reception of the built museum as Israel's ultimate masterpiece of contemporary architecture, do not contradict the museum's atavistic drive. Quite the contrary: the more self-consciously modernist a work of architecture is, the more unmediated access to subconscious formations of the vernacular it seeks. According to the *Fontana Dictionary of Modern Thought*, vernacular in architecture is "an adjective referring to an indigenous building style, generally the work of builders with no professional formation, which is nonetheless considered to have special attributes and to be linked to a certain degree to a glorious past. [...] Modern architecture has often set as one of its goals the establishment of a new vernacular."

The oxymoron of a "new vernacular" is visually illustrated in a photocollage created by Willem Sandberg, a renowned Dutch typographer and the first director of

(14)

(14) Yitzhak Frenkel, director of the Academy of Arts, in the Old City of Safed, 1952.
(15) Exhibition poster merging the Israel Museum with a ruinous Palestinian village, 1979. Willem Sandberg. Photocollage.

(15)

the Israel Museum. In his photocollage, the white cubes of the new museum and the masonry volumes of a Palestinian village (seemingly either Malha or Lifta) are flattened and fused into one seamless and painless continuum. Such captivating surrealism could offer a reflexive critique of modernism's Orientalist gaze, of the politics of simulacra at play, or of the very technique of photomontage (misleadingly called photocollage by Sandberg). Regrettably, it remains an exercise in graphic design, expressing trivial fascination with the effects of architectural masquerade and allowing the blurring of historical narrative into a timeless and painless poster sold at the museum's souvenir shop.

The actual appropriation and gentrification of Malha was by no means exceptional. The emerging Israeli "creative class" explored "absentees' property" in the established Arab neighborhoods of Jerusalem, Haifa, Safed, and Jaffa, as well as in pictorial villages such as Ein Hud and Ein Karem.

The first squatter "artists' colony" was established as early as 1949 in the ruins of the Old City of Safed by a group of painters including Shimshon Holzman, Hannah Lerner, Yitzhak Frenkel, and Moshe Castel. They were locally known as a rebellious modernist group rejecting the nostalgic Jugendstil and Orientalism of the Bezalel art circles. In 1953, a more radical group of artists, led by the Dadaist painter and architect Marcel Janco, settled in the "abandoned" stone houses of the Palestinian village of Ein Hud, on the southwestern slopes of the Carmel. Ein Hud had been evacuated in 1948 and was initially repopulated by Jewish immigrants from Algeria. The latter were relocated after it became clear that the hilly topography was not conducive to intensive agriculture and the parcelization of even plots.

(16)

Janco stumbled upon the ruins of Ein Hud in 1953 while working for the government as the architect in

⑰

⑱

charge of the establishment of national parks. He became aware of plans for the destruction of an abandoned village in the Carmel Forest that was being used as shelter by "infiltrators" (a term referring to Palestinian refugees who were trying to return to their native villages). He ordered a cessation of the demolition ruling and began to research the village, where he found historical remains from the Roman period; this led him to assume that Jews had lived there in ancient times. The Jewish Agency and the Israeli government gave their approval for the preservation of the village on the condition that it be settled. Thus the decision was made to establish an artists' colony there under the Hebrew name of Ein Hod. Janco, who believed in a synthesis of contextual localism and the universal language of modernism, wanted to establish the foundations of a popular Israeli arts and crafts movement upon the architectural and agricultural remains of the village. The movement would combine painting and sculpture with crafts such as pottery and jewelry-making. In this connection between arts and crafts, he saw the continuation of the Dada tradition.

Ein Hod remains a prosperous colony of Jewish artists and artisans to this day. It is considered one of the most pastoral living environments in Israel, in spite of the crowds of tourists on weekends and the spooky company of the spirits of the native homeowners among tasteful objets d'art and decorative gardens. The market value of the refurbished houses has increased dramatically. The old village mosque has been creatively adapted into a restaurant. A Dada museum was installed in the 1980s to commemorate Janco's endeavors. Apparently, at least one extended family from the original village of Ein Hud, Abu el-Hija, did not flee far in 1948. They relocated on an overlooking hill several kilometers away, established a new village off the Israeli grid, and watched their artistically transformed village all those years. In 2005, after a long legal battle and a public campaign, the surrogate village of Ein Hud was officially recognized and connected to the electrical grid.[1]

Even before his discovery of Ein Hud, Marcel Janco had been instrumental in preventing the total demolition of the old district of Jaffa. After the expulsion of the Palestinian residents during the war and the partial destruction of the district, new Jewish immigrants were housed in the dilapidated buildings. An impoverished neighborhood

⑲

⑯ Café Tarshish, Old City of Jaffa, mid-1960s. Eliezer Frenkel.
⑰ Old City of Jaffa, view from Pasteur Street, prior to 1959.
⑱ Old City of Jaffa after preservation works, view from Pasteur Street, late 1960s. Ora and Yaacov Yaar, Saadia Mendel, Eliezer Frenkel.
⑲ Tents and tin shacks of a transit camp located in the ruins of a Palestinian village in the Jerusalem Hills, early 1950s. Government Press Office.

arose in this area, becoming infamous as a hotbed of crime and prostitution. In 1953, after an attempt by some of the Palestinian residents to return to their homes, Prime Minister Ben-Gurion ordered the demolition of any home that had not been populated by immigrants. Consequently, vast areas of dense historic urban fabric were razed. Janco, who immediately recognized the exceptional natural beauty of Jaffa's shore and the distinctive architectural merit of the Old City, wanted to establish there an artists' quarter like the one that had already been set up at Safed. He managed to argue for the rescue of 20 dunam out of 100 that were set for demolition. The demolitions works were halted at the order of Teddy Kollek, then chief of the prime minister's bureau, and the site stood in ruin for eight years.[2]

In the early 1960s, the Old Jaffa Development Company was founded. The company's task was the rehabilitation and gentrification of the Old City through the formulaic mix of art, craft, tourism, and leisure—a complete turnabout of the historic city, which evolved around the fishermen's and merchants' port. In the first stage of the project, the Jewish provisional occupants were enticed to move out to new housing projects in other areas of Jaffa and in nearby Bat Yam. A survey conducted by the Housing Ministry determined that "given the unacceptable state of living conditions [in old Jaffa], the physical relocation of the residents to suitable housing seems a most urgent and essential need." In the second stage, young architects were mobilized for the entirely new and ostensibly counter-modernist professional assignment of historic renovation, preservation, conservation, restoration, and so on. Among these architects was Eliezer Frenkel (son of the painter Yitzhak Frenkel, one of the founders of the artists' colony in Safed), who recounts the instrumental role of artists and bohemians in the process of gentrification:

⑳

> It took some time to look around and see the prickly pear cactus and the fig trees. The first to see it were the artists—Anna Ticho, Leopold Krakauer—trendsetters, the bohemians of the 1950s and '60s, artists' communities, architects, and their milieu. Despite the touristic quality of the place, they tried to turn it into a center for important artists. This appeal to the artists, to the bohemians, to the avant-garde, was intentional, as an impetus for the development of Jaffa. Why the return to the historical city? Because there is no future without a past, even if it is borrowed. We were asked to rehabilitate Jaffa so that Tel Aviv could have a past.[3]

(21)

(20) New immigrants waiting to enter abandoned houses in Ein Karem, 1949. Photographer: Hugo Mendelssohn. Government Press Office.
(21) New immigrants in Jaffa, 1949. Photographer: Zoltan Kluger. Government Press Office.
(22) New immigrants entering an abandoned house in Jaffa, 1949. Photographer: Zoltan Kluger. Government Press Office.

So alleged artists and aesthetes provided the necessary impetus and pretense for a dual rehabilitation: both that of the ruinous urban matter itself and that of the war and the postwar crimes that generated the ruins and turned the living city of Jaffa into a phony historical site. The praxis of "preservation" that would henceforth gain momentum and pedantry in Israeli architecture was uncanny: by simulating, mutatis mutandis, an urban organism or an architectural organ, it did nothing but dissimulate, decontextualize, and defamiliarize the origin, in effect merely embalming its catastrophe. Preservation does preserve, but certainly not the space and performance of everyday life. It converts, it salvages, it redeems—that is precisely its proclaimed purpose—and in this sense, it is evidently just another form, or phase, or technique in an unfolding course of destruction, confiscation, and appropriation of both tangible property and cultural intangibles. In this case, as candidly confessed by Frenkel, Jaffa was literally conflated with Tel Aviv to serve as its surrogate past.

In the old district, the discriminatory regulations initially set up by the Development Company and backed by urban bylaws, restricting the purchase of property and the dwelling in the luxurious "preservation" to committee-screened artists only, are still valid today. They not only effectively prevent the hypothetical return of the original inhabitants of Jaffa, but have eventually also come to ridicule the wannabe artists of the colony. ■

(22)

1 On the confiscated Palestinian villages, see Walid Khalidi, *All That Remains: The Palestinian Villages Occupied and Depopulated by Israel in 1948* (Washington, DC: Institute for Palestine Studies, 1992); Meron Benvenisti, *Sacred Landscape: The Buried History of the Holy Land since 1948* (Berkeley: University of California Press, 2000). On Ein Hud, see Susan Slyomovics, *The Object of Memory: Arab and Jew Narrate the Palestinian Village* (Philadelphia: University of Pennsylvania Press, 1998); Malkit Shoshan and Maurizio Bortolotti, *Village: One Land Two Systems and Platform Paradise* (Bologna: Damiani, 2014).

2 On the urban history of Jaffa, see Mark LeVine, *Overthrowing Geography: Jaffa, Tel Aviv, and the Struggle for Palestine, 1880–1948* (Berkeley: University of California Press, 2005); Daniel Monterescu, *Jaffa Shared and Shattered: Contrived Coexistence in Israel/Palestine* (Bloomington: Indiana University Press, 2015); Sharon Rotbard, *White City, Black City: Architecture and War in Tel Aviv and Jaffa* (Cambridge, MA: MIT Press, 2015).

3 Eliezer Frenkel, in a discussion with the author, 1998.

㉓

㉔ ㉕ ㉖

㉗

㉘

㉓ General view of Ein Hud (now Ein Hod), 1956. Photographer: Hella Fernbach. Central Zionist Archives.
㉔ – ㉖ Artists at work, Ein Hod, 1950s. Photographer: Hanan Sade. Central Zionist Archives.
㉗ Hollywood actor Jeff Chandler visiting Ein Hod artists' colony, 1959. Photographer: Moshe Pridan. Government Press Office.
㉘ Artist at work, Ein Hod, 1950s. Photographer: Hanan Sade. Central Zionist Archives.

㉙ ㉚
㉛ ㉜

㉝

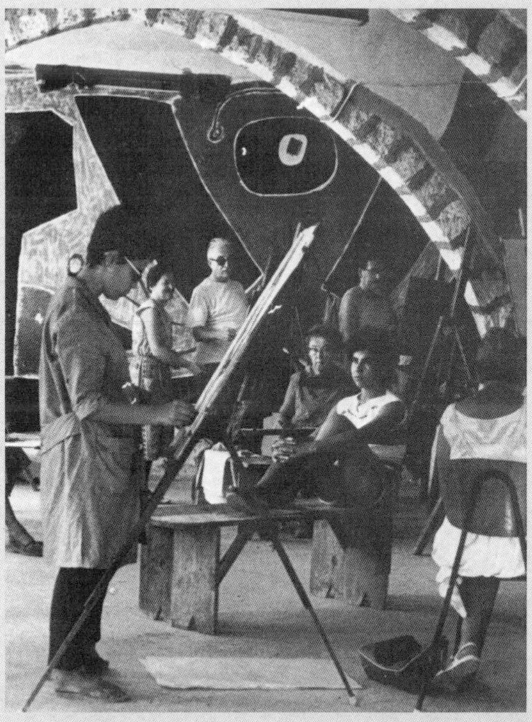

㉙ Moshe Mokady in his studio, Ein Hod, 1967. Photographer: Anna Rivkin-Brick. Central Zionist Archives.
㉚ Gertrud Kraus in her studio, Ein Hod, 1967. Photographer: Anna Rivkin-Brick. Central Zionist Archives.
㉛–㉜ Artist at work, Ein Hod, 1950s. Photographer: Hanan Sade. Central Zionist Archives.
㉝ Marcel Janco giving a painting class, Ein Hod, 1950s.

# Camps

## State of Emergency

The supply of "abandoned property" (see chapter "Ruins of War") proved limited. In 1949, a record number of Jewish immigrants—about a quarter of a million—entered the country. Many of these would be housed in absorption and transit camps, mostly converted British military barracks. By the end of 1949, about 100,000 immigrants, most of them unemployed, were living in such camps, often for years. The shift from ad hoc appropriation of Palestinian masonry buildings to the systematic distribution of provisional camps based on lightweight structures such as tents, canvas huts, tin shacks, and wood barracks accelerated the absorption process and created an instantaneous network of proxy settlements, many of which functioned either as labor camps for national infrastructural works or as nuclei for permanent towns prescribed by the 1950 national master plan.[1]

One of the most thoughtful responses to the challenge of large-scale lightweight construction came from Louis Kahn. In 1949, the Palestine Economic Corporation invited a number of international figures, including Kahn, who was already involved with the issue of postwar low-cost housing in the United States, to a meeting with the Israel Housing Survey Committee. Kahn researched technologies for industrialized lightweight construction and prepared a proposal that included sketches and explanations for the building of temporary camps. He maintained that by developing an industry of inexpensive construction components, Israel could become a center for the production and export of prefabricated building parts to the Near East, and thus make its way toward economic independence.

Six weeks after the first elected government was inaugurated, Prime Minister David Ben-Gurion announced the installment of an emergency apparatus, anchored in an "austerity regime," in order to reduce the State's dependence on imports and foreign currency, minimize luxury consumption, and "allow every family to reduce their expenses without harming their standard of living, while fulfilling their essential material and spiritual needs."[2] However, hopes to quickly overcome the economic crisis were dashed and the housing section of the Jewish Agency's Immigration Department seemed to lag behind its mounting mission. Likewise, the solutions proposed by the Ministry of Labor (which was responsible for employment and public works) during 1949 were deemed unsatisfactory. It became clear that the pace of construction could not keep up with demand and that the relocation of the immigrants to permanent settlements would be delayed.[3]

In March 1950, Levi Eshkol, head of the Land Settlement Department of the Jewish Agency, presented his "Transit Camp [Heb. *ma'abarot*] Plan." The purpose of the plan was to establish new absorption camps with the goal of integrating immigrants into the productive workforce in the cities and rural settlements. Unlike other or previous solutions, the Transit Camp Plan signified the beginning of a calculated settlement and integration enterprise based on comprehensive public works as a source of employment for the immigrants and as a stimulus for the development of the country. Eshkol's proposal was:

> [...] to thus dismantle the immigrant camps throughout the country. Wherever there is a settlement, we will attach an immigrant project to it. From Dan [in the north] to beyond Nir-Am [in the south], in every place where we have an economic foothold, we

> will establish sixty projects that will house up to a thousand people. The immigrants will be employed in forestry and planting fruit trees, preparing, terracing, and clearing out the land. We must encourage the building plans.[4]

Eshkol did not foresee the grievances and opposition that would come from the established settlements via the regional committees, municipalities, and village councils. The primary incentive behind his plan was to free the government's Immigrant Absorption Department from the burden of the immigrant camps. He tried to bring Ben-Gurion on board: "This new approach demands financial means for purchasing tents, putting together groups of immigrants, setting up water and sanitation systems, and building the appropriate amount of wooden shacks for public services. [...] We must find the immediate means, before the next rainy season, for the construction of at least another 15,000 to 20,000 wooden shacks or houses, in addition to the government's existing building plans."[5]

Beginning in the summer of 1950, most of the new immigrants were sent to the newly erected transit camps. The first of these were established in 1950 in the center of the country; from 1951 onward they were dispersed throughout the country. The transit camps could be divided into three primary types: those adjacent to or within existing settlements, wherein the residents of the camps were expected to work as salaried employees in the area of the camp; those established in the designated development regions (the Negev, the Galilee, and the Jerusalem corridor), which were meant to constitute the core of future settlements (in the first stage, 300 families were to be directed to each of these camps and employed in public works; some of these were called "Jewish National Fund transit camps," since they were based on forestry and land preparation); and those which used the facilities of existing immigrant camps, with the goal of eventually being transformed into permanent neighborhoods.[6]

A large supply of tents was needed for the establishment of the transit camps: the entire plan to evacuate the tenants from the initial immigrant camps depended on this. The leadership of the Jewish Agency decided to purchase 50,000 tents, and in May and June 1950 its agents were dispatched around the world on a vigorous search for suppliers of high-quality, inexpensive tents—primarily those left in the military storehouses of the Allied forces after World War II, but also tents from Japan and Iraq.[7] The lessons of the winter of 1949 to 1950 motivated the Immigrant Absorption Department to build dozens of wooden structures for emergency services and health clinics in every transit camp.

The Transit Camp Plan went awry in its early implementation stages. Many of the 100,000 tenants who had already settled in the earlier immigrant camps refused to leave, either because they wanted to remain near the big cities or in order to save money. Police records and daily newspapers from the period are full of reports of clashes between law enforcement officers and camp residents who refused to be evacuated and move to the new locations. To avoid the inconvenience (and associated waiting period) of transferring the immigrants from immigrant camps to transit camps, Labor Minister Golda Meir exhorted all the parties involved to build new transit camps for the direct absorption of immigrants upon their arrival. In March 1951, 42 new transit camps were built throughout the country, from Halsa (Kiryat Shmona) in the north to Beersheba in the south. In November 1951, there were 112 transit camps, housing 227,000 immigrants.

The interim plan of the transit camps lingered much longer than anticipated. Many camps continued to exist for several years, nurturing deprivation and bitter criticism that would lastingly blemish the permanent settlements built on their foundations. The population of the transit camps reached its height (257,000 people) at the end of 1951, at which point the immigrants began to leave the transit camps, whether of their own initiative or at the encouragement of the Jewish Agency. In order to leave the transit camps for the housing projects, one had to place a down payment on an apartment and commit to regular payments. Only the very weakest segments of the Jewish population—those who could not manage this financial burden—remained in the transit camps for several more years.

In mid-1952, about a quarter of a million people, one-sixth or so of the Jewish population in Israel, was still living in the transit camps.[8] Of these, 11,500 families lived in tents, 11,000 in canvas huts, 9,500 in tin shacks, 15,000 in wood cabins, and 4,500 in British military camps. Back in 1951, the prime minister had announced that the tents would be done away with and exchanged for stable structures—but the plan was slowed due to the large wave of immigrants from Iraq and the delay in the shipping of cabins.

Only at the end of 1952, when immigration subsided, did the transfer of most of the immigrants from the transit camps to neighborhoods in the development towns and new frontier settlements around the country begin, with the emphasis shifting from public works to agriculture. Golda Meir, in her autobiographical book *My Life,* recounts the shortcoming of this phase:

We made mistakes about that, too. We tried, probably too soon, to turn the pressure cooker into a melting pot. We created villages populated by combinations of people like the road-building crews. They had nothing much in common with each other and found it difficult (sometimes impossible) to live together in a totally isolated part of the country, and they usually had neither any experience nor any taste for farming.[9]

At the end of 1952, the government decided to appoint a ministerial commission on budgetary matters to audit the program of the Ministry of Labor for the liquidation of the transit camps. The program was meant to be implemented during the 1953–1954 and 1954–1955 fiscal years. The Jewish Agency decided that those thirty-five years old and under would be sent to agricultural settlements, while the older immigrants would be sent to development areas and towns.[10]

At the beginning of 1953 about 157,000 people remained in the transit camps. At the beginning of 1954 it was 108,000; and at the end of that year 88,000.[11] Despite the relatively low numbers of immigrant arrivals from 1953 to 1954, it was impossible to liquidate the transit camps entirely, since no more than about 30,000 immigrants could be provided with permanent housing each year. But the lessons learned from the transit camp experiment were implemented with the new wave of immigration that began to flow into Israel in 1954, with the new immigrants sent directly to permanent residences. The liquidation of the transit camps, which continued to scar the landscape, would preoccupy the authorities for years to come. Most of the residents of the camps were transferred to permanent housing between 1957 and 1960—but despite all efforts, 15,300 people were still stranded in the camps at the end of 1963.

Some of the transit camps turned into new towns (or "development towns," as they were called): Yeruham, Kiryat Malakhi, Sderot, Netivot, Bet She'an, Migdal Ha'Emek, Kiryat Shmona, and Yavneh. Others became suburb neighborhoods: Givat Olga in Hadera, Amishav in Petah Tikva, the Katamonim in Jerusalem, Ramat Eliyahu in Rishon LeZion. Yet others became agricultural settlements. Many transit camps—such as Tzemach, Zar'in, Nuris, Ne'eman, Hiriya, Ein Shemer, Mahane Yisrael, and Kadouri—were entirely wiped off the map. ■

1 See David Zaslavsky, *Immigrant Housing in Israel: Construction, Planning, and Development, 1950–1953* [in Hebrew] (Tel Aviv: Am Oved, 1954), p. 7.

2 The "austerity regime," an expression borrowed from the postwar British model, implemented a system of supervision on essential products, headed by the minister of agriculture, supply, and rationing, Dov Yosef, to restrain private consumption for the sake of security and development expenses. Ben-Gurion emphasized that the emergency regulations were only "temporary regulations, until we reach the plateau." See Mordechai Naor, ed., *Immigrants and Transit Camps, 1948–1952* [in Hebrew] (Jerusalem: Yad Izhak Ben-Zvi, 1986), p. 97.

3 In 1950, Israel was hit by a harsh winter that caused heavy damage to the temporary camps. In May 1952, the Film and Arts Union released a silent movie, *Boy in the Flood*, which portrayed the floods in the camps, montaging fictional footage and neorealist-style documentary clips.

4 Cited in Dvora Hacohen, *Immigrants in a Storm* [in Hebrew] (Jerusalem: Yad Izhak Ben-Zvi, 1994), p. 210.

5 Letter from Levi Eshkol to David Ben-Gurion, April 10, 1950 (Central Zionist Archives, Jerusalem, 4406/S30). Cited in Hacohen, *Immigrants in a Storm*, p. 205.

6 Haim Darin-Drabkin, *Housing and Immigrant Absorption in Israel, 1948–1955* [in Hebrew] (Tel Aviv: Gadish, 1955).

7 Hacohen, *Immigrants in a Storm*, p. 207.

8 Ibid., p. 299; see also State of Israel—Ministry of Labor, *Wood Shack Camps: A Dwelling Plan* [in Hebrew] (Jerusalem, 1957).

9 Golda Meir, *My Life*, 6th printing (London: Futura, 1978), p. 220.

10 Hacohen, *Immigrants in a Storm*, p. 301.

11 Ibid.

①

②

③

① Transit camp (ma'abara) in the center of the country, 1948. Photographer: Hans Pinn. Government Press Office.
② Light canvas huts toppled as a result of storms, Beit Lid, 1949. Photographer: Teddy Brauner. Government Press Office.
③ Grocery store, former British barracks ("Nissen huts") transformed into transitional camps, Tel Aviv, 1948. Photographer: Zoltan Kluger. Government Press Office.
④–⑤ Former British barracks ("Nissen huts") transformed into transitional camps, Tel Aviv, 1948. Photographer: Zoltan Kluger. Government Press Office.
⑥ New immigrants in an abandoned British military camp, early 1950s. Government Press Office.

④

⑤

⑥

⑦

⑨

⑩

⑧

⑪

⑦ Tin shacks, Har Toov Transit Camp, Beit Shemesh, 1956. Photographer: Fred Chesnik. Jewish National Fund Archive.
⑧ General view of Athlit immigrant reception camp, near Haifa, 1949. Government Press Office.
⑨–⑩ Transit camp near Tiberias, 1951. Photographer: David Eldan.
⑪ Still from a film documenting the foundation day of a transit camp, Kisalon Immigrant Village, on the outskirts of Jerusalem, 1950. The Lavon Institute for Labor Movement Research Archives.

# DOSSIER:
# LOUIS KAHN'S PREFAB DWELLINGS

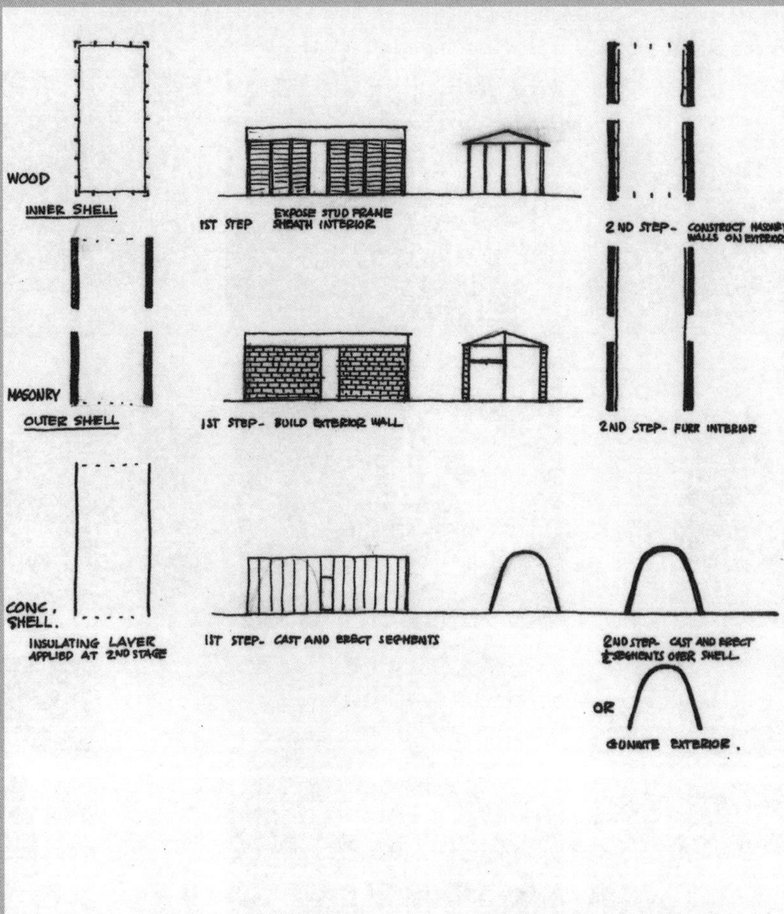


⑫ Proposal to relieve the housing shortage in Israel, 1949. Sketch. Louis Kahn. Louis I. Kahn Collection, University of Pennsylvania.

Louis Kahn visited Israel in April 1949, a year after the establishment of the State, and spent a month there as a member of a study team of the Israel Housing Survey Committee.[1] This advisory forum was established by the Palestine Economic Corporation (PEC)[2] to provide professional counsel on Israel's escalating housing crisis, the proliferation of emergency transit camps, and the need for a long-term national housing policy. In Israel, the study team systematically examined existing conditions, local material resources, and political apparatuses; met with planning authorities and building companies; and evaluated technical know-how. The team worked closely with the National Planning Office, led by Arieh Sharon, which was already in the process of devising a national master plan (see chapter "Project"). The scope of Israel's housing crisis was presented to the team by Yaakov (Shiffman) Ben-Sira, the municipal engineer of Tel Aviv, who stated that 50,000 houses were needed immediately and projected that 400,000 houses would be required within a decade.

The only architect on the committee, Kahn found himself in a minority position on several issues, especially regarding the core strategic dilemma of investing in temporary or permanent structures. His analysis and recommendations, assembled in his "Preliminary Report on Housing in Israel" of June 7, 1949, were attached to the Survey Committee's documents as an "Alternative Report."[3]

Kahn's report can be read not only as a highly pragmatic proposal addressing the crisis at hand on all scales—from national production infrastructure to the details of pre-casting methods—but also as an inspiring effort to establish the ethical commitment of architecture and to prove its competence in handling massive emergency situations. In this regard, it is particularly relevant to today's global refugee absorption issues and may serve as a rappel à l'ordre for architects.

Kahn was critical of transitional camps (ma'abarot) made up of tents or provisional shacks that could neither provide an "essential space"[4] nor develop into a sustainable community. Instead, he proposed a modular method of mass-produced, semipermanent homes which could be incrementally enlarged according to a prescribed modular urban layout. Practically, he proposed an efficient system to accommodate both urgent demand and long-term planning. Speculatively, he presented the acute housing crisis as a singular opportunity to reform the entire local building industry and turn it into a source of national livelihood. According to Susan Solomon,

> he recommended that Israel become a "center of building fabrication in the Near East," thereby turning the "Building Emergency into a Major Industry." Kahn envisioned an industry that would spawn its own company towns, what he termed "operational centers," and make Israel the economic heart of a reconstituted Near East. [. . .] Kahn's research led him to the vacuum-formed concrete method, a type of precast construction that depended on applying unusual pressure to molded concrete in order to speed drying time while increasing strength.[5]

The drawings attached to Kahn's "Preliminary Report" almost seem to be part of a do-it-yourself building manual, encompassing a kit of parts with precise measurements, a step-by-step assembly process, and an urban scheme with lot dimensions. The domestic unit described in the drawings is a parabolic shell, 12 feet (4 meters) wide and extendable to various lengths, which integrated "roof and wall as a single unit"[6] and could be built in one piece by unskilled workers. Kahn produced these drawings within about a month of his visit to Israel, but they reflect his long incubating experiments with minimal dwellings and mass prefabrication—experiments that could not possibly be implemented in "stable countries," as he acknowledged before embarking for Israel:

> In the style conscious and economically complex stable countries these methods are still meeting resistance. [. . .] The fluid state of Israel, faced with the stark reality of its emergency, braced by its will and aim to be self-sufficient, [. . .] should be prepared to make as courageous a plan for solution of its living places as it has to create a State. Fragmentary stabs at solution can result in waste and debt.[7]

After a month with the newly born yet already convoluted Israeli planning apparatus, Kahn seems to have realized that his concern with mass "living places" and efficient building techniques was destined to drown in a more primal territorial preoccupation. On the first page of his report, composed of recommendations and remarks, he boldly wrote:

> Advised:
> That the N.P.O. [National Planning Office] reduce its present activity in overall country planning, in order to put all effort into planning of housing types and sites.[8] ■

1 The full story of Kahn's involvement in Israel's housing crisis is told in Susan G. Solomon, *Louis I. Kahn's Trenton Jewish Community Center* (New York: Princeton Architectural Press, 2000), pp. 13–28. This brief is based on Solomon's book.

2 The PEC was a Jewish-American investment holding company that had financed industrial projects in Palestine since the 1920s.

3 Solomon, *Louis I. Kahn's Trenton Jewish Community Center*, p. 25.

4 This term was coined in Louis Kahn, George Howe, and Oscar Stonorov, "Standards versus Essential Space: Comments on Unit Plans for War Housing," *Architectural Forum* 76 (May 1942), pp. 308–311. Quoted in Solomon, *Louis I. Kahn's Trenton Jewish Community Center*, p. 17.

5 Solomon, *Louis I. Kahn's Trenton Jewish Community Center*, p. 15.

6 Cited in ibid., p. 27.

7 Louis Kahn, "Outline Report," March 1949, cited in Solomon, *Louis I. Kahn's Trenton Jewish Community Center*, p. 16.

8 Louis Kahn, "Preliminary Report on Housing in Israel," June 7, 1949, p. 1. Louis I. Kahn Collection, University of Pennsylvania.

⑬

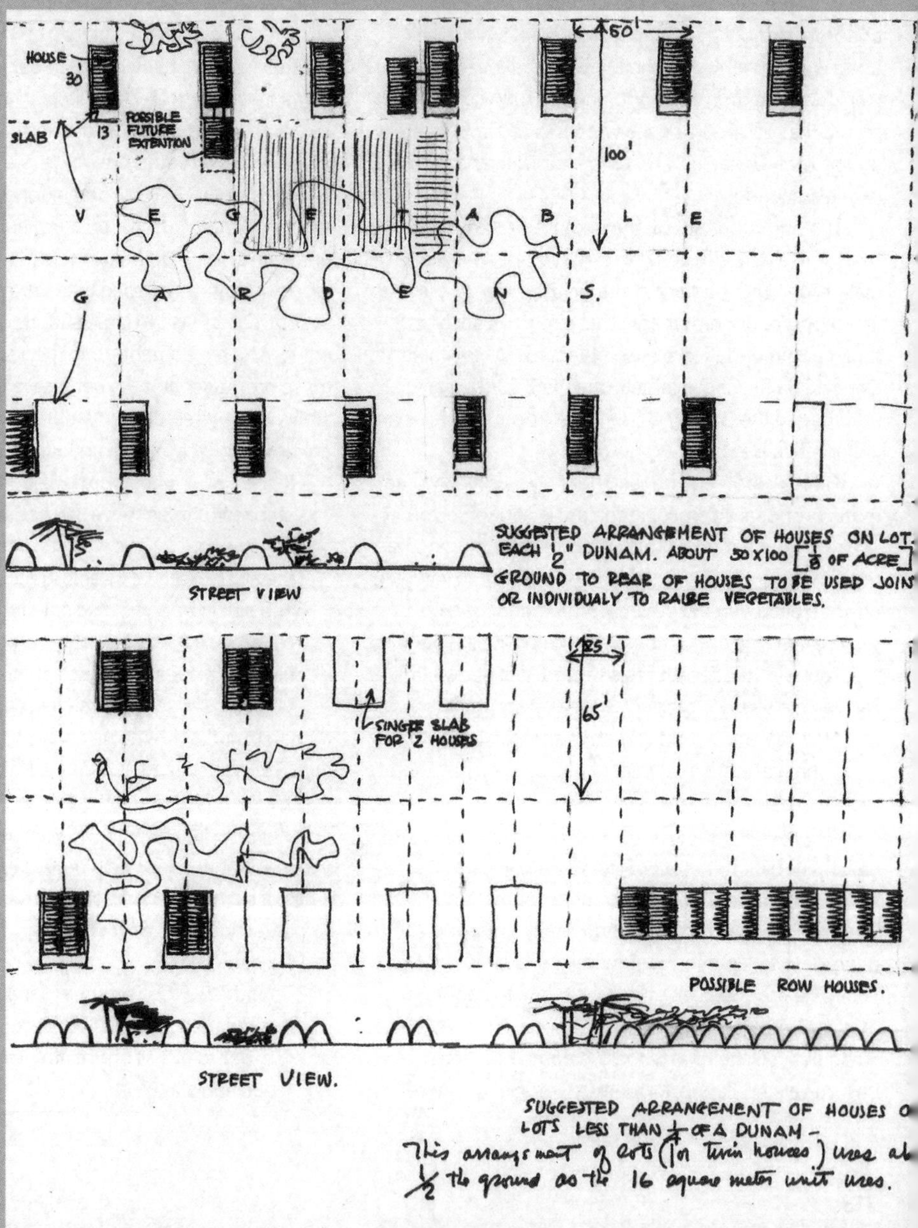

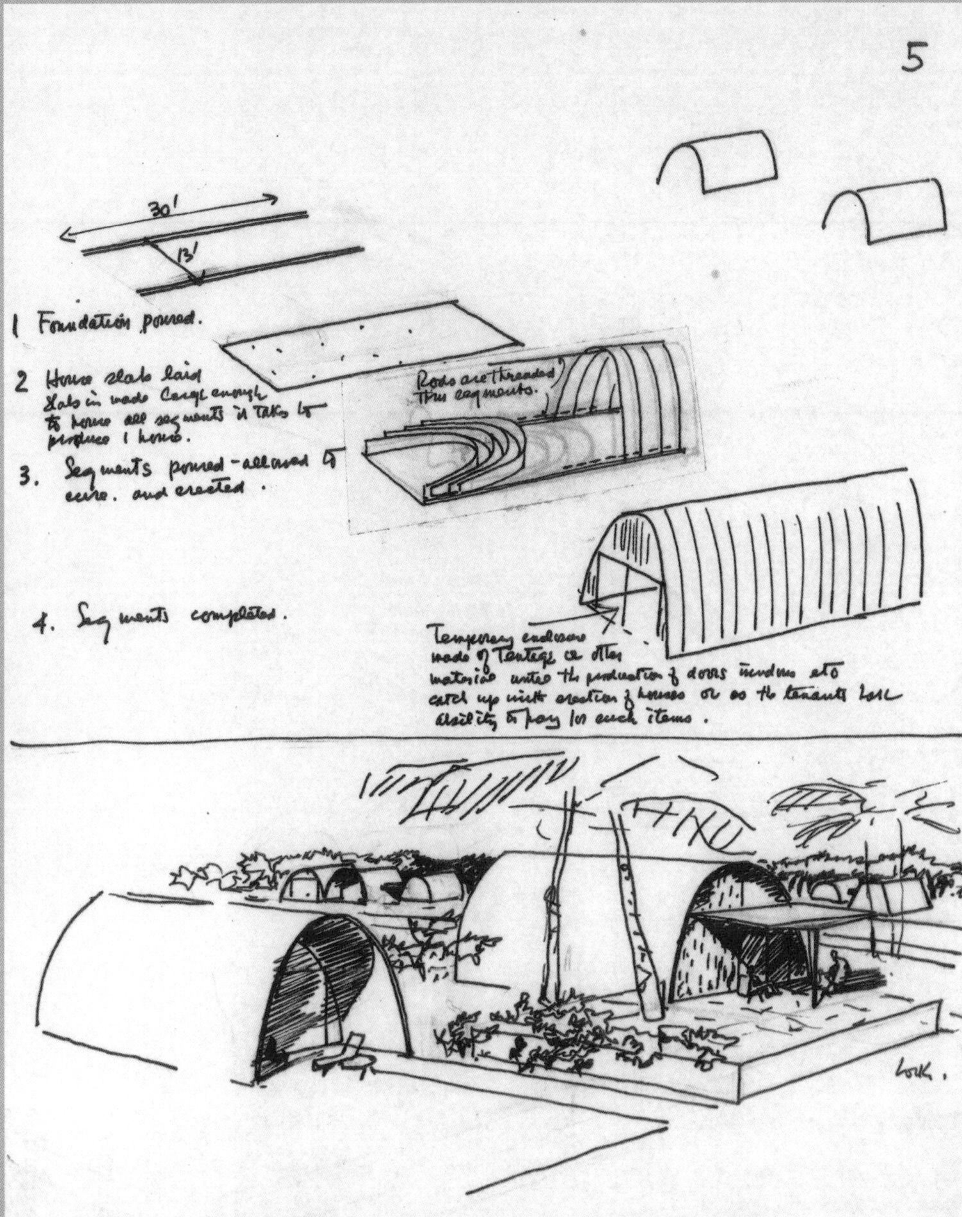


⑭

⑬ – ⑭ Proposal to relieve the housing shortage in Israel, 1949. Sketch. Louis Kahn. Louis I. Kahn Collection, University of Pennsylvania.

PRELIMINARY REPORT ON HOUSING IN ISRAEL

JUNE 7, 1949 - LOUIS I. KAHN, ARCHITECT

Israel, a new state of ancient beginnings, absorbing a tremendous flow of population from many countries, provides in its housing emergency opportunity for achievement of historical importance.

⑮ "Preliminary Report on Housing in Israel" by Louis Kahn, June 1949. Louis I. Kahn Collection, University of Pennsylvania.

Because of the unprecedented amount of housing and housing facilities needed, the full resources of financing, construction and planning would be involved. Duplication of effort, time and money with the limited resources directly available would seriously demoralize and retard the housing goal and damage the present remote economic feasibility of the whole effort.

The technical personnel of Amidar, Shikun, Jewish Agency, the National Planning Office and other organizations in Israel are working independently of each other on housing plans. Construction organizations are limited in their production by the depletion and the character of the construction labor force, unmechanized construction methods, the high cost of materials and transportation, lack of standardization, limited choice of materials, and import duties on essential materials.

Government funds are not fully realized thru the present taxation methods, Jewish Agency funds are decentralized from the Government, and the peoples' savings are not reflected in available construction, mortgage, or investment money in the midst of an acute inflationary condition.

RECOMMENDATIONS FOR A CENTRAL HOUSING AUTHORITY

| Recommended: | Remarks: |
|---|---|
| That a Central Housing Authority be created under the Ministry of Labor & Reconstruction, now the provisional authority for the agencies of Social Security, Public Works & Planning. | |
| That the Central Housing Authority be set up with 3 major divisions of 1- financing 2- construction 3-planning, with a director as expediting head of all these divisions, and that each division have its own expeditor answerable to the director. | It has been suggested by nearly all the people who understand the political and technical situation that the director of housing should come from the U.S. |
| That the National Planning Office (Ha Kir'ya), under the Central Housing Authority, take over the sole responsibility of physical planning for housing. | |
| Advised: | |
| That the N.P.O. reduce its present activity in overall country planning, in order to put all effort into planning of housing types and sites. | The enlistment of the National Planning Office is necessary in view of the shortage of technical men in Israel. |

Recommended:

That Shikun, Jewish Agency and the Jewish National Fund be retained as advisors to the Central Housing Authority.

That Amidar relinquish its responsibilities in housing to the Central Housing Authority.

That an American Foundation be set up to support the residence of U.S. Architects, Engineers and Site Planners to aid the Planning Department.

That Architects in the major cities of Jerusalem, Haifa and Tel Aviv, now not engaged in the specific plot planning and unit planning problems of this emergency, be immediately employed and be directed as to policy and standards by the National Planning Office.

RECOMMENDATIONS TO REDUCE BUILDING COSTS

Recommended:

That imported raw and finished materials, building machines and equipment be duty free, and that an effort be made by the Government to obtain long term credit agreements.

That the transportation of all material pertaining especially to the emergency housing be handled directly by the Government.

That a government committee establish fair prices for local materials.

Sharon's and Banett's offices are very limited in space and manpower to do the job entrusted to them. They must resort to the minimum of study to keep up with the demands put upon them. There are also a limited number of Architects not employed who have a thorough knowledge of site planning and all its implications. There are only a few Site Planning Engineers and their time is being taxed to the maximum.

Mr. Sharon enjoys the respect of all Architects in Israel and I believe that working under his direction would cause no friction on the part of other Architects throughout the country.

Sand, crushed stone and cement are natural resources of Israel. Still concrete costs $18.00 in Israel and $7.00 in the U.S., while labor rates are 60% of those in the U.S.

⑯ Proposal to relieve the housing shortage in Israel, 1949. Drawing. Louis Kahn. Louis I. Kahn Collection, University of Pennsylvania.

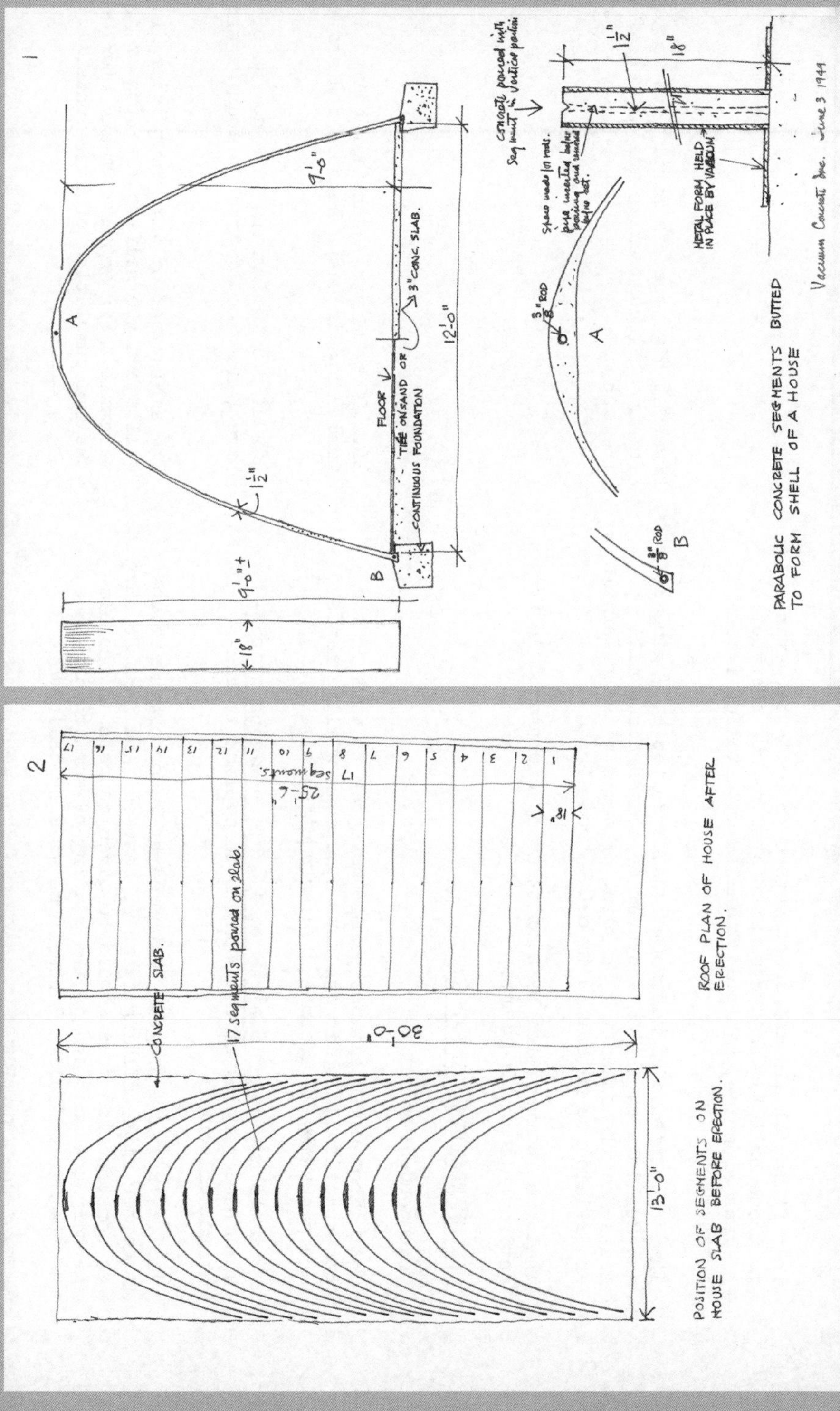

That financial aid and construction priority be given to those building products manufacturers now obstructed by lack of space, equipment, and transportation facilities.

That a committee of Manufacturers, Architects, Engineers and Builders establish a system of standardized mill sizes for the essential building products made in Israel and related to materials imported from abroad.

Present high cost is partly due to the present demand for uncatalogued sizes and shapes of essential building items.

That free competition be permitted and encouraged in the entire building industry.

## RECOMMENDATIONS ON LABOR

Recommended:

That labor organizations permit refugees to work on the construction of their own houses, as all willing hands are necessary to accomplish construction aims.

IL.1,000,000 per month is required to keep 50,000 immigrants in camps housed, fed and clothed.

That the device of Basic Rate + Cost of Living adjustment used for industrial workers be applied to construction workers.

50% of the immigrants have no funds. The remaining have funds too limited to acquire shelter.

That a training program sponsored by labor organizations together with building firms be renewed, and that foremen on construction jobs should be given courses in the elementary sciences and in the reading of working drawings, so that an efficient labor force will be trained.

The employment of immigrant labor in construction work will speed the self-sufficiency of the immigrants, maintain their enthusiasm and shorten their stay by their accumulation of some funds.

## SITE RECOMMENDATIONS

The National Planning Office is now considering new sites for towns and settlements and studying the extent to which existing towns should be increased. It is making a serious study of the national picture as regards the availability of water and power, the characteristics of the land and weather. Sites are being studied for the feasibility of Industry. The National Planning Office has the authority to approve or disapprove sites for all developments.

The Jewish Agency and the N.P.O. have been working together in the determination of housing sites for the immigrants and are in general agreement on location. There is still much work to be done in determining specific sites. (See maps A & B) Site plans are being drawn by the Jewish Agency for its temporary wood structures. Site plans are being made by the N.P.O. for dwellings of masonry construction intended for permanency.

Site development is being studied from inadequate surveys. Full utilities for either temporary or permanent sites are not being considered. Latrines are provided some distance from the dwelling sites. Space is left for community facilities to be provided under tents. (See Typical Plot Plan for Tempos by Jewish Agency). Photostat 7.

CAMPS: The camps, in spite of their complete undesirability, cannot be liquidated because economic planning and construction cannot keep pace at present with the steady flow of newcomers being added to the already existing backlog. Camps should therefore be improved and, if any temporary houses or accommodations must be built, they should be placed in these camps.

Recommended:

That tents be dispensed with entirely and that strictly temporary screened barracks be built in their stead.

That screen-enclosed bathing and toilet facilities be installed in place of the present insanitary facilities prevalent in camps.

That strict discipline be enforced for the maintenance of sanitary conditions. Flies and vermin must be exterminated.

That the personal belongings of refugees be stored in storage lofts in order to free the space available for living.

That the refugees themselves be employed in the building of new temporary space and the maintenance of such space against insanitation.

That new camps, if absolutely necessary, should not be built on sites intended for permanent developments. New camps, however, should be built close to possible employment and recreation.

Open latrines, fly density, uncleanable floor surfaces, unbathed people and sardine arrangement of beds are existing conditions seen in the present camps.

The refugees do not like to part with their personal belongings, consequently the already limited quarters for sleeping are cluttered with bags, trunks, bundles, etc.

People walk about aimlessly with nothing to do for the entire day. Some managers have shown imagination enough to devise some means of employment for pay or work in the fields, but a general policy of refugee employment is absent.

That olim be educated on the characteristics and work opportunities of the various locations of Israel being planned for permanent settlement.

That camp sites be progressively liquidated.

TEMPOS

Recommended:

That the present extensive program for the building of temporary structures be abandoned in favor of a program for improving camps and the building of permanent houses. (See map C for present camp sites.)

That sites approved or under consideration for "Tempos" (see map A) be abandoned in favor of permanent settlements projected by the National Planning Office.

The allocation of IL.3,605,000 to be spent over a period of a year starting from May, 1949 for 20,000 wood temporary shelters by the Jewish Agency could be used more effectively to improve the camps for only a portion of that sum, and use the remainder for the erection of permanent structures on permanent sites. (See page 12)

The cost of the J.A. 16 square meter unit - IL.181.0 - is about 75% of the cost of permanent construction. (See page 13)

Much needed improved space could be provided in camps for less money per sq. meter since water and other improvements are unnecessary.

PERMANENT HOUSING

Recommended:

That complete site plans be designed at the outset for the economic completion of all facilities in the future.

That road construction, except where it is indispensable for construction purposes and access to community facilities, may be deferred.

Recommended Procedure:

| | | |
|---|---|---|
| Shelter: (1st stage) | walls - masonry bearing walls-silica brick or concrete block on concrete foundation. | Refugee labor should be used for this construction. A few experienced superintendents can teach inexperienced workers to lay blocks or bricks. Blocks machined for dry construction would require the minimum of supervision. |
| | floor - concrete slab | Experienced labor will be required for the pouring of slabs, foundations, roof framing and plumbing installation. |
| | roof - wood rafters and nailers, and roofing of either concrete tile or corrugated asbestos. | Wood structural members should be eliminated in future construction as the manufacture of precast concrete beams is developed. See suggestions under CONCRETE CONSTRUCTION. |
| | Door & window openings - canvas coverings | |
| | Partitions - only enclosing bathroom | |
| | Bathroom - shower (or tub) w.c. and lavatory | |
| | Kitchen - work top with built-in sink | |
| Completion: (2nd stage) | Fur masonry walls on the interior with board or sheet material. | As far as possible, completion of the house should be done by refugee labor. |
| | Install windows and doors | |
| | Install full partitions | |
| | Install electricity for lighting and possibly for cooking. | |

Recommended:

That Purchasing Centers shall be established especially for the purpose of providing finishing materials and equipment - lumber, sheet material, doors, windows, hardware and tools - for the use of refugees in completing their own houses.

## CONCRETE CONSTRUCTION

Recommended:

That concurrent with both 1. Frame and 2. Masonry construction, techniques of construction in concrete be designed and tested in an effort to derive the most economical construction methods and the wider use of materials found in Israel to take the place of imported material now necessary.

The potentialities of advanced design in concrete is evident in the new systems of forming, stripping and curing by use of vacuum and boiling. In the vacuum system, the same equipment used for applying vacuum to the forms is also being employed for the lifting of castings, which simplifies the handling of large castings and provides greater possibilities in concrete design.

Concrete products, such as precast lumber for posts, beams, arches, trusses, roofing, planks, flooring, wall panels (of nailing and non-nailing type) should be developed. Insulating light-weight concrete blocks laid with or without mortar, now available in the U.S. should be studied for manufacture in Israel.

In France, Belgium, Switzerland and South America, where concrete has been used extensively for buildings and bridges, concrete is asserting itself as a material of beauty born of necessity and economy.

That the U.S. Housing Committee for Israel undertake or sponsor a project to erect an experimental enclosing concrete shell structure directly applicable to the present building needs of Israel. That such outstanding concrete engineers as Carl Billner and Severud be retained to work with a U.S. contractor and a U.S. architect together with a chosen architect and contractor from Israel on the design development and erection of such a structure.

In Israel, excellent work is performed in concrete finishing, making worktop slabs, floor tile, hand rails, and terrazzo work. Because forms are expensive, structural concrete work is done roughly, and is covered with cement plaster. Skeleton forms of exposed concrete - a logical perfection in the use of concrete - are not seen in Israel.

That Technion of Haifa be given funds and equipment to continue their present investigation of the potentialities of concrete products and concrete methods for Israel.

Technion (Haifa) lacks space, funds and equipment.

## SUGGESTED CONCRETE SHELL FORMS

The following pages of diagrams (photostats 1-6) suggest a system of shell construction which is believed to be immediately applicable to building needs of Israel. The parabolic shaped shell form is based on the integration of roof and wall as a single unit. Each shell is composed of segments fitted and tied together to form an enclosure of required length and about twelve feet wide. Enough segments are cast on the house floor slab to complete the shell of the house.

It is assumed that the mixing of concrete is done by hand and the erection of the structure is done by the use of a windlass. Six ordinary laborers can, after being given proper instruction, set the vacuum forms, mix and place the concrete and apply the vacuum for one complete structure in one day. The vacuum forms can be released five minutes after the concrete is in place. With proper scheduling, the same form can be reused every 20 minutes. There are 17 to 20 segments to one complete shell, therefore all these segments can be made by six men in one working day.

Erection - Two men can erect 20 segments in one working day. The attached estimate of cost (page 11) is based on costs in the United States with assumed costs in Israel noted.

Since the machinery can be used for the production of 3 houses per day, three sets of forms should be required. It is calculated that the forms and machinery are good for 10,000 houses. This segmental method of construction was suggested by Mr. Carl Biliner of Vacuum Concrete after reviewing the concrete shell ideas developed by the Committee. Also see newspaper article by Leo Kaufmann, Director of Shikun and Amidar, who explained the concrete shell idea of the Committee, and developed a thesis on its feasibility.

---

A comparative estimate made on casting the segments at a central plant to be transported to the site and segments cast on the house slabs at the site using smaller machinery shows the latter method to be more economical. The factory shed, and the cost of larger mixers, trailers, trucks, pumps, forms, lifters, straight edges, vibrators, etc., calls for an investment of $370,000. It would also require more experienced men. At that rate it would require a single operation of 4,000 houses to reduce the cost of forms to $100 - per house. Very few developments are contemplated of this size and in addition such an operation would involve the building of roads not contemplated in the first stage of construction.

# Ruins of Time

## A Sense of History

The ruins scattered around Israel and Palestine are a mute testimony not only to violence along their terrain, but also to below-grade attacks on the region's historical narrative. Revered by Jews and Arabs alike, archaeological relics are considered forensic metonymies of national disasters and conquests, as well as theological allegories of wrath, annihilation, and redemption. The material possession of ruins—the victor's trophy—is always an ostensible license to produce "a sense of history" and stimulate the collective memory with partial objects and fragments from past adventures.

In the newborn State of Israel, the impetus to dig, to unearth the biblical geography and authenticate the formative story of national Return, had a particular urgency and demanded special resources. Archaeology became a coordinated and supervised State project well before more vital infrastructural ventures took off. The numerous excavation sites across the country — those, for instance, in Masada, Hatzor, Megiddo (Armageddon), Sha'arayim, or Capernaum—were often orchestrated by retired generals, with the support of the army. This bolstered the epic dimension of heroism and sacrifice, as may be learned from the words of the retired chief of staff and archaeology professor Yigael Yadin, who was in charge of the excavations:

> The scientific significance of the Masada excavations is great; however for all of us—for the archaeologists and non-archaeologists among us—Masada is first and foremost a symbol, a memorial of the martyrs of the nation, the heroes who chose death over a life of slavery and bondage of body and spirit.[1]

If recruited archaeologists and scholarly generals took command of the symbolic and the imaginary, state architects were commissioned to lay out the real, embedding the scattered digs and ruins in a network of intertwined cultural and natural landscapes which would define the overall national pastime.

In a lecture broadcast on the Kol Israel radio station on August 2, 1949, architect Arieh Sharon, head of the State Planning Department, spoke of the didactic value of the ruins and of his intention to interlace in the future national master plan a "network of protected heritage monuments and national parks, and to combine the historic places [...] with forestation acts, paths and routes for hikers and tourists."[2] Sharon detailed the findings of the research that his team, with the cooperation of the Archaeology Department of the Hebrew University, had carried out concerning the archaeological and historical sites in Israel and declared that emphasis had been given to "holy places of the Jews, Christians, and Muslims with special concern toward the religious sentiments of the three world religions."[3]

③

④

①–② Tour by the Israel Exploration Society through ruins in the ancient city of Shivta, 1953. David B. Keidan Collection, Central Zionist Archives.
③ Yehiam fortress before its restoration by the National Parks Authority, early 1960s.
④ Holiday resort, Achziv National Park, early 1970s.

⑤ 

 ⑥

In October 1955, the Israeli government established the Authority of National Gardens, whose aim was to preserve and cultivate sites of historical heritage and those of singular natural beauty. The initiatives and actions of this Authority channeled state resources toward the development of recreational landscapes that would create a new bond between the people, the terrain, and the official narrative of homecoming. In 1963, the National Gardens Law was confirmed by the parliament; it mandated the Authority to allocate sites for national gardens. Forty-eight sites were selected which diachronically unfurled the history of Israel—from the time of Joshua ben Nun to the Kingdom of Judah and Israel, through the Roman conquests and the Great Revolt, to the Mishnah, the Talmud, and the Islamic conquests. The excavation sites provided vertical shortcuts in the frantic quest for biblical depth and allowed for the removal of the upper layers of "rubble," centuries of erasable history.

The State's special interest in patently Jewish ruins, and as such in material evidence of Jewish victimization, did not necessarily entail archaeological neglect of other cultures as long as these did not complicate the official narrative. Thus, digging and research also took place at Nabatean sites (Avdat and Shivta among them), Roman sites (Bet She'an), and Byzantine and Crusader sites (Acre, Caesarea). Sites encrypting the closer Arab history, such as Lydda, Ramle, Jaffa and Tiberias, were not excavated and preserved. Even sites with palpable Christian hallmarks were often endowed with a Hebrew record. About Caesarea, for instance, the archaeologist Dan Tanai claimed that "during antiquity it had been mostly a Hebrew city with a Jewish majority, a city of rabbis and geniuses. There began the rebellion against the Romans. The question before us is how to present a historical truth on the site where physically only Roman and Crusader ruins remained."[4] Politically sensitive sites, such as the one designated for the parliament in Jerusalem on the confiscated lands of the Arab village Sheikh Badr, required archaeological affirmation, even if it was somewhat speculative. In a 1955 statement to the press about the decision concerning the location of the future parliament, Joseph Sprinzak, chairman of the parliament, remarked that the designated site had been a Jewish settlement toward the end of the Second Temple Period, and that graves and caves from the Sanhedrin Period were found nearby. More recent ruins of war were not mentioned in the chairman's statement.[5]

The political boundaries outlined in the cease-fire agreements following the War of 1948 did not enable the Israeli archaeologists to excavate in major sites of prime national and religious significance such as Jerusalem and Bethlehem. As compensation for the loss of control over the Old City of Jerusalem and the inaccessibility of the Western Wall—the ultimate ruin—a miniature "historic city" was built in 1963 at the estate of the Holy Land Hotel in Jerusalem, reconstructing Jerusalem at the peak of its splendor, at the end of the Second Temple Period. This miniature, built under the supervision of Professor Michael Avi-Yonah of the Hebrew University, became a site of pilgrimage, exposing the Israeli public to the monumental building style of Herod and stirring yearnings for glorious Jerusalem. Just four years after its completion, however, the mock-up city became redundant with the conquest of the Old City of Jerusalem by the Israeli army during the 1967 War and the ensuing excavations on Temple Mount.

Yet another proxy object was the Shrine of the Book (see chapter "The National Museum and The Shrine of the Book"), designed by Frederick Kiesler and

⑦

⑧

⑨

(10)

Armand Bartos to contain the Dead Sea Scrolls, indisputably the most important archaeological discovery in Israel. The Shrine, which was eventually located in the gardens of the Israel Museum, was deliberately designed as a relic from the future, an ambiguous vessel with a gleaming shell and curvilinear shape, reminiscent of cultic structures and alluding to the actual clay urns which housed the scrolls. According to Kiesler, the intention had been to create a structure that would signify the historical depth of the Jewish people and the energetic rebirth of the State of Israel following the wars of "sons of light" (represented by the white dome) and "sons of darkness" (represented by a freestanding black wall). Upon the Shrine of the Book's completion in 1965, it became one of the most popular icons of Jerusalem, and the black wall functioned symbolically, at least until 1967, as the dark monument of the city's actual and spectral ruins.

With the Israeli conquest of the Old City of Jerusalem in 1967, the "Western Wall," believed to be the ancient retaining wall of the ruined Temple, became the national totem and the site of mass religious gatherings. Immediately after the fighting ended, volunteer contractors, backed up by military troops, bulldozed the neighborhood blocking the view to the Wall in a hasty operation, turning a 3.6-meter alley into a piazza of 20,000 square meters intended to contain the hundreds of thousands of pilgrims who were destined to journey to the Wall for Pentecost.

The newly cleared and sanctified space prompted design proposals, and a number of local and international architects submitted their visions for the site. In 1972, just a few years after his avant-garde Habitat in Montreal, Moshe Safdie suggested excavating the base of the Wall in order to expose the Herodian foundation of the structure, and in so doing raising the Wall another 9 meters. A square was to be built in front of the Wall with terraces surrounding it to create a colossal amphitheater encircled by buildings of the religious establishment such as the High Rabbinical Court and the Porat Yosef Yeshiva, as well as an unspecified national secular building.[6]

Safdie's plan was not carried out, and to this day the Wall area remains a brutal mise-en-scène of quasi-theological and political eccentricity. The Jewish Quarter of the Old City, however, underwent extensive rehabilitation and soon became an international showcase of architectural preservation in the context of historical complexity and contradiction. The rather masterly mix-up of procedures of conservation, restoration, adaptive reuse, and new masonry construction in the Jewish Quarter may not measure up to current preservationist standards, but in the late 1960s and early 1970s it opened up—for the first time in Israel on such a scale and with such intricacy—a Pandora's box of historicist adaptation, interpretation, and manipulation. As such, it may be construed in retrospect as a requiem for the modernist phase of the Israeli project and as a marker of the "redemptive" postmodernism that would plague local architectural production henceforth. ■

1 Yigael Yadin, *Masada* [in Hebrew] (Tel Aviv: Maariv Library and Shikmona, 1962).
2 Arieh Sharon, "Archaeology and Planning," radio lecture, Kol Israel [in Hebrew], August 2, 1949.
3 Ibid.
4 Dan Tanai, "Symposium about Caesarea," *Architecture* 2 [in Hebrew] (August 1971).
5 Palestinian ruins that remained partially intact were often preserved as memorials for victors, especially on battle sites, as was the case in the Kastel village. Most of the remains of Palestinian daily life were removed. Entire villages were erased or covered by national parks and extensive forestation. Large stone buildings, including mosques, were adapted and reused as service or storage facilities. See Walid Khalidi, ed., *All That Remains: The Palestinian Villages Occupied and Depopulated by Israel in 1948* (Washington, DC: Institute for Palestine Studies, 1992); Meron Benvenisti, *Sacred Landscape: The Buried History of the Holy Land since 1948* (Berkeley: University of California Press, 2000).
6 "The Design of the Western Wall Plaza and Its Surroundings," in David Cassuto, ed., *The Western Wall: Essays Regarding the Design of Its Plaza* [in Hebrew] (Heb. AAAI), pp. 69–70.

(5) Masada fortress, 1972. Photographer: Yitzhak Amit. Judaica Collection, Harvard Library.
(6) Herodion, 1980. Photographer: Yitzhak Amit. Judaica Collection, Harvard Library.
(7) Excavations in the Old City of Jerusalem, 1970. Photographer: Yehuda Eisenstark. Israel State Archives.
(8) Excavations at the foundation walls of Temple Mount, the Old City of Jerusalem, 1968. Photographer: Yehuda Eisenstark. Israel State Archives.
(9) Excavations at the foundation of Robinson's Arch, connecting the upper town of ancient Jerusalem with Temple Mount, 1969. Photographer: Moshe Milner. Government Press Office.
(10)–(11) Western Wall Plaza, 1972–1975. Model. Moshe Safdie.

# DOSSIER: MOSHE DAYAN'S ARCHAEOLOGICAL FETISH

⑫

⑬

⑭

⑫ Moshe Dayan and his collection of antiquities, 1969. Digital image of photograph by Giora Shalmi/Israel Sun Ltd., from the Judaica Collection of the Harvard Library, Harvard University.
⑬ Moshe Dayan in his backyard, 1968. AP.
⑭ Moshe Dayan and his collection of antiquities, 1969. Digital image of photograph by Giora Shalmi/Israel Sun Ltd., from the Judaica Collection of the Harvard Library, Harvard University.

The blurred boundaries between military protocol and civilian propriety, as well as the circumstantial confusion between recent war ruins and historical relics, during Israel's formative decades are best illustrated by the looting and collecting hobbies of Moshe Dayan. Dayan was a bohemian soldier of mythic proportions (chief of staff of the armed forces from 1953 to 1958 and minister of defense in 1967) who accumulated archaeological artifacts and displayed them as trophies in his domestic antiquarium. Dayan's archaeological disorder is described and diagnosed by the archaeologist and scholar Raz Kletter in his essay "A Very General Archaeologist: Moshe Dayan and Israeli Archaeology":

> During three decades between 1951–1981, Dayan established a vast collection of antiquities acquired through illicit excavations; as well as bought, exchanged and sold antiquities in Israel and abroad. [...] In his footsteps, Dayan left a huge legacy of gossip, anecdotes and rumors, and it is often difficult to separate these from facts. Even certain facts were deemed for many years to be too embarrassing to expose publicly. [...]
>
> At first, Dayan was helped by family members, but soon he became involved with amateur and professional robbers, dealers and smugglers. I have documented 35 sites where evidence of robbing and illegal digging by Dayan exists. No doubt, this is only the tip of the iceberg, but it testifies to the scale and temper of his activities. The distribution of sites fits his arena of activities, first in the south when he commanded the southern front, then in [the] whole [of] Israel until 1967, later extending to the Occupied Territories. [...]
>
> Probably most of Dayan's looting was done in areas conquered after 1967 and under his own military rule. There he faced no democratic institutions to oppose him. For exactly this reason, we know very little about his deeds in the West Bank and Gaza after 1967. [...]
>
> Apart from looting antiquities on his own, or with army comrades, professional robbers or personal friends, Dayan also received and gave antiquities. In many cases the lines between gift, acquisition or looting [are] blurred. During earlier years of his "hobby," Dayan received considerable help from army comrades and friends. This was an improvised net based on personal ties and appreciation or sometimes on dependency of lower ranks on their commander. Dayan also used personnel and equipment of the army for his private hobby. [...]
>
> Dayan turned his Zahala [in northern Tel Aviv] house into an archaeological garden. At first, the collection was a source of joy, but it gradually became an obsession. Pictures of the garden were published, e.g., "In the family circle, [in] uniform and in a civilian [dress]"—Dayan holding an ancient bowl. Another photo states that "archaeology requires not only patience, but also wisdom-of-hands," showing Dayan restoring a clay jar. In fact, museum workers had to re-treat many objects, because Dayan's restorations were not good. [...]
>
> Dayan was eclectic in his collection. What allured him was the "hunting," the sense of danger and excitement, the pride in doing it himself and the desire to possess.[1] ■

1 Raz Kletter, "A Very General Archaeologist: Moshe Dayan and Israeli Archaeology," *The Journal of Hebrew Scriptures* 4: Article 5 (2003), http://www.jhsonline.org/Articles/article_27.pdf. See also Tallay Ornan, *A Man and His Land: Highlights from the Moshe Dayan Collection* [in Hebrew and English] (Jerusalem: Israel Museum, 1986).

# Forests

## "Facing the Forests"[1]

A short paragraph in the 1950 national master plan casually mentions the most extensive geographic operation of the Zionist movement before and especially after Israeli Statehood:

> The National Plan provides for afforestation areas on the mountains and hill slopes which are at present desolate on account of neglect and soil erosion for many generations.[1]

This prosaic launch of a countrywide afforestation campaign, encompassing practically all territory not designated for agricultural use or construction, is but another formality in an already thoroughly designed and ideologized land occupation and transformation project entering its phase of uninhibited acceleration. In a 1949 meeting with "Father of Forests" (head of the Jewish National Fund) Yosef Weitz, Prime Minister Ben-Gurion urged him to increase the quota of tree plantings from a million a year to a hundred million a year, arguing that before the war, the Jewish community had dedicated its resources and efforts mostly to colonizing the land and establishing a State, and now, with sovereignty attained, it was time to commit to the eradication of the wilderness. Forestry was the most effective means to achieve this.

Ben-Gurion's phantasmagoria was never fully accomplished, but it is still under way, as can be gathered from the numbers provided on the official website of Keren Kayemeth LeIsrael – Jewish National Fund (KKL–JNF), as well as its general tenor:

> KKL plants and maintains over 240 million saplings and manages more than 100 thousand acres of natural woodland. Israel is the only country that entered the 21st century with a net gain in its number of trees.[2]

The Jewish National Fund, founded by the World Zionist Organization in 1901 during the Fifth Zionist Congress in Basel as its land-acquisition agent in Ottoman Palestine, proved to be one of the most consistent and effective infrastructural forces during Israel's formative decades. All told, it developed over 250,000 acres of land, built 180 dams and reservoirs, created over 1,000 parks, and assisted in the formation of hundreds of rural settlements. As such, it was also—and still is—the cover-up outfit for the ongoing Jewification of the land and the corresponding active erasure of the traces of indigenous Palestinian architecture and agriculture.

According to the JNF website, "in light of Statehood [...] and the growing need to prepare infrastructure for urban and agricultural settlement," its board of directors rephrased its mission statement and decided to take a greater role in the national effort. The JNF became the largest employer in the country, and remained so throughout the 1950s.

> Thousands of immigrants were employed in land development and afforestation at the time, "relief work" that made it possible to prepare land for settlement and provide newcomers with an initial livelihood. It was the belief of the Head Office that such work would bond new immigrants to the land, training them in farming for the establishment of rural communities.
>
> Weitz, who had hit upon this response to the twin challenges of immigrant employment and making the land bloom, dubbed the period "the blossoming of the wilderness," and promoted the establishment of "labor villages" which subsequently became moshavim [collective villages].[3]

The official narrative above does not account at all for the hundreds of destroyed Palestinian villages and the countless orchards and agricultural terraces subjected to monoculture (mostly pine) afforestation by the JNF. There is no mention of the fact that the Jewish National Fund joined forces with other environmentally minded organizations—such as the Israel Land Authority, the Israel Nature and Parks Authority, the Agriculture Department and the Land Settlement Department of the Jewish Agency, the Ministry of Agriculture, kibbutz archives, the Government Names Committee, and the Survey of Israel—in activating what Noga Kadman, who has studied the depopulated Palestinian villages of 1948, defines as "institutionalized ignorance" and "manufactured oblivion." The actual erasure of the villages, according to Kadman, was followed by a procedure of cognitive erasure whereby the remains of the villages were removed from official maps, documents, and histories. She writes:

> Failure to name places is tantamount to a deliberate act of disregard, which sentences these places to oblivion. Places without names do not latch onto the consciousness of people living nearby, traveling through them, or passing by them.[4]

In her essay "On Forests as Commemorative Sites," landscape theorist Sigal Barnir clarifies the obsessive afforestation campaign of the JNF as an ongoing performance of actual and symbolic appropriation:

> The Jewish National Fund forests cover the landscape's contour, the surface of the land. From the north to the south, from east to west, from the mountain to the desert, a mask of vegetation has been planted, forests consisting solely of pine trees hide the natural diversity of the landscape—a million square meters of planted forest, the work of the Zionist enterprise, a result of the "conquering of the desert" and the "redemption of the land" effort. [...] The tree has become the corner stone in building the Zionist narrative after the founding of the State.[5]

Barnir elaborates on the double function of the JNF forests in simultaneously manufacturing national oblivion and nationalist pathos: practically all the newly planted forests functioned as memorial sites—honoring individuals and communities, victims of the Holocaust and the fallen in Israel's wars—while also covering, "naturalizing," or "antiquating" the war ruins on their premises:

> Today, forests cover dozens of Palestinian villages, so much so that it appears to anyone walking through them that these are ancient and anonymous ruins, romantic objects that had undergone natural processes of erosion and disintegration. The village, having no commemoration rites of its own, disappeared from the landscape and its memory remains enigmatic.[6]

While physically obliterating or pictorially fetishizing the remains of the Palestinian villages—suppressing the memory of the *Nakba* altogether—the JNF forests established, according to Barnir, a martyr rite uniquely Israeli (with the exception of the German post–World War I *Heldenhain*, or Heroes' Forest). Indeed, the rite of passage of the new Jew:

> Commemorative forests had the pragmatic meaning of glorification and strengthening of national identity. It was then that the characteristics of the new Jew, the "Israeli," were molded, and commemorative forests had become a vehicle to sublimate fears of the wilderness [...] and at the same time, to repress Jewish-Diasporic traits.[7]

In the context of Zionism's epic communion of man and landscape—as engraved in the Israeli collective sense by the words of Shaul Tchernichovsky, the foremost Zionist poet of nature, "Man is nothing but the soil of a small country/ Nothing but the shape of his native landscape"[8]—the JNF's writing of the forests only marks the returning haunt of the Jewish and the Palestinian Diaspora. ■

1 Arieh Sharon, "Outline of the National Plan," English abstract attached to the Hebrew publication *Physical Planning in Israel* (Jerusalem: Government Printing Press and Survey of Israel Press, 1951), p. 6.

2 "KKL-JNF: For a Sustainable Future for Israel," Keren Kayemeth LeIsrael – Jewish National Fund, accessed June 6, 2017, http://www.kkl-jnf.org/about-kkl-jnf/kkl-jnf-id/goals-actions/.

3 "Fifth Decade: 1941–1950," Keren Kayemeth LeIsrael – Jewish National Fund, accessed June 6, 2017, http://www.kkl-jnf.org/about-kkl-jnf/our-history/fifth-decade-1941-1950/.

4 Noga Kadman, *Erased from Space and Consciousness: Israel and the Depopulated Palestinian Villages of 1948* (Bloomington: Indiana University Press, 2015), p. 111.

5 Sigal Barnir, "On Forests as Commemorative Sites," in *Borderline Disorder*, ed. Zvi Efrat, catalogue of the Israeli pavilion, 8th International Architecture Biennale in Venice, 2002, p. 134.

6 Ibid.

7 Ibid.

8 Shaul Tchernichovsky, "Man Is Nothing But" [in Hebrew], partially translated in Adam Zachary Newton, *The Elsewhere: On Belonging at a Near Distance; Reading Literary Memoir from Europe and the Levant* (Madison: University of Wisconsin Press, 2005), p. 73.

① Tree-planting ceremony of Ya'ar HaKdoshim (Holocaust Memorial Forest), Kisalon, 1955. Photographer: Avraham Malevsky. Jewish National Fund Archive.
② Detail.

②

③

④

PLAN OF THE BNAI BRITH MEMORIAL CENTER
IN THE MARTYRS FOREST

5

6

KEREN KAYEMETH LEISRAEL
קרן קימת לישראל
"וכי תבואו אל הארץ ונטעתם כל עץ"
"QUAND VOUS SERES ENTRES DANS LE PAYS AT QUE
VOUS Y AUREZ PLANTE TOUTES SORTES D'ARBRES"...
"AND WHEN YOU COME INTO THE LAND
YOU SHALL PLANT ALL MANNERS OF TREES"...
PLANTEZ UN ARBRE EN ISRAEL DE VOS PROPRES MAINS
PLANTEZ UN ARBRE POUR CHAQUE MEMBRE DE VOTRE FAMILLE
PLANTEZ UN ARBRE POUR VOS AMIS
PLANT A TREE IN ISRAEL WITH YOUR OWN HANDS
PLANT A TREE FOR EACH MEMBER OF YOUR FAMILY
PLANT A TREE FOR YOUR FRIENDS AT HOME
IN THE JEWISH NATIONAL FUND · BIRIYA FOREST – NEAR SAFAD · ISRAEL

7

⑧

③ Tree-planting ceremony in memory of the fallen soldiers of the Sinai Campaign, Memorial Day, May 1958. Photographer: David Gurfinkel. Government Press Office.
④ Plan of the "B'nai B'rith Commemoration Cave," posted on a sign in Ya'ar HaKdoshim, Kisalon, 1958.
⑤ Hoisting the flag in a tree-planting ceremony in memory of the fallen soldiers of the Sinai Campaign, Arbor Day, Bab El Wad, February 1949. Photographer: David Eldan. Government Press Office.
⑥ Biriya forest, 1962. Photographer: Fred Chesnick. Jewish National Fund Archive.
⑦ Tree-planting ceremony in honor of the fallen soldiers of the Egoz Military Unit, Golan Heights, 1977. Art event by Yitzhak Danziger.
⑧ Forestation in the Galilee, 1964. Photographer: David Hirschfeld. Jewish National Fund Archive.
⑨ Land reclamation for forestation in the Negev, 1961. Jewish National Fund Archive.
⑩ The newly planted Angels' Forest, Kiryat Gat. Jewish National Fund Archive.
⑪ Land reclamation for forestation, 1953. Jewish National Fund Archive.
⑫ Forestation at Biriya, 1953. Jewish National Fund Archive.

⑨

⑩

⑪

⑫

⑬ Pages from Forest and Forestation in Israel by Yosef Weitz, 1970.

54. אלונים בחורש טבעי שדולל בשנת 1955/56, צילום 1967

55. אורן ירושלים זריעים משנת 1926, צילום 1967

56. אורן הגלעין זריעים משנת 1926, צילו

# Desert

## Scene of Origin

> *If you look at the map you will see that the South contains many empty places, and nothing causes me so great a horror as this emptiness—not because nature cannot withstand emptiness, but because people cannot stand it and politics cannot withstand emptiness.*
> David Ben-Gurion[1]

The following excerpts from David Ben-Gurion's statements and writings about the wilderness document not only his illustrious horror vacui, but the way in which this mesmerizing rhetorician constructed the desert as the originary scene of the people of Israel and the site of redemption of modern Israel. Swaying between doomsday prophecies and futuristic visions, and employing reciprocally biblical hermeneutics, psycho-historical arguments, strategic analyses, pseudo-ecological observations, anthropological fabrications, scientific bravado, and patriotic fervor, Ben-Gurion invented simultaneously the Israeli project and the Israeli persona—a crossbreed of the savvy Bedouin and the Diasporic Jew.

①

*In the South and the Negev stood the cradle of our people; they are the country's weak points and danger zones; they are also its greatest hope. [...]*

*It is obvious why the forefathers of our nation went to the Negev: this was the most sparsely settled and populated part of the country, as it is in our own days. [...]*

*Then, as now, the Negev was the great empty space of Israel. Since the feet of the Patriarchs trod there, many changes and transformations have passed over it, and its ruined cities are evidence of the efforts of generations [...].*

*The small State of Israel [...] cannot long tolerate within its bounds a desert which takes up over half its territory. If the State does not eradicate the desert, the desert may well eradicate the State. [...]*

②

*The Southern half of the country remained desolate, as it had been for centuries, ever since the Arab conquest. Neither the Turks nor the British attempted to make this desert flourish, for they had no need to do so, and the Negev continued to lie under the curse of the prophet Jeremiah: "The cities of the Negev shall be closed up—and none shall open them." From the time when the Chamberlain Government's White Paper was issued in 1939, the Jews were forbidden to obtain a foothold in the Negev and the greater part of the South.*

*It is absolutely vital for the State of Israel, for both economic and security reasons, to move southwards: to direct the country's water and rain, the young pioneers and the new immigrants, and most of the resources of the Development Budget, to the South; to uproot a considerable proportion of our workshops and factories and transfer them to the South; to move a number of our scientific and research institutions [...] to the South. We must concentrate the attention of Israel's scientists and research workers on the investigation of the forces, whether known or latent, with whose assistance we shall be able to make the lands of the South and the Negev thrive and flourish.*

*Without the settlement of the South and the Negev this country cannot be secure, and we shall not succeed in attaining economic independence. They cannot be settled without the transformation of the facts of Nature, which is not beyond the capacity of science in our day or the pioneering energy of our youth. Science and pioneering will enable us to perform this miracle. [...]*

*Now, in the very hour when we have gained free and sovereign control over all the lands and resources of the State, we have come face to face with the greatest difficulty: the curse of nature and the fate of barrenness and desolation which has held the greater part of our soil in its grip ever since Creation. [...]*

*[...] The irrigation of the desert with purified sea water will appear a dream to many, but less than any other country should Israel be afraid of "dreams," which are capable of transforming the natural order by the power of vision, science and pioneering capacity. All that has been accomplished in this country is the result of "dreams" that have been made to come true by virtue of vision, science and pioneering capacity. [...]*[2]

*We need men of the desert who will know it in all its secrets and will lead us in transforming the wasteland into a blessing, a place in which to work and live. Unless we conquer both the sea and the desert by creating Jewish sailors and even Jewish Bedouin tribes—we cannot succeed in the tasks of immigration and resettlement that we must shoulder after the war. [...] The deserts of Israel were once inhabited in ancient times and even today are not entirely unpopulated. A beginning toward reclamation should be made by Jewish desert-dwellers, Bedouins, who will know how to live and work in tents and will be able to support themselves like the Arab, but who along with possessing primitive Bedouin skills will also be familiar with modern cultural, scientific, and technical knowledge. This combination will enable them to find a way of making the wilderness bloom and making the desert into a place of settled habitation.*[3]

(3)

④

1 Minutes of Israeli Government Session #12, May 3, 1949 (Israel State Archives).
2 David Ben-Gurion, "Southwards" (1956), in *Like Stars and Dust: Essays from Israel's Government Year Book* (Sde-Boker Campus: Ben-Gurion University of the Negev, Ben-Gurion Heritage Institute, 1997), pp. 174–187.
3 David Ben-Gurion, "The Imperatives of the Jewish Revolution" (1944), in *The Zionist Idea*, ed. Arthur Hertzberg (Philadelphia: Jewish Publication Society, 1997), p. 209.

① Eilat Bay, 1950s. Photographer: Ami Erev.
② Judean Desert around Jericho. Palestine Information Office (PIO) collection, Israel State Archives.
③ Sinai Desert, 1968. Photographer: Ami Erev.
④ Hike in the Negev, 1950s. Photographer: Ami Erev.

1

Bien qu'Israël compte de très no
artistes (une ancienne cité, Safed, leur a
été réservée), on n'y voit guère d'exem
synthèse des arts et l'architecture ne f
appel aux autres arts plastiques.

Par contre, une expérience insolite e
taculaire vient d'être entreprise : une
tion de sculptures au cœur du dés
Neguev, dans une petite cité en voie d
loppement, Mitze Ramone, à 200 km
Aviv. Il ne s'agit pas de synthèse de
mais bien d'une intégration d'œuvre
dans un paysage, renouant ainsi av
très ancienne tradition et créant u
d'attraction dans une région sauvage
de laquelle se dressent maintenant de
gnes » de la présence humaine.

Cette initiative est due, à l'origine, au
teur israélien Kosso qui, après avoir p
à des congrès internationaux en Autrich
Yougoslavie, suggéra d'organiser une m
tation analogue en Israël.

Neuf sculpteurs étrangers furent invit
un séjour de deux mois au cours du
devaient créer une œuvre en utilisant l
extraite sur place, œuvres qui, bien e
resteraient dans le site. Sur les neuf
étrangers l'Italien San Gregorio et l

# SCULPTURES DANS LE DÉSERT

3

**1. Vue d'ensemble des sculptures dans le
premier plan, l'œuvre d'Augustin Carde
celle de Kosso. Au fond, à gauche, celle
Mizui. 2. Augustin Cardenas. 3. Sternsch
5. Kosso. 6. Yasmo Mizui. 7. Mme Kyoko**

⑤

5

6

7

furent obligés de retourner dans leurs
out de quelques jours. Les sept autres
ovisèrent en plein désert étaient :
pon), Cardenas (Cuba), Prantl (Autri-
ss (Suisse), Lenassi (Yougoslavie),
(Belgique) et l'Américaine Diska, aux-
taient joints trois sculpteurs israé-
sso (qui créa deux œuvres), Feigin et
ss. Mme Mizui qui, venue simple-
mpagner son mari, réalisa, elle aussi,
e.

ence est curieuse et d'un intérêt cer-
hissante pour Israël, elle ne l'est pas
r les artistes qui ont pu ici se me-
une tâche des plus difficiles : s'im-
s un espace infini. L'idée ne manque
andeur.

stes ont-ils réussi ? Sauf le Belge
qui a coulé en béton armé une sorte
de 9 m de haut, les autres sont
siblement à l'échelle humaine. Tous
our l'abstraction et pour une certaine
rchaïsme qui s'insère bien dans le
-être aurait-on souhaité une moins
persion des œuvres dans le paysage,
ntative d'un groupement spatial plus
e quelle l'expérience pourrait être
reprise aussi bien en Israël qu'ail-

⑥

⑦

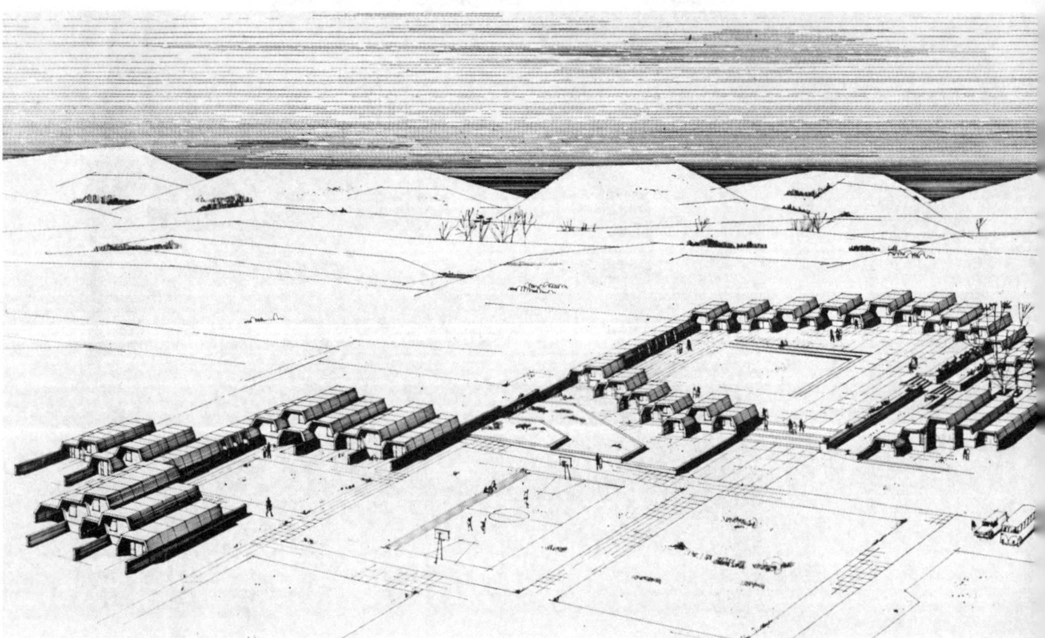

⑧

⑨

⑤ “Sculptures dans le désert,” spread from *L’Architecture d’Aujourd’hui* 106 (February 1963).
⑥ Visitors’ Center, the archaeological site of Ein Avdat, Negev, 1962. Nahum Zolotov.
⑦ Hatzeva field school, perspective drawing, 1968. Israel Goodovitch.
⑧ Climate-controlled elementary school with wind-catching chimneys, Eilat, 1968. Theodore Kisselov.

⑩

⑪ ⑫

⑬

⑨ Neptun Hotel, Eilat, 1969. Theodore Kisselov
⑩ Dead Sea Youth Hostel, Neve Zohar, early 1960s. Shmuel Mestechkin.
⑪ Field school, Ein Gedi, 1962. Rooftops. Nahum Zolotov.
⑫ Field school, Ein Gedi, 1962. Detail. Nahum Zolotov.
⑬ Masada Youth Hostel, 1959. Meir Levy.
⑭ Field school, Ein Gedi, 1962. Nahum Zolotov.
⑮ Dead Sea Works Museum, Neve Zohar, early 1960s. Shmuel Mestechkin.
⑯ Field school dormitories, Sde-Boker, 1961–1962. Yohanan Ratner, Mordechai Shoshani.

⑭

⑮

⑯

⑰

⑱

⑲

Apartments, Houses, Offices
Industrial Properties, Acreage
Rooms and Board

The New York Times

REAL ESTATE Sunday, June 1, 1969

New Towns Bloom in Israeli Desert

"Pyramid" apartment block in Beersheba, Negev desert town that was planned as a "garden city" 20 years ago

By ADA LOUISE HUXTABLE

Continued on Page 7, Col. 1

A Bedouin rides to market past Beersheba's new 14-story apartment building

⑳

㉑

⑰ Eilat, mid-1950s.
⑱ First housing blocks in Mitzpe Ramon, Negev, late 1950s.
⑲ Ophira, Sinai, 1972. Nahum Zolotov.
⑳ “New Towns Bloom in Israeli Desert,” *New York Times*, June 1, 1969.
㉑ “Prairie Houses,” Eilat, 1955. Moshe Kofman.

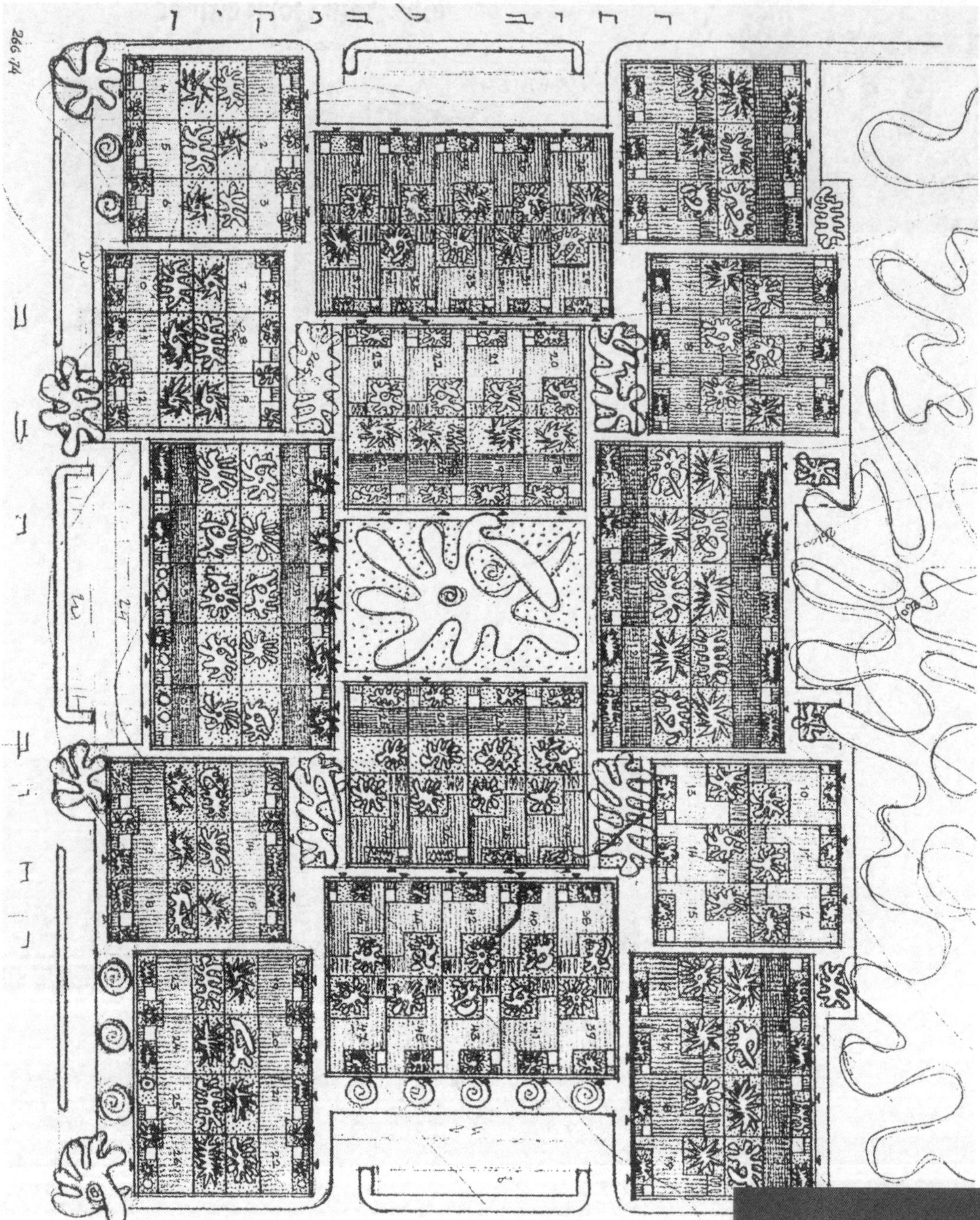

㉒

㉓

㉒ Patio mat housing, Beersheba. Plan of neighborhood, 1960s. Theodore Kisselov.
㉓–㉔ Patio mat housing, Eilat, 1956–1958. Theodore Kisselov.
㉕ Patio mat housing, Eilat. Plan of two adjacent units, 1956. Theodore Kisselov.

㉔

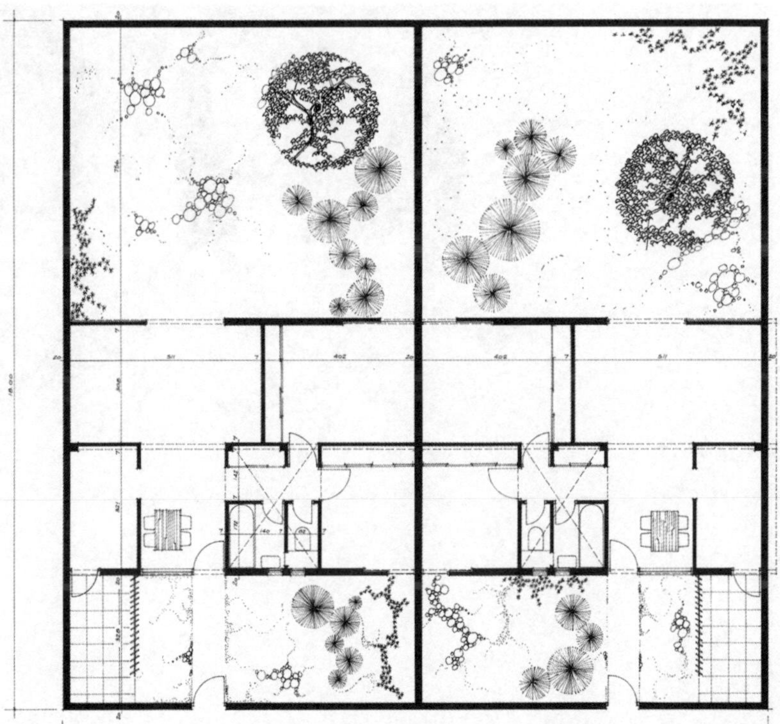

㉕

# DOSSIER: MOSHE NOVOMEYSKY'S SODOM

㉖ Salt mines, Sodom, 1964. Central Zionist Archives.

Zionist Sodom was to be the redemption of biblical Sodom. In the first Hebrew utopia, written in 1892 by Elḥanan Leib Lewinsky, the grotesque punishment of petrification in salt was inverted into a bustling spectacle: "And the city of salt teems with activity. Machines pound and whistle, funnels emit smoke, and thousands of workers toil there."[1] Eros at the Dead Sea, resurrection at the lowest point on earth: "A land no man has stepped foot on now transformed into a godly paradise."[2] And ten years later, in his illustrious *Old-New Land*, Theodor Herzl ignited the imagination of entrepreneurs:

> Twenty years ago any student of chemistry would already have known that the soil of Palestine contains great treasures, as demonstrated by samples brought to class from the Jordan Valley and the Dead Sea.[3]

Zionism's poetic license began to materialize in a visionary project in 1906, when the scientist and Zionist leader Otto Warburg met Mikhail Novomeysky, a mining engineer from Siberia, and introduced him to a report about the Dead Sea by the German geologist Max Blankenhorn.

Novomeysky visited the Dead Sea in 1911. In 1920 he immigrated to Palestine, and in 1922 he purchased land on the northern shore of the Dead Sea, near Jericho, as well as the rights to mine salt at Mount Sodom, near the southern shore. He founded the Palestine Mining Syndicate in 1924, and in 1929 the British Mandatory authorities granted a seventy-five-year concession to his Palestine Potash Company. Novomeysky entrusted Richard Kauffmann with the design of the company's facilities and its housing for workers. This project is perhaps the earliest significant display of modern architecture in Palestine—and it is certainly one of the most notable attempts to adapt it to the extreme local climate.

By 1940, the Palestine Potash Company was responsible for half of the country's industrial export, and it supplied half of the British demand during World War II. This epic storyline took a dismal turn with the establishment of the State of Israel, the dismissal of Novomeysky, and the conversion of the Palestine Potash Company into a state-owned enterprise, Dead Sea Works Ltd., which was gradually privatized and eventually became the suspected accelerator of a horrific ecological disaster in the region: the rapidly receding shoreline of the Dead Sea and the appearance of hundreds of sinkholes around it. "The place now looks like a set for a war movie, full of old props: large craters, shattered buildings that collapsed into the sinkholes, dead trees, pipes and cables hanging in midair," a recent newspaper article reports.[4] Sodom's Zionist utopia is collapsing into apocalypse. ■

1 Elḥanan Leib Lewinsky, "Voyage to the Land of Israel in the Year 2040," in *Yesterday's Tomorrow: The Zionist Utopia, vol. 2*; ed. Rachel Elboym-Dror [in Hebrew] (Jerusalem, 1993), p. 78. (Quotation translated by Tamar Cohen.)

2 Ibid.

3 Theodor Herzl, *Old-New Land*, trans. Lotta Levensohn (New York: Bloch Publishing, 1960). Originally published as *Altneuland* (Leipzig: Seemann, 1902).

4 Nir Hasson, "The Dead Sea: A Dramatic Look at Israel's Endangered Natural Wonder," *Haaretz*, February 24, 2016.

(27)

(28)

(29)

(27) Palestine Potash Company camp, Sodom, 1934–1937. Matson Collection, Library of Congress.
(28) Salt deposits, Dead Sea, 1964. Central Zionist Archives.
(29) Conveyor, Palestine Potash Company, Sodom, 1934. Central Zionist Archives.
(30) Salt formation, Sodom. Matson Collection, Library of Congress.
(31) Dead Sea Works, Sodom, 1950. Central Zionist Archives.
(32) Makeshift cinema in workers' camp, Palestine Potash Company, 1959. Central Zionist Archives.

⑳

㉜

㉛

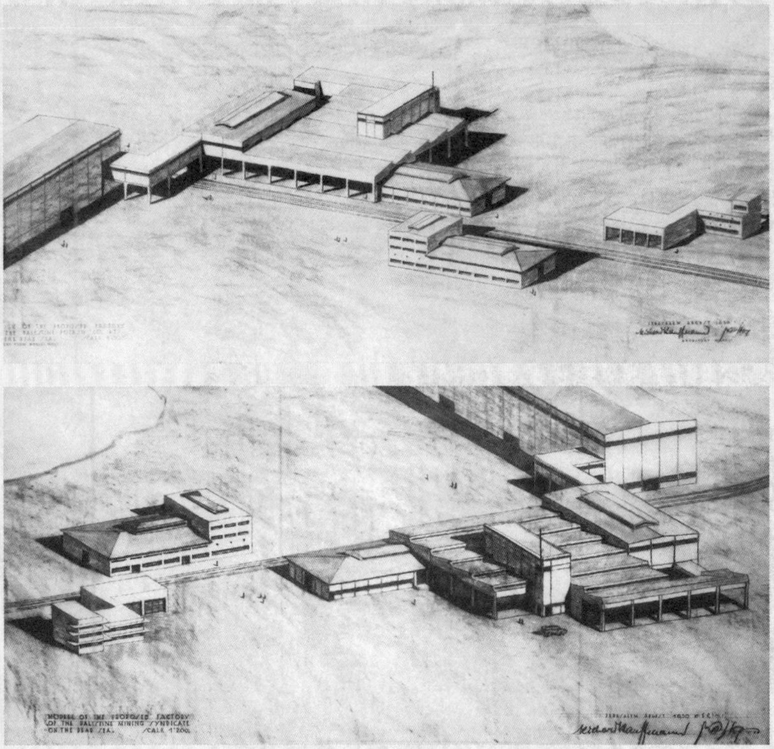

33

34

35

33 Palestine Potash Company, 1930. Perspective.
Richard Kauffmann. Central Zionist Archives.
34 Palestine Potash Company, workers' housing, 1932.
Richard Kauffmann. Central Zionist Archives.
35 Palestine Potash Company, workers' housing, 1929.
Perspective. Richard Kauffmann. Central Zionist Archives.
36 Palestine Potash Company, workers' housing, 1932.
Richard Kauffmann. Central Zionist Archives.
37 Palestine Potash Company, workers' housing, 1932.
Richard Kauffmann. Central Zionist Archives.
38 Palestine Potash Company, workers' housing on the north shore of the Dead Sea. Matson Collection, Library of Congress.

36

37

㊳

# Rural

## Instant Villages

> Once every 25 years, a ship named "Futuro" will bring us a select group of intellectuals. For us, their words will be like an oracle. We do not intend to create model villages in the land like the impressive fantastic villages of Catherine the Great's lover, Potemkin. All of the land will be open to visitors, and the guests of the "Futuro" will be our distinguished judges.
> Theodor Herzl, *Old-New Land (Altneuland)*, 1902[1]

During the 1948 War, Israel's isolated frontier settlements functioned as strategic strongholds and outposts in the territorial battleground. In many instances, these civilian bastions proved effective in deflecting attacks and changing the course of battle. After the war, the idea behind the establishment of these outpost settlements became both the rhetorical springboard for the country's continuing settlement project and an essential part of the national policy of demographic dispersal and militarized settlement. The possibility of an inverse process was also discussed, one in which agricultural settlements would develop out of military camps and outposts. In the words of Yosef Weitz, director of the Jewish National Fund's Land Development Authority:

> From the creation of a front-line of military outposts arose the idea to create permanent outposts, whose initial military role would eventually transform into one that advances the settlement project.[2]

The Israel Defense Forces' Nahal ("Fighting Pioneering Youth") units were regular army units trained for both farming and soldiering. These units were sent out to settle strategic locations along the borders. David Ben-Gurion, Israel's first prime minister, described the advantages of the soldier-farmer crossbreed:

> The frontier villages will not be cantonments of soldiers, but farm settlements like any other, in which a man will live his own life, raise his family and bring up his sons. We need men and women pioneers in equal measure. The inhabitants of these settlements, likely to be among the first attacked in any invasion by regular troops or bands of irregulars, must know how to carry and how to use firearms.[3]

The War of 1948 left a large number of abandoned Palestinian villages and already-primed agricultural lands which were confiscated by the State and which facilitated the establishment of ever more new settlements. The massive Jewish immigration during the first years of the State, the collapse of the Arab agricultural economy within the borders of Israel, the severing of commercial ties with the neighboring Arab countries (which before the establishment of the State had been the major source of agricultural imports to Palestine), the completion in 1950 of the national master plan with decentralization as its main objective, and the ensuing vigorous "From the City to the Village" campaign—all of these effectively catalyzed and accelerated the rural settlement movement in the new State.

Initially, the principal forms of rural settlement were the kibbutz and the workers' moshav. The communities in the new settlements were made up of pioneering youth from the various youth movements, or of decommissioned soldiers. In the first two years of the State some eighty such settlements were established.

①

At the outset, new immigrants, after their prolonged stay in transit camps, were not deemed suitable for agricultural work, let alone for the pioneering mission of guarding the borders of the country. Furious debates on this issue took place in the Land Settlement Department of the Jewish Agency, in the Agricultural Division of the National Labor Federation, and in the settlement movements themselves.[4] The severe housing shortage for the masses of immigrants flooding the country, coupled with the need to strengthen the existing settlements, gave way to a change in strategy, however.

The first waves of immigration right after the establishment of the State flowed primarily to the cities. The populations of the three large cities—Tel Aviv, Jerusalem, and Haifa—grew by 55 percent (from 413,000 to 641,000) between 1948 and 1954. The smaller cities expanded as well: urban and semi-urban settlements tripled their population during this period, from 163,000 to 519,000. Urbanization intensified in the early Jewish colonies (Petah Tikva, Rishon LeZion, Rehovot). Factories and workshops were established in the cities, but industry developed at a slower pace than anticipated. The housing and employment shortage generated an urgent need for population dispersal and for stimulating the agricultural settlement project.[5]

In an appeal by Levi Eshkol, then director of the Land Settlement Department of the Jewish Agency (and later prime minster), to dismantle the immigrant camps in order to put a stop to the bureaucratic ills of immigrant absorption, a new term appeared. "Immigrant fields" (*sedot olim* in Hebrew; eventually "transit camps," or *ma'abarot*) became the designation for new settlements that were to be established in the vicinity of existing ones:

> This is how we will dismantle the immigrant camps: throughout the country, wherever there are settlements, we will append immigrant neighborhoods to them. [...] The immigrants will be employed in forestation and planting fruit trees, infrastructure works, terracing, and clearing.[6]

By the end of 1948, Eshkol had come to the conclusion that the houses of the so-called "abandoned" Arab villages could provide a partial solution to the housing crisis while being an impetus for Jewish settlement:

> I have an idea that may well help us out of this predicament. [...] As we know, there are hundreds of abandoned villages throughout the country. [...] We must grab them, plan them, and prepare them for the approaching winter; into each of them we will transfer dozens of families, along with guides from the established co-operative moshavim and kibbutzim. Every such group will be given work tools and will begin to work the fields. What do we have to lose?[7]

In February 1949, a special session of the Moshav Movement Council was held in the city of Ramle, under the slogan "From the

Camps to the Village." To this day, members of the moshav movement see the Ramle Convention as a turning point in the integration of immigrants into agriculture, since it spurred the reorganization of the Land Settlement Department.

The settlement movement now ceased to be voluntary and was opened up for incoming immigrants, most of whom were arriving from Muslim countries. A new rural typology of "immigrant villages" (Heb. *kfarei olim*)[8] was established and an astonishingly efficient system of reproducing instant villages was devised, dramatically changing the face of agricultural settlement in Israel. Quantitative precedence shifted from the kibbutz to the immigrant village. Over the course of just a few years, some 25,000 families settled in about 400 newly erected immigrant villages.[9]

Many of these instant villages, however, suffered from organizational and administrative difficulties, security problems, lack of familiarity with cooperative marketing methods, and educational problems. About 30 percent of the inhabitants left the villages within a decade of settling there. Sometimes entire settlements were abandoned, and the Jewish Agency had to repopulate them, often two or three times, before a stable population was established.

During the years of the slowdown in the momentum of settlement, lessons were drawn from the failed planning of the hastily established immigrant villages. A few more years of experience and familiarization with the new population enabled a shift to a more accurate form of economic and physical planning that took into account the unique character and needs of each settlement, while uniting them under regional and national rural networks. For this purpose, in the spring of 1952, the Planning Division of the Land Settlement Department was established, cooperating closely with the Center for Agricultural Planning. Now each region in the country submitted statistics about the land and the population, and this data was translated into economic, agronomic, and architectural plans.

This specialization trend in farm planning accelerated between 1956 and 1967, thanks to the large quantities of water that became available to the farmers with the completion of the national water carrier. Specialization required an economic home front and led to increased interdependence between village and city. The market demand for high-quality produce, properly sorted and attractively packaged, brought about the establishment of regional service centers and triggered changes in the morphology of the villages. The elongated form, also known as "towel settlements" —rectilinear settlements built on a single altitude, with a main road, houses on either side, and a public square, grocery store, and "U-turn" at one end—proved to be socially alienating and unsuitable for specialized farming. Planners began to return to the concentric-circle format of the early cooperative moshavim, such as Nahalal or Kfar Yehezkel, placing the houses within a small distance from the village center. The public area became smaller, as some of its functions were transferred to inter-village and district centers. The arrangement of the houses came to be calculated more and more often according to topographical data. This resulted in settlements that were amorphous in form but similar in function to the original cooperative moshav model. Adjacent to the houses was a relatively small area for household crops, while most of the

① "Where To? To the Village!" Propaganda poster in Yiddish, early 1950s. Lavon Institute for Labor Movement Research Archives.
②–⑦ New immigrant villages, Lachish district, 1950s. Aerial view. Central Zionist Archives.

② ③
④ ⑤
⑥ ⑦

territory was centralized in accordance with the characteristics and uses of the land.

The new national master plan proposed a geographic subdivision into three types of agriculture, based on the experience of the prior years: dairy farms and citrus groves along the coast; field crops on the inland plains; and mountain farms for the hilly area, varying according to the quality of the soil and the topography.

With the end of the initial settlement drive came the period of consolidation of the hundreds of new settlements. The subsiding of the waves of immigration and the great capital necessary to complete the building and development of the existing settlements led to a drop in the construction of new settlements. Furthermore, agricultural yield grew from year to year in both new and old settlements: by the beginning of the second decade of the State, the new settlements were producing about half of Israel's agricultural product. Surpluses led to a decrease in profits.

In spite of the figures, settlement organizations did not cease to expand settlement in areas where it was deemed necessary for political and strategic purposes. In the first decade, new settlements were established primarily in the Lachish and Ta'anakh regions. In the second decade of the State and up to the 1967 War, the thrust of the settlement effort was focused in the Galilee and Besor regions.

The conclusion of the 1967 War brought with it a whole new set of issues, and political considerations quickly came to trump any economic, agronomic, or architectural consideration. The Israeli government launched a planned settlement campaign in the newly occupied territories (Heb. *ha-shetahim*; lit. "the territories"). But even before this policy materialized, unauthorized Jewish settlements began to appear in "the territories"—settlements that only retroactively received governmental endorsement.[10]

In early 1970, the government, in collaboration with the Jewish Agency, established a settlement committee to manage the establishment of the new settlements—rural and urban—on either side of the Green Line.[11] The criteria for the establishment of these settlements included meeting strategic political and economic needs, as well as compliance with the everlasting policy of population dispersal. Plans that had already been prepared before 1967 to position Jewish settlements on high ground in sections of the Galilee for optical and military control were reactivated between 1977 and 1984 with the establishment of thirty lookout settlements (Heb. *mitzpim*) in the Galilee and the Golan Heights.

The continuity of policies regarding settlement networks, population dispersal, and civilian occupation before and after 1967 should not be overlooked. It may be argued that practically all land occupation policies, legal maneuvers, and architectural whims were already in practice before the occupation of the West Bank, as S. Ilan Troen explains:

> In an effort to establish a significant "Jewish presence" in outlying areas, in the mid-1960s planners invented the rurban village, a nonagricultural community set in the countryside. This innovation was originally designed to "Judaize" predominantly Arab sections of the Galilee where an agricultural economy was impractical. The most extensive use of rurban villages has been in Judea and Samaria, the areas of the West Bank captured from the Jordanians in the 1967 Six-Day War. These settlements [...] are intentionally bourgeois communities based on white-collar occupations and usually driven by religious-nationalist imperatives.[12]

The rurban type, or the community settlement (Heb. *yeshuv kehilati*), reproduced within, beyond, and all along the Green Line. By the mid-1980s sixty such settlements had been built in the West Bank, many of which began as quasi-military camps and were naturalized retroactively. An ever-expanding network of civilian outposts and colonies of various sizes and with varying degrees of urbanity spread out across the hilltops of the West Bank, housing growing numbers of inhabitants. Today the population is over 300,000 (excluding the Jewish neighborhoods in the occupied areas now part of the Jerusalem municipality). Much like the kibbutz ideologues who spearheaded the Zionist settlement movement in its early decades, it was now the religious settlers of *Gush Emunim* (The Bloc of the Faithful) who pioneered Jewish settlement of the West Bank, triggering an ever-increasing migration drift away from the old dreary

(8) A new immigrant village, Lachish district, mid-1950s. Central Zionist Archives.
(9) The new village of Kisalon, Jerusalem Mountains, 1950. Central Zionist Archives.
(10) A new immigrant village, Lachish district, mid-1950s. Central Zionist Archives.
(11) A new immigrant village, Lachish district, mid-1950s. Central Zionist Archives.
(12) A new immigrant village, Lachish district, mid-1950s. Central Zionist Archives.
(13) Rural housing units, Beit Shemesh, 1956. Photographer: Fred Chesnik. Jewish National Fund Archive.

⑧ ⑨
⑩ ⑪
⑫ ⑬

frontier of the Labor governments, toward and across the Green Line, the new wild frontier of the Likud governments.

Unlike their predecessors, the new settlements in the Occupied Territories could no longer rely on social engineering or the mass mobilization of populations in order to grow and multiply. Nor could they expect State-owned industries to instigate workers' towns, or market forces to generate company towns. Beyond fundamentalist zeal, extravagant governmental funding, and generous tax benefits, they had to fabricate their raison d'être, their civic appeal, their urban typology, their scenography—even if, or precisely because, they were pop-up postcard communities, hollow architectural setups that could hardly conceal the violence inherent in their very inception.

While the ideological settlers took control of the inner West Bank hilltops overlooking Palestinian towns and villages, "quality of life" settlers inhabited the new towns closer to the pre-1967 border, which were in effect suburban satellites of the greater metropolitan area of Tel Aviv. For the price of a small apartment in Tel Aviv, and at a distance of a twenty- to thirty-minute drive from the big city, settlers could get hold of their own red-roofed house and benefit from massive government subsidies.

Eyal Weizman, in his landmark books *Hollow Land* and *A Civilian Occupation*,[13] clarifies the ostensible mimesis between geography and urban layout in the new settlements.

> The mountain settlement is typified by a principle of concentric organization in which the topographical contours of the map are retraced as lines of infrastructure. The roads are laid out in rings around the summit with the water, sewage, electricity and telephone lines buried under them. The division of lots is equal and repetitive, providing small private red-roofed houses positioned along the roads, against the backdrop of the landscape. The public functions are generally located within the inner most ring, on the highest ground.[14]

Indeed, unlike the old settlements and new towns of the 1950s and 1960s, which were often located in a desolate countryside with dull scenery and therefore had to assume an arbitrary form and fake their own organicity, the new rurban settlements of the West Bank were "the end results of tactical land use and topographical constraints."[15] And while the old settlements were conceived within a regional network (or at least a regionalist vision), the new settlements were devised as "cul-de-sac utopias," as Weizman puts it: a typology of their own, within a cartographic patchwork of isolated nodes and oversized infrastructure. Sociology, as we read in Weizman's work, comes with the territory and takes its proper shape. Again, unlike the reluctant pioneers of the 1950s and 1960s, proactive settlers organized in bedroom communities were now conducting a quality-of-life public relations campaign for a policy of territorial sprawl.

> Socially, the "community settlement" [...] is in effect an exclusive members' club with a long admission process and a monitoring mechanism that regulates everything from religious observance through ideological rigor. Furthermore, they function as dormitory suburbs for small communities who travel to work in the large Israeli cities. The hilltop environment, isolated, overseeing and hard to reach, lent itself to the development of this newly conceived utopia. The community settlements create cul-de-sac envelopes, closed off from their surroundings, utopian in their concentric organization, promoting a mythic communal coherence in a shared formal identity.[16]

A new rural iconography, then, is in the making. *Neudorf*, the imaginary New Village of utopian Zionism, is not the metonymy of a science-fiction physiocratic civilization of benevolent auto-colonizers, aspiring to radical social reform and soft harmony with the native land, as written. Nor is it the instant Potemkin village of the premature welfare state, an agonizing trace of its efficient self-annihilating project of social engineering, as tested. It is eventually but a dismal metaphor of pastoral masquerade, horror-film footage portraying a lethargic dormitory community of armed settlers engaged in lawn-mowing and territorial warfare. ■

⑭ ⑮
⑯ ⑰
⑱ ⑲
⑳ ㉑

⑭ Prototype public building, Lachish district, mid-1950s. Central Zionist Archives.
⑮ Generic health clinic, Lachish district, mid-1950s. Central Zionist Archives.
⑯ Generic health clinic for new villages, Jewish Agency, Settlement Department, mid-1950s. Model. Central Zionist Archives.
⑰ Building designated for public functions, Lachish district, mid-1950s. Central Zionist Archives.
⑱ School in the village of Zohar, Lachish district, 1956. Photographer: Yehuda Eisenstark. Israel State Archives.
⑲ Generic cultural center for new villages, Jewish Agency, Settlement Department, mid-1950s. Model. Central Zionist Archives.
⑳ School building in Lachish, 1956. Photographer: Yehuda Eisenstark. Israel State Archives.
㉑ Youth club for a rural village, Jewish Agency, Settlement Department, mid-1950s. Model. Central Zionist Archives.

1 Theodor Herzl, *Old-New Land*, trans. Lotta Levensohn (New York: Bloch Publishing, 1960), p. 223. Originally published as *Altneuland* (Leipzig: Seemann, 1902).

2 Cited in Alex Bein, *Immigration and Settlement in the State of Israel* [in Hebrew] (Tel Aviv: Am Oved, Hasifriya HaZionit, 1982), p. 76; see also Elisha Efrat, *Settlement Geography in Israel* [in Hebrew] (Tel Aviv: Ahiasaf, 1981).

3 David Ben-Gurion, *Like Stars and Dust: Essays from Israel's Government Year Book* (Sde-Boker Campus: Ben-Gurion University of the Negev, Ben-Gurion Heritage Institute, 1997), pp. 46–47. Cited in S. Ilan Troen, *Imagining Zion: Dreams, Designs, and Realities in a Century of Jewish Settlement* (New Haven: Yale University Press, 2003), p. 214.

4 Bein, *Immigration and Settlement*, pp. 77–78.

5 See Moshe Lisak, *The Extensive Immigration of the 1950s: The Failure of the Melting Pot* [in Hebrew] (Jerusalem: Bialik Institute, 1999).

6 Cited in Bein, *Immigration and Settlement*, pp. 67–68.

7 Cited in ibid., p. 81.

8 See Lisak, *Extensive Immigration*, p. 33.

9 Ibid., pp. 33–37.

10 Among these was the settlement in the abandoned Syrian town of Kuneitra, which eventually became Kibbutz Merom Golan. Three months after the war, Kfar Etzion was reestablished in the West Bank on the ruins of the Jewish settlement that had been destroyed in the 1948 War; a pioneering group of the Shomer Hatzair Zionist-socialist youth movement settled in the Banias Heights, and a group of Nahal-Golan settled near them. In the northern Sinai two Nahal outposts were also established —Nahal-Yam and Nahal-Sinai—whose goal was to demonstrate a Jewish presence in the region.

11 The term "Green Line" refers to the demarcation lines set out in the 1949 Armistice Agreements after the 1948 Arab-Israeli War. The "Green Line" is also used to mark the line between Israel and the territories captured in the Six-Day War—the West Bank, the Gaza Strip, the Golan Heights, and East Jerusalem.

12 Troen, *Imagining Zion*, p. 209.

13 Eyal Weizman, *Hollow Land: Israel's Architecture of Occupation* (London: Verso, 2007); Rafi Segal and Eyal Weizman, eds., *A Civilian Occupation: The Politics of Israeli Architecture* (Tel Aviv and London: Babel and Verso, 2003).

14 Rafi Segal and Eyal Weizman, "The Mountain," in Segal and Weizman, *Civilian Occupation*, p. 83.

15 Ibid., p. 83.

16 Ibid., pp. 83–84.

㉒ "The Histadrut (Labor Union Federation) Calls: From the City to the Village." Propaganda poster, 1950s.

# DOSSIER: RICHARD KAUFFMANN'S ZIONIST GARTENSTADT

On Richard Kauffmann's rural work, see chapters "Object" and "Communal" in this volume.

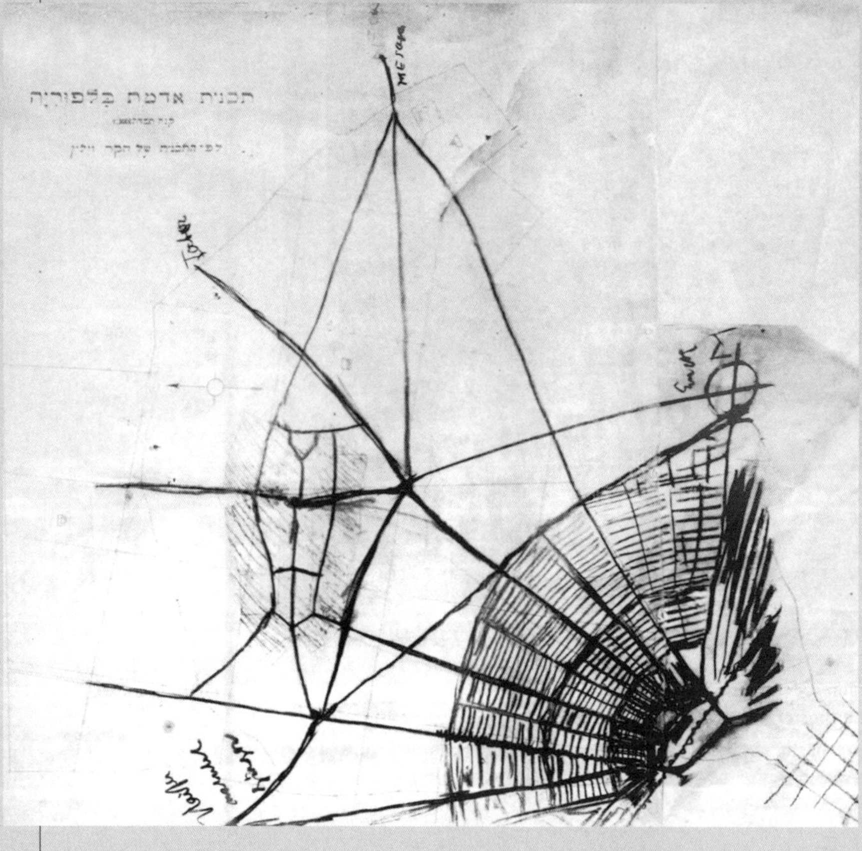

㉓ "Balfuria." Sketch for a rural settlement. Ca. 1930. Richard Kauffmann.

(2)

RICHARD KAUFFMANN
ARCHITECT AND TOWNPLANNER
JERUSALEM
ריכרד קאופמן
אדריכל ובונה ערים
ירושלם

# PLANNING JEWISH AGRICULTURAL SETTLEMENTS IN PALESTINE

## A BRIEF SURVEY OF FACTS AND CONDITIONS

by RICHARD. KAUFFMAN., M.T.P.I.

TO understand the layout and structure of the national Jewish agricultural settlements in Palestine, some knowledge is essential of the character and objects of the Jewish settlers in Palestine. This important basis of Jewish colonisation can, however, be only briefly touched upon here.

The driving force of the Jewish movement is founded in an inward rejuvenation and concentration of the Jewish masses. The only people in the world, which for centuries had to live without a country of its own, without a national culture and therefore without freedom, is now striving in Palestine towards the self-realisation necessary for the existence of a free and creative body of people. The first essential in this direction is their conscious turning towards the productive spheres of agriculture and industry, nothing less than the process of building their home. This reversal from previous modes of existence set in with force when the later Zionist colonisation began and the younger generation in particular have returned in large numbers to agriculture.

That this violent reaction of recent times should have called forth passionate attempts to find new forms of social life is only too easily understood in the case of a people which has such strong religious leanings as the Jews, the people who from Palestine gave mankind the Bible.

*Economic Possibilities.*

Palestine was at one time a very fertile country. The neglect of centuries has greatly damaged its economic possibilities, and the most resourceful and devoted work is needed to bring it back again to its agricultural zenith. Herein, as well as in the industrial manufacture of its agricultural products, of the natural raw materials of the country and its hinterland, as well as of imported raw materials, lie the potentialities of productive activity. The economic and geographical conditions of Palestine, in the region of the borderline of three continents, already made the country famous in olden times as a prominent centre for international traffic, trade and commerce. With progressive agricultural and sound industrial and commercial development, great possibilities have arisen again.

*Land Colonisation Organisation.*

The Jewish people have created various public organisations for the acquisition, tenure, amelioration and cultivation of land, the most important of which may be mentioned here. The Jewish agricultural settlements are mostly established on land acquired and held by the Jewish National Fund, a donation fund which holds the land as an inalienable property of the whole Jewish people. It grants the land on heredity tenure, and is thus not only a land-reforming institute in the most radical and idealistic sense, but by this solution of the land question, lays the first and most essential foundation for a satisfactory system of town planning in the settlements. The Jewish colonising authority is the Agricultural Colonisation Department of the Jewish Agency for Palestine, which established the first agricultural settlements by long-term loans provided by the Palestine Foundation Fund. Later on, long-term loans have also been obtained from other public or private institutions and the settlements themselves have contributed their own investments. The establishment and running of most of the villages is to a large extent aided by the Central Agricultural Organisation—"Mercaz Heclai" of the Agricultural Workers Organisation and its various branches.

*Aspects of Rural Planning Development in Palestine.*

Planning and layout for Jewish settlements started under far more favourable aspects in Palestine than elsewhere. Here, virgin soil awaited cultivation, very little and poor work of any sort existed, and the mistakes committed elsewhere served as a warning example and helped to further an organic growth adapted to the special needs of the country.

It may be mentioned that the special conditions attending Jewish settlement in Palestine, also brought the town planner a mass of fresh tasks and problems which were not lessened by the absence of previous material to work upon in modern village designing, or in earlier work of a general kind such as agricultural settlement and so forth. This will receive mention further on. Suffice it to say that these conditions increased the attraction for labour.

Probably the hardest problems confronting the Jewish Agency in respect of colonisation were those of agricultural settlement. Such problems have a general and special character.

Some of the most important problems are best described by the founder and director of the Colonisation Department of the Jewish Agency, the late Dr. Arthur Ruppin, in his book "The Agricultural Colonisation of the Zionist Organisation in Palestine."

In the introduction Dr. Ruppin mentions a few of his fundamental ideas of which I wish to quote the following :—

"1. That for the success of the Zionist colonisation, sociological no less than economic factors have to be taken into account.

2. That the peculiar nature of the problem, which is to bring back townsmen, and Jewish townsmen, to agricultural life in Palestine, renders a solution on the lines of any existing model impossible.

3. That the great sacrifices demanded by the work of colonisation are repaid not only by the immediate results, but by the fact that the experience acquired in the process is the indispensable basis for colonising on a larger scale in the future."

These fundamental ideas underlying the agricultural colonisation of the Jewish Agency are naturally bound to have a definite influence on the planning of the settlements. Added to this, the Planner has to contend against the peculiarities of the climate, and often those of the land and its configuration.

As regards the problem of town-planning in connection with agricultural settlements in general, mention should be made of the fact that when these were started upon no previous work or layouts whatsoever were available which could have served as a model. Villages and rural settlements in the whole world had sprung up in an almost haphazard way and even today they are very rarely planned beforehand anywhere.

The definition of the science and art of "town planning" in English ; "urbanisme" in French and "Staedtebau" in German very characteristically shows that *rural* planning has been in the past, and is even at present, the most neglected step-child of modern physical planning, still young in itself. Accordingly, designing and layout had to be started entirely anew and had to be developed and improved upon by new initiative, knowledge and experience.

Moreover, this mode of procedure in village design seems to be imperative on account of other—and for planning purposes almost revolutionary—facts.

As mentioned above, villages and agricultural settlements throughout the world have sprung up in a most haphazard way and not to a preconceived plan, usually in the vicinity of some road crossing, sacred edifice or wayside inn. Farms have been built and added to in the course of time, more or less by chance. According to the varying means of the individual peasant or farmer sometimes small, sometimes large farms have joined one another. The result of this sprawl has been the traditional village, which, in its picturesque appearance forms the cherished beauty-spots in the rural landscape all over the world, especially in ancient countries with old culture. A further characteristic for this development is the growth of the villages spreading over decades and even centuries.

In our case all these presumptions of historic village growth did not exist. On the contrary, the task has been an entirely different and unprecedented one. A previously stated number of farmers had to be settled, each under identical conditions regarding size, buildings and implements of each individual farm. The whole village had to be erected at once or at least in a very short time in its entirety.

This task became a more responsible and daring undertaking because it meant the adjustment of an entirely new, unprobed, and possibly alien type into the rural landscape. From the start it had been clear that on account of their very foundations, these settlements would be more rigid in appearance than the historic picturesque village, while one of the most important aims of planning should be to preserve the rural character of the landscape. The beginning, to a large degree, of this new kind of previously planned agricultural settlements was made in 1920 and it may be safely said now that these new types of villages are definitely augmenting and benefiting the rural character of the landscape.

In designing the layout for the different types of our villages, the aim should always be borne in mind to create a functional organism fulfilling to the utmost the task it is expected to perform. It should be as efficient as a biological organism or a machine, where each individual part as well as the whole is being so composed within a well balanced body as to fulfil its appropriate purpose. This primary aim in conceiving the settlement as a functional, dynamic and efficient organism provides in itself the foundation of its satisfactory appearance and the harmoniously balanced shape of the village.

All Jewish agricultural settlements are either co-operative, collective or communal. They are based on the entity of the individual farmer-family which receives as much land, farm buildings, livestock, implements etc., as is needed to ensure the family a reasonably decent standard of living by means of their own work. This aim is not only attaching the Jewish farmer to the soil, but beyond and above that preventing any form of exploitation of hired labour. In most cases only the settler and his family work the farm.

It may well be worth mentioning here that the sociological structures of our settlements have sprung up entirely from within, from the voluntary creative will of the farmers themselves, emanating from their ideas of social life and work. It has never been dictated by decree from above as is the case in other colonisations, where, outwardly, the settlements may have a similar appearance.

*Type of Farms.*

The type of farming in our agricultural settlements varies in accordance with the different natural conditions of soil, climate and irrigation possibilities. Common to nearly all our settlements is the principle of mixed farming, embracing cattle breeding, dairying, poultry-rearing as well as sheep raising, intensive and extensive cultivation and afforestation. Obviously the type of farming varies according to natural conditions existing in each case. In areas where available favourable soil conditions and irrigation possibilities allow for total intensive cultivation, the unit allotted to each settler is generrally 25 dunams, ( 1 dunam =1000 square metres). Where additional land for extensive farming and afforestation is being provided, the area for intensive cultivation is usually being decreased. Small industries, mostly those incidental to agriculture are being attached to quite a number of villages especially to the communal group settlements.

*Site for the Village.*

The selection of the site on which to erect the village is exceedingly important. The ideal spot would be approximately in the midst of its cultivated fields, on a moderate hill, near a spring and a main road. Care should always be taken that the settlement site is situated at a convenient distance from the main road in order that the approach road to the settlement should not be too long, but in any case at such a distance from the high-way that the village should not be disturbed by overland traffic. In the case of the smallholders' settlements, as described further below, the soil condition should be such as to allow for good land for growing garden produce, whereas for the site of the communal group (Kvutza or Kibbutz) a less valuable soil, from the agricultural point of view, and even rocky or waste-land could be chosen for the settlement proper. In practice it is not always possible to realise these ideas and it is the duty of the settlement commission to select the best site under the special conditions prevailing in each case.

*The Different Types of Jewish Agricultural Settlements.*

In general there are four different types of Jewish villages in Palestine as follows :—

1) The "Moshava", a village type with individual and privately-owned farms, mostly situated on privately owned land, comparable with the commonly known traditional type of village.

2) The "Moshav Ovdim", the smallholders' co-operative village with individual farms.

3) The "Kvutza" and "Kibbutz", the communal village.

4) The "Meshek Shitufih," the collective village. All three latter types are being erected on publicly-owned land, mostly of the Jewish

1. *Nahalal. Photographs: Keren Hayesod.*

National Fund, and are not employing hired labour.

The "Moshava" is not being dealt with in this article.

*The "Moshav Ovdim"*
*Smallholders' Co-operative Village.*

The original type of the "Moshav Ovdim" comprises approximately 80 to 100 families, and in addition about 20 families whose main occupations are not agricultural, such as artisans and craftsmen, teachers, doctors, etc. Every farmer is allotted agricultural farm-land according, to the key mentioned above, whereas the non-agricultural settlers are provided with a much smaller plot to enable them to produce their own requirements. The farm and adjoining intensive gardens are worked by the settler himself, with the aid of his family, whereas the extensive farming or dry culture is often done in common.

In the settlements of this type every settler works his farm individually. In most of the other branches of the work, as also in the life of the village, the social idea predominates. Accordingly the purchase of food supplies, tools and agricultural stocks as well as the sale of produce are undertaken in common through special buying and selling co-operative societies of the organised Workers' Association. The village has a co-operative dairy, co-operative machine shed, workshops, stores and shops, as well as a common dispensary provided and runs by the Workers' Sick Fund.

The internal structure of the "Moshav Ovdim" as scheduled above already indicates the task for the Planner in shaping this village. Obviously, all public buildings and co-operative institutions have to be arranged within easy reach of the individual farms and should therefore be located as far as possible in the centre of the village.

Such an arrangement emphasises the dominating character of the common and public over the individual purposes. It results in a functional structure in the outward appearance of the village, culminating from the outskirts to its crowning centre, and in the reverse sense, descending from this centre to the periphery.

Practically all the layouts for the co-operative smallholders' villages ("Moshav Ovdim") show this most typical character and need therefore not be dealt with in detail in the examples shown here. It is only proposed to describe more fully the first "Moshav Ovdim", Nahalal, established at the beginning of 1921.

## NAHALAL

Nahalal is situated on a gently rising oval-shaped hill in the Plain of Esdraelon near two springs. The chief approach road to the "Moshav" leads from the Haifa-Nazareth highroad direct to the summit of the hill which embraces the central part of the settlement. Following the contours of the hill, an oval road was built, the farmsteads being placed on its outer side. In the heart of the settlement, on the highest point of the hill, are found the most important cultural and economic communal buildings, crowning the settlement and at the same time outwardly embodying the principle of co-operation. Here stands the "Beth Haam" (Community Hall), the school, the dispensary, the central dairy, the communal stores, post office, water-tower, stores and sheds for agricultural produce and machinery, etc., focussing at its central point the communal life of the village. A communal public garden adjoins the Community Hall, and roads or paths radiate from this point to all parts of the settlement. Between the ring formed by the farms and the heart of the settlement, are placed the homesteads of the non-agricultural settlers, the teachers, artisans and craftsmen.

In this way it was sought to create a living organism with a natural culminating centre in harmony with the spirit of this particular type of settlement.

### TAMRAH

Tamrah is the most typical example of one of our recent co-operative villages situated very favourably on a protruding hillock. A bell-shaped road circumscribes the practically flat inner kernel, with the individual settlers' farmsteads being arranged on its outer edge with slightly sloping grounds. Between the two approach roads to the east of the village, workshops and co-operative stores etc. are being arranged, whereas public buildings, such as the community hall and school, lie further to the east away from traffic and close to the central community garden. Between this public garden and the inner road the smaller plots of the artisans and craftsmen are being arranged.

### *The Kvutza and the Kibbutz*
### *The Communal Village.*

The Kvutza and the Kibbutz are distinctly a communal form of village. The Kvutza is usually the smaller unit comprising from 80 to 100 agricultural families, whereas the Kibbutz is the larger communal group comprising from 100 to 200 agricultural families and even more.

*2. Tamrah*

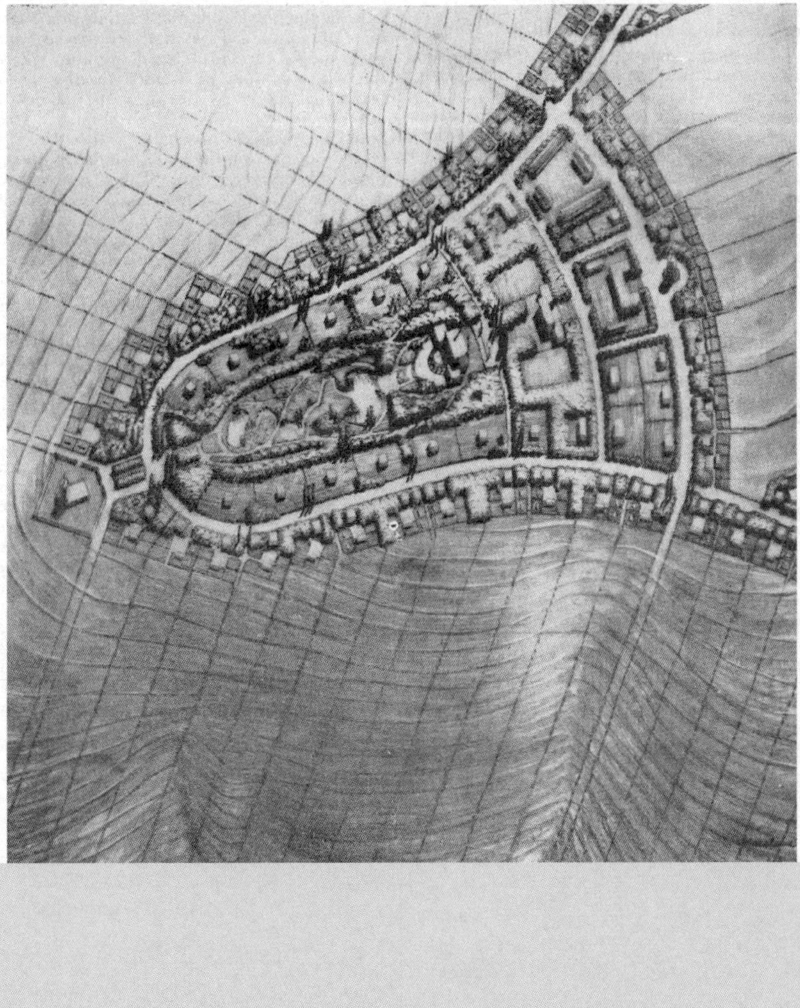

The collective principle finds expression in all aspects of daily life and work. The members of a Kibbutz or Kvutza pool their earnings and keep a common household. In most of the communal villages the children grow up, live, feed and are educated together. The families live in communal houses, each married couple is generally allotted one room in a one-storey dwelling-house, mostly containing four rooms. The members take their meals together in a common dining hall. Work in the communal group is divided amongst the members with due regard to special fitness, ability and leaning. The working hours are usually limited by common decision, unless seasonal exigencies demand a longer working day. This is in contrast to the "Moshav Ovdim" (collective smallholders' village) where working hours are practically unlimited and the farmer and his family work in all branches of the farm.

It also seems desirable to mention here that experience has shown definitely that this communal life not only does nothing to loosen the bonds between parents and children but, if anything, seems to draw them even closer. Children are the first concern of every Kibbutz, the whole community striving to provide the best possible conditions for them.

The joint ownership of implements and livestock and the application of the collective principle to life and work naturally express themselves also in the structure of the settlements. If the "Moshav" may be compared to a village with rhythmically arranged individual farms, the outward appearance of the Kibbutz resembles rather an enormous farm. The "Moshav" is more loosely knitted, even slightly scattered, whereas the Kibbutz shows itself as a more rigidly composed structure.

The body of the Kibbutz or Kvutza, designed for providing the best possible living conditions and most rational working facilities, comprises different units, each of them fulfilling its own function. In planning the groupment and structure of a Kibbutz or Kvutza the essential point is that its different units should form an organic entity retaining the interconnection between the individual parts and the correlation of the whole.

There are in general three main parts which form the body of the communal village.

1. The Living Quarters.
2. The Central Workshops and Stores.
3. The Farmyard proper.

In several cases a fourth part, namely an industrial establishment, is provided for.

Each of the above three parts again contains divisions as follows :—

1. Living Quarters.
   (*a*) Residential quarters for adults.
   (*b*) Living quarters for the small children up to 6 years.
   (*c*) Living quarters for the school children up to 14 and 16, respectively.
   (*d*) The public communal buildings *i.e.*, central dining hall, the community building containing assembly hall, library, reading room and music room (both of these usually located within the central community garden), the dispensary, secretariat, school, bakery, water-tower, laundry, sewing-room, etc. Sometimes a synagogue is built.
2. The Central Workshops and Stores.
   (*a*) Carpenter, locksmith, smith, etc.
   (*b*) Machinery sheds, garages, waggon shed, etc.
   (*c*) The central granary or silo, grain stores, vegetable and fruit stores, cold storage etc.
3. The Farmyard proper.
   (*a*) Cattle sheds, calf and cow sheds, bull barn, dairy, etc.
   (*b*) Stable
   (*c*) Incubator and brooder sheds, poultry sheds and poultry runs, etc.
   (*d*) Sheep fold.

In designing the layout of a Kibbutz or a Kvutza these three, or four, as the case may be, main parts should each form a definite unit, whereas the whole should be welded together as one functional body. Care must be taken that possible enlargements of the communal village could be effected organically so that the village would be able to grow from its nucleus and still retain its organic unity. Taking into account that with growing experience nearly all building types of the different parts, such as dwelling houses, children's houses, farm-buildings etc. have undergone many changes and improvements in course of time, this has been far from being an easy task. The whole plan had to be conceived in such a way as to provide for all its development stages, a rational structure, yet being on the other hand elastic enough to allow for necessary changes and additions.

One of the main conditions which has always to be considered is the cool breeze which not only provides the best opportunity for cooling the buildings by means of through ventilation, but which, moreover, must have a definite effect on the general layout. These winds sweep usually from a south-western direction in the winter to a north-western direction in the summer. Accordingly the layout of the different parts has to be effected in such a way that the living quarters are placed to the west, the workshops and machinery sheds further to the east and the farmyard proper with its cowsheds and poultry-yards still further to the east. The community buildings serving all the members, such as dining hall and cultural centre, are

3. *Kvutza Geva Photo. Keren Hayesod*

usually laid out abutting the community garden ("Village Green") in the centre of the village. Such an arrangement guarantees that the fresh cool breezes reach the living quarters at first and sweep from there to the workshops and farmyard taking with them noise, dust, odours and possible flies.

All buildings destined for living purposes or work, as well as the sheds for animals, should best be placed with their long sides facing north-west or north in order to get the maximum benefit of the cool breezes as well as the minimum of the hot sun-rays.

The road system should be so conceived that the main and general thoroughfares are well separated from the internal lanes of the living quarters as well as from the local connections within the various subdivisions of the individual parts of workshops and farmyard. In recent layouts the different parts of the settlements are enclosed, and thus separated from each other, by means of narrow green belts, preferably consisting of rows of compact trees, closely planted.

Similar conditions for the layout of the communal village might bear in themselves the danger of a certain monotony in their appearance, but not only are those exigencies mostly varying in detail, but natural conditions changing with almost all the settlements offer the possibility and need of introducing a most welcome variety of layout and appearance. This concerns not only the topographic configuration of the site and its environment, but also the introduction of vistas within the surrounding landscape.

Below are a few examples of the design and layout of different communal villages. The shortage of space does not permit detailed description of each case, but the general description as given above facilitates the understanding of the schemes.

## KVUTZA GEVA

Founded in 1921. First example of designing. Large central farmyard. Subdivision still lacking. In recent years a more elaborate plan has been worked out.

### *Kfar Ruppin*

Established in 1938 south of Maoz. Recent enlargement plan being shown. Of the two small hillocks within the settlement, the central one is being crowned by the cultural centre, whereas on the one north-east the school building has been arranged.

### *Kibbut Ein Zeitin*

Established in 1946. Situated on the hills of northern Galilee at a height of approximately 800 metres. The configuration of the site, on two neighbouring hillocks, with rather steep slopes, has been defining the layout to a large extent, the living quarters situated on the western hill, the farmyard proper on the eastern hillock, the stores and workshops on the saddle between the two.

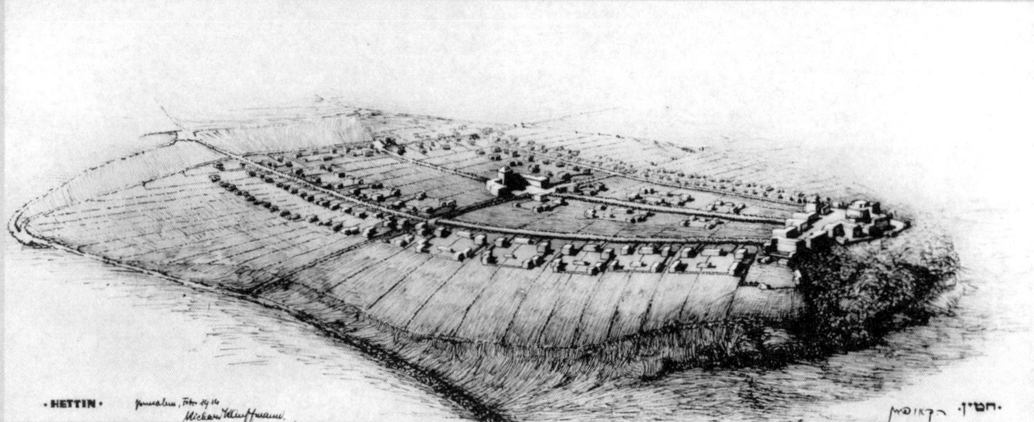


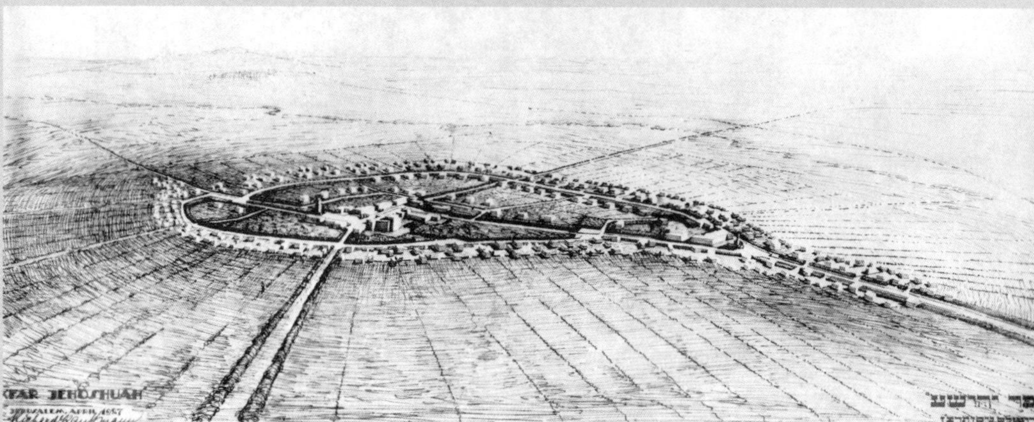

㉕ ㉖ ㉗

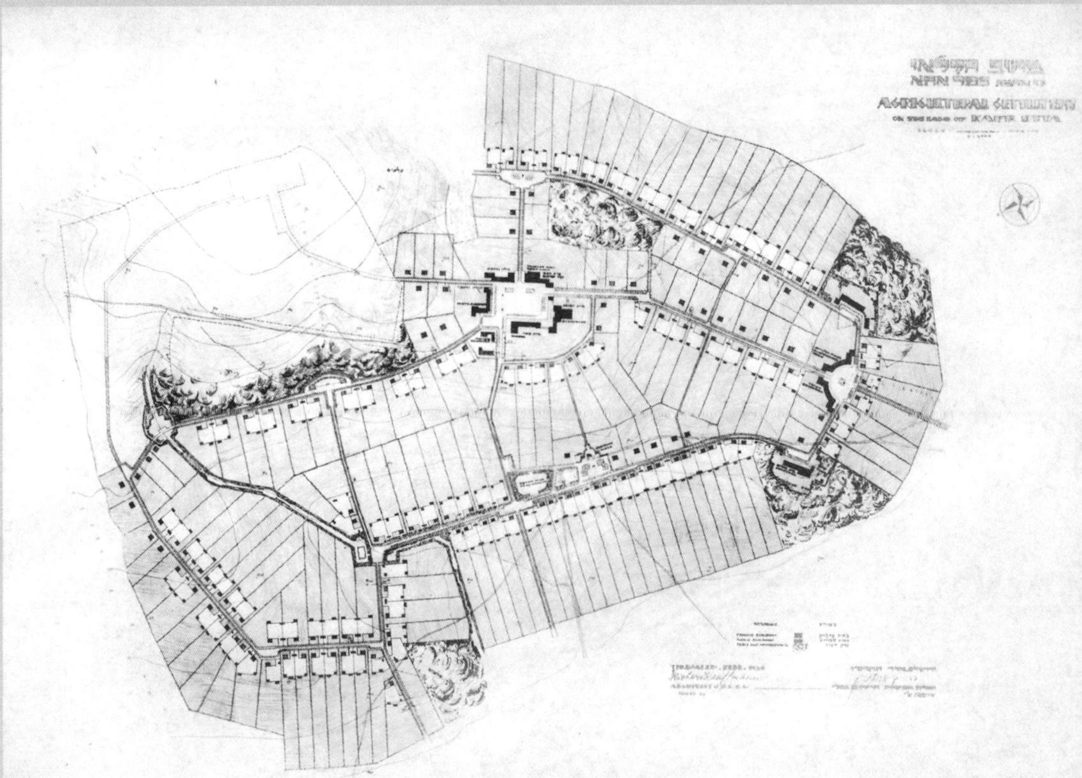

㉘

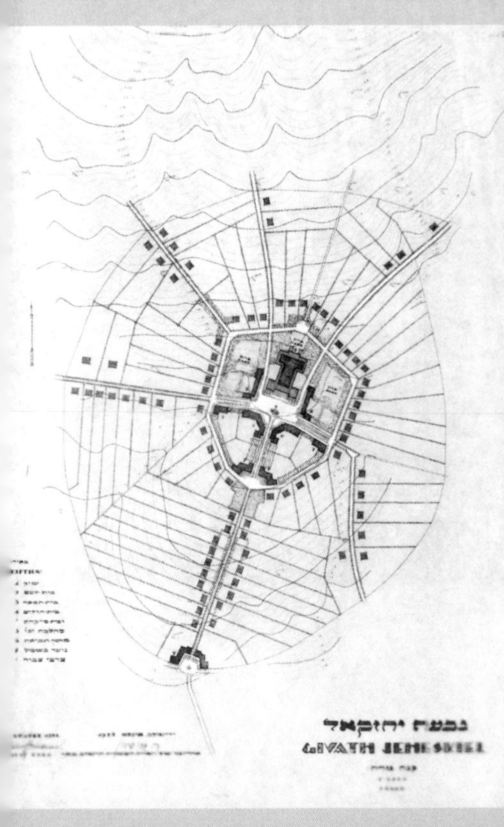


㉙

㉔ Richard Kauffmann, "Planning Jewish Agricultural Settlements in Palestine," Town Planning Review 12, no. 2 (November 1926). Central Zionist Archives.
㉕ Kfar Hettin, 1924. Perspective. Richard Kauffmann. Central Zionist Archives.
㉖ Kfar Yehoshua, 1927. Perspective. Richard Kauffmann. Central Zionist Archives.
㉗ Kfar Yehoshua, 1930s. Aerial view. Richard Kauffmann.
㉘ Kfar Etta, 1926. Plan. Richard Kauffmann. Central Zionist Archives.
㉙ Givath Jeheskiel, 1922. Plan. Richard Kauffmann. Central Zionist Archives.
㉚ Afula, aka Emek Stadt, urban settlement in Jezreel Valley, 1925. Master plan. Richard Kauffmann. Central Zionist Archives.
㉛ Detail.
㉜ Afula, aka Emek Stadt, urban settlement in Jezreel Valley, 1925. Bird's-eye view. Richard Kauffmann. Central Zionist Archives.
㉝ Afula, aka Emek Stadt, urban settlement in Jezreel Valley, 1925. Perspective of the city center and train station. Richard Kauffmann. Central Zionist Archives.

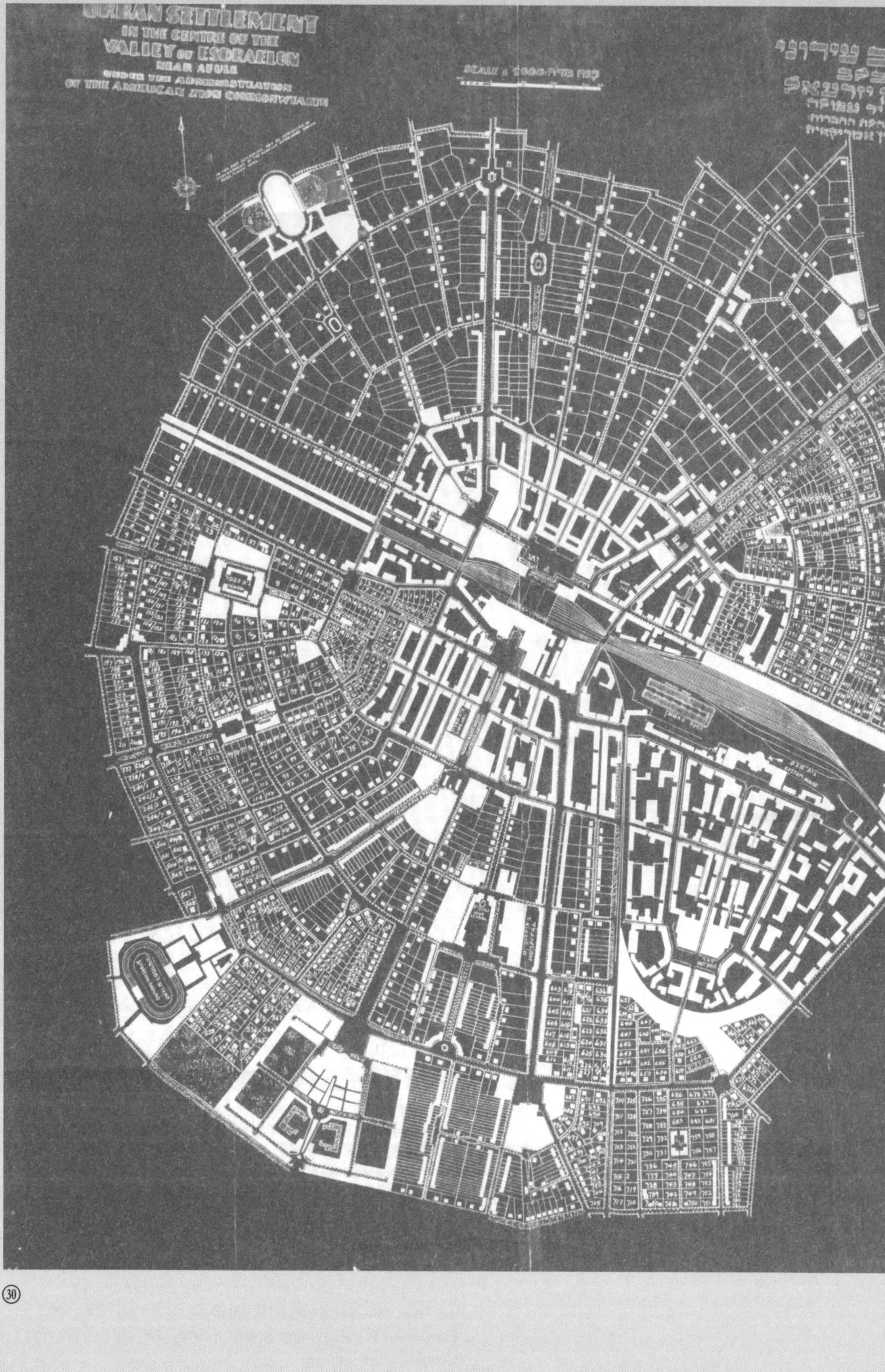
URBAN SETTLEMENT
IN THE CENTRE OF THE
VALLEY OF ESDRAELON
NEAR AFULE
UNDER THE ADMINISTRATION
OF THE AMERICAN ZION COMMONWEALTH

㉚

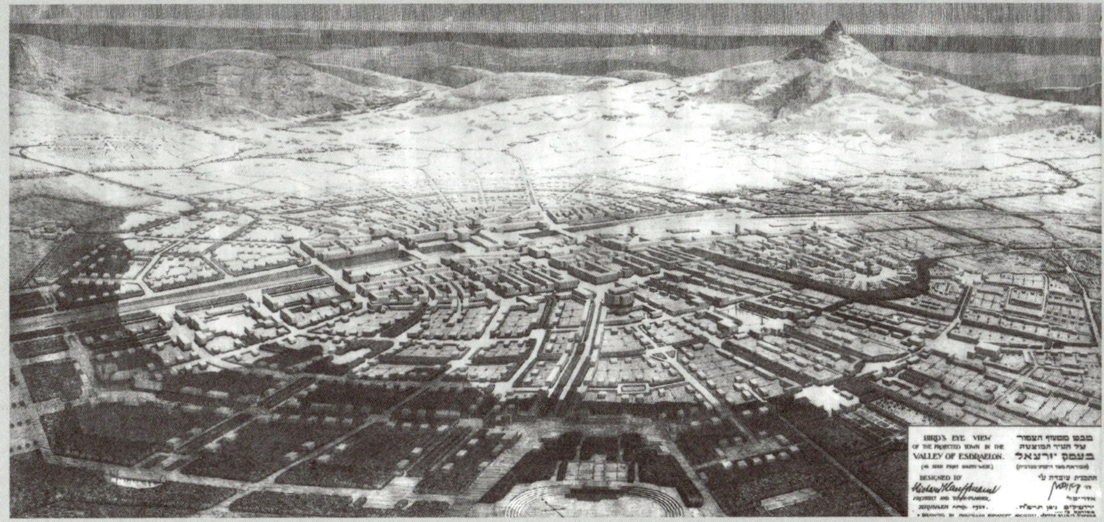
BIRD'S EYE VIEW
OF THE PROJECTED TOWN IN THE
VALLEY OF ESDRAELON.
(AS SEEN FROM SOUTH-WEST.)
DESIGNED BY
ARCHITECT AND TOWN-PLANNER,
מבט ממעוף הצפור
על העיר המוצעת
בעמק יזרעאל

㉜

㉛

BANK
בנק

㉝

# Communal

① Harvest Festival (Shavuot), Kibbutz Geva, 1960s.

## Kibbutz Architecture

A social construct rooted in Marxist and anarchist negative dialectics—neither a village nor a city, neither a community (*Gemeinschaft*) nor a society (*Gesellschaft*)—the kibbutz reveals itself as an architecture with no direct historical precedents. The briefest definition of kibbutz as a praxis is Lenin's aphorism "to each according to his needs, from each according to his abilities."

A full abstract of kibbutz may be as follows: a voluntary commune of individuals, organized for the purposes of settlement, self-labor, economic equality, mutual accountability, cooperation in all means of production and consumption, and provision of full health and education services throughout the entire life cycle of its members. No money is involved in kibbutz internal affairs. Ownership of all property is collective and all spaces are common (transcending, as it were, the commonplace dichotomy of private/public). There is no social hierarchy or official leadership, and all decisions are made collectively by vote in the general assembly. Daily dining is communal, as are all holidays and festivities. Children live not at home, but communally in a "children's society." Indeed, "home" and "family" do not exist as such in the kibbutz vernacular. Members' dwellings are called "rooms" or "apartments" and are accordingly minimal and spare. Conceptually, the kibbutz is a single unified space containing all dimensions of life. There is no parcelization, nor are there fences or any other markers of territorial ownership. The central arena of kibbutz life is the large lawn and the surrounding public facilities—the dining hall, the culture house, the library, the members' club, the swimming pool and sports facilities, etc.

From 1910, the year in which the first such commune, Degania, was founded, until the end of the twentieth century, kibbutz settlements proliferated across the country and came to number about 280 settlements with 230,000 members. There are several kibbutz movements, each with its own founding theories and doctrines; political and cultural agenda; and somewhat differing spatial layout, design of public facilities, and arrangement of dwellings.

We may begin our brief history of kibbutz planning where we left off with Franz Oppenheimer and the failing experiment of Merchavia (see chapter "Object"). The wish of the World Zionist Organization (WZO) for centralized planning and control of the agrarian training farms and the cooperative settlements, as laid out in Oppenheimer's model (and personified in the figure of the managing agronomist), led to a confrontation with the immigrant farm workers, especially those belonging to revolutionary circles such as the Young Worker's (Heb. *Hapoel Hatzair*) Party. These indoctrinated workers considered the official Zionist attitude a betrayal of the class struggle and began to argue for independent communist workers' settlements, independent of the Zionist institutions.[1] The first training farm taken over by its workers and reconstituted as an autonomous commune was Degania, located in the Jordan Valley. The new self-managed autarchic settlement type was called a kvutza (lit. "group"). It advocated close-knit community life based on a small, predetermined number of members and manual agricultural labor.

The most profound intellectual of the kvutza, or the "small kvutza," as it was initially referred to, was Aharon David Gordon, who emphasized the importance of humanistic self-education and negated what he called "mechanistic socialism."[2] Gordon's teaching, drawing on Jewish mystical texts but corresponding as well with Tolstoy and Nietzsche, criticized modern society for its increasing alienation from nature, sterilization of creative powers, and weakening of man's intrinsic moral fiber.

The architecture of the small kvutza, an adaptation of the aforementioned Prussian farm, sought to anchor the intimate spiritual partnership of the group members in its tight spatial scheme. This was based on two principal zones—one residential and one agricultural—connected to one another as a large farm, at the center of which was the common yard. The notion of a fixed-size community was manifested in a fixed-shape hermetic structure. However, the small kvutza was much too exclusive and spiritual to meet the growing demand among young immigrants for collective settlements. Therefore, various spontaneous communal associations, or "labor battalions," soon began to emerge.

The most significant proposal for the organization of a larger and more diversified community, numbering hundreds and even thousands of members, was the idea of the "large kibbutz" (lit. "grouping"), first proposed in 1923. Unlike the unmediated monoculture ideology of the small kvutza, the large kibbutz envisioned a community engaged in a variety of fields, including industry, culture, intellectual life, and education. Such a community required the establishment of a new settlement form with flexible boundaries for a "large and growing" settlement that is not circumscribed from the outset, but that can expand and develop continuously. Evidently, the proponents of the large kibbutz were aware of the need for a paradigm shift and articulated their project in relation both to the Marxist dialectical bind of agriculture and industry, and to the anarchist notions of a society based on voluntary associations.[3]

Yitzhak Tabenkin, the leading ideologue of the large kibbutz, wrote an inspiring treatise entitled "On the Problems of Kibbutz Building," initially delivered as a speech at the opening of the first building course of Kibbutz Ein Harod. (Established in 1921, this was the first communal settlement to be called a "kibbutz.") He lectured as follows to the future construction workers:

> The important thing for us when studying the forms of human habitats is to arrive at the recognition that the city and the village are not natural, eternal forms, that they are transient forms. [...]

DIE KOLONIE NEU UMDJUNI.

KOLONIE ALT UMDJUNI.

KINERETH: WIRTSCHAFTSHOF.

②③④⑤

> [...] And a new type of settlement will evolve in the future: neither a city [n]or a village, but an integration of both. This view was supported by Fourier, Owen, Chernyshevsky and others. *The Communist Manifesto* of Marx and Engels predicted the "combination of agriculture with manufacturing industries; gradual abolition of all the distinction between town and country". [...]
>
> [...] We said: We want to build a settlement that is neither a city nor a village. We called this ideal a communistic settlement. At first they used to speak of "battalions of the regiment". After this they called the settlement unit a farmhold (*meshek*). Already then we struggled for the name *yishuv* [settlement], because to us it alone designated the complete attitude of the people to the commune all the days of their lives. Not a *moshav*, not a village and not a city, not a battalion, not a camp, and not a farmhold.
>
> We aspire to a communistic settlement, that is the definition.[4]

Zionist discourse, as I have argued, has aspired since its inception to reform and rearticulate both the city and the village, but has yet to come up with a practicable proposal for the hybridization-by-obliteration of the two. What makes the double-negation of Tabenkin and his fellow kibbutzniks ("we want to build a settlement that is neither a city nor a village") so revolutionary is precisely the resulting logic and sequential image of a perfectly synthetic community, fabricated as an organic/organismic whole, instantaneously integrated in the (carefully designed) terrain, wiping out all traces of architectural labor.
The negation of traditional habitat formations seems instrumental not only for generating novel structures and fabrics, but also for

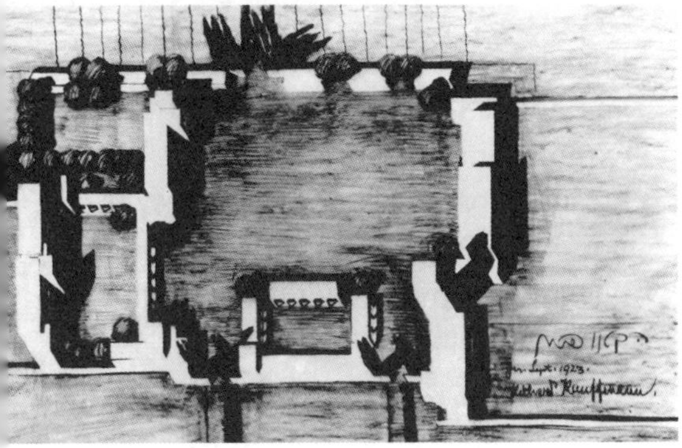

⑥

suggesting the necessary continuum between socialist and Judaic thought, as can be gathered from a text by Shabtai Be'eri, director of the Building Department of the United Kibbutz Movement. In "The Planning of Construction in the Commune in Socialist Thought," a 1952 architectural survey based on the 1930 book *Sotsgorod* ("Socialist City") by Milyutin, Be'eri quotes Nachman Syrkin, one of the most influential intellectuals of the kibbutz, who composed a new ideological program for Zionism that based its authority on the moral and socialist elements in Judaism:

> Nachman Syrkin, who wrote about "The Jewish Question and the Socialist Jewish State," thought the realization of Zionism would create a "socialist utopia." He imagined socialist settlement as an alliance of communal groups. He wrote: "within this union there will be no cities and villages, in the sense that industry and commerce would be concentrated in the cities and agriculture would be concentrated in the villages. The village will actually be a kind of immense village of industry, in which industry and agriculture are practiced side by side. The contrast between the city and the village will be no more. At the same time there will also be some centers where the administration of the economy will be located, as well as the big theaters, museums, the higher education institutions, the permanent exhibitions, etc."[5]

Clearly, such a sweeping crossbreeding of conventional taxonomy required architects to sketch the possible structure and shape of the new hybrid type. The preliminary kvutza and kibbutz structures of the 1910s could no longer accommodate the emerging aspirations of the "immense" and hypothetically ever-expanding "village of industry." The 1920s, therefore, witnessed the emergence of the "architectural" kibbutz, a kibbutz conceptualized and drawn to detail by a professional architect. From that point on, the kibbutz would be a total work of architecture. Nonetheless, kibbutz members themselves never relinquished full participation in the design process of their own habitat, nor did they cease to express their skepticism regarding the moral or intellectual capacity of professionals, as is evident, for example, in Tabenkin's words:

> Our task of building is not a matter of a profession that has to be learned from what is already there. Architecture for a socialist city will grow out of socialist thinking. The profession alone cannot solve problems of the goal. It is incapable of determining the form of "what we will build and how we will build it."[6]

② The commune in Degania (Umdjuni), 1912. Photographer: Leo Kahn. Degania Alef archive.
③ The commune in Degania (Umdjuni), 1911. Degania Alef archive.
④–⑤ The communal workers' farm in Kinneret, 1912. Kinneret archive.
⑥ Communal courtyard, Geva, 1923. Rooftop perspective. Richard Kauffmann. Central Zionist Archives.

It was Richard Kauffmann, director of the Architecture Department of the Palestine Land Development Company and planner of the cooperative Moshav Nahalal, who was destined to become the first kibbutz architect. It was he who was accredited with developing a work method that would enable the settlers' participation in the preparation of the program and the actual planning. In retrospect, we may ascertain that, attentive as he may have been to the settlers' notion of "what we will build and how we will build it," he was also responsible for introducing a highly formalized scheme which would dominate kibbutz design throughout the 1920s and have a lingering effect on the spatial organization of kibbutzim throughout the century.

In his essay "Planning Jewish Agricultural Settlements in Palestine," Kauffmann described the theoretical vacuum that existed in the field of rural planning. His Zionist mission, as he construed it, began ex nihilo:

> The definition of the science and art of "town planning" in English; "urbanisme" in French; and "Städtebau" in German, very characteristically shows that *rural* planning has been in the past, and remains in the present, the most neglected step-child of modern physical planning, still young in itself. Accordingly, design and layout had to be started entirely anew and had to be developed and improved upon by new initiative, knowledge, and experience.[7]

Despite the lack of disciplinary knowledge and experience in rural planning, Kauffmann realized that there was already a profound and fairly accepted program to which he was to apply a form:

> All Jewish agricultural settlements are either cooperative, collective, or communal. [...] The aim is not only attaching the Jewish farmer to the soil, but beyond and above that, preventing any form of exploitation of hired labor. [...] All the presumptions of historic village growth did not exist. On the contrary, the task has been an entirely different and unprecedented one. [...][8]

The task, according to Kauffmann, was unprecedented, but apparently he set to it by applying a well-established and fast-spreading precedent—an essentially urban one, that of the garden city—to the Palestinian landscape and the Zionist imaginary.

If Kauffmann's first Zionist rural archetype, Nahalal, was a derivative of the British garden colony, as related before, then his kibbutz prototype would be drawn from the garden city itself, or more precisely, from the German dialect of *Gartenstadt.* The British original version had accentuated romantic and picturesque references and displayed a distinctive arts-and-crafts taste that could hardly be applicable in the kibbutz. The Deutsche Gartenstadt-Gesellschaft—with Camillo Sitte's and Hermann Muthesius's "enlightened eclecticism" and Heinrich Tessenow's "proto-modern" housing, grounded in conservative *Heimat* sentimentality and at the same time in a more engineered pre-*Werkbund* instrumentality—was apparently a more relevant source for Kauffmann's vision of kibbutz architecture.[9] Indeed, his 1920s kibbutz schemes could appropriately be described as "proto-modern": transitional forms, somewhere between tight neoclassical layouts and modernist free-plan schemes. By the 1930s and 1940s, these transitional forms would seem utterly obsolete in the light of the new internally prepared master plans of the Kibbutz Movement architects.

Kauffmann's first master plan for a large kibbutz was that of Ein Harod and Tel Yosef, two adjacent settlements sharing a common service and education zone. This plan is striking because of its conspicuous urban manifestation; it looks like a formalized city fragment projected on the raw landscape. It seems to emerge already complete, fully equipped with a zoning scheme, axes of symmetry, internal thoroughfares, and an array of public facilities. A close examination of the plan reveals some principles that would prove durable throughout the various permutations of kibbutz architecture: the residential zones are situated in a fan structure around the common public zone and dining hall (a multifunctional building that also served as an administrative center), the "collection room" (perhaps a reference to a museum?), and a large plaza and lawn, which serve as gathering places for the entire community. Industrial and agricultural zones are located down the slope from the settlement, and the district-level culture, health, and education institutions are located higher up the hill.

In order to better grasp the perplexing phantom of the urban-in-the-rural, let us briefly digress to its inverse specter, that of the rural-in-the-urban, as it appears in what could be described as the first planned Zionist city, the Nordau Garden City, designed by architect Alexander Bärwald.[10]

The story of the Nordau Garden City begins in 1919, at the Zionist movement's celebration of the seventieth birthday of its veteran leader, Max Nordau—philosopher, writer, and close collaborator of Herzl's. On this occasion, a proposal to establish a garden city in Palestine bearing Nordau's name was presented under the title *Eine Gartenstadt für Palästina*. The proposal included a bird's-eye perspective sketch of a small town set up on a plain against a backdrop of low hills. Alongside this

⑦

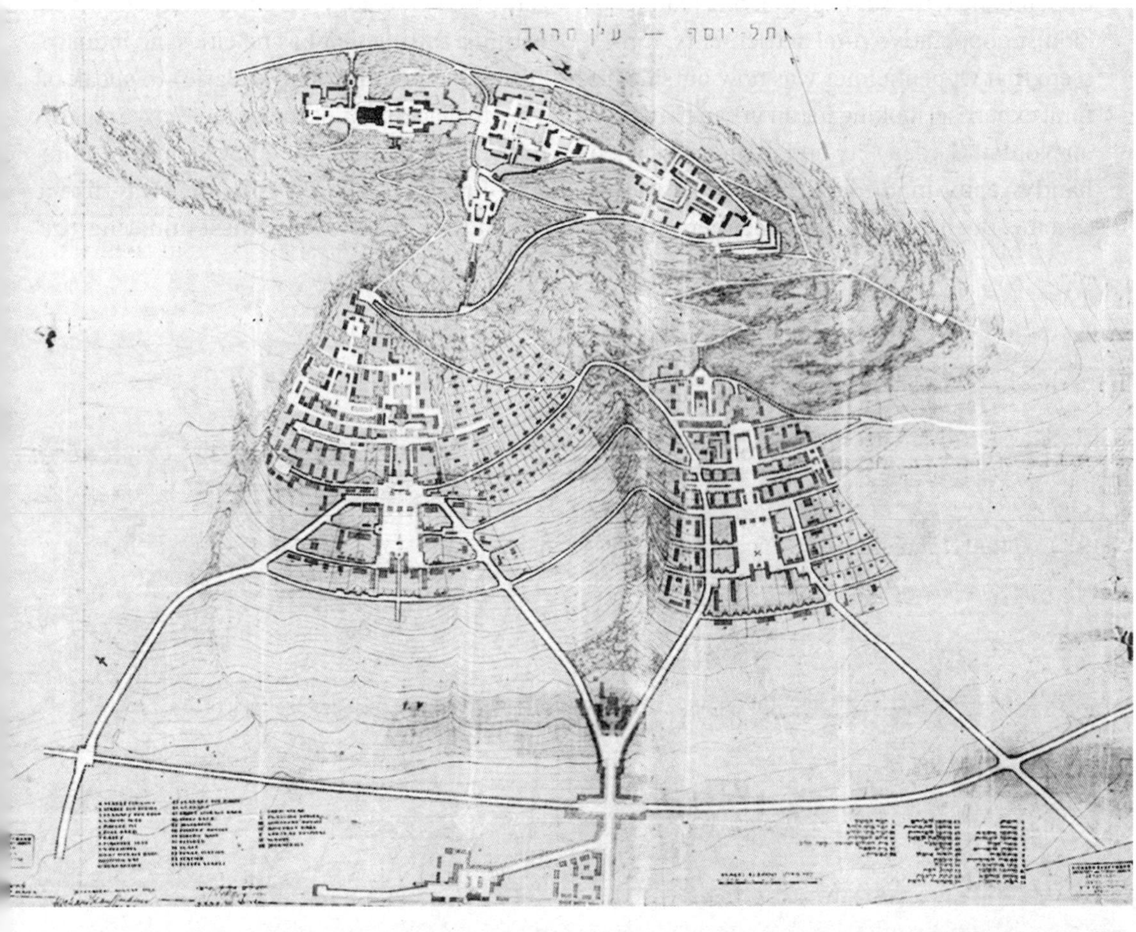

was a descriptive text, written as a dialogue, almost a play script, between a fictional Zionist official who explained the principles of the garden city and a family of settlers. The settlement is designed for a complete community, a defined social unit of 400 families and 300 single people (only somewhat larger, in fact, than an average "large kibbutz"). The physical structure of the settlement is supportive of community life, with a mix of standard housing-types of varying size and density, a defined urban core, and a full range of institutional buildings. It has an abundance of internal open space and is surrounded by an agricultural zone of arable countryside. There is also a zone designated for industry. The urban plan is highly formal and the buildings are cubical, reflecting regional characteristics.

Bärwald's proposal was accompanied by a paper, plainly titled "Gartenstadt," written by none other than the sociologist Franz Oppenheimer, the same pioneering planner of Zionist cooperative rural settlements. It may seem that Oppenheimer was now outside his rural expertise, looking for an urban paradigm for Nordau Garden City and finding an all-too-handy ready-made in Ebenezer Howard's scheme. But in fact, to Oppenheimer, city and village belonged to the same spatial order, as long as they maintained the core principles of planned communities, cooperative functioning, public ownership of land, and harmony between the urban and the rural. These principles were so identical in Howard's and Oppenheimer's theories that Oppenheimer believed himself to be "flesh of Howard's flesh."[11]

Nordau Garden City was never built, but partial garden cities and various garden suburbs were disseminated by the official Zionist agencies in rural and urban settings to such a degree that Zionist spatial planning, certainly during the 1920s, can be considered to be a direct implementation of garden-city precepts.

Returning to the kibbutz, we should note that the garden city's underlying impetus of social and environmental reform indeed seems to share common ground with kibbutz values, but its particular critique of congested, industrial metropolitan life—the bedrock of garden-city ideology—is completely contrived within a setting that has no cities, no industrialization, and no "urban malaise" to speak of. The displacement of the garden-city remedy to the countryside obviously cannot be curative. In effect, it works the other way, like a (Derridean) *pharmakon*, disseminating the

⑧

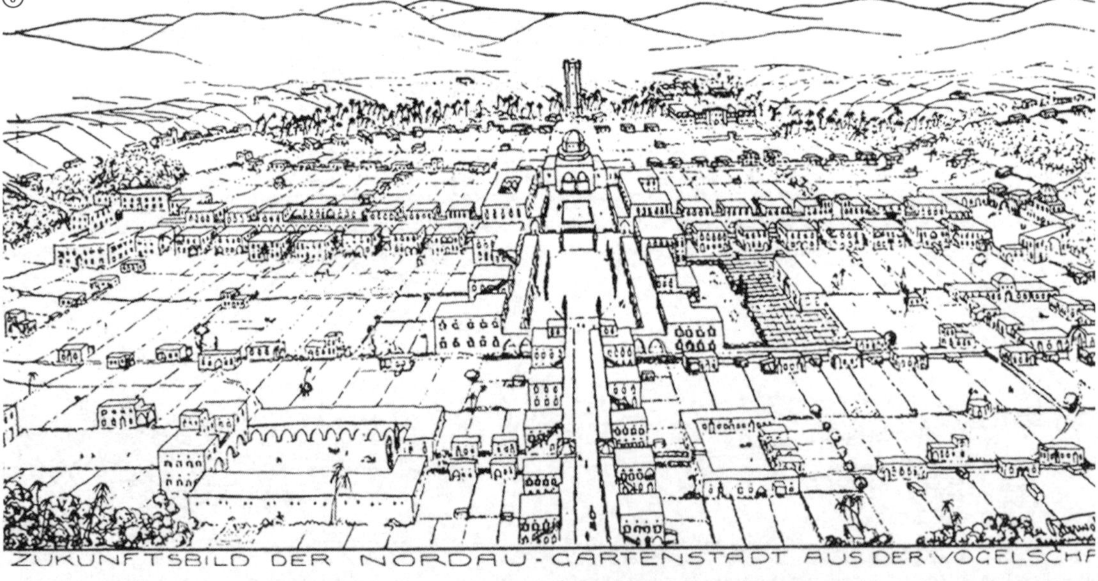

"poison" of urban planning in the rural. As a result, throughout the formative decade, the social agnosticism of the rural communes had no corresponding spatial iconoclasm. Instead, it was constrained by an overtly conservative and overly designed urban scheme, based on axial geometry, hierarchical order, programmatic zoning, formal gardening, and (sub-urban) parcelization. Against the grain of its revolutionary fiber, the kibbutz of the 1920s crystallized as a new rural archetype, made up of reprocessed and dislocated urban conventions. Kauffmann's initial complaint concerning the lack of precedents was hastily answered with architectural overkill.

The implementation of garden-city layouts in the open landscape was not a matter of internal planning discourse alone, but a directive of the World Zionist Organization, reflecting the latter's preference for the cooperative moshav type, with its incorporation of individual initiative and its skepticism about the odds of the kibbutz's survival as a commune (hence Kauffmann's imposition of parcelization in his kibbutz master plans as a way to facilitate an easy transformation of communal space into individually leased and cultivated properties). Beyond a genuine skepticism, there was also a constant ideological objection to the kibbutz among certain Zionist representatives, principally from within American Jewry, who feared that settlements of the communal type would lead to the consolidation of a "communist" or anarchist force.[12] In 1926 Franz Oppenheimer wrote a devastating report on the kibbutz to the WZO, as quoted and analyzed by Galia Bar Or in *Kibbutz: Architecture without Precedents*:

> Oppenheimer [reported that] communistic [i.e., cooperative] settlement has not been successful anywhere in the world, and would not be successful here either: "We speak not on [the] ground[s] of a preconception but after a thorough reflection [based] on the [vast] experience of all contemporary civilized peoples. And we declare that these associations could not be [led] to success even under the most favorable outer conditions and never will be brought to success". He argued that communism had long since proved its bankruptcy, "not only theoretical, but also practical", throughout the world, and reiterated his view that the workers' villages are the ideal form of settlement [...] and that "small *kvutzot*" could be tolerated: these are enlarged families, and "thus they are a kind of religious sect." As for the "large *kvutzah*", Oppenheimer claimed that this was a "socialism of feeling" and that the demands of its members are "pseudo-socialistic, an unclear mixture of 'utopian communism' (condemned by Marx) and an Anarchism of Kropotkin's or Bakunin's kind".[13]

Oppenheimer's forecast proved incorrect; during the 1930s the kibbutz flourished and proliferated. Dozens of new settlements were established, and the various kibbutz movements began to establish their own planning and building departments. Kibbutz architecture gradually took on its distinctly communal form, while reflecting the specific political and structural singularities of the respective movements. But it was the cumulative territorial impact of the kibbutz during the 1930s that turned out to be of greatest consequence.

(7) The twin communes of Ein Harod and Tel Yosef, 1926. Master plan. Richard Kauffmann. Central Zionist Archives.
(8) Nordau Gartenstadt, 1919. Perspective. Alexander Bärwald.

⑨

⑩

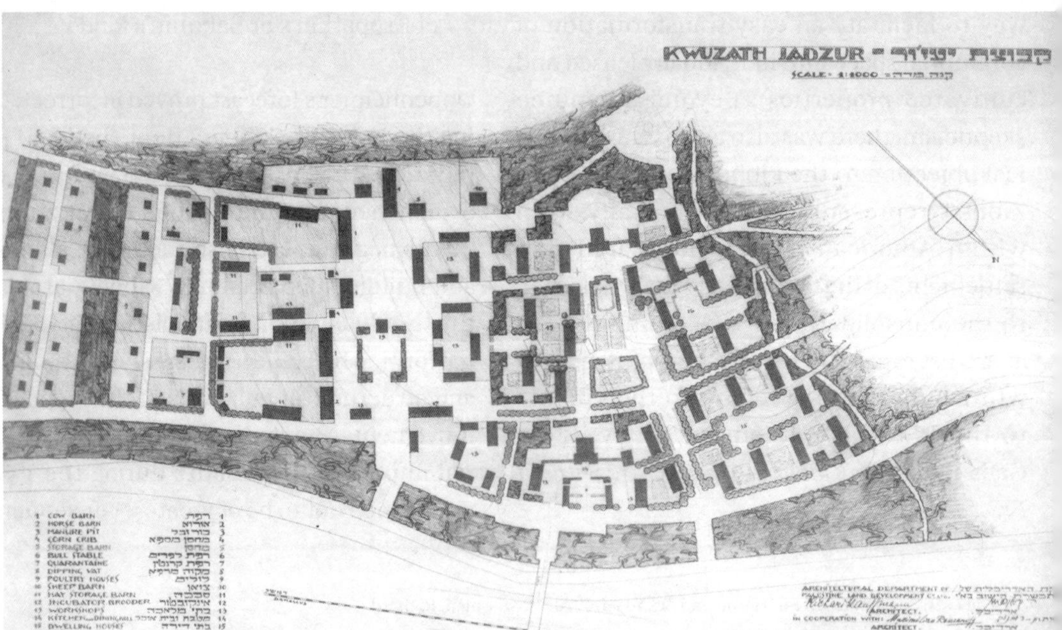

KWUZATH JADZUR
SCALE 1:4000
1 COW BARN
2 HORSE BARN
3 MANURE PIT
4 CORN CRIB
5 STORAGE BARN
6 BULL STABLE
7 QUARANTAINE
8 DIPPING VAT
9 POULTRY HOUSES
10 SHEEP BARN
11 HAY STORAGE BARN
12 INCUBATOR BROODER
13 WORKSHOPS
14 KITCHEN DINING HALL
15 DWELLING HOUSES
16 CHILDRENS
17 MACHINERY SHED
18 WAGON SHED
19 DAIRY
ARCHITECTURAL DEPARTMENT OF
PALESTINE LAND DEVELOPMENT C.
ARCHITECT.
IN COOPERATION WITH:
ARCHITECT.
JERUSALEM SEPTEMBER 1926.

⑪

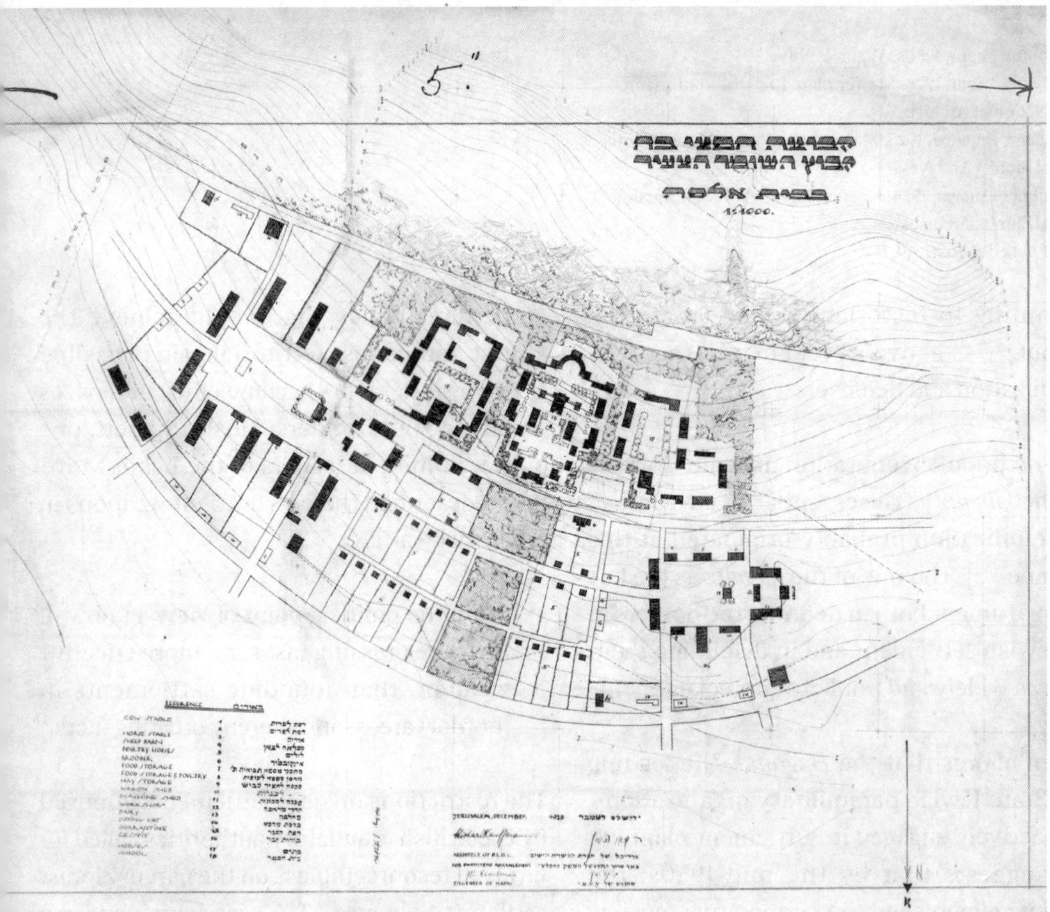

⑫

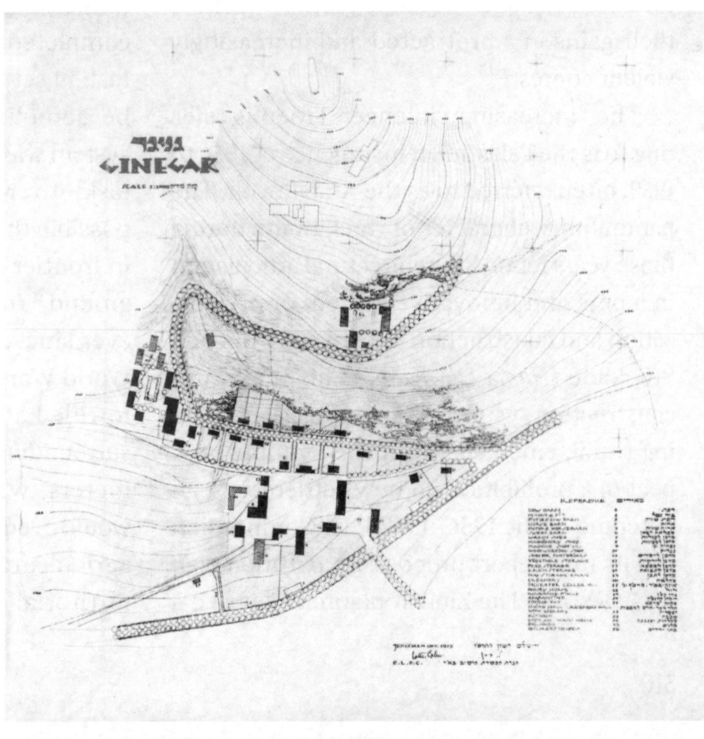

⑨ Kibbutz Yagur, 1930s. Yagur Archive.
⑩ Kibbutz Yagur, 1926. Master plan. Richard Kauffmann. Central Zionist Archives.
⑪ Kvutzat Heftziba, 1925. Master plan. Richard Kauffmann. Central Zionist Archives.
⑫ Kibbutz Ginegar, 1925. Master plan. Richard Kauffmann. Central Zionist Archives.
⑬ Kibbutz Tel Yosef, 1930s.

According to historian S. Ilan Troen, the kibbutz was above all an effective agent of colonization and defense:

> The popular reputation and the myth of the *kibbutz* as the essential avant-garde of colonization probably originated at this time [...]. The role of the *kibbutz* as the key instrument both in defining the borders of Jewish settlement and in defending them was widely and publicly appreciated.[14]

Troen claims that the *Hagana*—the leading pre-State Jewish paramilitary organization—was actively engaged in settlement planning. He suggests that by the mid-1930s, the kibbutz superseded the cooperative moshav as the preferred settlement type because it was "well suited to perform police and security functions [...] and to enable pioneers to hold their gains in a protracted and increasingly violent contest."[15]

The "increasing violence" Troen is referring to is the Palestinian insurgence of 1936 to 1939, often referred to as the Arab Revolt. The paramilitary character of the kibbutz during those years found its architectural articulation in a new and innovative system of prefabrication and construction known as Tower and Stockade (*Homa U'Migdal*). This makeshift construction system, or, more precisely, building ritual, emerged out of the looming prospect of a prohibition on new settlements, an outcome of the 1936–1937 Peel Commission and its final report proposing a partition plan for Palestine. The Zionist planners devised a settlement policy that would achieve the largest and fastest territorial gains possible. Civilian settlements became efficient devices for staking out frontiers. Moshe Sharett, one of the prominent leaders of the Labor Movement, described them as outright weapons in territorial warfare:

> From the political point of view, I know of no more pressing tasks, no more effective weapon, than founding settlements in [border] areas, and thereby creating facts.[16]

The restrictions on new settlements imposed by the British Mandatory authorities called for juridical resourcefulness on the part of Zionist settlement planners. This was soon found in a prior Ottoman law, still in effect during the Mandate period, which stated that a structure may not be demolished if the roof has been completed. According to this legal loophole, instant settlements, built overnight, could not be demolished. The Tower and Stockade system was invented to perform precisely this task—to erect as many instant settlements as possible throughout the country, particularly in frontier areas, and to create "facts on the ground," the slogan of expansionist Zionism ever since. From 1936 until the outbreak of World War II in 1939, nearly fifty-seven such fortified structures (about two per month), surrounding a square-shaped area of 35 square meters, were established. These outposts would eventually be transformed into fortified agricultural settlements, creating Jewish territorial contiguity that would later help

⑬

determine the borderlines of the United Nations Partition Plan.

The invention of the Tower and Stockade system is accredited to Shlomo Gur-Gerzovsky, a founding member of Kibbutz Tel Amal (the first Tower and Stockade outpost), and to the acclaimed architect-soldier Yohanan Ratner.[17] The system was based on the assembly of prefabricated wooden molds, which were then filled with gravel and enclosed with barbed-wire fencing. A prefabricated wooden observation tower and four shacks were erected in the inner yard, providing housing for a "conquering troop" of around forty people. The location of an outpost was determined by eyeshot from a neighboring settlement and accessibility for motor vehicles. Tactically, the idea was to create a spatial matrix, or local clusters of provisional strongholds, in order to swiftly cover as much ground as possible and to establish political realities.[18]

In the wake of the Tower and Stockade onslaught, the bucolic fancy of the Zionist rural would never be the same. The proliferation of makeshift strongholds, domesticated barracks, and panoptic networks transformed the landscape into an imminent battleground and the settlements into awkward military hardware penetrating and holding on to territory in the midst of a hostile countryside. Zionist inner colonization was compelled to produce ever more introverted and fenced communities. While kibbutz architecture would take a remarkable turn and adopt the "free plan," the Tower and Stockade remained its essential iconography. As open, shared, loose, flexible, and plentiful as it would be internally, kibbutz was ever to be a rather gated and vigilant community.

From the mid-1930s into the 1940s, the various kibbutz movements established their own independent planning, engineering, and building departments, in which the theoretical model for the physical planning of the kibbutz was debated and developed. The formalized garden-city schemes that had informed early kibbutz settlements were found conceptually unsuitable and spatially inflexible. The general urban propensity and the principle of zoning, as devised by Richard Kauffmann, were already axiomatic, though now they were transformable into more organic designs based primarily on the integrity and fluidity of the communal open space, or gardenscape, as it would now be referred to.

From the mid-1930s onward, kibbutz master plans were functionally divided into a residential zone and a farm-economy zone. The residential zone included several subzones, such as dwelling quarters for adults and children,[19] sanitary services, educational facilities, and a central social area. The farm zone included a livestock sector and an industrial and artisans' district.[20]

Formally as well as symbolically, kibbutz architecture was now crystallized as a single indivisible space, with no inner boundaries, separation fences, or any other hallmarks of property parcelization and private ownership. The integrated space framed all dimensions of

⑭

⑮

⑭–⑮ The erection of Tower and Stockade settlements, Jezreel Valley, 1936–1937. Central Zionist Archives.
⑯ Tower and Stockade settlement, Beit Yosef, 1937.

life and was collectively owned and activated by the members of the commune. The central arena of kibbutz life consisted of the large lawn and the public facilities (dining room, culture house, library, members' club), which were situated around the lawn like a "forum" or "agora" (terms invoked by the kibbutz planners themselves).

The modernist doctrine of zoning—often criticized for mechanically decomposing the city and deflating the vitality of the mixed-use street—had the opposite effect on the small scale and cohesive social fabric of the rural community. It was the principle of zoning, in fact, which allowed the kibbutz to replace the rigidity of the garden-city layout with the elasticity of the free plan, to do away with internal subdivision, and to operate as a unified performative space. Allegorically, kibbutz zoning drew a simple theatrical scheme of production/consumption, backstage/frontstage—but producers and consumers, actors and spectators, were one and the same here, and the only genre tolerated was that of social realism. Indeed, as is often the case with social realism, planning acquired a mythical quasi-scientific status, and every aspect of collective life was calculated down to the smallest detail. In the rural, the free plan appears to be a painstakingly thought-out doctrine.[21]

Architect Samuel Bickels was the most prominent theorist and practitioner of (large) kibbutz architecture: his lifework included more than sixty kibbutz master plans, dozens of social and cultural institutions, and several essays published in local periodicals between 1940 and the 1960s. He gradually articulated a spatial theorem of kibbutz, formulated around the notion of the internal space, or the "inclusive garden":

> Our planning has to be organic: neither an autonomous suburb nor a rural body. The kibbutz expression of internal gardenscape is an "inclusive garden," in which the individual lives in the framework of the commonality, and not of a parceling for "private" enterprise.[22]

⑯

The "framework of the commonality" mentioned above was a system of open spaces, organized in a continuous hierarchical manner, emanating from the large lawn at the heart of the kibbutz and penetrating into the residential, educational, and service zones. Circulation in the garden occurred along a system of walking paths: main paths leading from the center to the zones around it, and a system of secondary paths leading to the various buildings within the kibbutz territory. Vehicular traffic was restricted to limited areas in the center of the kibbutz and at the perimeter.

The gardenscape was not perceived as a merely decorative backdrop devised to beautify the settlement, but rather as a structuring and distributing system, framing the space itself. Traditional figure-ground relationships were inverted, since the terrain, rather than the buildings, became the main object of design and the major factor in defining what Bickels called "an architectonic interior." The notion of "architectonic interior" provides a tautological key for deciphering the kibbutz setting, since it signifies that architecture is essentially interior: it is a household; it has no outside. Bickels consistently accentuated this spatial split: "The landscape is a regional space in which man is not a criterion. In contrast, in the gardenscape, man is the sole criterion."[23] The gardenscape, then, is the ultimate kibbutz artifact—the all-inclusive product of the entire community's participation in the creative process, the mutual scene of action whereon not only the ordinary pattern of daily life, but also the aesthetic experience of the commune is displayed.

Conceptually, the notion of gardenscape indicates a patchwork rather than axial geometry; diffusive rather than contoured prospects; a textural rather than a structural sensation; a well-balanced biosphere rather than a well-decorated sanctuary. The private and the collective are liberated from their polarity, falling into a seamless continuum in a manner unknown elsewhere. The informal is embedded in the system. The "camp" area is always in flux, and the communal ownership of property allows for great flexibility and alternation of land uses.

There exist about 280 kibbutz settlements, sharing more or less the same architectural principles and organizational parameters as outlined above. Yet this seriality is devoid of any modularity. There are no two identical, or even similar, kibbutz settlements; each bears its own singular and distinctive physiognomy and character. Such phenomenal differential repetition has two explanations: First, kibbutz is conceived as anathema to utopian idealism and its diagrammatic purism. Its selective intellectual roots in dialectical materialism and anarchism dictate a more intricate and open-ended set of guiding principles that allow for greater adaptability to concrete geographic, economic, and political settings by which each settlement is nourished and into which it integrates. Second, since the members of the commune are active participants in the planning process of their settlement, each master plan, though mastered by an architect, is a superimposed tracing not only of the unique group character, but also of individual backgrounds, alignments, and sensibilities. In this respect, kibbutz planning has developed away from the transplanted garden-city diagram toward what might be considered today to be a softer "landscape urbanism."

Regarding the architecture of kibbutz buildings, as Galia Bar Or points out, Bickels underlined the notion of the "built collective" in contrast to the principle of the "commune house," which he described as "an idealistic solution desired by visionaries of collective settlement forms, from the '*phalanstère*' to

⑰

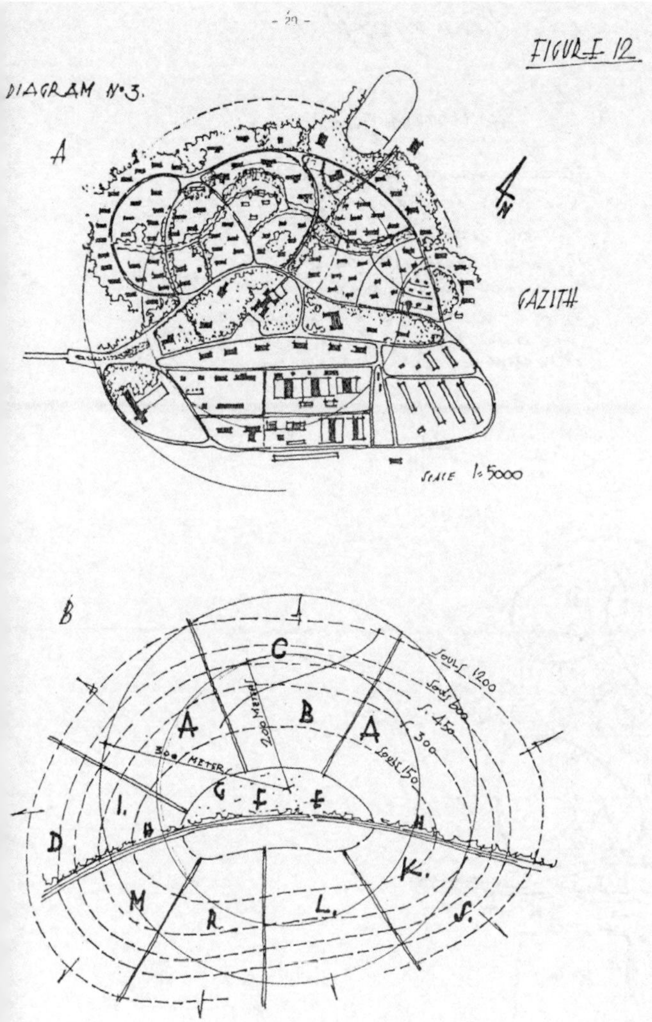
FIGURE 12
DIAGRAM N°3.
A
GAZITH
SCALE 1:5000
B
SOULS 1200
S. 450
S. 300
SOULS 150
200 METER
300 METER

⑱

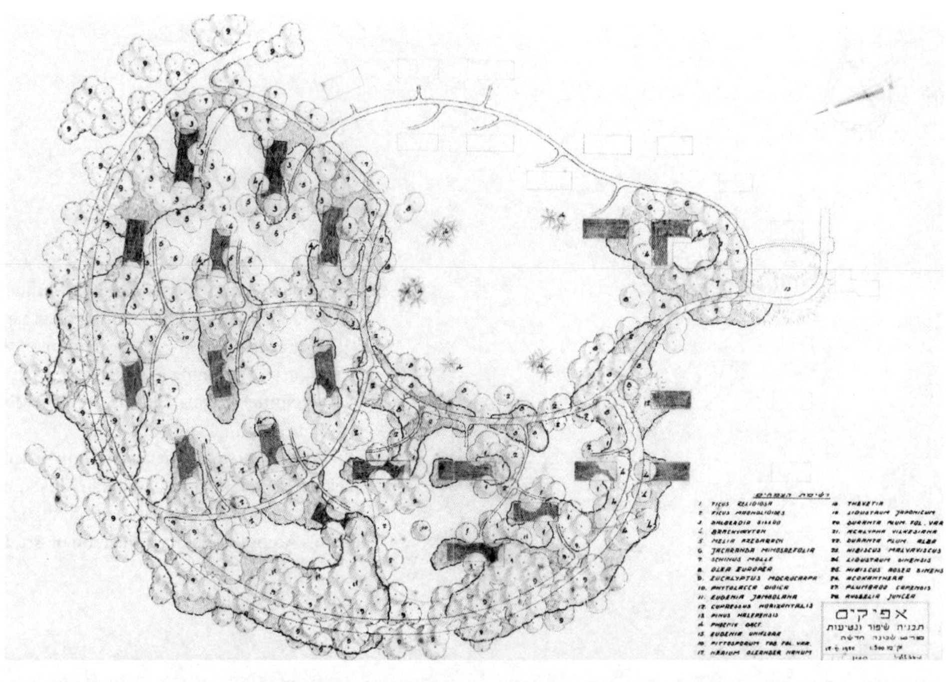

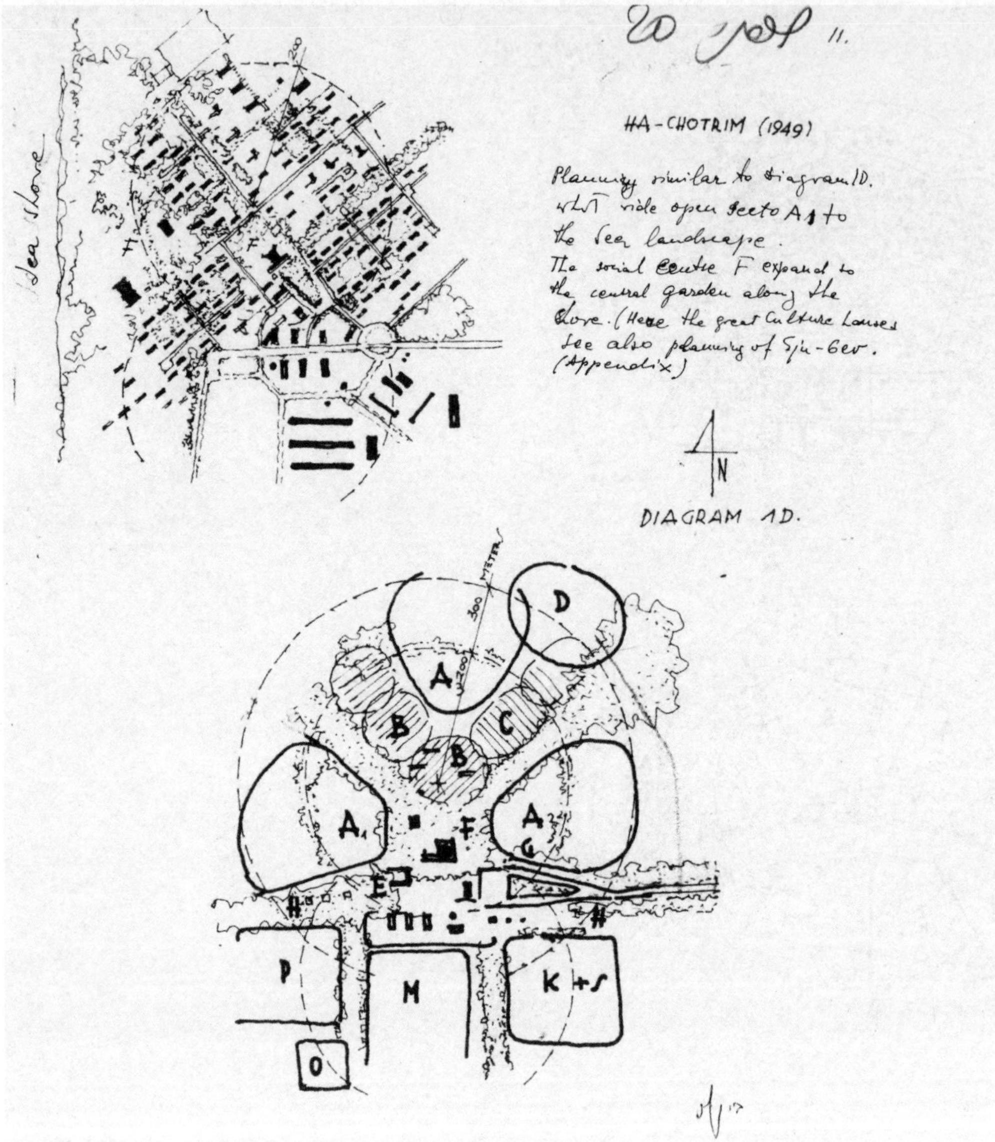


⑲

⑰ Kibbutz Gazit, 1930s. Diagrams. Shmuel Mestechkin.
⑱ Kibbutz Afikim, 1950. Planting plan. Lipa Yahalom.
⑲ Diagrams of kibbutz plans, demonstrating the principles of zoning and planning a unified space without parcellation, 1940s. Samuel Bickels. Bickels Archive, Mishkan Museum of Art, Ein Harod.
⑳ Residential free-plan distribution schemes, 1940s. Samuel Bickels. Bickels Archive, Mishkan Museum of Art, Ein Harod.
㉑ Diagrams of kibbutz circulation, 1940s. Samuel Bickels. Bickels Archive, Mishkan Museum of Art, Ein Harod.

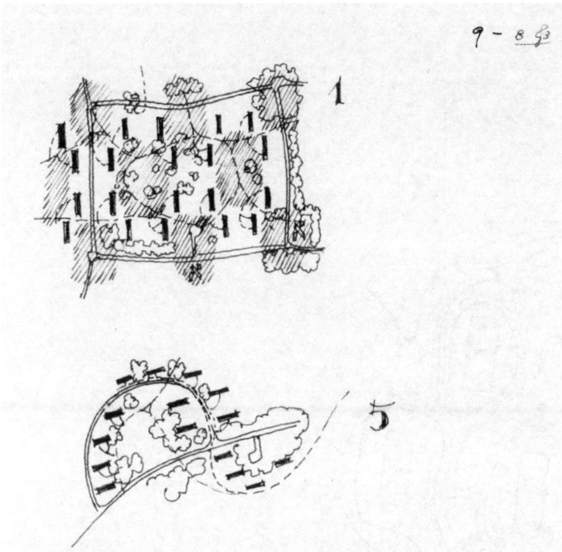
9 - 8 53
1
5

⑳

㉑

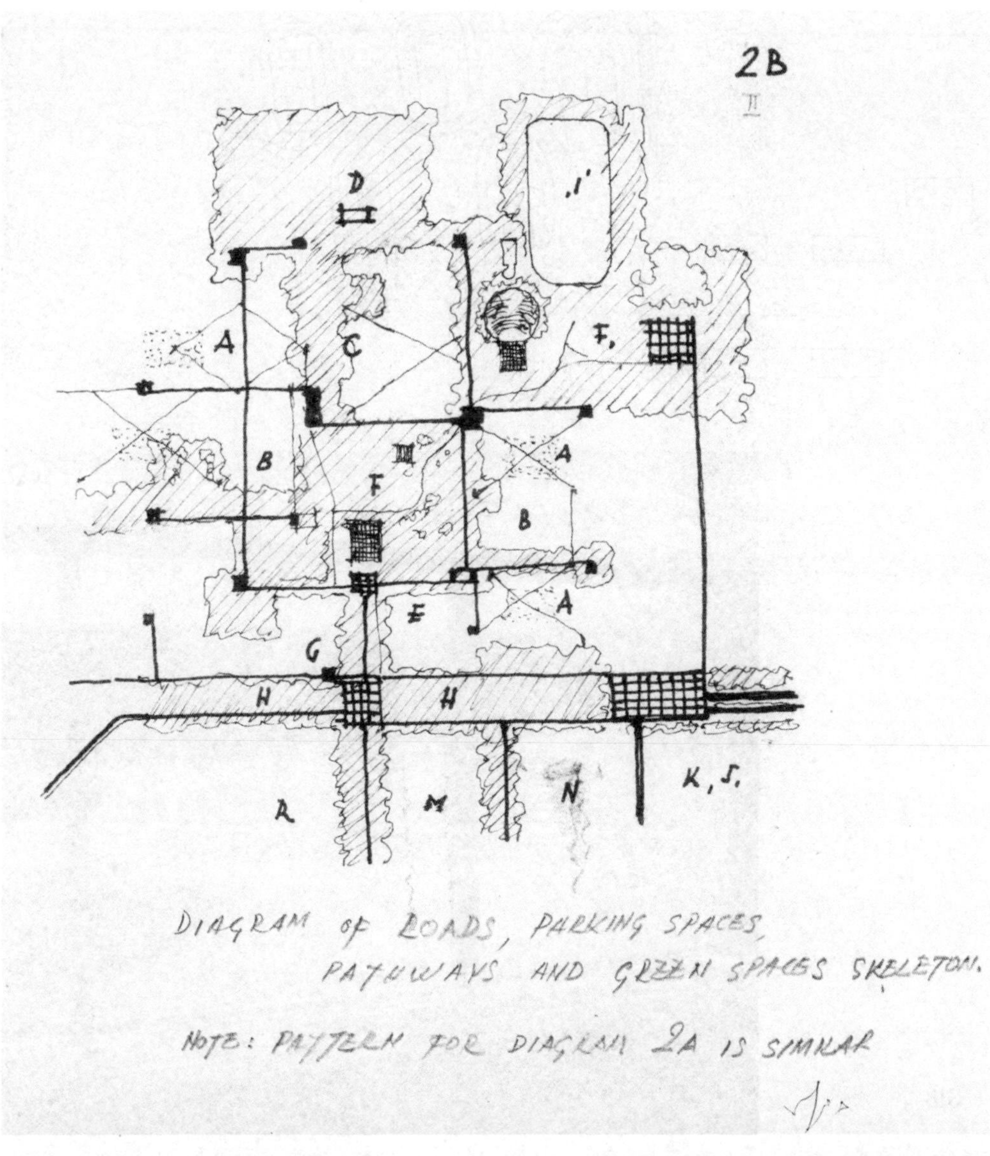
2B
II
D
A
C
F.
B
F
A
B
A
E
G
H
H
R
M
N
K, S.
DIAGRAM OF ROADS, PARKING SPACES,
PATHWAYS AND GREEN SPACES SKELETON.
NOTE: PATTERN FOR DIAGRAM 2A IS SIMILAR

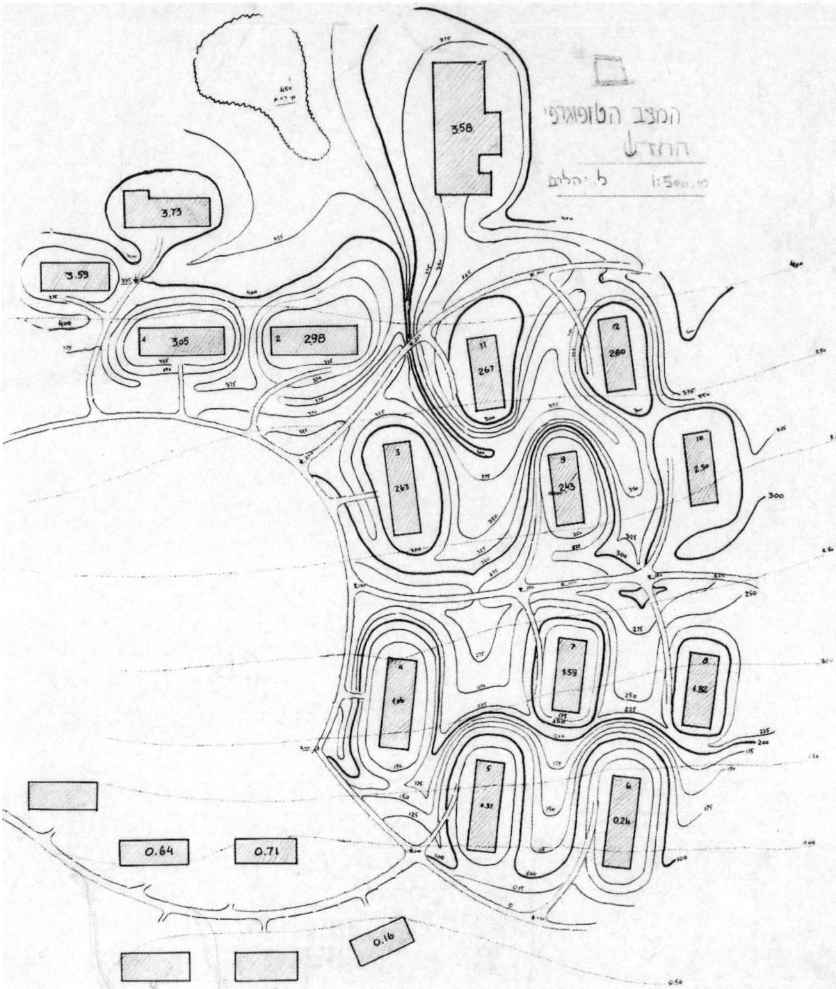

המצב הטופוגרפי
החדש
ל. יהלים
1:500
3.58
3.73
3.59
3.05
2.98
0.64
0.71
0.16


㉒

㉓

㉔

㉕

㉖

㉒ "The new topographic condition," Kibbutz Afikim, 1950. Lipa Yahalom.
㉓ Kibbutz Mishmar Haemek. View from the dining hall, 1970s.
㉔ Kibbutz Geva, 1970s. Geva archive.
㉕ Kibbutz Mishmar Haemek, 1960s. Mishmar Haemek archive.
㉖ Kibbutz Yagur, central garden, 1940s. Landscape: Shlomo Oren-Weinberg. Building (The Titz Vocational School, 1937): Erich Mendelsson.

Le Corbusier."[24] In later correspondence with Anatole Kopp, the eminent scholar of socialist architecture, Bickels asserted that "the kibbutz does not belong to the past. It is perhaps the sole actual architectural form in the world that may be described as an 'architecture of the left.'"[25]

The architecture of the built collective has two facets: that of dwellings that strive for *Existenzminimum* and minimal privacy, in both size and form (25-square-meter apartments with no private toilet, shower, or kitchen were quite common in kibbutz settlements for decades); and that of overdetermined communal buildings, functioning and signifying as "social condensers." In this respect, kibbutz is a somewhat peculiar index of excessive public facilities—dining hall, culture house, members' club, sports courts, swimming pool, library, archive, music room, performance hall, and often a museum or gallery. The formative dictum "neither a city nor a village," denoting a rejection of the cultural deficiency of the village and the lack of solidarity in urban life, generated an architecture with vast civic space and a colossal public sphere.

The dining hall, the most iconic of kibbutz architecture, was historically also its first public building type. It evolved spontaneously from the makeshift collective kitchen of the transient workers' communes into a meeting space where daily assemblies and occasional festivities took place.[26] From the 1920s onward, the dining hall was institutionalized as a building type of its own, accommodating three shared meals a day for the entire commune. It was also used for daily gatherings for discussions, organization of the work roster, and even memorials and holiday ceremonies. The symbolic significance of the dining hall is manifested in its central location in the kibbutz, forming an elevation to one side of the large lawn and constituting the terminus of the main pathway.

Most of the dining halls were financed by the WZO, in spite of its ideological and pragmatic misgivings, and the first permanent dining halls were designed by its chief architect, Richard Kauffmann. Interestingly, at the insistence of kibbutz members, the dining hall was the first communal building type that the WZO agreed to outsource to private architects, often those of exceptional merit, such as Leopold Krakauer, Fritz Kornberg, and Zeev Rechter. These architects represented the cultural elite of the time and were the local propagators of the discourse and praxis of modern architecture. Bauhauslers who studied with Meyer, Hilberseimer, and Mies, such as Munio Gitai Weinraub, Arieh Sharon, and Shmuel Mestechkin, were extensively involved in kibbutz architecture.

The kibbutz became a platform for innovative experiments in new building types that were distinctively modernist and displayed structural ingenuity, since they were based on large open spans to allow the assembly of the entire community. The pastiche of the Zionist rural assumed its incongruous iconography: amidst the rustic agrarian scenery, the crude agricultural structures, and the austere dwellings—often tents or wood cabins, and later on plain red-roofed *Heimat*-style houses—gleaming masterworks of International Style

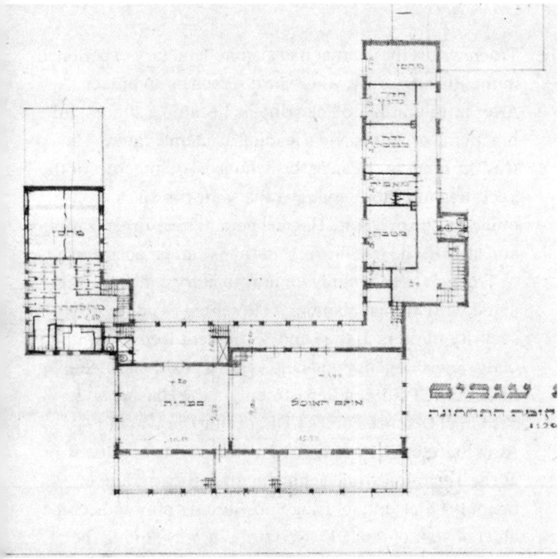

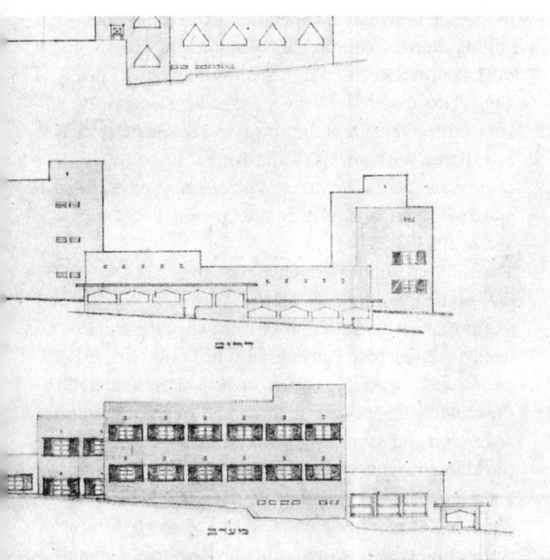

㉗ ㉘

architecture sprouted and claimed their aesthetic authority.

Modern architecture indeed found inspiration in the rural, especially in monolithic silos and light sheds, but it rarely returned to the rural to actually build there and articulate new technologies, typologies, or styles. Perhaps only in the Zionist rural of the 1920s to the 1960s did modern architecture proliferate, evolve, and signify so profoundly. While in the cities of Tel Aviv and Haifa modernism became the language of domesticity, in the rural it was distinctively the marker of publicity. The image of the (architectural) "machine in the garden," recurrent in official Zionist graphics and visual art, suggested an idealized symbiosis of nature and artifice, but at once also manifested Zionism's designed otherness, its estrangement from the native surroundings, its preeminence as émigré culture, and, above all, its transformative energy. The rural of Zionism should therefore be read as such: a staged setting, a radical concept, an emblem of national reincarnation, a mold for a model society working the land while cultivating communal *Bildung* and architectural savoir faire. Arieh Sharon's autobiography, *Kibbutz + Bauhaus,* published in the mid-1970s,[27] captured in retrospect the quintessence of this peculiar imaginary by hybridizing its two foremost form-related icons.

Incidentally, it was Arieh Sharon who in 1948, with the establishment of the State of Israel, would take Richard Kauffmann's place as the official architect of the Zionist movement and would push the rural doctrine even further, backing it up with regional planning theories, embedding it in the 1950 national master plan, and turning it into a State policy still operative, mutatis mutandis, today. ■

㉗ Proposal for communal building integrating dwellings, dining hall, and public amenities, Kibbutz Kiryat Anavim, 1922. Plan. Richard Kauffmann.
㉘ Proposal for communal building integrating dwellings, dining hall, and public amenities, Kibbutz Kiryat Anavim, 1922. Elevations. Richard Kauffmann.

1 Young refugees engaged in construction and road-building for the British Mandate authorities organized themselves in various forms of egalitarian partnership. Two thousand of them joined together in "labor battalions"; groups of women established "women-workers' farm-economies."

2 Galia Bar Or, "The Initial Phases: A Test Case," in *Kibbutz: Architecture without Precedents*, ed. Galia Bar Or and Yuval Yasky, catalogue of the Israeli pavilion at the 12th International Architecture Biennale in Venice, 2010, p. 19.

3 In her discussion of the influence of the Russian anarchist geographer Pyotr Kropotkin (1842–1921) and his 1898 book on discourse within the kibbutz movements, *Fields, Factories and Workshops*, Galia Bar Or writes that "the ideological circle at Ein Harod held discussions on [Kropotkin's] books [...] and raised questions about relations between agriculture, artisanry and factory work, the centralization and noncentralization of industry, manual work and mental work, and the nature of cooperation. They also read from Kropotkin's book *Mutual Aid: A Factor of Evolution*, which was based on his observations of animals during his long sojourn in eastern Siberia." Galia Bar Or, "Initial Phases," p. 30.

4 Yitzhak Tabenkin, "On the Problems of Kibbutz Building" (1921), in Bar Or and Yasky, *Kibbutz: Architecture without Precedents*, pp. 51–63.

5 Shabtai Be'eri, "The Planning of Construction in the Commune in Socialist Thought" (1952), in Bar Or and Yasky, *Kibbutz: Architecture without Precedents*, p. 66. Be'eri quotes from *The Writings of Nachman Syrkin* (Tel Aviv: Davar, 1939), p. 57.

6 Tabenkin, "On the Problems of Kibbutz Building," p. 56.

7 Richard Kauffmann, "Planning Jewish Agricultural Settlements in Palestine" (unpublished article found in his estate, late 1940s), p. 22.

8 Ibid.

9 Kauffmann was a direct disciple of Theodor Fischer, who was one of the planners, along with Hermann Muthesius, of the first German garden city, Dresden-Hellerau, from 1909 to 1910.

10 The discussion here of the Nordau Garden City is based on Gilbert Herbert and Silvina Sosnovsky, *Bauhaus on the Carmel and the Crossroads of Empire* (Jerusalem: Yad Izhak Ben-Zvi, 1993), pp. 68–72.

11 Cited in Herbert and Sosnovsky, *Bauhaus on the Carmel*, p. 71. According to Herbert and Sosnovsky, Oppenheimer's identification with Howard went back to his 1907 foreword to the German translation of Howard's *Garden Cities of Tomorrow*.

12 On the tension between the WZO and the Kibbutz Movement, see Bar Or, "Initial Phases," pp. 34–39.

13 Ibid., pp. 35–36.

14 S. Ilan Troen, *Imagining Zion: Dreams, Designs, and Realities in a Century of Jewish Settlement* (New Haven: Yale University Press, 2003), p. 76.

15 Ibid., p. 63.

16 Cited in ibid., p. 69.

17 Troen writes that Ratner had acquired military experience in the Russian army, where he'd served as an officer. After immigrating to Palestine he became a successful practicing architect and a leading academic figure. He was the founding dean of the School of Architecture at the Technion in Haifa, serving at the same time as a senior officer in the pre-State Hagana paramilitary organization, and later in the Israeli army. Ratner's career, according to Troen, is "a case study for how military concerns interacted with Zionist planning." He served as adviser for security matters in the Land Settlement Department of the Jewish Agency and held various positions, including head of the Planning Department, in the Hagana and the Israel Defense Forces (IDF) during the War of 1948. After Statehood, he remained a professor of architecture at the Technion while achieving the military rank of major general (and refusing Ben-Gurion's offer to become chief of staff of the IDF). Certainly, he was among the relatively limited professional corps of officers who shaped the Israeli army and its operational doctrines, and among even fewer professional architects who shaped the Israeli architectural education system and its pedagogical doctrines. See Troen, *Imagining Zion*, pp. 79–80.

18 For a critical reading of the Tower and Stockade system, see Sharon Rotbard, "Wall and Tower," in *A Civilian Occupation: The Politics of Israeli Architecture*, ed. Rafi Segal and Eyal Weizman (Tel Aviv and London: Babel and Verso, 2003), p. 39.

19 The children's house (which in the early stages was the only house in the kibbutz built from concrete) was planned as an "inclusive" space that satisfied all of the children's needs: a dining room, an infirmary, bedrooms, playrooms, a yard, and a vegetable garden. In most of the kibbutzim the children slept in the children's houses and spent the afternoon and evening hours with their parents. For the kibbutz architects, the "children's society" presented a unique planning challenge. In the kibbutzim of the Shomer Hatzair movement, children between the ages of twelve and eighteen were generally sent to a regional "institution" which absorbed youngsters from several kibbutzim in the surrounding area. In these cases the children's society was planned as a sort of miniature kibbutz, with a dining hall and school wings around a central lawn. The residential rooms for the children and the staff were built around this inner nucleus, and beyond them were the agricultural zones, such as orchards and stables. The small scale of the children's society provided an opportunity to plan a purer kibbutz model than was possible in the planning of large kibbutzim with complex needs. In the 1970s and 1980s many kibbutzim began to abandon the idea of "collective sleeping," and the children returned to living in their parents' homes.

20 See Samuel Bickels, "On Some Problems of Gardening in Kibbutz Settlement Planning" (1960) in Bar Or and Yasky, *Kibbutz: Architecture without Precedents*, p. 147.

21 According to Yuval Yasky, in his analysis of the kibbutz planning mechanism, "Tens of architects, planners,

and engineers, among them some of the best and most talented professionals, worked in and for these planning departments over the years. These kibbutz planning departments operated continuously until the early 1990s, and the office that was established after their privatization was for many years the largest engineering and architectural firm in Israel." Yuval Yasky, "Neither City, Nor Village – A Kibbutz," in Bar Or and Yasky, *Kibbutz: Architecture without Precedents*, p. 91.

22 Bickels, "Some Problems of Gardening," p. 147.

23 Ibid., p. 149.

24 From Samuel Bickels's handwritten notes (Bickels Archive, Ein Harod Museum of Art). Cited in Bar Or, "Initial Phases," p. 44.

25 Letter from Bickels to Kopp [in French], May 1970 (Bickels Archive, Ein Harod Museum of Art). Cited in Bar Or, "Initial Phases," p. 44.

26 See Emmanuel Tal, "Chapters in the Evolution of the Kibbutz Dining Hall, 1926–1935," *Cathedra* 70 (January 1994).

27 Arieh Sharon, *Kibbutz + Bauhaus: An Architect's Way in a New Land* (Stuttgart and Tel Aviv: Karl Kramer Verlag and Massada, 1976). In the introduction to the book, on p. 6, Bruno Zevi writes: "The fascinating, sometimes almost hypnotic, peculiarity of this volume is that it blends and synthesizes three books into one. Firstly, there is the biography of a life made up of rare ingredients: Zionism, kibbutz, Bauhaus, national planning, professional activity on a local, then on an international scale. In the second place, there is the story of a building of a country, agricultural settlements, urban housing, hospitals, universities, up to the reconstruction of a united Jerusalem. Finally, we have the achievements of an architect, his creative products, his space-time language in the dynamics of its numerous modern trends."

㉙ Arieh Sharon, Kibbutz + Bauhaus (Karl Kramer Verlag, Stuttgart and Massda, Tel Aviv, 1976).

㉚

㉛

㉜

(30) Dining hall, Kibbutz Tel Yosef, 1930. Leopold Krakauer.
(31) Dining hall, Kibbutz Tel Yosef, 1930s. Leopold Krakauer.
(32) Dining hall, Kibbutz Ein Harod. Reception for the youth society, 1930s. Richard Kauffmann.
(33) Dining-hall competition entry, Kibbutz Yagur, 1930s. Arieh Sharon.
(34) Dining hall, Kibbutz Kfar Masaryk, 1962. Elevations. Munio Gitai Weinraub.

(33)

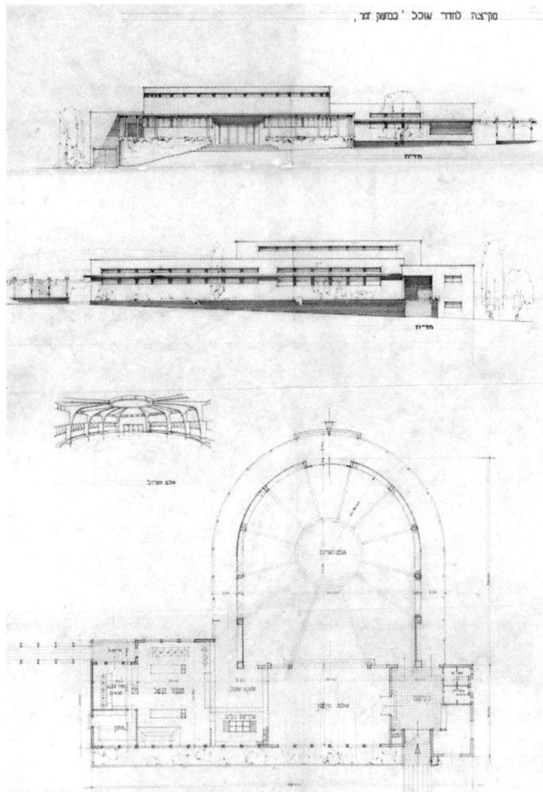

(34)

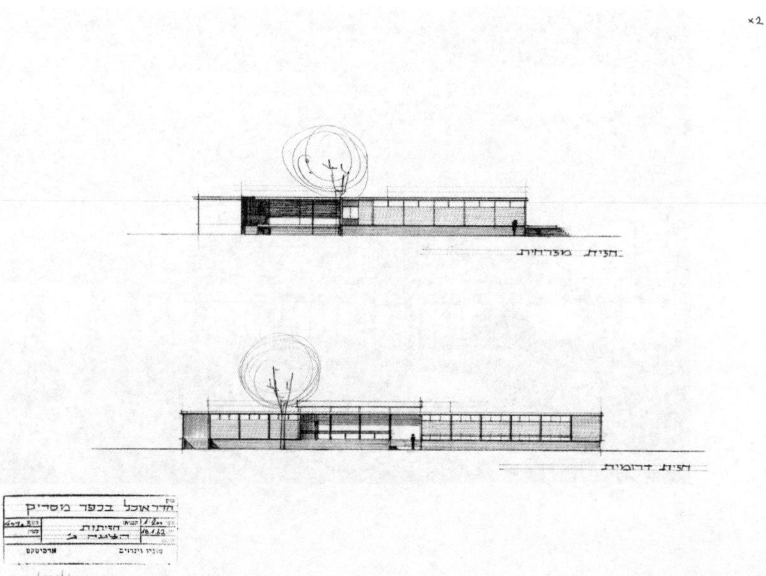

(35)

(36)

(38)

(37)

㉟ Dining hall, Kibbutz Givat Brenner, 1962. Robert Bennett.
㊱ Dining hall foyer, Kibbutz Mizra, 1950s. Shmuel Mestechkin.
㊲ Dining hall, Kibbutz Yagur, 1940s. Interior. Joseph Idelman.
㊳ Dining hall, Passover meal, Kibbutz Mishmar Haemek, 1953.
Mishmar Haemek archive.
㊴ Dining hall, Passover meal, Kibbutz Givat Brenner, 1950. Givat Brenner archive.
㊵ Marking Stalin's death in the dining hall, Kibbutz Gaash, 1953.

㊴

㊵

41

42

43

44

41 A concert by Jascha Heifetz, Ein Harod quarry, 1926.
42 Members' meeting, Kibbutz Geva, 1940s. Geva archive.
43 Women exercising by the pool, Kibbutz Mishmar Haemek, 1970s.
44 Harvest festival (Shavuot), Kibbutz Geva, 1960s. Geva archive.
45 First-fruit celebrations (Shavuot), Kibbutz Neve Yam, 1964. Family album. (The author is second from the left.)
46 First-fruit celebrations (Shavuot) around the silo, Kibbutz Ein Hashofet, 1945. Ein Hashofet archive.
47 Open swimming pool, unidentified kibbutz, 1960s.

45

46

47

(48)

(49)

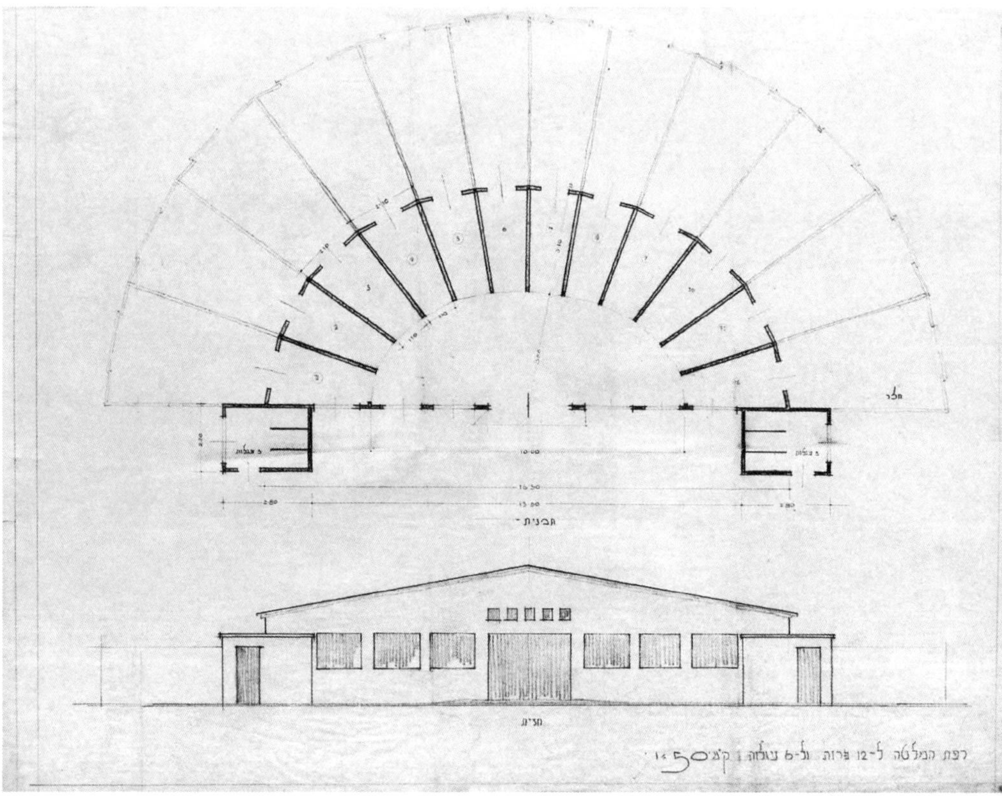

(50)

(48) Old cowshed, with a second floor for dwellings, Kibbutz Gan Shmuel, 1930s. *Kibbutz + Bauhaus*, Arieh Sharon.
(49) Calving shed, Kibbutz Gan Shmuel, 1930s. Plan and elevation. Arieh Sharon.
(50) Chicken coop, Kibbutz Mizra, early 1950s. Shmuel Mestechkin.
(51) First permanent dwellings, Kibbutz Nir David, late 1920s.
(52) Dwellings, Kibbutz Tel Yosef, 1928. Richard Kauffmann.
(53) Dwellings, Kibbutz Ein Shemer, 1930s.

(51) (52) (53)

⑭

⑮

⑯

⑰

(58)

(54) First permanent dwellings and dining hall, unidentified kibbutz, late 1920s.
(55) Water tower, unidentified kibbutz, 1930s.
(56) Residential building for four families, Kibbutz Geva, view in the 1930s.
(57) Kibbutz Mizra, late 1950s. Shmuel Mestechkin.
(58) Dwelling unit (heder), Kibbutz Givat Brenner, 1930s. Givat Brenner archive.
(59) Dwellings, bathroom door facing the public path to allow passersby to use it, Kibbutz Sarid, 1949. Plan and elevation. Arieh Sharon. Sarid archive.
(60) Residential room, Kibbutz Hazorea, 1950s. Shmuel Mestechkin. Hazorea archive.
(61) Residential room, Kibbutz Beit Hashita, 1960s. Azaria Alon family collection.

(59)

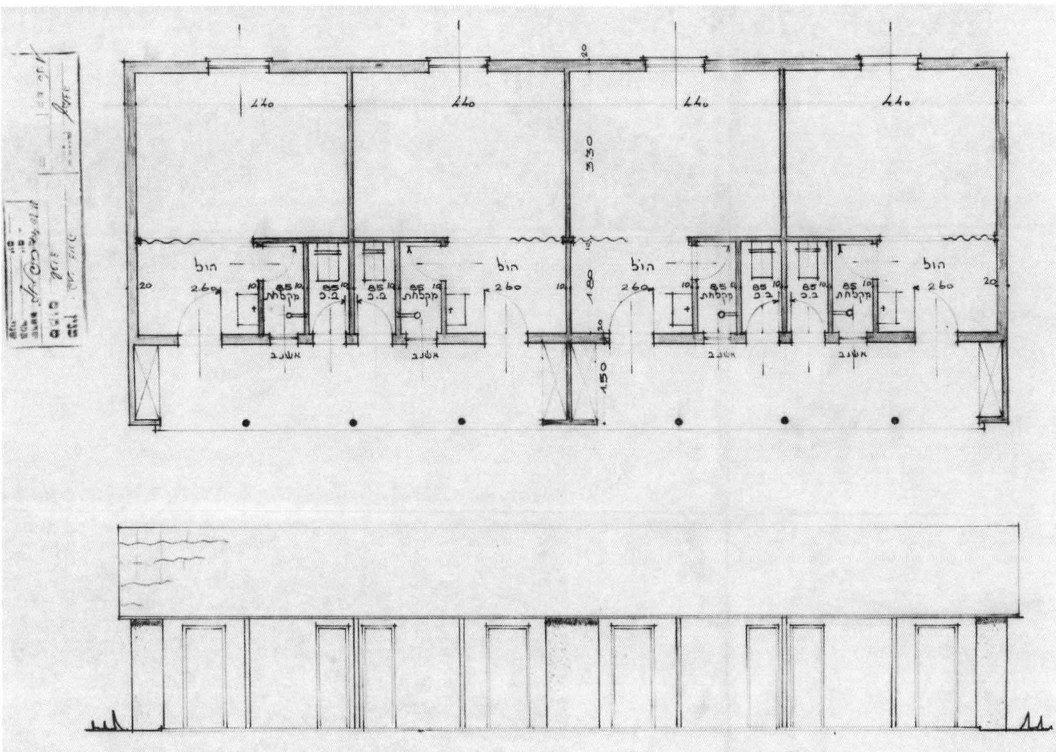

(60)

(61)

(62)

(63)

(64)

(65)

(66)

(62) Dining hall, Kibbutz Ein Hashofet, view in the 1940s
(63) Kibbutz Ein Gedi, early 1960s.
(64) School, Kibbutz Degania Alef, 1930s. Richard Kauffmann.
(65) Kibbutz Ein Harod, 1930s. Matson Collection, Library of Congress.
(66) Youth society area, Kibbutz Yagur, 1950s. Richard Kauffmann.

(67)

(68)

(69)

(70) (71)

(67) Unidentified structure, 1930s. Central Zionist Archives.
(68) The dining hall, Kibbutz Heftziba, view in the 1930s. Architect: Richard Kauffmann. Central Zionist Archives.
(69) Children's house, unidentified kibbutz, view in the 1930s. Architect: Richard Kauffmann. Central Zionist Archives.
(70) Dining hall, Kibbutz Beit Alpha, 1933. Leopold Krakauer. Central Zionist Archives.
(71) Unidentified structure, 1930s. Central Zionist Archives.
(72) Culture house, Kibbutz Heftziba, early 1970s. Ziva Armoni.
(73) Kolin House, Kibbutz Neve Eitan, 1960s. Samuel Bickels.

⑫

⑬

⑭

⑮

⑯

(74)–(76) Children's house, Kibbutz Mishmar Haemek, 1930s. Joseph Neufeld. Mishmar Haemek archive.
(77) Children's house, Kibbutz Geva, 1930s. Geva archive.
(78) Playpens in the yard of the children's house, Kibbutz Givat Brenner, ca. 1950. Givat Brenner archive.
(79) Children's houses, Kibbutz Yagur, 1950s. Richard Kauffmann. Yagur Archive.
(80) Children's house, Kibbutz Ein Shemer, 1938. Early sketches. Arieh Sharon.

(77)

(78)

(79)

(80)

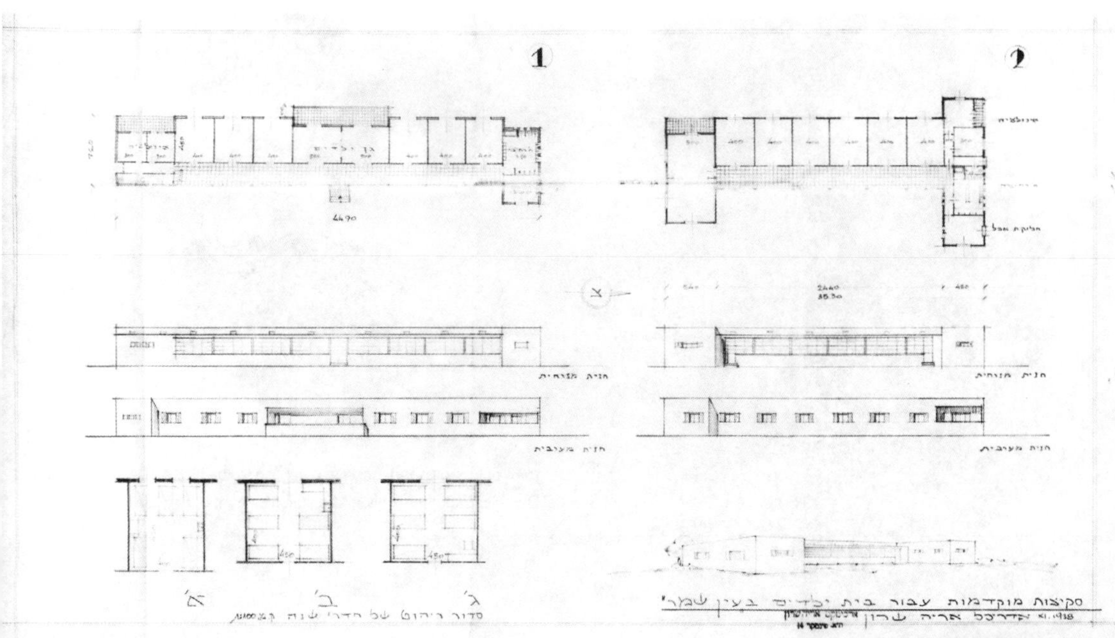

# DOSSIER:
# SAMUEL BICKELS' KIBBUTZ GARDENSCAPE

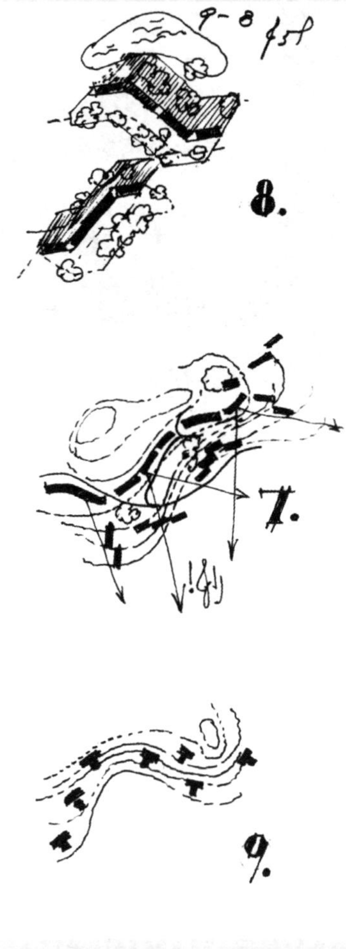


(81) Diagram of kibbutz landscape and gardenscape types, 1940s. Samuel Bickels. Bickels Archive, Mishkan Museum of Art, Ein Harod.

## On Some Problems of Gardening in Kibbutz Settlement Planning[1]

*By Samuel Bickels*

### The Kibbutz Settlement and the Kibbutz Gardenscape

Town planning theory deals with many problems of settlement planning and seeks perfect solutions for them on both the functional and the formal level. Planning a settlement entails a mixture of both practical and experiential values: love of landscape and space, aspirations for aesthetic harmony, satisfaction of cultural demands, and creation of conditions for both personal and public hygiene. These are inseparable values in all planning. The mode of life in every society determines the form of the settlement and shapes its character. The settlement is the fruit of a creative and organized society. It becomes a symbol of the society, the quintessence of its creative activity.

In the planning of settlements we make use of terms that define the framework of the planning: "city," "village," "farmhold" (*meshek*), etc. The kibbutz is a planned settlement of a communal society that has clear social aspirations. In the general planning of a kibbutz settlement, we use the word "kibbutz" as a planning term. Likewise, in the planning of each detail within it—a building, a neighborhood, a zone, and even its decorative garden (*gan noi*)—we will speak about a "kibbutz garden," a "kibbutz gardenscape," with everything that characterizes it.

A kibbutz is neither a village nor a city, and the gardenscape (*noi*) within it is not that of a village or of a city suburb. Nor is it a park in the traditional sense of a place for recreation. With the urbanistic development of the kibbutz settlement, the concept of the gardenscape has developed as a value of increasing importance. A settlement's demographic problems, such as those of density, are solved together with the solving of problems of dispersion, the impact of which is discernible in the emotional/experiential dimension of the inhabitants' lives. This development is gradually leading to the penetration of the gardenscape into the grounds of the buildings, to an organic connection of the two of these together. The kibbutz settlement as a complete creation finds its full expression in the specific kibbutz gardenscape.

### The Relation Between the Buildings and the Flora

Before we move on to a more detailed description of the problems of the kibbutz gardenscape, we need to clarify a number of concepts and outline some general problems of gardenscape planning in any kind of settlement: the problem of the equilibrium between the buildings and the gardenscape areas, and the organic integration of these in the planning. The connection between a building or group of buildings and the flora can create:

1. problems of preference of gardenscape over the building/s, or vice versa;
2. problems of autonomy, i.e., an autonomous building, autonomous gardening;
3. organic problems, i.e., the organic integration of the constructed building into a green structure.

It is only by a general integration that a fundamental solution can be achieved in the planning of a kibbutz gardenscape.

### The Regional Landscape and the Local Gardenscape

The settlement is situated in a region. A regional landscape encompasses it. In the description of the general plan we will progress from the general to the particular, from the region to the settlement area, and from that area to the immediate vicinity of the house. We progress from the landscape to the general gardenscape, and from there to the gardenscape around the house, from the landscape space to the gardenscape space.

We say: The gardenscape planning is expressed in the creation of the connection between defined spaces: even the free space in the region is quite defined. The landscape is a regional space in which man is not a criterion. In contrast, in the gardenscape, man is the sole criterion. The "space" is an architectonic interior that is created by buildings, flora, and other accessory factors, in their integration together.

Every architectonic interior has three dimensions: depth, breadth, and height. The region has an additional dimension—time. Every garden constitutes a combination of these spaces. [...]

The gardenscape we create is an autonomous element in the landscape that surrounds it. Elements

(82) Diagram of a radial kibbutz, 1940s. Samuel Bickels. Bickels Archive, Mishkan Museum of Art, Ein Harod.
(83) – (84) Diagram of a kibbutz planning type, 1940s. Samuel Bickels. Bickels Archive, Mishkan Museum of Art, Ein Harod.

of the landscape "penetrate" and become integrated into it. In figure X we see the settlement from an elevation, from a viewpoint that encompasses the entire region. In this general picture we see the area of the kibbutz settlement from Level 1 as a patch that stands out from the landscape around it. This patch can either integrate organically into the landscape or stand out from it, for the region has a specific landscape of its own. Every landscape has a physical dominant, characteristic flora, characteristic topography, and sometimes there are buildings or concentrations of buildings in it that may constitute an emphasis in the region's overall landscape. Not infrequently, the settlement creates the first motif in the landscape, even its dominant, and what applies to the settlement applies equally to its gardenscape.

When we descend lower, to Level 2, and our angle of vision narrows, our gaze will encompass the area closest to the settlement, its total gardenscape. Here we will see the connection between the surrounding landscape and the interior of the gardenscape of the smaller area, i.e., the reciprocal relations between the landscape and the total gardenscape.

From Level 3 we will see the connections between the various zones within the settlement, i.e., the interior space of the kibbutz garden. In the plan, we will see the structure of its external lines, the flora in its overall composition, the paths and thoroughfares, and we will learn about the reciprocal relations between the built space and the gardenscape surrounding it. This is the place to distinguish between an autonomous building and an autonomous garden, or acknowledge the organic connection between them.

At Level 4 we will see the relations between the interior of the constructed building and the gardenscape adjacent to it, between the architectonic "space" of the building's interior and that of the garden beside it.

Even Level 5 is of major importance, and is needed to give us a complete picture of the plan. This is the level beneath the ground, where the sewage, water supply, and electricity lines are. This level has a major influence on the planning of a kibbutz settlement (as of any other kind of settlement).

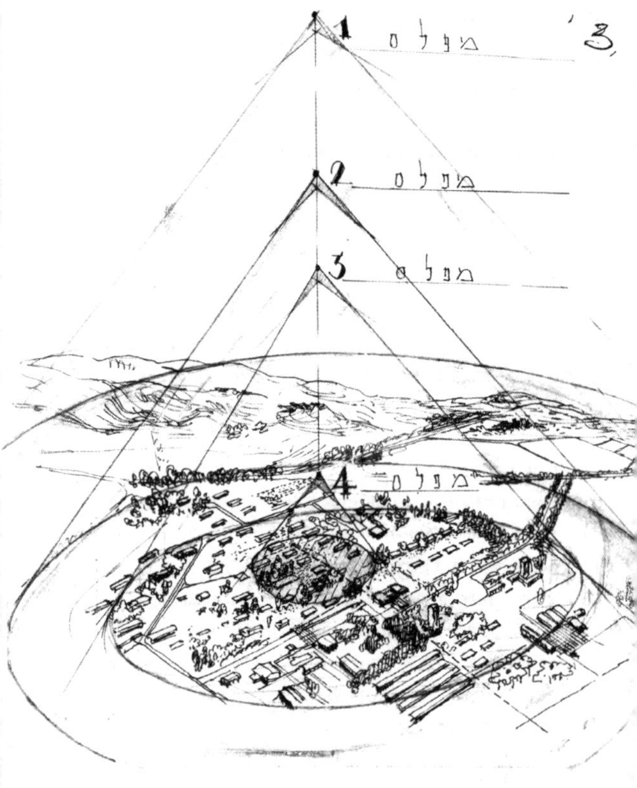


(82)

In giving all the pictures from these five levels together, one on top of the other, we obtain a uniform picture: the plan of the kibbutz settlement with its gardenscape values.

## The Emphasis in the Landscape

In every landscape there is a dominant—its emphasis. It is produced by objective values of the region, such as topography, flora, water, or buildings, a road, a house, etc. Every region has its specific climatic conditions, and we have to exploit these in planning the gardenscape in the settlement and its surroundings.

All the abovementioned factors have a major influence on the selection of the flora and the positioning of the houses, on determining the distances between them, their height, their location in the area, and even the selection of a place for the settlement, and of course its gardenscape. Elements of flora in the region's landscape also constitute a desirable element for its penetration into that landscape (groves, avenues of trees leading to the settlement).

The landscape penetrates into the gardenscape by means of construction that takes into account the flora and emphasizes the depth of the gardenscape that faces the landscape. In this case the landscape is the determining factor, and the gardenscape has to create a secondary emphasizing frame. [...]

## "An All-Day Garden"

In functional terms, the general plan of a kibbutz settlement is divided into two major zones:

> *The residential zone*, which includes several subzones, such as residential neighborhoods for adults, children, and youth; sanitary services, a school, a central zone.
>
> *The farm-economy zone*, which is also divided into a livestock zone and an artisanry and industrial zone.

The various zones generally appear as *integrated* in the older kibbutz settlements, or as *adjacent* in settlements from the '40s, or as *partially separated*.

The residential zone and the farm-economy zone are separated by a broad expanse of gardenscape, which is commonly seen as a "separating" zone. An external traffic artery leads to this zone. In most cases this is planned as a broad avenue of trees. [...]

In formal and planning terms, these zones with their different functions create a unified value, a unified kibbutz. The specific gardenscape within them, with its specific functions in each zone separately, creates a unified value, a unified garden. Its function is not solely utilitarian—although this is "an all-day garden," not a park for recreation—but at the same time it has to serve as a distinctive formal frame, visually and experientially. These formal functions, reciprocally integrated, create a homogeneous kibbutz garden. Only in rare cases is the garden in the residential zone separate from the garden in the farm-economy zone. ■

1 This article by Samuel Bickels was originally published in *Gan VeNof* 5–6 (February 1960), pp. 229–239. The complete article was also printed in *Kibbutz: Architecture without Precedents*, ed. Galia Bar Or and Yuval Yasky, catalogue of the Israeli pavilion at the 12th International Venice Biennale, 2010. Excerpts are given here.

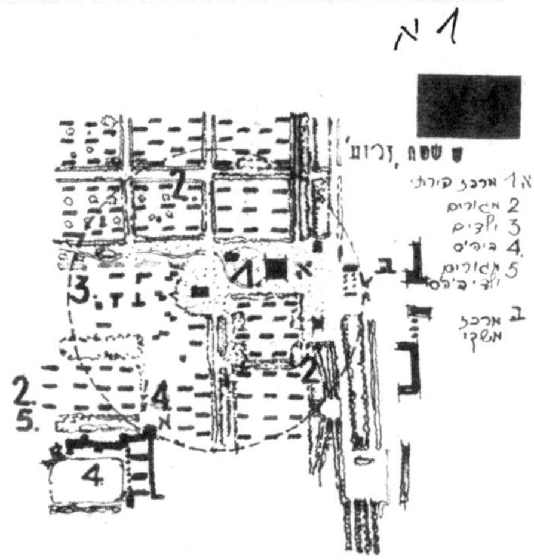

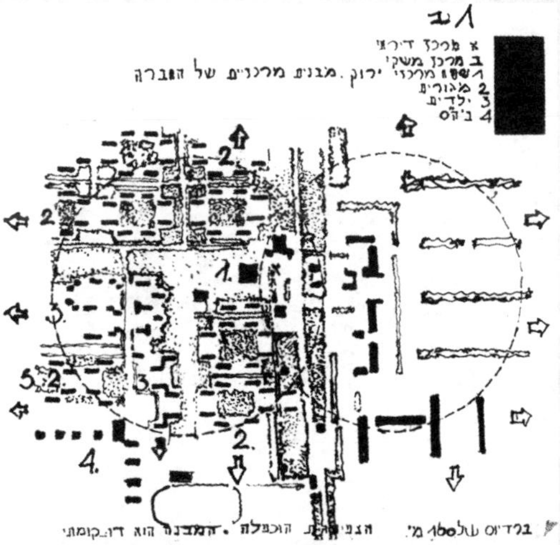

85

86

87

(88)

(89)

(85)–(89) Mishkan Museum of Art, Kibbutz Ein Harod, 1948. Samuel Bickels. Bickels Archive, Mishkan Museum of Art, Ein Harod.

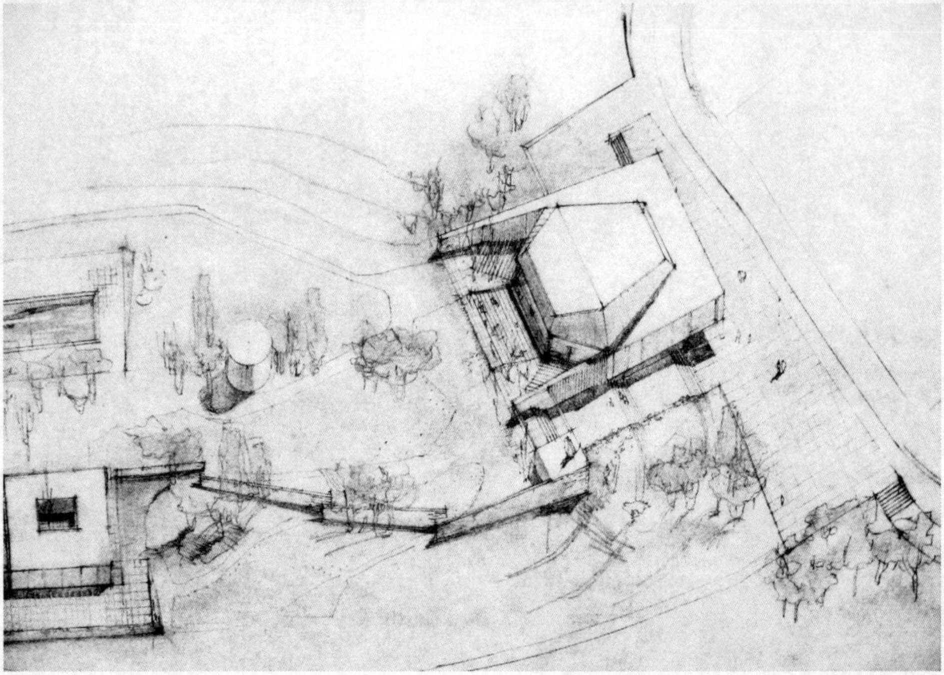

⑨⓪

⑨①

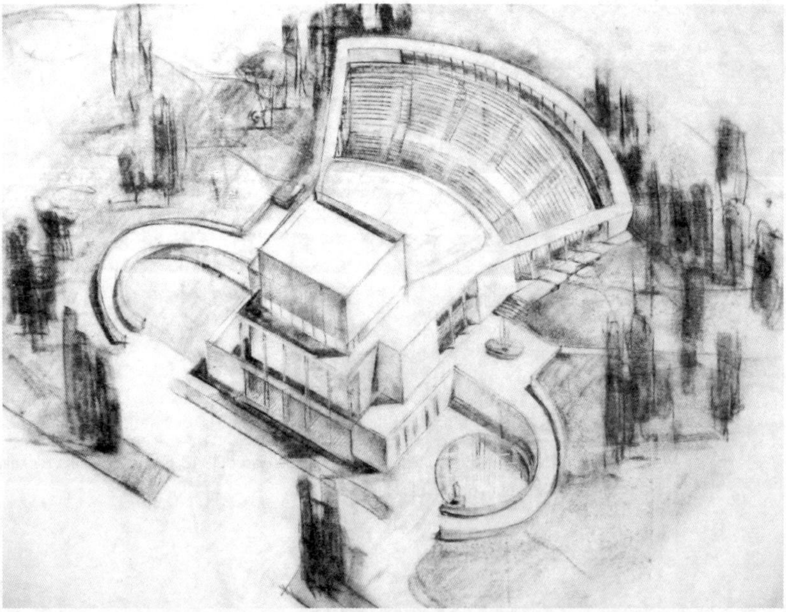

⑨②

(90) Yitzhak Sadeh Memorial, Kibbutz Mashabei Sadeh, 1965. Perspective. Bickels Archive, Mishkan Museum of Art, Ein Harod.
(91) Borochov House, later proposal, Kibbutz Mishmar Hanegev, 1953. Perspective. Bickels Archive, Mishkan Museum of Art, Ein Harod.
(92) Regional amphitheater, Kibbutz Ayelet HaShahar, 1950s. Bickels Archive, Mishkan Museum of Art, Ein Harod.
(93) Beit Banduri, Kibbutz Givaat Hashlosha. Samuel Bickels. Bickels Archive, Mishkan Museum of Art, Ein Harod.
(94) Kolin House, Kibbutz Neve Eitan, 1961. Samuel Bickels. Bickels Archive, Mishkan Museum of Art, Ein Harod.
(95) Tzisling House, Kibbutz Ein Harod, Jezreel Valley, mid-1940s. East elevation. Samuel Bickels. Bickels Archive, Mishkan Museum of Art, Ein Harod.
(96) Members' clubhouse, Kibbutz Beit Hashita, 1960. Samuel Bickels. Bickels Archive, Mishkan Museum of Art, Ein Harod.

(93)

(94)

(95)

(96)

# Pasolini's Travelogue

## Pasolini's *Sopralluoghi in Palestina*

In 1963 Pier Paolo Pasolini arrived in Israel to scout for shooting locations for his film *The Gospel According to St. Matthew*. Along with the Reverend Andrea Carraro and a film crew, he ascended to the holy sites of Christ's life, traveled across the landscape, and spoke to the indigenous people and immigrants who inhabited the actual *Terra Santa*.

Pasolini was instantly and deeply disappointed. He dismissed any possibility of shooting his film in 1960s Israel-Palestine, eventually choosing Italy's Basilicata region instead. We are left with a fifty-five-minute travelogue which was later given the title *Sopralluoghi in Palestina* and was released in 1965 as a promo for *The Gospel*. Watching the roughly cut footage two years later, Pasolini recorded a voice-over narration in which he described the smallness and humbleness of the Israeli scenery and its uselessness for the reconstruction of the biblical mise-en-scène. His retrospective commentary, along with several dialogues and a monologue filmed on-site, transmits the poignant discrepancy between the literary and pictorial layers of the Holy Land and its stark natural and cultural geography. ■

① Pier Paolo Pasolini, *Sopralluoghi in Palestina per il vangelo secondo Matteo (Location Hunting in Palestine)*, 1965. Film-still collage by Gili Merin.

I confess...
the brutal, physical reality of the Jordan
... makes me feel a lack of respect
something inaccessible.
For me it's here
And I'm embarrassed
for aesthetic reasons
Yes, a poor, humble,
desperate little stream

Still en route to Nazareth, across

zones, shall we say, colonized

by Israelis: kibbutzes

... resembling a corporation for social

... reform

All these trees are reforestation

when Christ begins preaching

Probably the first men
who heard Him speak

similar to the European sub-proletariat

they're a cross between
Arabs and crusaders

The towns where Christ's
miracles will occur

and I repeat, they closely resemble
places in Puglia

I stopped in a kibbutz to talk

Every mother...

intellectual way, thinking about it

The most startling thing in Israel

and the same ideals regarding society

We're on the shore of the Dead Sea

There it is

This is the only landscape

in all my search

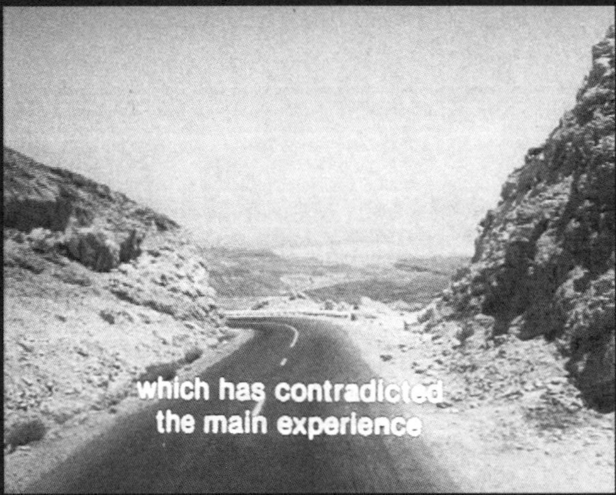
which has contradicted
the main experience

of my trip

This is Jerusalem

the most exciting place of our trip

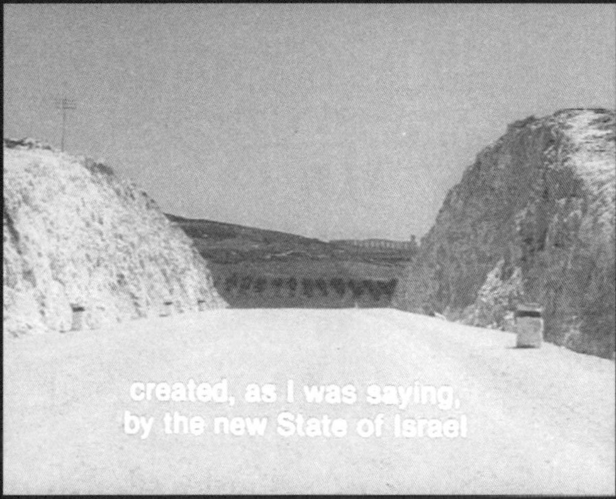
created, as I was saying,
by the new State of Israel

In reality...

A huge ruin.
That's how the Arab world is:

... wretched, pastoral

a kind of dignity, probably...

... archaic, fragmented

as it appears to the modern world

Nazareth is a modern city

There it is

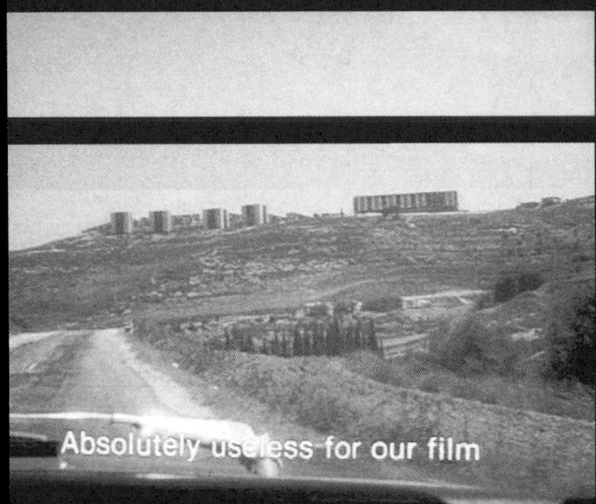
Absolutely useless for our film

the shape of grandeur

is sublime and solemn in its smallness

but never grandiose

Where Sodom and Gomorrah stood

An awful, lunar landscape

... Industrial plants

that fence is the border
between Israel and Jordan

From here we see the main place

of the last days of Christ's passion

... the Mount of Olives,
the Valley of Cedron

Israel's Palestine

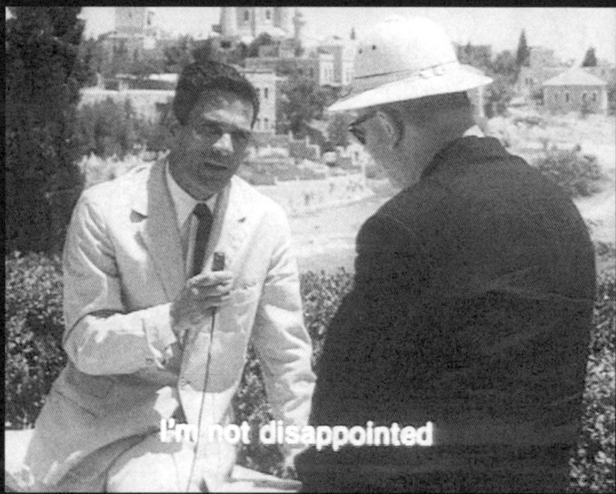
I'm not disappointed

I've found nothing useful for the film

neither landscapes, nor characters

The landscapes are bare hills

What intrigues me in the landscape

so empty of any amenity

a gloomily hot lake... nothing else

Beyond, Jordanian Jerusalem

Jerusalem is a special...

a world within a world

my stylistic ideas for the film

seeing Jerusalem

There's something...

Obviously in the film when...

Jerusalem appears

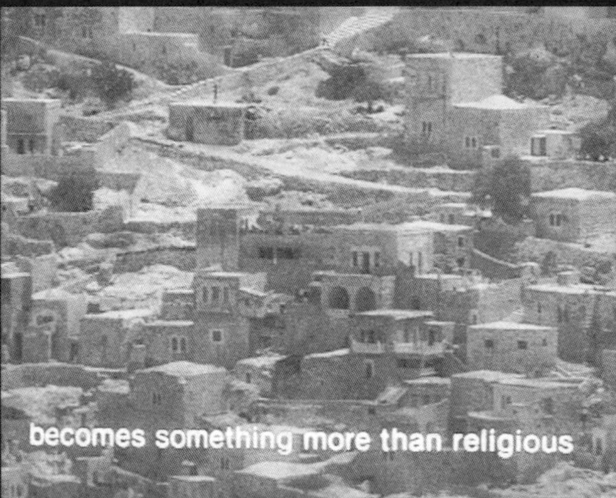
becomes something more than religious

or Israeli Jerusalem, but it's a modern

re-emerges like a wreck

# 6: Sopraluoghi in Palestina and The Gospel According to St Matthew

*When you made* Sopraluoghi in Palestina *did you envisage showing it in public, or was it initially conceived as a private research film?*

It came about very casually, and in fact I never took any part in the camera set-ups or the shooting or anything else. When we went to the Middle East there was a cameraman with us who was sent along by the production company. I never suggested a thing to him, because I wasn't thinking of using the material to make a film, I just wanted some documentation which would help me set *The Gospel*. When I got back to Rome the producer asked me to put together some of the footage and put a commentary on it so it could be shown to a few distributors and Christian Democrat bosses to help the producers. I didn't even control the montage. I had it put together by someone and then just looked over it, but I left everything, including some very ugly cuts which this person had made – who anyway wasn't even a qualified editor. I had it put on in a dubbing-room and improvised a commentary, so altogether the whole film is rather improvised.

*The conversations between you and Don Andrea must have been done at the time.*

Yes, those are real, but it was the cameraman who decided whether or not to record them.

*Sopraluoghi in Palestina:* 'These won't do for the film'; 'I realized it was all no use'

74

*After the business with* La Ricotta *you must have had some trouble re-establishing good relations with representatives of the Church?*

I had good relations with Don Giovanni Rossi and the others from the Pro Civitate Christiana organization and with some other people from the Catholic left, let's say, before the *La Ricotta* affair. But everything was made easier by the advent of Pope John XXIII who objectively revolutionized the situation. If Pius XII had lived another three or four years I'd never have been able to make *The Gospel.*

*One thing that seemed a bit odd to me in* Sopraluoghi *is where you meet some Arab children and you say something like 'These won't do for the film because you can see that Christ's preaching has not passed across their faces'; I didn't quite get this.*

That's a bit difficult to explain because it is one of those things which come from the heart. But historically it is true – you can't say it isn't. It's something I said from inspiration, yet at the same time it is something banal; it is true in the most practical and brutal sense of the word, just as it is true of the Italians in Southern Italy – you can see that Christ's preaching hasn't passed by there either because their morality is not evangelical, it isn't founded on love but on honour; there's no pietism; there isn't even piety at bottom, in the Christian sense of the word – i.e. in the slightly blackmailing sense. If there is piety it's because it's there, not because it is supposed to be there. You can see this better in the Arabs than in Southern Italians.

*How long did it take you to realize there was nothing you could use? In the film I think it's Don Andrea Carraro who says it first, but one gets the distinct impression that you'd been feeling it before that.*

When I landed at Tel Aviv, naturally, I couldn't make out anything. It was night-time. All I could see was an airport and a city. I got a car and went in towards the interior. Right at the beginning I got a few images of an ancient world, which was mainly Arab. I thought at first I might be able to use them, but then immediately afterwards the kibbutzim began to appear, and reafforestation works, modern agriculture, light industry, etc. and I realized it was all no use – that was after a few hours driving.

*Recently, after the June War you published*[1] *some poems which you wrote while you were in Palestine but didn't publish at the time, along with a text about Israel which was more or less an attack on* L'Unità. *It's a bit difficult to see from these what you thought of Israel as a society: what did you think of it?*

The poems in *Nuovi Argomenti* are poems I didn't include in *Poesia in Forma di Rosa*, where there's a section called 'Israel' which gives an idea of the impression the society gave me: it's a contradictory one, in the sense that I disapprove of it fundamentally because it's founded on a basically racist, messianic and religious idea – the idea of a promised land based on religious reasons which go back three thousand years, which is all completely mad. I don't accept the premise, which is a nationalistic-religious one – it's horrible, although it's basically the same principle on which all states are based. But on this premise has been built a nation which inspires great sympathy – for example, the kibbutzim although they are profoundly sad and recall the concentration camps and the Jews' tendency towards masochism and self-exclusion are at the same time something extremely noble, one of the most democratic and socially advanced experiments I've ever seen. Moreover, I have always loved the Jews because they have been excluded, because they are objects of racial hatred, because they have been forced to be separate from society. But once they've founded their own state they are not different, they're not a minority, they're not excluded: they are the majority, they are the norm. And that was a bit of a disappointment, I don't quite know how to put it. They, who had always been the champions of difference, of martyrdom, of the fight of the other against the normal had now become the majority and the normal and that was something I found it a bit hard to swallow.

② Oswald Stack, "*Sopraluoghi in Palestina* and The Gospel According to Matthew," in *Pasolini on Pasolini: Interviews with Oswald Stack*, 1969.

# Model State

①

## Miniatures

Architecturally speaking, the State of Israel was launched in a curatorial project. An exhibition accompanied by a handbook, *The Planning of Israel* (or, in some Hebrew and English versions, *Physical Planning in Israel*), took place at the Tel Aviv Museum in 1950, curated by Arieh Sharon (see chapter "Project"). The medium of the exhibition was by no means out of the Zionist ordinary. Indeed, propaganda exhibitions of various means and ends trailed the Zionist project from its formative years throughout the entire twentieth century.[1] Many of these exhibitions contained utopian scenarios and elaborate optical constructs, but none of them went as far as projecting an instantaneous and complete model state, as the 1950 planning exhibition did, and none relied on a rhetorical strategy of willfully giving up visual and tactile pleasure altogether in favor of a quasi-empirical rigor mediated by social-realist graphics. Abstinence from the usual collage of photogenic pioneers and their laborious achievements cleared the museum walls for the depiction of the entire country as a crafted object—as a total work of engineering and architecture—and produced an effect of monumental emptiness. The glorifying documentaries of former Zionist exhibitions were overtaken by an overwhelming fiction of a vacant and amorphous ground awaiting its configuration, "a land without a people" in anticipation of "a people without a land" (but with scores of visionary modelers).

The 1950 planning exhibition included no physical models.[2] These would only inhibit the national imagination and belittle the territorial scheme. But throughout the 1950s and 1960s, the government and its planning authorities habitually used urban and architectural models for design and presentation purposes. Many of the hundreds of rural settlements, new towns, typical neighborhoods, serial housing estates, administrative compounds, and public buildings of the period would make their initial appearance as toylike replicas. In effect, despite the strategic urgency and austerity measures, a cardboard (and/or gypsum) proxy State was initially contrived, black-and-white photographs of which could easily be mistaken for aerial images of existing towns, villages, and landscapes.

Why was model-making so prevalent during Israel's formative decades? Why bother with such craftsmanship when the State was its own proprietor, planner, financer, builder, and occupant?

Perceptually, because the elusive tangibility of models seems to diminish the distance between the fascination of visionary master plans and the banality of standardized design.

① Model-maker Chaim Heller working on the model of the Old City of Jerusalem, early 1940s. Heller brothers' archive.
② Model-making for the Jewish Palestine pavilion, New York World's Fair, 1939. Photographer: Zoltan Kluger. Israel State Archives.

Practically, because model-making saves time spent on meticulous land surveys, construction documents, and shop drawings, and probably speeds up permit procedures and fund-raising.

Tactically, because models, especially large-scale urban and regional models, naturalize the new, authenticate the superficial, and validate the superfluous. It was this patent quality of models that made them so instrumental in advancing the logistics of Zionism and in manufacturing a peculiar time-space whereby old/new settlements could be erected/erased overnight; entire towns could be fabricated/evacuated in an instant; and émigré/native populations could be displaced/replaced according to strategic blueprints or *Raumplanung* diagrams (see chapter "Theory").

The model of the desert "garden city" of Beersheba illustrates the illusory construct at work here: The loosely spread urban organs with biomorphic contours, which appear to have been softly shaped by time and gently embedded in the topography, are actually signifiers of "enclave urbanism," based on synthetic "neighboring units" and mass-produced housing blocks (in reality, some of these, known as "canon houses," were poured on-site overnight by gigantic cement mixers). In contrast, the dense orthogonal grid at the center of the model, which appears like a fragment of speculative generic urbanism forced upon the terrain (or, alternatively, like an archaeological excavation of a Roman camp), is in fact the ghostly image of the indigenous Arab town of Bir Seb'a, efficiently designed and built to sustain desert conditions and razed just a few years before, in October 1948, in a military operation (see chapter "Ruins of War").

Between the twists and folds of imported "garden city" schemes (the first generation of Israeli new towns was modeled after the British postwar new towns), such figures of speech as "organic forms," "eggs plan," "free flow," "green belts," and "natural growth" proliferated and became buzzwords. Counterintuitively, they signified not a-formality,

②

③

spontaneity, or vernacular sensibility, but, quite the opposite, the rise of a local dialect of settler colonialism equipped with an architectural doctrine that was organic in only one sense: its incessant transformative and expansionist drive. (Note that the size of the prosthetic town of Beersheba is about ten times the size of the original body of Bir Seb'a.) The plaster model of the Old City of Jerusalem represents a different order of things, since it merely depicts an existing city (and substitutes the omniscient gaze of the architect with the manual care of the modeler). The precise date and whereabouts of the model are not known, but it was probably made in the late 1940s or early 1950s, when the Old City of Jerusalem was under Jordanian control—an out-of-reach object of longing for Israelis. This labor-intensive object, of which there were several versions, according to the photo albums of the model-ers,[3] served no apparent professional, political, military, entrepreneurial, touristic, or religious purpose. It is therefore left for us to speculate that in this context the art of model-making was primarily an allegorical act of appropriation and reification. (Perhaps a similar argument could be made regarding the model of the Old City of Acre.) During the 1960s the fetish attributes of the model, as well as its caricatural allure, were publicly acted out with another model of Jerusalem, a dubious "historical" reconstruction of the city from the time of the Second Jewish Temple (between 516 BCE and 70 CE), created by Israeli archaeologists. This mock-up, built to a scale of 1:25, the very same as that used for uncanny entertainment parks such as Madurodam and Mini Israel, was venerated as an authentic relic of the destroyed Temple Mount. After the War of 1967 and the conquest of the Old City of Jerusalem, this model

③ Beersheba, the Old and New City, mid-1950s. Model. Model-makers: Chaim and Arieh Heller. Heller brothers' archive.
④ The Old City of Acre, mid-1950s. Model. Model-makers: Chaim and Arieh Heller. Heller brothers' archive.

became the crude blueprint for messianic proposals to reinstate Jewish hegemony on Temple Mount. Initially installed at the premises of the Holy Land Hotel in West Jerusalem, it was relocated in 2006 to the gardens of the Israel Museum, next to the Shrine of the Book, acquiring more of a cultural aura but losing some of its pagan mystique. Meanwhile, some Jewish militant groups are working on detailed models of a future Third Temple, occasionally showing them off in sinister processions.

Most architectural models produced in Israel, however, were worldly demonstrative objects, as could be gleaned from a series of miniatures of rural settlements. Evidently, these miniatures are not just site-specific simulations of certain settlements (Kibbutz Yehiam, Kfar Yehezkel, the Ben Shemen Youth Village, etc., as their labels indicate), but actually preliminary architectural studies for new social forms situated in different geographic settings (highland kibbutz, lowland moshav, desert garden suburb, etc.).

The models of standard rural dwellings and public facilities, known locally as "Jewish Agency Types," formulated the norms and standards of rural domesticity and provided ample prototypes for schools, synagogues, clinics, libraries, and administrative buildings which would be reproduced and disseminated ad nauseam in the immigrant villages of the 1950s and 1960s.

The models of national or municipal institutions renounce in advance the elaboration of formal elements and stylized details in order to consolidate their generic status and serial resemblance. Within the welfare state's visual field, architectural authority could be built up mainly by crystallizing a core vocabulary and disseminating emblematic images that would eventually constitute the national lexicon of forms. Models scaled at 1:100 and 1:200 proved to be the most effective means to this end. They iconicized the ordinary and presented the entire State apparatus—from government administrative compounds and post office buildings to central cultural institutions such as museums, theaters, and concert halls—as a productive-reproductive workshop for white objects and modernist architectural paradigms, cut off from the genius of the place and swept up in the spirit of the moment.

④

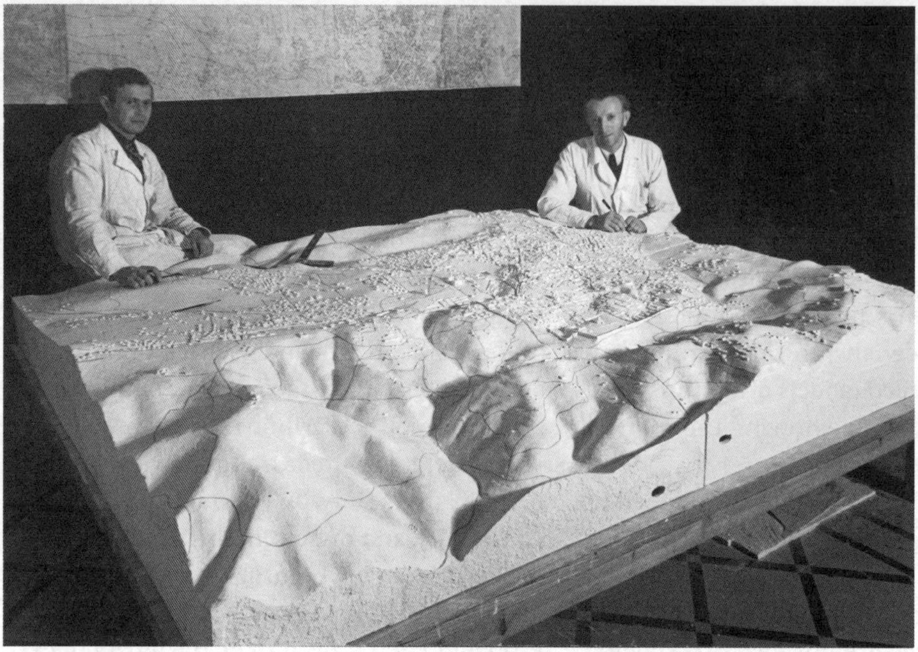

(5)

If a certain poetic license in terms of scale, articulation, or display is noticeable in models of over-plastic Brutalist or extra-modular structuralist projects such as dwelling habitats or experimental public buildings, it is essentially because the avant-garde margins, sponsored mostly by the State, the Labor Union, the military, or the academy, bolstered the vitality of the national project and enunciated the State's (momentary) self-image as an exploratory architectural lab. ■

1 See Iddo Ginat, "The Representation of Zionist Landscape in World Fairs and Exhibitions" (PhD diss. in progress, Tel Aviv University).
2 As far as we know, that is, from original graphic material found at Sharon's archive, from newspaper articles and personal reports, and from a few partial photographs of the exhibition itself at the Tel Aviv Museum.
3 The albums of the modelers, the brothers Haim Heller and Arieh Heller, were kept by the family. The models themselves did not survive.

⑤ Model of the Old City of Jerusalem and its surrounding landscape with model-makers Chaim and Arieh Heller, early 1940s. Heller brothers' archive.
⑥ Tourists looking at the model of the "City of David", Holy Land Hotel, Jerusalem, 1965. Photographer: Moshe Pridan. Government Press Office.
⑦–⑧ Model of Jerusalem during the Second Temple Period (66 CE), Holy Land Hotel, Jerusalem, 1962–1966. Concept: Michael Avi Yonah.

⑥

⑦ ⑧

⑨ ⑩

⑪

⑨ Youth Cultural Center, Jerusalem, 1956. Architects: Shulamit Nadler, Michael Nadler. Model: Paul Verberne.
⑩ Children look at a model of Tel Aviv City Hall, 1957. Architect: Menachem Cohen. Model: Paul Verberne.
⑪ Yaacov Rechter at the unveiling ceremony of the Hilton Hotel model, Tel Aviv, 1962. Model: Paul Verberne.
⑫ Winning proposal for Yad Vashem Holocaust Memorial Center, Jerusalem, 1957. Model. Arieh Elhanani, Arieh Sharon, Binjamin Idelson. Model-makers: Chaim and Arieh Heller. Heller brothers' archive.
⑬ Binyenei Ha'Uma convention center, Jerusalem, 1949–1959. Model. Zeev Rechter, Moshe Zarhi, Yaacov Rechter. Model-makers: Chaim and Arieh Heller. Heller brothers' archive.
⑭ Nuclear research reactor, Soreq, 1956. Model. Philip Johnson.
⑮ Proposal for a hotel in Caesarea, early 1960s. George Candilis, David Best.

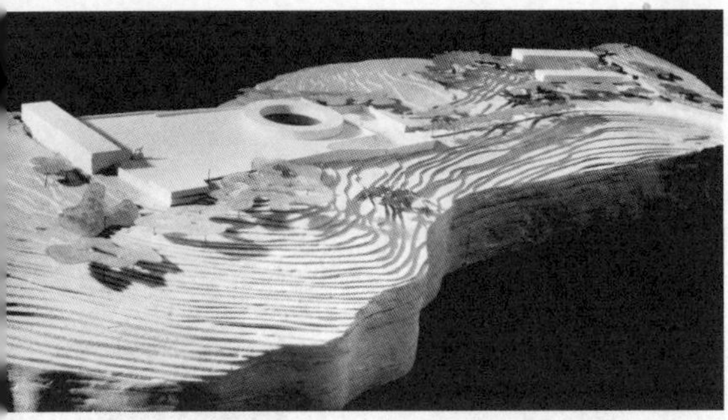

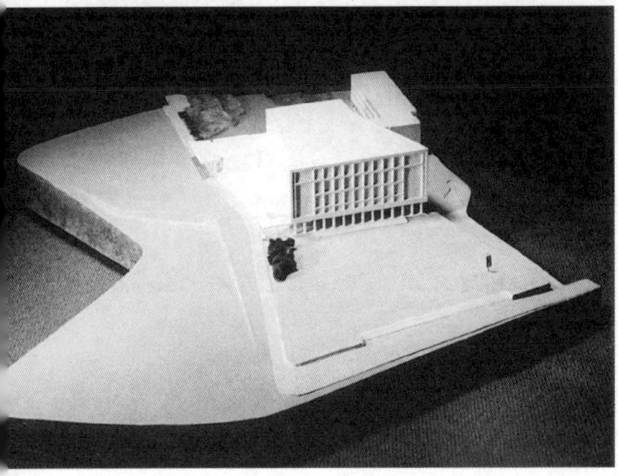

⑫ ⑬

⑭

⑮

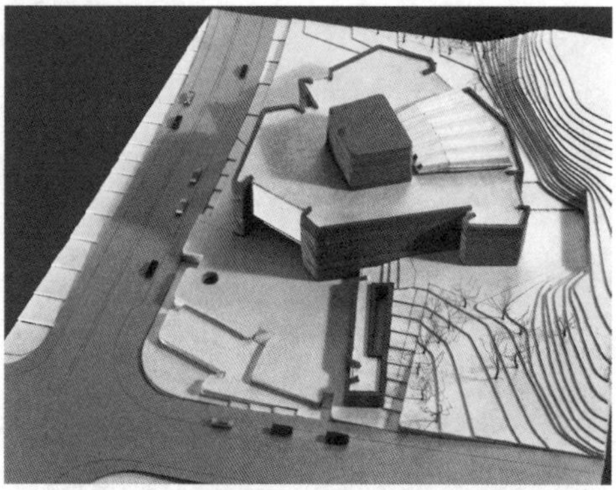

⑯ ⑰

⑱

⑲

⑳

㉑

⑯ Early version of the Jerusalem Theater, 1958. Model. Shulamit Nadler, Michael Nadler. Model-maker: Paul Verberne.
⑰ Mann Auditorium, Tel Aviv, 1953–1959. Model. Detail. Zeev Rechter, Dov Karmi, Yaacov Rechter. Model-maker: Paul Verberne.
⑱ Model-maker Paul Verberne examines a model of an early version of the Jerusalem Theater, 1958. Shulamit Nadler, Michael Nadler.
⑲ Proposal for housing in Eilat, early 1970s. Arieh Sharon, Eldar Sharon.
⑳ Military Academy, Mizpe Ramon, 1963–1967. Alfred Neumann, Zvi Hecker, Eldar Sharon.
㉑ Prefab "saddle" housing, 1957. Israel Goodovitch.

(23)

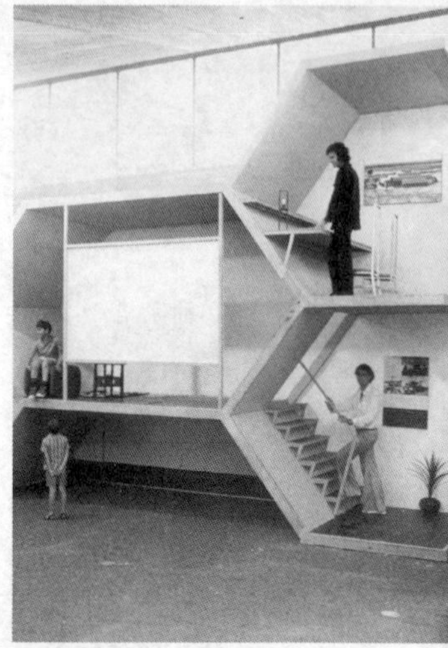

(22)

(24)

(22) Prime Minister Ben-Gurion examines a model of the Israel Trade Fairs & Convention Center, Tel Aviv, mid-1950s. Aba Elhanani.
(23) Exhibition dedicated to the work of architect Israel Goodovitch, Israel Museum, Jerusalem, 1972.
(24) Model of a neighborhood in Kiryat Gat, Public Housing pavilion, Levant Fair, 1959. Model-makers: Michael Hefetz, Dan Ogen, Abraham Hasson.
(25) New Towns pavilion, trade fair, Tel Aviv, 1968.
(26)–(29) Neve Oved housing company exhibition, 1950. Photographer: Moshe Raviv. Shikun & Binui historical archive.

(25)

(26)

(27) (28)

(29)

+ ~~T 336~~ CUL. 108. Palestine at War Exhibition London, 1944. MR. ROSETTÉ. D

(30)

(31)

(32)

CUL. 86.
Pictorial representation of Jewish coloni-
sation in Palestine, on the walls of the
Palestine pavilion at the Paris World Ex-
hibition 1937.

(29) *Palestine at War* exhibition, London, 1944. David B. Keidan Collection, Central Zionist Archives.
(30) Representation of Jewish colonization, unidentified exhibition. Display captions: "Palestine: the Land of Refuge," "From Dawn to Midnight: A New Settlement." David B. Keidan Collection, Central Zionist Archives.
(31) Palestine at War exhibition, London, 1944. David B. Keidan Collection, Central Zionist Archives.
(32) Representation of Jewish colonization, the Palestine pavilion, Paris World Exhibition, 1937. David B. Keidan Collection, Central Zionist Archives.

# State Architecture

①

## The Official Object without Qualities

In present-day spoken Hebrew, the notion of "statism" (*mamlachtiut*) is a signifier devoid of ideological content, political conviction, or actual operative relevance—an idiomatic cloud of neutrality and respectability hovering over the ethnic, religious, and political divide. In the 1950s and 1960s, by contrast, this same Hebrew term denoted a political doctrine that was meant to dictate and monitor the relationships, or at least ease the tensions, between three vectors: nation-building, the welfare state, and centralist rule.

Functionally, statism was, first, code for a sweeping campaign initiated and commanded by Prime Minister David Ben-Gurion to dismantle, restructure, and nationalize all pre-State production, service, and management organs, especially the paramilitary organizations, the Labor Federation's health and welfare services, and the sectarian education systems. Second, statism was a unifying, flattening, and hollowing slogan, providing a common meta-cultural objective and an instant collective identity to an emerging society of immigrants, exiles, and settlers, a group allegedly too heterogeneous and feeble to survive as a body politic.

In his seminal book *Immigrants, Settlers, Natives*, sociologist Baruch Kimmerling analyzes the failed attempt to constitute a continuous political hegemony and a consensual cultural uniformity in Israel. His account begins with the fabrication of the statist ideology:

> Out of awareness of the growing heterogeneity of the social structure of the newly

① The Knesset building under construction, Jerusalem, 1963. Yosef Klarwein, Dov Karmi. Builder: Solel Boneh. Shikun & Binui historical archive.
② "Binyenei Ha'Uma—International Convention Center," a sign with an image of the prospective building, Jerusalem, 1949–1959. Zeev Rechter, Moshe Zarhi, Yaacov Rechter.

> established state, and in the interest of not endangering the cultural, class, and political structure of the state as it had taken shape in the pre-sovereign communitarian period, mechanisms of homogenization and Israelization were put into place—according to the American model, though more sophisticated and aggressive, by virtue of the fact that individual rights were not placed at the center. The intention was to create a mono-cultural, monolithic, homogeneous, but hierarchically stratified system. The need for this homogenization was argued not only in the ideological terms of nation-building and creation of the "new man" (as opposed to the "degenerate Diaspora Jew") but also in the instrumental and existential terms of the need for social cohesion because of their position as "the few against the many" in the ongoing conflict—which came as a kind of decree, accompanied by periodical existential wars against the Arab surroundings.[1]

Such determination of the State apparatus to instantaneously solidify a common ground and a national character brings up a number of questions: What representational role did architecture play in promoting the political precepts of the new State and in substantiating the national *habitus*? What was the actual investment, rhetorical and tangible, of the Israeli regime in the construction of government institutions, monuments, and other national symbols? And, finally, did statism outfit itself with a distinct language, a particular style, or any iconography whatsoever in order to broadcast its doctrine at home and abroad?

The preliminary answer to these questions distinguishes Israel from the outset; the planning professions, architecture included,

②

were literally recruited for the logistical tasks related to the enterprises of mass immigration, mass settlement, and mass housing. All prior preoccupation with language, expression, and style (Bauhaus, etc.) came to an immediate halt, certainly in those public projects (the vast majority of the built fabric) initiated and supervised by the State. The option of symbolic, ritual, monumental, or merely ornamental architecture was routinely disqualified, whether for ideological or pragmatic reasons. Statism presented itself as a remedy for architectural ambition and excessive design. Pretense and extravagance were decried in official government propaganda and in the discourse of the cultural community, not only as bad taste, but also as moral degeneration and a direct affront to the collective pocket. The spartan huts inhabited by Prime Minister Ben-Gurion and President Izhak Ben-Zvi provided a plain-faced iconography of the ethos of self-sacrifice and popular solidarity, signifying the willing suspension of the architectural moment.

In this chapter, I will examine the official Israeli State architecture of the formative decades through a series of emblematic projects and prevailing typologies produced

③

④

③ Binyenei Ha'Uma convention center, under construction, Jerusalem, 1953. The building was covered with Celotex boards during the *Conquest of the Desert* exhibition, also known as the "Jerusalem Expo." Zeev Rechter, Moshe Zarhi, Yaacov Rechter. Photographer: Yitzhak Kalter.
④ Binyenei Ha'Uma convention center, 1950s. Elevation with stained-glass artwork. Zeev Rechter, Moshe Zarhi, Yaacov Rechter. Artists: Yitzhak Danziger, Joseph Zaritsky.
⑤ Binyenei Ha'Uma convention center, early 1960s. Interior with ceiling artwork by Yaacov Agam. Zeev Rechter, Moshe Zarhi, Yaacov Rechter. Photographer: Yitzhak Kalter.
⑥ Binyenei Ha'Uma convention center, 1960s. Zeev Rechter, Moshe Zarhi, Yaacov Rechter. Photographer: Yitzhak Kalter.

⑤

⑥

directly by the State apparatus and realized in government buildings, post offices, public schools and universities, security installations, public hospitals, and so on. These will be compared to corresponding buildings produced simultaneously in the parallel system of the Histadrut, or Federation of Labor Unions, in the next chapter, "Union Architecture." The national mass-housing project, the remarkable centerpiece of the welfare state, will be discussed in the chapters "Public Housing" and "Serial Blocks."

## Binyenei Ha'Uma

The Binyenei Ha'Uma (lit. "Buildings of the Nation"[2]) building, located on the outskirts of the government compound at the main entrance to Jerusalem, is an appropriate object with which to begin, as it represents the first effort of note to articulate and realize a symbolic landmark that would assert Jerusalem as the epicenter not merely of the Israeli State, but of the entire Jewish nation. The vigorous public and governmental debate and the oft-expressed contempt throughout the protracted period of its construction give us a sense of the spontaneous public resentment of architectural exploits—and even more so of official anti-monumental taste during the first years of Statehood.

Binyenei Ha'Uma was designed to host the Zionist Congresses, to serve as a center for national conferences and international conventions of Diaspora Jewry, and to bolster Jerusalem's status as the nation's capital. The need to establish such an authoritative edifice, which trumped statist priorities for the sake of a wider gesture of Jewish pride, stirred arguments around the government table over matters of principle. These arguments continued until the very end of the construction and cast a shadow on all such emblematic projects from the first decade of the State. The minutes of the 34th Government Session, held on March 8, 1951, in which the allocation of construction material for the completion of Binyenei Ha'Uma was discussed, reveal some of the misgivings and unease the building stirred:

> David Remez [Minister of Education and Culture]: "There is the matter of honoring the Jewish people, and I suggest this not be put up for negotiation. We receive millions of dollars from this people [...]. Let's not bicker with them about 88,000 pound sterling, *und Gott vet helfen* [Yiddish: 'and may God help us']."
>
> Golda Meirson [Meir] [Minister of Labor]: "I am not an anti-Zionist, but I would like us to make a decision based on the facts. I am not even talking about new immigrants at this point, but there are thousands of families whom the government promised housing to [...] and this looks like it may turn out to be the country's greatest scandal."

Yaakov Garry [Minister of Commerce and Industry]: "Can we allocate them enough wood to complete the roofs of 5,000 housing units?"

Golda Meirson: "That is precisely the number of housing units currently in need of roofs."[3]

The plans for Binyenei Ha'Uma were prepared by architect Zeev Rechter, who won the design competition for the project in early 1949. In this project, Rechter tried to blend ceremonial classical splendor with calm modernist efficiency. The interior of the building, a labyrinthine complex of foyers and columned halls (in explicit reference to Greek architecture), is packaged in a smooth, monolithic trapezoidal box, whose main façade became, in more advanced versions of the project, a transparent screen wall.

The construction of Binyenei Ha'Uma, which began in 1950, was frozen by government ordinance as part of the emergency economic measures. The building was inaugurated only at the end of the decade, after standing for years as a skeleton and being dubbed "Khirbet al-Umma" (a hybrid of Arabic and Hebrew meaning "The National Ruin"). Journalist Theodor Hatalgi offers a particularly picturesque description of the "ruin":

> To the left of the gray concrete mound, the skeleton of an elongated wooden hut is taking on flesh and blood. The concrete mound—a giant eyesore for all who reach the capital on the main road from the lowlands—is the Binyenei Ha'Uma center. The immense building remains forlorn, miserable, and orphaned, as if the bold plans for its completion were abandoned midway, as if its contractors recoiled

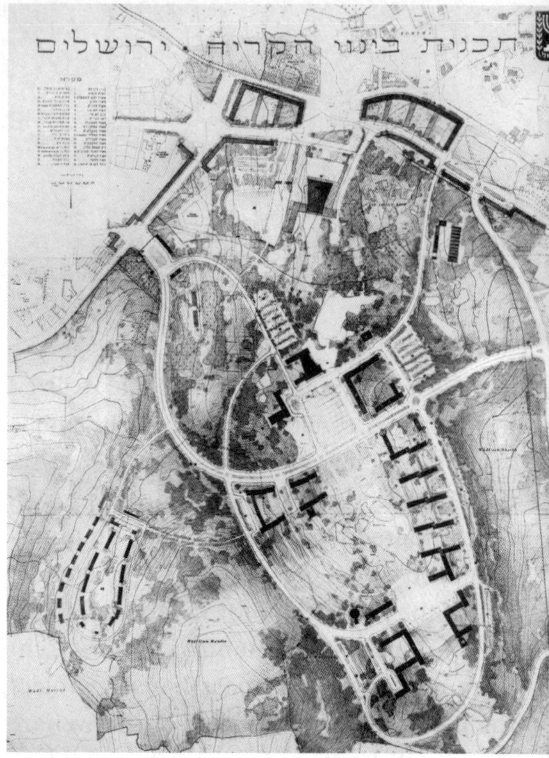


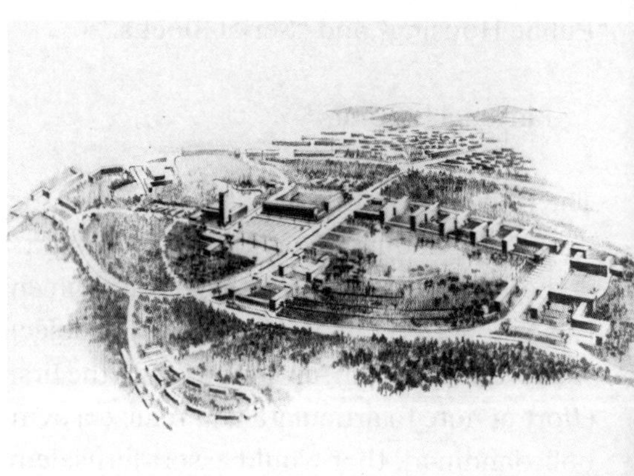

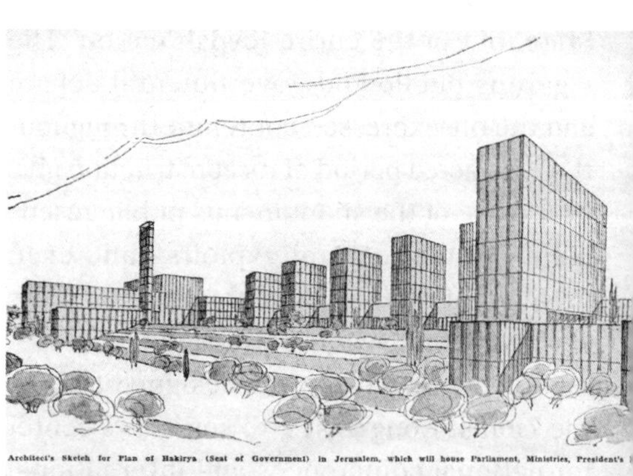


⑦ ⑧ ⑨

⑦ Winning proposal for planning the government district (Hakirya), Jerusalem, 1950. Master plan. Munio Gitai Weinraub, Al Mansfeld.
⑧ Winning proposal for planning the government district (Hakirya), Jerusalem, 1950. Aerial perspective. Munio Gitai Weinraub, Al Mansfeld.
⑨ Proposal for planning the government district (Hakirya), Jerusalem, 1950. Perspective. Arieh Sharon.

from the realization of the much-touted idea of establishing "the largest building in the Near East," a center for Zionist Congresses, worldwide conferences, and international exhibitions.

This is how the large and unfinished building looks from the outside, and the same can be said of the vast halls on the inside [...] its dozens of rooms with unfinished walls, stairways with no banisters, [...] piles of boards and rocks strewn around the empty and strange chamber.[4]

The Government District

The reservations that accompanied the construction of Binyenei Ha'Uma intensified when planning began for the government district in Jerusalem, the future administrative heart of Israeli statism. The question of the location of the government district was decided in April 1949, when, at the advice of Arieh Sharon, head of the Planning Department, lots in the center of West Jerusalem were appropriated. These lots comprised a total area of 600 dunam (for the sake of comparison, the British Mandatory authorities planned their government compound in Jerusalem on 30 dunam); a few of them had been under Jewish ownership, but most belonged to the Arab villages of Sheikh Badr and Kafr Sil. This huge compound would remain mostly empty even after fifty years of political sovereignty.

The issue of the allocation of land for the government buildings in Jerusalem is documented for the first time in the protocol of the 8th Government Session, held on April 11, 1949:

Eliezer Kaplan [Minister of Finance]: "Now we have started to use abandoned houses, Arab houses, and there are many demands, but we said that we will put aside a certain area in Jerusalem for the future construction of the government compound, and we will not designate this land for any other use."

Prime Minister D. Ben-Gurion: "This means designating enough land for the likelihood that we will transfer the government to Jerusalem, such that the entire area will be at the disposal of the government buildings. [...] The main idea is that we designate land in Jerusalem for a government center for the time at which we will transfer the government there, and steps must be taken for this land to be reserved for us."

The decision: The area, found within the Green Line and marked on the map of Jerusalem, signed by the Prime Minister, and carrying today's date, is found suitable to be the central seat of the government of the State and its related institutions.

And thus the government decides to empower the Minister of Finance to take steps in order to attain the designated area for the government—via purchase, expropriation, exchange, or any other means, as the situation requires.[5]

At the beginning of 1950 a closed competition was held for the planning of the government district, and in April of that same year the winners were announced: the architects Munio Gitai Weinraub and Al Mansfeld.

⑩ ⑪

Their proposal is based on the premise of an autonomous formal campus, cut off from the urban fabric and imposed on the landscape. Their site plan brings together seemingly conflicting planning traditions: that of the mall, based on a monumental axis; and that of the garden city, circumscribed within picturesque outlines. It succeeds in "covering" the overly large compound, achieving a reasonable balance between built density and a surplus of open spaces, and proposing a convincing fusion of authoritarian decorum, bureaucratic competence, and civilian calm. An open ceremonial courtyard, surrounded by buildings for the parliament, the prime minister, and the president, provides a stable focus. Bisected by a road that connects to a system of routes and pathways, the site dictates an architecture that is experienced in motion.

Gitai Weinraub and Mansfeld's plan underwent a number of alterations before it was finally shelved. Such was also the fate of other master plans proposed for the complex during the 1960s and 1970s. Mordechai Shoshani, head architect of the Israeli Public Works Department (PWD), wrote about this in hindsight:

> Eventually it was decided that a government compound would be built on the site, and that most of the ministries would be concentrated there; three office buildings were built. They were "sown in the land" just as thousands of housing blocks were sown around the country; lands were delegated to many parties—the Knesset (Parliament), Beit Ha'Hayal (Soldiers' House), Yad Lebanim (Memorial for the Fallen Soldiers), Binyenei Ha'Uma, the Hilton Hotel, the Bank of Israel, the Archaeological Institute, the Stadium, and the Israel Museum. A number of master plans were drawn up, and all of them ended up collecting dust.[6]

Beneath Shoshani's belittling comparison between the government buildings that were eventually constructed (for the Ministry of the Interior, the Treasury, and the Prime Minister's Office [architect: Yosef Klarwein]) and the housing blocks that were arbitrarily "sown," as it were, around the country, one can detect a rather comforting banality. After all, the conscious choice of the commonplace over the authoritative, the generic over the iconic, is not the worst option for a statist district.[7]

⑫ ⑬ ⑭

## The Israeli Public Works Department

The network of public institutions with which the citizen comes into daily contact —post offices, social security bureaus, local councils, schools, tax authorities, etc.—was designed for the most part by the Israeli Public Works Department, successor to the British Mandatory PWD, in a style that was dubbed "democratic functionalism." The Israeli PWD was involved in two main fields: paving roads and constructing public buildings. The architectural Planning Department in charge of public buildings had three branches: one for the post office, another for the department of health, and yet another for other governmental and semi-governmental offices such as the Social Security Bureau and various other authorities. Gad Asher was head architect of the PWD after the establishment of the State; he had previously worked in the pre-State offices of Erich Mendelsohn (where he co-designed the British Government Hospital in Haifa) and in the Public Works Department of the British Mandate (where he participated in the design of British Tegart forts[8] and military barracks, among other things).

Gad Asher would later be described as one who sacrificed his professional talents in order to "design a functional architecture of the everyday."[9] The style in the period of his tenure as head of the Planning Section of the PWD (1948–1965) was characterized as "functionalism and aestheticism with a modesty befitting of a small and not particularly

⑩ Post office in the Lessin Culture House, Tel Aviv, 1950s. Gad Asher, Motello Puck, Public Works Department.
⑪ Post office, Ra'anana, 1950s. Gad Asher, Public Works Department.
⑫ HaYarkon post office, Tel Aviv, 1950s. Gad Asher, Public Works Department.
⑬ Post office, Ness Ziona, 1950s. Gad Asher, Public Works Department.
⑭ "Bituach Leumi" (National Social Security), Nahariya, 1959–1960. Shmuel Rosov, Arie Rosov.

⑮ Standard state school in a new town, 1960s. Unknown architect.
⑯ Standard state school in the new town of Dimona, 1960s. Unknown architect.
⑰ Primary school, Kiryat Ono, 1964. Moshe Kofman.
⑱ Primary school, Jerusalem, 1963. Avraham Yasky, Amnon Alexandroni.
⑲ State school, Kiryat Gat, 1960. Unknown architect.

wealthy state" which "resisted the temptation to establish ostentatious public buildings."[10]

The ordinariness of this "minor architecture"—manifested in efficient and accessible design, usually without the ceremonial mediation of wide steps or monumental entrance halls—signified the State's contribution to the national effort, which demanded of the population material concessions and complete identification with the building missions of the time. However, the PWD Planning Department's role as the national architecture commissioner was primarily defined not by attempts to dictate public taste, but by the department's decisive contribution to the development of standardized construction details and the establishment of sets of regulations for public buildings. The PWD's construction-detail booklets, laid out and bound in hardcover by the government printer, were distributed to architecture firms and were an indispensable tool for generic architecture, both public and private, until the 1980s. This local professional tradition continues to this day in certain items such as steps, handrails, door frames, and sealing. To a large extent, the PWD booklets document the critical transition from the culture of "high" architecture of the 1930s, which created one-off buildings whose custom-designed and fabricated parts were meant to create a new whole, to the "low" architecture of the 1950s and 1960s, which aspired to establish minimum standards, Taylorite work processes, and serialized shelf products in order to ensure the realization of the national building project. The god of statism is in the (standardized) details.

## State Schools

State schools were the only facilities under direct government jurisdiction that also bore the mark of statism in their title. In the British Mandatory period, great importance was attached to the exemplary appearance of educational establishments (especially in urban plans deriving from garden-city precepts), often more so than with government buildings, and they therefore played a central role in urban planning. Schools, gymnasia, colleges, research institutes, and academies were elegantly designed to serve as focal points along central urban axes, or as monumental objects projecting onto their surroundings. With the establishment of the Israeli public school system, the urban prestige of schools changed entirely, and their design was stripped of all ceremonial and symbolic trappings. The bulk of the architectural effort was aimed at technical and functional research for the development of building prototypes that would be economical to produce (and reproduce), convenient to maintain, and suitable for study. Government publications from the 1950s about the

⑲

⑮ ⑯ ⑰ ⑱

planning of schools are full of graphs and scientific formulae trying to solve acoustical, optical, and climatic problems, and to identify optimal organizational and circulation patterns, while demonstratively ignoring questions of design, appearance, and urban context. Typology trumps object-making; national uniformity trumps urban fabric-making. The new planning dogma of zoning, which championed the taxonomic breakdown of urban functions and services, dictated the detachment of the school from the street and from urban centers of activity.

## State Hospitals

The official approach to the design of State hospitals in Israel reveals an even more radical and moralizing pragmatism. In this matter, not only is architectural design superfluous, but so is the very pretense of creating permanent structures according to long-term forecasts and operational standards. This official attitude begs comparison with the policy of the Federation of Labor Unions (Histadrut), which, in the first decade of the State, established a parallel network of hospitals, all designed by outstanding architects, celebrating the Histadrut's ubiquity and omnipotence. A public debate between Dr. Chaim Sheba, general director of the Ministry of Health, and Moshe Soroka, the Histadrut's great builder, sharply sums up the contrasting approaches to the building of hospitals and the ramifications for all of public architecture:

> Soroka: "All of the government hospitals [built in the cabin method] are in dire distress, because the Treasury has clung to Sheba's flawed reservations and preferred the temporary over the permanent,

(20) (21) (22)

the cheap, the superficial, and the fast over the good and the stable. 'Here we have no luxury. Here everything is functional.'"

Sheba: "But for this cost [of building the Herzfeld Hospital—the pretext for the debate] we could have solved the problem of washing machines and refrigerators for 20,000 poor families with many children. [...] Soroka's right to build is an imagined right. Every dictator builds majestic halls for himself, but the construction is not a measure of the service. He is building himself [...]."[11]

### Immigrant Absorption Hostels

In contrast to the didactic commonness of the public schools and the therapeutic transiency of the State hospitals stood an exceptional, entirely original, and no less official typology that signified a new openness to architectural expression and experimentation on the part of the State.

In 1957, the government immigration absorption authorities began developing a new method for absorbing immigrants. This was based on a network of hostels, located in the cities, in which the immigrants could reside, become acclimated, learn Hebrew, and search independently for work and housing. Twenty-three such immigrant hostels, or "absorption centers," as they were also called, had been built around the country by 1969. Their design, though based on a rather uniform and strict program and produced on a tight budget, was entrusted to eminent veteran architects or to young "stars"; this yielded exceptional and even masterful works, some of which received exposure in professional journals in Israel and abroad. The idiosyncrasy of this typology—literally building a transitional object, or devising a transformation machine that converts immigrants into citizens—became the showcase of Israeli civic culture. Many of the hostels were erected in central urban locations, as focal points of Israeli community life and as a symbolic reminder of the "melting pot" rhetoric of the Labor governments.

### Security Facilities

Although it is not a bona fide typology, there is an additional subcategory of State architecture in which a relatively "excessive" design is apparent: that of the various "invisible" buildings and compounds serving security or military purposes. Hidden from the public eye—or, in fact, so secretive that their very existence was and often still is officially denied—these installations did not have to heed the dictates of propagandistic restraint or the tight budgets of public facilities. Consequently, perhaps incongruously, and certainly remarkably, some of the finest works of architecture sponsored by the State during Israel's formative decades are inaccessible, often non-photographable structures designed by renowned architects. These include the nuclear research centers in Nahal Soreq, designed by Philip Johnson, and Dimona, designed by Dan Eytan and Yitzhak Yashar; the officer-training school in

㉓ ㉔

㉕ ㉖

⑳ Kaplan state hospital, Rehovot, 1953. Zeev Rechter.
㉑ State hospital, 1960s. Gad Asher, Public Works Department.
㉒ Maternity ward in a state hospital, Nahariya, 1960s. Gad Asher, Public Works Department.
㉓ Hostel for academic immigrants, Beersheba, 1956–1957. Avraham Yasky, Amnon Alexandroni.
㉔ Hostel for new immigrants, Upper Nazareth, 1956–1957. Avraham Yasky, Amnon Alexandroni.
㉕ "Brodetsky House," hostel for new immigrants, Ramat Aviv, Tel Aviv, 1956–1960. Robert Bennett
㉖ Hostel for new immigrants, Hertzelia, 1965. Robert Bennett.

㉘

㉗

㉙

Mitzpe Ramon, designed by Zvi Hecker and Eldar Sharon; the Israeli General Security Agency Headquarters, designed by Nahum Zolotov (a building that won the Rokach Prize for Architecture, despite its secrecy); buildings in the Mossad headquarters, designed by Avraham Yasky and Yaacov Rechter, and the Army Headquarters in Tel Aviv (aka "the pit"), designed by Mazor-First.

㉚

㉛

## The Knesset Building

The Knesset (Israeli parliament) building exemplifies the climax of debates on the proper architectural representation of the Israeli regime. More than anything, this building indicates the absence of architectural or administrative "threads"—iconic precedents, collective symbols, tectonic traditions, a constitution, a clear structure of governance—that might lead to the design of a canonical Israeli building. And yet the account of the design and construction of the Knesset building, which spans almost the entire formative period of the State, beginning in 1950 and ending some eight months before the outbreak of the 1967 War, marks the awakening of a critical discussion among the local architectural community and the general public. In this discussion, which addressed questions of style, expression, authority, identity, and patriotism, it is possible to identify the first conceptual buds of post-1967 Israeli architectural discourse and praxis (which is more or less concurrent with, or even prior to, European and American architectural postmodernism, except that it emanates to a large extent from the experience of the glorified 1967 War and the ensuing occupation of the Palestinian territories). More specifically, the Knesset building paradoxically signifies a change of representational paradigm: the end of modernist iconoclasm as the official Israeli vernacular, and the beginning of a new cycle of historicist and "regionalist" pastiche.

㉗ Nuclear Research Center, central building, Dimona, 1961–1963. Dan Eytan, Yitzhak Yashar.
㉘ Detail.
㉙ Soreq Nuclear Research Center, lab building, 1960–1968. Moshe Zarhi.
㉚ Shin Bet (Israeli Security Agency) headquarters, Tel Aviv, 1967–1968. Nahum Zolotov.
㉛ Detail.

㉜

The design and construction of the Knesset building is documented in a detailed and riveting account by Susan Hattis Rolef, the official archivist of the Knesset, in an article published in the journal *Cathedra*.[12] Following is a brief description based on Rolef's article. In the first years of the State, the Knesset wandered between several addresses in Tel Aviv and Jerusalem. In March 1950 it was housed in the Frumin House on King George Street in Jerusalem, where it remained until 1964. None of the various proposals for a new temporary location—Beit Ha'Am or Binyenei Ha'Uma in Jerusalem, or any of the other structures designated for government ministries—came to fruition. The delay in the construction of the permanent building and the tight quarters at Frumin House aroused complaints on the part of ministers and members of Knesset, but these were also instrumentalized for the formulation of the rhetoric of national sacrifice. At the 55th Government Session, held on August 17, 1952, there was a discussion on "determining a place for the Knesset building":

> Levi Eshkol [Minister of the Treasury]: "Several of us ministers held a meeting with the chairman of the Knesset and his aides on the matter of the Knesset building. Three alternatives stand before us, and all take into account that the situation as it is today is untenable [...]. So far, no conclusive deal has been struck with another building; some money was invested in Beit Ha'Am but in the meantime construction is not being continued there [...]."
>
> Prime Minister David Ben-Gurion: "Why can't we just continue in the present building, what's the problem? None of us are working in ideal conditions."
>
> Moshe Sharet [Minister of Foreign Affairs]: "I think that the current situation is untenable [...]. Every day I am there —and this is the feeling of most of the people—there is a constant feeling of revulsion. The place is unbearable. The place, the location in the middle of town, is impossible; it is detrimental to any attitude of reverence for the Knesset [...]."
>
> Peretz Naftali [Minister of Agriculture]: "I think that poverty is not something to be ashamed of [...]. If I explain to a guest from abroad that we are living in difficult conditions and that it is a matter of years until we can live comfortably as they do in other countries—I think that is respectable. I have always encountered understanding on this matter."
>
> [The government decides by majority vote to remain in the building].[13]

Gitai Weinraub and Mansfeld's proposal from 1950 for the master plan of the government compound had included a plan for the Knesset building at the center of the compound, on the northwest side of the ceremonial courtyard, along with the president's office and that of the prime minister. Their plan favored efficiency over the civic principle of separation between the legislative and executive branches. Only in 1955 was it decided to construct an independent building for the Knesset on a separate hill on the southeastern side of the compound.

In 1956 a public competition was announced, in collaboration with the Union of Engineers and Architects in Israel, for the design of the permanent building of the Knesset in the government compound.[14] The winning plan, by architect Yosef Klarwein,[15] proposed a simple rectangular structure surrounded by a colonnaded portico. Klarwein placed the assembly hall at the building's center, with internal courtyards on either side; it was a reductivist neoclassical building and a direct reference to Karl Friedrich Schinkel's Altes Museum in Berlin (built 1823–1830). The jury explained its choice by saying that Klarwein's building "nicely expresses and serves its special purpose by positioning it on a level whose dimensions are not exaggerated [...] and through the noble appearance of the body of the building from all sides [...] the use of classical symbols in the architectural composition makes the building inspire awe and respect for all who approach it."[16]

The jury did not find a suitable project for second place and thereby reinforced their absolute preference for Klarwein's "classical symbols." The plans that were chosen for third and fourth places were modernist in scheme and appearance. One of them, that of Aba Elhanani, Mordechai Ben Horin, and Hannah Elhanani, even included an office tower of sixteen storeys—a "skyscraper" on the 1950s Jerusalemite horizon.

The publication of the competition's results infuriated members of the professional community, who expressed open criticism in the *Journal of the Union of Engineers and Architects in Israel* and in the general press. They also began to devise plots and lobbies to try to disrupt Klarwein's plan. The young generation of local architects categorically rejected the regression to a conservative style at odds with the progressive spirit of contemporary international architecture. The plan's detractors described it as "an echo of the past" that ignored (what they saw as) the "new dawn in contemporary architecture."[17] There were even those who found the building to contain fascistic imagery and a stylistic affinity with Albert Speer's works for the Nazi regime.[18]

Due to pressure from the Union of Engineers and Architects in Israel, a committee of experts was established that included the

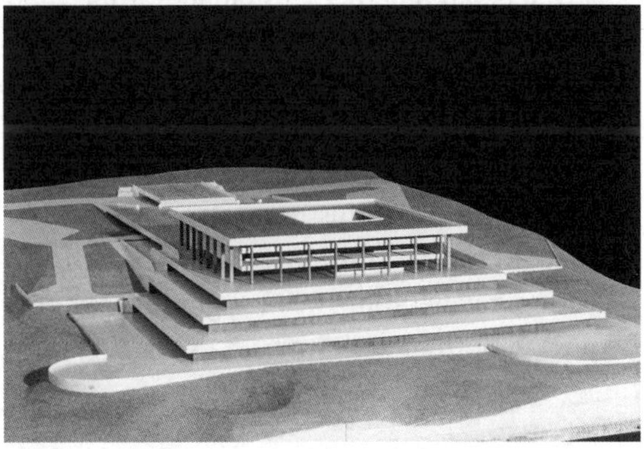

(33) (34)

㉜ Winning entry, the Knesset building design competition, Jerusalem, 1956–1957. Model. Yosef Klarwein. Photographer: Yitzhak Frenkel.
㉝ Joint proposal for the Knesset building, Jerusalem, 1959. Model. Yosef Klarwein, Shimon Powsner. Photographer: Yitzhak Frenkel.
㉞ Compromise proposal for the Knesset building, Jerusalem, 1959. Model. Dov Karmi, Ram Karmi.
㉟ The Knesset building, Jerusalem, 1956–1966. Yosef Klarwein, Shimon Powsner, Dov Karmi.

architects Max Abramovitz from New York (one of the designers of the United Nations building, whose construction was completed in 1950) and Sir Howard Morley Robertson from London, as well as Leo Arye Meir, a professor of archaeology and art history from Jerusalem. The decision of the expert panel is formulated in arcane and lofty language, as befits the object of their judgment:

> The concept of the winner, Mr. Klarwein—which proposed a building that excels in great simplicity and unity of form, built on an elevated site that expresses a feeling of movement, and placed within a landscape of existing buildings with varying silhouettes—deserves to be accepted. It can provide an excellent and powerfully expressed solution by emphasizing the contrast with the background, while being of an exalted stature that encompasses the possibility of being the most noticeable spot in the area.[19]

Despite the recommendations of the external committee, an executive committee was appointed, comprised of local architectural advisers, among them Yohanan Ratner, then dean of the Faculty of Architecture at the Technion Institute of Technology, and engineer Shlomo Gur-Gerzovsky, manager of the projects on the Givat Ram campus. Rejecting Klarwein's plan, this committee suggested that architect Shimon Powsner, from the younger generation, be brought into the project. According to Ratner, "[...] Mr. Klarwein agreed to the establishment of an office headed by Powsner [...]. Klarwein could not make a good building out of his plan [...] therefore Powsner was an intermediary who could make something more reasonable out of Klarwein's concept."[20]

Klarwein and Powsner presented two separate proposals to the Knesset Construction Committee. Abramovitz and Robertson were of the opinion that Powsner's plan was too transparent and light, while Klarwein's was too heavy, and suggested combining the two. Powsner and Klarwein prepared a joint plan that preserved the original geometrical simplicity but shed the monumentality and symmetry. One of the inner courtyards was omitted. The assembly hall was transferred from the center to the eastern side of the building. The colonnades on the sides were removed, and the number of columns on the front and back façades was reduced from twenty to ten. The front entrance remained, as in Klarwein's plan, at the south.

Architect Dov Karmi, who was invited by the executive committee as an adviser and mediator, prepared a new plan for the building that transferred the entrance to the north. He and his son, Ram, also an architect, turned the rectangle into a square, reduced the perimeter of the building, and reduced the number of columns. Dov and Ram Karmi's entrance into the project marked the end of Powsner's involvement. In 1960, their plan was approved and they became the main planners of the building. Ram Karmi wanted to get rid of the columns altogether, or reduce their number to

35

"no more than seven on each side," but his father refused, saying that he had promised to leave the columns.[21] Following this, Ram Karmi resigned from the project and took upon himself the planning of another parliament building—in Sierra Leone. When Dov Karmi died in 1962, the completion of the building returned to Klarwein's hands. On August 30, 1966, the building was inaugurated.

Following the inauguration of the building, a new journal of architecture with more intellectual aspirations, called *Tvai* (lit. "contour" or "outline") and edited by Aba Elhanani (whose team had won third place in the Knesset competition), initiated a symposium on the subject of monumentalism. The discussion was published in the third issue of *Tvai* (Spring 1967), alongside dozens of plans and photographs of the Knesset building. The voices recorded in the discussion reached an unprecedented (albeit still timid) professional consensus in favor of pomp and pretense:

> A. Elhanani [*Tvai*'s editor]: "The fact is that almost every important public building built in Israel with any monumental pretense has caused a storm. The Tel Aviv Municipality, the Bat Yam Municipality, Binyenei Ha'Uma, The Palace of Culture, and more and more. The same can be said of monumental public buildings that were built in the last twenty years around the world, beginning with the UN buildings, the Brasília buildings, the Toronto Municipality, etc. [...] The essence of the concept of monumental architecture can have different definitions. I will try to define it simply: monumentalism is an exaggerated, overblown, pretentious thing—and these are negative definitions. However, the concept can also be defined positively: a building

that is an apex in a hierarchy of the ladder of architecture, which begins with a residential home at the bottom and ends with a parliament building. Given the need for such a hierarchy, perhaps one can create a defense for monumental architecture."

Shlomo Gilad: "Our subject here is monumental architecture and not public architecture. A kind of provocation exists in the very name of the subject, since in recent years, monumentalism has been anathema when it came to modern architecture [...]. It seems that the time has come for modern architecture to be able to avail itself of monumentalism. To the extent that we agree that monumentalist architecture always expressed something essential about what the generation wanted to express, we can agree that today, too, it must also express the essence of our lives and the will of the people. Function is one of the fundamental concepts of modern architecture [...] but it seems that one of the functions is for the building to be impressive and to express itself, its needs, and its goals."

Abraham Erlick: "We have reached the conclusion that monumentalism can be considered a function of buildings of a certain kind—a social need that should be realized. The Knesset building is of the kind that must be a monumental building. The question that follows is, how should it be made monumental? We live in a time in which this question has become very difficult to answer. We have no obvious forms—no distinctiveness of form. One of the main things is placing the building within the urban landscape, of the street, or in the texture of the city. In this sense we are doing our utmost. The building is too well-placed! I do not know if the replanning of the government compound will solve this. *Today pathos 'dresses' differently.* We prefer introverted pathos over declarative pathos. Here we are, a people and a state with no consciousness of hierarchy. Besides a certain functional hierarchy, we are all equal. Whichever way you look at the building you see it on the backdrop of the sky. It's good and not good. It's monumental, it's domineering, it creates a division, and perhaps this needs to be rectified. A parliament building does not need to stand aloof—'I live among my people.'"[22]

A new era of Israeli architecture had begun. In retrospect, we may suggest that the local dialect of postmodern architecture was generated and has evolved within the framework of what was postulated here as official State architecture. The Knesset building, and the debate it generated, marks not merely a paradigm shift within the local culture of architecture, but an outright rejection of the modernist premise and the building practices associated with it.

Whatever happened to the bare, plain concrete architecture of the first two decades of Statehood? With the same determination with which it emerged out of the national pride of the War of Independence in 1948, so it disappeared with the nationalist arrogance born of the Six-Day War in 1967. During the decade following that war, Israeli society underwent a dramatic transformation in which the modernist text and the social-realist subtext of the formative era became an unintelligible and much-despised anachronism.

Architecture is never much more than an awkward, albeit credible, embodiment of the political. So long as the Labor Party hegemony endured in Israel, solidarity—indoctrinated and rhetorical as it may have been—was the primary survivalist strategy, often more captivating than patriotism. Under the spell of solidarity, architectural austerity and rigor could be readily enforced (or self-disciplined). Once the mechanisms of the "workers' society" began to malfunction and the foundations of the "welfare state" were shaken, however, all those repressed sectoral interests, distinct folklores, and personal pretenses emerged out of the cloak of statism and demanded their spatial manifestation. The decorum of the Left was rapidly lapsing, while that of the Right had yet to take form. Eventually, the political slide would produce new architectural habits, even as, or precisely because, the passive-aggressive rhetoric of an "asylum country" (for Jews) was maintained and new habits of territorial takeover and military control over a neighboring population were cultivated.

In the late 1950s and early 1960s one could already detect the first, rather bold, architectural attempts to transgress the austere framework dictated by the State—through a surplus of size, form, or ornamentation. But only after the 1967 War and the end of a prolonged recession did the "return of the repressed" copiously surface. Its outburst was most clearly and bluntly manifested in the new neighborhoods built around Jerusalem—but not only there. Within a decade, the entire country filled up with agglomerated, stepped, or suspended clusters, rife with cantilevers, slopes, and creased corners and covered with an assortment of coatings and claddings. With no prior warning, the era of the Israeli "formless" had begun. Architects who until a moment prior had been devout modernists, committed to the aesthetic of efficiency and commonality, were reincarnated in the post-Six-Day-War euphoria as sentimental regionalists, historicists, or Orientalists. They began making ostensibly "authentic," "contextual," and "open-ended" clusters that spread out boundlessly and enveloped the topography in colossal superstructures, infested with overt references to Herodian, Crusader, and Mediterranean architecture, or any other motif that aroused associations of historical depth, geographic rootedness, or appropriable folklore. ■

1 Baruch Kimmerling, *Immigrants, Settlers, Natives: The Israeli State and Society between Cultural Pluralism and Cultural War* [in Hebrew] (Tel Aviv: Am Oved, 2004), p. 11.

2 The name "Binyenei Ha'Uma" should be read as a reference to the common socialist typology of Beit Ha'am (People's House). "Buildings" (*Binyenei*) appears in the plural here, perhaps to indicate a future campus, while the word *Ha'Uma*, for the first and the last time in the context of an institutional title, denotes a nation, or even The Jewish Nation, in contradistinction to the word *Ha'am*, which signifies The People.

3 Minutes of Israeli Government Session #34, March 8, 1951 (Israel State Archives).

4 Theodor Hatalgi, "An International Exhibition Is Under Construction in Jerusalem," *Yedioth Ahronoth* [in Hebrew], July 19, 1953.

5 Minutes of Israeli Government Session #8, April 11, 1949 (Israel State Archives).

6 Cited in Susan Hattis Rolef, "The Knesset Building at Givat Ram—Planning and Construction," *Cathedra for the History of Eretz Yisrael and Its Yishuv* 96 [in Hebrew] (July 2000), p. 134.

7 After 1967, the centralized conception of the government compound was abandoned when a new political agenda dictated the dispersal of the government offices adjacent to and on both sides of the old seam line between West and East Jerusalem.

8 "Tegart forts" were reinforced concrete militarized police structures named after their designer, British police officer and engineer Charles Tegart. Dozens of these structures were built along the so-called "Tegart Wall" of the northern border with Lebanon and Syria.

9 M. Golan, "Public Architecture and Construction for Government Programs," *Engineering and Architecture: The Union of Engineers and Architects in Israel* 2 [in Hebrew] (1967), p. 5.

10 Ibid.

11 Idith Zertal, *Days and Deeds: A Life of Moshe Soroka* [in Hebrew] (Tel Aviv: Hotsa'at Maḥbarot le-sifrut, 1975), p. 175.

12 Rolef, "Knesset Building," pp. 131–170.

13 Minutes of Israeli Government Session #55, August 17, 1952, Item 556: "Determining a place for the Knesset building" (Israel State Archives).

14 According to Susan Hattis Rolef, the guidelines for the competition included only a list of areas, facilities, and spaces, without any instructions as to the essence or form of the activities in the building, and with no preference for any architectural style. A discussion was never held in the Knesset itself about the guidelines (Rolef, "Knesset Building at Givat Ram," p. 136). Due to the vague guidelines and lack of sources of funding at the time the competition was announced, rumor spread within the architectural community that the competition was bogus. For this reason, most of the veteran architects in Israel did not participate. A number of days before the announcement of the results of the competition, it became known that Baron James de Rothschild had bequeathed 1.25 million pounds sterling for the construction of the Knesset building (additional funds for the completion of the building were later provided by his widow). As a rule, one can say that emblematic public architecture was not a high priority in the routine budget of the state and was seen as a philanthropy-dependent luxury.

15 Klarwein participated in the competition despite the fact that he had served in the early 1950s as architectural adviser to the committee for the Knesset compound. This ethical blemish may well have been one of the factors that ignited the blanket opposition of the local professional community to his proposal. The protocol of the 48th session of the Knesset Compound Committee (May 13, 1950) documents Klarwein's own erstwhile opposition to the construction of a permanent building for the Knesset: "I think that the time has not come to build a Knesset building so long as we don't yet have a constitution in the state that determines the form of representation of the people: one house or two?" (cited in Rolef, "Knesset Building at Givat Ram," p. 134). During the competition, of course, this lucid statement was forgotten, and the building was planned in the absence of a constitution.

16 Jury's Decision, July 24, 1957, file 2183 a2, canister 3. Cited in Rolef, "Knesset Building at Givat Ram," p. 138.

17 From an editorial on the results of the competition, published in the *Journal of the Union of Engineers and Architects in Israel* (October 1957), p. 1.

18 Heintz Rau claimed that the building was fascist and that it reflected neither a democratic regime nor the free and direct connection between the citizen and his elected representatives. Cited in David Kroyanker, *Architecture in Jerusalem – Periods and Styles: Modern Buildings 1948–1990* [in Hebrew] (Jerusalem: Keter, 1991), p. 107.

19 Protocol of the concluding session of the Special Commission for verifying the plan of the Knesset building, April 13, 1958. Cited in Rolef, "Knesset Building at Givat Ram," p. 141.

20 Protocol 29 of the Executive Committee, May 13, 1959, file 2182, canister 26. Cited in Rolef, "Knesset Building at Givat Ram," p. 143.

21 Ram Karmi describes the argument with his father: "When we reached the point where we had to design the façade, Klarwein insisted that there be columns all around the building, despite the fact that they, in my opinion, don't at all express what goes on inside the building. I wouldn't have it and I yelled. My father interrupted me and said, 'Rami, you have to give in.' So I agreed that it could be like the Palace of Assembly in Chandigarh, India [...]. I said, seven columns, that's the maximum, because that's what the human eye can capture and still identify as a distinct number. And then my father said to me, 'You're a jackass.' I was insulted, I closed the door and quit." Interview with Chen Shalita, *Kol Ha'ir,* December 5, 1997. Cited in Susan Hattis Rolef, "The Chronicles of the Knesset's Design," *Israeli Architecture* 37 [in Hebrew] (1999).

22 Aba Elhanani (moderator), "Monumental Construction" roundtable discussion, *Tvai* 3 [in Hebrew] (Spring 1967), pp. 17–22.

# DOSSIER: THE HEBREW UNIVERSITY CAMPUS

(36) Ground breaking ceremony of Givat Ram Campus, Hebrew University, Jerusalem, 1954. Photographer: Werner Braun. Hebrew University Photography Archive.

(The Hebrew University Campus at Givat Ram, Jerusalem)

The idea of establishing a Jewish university in Palestine was initially discussed at the First Zionist Congress, held in Basel in 1897. In April 1925 the opening ceremony of the Hebrew University on Mount Scopus in Jerusalem was held. Chaim Weizmann, who would later be the first president of the State of Israel, was chairman of the university's first board of trustees, which also included such figures as Albert Einstein, Sigmund Freud, and Martin Buber. At the end of the War of 1948, the Mount Scopus campus remained under Israeli control but lacked territorial contiguity with the Jewish part of Jerusalem. The university thus had to move to a different location for a time.[1]

The location chosen for the new campus was a barren hill in West Jerusalem, adjacent to Givat Ram, the national institutions compound. Construction of the Givat Ram campus began in 1953; it functioned as the main Hebrew University campus for about twenty years. In 1967, with the reunification of Jerusalem under Israeli control following the so-called Six-Day War, the restoration and expansion of the Mount Scopus campus began. By 1981 most of the faculties had moved to Mount Scopus, with the Givat Ram campus continuing to house the faculty of natural sciences and the National Library of Israel.

The master plan of the Givat Ram campus was designed in 1953 by Richard Kauffmann, Heintz Rau, and Yosef Klarwein. It depicts a linear array of parallel buildings connected by a covered arcade, open to a picturesque garden, and anchored by the university's administrative building at the entrance side. The National Library, the apex of intellectual activity, is at the end of the arcade. This scheme echoes Munio Gitai Weinraub and Al Mansfeld's proposal for the government compound, though it presents a more reductive and compact version, without biomorphic contours, hierarchical organization, or ceremonial plazas.

The Givat Ram campus marks a milestone in Israeli architecture for a number of reasons:

First, it was during this project that "schnorr" techniques were developed for the funding of public buildings, in particular academic institutions, by donations from Diaspora Jewry. These earmarked donations enabled planners and builders to bypass government-dictated budgets and to invest relatively disproportionate resources in their work; as a result, they gained valuable professional experience in the design of complex landmark projects, and the cultural status of public architecture was solidified.

Second, the introverted setup of the Givat Ram campus—its design as an exterritorial domain, attached to but isolated from the city—would become a recurring element in the planning of all the academic institutions in Israel.[2]

Third, the Givat Ram campus was, in effect, the initiation site for the architectural "generation of 1948," a generation that became dominant during the 1950s, dictated the ethics and aesthetics of Israeli architecture until 1967, and instilled its hegemony in the professional market for decades afterward. The establishment's wholehearted embrace of the young generation (a phenomenon that would not be repeated in Israel) can only be interpreted as a conscious choice of the International Style as a guiding framework for the formulation of official architecture. The attributes of this style—clarity, efficiency, transparency, and elegance—represented the acquired decorum and desired look of the new State.

This manifest choice of fashionable ordinariness—eschewing any fancy to erect iconic buildings, to endow monumentality, to reconstruct classical motifs, to produce regional textures, to appropriate Oriental ornamentation, or to fabricate a surplus of weight and plasticity (a moment before Brutalism became the new Israeli taste)—is hardly imaginable in contemporary Israeli institutional or academic architecture. The clustered monumentality of the post-1967 Mount Scopus campus is a testament to the fact that the architecture of the formative Israeli era, which found its refined expression in the showcase modernism of the Givat Ram campus, has lost its rhetorical power and remains a poignant relic of sixties youth culture. ■

1 For a comprehensive study of the Hebrew University's Mount Scopus campus, see Diana Dolev, *The Planning and Building of the Hebrew University, 1919–1948: Facing the Temple Mount* (Lanham, MD: Lexington Books, 2016).

2 The Negev University in Beersheba, which was built in the early 1970s, was located near the city center as a critical response to the urban seclusion of the former campuses, but given Beersheba's structure of "enclave urbanism" (see chapter "New Towns"), the university campus remained a gated domain, just like the ex-urban campuses.

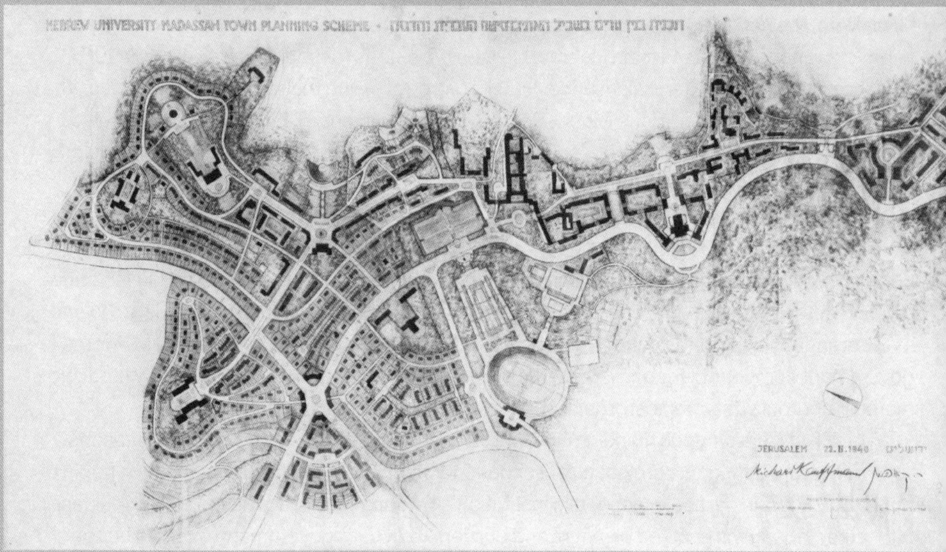


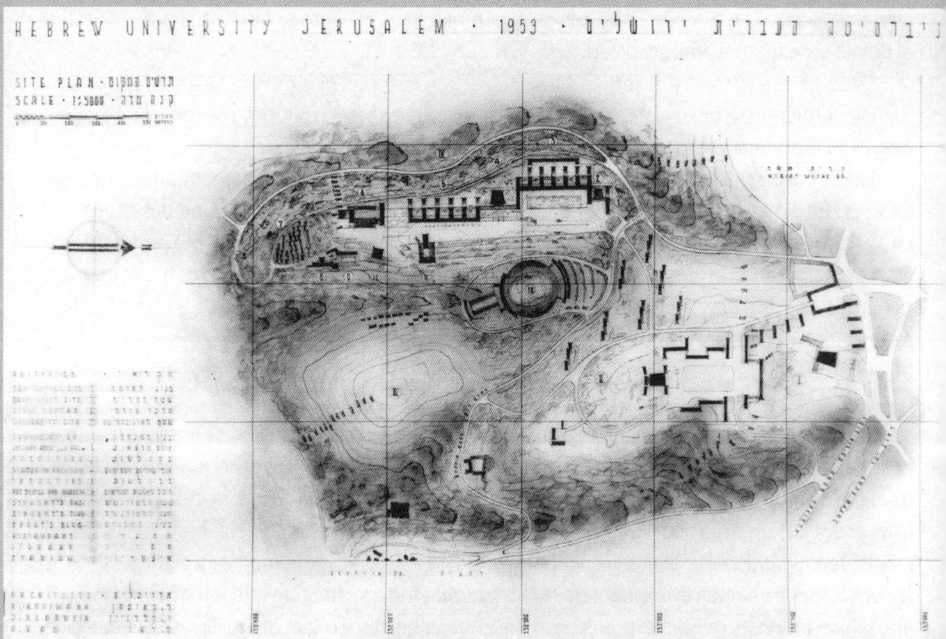


㊲ ㊳

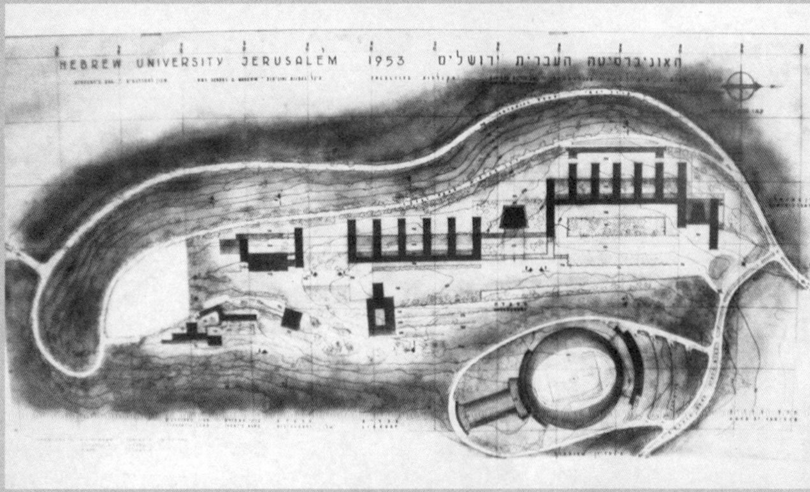

(39) (40)

(37) Mount Scopus campus, Hebrew University, Jerusalem, 1948. Master plan. Richard Kauffmann. Hebrew University Central Archive.
(38) Givat Ram campus, Hebrew University, Jerusalem, 1953. Master plan. Richard Kauffmann, Yosef Klarwein, Heintz Rau. Hebrew University Central Archive.
(39) Givat Ram campus, Hebrew University, Jerusalem, 1953. Master plan. Richard Kauffmann, Yosef Klarwein, Heintz Rau. Hebrew University Central Archive.
(40) Givat Ram campus, Hebrew University, Jerusalem, 1953. Model. Richard Kauffmann, Yosef Klarwein, Heintz Rau. Photographer: Alfred Bernheim. Hebrew University Photography Archive.

האוניברסיטה העברית בירושלים
THE HEBREW UNIVERSITY JERUSALEM
נולוגי לישראל
TECHNION - ISRAEL I

41

42

אדריכלים מ.וינראוב א.מנספלד חיפה
ARCHITECTS M.WEINRAUB

HEBREW UNIVERSITY JERUSALEM 1953 האוניברסיטה העברית ירושלים
ARCHITECTS: R. KAUFMANN
J. KLARWEIN
H. RAU

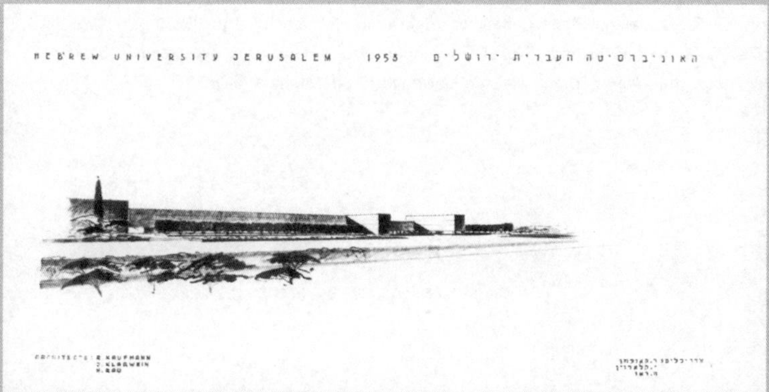
HEBREW UNIVERSITY JERUSALEM 1953 האוניברסיטה העברית ירושלים
ARCHITECTS: R. KAUFMANN
J. KLARWEIN
H. RAU

(43) (44)

(45)

㊶ Givat Ram campus, Hebrew University, Jerusalem. Master plan. Richard Kauffmann, Yosef Klarwein, Heintz Rau. Hebrew University Central Archive.
㊷ Givat Ram campus, Hebrew University, Jerusalem, 1955. Donors to the Institute of Jewish Studies at the building's construction site, with architect Munio Gitai Weinraub sitting on the left. Munio Gitai Weinraub, Al Mansfeld. Photographer: Werner Braun. Hebrew University Photography Archive.
㊸–㊹ Givat Ram campus, Hebrew University, Jerusalem, 1953. Perspective. Richard Kauffmann, Yosef Klarwein, Heintz Rau. Hebrew University Central Archive.
㊺ Givat Ram campus, Hebrew University, under construction, Jerusalem, 1954. Local stone is used as the main facing material. Photographer: Werner Braun. Hebrew University Photography Archive.
㊻–㊼ Chemistry Building auditorium, Givat Ram campus, Hebrew University, Jerusalem. 1956. Arieh Sharon, Benjamin Idelson. Photographer: Werner Braun. Hebrew University Photography Archive.
㊽ Student lounge, Givat Ram campus, Hebrew University, Jerusalem. 1957. Arieh Sharon, Benjamin Idelson. Photographer: Werner Braun. Hebrew University Photography Archive.
㊾ Student dormitories, Givat Ram campus, Hebrew University, Jerusalem. 1957. Photographer: Werner Braun. Hebrew University Photography Archive.

㊻

(47)

(48)

(49)

⑩ ⑪

⑫

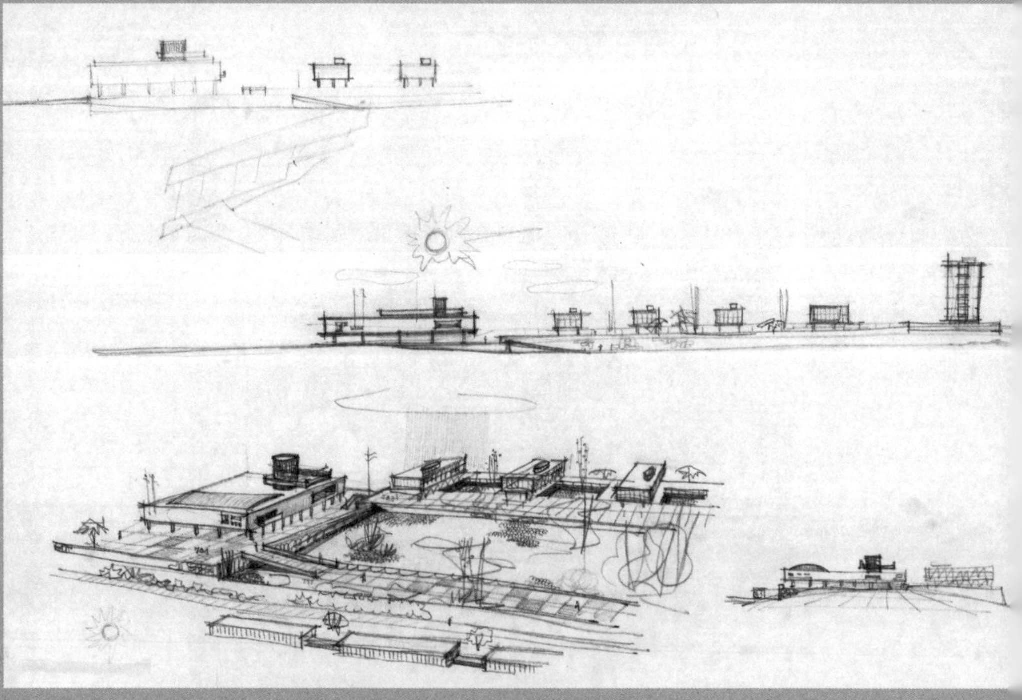

(53)

(54) (55)

(56)

(57)

(58)

(50) Entrance plaza, Givat Ram campus, Hebrew University, Jerusalem, 1956–1957. Shimon Powsner.
(51) Faculty of Humanities and Social Sciences, Givat Ram campus, Hebrew University, Jerusalem, 1954–1958. Avraham Yasky, Shimon Powsner.
(52) The National Library and adjacent buildings, Givat Ram Campus, Hebrew University, Jerusalem. Perspective and elevation sketches, Hanan Hevron, late 1950s. Hanan Hevron's collection, Yad Tabenkin Archives.
(53) National Library, Givat Ram campus, Hebrew University, Jerusalem, 1956–1960. Ziva Armoni, Hanan Hebron, Shulamit Nadler, Michael Nadler, Shimon Powsner, Avraham Yasky, Amnon Alexandroni. Hebrew University Photography Archive.
(54)–(55) National Library, interior. Givat Ram campus, Hebrew University, Jerusalem, 1956–1960. Ziva Armoni, Hanan Hebron, Shulamit Nadler, Michael Nadler, Shimon Powsner, Avraham Yasky, Amnon Alexandroni. Hebrew University Photography Archive.
(56)–(57) Medical Research Institute, Givat Ram campus, Hebrew University, Jerusalem, 1957. David Anatol Brutzkus. Photographer: Bodin. Hebrew University Photography Archive.
(58) Institute of Archaeology, Givat Ram campus, Hebrew University, Jerusalem, 1958. Zeev Rechter. Photographer: Orient Press. Hebrew University Photography Archive.

⑲

⑳

㉑ ㉒

⑥③

⑥⑤

⑥④

(59) Administration Building, Givat Ram campus, Hebrew University, Jerusalem, 1956. Dov Karmi, Zvi Meltzer, Ram Karmi.
(60) Bus station, Givat Ram campus, Hebrew University, Jerusalem, 1957. Avraham Yasky and Amnon Alexandroni with artist Yitzhak Danziger.
(61) Bus station, Givat Ram campus, Hebrew University, Jerusalem, 1957. Avraham Yasky and Amnon Alexandroni with artist Yitzhak Danziger.
(62) Bus station, Givat Ram campus, Hebrew University, Jerusalem, 1957. Avraham Yasky and Amnon Alexandroni with artist Yitzhak Danziger.
(63) Givat Ram campus, Hebrew University, under construction, Jerusalem, 1956.
(64) University synagogue, Givat Ram campus, Hebrew University, Jerusalem, 1957. David Resnick, Heintz Rau. Photographer: Werner Braun. Hebrew University Photography Archive.
(65) University synagogue, Lobby. Givat Ram campus, Hebrew University, Jerusalem, 1957. David Resnick, Heintz Rau. Photographer: Werner Braun. Hebrew University Photography Archive.
(66) Detail, the synagogue's Torah ark.
(67) The synagogue's interior, Givat Ram campus, Hebrew University, Jerusalem, 1957. David Resnick, Heintz Rau. Photographer: Gross. Hebrew University Photography Archive.

(66)

(67)

(68)

(69)

(68) Swimming pool and gymnasium, Givat Ram campus, Hebrew University, Jerusalem, mid-1960s. Elevation. Shmuel Mestechkin.
(69) Gymnasium, Givat Ram campus, Hebrew University, Jerusalem, mid-1960s. Interior. Shmuel Mestechkin.
(70) Amphitheater, Givat Ram campus, Hebrew University, Jerusalem, 1958. Shmuel Mestechkin. Hebrew University Photography Archive.
(71) Aerial view of stadium and amphitheater. 1958. Photographer: Alfred Bernheim. Hebrew University Photography Archive.
(72) Swimming pool, Givat Ram campus, Hebrew University, Jerusalem, mid-1960s. Interior. Shmuel Mestechkin.
(73) Outdoor Concert, Givat Ram campus, Hebrew University, Jerusalem, 1957. Shmuel Mestechkin. Photographer: Werner Braun. Hebrew University Photography Archive.

⑦⓪

⑦①

⑦②

⑦③

# Union Architecture

## The Architecture of the *Histadrut*

At the inauguration ceremony of the Executive Committee Building of the Histadrut General Labor Federation[1] on July 1, 1953, the keynote speaker, Prime Minister David Ben-Gurion, former head of the Histadrut, publicly expressed ambivalence:

> I do not know if I am permitted to say this, for today is unarguably a happy day, but if I had remained to this day a member of the Executive Committee, you would not have built this building without a fight from me. Perhaps I would have been outnumbered, as happened on a number of occasions, however, since it has been built—congratulations to the builders. [...] It has been more than fifteen years since I have been distanced from the work in this building, but it seems to me that nothing has changed. [...] The Histadrut has not taken the high road in either framework or content, and to this day I doubt if this union has a counterpart in the world. [...] We were not a trade union like other trade unions. Nor were we a cooperative organization like other cooperative organizations. We were something more. The founders of the Histadrut, and those who designed its infrastructure and modes of practice, saw this organization not only as a professional, cooperative, cultural, and settlement-oriented organization—but as something deeper: a covenant of the founders of the State and the revivers of the homeland. [...]
>
> I really do not know whether to be truly happy—and I am truly happy for this building and its splendor—or to be slightly regretful for the [lost] austerity with which we acted in those early days.[2]

①

This inauguration ceremony is a particularly demonstrative event with which to begin unraveling the intricacies of Israeli institutional architecture in its early days. More than any other building of the period, the Histadrut's Executive Committee Building—which was the first notable post-1948 attempt at emblematic institutional architecture—exemplifies both the remarkable duality and the incredible polarity of two executive superstructures: the State and the Histadrut. The first was a new organization whose very existence and routine performance were dependent on the dismantling of all its forerunners and the fusing of their shards into a cohesive sovereign body. The second was a veteran organization, profoundly entrenched in the local economy and politics, which saw the State as its immature offspring—a formal and as of yet empty administrative framework. Such an outlook can be detected, for instance, in the "historiography" offered by *The Histadrut Lexicon* under the entry "The Prime Minister of Israel":

> There was more than symbolism involved in the fact that the first General Secretary of the Histadrut Labor Federation, David Ben-Gurion, was also the first Prime

> Minister of the State. For State and sovereignty are nothing more than a form for the content of independence—and this content is determined by powerful economic, social, moral, and cultural achievements. All these were created, formed, and made available by the General Federation of Workers for the enterprise of Jewish revival in the Land of Israel.[3]

For the "Labor Federationists," the Executive Committee Building signaled the Histadrut's refusal to be co-opted into the "empty" statist framework and celebrated its reinvigorated infrastructure, which allowed it to triumphantly build a colossal edifice in the terms of the time.

For the "statists," the inauguration ceremony was an opportunity to cling to the pioneering past of the "covenant of the founders," to force the severing of protracted sectoral kinships, and to demonstrate leadership. The magnificent building is built. The battle is lost. Ben-Gurion is left with a final venomous comment: "this building and its splendor"—more than enough to imply the bankruptcy of the Labor Movement's values.[4]

Just as the Labor Federation, reluctant to give up its old position and its involvement in all areas of pre-State life, reacted to the new situation of sovereignty with architectural overkill, so did Ben-Gurion find it difficult to part with the pioneering ethos of sacrifice dating from the first days of settlement, and to adapt—for himself and for the State—new forms of institutional representation.

As Ben-Gurion aptly stated, the Labor Federation indeed had no counterpart and no precedent: During the formative decades of Statehood, the Histadrut was a trade-union umbrella that united the majority of workers in the country, protecting their rights and working conditions. At the same time, it was a monopolistic employer, the largest in the State, with its hand in every economic sector: industry, construction, commerce, export, import, banking, and services. Through its economic arm, Hevrat Ha'Ovdim ("Society of Workers"), the Labor Federation owned and operated a number of enterprises, including the country's largest industrial conglomerates and largest bank, Bank Hapoalim ("The Workers' Bank"). In addition to its colossal "pyramidal" economic constitution, the Labor Federation was also a comprehensive social system, with branches providing housing, social welfare, health care, education, and cultural activities for its members (and often also for immigrants who were not yet members).

Just as it touched every aspect of the economy and society and every part of its members' lives, the Histadrut also spread itself throughout the country by means of an intricate network of administrative and public buildings: workers' councils and dues offices, cooperatives, wholesale markets, department stores and groceries, clinics and hospitals, convalescent homes and cultural centers, community centers, youth centers, academies, colleges, theaters, cinemas, libraries, and museums. The accumulation of these architectural objects created a spatial and mental matrix no less ubiquitous than that of the State.

At a time when the State apparatus was not fully formed, or was demonstratively refraining from the consolidation of building types and from the design of architectural hallmarks, the Labor Federation focused on developing an architectural language that would express its organizational efficiency and amplify its presence in practically every town and settlement across the country. For a workers' council building, a health clinic, or a workers' theater, the identification with the corporate identity of Histadrut always came before any site-specific consideration.

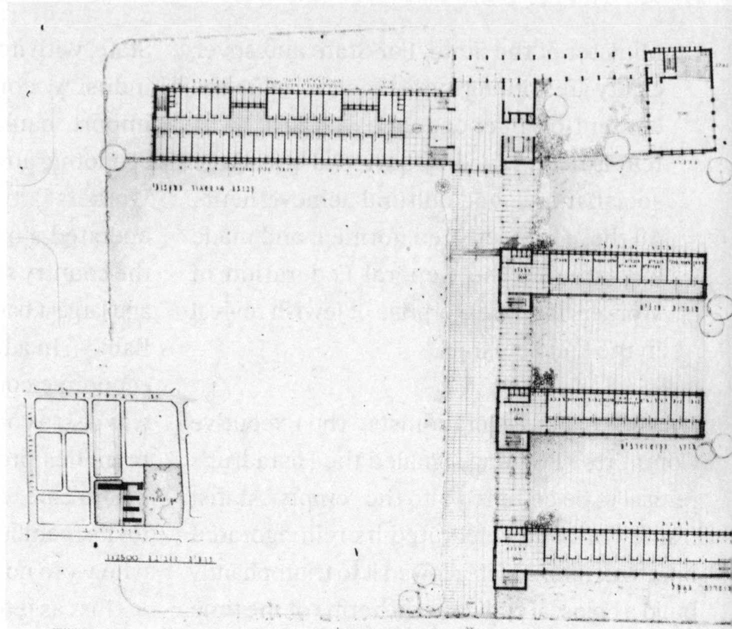

②

③

① Histadrut (Labor Union) Executive Committee building, entrance lobby, Tel Aviv, 1949–1953. "Chever" Architects' Cooperative: Dov Karmi, Zvi Meltzer, Marian Grynhaus, Malkiel Kotlowitz, Yitzhak Yashar, Yitzhak Levkovich, Meir Sarfati, Mark Pintel. Artwork: Yohanan Simon, photographer: Fritz Cohen. Government Press Office.
② Histadrut Executive Committee building, Tel Aviv, 1949–1953. Floor plan. "Chever" Architects' Cooperative.
③ Histadrut Executive Committee building, view from the southeast, Tel Aviv, 1949–1953. "Chever" Architects' cooperative. Photographer: Fritz Cohen. Government Press Office.
④ Histadrut Executive Committee building, main entrance, Tel Aviv, 1949–1953. "Chever" Architects' Cooperative. Photographer: Fritz Cohen. Government Press Office, Photography Department.
⑤ Histadrut Executive Committee building, members' tax cards hall, Tel Aviv, 1949–1953. "Chever" Architects' Cooperative. Photographer: Fritz Cohen. Government Press Office.
⑥ Histadrut Executive Committee building, archive room, Tel Aviv, 1949–1953. "Chever" Architects' Cooperative. Photographer: Fritz Cohen. Government Press Office.

④

⑤

⑥

The political clout of the Labor Federation—stemming from its ability to garner the support (and the constant striking potential) of the workers and immigrants, and from its blood ties to the ruling Labor Party—enabled it to function for years as a proxy state-within-a-state, running parallel systems that were equally symbiotic and competing. The Labor Federation had its own "Foreign Office" (at a time when the Soviet Union was a supporter and the Socialist International was a proxy for the United Nations); its own "Treasury" (banks, independent tax offices); its own "Ministry of Health" (hospitals, clinics, convalescent homes); its own "Ministry of Education" (networks of vocational schools and teachers' academies); its own "Ministry of Sport" (Hapoel ["The Worker"] amateur and professional sports clubs, with leading teams in most team sports); and even its own "Ministry of Housing." The boundaries between the State and Labor Federation economies were blurred, with the Labor Federation often taking upon itself national tasks of housing, immigrant absorption, and public works. At a time when Israeli society operated according to sectoral affiliation and every political party had its own public-housing company and its own bank, the Histadrut was the favored sector, large enough and close enough to play the State's doppelgänger.

In the field of public housing, the Labor Federation was the largest developer and builder, second only to the Housing Department of the government's Labor Ministry. Through housing companies such as Neve Oved ("Worker's Oasis") or Shikun ("Housing"), which merged in 1954 to form Shikun Ovdim ("Workers' Housing"), the Labor Federation provided dwellings not only for its veteran members, but also for the influx of immigrants: out of 18,000 housing units built by Shikun and 13,000 built by Neve Oved by

1954,[5] 1,960 and 7,314 units, respectively, were designated for new immigrants through the Shikun Olim ("Immigrant Housing") initiative.[6]

In terms of architectural innovation and merit, the Labor Federation's housing projects provided pioneering prototypes that were soon adopted in State projects and circulated across the country. The popular and affordable building types developed by the Histadrut during the 1930s and 1940s in the Me'onot Ovdim (workers' housing compounds), the Krayot Amal (labor estates), and the serial housing blocks were indeed materially and aesthetically inferior to the bourgeois "Bauhaus" apartment buildings in the cities, but they were superior in terms of urban design, community planning, and standardized production. As such, they could properly become models for the State's public housing after 1948 and define the characteristics of the emergent Israeli culture of construction and housing. But beyond its entrepreneurial and architectural contribution in the field of public housing, the Labor Federation was also the organization with the largest construction company in the country, Solel Boneh. This company worked directly for the Labor Federation, while also functioning as a regular contractor. Between 1949 and 1957 it was responsible for over half of the residential units built in Israel.[7]

In addition, most of the national infrastructure—ports, roads, railways, nuclear installations, and water systems—were built by this same "State contractor," which also had a monopoly on raw materials (stone quarries, cement factories, glass and steel industries, etc.). The Solel Boneh conglomerate became so large that it began to threaten the economic independence of the State. In 1958 it was decided to divide it into three separate companies: the Construction and Public Works Company; Kur (meaning "furnace"), responsible for factories and industry; and the Ports and External Works Company, responsible for infrastructural work in Israel and abroad.[8]

The importance the Labor Federation attributed to public buildings was obvious from the first decades of its existence. In 1935 it established the Public Buildings, Ltd. company, through which it built the first workers' council buildings and other public buildings planned by prominent pre-State architects. With the founding of the State, the organization's Committee of Public Buildings decided on an ambitious plan to construct hundreds of Histadrut public buildings throughout the country—a veritable nervous system whose goal was to convey messages to veteran members and to bring in new immigrant members who had not yet chosen their political affiliation. This plan aimed at creating—within the fabric of existing towns, in the empty centers of new towns, and in regional and village centers—an accumulation of architectural signs perpetuating the particular society of the Israeli labor union.

During the 1950s and 1960s this plan was translated into a national network of no less than sixty-eight workers' council buildings, dozens of cultural centers,[9] about 850 health-fund infirmaries (one in almost every settlement in the country), eleven retirement homes, a chain of educational and research institutes in cities and rural settings,[10] and, finally, over twenty museums, located mainly in rural settlements.[11]

Histadrut architecture relied on complicated funding systems that directed funds to the Public Buildings, Ltd. company in different ways: voluntary collection drives for contributions of a day's salary (this "Public Building Drive" was accompanied by a motivational campaign with colorful posters and radio

⑦ ⑧ ⑨

⑦ Histadrut House, Eilat, 1955. Aba Elhanani.
⑧ Histadrut center, Eilat, early 1950s. Unknown architect.
⑨ Labor council and culture center, Dimona, 1950s.

programs); various Labor Federation dues (both "parallel dues," paid by the employer and mainly forwarded to the health funds, and "individual dues," paid by the member, with a regular sum being set aside for the "Building Fund"); money from the workers' pension plans; and loans from the Worker's Bank. There were also donations from overseas worker's organizations (Soroka Hospital in Beersheba, for example, was built with a donation from the American Ladies' Garment Workers' Union) and various private donors (Frank Sinatra, through his special contacts with heads of American unions, made a donation for the Histadrut offices and for a cultural center in Nazareth).

As mentioned above, the Labor Federation strategically emphasized its own cumulative trademark and influence by creating service networks. But no less importantly, it saw itself as an enlightened patron of architecture, as the dictator of public taste. Unlike many long-established organizations that commemorate their status with conservative architecture, the Israeli Labor Federation consistently supported the architectural fashions and fashionable architects of the day.

Returning to the Labor Federation's headquarters, the Executive Committee Building was launched in an architectural competition in 1949 which was won by "The Architects Group," a short-lived collective headed by Dov Karmi, who up to that point had been identified with the petit bourgeois International Style, or the so-called "white architecture" of Tel Aviv. The built compound of the Executive Committee Building is a branched array of parallel slab buildings positioned along a central axis that marks the official entrance.

The main building, eight storeys high, dominates the street from behind a large open lawn, symbolizing bureaucratic distance and staging theatrical authority.

An innovative architectural device on the façade of the Executive Committee Building is what makes this building revolutionary: it was the first Israeli building to make considerable use of prefabricated concrete elements for shading and light filtration.[12] This industrialized shading element was directly inspired by the brise-soleil façade of Le Corbusier, Lucio Costa, and Oscar Niemeyer on the Ministry of Education building in Rio de Janeiro (1937–1943)—though here it was placed vertically, as opposed to the horizontal placement of the original. The brise-soleil, and the tight weave it created over the building's façade, was developed in the 1930s but became a common practice and an architectural trademark only after World War II. In Palestine, the architects of the 1930s adapted the early International Style to the local climate and solar conditions, mainly by the pliable plastic treatment of the body of the building (creating cantilevered and recessed volumes) and by protecting the apertures using various sorts of operable shutters. In the 1950s, following the precedent set by the Executive Committee Building, Israeli architects now had the option of using a built-in screen or radiator-like grid over entire sun-facing façades. Israeli modernist architecture could finally be produced, distributed, and perceived as a standard off-the-shelf product.

⑩ "Keren" workers' theater, Beersheba, 1950–1954. Shulamit Nadler, Michael Nadler.
⑪ Lessin culture house, Tel Aviv, 1948. Arieh Sharon. Arieh Sharon digital archive.
⑫ Lessin culture house, Tel Aviv, 1948. Arieh Sharon. Arieh Sharon digital archive.
⑬ Lessin Culture House, Tel Aviv, 1948. Interior. Arieh Sharon (holding camera). Arieh Sharon digital archive.

⑩ ⑪ ⑫ ⑬

⑭

⑮

The brise-soleil façade would be repeated on other Histadrut buildings,[13] to the point that it can be identified as a marker of Labor Federation architectural physiognomy. The relative lightness of the screen façades differentiates Histadrut buildings from State public buildings, which are often solid and opaque—whether built in the pre-State era (for example, the National Institutions House in Jerusalem, a massive stone building with small, narrow windows, designed by Yohanan Ratner from 1928 to 1932) or after Statehood (the government offices in Jerusalem designed by Yosef Klarwein in the early 1950s are another permutation of the solid presence of stone architecture). To make a sweeping generalization, the impression created by Labor Federation architecture is one of repetitive framing devices and shading screens, while that of State architecture is based on imposing compositions of freestanding monoliths. During the 1960s, the "union look" of the Labor Federation buildings circulated and became popular in all sectors of public and private architecture. The prefab concrete brise-soleil and its various offspring, above all the notorious aluminum-and-PVC Trisol, loomed as both leitmotif and distinctive insignia of Israeli architecture (for a discussion of these elements, see chapter "Detail").

The most heated architectural battle between the Labor Federation and the government unfolded around the Labor Federation's health institutions and hospitals. With its many hospitals, clinics, vocational training centers, and office buildings, the efficient system of Kupat Holim ("Health Fund") is

⑭ Bank Hapoalim ("The Workers' Bank") headquarters, 1959–1960. Arieh Sharon, Benjamin Idelson. Iron grille designed by Bezalel Schatz. Arieh Sharon digital archive.
⑮ Beit Elisheva, Jerusalem, 1961–1963. Shulamit Nadler, Michael Nadler, Shmuel Bixon.

without a doubt the most impressive of the Labor Federation's architectural endeavors. Moshe Soroka, administrative director of the Health Fund, stood behind this vast network and oversaw its construction projects.

At a time when the State was building temporary health facilities in bungalows and huts—following the doctrine of Chaim Sheba, managing director of the Ministry of Health—the buildings of the Labor Federation's Health Fund were notorious for their architectural merit. Recall Soroka's rebuke in his debate with Sheba, discussed in the chapter "State Architecture":

> All of the government hospitals [built in the cabin method] are in dire distress, because the Treasury has clung to Sheba's flawed reservations and preferred the temporary over the permanent, the cheap, the superficial, and the fast over the good and the stable. "Here we have no luxury. Here everything is functional."[14]

In the name of "the good and the stable," Soroka worked with the best architects in the country to create the public buildings that he saw as essential for an advanced health system. He traveled the world with his architects—among them Arieh and Eldar Sharon, Zeev and Yaacov Rechter, Avraham Yasky, and Amnon Alexandroni—in order to keep abreast of the latest advances in hospital construction.

In Soroka's eyes, the Histadrut hospitals were strongholds designed to stave off attempts by Ben-Gurion and Sheba to take over

⑯ ⑰

⑯ Beit Cur – Agricultural Co-op headquarters, Tel Aviv, 1965–1968. Interior. Arieh Sharon, Eldar Sharon. Arieh Sharon digital archive.
⑰ Beit Cur – Agricultural Co-op headquarters, Tel Aviv, 1965–1968. Arieh Sharon, Eldar Sharon. Arieh Sharon digital archive.

the Health Fund as a way of enforcing centralized control of health services:

> We had a serious argument [...] about the transfer of Kupat Holim to the State, and it was decided not at the table and not by committees. It was decided by the fact that during those days Kupat Holim committed, even dared, to spread and create certain facts. [...] Then they saw that the baby was so large it couldn't be swallowed.[15]

The climax of the conflict between Soroka and Ben-Gurion materialized with the founding of a central hospital in Beersheba, in the Negev Desert region. Even when Ben-Gurion finally agreed to the facility being founded by Kupat Holim, he expected to control all details of the architecture and planning, as Teddy Kollek, Ben-Gurion's office manager, made clear in a letter to Soroka in 1956:

> The Prime Minister's request with regard to the building is that it be done with the austerity befitting of our country, therefore I propose that perhaps you make the building plans available for an additional inspection so they can be approved for austerity construction.[16]

Soroka did not submit the plans for State censorship—he carried on building according to the plans drawn up by Arieh Sharon for the construction of the Beersheba hospital, which was later named after him. ■

1 Originally the General Federation of Jewish Workers in Palestine, founded in 1920 under the British Mandate.

2 David Ben-Gurion, "One Histadrut: One Socialist-Zionist Party," *Davar* [in Hebrew], July 2, 1953.

3 Dov Ben-Meir, "The Prime Minister of Israel," in *The Histadrut Lexicon* [in Hebrew] (Tel Aviv: Am Oved – Culture and Education Series, 1980), p. 370.

4 The public criticism of the Labor Federation's "ostentation," in the same spirit as Ben-Gurion's speech at the opening of the Executive Committee Building, crept into internal discussions held by Labor Federation bodies on more than one occasion. For example, during a meeting of the Supreme Committee for Public Building Supervision to discuss the founding of a Bank Hapoalim branch on Rothschild Boulevard in Tel Aviv (designed by Arieh Sharon and Benjamin Idelson), comrade Soroka was indecisive about the consequences of building five or seven storeys: "We are discussing this from the public angle, and we must give public validity to institutional activity. The building will be finished, as far as the public is concerned, at a most difficult time—election time. The public will perceive this building not as a cultural-public service, but as a bank. Therefore you must explain to us what is so important that makes the 'what will they say' less so." Comrade Zack, one of the bank's representatives, was not upset by this: "If we consider this only from the point of view of public opinion, the entire bank should not have been allowed to be built. Every new building is an eyesore, and it is hard for the public to accept it." And comrade Rosen added: "Public opinion will not differ whether there are five or seven storeys." In the end it was decided to authorize the complete building, with the claim that "the concentration of institutions is to the public's benefit." Protocol No. 13-A of the Supreme Committee for Public Building Supervision, April 2, 1958 [in Hebrew] (The Histadrut's Lavon Archive).

5 See Itzhak Greenberg, "The Reforms on the Member's Company Following the Great Immigration," in *Between Immigrants and Veterans*, ed. Dalia Ofer [in Hebrew] (Jerusalem: Yad Izhak Ben-Zvi, 1996).

6 See Haim Darin-Drabkin, *Housing and Absorption in Israel* [in Hebrew] (Tel Aviv: Gadish, 1955), p. 54.

7 268,000 housing units were built in Israel up until the end of 1957—154,000 of them by Solel Boneh. Of these, 74 percent were designated for new immigrants and 25 percent for veteran Israelis, leaving only 1 percent for the private sector. Solel Boneh's part in public building in Israel is therefore enormous. See Greenberg, "Reforms on the Member's Company."

8 See Hillel Dan, *On an Unpaved Road: The Legend of Solel Boneh* [in Hebrew] (Jerusalem and Tel Aviv: Schocken, 1963).

9 Among these are Beit Lessin in Tel Aviv, designed by Arieh Sharon (1951–1954); Beit Philip Murray in Eilat, designed by Aba and Hannah Elhanani (1955–1956); and the Keren Theater in Beersheba, designed by Shulamit and Michael Nadler (1951–1954), who also designed the

Rachel Cinema in Ashkelon (1956) and Beit Elisheva in Jerusalem (1961–1963).

10 For example, Beit Berl, planned by Mordechai Shoshani and Yohanan Ratner (1946–1960); Ruppin Agricultural College in Emek Hefer, designed by Shulamit and Michael Nadler (1946–1950); and the Givat Haviva Seminar Center, designed by Shmuel Mestechkin (1960–1965).

11 Among these are the Ghetto Fighters' Museum in the Ghetto Fighters' Kibbutz, designed by Samuel Bickels (1956–1959), who also designed the Ein Harod Art Museum (1948); and the Caesarea Antiquities Museum at Sdot Yam, planned by Shmuel Mestechkin (1947).

12 In general, a façade design based on a structural or decorative grid was extremely rare in the modernist architecture of the first decades of the century, in both Palestine and Europe. A local exception is the State hospital in Haifa, designed by Erich Mendelsohn (1936–1938)—although there it is an open grid that emphasizes the building's division into cells, and not a brise-soleil tight weave creating a continuous surface.

13 To name just a few examples: the Beit Lessin Theater in Tel Aviv, the Keren Theater in Beersheba, the Soroka, Beilinson, and Meir hospitals, and the Misha'an retirement home in Ramat Aviv.

14 Idith Zertal, *Days and Deeds: A Life of Moshe Soroka* [in Hebrew] (Tel Aviv: Hotsa'at Maḥbarot le-sifrut, 1975), p. 175.

15 Ibid.

16 Letter from Teddy Kollek to Moshe Soroka, 1956. Published in Shifra Shwartz, "The Political Struggle of Founding the Central Negev Hospital," *Theories of the Founding of the State* 5 [in Hebrew] (1995), p. 410.

⑱ Beilinson Hospital, Petah Tikva, 1949–1956. Arieh Sharon, Benjamin Idelson. Photographer: Yitzhak Kalter.
⑲ Meir Hospital, Kfar Saba, 1946–1956. Zeev Rechter, Moshe Zarhi, Yaacov Rechter.
⑳ "Abolish the Martial Law!" Graffiti at Ichilov Municipal Hospital, Tel Aviv, 1954–1960. Arieh Sharon, Arieh Sharon digital archive.

⑱ ⑲ ⑳ ㉑

㉒ ㉓ ㉔

㉑ Yoseftal Hospital, Eilat, 1964. Arieh Sharon, Benjamin Idelson, Avraham Yasky, Amnon Alexandroni.
㉒ Mental hospital, Ezrat Nashim, Jerusalem, 1961. Architects: Arieh Sharon, Benjamin Idelson; architects in charge: J. Hertz, G. Zippor. Arieh Sharon digital archive.
㉓ Medical clinic, Petah Tikva, 1950–1954. Zeev Rechter.
㉔ Soroka Medical Center, Beersheba, 1954–1964.
Arieh Sharon, Benjamin Idelson, Micha Amitai. Photographer: Photo Sadeh.

# DOSSIER:
# THE RECHTERS' PROLETARIAN RETREATS

㉕

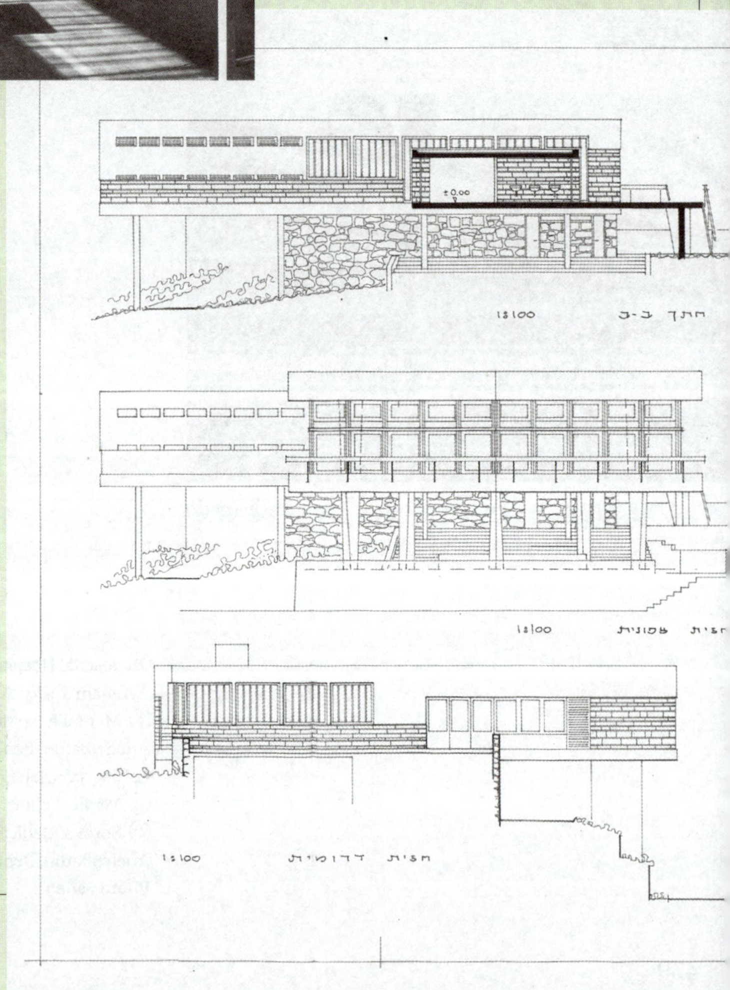

The chain of Margo'a Le'oved ("Worker's Calm") and Mavtihim ("Surety") convalescent homes completed the Labor Federation's network of production, service, representation, and control: rewarding workers with the small pleasures of a convalescent home was an effective way of ensuring the maintenance of their physical and mental productivity. The privilege of work entailed the obligation of rest (organized, controlled, and, most importantly, not private). The Labor Federation's convalescent homes were run like hospitals: the staff wore white gowns, and guests were weighed on arrival and departure to make sure they gained weight and became stronger. Meals and social activities took place promptly on schedule. Yet, given the natural beauty of their chosen locations and the poetic license accorded to them, these proletarian "pleasure boats" became the flagships of the Histadrut's architecture of spectacle—and landmarks of the Israeli welfare state.

Outstanding among the convalescent homes are those in Nazareth (1956–1960), Zichron-Ya'akov (1966–1969), and Safed (1970–1972), designed by the office of Rechter-Zarchi-Rechter. Beyond Labor Federation dogma, these architectural masterpieces demonstrate considerable creative freedom in their working out of figure-ground relationships, in their volumetric composition, and in their sensuous materiality. In the context of the 1960s, these structures—fashionable and stylized as they may have been—should be considered as the most significant architectural attempts to develop an exceptional localized or "critically regionalist" architectural dialect. ■

26

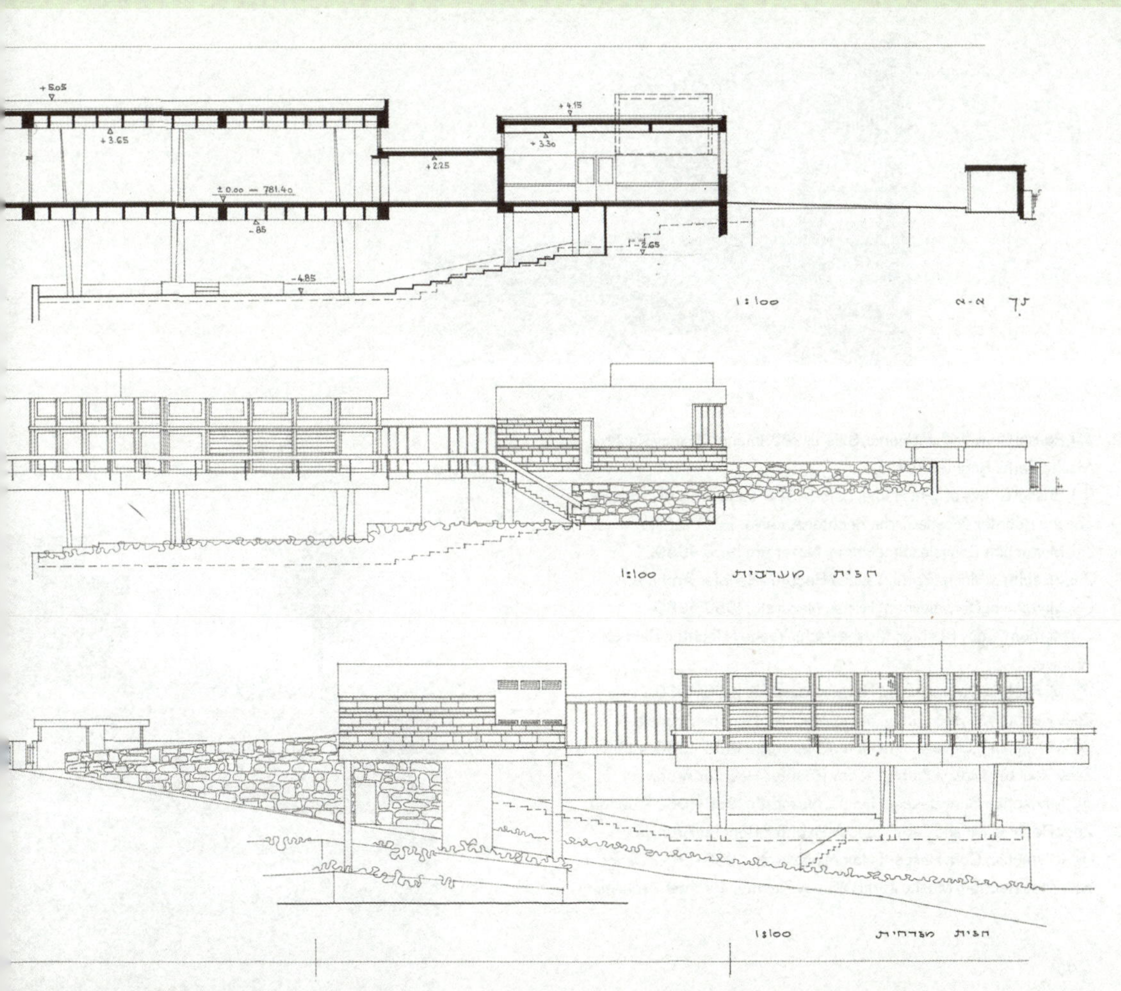

㉗

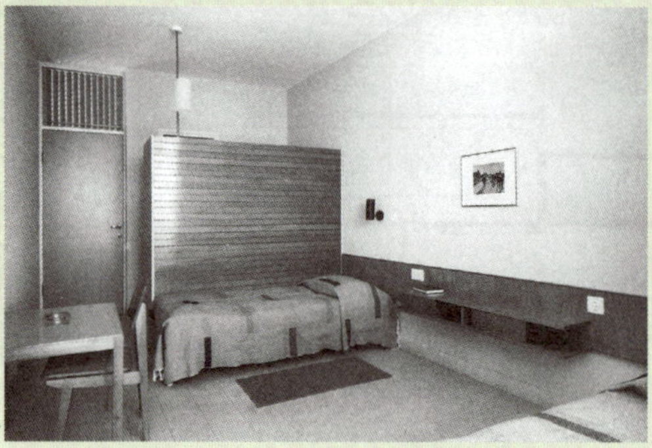

㉘

㉕ Bussel Convalescent Home, Safed, 1962. Interior. Yaacov Rechter, Moshe Zarhi. Rechter Archive.
㉖ Bussel Convalescent Home, Safed, 1962. Façades and sections. Yaacov Rechter, Moshe Zarhi. Rechter Archive.
㉗ Mivtachim Convalescent Home, Nazareth, 1956–1960. Zeev Rechter, Moshe Zarhi, Yaacov Rechter. Rechter Archive.
㉘ Mivtachim Convalescent Home, Nazareth, 1956–1960. Guest room. Zeev Rechter, Moshe Zarhi, Yaacov Rechter. Rechter Archive.
㉙ Mivtachim Convalescent Home, Nazareth, 1956–1960. Zeev Rechter, Moshe Zarhi, Yaacov Rechter. Rechter Archive.
㉚ Mivtachim Convalescent Home, Nazareth, 1956–1960. Interior. Zeev Rechter, Moshe Zarhi, Yaacov Rechter. Rechter Archive.
㉛ Mivtachim Convalescent Home, Nazareth, 1956–1960. Lounge. Zeev Rechter, Moshe Zarhi, Yaacov Rechter. Rechter Archive.
㉜ Mivtachim Convalescent Home, Nazareth, 1956–1960. Dining hall. Zeev Rechter, Moshe Zarhi, Yaacov Rechter. Rechter Archive.

㉙

30

31

32

㉝

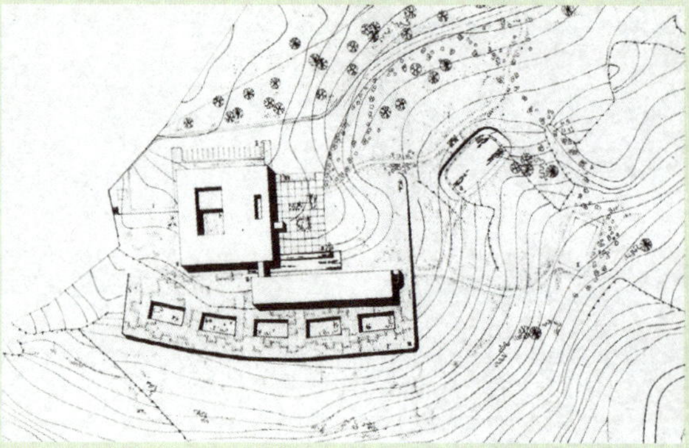

㉞

㉟

㊱

㊲

㊳

㉝ Mivtachim Convalescent Home, Nazareth, 1956–1960. Patios. Zeev Rechter, Moshe Zarhi, Yaacov Rechter. Rechter Archive.
㉞ Mivtachim Convalescent Home, Nazareth, 1956–1960. Site plan. Zeev Rechter, Moshe Zarhi, Yaacov Rechter. Rechter Archive.
㉟ Mivtachim Convalescent Home, Nazareth, 1956–1960. Patios. Zeev Rechter, Moshe Zarhi, Yaacov Rechter. Rechter Archive.
㊱ Mivtachim Convalescent Home, Nazareth, 1956–1960. Zeev Rechter, Moshe Zarhi, Yaacov Rechter. Rechter Archive.
㊲ Mivtachim Convalescent Home, Nazareth, 1956–1960. Balcony. Zeev Rechter, Moshe Zarhi, Yaacov Rechter. Rechter Archive.
㊳ Mivtachim Convalescent Home, Nazareth, 1956–1960. Patios. Zeev Rechter, Moshe Zarhi, Yaacov Rechter. Rechter Archive.

(39) Mivtachim Convalescent Home, Zichron Yaacov, 1966–1969. Side elevation. Yaacov Rechter, Moshe Zarhi. Rechter Archive.
(40) Mivtachim Convalescent Home, Zichron Yaacov, 1966–1969. Yaacov Rechter, Moshe Zarhi. Rechter Archive.
(41) Mivtachim Convalescent Home, Zichron Yaacov, 1966. Floor plan. Yaacov Rechter, Moshe Zarhi. Rechter Archive.
(42) Mivtachim Convalescent Home, Zichron Yaacov, 1966–1969. Yaacov Rechter, Moshe Zarhi. Rechter Archive.
(43) Mivtachim Convalescent Home, visitors' activity, Zichron Yaacov, 1972. Digital image of photograph by Yisrael Simionski/Israel Sun Ltd., from the Judaica Collection of the Harvard Library, Harvard University.

(39)

(40)

(41)

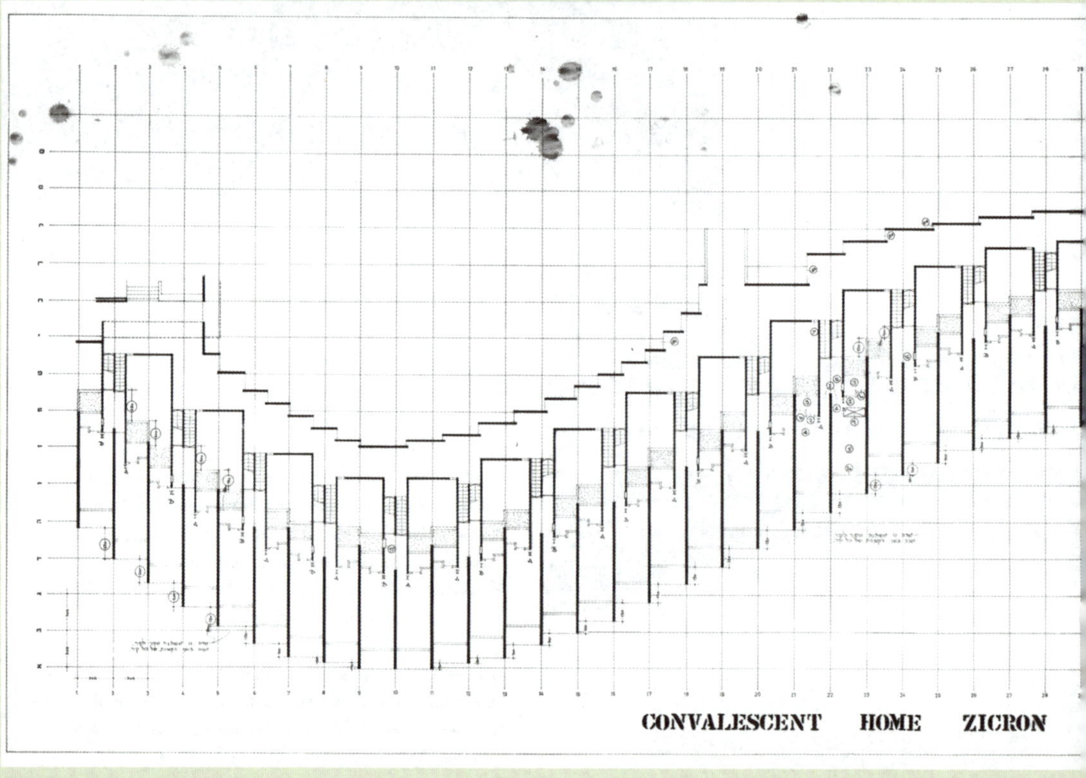

(42)

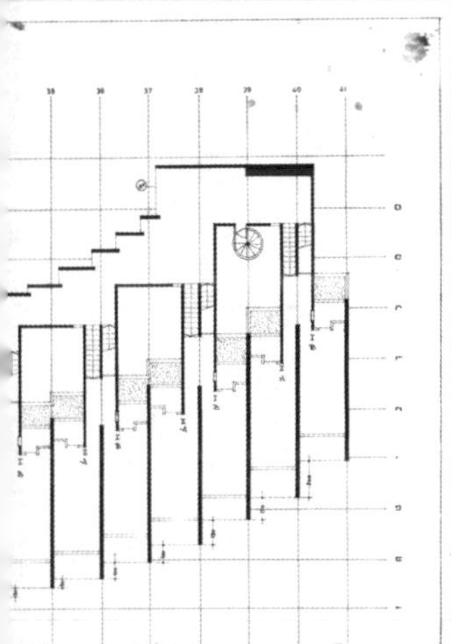


(43)

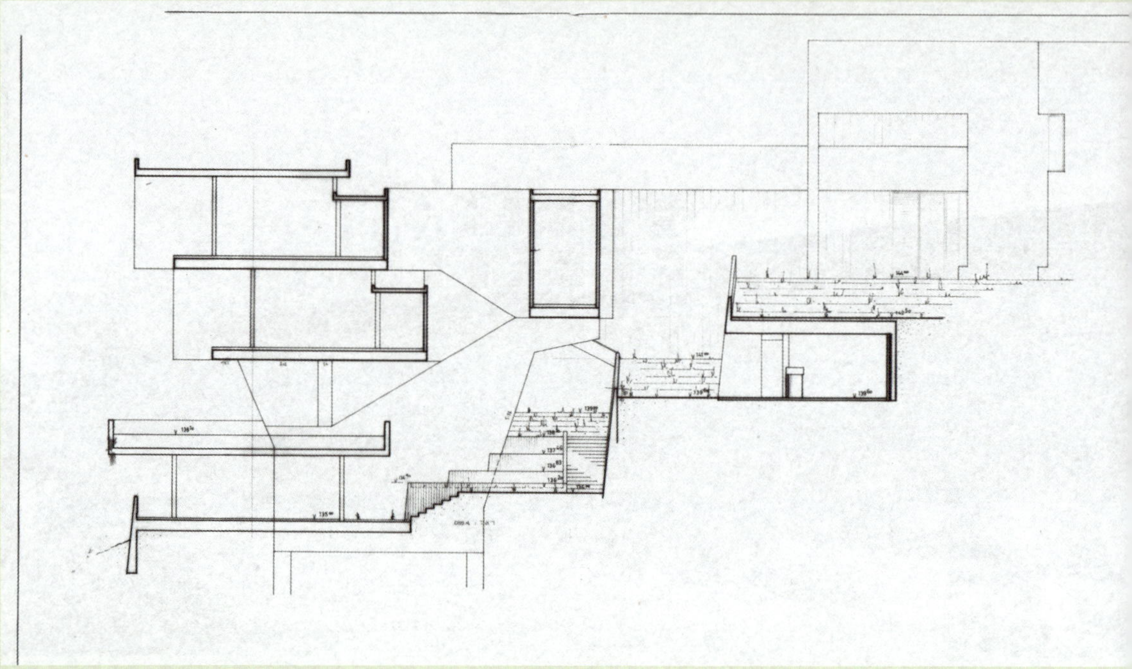

(44)

(45)

(44) Mivtachim Convalescent Home, Zichron Yaacov, 1966. Section. Yaacov Rechter, Moshe Zarhi. Rechter Archive.
(45) Mivtachim Convalescent Home, Zichron Yaacov, 1966–1969. Shaded space below structure. Yaacov Rechter, Moshe Zarhi. Rechter Archive.
(46) Mivtachim Convalescent Home, Zichron Yaacov, 1966–1969. Interior. Yaacov Rechter, Moshe Zarhi. Rechter Archive.
(47) Mivtachim Convalescent Home, Zichron Yaacov, 1966–1969. Interior. Yaacov Rechter, Moshe Zarhi. Rechter Archive.

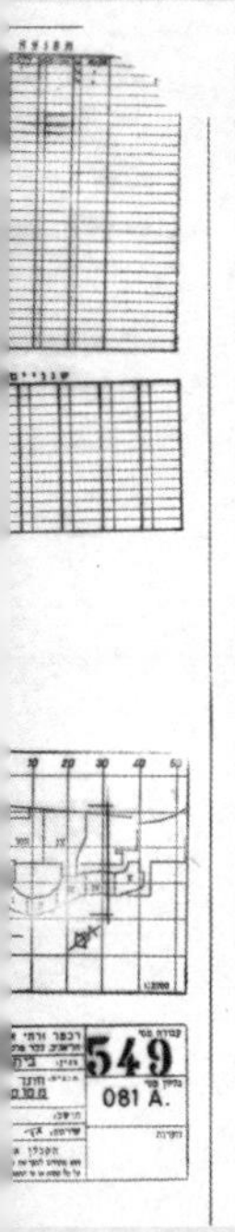

46

47

# New Towns

①

## The Garden Cities of Yesterday

Since its inception as a State, Israel has been one of the most prolific proliferators of new towns. In principle, civilian occupation and the setting up of new settlements have always been construed as Israel's most effective weapon in the ongoing territorial and ethnic warfare. Against all economic and civic sense, and often by various means of population engineering, dozens of new towns were built and are still being built today, albeit at a slower rate. Much like any mass armament protocol, new-town policy is a mystified strategy imbued with survivalist overtones and redemptive undertones. It is therefore safe to assume that Israel is highly unlikely to sign any new-town nonproliferation agreement in the foreseeable future. This would counter its instinctive predisposition toward continuous manipulation of its own boundaries as well as constant territorial disintegration of a possible Palestinian state.

The Israeli doctrine of new towns—within or beyond the Green Line[1]—consolidates numerous Zionist psycho-spatial precepts, programs, itineraries, and modes of operation, which can be synopsized in three fundamental principles:

First is the principle of territorial diffusion, or borderline disorder, to the degree that the entire land, and later on the entire country, is perceived as frontier (Heb. *sfar*), an ever volatile zone stirring apprehension and dictating routine vigilant measures throughout both public and private realms.[2] This principle empties the concept of border of its geopolitical meaning, blurs the distinctions between "internal" and "external," and draws a fluid cartography based not on

① Site allocated for the new town of Karmiel by the Ministry of Housing. Photographer: Fritz Cohen. Government Press Office.
② Map of planned new towns, Planning Department, 1951.

bilateral agreements, but on the ritualized dissemination of "facts on the ground." The open-ended process of colonization in itself, rather than the finite contour of the nation-state, is the Zionist apotheosis, since it generates the desired force of enduring proactive patriotism.

Second is the principle of gradual ethnification or Jewification of nationalized space, in ways subtle or blunt. The Israeli new towns of the 1950s and 1960s were not only low-cost housing depositories for waves of new immigrants; modernist workers' towns, and occasionally company towns based on reformist urban theories; or regional service centers synchronized with a national master plan. They were also an effective system of confiscation, obliteration, and substitution of an existing Palestinian rural and urban infrastructure. If the violence of new towns was initially masked in regionalist and socio-realist rhetoric, in later decades this rhetoric was disavowed altogether and replaced by a rather open endorsement of discriminatory "demographic equilibrium" campaigns within the State's recognized boundaries,[3] or by the colossal operation of "civilian occupation" in the Occupied Territories.[4]

The third, and presumably the softest, principle informing the rate of production and the particular character of Israeli new towns is the dogma of de-urbanization (not to be confused with suburbanization). According to this principle, the new town is devised as a machine (in the garden), programmed to dissolve not only the native town of the past, but even more so the big city of the future, or the future of metropolitan life altogether. On a national scale, this principle implied the rapid settling of a network of as many rural towns as possible. On a local scale, it required the adaptation and amalgamation of various urban reform theories in order to shape the distinctive structure and look of the Israeli new town.

②

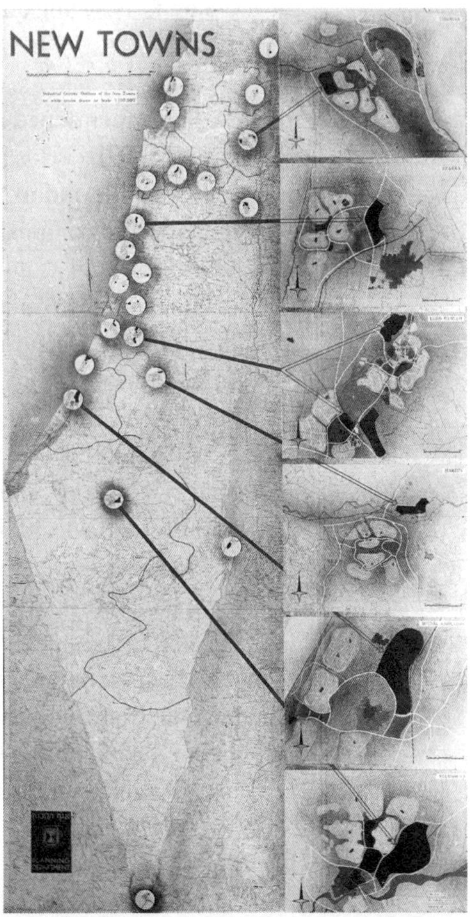


The maintenance of these principles across the Israeli ideological spectrum—keeping them afloat between "Left" and "Right"; between the alleged welfare state of the formative decades and the hypothetical neoliberal order of the last decades; between the workers' garden cities of yesterday and the gated bedroom communities of today—ensures a steady production of new built settings, but it also accelerates a brutal process of deterioration. After all, new towns are doomed to quickly grow old, become dilapidated, and be partially abandoned in favor of newer towns with ever-more-enticing tax exemptions, ever-more-indulging infrastructures, and ever-more-seductive sunsets.

Chronologically, the Israeli new town was born in 1950 as an integral component—indeed, as the apotheosis—of the national master plan. During the 1950s and 1960s over thirty new towns, professionally referred to as "district towns" and better known by the public as "development towns," were planned and built across the country. Typologically, these new towns adhered to the primary garden-city formula of a "town for healthy living and industry; of a size that makes possible a full measure of social life, but not larger; surrounded by a rural belt; the whole of the land being in public ownership or held in trust for the community."[5]

The design of the new town was based on a conceptual crossbreeding between mechanistic planning methods on the one hand (striving to render the traditional city more efficient in terms of affordable mass housing and the flow of motor vehicle traffic) and picturesque conceits on the other (aiming to tone down the city by decomposing it into small autonomous communities protected from street life, zoned off from industrial sectors, and wrapped by green pastoral surroundings). The Israeli planners believed that through their critical observation of urban history, they had managed to develop an innovative method for ideal city planning, as can be gathered from the writings of Eliezer Brutzkus:

> The structure of the new towns is determined by their division into neighboring units. This method differs from conservative methods of urban planning still prevalent in the old cities in Europe, as well as in Israel. These cities are built as a monotonous continuum of houses, streets, and residential neighborhoods, dragging on endlessly and making the lives of their residents gray and dull.[6]

The abovementioned neighboring units, or "eggs"—a popular postwar term imported from the British new-town jargon, specifically from Patrick Abercrombie's 1943 Greater London "bubble" or "egg" plans—were deployed as the foremost semantic and compositional device of the local new town. The neighboring unit was interpreted as an autonomous module consisting of a limited number of building and apartment types, relatively self-sufficient in terms of commerce, education, and leisure services. The town was construed as a cluster of neighboring units, assembled around a civic center with municipal institutions. The evolving town accumulates modular units, thus preserving its neighborly character. The actual size of each unit is determined in relation to the estimated capacity of schools and kindergartens, the optimal dimensions of the commercial center, and the desirable length of paths in the neighborhood. The primary planning task is to isolate motor traffic from the internal pathways of the neighborhood, enabling pedestrians to access all daily services at a distance of no more than 250 meters, without ever having to cross the street.

On paper, the neighboring unit seemed like a pleasant urban cell, with biomorphic contours defying orthogonality and endowing the new town with instant elasticity and vibrancy. In reality, however, carving out self-contained sectors, each equipped with its own facilities of commerce, education, services,

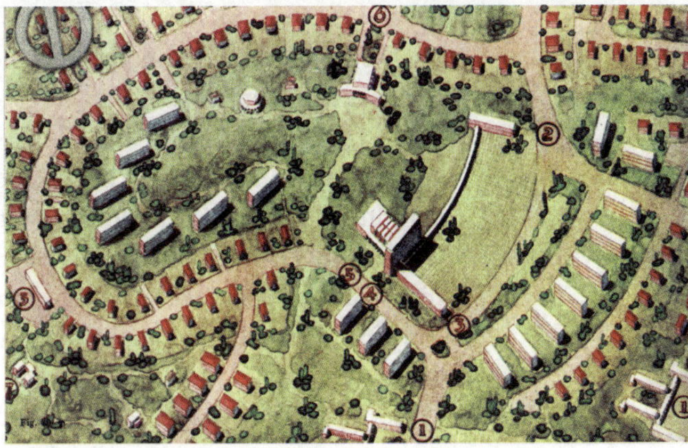

③

and leisure, turned the new town into a cluster of disjointed and dysfunctional urban organs.

The smooth, flexing lines of the neighboring units; the abundance of open space within and between them; the placement of educational and recreational facilities at the heart of the units, amidst lawns or woods; the removal of industrial areas from living quarters and their separation by green belts; the design of repetitive social housing on undivided land, rather than normative parceling and free-market development—all these forged a peculiar, and rather deceptive, illusion: the Israeli new town was meant to be a blown-up kibbutz based on homogeneous community, collective and egalitarian, without private property or speculative market forces. However, unlike the kibbutz, which was created (and perfected over several decades) as exclusive and hegemonic architecture by and for the members of a social cult, the new town came into being abruptly, expediently, and coercively. It was a premature urban doctrine tested on a population of immigrants and refugees, "reluctant pioneers" maneuvered to activate a national project.

With the foundation of the first new towns, it became apparent that the progressive zoning principles and the generous ecological attitude simply did not work. The detached, sparsely populated, ready-made towns weighed disproportionately on the national budget due to the huge amounts of infrastructure they demanded.

The supply of capital and entrepreneurship required for the creation of jobs in out-of-the-way locations lagged behind the pace at which new immigrants were sent there (in Kiryat Shmona, for instance, the first factory was built a full decade after the town was created). The veteran urban population remained in the cities and had little interest in the national challenge—and the veteran population in the rural collective and cooperative settlements, which had well-organized marketing networks of their own, had no use for the services provided by the new towns and completely discounted the planners' regionalist vision. Or, worse still:

> The well-established kibbutzim and moshavim were mostly indifferent and sometimes even hostile towards the introduction of urban centers into their region, and had little use for the very elementary and low-quality services that such immigrant towns could provide. In effect, the towns did not become part of their regions, and were far from becoming regional centers. They remained a foreign body in the agricultural surroundings and at best served as a pool of

seasonal agricultural labor, which the cooperative and collective settlements consented to employ.[7]

The vast open public spaces that had been watercolored green on paper proved totally inappropriate to the climate, water resources, and maintenance facilities in the country. They became dead zones, further dissolving the urban fabric, which had been porous anyway. The introverted neighboring units and the separation of motorways and walkways obstructed the development of common mixed-used streets.

The "alienation, degeneration, and low quality of life" in the big city, so consistently denounced by official State propaganda, was replaced in no time with homogeneity, remoteness, and deprivation.

Bitter criticism soon replaced the prophetic positivism of both planners and politicians. Some of it referred to the hasty application of imported models without proper adjustment, and to the ensuing problems of excessive scale and climate control, as can be gathered from the minutes of a 1964 architects' discussion on the planning of the Israeli new towns:

> There was an industrial world, there were enormous cities, but they sought dispersal there. It was in the center of London—where you cannot go in and you cannot go out, where traffic and noise are tremendous, where there is neither sunlight nor greenery—that the concept was born. The very same idea—not only in its qualitative but also in the quantitative sense, in its formal sense—was shifted to Beersheba. And in Beersheba, where one searches longingly for traffic and commotion, for a bit of social gathering—there, in the middle of the desert, we solved the problems of London. [...] But obviously, what is good for five or eight or ten million people is catastrophic when you have a mere ten thousand in the desert.[8]

④

But most of the criticism was pointed at the very conceptual makeup of the new towns, with their theoretical foundations in hierarchical regionalism and pastoral urbanism. According to the sociologist Erik Cohen, the Israeli new towns were not just garden cities in the countryside, but in fact semi-agrarian constructs:

> Their population had to be small, and set in agricultural surroundings. They were planned for a very low population

③ Neighborhood in Beersheba. Arieh Sharon, *Physical Planning in Israel*, 1951.
④ Cornerstone ceremony for the new town of Arad, 1961. Photographer: Yehuda Eisenstark. Israel State Archives.
⑤ The new town of Mitzpe Ramon, 1960s.
⑥ The new town of Migdal Gad, Ashkelon. Master plan. Arieh Sharon, Physical Planning in Israel, 1951. The orange enclaves indicate the neighboring units; the purple designate industrial zones; the brown mark the existing, often ruinous, fabric of a Palestinian town.
⑦ The new town of Hadera. Master plan. Arieh Sharon, *Physical Planning in Israel*, 1951.
⑧ The new town of Beersheba. Master plan. Arieh Sharon, *Physical Planning in Israel*, 1951.
⑨ The new town of Ramla. Master plan. Arieh Sharon, *Physical Planning in Israel*, 1951.

> density, and were thus dispersed on a relatively large area. The houses were small and low, usually one-story buildings, often inhabited only by two families. Outwardly, these settlements resembled big villages more than towns. [...] The settlers of the new towns were expected to be part-time farmers, living in towns.[9]

Cohen offers two explanations for the confounding hybridity of the new towns. The first is attributed to the lack of experience of the planners, who "approached the idea of [Walter Christaller's] 'hierarchy of settlements' too formalistically and did not try to adapt it to Israel's conditions, or to experiment with it before applying it on a nationwide scale."[10] This explanation seems to me self-defeating, since it implies that the pseudoscientific methods of centralized planning "by the numbers" and by geometrical gridirons could have actually worked out had they been applied carefully enough. Cohen's second explanation returns to what he defines as the Zionist "agricultural bias," or what I suggest describing as its "rural imaginary," which still had an alluring grip on the planners. The transition during the 1950s to a more rapid, and hence urban, colonization was circumstantial, according to Cohen:

> Urban settlement was still considered second best; a course unwillingly taken for lack of opportunities for large-scale agricultural settlement. Thus the idea was conceived to make the new urban centers as similar to agricultural settlements as possible.[11]

Such ideas seem close enough to contemporary concepts of rural urbanism, urban farming, landscape urbanism, or communal urbanism. However, in the Israel of the 1950s and 1960s they were not at all marginal infill, reuse, mixed-program, participatory, or bottom-up projects, but rather the directive of the national master plan and the hallmark of State architecture.

⑤

## Epilogue

Over sixty years after its official publication, the national master plan still holds its own. The vision of colonization and modernization laid out by the plan has, for the most part, been implemented. The country has developed at an unprecedented rate of growth. The new towns of the 1950s and 1960s still exist more or less as originally (mis)conceived: barren garden cities; bypassed regional centers; homogeneous melting pots; gray industrial towns left with the ruins of forsaken factories; underdeveloped urban odds and ends struggling to preserve their special class-A tax-reduction status, granted by the various governments to "areas of national preference." The newtowners, those compliant protagonists of the national master plan, became the adversarial propagators of the social unrest and political turnabout of the 1970s that terminated the long political hegemony of the Labor Party and instigated the even longer ascendancy of the rightist Likud Party.

The urban scheme and the architectural iconography of the Israeli new town have changed considerably—mirroring shifting political and consumerist trends—but the very policy of proliferating new towns has always been kept alive. Since the late 1970s, a series of successive rightist governments radicalized this policy and used it effectively to push forth an expansionist agenda, mostly but not only beyond the Green Line. Emptied of its socialist "melting pot" rhetoric, wrenched from its origins in garden-city reformist schemes, and cut off from the regionalist vision of equilibrium between city and hinterland, the new wave of Israeli "rurbanism" developed a hostile type of dormitory settlement, designed as a fenced-in hilltop "cul-de-sac community" for the single function of sustaining an ongoing civilian occupation of the militarily occupied Palestinian territories.[12] By the 1980s, about 120 such settlements were already established. Today they are populated by more than 300,000 settlers. If these settlements thrive economically and consistently receive some of the highest ratings in Israel in terms of standard of living, municipal services, education, and, indeed, security, this is due to excessive government spending on infrastructure, services, and subsidies (at least three times the average per capita in Israel). Tellingly, these ready-made settlements are never referred to as new towns; they are seen as having been instantaneously naturalized and ingrained in the Israeli fabric. ■

1 The “Green Line” was set out in the 1949 Armistice Agreements after the 1948 Arab-Israeli War, and was the de facto border of Israel from 1949 to 1967.

2 Building regulations in Israel require a public shelter in every public building, a common shelter on each floor of office buildings, and a private shelter in each new or remodeled apartment.

3 See, for example, the newest new town of Harish, now under construction at the heart of the predominantly Arab area of Wadi Ara, which was initially designed for the particular needs of the fastest-growing population of Orthodox Jews. See also the ongoing efforts to eradicate the Bedouin “unrecognized villages” in the Negev region and the current plans to build there the new Jewish towns of Kasif, Heletz, and Beit Guvrin.

4 According to a B’Tselem report from 2010 (see chapter “Occupation”), some half million Israelis are living beyond the Green Line in total. Eyal Hareuveni, *By Hook and by Crook: Israeli Settlement Policy in the West Bank*, trans. Zvi Shulman (Jerusalem: B’Tselem, July 2010), accessed May 26, 2017, http://www.btselem.org/download/201007_by_hook_and_by_crook_eng.pdf.

5 This was a short definition adapted by the Garden Cities and Town Planning Association in 1919. Cited in Gilbert Herbert and Silvina Sosnovsky, *Bauhaus on the Carmel and the Crossroads of Empire* (Jerusalem: Yad Izhak Ben-Zvi, 1993), p. 60.

6 Eliezer Brutzkus, “Changes in the Network of Urban Centers in Israel,” *Engineering and Architecture: The Union of Engineers and Architects in Israel* 3 [in Hebrew] (1964), p. 43.

7 Erik Cohen, “The City in the Zionist Ideology,” *Jerusalem Urban Studies* 1 (1970), p. 135.

8 Eliezer Brutzkus, “A Discussion of New Towns,” *Engineering and Architecture: The Union of Engineers and Architects in Israel* 3 [in Hebrew] (1964), p. 15.

9 Cohen, “City in the Zionist Ideology,” p. 134.

10 Ibid., p. 133.

11 Ibid.

12 For a comprehensive architectural account and analysis of the Jewish settlements in the Occupied Territories, see Eyal Weizman, *Hollow Land: Israel’s Architecture of Occupation* (London: Verso, 2007).

⑥

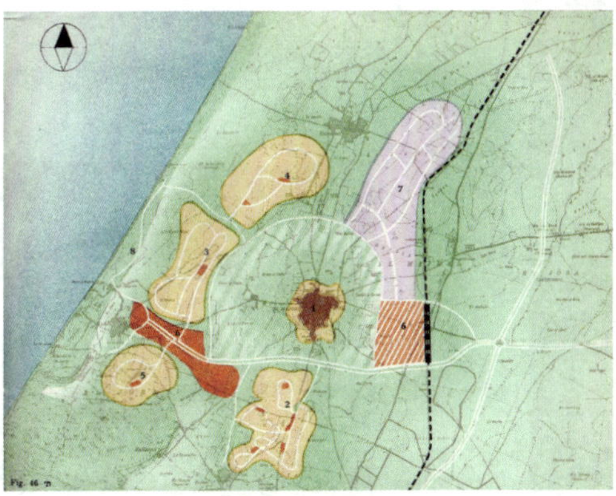

⑦

⑧

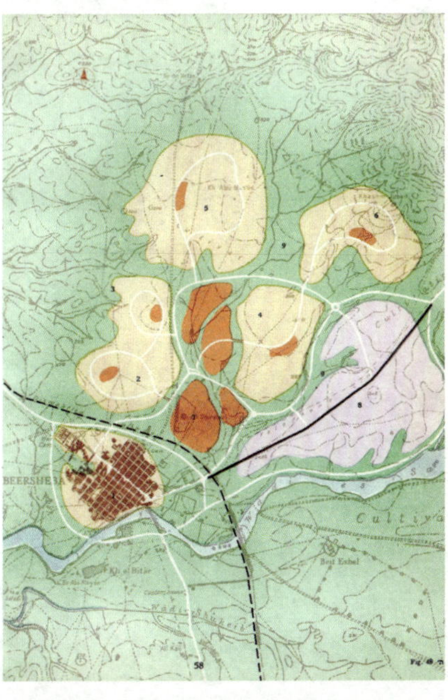

⑨

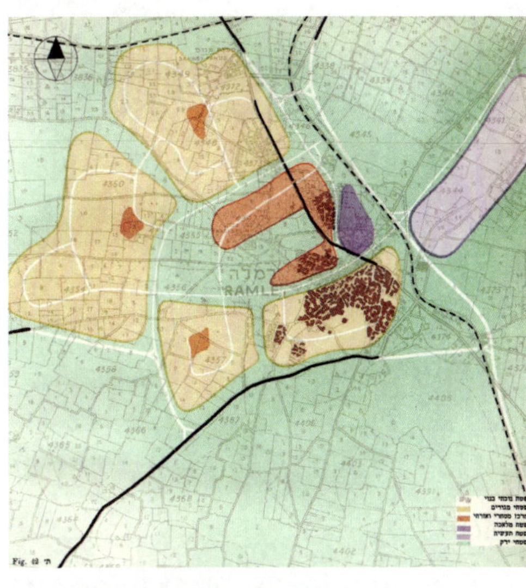

⑩ Transit camps and newly built housing blocks in the new town of Yokneam, early 1950s. Photographer: Amiram Erev.
⑪ Neighboring units in the new town of Migdal Gad, Ashkelon. Arieh Sharon, *Physical Planning in Israel*, 1951.
⑫ Old (grid layout) and new (amorphous) Beersheba, early 1950s. Aerial view.
⑬ Gessi Cohen neighborhood, Holon, 1950s. Aerial view.
⑭ Kiryat Shalom, Tel Aviv, early 1950s. Aerial view.
⑮ The new town of Dimona, 1960s. Aerial view.
⑯ The new town of Karmiel. 1960s. Photographer: Ami Erev.

⑩

⑪

⑫

⑬

⑭

⑮

⑯

⑰ The new town of Yamit. Promotional brochure for prospective residents, 1973.

⑱

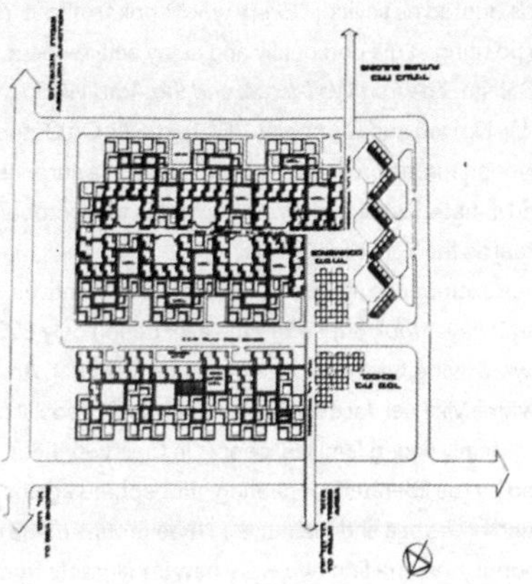

*Please clip and mail to:* **GARIN YAMIT** c/o AACA
515 Park Avenue, New York, New York 10022

I am interested in **YAMIT**. Please contact me.

NAME ____________

ADDRESS ____________

____________

Telephone ____________ Age ____
(area code)

Marital Status ________ Childrens' Ages ________

Husband's Profession ____________

Wife's Profession ____________

Yamit, a Mediterranean seaside town on the shores of the Rafah Salient, set several precedents in the local annals of colonization, only to become Zionism's haunting doomsday icon.

Yamit may hold the ignoble record of being the most dispensable town ever built: conceived during Israel's occupation of Sinai (1967–1982)[1] by visionary generals;[2] decriminalized by the Israeli High Court's first deliberation on the issue of land grabbing in a militarily occupied territory;[3] secretly designed in 1972 by the architects Yehuda Drexler and Ze'ev Drukman as a port city of up to 200,000 inhabitants;[4] retroactively approved by the government and inaugurated in September 1973;[5] immediately denounced as a casus belli by Egyptian president Anwar Sadat ("Yamit means war, at least for Egypt"[6]); nevertheless constructed in 1975; written off in the Egypt-Israel Peace Treaty of March 1979; and finally evacuated and destroyed in April 1982.[7]

For its architects, however, Yamit offered the opportunity of a lifetime, allowing them to implement their critique of modernist planning, to simulate newly acquired regionalist theories, and to finally fabricate an easygoing Mediterranean town in Israel. Architect Ze'ev Drukman later recalled:

> I thought it would be desirable to build a kind of interpretation to the Greek village: many shades of white, separation between pedestrian and vehicular flow, courtyards and balconies for people to sit in, to eat watermelon and throw the seeds at each other. We planted many trees along the streets and people indeed strolled outdoors a lot. During its last days, Yamit looked like a recreation camp [...].
>
> The design process was intriguing. We took [prefab] building components that we found in the catalogue of the ministry of housing, took them apart and reassembled them so that the houses would fit our ideas.[8]

The architectural writer Michael Jacobson observes that the inspiration for Yamit's minor urbanism may have been the "mat housing" quarters designed across the country during the 1960s. But while these quarters were essentially segregated and introverted urban sections without any real public space, Yamit's planning presented an improved version based on houses built in clusters of four around a common courtyard that was integrated into a larger system of streets, alleys, and public squares: "The open urban space functioned as the real living room of each resident and family and was the closest thing to Mediterranean street life."[9]

With the demise of Yamit, the Mediterranean fancy lost its currency in Israeli town planning, unleashing a furor of sprawling suburbia and proliferating dormitory communities.[10] ■

1 As part of an architectural blitz to establish a buffer zone between the Gaza Strip and the Sinai Peninsula by building twenty-one settlements (sixteen of them in the Rafah Salient) in a span of seven years (1971–1978).

2 Yamit's site and its surroundings were cleared by an unauthorized military operation in January 1972. According to *Haaretz* correspondent Amira Hass, 1,500 Bedouin families of the Al-Ramilat tribes were expelled under the direct orders of Defense Minister Moshe Dayan and Southern Command Head Ariel Sharon. Amira Hass, "From Yamit to the Jordan Valley, the IDF Continues to Force Arabs from Their Homes," *Haaretz*, April 16, 2012. According to Eyal Weizman, the operation was part of Sharon's counterinsurgency campaign in Gaza: "In the winter of 1972, acting without an explicit government order, but very likely in response to an indirect oral suggestion by Dayan, Sharon ordered the destruction of the orchards, the blocking up of the water wells and the deportation of the villagers." Eyal Weizman, *Hollow Land: Israel's Architecture of Occupation* (London: Verso, 2007), p. 98.

3 Weizman writes, "The eviction of the Bedouin from their lands provoked outrage in a nearby kibbutz, whose members commissioned a human rights lawyer to represent the villagers via their tribal elder, Suleiman Hussein Uda Abu Hilo, in an HCJ [High Court of Justice] petition against the State of Israel in general and against Ariel Sharon as the military commander in particular." Weizman, *Hollow Land*, p. 98.
The Yamit ruling determined that the Geneva Convention was not violated by the act of expropriation. The convention's prohibition on transferring civilian populations of the occupier to an occupied territory was dismissed as irrelevant since in this case it was allegedly expropriation for military needs. Another prohibition, on forcefully transferring civilian populations from occupied territories to the occupying state, was inapplicable here, since the petitioning deportees were transferred from place to place within the occupied territories. For a discussion of the Yamit court hearings and ruling, see Idan Landau, "The Expulsion from Rafah and the Theory of Zionist Non-Knowledge," Do Not Die Stupid (blog), https://idanlandau.com [in Hebrew].

4 During the High Court trial, while the case was still pending, it was inadvertently exposed that Dayan had commissioned the architects Drexler and Drukman to produce a brochure with urban plans for a new town on the expropriated lands, without government authorization. The brochure was sequestered by the IDF to ensure that the material would not be discussed in court.

5 Noam Chomsky writes, "In September 1973, the Labor Party approved the 'Galili Protocols' which called for extensive additional rural and urban settlement and commercial and industrial development in the territories, including Golan, the West Bank, Gaza, and northern Sinai, where the city of Yamit was to be established." Noam Chomsky, Fateful Triangle: The United States, Israel, and the Palestinians (Cambridge, MA: South End Press, 1999), p. 105.
According to Landau, "Finance Minister Sapir slammed the plan and claimed that a city in Sinai was a waste of money and an obstacle to peace. Dayan insisted on the plan and in the end he had the upper hand." Landau, "Expulsion from Rafah."

6 Cited in Chomsky, *Fateful Triangle*. According to Avi Shlaim, Sadat was quoted as saying, "Every word spoken about Yamit is a knife pointing at me personally and at my self-respect." See Avi Shlaim, *The Iron Wall: Israel and the Arab World* (New York: W. W. Norton and Company, 2001), p. 317. On October 6, 1973, Egyptian forces crossed the Suez Canal in a surprise attack and initiated what is known in Egypt as the October War and in Israel as the Yom Kippur War.

7 Despite tax exemptions and other government incentives, the city of Yamit never took off; before the evacuation only 625 families were living there (the size of a large kibbutz). Architectural writer Michael Jacobson describes Yamit's social composition: "Mainly young families, people in their twenties enchanted by the liberated pioneering atmosphere against the background of the sea and the dunes. Three groups made up Yamit's population: the first two were new immigrants from the Soviet Union and the United States, eager to settle the land of Israel and make the desert bloom. To these were added Israeli families, some of military personnel serving in the area, others ordinary civilians. The latter had to go through a selection process by a committee. Priority was given to doctors, policemen, teachers, social workers, etc. The State endowed both new immigrants and veteran Israelis with especially generous grants and loans." Michael Jacobson, "Yamit Days: The Seven Good Years and the Bitter End," April 8, 2012, Xnet [in Hebrew].
As for the demolition of Yamit, it was initially agreed that Egypt would pay $80 million for the houses and infrastructure, but Ariel Sharon decided to destroy the town and the other rural Jewish settlements in the Rafah Salient. According to Shlaim, Sharon deliberately made the evacuation more traumatic so that the Israeli public would contest possible dismantling of other settlements in the future. Shlaim, *Iron Wall*, pp. 399–400.

8 Drukman, interviewed by Jacobson. In Jacobson, "Yamit Days."

9 Jacobson, "Yamit Days."

10 See Roy Brand and Ori Scialom, eds., *The Urburb: Patterns of Contemporary Living*, catalogue of the Israeli pavilion at the 14th International Architecture Biennale in Venice (Montreal: Sternthal, 2014).

⑱ The new town of Yamit. Promotional brochure for prospective residents, 1973.
⑲ Civic center, the new town of Yamit. Axonometric drawing. Yehuda Drexler and Ze'ev Drukman. Brochure issued by the Ministry of Housing, Department of Rural Settlements, 1976.
⑳ Civic center, the new town of Yamit. Plan. Yehuda Drexler and Ze'ev Drukman. Brochure issued by the Ministry of Housing, Department of Rural Settlements, 1976.

⑲

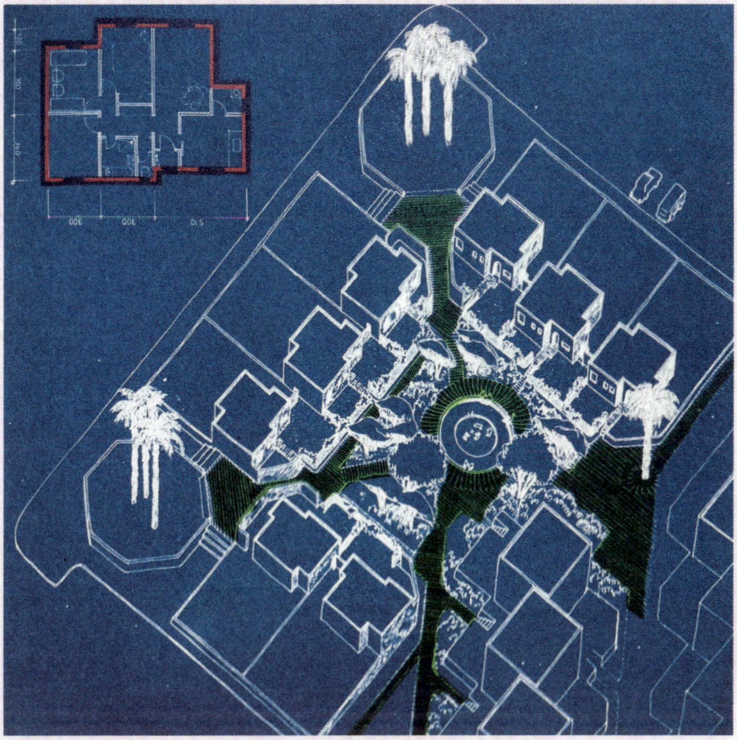

⑳

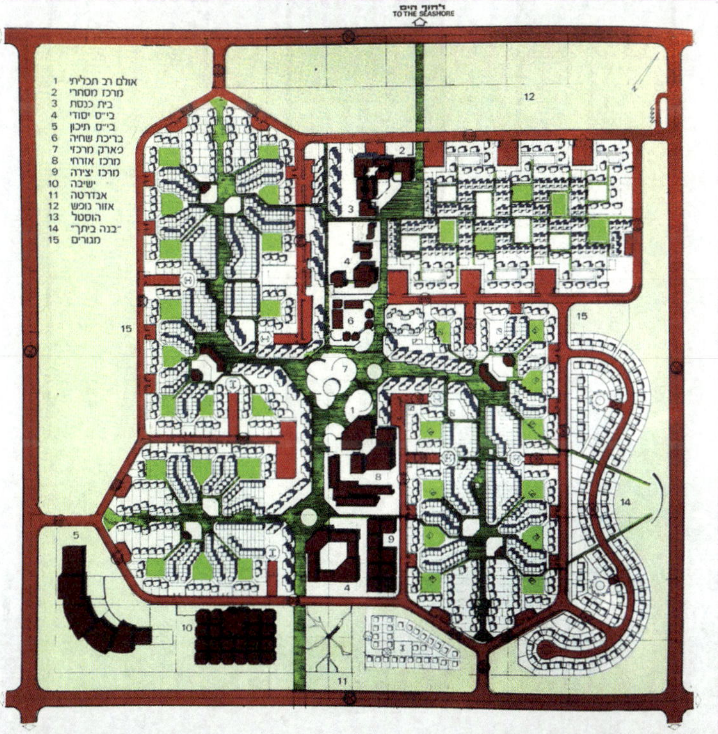

(21)

## WHAT IS YAMIT.

Yamit is a new town being built by the Israeli government on the Mediterranean Coast at the point where the old Sinai-Negev border met the sea. The entire region known as the "Rafah Approaches" is being developed as an urban-agricultural area and already comprises several flourishing moshavim and kibbutzim. The site is one of great physical beauty, overlooking a palm tree studded stretch of clean, sandy coast line. The climate combines the dryness of the desert with pleasant sea breezes to make it perfectly delightful nearly year round.

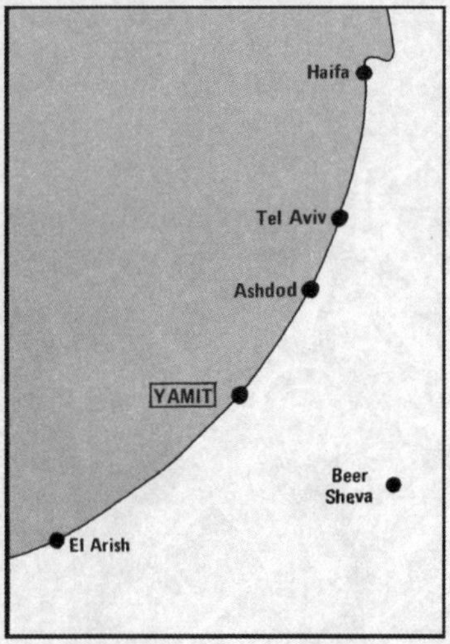


Yamit has been designed by the Israeli Ministry of Housing according to the latest principles of town planning, with an eye to ecological considerations and toward its esthetic integration into the natural landscape. Industry will be located a good distance from the living area, sewage from the city will be dried in the desert and recycled for agricultural uses, and no cars will enter the living area but will be parked on the fringes of the neighborhood in special parking areas.

In accordance with the policies of the Israeli government, Yamit is to be settled initially by families who meet criteria of employability, physical and mental health, age, and a preparedness to meet the as yet unforseen challenges that starting a new town entails. A selection committee of government representatives, which includes members of the group already in Israel, will consider new applications to live in Yamit. Much of the future character of Yamit, its economic bases and conditions of life there, will, in effect, be determined by the original settlers. The group presently in Israel is hoping to make Yamit a center of culture, education, and beauty on the Mediterranean Coast.

The government provides the basic physical needs such as housing, public buildings and the necessary infra-structure of roads, electricity, water supply, and sewage disposal, and the settlers set up their own business or work at jobs in the area and in the town itself and establish the local government for Yamit.

In all these first steps, the Israeli government and the Jewish Agency provide help to both individuals and the group as a whole so as to guarantee everyone a living income until the town becomes self-sufficient. Possibilities exist for the person with initiative to develop business and enterprises with the help of the Ministry of Absorption. Jobs and opportunities to join in already existing businesses will be offered to the new immigrant through the American garin.

(22)

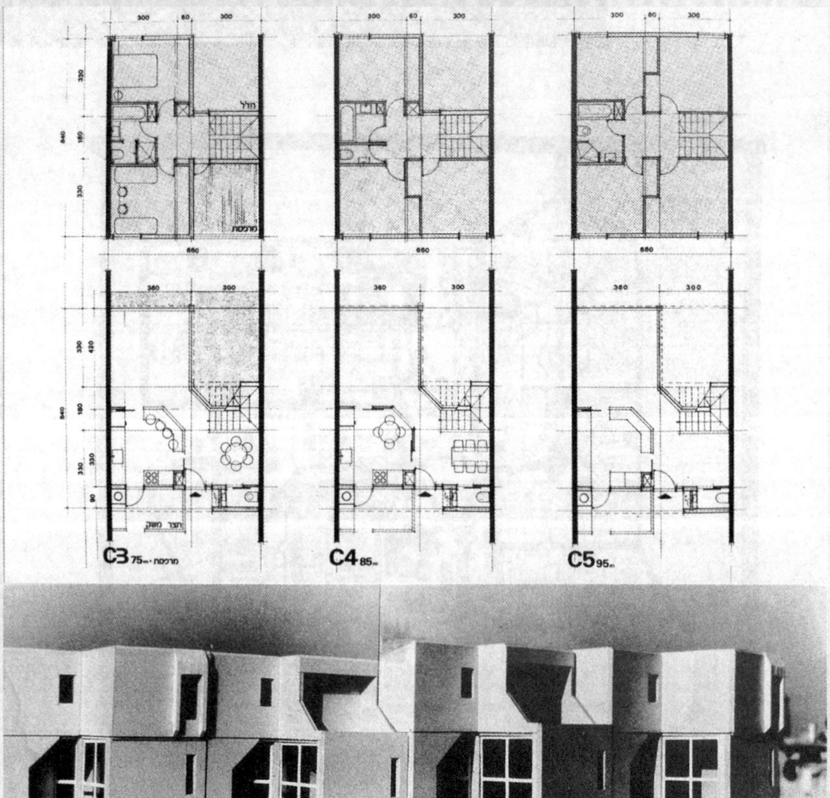

Architect's Model of
Residential Area

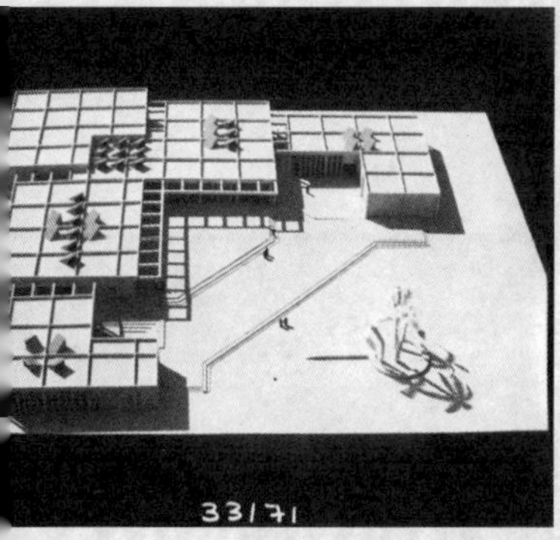


㉓

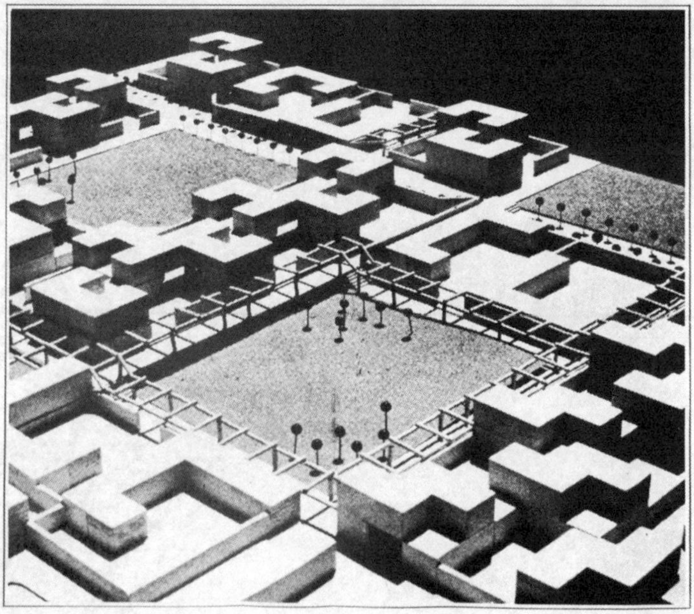

㉔

㉕

㉖

㉗

㉘

㉑ The new town of Yamit. Promotional brochure for prospective residents, 1973.
㉒ The new town of Yamit. Promotional brochure for prospective residents, 1973.
㉓ The new town of Yamit, 1973. Model of residential units. Ze'ev Drukman.
㉔ The new town of Yamit. Promotional brochure for prospective residents, 1973.
㉕ Civic center, the new town of Yamit. Yehuda Drexler and Ze'ev Drukman.
㉖ Civic center, the new town of Yamit. Yehuda Drexler and Ze'ev Drukman.
㉗ The new town of Yamit, late 1970s. Aerial view. Yehuda Drexler and Ze'ev Drukman.
㉘ The demolition of Yamit by the Israel Defense Forces, April 1982.

# Public Housing

① Family examining model apartments, housing exhibition, late 1950s.

② ③

## The Israeli *Shikun*

The Hebrew term *shikun* epitomizes both the efficiency and benevolence of the welfare-state apparatus and the coercive policy of social engineering associated with the ambitious project of housing hundreds of thousands of new immigrants and veteran citizens in the first years of Statehood. The term is also the proper name of a workers' housing company founded by the Israeli Labor Federation, or Histadrut. The Shikun Company, active in the housing industry since 1928, germinated the architectural precedents that were to refashion the country's landscapes, determine the generic Israeli look, alter the local building and dwelling culture, and diagrammatically illustrate oscillations in political taste.

The British Mandatory government (1917–1948) took no active role and had no centralized policy in the field of public housing. The first organized public-housing projects in pre-State Israel were initiated by the Labor Federation in order to provide an institutional response to the growing housing shortage affecting workers and municipal employees. The Labor Federation's enterprise in this domain yielded two main architectural typologies: Cooperative Workers' Housing projects (Heb. *me'onot ovdim*), located in the center or at the margins of the cities and mostly populated by Histadrut elites; and Labor Townships (Heb. *krayot amal*), garden suburbs for low-income unionized workers. Together, these two prototypes paved the way to the residential "block" and the "neighboring unit" (a compound of blocks)—as they were referred to in the professional literature of the 1950s and 1960s—which proliferated during the first decades of Statehood in Israel.

In matters of settlement and housing, the Labor Federation's activities were a direct manifestation of the agenda and taste of the hegemonic streams in the Zionist movement. In general terms, the rural penchant of both literary and political Zionism generated a profusion of agrarian villages and pastoral suburbs. In 1912, for instance, Nachman Syrkin, a prominent Zionist ideologue, recommended establishing in Palestine "cooperative garden cities, factories, urban quarters, shops, food houses and cultural institutions—and all upon cooperative foundations, so there would not be a place for capitalist exploitation, nor barbaric distinctions between the landlords and the workers."[1]

The rhetoric enveloping the formation of the Labor Federation workers' projects was not so different in its Marxist overtones from texts like Syrkin's, but the architecture of these neighborhoods marked a significant deviation from both rural Zionist layouts and urban prototypes. In the petit bourgeois urban fabric of the 1920s and 1930s, which was based on parcelization into small private lots and freestanding buildings (ownership being a key factor, since only property owners had the right to vote in municipal elections), the cooperative housing compounds of the Labor Federation alone signified an ideological correlation between architectural modernism, working-class ethics, and union logistics. Reliance upon established European types (the perimeter block or, alternatively, parallel row housing) and exploitation of the Labor Federation's political and organizational capacities made possible a concentrated acquisition of large lots, as well as the design of a continuous site plan up to the zero lot line. The big lots with unified design enabled the efficient merging of the unbuilt remainders of lots, usually surrounding an individual apartment building, and the creation of large internal common spaces—protected and protective. In comparison with the rather porous existing urban building patterns, which emphasized the autonomy of the single building and fragmented the street elevation, the elongated façades of the workers' projects provided the missing urban dimensions of size, contiguity, density, efficiency, and homogeneity, as it were.

But far from invigorating the city, these cooperative housing projects drained its public performance. The continuous elevations, rather than enhancing the street, screened it off and defined its own exclusive internalized existence. Indeed, unlike their early precedents, such as Charles Fourier's phalansteries, which developed communal prototypes in order to facilitate urban life for the workers and amplify the new metropolitan experience, the Zionist cooperative workers' projects aimed to construct a communal urban cell that would be impervious to the modern city and its social malaise, or would at least tone it down.

Following the establishment of the State in 1948, this contempt for the big city assumed a different—less privileged and more efficient—expression in the second housing typology, that of the Labor Township. The large block of the Cooperative Workers' Housing projects, which had been transplanted like a Trojan horse into the city, was exiled far beyond the city's boundaries to carry the message of class solidarity to more remote regions, cloning itself endlessly

② Housing for new immigrants, Kiryat Yovel, Jerusalem, 1957. David B. Keidan Collection, Central Zionist Archives.
③ Housing for new immigrants, Kiryat Yovel, Jerusalem, 1957. David B. Keidan Collection, Central Zionist Archives.

in perfectly isotropic grids, freeing itself from the habits and memories of the Old City. The Labor Township, though sharing ideological common ground with the Cooperative Workers' Housing estate, suggested an entirely different spatial model: diffuse, scattered, pastoral, and pronouncedly ex-urban. About three decades before the first Labor Townships were actually built, they were already envisioned in Theodor Herzl's *The Jewish State*:

> The workers' dwellings (which include the homes of all manual laborers) are to be erected by the Company itself. I am certainly not thinking of the dismal workmen's barracks of European towns nor of the miserable shanties that are lined up around factories. Our workmen's homes must also present a uniform appearance, to be sure, because the Company can build cheaply only if it produces the materials in large quantities—but these detached houses with their little gardens shall be combined into attractive groups in each locality. The natural qualities of the surroundings will inspire the happy genius of our young architects which has not yet been sapped by routine, and even though the people may not understand the great outlines of the plan, they will at any rate feel comfortable in this uncrowded arrangement.[2]

The distance between visionary literature and advertisement leaflets diminishes upon glimpsing the bulletin of the Shikun Company, which built numerous Labor Townships on the outskirts of Haifa, Holon, Ramat Gan, and Tel Aviv. The bulletin proclaims that the company

> is guided by the social ideal of spacious garden cities for workers, offering a basis for a pleasant and healthy life and cooperative public responsibility, as well as education and culture for all of its residents, [cities] designed for the purpose of aesthetics and comfort and planned for the well-being of the individual and the community.[3]

The casual use of the term "garden cities" in this document is a trace of the long-standing reciprocal relations, ideological and practical, between the World Zionist Organization and the International Garden City Movement. As a matter of fact, Shikun's branding, just like so many other Hebrew commonplace bulletins or lofty manifestos from the early 1920s to the late 1950s, was no more than a transliteration of the definition adopted in one of the charters of the founders of the Garden City Association.

It should be pointed out, however, that the all-too-facile adaptation and dissemination of the notion of garden city, or *Gartenstadt*, does not indicate a direct appropriation of European models of garden cities and garden suburbs. Generally speaking, the Zionist workers' townships of the 1920s and 1930s, as well as the State's network of new towns of the 1950s and 1960s—all rhetorically construed as garden cities—were far more schematic, *sachlich*, and serial than their originators, entirely devoid of the cultural nostalgia, folkloric ambience, and rustic domesticity characterizing both English Arts and Crafts and German *Heimat* architecture. They were perhaps less a retreat and more an outpost; less "back to nature" and more "occupying the land" and "cultivating the wilderness"; fewer lawns and flower gardens and more housing estates with farm allotments; less an ideal image of the familial property and more a transformative and crystallizing experience of the community, and by extension, of the society.

Berl Katznelson, the ideological leader of the Hebrew Workers' Movement during the 1920s and 1930s, referred to the subject of Labor Townships in the Council of the Labor Federation in 1924:

> If we cannot offer him [the urban and agrarian worker] the creation of a complete settlement, an orderly farm and a new industry, we will give him, in the vicinity of the city, a plot, to enable him to establish his hut or cabin and his basic domestic farm; we will give him the Workers' Suburb [...].[4]

At the Third Convention of the Labor Federation, in 1927, Katznelson further said:

> The forthcoming period is not a time for heavy but for light settlement. If, during the coming year and the year following, our strength is not sufficient for large settlement projects, we should attain a maximum of light settlements, meaning farm allotments for the employed worker, a workers' neighborhood for the country laborer, a workers' neighborhood for the city laborer.[5]

It should be emphasized that the interests of the Labor Federation were not always identical to national goals. From the perspective of the Labor Federation, the largest and most urgent task was to supply housing for the workers and employees in the central cities and townships. These workers could not live a great distance from their places of work, and thus large plots (under Jewish ownership) on the outskirts of cities were required. The Jewish National Fund (JNF) and the Jewish Agency, however, gave priority to the "redemption" of land that was not yet under Jewish ownership and to its cultivation by agriculture and forestry. For this reason, national institutions underplayed their role in the Labor Federation's building projects. With the establishment of the State, the conflict of interests was resolved when the JNF received large areas of "abandoned lands" and "absentee property" in the vicinity of the Labor Townships and handed them over to the Labor Federation housing companies, which were already skilled in the "rational planning of large areas." In addition to the land they accepted from the JNF, the Labor Federation companies received lease concessions from the development authorities: government land in the areas of the "abandoned" villages and parts of cities (mainly Lydda, Ramle, Yahud, Akir, Beit-Dagon, and Yavne). Here it was proved that the "planning conception" of the Labor Federation was good not only for the creation of settlements and model neighborhoods ex nihilo, but also for the pioneering "rehabilitation" of destroyed settlements, as may be learned from the anniversary bulletin of the Neve Oved (lit. "Worker's Oasis") Company:

> The company took upon itself the rehabilitation of several abandoned villages that were populated by families of new immigrants. The Arab village, with winding alleys and wild buildings, is not suitable for any planning conception. Therefore, our planning included plots of land that were integrated with the village, upon which the company built the extended village; among these are Yahud, Beit-Dagon, Akir, Yavne. The village centers, in which there still exist inhabited buildings, were planned for public establishments and for gardens—and with time, the citizens will be relocated to the new quarters, and the old buildings, usually inappropriate for residence, will be destroyed.[6]

The State's responsibility for the planning and building of public housing was formally institutionalized in 1949 with the establishment of the Housing Department in the Labor Ministry. This department dealt mostly with systemic and infrastructural solutions to the problem of housing the new immigrants (administrative responsibility fell entirely upon the State, while the execution was divided between the Housing Department, which built 29,645 apartments between 1949 and 1955, and the public companies, many of which belonged to the Labor Federation, which built 29,630 apartments during that time period).

The dilemma of "heavy" versus "light" settlement, as defined by Berl Katznelson—or the various attempts to merge the two approaches—stands at the core of the State's building strategy. Conceptually, we may suggest that the Cooperative Workers' estate paradigm endowed the State's generic housing type, the *shikun*, with its volumetric crudeness and distinctive horizontality, while the Labor Township paradigm paved the way for rural or suburban mass-housing projects on national(ized) land.

Initially, the State adopted, quite directly, the pastoral model of the Histadrut's Labor Townships, assuming that the uniform little houses (which in the State version were named *blockonim* [lit. "mini-blocks"; sing. *blockon*]), with their generous farming allotments, would be a quicker and cheaper response to the urgent housing shortage. This form of housing would encourage the production of basic foods for personal consumption in times of crisis, facilitate the employment of an unskilled labor force (the tenants themselves) in construction, and be the core from which the future growth of the houses would extend.

Typologically, the *blockonim* were slightly more diverse than the houses of the Labor Townships. There were single-level, two-family houses, with

④ ⑤

apartments of 24 square meters; two-level, four-family houses, with apartments ranging from 25 to 29 square meters with a shared staircase; or single-level row houses of varying lengths. Yet these simple houses were not built at a satisfactory pace, and they remained anecdotal in satisfying the immediate needs for mass housing during the first years of Statehood. In most cases, the spacious *blockon* neighborhoods did not develop into the coveted garden suburb "designed for the sake of aesthetics and comfort," the notion of "the growing house" did not work, and the farm allotments became junkyards.

While the State was adopting the diminutive housing prototype of the Labor Townships for new immigrants, the Labor Federation launched its own "Veteran Citizens" projects, in which it reproduced and refined the elongated housing block. The first such "block neighborhoods" in the country—rows of three- to four-storey houses on the outskirts of big cities—were built in Yad Eliyahu (near Tel Aviv), Kiryat Eliezer (near Haifa), and Kiryat Moshe (near Jerusalem). Within these new compounds, the Labor Federation crossbred its two pre-State typologies into a new local type, the Israeli housing block, at once vague and radical: vague in its attempt to negotiate between the idyllic suburban lifestyle and the efficiency of urban living; and radical in its abandonment of the block as an urban marker that demarcates the borders between public and private, turning it instead into an autonomous, suspended object, distributed randomly, as it were, on-site and signifying no more than its own schematic orientation, repetitive spacing, and routine serial reproduction.

The drafting of the site plan of a block compound is a seemingly trivial task. After all, the site is customarily construed as a tabula rasa, a bare surface free of any traces of existing structures, upon which sparse rectangular blotches, identical or at least similar, must be positioned according to a given index of density, direction, spacing between elevations, and distancing from access routes. There is no style, no custom, no experience, no historical conditioning, no irregularity of an existing fabric, no "genius loci," no view to speak of, no topography (only as a hurdle to be overcome in the section), no time. There is only a sketchy composition that needs to articulate, over and over again, with slight alterations, not the figure of the buildings themselves but their ground—

⑥

the constructed plainness upon which they will be placed; their liberating detachment from origin and originality; their ability to generate a wealth of imprints, outlines, fabrics, numbers, and names, without divulging their relentless sameness and exhausting seriality.

It is not inconsequential that the Zionist housing block initially came into being as a status symbol. The Labor Federation first made use of it in its Veteran Citizen Housing (Heb. *shikun vatikim*) projects, through which the Federation asked to maintain its position as a prominent housing authority in the face of the State agencies' efforts to dictate generic standards. The area of an apartment in the Veteran Citizen Housing buildings was between 55 and 75 square meters, twice the area apportioned to new immigrants by the State. This sizable difference enrooted the notion of "luxury apartment," defined "veterans" and "newcomers" as distinct sectors in Israeli society, and enriched the lexicon of designated housing projects, with eligibility determined according to a highly idiosyncratic index of interest groups developing under the carpet of the egalitarian welfare state: engineers, Foreign Office officials, military officers, Krakow-ites, war veterans, Anglo-Saxons, agricultural workers, and so forth.

Following the initial period of austerity, along with the launch of the Transit Camp Plan, the block became the "philosopher's stone," self-generating and automatically distributed, solving by itself, as it were, the predicament of mass housing and regulating center-periphery relationships. What had begun as the "luxury" of privileged socialists quickly turned into the "housing machine" of the modern welfare state.

The paradox that best epitomizes Israeli society of the 1950s—the phenomenon of increasing statism, on the one hand, and deepening sectorality, on the other—assumed its most apparent embodiment in the *shikun*, the public-housing block. Uniformity became the masquerade of ethnic segregation and political discrimination.

In the local race to attain affordable housing, those who could not be labeled as workers of unionized workplaces, refugees of specific traumatized countries,

④ Kiryat Haim, Haifa Bay, 1937. Richard Kauffmann. Photographer: Zoltan Kluger. Central Zionist Archives.
⑤ Kiryat Haim, Haifa Bay, 1937. Richard Kauffmann. Photographer: Zoltan Kluger. Central Zionist Archives.
⑥ Workers' neighborhood, Tel Aviv, 1934. Arieh Sharon. Yael Aloni Photo Collection. Courtesy of the Azrieli Architectural Archive, Arieh Sharon Collection.

or veterans of official organizations remained behind. For them, another sector—the "popular"—was invented, which, against the grain of Labor politics, set in motion the process of privatization and commodification of the Israeli housing project.

The category of "popular housing" (Heb. *shikun amami*) is neither an architectural typology nor a class distinction, but a process of financing based upon various degrees of participation of the tenants. The question of financing became central following the rapid increase of construction costs. In 1948, the price of one square meter was 19.4 Israeli lira, and by 1953, it had risen to 74.4 Israeli lira—an increase of nearly 400 percent in five years. At the same time, the amount that banks were willing to give in mortgage loans rose only slightly. Thus, if in 1948 the value of the loan made up about 40 percent of the cost of the apartment, in 1952 it was only 16 to 20 percent. These circumstances demanded greater intervention on the part of the government by way of funding—but they also led to a gradual decline in the State's position as the central building and housing body. In the first phase of the Popular Housing Project, the State provided attractive government loans constituting 51 percent of the total building expenditure. In effect, the government was now a provider of securities, both to a growing number of potential tenants and to public and private companies, which could now increase their production. Thus began the shift of the public-housing project from the ideological left to the economic right. From a crowd lacking means and choice, the tenants became a community of consumers with options to choose from and decisions to make concerning their homes (for instance, 60 percent of those who signed up for the Popular Housing Project abandoned their rights to be housed by it and eventually withdrew their deposits).

The "popular" doctrine was perfected in various savings-and-loan programs which habituated Israelis to a mortgage culture. Governmental and Histadrut housing companies were gradually privatized or replaced by entrepreneurial contractors who lacked (or, alternatively, were free of) the ideological rigor and puritan taste of their predecessors. The privatization of Israeli domesticity accelerated until it found its ultimate discharge in the "Build Your Own Home" sprawls of the 1970s, the flagship project of the first right-wing government in Israel, headed by Prime Minister Menachem Begin (see chapter "Privatization"). ■

1 Nachman Syrkin, "Brotherhood," in *Yalkut Ha'ahdut* [in Hebrew] (Tel Aviv, 1962). Originally published in the periodical *Ha'ahdut* (The Solidarity), no. 33 (1912).

2 Theodor Herzl, *The Jewish State*, trans. Harry Zohn (New York: Herzl Press, 1970). Available online (accessed April 18, 2017): http://library.gayhomeland.org/0001/EN/content_index.htm. Originally published as *Der Judenstaat* (Leipzig and Vienna: Breitenstein, 1896).

3 Shikun Company, *Housing in Israel Bulletin* [in Hebrew] (1953).

4 Cited in Neve Oved Company, *A Decade of Neve Oved: A Company for Workers' Dwelling in Moshavot* [in Hebrew] (1954), p. 68.

5 Ibid.

6 Ibid., p. 15.

⑦

⑧

⑩

⑨

⑦ “Cannon houses” built with the Tournalayer construction system, which produced two houses per day, 1951.
⑧ Tournalayer construction system, 1949. Max and Celia Leavitt Book Fund, Harvard Library.
⑨ Tournalayer construction system, 1949. Max and Celia Leavitt Book Fund, Harvard Library.
⑩ Public-housing project built with the Tournalayer construction system, Beersheba, 1950. Central Zionist Archives.

⑪

⑫

⑬

⑭

⑪ Public-housing projects for new immigrants, Beersheba, 1950–1959. David B. Keidan Collection, Central Zionist Archives.
⑫ New immigrants moving into a new housing project, Beersheba, early 1950s.
⑬ Public-housing projects for new immigrants, Beersheba, 1950. David B. Keidan Collection, Central Zionist Archives.
⑭ New housing project, Beit Shemesh, early 1950s.

# DOSSIER:
# BRIEF TYPOLOGY OF THE *SHIKUN*

⑮ ⑯ ⑰ ⑱

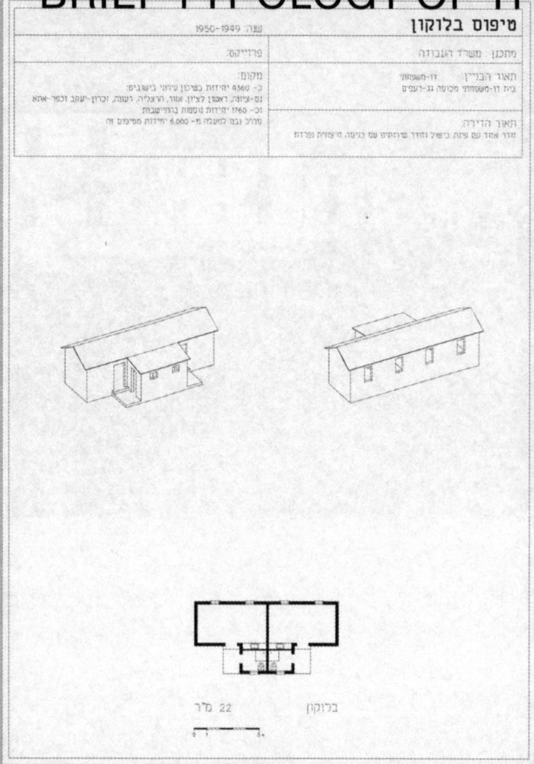


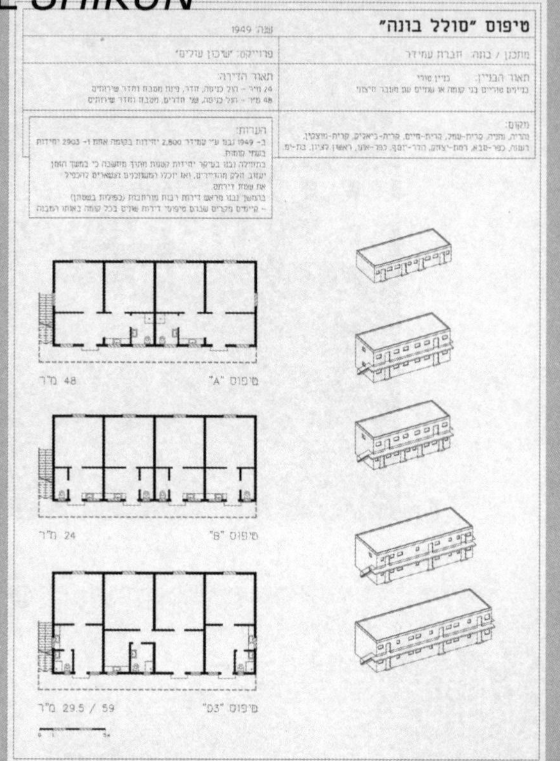


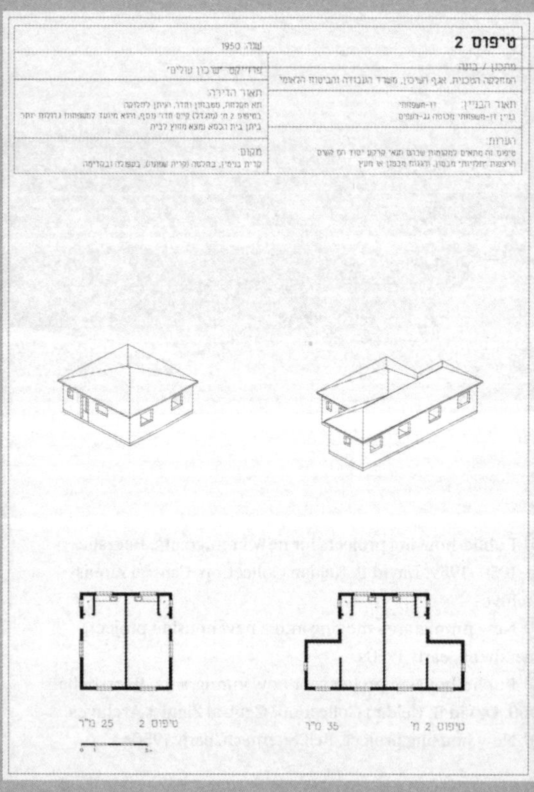


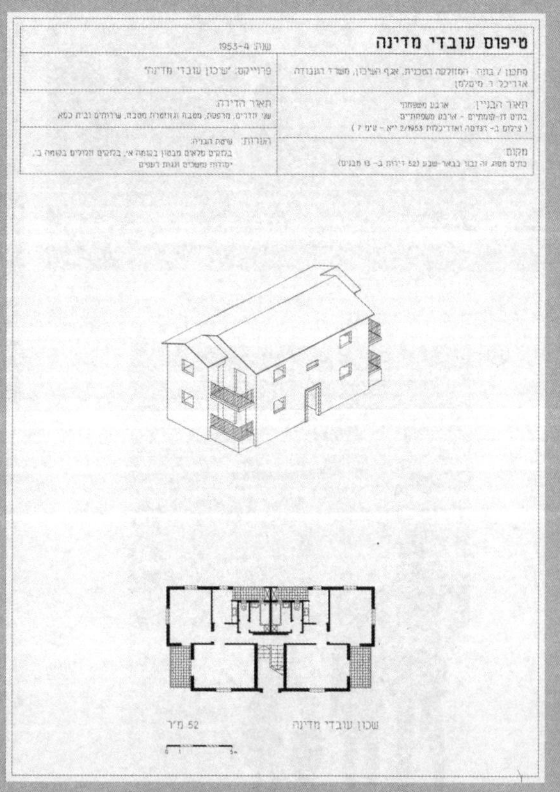

⑲ ⑳

㉑ ㉒

## טיפוס באר-שבע

שנה: 1953-4

מתכנן / בונה:

פרוייקט: "שיכון עממי - שלב א'"

תאור הבניין: בניין טורי
בתים בני 3 קומות, 2-3 כניסות
שיטת הבניה: שלד בטון מזויין, קירות מבלוקי-בטון חלולים, תקרות צלעות

תאור הדירה:
הול כניסה, מטבח וגומחת מטבח, חדר אמבטיה, בית שימוש, שני חדרים ומרפסת

מקום:
באר שבע (9 בלוקים - 150 דירות), חולון

צילומים:
הנדסה ואדריכלות 1953/2 י"א - עמ' 7
זנדבנקר / שיכון עולים בישראל - ע"מ 118

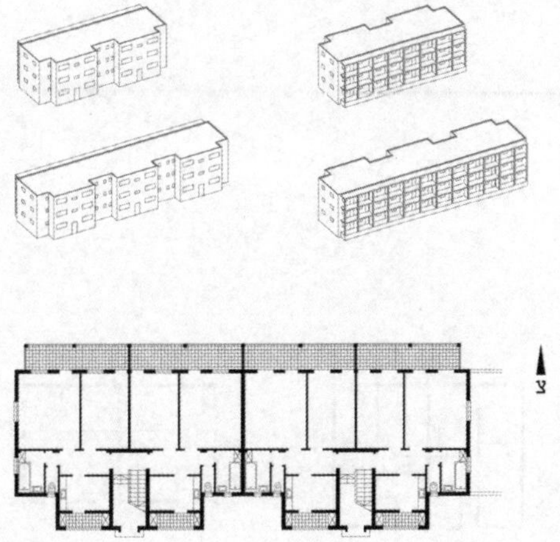

שיכון עממי
62 מ"ר

## טיפוס השיכון העממי

שנה: 1953-4

מתכנן: המחלקה הטכנית של אגף השיכון - אדריכל ד. ברוצקוס
בונה: "ירסקו" - חברה להתיישבות חקלאית ועירונית

פרוייקט: "שיכון עממי - שלב א'"

תאור הבניין: בניין טורי
בתים בני 3-4 קומות, 3-5 כניסות (18-30 דירות) - גג שטוח
בתים בני 2-3 קומות, 2 כניסות (8-12 דירות) - גג רעפים

תאור הדירה:
הול מואר, שני חדרים ומרפסת, מטבח וגומחת מטבח, חדר אמבטיה ובית שימוש

מקום:
ירושלים (בשכונות קרית-היובל וקטמון), חולון

הערות:
כל יחידות הדיור פונות באופן כללי צפון-דרום (עם התאמות לטופוגרפיה) המרחק בין הבניינים הוא 22 מ' (בחולון), 25-30 מ' (בקרית היובל)

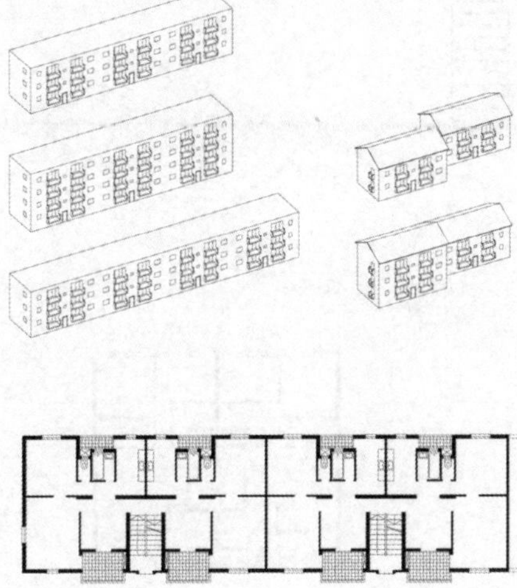

שיכון עממי
63 מ"ר
(קיימים הבדלים קטנים בין תוכניות באזור ושל מרפסת המטבח)

## טיפוס "בניין צלב"

שנה: 1961

מתכנן / בונה: שיכון עובדים

פרוייקט:

תאור הבניין: בניין צלב
בניין בן ארבע קומות, ארבע דירות בכל קומה

תאור הדירה:
חדר מגורים עם פינת אוכל, חדר פינה, נשבה, חדר אמבטיה, בית שימוש, מרפסת מגורים ומרפסת מטבח

מקום:
קרית המיינים (תל-אביב)

הערות:

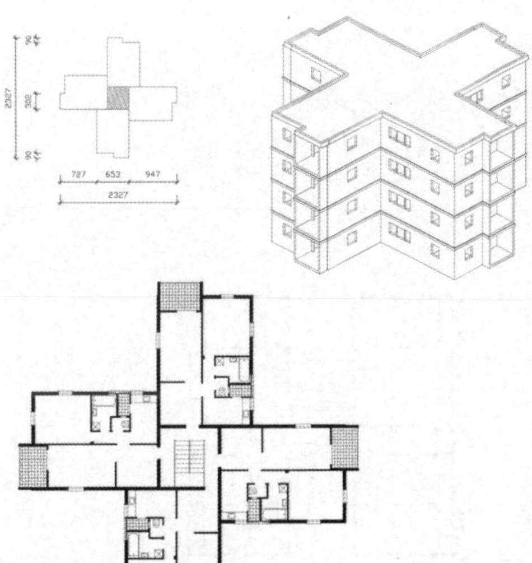

טיפוס "צלב"
61 מ"ר

## טיפוס 206

שנה: 1958-9

מתכנן / בונה: שיכון עובדים

פרוייקט: "מפעל החיסכון לבניין"

תאור הבניין: בניין טורי
מופיע בוריאציות של 2-4 קומות וב-2 או 3 כניסות (8-24 דירות)
גג בטון שטוח (יתכן והוקמו גם בניינים עם גג רעפים)

תאור הדירה:
חדר מגורים, עם מרפסת, שני חדרי שינה, הול כניסה מואר, חדר שרותים, מטבח וגומחת מטבח

מקום:
חולון, סלמה ב' (במזרח ת"א) תקוה (שד' ויצמן)

הערות:
לעתים מופיע שילוב של דירות מטיפוסים 206 ו-210 באותו בניין

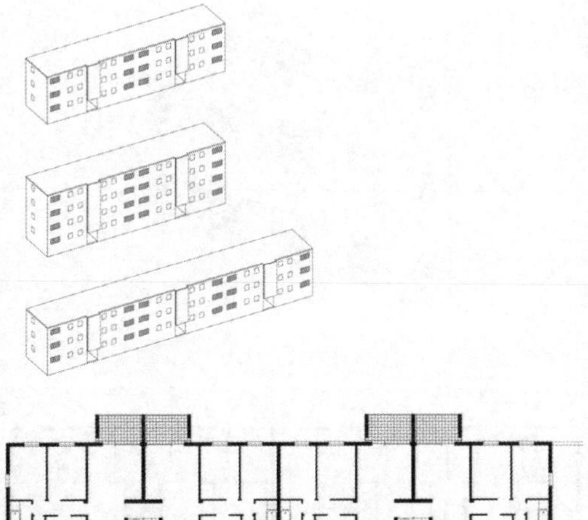

טיפוס 206
72 מ"ר

23 24

25 26

## טיפוסי רמת-הדר - בניין "ס"

שנה: 1957–1960

אדריכלים: מוניו וינרויב, אל מנספלד    בונה: "רסקו"

פרוייקט: "רמת-הדר"

תאור הבניין: בניין גשר
גשר חיצוני מוביל ממפלס הרחוב אל קומת עמודים מפולשת.
7 פירי מדרגות אנכיים מובילים אל דירות ב-10 קומות מגורים – 6 מעל קומת הכניסה ו- 4 מתחת לקומת הכניסה (ראה חתך)
בקומת הכניסה גם תא-שוער, קיוסקים, חנויות, תאי טלפון ומספלים
בבניין 140 דירות – כולן זהות.

תאור הדירה:
חדר מגורים המקושר למרפסת, מטבח, פנת אכל ומרפסת שרות,
שני חדרי שינה, חדר ארונות, חדר אמבטיה ובית שמוש

מקום: בניין יחיד מסוג זה נבנה ברמת הדר שבחיפה (רחוב ליאון בלום)

הערות: קיר צפוני עבה ואטום יותר מהקיר הדרומי - לצורך בידוד

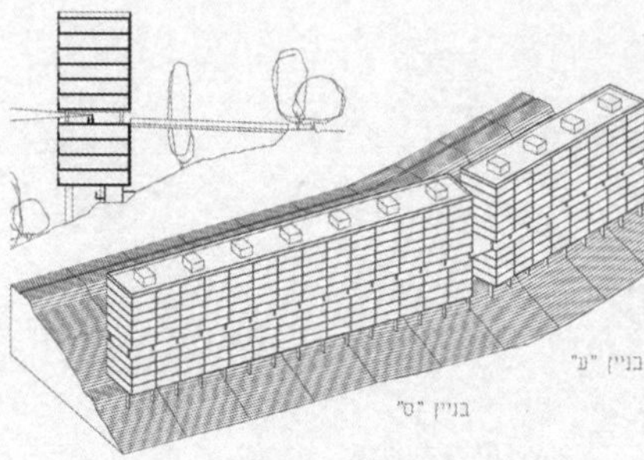


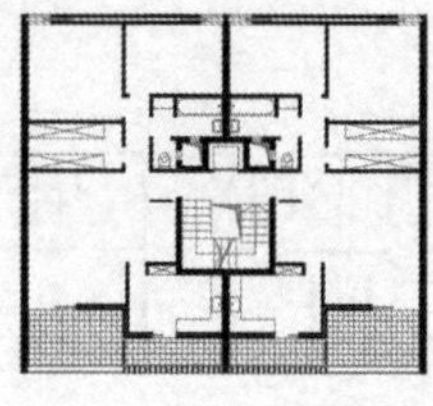

טיפוס בניין "ס"    94 מ"ר

## טיפוס גליקסון 3

שנה: 1964

מתכנן: אדר' ארתור גליקסון

פרוייקט: "שכונת הצפון בקרית-גת"

תאור הבניין: ארבע משפחתי
מבנים ארבע משפחתיים, המשורים ביניהם בגשרים (מסכן במדרגות)
מופיעים בשרשרת של בין 3–5 בניינים

תאור הדירה:
דירה תחתונה: 3 חדרי מגורים, מטבח, חדר שרותים וחצר אחורית
דירה עליונה: סלון עם פנת אכל ומרפסת, מטבח, חדר שינה וחדר שרותים

מקום:
שכונת הצפון בקרית-גת
48 בניינים (בשרשרות שונות) - 192 דירות

הערות:

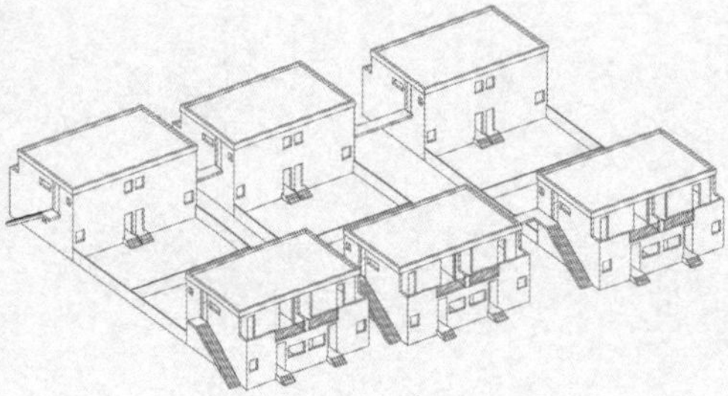

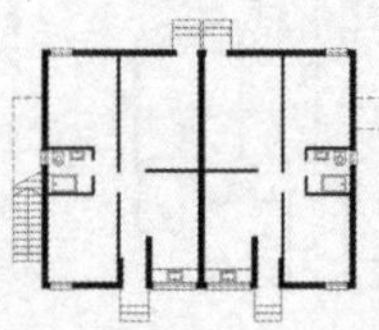

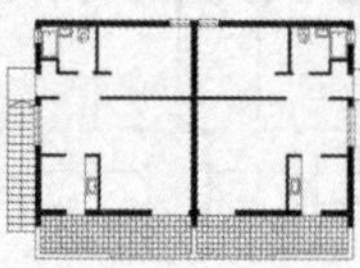

קומה א'    53 מ"ר

קומה ב'    53 מ"ר
(כולל המרפסת)

## טיפוס 217 (הבית הגדל)

שנה: 1958–9

מתכנן / בונה: שיכון עובדים

פרוייקט: "מפעל המיסכון לבניין"

תאור הבניין: בניין טורי
מופיע בואריאציות של 3 כניסות בשתי קומות (12 דירות)
ו- 4 כניסות ב- 3–4 קומות (24–32 דירות)

תאור הדירה:
החלק המושלם של הדירה כולל:
חדר, הול, מטבח ומרפסת מטבח וחדר שרותים
החלק הבלתי מושלם מוכן עבור שני חדרים נוספים ומרפסת
(ע"פ התוכנית ניתן להפריד את חדר השרותים לבית-כסא ולחדר אמבטיה)

מקום:
אור-יהודה, בת-ים, רחובות, נתניה, חולון (קרית עבודה),
קרית-חיים, וחיפה

הערות: קיימים הבדלים קטנים בתוכנית בין פרסומים משנים שונות

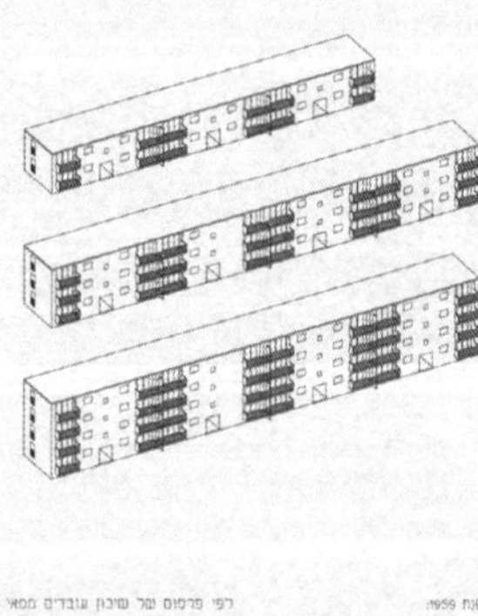

לפי פרסום של שיכון עובדים משנת 1959:

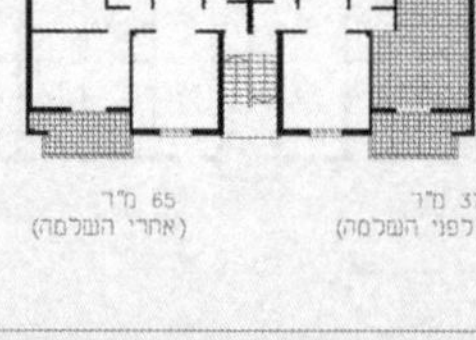


לפי פרסום של שיכון עובדים ממאי 1964:

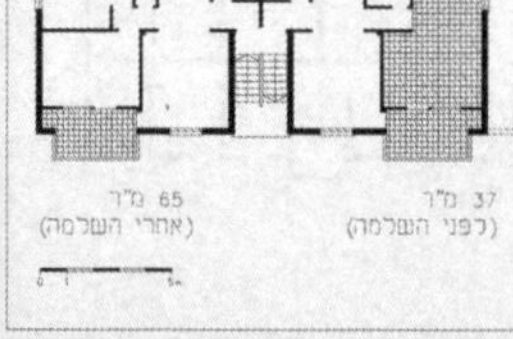


37 מ"ר (לפני השלמה)    65 מ"ר (אחרי השלמה)    37 מ"ר (לפני השלמה)    65 מ"ר (אחרי השלמה)

## טיפוס 211

שנה: 1958–9

מתכנן / בונה: שיכון עובדים

פרוייקט: "מפעל המיסכון לתושבי הצריפונים"

תאור הבניין: בניין "א"
3–4 קומות, 2 דירות כל חצי קומה

תאור הדירה:
3 חדרים, הול מואר, מטבח, חדר אמבטיה, בית שמוש,
מרפסת לחדרים ומרפסת מטבח

מקום:
שכונות הפועלים בבני-ברק

הערות:

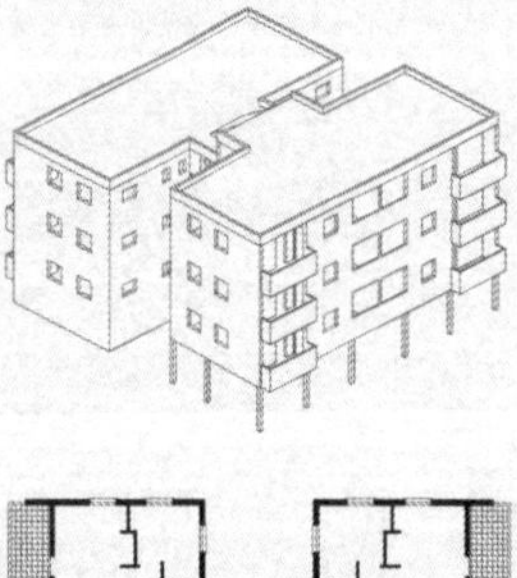

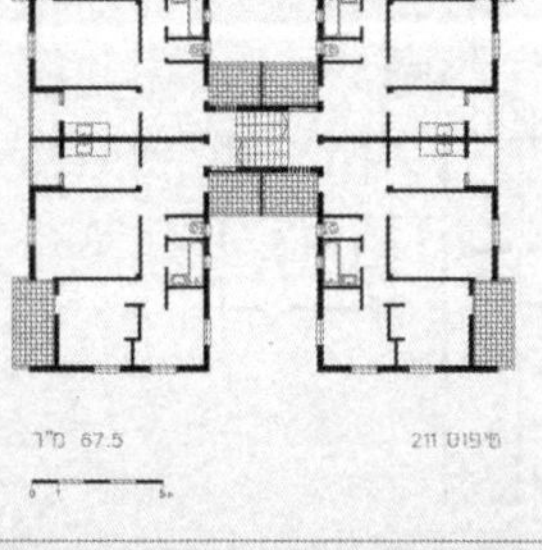

טיפוס 211    67.5 מ"ר

(27) (28)

(29) (30)

## טיפוס ק-51

שנה: 1961

מתכנן / בונה: מינהל השיכון
צוות ירושלים בראשותו של אדר' שמואל שקד

פרוייקט:

תאור הבניין: בניין שמות מורי
בניין עורי - 6 כניסות, 3 קומות מעל קומת עמודים (36 דירות)
בניי משלד בטון ומילואות מתועשות

תאור הדירה:
שני חדרים, מטבח, מרפסת וחדר שרותים, המואורר דרך פיר

מקום:
ירושלים

הערות:
ניסיון לחסוך באורך חזית - אורך חזית ממוצע לדירה: 4.25 מ'
הבדל בין חזיתות נגדיות בעובי הקירות בלבד

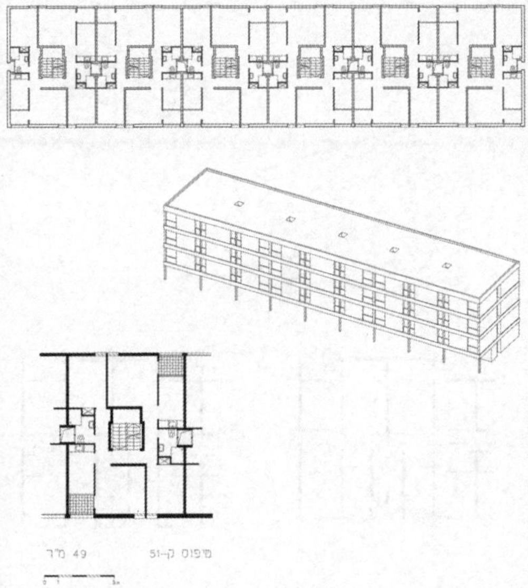


## טיפוס 64

שנה: 1960

מתכנן / בונה: י. פרלשטיין

פרוייקט:

תאור הבניין: בניין מרובע
4-3 קומות, 4 דירות בקומה
ואריאציות של קומת הכניסה
א. קומת עמודים המכילה מקלט עליון
ב. קומת עמודים המכילה 2 דירות
ג. כניסה לבניין ו-4 דירות

תאור הדירה
שני חדרים עם מרפסת, מטבח עם גזוזטרה, פינת אוכל וחדר שרותים
השרותים מאווררים דרך פירים במרכז הבניין
(בטיפוס 64 ב' השרותים מאווררים דרך גזוזטרת המטבח)

מקום: אשדוד

הערות

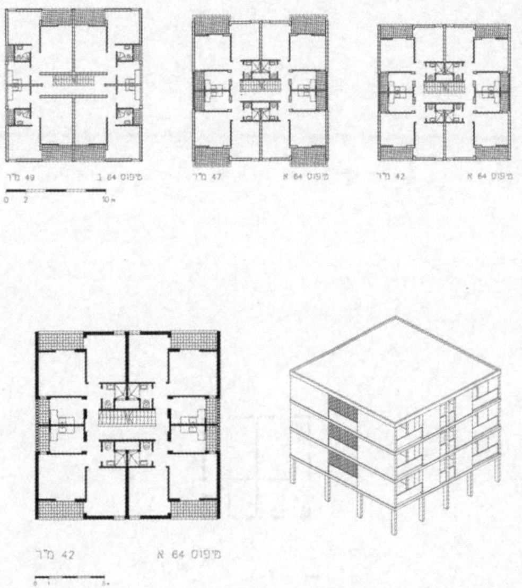


## טיפוס גליקסון 1

שנה: 1964

מתכנן : אדר' ארתור גליקסון

פרוייקט: "שכונת הנסיון בקרית-גת"

תאור הבניין: מבנה שטיח
מבנה שטיח בן שתי קומות
בניין קצר מכיל 16 דירות ובניין ארוך מכיל 24 דירות

תאור הדירה:

מקום:
שכונת הנסיון בקרית-גת
13 מבנים קצרים ו-2 מבנים ארוכים : 256 דירות

הערות:

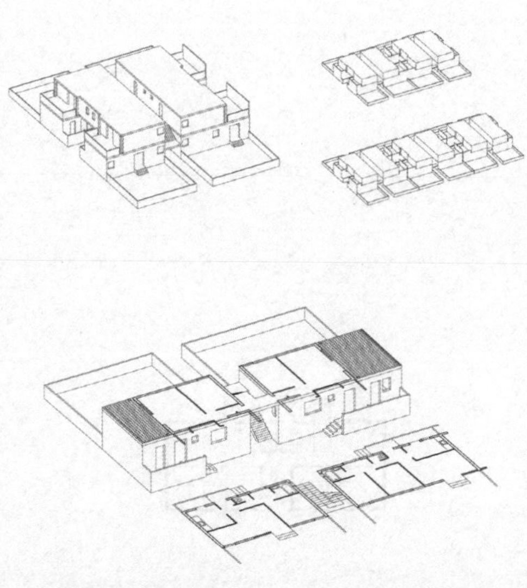

## טיפוס 247

שנה:

מתכנן / בונה: י. פרלשטיין

פרוייקט:

תאור הבניין: בניין "א"
4 קומות מעל קומת עמודים - 4 דירות בקומה (16 דירות)
אחד מקצוות ה-"א" או שניים הינם סגורים (בעלי חזית אטומה),
וכך יכולים הבניינים להתחבר - קצה סגור לקצה סגור וליצור מבנן רציף

תאור הדירה:
הול כניסה, חדר מגורים עם מרפסת, מטבח ומרפסת מטבח,
שני חדרי שינה (חדר וחצי), חדר אמבטיה וחדר שירות

מקום:
רמת-יוסף

הערות:

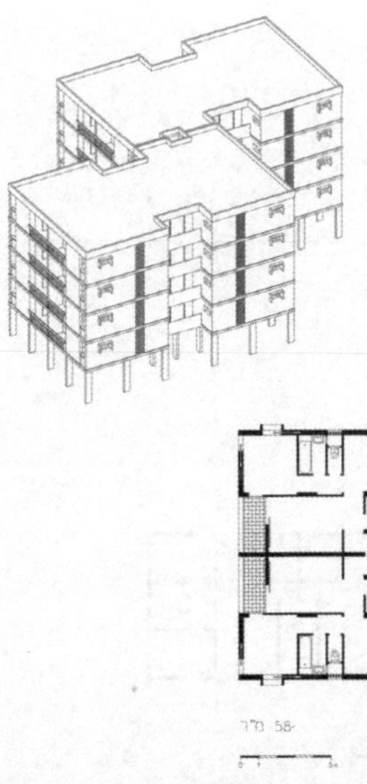

(31) (32)

(33) (34)

## טיפוס "נוה-עובד"

שנה: 1949

| מתכנן / בונה: חברת "נוה-עובד" | פרוייקט: "שיכון עולים" |
|---|---|
| תאור הבניין: דו-משפחתי<br>בניין דו-משפחתי עם גג רעפים | תאור הדירה:<br>חדר אחד, מטבח וחדר שירותים |
| מקום:<br>חורה, יוקנעם, הרצליה, מגדל, יהוד, נס-ציונה, רחובות ועקיר (עקרון) | הערות:<br>צילום בספרו של זסלבסקי דוד / שיכון עולים בישראל, עמ' 56 |

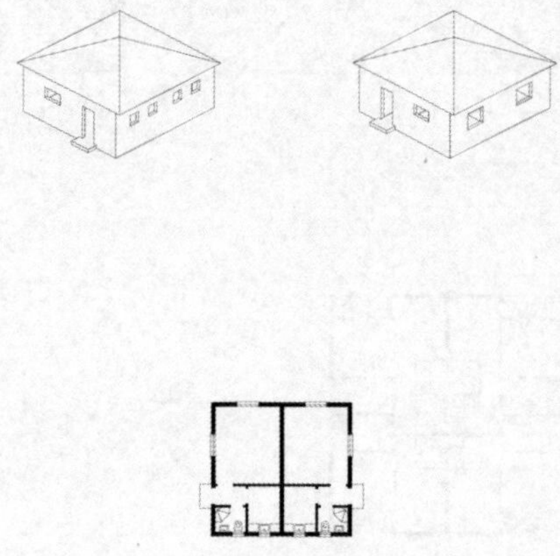

נוה-עובד 28 מ"ר

## טיפוס ק-54

שנה: 1961-4

| מתכנן / בונה: מינהל השיכון<br>צוות ירושלים בראשותו של אדר' שמואל שקד | פרוייקט: |
|---|---|
| תאור הבניין: בניין גשר טורי<br>בניין טורי - 6 כניסות, 3 קומות מעל קומת עמודים (36 דירות)<br>בנוי משלד בטון ומילואות מתועשות | תאור הדירה:<br>חדר מגורים ושני חדרי שינה, מרפסת מגורים, מטבח ומרפסת מטבח, חדר אמבטיה ובית שימוש (המאווררים דרך פיר) |
| מקום:<br>ירושלים (קרית יובל - 8 בניינים ברחוב ברזיל) | הערות:<br>הבניינים תוכננו לאזורים בהם השיפוע הוא כ-30% |

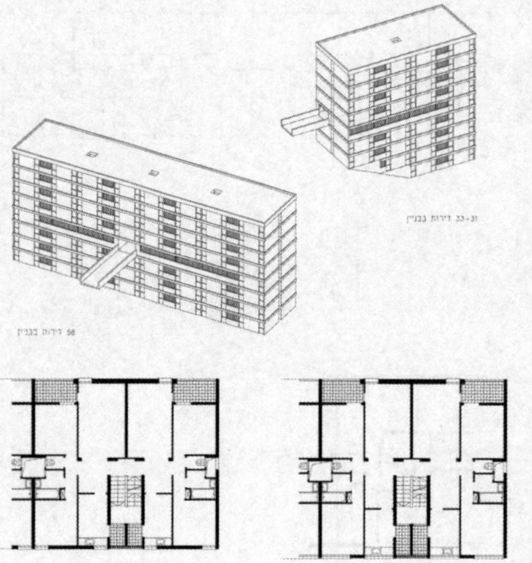


טיפוס ק-54 71 מ"ר

טיפוס ק-54 67 מ"ר

## טיפוס 4301

שנה: 1958-9

| מתכנן / בונה: שיכון עובדים | פרוייקט: "שיכון עולים" |
|---|---|
| תאור הבניין: ארבע משפחתי<br>בתים ארבע-משפחתיים דו-קומתיים בעלי גג-רעפים | תאור הדירה<br>חדר מגורים, הכולל פינת אוכל, מטבח וגזוזטרת מטבח, שני חדרי שינה, מרפסת, חדר אמבטיה ובית שימוש |
| מקום:<br>רחובות (בשכונת אפרות), חדרה (בשכונת רמות אפריים), נס-ציונה (בשכונת "ויצמן" ובשכונת יד-אליעזר) | הערות: |

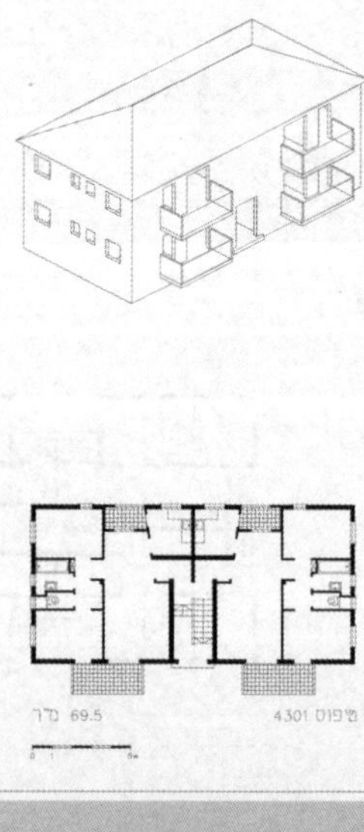

טיפוס 4301 69.5 מ"ר

## טיפוס 139

שנה: 1958-9

| מתכנן / בונה: שיכון עובדים | פרוייקט: "שיכון עולים" |
|---|---|
| תאור הבניין: בניין ארבע-משפחתי / בניין טורי<br>בדרך כלל מופיע כבית ארבע משפחתי, בן שתי קומות. מכוסה גג-רעפים<br>במקרים אחדים מופיע כדירה בבניין טורי עם גג-רעפים או גג שטוח | מקום:<br>רמלה (שיכון פועלים ליה"ב), בנוף-ים ובנס-ציונה (יד-אליעזר)<br>ברעננה (משכנות הפועלים) מופיע כיחידת כפולות - שמונה משפחתי<br>בנתניה (שיכון טורים) מופיע כבניין טורי, גג שטוח, 2-8 כניסות, 3 קומות<br>באור יהודה מופיע בבניינים של 2 כניסות בשילוב עם טיפוס 1-138<br>כיחידות הצד משקפת |
| תאור הדירה:<br>חדר מגורים עם מרפסת, שני חדרי שינה קטנים,<br>מטבח מנוע, וחדר שירותים | |

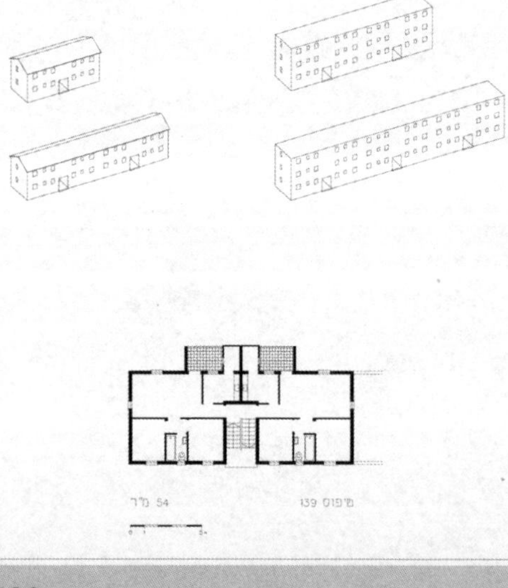

טיפוס 139 54 מ"ר

35 36

37 38

# טיפוס 2112 / 2113

שנה: 1958-9

| מתכנן / בונה: שיכון עובדים | פרוייקט: "שיכון עולים" |
| --- | --- |
| תאור הבניין: דו-משפחתי<br>בתים דו-משפחתיים חד-קומתיים בעלי גג-רעפים | מקום:<br>טיפוס 2112: בראשון לציון (נחלת בנימין), ברמת השרון, ברמתיים (נוה-נאמן) וברעננה<br>טיפוס 2113: בקריית אונו, ברמלה (שכ' נוה דוד), בזרנוגה, במזכרת-בתיה, בפרדס-חנה, בראשון-לציון (נחלת בנימין), ברמת השרון, ברמתיים (נוה נאמן) וברעננה |
| תאור הדירה:<br>חדר מגורים, שני חדרי שינה, מטבח וחדר שירותים | |

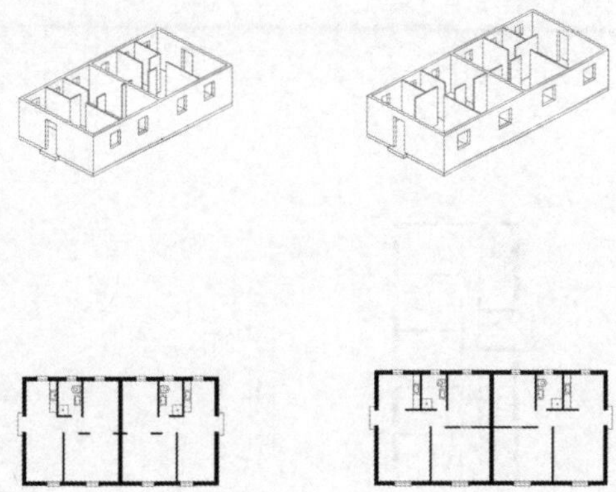

טיפוס 2113 46 מ"ר

טיפוס 2112 36 מ"ר

# טיפוס 2233

שנה: 1958-9

| מתכנן / בונה: שיכון עובדים | פרוייקט: "שיכון עולים" |
| --- | --- |
| תאור הבניין: דו-משפחתי<br>בתים דו-משפחתיים חד-קומתיים בעלי גג-רעפים | תאור הדירה:<br>חדר מגורים, שני חדרי שינה, מטבח עם פינת-אוכל וחדר שירותים |
| מקום:<br>קרית-אונו, זרנוגה, מזכרת-בתיה, פרדס-חנה, ראשון לציון (נחלת בנימין) | הערות: |

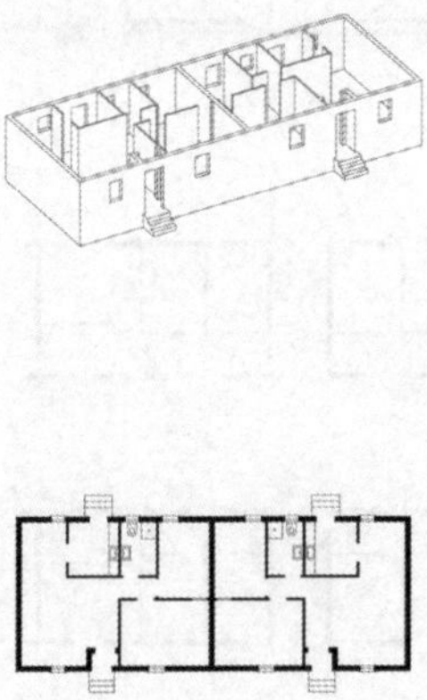

טיפוס 2233 54 מ"ר

# טיפוס 210

שנה: 1958-9

| מתכנן / בונה: שיכון עובדים | פרוייקט: "מפעל החיסכון לבניין" |
| --- | --- |
| תאור הבניין: בניין טורי<br>מופיע בוריאציות של קומה עד שלוש, וב-3 עד 4 כניסות (24-6 דירות)<br>גג בטון שטוח (יתכן והוקמו גם בניינים עם גג רעפים) | תאור הדירה:<br>חדר מגורים, המקושר למרפסת ומשמש כפינת אוכל,<br>חדר שינה אחד, חדר שירותים, מטבח ומרפסת מטבח |
| מקום:<br>חולון, מגמה ב' (במזרח ת"א), בת-ים ובני-ברק | הערות:<br>לעתים מופיע שילוב של דירות מטיפוסים 206 ו- 210 באותו בניין |

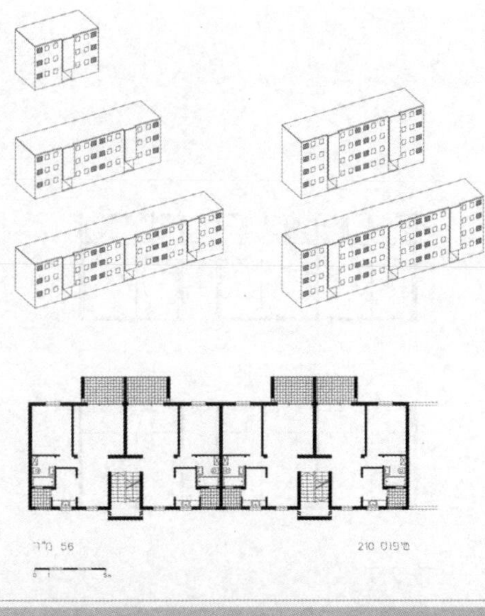

טיפוס 210 56 מ"ר

# טיפוס "רסקו"

שנה: 1950-1949

| מתכנן / בונה: חברת רסקו | פרוייקט: "שיכון עולים" |
| --- | --- |
| תאור הבניין: ארבע משפחתי<br>בניין ארבע-משפחתי בשתי קומות עם גג רעפים | תאור הדירה:<br>הול כניסה, 2 חדרים, מטבח וחדר שירותים |
| מקום:<br>כפר אונו, עפולה, עליה, ראשון לציון ועוד | הערות: |

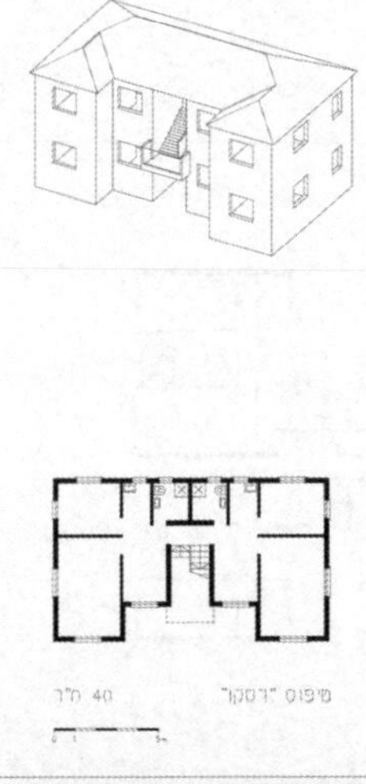

טיפוס "רסקו" 40 מ"ר

(39) (40)

(41) (42)

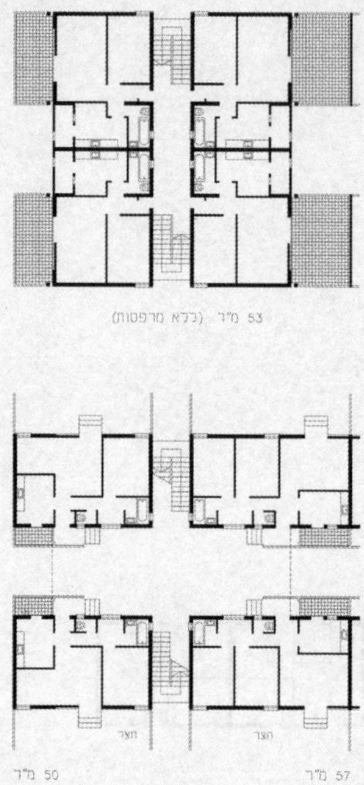


גליקסון – טיפוס 1

## טיפוס "שיכון רזניק"

שנה: 1959-62

מתכנן / בונה: אדר' דוד רזניק (עבור משרד השיכון)

פרוייקט: "קרית היובל - מערב"

תאור הבניין: בניין גשר
שלושה בנייני גשר, המחוברים ביניהם בגשרים

תאור הדירה:
דירה גדולה: הול, 3 חדרים, מטבח ומרפסת מטבח, חדר אמבטיה ושרותים
דירה קטנה: שני חדרים, מטבח ומרפסת מטבח וחדר שרותים

מקום:
קרית היובל – מערב (רחובות הגפקה וברזיל)

הערות:
קירות מטבים יותר לכיוון מערב (כיוון הרוח והגשם) לעומת כיוון מזרח
הפתחים הגדולים יותר מופנים לכיוון דרום, ואילו החזית המערבית אטומה

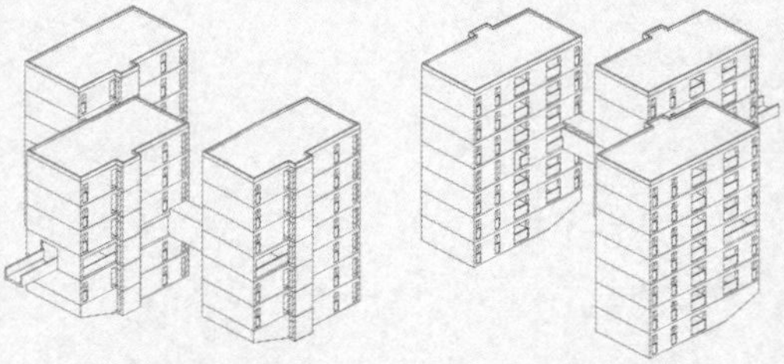

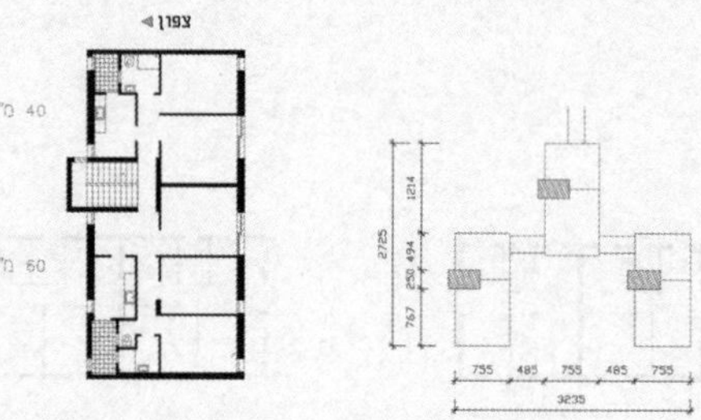


שיכוני רזניק – קרית היובל

## טיפוס גליקסון 6

שנה: 1964

מתכנן: אדר' ארתור גליקסון

פרוייקט: "שכונת הנסיון בקרית-גת"

תאור הבניין: בניין "אי"
3 קומות מעל קומת עמודים - 4 דירות בקומה

תאור הדירה:
3 חדרי מגורים ומרפסת, מטבח עם מרפסת שירות, פינת אוכל,
חדר אמבטיה ושרותים

מקום:
שכונת הנסיון בקרית-גת
14 בניינים - 168 דירות

הערות:

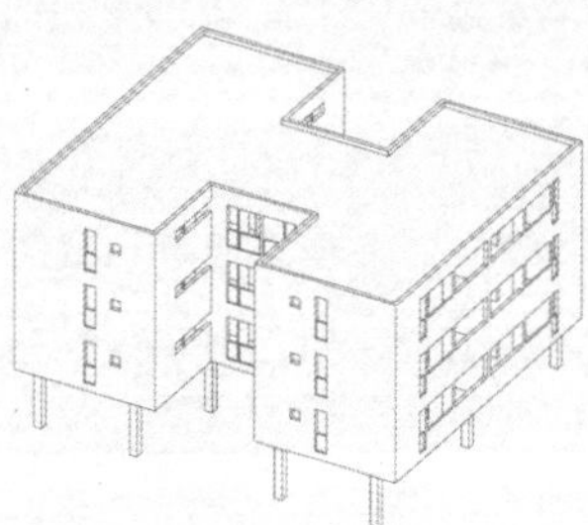

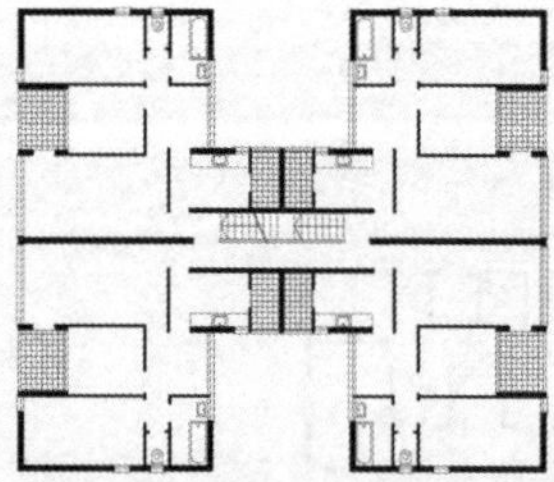


טיפוס 6 (גליקסון)

## טיפוס גליקסון 5

שנה: 1964

מתכנן: אדר' ארתור גליקסון

פרוייקט: "שכונת הנסיון בקרית-גת"

תאור הבניין: ארבע משפחתי
מבנים ארבע משפחתיים, המסודרים ביניהם בגשרים (מסכן במדרגות)
מופיעים בשרשרות של בין 1.5-2.5 בניינים

תאור הדירה:
דירה תחתונה: 2 חדרי מגורים, מטבח, חדר שרותים וחצר אחורית
דירה עליונה: 2 חדרי מגורים, מטבח, חדר שרותים ומרפסת

מקום:
שכונת הנסיון בקרית-גת
22.5 בניינים (בשרשרות שונות) - 90 דירות

הערות:

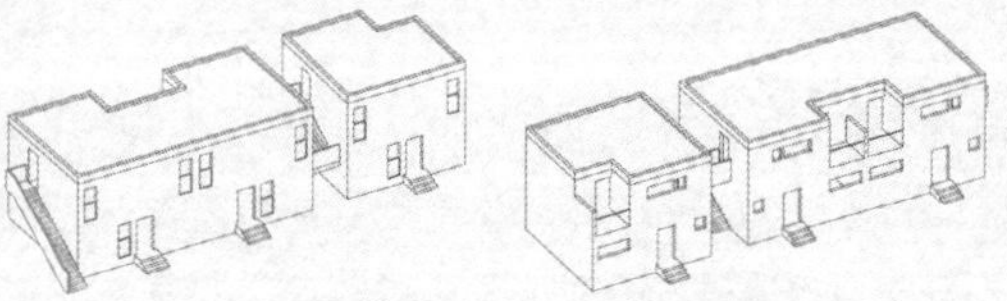

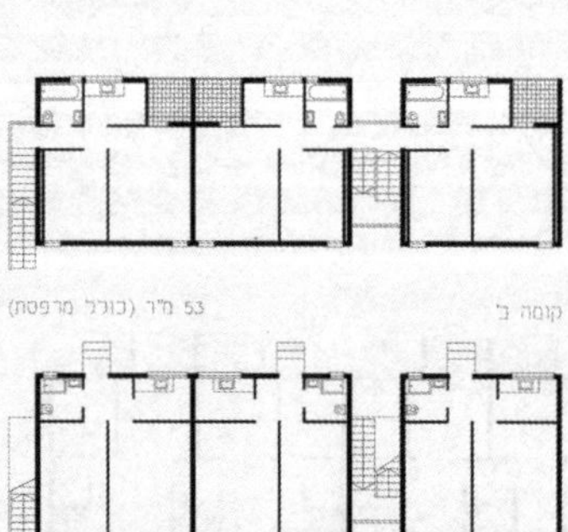

⑮ "Blockon type": detached two-family house with tiled roof, built by the Ministry of Housing, Technical Department, 1949–1950.
⑯ "Solel Boneh type": row house, single-storey or two-storey unit with external entrance hall. Project: Housing Project for New Immigrants, 1949. Built by Amidar (National Housing Company).
⑰ "Type two": detached two-family house with tiled roof. Project: Housing Project for New Immigrants, 1950. Built by the Ministry of Housing, Technical Department.
⑱ "Civil-servant type": detached two-storey, four-family house. Project: Civil Servant Housing, 1953–1954. Built by the Ministry of Housing, Technical Department. A. Mittelman.
⑲ "Public-housing type": serial apartment blocks. Type A: three to four storeys high, three to five entrances, with flat concrete roof. Type B: blocks of two to three storeys, two entrances, with tiled roof. Project: Public Housing, 1953–1954. Phase I built by the Ministry of Housing, Technical Department.
⑳ "Beersheba type": three-storey horizontal block.
㉑ "Type 206": three- to four-storey horizontal block.
㉒ "Cross-house type": four-storey building with four apartments on every level. Built by the Shikun Ovdim (Workers' Housing) Company, 1961.
㉓ "Glikson 3 type": semidetached, four-family buildings, interconnected by bridges. Comes in a series of three to five buildings. Project: Model Neighborhood Kiryat Gat, 1964. Artur Glikson.
㉔ "Ramat Hadar – 'S' Building": ten-storey apartment building, with external bridge leading to open entrance level connected to seven vertical circulation shafts, 1957–1960. Munio Gitai Weinraub, Al Mansfeld. Contractor: Rassco (Rural and Suburban Settlement Company).
㉕ "Type 211": H-shaped building with three to four storeys, with a mid-level offset. Project: Construction Cost Savings Project for Transit Camp Residents, 1958–1959. Built by the Shikun Ovdim Company.
㉖ "Type 217" (the expandable house): block type constructed in rows, enabling variations of three entrances for two-storey buildings or four entrances for three- to four-storey buildings. Project: Construction Cost Savings Act, 1958–1959. Built by the Shikun Ovdim Company.
㉗ "Type 64": square building, three to four storeys, four apartments per storey, 1960. Yitzhak Perlstein.
㉘ "K-51 type": three-storey block on pilotis, constructed in rows, containing six vertical circulation shafts, 1961. Shmuel Shaked. Built by the Jerusalem Division Housing Authority.
㉙ "Type 247": H-shaped, four-storey building on pilotis, 1960. Yitzhak Perlstein.
㉚ "Glikson 1 type": semidetached, two-storey buildings. Project: Model Neighborhood Kiryat Gat, 1964. Artur Glikson.
㉛ "K-54 type": nine-storey building containing six vertical circulation shafts, with street-level bridge connection, 1961. Shmuel Shaked. Built by the Jerusalem Division Housing Authority.
㉜ "Neve Oved type": detached two-family house with tiled roof. Project: Public Housing for New Immigrants, 1949. Built by Neve Oved.
㉝ "Type 139": block series with flat concrete roof or tiled roof. Comes in varieties of three to four storeys and two to three entrance halls. Project: Housing Project for New Immigrants, 1958–1959. Built by the Shikun Ovdim Company.
㉞ "Type 4301": detached, two-storey, four-family house. Project: Housing Project for New Immigrants, 1958–1959. Built by the Shikun Ovdim Company.
㉟ "Type 2233": detached, one-storey, two-family house with tiled roof. Project: Housing Project for New Immigrants, 1958–1959. Built by the Shikun Ovdim Company.
㊱ "Type 2113/2112": detached, one-storey, two-family house with tiled roof. Project: Housing Project for New Immigrants, 1958–1959. Built by the Shikun Ovdim Company.
㊲ "Rasco type": detached, two-storey, four-family house. Project: Housing Project for New Immigrants, 1949–1950. Built by Rasco.
㊳ "Type 211": serial block constructed in rows enabling variations of three entrances for two-storey buildings or four entrances for three- to four-storey buildings. Construction Cost Savings Act, 1958–1959. Built by the Shikun Ovdim Company.
㊴ "Resnick type": seven-storey block in clusters, containing three vertical circulation shafts, with street-level bridge connection. David Resnick, for the Ministry of Housing.
㊵ "Glikson 1 type": semidetached, two-storey buildings. Floor plan. Project: Model Neighborhood Kiryat Gat, 1964. Artur Glikson.
㊶ "Glikson 5 type": semidetached, two-storey, four-family buildings. Project: Model Neighborhood Kiryat Gat, 1964. Artur Glikson.
㊷ "Glikson 6 type": H-shaped building, three storeys, four apartments per storey. Project: Model Neighborhood Kiryat Gat, 1964. Artur Glikson.

# Serial Blocks

① Theodor Marmorstein presenting his model for Yad Eliyahu Neigborhood, Tel Aviv, planned for World War II ex-servicemen, 1945. Steinpres-Marmorstein album, "Israel Revealed to the Eye" project, Yad Izhak Ben-Zvi Archives.

②

## The Logistics of Horizontality

The morphological naïveté of the postwar serial housing block is deceptive. Commonly associated with aesthetic homeliness, urban indifference, technological ineptness, social belligerence, and domestic unseemliness, the block is in fact the most political architectural object of Left and Right alike. To the Left, it is the apotheosis of Marxist materialism and the embodiment of Engels's *Wohnungsfrage*. To the Right, it is the inevitable end product of Taylorite and Fordist "sciences" of management, efficiency, ergonomics, mass production, and profit engineering.

The scene of origin of the modern housing block may be the nineteenth-century industrial city, but its political and intellectual premise was manifested only in early twentieth-century pursuits of new architectural objecthood, exempt of surplus manners and rationally designed according to lexical definitions of type-needs or type-programs and their correlation to type-bodies or type-forms. While most early modernists were still updating traditional preoccupations with questions of form, expression, imitation, and representation, several "objectivists," "materialists," or "post-humanists" began to polemically contest and politicize the purist, formalist, and allegorically functionalist discourse in order to accelerate the entry of architecture into the age of mechanical reproducibility and ethical affordability. Prominent among these, and most relevant to the genealogy of the housing block, were the *Neue Sachlichkeit* radicals Hannes Meyer and Ludwig Hilberseimer, who formulated a manifesto of *Marxist Architecture* that was entirely exposed to the market economy and to statistical analysis, rigorously confined to production and assembly modules, and piously reduced to the poiesis of banal solutions for banal problems. The housing block—never more than a plain diagram of an oversimplified program, a serial item building up an urban section, an optimized container arranged in patterned fields—was the metonymy of this architecture.

Prior to World War II, the serially reproduced housing block had mainly been a subject of theoretical discourse. The various workers' neighborhoods built on the outskirts of cities in Germany, Austria, Russia, and Palestine during the 1920s and 1930s certainly marked a new architectural commitment to the issue of public housing—but most remained little more than local laboratories, forgoing, a priori, any massive-scale generic, organizational, or technological solutions. Only after the war, and especially in nations with a centralist planning apparatus and settlement policy, did the housing block become an essential tool in the process of rehabilitation of the "Old World" and fabrication of the "New World." Architecture had reached its utmost minimum. Concurrently, the first phase of the Zionist colonization project ended and the new phase of the Israeli sovereign nation-state began.

The European experience in postwar mass building served as both an exemplary model and a cautionary tale for the Israeli architects. The recognition that the logistical preparation for an instant mass-scale housing project was in order had sunk in even before the political future of the Jewish population in Palestine was known. Centralization, serialization, standardization, reductivism, and ergonomic efficiency were not merely the idealized concepts and modes of operation of the Zionist establishment; they were its only option. Between the drafting boards and the writing desks, a new agenda had developed. Munio Gitai Weinraub, a Bauhaus graduate, wrote:

> When the war ends, mass construction—using limited resources—will be necessary. This condition will force us to construct buildings as simply as possible and to search for new building types. There is nothing wrong with such a necessity when it leads to simplicity, but boring monotony should be avoided. [...] The design's aim should always be to unify and not separate. It would be wise to plan larger buildings in various places.[1]

As Gitai Weinraub had anticipated, the war and its aftermath created an urgent need for mass construction and new housing prototypes in Israel. For architects such as Gitai Weinraub, this new scale was not necessarily perceived as a predicament, but rather as an opportunity for the materialization of a continuous urban environment and for a new experimentation with surface compositions.

Gitai Weinraub and Al Mansfeld designed an elongated block (*Zeilenbau* type, or "Type M" in their lexicon) which was preferred for flat or moderate topographies and was applied in the suburbs of Kiryat Yam (1952–1955), Kiryat Eliyahu (1954), and Kiryat Sprinzak (1956). A distinctive articulation for the hilly terrain of Ramat Hadar in Haifa, "Type T" (1959–1963)—inspired by Le Corbusier's Unité d'Habitation in Marseilles—connected four elongated blocks into a single complex, only half of which is above street level.

Hannes Meyer and Ludwig Hilberseimer provoked an intellectual turn, wishing to entirely release architectural practice from the habits of humanist-formalist discourse. Two decades later, when mass industrialized construction was no longer a theoretical issue, their student, Gitai Weinraub, pointed out the need to resort to architecture of sensual perception:

> When a building is large it is easier to locate its rhythmic lines, the integration or opposition of which creates all architectural compositions. In a large building the rhythm of details repeats itself—in a Classical building the rhythm of columns, in a Modern building, the exposed construction and the repetition of windows—whereas a small neighborhood house constitutes a cell, and cannot be divided into additional architectural components. [...] Why do longer buildings, approximately fifteen meters long and four meters tall, affect us so much more pleasantly and positively than short buildings do? The pleasant optical impressions are probably those that allow our eyes to glide along a building's body for some time.[2]

Gitai Weinraub took upon himself the didactic mission of fashioning public taste in order to prepare for the cultural reception of the elongated serial building. In fact, during the formative years after the establishment of the State, most leading figures of the professional community acted in a similar way to cast cultural content into the official building project. The spatial order that was dictated by the State's planning policy was stripped of its strategic and ideological motives and was often represented as the appropriate marker of the zeitgeist: a progressive architecture for a progressive state.

However, architects' discourse must not confuse the order of things: the serial block was, first and foremost, a political symptom; only later was it an exercise in design. Regardless of its architectural performance, the hegemony of the horizontal block—and of architectural horizontality in general—is both the chronic aftereffect and the most concise emblem of a regime of centralist control over lands, infrastructure, planning and legislative processes, production and construction systems, propaganda mechanisms, demographic engineering, and mobilization methods. A normative decentralized real estate market, based on private ownership and profit, does not produce low, elongated buildings. Only an authoritative state apparatus (or a proto-state monopolistic organization such as the Labor Federation) has the territorial drive and the administrative capability to seize and nationalize lands; to annul existing parcelizations; to disperse ad hoc "facts on the ground"; to lay wasteful infrastructure across the landscape; to devise random urban and architectural compositions; to dictate and regulate zoning and building standards; to duplicate, replicate, and mutate at every scale; to reduce building costs through height restrictions (saving on skeletons and elevators) and minimization of exterior surface area (the elongated building has fewer exterior elevations per square meter than several short buildings); and to charge baseline generic architecture with patriotism ("ingathering of the exiles") and welfare-state ("melting pot") rhetoric.

The local architects, especially those of the so-called "Generation of '48," spontaneously mobilized for the national project, most of them out of total self-identification with the edifice of the welfare state. The elementarity dictated by the State was perceived not as a temporary default, but as a moral stipulation and a professional challenge. Contrary to popular opinion, the block of the 1950s (as opposed, for instance, to the "contractor's apartment building" of the 1970s) was not the product of an architect-free market vernacular. Quite the contrary, the leading architects of the time were preoccupied with the development of simplified building details and with the virtuoso perfection of minimal apartments of 25, 28, 34, and 39 square meters, as well as "luxury apartments" of 60 and 65 square meters. The morphological limitations of the block, its uncompromising monolithic form and contextual indifference, rendered obsolete the traditional expertise of tectonic composition and narrowed graphic skill to the design of the block's façades and the drafting of the neighborhood site plan.

The topic of façades exposes the "double standards" of the block: its tendency to appear at once as an autonomous and detached object and as a segment of a continuous, randomly sliced bar. This ambivalence is due to the fact that the freestanding block has four façades, but only two expressive facets, or active interfaces ("air directions" in Hebrew). The short sides of the block are usually "blind," without openings—stumps of sorts that do not allow the longer façades to fold over and wrap the building. The flat, elongated frontality, as a rule facing north and south, is supposed to bear the identifying marks of the block (the series to which it belongs) and exhibit its (only) environmental sensibility: the various shading and ventilation devices that developed upon its surface in relation to the angles of the sun and directions of the wind (a local proficiency whose match could be found only in Brazilian architecture of the time, and which was lost almost entirely after 1967).

The exigencies of providing instant shelter for untold masses turned the Israeli project in its early years into a provisional scene of imported reused tents and makeshift tin or wood shacks assembled in so-called transition camps (Heb. *ma'abarot*) and labor camps dispersed across the country. The trauma of these notorious camps, many of which subsisted for over a decade, delayed the prospects of a local industry of prefabricated construction for several years. It also ruled out for good the option of light construction, which could be advantageous climatically and logistically and already had an epic precedent in the Zionist 1930s blitz-colonization model of the Tower and Stockade (see chapter "Communal").[3] From the late 1950s through the 1960s and much of the 1970s, cement was raved about as the "Israeli material": wet on-site concrete casting became a local expertise, and bulky *béton brut* buildings allegorized a collective sense of solidity, integrity, sensuality, and ingenuity (see chapter "Brutalism").

Parallel to the proliferation of customized (mostly public) Brutalist buildings, a routine of industrialization was taking over the local housing industry, placing Israel, if somewhat belatedly, abreast of other modernized countries. The scope of work involved in this put Israel at the top of world statistics on per capita construction starts.

The transition to industrially produced buildings and prefab methods at the end of the 1950s compensated for the lack of skilled workers, answered the need for the standardization of housing units and components, helped consolidate governmental multiyear plans, and bailed the country out of economic depression. During the 1960s the prefab plants supplied some 20 to 25 percent of the country's overall construction needs, and by 1973 prefab construction covered 44 percent of projects initiated by the Ministry of Housing.

In the southern new town of Eilat, due to its geographic remoteness and an acute shortage of construction workers, prefab plants were put up as early as 1958. In the course of the 1960s and 1970s, the pattern of setting up such local town-building plants (and providing jobs for the new-towners) was repeated in several new towns (Ashdod, Sderot, Ashkelon, Karmiel, etc.). The particular prefabrication methods, standard elements, and assembly techniques of these plants often determined the distinctive architectural detail and overall look of the towns.

The variety of prefab systems and scales—from detached walls to ready-made sanitary units, from experimental polygonal building components (see chapter "Structuralism") to entire cubic units—offered architects and contractors patented design and construction benchmarks and allowed a certain leeway for aesthetic judgment. Prefabrication, which had initially been identified with low-quality construction, was soon adopted by building companies catering to the middle class. However, profound changes in the local construction industry, emanating from the influx of a "cheap" Palestinian workforce in the aftermath of the 1967 War, brought about the decline of the closed prefab methods—those with all building components produced in the same factory—in the early 1970s. The open prefab method, in which different factories specialize in producing building components that can be integrated on-site in a conventional construction method, became dominant in Israel and remains in force in commercial construction to this day. ■

1 Munio Gitai Weinraub, “The Neighborhood’s Street: Its Planning and Image.” Cited without a date in Richard Ingersoll, *Munio Gitai Weinraub: Bauhaus Architect in Eretz Israel* (Milan: Electa, 1994), p. 226.

2 Gitai Weinraub, “Neighborhood’s Street,” cited in Ingersoll, *Munio Gitai Weinraub*, p. 224.

3 See also Sharon Rotbard, “Wall and Tower,” in *A Civilian Occupation: The Politics of Israeli Architecture*, ed. Rafi Segal and Eyal Weizman (Tel Aviv and London: Babel and Verso, 2003), pp. 39–56.

② Housing for military personnel, Kiryat Yam, 1957. Munio Gitai Weinraub, Al Mansfeld. Munio Gitai Weinraub archive.
③ Public housing for military personnel, Ramat Aviv, Tel Aviv, 1953–1955. Zeev Rechter, Moshe Zarhi, Yaacov Rechter. Photographer: Boris Carmi.
④ Public housing for military personnel, Ramat Aviv, Tel Aviv, 1953–1955. Zeev Rechter, Moshe Zarhi, Yaacov Rechter. Photographer: Boris Carmi.
⑤ Housing for military personnel, Kiryat Yam, 1957. Munio Gitai Weinraub, Al Mansfeld. Munio Gitai Weinraub archive.

③ ④

⑤

⑥

⑦

⑧ Public housing, Beersheba, 1955. A. Mittelman.
⑨ Housing block, 1960s. Plans and elevation. Moshe Zarhi. Zarhi archive.
⑩ Prefabricated housing blocks, Module-Beton company, Karmiel, 1965–1966. Moshe Zarhi. Photographer: Moshe Gross, Keren Or Studio. Zarhi archive.
⑪ Prefabricated housing blocks, Module-Beton company, Karmiel, 1965–1966. Moshe Zarhi. Photographer: Moshe Gross, Keren Or Studio. Zarhi archive.

⑥ Public housing, Ein Hayam, Haifa, early 1950s.
⑦ Prefabricated housing blocks, Eilat, mid-1960s. Photographer: Ami Erev.

⑧

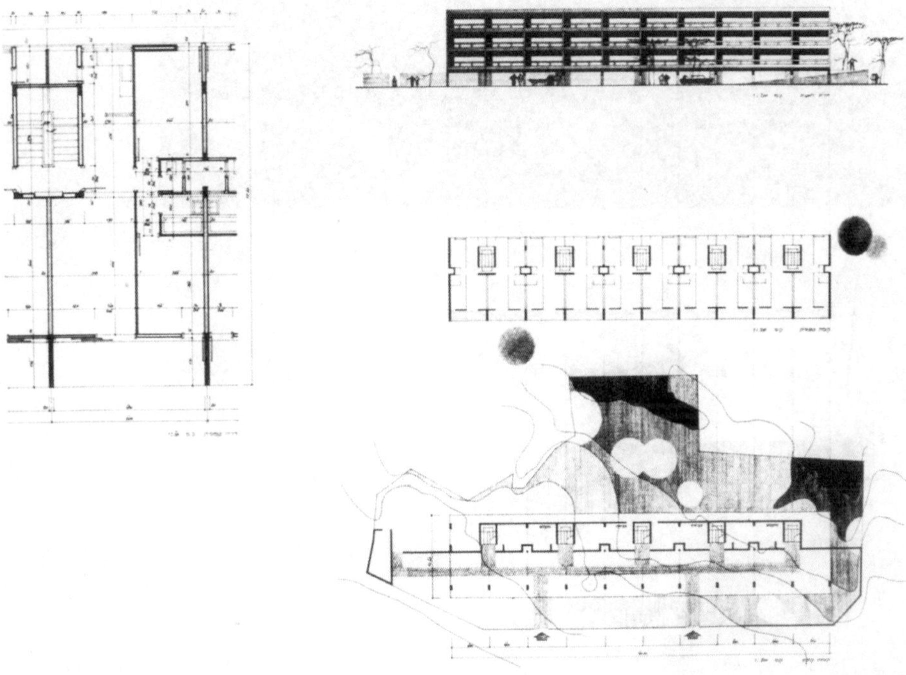

⑨

⑩ ⑪

⑫

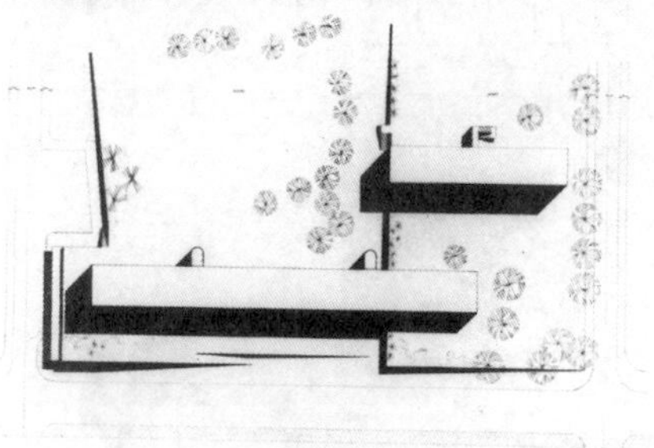

⑬

⑭

⑫ Kiron neighborhood, Kiryat Ono, 1962–1967. Israel Lotan. Lotan Archive.
⑬ Housing block, Ramat Aviv, early 1960s. Roof plan. Moshe Zarhi.
⑭ Housing block, Ramat Aviv, early 1960s. Moshe Zarhi. Zarhi archive.
⑮–⑯ Unidentified housing block, 1950s. North elevation.
⑰ Public housing block, Ashkelon, early 1960s. Nahum Zolotov.

⑮ ⑯

⑰

⑱

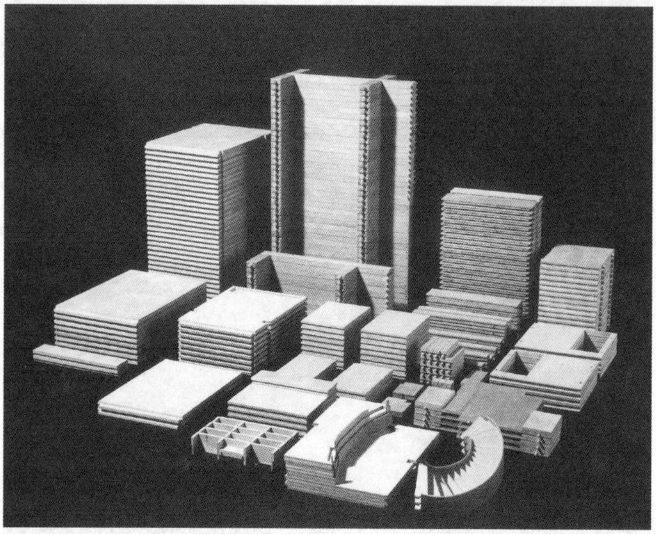

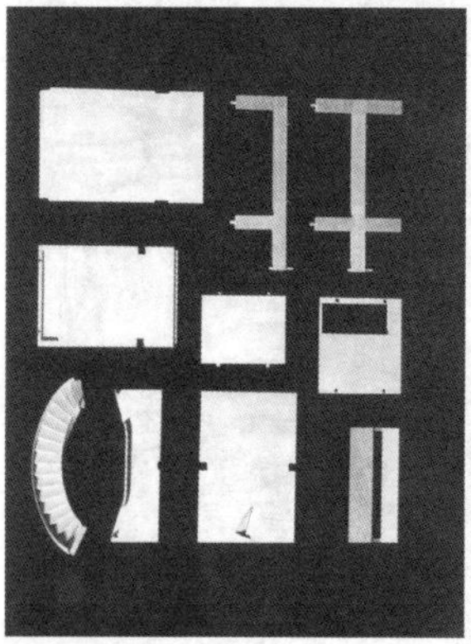

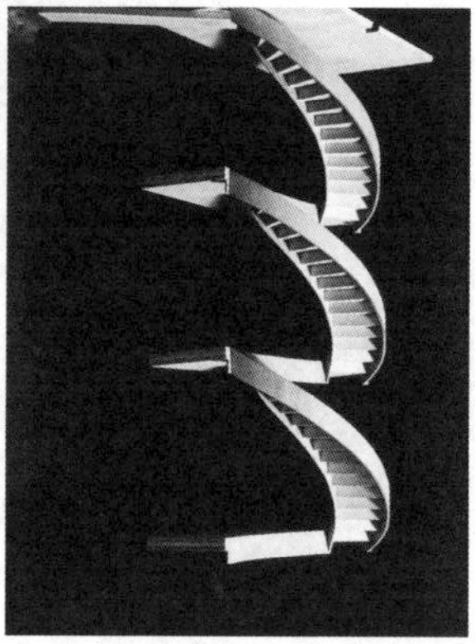

⑲ ⑳ ㉑ ㉒

㉓

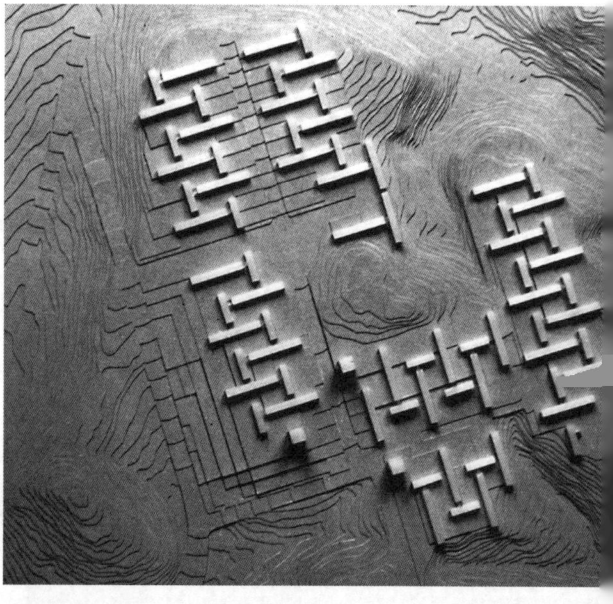

㉔

㉕

㉖

㉗

⑱ – ㉒ Kit of prefabricated elements, proposal for model housing, 1964. Yaacov Rechter, Moshe Zarhi. Prefab consultant: Y. Weinstein. Zarhi archive.
㉓ Prefabricated housing blocks under construction, Mitzpe Ramon, 1958. Zeev Rechter, Moshe Zarhi, Yaacov Rechter. Zarhi archive.

㉔ Prefabricated housing blocks, view from the courtyard, Mitzpe Ramon, 1958. Zeev Rechter, Moshe Zarhi, Yaacov Rechter. Zarhi archive.
㉕ Prefabricated housing blocks, view from the courtyard, Mitzpe Ramon, 1958. Zeev Rechter, Moshe Zarhi, Yaacov Rechter. Zarhi archive.
㉖ Tichnun ("Planning") company building housing in the Bonnet-Callad method, Eilat, 1958–1964.
㉗ Construction of prefab housing according to Ash-Trom system (the Ash-Trom Company was located in Ashdod and built the city), Ashdod, mid-1960s.

# Exemplary Neighborhoods

## The Housing Laboratories

Toward the end of the 1950s, the Housing Department of the Ministry of Labor initiated an experimental building campaign. Called the Model Housing (Heb. *shikun le'dugma*[1]) Campaign, its stated goal was to upgrade the quality of the affordable residential unit and to restructure the relationships between the various elements of the neighborhood. The campaign displayed an intrinsic, and rather productive, duality: on the one hand, an aspiration to create a new prototype, a standard module, a mold for serial reproduction; and on the other hand, a willingness to stray from the paradigm, or at least to test the limits of existing systems and methods by placing special planning efforts into a singular project. Such an institutional and controlled experimentalism is not foreign to the history of modern architecture; it can often be seen as a mediator between architectural expositions and fairs and conventional construction industries and real estate markets. In retrospect, one can say that even if in reality this format never proved itself as an efficient means for the dissemination of building prototypes, it did become a prestigious mechanism for minting the architectural icons of an era and for laying down new planning and design norms.

Israel has a rich history of experimental architecture, from makeshift Tower and Stockade settlements, collective and communal moshav and kibbutz settlements, and the Labor Townships and Cooperative Workers' Housing of the pre-State period to frontier settlements, paramilitary outposts, edge towns, desert mat-housing, polyhedral habitats, "ziggurats," terraced structures, and prefab vertical casbahs, all ostensibly adapted to the local climate, landscape, and means of production.

The Model Housing Campaign was innovative both in the scope of its projects and in its stipulation of coordination between teams of architects, most of them young Brutalists with little experience in housing. In contrast to its tentative local precursors, the explicit objective of this campaign was to redefine the very notion and perception of public housing and to establish new standards of building and dwelling.

Evidently, the limited means dictated the limits of the experimentation, and the projects executed in the framework of the Model Housing Campaign were still essentially a variation on an existing typology, that of the housing block (or "super-block") combined with a (locally) new typology, that of the "mat." In the 1959 issue of *Engineering and Architecture: The Union of Engineers and Architects in Israel* on the subject of public housing, editor Yaakov Ben-Sira wrote:

> Israel's image hangs on the housing endeavors of the last ten years and on the implementation plans for the coming years. This image is being shaped before our very eyes and it will be the pronouncement of both our achievements and our failures. [...] In the public-housing project, where the budget

> is restricted and the variety limited, a large dose of creative imagination is needed to solve the problem, and still it remains for the most part in the realm of experimentation.[2]

Later in the same article, Ben-Sira cast doubt on "buildings of 15 storeys and their like, super-blocks hundreds of meters in length," but agreed that "these experiments contributed greatly to bringing problems to light and presenting them within the constraints that will enable a correct and wise assessment."[3]

In his book *The Struggle for Independence: Israeli Architecture in the Twentieth Century*, Aba Elhanani mentioned several clusters from the early 1950s that, "even if they were not yet named model-housing projects," tried to deliver an architecture that went beyond the routine. These include the neighborhood of Maoz Aviv in Tel Aviv (1952), designed by the office of Rechter-Zarchi (a single unit with public areas, unique internal spaces, and distinctive apartments, which, according to Elhanani, marked a shift in the "anatomical structure" of the Israeli residential unit); the housing project in Kiryat Yovel in Jerusalem (1954), designed by David Anatol Brutzkus; the Engineers' Compound in Neve Sha'anan in Haifa (1955), designed by Dan Eytan; and the Neve Magen neighborhood in Ramat Hasharon for career military people (1956), designed by Rechter-Zarchi.[4]

However, the direct precedent and reference for the Israeli model-housing projects of 1959 was not local; it was actually the Interbau international building exhibition held in West Berlin in 1957. Fifty-three architects from thirteen countries participated in this exhibition, among them Alvar Aalto, Walter Gropius, Le Corbusier, and Jaap Bakema (who a few years later participated in design competitions in Tel Aviv, Jerusalem, and Ashdod), Oscar Niemeyer (whose résumé for the year 1964 is devoted almost entirely to projects in Israel; see dossier "Oscar Niemeyer's Exile" in chapter "Speculation"), and Pierre Vago (later editor of the journal *L'Architecture d'Aujourd'hui* and winner of the first prize in the planning competition for Ashdod). Interbau focused on the experimental construction of housing projects and public buildings in the Hansaviertel in Berlin, which had been severely damaged by bombing during World War II. The design of the neighborhood at the heart of Berlin was based on freestanding

① Hansaviertel, Interbau 1957, Berlin. Model.

vertical and horizontal apartment buildings and a compound of low detached and semi-detached homes, interspersed with green areas that blended into the Tiergarten park; pedestrian paths; an underground station with a small commercial center; an art academy; a library; an exhibition pavilion; and two churches.

Architect Aviya Hashimshoni, who in 1963 wrote about the state of architecture in Israel, found that at the beginning of the 1960s one could detect a greater freedom and daring in the design of the open public spaces of the residential neighborhoods. This was in contrast to the arbitrary "barrack-like" placement of buildings that characterized the housing blocks of the first decade of the State. According to Hashimshoni, the model-housing projects were the most outstanding example of architectural design as an integral framework for human cultural and social life:

> In Israel, too, three housing projects were built according to the international model-housing scheme. These were planned with lesser or greater freedom by a group of architects. In addition to these were many other projects that also attest to the search for new solutions in the organization of residential neighborhoods and in infusing new housing typologies.[5]

The three housing projects mentioned by Hashimshoni are the model-housing projects in Ramat Aviv and Beersheba and the residential neighborhood in Ramat Hadar in Haifa. Together, these were portrayed as breakthrough projects in that same 1959 public-housing issue of *Engineering and Architecture: The Union of Engineers and Architects in Israel.*

The master plan for the Ramat Aviv model-housing project was prepared in 1959 by architects Robert Bennett and Yitzhak Perlstein. Established as part of

②

the "building savings" initiative, it was built as the first part of neighboring unit B in north Tel Aviv, intended to include 500 housing units and all the essential public services. The Housing Department of the Labor Ministry, which had initiated the enterprise, encouraged experimentation with different building types. According to the issue of *Engineering and Architecture*, "each architect is given planning freedom and choice regarding the form of the apartment and building plans, materials, and construction methods."[6] The intentions were lofty. All of the infrastructure and landscaping was planned by a team of engineers from the Housing Department and the Municipality, as well as by private engineers.

Here, too, there was an attempt to take the field in new planning directions, which were acknowledged as both economically and aesthetically progressive in relation to the norm in public housing until that time. [...] One can see this attempt as both positive and justified, in terms both of the quality of planning and the diversity of buildings, which are integrated into a coherent architectural composition. But the most important contribution of this experiment will certainly be in the comparison between the different kinds of apartment types that were built in a single place under equal circumstances.[7]

The architects in Ramat Aviv had to adhere to a fixed budget for each apartment and to incorporate the buildings into the neighborhood master plan.

The purpose of this constraint was to maintain the unity of the entire housing project and not to give the impression of being an exhibition of unrelated experimental buildings.[8]

This refutation of the trappings of an exhibition (which contained an explicit criticism of Interbau) changes after a few lines:

> The Housing Department intends to furnish the various apartment types and to use the model-housing project as a temporary housing exposition, which is of great interest for those engaged in and concerned with housing enterprises, as well as a tool for educating the general public about housing culture.[9]

In effect, the model-housing project in Ramat Aviv had a didactic function not only for the local public, but also for many visitors from developing countries, including those who came to Israel for an international conference on public housing held in 1960.

Bennett and Perlstein were critical of the policy of replicating identical building patterns throughout the country. They tried to restore the role of the organic neighborhood in the process of social and cultural development—a role that had been evident, in their opinion, in the Cooperative Workers' projects of the Mandatory period. In order to ensure the success of the neighborhood, they would need sociological bait, as can be inferred from Bennett's words:

> Architectural planning is capable, notwithstanding the most limited budget, of making a place of residence more pleasant, more functional, and maybe even simply better. [...] We wanted to turn this neighborhood into a diverse, living organism. The population was comprised of the evacuees of Jaffa [i.e., Jewish immigrants initially settled in Arab "abandoned" property]. We therefore had to make an effort to bring in a socio-economically stronger population as well. [...] This was one of the places that people didn't want to move to at first. And then we suggested building clusters of two-family homes for artists. We thought that artists would bring in their wake a stronger population, socio-economically speaking. This went off very well. [...] The place became more desirable, and we could continue to build better houses.[10]

The critics were not convinced. In Hashimshoni's opinion, the model-housing project in Ramat Aviv primarily emphasized harmony between blocks and upgraded apartment types based on the tradition of apartment design that had developed in Israel—and showed no sign of new directions.[11] Elhanani also claimed in his book that the experiment in Ramat Aviv had failed: "Mansfeld admits that he is not satisfied with his work on that model-housing project. Neither is Rechter's office boasting about the results, despite the fact that they tried—perhaps for the first time in Israel—to build duplex apartments in a four-storey structure on columns." In a sarcastic aside, Elhanani added that dissatisfaction is a typical phenomenon when several respected architects meet to build alongside one another. He dubbed this phenomenon "prima-donna-ism."[12]

Immediately after planning for the Ramat Aviv project began, so did another experiment. According to architect Avraham Yasky:

> Within a short time it was decided that, politically speaking, [...] there was no way we could build a model-housing project in Tel Aviv without doing the same thing in a development town. Therefore it was decided to repeat this experiment in Beersheba.[13]

The model-housing project in Beersheba was planned as part of a large urban quarter on the western outskirts of the city. At the beginning of the 1950s, 650 immigrant apartments had been built in the older part of the neighborhood, most of them low-density two-family homes or row houses built to a low standard. The second group of buildings—those making up the model-housing project—were constructed between 1960 and 1964 and included about 1,000 housing units. These units were built to a higher standard and constituted the first stage of the area's transformation into one coherent residential neighborhood unit.

The planning team for the model-housing project in Beersheba was made up of six architectural firms.[14] The planners defined their goals as follows: to find solutions to the basic problems of neighborhood design, to propose prototypes for housing in the Negev Desert, and to stimulate growth in low-cost mass housing. In light of the limited budgets and schedule, and in order to propose an authoritative model for housing in the desert, secondary importance was given to the design of the apartments themselves.

Unlike its predecessor in Ramat Aviv, which adhered to the building-exhibition or competition model, the model neighborhood in Beersheba proposed an integrative systemic approach from the outset. The head of the team and planning coordinator, architect Avraham Yasky, clarifies the essential difference between the two approaches:

> The directives for this neighborhood in Beersheba were exactly like those in Tel Aviv. Six or seven architectural firms would make the same houses, only in Beersheba, and for new immigrants. The first decision in the planning team's initial discussion was that we do not want model houses. We want to create an environment in which no one will be able to tell who did what and in which the entire complex has meaning. [...] It seems to me that the experiment in Beersheba was successful primarily in this sense; we created a complete environment and not a collection of exemplary buildings, even though the buildings themselves are distinct.[15]

Soon after the urban planning and design work began, the architectural team realized that the program was too sparse. The 650 existing apartments in the older quarter, with the addition of the 550 apartments that they were asked

③

to plan, could not serve as a sufficient model for a desert neighborhood. The planners worked according to the assumption that it was possible and even necessary to significantly increase the footprint and the density; to reduce the green areas to a minimum; and to use the project to articulate a radical counter-response to the garden-city paradigm that had dictated the planning of the new towns in Israel, including desert cities such as Beersheba, in the 1950s. Based on this stance, they prepared a master plan for a neighborhood of some 3,000 families. In 1966 the plan was reassessed and adapted to the most recent master plan of Beersheba, the borders of the neighborhood were expanded, and it was determined that at the final stage it would contain 4,400 housing units (including the older quarter, which would undergo renovations) for about 16,000 people. Eventually, the directives regarding the size of the apartments were changed from 50 square meters to 70 and even 100.

Three architectural principles underlay the Beersheba model-housing project: demarcation by long four-storey "super-blocks" to create a sort of perimeter wall that clearly defines the borders of the neighborhood and its interior/exterior relations while also protecting it from desert sandstorms; design of a central axis that unites the social and public activities of the neighborhood; and spreading dense "mat" housing units between the super-blocks.

The "wall" buildings also dictated the subdivision of the project into three smaller neighborhoods, each of a scale that could be apprehended by the human gaze. Every sub-neighborhood was given a unique characterization and was to have its own high-rise landmark (these were not ultimately built). The "mat" was designed as an orthogonal weave with the goal of creating comfortable dwelling conditions in the Negev Desert: each of the housing units has a separate entrance at street level and is surrounded by a fence enclosing a small private garden and an agricultural plot. The second floor of apartments alternately covers the neighborhood paths, achieving a shading effect without having to rely upon trees, which were hard to grow and cultivate in the Negev climate.

The Beersheba model-housing project was received with great enthusiasm, in particular within the architectural community, where it gained broad international exposure and was hailed as one of the important achievements of the era in the field of public housing. According to a sociological survey by the Housing Ministry after the neighborhood was populated, the "mats" enjoyed prestige and popularity in Beersheba, despite the small size of the apartments. The idea resonated, and similar attempts were made in the new towns of Eilat, Karmiel, and Ashkelon. Architect Aviya Hashimshoni praised the departure from the garden-city tradition and the attempt to reach an urban articulation that was suited to the region:

> In this project we see a new eclectic impulse manifested in the use of two kinds of desert construction, in particular that of North Africa—the "vertical

casbah," which is made of multi-storeyed buildings arranged like a fortress wall, and the "horizontal casbah," made of low, densely arranged houses, which sometimes even hover over the streets.[16]

It should be noted that this allegedly new regionalist sensibility of Israeli architects did not rely on any local environmental research or inquisitive observation of the neighboring Arab or Bedouin building types and methods, but rather on their heightened awareness of international architectural fashions of the day. The "vertical casbah" is none other than the Corbusian Unité d'Habitation, whose innovative plans and cross-sections, as well as Brutalist skeleton and textures, were studied with diligence and transposed, almost verbatim, to the desert city of Beersheba. The Israeli "horizontal casbah" reenacts, or at best reinterprets, the quasi-anthropological studies of members of Team 10, primarily Aldo van Eyck and Candilis-Josic-Woods, who in the early 1950s produced designed variations on North African, Mediterranean, and Middle Eastern indigenous urban and rural cluster formations.

The fleeting mirage of the Beersheba model-housing project—the prospect of a top-down avant-gardism that effortlessly emanates the zeitgeist and conveys the genius loci—dissipated as forcefully as it appeared. The neighborhood was never completed according to the plans. The high-rises, as well as some of the super-blocks, were not built at all. Some of the "mat" compounds did retain their prestige, but most of them devolved into slums, cluttered with the improvised building additions of residents who had either not read the manifestos of Team 10 or did not particularly care about the concept of the Israeli team. The "quarter-kilometer" super-block, a colossal desert ship housing 135 families on four stairwells, was defaced and reluctantly transformed into an immigrant dormitory. Its architect, Avraham Yasky, described it in retrospect as "a conscious attempt that failed completely."[17] In the year 2000, the bridge that connected this structure to the "mat" was also destroyed, thus severing once and

④

for all the "architectural axis" whose purpose was to connect the Corbusian apartment block, "which adheres very seriously to the elongated lines of the horizon," and the labyrinthine casbah, "which seems to spill the entire built-up area onto the topography."[18]

The predisposition for maximum density which characterized the model-housing project in Beersheba was replaced by the principle of "concentration without density" in the Ramat Hadar neighborhood in Haifa (which was called not a "model-housing project," but a "new residential district"). The neighborhood was designed by a team of architects[19] and built on an isolated extension off the northern Carmel ridge. The plan included a ring of tall buildings which were tucked into the slope, leaving the top of the mountain free for future public facilities. The plan's uniqueness rests in the fact that it is based almost entirely on "vertical slabs"—large apartment buildings, each constituting a kind of autonomous neighborhood connected by an entry bridge to the perimeter road system. The use of blocks of tall buildings on the sloping topography of Ramat Hadar was meant to enable the opening of the road to the sea view; the clearing of vast areas for parks and forestation; and the provision of all of the apartments with a visual field that is not disrupted by neighboring houses. Efficient central services were to be facilitated in the buildings: elevators, the supply of hot water and gas, waste removal.

The actual result was a collection of oversized buildings whose lowest floors were placed below street level, doubtfully fulfilling the initial promise of the project: "the team of architects that prepared the plans aspired to create a coherent urban residential neighborhood and by no means a *shikun* or a row of *shikunim*."[20]

In order to achieve the greatest possible diversity, the housing units—some 14,000 in all—were divided into several building types: high-rises of fifteen to

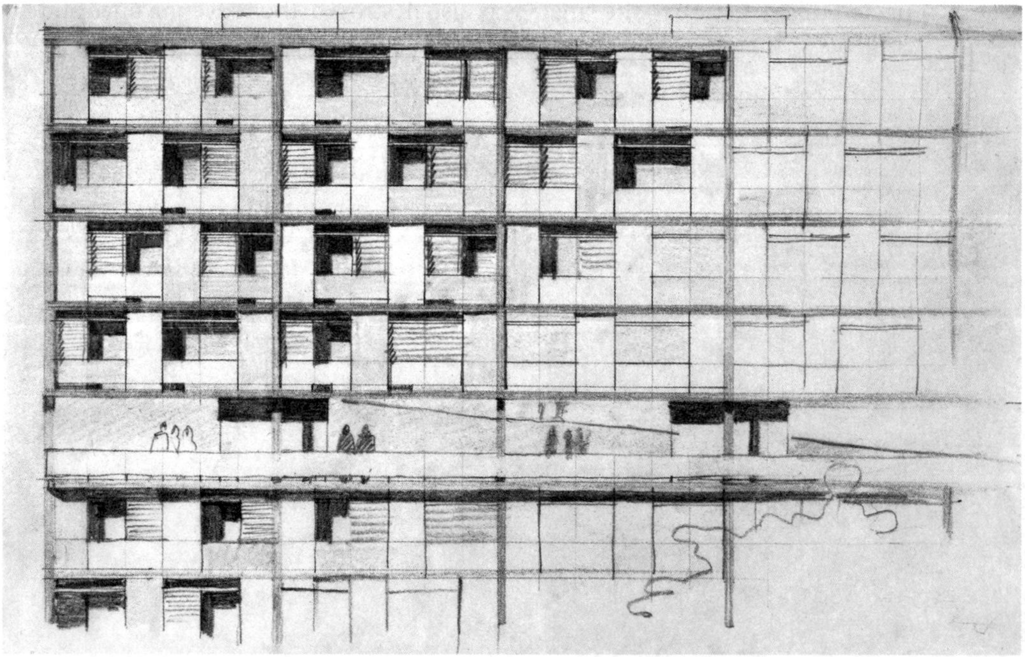

(5)

seventeen storeys, mid-rise buildings of twelve storeys, and eight-storey buildings with passageways connecting the buildings on the middle floor, as well as "mat" types of one or two storeys.

The "new residential district" of Ramat Hadar influenced the design of housing projects in the steep topography of Haifa and Jerusalem during the 1960s and 1970s. These projects were generally built to lower construction standards, but used the idea of having the middle level of the building at street level, thus dividing the building in two, so as to save on elevators (an eight-storey building thus became two four-storey buildings, which do not necessitate an elevator).

In retrospect, the experiments of the model-housing projects may seem anecdotal. Their main contribution was in stimulating local public debate and professional discourse around the question of public housing, and in setting new polemical building types and work methods against the automatism of the State housing apparatus. At a professional conference on the subject held in 1972, architect Al Mansfeld, who participated in both the Ramat Aviv and Ramat Hadar projects, raised doubts about the conceptual validity of the model-housing venture and about the possibility of "repeating this exercise":

> What is this method, after all? It is not really clear whether these are experimental neighborhoods or model neighborhoods, and there is a big difference between the two. You build an experimental neighborhood in order to check some things, and then you build them in an unauthorized, experimental way—and you draw conclusions. If you build a model neighborhood, then you are always confronted with the desire to do something exemplary and emblematic. We shouldn't forget that this neighborhood (Ramat Aviv) was built in 1959, two years after Interbau, the foundation stone for model neighborhoods, was built in Berlin. It was built according to the same format. The trends were exactly the same trends, meaning, a group of planners defined some planning framework, so that they wouldn't be bored and so that each of them would show their strengths and thereby prove to the Housing Ministry that things can be done better. [...] If I may dare say so, the results in Ramat Aviv were very similar to those in Berlin. Part of it looks pretty bleak. One thing is clear: this is by no means a planned neighborhood or a part of a city; it is a collection of forms, of images, perhaps of methods.[21]

Successful or not, this "collection of forms" would remain iconic for the Israeli architectural community as decaying memorabilia of a transgressive defiance against the State apparatus, carried out under its patronage. ■

1 The Hebrew term shikun le'dugma refers both to model housing and to exemplary neighborhood projects.

2 Yaakov Ben-Sira, "A Portrait of the Israeli Public Housing," *Engineering and Architecture: The Union of Engineers and Architects in Israel* 7–8 [in Hebrew] (1959), p. 172.

3 Ibid.

4 Aba Elhanani, *The Struggle for Independence: Israeli Architecture in the Twentieth Century* [in Hebrew] (Tel Aviv: Ministry of Defense, 1998), p. 71.

5 Aviya Hashimshoni, "Architecture," in Binyamin Tamuz, ed., *Israeli Art* [in Hebrew] (Tel Aviv: Massada, 1963), pp. 213–246; Hashimshoni writes that Interbau took place in 1958, and he mentions another building exposition that took place in Berlin in 1927, which also had a great influence on the construction of housing projects. He was apparently referring to the Weissenhof neighborhood, which was built in 1927 in Stuttgart, and not in Berlin.

6 Ben-Sira, "Portrait of the Israeli Public Housing," p. 180.

7 Ibid.

8 Ibid.

9 Ibid.

10 Robert Bennett, in "Discussion on the Subject of Residential Neighborhoods," conference of the Union of Engineers and Architects in Israel. The discussion was published in the first issue of the journal *Adrikhalut* ("Architecture") in 1973. Cited in Aba Elhanani, *The Struggle for Independence: Israeli Architecture in the Twentieth Century* [in Hebrew] (Tel Aviv: Ministry of Defense, 1998), p. 71.
The mobilization of artists as generators of property reuse and gentrification was extensively practiced in Israel during the phase of populating the "abandoned property" of Arab villages and neighborhoods (see chapter "Ruins of War").

11 Hashimshoni, "Architecture."

12 Elhanani, *Struggle for Independence.*

13 Avraham Yasky, in "Discussion on the Subject of Residential Neighborhoods," *Adrikhalut* [in Hebrew] (1973), pp. 4–9.

14 Avraham Yasky and Amnon Alexandroni; Nahum Zolotov and Daniel Havkin; Dov Karmi, Zvi Meltzer, and Ram Karmi; the "Tichnun" company (Theodor Kisselov and Aharon Bareli); M. Chechik and B. Conforti (the Housing Department's Negev team); and landscaping architects Zvi Miller and Moshe Blum.

15 Yasky, "Discussion on the Subject of Residential Neighborhoods."

16 Hashimshoni, "Architecture."

17 Avraham Yasky, in a recorded discussion with the author, 1999.

18 Ibid.

19 Including Shemi Almosnino, Shlomo Gilad, Aviya Hashimshoni, Munio Gitai Weinraub, Daniel Havkin, and Al Mansfeld.

20 *Engineering and Architecture: The Union of Engineers and Architects in Israel* 7–8 (1959), p. 191.

21 Al Mansfeld, in "Discussion on the Subject of Residential Neighborhoods," *Adrikhalut* [in Hebrew] (1973), pp. 4–9.

② Members of the international conference on public housing tour the exemplary housing project in Ramat Aviv, Tel Aviv, 1960. Robert Bennett, Yitzhak Perlstein.
③–⑤ Exemplary housing, Ramat Hadar, Haifa, 1959–1963. Munio Gitai Weinraub, Al Mansfeld.
⑥ Exemplary neighborhood, Beersheba, 1956. Preliminary model. Avraham Yasky, Amnon Alexandroni, Ram Karmi, Nahum Zolotov, Daniel Havkin, Bitush Comforty, Theodore Kisselov, Meir Chechik, Aaron Bareli, David Zaslavsky, Zvi Miller.
⑦ Exemplary neighborhood, Beersheba, 1956. Final model. Avraham Yasky, Amnon Alexandroni, Ram Karmi, Nahum Zolotov, Daniel Havkin, Bitush Comforty, Theodore Kisselov, Meir Chechik, Aaron Bareli, David Zaslavsky, Zvi Miller.
⑧ Exemplary neighborhood, Beersheba, 1956. Master plan. Avraham Yasky, Amnon Alexandroni, Ram Karmi, Nahum Zolotov, Daniel Havkin, Bitush Comforty, Theodore Kisselov, Meir Chechik, Aaron Bareli, David Zaslavsky, Zvi Miller.

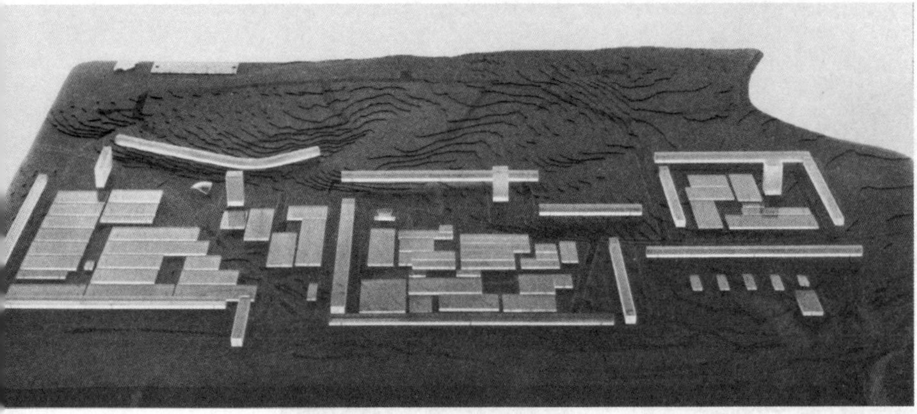

⑥

⑦

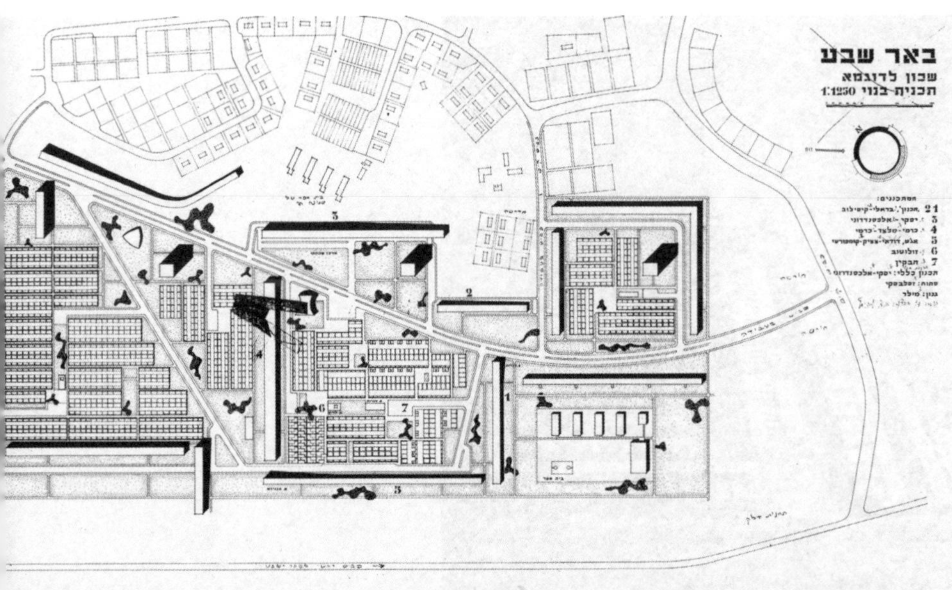
באר שבע
שכון לדוגמא
תכנית בנוי 1:1250
N
המתכננים:
3 יסקי-אלכסנדרוני
4 כרמי-מלצר-כרמי
6 זולוטוב
7 חבקין
תכנון כללי: יסקי-אלכסנדרוני
גנון: מילר

⑧

⑨

⑩

⑪

⑫

⑬

⑨ Exemplary neighborhood, Beersheba, 1956–1959. View at perimeter block.
⑩ Exemplary neighborhood, Beersheba, 1956–1959. View at mat housing.
⑪ Mat housing, exemplary neighborhood, Beersheba, 1956–1959. Nahum Zolotov, Daniel Havkin. Aerial photo by Nahum Zolotov.
⑫ Exemplary neighborhood, Beersheba, 1956–1959. View from perimeter block.
⑬ Mat housing, exemplary neighborhood, Beersheba, 1956–1959. Nahum Zolotov, Daniel Havkin.

⑭ “Quarter-kilometer” super-block, Beersheba, 1959. Avraham Yaky, Amnon Alexandroni.
⑮ “Quarter-kilometer” super-block, Beersheba, 1959. Floor plans. Avraham Yasky, Amnon Alexandroni.
⑯ “Quarter-kilometer” super-block, Beersheba, 1959. Avraham Yasky, Amnon Alexandroni.
⑰ “Quarter-kilometer” super-block, Beersheba, 1959. Detail. Avraham Yasky, Amnon Alexandroni.
⑱ “Quarter-kilometer” super-block, Beersheba, 1959. Staircase. Avraham Yasky, Amnon Alexandroni.

⑭

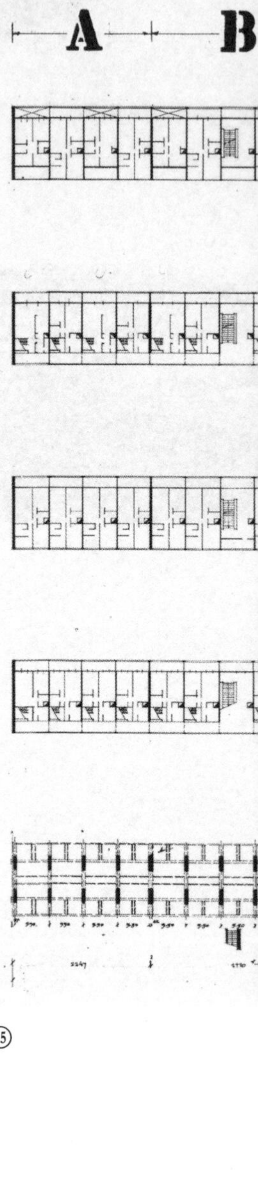


⑮

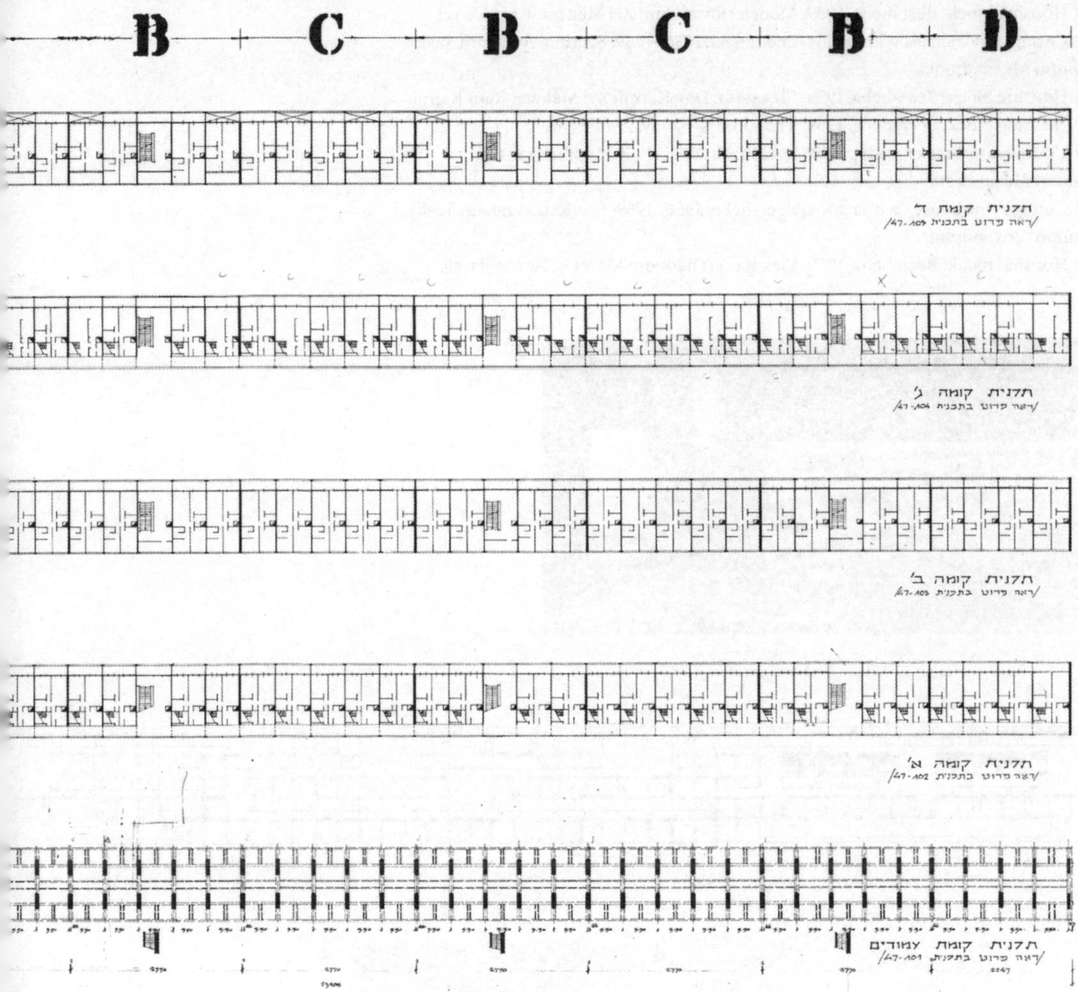
B C B C B D
תכנית קומת ד'
/ראה פרוט בתכנית 47-105/
תכנית קומה ג'
/ראה פרוט בתכנית 47-104/
תכנית קומה ב'
/ראה פרוט בתכנית 47-103/
תכנית קומה א'
/ראה פרוט בתכנית 47-102/
תכנית קומת עמודים
/ראה פרוט בתכנית 47-101/

⑯

⑰

⑱

⑲ Housing block, Beersheba, 1959. Model. Dov Karmi, Zvi Meltzer, Ram Karmi.
⑳ Cottage row houses with patios, Beersheba, 1956–1959. Section. Avraham Yasky, Amnon Alexandroni.
㉑ Housing block, Beersheba, 1959. Elevation. Dov Karmi, Zvi Meltzer, Ram Karmi.
㉒ Housing block, Beersheba, 1959. Theodore Kisselov, Aaron Bareli.
㉓ Cottage row houses with patios, Beersheba, 1956–1959. Avraham Yasky, Amnon Alexandroni.
㉔ Cottage row houses with patios, Beersheba, 1956–1959. Section. Avraham Yasky, Amnon Alexandroni.
㉕ Housing block, Beersheba, 1959. Elevation. Theodore Kisselov, Aaron Bareli.

⑲

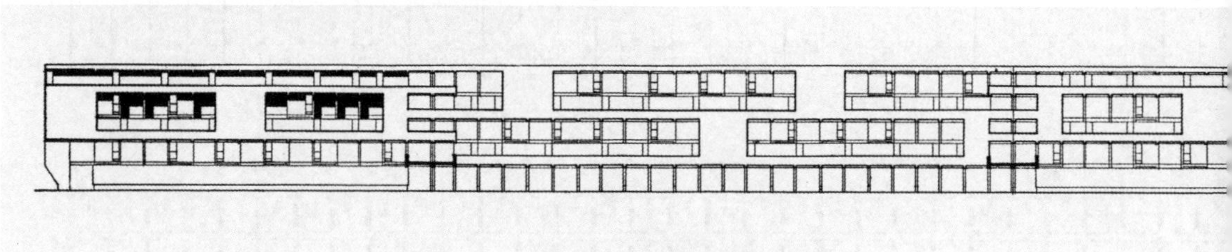

㉒

㉕
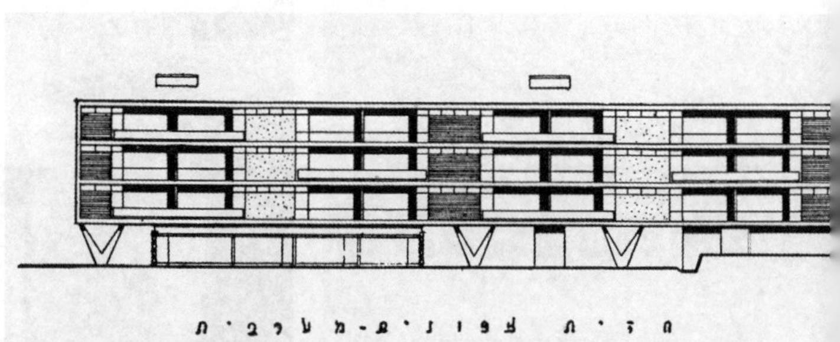

⑳

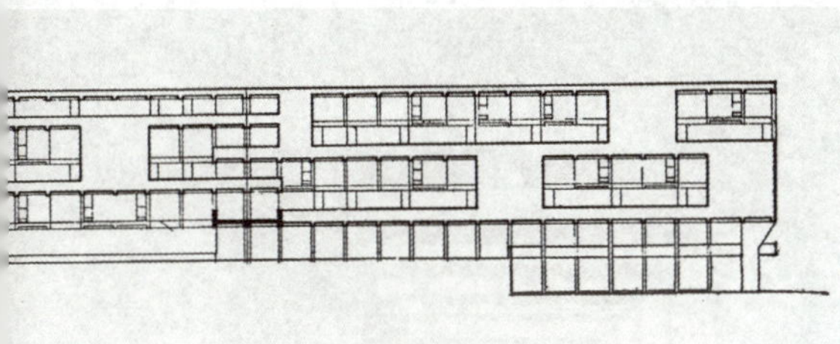

㉑

㉓

㉔

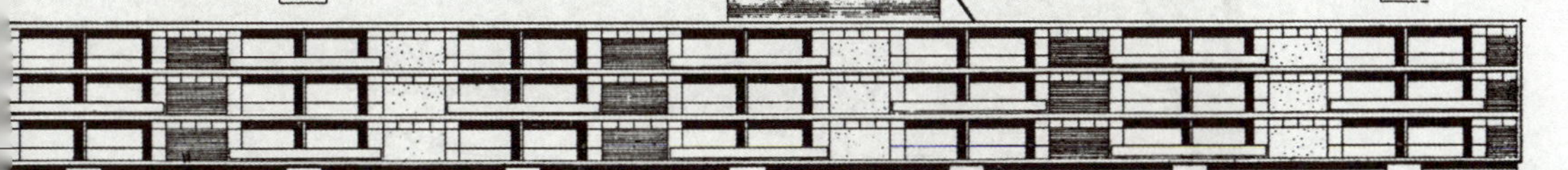

㉖ Alley and synagogue, exemplary neighborhood, Beersheba, 1956–1959. Nahum Zolotov, Daniel Havkin.
㉗ Mat housing, exemplary neighborhood, Beersheba, 1956–1959. Nahum Zolotov, Daniel Havkin.
㉘ "Housing Block 40," Beersheba, 1956–1959. Avraham Yasky, Amnon Alexandroni.
㉙ Mat housing, exemplary neighborhood, Beersheba, 1956–1959. Plans. Nahum Zolotov, Daniel Havkin.
㉚ Mat housing, exemplary neighborhood, Beersheba, 1956–1959. Nahum Zolotov, Daniel Havkin.

㉗

㉖

㉘

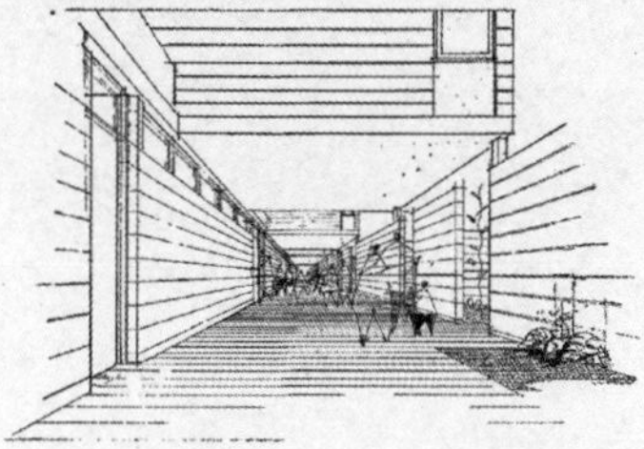

Pedestrian Alley מראה שביל הולכי הרגל

## 6 ארכ׳ ד. חבקין
D. Havkin, Arch.

הבניה הנמוכה מבוססת על עקרון של „פתוח — שטיח״. הכניסה ל־בתים היא משביל של הולכי רגל ברוחב 3 מ׳. מצד אחד של השביל בית בן קומה אחת ומעברו השני בית בין שתי קומות. חלק מהבית בן שתי הקומות עובר מעל השביל ויוצר הצללה (ראה ציור למעלה מ־ימין). חצרות הבתים סגורות בקיר היוצר שטח פרטי לכל בית.

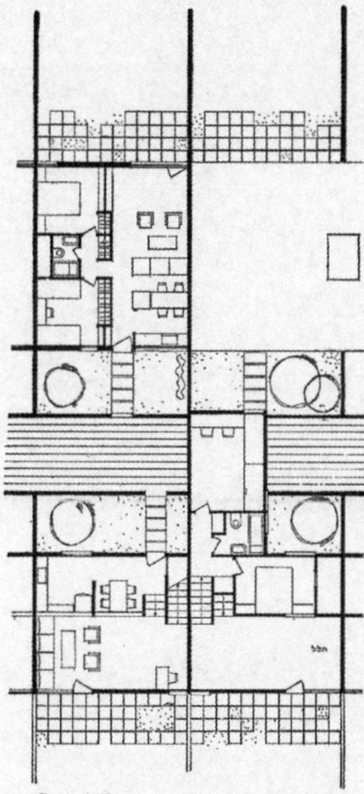

Ground Floor תכנית קומת קרקע 1:200

Upper Floor תכנית קומה עליונה 1:200

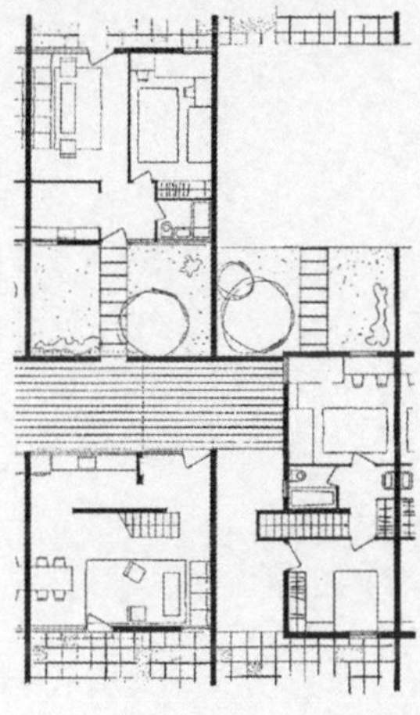

## 7 ארכ׳ נ. זולוטוב
N. Zolotov, Arch.

General Plan, Carpet Developement תכנית כללית של השטיח

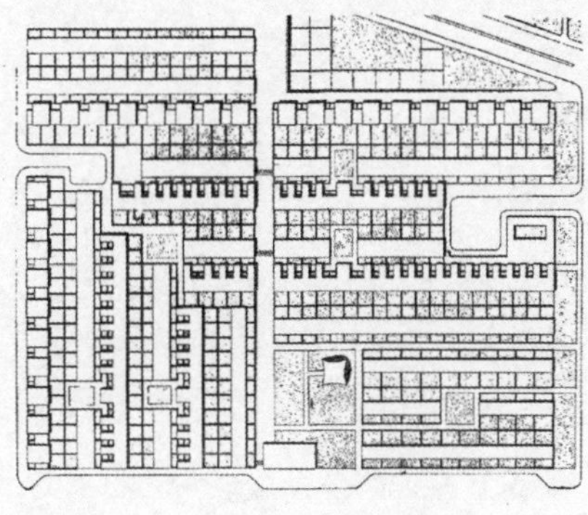

(29)

(30)

# Hyper-Urbanism

①

## The Planning of Ashdod

In the context of the Israeli welfare state of the 1950s and 1960s, the planning of Ashdod introduced the most radical urban model possible—that of the entrepreneurial city. Initially planned from 1950 to 1952 as a new port town on the Mediterranean according to the national master-plan directives, it was redesigned from 1957 to 1959 according to the prescription of a group of Jewish-American investors who began to look into Ashdod as a site for their real estate activities. The investors' request for a franchise to build and develop the new city in the open dunes was supported in principle by the Planning Department and enjoyed full sympathy within the Treasury. Eliezer Brutzkus, a former member of Sharon's team at the Planning Department, took a critical view of the way events unfolded:

> They were given a franchise territory of 40,000 dunam—too large an area even in the best case scenario for the city's future growth and development. The contract vested the group with broad authority as the "Ashdod Development Corporation" while burdening it with very few obligations. Meanwhile, it was the government of Israel that would in effect remain responsible for development and implementation. The contract left a large opening for quick profits for the company through the sale of real estate properties while [requiring] little investment in development.[1]

① Developers and planners surveying the site of the new town of Ashdod, 1956.
② Ashdod, master plan drafts, 1949, 1959, 1969. Yitzhak Perlstein, Arieh Dudai. Ashdod's port, 1963.

Just as the area of the city allotted in the franchise was excessive, so was the long-term urban program. The demographic goal of 250,000 residents, which governed the planning, surpassed any reasonable demographic forecast for twenty, thirty, or even forty years. Brutzkus once again expressed his skepticism:

> The results of this flight of fancy regarding the end goal are clearly felt in the city plan—whether it be by grabbing unnecessary areas as reserves for urban development, or placing the city center at too great a distance from the port and from the already existing city. If the town center is built in the planned location it will be destined to remain exogenous to the existing city.[2]

Architects Yitzhak Perlstein and Arieh Dudai, who were entrusted with the preparation of Ashdod's master plan, defined it as "an attempt to liberate ourselves from the concept of the garden city" that was still favored at the time, and instead to propose "a contiguous urban fabric, defined quarter by quarter and distinguished by its system of roads and traffic principles."[3] Accordingly, the new city was planned based on an orthogonal gridiron system of longitudinal roads that defined the various residential neighborhoods and quarters of the city, and a secondary system of streets within the neighborhoods and quarters. The plan's approach was to disconnect the fast automobile traffic, which would move along the long axes, from the slow traffic running along the smaller

②

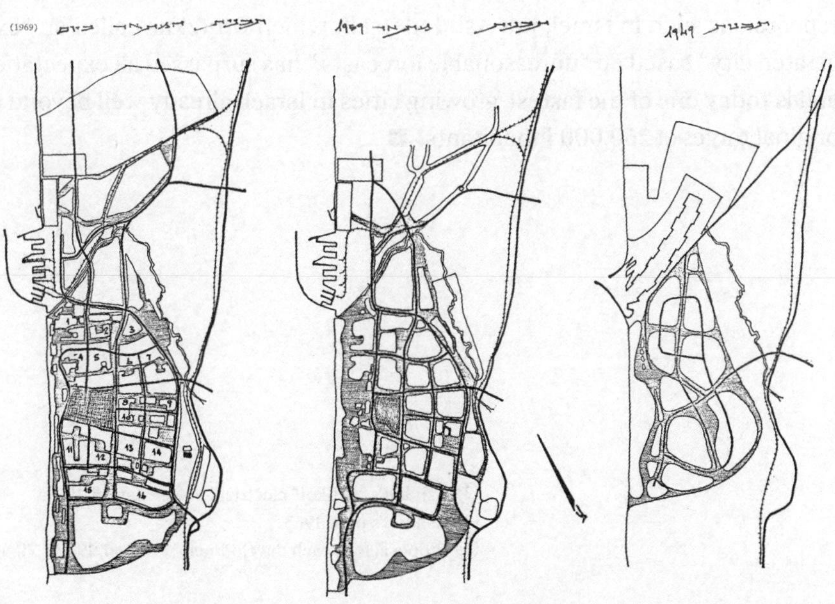

streets. The network of longitudinal streets defined sixteen fairly high-density residential quarters of 12,000 to 20,000 residents each (the size of a typical 1950s new town). Each quarter had its own subcenter, and the activity in the quarter was aimed inward.

The city center remained unplanned, awaiting the launch of an international competition in 1965. The competition aroused great international interest and the enthusiastic participation of leading architects from around the world. The winning proposal, submitted by Jean Ginsberg and Pierre Vago (editor of *L'Architecture d'Aujourd'hui*), imported to Ashdod the principles and the spirit of the "charter" that had been adopted at the eighth CIAM congress in 1951.[4] Ginsberg's and Vago's project was never implemented, but the remarkable international competition and the subsequent professional and public debate on urbanism in Israel put an end to the era of the idealized garden city with its socialist and environmentalist penchant and marked a new horizon of free enterprise and corporate architecture within the cities and around their ever-sprawling suburbia. Curiously, the precedent of the generic city was not repeated as such in Israel, but Ashdod itself, which Brutzkus called an "exaggerated city" based on "unreasonable forecasts," has surpassed all expectations and is today one of the fastest-growing cities in Israel, already well beyond the original target of 250,000 inhabitants. ■

③ Ashdod's "Eshkol" electrical power station, 1959.
④ Ashdod's port, 1963.
⑤ Proposal for beach development, Ashdod, 1960s. Yitzhak Perlstein.

1 Eliezer Brutzkus, "Ashdod: An Idea and Its Materialization," *Bulletin of the Environmental Planners' Union* 10 [in Hebrew] (1969).

2 Ibid.

3 Cited in ibid.

4 The text of the winning proposal by Ginsberg and Vago reads as follows:
The problem of the "core" of the new city, namely, that it is created out of nothing, is without a doubt one of the most difficult for the urban planner to solve. Our plan is guided by three basic principles:
– Dynamic density: Analyzing the very few achievements of the past decades, we immediately see that one of the reasons for the failure [of cities] is insufficient density. [...] One can argue about the advantages and disadvantages of "green cities" or of "monumental cities," but one cannot deny that the failure of a "core" is due to lack of density—"masses" of people pulling, reviving, and creating a feeling of the city.
– A human scale: [...] When architects plan the centers of cities, they often exaggerate in terms of scale. We must always remember that the measure has always been and will always be—the human being. [...] We do not create a city so that it may be observed from an airplane, but for the good of its inhabitants, who will look at it at eye-level, 1.60 meters from the ground.
– Collaboration: When an urban planner prepares plans for the center of a new city, he often simply thinks like an architect. He sees his city, or its center, as the work of an architect, while in fact it is the collective work of many architects. In order for it to have a real life, a city center of hundreds of thousands of inhabitants must be a collective work. The general plan must enable, prepare, and encourage cooperative work.
From: "Summary of the Town Planning Competition for the Development of the Central Area of Ashdod" (Hebrew/English booklet, Tel Aviv: "Ashdod" Company, 1965).

(5)

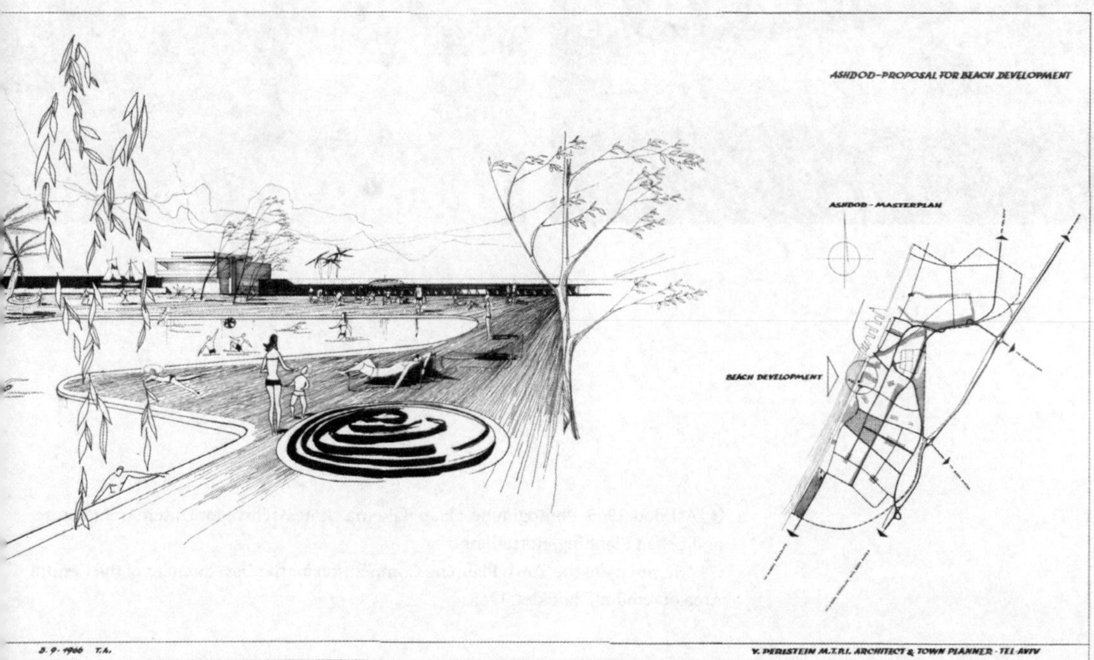

⑥

⑥ Ashdod, 1965. Photographer: Jaap Bakema. State Archive for Dutch Architecture and Urban Planning, Rotterdam.
⑦ "Summary of the Town Planning Competition for the Development of the Central Area of Ashdod," booklet, 1965.

# SUMMARY OF THE TOWN PLANNING COMPETITION FOR THE DEVELOPMENT OF THE CENTRAL AREA OF ASHDOD

The open competition for a town-planning scheme for the development and building of the central area of the town of Ashdod was announced on January 1965 by the State of Israel and the Ashdod Company, in agreement with the central competitions committee of the Association of Engineers and Architects in Israel and with the approval of the U.I.A. This competition was an open one with invitees, and the participants included architects, town-planners and engineers (six from Israel and four from abroad).

Ashdod, bordering on the Mediterranean coast in the southern part of Israel, is a new town established on the former site of an historical city with a rich past. At the time of the birth of the State of Israel there was nothing in the locality but shifting sand-dunes. Today the town numbers 25,000 inhabitants and is planned for a population of 350,000, but its economic and regional features may well turn it into a city of half a million or even more. The deep-water harbour, the construction of which is proceeding rapidly, is intended to serve the requirements of the intensive development of the industry, quarries and agriculture in central and southern Israel.

Ashdod, the sea-gate to Jerusalem and the south of the country, is situated half-way between Tel-Aviv — the largest city in Israel — and Ashkelon — the southernmost city on the Mediterranean coast — abont 50 kms. west of Jerusalem. In addition to its function as a port and industrial town, it serves as the centre of a fertile and populous agricultural region.

The master plan of Ashdod is based on two road-systems: a network of arterial roads delimiting residential quarters and other districts, and a system of secondary roads passing through and linking together the various districts. The city centre is situated at the geographical centre of the city, at the intersection of its two major traffic axes: the north-south axis, linking the centre with the industrial zone and the port (and also forming the main entry to the city from the north), and the east-west axis, linking the transport centre to the city (and also forming the main entry from the south-west).

Prof. Y. Ailon    Mr. I.M. Pei    Mr. O. Ben Ami

חבר השופטים דן ביולי 1965, ב־31 תכניות שהובאו לפניו. הפרסים והקניות נקבעו פה אחד.

The purpose of the competition was to obtain a town-planning proposal for the development of the central area of the new city, within the framework of the approved master plan of the city. This centre will be an administrative, financial, commercial, cultural and recreational meeting place for the inhabitants of the town and the region, and for the port. The solution was required to be practical and economically feasible, to provide for the possibility of immediate implementation of the first stage, and to constitute the framework for the future development of the centre.

The scope of the competition included the urban centre with its services; dwellings with their services, and their integration in the central area; a park linking the centre with the sea; a stretch of bathing beach.

The urban centre and its services include: retail trade (50,000 square metres); administration and office services (100,000 square metres); religious, cultural, and recreational services; public buildings and the central bus station of the city.

Dwellings in the centre (7,000 apartments with services), most of which should be integrated with the urban centre, together constituting a quarter of intense activity, without the character of merely another residential neighbourhood.

A park (40 hectares), integrating the beach with the centre.

The jury considered 31 plans which were submitted to them. The prizes and purchases were unanimously decided (July 1965).

⑧

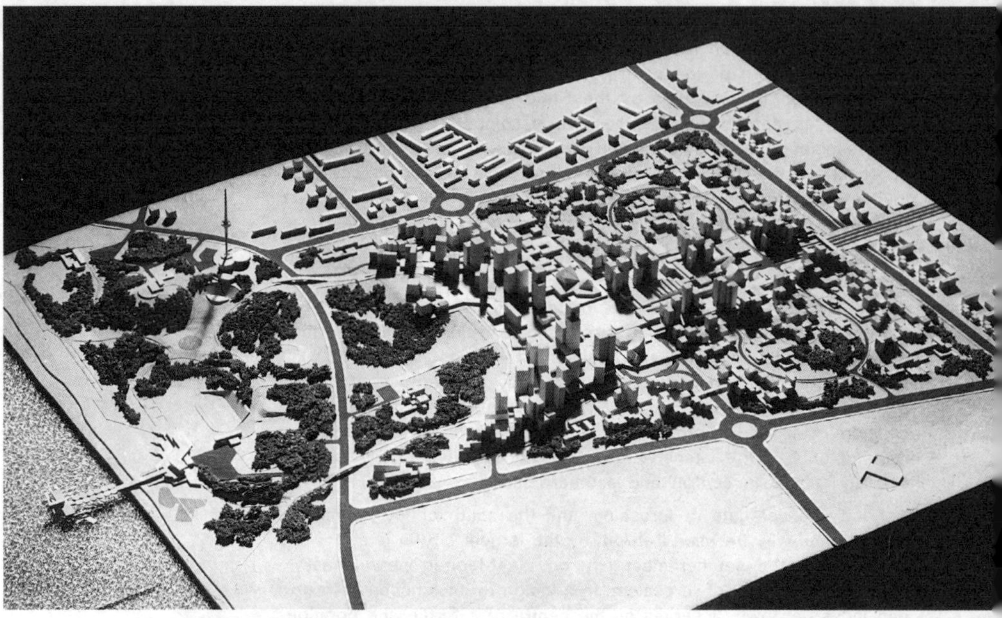

⑨

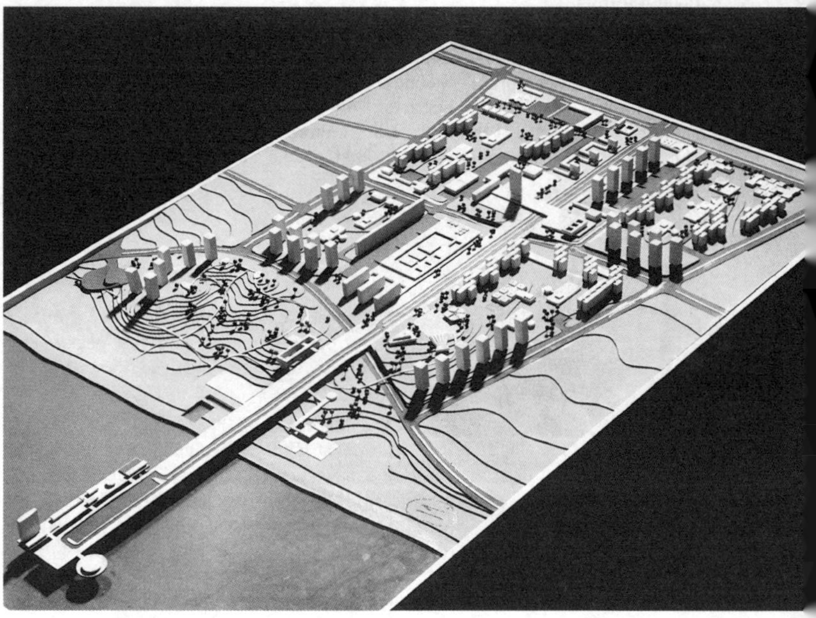

⑧ Winning entry for the town-planning competition for the development of the central area of Ashdod, 1965. J. Ginsberg and P. Vago, in association with M. Van Treeck (France).
⑨ Entry for the town-planning competition for the development of the central area of Ashdod, 1965.

⑩

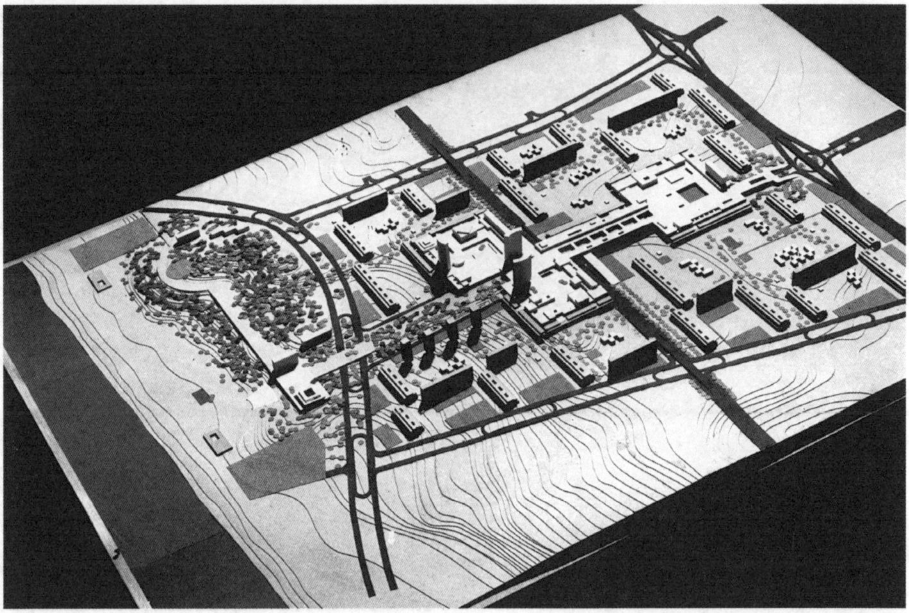

⑪

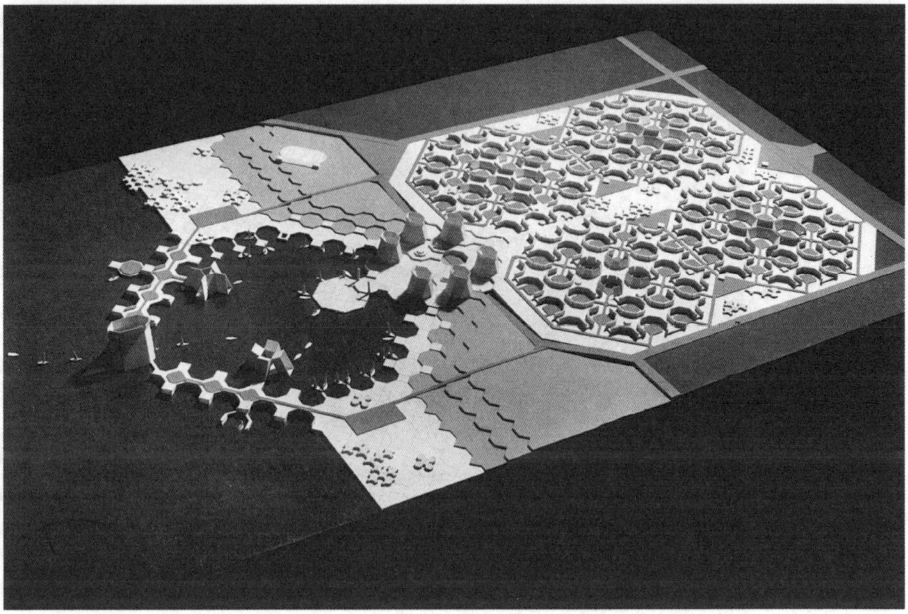

⑩ Entry for the town-planning competition for the development of the central area of Ashdod, 1965.
⑪ Town-planning competition for the development of the central area of Ashdod, 1965. Fourth prize. Al Mansfeld, in association with D. Havkin (Israel).

⑫

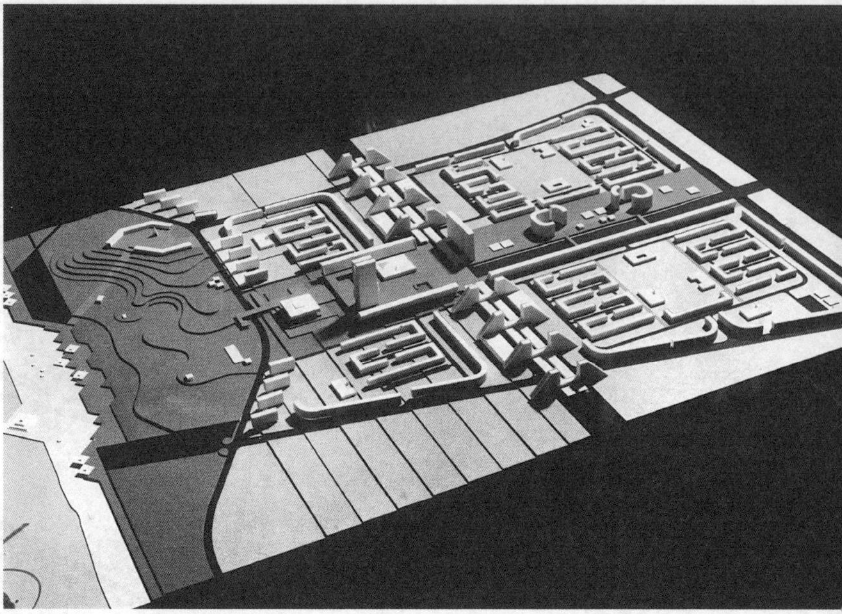

⑬

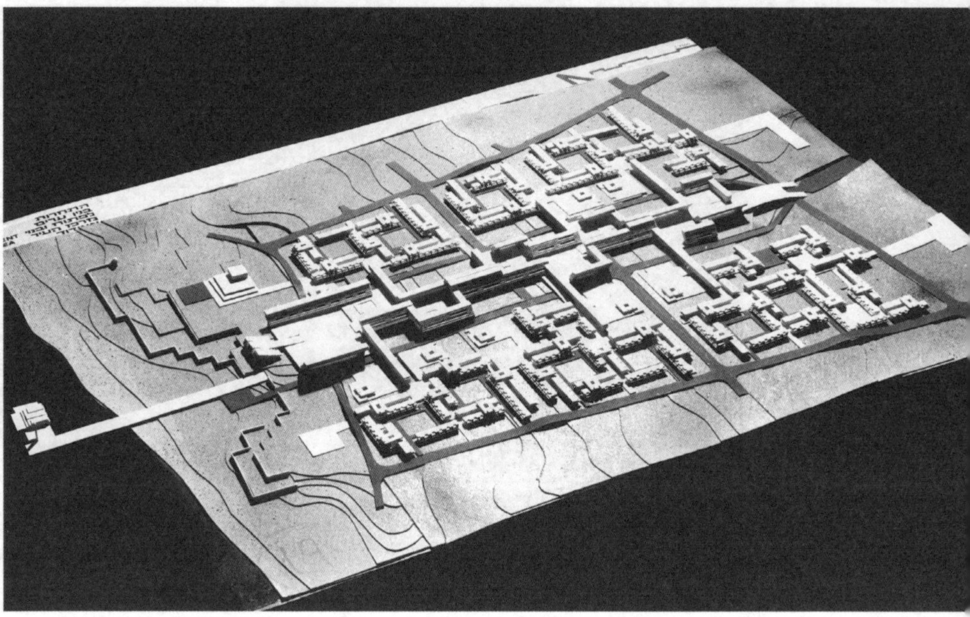

⑫ Entry for the town-planning competition for the development of the central area of Ashdod, 1965.
⑬ Entry for the town-planning competition for the development of the central area of Ashdod, 1965.

⑭

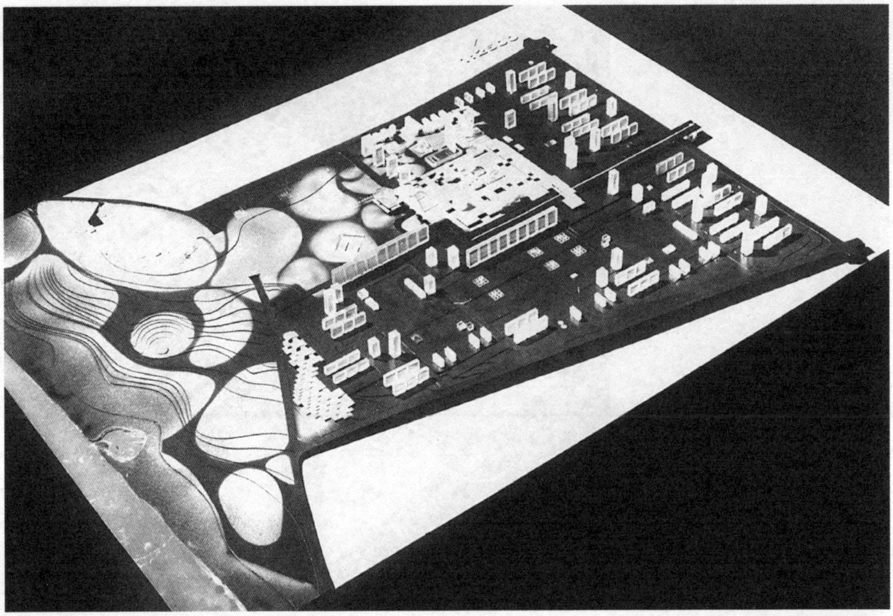

⑮

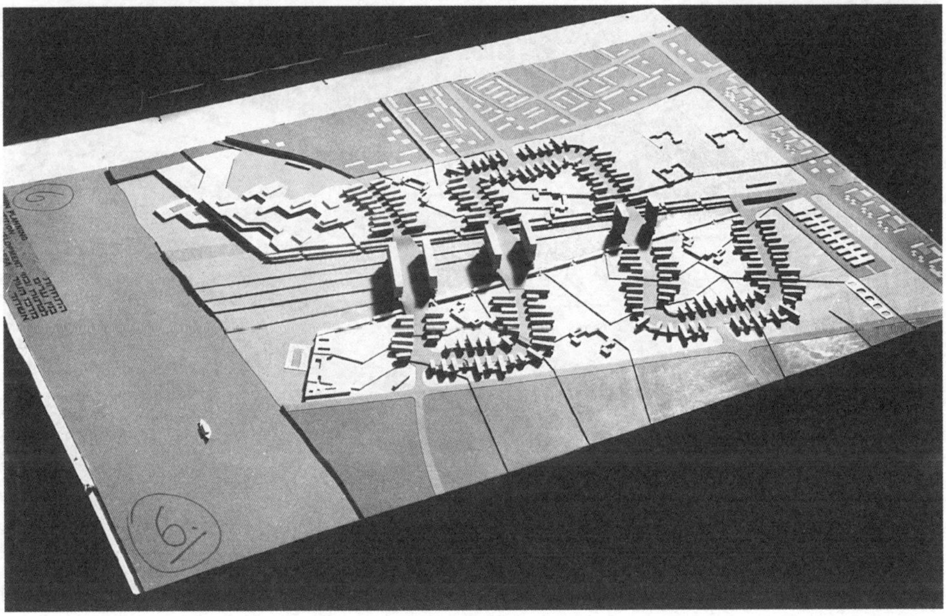

⑭ Entry for the town-planning competition for the development of the central area of Ashdod, 1965. Third prize. A. Elhanani and E. Lipsky, in association with I. Bracha, A. Man, and S. Zolitsky.
⑮ Entry for the town-planning competition for the development of the central area of Ashdod, 1965.

⑯

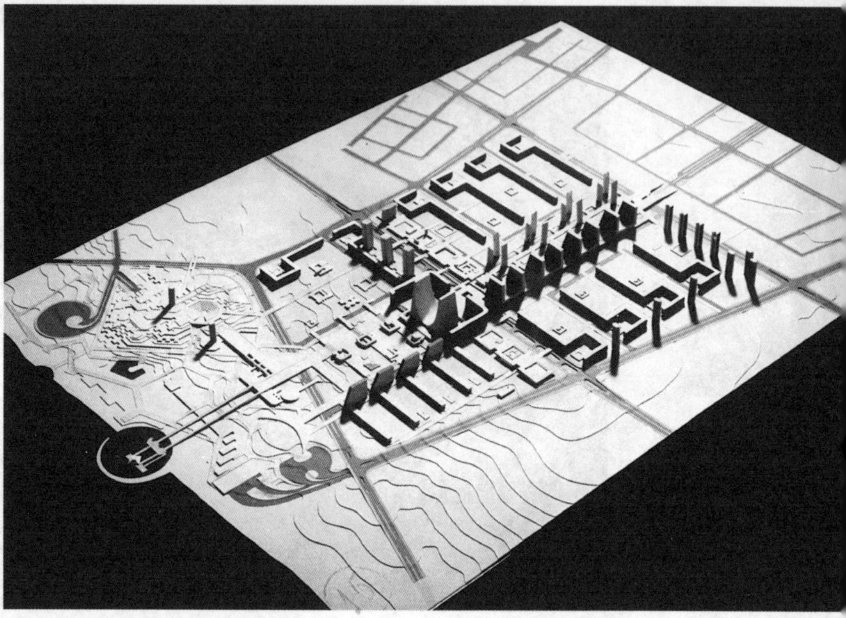

⑰

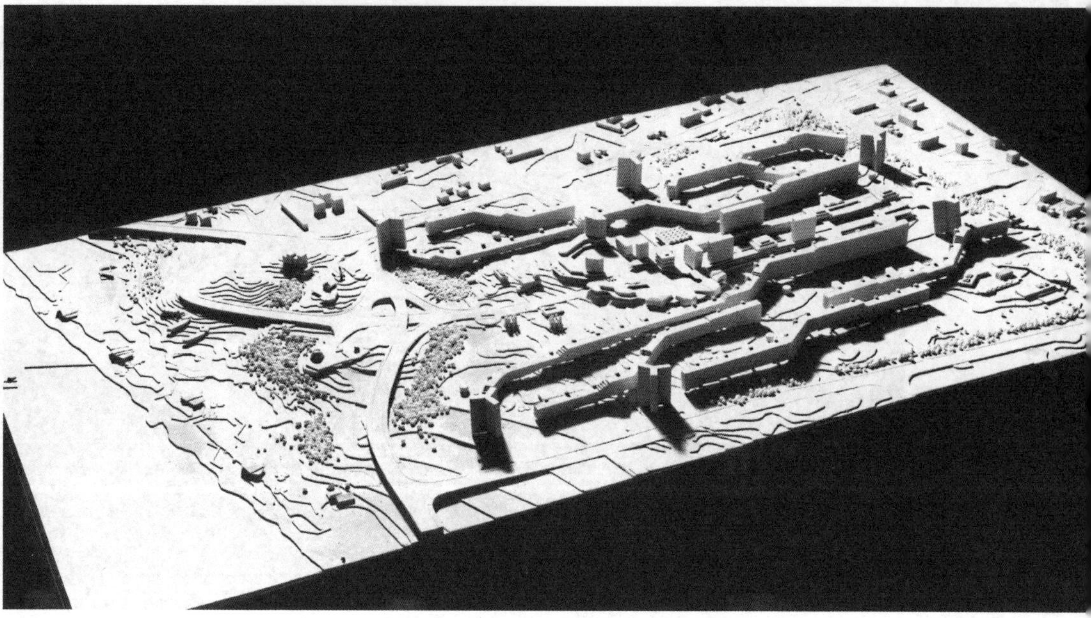

⑯ Entry for the town-planning competition for the development of the central area of Ashdod, 1965.
⑰ Entry for the town-planning competition for the development of the central area of Ashdod, 1965. Second prize. Y. Carmi, engineer, and Winogard, J. M. Y. Vedia, and G. L. Peani, architects (Argentina).

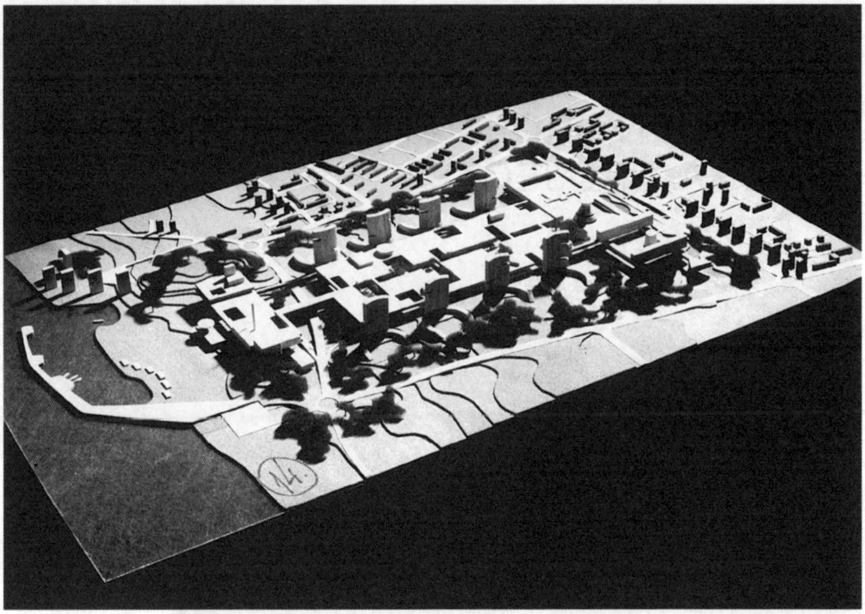

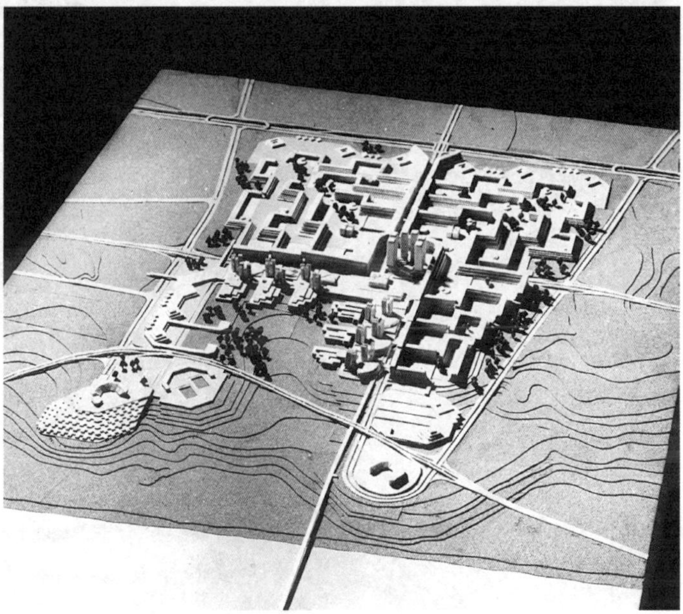

⑱ Entry for the town-planning competition for the development of the central area of Ashdod, 1965.
⑲ Entry for the town-planning competition for the development of the central area of Ashdod, 1965. Third prize. Karmi and Partners, Architects (Israel).

# DOSSIER: VAN DEN BROEK AND BAKEMA'S MEGA-PROJECTS

⑳ Entry for the Jerusalem city hall competition, 1963. Perspective. Van den Broek & Bakema. State Archive for Dutch Architecture and Urban Planning, Rotterdam.

The Dutch firm Van den Broek and Bakema participated in three major international competitions in Israel during the 1960s: the 1963 Jerusalem city hall competition, the 1963 competition for Tel Aviv's central business district at Manshiya, and the 1965 town-planning competition for the development of the central area of Ashdod. These competitions, which displayed spectacular urban visions and oversized vertical and horizontal artifacts, attracted much local and international publicity, but the winning entries were never actually built or conceptually implemented. For Jerusalem, Jo van den Broek and Jaap Bakema proposed an ensemble of three towers rising above the city's central park and staring at the Old City. In Tel Aviv, they stretched the competition brief and superimposed a colossal infrastructural web of roads, squares, "citygatebuildings" and "backbonebuildings" on the entire city. In Ashdod, their guiding concept, as quoted by the competition's jury, who gave them second prize, was designing a "cityroom in the form of a tree."

In an abstract published in the Dutch magazine *Katholiek Bouwbald*, Van den Broek and Bakema posed the following rhetorical question:

> How to produce the visual reality called core, respecting both the permanent small scale of table and bed and desk and on the other hand the ever-increasing scale of administration and traffic and (perhaps the most important thing to do) harmonizing the relationship between the two of them.[1]

The question is followed by proclamations such as: "Let's intensify the coastline, thus making the land embrace the water, without interrupting the natural flow of it, however, and making it a part of the interior of the city."[2] Or, a few paragraphs later:

> The transitional scale elements go like ribs into the structure of the existing town. Along the backbonebuilding are elevators and staircase towers connecting the interior streets of the building with the townscape levels for traffic and parking.[3]

Two years later, in Ashdod, Van den Broek and Bakema reconfigured the "visual reality called core" as a metaphorical tree and exquisitely drew it in the shape of a concrete poem. Their competition abstract claims:

> City room (trunk, branches, twigs, leaves): Long buildings are going from the heart (focus) of the town along the main roads like branches from a tree. From these branches, like twigs, transitional types of dwellings going to the patio-houses, which are like leaves. [...] The highest, wall-like, buildings make visually clear where the heart is of the city. In these cityrooms are also towerlike buildings of up to 25 floors. At the foot there are connections with the multi-level of the focus of the town [...].[4]

The competition's jury was impressed by the proposal's "strong architectural form" and "fully developed urban atmosphere," but commented that "the excessive dispersal of offices and other services results in inordinate walking distance."[5] ■

1 Jo van den Broek and Jaap Bakema, "Toelichting ontwerp v.d. Broek en Bakema," *Katholiek Bouwbald* (1965), p. 64.
2 Ibid.
3 Ibid., p. 65.
4 From: "Summary of the Town Planning Competition for the Development of the Central Area of Ashdod" (Hebrew/English booklet, Tel Aviv: "Ashdod" Company, 1965).
5 Ibid.

(21)

(22)

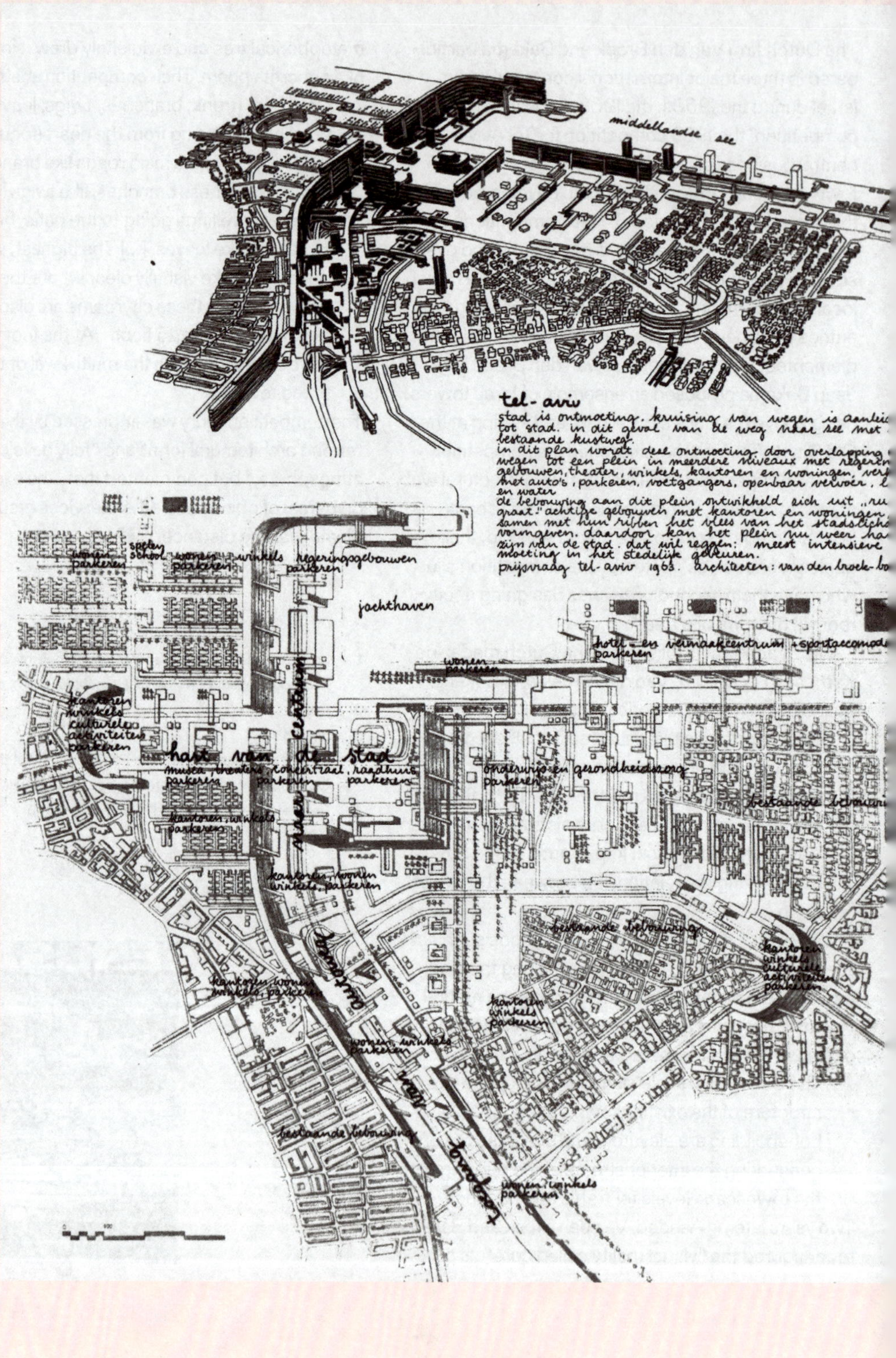


㉓

㉑ Entry for the Jerusalem city hall competition, 1963. Model. Van den Broek & Bakema. State Archive for Dutch Architecture and Urban Planning, Rotterdam.

㉒ Entry for the Jerusalem city hall competition, 1963. Elevation. Van den Broek & Bakema. State Archive for Dutch Architecture and Urban Planning, Rotterdam.

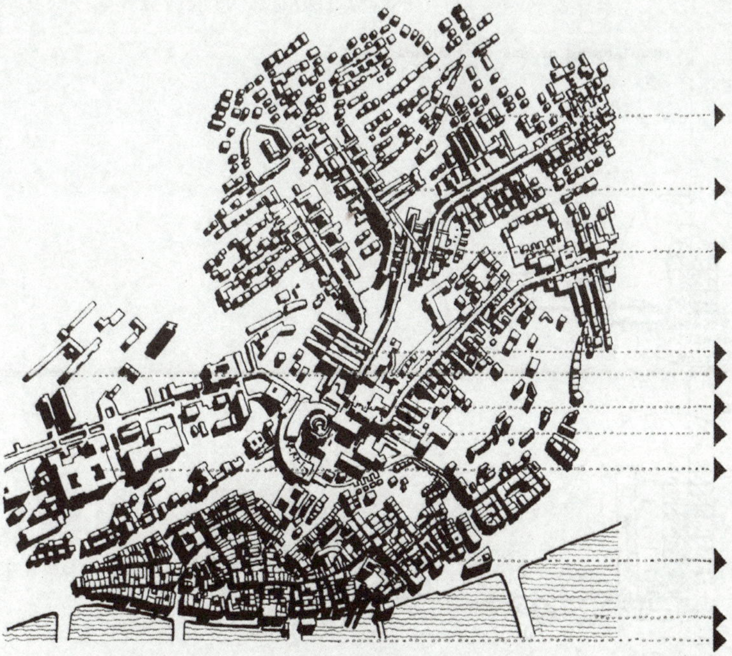

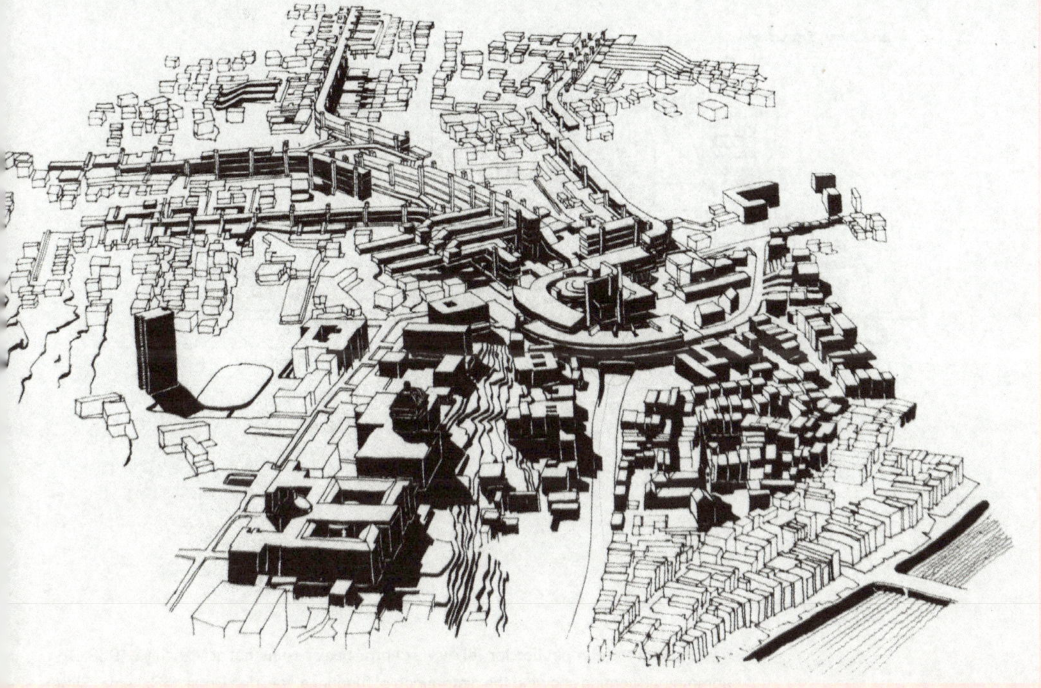

㉔

㉓ Entry for the competition for Tel Aviv's central business district at Manshiya, 1963. Plan and perspective. Van den Broek & Bakema. State Archive for Dutch Architecture and Urban Planning, Rotterdam.
㉔ Entry for the competition for Tel Aviv's central business district at Manshiya, 1963. Plan and perspective. Van den Broek & Bakema. State Archive for Dutch Architecture and Urban Planning, Rotterdam.

㉕

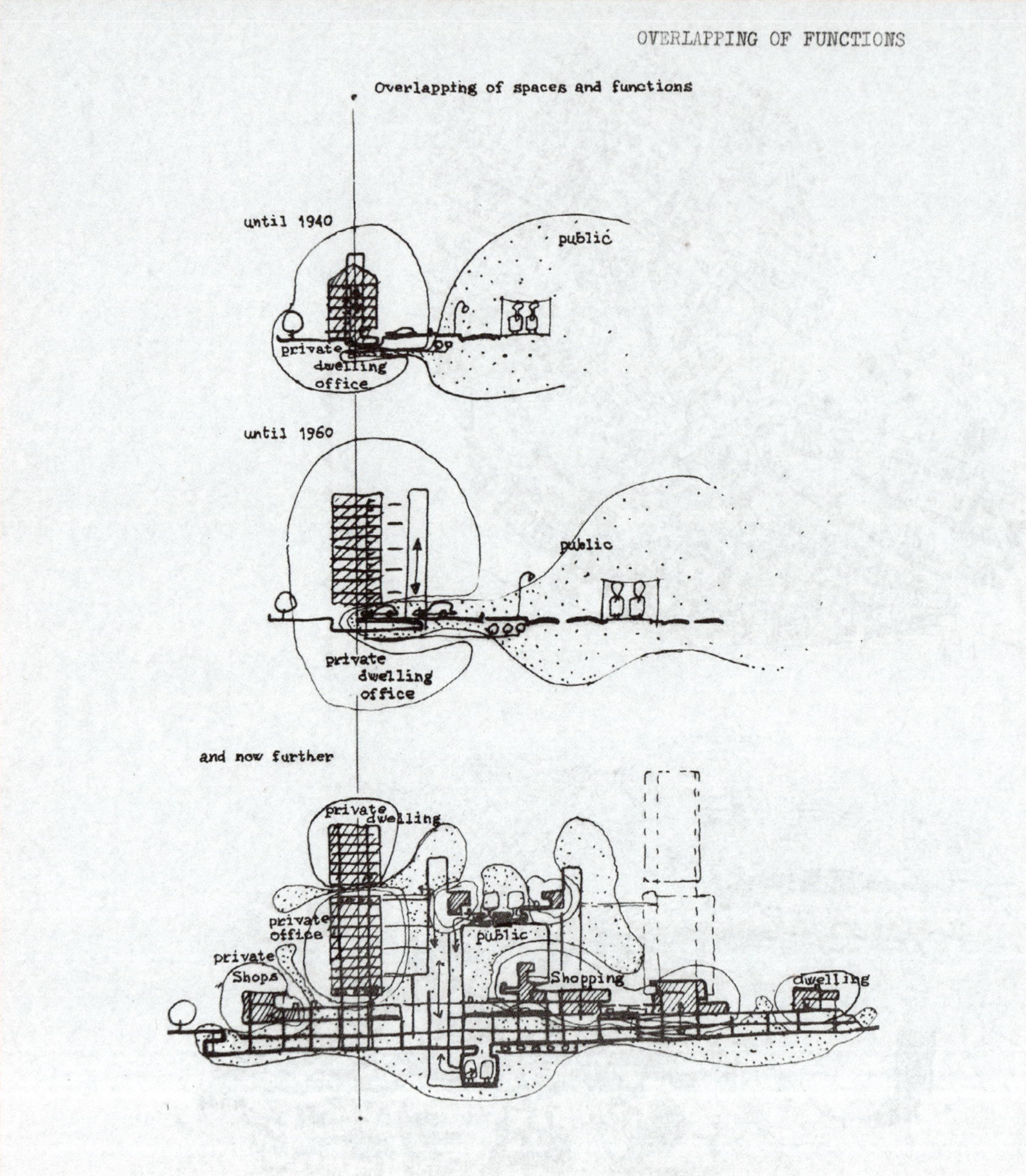


㉕ Entry for the competition for Tel Aviv's central business district at Manshiya, 1963. Diagrammatic section showing the distribution of functions. Van den Broek & Bakema. State Archive for Dutch Architecture and Urban Planning, Rotterdam.
㉖ Entry for the competition for Tel Aviv's central business district at Manshiya, 1963. Model. Van den Broek & Bakema. State Archive for Dutch Architecture and Urban Planning, Rotterdam.
㉗ Entry for the competition for Tel Aviv's central business district at Manshiya, 1963. Model. Van den Broek & Bakema. State Archive for Dutch Architecture and Urban Planning, Rotterdam.

㉖

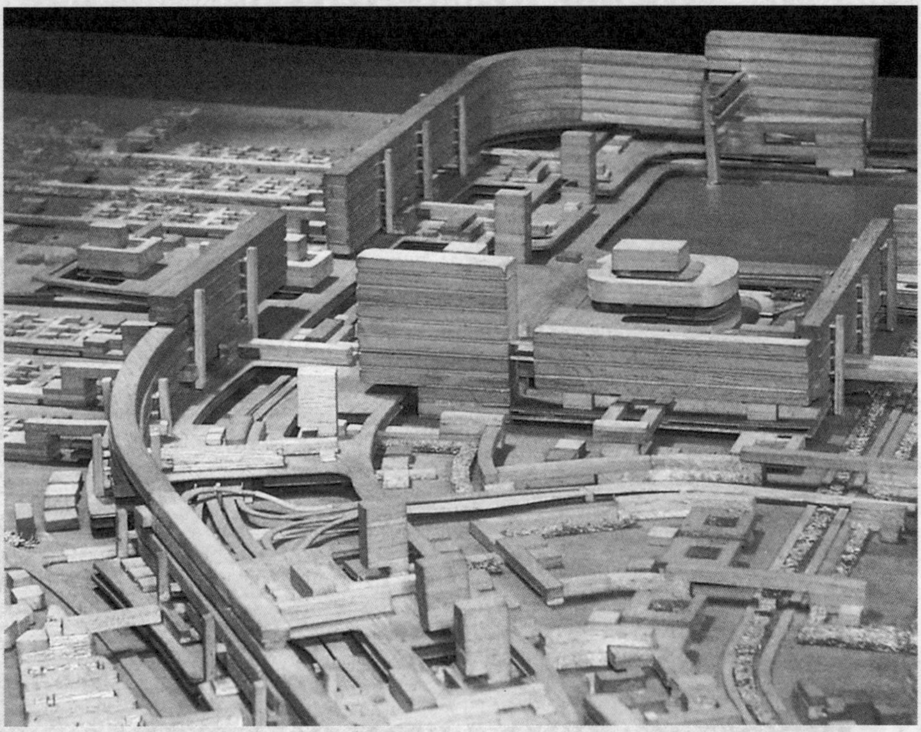

㉗

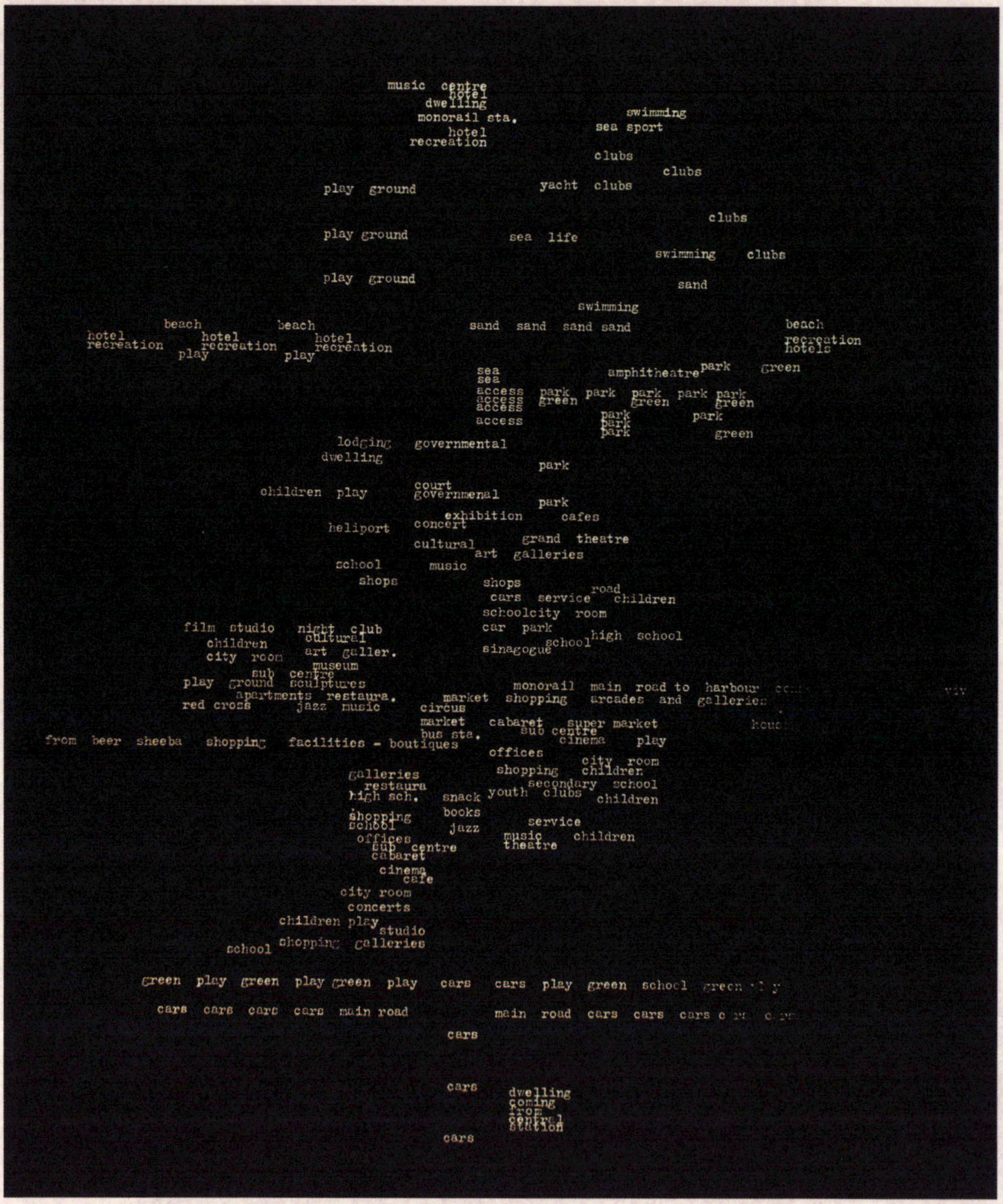
music centre
hotel
dwelling
monorail sta.
hotel
recreation
swimming
sea sport
clubs
clubs
play ground
yacht clubs
clubs
play ground
sea life
swimming clubs
play ground
sand
swimming
beach
beach
sand sand sand sand
beach
hotel
recreation
hotel
recreation
play
hotel
recreation
play
recreation
hotels
sea
sea
amphitheatre park green
access park park park park park
access green green green
access
access
park
park
park
park
green
lodging governmental
dwelling
park
children play
court
governmenal
park
exhibition cafes
heliport concert
cultural grand theatre
art galleries
school music
shops shops
road
cars service children
schoolcity room
film studio night club
cultural
car park
children art galler.
high school
city room
sinagogue school
museum
sub centre
play ground sculptures
monorail main road to harbour
apartments restaura.
red cross jazz music
market shopping arcades and galleries
circus
market cabaret super market
bus sta. sub centre
from beer sheeba shopping facilities - boutiques
cinema play
offices
city room
galleries
shopping children
restaura
secondary school
high sch. snack youth clubs children
books
shopping
school
jazz service
offices
music children
sub centre
theatre
cabaret
cinema
cafe
city room
concerts
children play
studio
school shopping galleries
green play green play green play cars cars play green school
cars cars cars cars main road main road cars cars cars
cars
cars dwelling
coming
from
central
station
cars

㉘

(28) Entry for the town-planning competition for the central area of Ashdod, 1965. Program distribution diagram. Van den Broek & Bakema. State Archive for Dutch Architecture and Urban Planning, Rotterdam.
(29) Entry for the town-planning competition for the central area of Ashdod, 1965. Program distribution diagram. Van den Broek & Bakema. State Archive for Dutch Architecture and Urban Planning, Rotterdam.

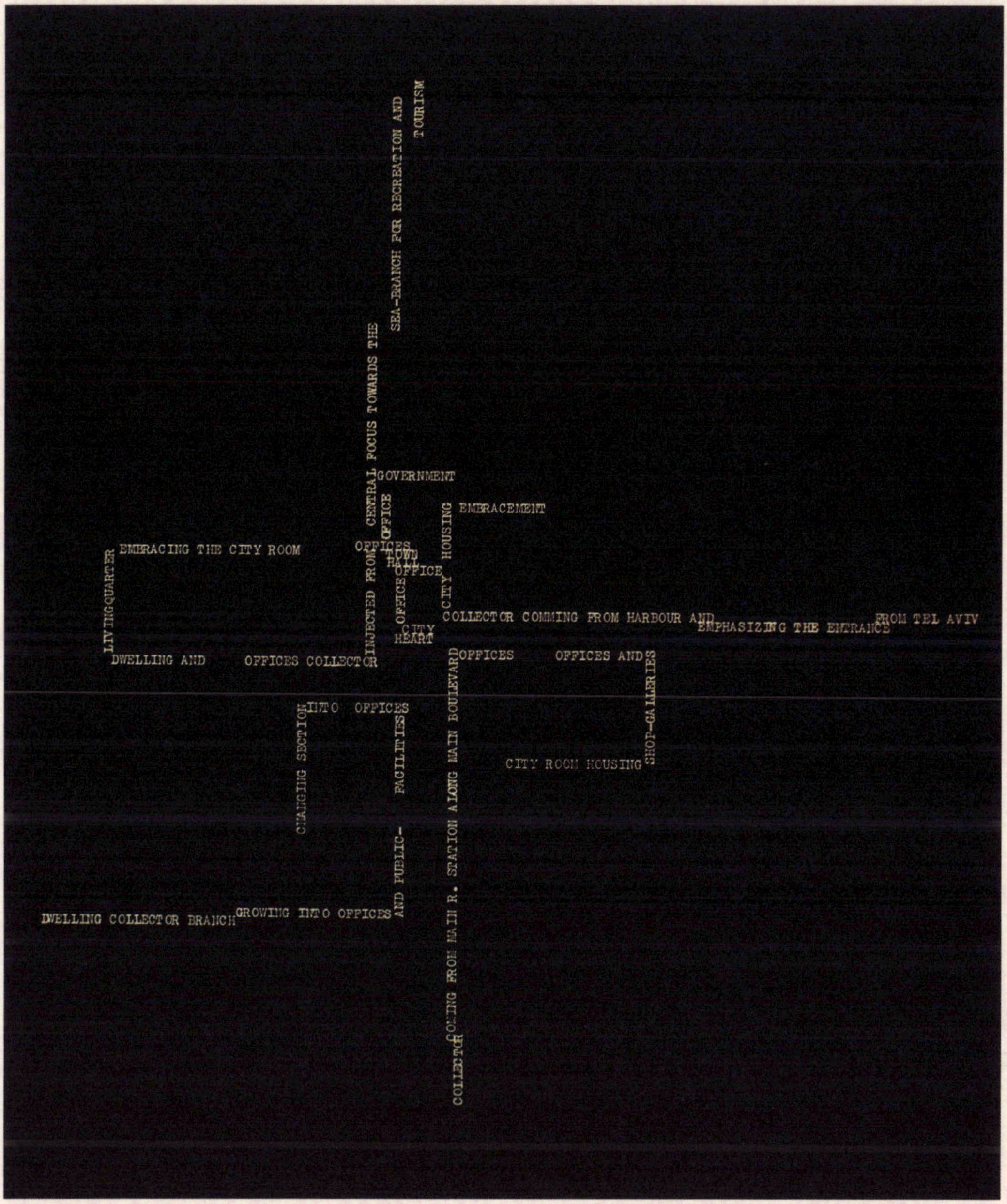

(29)

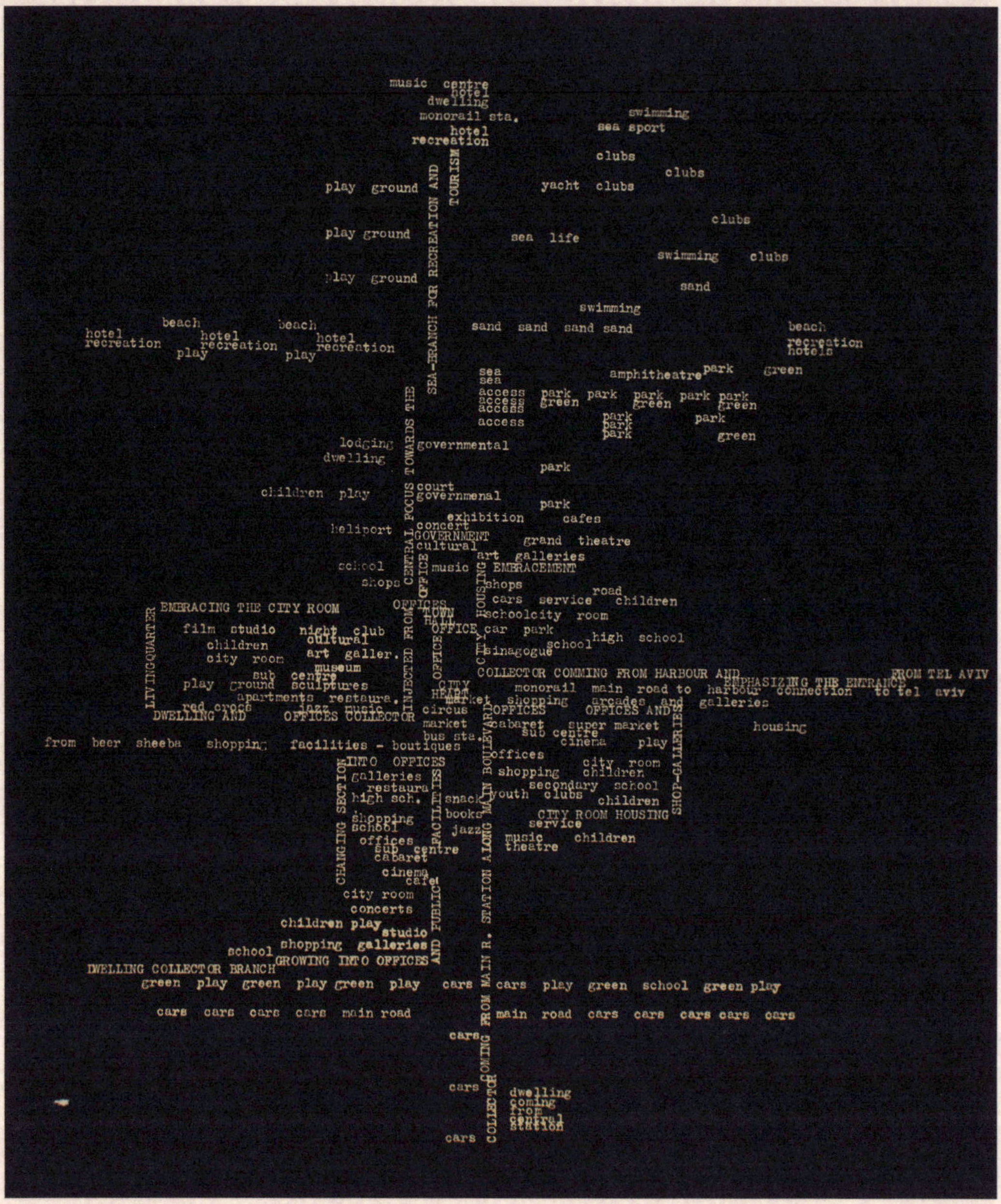

music centre
hotel
dwelling
monorail sta.
hotel
recreation
TOURISM
SEA-BRANCH FOR RECREATION AND
swimming
sea sport
clubs
clubs
yacht clubs
play ground
play ground
play ground
clubs
sea life
swimming clubs
sand
swimming
sand sand sand sand
beach
hotel
recreation
hotel
recreation
play
beach
hotel
recreation
play
beach
recreation
hotels
sea
sea
access
access
access
access
amphitheatre
park
green
park
green
park
park
green
park
park
green
park
park
park
park
green
lodging
dwelling
governmental
park
children play
court
governmenal
park
exhibition
concert
GOVERNMENT
cultural
cafes
heliport
grand theatre
art galleries
school
music
EMBRACEMENT
shops
shops
CENTRAL FOCUS TOWARDS THE
INJECTED FROM
OFFICE
road
cars service children
schoolcity room
car park
high school
school
sinagogue
EMBRACING THE CITY ROOM
LIVINGQUARTER
film studio
night club
cultural
children
art galler.
city room
museum
sub centre
play ground
sculptures
apartments
restaura.
red cross
jazz music
DWELLING AND
OFFICES COLLECTOR
OFFICES
TOWN
OFFICE
CITY
HEART
market
circus
market
bus sta.
COLLECTOR COMMING FROM HARBOUR AND
EMPHASIZING THE ENTRANCE
FROM TEL AVIV
monorail main road to harbour connection to tel aviv
shopping
arcades and
galleries
OFFICES
OFFICES AND
cabaret
super market
sub centre
cinema
play
housing
from beer sheeba shopping facilities - boutiques
offices
INTO OFFICES
galleries
restaura
high sch.
snack
books
jazz
shopping
school
offices
sub centre
cabaret
cinema
cafe
city room
concerts
children play
studio
school
shopping galleries
GROWING INTO OFFICES
CHANGING SECTION
FACILITIES
AND PUBLIC
shopping
city room
children
youth clubs
secondary school
children
CITY ROOM HOUSING
service
music
theatre
children
SHOP-GALLERIES
DWELLING COLLECTOR BRANCH
green play green play green play
cars cars play green school green play
cars cars cars cars main road
main road cars cars cars cars cars
cars
COLLECTOR COMING FROM MAIN R. STATION ALONG MAIN BOULEVARD
cars
dwelling
coming
from
central
station
cars


㉚

(30) Entry for the town-planning competition for the central area of Ashdod, 1965. Program distribution diagram. Van den Broek & Bakema. State Archive for Dutch Architecture and Urban Planning, Rotterdam.

(31) Entry for the town-planning competition for the central area of Ashdod, 1965. Urban tree diagram. Van den Broek & Bakema. State Archive for Dutch Architecture and Urban Planning, Rotterdam.

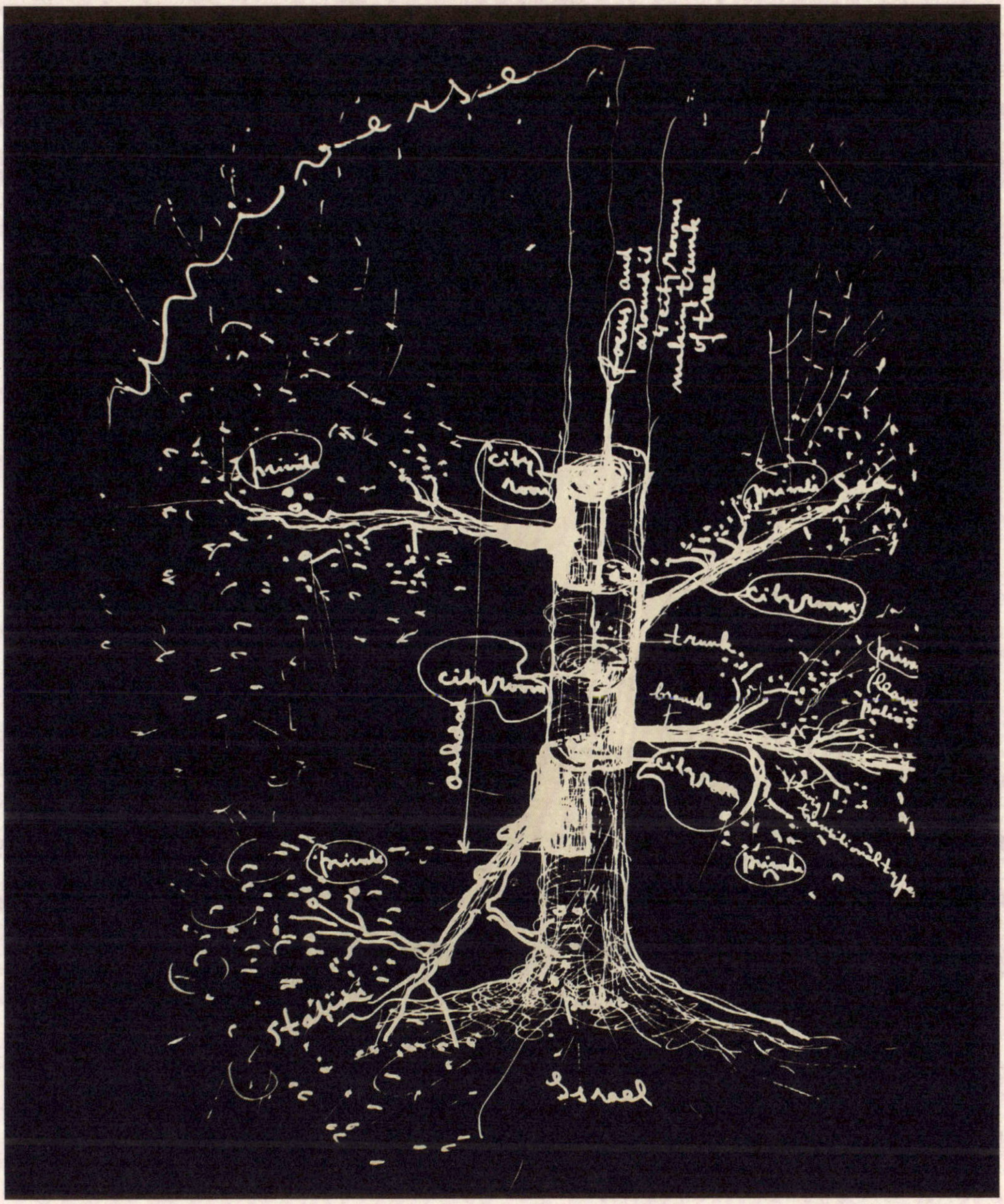


(31)

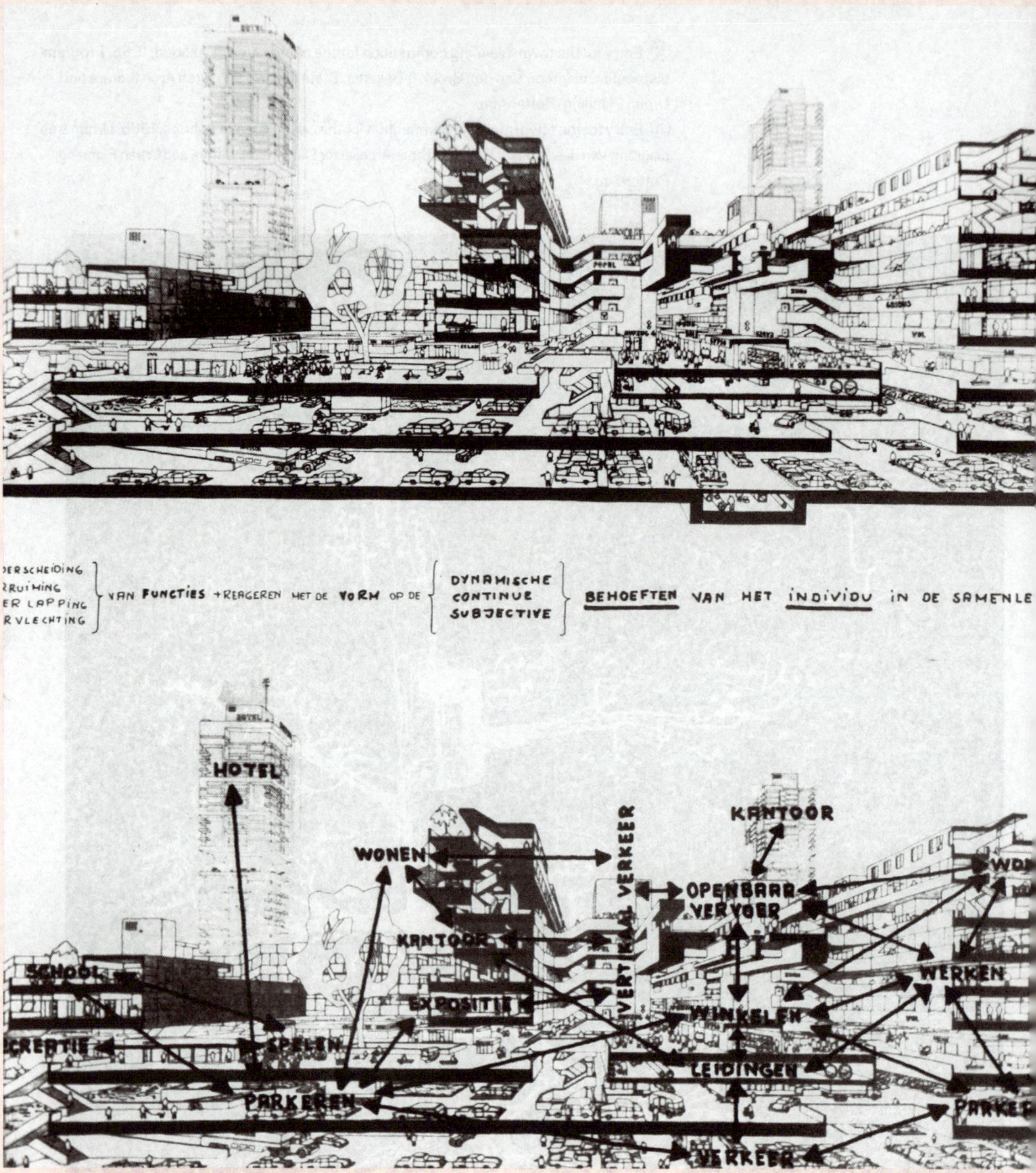


(32)

(32) Entry for the town-planning competition for the central area of Ashdod, 1965. Perspectival sections. Van den Broek & Bakema, State Archive for Dutch Architecture and Urban Planning, Rotterdam.

(33) Entry for the town-planning competition for the development of the central area of Ashdod, 1965. Second prize. Van den Broek & Bakema, Architects in collaboration with A. Eidelman (Holland).

(34) Entry for the town-planning competition for the central area of Ashdod, 1965. Perspective and urban section. Van den Broek & Bakema. State Archive for Dutch Architecture and Urban Planning, Rotterdam.

33

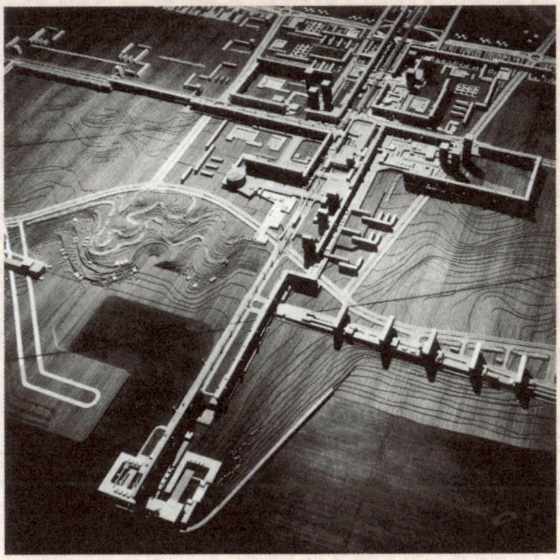

34

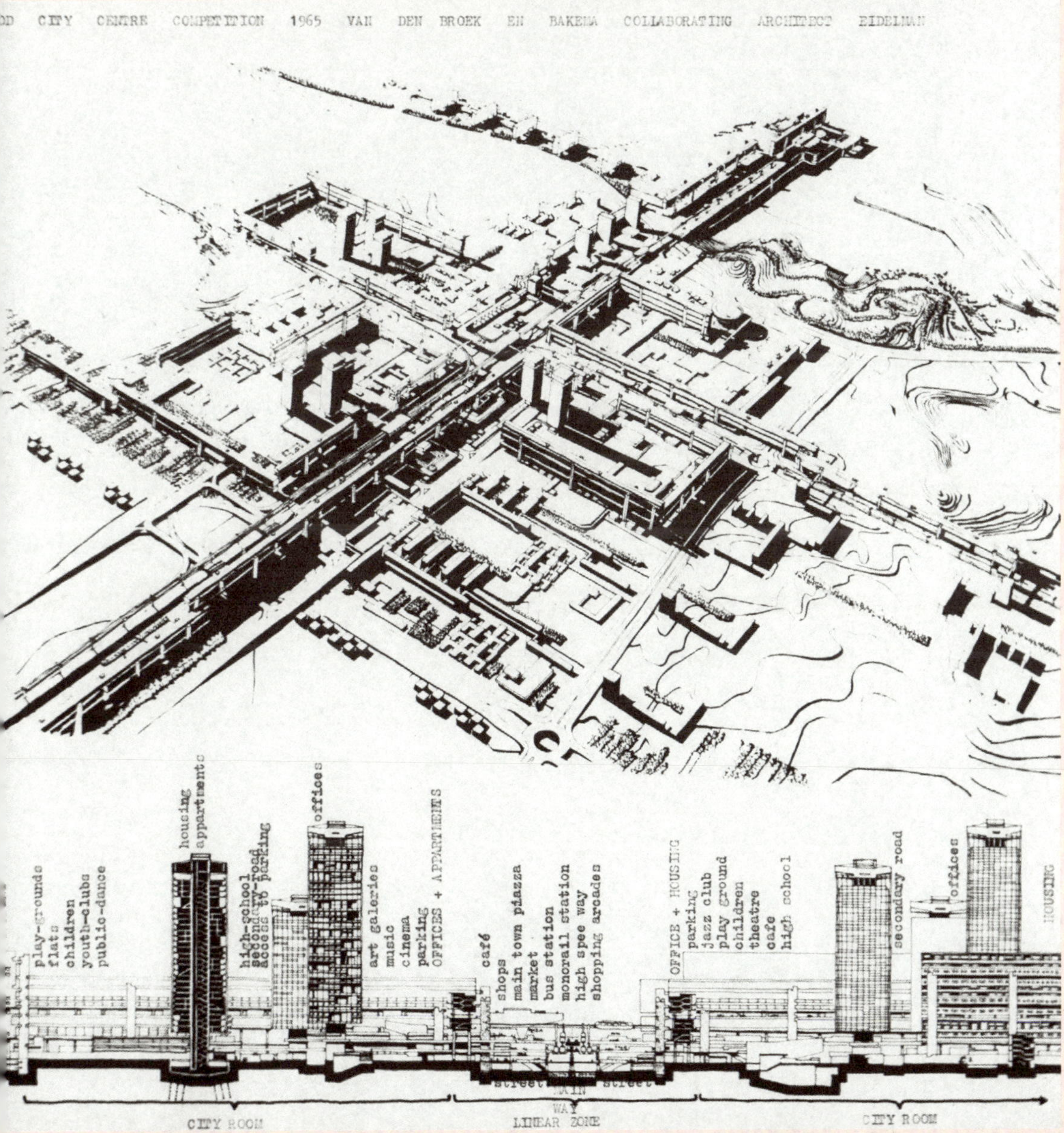
OD CITY CENTRE COMPETITION 1965 VAN DEN BROEK EN BAKEMA COLLABORATING ARCHITECT EIDELMAN
play-grounds
flats
children
youth-clubs
public-dance
housing
appartments
high-school
secondary-road
access to parking
offices
art galeries
music
cinema
parking
OFFICES + APPARTMENTS
café
shops
main town piazza
market
bus station
monorail station
high spee way
shopping arcades
OFFICE + HOUSING
parking
jazz club
play ground
children
theatre
cafe
high school
secondary road
offices
HOUSING
street
MAIN
street
WAY
CITY ROOM
LINEAR ZONE
CITY ROOM

# The National Museum and the Shrine of the Book

## The Iconic Architecture of the Israel Museum and the Shrine of the Book

Jerusalem's museum hill, built in the early 1960s, has acquired an aura normally reserved for sacred sites and historical monuments. Although venerated as an "organic whole," it consists of two somewhat incongruous architectures and a third that inadvertently mediates between them. The first architecture, that of the Israel Museum, designed by Al Mansfeld and Dora Gad, is a megaform disguised as minor architecture; the second, that of the Shrine of the Book, designed by Frederick Kiesler and Armand Bartos, is a compact garden folly invested with endless monumental aspirations; and the third, that of the sculpture garden, designed by Isamu Noguchi, is an artful take on indigenous terraced landscapes. The first and last were planned for the specific hill site they occupy and exhibit the organic propensity and picturesque—or rather arabesque—allure of quasi-cybernetic design systems, whereas the second was initially conceived for another site. It only happened to land on the museum hill, where it enacts the formal autonomy of hallowed structures.

### The Museum

The Israel Museum, originally the Bezalel National Museum,[1] was conceived during the 1950s as a national art and archaeology museum. It was programmed to be the ultimate stockroom of tangible historical evidence of a rejuvenated nation and its glowing showcase, embodying its creative force.

In 1959 an architectural competition was set up to determine the museum's architect. Ten of the foremost Israeli architects of the time were invited to submit their proposals. Most of the entries were based on ceremonial schemes, a pastiche of International Style layouts with neo-Mesopotamian sections of ziggurats and stepped pyramids. The winning entry, however, by architect Al Mansfeld and designer Dora Gad, was remarkably reductive, free of epic allegories and archaic motifs (well, there was no figural archaism whatsoever, yet the entire setup recalled a spectacular assemblage of ruins). It effectively proposed that the national museum be no object, no form, no façade; that it have no compositional hierarchy, no axial stature, nor even any useful spaciousness. Instead, it austerely described an infrastructure of modular probabilities and sketched a captivating silhouette.

The silhouette, located at the top of the design principles board of the competition entry, was equipped with the inscription "General View of Malha near Jerusalem." Below, it appeared as a mirror image: a perspective view of the proposed museum. As we learn from the competition proceedings, it was this quick doodle, this nonchalant analogy, which caught the attention of the jury

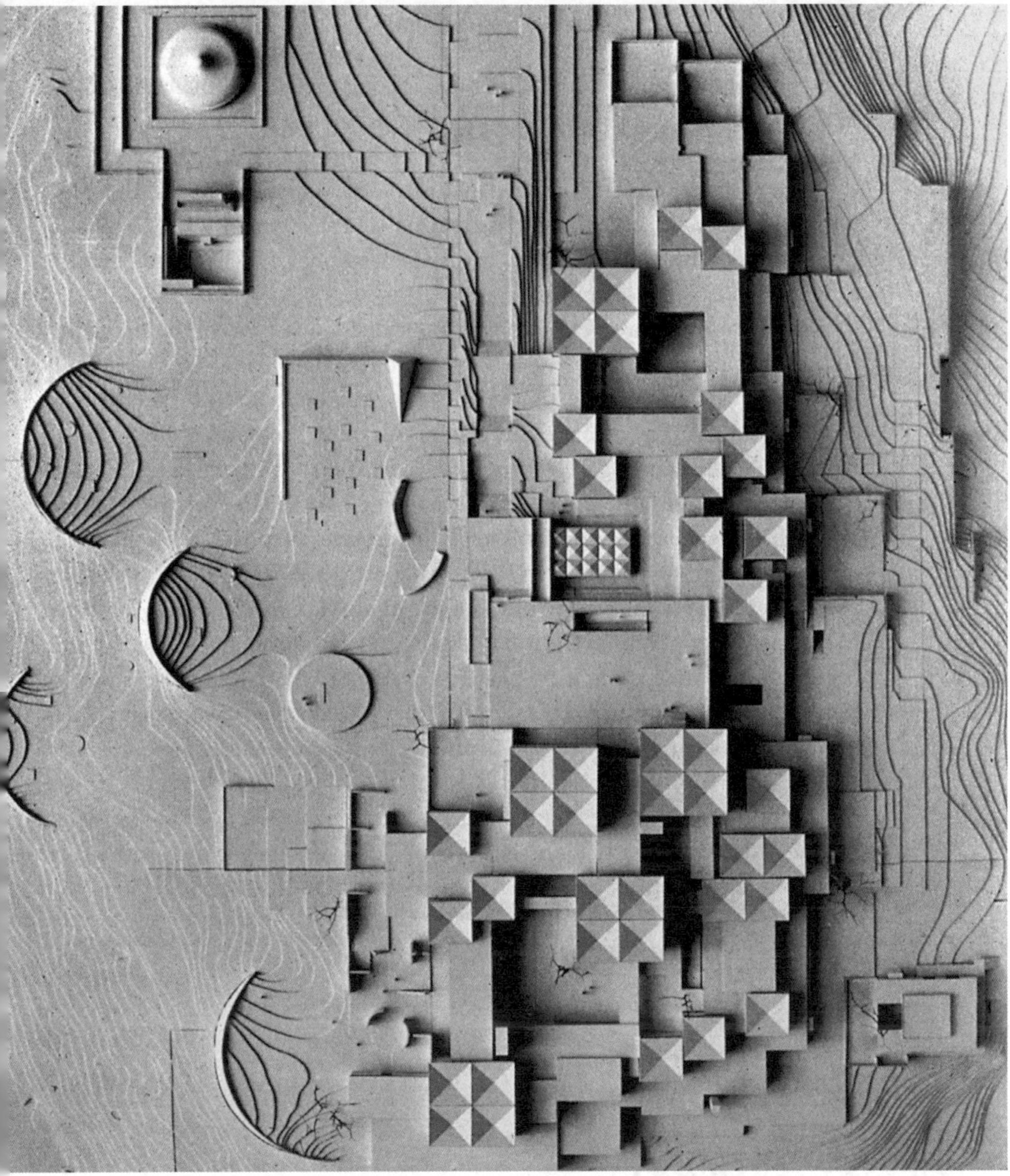

① The Israel Museum, Jerusalem, 1959. Model. Prof. Al Mansfeld, Dora Gad. Israel Museum Archives, courtesy of the Mansfeld Family.

and was the irrefutable factor in their choice of this project. Later analogical drawings by Mansfeld—most illustrious among them a double image of "an Arab village near Jerusalem" and a view of the "Israel National Museum from the Valley of the Cross," with a diagram of the museum's plan at the bottom of the image—as well as a "photocollage" made by Willem Sandberg, the museum's first director, further established the native Palestinian village (see dossier "Marcel Janco's Bohemian Colony" in chapter "Ruins of War") as the myth of origin of the Israel Museum.

A brief study of drawn elevations in Mansfeld's and Gad's competition entry reveals that alongside the spontaneous contour of the village, their museum is haunted by a counterimage, that of Mies van der Rohe's Brick Country House of 1923, an unbuilt project which was presumably modeled after Theo van Doesburg's 1918 painting *Rhythm of a Russian Dance* and which was retroactively iconized by Peter Eisenman as "the first indication in Mies's work of textual notation."[2] The clear import of this image to Jerusalem exposes the architecture of the museum to speculations about "the reduction of symbolic objects to mere objects"[3] and the setting up of radical figure-ground relations. According to Eisenman, "the walls in the Brick Country House are merely object presences, divisions where there is no space to divide or where the space has been removed and only surfaces exist. [...] For Mies, the absence of space eliminates a major classical element—the ground—leaving the walls as suspended figures."[4]

The "suspended figures" of the walls are seemingly illustrated in Mansfeld's technical drawings, particularly in the exploded axonometric of the structural system, which is based on central columns, cantilevered hypar ceilings, and

②

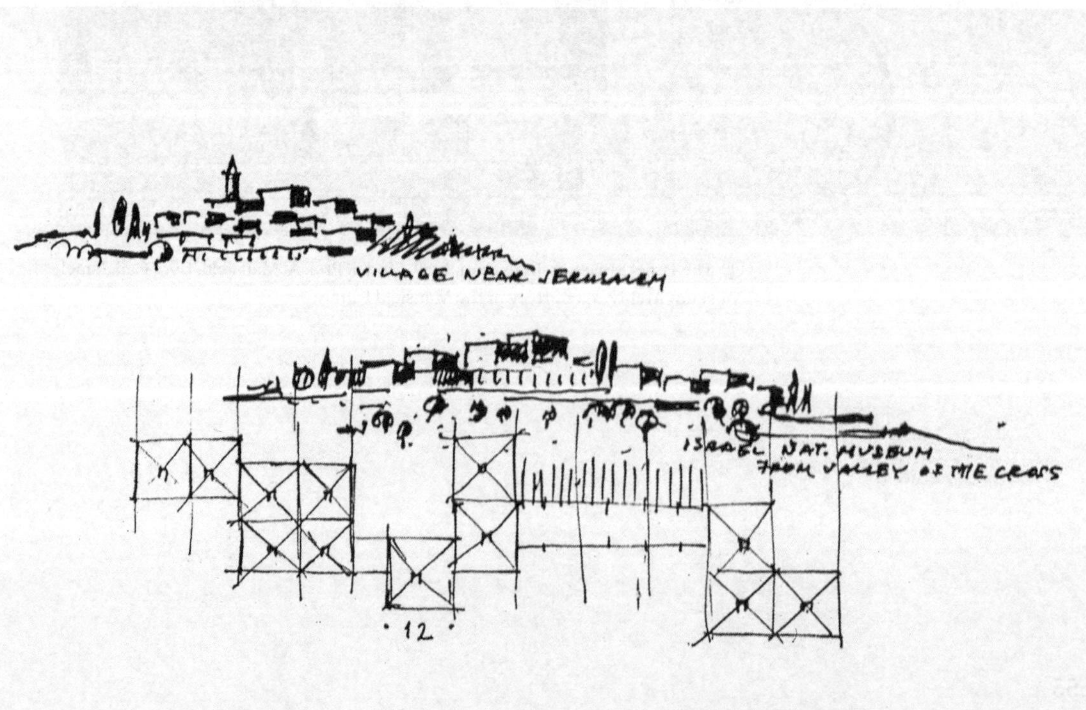

③

④

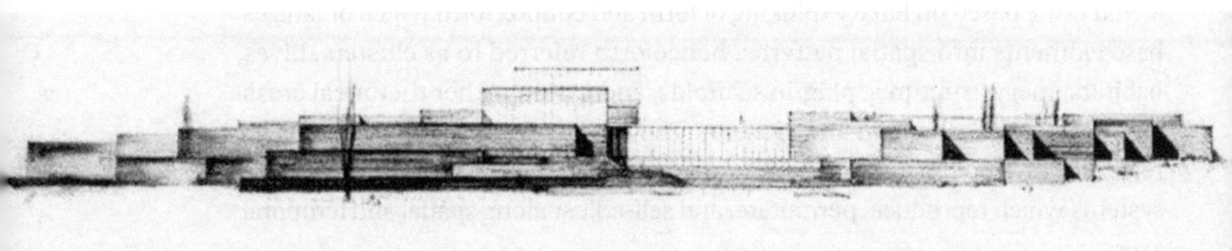

detached nonbearing walls. Indeed, the entire setup of fluctuating floors and topographical roofscape suggests an intricate mat-building designed to blur typical figure-ground distinctions. However, a second look at the museum's overall plans reveals the extent of misappropriation at work here. In Mansfeld's scheme, the Miesian "notational" field of free walls and floating planes becomes a matrix of modular boxes and enclave spaces, clustered in various groups and distributed spontaneously, as it were, on the terrain. Such modular "randomness" was also referred to in 1950s and 1960s architectural discourse as "New Humanism," or more commonly as "structuralism." "New Humanism" because of its empathic anthropological gaze and probing studies of native pueblos in Central America or casbah formations in North Africa. "Structuralism" because of its reliance on Gestalt theory, and especially on the new trends of system theory and cybernetics. The logic and logistics of this architecture are succinctly described by Mansfeld (who preferred the structuralist title):

> The system generates design; design sustains the system. Thus, for us design is the act of preservation and enhancement of the intrinsic character of the system. [...] At the same time, we should always bear in mind that a

② "Israel National Museum, [seen] from Valley of the Cross" and "Village Near Jerusalem," 1960s. Analogical sketch. Prof. Al Mansfeld. Israel Museum Archives, courtesy of the Mansfeld Family.
③ Brick Country House, 1923. Perspective. Mies van der Rohe.
④ Second-stage competition entry for the Israel Museum, Jerusalem, 1959. Elevation. Prof. Al Mansfeld, Dora Gad. Israel Museum Archives, courtesy of the Mansfeld Family.

⑤ Ada Louise Huxtable, "Museums A La Carte," *New York Times*, June 15, 1969.
⑥ "Luda" model for modular design, 1974. Al Mansfeld, Michael Mansfeld, Haim Kehat, Yehudit Mansfeld. Top: Israel Museum. Middle: proposal for the Jerusalem municipality. Bottom: proposal for residential neighborhood.

> system is merely a tool. In other words, it is the language. Architecture created with its help becomes the speech.[5]

The tautological circuits created by structuralist architecture cannot be fully explored here. Suffice it to point out that what appears is a new diagrammatic architecture based on binary thinking of form and counterform which organizes base elements into spatial patterns, henceforth referred to as clusters, hives, habitats, megastructures, plug-in scaffolds, and various other rhetorical crossings between mechanism and vitalism. The novelty of this architecture is its rejection of predetermined objects and fixed forms in favor of auto-generic systems which reproduce, permutate, and self-adjust along spatial and temporal axes.

Architecture critic Ada Louise Huxtable described the Israel Museum in 1969, four years after the official opening, as "a series of connected but separate pavilions at stepped levels that sit without undue disturbance in the Jerusalem hills. [...] [The museum's] clustered volumes clearly demonstrate a proper alternative to the violence that would be wreaked by a conventional blockbuster on a landscape that is at once surprisingly strong and subtle and surpassingly beautiful in the almost oriental intricacies of its contours."[6]

Four decades later, architectural scholar Philipp Misselwitz elaborates: "The museum's architecture embodies a spatial and temporal concept that is situated on the line between urban and pastoral, fusing the metaphor of the historical Arab village with the planning language of British garden city planning and structuralist philosophy. Today, after forty-four years of permanent growth in which the museum spaces have expanded ten times, the Israel Museum remains one of the most important yet little known examples of field architecture in the world."[7]

We realize, then, that the most useful quality of structuralist architecture is its elasticity (in contradistinction to plasticity) and expandability on a prescribed matrix and according to a predetermined code, without changing its "genetic" character and scenic image. Misselwitz describes the parameters and dimensions of the matrix in detail:

> Mansfeld and Gad devised a modular planning grid based on variables of 0.7 $m^2$ in order to locate and proportion all subsystems ranging from public space furniture, infrastructural grids (power supplies, fittings, lighting), and mechanical engineering to all larger building components. In this way, grid points determine even the smallest details [...] and the larger spatial units of the exhibition pavilions.

**Architecture**

# Museums A La Carte

By ADA LOUISE HUXTABLE

THERE'S nothing like a dame and there's nothing like a museum; both are calculated displays of beauty. Define your woman or define your museum — no two definitions will match. And no greater range of definitions could be offered than this recently returned traveler's experience of museums in Turkey, Israel, Greece, Yugoslavia and England.

Frankly, it is hard to get me into a museum. Cities are the best museums and until I have exhausted the life and art of their streets I am loath to leave that rich record and fabric of the real, living thing for the embalmed treasures of the galleries. But this time I did, and it was worth it. A report, herewith.

We opened in Istanbul with Topkapi, and if your interests extend no farther than emeralds the size of ostrich eggs, O.K. But there is a lot more to see. If your interests include how the kitchens of the palace buildings that make up the museum can be used to accommodate a remarkable collection of Chinese ceramics, breaking every current rule of selective installation, this is the place.

*

Restored from partial ruin, this series of typically Turkish arched masonry rooms with their characteristic thick-walled, high-vaulted spaces — always taller than they are wide which seems to suit the spirit better than the reverse — now house grosses of dozens of plates on their handsome stone walls, in addition to jam-packed cases. A room papered, or rather plattered, floor-to-ceiling with Celadon is a pretty great thing. There is the nice touch of the smoke-blackened domes that have been left as the royal cooking fires darkened them. All wrong, of course. And all right.

On to Israel and the celebrated, four-year old Israel museum, which, like Gaul, consists of three parts. There is the main museum of art and archeology, designed by Alfred Mansfeld and Dora Gad, a series of connected but separate pavilions at stepped levels that sit without undue disturbance in the Jerusalem hills.

Connected to this is the Shrine of the Book, by Arnold Bartos and the late Frederick Kiesler, an architectural conceit of depressingly involved symbolism that contains the famous Dead Sea scrolls. The third part is the now almost equally famous Billy Rose sculpture garden, designed by Isamu Noguchi.

In the press coverage, the Shrine of the Book has gotten all the lines. It has the advantage of being an aggressively photogenic oddity, something that is often confused with great architecture. The sculpture garden has been acclaimed by more astute critics than I. The main museum has been largely passed over.

I would reverse that order. The museum building— a group of 35-foot square units topped by hyperbolic parabaloid shell roofs supported on a central column that holds all services — works remarkably well. The avowed purpose of the design, which won an international competition, was to respect the landscape at the same time that it makes a restrained monumental statement.

It works, because it is at once elegant and unpretentious. It works because it serves its purpose honorably. Its clustered volumes clearly demonstrate a proper alternative to the violence that would be wreaked by a conventional blockbuster on a landscape that is at once surprisingly strong and subtle and surpassingly beautiful in the almost oriental intricacies of its contours.

It also works for the museum visitor, because the pavilions break the fatigue of the traditional endless gallery or the rat's maze that directors like to make of their modern factory-style boxes. The quality of installation in both exhibits and equipment (by the architects) is kept admirably high.

> The grid system proportioned the dimensions of 11.2 $m^2$ hyperbolic, paraboloid concrete shells, [...] [which are] supported from a pre-stressed central column with a hollow core that contains all services [...]. The so-called "mushrooms" would occur as single units or [*sic*] joined up in predetermined combinations: doubled, combinations of three or forming a large square cluster of four in order to accommodate larger public functions.
>
> [...] On the one hand, growth became the product of an essentially mechanical, cybernetic process: the reproduction of sameness where predefined elements are rearranged and reorganised in a non-hierarchical arrangement, like automatic writing on the landscape. On the other hand, the overall appearance remained a question of subjective composition. In order to realise and retain the desired pastoral appearance, both mushrooms and linking elements vary in height, following the local topography.[8]

The successful implementation and actual performance of "open-ended accumulative systems" or "growth theories" at the Israel Museum have hardly any precedent. After all, most of the built versions of "field architecture" (such as

⑥

Candilis-Josic-Woods's 1963 Free University of Berlin) were circumscribed projects that never really altered their configuration and certainly did not continually grow over decades. The exceptionally rigid mathematics of the Israel Museum, backed up by a playful design system[9] and a masterful sketchbook, created a mutable national (anti)monument which oscillates between the Arab village and the canonic acropolis; between the hilltop bunker and the last site of aesthetic relief; between a reductive mold of local "Bauhaus" and a prolific model of the structuralist avant-garde. As such, it embalms both the Zionist quest of the rural and the displaced phantom of the native.

According to Roland Barthes, structuralism can be defined historically as the passage from symbolic to paradigmatic consciousness. Let us now journey backward, from the paradigmatic to the symbolic, to what was described by Ada Louise Huxtable as an "architectural conceit of depressingly involved symbolism that contains the famous Dead Sea scrolls [...] an aggressively photogenic oddity, something that is often confused with great architecture."[10]

## The Shrine

The Shrine of the Book, a folly transplanted in the museum garden, was initially conceived in 1957 (it had no relation to the national museum competition, which was launched two years later). Its original site was a hill near the museum grounds, Givat Ram, where the new campus of the Hebrew University and the National Library was being built.

The Shrine was designed to display the Dead Sea Scrolls, discovered in 1948 by Bedouins in the Qumran caves in the Judean Desert. The thrill of the discovery and purchase of the Scrolls and the ensuing scholarly debate regarding their actual writers cannot be elaborated here. Let us simply recall that these scrolls, among the oldest original documents in Hebrew ever found, include biblical texts and historical testimonies written from the third century BCE to the second century CE by members of an ascetic cult hiding in the caves of the Judean Desert. The Scrolls, then, are relics from the last period of Jewish culture in the Land of Israel before two millennia of Diaspora. The first discovery of the Scrolls in 1946/1947 and the new discoveries from 1948 to 1951 coincided with

(7)

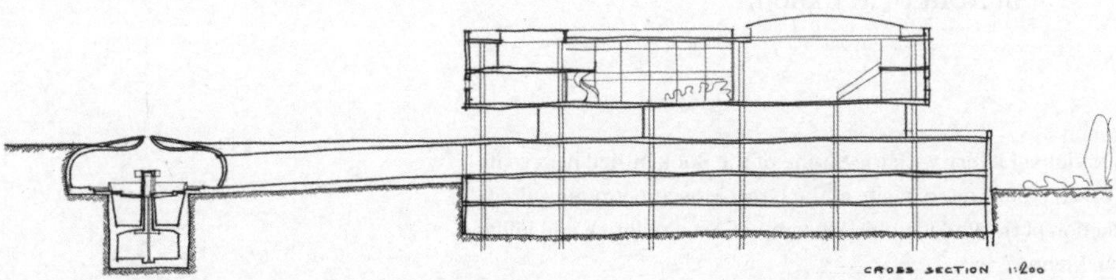

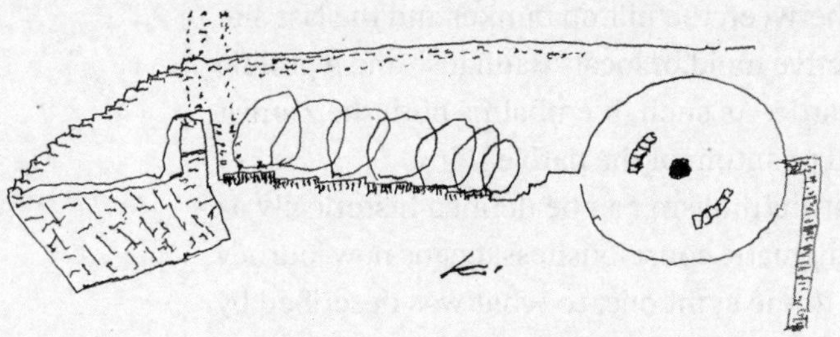

⑧

the end of the British Mandate in Palestine and the United Nations' recognition of the sovereign State of Israel, endowing the archaeological finding with a miraculous redemptive dimension and suggesting a historical shortcut between the newly founded State of Israel and the ancestral desert mystics.

This revisionist narrative of resurrection was magnificently formalized by Frederick Kiesler and Armand Bartos, who were initially commissioned to design the Shrine as an integrated yet self-contained edifice within, or rather below, the premises of the planned National Library, which was to be the centerpiece of the modern Hebrew University campus. Their proposal sketched a round vessel buried underneath the library, with a light chimney penetrating vertically through the building. The Israeli architects of the campus, and especially those of the National Library, were taken aback by the odd structure and considered it offensive in the context of what they perceived as the local showcase of International Style architecture. (The library itself was designed by a group of young architects as an inflated Villa Savoye.[11]) In *Inside the Endless House*, Kiesler recollects:

> The shrine was gently pushed out
> from the interior of the new
> library building to the outside
> in front of it. Exiled.[12]

⑦ Section of the National Library with the Shrine of the Book buried next to it.
⑧ Shrine of The Book, 1958. Sketch of site at the Israel Museum grounds. Frederick Kiesler. Collection of the Philadelphia Museum of Art. Frederick and Lillian Kiesler Foundation, Vienna.

Mediators proposed that the Shrine be separated from the library and relocated on the campus. A 1:1 model was actually built in situ to test its probability, and after several locations were attempted, it still proved to be a misfit in the otherwise modernist ensemble. In the end it was decided to move the Shrine, as-is, to the nearby museum hill, which was under construction at the time. Kiesler denounced Mansfeld and Gad's museum as an "Arab village in the International Style," alluding unambiguously to the Nazi photomontaged mockery of the Weissenhofsiedlung as *Araberdorf*. Nevertheless, the new site offered the Shrine a heightened presence and aura, which evidently pleased Kiesler. In his diaries he recounted his first impressions of Israel; his encounters with the architects of Givat Ram and later with Mansfeld; and the birth of the ideas for the parabolic shape of the Shrine and the addition of the black basalt wall to balance the white dome and circumscribe his project in the museum's open garden.

October 25, 1957

Our firm was chosen to design a shrine for the Scrolls, a shrine on the campus of the new university under construction. My partner Bartos and I flew to Tel Aviv. We rode up the hilly road to Jerusalem and on the following day we sat with many of the faculty heads as well as the president of the university and listened to the story of the origin and discovery of the precious documents. The account seemed to me beyond belief but, as I learned later, was factual indeed. The earth had given forth seeds of truth.

October 27, 1957

Two days later, on the flight back to New York, unable to sleep, I turned the overhead light on. I quickly designed: a double parabolic dome. The drafting went rapidly and when it was finished, it spoke to me with conviction as a plastic representation of "rebirth."

Spring 1958

When we returned to Jerusalem, the concept was fully approved by the faculty. The gratifying fact was that no further explanations were necessary. The plans were exhibited on the walls. Everybody seemed to understand.

[The following pages describe the rejection by the local architects and the new location on the museum grounds.]

October 13, 1959

We went to Haifa, invited by Al Mansfeld, the architect of the new art museum in Jerusalem, whose neighbor, the Shrine, will soon be within the galaxy of museums. In Haifa one can practically hear the growing pains of this city, squeezed between Arabian culture and Western industrialism.

Fall 1959

Today was another victory in the making. It concerns a new type of a giant freestanding wall, with an unusual method of joining the chunks which form it. This huge barrier would be built up of boulders of basalt in the raw, just as they came from the crater [...]. This concept was the result of the new location [the museum] since the plot is entirely open on all sides to the views of the hills. In addition, the white dome demanded a counterbalance in shape and color [...].

April 20, 1965

The Shrine of the Book opens today with a gala ceremony.

Surfacing as a miniature curvilinear monument in the museum's grounds, the Shrine was a half-buried "sanctuary of silence" designed to inspire a spiritual experience and mediate between a legendary past and a fanciful future. If the museum itself was, as described above, a system of accumulative particles, a metonymic diagram tracing at once indigenous formations and modernist functionalism, the Shrine of the Book, by contrast, was pure metaphor, an autonomous and finite object, sterile and scaleless, untouched by time and circumstance, indifferent to geography and language. Its symbolic amplitude is well described in an in-situ exhibition on the occasion of the museum's fiftieth anniversary:

The staircase and plaza leading to it have a ceremonial quality, so that visitors have the sense of making a procession toward something sacred. The monumental entrance resembles the portals of ancient temples or burial structures, and the three interior spaces parallel divisions such as the various

⑨

courts of the Jerusalem Temple, which culminated in the inner sanctum, the holy of holies. The white dome [tiled in glossy porcelain], sunk somewhat below ground level, and the black basalt wall facing it balance each other in terms of color, shape, and meaning. The dome represents the revival of the Jewish people in the State of Israel, while the wall represents their suffering in the Diaspora. Its form recalls the lids of jars in which three of the Scrolls were found. Its color is said to allude to the Sons of Light (followers of the Judean Desert sect), destined to fight the Sons of Darkness, represented by the black wall. The water on which the dome seems to float represents purity, which played a key role in the sect's way of life.

The architects originally planned to install permanent torches of fire on top of the basalt wall, as a counterpoint to jets of water emanating from the dome, but the plan was abandoned for technical reasons. Constructing this unique Shrine demanded unconventional solutions. Cast concrete slabs were attached to a wood structure to shape the double parabolic dome.[13]

For Kiesler, the carefully calculated and coordinated contrasts—light and dark, curved and straight lines, water and fire, archaism and futurism—build up the ultimate dialectical image to modernist dogma. In his article "Eine neue Akropolis," he offers his anti-functionalist and anti-formalist formal ideology:

> The Shrine of the Book [...] represents an ideologically new type of architecture and goes far beyond being merely functional. It reflects its contents and is not formalistic like buildings of Corbusier or à la Bauhaus. This style has nothing to do with the new houses on Park Avenue and the Avenue of the Americas, but leads us in a continuous sequence from biblical times into the future.[14]

On-site, the sequence of space-time experience is actually the reverse: from the post-Bauhaus future down to the pre-architectural grotto. The Shrine's exterior smoothness, blinding brightness, and excessive hygiene contrasts with

⑩

its dark and tactile interior, which invokes the womb-like spaces dreamed of by the surrealists. Once underground, the visitor is led on a journey from a claustrophobic tunnel to a monumental cupola; from the ritualized stone wall outside to the fetishized text inside. The Isaiah Scroll, the collection's centerpiece, is positioned at the geometric center of the building, under its nipple, connected to the heavens by a column of light and—so the tale goes—transportable to a quarried nuclear shelter by a sliding hydraulic column in case of an emergency.

The Shrine of the Book is the only freestanding building achieved by Kiesler, and it should be considered in relation to the holistic spatial theory he developed from the 1930s under the enigmatic title "Correalism." According to Correalism, forms were presumably the outcome of interplay between visible and invisible forces driven by the needs and aspirations of people in relation to their environment. The most elaborate and well-known architectural vision to emerge from Correalism was Kiesler's Endless House, which was "called the 'Endless' because all ends meet, and meet continuously. [...] There is no beginning and no end to it."[15] The Shrine of the Book's Correalist credo is its illusive non-photogeneity, as can be gathered from Kiesler's phenomenological verse:

> The entire Shrine is a matter of continuity.
> You cannot photograph the spaces.
> You have to go through them.
> The architecture takes you by the hand
> and guides you through.[16]

In 1958, while working on the plans for the Shrine of the Book, Kiesler was invited to build a full-scale prototype of the Endless House for the sculpture garden of The Museum of Modern Art in New York. Since the project was never
⑪ executed, we are left with the Shrine in Jerusalem to experience Kiesler's built

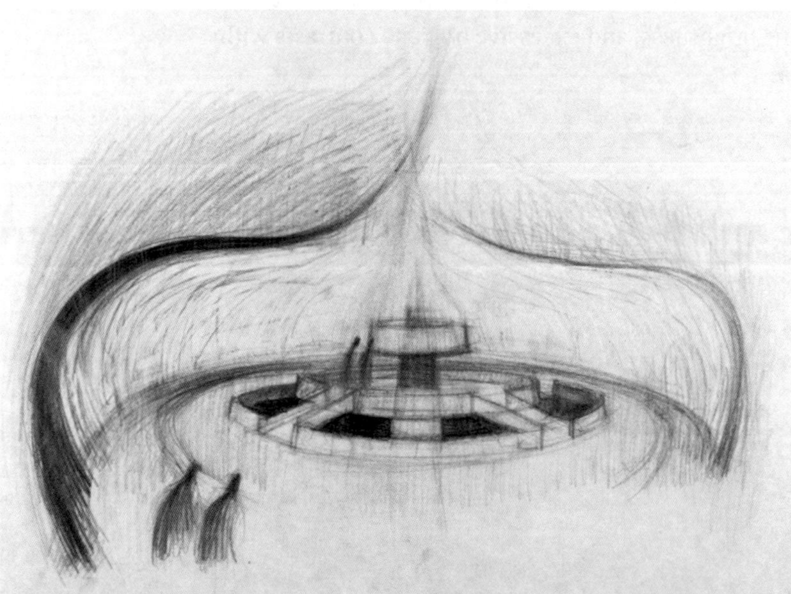

endlessness and amass it with signification. It is perhaps not at all surprising that while the local professional and artistic milieu remained indifferent — or rather, speechless—about the eccentric architecture of the Shrine, the general public was inspired to release figurative associations and historical connotations triggered by the building. And the international print media was instantaneously charged by it, as reported by *Progressive Architecture*:

> In the first five months since its opening, this building has been enthusiastically praised and vociferously panned. *Vogue* has called it "instantly one of the most beautiful buildings in the world." Nelson Glueck of the Hebrew Union College has said, "a book is a shrine in itself, but it is doubly so when housed in a shrine like this. Time has become timeless here." And *The New York Times* carried a reverent review by Sam Hunter [...] who said: "It is sculpture and architecture at once, the summation of Kiesler's considerable plastic genius." The negative position was taken by the [...] *Jerusalem Post*, whose architectural correspondent observed acidly that "internally it has the atmosphere of an electricity-generating turbine station." These views are supplemented by the breast vs. onion argument, which is becoming ever more involved as more viewers indulge their fantasies (Chinese pagoda, coolie hat, child's top, etc.).[17]

In a letter of reply to the abovementioned *Jerusalem Post* article, Kiesler argued that the Shrine had no symbolic meaning at all. Curiously, however, his insistence all along on the purely conceptual origin of the shrine only reaffirmed its epic ambition to objectify timelessness:

> This is the first ideological building
> in our time.
> It is not a symbolic building at all.
> It is neither a woman's breast,
> nor an onion, nor a jar.
> The Shrine comes from its inner concept,
> which has grown into a structure.
> It is the first building anywhere today
> that in its totality and in every detail
> is related to its own basic ideology.[18] ■

⑨ Shrine of the Book, 1960. Conceptual drawing. Frederick Kiesler. Collection of the Philadelphia Museum of Art. Frederick and Lillian Kiesler Foundation, Vienna.
⑩ Endless House, 1958. Model. Frederick Kiesler.
⑪ Shrine of the Book, 1962. Conceptual drawing. Frederick Kiesler. Collection of the Philadelphia Museum of Art. Frederick and Lillian Kiesler Foundation, Vienna.

⑫ Shrine of the Book, 1965. Photographer: Hillel Burger. Israel Museum Archives.

1 The Bezalel museum was instituted in 1906 as part of the Bezalel Arts and Crafts School in Jerusalem and was opened to the public in 1912. It operated until 1965, when it was reincarnated as the Israel Museum.

2 Peter Eisenman, "miMISes READING: does not mean A THING," in *Mies Reconsidered: His Career, Legacy, and Disciples*, ed. John Zukowsky (Chicago and New York: Art Institute of Chicago and Rizzoli, 1986), p. 88.

3 Ibid.

4 Ibid.

5 Al Mansfeld, reading from notes in a discussion with the author, 1997.

6 Ada Louise Huxtable, "Museums A La Carte," *New York Times*, June 15, 1969, Section D, page 23.

7 Philipp Misselwitz, "Landscape of Change, Growth and Uncertainty – Reworking the Israel Museum," *Quaderns, no.* 243 (October 2004), p. 20.

8 Ibid., pp. 21–22. Misselwitz's account here is based on technical information supplied in interviews with Efrat-Kowalsky Architects, who were in charge of the museum's renewal project from 2002 to 2010.

9 The museum's constant requests for additional spaces led to the invention of the Luda Model system in the 1970s. This modular system, developed by the office of Mansfeld-Mansfeld-Kehat, examined the various possible compositions of building elements and their effect on the whole. Luda Models were made from square and triangular pieces of wood, based on the mathematical modules used for the museum. All elements could move and change horizontally and vertically, and be added to horizontally. Luda became an effective working tool for the office, enabling the quick simulation of growth scenarios which could be demonstrated to curators and donors by means of photographic documentation. See Misselwitz, "Landscape."

10 Huxtable, "Museums A La Carte."

11 On the architecture of the Hebrew University campus and the National Library, see chapter "State Architecture."

12 Frederick Kiesler, *Inside the Endless House; Art, People, and Architecture: A Journal* (New York: Simon and Schuster, 1966), p. 318. Cited in Jill Meissner, *Kiesler and Bartos: The Shrine of the Book*, exh. cat. (Vienna: Austrian Frederick and Lillian Kiesler Private Foundation), p. 29. (The exhibition was curated by Jill Meissner and Gerd Zillner and ran from June to October 2015.)

13 Text in the exhibition *The Architecture of the Shrine of the Book*, curated by Osnat Syrkin and Judith Kaplan, The Israel Museum, April–December 2015.

14 Frederick Kiesler, "Eine neue Akropolis," in *Aufbau*, May 28, 1965, p. 16. Cited in Meissner, *Kiesler and Bartos*, p. 31.

15 Kiesler, *Inside the Endless House*, p. 566. Cited in Dieter Bogner, *Friedrich Kiesler, 1890–1965: Inside the Endless House* (Vienna: Böhlau, 1997), p. 19.

16 Kiesler, "The Shrine of the Book," *Progressive Architecture* 46 (September 1965), p. 130.

17 Editorial, *Progressive Architecture* 46 (September 1965), p. 133.

18 Kiesler, "Shrine of the Book," p. 127.

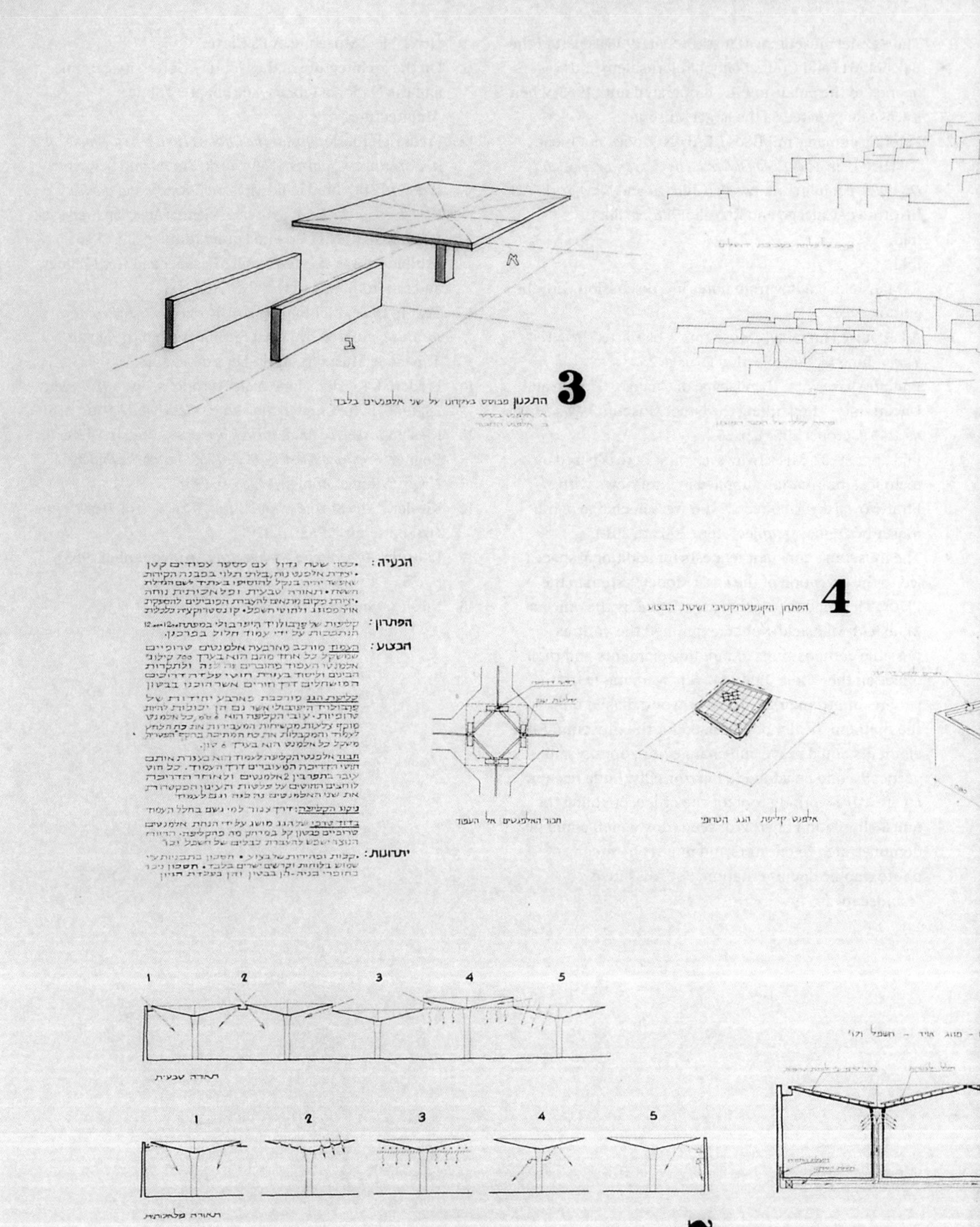

3
התכנון מבוסס בעיקרו על שני אלמנטים בלבד
א
ב
4
הבעיה:
הפתרון:
הבצוע:
יתרונות:
1
2
3
4
5
7

**2**

התאמה לסביבה הירושלמית האופינית

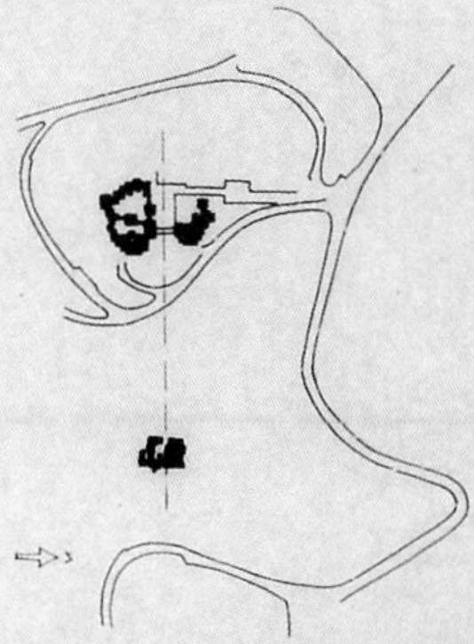

**1** **אתר:** הפניה אל ירושלים העיר וקשר פורתי לסביבה

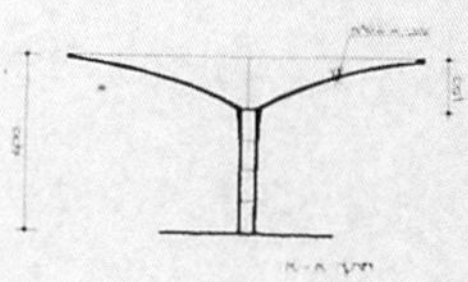

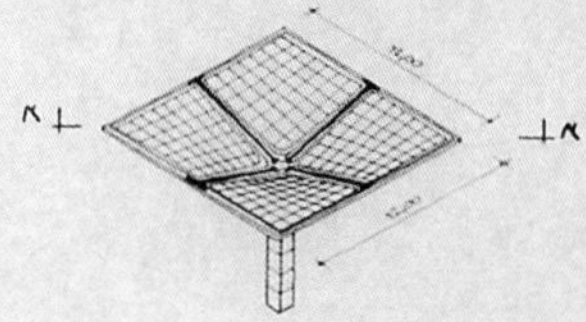

הפרבולויד ההיפרבולי

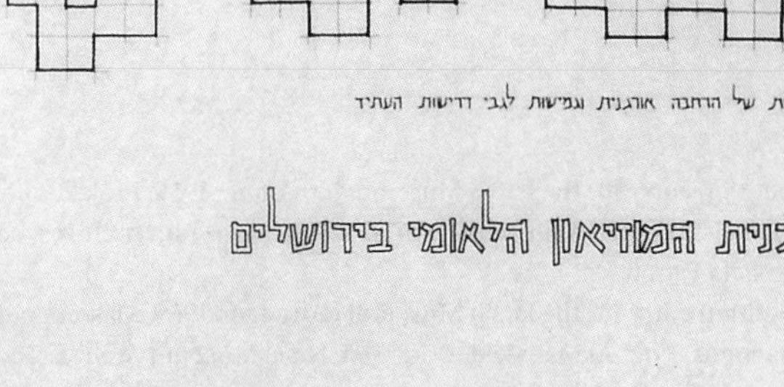

**5** אפשרויות של הרחבה אורגנית וגמישות לגבי דרישות העתיד

# התחרות לתכנית המוזיאון הלאומי בירושלים

## עקרונות התכנון

⑬

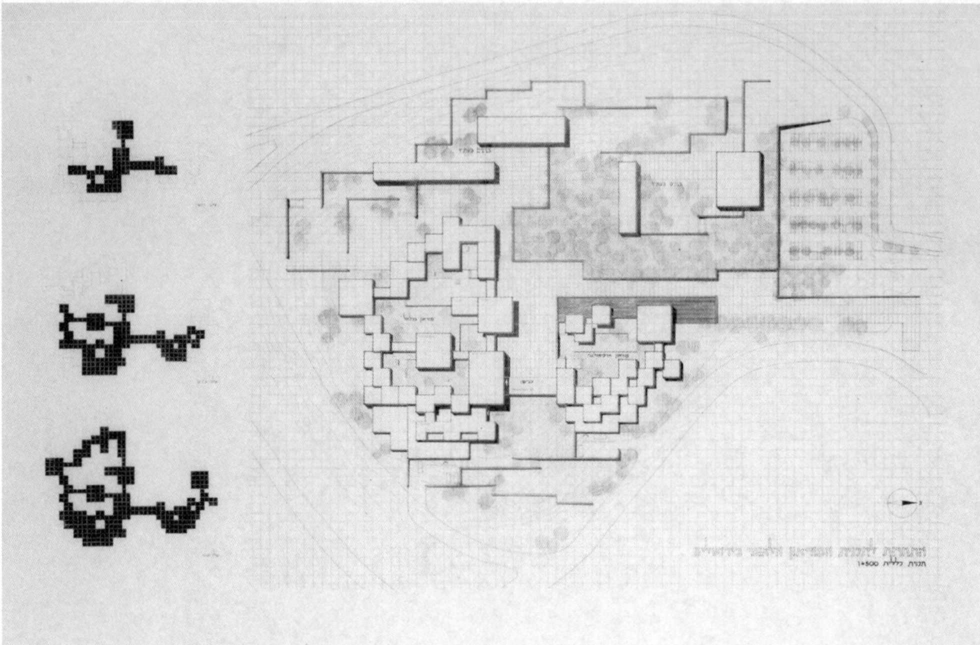

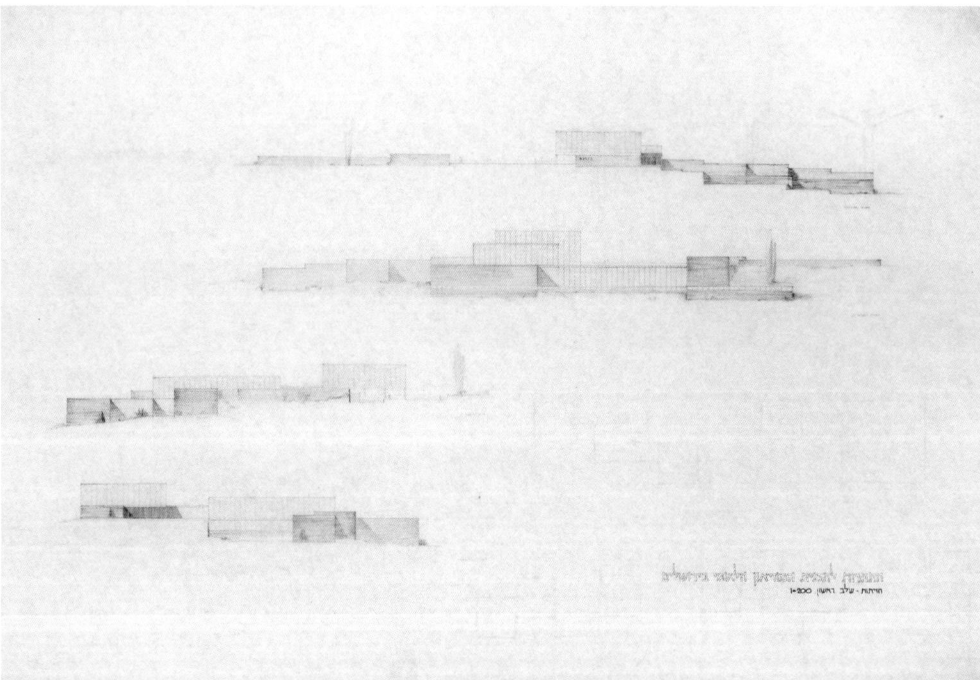

⑭ ⑮

⑬ Competition entry for the Israel Museum, Jerusalem, 1959. Project's concept and components. Prof. Al Mansfeld, Dora Gad. Israel Museum Archives, courtesy of the Mansfeld Family.
⑭ Competition entry for the Israel Museum, Jerusalem, 1959. Master plan and growth diagrams. Prof. Al Mansfeld, Dora Gad. Israel Museum Archives, courtesy of the Mansfeld Family.
⑮ Competition entry for the Israel Museum, Jerusalem, 1959. Elevations. Prof. Al Mansfeld, Dora Gad. Israel Museum Archives, courtesy of the Mansfeld Family.

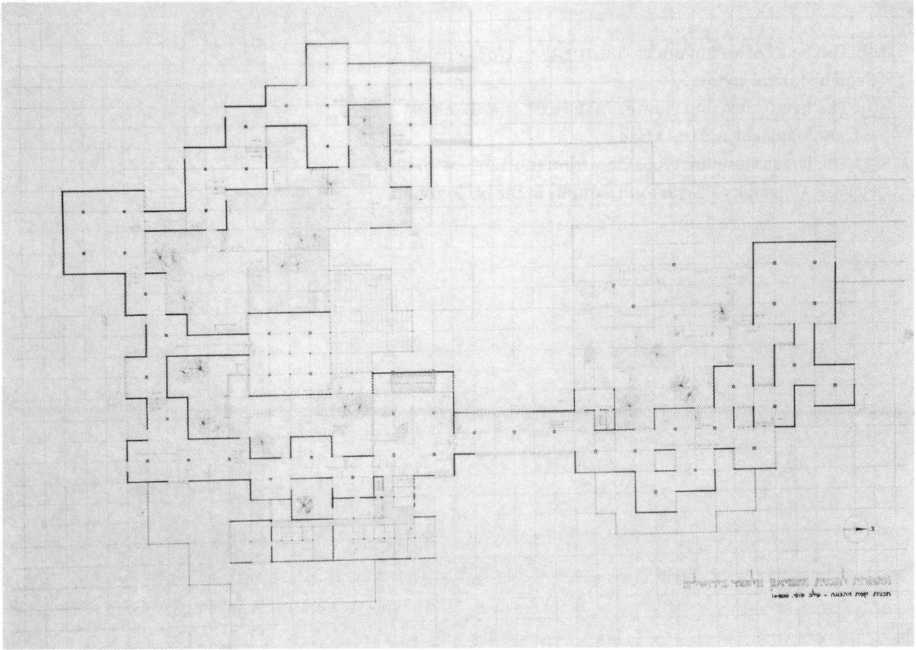

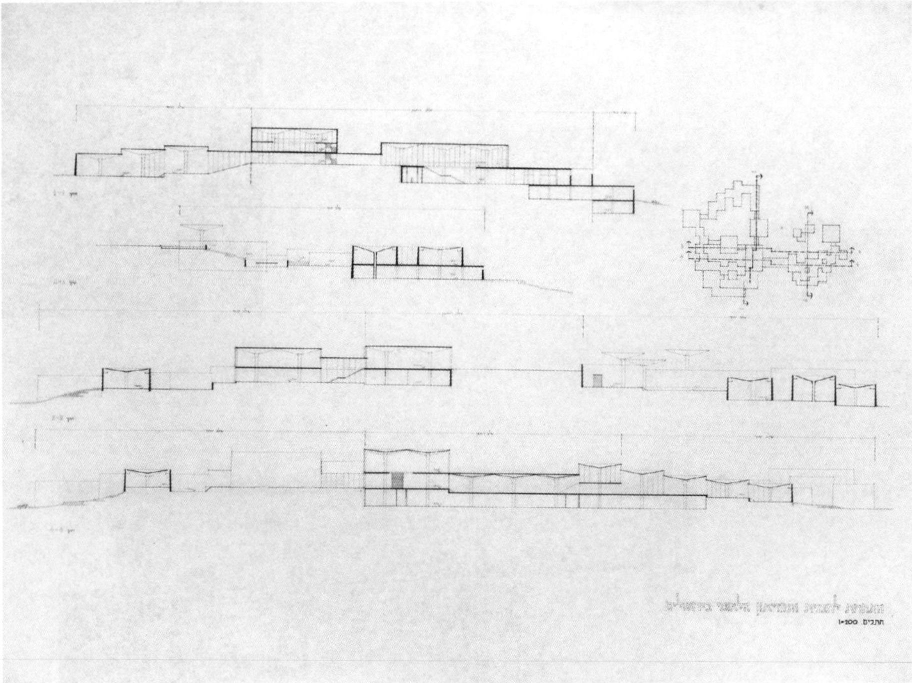

⑯ ⑰

⑯ Competition entry for the Israel Museum, Jerusalem, 1959. Floor plan.
Prof. Al Mansfeld, Dora Gad. Israel Museum Archives, courtesy of the Mansfeld Family.
⑰ Competition entry for the Israel Museum, Jerusalem, 1959. Sections.
Prof. Al Mansfeld, Dora Gad. Israel Museum Archives, courtesy of the Mansfeld Family.

⑱ The Israel Museum under construction, 1962. Shikun & Binui historical archive.
⑲ The Israel Museum: view from the east, mid-1960s. Prof. Al Mansfeld and Dora Gad.
⑳ The Israel Museum, 1965. View from the north, with the Hebrew University's Givat Ram campus in the background.

⑲

⑱

⑳

㉑

㉒

㉓

㉔

㉕

㉑ The Israel Museum, Jerusalem. Perspective of exhibition spaces. Prof. Al Mansfeld. Israel Museum Archives, courtesy of the Mansfeld Family.
㉒ The Israel Museum, Jerusalem, 1960s. View of the main entrance hall with four hypar "mushrooms."
㉓ The Israel Museum, Jerusalem, 1960s. Interior view.
㉔ The Israel Museum, Jerusalem, 1960s. View from the archaeology wing.
㉕ The Israel Museum, Jerusalem. Perspective and collage of exhibition spaces. Prof. Al Mansfeld. Israel Museum Archives, courtesy of the Mansfeld Family.

The hope was to have something miraculous,
in the sense of surprises,
like entering a beautiful garden that you
have never seen before,
and could never have known in advance.
The trouble with most architecture is
that we know it all in advance.

The Shrine is nothing but scale
in all its parts.

And so you have been in the past,
and you skip the present,
and you look toward the future.
That is the magnificent experience
of the Shrine.
People feel that they have gone back
thousands of years into the past,
but when they come out
they see the future in front of them.
People go in with doubts.
They do not understand what it is.
But they come out with stars in their eyes.
You can go to church on Sunday,
or temple on Yom Kippur,
but as someone says, a very religious
man, you sit there,
but you are not there.
At the Shrine of the Book,
you are really there.

1

2

3

4

PHOTO: DAVID RUBINGER

5

ALL PHOTOS THIS PAGE, EXCEPT AS NOTED: ALFRED BERNHEIM

6

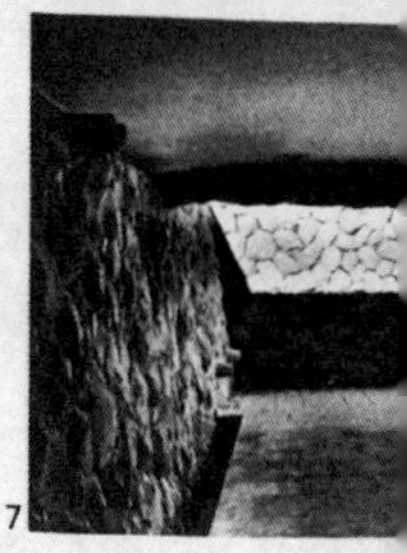
7

8

9

10

*Before going through the Shrine, one can rest in a shaded area first* **(1)**. *The earliest of the many spatial experiences is in the patio* **(2)**, *from which the research library leads off in one direction, the exhibit areas in the other. Since stone architecture of the past did not have railings for a stair along a wall, the solution here was to place a 6" square block at the end of each tread (shown at larger scale, page 126). Along the wall itself, one can grasp the polished stones that protrude at intervals. Once in the building, at the basalt wall, the setting is sombre except for the bright daylight filtering down from above* **(3)**, *and the gleaming brass of the gate* **(4)**. *The display corridor (page 129, bottom), with its variously shaped openings, leads finally to the sanctuary* **(5)** *and the central Isaiah Scroll. Around the interior are other displays, in 10-ft-wide vitrines that are removable for safekeeping to a vault outside the dome. Downstairs* **(6)**, *there are further artifacts displayed in niches along the masonry walls, in a crypt that intensifies the image of a cave. The only source of light here comes from the display cases, or filters down from above. Journeying up again (a balustrade has been added to this staircase), one leaves by a short exit corridor* **(7)**, *a neutral space that gives time to absorb the whole experience. Then an open-air corridor, 200-ft long* **(8)**, *makes possible a further meditation period, with three views out towards Jerusalem* **(9, 10)**. *The polygonal stone of these walls is the native stone of Jerusalem, found lying on any hillside.*

APPRAISAL

the first five months since its opening, this building has n enthusiastically praised and vociferously panned. *Vogue* called it "instantly one of the most beautiful buildings the world." Nelson Glueck of the Hebrew Union College said, "A book is a shrine in itself, but it is doubly so en housed in a shrine like this. Time has become timeless e" (quoted in *Time* magazine). And *The New York Times* ried a reverent review by Sam Hunter, now director of w York's Jewish Museum, who said, "It is sculpture and hitecture at once, the summation of Kiesler's considerable stic genius." The negative position was taken by the glish-language newspaper *The Jerusalem Post*, whose hitectural correspondent observed acidly that "internally has the atmosphere of an electricity-generating turbine tion." These views are supplemented by the breast vs. onion ument, which is becoming ever more involved as more wers indulge their fantasies (Chinese pagoda, coolie hat, d's top, etc.).

here are, of course, more specific evaluations that can be de. The Shrine is nominally part of an entire hillside com-x, but it remains ill-coordinated with the other two parts the complex, each of which—like the Shrine—is a strong ign (the art garden of sculptured earthworks by Isamu guchi, and the large museum, an International-style "Arab age," by A. Mansfeld and Dora Gad). The shrine is a ll, self-contained unit at the edge of the hill, in some npetition with the other two elements, and from certain les so low as to be effectively out of the running.

n the Shrine itself, some critics have pointed to an uneasy nbination of forms—what one writer calls the difficulty of uaring the circle." Others have looked at various materials "special effects," and found them jarring: the line of gas atop the black basalt wall, the automatic door at the rance to the sanctuary (suggesting to *The Jerusalem Post* ic the "gimmickry of International Fairs"), and a com-ation of materials that verges on the "bewildering."

ome have said that the Shrine is extravagant, in a land re new schools and housing are urgently needed. But the ds came from a private source—the D. S. and R. H. Gottes-n Foundation; the late Samuel Gottesman had purchased r of the seven Dead Sea Scrolls in 1954, and then decided provide for their permanent safekeeping in Israel. In any e, a shrine cannot be compared with a school by any aningful criteria; each has its own validity on its own terms.

erhaps adding to the rumble of negative comment is one troversial question. There is an elaborate design—not yet lt—for a plastic cone to protect the case of the Isaiah oll against backsplash from the central water jet. But the is already functioning (intermittently, when good weather mits removal of the present plastic cover at the apex of sanctuary), and the Isaiah Scroll is already fully protected. haps it is the *idea* of water that is disturbing; the scrolls, r all, were only preserved for 2000 years because they were he dry climate of the Dead Sea, sealed in jars in caves. It ıld be emphasized, however, that the water in no way angers the scroll; the architects worked for four years the British Museum, Smithsonian Institute, and Metro-tan Museum, studying techniques for preserving rare documents, and have applied them rigorously in the Shrine. The water is questioned here purely as an idea (although Kiesler replies that "fire and water are the very symbols of rebirth").

And, with all this, one returns to the *idea* of the Shrine, as expressed in Kiesler's words. The strength of the idea of rebirth is undeniable. Here is a powerful vision, echoing the great moral cry of the priceless items now housed in the Shrine. Among these are 2000-year-old letters from the fortress of Masada, the remote rock overlooking the Dead Sea where the last group of Jews held out against the Romans after Jerusalem fell in 70 A.D. After three years, when defeat was a certainty, these 960 men, women, and children died by their own hand rather than let themselves be taken captive. And in the Isaiah Scroll, now the oldest of any existing Biblical manuscript, is the prophet's vision:

> And they shall beat their swords
> into plowshares,
> And their spears into pruninghooks;
> Nation shall not lift up sword
> against nation,
> Neither shall they learn war anymore.

If anything, the world needs these ideas more today than ever before, when brutality and arrogance and hypocrisy seem to be feeding on themselves and growing stronger.

If, as is the judgment of some, the execution of the Shrine is less than equal to its idea, perhaps it is because ideas are inevitably stronger than objects. Abba Eban, Deputy Prime Minister of Israel, spoke about this duality when the Israel Museum was opened this spring. "The Jerusalem in which we stand is a dual concept. Above the material Jerusalem of streets and buildings, bricks and mortar, there is the ideal Jerusalem that lives forever in the heart and hopes of men —symbol, in every land and every tongue, of man's unfinished quest for individual and social perfection."

Life, and the works of man, must always be imperfect. And the Shrine of the Book is a statement about life—it is more than a repository for ancient documents and historic artifacts. History and archeology are already living subjects to the people of the State of Israel, and Kiesler and Bartos have enshrined these objects of the past in such a way as to make them even more vitally and dramatically meaningful. Kiesler has always had a feeling for drama; among his innovations were the startling settings for Capek's *R.U.R.* and the kinetic space-stage for *The Emperor Jones*, and his Endless House was originally conceived as a vast space-theater. The Shrine of the Book is theater in its own way. There is architectural drama in the structuring of space, and in the extreme sensitivity to the tension and resolution of opposites. It demands more than passive viewing; it wills an active response from "mind and heart and guts."

There are few buildings for which an ideological architecture is appropriate, or even possible. And few architects who would dare to attempt it. Whether Kiesler and Bartos have, in fact, given plastic expression to an idea—the idea of rebirth—will be debated by all who feel strongly about this building. —EP

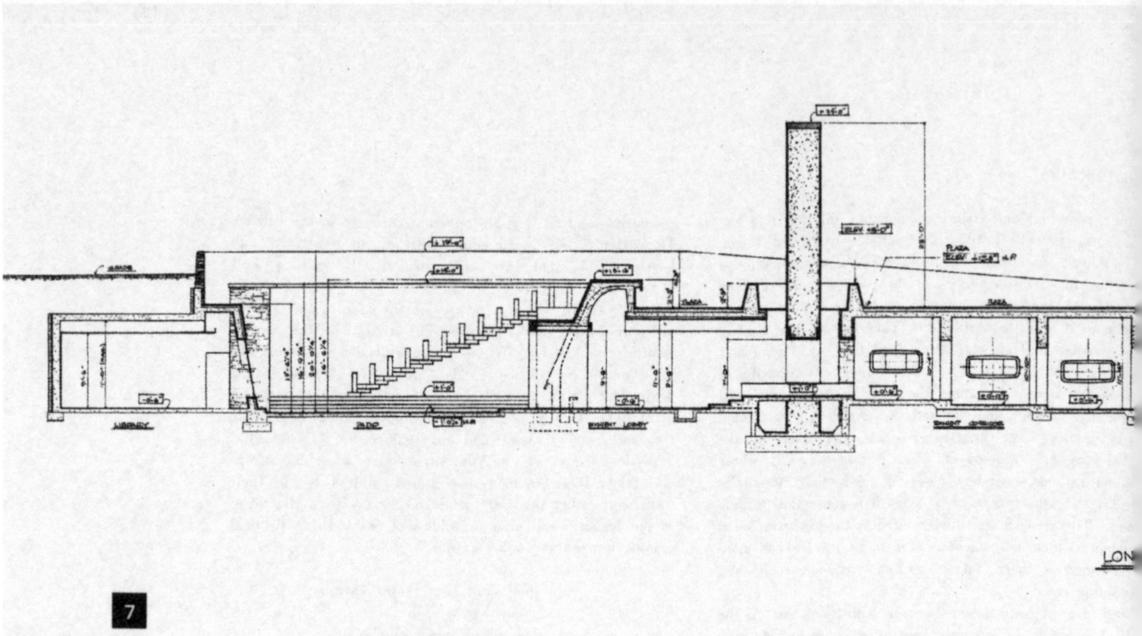

(27)

(28)

(29)

(26) Spread from *Progressive Architecture*, September 1965.
(27) The Shrine of the Book, early 1960s. Longitudinal section. Armand Bartos and Frederick Kiesler.
(28) The Shrine's dome under construction, early 1960s. View of the crypt below the dome. Photographer: Alfred Bernheim. Israel Museum Archives.
(29) The Shrine's dome under construction, early 1960s. Photographer: Alfred Bernheim. Israel Museum Archives.
(30) The Shrine of the Book, 1958. Conceptual drawing. Frederick Kiesler. Collection of the Philadelphia Museum of Art. Frederick and Lillian Kiesler Foundation, Vienna.

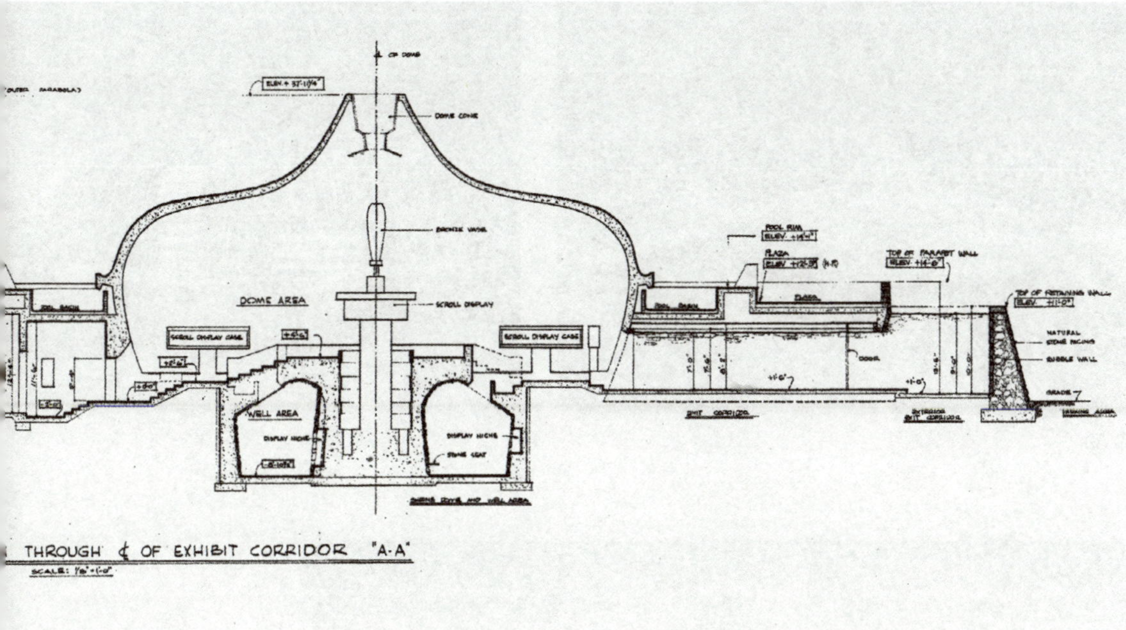
DOME AREA
SCROLL DISPLAY CASE
SCROLL DISPLAY CASE
WELL AREA
TOP OF PARAPET WALL
TOP OF RETAINING WALL
THROUGH ℄ OF EXHIBIT CORRIDOR "A-A"

30

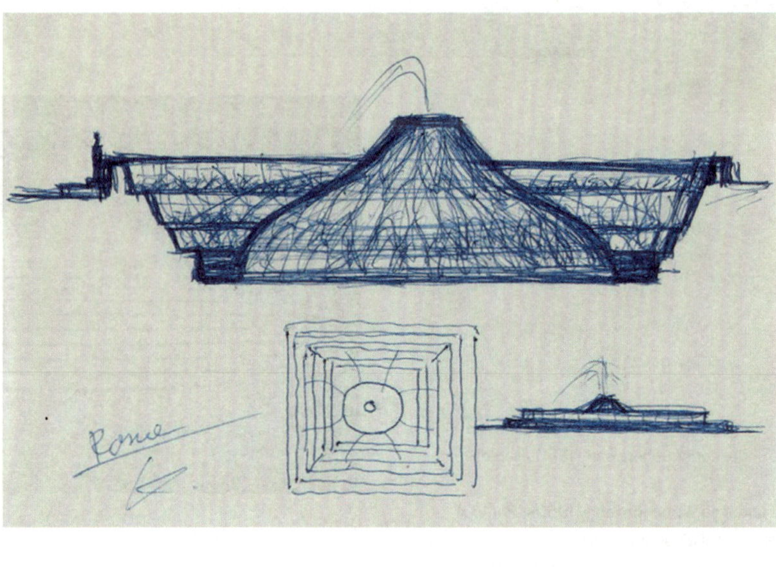
Rome

(31) (32)

(33)

(34)

(31) The Shrine's dome under construction, early 1960s. Israel Museum Archives.
(32) The Shrine's dome under construction, early 1960s. Photographer: Alfred Bernheim. Israel Museum Archives.
(33) The Shrine's dome under construction, early 1960s. Photographer: Alfred Bernheim. Israel Museum Archives.
(34) The Shrine's dome under construction, early 1960s. Israel Museum Archives.

(35)

(36)

(35) Frederick Kiesler before the Shrine's inauguration ceremony, 1965. Photographer: David Harris. Israel Museum Archives.
(36) Armand Bartos and Frederick Kiesler in front of the Shrine of the Book, 1965. Photographer: Alfred Bernheim. Israel Museum Archives.

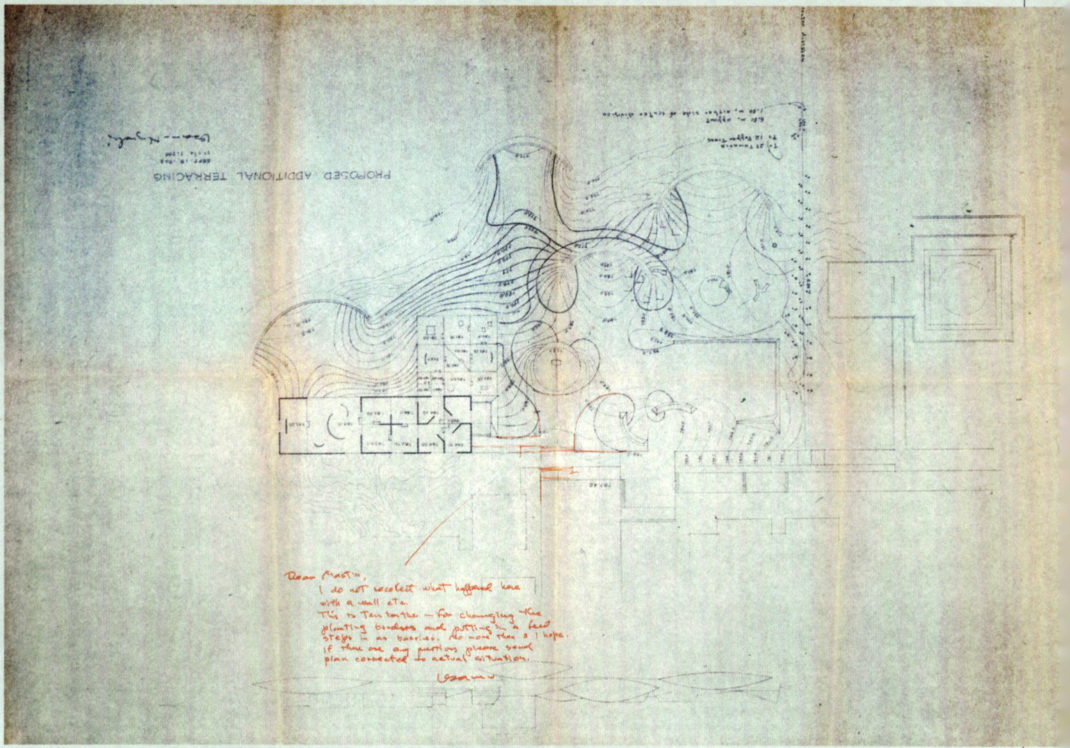

(37) Proposed additional terracing for the Billy Rose Sculpture Garden, Jerusalem, 1960–1965. Plan. Isamu Noguchi. Isamu Noguchi Foundation and Garden Museum, New York.

In 1960 Isamu Noguchi was asked by Billy Rose, the American impresario, to design a sculpture garden for his collection on the premises of the Israel Museum in Jerusalem. To acquire Rose's collection, the museum had agreed to designate a vast outdoor site as the Billy Rose Sculpture Garden. Noguchi reflected on the circumstances of this commission and its spiritual significance to him:

> Jerusalem is not a city; it is a place of the emotions. There is a hill there called Neve Shaanan, "The Place of Tranquility." Here was to be built the New National Museum of Israel—and here I was asked to build a garden for sculpture.
>
> It was the idea of Billy Rose that he would present his collection of Western European sculpture since Rodin as a nucleus to which would be added the sculptures of our time—the significance of which would be pointed through the setting: a garden tied to history, reverse-wise, as it were.
>
> In the new Jerusalem of the new state of Israel, facing its parliament (Knesset), still to be built, and its new Hebrew University, this would be the place of quiet and contemplation. The garden is between the archaeological museum, the Bezalel National Museum, and the domed repository of the Dead Sea Scrolls, designed by Frederick Kiesler.
>
> About five acres of walkable space is to be made through the device of large, curved, retaining walls, which are like great wings seen from the university, or like vast ship prows from within the garden. There are to be no roads or paths, only free areas of gravel and planting, wherein the sculptures by their placement will themselves act as the delineators of an abstract space, formal and informal in counterpoint to the various walls and the blue sky [...].[1]

Martin Friedman, the director of the Walker Art Center, elaborated on Noguchi's design concept for the sculpture garden in Jerusalem on the occasion of the 1978 exhibition *Noguchi's Imaginary Landscapes*:

> His concept for the sculpture garden was a series of huge, curved retaining walls formed of local rubble to create spacious outdoor galleries. [...]
>
> The heroic process of earth moving soon began. The great, curved walls became imposing sculptural forms that echoed the surrounding hills and seemed always to have been part of the landscape. Of their appropriateness to the site, Noguchi says:
>
> "Everybody seems to think my walls were evocative of Israel, but all around Jerusalem and all through the Near East you have these retaining walls because of the dryness of the land. But those are all straight, not curved."
>
> [...] The Rose collection, which includes examples by 19th and 20th century European and American masters such as Rodin, Bourdelle, Moore, Calder, David Smith and Noguchi himself, as well as works by a group of contemporary Israeli sculptors, was comfortably deployed within Noguchi's commodious spaces.
>
> Impressive as the venture is, the relationship of the sculptures to their surroundings is not without problems. Many massive works manage to hold their own within Noguchi's idiosyncratic spaces, but smaller sculptures are sometimes diminished by them. Noguchi is the first to assert that his curved, rubble-formed walls are not always hospitable to traditional, base-oriented sculpture. His spaces, he feels, serve best as backgrounds for tall, linear shapes that can work against rough mass; the ideal form for exhibition in these, he wryly suggests, might be a lunar lander. [...]
>
> The overall result, nevertheless, is an awesome space in which sculptures, representative of diverse styles, interact vividly with their surroundings.[2] ■

1 Isamu Noguchi, "Sculpture Garden of the New National Museum in Jerusalem," undated manuscript, possibly a draft for the garden's inauguration speech (Document MS_PROJ_106_024, The Noguchi Museum Archives, Long Island City, NY).

2 Martin Friedman, "Noguchi's Imaginary Landscapes," *Design Quarterly* 106/107 (1978), pp. 1, 3–99.

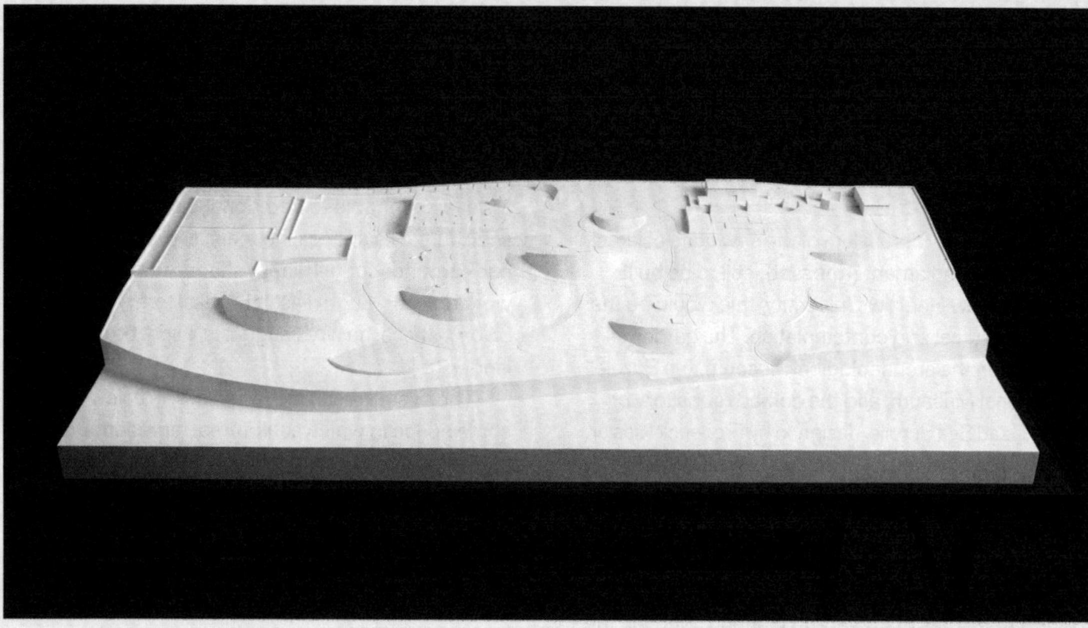

㊳

אל. מנספלד, ארכיטקט
AL. MANSFELD, ARCHITECT

Haifa, April 9, 1960

Dear Isamu,

Enclosed two copies of the General Layout of the Sculpture Garden, the Museum and the Shrine of the Book. Could you please give one of the copies to Kiesler + Bartos?

You have probably heard that there is quite an uproar of the orthodox people against a sculpture garden in Jerusalem, but as the "indignation" is artificially built up for political reasons, I hope it will quiet down in a while, and that everything will turn out all right in the end. I ignore to what extent Billy Rose has been informed of the position, but I am sure that his intervention could help a lot to clear up the situation.

With best wishes

Yours

Al

HAIFA, MT. CARMEL, 5, KELLER ST., PHONE 84102 חיפה, הר הכרמל, רחוב קלר 5, טלפון 84102

(39)

⑩

⑪

(42)

(43)

(38) The Billy Rose Sculpture Garden, Jerusalem, 1960–1965. Model. Isamu Noguchi Foundation and Garden Museum, New York.
(39) Letter from Al Mansfeld to Isamu Noguchi, 1960. Isamu Noguchi Foundation and Garden Museum, New York.
(40) – (41) The Billy Rose Sculpture Garden, 1960–1965. Detail of a model. Isamu Noguchi Foundation and Garden Museum, New York.
(42) Isamu Noguchi working on a model of the Billy Rose Sculpture Garden, March 1960. Isamu Noguchi Foundation and Garden Museum, New York.
(43) – (46) The Billy Rose Sculpture Garden, The Israel Museum, Jerusalem, 1960–1965. Isamu Noguchi Foundation and Garden Museum, New York.

(44)

(45)

(46)

㊼

㊽

㊾

㊼ Isamu Noguchi at the construction site of the Billy Rose Sculpture Garden, 1965. Photographer: R. M. Kneller. Isamu Noguchi Foundation and Garden Museum, New York.
㊽–㊾ The Billy Rose Sculpture Garden, The Israel Museum, Jerusalem, 1960–1965. Isamu Noguchi Foundation and Garden Museum, New York.

# Ein Rafa

① The village of Ein Naqquba, 2016. Photographers: Sharbel Halloun, Nagham Copty, Fouad Habash.

## The Story of Ein Naqquba (aka Ein Rafa)[1] by Sharbel Halloun, Nagham Copty, Fouad Habash

On the south side of the Jerusalem–Tel Aviv highway, ten kilometers from the Old City of Jerusalem, lies the village of Ein Naqquba. This village did not exist until the year 1962, when it was built to house the refugees of the Palestinian village of Beit Naqquba.

In 1945, Beit Naqquba consisted of 55 houses and 240 people. Its residents relied mainly on agriculture; they owned vast lands on which they grew olive trees, grape vines, and grains. Like most other Palestinian villagers, the people of Beit Naqquba were displaced by the Arab-Israeli War of 1948. Today, the site of their village is occupied by the Jewish moshav Beit Nekofa.[2]

During the years 1961 and 1962, a number of articles were published in Israeli newspapers concerning the fate of Beit Naqquba and the resettlement of its inhabitants. In one article, bearing the headline "An Arab Village is Born," the mukhtar of the village, Ahmad Hussein, recalls that one day during the War of 1948, his Jewish friend Yaakov Lisser, from the nearby kibbutz Kiryat Anavim, advised him and his people to flee from their village.[3] After the war, the mukhtar received a letter from Lisser calling the people of Beit Naqquba to return to their lands, but not to their houses. However, "one day, in the middle of work, Mr. A. Biderman, a messenger from the Custodian of Absentee Property, appeared" and ordered that cultivation of the land be stopped.[4] Soon afterward, the villagers' houses were settled by Jewish immigrants from the Balkans, and their lands were confiscated and handed over to the newcomers as well.

Mukhtar Hussein expressed his opposition in the Israeli parliament, requesting that the property be returned to its original owners, but his call was not answered. For fourteen years the people of Beit Naqquba lived as refugees, engaged in a legal battle and negotiating with the authorities. In 1962 they were resettled in a new village planned by the architectural team of Alfred Neumann, Zvi Hecker, and Eldar Sharon, one kilometer south of their original home, next to the existing Arab village of Ein Rafa. The newspaper reporter Aharon Dolev attempted to convey the complexity of the moment:

> A mountain terrace. A row of cast concrete boxes and an enlightening sign: Housing Department, Dwelling Units for Arab Citizens. A new village is born in the Judean Mountains. A sense of anxiety is in the air. A strange and unnatural tranquility. No breaking-ground celebration. At the mukhtar's house [are] sitting a few "new settlers" who were privileged to receive from the Housing Department the keys for their new homes, but agony is reflected in their eyes. [They are] the exiles of the former Arab Beit Naqquba.[5]

As one of the original maps signed by the architects shows, the project for the new village consisted of two phases, A and B. Twenty housing units, surrounded by open yards, were planned for each phase. The two phases are shown to be connected by two main roads, and the houses are categorized into two types, rectangular and square.[6] The original design depicts small units of about 36 square meters each, based on load-bearing stone walls that hold roofs made of corrugated metal sheets. With time, these core houses were swallowed up —to the point of almost disappearing—by the massive expansion of the village. The remains of two of them can still be detected today.

A topographic map of the area has the caption "Prepared for the Housing Department" (Agaf Hashikun),[7] indicating that the project for the new village was commissioned by the governmental Housing Department, which was under the Ministry of Labor at the time. However, archival letters related to this issue show that the Israeli Ministry of Agriculture and the Jewish National Fund (JNF) were also involved. On March 4, 1960, Shalom Sverdlov from the Landholdings Department at the Ministry of Agriculture received a letter from the Department of Housing, replying to his inquiry regarding the "*shikun* [Hebrew for "housing"] in Ein Rafa" and reporting that the planning was complete. Two days later, Sverdlov sent a letter to Yididya Eisenstadt from the JNF, asking him to hand over the area designated for the Arabs of Beit Naqquba. The same day, as another letter shows, Eisenstadt had received two

2

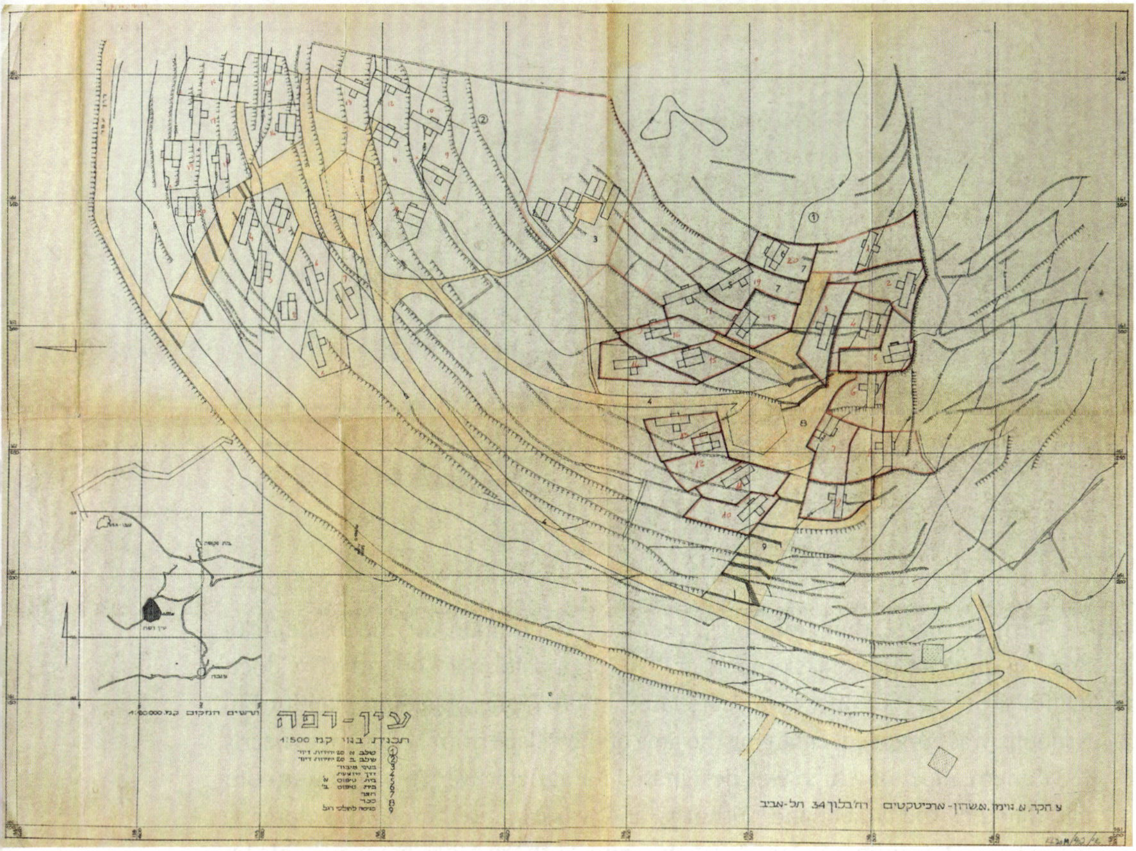


③

topographic maps of the area of Ein Rafa from the department of mapping in the JNF.[8]

Considering the fact that no other village was planned in Israel for Palestinian refugees, the question hovering above the story of Ein Naqquba is why the governmental Housing Department commissioned such a project.

The abovementioned newspaper article reported that the village was established within the legal framework of the Land Acquisition Law of 1953.[9] This law allowed the Minister of Finance to approve the expropriation of land and allot it to the Land Development Authority (Rashut Hapituah) if those lands were not in the possession of their owners on April 1, 1952, due to the State's use of the land for development, settlement, or security purposes. However, section 3 of the law states that owners of expropriated properties are entitled to financial compensation, or to alternative lands if they relied mainly on agriculture.[10]

② Ein Naqquba, 1961. Plan prepared for the Housing Department, Ministry of Labor. Zvi Hecker, Alfred Neumann, Eldar Sharon. Central Zionist Archives.
③ Ein Naqquba, 1961. Plan prepared for the Housing Department, Ministry of Labor. Zvi Hecker, Alfred Neumann, Eldar Sharon. Central Zionist Archives.

④

The new village, then, may have been built to compensate the residents of Beit Naqquba for their lost properties. This supposition is supported by documents showing that only two years later, in 1964, an expansion plan for Ein Naqquba was approved, enlarging the area of the village from 14 dunam to nearly 450 dunam, most of which was designated for agriculture. This plan was commissioned by the Israel Land Authority and was executed on lands belonging to the Land Development Authority, the same authority legally responsible for compensating landowners.

The mystifying disappearance of the acclaimed project by Neumann-Hecker-Sharon is now clarified: it was first planned as an extension to the village of Ein Rafa, with the purpose of resettling the displaced residents of Beit Naqquba. While referred to in architectural publications as Ein Rafa, it was actually called Ein Naqquba, commemorating by name the lost village of its origin and covering by rapid growth its exceptional history. ■

④ The new village of Ein Rafa/Ein Naqquba, early 1960s. Dwelling unit. Zvi Hecker, Alfred Neumann, Eldar Sharon.
⑤ Ein Naqquba, 2016. View of transformation of original dwelling unit. Photographers: Sharbel Halloun, Nagham Copty, Fouad Habash.
⑥ Refugee family from Beit Naqquba resettled in the new village of Ein Naqquba, early 1960s. Central Zionist Archives.
⑦ Ein Naqquba, 2016. View of transformation of original dwelling unit. Photographers: Sharbel Halloun, Nagham Copty, Fouad Habash.
⑧ Ein Naqquba, 2016. View of transformation of original dwelling unit. Photographers: Sharbel Halloun, Nagham Copty, Fouad Habash.

⑤

1 Sharbel Halloun, Nagham Copty, and Fouad Habash are architecture students at the Bezalel Academy of Arts and Design. Their research about Ein Rafa / Ein Naqquba was done in the framework of a course on the history of Israeli architecture. Their astounding findings finally bring to light a long-silenced episode of expulsion (one of many) and return (one of few) which was enigmatically veiled by a scenic architectural assemblage put up by the avant-garde team of Neumann-Hecker-Sharon. By unraveling the story of this project, their text only amplifies the question of why it was such an exceptional enactment of the right to return.

2 For further information about the appropriation and renaming of Beit Naqquba, see Walid Khalidi, *All That Remains: The Palestinian Villages Occupied and Depopulated by Israel in 1948* (Washington, DC: Institute for Palestine Studies, 2006), pp. 601–602.

3 Aharon Dolev, "Beit Naqquba: An Arab Village Is Born," *Maariv* [in Hebrew], August 10, 1962, p. 6 (Historical Jewish Press of the National Library of Israel and Tel Aviv University).

4 Ibid.

5 Ibid.

6 Ein Rafa Map, KL20M/402/46, Central Zionist Archives, Jerusalem.

7 Ein Rafa Map, KL20M/402/42, Central Zionist Archives, Jerusalem.

8 Letters from file KL20M/402/60, Central Zionist Archives, Jerusalem.

9 "Beit Naqquba: An Arab Village Is Born," p. 6.

10 Land Acquisition (Validation of Acts and Compensation) Law, 1953. Available online (accessed August 1, 2017): https://jewishvoiceforpeace.org/wp-content/uploads/2016/06/Israeli-Land-Acquisition-Law-1953.pdf.

⑥

⑦ ⑧

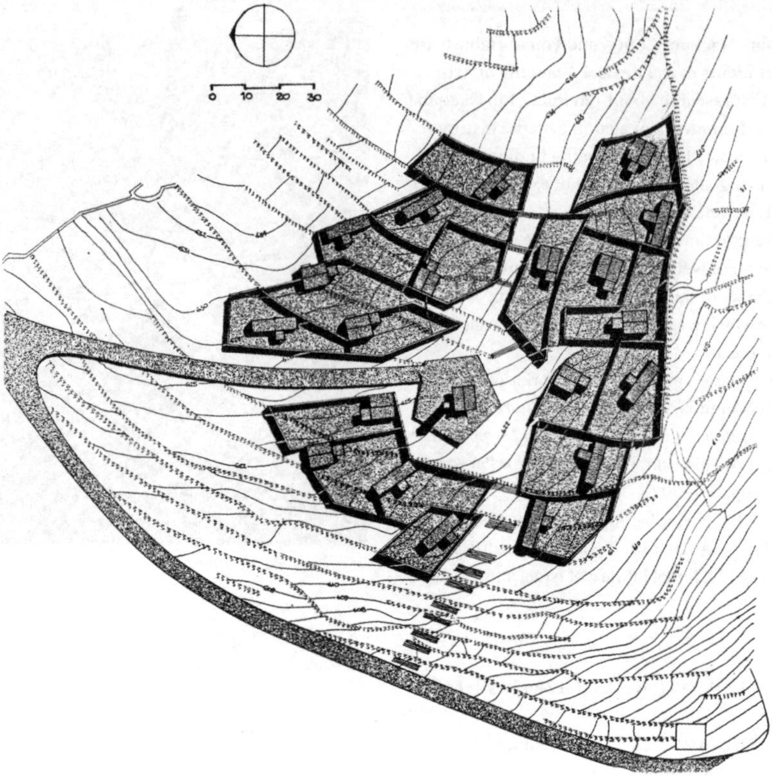


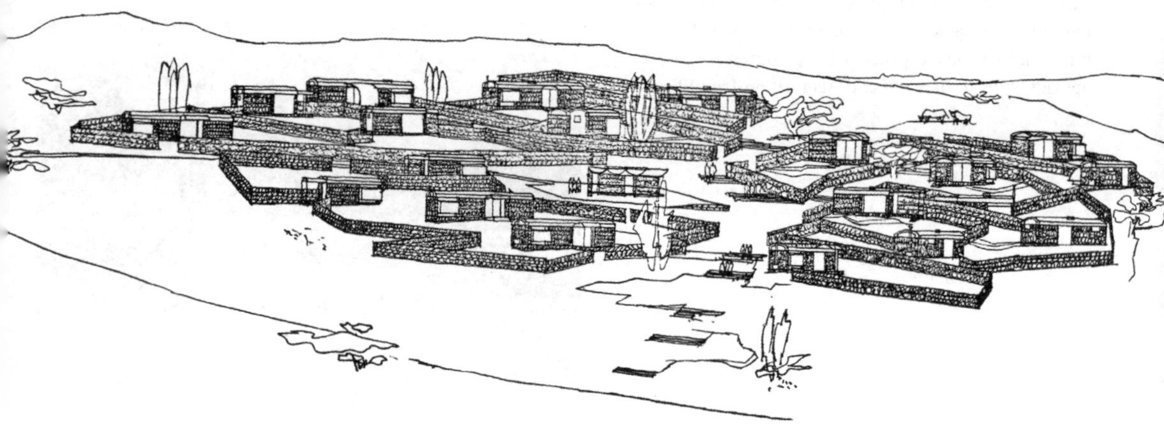

⑨ The new village of Ein Rafa/Ein Naqquba, 1961–1962. Plan. Zvi Hecker, Alfred Neumann, Eldar Sharon. Zvi Hecker archive.
⑩ The new village of Ein Rafa/Ein Naqquba, 1961–1962. Perspective view. Zvi Hecker, Alfred Neumann, Eldar Sharon. Zvi Hecker archive.
⑪ The new village of Ein Rafa/Ein Naqquba, 1961–1962. Model and prefabricated roof elements prepared in situ. Zvi Hecker, Alfred Neumann, Eldar Sharon. Zvi Hecker archive.
⑫ The new village of Ein Rafa/Ein Naqquba, 1962. Built dwelling units. Zvi Hecker, Alfred Neumann, Eldar Sharon. Zvi Hecker archive.

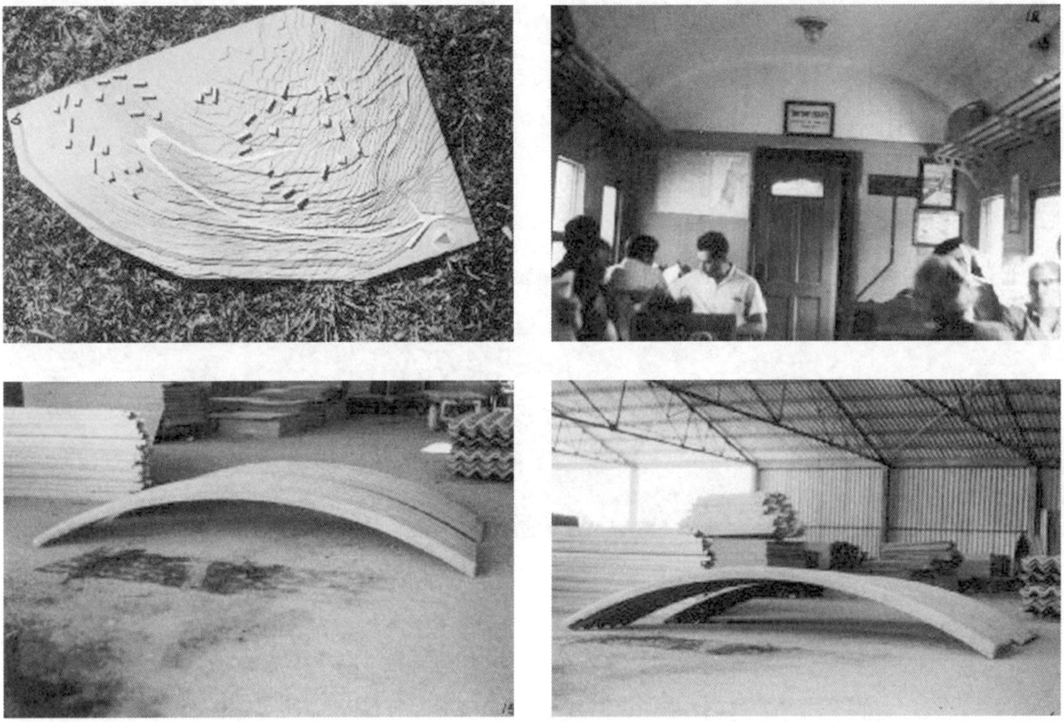

⑪

⑫

⑬

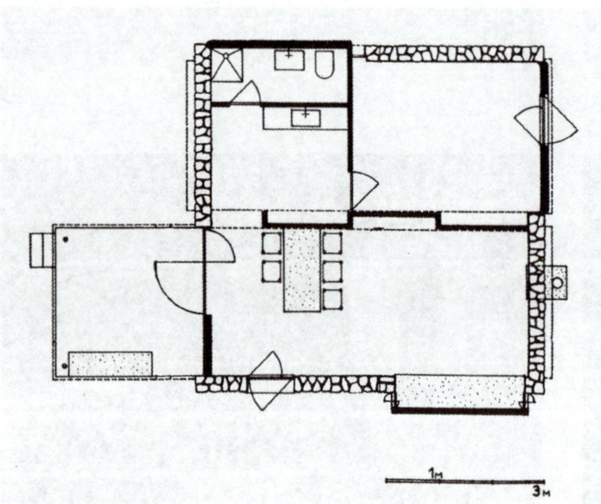


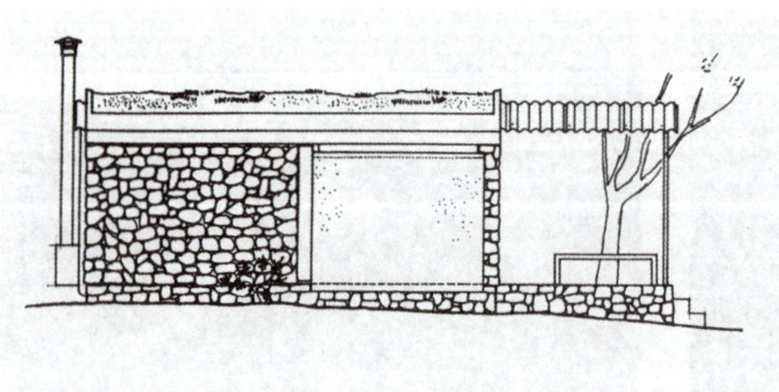

⑭ ⑮

⑬ Ein Rafa/Ein Naqquba, 1962. General view of the village.
⑭ The new village of Ein Rafa/Ein Naqquba, 1961. Plan of a minimal dwelling unit. Zvi Hecker, Alfred Neumann, Eldar Sharon. Zvi Hecker archive.
⑮ The new village of Ein Rafa/Ein Naqquba, 1961. Elevation of a minimal dwelling unit. Zvi Hecker, Alfred Neumann, Eldar Sharon. Zvi Hecker archive.
⑯ The new village of Ein Rafa/Ein Naqquba, built dwelling unit, 1962. Zvi Hecker, Alfred Neumann, Eldar Sharon. Zvi Hecker archive.

⑯

⑰

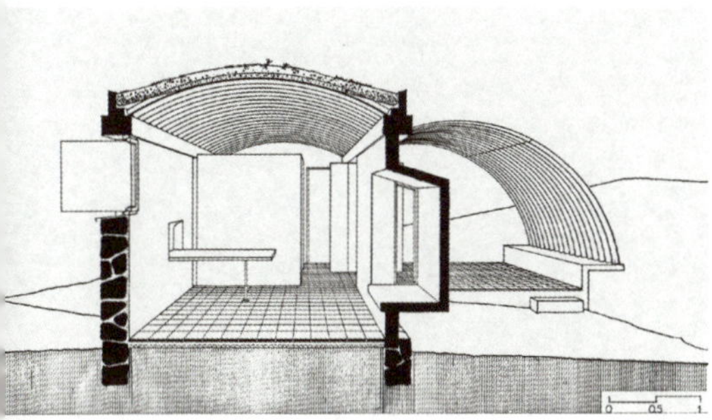

⑱

⑲

⑰ The new village of Ein Rafa/Ein Naqquba, built dwelling units, 1962. Zvi Hecker, Alfred Neumann, Eldar Sharon. Zvi Hecker archive.
⑱ Section of a minimal dwelling unit showing the prefab roofing elements. Zvi Hecker, Alfred Neumann, Eldar Sharon. Zvi Hecker archive.
⑲ Perspective of a longer dwelling unit. Zvi Hecker, Alfred Neumann, Eldar Sharon. Zvi Hecker archive.
⑳ Ein Naqquba, 2016. View of transformation of original dwelling unit. Photographers: Sharbel Halloun, Nagham Copty, Fouad Habash.

⑳

# Brutalism

① Construction site, "quarter-kilometer" super-block, Beersheba, 1959. Avraham Yasky, Amnon Alexandroni.

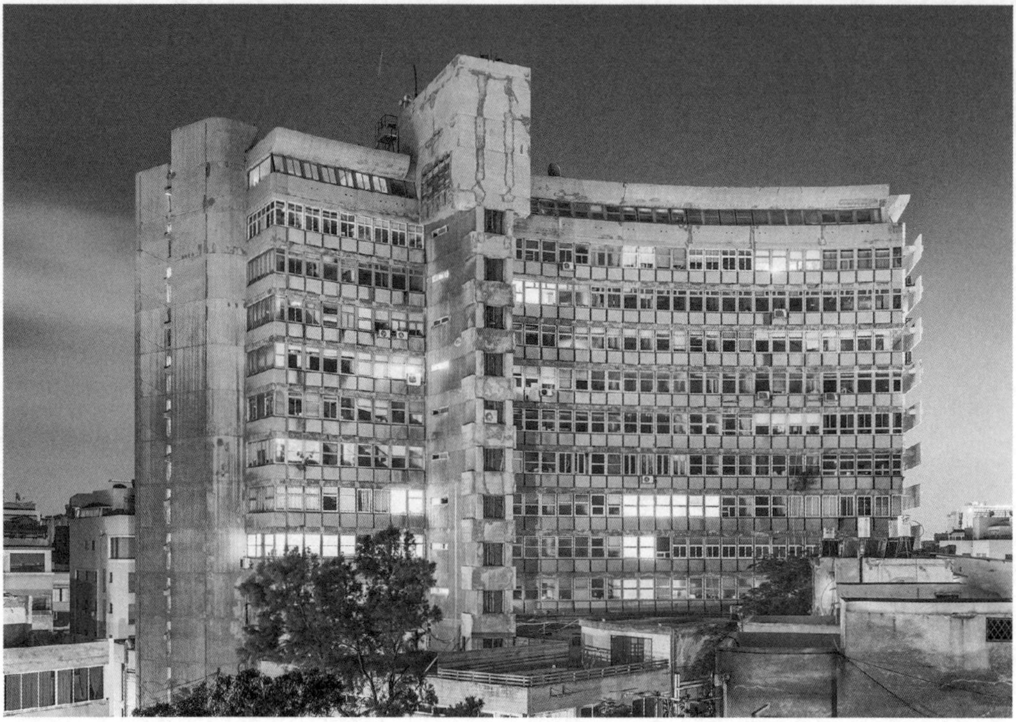

② El Al Building, Tel Aviv, 2015. Eli Singalovski.

## The Architecture of Israeli Patriotism

Concrete, according to *The Hebrew Encyclopedia*, is "the most important building material that may be produced entirely of the land [of Israel]'s crude resources."[1] A document dating from 1951, from the Research and Statistics Department of the Israel National Planning Office, affirms that:

> All of our considerations need to derive from the fact—established in many other countries as well—that cement is the most important of building materials. For us it is especially important, seeing as the raw material is available inexhaustibly in our homeland. The accessibility of the material and its availability in different regions is of great importance both geographically and transportation-wise. One prominent expert, who visited here upon invitation from our government, accurately expressed our fortunate condition in this field: "Your entire land is one big cement factory."[2]

Although it was already commonly in use in the pre-State era, concrete gained its unassailable reputation as the "Israeli material" only following Statehood. Its components—limestone, clay, sand, and gravel—were officially declared "nature's great treasures, available for immediate use."[3] The low technology required for its production in situ seemed appropriate for a national building project whose highest aspiration—both practically and ethically—was to be as rudimentary, solid, and concrete as could be.

Was the situation in the first years of Statehood indeed as fortunate as may be inferred from the official document of the Planning Office? Contrary to the impression of the visiting expert, the entire land was not a cement factory. In fact, there was only one functioning cement factory in the country: Nesher-Portland Cement Factories of Israel, which was established in Haifa in the early 1920s and moved to Ramla in 1953. With the onset of the large waves of immigration, the Nesher factories nearly doubled their production capacity from 241,000 tons in 1949 to 439,000 tons in 1951, but still did not manage to meet the demands of the civil and military construction boom. In spite of the severe shortage of foreign currency during the period of austerity,[4] it was necessary to import more than 200,000 tons of cement between 1950 and 1952. During this time a "cement regime" developed in Israel, arbitrating on matters of national interest (i.e., military shelters versus public housing) and sectoral disputes (labor unions versus municipal bodies)—and bringing with it a cement black market. The scarcity of cement topped the government's agenda, as we can learn from the Government Session of December 6, 1950, which discussed the question of how to allocate cement and set priorities. Following is the reaction of Dov Yosef, Minister of Supply and Rationing:

> To say that cement must be rationed but not to lay down priorities is to contradict oneself. When the subject is the rationing of rice and of sugar, it is understood that each man in Israel is to receive a portion, and there is no question of priority. But distributing and rationing cement—what does that mean? Not every man is in need of cement. Is it intended that each and every man in Israel is to receive a kilo of cement? [...] Rationing cement means determining precedence from among those requesting cement. There is no other way. Mr. Shapiro [Minister of the Interior and of Immigration] carries the burden of determining that one person gets more cement than another. Therefore, a system of prioritizing must be put into place.[5]

Pinkas Lavon [Lubienker], Minister of Agriculture, added:

> In the field of building, rationing is a function of priorities. Without this foundation of priority, rationing is certainly not justified. [...] You have a number of contractors, and one of them has sources for raw materials. Why does he need to share them with other contractors? When is this justified? Should we expropriate the goods from their manufacturer and say that there is a general interest with regard to matters that the State sees as its highest priority, and to this end it imposes the distribution of cement and the rationing, not only of cement, but also of other building materials? If we should refrain from

> doing so, the result would be nothing but ordinary competition between contractors.[6]

In addition to the quantitative difficulties in the production and supply of raw cement during the first austerity period, there were also questions regarding the quality of the concrete (the liquid mix to be cast) and its adaptability to local conditions. Throughout the 1950s, the "Israeli material" was the object of incessant research and experiments which tested its genuine "nativeness." The seal of approval finally came from the Building Research Station at the Technion, which in 1963 performed a comprehensive study of "the concrete casting problems in Israel's warm zones." This study tested the recommendations of the American Concrete Institute (ACI) in relation to the climatic conditions in Israel. Its conclusions were as follows:

> In light of the above results, concerning both strength and plastic fracturing [fractures appearing before the concrete is entirely dry], and even the acceleration of bonding, there is no justification for the restriction of the casting of concrete to the shade or to the evening hours each time air temperature surpasses 32 degrees Celsius, as is demanded by the ACI brief. If we were to follow this brief in Israel, we would have to abstain almost entirely from ordinary casting during the day during the summer in the southern half of Israel, and sometimes even in the northern half of the country.[7]

According to the study, the warm Israeli climate did not pose a problem for concrete castings, and was even an advantage in some cases. It was later discovered, however, that humidity does not benefit reinforced-concrete structures. Architect Avraham Yasky clarifies the problem thus: "Most of the concrete buildings that were built on the coastal plain absorbed humidity, and the steel reinforcements expanded and exploded the concrete after several years. This did not occur in the desert town of Beersheba. The dryness preserved the concrete in good condition."[8]

Despite the difficulties and limitations, local natural resources, along with local means of production, made concrete construction an "indigenous" Israeli building technology. However, it was the imported postwar fashion of Brutalism that facilitated the acculturation of concrete architecture as distinctive Israeli folklore.

Brutalism arrived in late 1950s Israel in its most reductive and literal sense: as a generic title for exposed-concrete architecture and as an architect's password for the ritual of material and constructional sincerity. The apparent discrepancy between Brutalism's quest for authenticity and its dissemination as a derivative global trend perplexed the older generation of Jewish émigré modernists. It thrilled the younger generation of native Israeli architects, however; they advocated Brutalism not merely as a new architectural culture, but as an allegorical embodiment of their own instantaneous autochthony, self-fabricated integrity, and contrived spontaneity.

The swift acculturation of Brutalism in Israel from the mid-1950s to the mid-1970s, and its diffusion throughout most public (and various private) architectural typologies and programs, evidently worked against the grain of Reyner Banham's insistence on Brutalism as an ethic rather than an aesthetic. Indeed, if the Israeli case is of interest, it is primarily because it unveils Brutalism's ethical malleability and political conformity; its aesthetic exuberance and fashionable currency; its range of cultural mannerism, structural masquerade, morphological fancy, and surface fetishism.

The post–World War II generational shift, engendering critical practices and fueling local Brutalist dialects across the globe, was overplayed in Israel, where the impetus of "youth culture" was sponsored and propagated by the State apparatus itself. Locally born and educated architects in their twenties and thirties, venerated as the "generation of the State," were commissioned to design new towns and new rural settlements, extensive housing estates and public buildings, industrial compounds and infrastructural facilities.

Expected to push forth a national building project and to articulate a decisive conversion from an allegedly drifting Diasporic culture to a seemingly sedentary nativism, the Israeli architects did not hesitate to borrow indiscriminately the objets bruts of the French, English, Brazilian, or Scandinavian architecture of the hour and adapt them as their own ready-made vernacular. The flow of citations and imitations liberated them from social-realist protocols of efficiency and reproducibility and unleashed a flurry of singular works of architecture, solid and hollow monoliths, casts of inflated plasticity, naked bodies of boasted sensuality, or clusters of space-packing polygonals.

Brutalism's material "poverty" and technical "honesty" rhetoricized the desired homogeneity and solidarity of the welfare state, signaled the passage from bourgeois whiteness to proletarian grayness, camouflaged the folkloristic diversity and ideological ruptures within the Israeli "melting pot," and effectively accelerated an idiosyncratic building culture idolizing structural originality and formal inventiveness. By the early 1960s, exposed-concrete buildings were praised for "not surrendering to mediocrity and anonymity" and for exhibiting "daring and unequivocal expression." Paradoxically, the more gestural local Brutalism appeared to be, the more common it became. The more eccentricities it accumulated, the more homely and recognizable it was. The more crafted and irreproducible it turned out to be, the more it was held to illustrate the "Israeli character" and to suggest a desirable subject-object bonding based on the common attributes of sincerity, ingenuity, and sensuality.

Architect and writer Aba Elhanani (perhaps the Israeli doppelgänger of Reyner Banham, and certainly the chief Hebrew exegete of the architectural zeitgeist of the 1950s to 1970s) brought up the predicament of honesty in a 1960 lecture:

> This honesty—instructing us to limit the use of plaster in order to expose the natural building materials, to accentuate the construction so that it will be visible and readable, to highlight expansion joints and even scaffolding holes—this honesty is without a doubt a new value in architecture and in art in general.[9]

Elhanani the architect, in his built works, was totally committed to the new diktat of corporeal honesty. Elhanani the critic kept a sarcastic distance:

> Today we are not to build in bricks and stone; the new material is reinforced concrete. Modism, rhyming with Snobism, devours every good lot, and woe to the one who attempts to rise against the mode.[10]

In the mid-1970s, summarizing Israeli Brutalism, Elhanani was still perplexed:

> Of course, the younger generation is not entirely to blame. [...] Even our veteran architects [...] have adopted this same sure and easy way of drawing from foreign wells, and in this way have turned into modish architects while pretending to be modern ones. [...] Of course it is convenient to believe in international architecture, because this dogma facilitates the widespread use of architecture journals. And so it happens that this or that famous building in Tel Aviv is in fact a copy, smaller and less successful than another, more

③

④

important, building somewhere else in the world. It is not that the building here is ugly, but it is sterile and out of place and it comes to teach a lesson to all who admire it.[11]

The talk about modism—always in the transition from one fashion to the next, always a denunciation, always tautological[12]—took on particular impetus in 1950s Israel, since with the establishment of the State and immediately following the first austerity period, fashionability for its own sake became both an expedient modus operandi and the marker of a generational *mentalité*. The generation of young, mostly native "architects under the influence," as Elhanani called them, did not in the least see itself as inept or insipid, but in fact as the bearer of a new gospel. Indeed, the formative decades of Israeli architecture enjoyed an extended, and rather prolific, adolescence, in which keeping up with international cultural centers and sensitizing the zeitgeist was perceived and performed as an act of resistance (to a peripheral state of being). The adoption of stepfather figures

③–④ El Al Building, Tel Aviv, 1958–1962. Dov Karmi, Zvi Meltzer, Ram Karmi. Photographer: Paul Gross.

(Le Corbusier, Peter and Alison Smithson, James Stirling, Alvar Aalto, Louis Kahn) was a declaration of mutiny against the biological fathers (the local generation of émigré architects that emerged under the British Mandate); blatant acts of mimicry and replication were construed as informed and somewhat critical intellectual maneuvers. Honesty, in this context, was overt forgery. Authenticity was crude appropriation. This was the petri dish of Israeli Brutalism.

Much as in post–World War II England, in Israel, too, the "new situation" sharpened intergenerational differences and rendered everyone who came "before" old, and all who were trained during or immediately "after" young. Most of the older "Diasporic architects," the modernists of the 1930s, were pushed to the sidelines. Those who survived professionally (Arieh Sharon, Zeev Rechter, Dov Karmi) hired and trained the graduates of the local Technion who would replace them within a decade. No project was too big for these neophytes, no program too complex. Hardly a competition was lost. By the 1960s the professional market was almost entirely in their hands.

The velocity and extent of this generational takeover is unique to Israel and could hardly be compared to sociological alterations within professional milieux in other countries. Indeed, many Israeli architects built in a single decade far more than their role models in Europe, as well as their direct tutors in Israel, built in their entire careers. Needless to say, such breathless architecture is inconceivable today.

Thanks to its youthfulness, the architectural flurry in Israel enjoyed unprecedented exposure in the international professional journals of the time in Europe, the United States, and Japan, which devoted regular reports, features, and sometimes even entire issues to the Israeli project or to projects in Israel. Over the course of nearly two decades, Israel was portrayed as the prodigal wunderkind of modern architecture: a newly born nation-state fighting for its territorial definition; growing and developing at an incredible pace; effectively assimilating and proliferating the architectural doctrines and styles of the moment; and even conducting its own distinctive experimentation in building technology and climatic construction, in morphology and space-packing, and in typology of rural settlements and new regional towns.[13]

The ambivalence of Aba Elhanani and other members of the older generation of émigré architects in Israel regarding Brutalism's fake honesty was eclipsed by the fervor of the Israeli-born architects of the younger generation, who advocated Brutalism not merely as a manifestation of a new culture or a new body politic, but actually as the architectural incarnation of their own self-image. The most outspoken of this generation of architects was Ram Karmi:

> Within the general stream of international architecture, here there sprouted a new generation—Israeli, native, not intellectual, very physical, linked to Danziger, to Canaanism, to the roots of this place—Zionist, patriotic. We wanted to be real. The International Style was not real. For us, concrete was

> the Israeli material. Concrete gave a sense of stability: once you implant it in place, nobody can move it. With those white pilotis you go "phoo!" and blow them away. Exposed concrete is the exposed truth of the material. White is the spirituality of the modernist idea. It is like a white dress shirt. Concrete is the flesh of the building.[14]

Here, then, we witness the operation of the concrete mixer: the aggregates—Canaanist, Zionist, "very physical," "Danziger-like" qualities (or any other trapping of the native Israeli: "frank," "instinctual," "sensual," "crude," "rude")—join the viscous mixture of individual and communal personifications and harden at once as a solid casting of Israeli identity.

Indeed, exposed-concrete architecture in Israel, derivative as it was, signified an ever-deepening local patriotism.[15] The contempt for "modernist spirituality" expressed above, the atavistic quest for pagan roots, and the portrayal of Brutalism as a regionalism anathema to the International Style, may be confusing: they do not at all indicate a predilection for indigenous structures or traditional techniques. Quite the contrary: they imply Brutalism's proxy authenticity; its "regressive" mode; its tectonic retreat from both dry construction and stonemasonry (related to indigenous Arab as well as British colonial architecture). Indeed, the momentary allure of this latest architectural fashion, at least for the Israelis, was the semblance of indifference to all native and colonial building traditions and the iconoclastic withdrawal to the muddy scene of casting.

The first signs of the patriotic naturalization of exposed-concrete architecture may be discerned in the comments made by the jury of the prestigious Rokach Prize for Architecture upon awarding it for the El Al Building in Tel Aviv (with twelve floors, the first high-rise office building in Israel), designed in 1958 by the architecture firm Karmi-Meltzer-Karmi and inaugurated in 1962:

> As in the rest of the world, here, too, we have seen a proliferation of office buildings in the last decade. These high buildings are taking over a substantial part of construction in the centers of cities, and may, in the future, determine no less than the entire face of Tel Aviv. Thus the question arises: will we follow the path of mere technological solutions and fill our streets with expressionless and almost identical glass boxes, or will we begin our search for the enrichment of architectural identity in our urban landscape?
>
> In this respect, the El Al Building plays the part of a highly important pioneer in this chapter of building our city. It is real proof that an office building, whose function is simple and common and within the confines of commercial construction, does not directly lead to mediocre and anonymous results. [...] With respect to material, it is indeed one of the more distinguishable buildings in our cityscape, a daring and unequivocal expression for concrete as construction and as a finishing material. In this way, the finish of the

building, which is usually the phase that blurs the clarity of the plan, becomes the phase that projects the real character of the building.[16]

Once more, the allegory of exposed-concrete architecture as a "daring and unequivocal expression" that "projects the real character" and does not surrender to "mediocre and anonymous results" suggests a desirable subject-object bonding based on the common attributes of originality, sincerity, and tangibility. The polarization in the above text between the artisanry of concrete casting and the generic reproduction of "technological solutions" or "glass boxes" reveals a profound ambivalence in late-1950s Israel regarding the inevitability and pervasiveness of the free-market economy, with its aesthetic of efficiency and standardized by-products that "may, in the future, determine no less than the entire face of Tel Aviv."

Against the particular background of modernism-without-modernization (pre-State "Bauhaus" architecture in Israel), Brutalism seemed to further propel an architecture of affect, expression, and identification, and to suggest a new perplexing image of modernism-against-itself. The El Al Building, the first local attempt at a sizable corporate building, is effectively an elaborate dialectical figure; a crossbreed of official State apparatus and entrepreneurial taste; a *béton brut* sculptural monolith with double-loaded corridors connecting two vertical shafts. If I consider it as the first illustrious embodiment of Israeli Brutalism, it is precisely because it appeared in the early 1960s as an oversized open signifier, reverberating simultaneously the exhilaration and "sincerity" of popular culture, the pomposity of national architecture, the emergence of a tentative corporate order, and, finally, the release of self-reflexive design pleasures, auteurist eccentricities, and object fetishisms.

The 1950s had seen the construction of relatively large office buildings in Israel, but these served mostly governmental, municipal, or Labor Federation institutions. Accordingly, their architecture expressed bureaucratic poise, civic transparency, and typological clarity (the ultimate archetype of this being Dov Karmi's Labor Federation Executive Committee House in Tel Aviv). Morphological creativity was considered to be irreverent mannerism and an indecent waste of collective resources. The means of expression available to the architect in adjusting the relationship between ceremonial formality and casual efficiency were limited to the positioning of the building in relation to the street, the design of the entrance procession, the distribution of open public spaces on-site, and the design of the envelope as a latticework, describing to some extent the organizational system and modulation of the building and, by extension, the institution. The public buildings of the 1950s indeed began to develop an aesthetic of exposed concrete, though, interestingly enough, mostly as the expression of schematization, rationalization, and surface patterning. Actually, it was on the envelopes of these buildings that the grid (whether structural or cladded) first

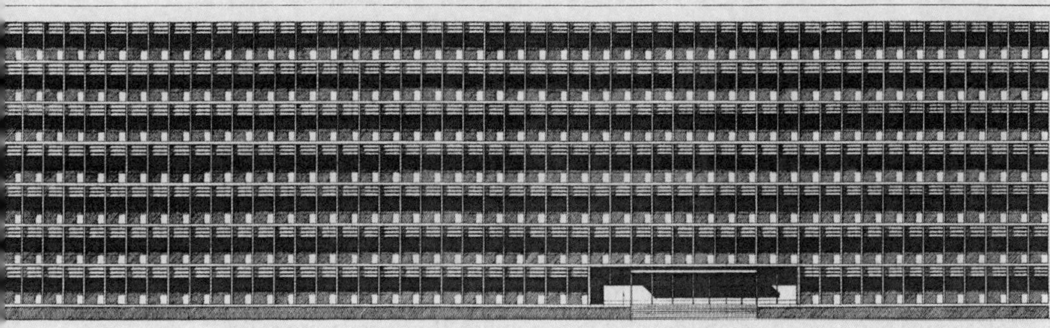

⑤

received a visible expression and became the conspicuous architectural trademark of the period.[17]

In relation to the formative decade of the 1950s, then, the El Al Building performed a double transgression: against the existing clerical mediocrity of Israeli welfare-state architecture, and against the ominous lightness and technical reproducibility of the pending corporate culture. It offered formal idiosyncrasy in place of off-the-shelf typology, and a contextual infill design (following irregular plot lines) in lieu of an autonomous object "floating" on the site (typical of 1930s urbanism in Tel Aviv). It boasted plasticity rather than rigid orthogonality; wet casts instead of dry joints; sensual heftiness rather than visual elegance; drama rather than show.

Henceforth, originality was not only a palliative for leftist dogmatism, but also a prophylactic for the plague of rightist pragmatism and the future of generic commodities it forecast. A work of Brutalist architecture—admittedly a blend of borrowed effects, faulty citations, and transliterated tributes—was considered an original, a singular one-of-a-kind that could be neither reproduced nor displaced. A multitude of originals was expected to accumulate into a new building culture, traversing social sectors, cultural traditions, and political agendas, and blurring conflicts of interest between corporate and collectivist identities. There was no competitive free market to speak of in Israel in the 1960s; the developing economy was run by public companies, trade unions, and a small oligarchy, all intertwined with the State institutions and the hegemonic apparatus of the Labor Party. Thus, the architecture of the period reproduced the same manners in order to designate an office building for travel agents, a hostel for new immigrants, a hotel for an American corporation, a convalescent home for Labor Union members, a synagogue in Jerusalem, a museum in a kibbutz, an academic campus in the desert, a town hall in a beach new town, an apartment building in the Galilee, a villa in an affluent suburb, a factory in a remote company town, a military officers' academy wherever. These were all singular works of architecture, all alike in their morphological inventiveness and "architectural character," all masquerading typological affinities for the sake of cultural solidarity, all representing a conscious retreat from technological efficiency toward manual on-site labor, all returning to the muddy scene of casting—the sensuous meeting ground of the architect and the builder.

The evolution of Israeli Brutalism can be traced by observing the public buildings of the 1950s, which used concrete work to expose the building's structural skeleton and the brise-soleil pattern. Such a tendency to expose a building's skeleton or to promote an aesthetic of scaffolding is regarded as a moment of noble coalescence between the architect and the engineer, thus triggering a discourse of honesty, transparency, and efficiency. A close scrutiny of the functional validity and structural honesty of Brutalist buildings reveals a gradual thickening of the constructive frames (columns, beams, floors, shadings) during the 1950s and 1960s, to the point that it becomes preposterous to refer to them as "skeletons." The Cartesian fabrics that tied and restrained the architectural object began to emit hitherto repressed desires. The previous modernist fetishism with regard to the building's skeleton sanctified instrumentalism and a longed-for dematerialization. The concrete frames demanded a body of their own, a mass with no bones and no skin, a physical state and a cultural stature that cut through

⑥

⑦

traditional tectonic distinctions and compressed the elements of building into a monochrome petrified blend.

As the architecture of exposed concrete in Israel gained in weight and monolithism, it drifted away from the frankness and concreteness attributed to Brutalism. I already mentioned the habits of replication (of layouts, motifs, and wall sections), exacerbation (of sensuality and pliability), and exaggeration (of size and weight). To this we should add the eccentric custom of refining the language of wet construction on-site with effects borrowed from the jargon of dry modular construction. These effects include assorted fake joints, stitches, and brackets that imitate industrial prefabrication. The accentuation of such fake joints entails a special design effort and complicates the casting work, but compensates, as it were, for the deficiency of concrete buildings, namely, their non-reproducibility. Moreover, against its proclaimed bareness, concrete's capacity to take on both the shape and the textural imprints of the mold into which it is poured triggered a new ornamental fervor and demanded a new professional skill. In addition to construction documents that detailed specific instructions concerning the type and arrangement of the (typically wooden) casting mold, the craftsmanship of the architect and his "eye" were required on-site as well. In many cases, the exposed-concrete walls were treated as reliefs—and soon they were perceived as nothing less than artistic murals. (These would be replaced in the 1970s by the mosaic and ceramic decorative works applied on interior and exterior façades of public buildings, corporate office buildings, and standard developers' apartment buildings.)

The increasing robustness of building had set off counter-attempts at hollowing, stretching, bending, and warping concrete surfaces. Curiously, Israeli Brutalism

⑤ Jewish Agency building, Tel Aviv, front elevation, 1960. Arieh Sharon, Benjamin Idelson.
⑥ Tel Aviv–Yafo City Hall, Tel Aviv, 1957–1965. Menachem Cohen.
⑦ Hilton Hotel, Tel Aviv, 1965. Yaacov Rechter.

was also an index of shell structures, barrel vaults, flat arches, polygonal domes, and a collection of hyperbolic paraboloids. The material and structural attributes of concrete, as well as its cultural signification, were represented inversely: tension rather than compression, elasticity rather than plasticity, porosity rather than density, lightness rather than massiveness, "tents" instead of "catacombs."

Concrete's material and rhetorical malleability, and its tolerance of a miscellany of uses, performances, embodiments, and significations, loosened up the uptight official State architecture in Israel and launched the first and possibly last atavistic mise-en-scène in which the presumably unmediated and uninhibited relationship between the architect and the architectural object could take place. Avraham Yasky, a prolific Brutalist, narrates this scene in retrospect:

> Concrete is both an art and a craft. By no means would anyone return to it today—not as a fashion, certainly not as something of technological interest. In all that concerns building, we are moving away from art and craft. With concrete, you cast a sculpture and attain a building, and if you make of the concrete something industrial, an elegantly smooth surface, it loses the basic principle of poured liquid.[18]

Indeed, Israeli Brutalism dissipated in the late 1970s with the rising euphoria of the neoliberal economy, postmodern architectural euphemisms, and the habitus of military and civilian occupation. The rhetorical figures of bareness, crudity, authenticity, and honesty had no more cultural, let alone ideological, currency whatsoever. During the 1980s and 1990s, Brutalist buildings became objects of public contempt and professional denial, monumental vestiges of the "shameful past" of the Israeli welfare state. Often too solid to be totally demolished, they were refurbished, redecorated, encased, plastered, or painted, usually with the consent of their original architects and sometimes even on the architects' own initiative.

In twenty-first-century Israel, Brutalism is gradually becoming a topos of connoisseurship, academic research, and curatorial projects, as well as recent preservation campaigns. Lists of hundreds of protected Brutalist buildings are now under preparation in various municipalities across the country. It seems that from our historical vantage point, Brutalism's secret as a double agent of righteous concreteness and sumptuous mannerism is ever more pleasing. ■

1 Rachel Schlon, "Concrete," *The Hebrew Encyclopedia* [in Hebrew] (Jerusalem: Massada, 1958).

2 Israel National Planning Office, Planning Department, "Promoting the Cement Industry" [in Hebrew] (1951).

3 Ibid.

4 The decision to instate a rationing policy was taken in the first session of the government in April 1949. In order to implement the policy, a special ministry was established: the Ministry of Supply and Rationing, with Dov Yosef appointed as minister. One reason for his appointment was his success in regulating the distribution of commodities in his role as military governor of Jerusalem during the siege in the War of Independence. The main reason for the austerity program was the need to absorb massive

immigration waves after the establishment of the State, along with the high cost of the war.

5 Minutes of Israeli Government Session #20, December 6, 1950, on the Distribution of Cement and Setting Priorities in Building [in Hebrew] (Israel State Archives).

6 Ibid.

7 Rachel Schlon, "The Problem of Casting Concrete in the Hot Regions of the Country," *Engineering and Architecture: The Union of Engineers and Architects in Israel* 3–4 [in Hebrew] (1963).

8 Avraham Yasky, in a discussion with the author, 1999.

9 Aba Elhanani, "Our Contribution to the New Architecture," transcript of a lecture given at a symposium entitled "Whither Israeli Architecture" in Jerusalem, October 28, 1960, published in *Engineering and Architecture: The Union of Engineers and Architects in Israel* 5–6 [in Hebrew] (1961), p. 133.

10 Ibid.

11 Aba Elhanani, "On Architecture in Israel," *Engineering and Architecture: The Union of Engineers and Architects in Israel* [in Hebrew] (July 1975), p. 8.

12 See Roland Barthes, *The Fashion System* (Berkeley and Los Angeles: University of California Press, 1990); Deborah Fausch, Paulette Singley, Rodolphe El-Khoury, and Zvi Efrat, eds., *Architecture: In Fashion* (New York: Princeton Architectural Press, 1994).

13 The local architectural community maintained contact with architectural editors and publishers through several architect-writers: Aba Elhanani was a regular contributor to the Swiss series *Architecture, Forms, Functions*; Moshe Zarhi reported regularly for the French journal *L'Architecture d'Aujourd'hui*; and Ram Karmi presented projects of Israeli architects in the British series *World Architecture*. A few books about architecture in Israel were published internationally. The most important of these was *New Towns in Israel*, written by Erica Spiegel after an extended research period in Israel and published in 1966 by Karl Kramer. A decade later, Kramer published (together with Massada Publishing) Arieh Sharon's autobiography, *Kibbutz + Bauhaus: An Architect's Way in a New Land*.

14 Ram Karmi, in a discussion with the author, 1998. The proposition that Israeli Brutalism was considered by its own practitioners to be an offshoot of Canaanism was mentioned for the first time in this discussion with Ram Karmi, but it was corroborated in interviews with other architects of the young generation, such as Avraham Yasky, Dan Eytan, Shulamit Nadler, and Mordechai Ben Horin.
Karmi's reference to Yitzhak Danziger and his attempt to relate Brutalism to Canaanism merits an elaboration: Canaanism was a cultural and ideological movement founded in 1939 by a group of Jewish intellectuals in Palestine, headed by poet Yonatan Ratosh. It reached its peak in the 1940s (the same decade of the adolescence of the "young generation" of local architects who would dominate the national building project of the 1950s). The Canaanite school advocated doing away with Jewish religious tradition, cutting off relations with Diasporic Jews and their culture, and adopting instead a "Hebrew" identity based on ancient Semitic heroic myths. Originally a pejorative term, "Canaanism" referred to a movement that grew out of Revisionist Zionism and had "its early roots in European extreme right-wing movements, notably Italian fascism." Ron Kuzar, *Hebrew and Zionism: A Discourse Analytic Cultural Study* (New York: Walter de Gruyter, 2001). Kuzar writes that the movement "exhibited an interesting blend of militarism and power politics toward the Arabs as an organized community on the one hand and a welcoming acceptance of them as individuals to be redeemed from medieval darkness on the other." Estranged both from Judaism and from mainstream socialist Zionism, the Canaanites argued that the State of Israel ought to be a Hebrew state, not a solution to the Jewish Question. Designating the Israeli People as a "Jewish People," the Canaanites argued, was misleading. A nation must be rooted in a territory and a language—things which Judaism, by its very nature, could not provide. Though it never gained mass support, Canaanism had a significant impact on the course of Israeli art, literature, and political thought. There were no architects active in the movement, and no work of architecture directly manifested its spiritual and political agenda, but it certainly enchanted the generation of young "Sabra" architects graduating in the 1950s. It should be noted that sculptor Yitzhak Danziger (1916–1977), whose iconic *Nimrod*, a statue depicting the biblical hunter, was taken up as the emblem of the Canaanite movement, was also the charismatic art teacher at the Technion's Faculty of Architecture, the only local breeding ground of Israeli architects until the 1980s.

15 Only two decades later, with the territorial expansion following the 1967 War and the political upheaval of the late 1970s, did stonemasonry come to signify authenticity and rootedness. To the first generation of Israelis, stone was but an external codex inherited from indigenous Arab tradition and British Mandate building bylaws.

16 Cited in *Engineering and Architecture: The Union of Engineers and Architects in Israel* 2 [in Hebrew] (1966), p. 14.

17 The latticed façade and the use of brise-soleil did not exist in Israeli modernist architecture until the 1950s and could hardly be found in early modernist European architecture. For the Israelis, the relevant source for surface treatment and shading was Brazilian modernist architecture.

18 Avraham Yasky, in a discussion with the author, 1999.

⑧

⑨

⑩

⑧ Institute of Metals, Technion, Haifa, 1964. Avraham Yasky, Amnon Alexandroni. Photographer: Avraham Yasky.
⑨ The Leon Recanati Graduate School of Business Administration, Tel Aviv University, 1967–1968. Benjamin Idelson, Yaakov Hertz, Gershon Tzipor.
⑩ Israel Electric Corp. Technical Center, Tel Aviv, 1960–1962. Tovah and Gideon Ziv.

⑪ Wix Central Library, Weizmann Institute of Science, Rehovot, 1957. North elevation. Arieh Elhanani.
⑫ Faculty of Engineering Sciences, Ben-Gurion University, Beersheba, 1970–1974. Avraham Yasky, Yaacov Gil.
⑬ Apartment building, Tel Aviv, 1961. Avraham Yasky, Amnon Alexandroni.

⑪

⑫

⑬

⑭

⑮

⑭ Herzfeld Geriatric Medical Center, Gedera, 1958–1965. Avraham Yasky, Yaacov Gil.
⑮ Lunenfeld-Kunin residence (staff dormitory), Weizmann Institute of Science, Rehovot, 1966–1967. Yaacov Rechter, Moshe Zarhi.
⑯ Carmel Forest Convalescent Home, Mount Carmel. 1966–1968. Nahum Zolotov.
⑰ Negev Center, Beersheba, 1956–1960. Interior. Ram Karmi.
⑱ Student dormitory, Tel Aviv University, 1968–1969. Interior. Avraham Yasky, Yaacov Gil.
⑲ Negev Center, Beersheba, 1956–1960. Ram Karmi.

⑯

⑱

⑰

⑲

⑳

㉑

⑳ Egged Building, Haifa, 2015. Eli Singalovski.
㉑ Amir Center, Jerusalem, 2014. Eli Singalovski.

㉒ Amphitheater stage building, Jezreel Valley, mid-1950s. Shmuel Mestechkin.
㉓ Student dormitory, Ben-Gurion University, Beersheba, 1972–1976. Ram Karmi.
㉔ Hostel for new immigrants, Upper Nazareth, 1959–1961. Avraham Yasky, Amnon Alexandroni.
㉕ Orot Cinema, Beersheba, 2015. Eli Singalovski.
㉖ Orot Cinema, Beersheba, 2014. Eli Singalovski.

㉒

㉔

㉓

㉕ ㉖

㉗

㉘

㉙

㉚

㉛

㉗ The Archaeological Museum of Hatzor, Kibbutz Ayelet HaShahar, 1962–1964. David Resnick.
㉘ Dining hall, Kibbutz Hazorea, 1954–1956. Munio Gitai Weinraub, Al Mansfeld.
㉙ Meir Hospital, Kfar Saba, stairs, 1960s. Moshe Zarhi. Photographer: Paul Gross. Zarhy Architects collection.
㉚ Nitzanim High School, Tel Aviv, 1960–1962. Yaacov Rechter, Moshe Zarhi. Photographer: Yitzhak Frenkel.
㉛ Hostel for new immigrants, Beersheba, 1956–1957. Avraham Yasky, Amnon Alexandroni.
㉜ Mexico building, Tel Aviv University, 1964. Yitzhak Yashar, Dan Eytan.
㉝ Kiron neighborhood, Kiryat Ono, 1962–1967. Israel Lotan.
㉞ School, Ben Shemen Youth Village, mid-1960s. Shulamit Nadler, Michael Nadler, Shmuel Bixon.

㉜

㉝

㉞

35

36

37

(35) Kreitman auditorium building, Ben-Gurion University, Beersheba, 1974. Avraham Yasky, Yaacov Gil.
(36)–(37) Student dormitory, Tel Aviv University, 1968–1969. Avraham Yasky, Yaacov Gil.
(38) Faculty of Engineering Sciences, Ben-Gurion University, Beersheba, 1970–1974. Avraham Yasky, Yaacov Gil.
(39) Kreitman Building, Beersheba, 2015. Eli Singalovski.

(38)

(39)

40

41

42

(40) Leo Baeck High School, Haifa, 1965–1970. Shulamit Nadler, Michael Nadler, Shmuel Bixon. Photographer: Moshe Gross, Keren Or Studio.
(41) Amal "Lady Davis" High School, Tel Aviv, 1965–1973. Ram Karmi, Chaim Ketzef, Ben Peleg.
(42) Amal "Lady Davis" High School, Tel Aviv, 1965–1973. Ceiling detail. Ram Karmi, Chaim Ketzef, Ben Peleg.
(43) Central Library, Ben-Gurion University, Beersheba, 1968–1972. Shulamit Nadler, Michael Nadler, Shmuel Bixon. Photographer: Hector Petroko.
(44) Central Library, Ben-Gurion University, Beersheba, 1968–1972. Shulamit Nadler, Michael Nadler, Shmuel Bixon. Photographer: Hector Petroko.
(45) Amal "Lady Davis" High School, Tel Aviv, 1965–1973. Ram Karmi, Chaim Ketzef, Ben Peleg.

(43)

(44)

(45)

㊻

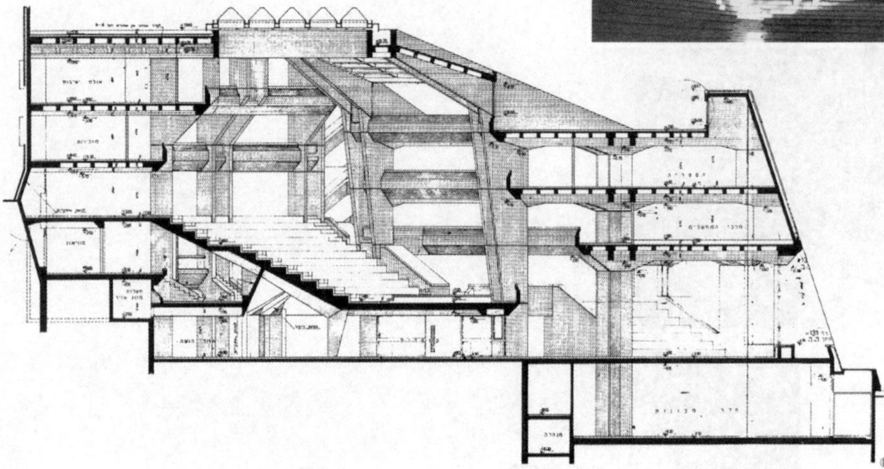

㊼

㊽

㊻ Auditorium, ORT School of Engineering, Jerusalem, early 1970s. Shulamit Nadler, Michael Nadler, Shmuel Bixon, Moshe Gil.
㊼ ORT School of Engineering, Jerusalem, early 1970s. Section. Shulamit Nadler, Michael Nadler, Shmuel Bixon, Moshe Gil.
㊽ The Jerusalem Theater under construction, Jerusalem, 1971. Shulamit Nadler, Michael Nadler, Shmuel Bixon.
㊾ The Institute for Oceanographic and Limnological Research, Bat Galim, Haifa, 1968. David Yanai.
㊿ Sourasky Central Library, Tel Aviv University, Tel Aviv, 1969. Shulamit Nadler, Michael Nadler, Shmuel Bixon. Photographer: Israel Sun. Harvard Library
51 Jabotinsky Institute, headquarters of the Likud Party, Tel Aviv, 1963–1964. Mordechai Ben-Horin.
52 Beit Yad Lebanim and Herzliya Museum of Contemporary Art, Herzliya, 1965–1975. Yaacov Rechter, Moshe Zarhi.

(49)

(50)

(51)

(52)

(53)

(54)

(56)

(55)

(57)

(58)

(59)

(60)

(61)

(53) Construction of the Central Synagogue, Upper Nazareth, 1967–1969. Nahum Zolotov.
(54) Central Synagogue, Upper Nazareth, 1967–1969. Nahum Zolotov.
(55) Parking shed for the Geophysics Institute, Azur, 1958–1959. Shmuel Mestechkin.
(56) Soroka Medical Center, Beersheba, 1954–1964. Entrance canopy. Arieh Sharon, Benjamin Idelson.

(57) Atarim Square, Tel Aviv, 1971–1975. Yaacov Rechter, Werner Yosef Witkover.
(58) Atarim Square, Tel Aviv, 1971–1975. Yaacov Rechter, Werner Yosef Witkover.
(59) Restaurant in Gan Hashlosha National Park, 1960s. Ora and Yaacov Yaar.
(60) Herzliya airport for light planes, 1961. Avraham Yasky, Amnon Alexandroni.
(61) The Babylonian synagogue, Beersheba, 1970s. Nahum Zolotov.

# DOSSIER: PHILIP JOHNSON'S REACTOR

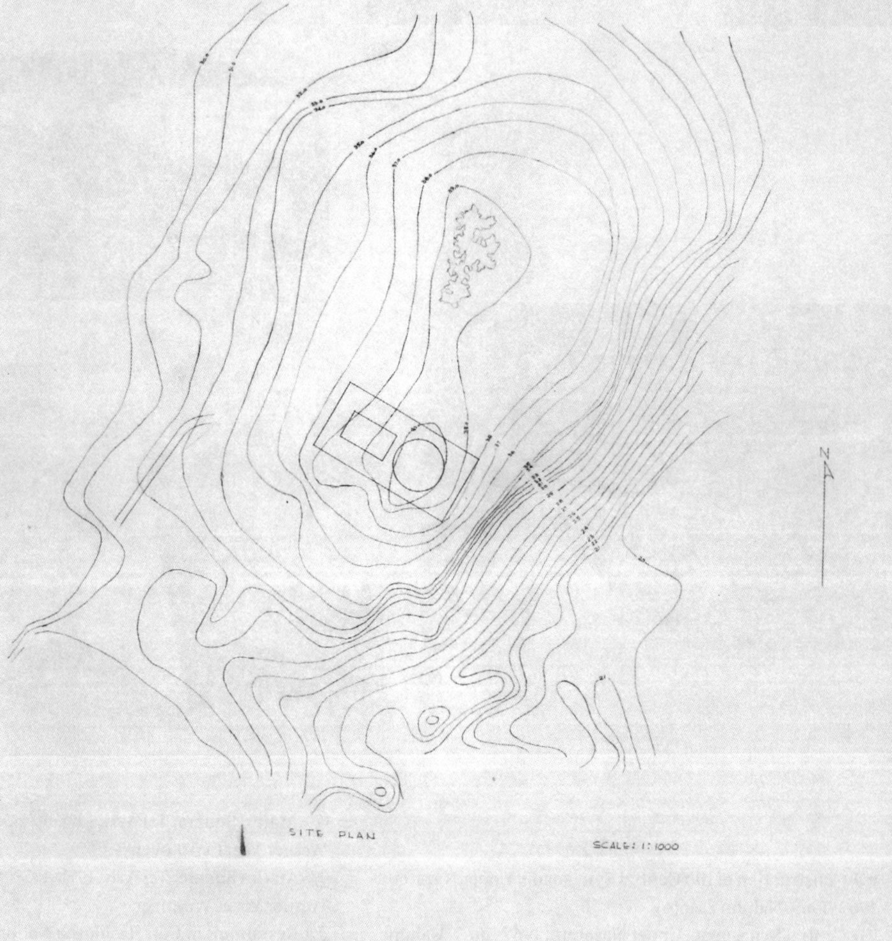


⑥②

The circumstances leading to the design of a nuclear power plant in the sand dunes of Soreq by the American architect Philip Johnson remain somewhat vague, though it seems that Johnson's built "temple in the desert" had a redemptive role in his biography.

In 1956 Philip Johnson was commissioned to design an experimental nuclear reactor by the Israeli government. Intended for training and research purposes only,[1] the reactor was part of the American Atoms for Peace program led by President Dwight D. Eisenhower; then Deputy Minister of Defense Shimon Peres solicited its construction. According to both Johnson's and Peres's official stories, a visit of the latter to New Canaan sparked the commission. Johnson later recalled: "Peres was always a fan of mine. He had been to the Glass House and one night he asked me, 'How come you've never done anything in Israel?' 'Nothing would please me more,' I said. Rehovot was the result."[2]

Johnson's biographer, Franz Schulze, elaborated on Johnson's friendship with Edward Warburg as instrumental in getting the commission and rectifying the architect's relationship with the New York Jewish community, which had been marred by his support of the Nazi party and his attempts to import fascism to America in the 1930s. "Beyond that lay the ultimate goal: to persuade Philip's American antagonists to recognize that he had at last and formally been washed clean of his sins, by no less an entity than the government of the Jewish State itself."[3]

The architecture of the reactor was described by Schulze as follows:

> The Rehovot reactor remains the most lasting thing Philip left to Israel. [...] A four-sided battered wall interrupted only by an entrance on one of its short faces surrounds an open court, with a single solid and powerful form looming up at the far end. That dominant latter object, also battered, is central in plan and ridged in its twenty-sided elevation [...].
>
> [...] It brings to mind an ancient Egyptian temple, in which a wall-girded courtyard, open to the sky, led to the sheltered hypostyle hall and the secret sanctuary.[4] ■

1 Avner Cohen, *Israel and the Bomb* (New York: Columbia University Press, 1998).

2 Philip Johnson, quoted in Franz Schulze, *Philip Johnson: Life and Work* (Chicago: University of Chicago Press, 1996) pp. 283–285.

3 Ibid.

4 Ibid.

(63)

(64)

(62) Soreq Nuclear Research Center, 1958. Site plan. Philip Johnson. Philip Johnson collection, Avery Drawings & Archives, Avery Architectural and Fine Arts Library, Columbia University, New York.
(63) Soreq Nuclear Research Center, 1959. Reactor. Philip Johnson.
(64) Soreq Nuclear Research Center, 1958. Perspective drawing. Philip Johnson. Philip Johnson collection, Avery Drawings & Archives, Avery Architectural and Fine Arts Library, Columbia University, New York.
(65) Soreq Nuclear Research Center, 1958. Studies for the reactor's dome. Philip Johnson. Philip Johnson collection, Avery Drawings & Archives, Avery Architectural and Fine Arts Library, Columbia University, New York.
(66) Soreq Nuclear Research Center, 1958. Axonometric drawing of reactor. Philip Johnson. Philip Johnson collection, Avery Drawings & Archives, Avery Architectural and Fine Arts Library, Columbia University, New York.

(66)

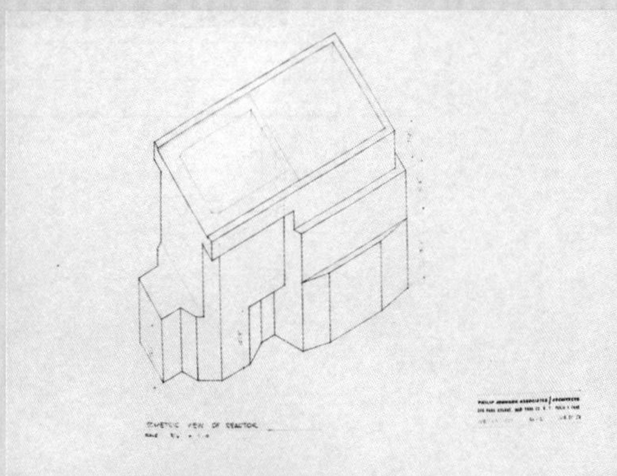

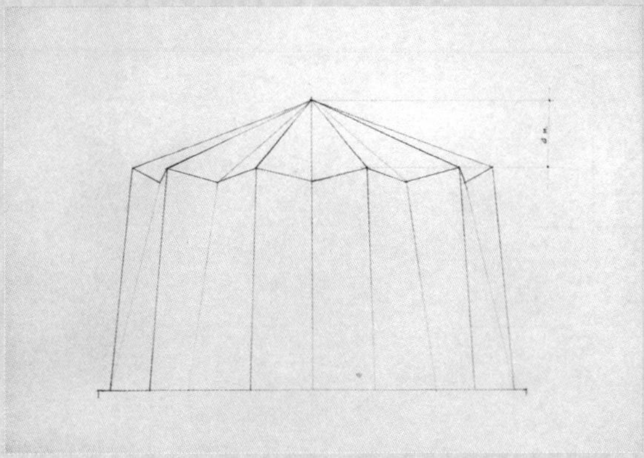

(65)

(67)

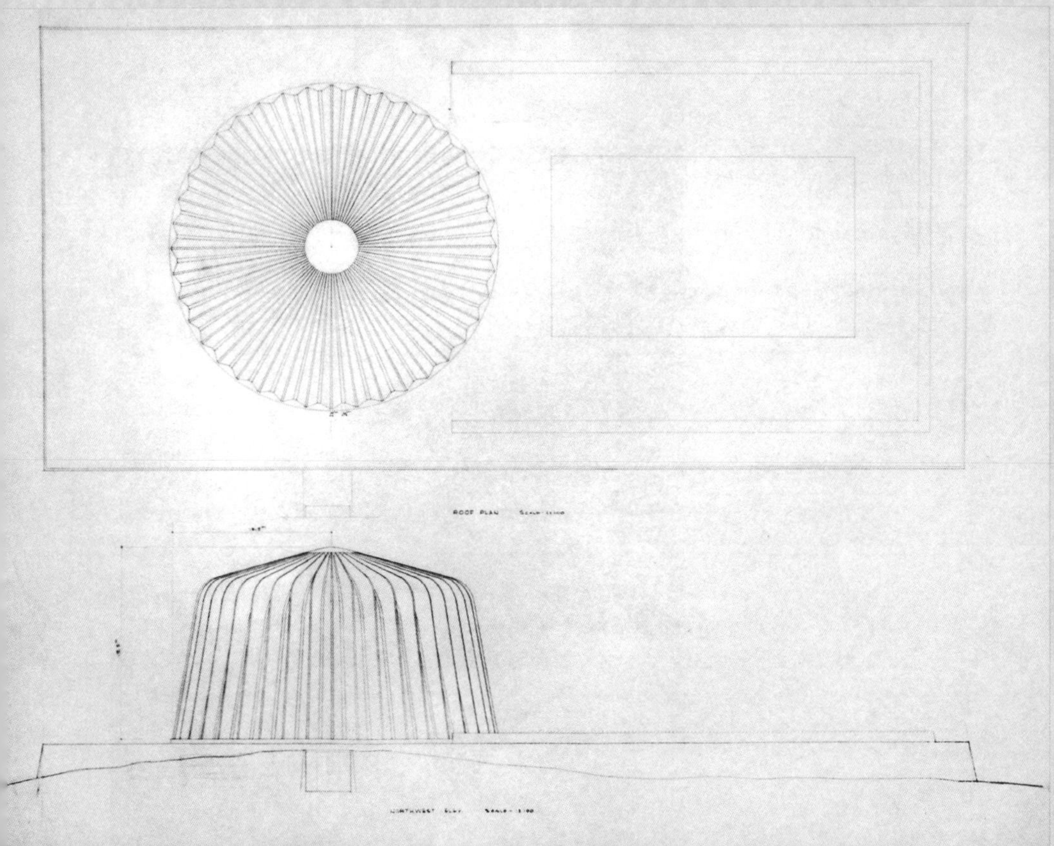

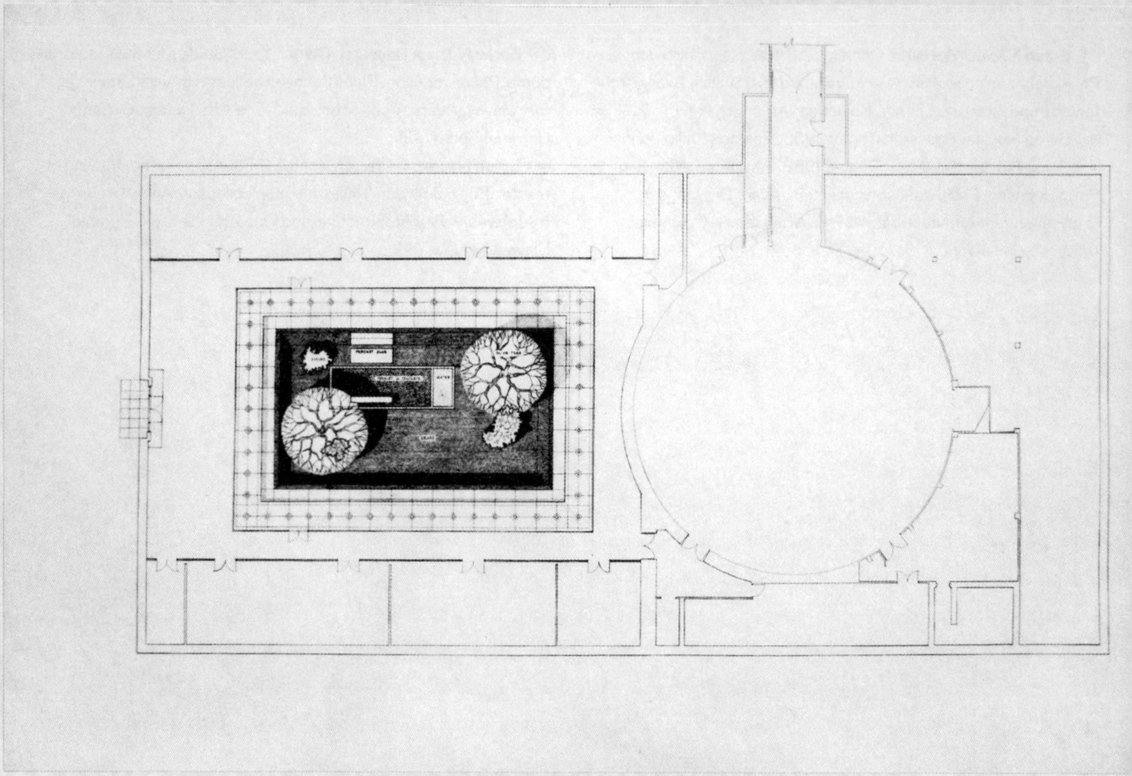

(68)

(69)

(67) Soreq Nuclear Research Center, 1958. Roof plan and elevation. Philip Johnson. Philip Johnson collection, Avery Drawings & Archives, Avery Architectural and Fine Arts Library, Columbia University, New York

(68) Soreq Nuclear Research Center, 1958. Plan of courtyard. Philip Johnson. Philip Johnson collection, Avery Drawings & Archives, Avery Architectural and Fine Arts Library, Columbia University, New York.

(69) Soreq Nuclear Research Center, 1959, under construction. Philip Johnson.

(70) Soreq Nuclear Research Center, 1958. Perspective drawing, interior. Philip Johnson.

(71) Soreq Nuclear Research Center, 1958. Reactor details. Philip Johnson. Philip Johnson collection, Avery Drawings & Archives, Avery Architectural and Fine Arts Library, Columbia University, New York.

(70)

(71)

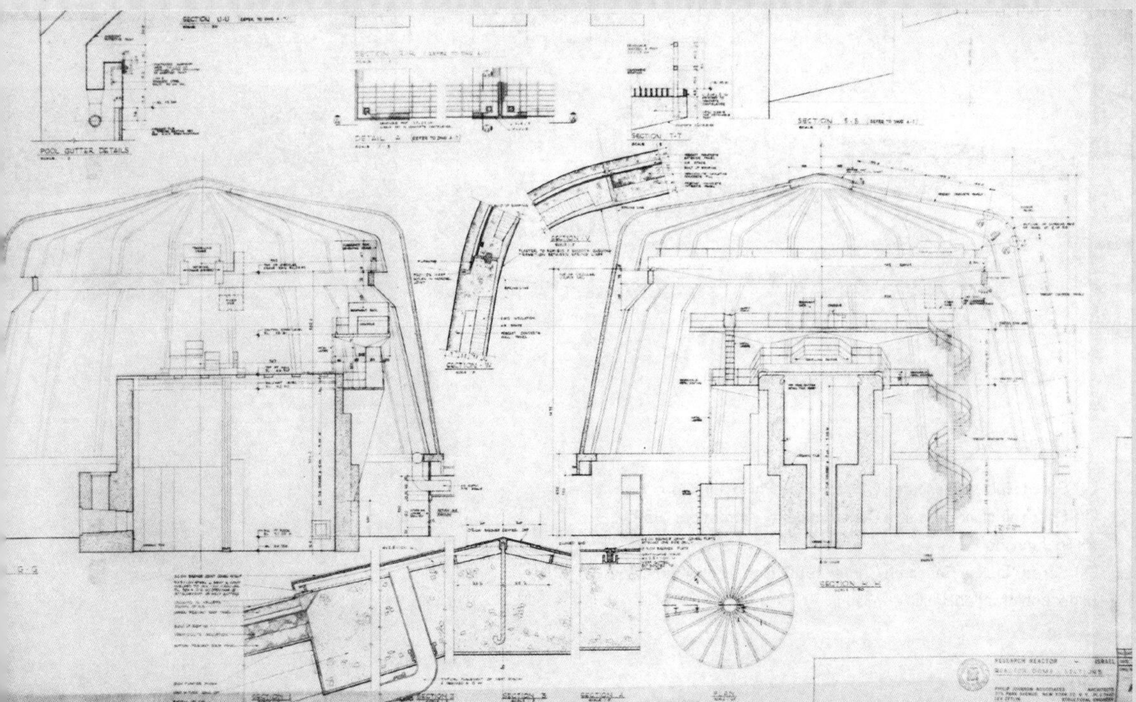

(72)

(73)

(74)

(72) Soreq Nuclear Research Center, 1959. Philip Johnson.
(73) Soreq Nuclear Research Center under construction. 1959. Philip Johnson.
(74) Soreq Nuclear Research Center, 1959. Dome and inner court under construction. Philip Johnson.

⑮

⑯

⑰

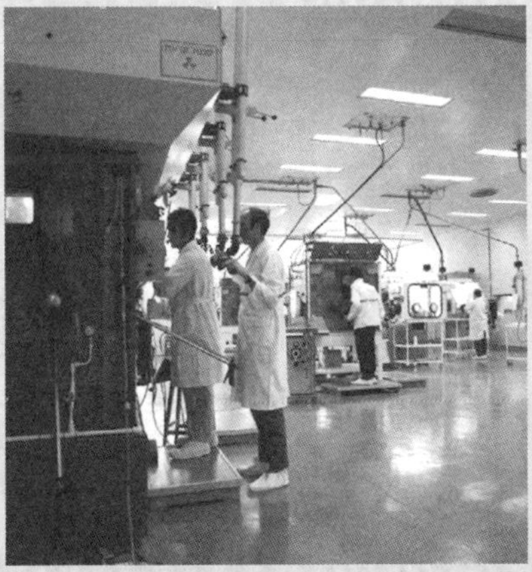

⑱

⑮ Soreq Nuclear Research Center, 1959. Interior. Philip Johnson.
⑯ Soreq Nuclear Research Center, 1959. Reactor. Philip Johnson.
⑰ Soreq Nuclear Research Center, 1959. Interior view toward the inner court. Philip Johnson.
⑱ Soreq Nuclear Research Center, 1959. Interior. Philip Johnson.

# Structuralism

① 

## The Avant-Garde and Its Discontents

In the late 1950s and early 1960s, a highly self-reflexive architectural avant-garde emerged in Israel. A group of architects converging at the faculty of architecture at the Technion Institute of Technology in Haifa—among them Alfred Neumann (the admired teacher), Leopold Gerstel, Yona Friedman, Al Mansfeld, Zvi Hecker, Eldar Sharon, and Israel Goodovitch—aimed to defy the solidity and authority of the autonomous object with a flux of random clusters, self-replicating and ever-mutating space modules, casbah-esque mats and ziggurats, polyhedral matrices, collapsible space frames, cybernetic contraptions, and various other crossbreeds of system theories and biomorphisms. This outburst of structural and metaphorical open-endedness proved to be an architectural impasse and no more than a fleeting epidemic of self-generating experimentalism. However, its exceptionally vigorous performance in Israel rendered it momentarily synonymous with local architectural culture, and the habits and peculiar scars it left behind lingered for decades. What could be clearly portrayed in retrospect as a highly derivative local dialect of international structuralist trends was occasionally referred to as a symptomatically Israeli,[1] or even Jewish, compulsion (see the discussion below of Robin Middleton's article "A Yiddish Grid," published in the September 1965 issue of *Architectural Review*). Publicity built up to the point that the Israeli structuralist architects, much like the Japanese Metabolists or the Dutch Forum group, seemed to briefly occupy the imaginary of architectural futures. The predictable climax came when the Israeli architect Moshe Safdie, representing Canada at Expo 67, etched the term "habitat" in architectural discourse, constructed a monumental icon of prefabricated compilation, and frivolously slipped between Israeli

① Ramot Polin housing, Ramot, Jerusalem, 2015. Gili Merin.
② *L'Architecture d'Aujourd'hui* 106 (February–March 1963), dedicated to structuralist architecture in Israel.

“space-packing” ingenuity and Mediterranean rural authenticity.

What, then, was the lure of Israeli structuralist architecture? Was there anything distinctive that created the impression of a feverish architectural laboratory? Perhaps the fact that Israel’s avant-garde was highly institutional—emanating almost exclusively from the academy—and routinely State-sponsored made it both more prolific and more perplexing. Statistically speaking, a relatively large number of structuralist buildings and compounds materialized in Israel in the 1960s and 1970s, and several of them were remarkable enough to draw international attention. Critically speaking, the phenomenon of a counterculture recruited to the national building project bewildered protagonists and antagonists alike and fueled superficial media hype.

Apart from its inherent institutional conformism and casual patriotism, Israeli structuralist architecture is quite similar to its international counterparts in its tentative swings between anthropological spontaneity and technological efficiency. At both ends, the result is always exacerbated serialism, be it clustered or stringed.

The twofold quest for a long-lost authenticity and a not-yet-achieved instrumentality was meant to defeat the traditional dichotomy of Vitalism and Mechanism by juxtaposing a new susceptibility to the biological and geological, to the social and ethnic, to mental spaces and patterns of everyday life, with pseudoscientific methodologies, complex geometries, self-generating processes, and hyper-industrialized construction techniques. However, this juxtaposition only rarely engendered meaningful urban or architectural spaces. All too often, the academic ambition to decode the cryptograms of vernacular formations—along with the megastructures of bees, ants, or spiders and the microstructures of plants or rocks—in order to crystallize and animate a new architecture produced scaleless, exorbitant prototypes, completely removed from the realities of production, cost, construction, and habitation in the Israeli welfare state of the 1960s.

This may in fact be the singularity of Israeli structuralist architecture: it is above all ceremonial; it quickly loses interest in its sociospatial contents and abandons altogether its technological aspirations in favor of a new addiction to the ritual of dismantling the object and objectifying the component. In the enacted absence of the object, of the figure, of the stable contour, Israeli architecture was destined to a course of relentless taking and losing shape, symptomatic of its perpetual borderline disorder.

## Beehives

Searching for an origin myth of the Israeli habitat, we may find it deeply embedded in the annals of productivist Zionism, most figuratively in the autobiography of Arieh Sharon,

②

published in 1976. "I received my first lesson in architecture from a bee," wrote the former Bauhausler and kibbutznik who literally became the architect of the State of Israel:

> I was working at the time as the beemaster of the hives on the young kibbutz, of which I was a founding member. I was naturally fascinated by the construction methods used by the bees, which are among nature's most successful architects and engineers [...].
>
> Honeycombs are composed of hexagons, which provide both living space for the bees and storage chambers for their product. [...] The solution of hexagons adopted by the bees was the most spacious, logical, comfortable and economic one, using beeswax as the basic building material. [...]
>
> I also learned about modular construction from the simple wooden cubes of the beehives, each containing dozens of hexagonal honeycombs—the neat homes of thousands of bees made possible their well-organized and organically constructed society, praised by Shakespeare in *Henry V* as a model for human beings.[2]

Sharon's beehive tale is a reenactment of his Bauhaus interview and initial meeting with Walter Gropius, but the hexagons resurfaced in his memoirs as the hallmark of his collaboration with his son Eldar toward the end of his professional career: "Much later, in my office we designed some buildings based on the hexagonal module—examples are the Yad Mordechai Museum and the Israel Pavilion at the '67 Expo."[3]

"In my office *we* designed some buildings." The ceding of authorship here cannot go unnoticed. Sharon's surrender to a generational shift can be detected in his most delighted lines: "A new architectural era began for me, my partnership with my son Eldar, the young Israeli avant-garde merging with the older Bauhaus avant-garde [...]."[4]

The son joined his father's office, as is often the case in Israel, but a formative split began at home, at the home office of doctrinaire State architecture:

> [Eldar] finished his architecture studies in the Haifa Technion and was decisively influenced by Professor Neumann, a former member of CIAM and an enthusiastic disciple of Le Corbusier. [Eldar] started to work at the Sharon-Idelson office together with his friend Zvi Hecker. But in the evening and nights, they continued to develop their own projects.
>
> They participated in architectural competitions and won the first prize for their project, submitted together with former professor, Alfred Neumann, of a town hall in Bat Yam, a small satellite city of Tel Aviv.[5]

Sharon goes on to approvingly describe the projects of the Neumann-Hecker-Sharon partnership, as well as its abrupt breakup upon the departure of Neumann to Canada in 1965, when Eldar, "the prodigal son," returned, joining his father again, bringing with him new, dynamic ideas on building and planning. Of course, we both had some doubts about the prospects of working together, but hoped that with some measure of goodwill and common effort, we would be able to find a synthesis between the two generations.[6]
The familial memoir is in fact a protocol of the formation of one of the most ingenious architectural teams ever to operate in Israel.[7] A team that was determined to deconstruct everything that Sharon the elder stood for—from the aesthetic truisms of the Bauhaus legacy that proliferated in Palestine in the

1930s to the ethical imperatives of the welfare state that molded Israel in the 1950s. The parable of the hexagon becomes ever more intricate.

## The EM-PHI System

The specter of the hexagon in Israeli regional planning was mentioned in the chapter "Project," in the discussion of the Sharon master plan and its allusion to Walter Christaller's central-place theory. However, a far more conspicuous manifestation of the hexagon and its polygonal offspring was triggered by the architect Alfred Neumann's 1949 arrival in Israel, and by his subsequent nomination as assistant professor and soon after dean of architecture (1953–1958) at the Technion.[8]

In Israel, Neumann expanded his research on architectural proportions and published a flurry of polemical statements: "Architecture itself has never been attacked scientifically, although there exist a multitude of scientific investigations of side issues to architecture (climatology, light, acoustics, sociology, ecology, etc.). [...] Tackling architecture itself is taboo. Of course, architecture is a creative activity, but so is physics [...]. There is a pronounced trend to withdraw into a foggy irrationalism, with plenty of humanitarian slogans as opposed to the platitudes of common-sense [...]."[9] His research, which was nonetheless entitled *The Humanization of Space*,[10] attracted a devout group of students and followers at home, as well as some noteworthy international attention. Walter Gropius, who met Neumann at the CIAM conferences, compared the latter's theory to Le Corbusier's *Modulor* and evaluated its scientific and comprehensive approach in contrast to Le Corbusier's intuitive proposition.

> The EM-PHI system (Humanization of Space) by Alfred Neumann represents, in my opinion, an important contribution to the entire field of design, planning,

architecture, and industrial design. It is the first attempt I know to create a modular system which comprehends the whole range of possibilities of proportion. [...] The only system akin to the new investigations of Alfred Neumann is Le Corbusier's *Modulor*, which has been conceived intuitively. Mr. Neumann goes beyond this system and gives it a comprehensive mechanical background.[11]

Le Corbusier himself referred to Neumann's theory in his *Modulor 2*, and was particularly impressed with his biologism:

> Alfred Neumann of Jerusalem is well acquainted with the whole question. He believes in the value φ. He has created a beautiful term: Humanization of Space [...]. Mr. Neumann has spoken to me about the beginning of the biological era, of the tendencies to place techniques within a biological line of thought, of a general tendency aspiring to a biological equilibrium, etc.[12]

In Neumann's humanized space, the last vestiges of anthropomorphism were removed together with the symbolism of the humanist tradition, as Rafi Segal explains:

> Neumann's thesis was a rational, abstracted approach to proportion systems. It lacked the symbolic aspect of theories of proportion, as evident in Renaissance theories (discussed at the time by Wittkower), and also to some degree, in Le Corbusier's *Modulor*.
>
> [...] The system remained abstract, presented almost as a reference chart, guidebook, a series of scales and numerical tables that expressed the mathematical logic and extent of his system. There was no explicit guidance on how to implement the system.
>
> [...] Neumann relied solely on the rationale of mathematics and the conviction of his theoretical argument. The degree to which the system was applicable was not a criterion in its validation. It was only in the years to follow that the EM-PHI system was used in practice, in Neumann's constructed and design work undertaken in the 1960s.[13]

Neumann's research evolved into pattern-making and space-packing studies as strategies for generating the built form. With the new title of "morphological architecture," his work in the 1960s proposed to trace in a parallel fashion the morphogenesis of design and the morphogenesis of biology, toward a history of the built form as guided by the natural evolutionary tendency toward grouping. Space was conceived as an aggregation of units that followed certain patterns of packing systems. Having no personal memories of beehives to speak of, Neumann offered his ontogenetic analysis:

> Wasps and bees and related insects build a cylinder with a horizontal rotation axis. As social beings they group themselves and build "skyscrapers," cell aggregates within which the cylinders are transformed into hexagonal prisms with half rhombic-

③ Alfred Neumann inspecting the construction of the Faculty of Mechanical Engineering, Technion, Haifa, 1964–1967. Alfred Neumann, Zvi Hecker.
④ Competition entry for the Netanya City Hall, 1963. "Morphologic Architecture," *RAIC Journal 40* (May 1963). Later republished in *Zodiac* 16 (1966). Alfred Neumann, Zvi Hecker, Eldar Sharon.

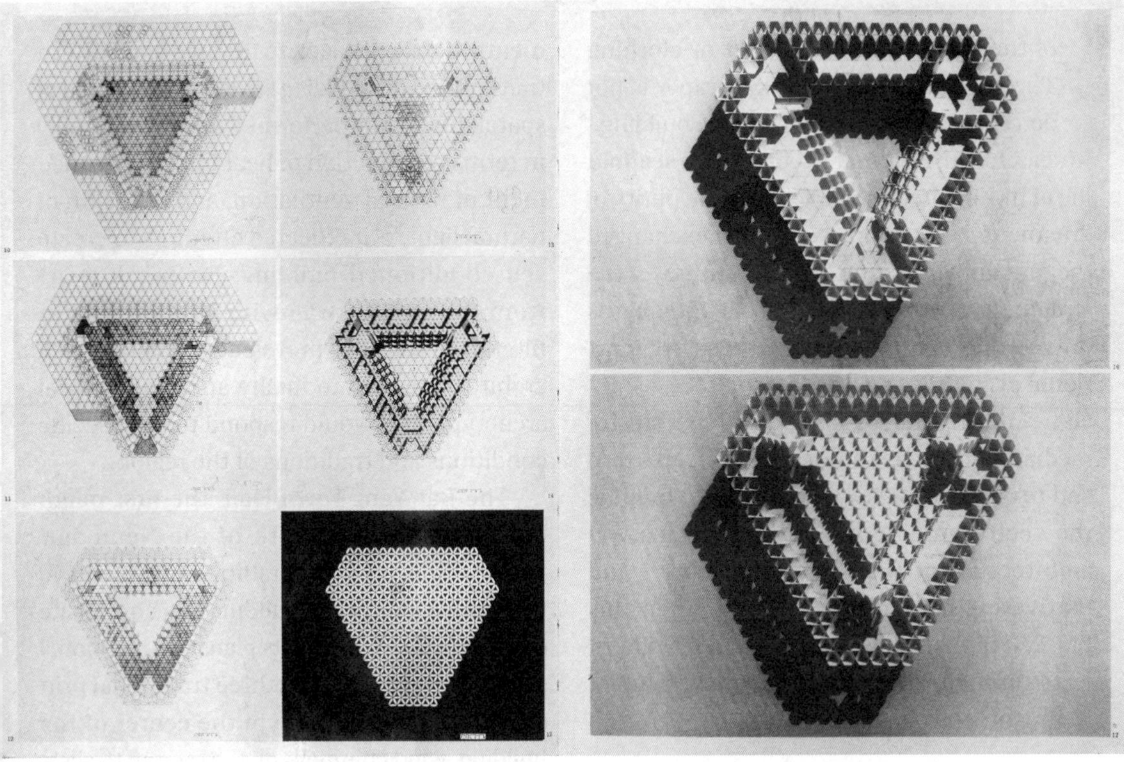

④

> dodeca-hedra at the end. It is a very rational, but restricted, building system. The architecture is as monotonous as the business architecture of today's evolution line.[14]

According to Neumann, the problems of space structures and sphere packing demand further analogical research in order to explore the large array of Platonic and Archimedean solids that have not yet found any architectural application. For instance, he found the field of crystallography to be especially pertinent, but warned against overly simplistic transfers: "It would be naïve to believe that one could mechanically transfer shapes from crystallography to architecture. This would mean a worse formalism than the application of historical forms. What is important is thinking in analogies."[15] In a 1967 lecture entitled "Architecture as Ornament," he further explained the significance of the crystallographic analogy for three-dimensional pattern-thinking and for rethinking the notion of ornament in architectural discourse. Here he made his decisive move against the proverbial prescriptions of functionalism:

> In their militant zeal, Loos and his followers have overlooked, or could not have seen in their time, that we are all submitted to the inescapable compulsion of ornament.
>
> [...] Crystallography deals amongst others with the regular division of space, a feature it has in common with ornament and architecture. [...] With the additional form-restricting conditions like the representational prohibition in Mohammedanism, the motif elements disappear completely, and only the geometric scaffolding remains. We obtain the ornament in pure state. The morphology of an object has nothing to do with its use, what one calls its function. The weaving process and the resulting structural pattern are independent

of the tissues used as carpet or clothing.
The steel structure of a skyscraper is not
determined by its use as an office building.[16]

In search of the ultimate geometrical scaffolding of the architectural object, for the purity of ornament as structure, Neumann exchanged the functionalist metaphorical routine for the structuralist metonymic mind-set. Building as ornament—as modular pattern, as organizational system, as space-packing tool, as machine, not figuratively for dwelling, but for mediating between body and space, pattern and texture, part and whole—this would be the vector guiding his critique of postwar architecture of *le plus grand nombre*[17] and motivating his attempts to implement his EM-PHI proportion system in actual built projects through the short-lived partnership of Neumann-Hecker-Sharon.

## The Building as Ornament

Most of the built work of Neumann-Hecker-Sharon, subversive as it may have been perceived locally and promoted internationally, was commissioned and executed by national, municipal, or academic institutions. The rhetorical attack on conventional practice, delivered with the promise of a new architecture—rationally produced and assembled and at the same time climatically efficient and responsive—had a special appeal in Israel in the 1960s, enough at least to entrust the partnership with the design of the Bat Yam Town Hall (1959–1963; competition winner), the Club Med Holiday Camp in Achziv (1960–1961), the Netanya City Hall (1963; unbuilt project), the Israel Defense Forces officer-training school (1963–1967), and the Mechanical Engineering Faculty at the Technion (1964–1967).

The exceptional morphological complexity of the designs was explained in a mix of scientific, aesthetic, historical, and regionalist arguments. If the approach to module and pattern "transformed the building envelope into a kind of spatial filter that performed environmentally in terms of reduction of heat intake, enhancement of natural ventilation, and diffusion of natural light,"[18] it reflected attempts to create self-conditioned buildings, to break away from the curtain wall with its various sun-filtering systems so prevalent in official Israeli architecture, and to finally articulate a local archetype that would respond to the specific conditions and traditions of the region.

The Bat Yam Town Hall, the first major built architectural work of the Neumann-Hecker-Sharon partnership, expressed the innovative idea of the building as a composite of volumetric units, but its planar and sectional schemes were based on three traditional principles: an interior patio in the center of the building, wind chimneys on the rooftop to allow for proper air circulation, and an inverted ziggurat shape, creating extended floors that made the building cast shadows on itself.

The Netanya City Hall design is triangular in plan and based geometrically on truncated tetrahedron space-packing units, with hexagonal panel walls and triangular window openings. In this project, with its large internal courtyard, the architects were explicit about their intention to "continue a Mediterranean tradition that has been largely ignored until now in modern architecture."[19]

Regionalist arguments were put forth to validate the morphology of the Mechanical Engineering Faculty at the Technion. This jagged *béton brut* monolith, with its rectilinear symmetrical plan and triangulated envelope, is described by the architects as an environmentally sensitive mechanism: "The exterior walls, which unified construction, fenestration, and climatic protection in one consistent system, consist of a continuous row of folded slab pre-cast elements (14 cm thick), triangular in shape, and a fill-in of narrow windows between the concrete elements. The saw-tooth overhang of each floor above the window openings protects it almost completely from the penetration of direct rain and sun."[20]

Of all the projects by Neumann-Hecker-Sharon, it was not a public project but a residential one that assumed the status of a new local archetype: the Dubiner House designed and built from 1960 to 1965 on a steep hill in Ramat Gan, a former garden city northeast of Tel Aviv.[21] This building, containing a mere eleven apartments of various shapes and sizes, aroused disproportionate professional and public attention and became an instant Israeli landmark. In the June 1965 issue of *Domus* magazine, the architects described the project as follows:

> The basic shape of the plan is an elongated hexagon, created by a prismatic hexagonal space-packing pattern. The pyramidal build-up of the lower three storeys follows the retreating profile of the hill, while the upper storeys project in overhanging layers. [...] The hexagonal inside space creates a kind of stepped interior piazza with small-scale landscaping. This space penetrates the whole building volume and contains the freely arranged vertical communications and the bridged accesses to the flats. The piazza has its own microclimate—shadowy cool in summer and sun-warmed in winter. [...] The main feature of the apartments is their half-covered and half-opened polygonal terraces, with major rooms facing and opening around it. The interpenetration of solid and void prismatic form, integrated into the stereometric structure of the stepped section of the building, is an external expression of the inner habitation activity. [...] The anonymity of the conventional accesses to apartments from staircase-landing and elevator lobbies is transformed into an open relationship providing identity for every flat. [...] This system, though providing maximum privacy, does not mean complete separation, but maintains visual contact with the surroundings and a constant change of view.[22]

⑤

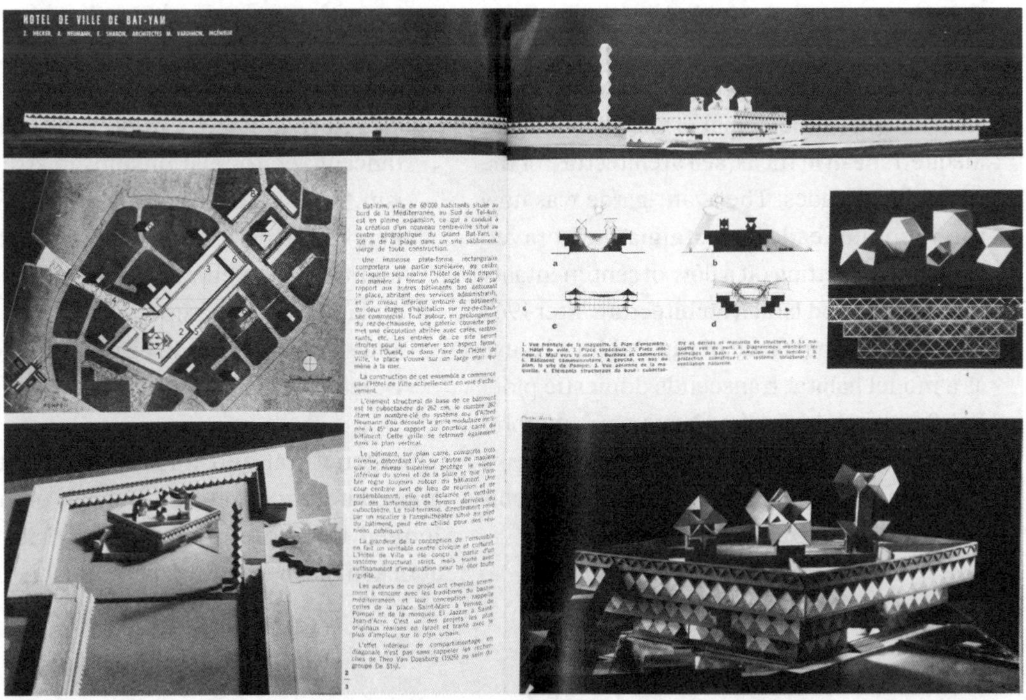
HOTEL DE VILLE DE BAT-YAM

Z. HECKER, A. NEUMANN, E. SHARON, ARCHITECTES M. VARDIMON, INGÉNIEUR

This text is too descriptive to become a sweeping architectural manifesto, but it certainly has the originality, the richness, and the conviction of a document aiming to instigate a paradigm shift. The essential ingredients for the articulation of a new habitat are all there: geometric sophistication and tectonic complexity; architectural idiosyncrasy and structural reproducibility; environmental sensibility and integral landscaping; urban precepts and communal life; open and interchangeable figure-ground relations; equilibrium between density and porosity, anonymity and identity. This is a future dwelling system posed as a spontaneous vernacular setting.

Zvi Hecker, the main protagonist of the Dubiner project and its resident for over five decades, recalls the diverse attributes applied to it.[23] According to Hecker, for Neumann, it was simply a rudimentary form of a city (a courtyard with surrounding houses). Some interpreted its piled-up form, stepped terraces, and erratic roofscape as a direct analogy of the Arab village, while others saw its interwoven communal and discrete spaces as a plausible model for an urban kibbutz. The more the Dubiner House became an object of contention, the more cultural authority it gained, triggering both a local trend of experimental (mostly paper) architecture and a wave of lamentation about the denial of the Oriental and Mediterranean in the Israeli architecture of the formative decades. The avant-garde was now the fountainhead of nostalgia and craved authenticity, setting off a flow of sentimentality that would flood Israeli architecture after 1967.

But the significance of the Dubiner House as a model habitat transcends domestic plots. Rafi Segal's study of Alfred Neumann's morphological approach clarifies the distinctiveness of the Dubiner project within the broader context of architectural structuralism:

> Neumann's pattern-thinking aimed to offer an alternative way of conceiving the assembly of the architectural object. His approach was not structuralist in the sense of Herman Hertzberger's architecture, where a structure was an overall organizational armature, and the unit an infill inserted within that structure. For Neumann, the unit composed the structure; its spatial repetition and assembly created the shape of the building. The unit was not an infill in a larger structural element but created the structure in itself. Counter to the importance given to relationships in structuralism, where the parts could be changed as long as the part-whole relationships were maintained, Neumann's units were non-replaceable. The properties of form, shape, and size of the unit in Neumann's designs were particular.[24]

The structural and formal peculiarity diagnosed in retrospect by Segal was often overlooked by contemporaneous critics, who attacked the overall work of Neumann-Hecker-

⑥

Sharon as too eccentric, nonindustrialized, and uninhabitable. Most skeptical, indeed disdainful, of the critics was Robin Middleton, whose articles in the leading international architectural magazines of the time were instantaneously translated into Hebrew and published in the leading local professional magazine, which was controlled by the hegemonic circles of "State Brutalists."[25] In a short review for the September 1965 issue of *Architectural Review*, entitled "A Yiddish Grid," Middleton suggested that a particularly radical (and rather infantile) faction of morphological architecture was developing in Israel:

> The first finished block of the town hall at Bat Yam [...] looks at first sight like a film set for "I was a Teenage Tange." Its violently triangulated geometry, its tortuous rooflights and its internal diagrid assert a personal flavor as intriguing as it may be distasteful [...]. Nor is this building an isolated freak, as the June issue of *Domus* revealed.[26]

Two years later, Middleton extended his critique, this time in *Architectural Design*, with the article "The Geometrical Straitjacket" (February 1967). Here, Middleton went so far as to analyze the architectural preoccupation with geometry from J. N. L. Durand and Viollet-le-Duc up to Le Corbusier, Scharoun, and Fuller, only to finally point at the Neumann-Hecker-Sharon partnership as the leading provocateurs of the latest architectural vanity. This article is quoted here at some length since it best illustrates the central and rather contentious place occupied by the Israeli avant-garde in the international scene of the 1960s.

> Alfred Neumann, Zvi Hecker, and Eldar Sharon have constituted themselves as the most determined exponents of this new architecture. During the past five years they have designed a spate of buildings in Israel based on polyhedral solids—rhomboid, hyperbolic paraboloids, truncated tetrahedra and octahedra, these are the words they used to describe the architecture. First was the Bat Yam civic center, then a series of elegant, light-hearted holiday camps [...], but they took up thereafter the ponderous administrative mode: the Faculty of Mechanical Engineering at Haifa, the Netanya civic center and the El Al terminal building in Tel Aviv. They have also designed housing in the new geometrical style at Ramat Gan. The buildings are not without felicities of climatic control and dramatic internal lighting effects, but these

⑤ Bat Yam Town Hall, *L'Architecture d'Aujourd'hui* 106 (February–March 1963). Alfred Neumann, Zvi Hecker, Eldar Sharon.
⑥ Dubiner House, under construction, Ramat Gan, 1961–1963. Alfred Neumann, Zvi Hecker, Eldar Sharon.

⑦ Robin Middleton, "A Yiddish Grid," *Architectural Review* (September 1965).
⑧ Robin Middleton, "The Geometrical Straitjacket," *Architectural Design* (February 1967).

⑦

# A YIDDISH GRID

The first finished block of the town hall at Bat Yam, 33, an industrial town close to Tel Aviv looks at first sight like a film set for 'I was a Teenage Tange.' Its violently triangulated geometry, its tortuous rooflights and its internal diagrid assert a personal flavour as intriguing as it may be

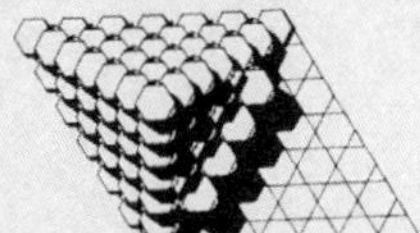

34

distasteful. Two of the architects, Zvi Heker and Eldar Sharon, are young, but the leader of the team, Alfred Neumann, is aged 65 and a former pupil of Behrens, Perret and Loos. Nor is this building an isolated freak, as the June issue of *Domus* revealed. For El Al they have designed a pyramidal air terminal on a triangular site in Tel Aviv, 34. Its single concourse, with a small gallery of offices projecting over the entrance, will be lit through each one of the prefabricated tetrahedrons, 35.

More important, Neumann and Heker only have designed a complex of three buildings, 36, for the engineering faculty at Haifa's famous Institute of Technology, and these are actually under construction, 37. The principal block of laboratories and lecture halls, 38, is built up with a series of triangular units, 39, with shuttered slit windows in the joints. The major part of the plan, 40, seems to satisfy at first sight, apart from some zig-zag corridors in the central link. The second main block, 41, containing electrical engineering workshops, has its units still further articulated.

The architects claim that their system is a completely integrated solution of the problems of heat, glare and rain. It will be interesting to see what use is made of the triangular bays along the perimeter.

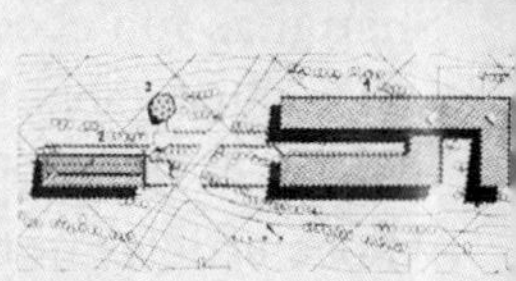

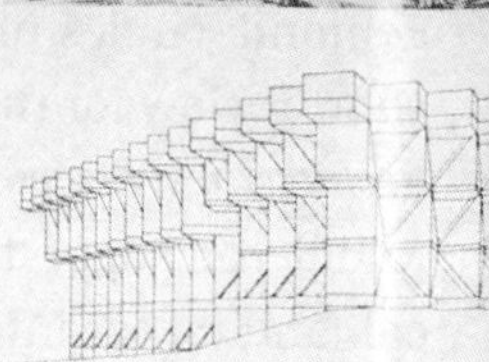

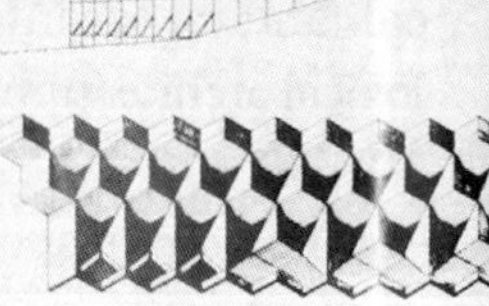

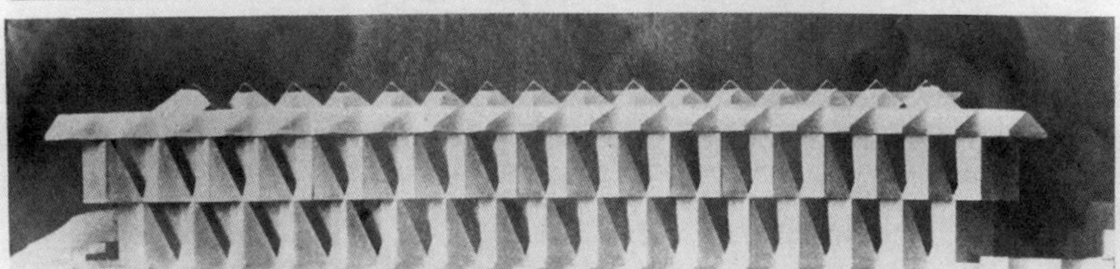

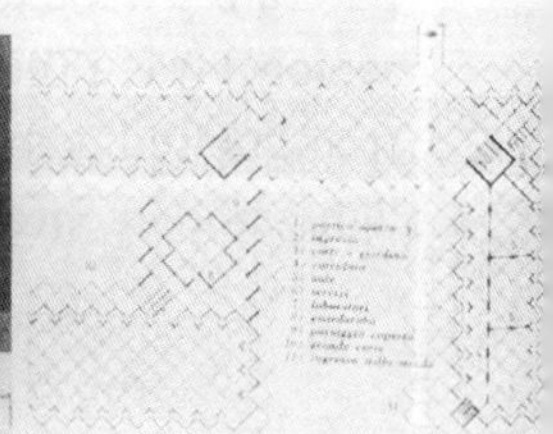

41

160

(8)

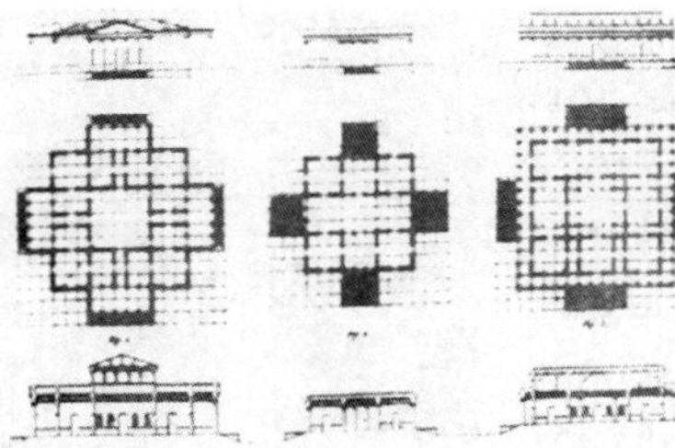

1

## The geometrical straitjacket

*Robin Middleton*

The great advantage of the Gothic Revival was that it restored common sense to architecture. By the end of the eighteenth century the disciplines imposed by the Classical style had become so rigid and codified and so restrictive that all ease of organization, all convenience of planning was impossible. The height, the breadth and the width of any room of any pretension was determined by rules; even the sizes of the door and window openings were controlled by these rules. Symmetry was *de rigueur*, so that one opening had to be balanced by another of the same size and each had to relate to a symmetrical scheme in adjoining rooms. Planning, at best, was an affair of geometric ordering. The grid came into its own. J. N. L. Durand, the greatest grammarian of Neo-classicism, reduced architecture to a geometric pattern **1**. He started, whenever possible, with a square, equally sub-divided in both directions. On this he arranged first his plan—strictly symmetrical in all its parts—then, projecting the grid vertically, he composed the section and elevation. There is a play of rationality in this method, but clearly, the logic has little to do with the objectives of architecture. Durand's vaunted logic is disingenuous. There was no question of convenience prompting an ideal.

When it came to detail, the formulas of the Neo-classical movement were even more inhibiting. The height of a column and all its related mouldings were fixed by its diameter, and the application of such Greek and Roman temple details was so unsuited to the complexities even of early nineteenth century planning that a crisis ensued every time a corner had to be turned or a junction effected. Very few architects could stand the strain. Sir John Soane determined to think out a new vocabulary for himself. But the Gothic Revival swept away these barriers. Henceforth, all arrangements, all plans, all mouldings even, could follow the apparently wayward pattern imposed by external limitations and—most important—by use. Rooms could be of the size and shape required, they could be set in relation one to another according to convenience, and openings could be placed exactly where they were needed. The particular and appropriate success of Alfred Waterhouse's vast and complex public buildings would have been impossible before the Gothic Revival.

The other inestimable contribution that the Gothic Revival made to architecture was freedom and honesty of structural arrangement. Structure could be designed as and where it was needed, and it was allowed, —indeed encouraged—to show. There was to be no more dissimulation. Viollet le Duc was the prophet of this movement; small wonder that the pupils of the Ecole des Beaux Arts swore *haine à Viollet le Duc* on their *Grand Durand*.

Viollet le Duc's theories largely conditioned the modern movement—Le Corbusier's *Vers une architecture* is little more than a paraphase of his ideas; Frank Lloyd Wright thought him a perfervid prodigy, while Mies van der Rohe continues still to lean heavily on verities that he propounded. Functionalism and structural honesty as ideals are a legacy of the Gothic Revival. The architects of the Heroic Period took full advantage of the freedom afforded by these commonsense goals. 'Free planning' is a phrase we associate still with the masterpieces of the twentieth century masters. But during the last twenty years there has not been much time for inventive experimentation. An architecture bathed in the concealed light of modernity has long been accepted. Most architects have been forced to build continuously, endlessly and at great pace in a known idiom. Formulas have had to be devised for architecture. And one of the most pervasive is that of space enclosed by planes at right angles to one another. The rectangle is taken for granted. Architects are scarcely conscious of it as a decisive and limiting factor in planning. Rather it appears a convenience. Certainly it simplifies problems of detailing, junctions and setting out and relates closely to the standard shapes and sizes of manufactured sheet materials and of furniture. There is no difficulty in making things fit.

But, of course, the rectangle has been found a constraint. Hans Scharoun has therefore continued serenely to design in exactly the same dynamic manner as in the twenties. Since the completion of the Berlin Philarmonie many architects in Germany have attempted to imitate the urgent angular lines of his plans. But uncontrolled by the master, they are rarely satisfying. Some less exacting and more certain method of achieving success has long been sought by architects tired of the rectangle; some planning formula not based on the right-angle. There is a range of other regular geometric figures—the triangle, the hexagon and the octagon are some of these—and one by one they have been adapted as an organizing motif. Frank Lloyd Wright was one of the first to use them with any degree of persistence. He drew and even built a number of houses based on these figures. But he soon found faults. Not only was the architecture unbearably self-conscious, but inconvenient. How was one to live in these spaces, how to arrange the furniture and relate it to the architecture. He was forced to re-design all furniture to the same insistent geometric pattern—to ludicrous resultant effect. Until a new mode of living was devised appropriate to the new geometric formula it was simply an embarrassment.

But the triangle, the hexagon and the octagon still seem to offer to restive architects a modicum of planning freedom withheld by the ubiquitous rectangle. Recently, Noel Moffet, stacking up an array of hexagonal boxes for an old age home in White City **9** (conceived as an occasional building between lumbering slabs of rectangular housing) demonstrated yet again how awkward that figure could be as a plan form. But there have been more sophisticated essays. For it has seemed to many inquisitive architects that a new planning formula might be linked inseparably to that other twentieth century dogma, the ideal of structural economy and honesty. Buckminster Fuller has proclaimed the static supremacy of the tetrahedron, the icosahedron and what-have-you. A new geometry seems to be upon us. One that could unite the desired planning formula and the refinements of structure. Alfred Neumann, Zvi Hecker and Eldar Sharon have constituted themselves the most determined exponents of this new architecture. During the past five years they have designed a spate of buildings in Israel based on polyhedral solids—rhomboid, hyperbolic paraboloids, truncated tetrahedra and octahedra, these are the words they used to describe the architecture **2**. First was the Bat Yam civic centre (*AD*, November, 1964), then a series of elegant, light-hearted holiday camps at Arhziv (*AD*, April, 1965), Michmoret and Kiriat Yam **3**, but they took up thereafter the ponderous administrative mode; the Faculty of Mechanical Engineering at Haifa **7** the Natania Civic Centre **4, 5, 6** and the El Al terminal building in Tel Aviv **8**. They have also designed housing in the new geometrical style at Ramat Gan, outside Tel Aviv. The buildings are not without felicities of climatic control and dramatic internal lighting effects, but these are secondary to and in any case not dependent upon the rigid adherence to a simple three-dimensional structural and spatial unit. The adventurousness and the spirit of intellectual honesty that must first have conditioned their use has been dissipated. The geometry has taken over and has the architects in thrall—indeed, in a stranglehold. They have abrogated all freedom and all common sense. Their planning has become progressively more rigid and their composition more hieratic. The later buildings have miserable pretentions to monumentality. Durand even, with all the formulae of Neo-classical composition at his command, offered more freedom of design. For Durand at least retained the rectangle as the basis of his design (the circle was an ideal only, not a seriously considered practical possibility) and the rectangle can, within its limits, be adjusted in size. Moreover it is neither obtrusive nor inconvenient. The truncated tetrahedron as adapted for use in Israel is not only grossly inconvenient for planning, but obsessive—an opinion with which Buckminster Fuller would certainly agree. The architecture has the quality of hallucination, far removed from the sanity needed to build in this teeming twentieth century.

are secondary to and in any case not dependent upon the rigid adherence to a simple three-dimensional structural and spatial unit. The adventurousness and the spirit of intellectual honesty that must first have conditioned their use has been dissipated. The geometry has taken over and has the architects in thrall—indeed, in a stranglehold. They have abrogated all freedom and all common sense. Their planning has become progressively more rigid and their composition more hieratic. Their later buildings have miserable pretensions to monumentality.

[...] The truncated tetrahedron as adapted for use in Israel is not only grossly inconvenient for planning, but obsessive—an opinion with which Buckminster Fuller would certainly agree. The architecture has the quality of hallucination, far removed from the sanity needed to build in this teeming twentieth century.[27]

Although the above depiction of Israeli morphological architecture as a "miserable pretension to monumentality" was aimed mainly at public or institutional buildings, it already indicated the early spillover of "the new geometrical style" to the housing industry. Indeed, during the 1960s and 1970s many housing projects in Israel would fake a modular reproducibility and frivolous accumulability in order to gain a fashionable "plug-in" look and a habitat ambience.

## Habitat

The change of tone of postwar architectural discourse was epitomized in the emergent notion of "habitat" in the early 1950s. Searching for the primal leap of the concept of habitat, Monique Eleb relates of her research on Casablanca with Jean-Louis Cohen: "I wanted

⑨

⑫

⑭

⑩

⑪

⑬

⑮

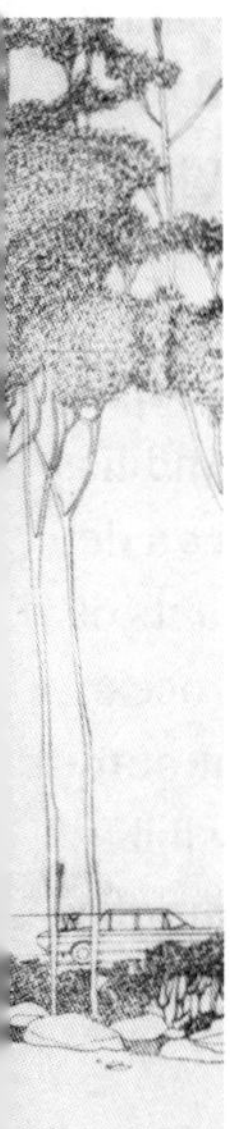

⑨ Apartment building spiral-square, Eilat, 1961. Theodore Kisselov.
⑩ Terraced housing in Upper Nazareth, 1957. Arieh Sharon, Benjamin Idelson.
⑪ Terraced housing, Upper Nazareth, 1976–1968. Avraham Ventura.
⑫ Apartment building, Netanya, 1970. Tov Strikovsky.
⑬ Stepped apartment Building, Ashkelon, 1957, Nahum Zolotov.
⑭ Apartment buildings, Netanya, 1970. Perspective drawing. Tov Strikovsky.
⑮ “Drawers” building, Beersheba, 1966. Moshe Lolenfeld, Giora Gamraman.

to know where the slogan 'habitat for the greatest number'—so commonly encountered in our research—had come from [...]. And how come the term 'habitat' suddenly appeared in the field of architecture, given that it had been entirely absent in France and elsewhere until the 1940s?"[28] Eleb's abridged account of habitat's "sudden appearance" is found in her essay "An Alternative to Functionalist Universalism," which gives a résumé of the sources and attributes of the term and its build-up as a softening elixir for the Charter of Athens:

> At the time, the theoretical study of the "housing function" was undergoing crisis within CIAM. The meeting at Bridgewater in 1947 aimed to "work for the creation of a physical environment that will satisfy man's emotional and material needs" and to "stimulate man's spiritual growth." Following a proposal made by the French, the notion of habitat, which served as the basis for CIAM discussions, was borrowed from geographers and anthropologists, the former stressing the geographical space and land, the latter the connection with civilization. "Habitat" thus replaced the terms *logis*, *machine à habiter*, *logement minimum*, and *function d'habiter*, which had been in use until then.[29]

Its etymology and ethology aside, habitat is genuinely embedded in the colonialist mindset and modus operandi. Eleb mentions that the term was "originally used to refer to 'other', non-Western societies,"[30] and recounts the urbanist background to Michel Ecochard's work in Morocco, as illustrated in the Medina district built in 1917 on the outskirts of Casablanca: "It was a mimetic district designed using techniques and patterns taken from Moroccan spaces, with their complex transitions between private and public areas, as well as their zoning."[31] Prewar "mimetic urbanism" metamorphosed into postwar "adaptive architecture" by Ecochard and his team at the Service de l'Urbanisme of the French protectorate and enabled a more effective *habitat pour le plus grand nombre*. The problem of mass housing was never *en bloc*, but always ethnically and economically specific. "The 'adapted' habitat was reserved for the 'poor' in the Muslim and Jewish communities. 'The greatest number' refers to the poor, the working class, people in shantytowns and rural people."[32] "Adaptive architecture," as practiced by Ecochard and endlessly appropriated and misappropriated by colonial and postcolonial modernists from the late 1950s onward, was both sympathetic and pedagogic. Its project was not merely accommodating, but noticeably missionary. Ecochard declared that he would create districts for the masses, "made of individual houses with courtyards, which were supposed to respect 'traditional customs' and enable a 'progressive lifestyle transformation.'"[33]

Paradoxically—indeed, characteristically—as the atavistic fascination with vernacular building and dwelling patterns became more explicit and the longing for architecture-without-architects became more prevalent, so did the figure of the auteur-architect, called upon to articulate a new decorum. Georges Candilis, head of *ATBAT-Afrique* from 1951 and probably one of the most prolific propagators of "mat" structures, extruded Ecochard's 8-by-8-meter infrastructural grid into a multi-storey "vertical casbah" and added his poetic supplement of the *dimension indicible*. For Candilis, whose task was to define and construct a decent standard of housing for the inhabitants of the *bidonvilles* scattered around the Moroccan cities, the modernist repository of minimum-existence schemes did not meet the sensibility to human dignity and to authentic traditions required of an architect. Captivated by the "inventiveness with which residents, who flooded into the *bidonvilles* from all over the country, managed to express their distinctive, primeval patterns of life and coordinate them with the most modest of means, [...] he recognized it as a stage in the process of growth towards a veritable habitat, as an authentic human ecology in gestation."[34] Following Candilis and his presentation at CIAM 9 in Aix (1953),[35] Aldo van Eyck developed his report to the CIAM committee on the synthesis of the visual arts, entitled "Attitude towards Natural Data and Archaic Civilizations." In this report, van Eyck expressed his appreciation of "primitive" civilizations, which, "through both their artifacts and their habitats [...] testify to the primal human capacity for self-expression in elementary forms charged with multiple meanings: pregnant forms that simultaneously voice the local natural conditions, a social structure and cosmological views."[36] To van Eyck, the commitment to the problem of mass housing was also an obligation to articulate a new aesthetic, an "aesthetic of number." In 1959 he wrote in the Dutch magazine *Forum*:

> Projects should attempt to solve the aesthetic problems that result through the standardization of constructional elements: through the repetition of similar dwellings within a larger housing unit; through the repetition or groupings of such housing units, similar or dissimilar (theme and its mutation and variation).[37]

By this time the framework for new architectural parables and paradigms was set. Through the conduits of Candilis, van Eyck, Team 10, a rejuvenated CIAM, *Forum*, *Architectural Design*, and *L'Architecture d'Aujourd'hui*, the aestheticization of authenticity, spontaneity, and bricolage gained swift momentum, and by the end of the 1950s, it held a certain grip on practically every conscientious affordable housing project in both developed and developing countries. The maxim "habitat," generally connoting a low-rise, high-density, low-income, high-State sponsorship, signified a desirable alternative to the commonplace horizontal and vertical slab housing.

In the Israel of the late 1950s and 1960s, the notion of habitat had a special appeal, though it had little to do with local anthropological studies or with a plausible architecture "for the greatest number." By the late 1950s, the rate of absorption of new (Jewish) immigrants and (Jewish) refugees in Israel may have slowed down, but the project of eradicating the transit camps and erecting permanent housing for all (Jewish) citizens became the most pressing national task. The standardization and dissemination of oversimplified housing blocks was a marker of the efficiency and integrity of the welfare state. There was little to be learned from the transit camps: they may have been reminiscent of the *bidonvilles* in terms of living conditions, but unlike those impromptu shantytowns, the camps were strictly designed barracks with no added folklorist value. On the other end of the local spectrum, the indigenous Palestinian communities and habitats—those which partially remained—were too devastated to be looked at and emulated as "pregnant forms." At best they posed as ruins for local painters or were appropriated by bohemian gentrifiers. Architectural production in Israel, when willing to transcend State indoctrination and engage in the intricacies of genius loci, had to look afar and draw upon well-established and well-published exemplars. The North-African casbah, mediated through the leading modernist colonial architects, provided such a perfect exemplar: it was remote enough to enable indulgence with native patterns, and contentious enough to suggest a progressive experimental activity at the margins of the national project. This experimental activity, it should be noted, was almost always initiated, supported, and materialized by the State apparatus itself as its dialectical outsider. After all, the state of utter denial when it came to Israeli colonialist practices (vis-à-vis both the native Palestinians and the immigrant North-African Jews) and the epic discourse of self-colonization required the invention and cultivation of otherness through the production of deviant projects and formalized habitats. These projects proliferated in Israel beginning in 1959 and continued well into the 1970s. They developed some noteworthy adaptations of "mat structures," "courtyard houses," and "expandable units." These projects were customarily called "model neighborhoods," not at all due to their status as reproducible prototypes, but, quite to the contrary, in order to indicate that they were done under controlled laboratory conditions. The synonymy in Israel between the terms "model housing" and "habitat" implied a double disavowal: first, a renunciation of the official housing-block typology; and second, a rejection of the fake elasticity and porosity of the garden city, the quintessential Israeli town-planning paradigm. Israeli "mat structures," therefore, should be considered not merely as ethnographic curiosities, but actually as prospects for overplaying the orthogonal grid, an urban setup never really trusted in Zionist planning.

## Yona Friedman's Beginnings

The Israeli habitat, then, was mostly flat. A few noteworthy exceptions (of which some remained on paper and some were realized in built projects) which explored the social, environmental, and technological performance of the spatial habitat will be described in what follows. Most of these instances incubated and developed within or around the circle of the Technion "radicals," led by Alfred Neumann, and most of them had a greater impact and longer afterlife internationally than they did locally. The exemplary hillside project, Neumann-Hecker-Sharon's Dubiner House, with its complex interior-exterior associations, has already been discussed at some length above. It was, in any case, too idiosyncratic to suggest a methodology or produce a consistent discourse. In fact, its only proclaimed successor is an outlandish housing project in Jerusalem which was designed in the 1970s by Zvi Hecker, and which will be mentioned in the concluding remarks of this chapter.

More prudent was the work of Yona Friedman, a student at the Technion and eventually Neumann's teaching assistant. His initial work retreated from the indulgent geometries of his colleagues and explored accessible resources for shelters. Friedman, born in 1923 in Budapest, survived World War II and immigrated to Palestine in 1945, but left Israel for Paris in 1957. The foundation for his life's work—first presented internationally at the 1956 CIAM meeting in Dubrovnik as *Manifeste de l'Architecture Mobile* and published in Paris in 1959—was laid during his early research in Israel. Conspicuously, his Israeli

(16) Temporary shelter prototype made of reused steel barrels, 1953. Photomontage. Yona Friedman (with Jean-Pierre Pecquet).
(17) Desert mat housing, 1960s. Plan and elevation. Yona Friedman.
(18) Desert mat housing, 1960s. Perspective. Yona Friedman.

⑯

experiments with provisional emergency structures present a dialectical image to his proverbial *ville spatiale*, with its hovering scaleless megastructure. In an interview with architect Daniel Rauchwerger for the Israeli newspaper *Haaretz*, Friedman referred to his Israeli chapter and showed the interviewer a photomontage "of an Israeli beach, with palm trees and sand and sun, on which has been overlaid a somewhat sloppy 'simulation' of cylindrical residential units that are arranged atop each other like a pile of barrels." Rauchwerger describes the image as a remnant of Friedman's farewell project:

> It's part of a series of sketches on which Friedman focused during his final days in Israel, in an attempt to find a use for hundreds of superfluous sections of water pipelines, concrete cylinders with a diameter of 2.5 meters. With the help of several rolls of toilet paper and several pieces of cardboard, he prepared wood and aluminum models of his improvised community.
>
> Friedman was unable to carry out the experimental project in Israel. In France, the idea was well received and was even partially implemented, becoming the "cheapest industrialized housing unit in Europe that year [1958]," he explains with pride.[38]

The subtext of postwar trauma and the direct experience of homeless refugees in Europe and in Israel are evident in Friedman's early projects and writings, but his minor architecture soon took a turn, becoming all-encompassing and fantastic. It radicalized the notion of habitat and endowed it with apocalyptic overtones of insurmountable future populations and urban infrastructures, contrasted with naïve drawings of "artificial topographies" and utopian nomad communities. In

⑰ ⑱

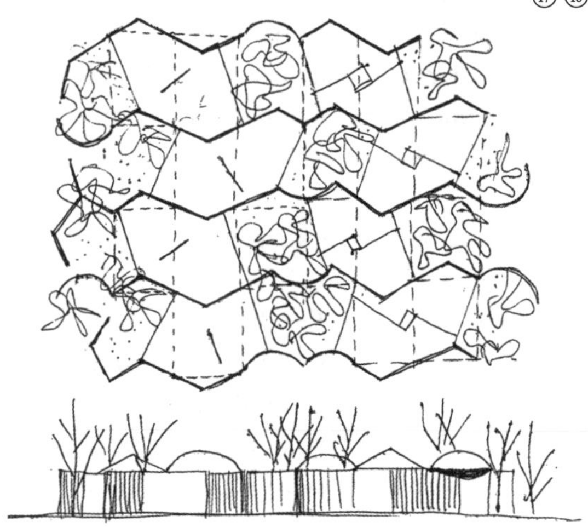

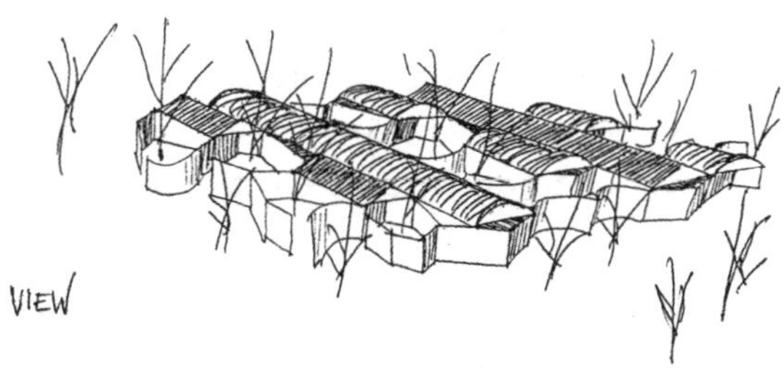

⑲ "The Horizontal Ziggurat," 1962. Model. Leopold Gerstel.
⑳ Proposal for a habitat, Ramat Yitzhak, Haifa, 1966. Leopold Gerstel.

Friedman's only text published in Hebrew during the 1960s, the apparent incongruity of gigantism and smallness, of mass industrialization and self-made dwelling, of expert and amateur architecture, is "resolved" in his proposition of "folklore-architecture":

> As a result of the new system for urban planning and the Spatial City, architecture will become a new folklore. Folklore means the creation of rules and codes by a group of people. The folklore-architecture will reaffirm our assumption: It will be determined by democratization and activation of the rules we defined.[39]

Enigmatic and amorphous as it may be, folklore-architecture shifts the rhetorical weight from the object to the subject of architecture. The suspended limitless grid abstracts the city and imagines a new kind of social ingenuity and mobility. Habitat is drawn back to its primal condition as human shelter, while being rescued from probable nostalgia for the native, the exotic, or the traditional. Folklore-architecture is back-to-the-future.

### Leopold Gerstel's Ziggurat

Leopold Gerstel, Friedman's colleague and friend, was also invested in constructing a sense of habitat around the notion of human mobility; however, unlike Friedman's airy infrastructural skeletons projected onto the future, his were colossal "mounds," or archetypal "ziggurats," designed as mass clustered housing for actual new towns in Israel. If Friedman seemed to be interested in spacing, suspending, and hollowing out his architecture, Gerstel experimented with compression, perforation, and agglomeration. His ziggurats (published internationally in *Architectural Design* in January 1964) consisted of a housing "shield" set back in tiers over a core of shops and car parks. The whole appeared as a solid mass, but it was perforated throughout by courtyards, light wells, streets, and alleys, so that sunlight and air could penetrate to the lower levels. For Gerstel, the ziggurat was a compact megastructure—and megastructure, for him, was an abridged catalogue of medieval or Mediterranean public spaces, "made up not of concrete walls, but of the motion of human crowds." "It is to be regretted," he wrote, "that the skyline of the ziggurat had a greater impact on architecture than its inner qualities and its very conceptual structure."[40] Inner quality, according to Gerstel, is the integration and layering of micro-situations created by

⑲

(20)

the movement and congregation of people in simulated traditional public spaces. There is no claim of authenticity in his work, only a quest for a tantalizing illusion, reminiscent of the experience described by Louis Aragon in *Le Paysan de Paris*. Gerstel, indeed, was the only Israeli architect of the 1960s who talked about *flânerie* as a rudimentary form of urban praxis and referred to the surrealists as his creative ancestors: "Not the anecdotal surrealism (exemplified in Dalí's work), [...] and not surrealism of rigid and immutable physical laws (as practiced by Escher, Duchamp and de Chirico)," but "[...] surrealism generated by an equivocal sense of orientation."[41] It is, then, a situationist surrealism that Gerstel was looking for, a surrealism that stages chance encounters and arbitrary trajectories on the backdrop of trivial sets. "I wish to emphasize," he wrote, "that the most surreal situations are triggered by the most ordinary—I would say plain, almost poor—circumstances, structures, and patterns [...]. Architecture begins to exist when it stimulates connotations and personifications."[42]

We can imagine Yona Friedman's slender matrix as a hyperactive cage whereby mobility, both social and individual, is always instrumental: assembling and dismantling, plugging in and deterritorializing. Leopold Gerstel's chunky ziggurat must be quite different. It is a cumbersome theater for existential plays and idle strolling. Its architecture has no survivalist agenda, no technological revelation, and no narrative to follow. If anything, habitat is what happens when architecture takes a leave of absence.

### Architecturology: The (Pre)Fabricated Course of I. M. Goodovitch

Situationist surrealism was far too frivolous for the Israeli project and went, in any case, against the grain of the structuralist teaching at the Technion. A rare comment on this school's atmosphere and a glance into Alfred Neumann's "court" is provided in Israel Goodovitch's book *Architecturology*,[43] perhaps the only architectural monograph composed in Israel in the 1960s (and published only in English):

November 1957
My last year in the 'incubator.' I have Professor A. Neumann as an instructor. It was he who —during this last year—gave me some moral support. We used to discuss Beckett and Prévert, Mozart and Hindemith, and our contemporary society. [...] "Your year's project will be: A FAIR. It has to be portable, moveable, storable and attractive. It has to represent contemporary technical progress. [...]" And to this 'Free Programme' he did not add a single word of explanation [...]. He went back

㉑

㉒

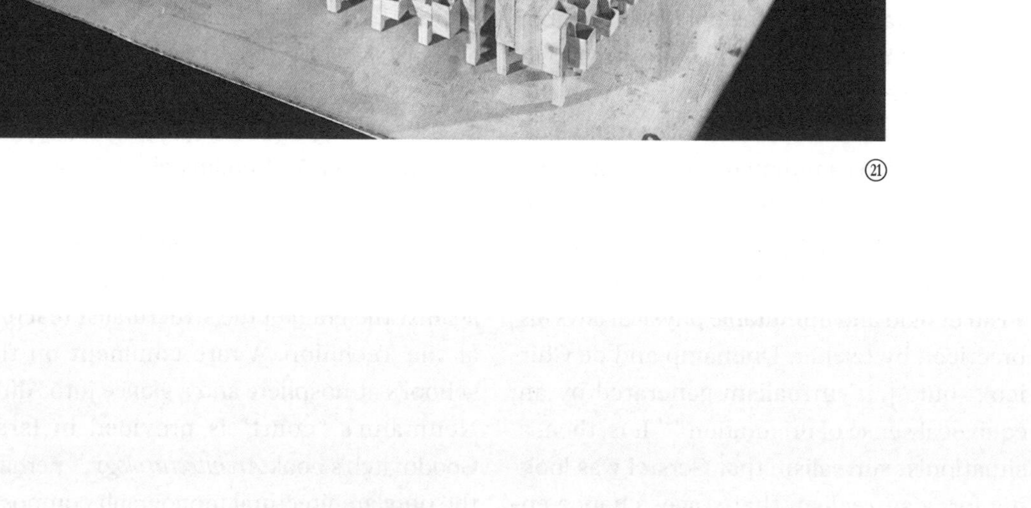

(21) "Ziggurat: An Experiment in Spatial Urbanism," 1962–1963. Model. Leopold Gerstel.
(22) "Ziggurat: An Experiment in Spatial Urbanism," 1962–1963. Section. Leopold Gerstel.
(23) Prefab Field school under construction, Hatzeva, 1968–1969. Israel Goodovitch.

(23)

to his room, leaving us students shocked and puzzled [...].

December 1957
A students' protest. "We cannot invent a project out of nothing." "We need instructions." All this time the Grand Inquisitor was sitting silently in his room. At least his assistant came out with a message: He wants you to prepare individual programmes [...] there is a vast field of possibilities, of variations, of experimentation. This field belongs to you, future architects.

January 1958
[...] The professor said that my idea was expressionistic and surrealistic architecture which fitted more to décor and setting. I am thinking.[44]

Goodovitch developed into an illustrious nonconformist, but he was certainly no expressionistic surrealist or set designer, at least not during the first decades of his professional activity. Unlike Neumann, Hecker, Friedman, and Gerstel, he remained in Israel (after a period of study in Japan, during which he mingled with Kenzo Tange and the younger Metabolist architects). He maintained a lifelong local private and public career; served as architect in charge of planning and rural development in the Ministry of Housing from 1964 to 1973;[45] returned as a senior civil servant for a two-year stint as city engineer of Tel Aviv (1999–2000); and gradually established himself as the local media's go-to agent provocateur on matters of public spaces and institutional bureaucracy.

Goodovitch's interest in morphology and space-packing was never primarily formal or aesthetic. To him, structuralism was above all a cultural and technical framework for investigating possibilities of prefabrication and pre-casting of structural components in order to reshape and reproduce the human habitat. Unlike most of his compatriot avant-gardists of the 1960s, he seriously explored industrial reproducibility, and he was genuinely political in his actions both within the academy and in the actual realm of affordable housing. In his monograph, he described plain social observations, stripped of any applied theory, as triggering his construction process and the architectural argument regarding his hexagonal desert habitat:

24

> In the developing countries, in countries of immigration—at certain stages of life—young couples, either alone, with children, or with parents—as in the natural state of society, with families of various types—creating a priori a similarly natural state—neighboring flats of different sizes—families of different sizes—children, adults, old people—all together, a flow of life. [...]
>
> Saddle vertebra shape construction—with no separation between vertical and horizontal elements—following the natural flow of forces—in a syncopated sequence—creating an inner network—prefabricated standard units combining to form a non-standard product, alterable according to needs, according to the landscape—[...] merging with nature—with a soft skyline echoing a changing topography—floating in various directions—*'panta rei'*.[46]

Goodovitch designed and exhibited several versions of his "saddle housing" (including a one-to-one mock-up of an exemplary interior shown at the Israel Museum, and a technologically complete cluster built as a model-housing project in Japan), but he chanced to actually build only one fully operative prototype, a field school for desert studies and hiking in Hatzeva, located in the arid Arava region. The failure of the "saddles" was definitive. The pre-cast concrete segments creating a "soft skyline echoing a changing topography" were climatically inhabitable and were never reproduced. Before giving up on habitat experiments altogether in favor of corporate curtain-wall architecture, Goodovitch proposed several other formats for affordable housing, most notably the "vertical shell structures" built in the new town of Or Yehuda, which offered young families the chance to buy hollow concrete envelopes in which they could build themselves and expand vertically with time. This project was not repeated either, although it seems to have evolved as envisioned by the architect and to function like a typical row house.

## Habitat Redivivus: Moshe Safdie at Expo 67

There is a moment in Reyner Banham's epic *Megastructure: Urban Futures of the Recent Past* when the notion of habitat and its polyhedral forerunners seems to insinuate a Jewish entrepreneurial conspiracy. "On Safdie's own

㉔ Prototype units according to the "saddle system," Japan. Israel Goodovitch.
㉕ – ㉗ Envelope housing for young families, designed to allow vertical expansion. Perspective sections showing stages of infill. Or Yehuda, 1970s. Israel Goodovitch.
㉘ – ㉛ Envelope housing for young families, designed to allow vertical expansion, under construction, Or Yehuda, 1970s. Israel Goodovitch.

㉘ ㉙ ㉚ ㉛

㉕ ㉖ ㉗

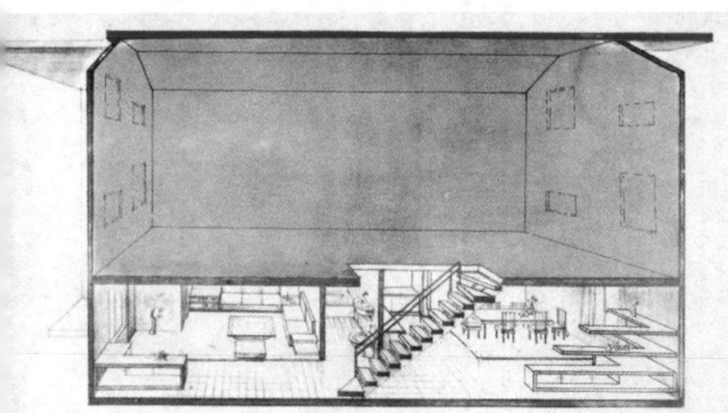

32

ELCO
ELCO
33
32

admission," reports detective Banham, having just deciphered the plot behind the construction of Habitat in Montreal,

> [Anne Tyng's] ideas [about tetrahedral and pyramidal geometries] had a crucial effect on the first project for Habitat, in which the house-capsules are stacked directly on one another in a staggered formation [...] giving a ziggurat or "stepped die" profile that was to rattle around for some years as a possible megastructure format. It occurs again in the projects of Kahn's fellow-Israelis Leopold Gerstel and Zvi Hecker (the latter came to Montreal in due course, cementing a kind of Montreal/Tel Aviv axis) [...] and indeed wherever there was any interest in the mathematics of closest-packing figures.[47]

Perplexed by the sensational hype around a format that had been circulating for some time, Banham could not but devote some of his most toxic pages to Safdie's project, expressing an outright contempt not merely for the derivative object, but even more so for the conservative climate it embodied. "Habitat was the most immediately accepted of all the Montreal megas because it was the least radical," asserts Banham,[48] going on to assault the vulgar production and consumption of cultural icons:

> The magazine coverage seems to suggest that most of the world's architectural correspondents got no further than Habitat before rushing back to write their reports on Expo. They cannot really be blamed; it was almost exactly the kind of thing they most wanted to see at such an occasion, a building that most neatly expressed the overt architectural ambitions of its time. If megastructure ever was the "child of informed opinion," then it was at Habitat, conceived in the academic groves of McGill, idolized by the magazines, and taken up by academics [...] as the model of the good urban architecture of the future.[49]

In *Beyond Habitat*—Safdie's own account of what Banham called the "saga of adventures and misadventures that led to the building's construction"[50]—Safdie established Habitat's myth of origin in his thesis project at McGill, entitled "A Three-Dimensional Modular Building System":

> It had all the ingredients that were eventually to make up Habitat. There were box-like space cells manufactured in the factory. The modules were combined in many different permutations to make up the variety of house types. Each house was an entity in itself, recognizable in space. The modules were grouped in spiral formations stepping back from each other, each roof forming a roof garden for another dwelling. I had developed three possible systems each with its own geometry and structural system, and I then made a model showing what a community of five thousand people would be like.[51]

In the annals of architecture, Habitat, with a capital H, is irrevocably Safdie's project for Expo 67. In retrospect, we may observe that its allure is precisely as a memorable image of both the index and the climax of 1960s

(33)

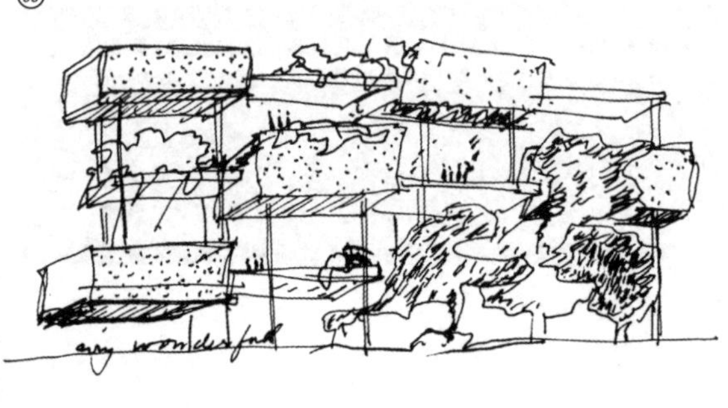

structuralist architecture. In comparison with its more "radical" predecessors, it was an ingeniously formulated, masterfully coordinated, and skillfully produced scheme that effectively summed up and displayed contemporary predicaments of urban density, serial production, public housing, and alternative building typologies. Habitat's overwhelming visual presence—generated by elementary modular units, essentially a single form, creating an impression of exceptional spatial complexity, endless structural variability, and awesome artificial landscape—not only turned it into an instant icon (to Banham's revulsion), but exalted it as the last totem of modernist culture.

If Habitat does not qualify as a paradigm shift, it is nevertheless the ultimate diagram of the structuralist binary objective of maximum repetition/maximum difference; or maximum prior exactitude/maximum random aftereffect.

By the mid-1970s, Banham already knew that beyond Habitat there would be no sustainable megastructures; that these "urban futures of the recent past" were rapidly becoming extinct; that all that remained was a persistent argument against the false promise of architectural deus ex machina, made precariously tangible by Safdie's Habitat:

> At a time when North American constructional theorists were about to go for broke on "system-building," "factory-built," "industrialized" or "prefabricated" housing, Habitat was, as *Architectural Forum* declared, "an idea whose time has come." *Forum*'s faith in "building with boxes" was

(32) Or Yehuda, 2015. Eli Singalovski.
(33) Sketch from graduation project at McGill University, Canada, 1961. Moshe Safdie.
(34) Habitat (built for Expo 67), prefab unit carried by crane, Montreal, 1964–1967. Moshe Safdie.

sustained and passionate; Habitat's justification was seen, in the last resort and in defiance of its elevated costs, as a necessary prototyping and research exercise for a new phase of North American constructional technology, as development work which the industry could or would not finance for itself.

What ultimately came out of this aspect of Habitat was an illusion, a myth, that heavy prefabrication would "solve the crisis of the American city." [...] Ultimately, [Habitat] delivered almost nothing commensurate with the size of the myth that had been built up.[52]

Safdie himself, it must be noted, never fully trusted the technical instrumentality and economic viability of Habitat, and soon after its completion he infused it with sentimental reflections on vernacular patterns and rural urbanism. His *Beyond Habitat* finally unravels as a personal quest for lost environmental and social authenticity:

In retrospect, I had set out on this trip with preconceived ideas, feeling suburbia was bad—after all, the Mediterranean cities were my background. But my conclusion was new: I felt we had to find new forms of housing that would re-create, in a high-density environment, the relationships and the amenities of the house and the village.[53]

Banham does not succumb to such gestural anachronism. He seizes on Safdie's autobiographical reflections to finalize his verdict on Habitat and, more significantly, to offer his own critical input to the larger discourse about the appropriation, reification, and consumption of the vernacular image in architectural practices:

It is clear from the last pages of *Beyond Habitat* that Safdie believed that this particular brand of cellular geometry could deliver a radically new kind of urban environment; but, looking at what he actually built, one cannot help feeling that he had merely backed up into his autobiography and built an image of his pro-Mediterranean prejudices, and that this was the real reason for its success, since that was about the most widely entertained prejudice then current in architecture. Even the admitted and clearly observed problems of exposed access and lack of privacy seemed to be excusable because these, after all, were the urban conditions that were supposed to lead to that desirable vitality displayed by the communities that inhabited real Mediterranean villages.[54]

It is time indeed to return, with Safdie, to our scene of origin. Expo Montreal coincided precisely, as it happens, with the 1967 War between Israel and the neighboring Arab states.[55] Thus, the year of Habitat and of Safdie's rapid ascent to the architectural pantheon is engraved locally as a geopolitical fault line that transformed the Middle East territorially and condemned the Palestinians to a military and civilian occupation that has now lasted for fifty years. In addition, it had immediate repercussions on Israeli national planning and building strategies, as well as on architectural praxis and taste.[56]

In post-1967 Israel, the mediatized image of Habitat, bouncing back from the World's Fair and spilling across magazine pages as the old-new architectural paradigm, seemed conveniently timely and homey. Jerusalem was to be "united" and greatly expanded soon after the war. Urban master plans were prepared, an international forum of prominent critics was established ("The Jerusalem Committee," formed by mayor Teddy Kollek, comprised about seventy experts, including such figures as Nikolaus Pevsner, Lewis Mumford, Bruno Zevi, Louis Kahn, Buckminster Fuller, and Philip Johnson),[57] and Safdie was invited to take part in reshaping the architectural character of the city. He was awarded significant commissions on sites of special symbolic resonance within the confines of the walled Old City (at the Porat-Yosef Yeshiva compound and at the Western Wall plaza) or just adjacent to it (in the area of Mamilla), and began constructing his "Habitat Israel."

Practically speaking, "Habitat Israel" made no sense. It came at the worst possible time for prefabrication in the Israeli construction industry. The occupation of the Palestinian territories had created a new economy based on an abundance of cheap labor and skillful traditional stonemasons. Industrialization was now superfluous and almost came to a halt for over a decade.

Metaphorically, however, Habitat became an effective marker of the postwar ambience. In Jerusalem, the hectic image of haphazardly piled-up harbor containers from Expo 67 morphed into a picturesque figure of Mediterranean composition juxtaposed with Oriental-Islamic motifs such as arches, domes, and local stonemasonry. The newfound regionalism of post-1967 Jewish-Israeli architecture was as contagious as it was uncritical. It quickly spread, in various configurations and outfits, throughout the sprouting neighborhoods of "Greater Jerusalem" and the urban settlements in the West Bank, and became the hegemonic style—the distinctive marker of cultural supremacy and territorial domination. Safdie's autobiographical nostalgia finally met its political salvation. Habitat slipped seamlessly from its earlier hyper-modernist phase into a manifestly postmodernist fairy tale of national(ist) domesticity.

The local structuralist and morphological discourse of the late 1950s and early 1960s had prompted much intellectual anticipation, through publications, exhibitions, competitions, and academic curricula, and seemed to be destined for the experimental margins of the building industry. Now it was resurrected as proper architecture, especially adaptable to the hilly topography of Jerusalem. Clustering became the catchphrase, replacing the former notion of "space-packing." In the jargon of the Ministry of Housing (which was in charge of virtually all post-1967 planning of new neighborhoods and settlements around Jerusalem), there were no more buildings (Heb. *binyanim* or *mivnim*), only clusters or agglomerates (Heb. *mivnanim*), idiomatic traces of the Israeli avant-garde legacy.

Many of the clustered habitats proposed for Jerusalem remained on paper, but some

(35)

(36)

(37)

were actually built and to this day commemorate the post-1967 chapter of the Israeli polymorphic phantasmagoria. Two of our early protagonists, Eldar Sharon and Zvi Hecker, now each on his own, were commissioned to design extensive housing projects in Jerusalem's satellite quarters of Ramot and Gilo. Both of these photogenic projects were extensively published in international and local magazines before and after construction—and both were utter failures. Their polygonal beehive qualities did not appeal to potential residents, who saw only badly built, awkwardly shaped, and frantically piled-up apartments. Having little value in the normative public-housing market, one project was converted to a dormitory for new immigrants and the other to student housing for an Orthodox yeshiva. The latter, designed by Zvi Hecker, is geometrically more ambitious and can be regarded as the final built outcome of Alfred Neumann's teaching: a full-scale, real-life polygonal colony (by now a shabby autoschediastic favela). It monumentalizes academicism's best shot at the most radical of all projects: an alternative layout for the standard housing block.

Israeli Habitat went awry. It could have chosen one of two diverging paths. The first of these is demonstrated by Hecker's rock 'n' roll housing project in Ramot, discussed above. The other is concealed in Neumann-Hecker-Sharon's vanishing project in Ein Rafa (1961–1962; see chapter "Ein Rafa"). Little is known about this project,[58] which was apparently initiated by one of the government's housing agencies with the explicit objective of rebuilding the destroyed Arab village of Ein Rafa and facilitating the return of its original inhabitants, refugees of the 1948 War. The enigma of this project is twofold: First, no other case is known in which the State of Israel initiated

(35) Habitat Israel, Jerusalem, 1969–1970. Model of clustered prefabricated units with cast glass domes. Moshe Safdie.
(36) Straw bungalow, Club Med resort, Achziv, 1961. Alfred Neumann, Zvi Hecker, Eldar Sharon. Zvi Hecker archive.
(37) Straw bungalows, Club Med resort, Achziv, 1961. Alfred Neumann, Zvi Hecker, Eldar Sharon. Zvi Hecker archive.
(38) Bungalows, Club Med resort, Achziv. In the background, the ruins of the village Az-Zibb. 1961. Alfred Neumann, Zvi Hecker, Eldar Sharon. Zvi Hecker archive.
(39) Club Med resort, Achziv. Master plan, hexagonal design next to the vernacular layout of the ruined village Az-Zibb. 1961. Alfred Neumann, Zvi Hecker, Eldar Sharon. Zvi Hecker archive.

(38)

(39)

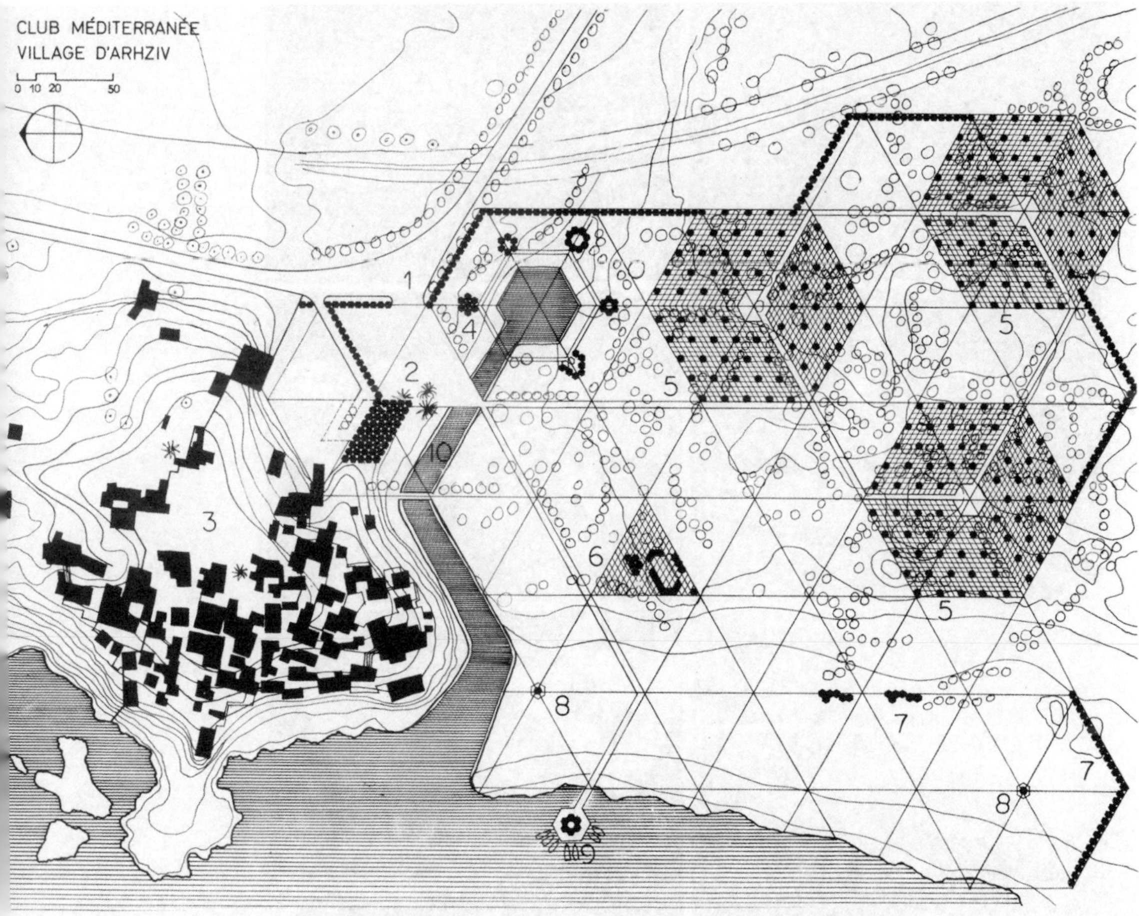
CLUB MÉDITERRANÉE
VILLAGE D'ARHZIV
0 10 20 50
1
2
3
4
5
5
5
6
7
7
8
8
10

40

(40) Ramot Polin housing, Ramot, Jerusalem, 1972. Zvi Hecker.
(41) Ramot Polin housing, Ramot, Jerusalem, 1972. Axonometry, plans and images of the building process. Zvi Hecker. Unidentified publication.

or even allowed the rehabilitation of a destroyed Palestinian village. It is an exceptional gesture that certainly was not motivated by propaganda needs, since the project had no self-aggrandizing promotion—and, indeed, no public exposure whatsoever. Second, the choice of the Neumann-Hecker-Sharon group for the execution of the project is perplexing. Why would a government agency commission the provocative enfant terrible of Israeli architecture, famous for its self-referential morphological studies, to work on this sensitive emergency project?

Enigmatic as the grounds for rebuilding the village of Ein Rafa may be, the result constitutes the most profound, humane, and resilient interpretation of the notion of Habitat. Neumann-Hecker-Sharon's project was not only ethically and politically just, but also tectonically inspired, environmentally appropriate, and culturally pertinent. Judging from photo albums and several drawings (the only remaining documentation of the project; more on this below), the architects established a makeshift workshop on-site to produce a kit of light prefab components such as corrugated metal sheets for roofing and water pipes for outdoor porches, as well as a series of pre-cast masonry walls and concrete barrel vaults. The drawn plan and perspective of the renewed village show an irregular distribution of the houses and organic adjustment to the topography. Irregularity here is clearly not a random aesthetic whim, but a tracing of the original

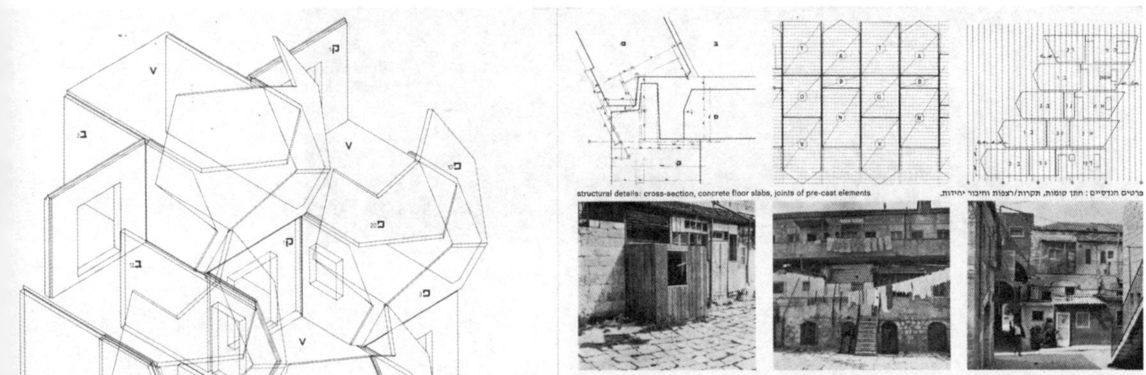


(41)

(42) (43)

(44)

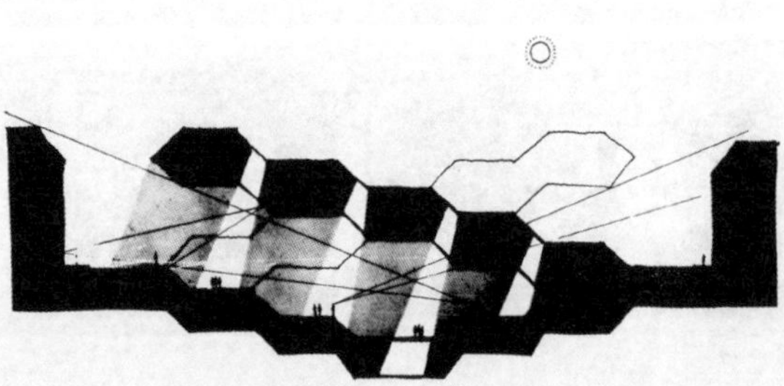

45

plotlines distinguishing family properties in the village. Architecture provides the bare minimum necessary for the return of the refugees and regeneration of the community—a small masonry core with a built-in oven, a porch, and a shaded storage area. It is by no means folklore architecture, nor is it a frivolous visual appropriation of vernacular Mediterranean or Oriental motifs, as was the case with most hyper-habitats described above. The tentative design of Ein Rafa is remarkably instrumental; it prudently utilizes modular production techniques as well as available local materials and the indigenous urban layout to put up immediate permanent shelters, to delineate land ownership, and, most admirably, to restrain architectural ambition in order to facilitate gradual and sustainable rehabilitation and self-expansion. Indeed, the best possible appraisal of the project is that, like a biodegradable habitat, ithas completely disintegrated into a prospering village where today the core shelter designed by the celebrated architects is no longer detectable.[59]

The Ein Rafa project should be contrasted with another "recyclable" project by Neumann-Hecker-Sharon, the Club Med resort in Achziv (1961). Here the (fresh) ruins of the former Arab village of al-Zib, visible in all the photographs of the project, appear as a film set for Club Med.[60] This set evidently is not décor for war tourism, but a hospitable construct of an "archaic" ambience, against which the beautifully designed and lightly constructed straw polygonal pavilions appear as the shape of decadent things to come.

Ein Rafa, to say the least, was the path not taken. Resilient planning and self-effacing architecture were not a practical choice for the zealous post-1967 machine-á-territorializer. After 1967, and well into the 1970s and 1980s, proliferating clusters, ziggurats, hives, and mats, dressed in pseudo-vernacular, quasi-organic, or ersatz-historical styles, constituted a double promise for the Israelis: First, to finally do away with all that modernist *Sachlichkeit*, the aggravating debris of the welfare state. And second, to get hold of a new philosopher's stone which would guarantee, as it were, a perpetual state of sui-generis "growth, change, and uncertainty"[61]—an incremental building process that by its very nature defies finite boundaries.

The experimental work of the Technion radicals turned against itself. Dispossessed of its sophisticated geometry and abstract patterns, it was deformed into fluctuating aggregates of haphazard monumentality. Prefabrication

(42) Prefab stepped housing in Gilo, Jerusalem, 1975. Eldar Sharon. Arieh Sharon digital archive.
(43) Hotel in Sharm-El-Sheikh, 1970. Arieh Sharon, Eldar Sharon. Arieh Sharon digital archive.
(44) Proposal for Centre Pompidou competition, Paris, 1971. Section. Moshe Safdie.
(45) Israeli pavilion, Expo 67, Montreal, perspective. Arieh Sharon, Eldar Sharon. Azrieli Architectural Archive, Arieh Sharon Collection.

remained a fabricated tale and never really stepped up the local construction industry. Space-packing theories, intended for densification, were distorted to serve expansionist and exclusionist ideologies. Israeli habitats, both modernist and postmodernist, were always introverted, always defensive—rarely "open-ended systems," as claimed. They were rarely integral to an urban fabric, rarely urban at all. They were in fact ongoing State-sponsored experiments in ruralizing, suburbanizing, or rurbanizing the city, a relentless affirmation of Zionism's anti-urban bias and strategic regional planning. ■

(46)

1 Ada Louise Huxtable, in "Tinker Toy City Hall in Israel is Space Packed," *New York Times,* June 5, 1969, p. 49, writes: "In Israel, the school of design theory that led to Habitat has produced a small, strange collection of buildings of intriguing appearance and—like Habitat—of debatable experimental value. They are undoubtedly some of the most striking and provocative buildings to be seen today." Cited in Rafi Segal, "Unit, Pattern, Site: The Space Packed Architecture of Alfred Neumann, 1949–1968" (PhD diss., Princeton, 2011), p. 2.

2 Arieh Sharon, *Kibbutz + Bauhaus: An Architect's Way in a New Land* (Stuttgart and Tel Aviv: Karl Kramer Verlag and Massada, 1976), p. 14.

3 Ibid., p. 15.

4 Ibid., p. 186.

5 Ibid.

6 Ibid.

7 Rafi Segal's dissertation, "Unit, Pattern, Site: The Space Packed Architecture of Alfred Neumann, 1949–1968 (PhD diss., Princeton, 2011), is the first thorough study of Neumann's theory and his joint venture with Zvi Hecker and Eldar Sharon. The description in this chapter of Neumann and the Neumann-Hecker-Sharon partnership has been modified in places according to Segal's dissertation.

8 The following biographical sketch is based on the biography outlined in Segal, "Unit, Pattern, Site": Alfred Neumann, a Czech architect who was born in Vienna in 1900, graduated from the Brno Technical University and studied under Peter Behrens at the Meisterschule für Architektur of the Vienna Academy. Later, under Auguste Perret, he studied at the Atelier du Palais de Boisin, Paris, and was frequently in association with Adolf Loos. Neumann was a member of the artist groups "Abstraction of Creation" and "Circle and Square." In the 1930s he worked on projects of various scales in Central Europe and North and South Africa. During World War II he was imprisoned in the Terezín Concentration Camp. In 1945, he returned to Brno to work for the Czechoslovakian planning offices on a large-scale regional master plan for the country. At the 6th CIAM International Congress, held in Bridgewater, England, in 1947, Neumann presented this work as representative of Czechoslovakia. He stayed in Brno until the rise of Czechoslovakian communism in 1948, when he decided to immigrate to Israel. In 1953 he represented Israel in the CIAM meeting in Aix-en-Provence. That same year he was appointed dean of the Architecture and Town Planning Faculty at the Technion; he maintained this position until 1958. He continued to teach as a professor at the Technion until his resignation in 1966, when he departed from Israel for a permanent position at Laval University, Quebec City. In 1959 he established a practice with his former students Zvi Hecker and Eldar Sharon. He died in Canada in 1968.

9 Alfred Neumann, "Morphologic Architecture," *RAIC Journal* 40 (May 1963), p. 42. Later republished in *Zodiac* 16 (1966).

10 Alfred Neumann, *L'Humanisation de l'espace: le système mφ*, Collection Espace (Boulogne-sur-Seine: Editions Architecture d'Aujourd'hui, 1956).

11 Walter Gropius, in a letter from 1953 published in the introduction to Neumann, *L'Humanisation de l'espace*.

12 Le Corbusier, *Modulor 2* (1955), trans. Peter De Francia and Anna Bostock, 2nd ed. (Cambridge, MA: Harvard University Press, 1958), pp. 86–88.

13 Segal, "Unit, Pattern, Site," pp. 42–43.

14 Neumann, "Morphologic Architecture," p. 43.

15 Ibid.

16 Alfred Neumann, "Architecture as Ornament," transcript of a lecture given at Laval University, Quebec City, Canada, 1967, published in *Zodiac* 19 (1969), pp. 90–98. Cited in Segal, "Unit, Pattern, Site," p. 336.

17 This term, coined by Michel Ecochard and adapted by Georges Candilis, relates to the problem of quantity and the need for a structural and visual paradigm of housing for the masses.

18 Segal, "Unit, Pattern, Site," p. 146.

19 "Natania City Hall and Civic Centre," *Zodiac* 16 (1966), p. 140.

20 Ibid.

21 Sam Dubiner, an industrialist and art collector who opened the first commercial art gallery in Israel in 1961 and exhibited works by the abstract artists of the "Ofakim Hadashim" (New Horizons) school, commissioned Neumann-Hecker-Sharon to do their first residential project. Rumor has it that the group was recommended to Dubiner by the renowned artist Yitzhak Danziger.

22 Cited in "Alfred Neumann, Zvi Hecker, Eldar Sharon," *Domus*, 427 (June 1965).

23 Zvi Hecker, in a recorded discussion with the author, 1999.

24 Segal, "Unit, Pattern, Site," p. 92.

25 Robin Middleton, "The Geometrical Straitjacket," *Tvai* [in Hebrew] (Winter 1967), p. 2.

26 Robin Middleton, "A Yiddish Grid," *Architectural Review* (September 1965).

27 Robin Middleton, "The Geometrical Straitjacket," *Architectural Design* (February 1967), p. 160.

28 Monique Eleb, "The Concept of Habitat: Ecochard in Morocco," in *Colonial Modern: Aesthetics of the Past, Rebellions for the Future*, ed. Tom Avermaete, Serhat Karakayali, Marion von Osten (London: Black Dog Publishing, 2010), p. 153.

29 Monique Eleb, "An Alternative to Functionalist Universalism: Ecochard, Candilis and ATBAT-Afrique," in *Anxious Modernisms: Experimentation in Postwar Architectural Culture*, ed. Sarah Williams Goldhagen and Rejean Legault (Montreal and Cambridge, MA: CCA and MIT Press, 2000), p. 55. Eleb adds: "So new to English-speaking architectural circles was the notion of habitat that in 1955 the Smithsons [...] found it necessary to define it in an article that attracted much attention: '"Habitat" is a word used by the French to describe not

only the home but also its environment and everything appertaining to it.'" Ibid., p. 56.

In the Doorn Manifesto, reprinted in the *Team 10 Primer*, "habitat" is a signifier of social and cultural idiosyncrasy: "'Habitat' is concerned with the particular house in the particular type of community. [...] To comprehend the pattern of human associations we must consider every community in its particular environment." However, the manifesto also contains the following provision vis-à-vis the perils of interdisciplinarity: "The appropriation of any solution may lie in the field of architectural invention rather than social anthropology." Alison Smithson, ed., *Team 10 Primer* (Cambridge, MA: MIT Press, 1968), p. 75.

30 Eleb, "Concept of Habitat," p. 156.

31 Ibid., p. 154.

32 Ibid., p. 155.

33 Ibid., p. 157.

34 Francis Strauven and Aldo van Eyck, *The Shape of Relativity* (Amsterdam: Architectura & Natura, 1998), p. 253.

35 The Smithsons declared Candilis's "*habitat marocain*" to be "the greatest achievement since Le Corbusier's Unité d'Habitation." Alison and Peter Smithson, "Collective Housing in Morocco," *Architectural Design* 1 (1955). Cited in Strauven and van Eyck, *Shape of Relativity*, p. 254.

36 Strauven and van Eyck, *Shape of Relativity*, p. 255.

37 Aldo van Eyck, in *Forum* 7 (1959), p. 223. Cited in Strauven and van Eyck, *Shape of Relativity*, p. 255.

38 Daniel Rauchwerger, "A Model Architect," Haaretz, November 18, 2011, http://www.haaretz.com/weekend/week-s-end/a-model-architect-1.396308.

39 Yona Friedman, "The Architecture in Motion," *Kav* 9 [in Hebrew] (Autumn 1968), p. 16.

40 Leopold Gerstel, "Thinking about Architecture," *Tvai* 20 [in Hebrew] (1980), p. 7.

41 Ibid.

42 Ibid.

43 I. M. Goodovitch, *Architecturology: An Interim Report* (Tel Aviv: AD Publishing Co., 1967).

44 Ibid., pp. 30–31.

45 This tenure coincided with the post-1967 territorial euphoria during which Israel tripled its size by annexing or militarily controlling the Occupied Territories (the West Bank, Gaza, the Golan Heights, and the Sinai) and pervading them with Jewish rural and urban settlements.

46 Goodovitch, *Architecturology*, p. 18.

47 Reyner Banham, *Megastructure: Urban Futures of the Recent Past* (New York: Harper and Row, 1976), p. 107.

48 Ibid., p. 11.

49 Ibid., p. 106.

50 Ibid., p. 105.

51 Moshe Safdie, *Beyond Habitat* (Cambridge, MA: MIT Press, 1970), p. 53.

52 Banham, *Megastructures*, pp. 110–111.

53 Safdie, *Beyond Habitat*, p. 53.

54 Banham, *Megastructures*, p. 111.

55 Expo Montreal took place from April 27 to October 29, 1967. The Six-Day War was in June 1967.

56 For the chronicle and analysis of the Israeli architecture of occupation, see Eyal Weizman, *Hollow Land: Israel's Architecture of Occupation* (London: Verso, 2007).

57 On the Jerusalem Committee, see Alona Nitzan-Shiftan, *"Frontier Jerusalem: The Holy Land as a Testing Ground for Urban Design,"* in *Frankel Institute Annual*, vol. 2008, University of Michigan.

58 Neuman-Hecker-Sharon's project in Ein Rafa (1961–1962) was published in several international publications of the period, but it was described primarily as technically innovative and environmentally sensitive architecture, without any information about the political and administrative circumstances leading to this exceptional project. The Ein Rafa project is mentioned, but the disturbing background to this commission is not explicated, in Rafi Segal's dissertation on Neumann. Zvi Hecker, in an interview I conducted in 1999, did not recall the circumstances of this project.

59 Just recently, after a careful "forensic" inquiry and a patient testimonial survey, a group of students of mine at Bezalel were able to locate and document the traces of the original structures designed by Neumann-Hecker-Sharon; see their report in the chapter "Ein Rafa."

60 See Peter Lagerquist, "Vacation from History: Ethnic Cleansing as the Club Med Experience," *Journal of Palestine Studies* 36, no. 1 (Autumn 2006), pp. 43–53.

61 This aphorism, a local version of Team 10 phrasing, was coined by architect Al Mansfeld (see chapter "The National Museum and the Shrine of the Book").

(46) Israeli pavilion, Expo 67, Montreal. Arieh Sharon, Eldar Sharon. Azrieli Architectural Archive, Arieh Sharon Collection.
(47) Youth Camp Beit Zait, near Jerusalem, 1969. Zvi Hecker. Zvi Hecker archive.

(47)

# DOSSIER: GOODOVITCH'S ARCHITECTUROLOGY

*Architecturology: An Interim Report by I. M. Goodovitch*, published in 1967 (London: Allen and Unwin), was the first architectural diary written by an Israeli architect. To this day, it remains a singular exposé of applied structuralist theory. The *Interim Report* begins in 1953 at the Technion (the "Incubator"), where Israel Goodovitch first sketched his speculations and experiments on modular prefab construction (the "saddle system"), and then embarks on a journey from the Israeli deserts to Japanese suburbia.

Goodovitch maintained his status as the enfant terrible of Israeli architecture even when he was in charge of rural planning at the Ministry of Housing (1967–1972); when he converted to corporate architecture in the 1980s; and, curiously enough, when he was appointed city engineer of Tel Aviv in 1999, a position he kept for about a year. ■

㊽ – ㊾ "Saddle system," diagrams, *Architecturology: An Interim Report* by I. M. Goodovitch, 1967. Courtesy of Israel Goodovitch.
㊿ "Saddle system," elevations of clusters, *Architecturology: An Interim Report* by I. M. Goodovitch, 1967. Courtesy of Israel Goodovitch.
(51) "Saddle system," roof plan, *Architecturology: An Interim Report* by I. M. Goodovitch, 1967. Courtesy of Israel Goodovitch.
(52) "Saddle system" under construction, *Architecturology: An Interim Report* by I. M. Goodovitch, 1967. Courtesy of Israel Goodovitch.
(53) "Saddle system," perspectives, *Architecturology: An Interim Report* by I. M. Goodovitch, 1967. Courtesy of Israel Goodovitch.
(54) – (60) "Sdom Subcity," *Architecturology: An Interim Report* by I. M. Goodovitch, 1967. Courtesy of Israel Goodovitch.

PANTA REI

In the developing countries, in countries of immigration – at certain stages of life – young couples either alone, with children, or with parents – as in the natural state of society, with families of various types – creating a priori a similarly natural state – neighbouring flats of different sizes for families of different sizes – children, adults, old people – all together, a flow of life –

Inner space suiting human life – suiting man's needs and movements – wider at mid-height, narrower at the top and bottom – when shelve widths are proportioned to man's reaching ability – when bed is cantilevered –

4 UNITS CREATE 1 CELL

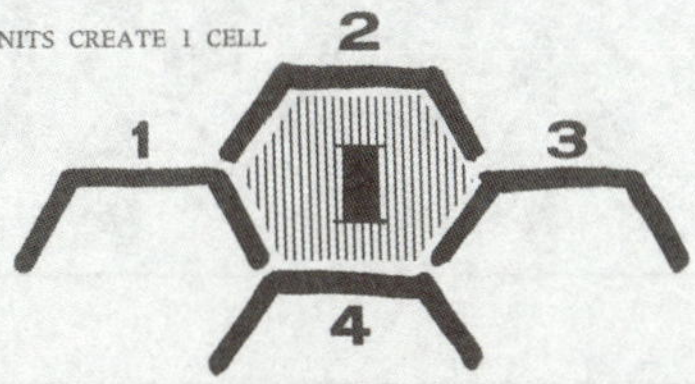

Saddle vertebra shape construction – with no separation between vertical and horizontal elements – following the natural flow of forces – in a syncopated sequence – creating an inner network – prefabricated standard units combining to form a non-standard product, alterable according to needs, according to the landscape –

A slope line from one flat to another – visual interconnection – as in the street, as in the open –

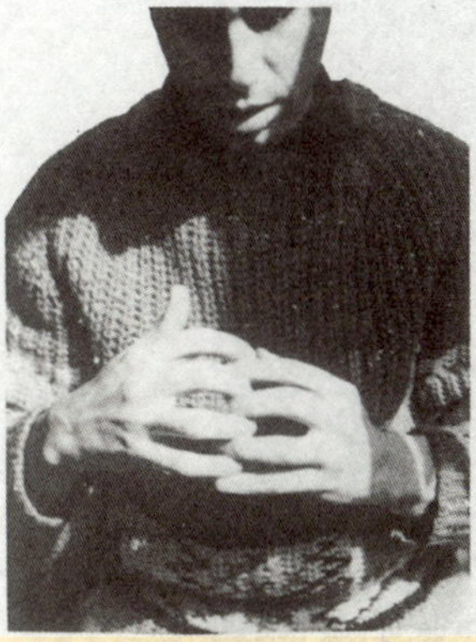

Merging with nature – with a soft skyline echoing a changing topography – floating in various directions – "panta rei" –

PR. C

I M G

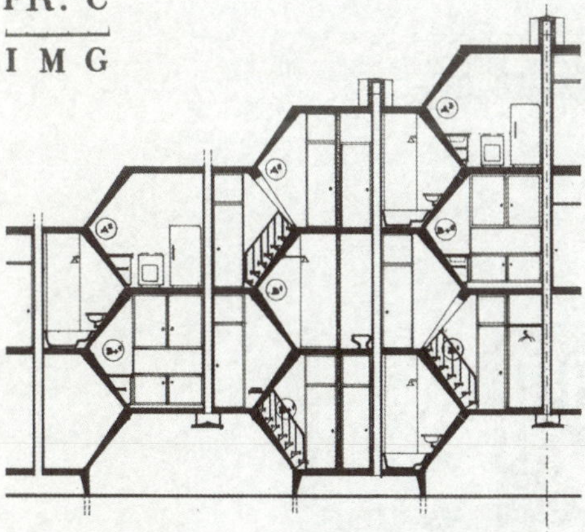

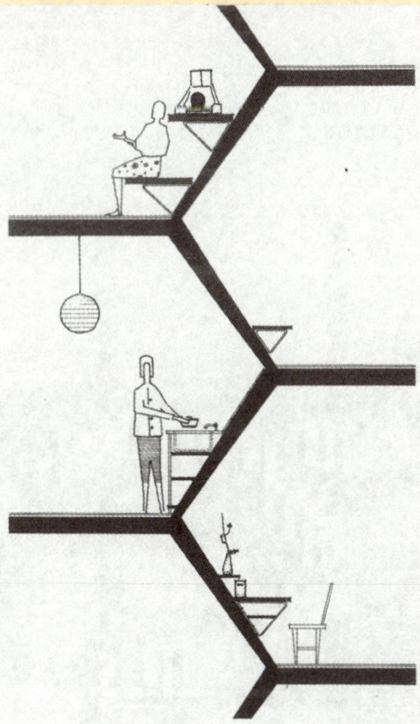

SECTION

PLAN

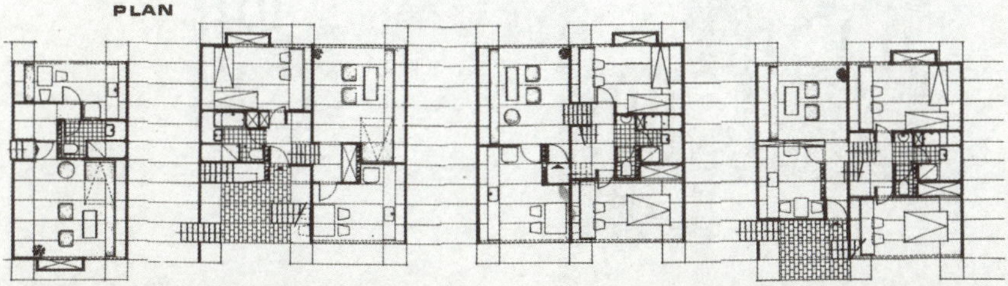

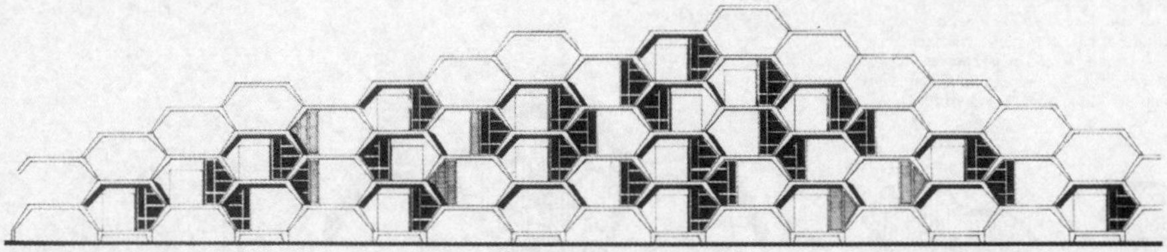

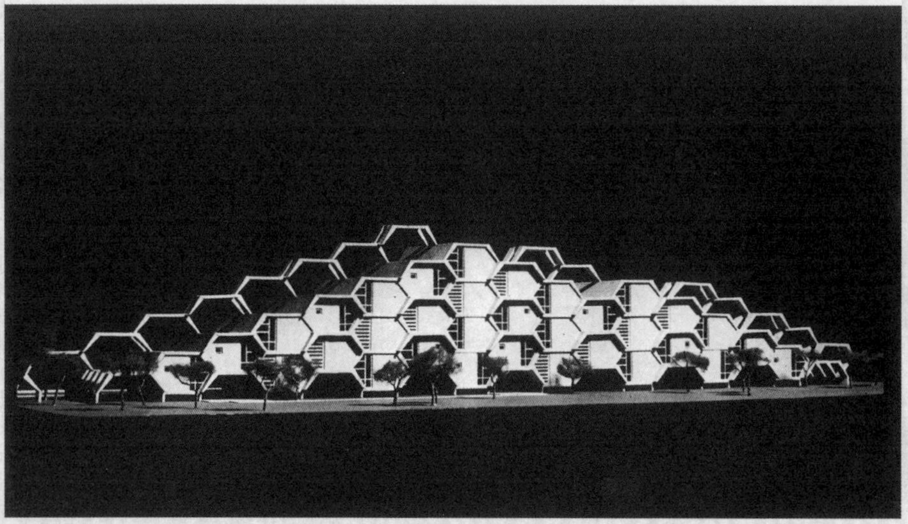

50

THE URBAM IMAGE

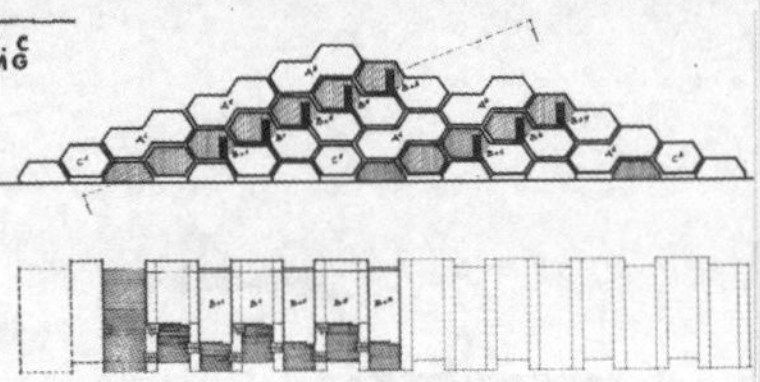

51

THE CONSTRUCTION METHOD

23

(52)

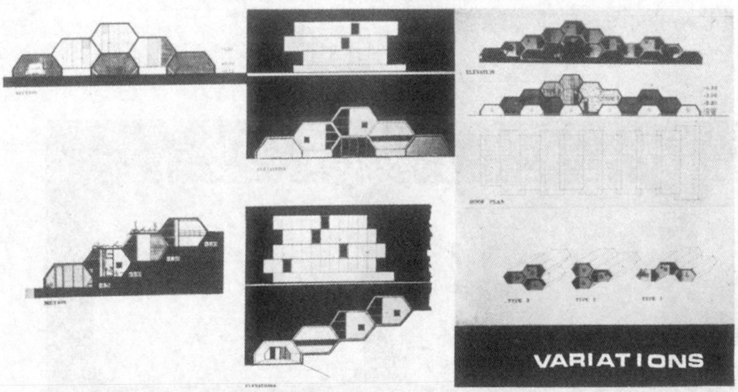


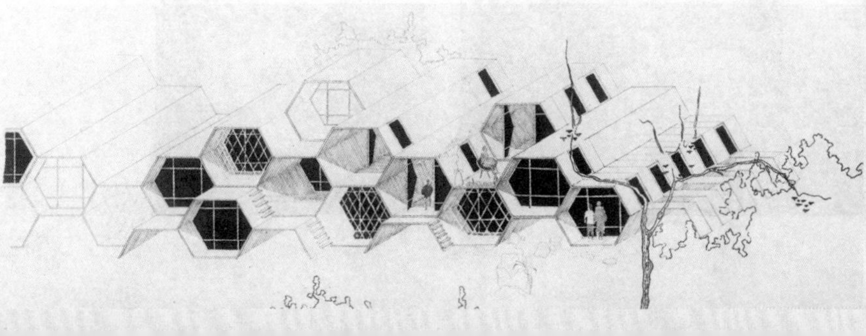

(53)

## March 1959

André Block, editor of L'Architecture d'Aujourd'hui has arrived in town. Everybody is busy courting the man in the hope of getting mentioned in the magazine.
He wishes to see what the young generation has in mind. All the way to my studio he is busy talking about the importance of searching for new ideas and non-conformist conceptions.
"But paintings need to be hung on walls, or on partitions", he stated, after a quick look at the preliminary sketches of the museum. For him there was no doubt that all my efforts to re-examine the conventional conceptions of the project and to analyse its essence – were a sheer waste of time; in his opinion, I would have done better had I applied my energy to design the plastic appearance of the building and its proportions. I gave up the whole thing: my researches on the relation between Time and the Human Perception, between the exhibition area and the storage needs, and the relation between the movement of the body and the eyes in the designed space – I put them all aside. I understood through the oracle of Mr. Block that research and analysis are not part of our profession: they belong to logic – whereas we are artists (or artisans?), and design under the star of inspiration, muse or whim.

## April 1959

The Governor of the Sdom Region was looking for a planner to work voluntarily on a research project for planning a new town in his region. The conditions were: 6 months work, maintenance and some pocket money. Additional note: complete freedom in planning and design was guaranteed.
I jumped at the offer. It gave me a chance to get away from the milieu that I detested, and it opened for me a new horizon.
For about six months I lived in the desert, travelling, taking photographs, collecting information, and designing.
I presented the following report:

## September 1959

Mr. Y. Almog, Governor,
Sdom Region.
S d o m, Israel.

Dear Mr. Almog,

I take pleasure in presenting this report on the problems of a regional planning policy and a development programme for the Sdom Region.
Though the region is not inhabitated at present, I have tried to collect the available information concerning climate, ecology, geology and the natural phenomena which are characteristic of this region. In addition to that – my own observation and comments on the area.
This survey geared my thoughts in several directions, concerning the prospective growth of the region, the land uses and the location of the various functions. Beside the general regional scheme, I included in the report my comments on the sequence (stages), and the physical appearance of the plan: The city and the sub-city.
I should like to thank all the people who have been of assistance to me in providing useful background material and information. And I would like to express my thanks to you, Sir, for the privilege and opportunity to work out the future image of this region.

Sincerely yours,
I. M. Goodovitch.





I devoted the first portion of my stay in the region to observe and to study the Dead Sea coast-line, the erosion and salt formations, the region's ecology, its climate and its fossil and fauna.

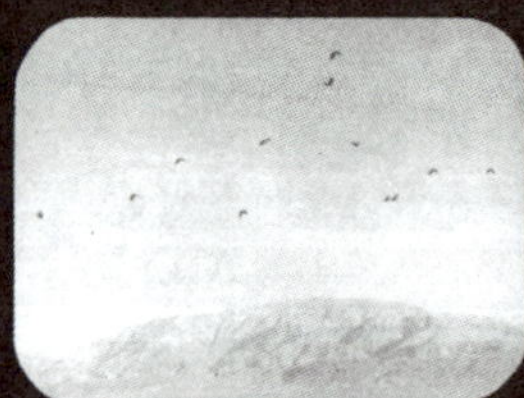

The next stage was to find out the economic potentialities and their possible uses:

DEAD SEA MINERALS

| | |
|---|---|
| Magnesium Chloride | 52.0% |
| Sodium Chloride | 30.0% |
| Calcium Chloride | 12.0% |
| Potassium Chloride | 4.3% |
| Magnesium Bromide | 1.4% |
| Calcium Sulphate | 0.3% |

The specific gravity of the Dead Sea water is high and varies from 1.16 to 1.23. The temperature at sea level is very high and suitable for the extraction of the basic raw materials with a minimum of workers. These raw materials could be transferred to the nearby cooler Mesa, where an industrial and residential settlement could develop.

IRRIGATION

Agriculture depends on water. Rainfall in the region is very scanty and irregular although the amount of water passing at a time can be enormous. The canyons are natural waterways but a stream of water in a canyon carries with it everything it meets on its way: stones, mud, tree-trunks – and thus can fill up and block any reservoir or dam. But a system of several sifting dams will separate the coarser particles and permit water to pass through.

RECREATION

The area is a major tourist attraction: dry climate; warm in winter; water sports; hot springs recommended by doctors for various ailments; beauty and historical treasures.

A sun-protected promenade along the coast-line, connecting the various centres of activity.

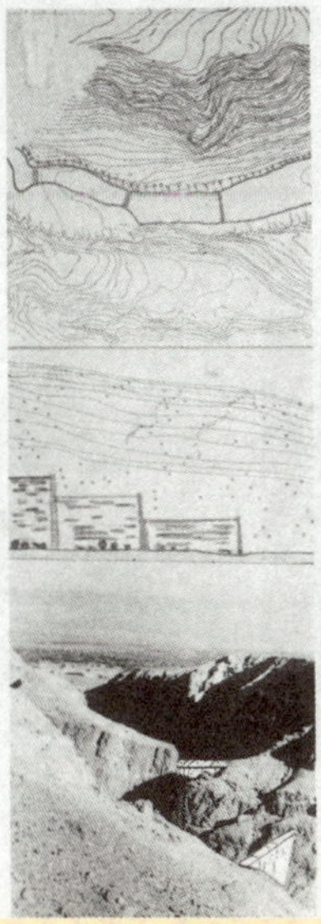

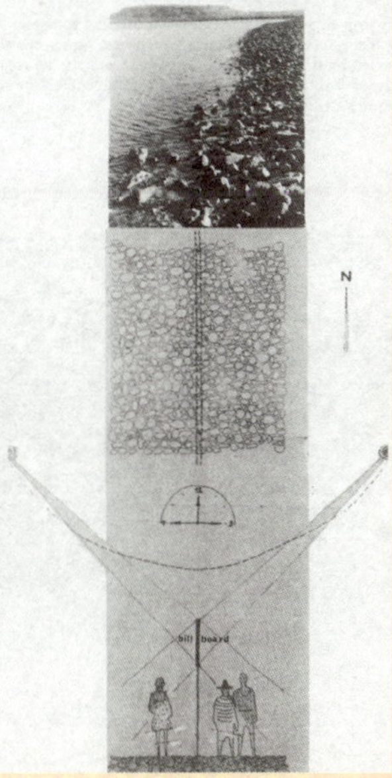


56

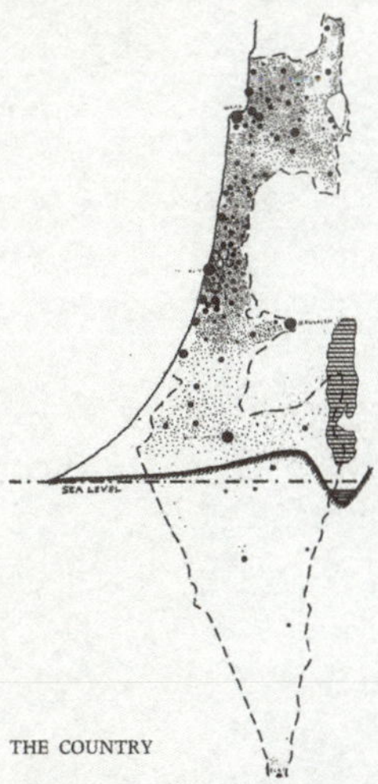


THE COUNTRY

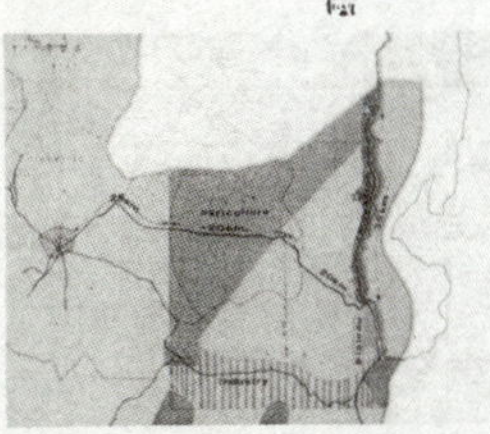

THE REGION

THE REGIONAL SCHEME

Communication system, location of the various functions and a typical section of the region.

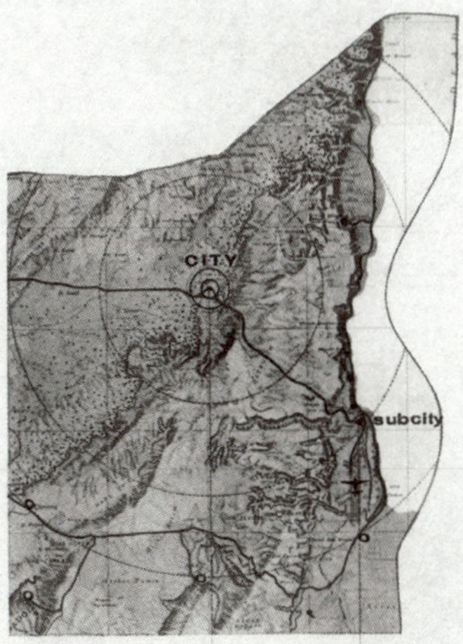


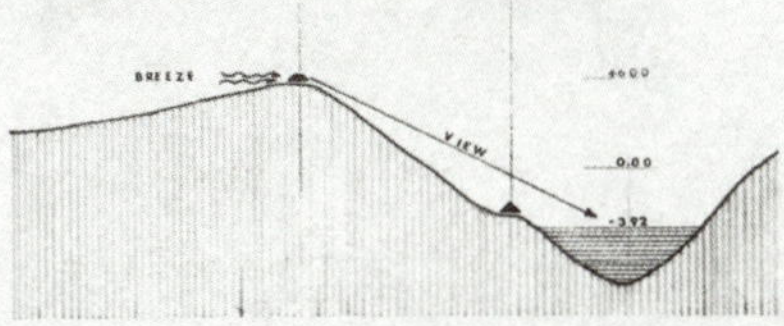




57

THE SUBCITY

Here I am concerned with what happens "in between" – not in the moment of birth, nor in the days of maturity, but with the transposition of an idea into a product, the evolutionary process from thought to creation. I want to watch what goes on backstage, at rehearsals, in the artist's atelier at the sculptor's workshop.
I want to observe the growing impact of the building site on the building itself; the impact of the workers dwellings (SUBCITY) on the image of the City. I am studying the influence of the Ciudad Libre squatters on the functioning of the new Brasilia, the methods and effects of creating temporary makeshift adobe structures for the Indian workers which will be gradually washed away with the rain and exist only for the time of their use.
My Subcity is in-between – between the industrial zone and the new city site; in fact, it is the very area reserved for recreation purposes. And when the time comes and the new city has passed its first stage of development and the workers' dwellings have become superfluous – my subcity will be the recreation centre. I have designed my subcity as a "solar pyramid" of dormitories.

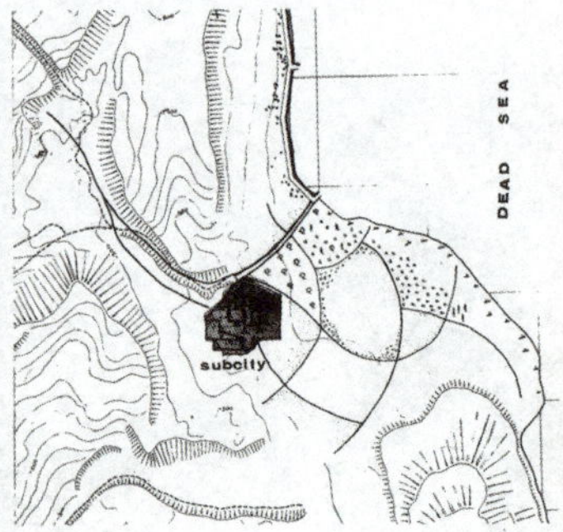






The solar pyramid is a spheric structure, constructed out of 35 prefabricated units. It is based on the daily and annual rotation of the sun. The exterior faces north at an angle of 53 degrees, which is equal to the angle of the sun in our latitude (53–87°). Thus, each dwelling unit is sun protected.

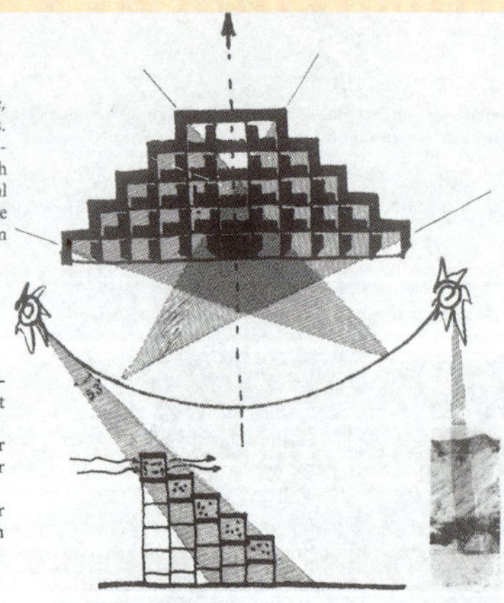

The ground-floor of the pyramid is always in shade (like the ground at the foot of the desert-tree).
Each unit opens on one side into the inner space of the pyramid, and on the other side towards the exterior.
The set-back of each unit to the other makes room for a balcony to cool off in the hot evenings.

Like an upside down canyon shape the inverted pyramid acts as a wind tunnel.

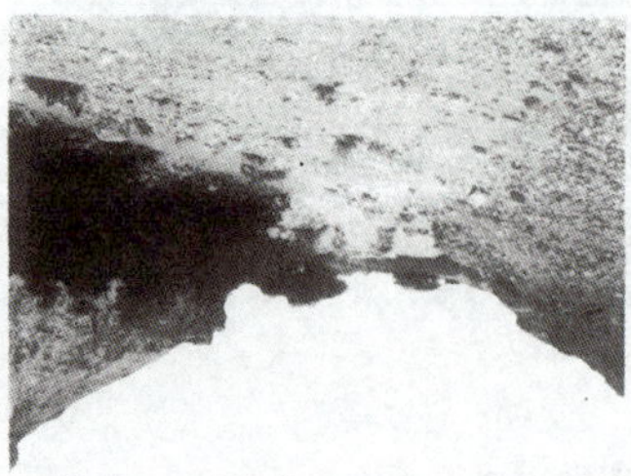

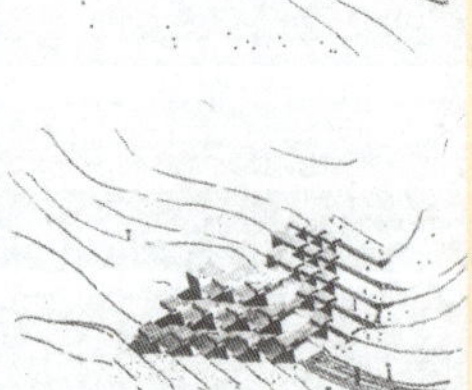

And thus, by incorporating the natural climatic phenomena I have created a natural controlled "medio-cosmos" – structure in the middle of the wild non-protected desert.

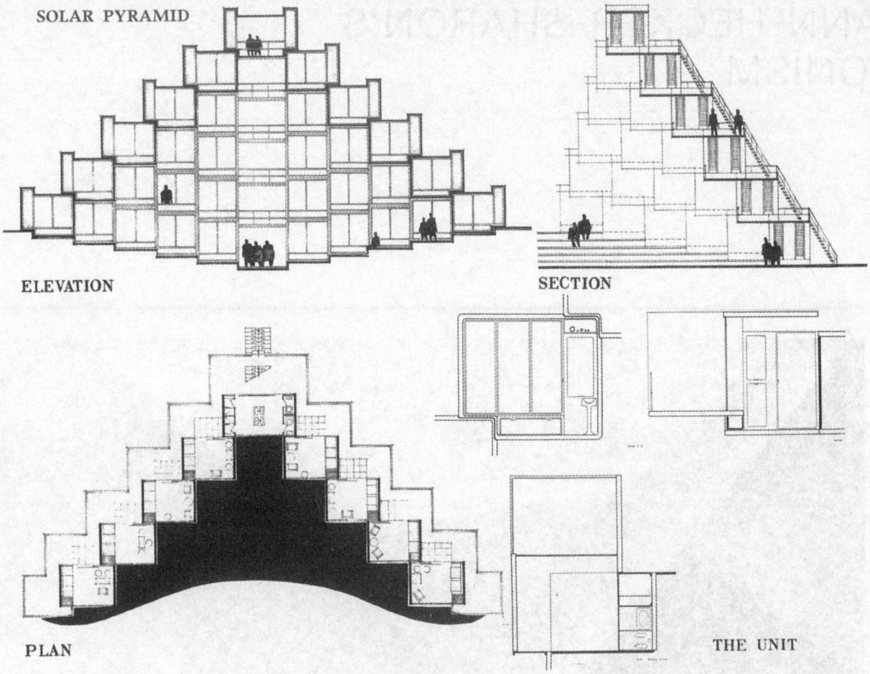


(60)

(61)

# DOSSIER: NEUMANN-HECKER-SHARON'S POLYGONISM

(62) Bat Yam Town Hall. Rooftop wind catchers, 1961.
Alfred Neumann, Zvi Hecker, Eldar Sharon. Zvi Hecker archive.

* For a description and evaluation of Neumann-Hecker-Sharon's work, see chapters "Structuralism" and "Ein Rafa" in this volume.

*The Bat Yam Town Hall, 1961–1963*
Alfred Neumann, Zvi Hecker, Eldar Sharon

The Bat Yam Town Hall was the first major project by Neumann-Sharon-Hecker to be executed. Despite its technological premise, the entire project was cast in situ. It thus constitutes a singular work of architecture rather than a modular building system.

The town hall is a freestanding inverted ziggurat composed of three volumetric units which are constructed of hollow concrete panels and supported by twelve columns. Its façades display diagonally rotated squares punctured by triangular openings. Inside, eighty office spaces line the perimeter of the structure, surrounding a central atrium which was originally ventilated by four tetrahedral rooftop chimneys. The building's deviant features add up to a seemingly paradoxical performance in which a morphological compulsion acts to diminish institutional authority and amplify civic informality. In effect, the building has no frontal orientation, no formal entrance, and presumably no solid walls at all, but only layers of perforated screens, alluding to vernacular latticework. Accessible from all sides, it seems to invite citizens coming from the nearby beach to enter its atrium barefoot or to relax on the bench extending from its rim and shaded by its stepped-out volumes.

Some critics found in the building's climatic section and surface porosity a promise for a new Mediterranean architecture: light, breezy, casual, and rather amused by its own monumentality. Others found it presumptuous. Two years after the town hall inauguration, architectural critic Robin Middleton dismissed the building as a rather juvenile geometrical experiment (see chapter "Structuralism").

In 1966 Neumann resigned from the Technion and departed for Canada, where he died in 1968. Eldar Sharon joined the firm of his father, Arieh Sharon, where he produced major Brutalist buildings during the following decade. Zvi Hecker established a Berlin-based practice and maintains his experimental fervor to this day.

Bat Yam has become one of the densest cities in Israel. Its inaugural town hall still functions as such and continues to stand out as a highly reflexive architectural "piece" amidst a generic residential plateau. With the rooftop ventilation shafts long removed due to hypothetical safety issues, and with new climate regulations and comfort codes, the building has become the subject of random additions and makeshift solutions: air-conditioning engines and ducts, external pipes and hanging wires have found their place within the façade's color scheme and angular cladding. While these would be visually intolerable in most buildings, in Bat Yam's town hall they merely add a random layer of accessories to the building's formalized informality. ■

(63)

(63) Bat Yam Town Hall, under construction, 1960. Alfred Neumann, Zvi Hecker, Eldar Sharon. Shkun U'binui Archive.
(64) Bat Yam Town Hall, 1960–1963. Interior. Alfred Neumann, Zvi Hecker, Eldar Sharon.
(65) Bat Yam Town Hall, under construction, 1961. Alfred Neumann, Zvi Hecker, Eldar Sharon. Zvi Hecker archive.
(66) Bat Yam Town Hall, 1963. Roof terrace and wind catchers. Alfred Neumann, Zvi Hecker, Eldar Sharon. Zvi Hecker archive.
(67) Bat Yam Town Hall, 1960–1963. Aerial view. Alfred Neumann, Zvi Hecker, Eldar Sharon.
(68) Bat Yam Town Hall, 2015. Gili Merin.

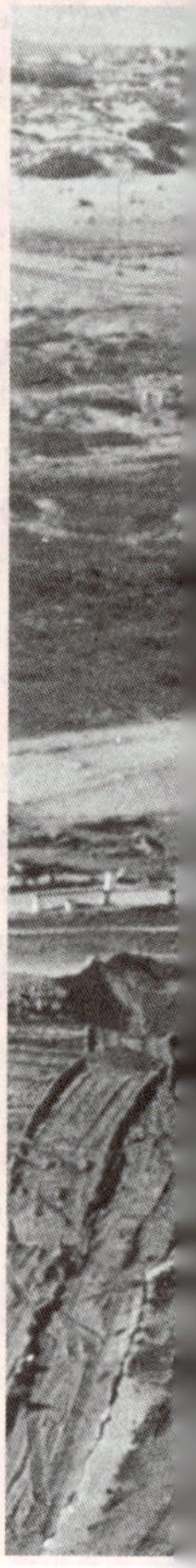

(64)

(65)

⑯

⑰

68

# MORPHOLOGIC ARCHITECTURE

**ALFRED NEUMANN**

*Even after long experience in teaching architectural design one cannot get rid of the unpleasant feeling of conveying a rather subjective know-how lacking theoretical justification. There are theories about many aspects of architecture but there is no single consistent theory of architecture. The vague term art is often evoked to cover the confusing situation. Sometimes one has the near certitude of touching the border of art. But the built human environment, seen as a whole in its geographical distribution and historical process, has almost nothing to do with art. To use an analogy — of all the spoken or written communication material very little represents poetry. It is obvious that, in building, a certain latent potential of art can be freed, but such a case represents more the exception than the rule.*

*I was repeatedly asked, by interested laymen, to recommend a book which explains the essence of architecture in a general, accessible way. To my own astonishment, I was unable to do so. The inadequacy of all architectural speculation goes back to its beginning. It is a case of heredity, and it is not easy to get rid of a negative tradition. The ten books on architecture by Vitruvius are a compilation of informations about building and related fields in the Mediterranean basin during the Augustean period. They do not form a coherent system but contain independent references on such topics as climatology, hydrology, building materials, proportion theories, and also recipes for conventional building types as well as for the construction of war machinery. Since the Renaissance, the expression Vitruve has become a collective term for architectural theory. All architects bowed before the authority of antiquity and pressed their own thinking into the traditional pattern.*

*This pluralistic approach has not changed up to the present. Under the influence of the general development of technology, the scientific methods replaced the trial and error phase in the mechanical aspects of construction. More recently, the life within the built structures, from the dwelling to town and region, underwent sociologic and ecologic analysis. But it remains doubtful whether there is direct interdependence between function and structure. Without having contributed to the understanding of architecture, those studies have widened the existing gap between architecture in the narrower sense and townplanning, which tends to become a super discipline where specific shape is without importance. Another field of study, History of Architecture, catalogued nearly the entire building production of the past and brought it into geographical and chronological order. The so-called science of art (Kunstwissernschaft) has attempted an interpretation of that accumulated material. The most important outcome of that work was the awareness of architectural space and its evolution.*

*The research lines mentioned have hardly any relation to each other. The possibility exists to conceive the whole man-made human environment from an unifying point of view by applying morphological criteria. Scientific domains, which have been developed up to now and which are predominantly of ecological nature, can easily be integrated into a morphological system, because they possess the value of selection factors only.*

*A science of architecture, like any other science, should describe the different phenomena by a common lawfulness. But until now, styles and periods of style have remained isolated phenomena. There were endeavors to demonstrate mutual influences of forms and to represent the flow of motives geographically. But styles, as such, remain enigmatic in this representation. Analogies with biological phenomena might contribute to a better understanding. Morphogenesis of design is analogous to morphogenesis of biology. It also is a science at its beginning, but since it moves in the accepted tracks of scientific methods, a normal evolution can be expected. Similarly in architecture, one could follow the way from cell to cell (aggregate) the transformation of shape and dimension which the element undergoes, the laws and symmetries determining the shape of the aggregations.*

*I do not believe that values can ever be entirely eliminated from architecture, as from any other human activity. As in any creative activity, whether in the domain of art, science or technology, the deciding contribution will always depend on intuition. But the mechanism of intuition works only if certain preconditions are given, the most important one being profound knowledge of the subject. Musical talent without thorough training will rarely become productive. In a certain stage of investigation the introduction of a scale of values is hampering. As known, there are again actual attempts to put value relations on an experimental mathematical basis, to « scientifice » them. (Hartman, New-Mexico). These endeavors continue earlier trends, for instance, Fechner's experimental esthetics « Esthetics from Underneath », using statistical methods. The results were rather primitive and even when further extended one doubts if they could do justice to so complicated a phenomenon that is involved in architectural esthetics, with its intricate interpenetration of logic, sentiment, function, structure, etc. In spite of the unsurmountable difficulties, architectural science has pursued this way. At the basis of architectural research stands architectural history, and architectural history is conceived as a part of the history of art. That implies that under the raw material offered by building history, a division into works of art and non-art was*

(69) Alfred Neumann, "Morphologic Architecture," *RAIC Journal* 40 (May 1963). Later republished in *Zodiac* 16 (1966).

*made. The development of works of art is discussed and the others ignored.*

*Thinking of biology, we often encounter in nature phenomena of astonishing beauty. Naturally the professional esthetician will strictly prove that an unbridgeable rift exists between beauty in nature and beauty in art. But where would biology stand if morphological research had introduced esthetic appreciation in advance? I do not know if morphologists and biologists are less receptive to beauty than architects and art critics, but the idea of a mixture of biology and esthetics in research seems deviative.*

*I believe that architecture can be investigated like any other phenomena. The cumulative efforts of scientific thinking, when approaching a phenomenon, have always helped to reach a conceptual order. Architecture itself has never been attacked scientifically, although there exist a multitude of scientific investigations of side issues to architecture (climatology, light, acoustics, sociology, ecology, etc.). Whenever architects devote their time to architectural research, they tackle these subject-matters; and one can rightly assume that non-architect scientists would do the job better, and as a matter of fact, they do. Tackling architecture itself is taboo. Of course, architecture is a creative activity, but so is physics, for the creative mind. There is a pronounced trend to withdraw into a foggy irrationalism, with plenty of humanitarian slogans as opposed to the platitudes of commonsense, common-sense being the label which the fake mystic but wildly efficient businessmen architects stick on any attempt at creative order. It is an advertising trick relying on the 19th century popular image of the irresponsible romantic artist, and which still appeals to the provincial taste. They discredit art and they discredit science.*

*The present views on architecture are distilled from highly complex works of the Baroque period where space had an absolute meaning and received a perfect expression. The concept of space as known today was first discovered through the investigation of Baroque architecture. That means that it has been abstracted from the final product of a long evolution. The thus derived concepts of space do not apply to simpler, earlier or less intricate structures. Although no coherent architectural theory has emerged through the discovery of space, the recognition of space as a constituting factor of architecture, unrecognized by previous generations, remains a lasting contribution.*

*Architecture is a projection of space images into material form. In the development of architectural space, the known parallelism of ontogenesis and philogenesis is equally present. Some insight into the space perception of children has been won. They go through a topological stage into a projective stage and arrive finally at the Euclidian space of the adult. The building activity of mankind all over the world follows this evolutional scheme. This is true not only for building alone but also for the whole man-made human environment, and particularly for the containers.*

*The artifacts of the whole human environment can be roughly divided into two groups, tools and containers. I do not wish to enter the domain of tools, which might by itself be a subject for extensive studies. All tools are a prolongation or multiplication of the human body. Tools and arms developed on the same pattern. When the human hand developed into the gripping organ, the primary tool came into being. Next a transfer of the teeth function to the hand, and from there to the primitive tools took place. All mechanical tools are a kind of mobile teeth connected to the hand. Knives, scissors, hammers, tongs, forks, shovels show this morphological relationship from the first glance. The lever bar is the prolongation of the arm. There is a third element, the handle, an adaptation to the human hand. Tools acquire artificial muscles, first, animal muscular power, then with the first industrial revolution, the mechanical muscle, the motor. A further evolutionary line prolongates the human sense-organs, prolongation of the eyes: microscope, telescope, television, X-rays; prolongation of the reach of the ear, telephone, radio, ultrasound; prolongation of the tactile senses: magnetic detectors, radar, thermometer, barometer, ionisation. Recently prolongation of the brain function forms an additional range of tools: cybernetics, automation, electronic computers.*

*Animals cannot take off or change at will their teeth, claws, saws, tongs, scissors, as nature developed them. Tools are extended, exchangable, removable organs which means a greater amount of freedom in evolution, therefore less constraint, less specialization. Man seems to be the least specialized being.*

*Man is a complex container with the head and the body as two conspicuous main containers, the whole equipped with tools — the limbs, for moving and grasping like a child's drawing. The containers next to man are an inexhaustible domain, which would merit a deeper investigation. Many connections lead to the neighbouring domains of clothing and building.*

*The container nearest to man is clothing. It is a container for a container, a reinforced skin, as many animals have developed, like sea shells. The armor of a knight is built on the same principle. Clothing hardly allows movement inside the container, only the wider container of the house allows this freedom. The snail leaves its shell to a certain degree, but is still bound to it. Man's clothing represents an extension of his skin and is removable and changeable. This feature puts clothing in analogy with tools. Man is the prisoner of neither his clothing nor of his tools.*

*One approach is to see man as a building animal. Building of most animals is guided by instinct. It is most obvious with insects. Instinct is characterized by narrowly bound reactions which do not admit deviations. It is orientated towards certain environmental stimuli. Once those stimuli change, the instinct no longer reacts purposefully. It is too specialized. Man is a learning being. He can adapt to a great extent his reactions to environmental changes, thereby heightening his chances of survival. His buildings are richer and offer great variety. But it is submitted to lawfulness, as is instinctive building. Wasps and bees and related insects build a cylinder with a horizontal rotation axis. As social beings they group themselves and build « skyscrapers », cell aggregates, within which the cylinders are transformed into hexagonal prisms with half rhombicdodeca-hedra at the end. It is a very rational, but restricted, building system. The architecture is as monotone as the business architecture of today's evolution line. The mole-hill has a vertical rotation axis. It is a complex pattern of a central space with a surrounding double ring system. The radical corridors show the numerical order of the Fibonacci series. Most birds nests also show rotational symmetry. If I were to name a further geometric property of those buildings, I would say those structures are round and that they approach, as far as execution in different building materials allows, the form of minimal areas. Building materials are deter-*

*mined by the environment; it is a factor that introduces minor changes but does not influence the basic shape. If we look for analogies to animal buildings in the man-made environment, our attention is drawn towards our containers, which show the same characteristics: rotational symmetry and enclosing minimal areas. One could say that they show a stylistic affinity. The contours of those containers are so called* plateau *figures, mainly roulettes of conics. Gravitation adds a further element, influencing the symmetry relations. Broadly speaking, one can divide our containers into two subgroups of soft and stiff containers. The soft container is a suspended construction, like the tent or clothing, and its prototype are the sacks and soft containers for liquids; for example, the pockets in clothing, the rucksack of the alpinist, the saddle bag of the horse man, the lady's hand bag, the tobacco pouch, luggage, kitbags, balloons, giant petrol tankers of plastic, and also the modern big tents and inflatable structures. Those containers are essentially mobile and are put on the ground for a certain time only. The stiff container has a different genealogy. It first sinks into the ground to lift itself out of the ground, and finally free itself into independent shapes. The first stiff containers are hollows in the ground; for example, grain storage of animals and man, water cisternes, with the typical narrow neck remiding the bottle shapes to reduce evaporation. Even after having detached itself from the ground, the stiff container sinks once more into the ground, like the Egyptian pointed vases. The shapes of the stiff and soft containers converge towards common shapes and their origin can no more be identified.*

*In the containers next to man the problem of grouping or packaging had no significance in the past. For a long span of time, and in different civilizations, those shapes had hardly changed. Mass transport of containers has brought the packing shape into being. Consider only jerrycans for petrol, and, above all, our over-production of paper packaging. The evolution of containers omitted an intermediate stage which could be called the projective stage, and can be detected in the evolution of houses. Modern package containers are mostly rectangular orthogonal. Of necessity, they should have straight edges and surfaces, but not necessarily right angles. But group containers were born into a rectangular civilization and architecture therefore had to assimilate itself. Problems of transport and storage have forced it. Interpreted into geometry, this means that the densely packed containers have undergone a topological transformation. In the topological rubber geometry, a sphere can be transformed into a cube. I simplify a bit. In analogy to biology one can see the house element as a kind of container cell with a smaller or larger group of men as the nucleus. This cell can develop in two directions:*

*a) change its size and create large spaces like large cells. Examples: the Syrian, Roman and Byzantine cupolas, and the big modern shell vaultings. The spans grow absolutely, the amount of material used diminishes. The building dematerializes.*

*b) lead to differentiated container aggregates, like cell aggregates. Examples: office buildings, flat block, hospitals, etc.*

*Architecture creates containers for man. It begins with the horizontal area as man moves optimally on horizontal areas. Where horizontal areas do not occur in nature, man introduces them by terrassing mountains and by creating stairs. He creates sunken and lifted horizontal areas, juxtaposes and superposes them.*

*The end of a linear movement is a rotation movement, creating a round area as an expression of rest. Animals like cats and dogs turn to prepare their resting place. Long after the house became rectangular, the resting place, the apsis, remained round. The house, the container cell, is primarily round, a hollow space with a rotation axis like the other containers next to man. There are cupolas both cylindrical and conical. In clothing similar shapes are found in the head cover. These shapes are very independent of environmental factors like building material and climate. The igloo of the eskimo is identical in shape with the equatorial round hut and the tent of the steppe. Excavations show the same house type in old China, India, Africa and the Near East. Like other containers, houses follow two evolutionary lines: that of soft containers, like tents, and that of stiff containers, starting with sunken floor caves, later rising out of the ground with forms lifting massive houses.*

*Grouping follows the same scheme. The huts are loosely arranged in a circle, sometimes enclosed by a round wall, which could either be elliptic or take any free round shape. The openings of these houses are also round. Cell growth of containers follows the same form structure, whether covered spaces like the Atreus tomb of Mykenae or the non-covered space of Stonehenge. Incidentally, the round shapes belong mainly to the pre-agricultural civilization stage. We could call this round structure stage a topological stage. But with the emergence of agriculture round shapes do not disappear but receive a sacral character.*

*Under social pressure, the cells move closer to each other and undergo topological transformations. Certain transitional forms come into being. These transformations could best be visualized by a film. The round cells move closer and closer, the shapes become oblong, only the corners remain round, occasionally an apsis remains, until a complete form transformation takes place. There are not yet rectangles or squares but straight lined figures with oblique angles. The Megaron type has been created. One could call this the projective stage of architecture.*

*Consequently this architecture transforms into a rectangular pattern. This rectangular architecture has, seen stereometrically, the advantage that area angles and dyhedral angles are identical of 90 degrees. Thus the final result of the topological transformation of loose round shapes is a tightly knitted rectangular pattern. This process provides matter for thought. Geometrically, it is not self evident that the round houses become rectangular. Remembering beehives, where the social structure formed the package into a hexagonal pattern having the advantage of being isotrop. The rectangular pattern is not isotrop but hexagonal houses are rare. It may be that the rectangular structure offers a greater degree of freedom; besides it allows the transfer of proportions of other polygons as the pentagon in the golden section.*

*The house as we know it from children's drawings is a synthetic form. It is a combination of the two evolutionary trends, of the soft and stiff container. Remember the drawing of a typical house section which Le Corbusier demonstrated as an obsolete example which is opposed to his new section. A typical house consists of a roof, which is a direct descendent of the ancient tent; then of a cellar, which is the descendent of the old sunken floor cave; and then the house proper, which is the central part and is the cave lifted from earth to the sun. The image of such a house has become a kind of archetype, deeply anchored in the individual and collective subconscience. Now we under-*

*stand the general popularity of this type of house and the emotional resistance against all attempts of reform. Obsolete shapes do not disappear even after having ceased to fulfill their function. The obsolete house type covers, in a growing measure, the suburbs of highly civilized industrial countries. Inside that house remains the old fireplace, which does not serve for heating anymore, and is another instance of the inertia of form.*

*The grammar of space developed gradually from euclidian to projective geometry and from there to the new discipline of topology. The evolution of architectural space took the inverse direction: at the beginning there was a topological stage tending towards space enclosure by minimal areas; for example, tholos-type round houses and clusters, absidial and round-cornered houses. Then came a projective geometric stage with undetermined angle lenght relations; for example, early Megaron-type houses in irregularly grown clusters. Finally architecture arrived at an euclidian organization with straight lined rectangular shapes; for example, building and town planning in high civilizations.*

*Except for the rectangular prismatic patterns, the possibilities of euclidian order in architecture are far from being fully exploited until now. The large array of space packing patterns, using the platonic and archimedian solids and their duals, prisms and antiprisms, has not yet found any architectural application. These patterns are related to the problem of sphere packing, where mathematical investigations are still in development. Besides the crystallographic space structures there is a whole range of little explored looser packing forms, some appearing in organic life. These forms could have repercussions on architecture. The architect entering this research field would find, to his surprise, that crystallographers had preceeded him. In the discovery of crystal structures, mathematical intuition anticipated later observed confirmation on the X-ray screen. The morphogenetic factors producing crystals operate on the molecular scale level, where gravitational forces are negligible. But, within the realm of container groups on the human scale, as in architecture, these forces strongly influence the configuration of space enclosure. A general science of space should reflect equally upon nature and human creation. The crystallographic discoveries remained without resonance in architecture. The cross-fertilisation between art and science, which one could normally expect after an important finding in the domain of form, did not set in. The inadequate state of tectonic and massive construction methods prevented a direct impact on architecture. With the actual development of 3-dimensional construction methods the transposition into another medium has become possible.*

*Space packing patterns are a geometrical abstraction only. In chemistry, many aspects besides the crystallographic ones enter the stage to perform the drama of matter in space time. Also in architecture, the geometric aspect covers only a part of the complex tissue. It would be naive to believe that one could mechanically transfer shapes from crystallography to architecture. This would mean a worse formalism than the application of historical forms. What is important is* thinking *in analogies. Geometric space patterns have to be transposed into human scale and put into a visually seizable order to be of architectural value. In traditional rectangular packing, questions of scale have found routine answers. Approved cooking recipes exist. In the non-traditional proposals they solicit new approaches. Because of the inherent difficulties a fresh awareness of scale arises.*

*Historic architecture was mainly concerned with the dramatization of statics. The restricted register of baroque space order soon became exhausted. We are now able to distinguish the possible elements constituting architecture. Like in crystallography, the elements are limited in number. Even so, 3-dimensional space packing offers far more possibilities than the 2-dimensional patterns, commonly called ornament (also 2-dimensional crystallography), on which architecture was mainly based until now. Different stages of civilization have different optimal population densities and use corresponding space packing. Hunting and fishing communities lived in loosely packed round houses, of the topological kind, in accordance with the low population density. Agricultural civilizations created the rectangular euclidean pattern. Industrial civilization with its high population density is still packed into an outlined agricultural frame work and has yet to create its appropriate pattern. The rotational symmetries of the new patterns which were meaningless before the space age now become the exact bearers of widely understood contemporary symbolism.*

*Particular design problems arise at the boundary portions of the new space packings, where different conditions prevail than in the homogeneous inside parts. One of the direct implications is the change of the shape of the openings. In the topological stage the openings followed the general character, and were consequently rounded, as in African huts. In the rectangular space pattern, doors and windows were rectangular, their distribution tending towards certain proportional orders. In the proposed packings rectangular openings are the exceptions. This evolution was forecast by cars and planes, where no more rectangular openings occur. A parallel evolution is noticeable in newer industrial and religious buildings.*

*Where does architecture as an art, with all the perfection for the senses, fit into? Where, Greece? Italy? Japan? Architecture is not so much a direct art of the senses, but is like music memory. The tone of the cord which I now hear does not exist in the next moment, nevertheless the synthesis of music forms in my memory. The space through which I passed I do not see anymore; even so, it is present in my memory and directly connected to my actual perception. Architecture is interwoven with reality and the stuff that dreams are made of. This is equally true for the interior of a building as well as the exterior. The façade of the Gothic dome does not reveal the nature of its nave. This remark shows our relation to the slogan « Form Follows Function », which characterizes the actual unwinding period of architecture. Stone minarets still tower above the cupolas of the mosques. Not far from them on some missile launching site rise identical shapes, the rockets, no more built of stone. These containers built of modern synthetic materials fly into outer space to destroy themselves and perhaps to spread destruction. Two identical shapes but what difference in function. The cupola might be one of the inflatable structures which blow off here today and there tomorrow. Tinguely, the Swiss sculptor, in the court-yard of the Museum of Modern Art in New York, fired his self-destructive sculpture symbolizing one aspect of architecture projected on the mind of the contemporary artists. Architecture has become aggressive and has conquered the dedivined heavens. The nostalgic longing for the stable, symbolic architecture of yesterday, and maybe of tomorrow, remains stronger than ever, the eternal polarity of all human endeavour.*

⑩70

⑪71

(72)

(73)

(74)

(70) Faculty of Mechanical Engineering, Technion, Haifa, 1964–1967. Interior. Alfred Neumann, Zvi Hecker.
(71) Faculty of Mechanical Engineering, Technion, Haifa, 1964–1967. Alfred Neumann, Zvi Hecker.
(72) Faculty of Mechanical Engineering, Technion, Haifa, 1964–1967. Alfred Neumann, Zvi Hecker.
(73) Faculty of Mechanical Engineering, Technion, Haifa, 1964–1967. Interior. Alfred Neumann, Zvi Hecker.
(74) Faculty of Mechanical Engineering, Technion, Haifa, 1964–1967. Interior. Alfred Neumann, Zvi Hecker. Zvi Hecker archive.

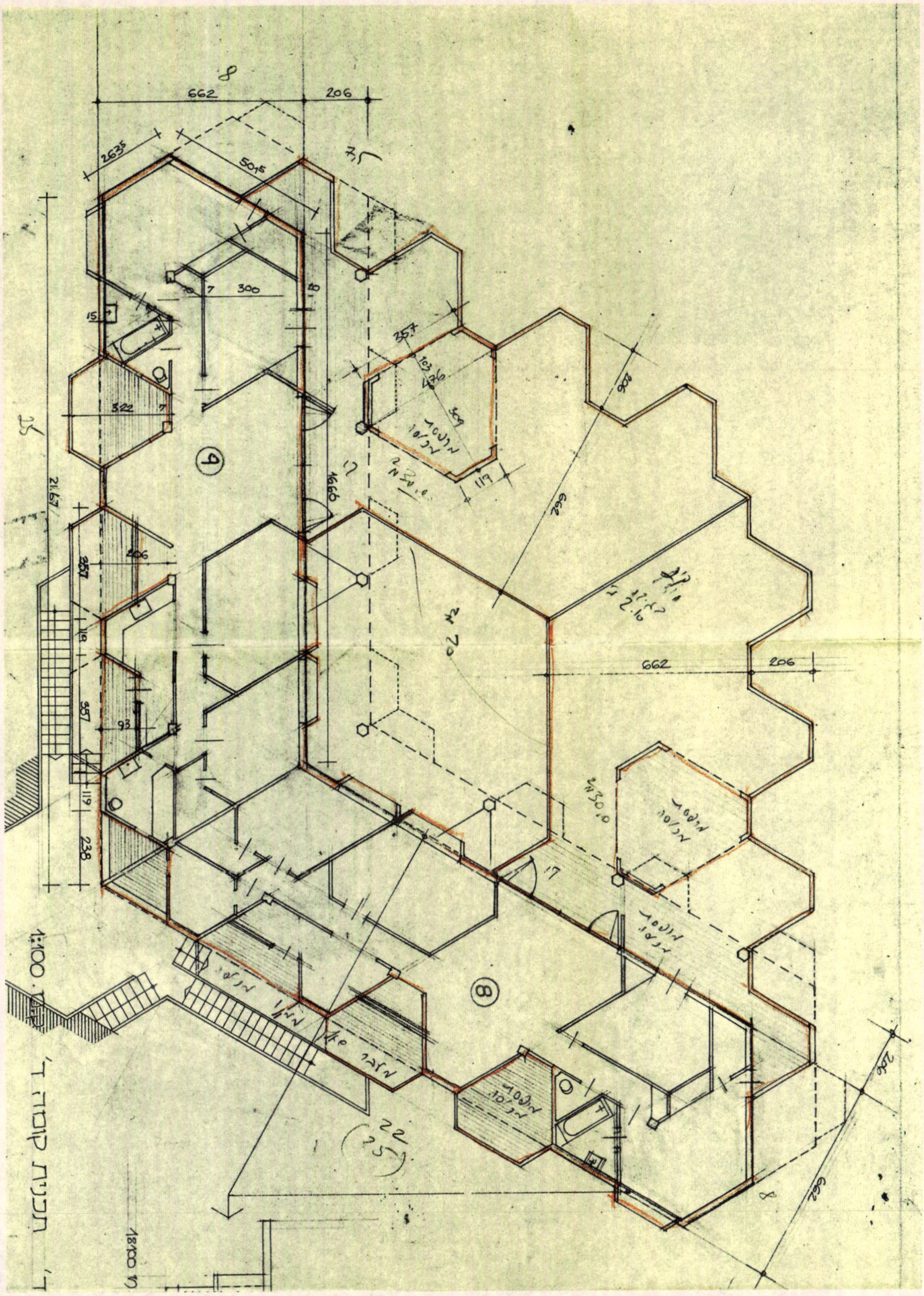


(76)

(75) Dubiner House, Ramat Gan, 1961–1963. Alfred Neumann, Zvi Hecker, Eldar Sharon.
(76) Dubiner House, Ramat Gan, 1961–1963. Floor plan. Alfred Neumann, Zvi Hecker, Eldar Sharon.

⑺

⑱

⑲

(77) Dubiner House, 2015. Eli Singalovski.
(78) Military Academy, Mitzpe Ramon, 1963–1967. Alfred Neumann, Zvi Hecker, Eldar Sharon.
(79) Military Academy, Mitzpe Ramon, 2015. Gili Merin.
(80) Military Academy, Mitzpe Ramon, 1963–1967. Alfred Neumann, Zvi Hecker, Eldar Sharon.
(81) Military Academy, Mitzpe Ramon, 1963–1967. Alfred Neumann, Zvi Hecker, Eldar Sharon.

(80)

(81)

(82)

(83)

(84)

(82) Synagogue at the Military Academy, Mitzpe Ramon, under construction, 1967. Alfred Neumann, Zvi Hecker.
(83) Synagogue at the Military Academy, Mitzpe Ramon, 1969. Alfred Neumann, Zvi Hecker. Zvi Hecker archive.
(84) Synagogue at the Military Academy, Mitzpe Ramon, interior view, 1969. Alfred Neumann, Zvi Hecker. Zvi Hecker archive.
(85) – (87) Michmoret recreation resort, 1961. Alfred Neumann, Zvi Hecker, Eldar Sharon.
(88) Ramot Polin housing, Ramot, Jerusalem, 2015. Gili Merin.

⑧⑤

⑧⑥

⑧⑦

⑱

# Public Works

①

## Infrastructuring

During the formative years of Statehood, the notion of "conquering the land" (Heb. *kibbush ha'aretz*) found its most literal manifestation in the laying out of the country's comprehensive infrastructure. Nationwide networks of roads and bridges, electric, water, and sewage grids, civil and military industries, nuclear power plants, ports and airports, national parks and forests—all these made up the foundation of the long-term physical development that would double and triple the country's capacity to receive massive immigration and enable the implementation of the policy of population dispersal (see chapter "Project").

In the first years, development budgets were funneled primarily into the agricultural sector. Only in 1955, with Pinchas Sapir's appointment as minister of trade and agriculture, did the emphasis shift to investment in the industrial sector; a new policy of setting up factories on the periphery in order to stimulate employment in these remote areas was launched. Until then, industry had been concentrated in the well-established regions and focused on the supply of basic services such as housing, food, and textiles. Due to inadequate planning in the first years, thousands of workshops and hundreds of factories were established in the center of the country. These ultimately failed due to a lack of raw materials (made-in-Israel was given top priority at the time, and the import of some products was prohibited in order to protect local manufacturing).

① New road to Sodom, April 1953. Prime Minister Ben-Gurion giving a speech at the road's opening ceremony.
② New road to Sodom by Israeli army engineers, 1954. Photographer: Fritz Cohen. 1954, Government Press Office.

The government created two coffers, or two parallel budgets, for funding its missions: a regular budget, prepared by the Treasury and approved by the Knesset; and a development budget, whose coffers were filled by donations, loans, and compensation funds from external sources and whose distribution did not require approval through the conventional channels. The Reparations Agreement signed with the Federal Republic of Germany in the autumn of 1952 channeled capital and merchandise into Israel over the course of about a dozen years. This proved to be a major factor in boosting the Israeli economy—and specifically in accelerating industrial and infrastructural projects. American aid in loans and grants through the American Ex-Im (Export-Import) Bank constituted a kind of miniature Marshall Plan for Israel. Until the mid-1960s, the development budget almost equaled the regular budget. A considerable part of the infrastructural work was conducted according to rational master planning, but many projects, some of them expensive, were motivated by political, strategic, and ideological considerations, often against all economic sense.

The Negev development project is an extreme example of the precedence given to ideology and strategy over cost-benefit analysis: Prime Minister David Ben-Gurion saw the development of the Negev region as the utmost pioneering challenge for the new State. "The disgrace of the wilderness" and "making the desert bloom"—propaganda code-language for the neglect of the land by its Arab inhabitants and its rehabilitation by the new citizens—motivated the drive to establish infrastructure projects that were huge by any measure. In the Negev Development Symposium, which took place in September 1953, Arieh Sharon, the chief architect of the national master plan (see chapter "Project"), explained the advantages of the desert's hypothetical "tabula rasa": "There is one encouraging factor [...] in the Negev, in particular for planners, and this is its empty and undeveloped space. It has not yet been burdened by densely populated cities, chaotic construction, or speculative parcelization. The vast majority of lands in the Negev are under public ownership, and the large

②

expanses are ready for agricultural and industrial development. For the planner, these facts involve great potential and many risks."[1]

Particular hopes were hung on the mineral industry, both as an export branch and as a source of foreign currency: the copper mines in Timna, the phosphate plant in Oron, the Dead Sea Works, and others were established in the 1950s and 1960s with the goal of exploiting the country's natural resources. These plants also stimulated the building of transportation infrastructure in the south of the country: train tracks were laid, roads were paved, and the ports in Ashdod and Eilat were built. Additional by-products of the mineral industry were the large textile plants in Dimona, Beersheba, and Yeruham, meant to provide employment for the wives of the miners.

Strategically speaking, the primary motivation behind the Negev development project was the necessity of settling the uninhabited regions in order to prevent any possible future territorial concessions, and of creating a link with the countries of Asia and Africa through Israel's southern border. Defense projects such as the nuclear plant in Dimona, as well as weapons and chemicals industries, were established in the Negev due to the sparseness of the population there. The Trans-Israel pipeline, whose very existence was a well-guarded secret, was Israel's final attempt to create a strategic substitute for the Suez Canal. After the closing of the canal in 1967, the pipeline was reinforced through distribution terminals, oil pumps, and reservoir tanks—the biggest of their kind in the world—and served the transportation of Iranian crude oil to Israel and Europe. The reopening of the Suez Canal in 1975 and the severing of ties with Iran in 1979 rendered this huge infrastructure project redundant.

The drainage of the Hula Valley, like the Negev development project, was at the top of the list of the young State's infrastructure projects. The operation to drain the 37,000-dunam swamp began in 1951 under the management of an American company. The works were accompanied by border disputes with Syria, culminating in a discussion in the United Nations, freezing of the development grant from the United States, and reprisal actions. Today, about five decades after its completion, the operation is considered an ecological failure.

The establishment of the national water carrier also summoned international opposition and border disputes, since its ambitions went well beyond just infrastructure: the national water carrier was meant to resolve the water shortage in the south of the country by diverting water from the Jordan River for Israel's exclusive use. Political and military pressure prevented the diversion of water from the Jordan in the most hydraulically suitable place, and ultimately the carrier's exit points were set at the Sea of Galilee, in underground pumping

③ National Water Carrier, works by the National Water Company, 1950s–1960s. Tahal Group. Mekorot archive.
④ National Water Carrier, works by the National Water Company, the Jordan (Yarden) Canal, 1950s–1960s. Tahal Group. Mekorot archive.

stations that were protected from Syrian attack. (A Syrio-Lebanese plan to divert water from the Jordan was forcibly stopped by Israel in 1966 and was one of the causes of the outbreak of the Six-Day War.) Dams, reservoirs, and groundwater enrichment plants were built as tributaries to the national water carrier. The water market enjoyed consistent support, as it was an essential resource for all the settlement projects. Sewage infrastructures, on the other hand, were neglected, and the rivers and coasts of Israel were gradually polluted over the years.

The Reparations Agreement with the Federal Republic of Germany provided a powerful impetus for the development of the State of Israel, since the means of production supplied to Israel as part of the agreement bolstered local planning initiatives with modern equipment that enabled efficient implementation. With the end of World War II, representatives of the Jewish Agency assessed that, despite the boycott of Germany, ties with that country were essential to Israel's development. The emergency bylaws that beset the country in its first years hastened the decision on the controversial subject, and the claim for reparations was presented to the German government as early as March 1951. A year later, negotiations opened in The Hague as to the amount and character of the reparations. Israel demanded that one-third of the reparations be given

③

④

⑤ Infrastructure works by the National Water Company,1956. Photographer: Hanan Sade. Central Zionist Archives.
⑥ Infrastructure works by the National Water Company, 1956. Photographer: Hanan Sade. Central Zionist Archives.
⑦ Prime Minister David Ben-Gurion with the CEO of Tahal Group and engineer Shimon Livyatan inside a water pipe, Eshed Kinorot factory, Tabkha. Mekorot archive.
⑧ Zohar artificial lake, Lachish region, 1960s. Tahal Group. Mekorot archive.
⑨ Water cistern under construction in the Bet She'an Valley.
⑩ Storage tanks and oil pipelines, Ashdod, 1973.
⑪ Infrastructure work by the National Water Company, 1960–1969. Photographer: Hanan Sade. Central Zionist Archives.
⑫ Infrastructure work by the National Water Company, 1960–1969. Photographer: Hanan Sade. Central Zionist Archives.

⑤

⑥

⑦

⑧

(10)

(11)

(12)

in hard currency, and the rest in merchandise and production means that would serve the establishment of nationwide public works. The agreement was signed in September 1952 and was passed by the Bundestag in March 1953. That same year saw the beginning of the flow of products and raw materials into Israel, amounting to about three billion German marks and divided as follows: 21 percent—iron and iron products, steel, and other metals; 36 percent—various machines, automobiles, train engines, train cars, boats, and building parts; 28 percent—chemical and other industrial products (rubber, wood, cement, pottery, glass, and leather); 3 percent—products and raw materials for agriculture; 12 percent—services (such as transport and insurance of merchandise). Israel entered into a decade of accelerated growth and industrialization. The external support enabled the establishment of a centralized economy, and it was often the government's preferences that determined the fate of this or that branch of the economy. Forty-one percent of the total reparations earmarked for industry were channeled into the peripheral zones.

(9)

In 1954 the Israeli government nationalized the Israel Electric Corporation, which had been a private company under the British Mandate. In 1921, two years before founding the Palestine Electric Company, Pinchas Rotenberg had obtained two exclusive concessions from the British high commissioner for the production, supply, distribution, and sale of electrical energy on the borders of Palestine, good until 1966. Jerusalem was not included under this jurisdiction, as the right to supply electric power to the city had already been granted to a

(13) (14)

Greek entrepreneur before World War I. In 1928 the Jerusalem Electric and Public Service Corporation was established in Jerusalem; it operated independently until its stocks were purchased by the Israel Electric Corporation in late 1954.

The development of nuclear energy in the late 1950s, with American and French aid, was probably the most expensive and technologically advanced single project undertaken by the young State in its drive to establish a long-term strategic advantage and to promote nuclear research for peaceful purposes (as officially declared to this day). Although they were invisible to the public eye, the nuclear plants in Dimona and Soreq—like many other security installations in Israel—benefited from special attention to architectural quality. Among their planners were the American architect Philip Johnson and the Israeli architects Gideon Ziv, Yaacov Rechter, and Moshe Zarhi (Soreq) and Yitzhak Yashar and Dan Eytan (Dimona).

Dictated by security and settlement needs, the land transportation infrastructure in Israel developed into a branched network of arteries connecting distanced settlement points that were being established in frontier areas as part of the policy of population dispersal.

The sharp rise in the number of cars in the 1960s did not bring with it the development of an advanced network of main roads, and transportation infrastructure continued to lag behind the constant growth of traffic on the roads. Highways were not paved until the end of the 1960s, and with the exception of a few bridges (primarily for pedestrians), interchanges were not built. The first such interchange, Rishon LeZion West, opened to traffic in 1967. The tender for the Ayalon Highway project, Israel's main transportation artery, was announced in 1971. In the 1970s the pace of paving roads in the country slowed, with the exception of those throughout the occupied and annexed territories of Sinai, the Jordan Valley, and the Golan Heights. The excess of infrastructure (apartheid roads and bridges, security fences, surround lighting and optical surveillance, over-landscaping, bypassing water and sewage systems, etc.) would henceforth become the hallmark of the Jewish settlements in the Occupied Territories and the symptom of their civilian and environmental hubris.

⑮

⑯

⑱

⑰

⑬ Reading Power Station, Tel Aviv, 1938–1953. Israel Electric Company archive.
⑭ Reading Power Station, with painted camouflage against air-raid bombing, Tel Aviv, 1938–1953. Israel Electric Company archive.
⑮ Power station, Hadera, 1973. Israel Electric Company archive.
⑯ Construction of a new section of the Jerusalem–Tel Aviv highway ("Road 1"), 1970. Public Works Department archive.
⑰ The new road to Sodom at sea level, April 1953. Public Works Department. Central Zionist Archives.
⑱ Passengers waiting in the Dimona train station after the inauguration of the Negev Railway, 1967. Central Zionist Archives.

Since the establishment of the State, trains have never been seen as a primary form of passenger transportation. With the exception of amendments to the Tel Aviv–Haifa line and connections to the city of Beersheba (1956) and the Ashdod port (1962), no new passenger lines were added to the Turkish and British system of tracks during the first decades. There were proposals to build an underground railway in the Tel Aviv metropolitan area as early as the 1930s, and actual plans for such a method of transportation resurfaced in the 1950s and early 1960s. (Now finally under construction, this project is estimated to be completed in the mid-2020s.)

The only underground railway project to actually be realized in the 1950s was the Carmelit in Haifa, a cable car tunnel 1,800 meters long, planned by French engineers and built by the Israeli Solel Boneh company. ■

1 Arieh Sharon, Negev Development Symposium, September 27–28, 1953.

⑲

⑳ ㉑ ㉒ ㉓

⑲ Skeleton of a new factory, 1960s. Built by Solel Boneh. Photographer: Ami Erev. Shikun & Binui historical archive.
⑳ Of-Ar textile factory, Ofakim, 1960. Yitzhak Rapoport, Asher Gleiberman, Zvi Frenkel. Built by Solel Boneh. Photographer: Ami Erev. Shikun & Binui historical archive.
㉑ Keizer factory under construction, Ashkelon, 1960. Built by Solel Boneh. Photographer: Ami Erev. Shikun & Binui historical archive.
㉒ Keizer factory, Ashkelon, 1960. Built by Solel Boneh. Photographer: Ami Erev. Shikun & Binui historical archive.
㉓ Skeleton of a new factory, 1960s. Built by Solel Boneh. Photographer: Ami Erev. Shikun & Binui historical archive.

(24)

(25)

(26)

(24) Shemen silos, Haifa, 1965. Built by Solel Boneh. Shikun & Binui historical archive.
(25) Silo, Ashkelon, 1965. Engineer: Josef Idelman. Built by Solel Boneh. Shikun & Binui historical archive.
(26) Hazera Grain Institute, Masmia, 1958. Engineer: Josef Idelman. Built by Solel Boneh. Shikun & Binui historical archive.
(27) Beit Dagon grain elevators, Haifa, 1953–1963. Yosef Klarwein. Built by Solel Boneh. Shikun & Binui historical archive.
(28) Grain elevator, Jaffa, 1956–1957. Engineer: Josef Idelman. Built by Solel Boneh. Shikun & Binui historical archive.
(29) Beit Dagon grain elevators, Haifa, 1953–1963. Interior view. Yosef Klarwein. Built by Solel Boneh. Shikun & Binui historical archive.
(30) Beit Dagon grain elevators, Haifa, 1953–1963. Yosef Klarwein. Built by Solel Boneh. Shikun & Binui historical archive.

(27)

(28)

(29)

(30)

(31) Underground auditorium under construction, Bet Shean, 1971.
(32) Shelter and ditches in Kibbutz Hamadia, 1969. Photographer: Yitzhak Amit. Harvard Library.
(33) Reading Power Station, underground power station under construction, Tel Aviv, 1952–1954. AEG company (as part of the Reparations Agreement between Israel and the Federal Republic of Germany). Israel Electric Company archive.
(34)–(35) Movable metal bomb shelter accommodating 45 people, 1975. Digital image of photograph by Yisra'el Simionski/Israel Sun Ltd., from the Judaica Collection of the Harvard Library, Harvard University.
(36) Prefabricated bomb shelter designed by the Technical Department of Hashomer Hatzair Kibbutzim, presented in Ashdod, 1976. Digital image of photograph by Yisra'el Simionski/Israel Sun Ltd., from the Judaica Collection of the Harvard Library, Harvard University.
(37)–(38) Prefabricated bomb shelter designed by the Technical Department of Hashomer Hatzair Kibbutzim, presented in Ashdod, 1976. Digital image of photograph by Yisra'el Simionski/Israel Sun Ltd., from the Judaica Collection of the Harvard Library, Harvard University.

(31)

(32)

(33)

㉞

㉟

㊱

㊳

㊲

# Detail

## The Local Genius of Shading

As a rule of thumb, most pre-State designed buildings in Mandatory Palestine were one-offs, and most of the visible building components, construction details, carpentry and metalware, surface coverings and decorative patterns —doors and windows, shadings and screens, handles and railings, wall and floor tiles, etc.—were designed and tailor-made for a particular building. In general, Bauhaus and British colonial architecture considered the building an autonomous object, an elaborate piece of public and domestic furniture. It was the master architect's prerogative to ensure that all the building's elements harmoniously came together in a total work of art and craft.

With the establishment of the State in 1948 and the nationalization of significant sections of the building industry, the integrative approach to design and construction was rapidly replaced by a differential one, which emphasized the building as an elementary, serial, reproducible product and effectively sabotaged the singularity of the architectural episode. The Israeli building of the 1950s and 1960s was thus a kit of mass-produced parts, serialized fittings, and generic details assembled at the site and repeated to the utmost in different variations. Accordingly, the Israeli architect exchanged the authority of the master builder and the aura of the *Gesamtkunstwerker* for generous tributes and commissions bestowed by the State and by the Labor Federation for diligent agents of the newly established social-realist aesthetic of efficiency.

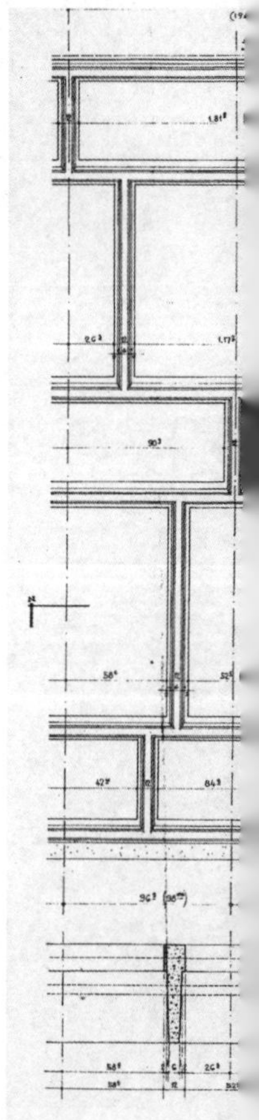

The massive scope of construction, commissioned by the housing authorities and implemented under great time constraints, led to the articulation of a "State-sanctioned" protocol of details which significantly streamlined design, production, and construction methods. The old routine of customizing details was now perceived as an unwarranted "luxury," detrimental to the general effort. A sense of the prudent rhetoric of the time can be gathered from the minutes of government or parliament sessions, such as the following report by the minister of agriculture, supply, and rationing, Dov Yosef, on August 2, 1949:

> Some time back we announced a competition for the submission of examples of furniture "for the masses": tables, chairs, and so forth. It was an utter failure. The judges wouldn't grant a prize to any of the competitors. The proposals included some nice samples, but they did not hit the target—that of reducing the cost of the furniture. We sat

our architects down and they worked out plans for the production of furniture "for the masses." By mid-month we hope to present examples to the public.[1]

The State in effect authorized itself to produce design norms, planning codes, building standards, built prototypes, and exemplary projects. The most comprehensive work in this field was done in the building details unit of the Housing Department (later the Housing Ministry) under the direction of architect Alexander Piekarczyk. This unit prepared a complete repertoire of building details which was advertised in brochures and books and thereby affixed in the Israeli building canon. At the beginning of the 1960s, the Housing Ministry, in collaboration with the Israel Standards Institution, began to issue standards certificates for the building industry. The criteria rapidly turned from a general guideline of simplicity and efficiency to a totalizing and binding code of conduct. Even contractors working in the private market had to align with the dogma of the specifications book of the Housing Ministry. As a result, the level of detail in "luxury" private housing was generally no higher than in the public-housing projects. The difference was generally in the quality and prestige of the materials—marble instead of regular floor tiles, imported fixtures, and so on.

(1) Courthouses, Tel Aviv, 1960–1965. Façade detail. Zeev Rechter, Moshe Zarhi, Yaacov Rechter.

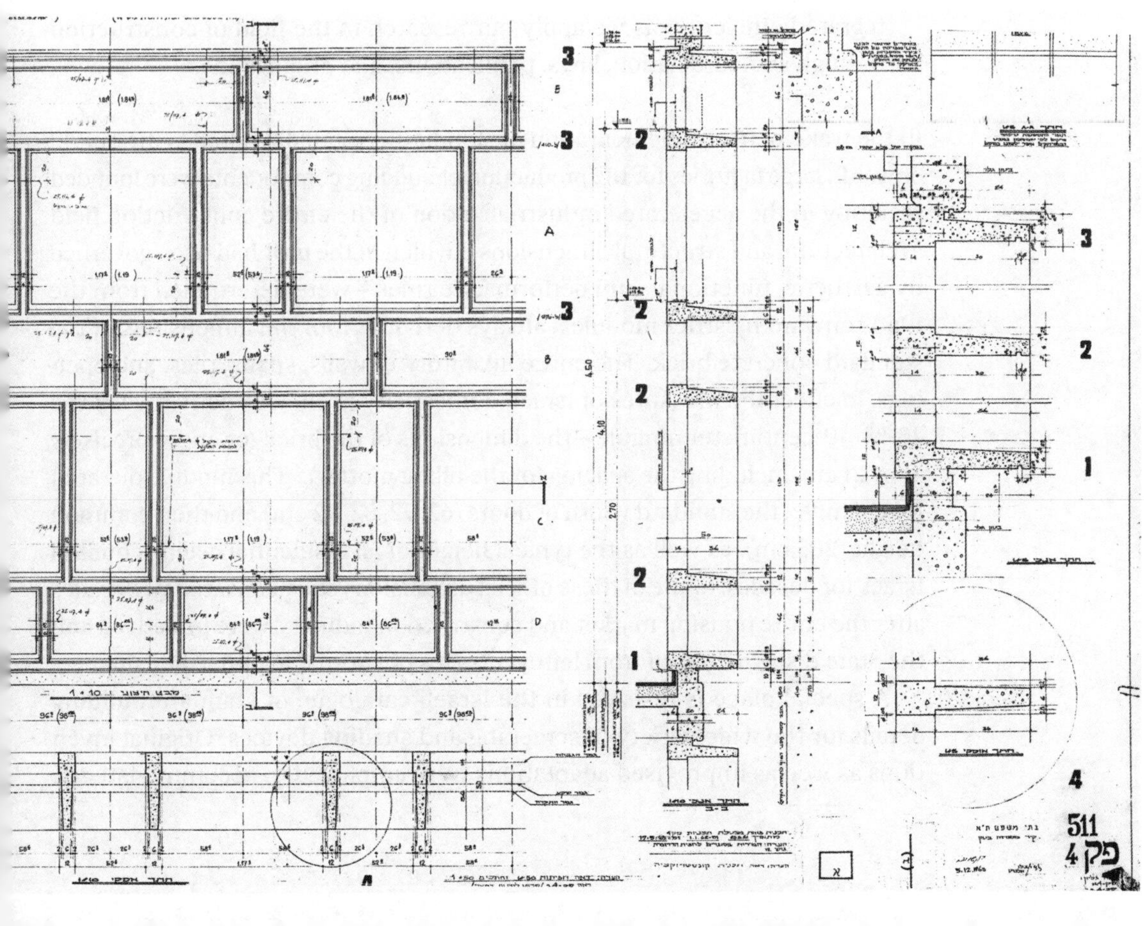

Sitting on the committee to determine Israeli building standards, alongside representatives of the Housing Ministry and the Standards Institution, were representatives of the Jewish Agency, the Union of Craftsmen and Small Industrialists, the Workers' Corporation, the Engineers' Board, the Public Works Authority, and the Israel Defense Forces. The Standards Institution regularly published the results of its tests and its new standards protocol in the professional press—primarily in *Engineering and Architecture: The Union of Engineers and Architects in Israel.*

The pragmatic and symbolic significance of standardization to the welfare-state apparatus is concisely expressed in the introduction to the first book in a series of publications about standard construction details, *Standard Carpentry for Residential Buildings*, written by David Tenne, general director of the Housing Ministry:

> At the Housing Ministry, we have come to the conclusion that we must quicken the pace of standardization of construction materials and products in Israel. Standardization in the field of construction will help improve the quality of buildings and lower construction costs.
>
> This subject is likely to be of great importance for the entire construction market in Israel. However, it is especially important as concerns the many housing and construction projects of the Housing Ministry. Therefore in the coming years we must emphasize this subject and ensure that it will be integrated efficiently as we apply our research in the field of construction, through standardization, laws, publications, and propaganda.[2]

In the wake of the implementation of standardized building details (from 1951 onward), large factories for the production of building components were founded, resulting in the accelerated industrialization of the entire construction field. Architectural and structural dimensions—which in the past had been governed by aesthetic, functional, and performative rules—were determined from the 1960s onward by strict modules, always deriving from the dimensions of the standard concrete brick. The entire inventory of walls, spans, tiles, and openings, in effect the measures of Israeli domesticity itself, was derivative of the 20-by-40-centimeter module—the dimensions of the brick (or, more precisely, 41 by 21 cm, including the spacing for the filling mortar).[3] This module dictated, for example, the standard width of doors (62, 72, 82, 92 cm) and their common height (205 cm), as well as the typical height of all residential ceilings built in Israel, for decades. Some of these official dimensions still persist today, decades after the entire housing market and construction industry were privatized and the State disowned itself from leftover traces of affordable public housing.

A special place is reserved in the Israeli catalogue of standard building details for the wide variety of screening and shading devices. Original inventions as well as improvised adaptations were employed to accommodate the functional and aesthetic norms of modern architecture to the climatic and solar conditions in Israel. These surface features quickly became a prevalent symptom of the local bricoleur culture and the unmistakable visual hallmark of Israeli architecture.

Following is a brief history of architectural shading and ventilation devices in Israel.

Pre-casts:

These prefabricated concrete units, which came in a variety of sizes and stippled patterns, were designed to be assembled as an integral and permanent part of the building. One could order a special design, but in order to justify the cost of the mold, a large series had to be cast. Some local architects worked in conjunction with the brick-casting factories on the development of special elements (one of the best-known of these was the collaboration in Haifa between the Beton Mechanical Factory for Cement Products and the architectural firm of Shmuel Rosov). The austerity bylaws and the design directives of the 1950s limited creative expression and channeled design initiatives into rudimentary geometric latticework applied on balconies, kitchen openings, and ground-floor barriers.

②

③

Brise-soleil:

The brise-soleil is a prefabricated blind that is not an integral part of the building envelope, but an independent fixture attached on the outside to openings or even to entire façades for shading purposes. The Executive Committee Building of the Labor Federation, on Tel Aviv's Arlozorov Street, was the first building in Israel to use large industrialized shading elements (see chapter "Union Architecture"). A product of international fashions of the time, most distinctively of modern Brazilian architecture, the brise-soleil was well suited to the Israeli climate and was applied extensively on institutional buildings. Whether made of concrete or asbestos, whether dense or sparse, the brise-soleil was always placed matter-of-factly in relationship to the direction of the building façade (horizontally on the southern façade to protect from the high-altitude sun rays; vertically on the eastern and western façades to block low rays; and almost never used on the northern façade). This architectural practice, perhaps the most basic that one can think of, is no longer to be taken for granted. Such a conspicuous "contextual" attitude to climatic parameters is rarely in practice nowadays in Israel.

Brisol:

One of the most original Israeli inventions in the field of shading was the "brisol," developed in the early 1950s. This patent, filed by architect Shmuel Rosov, combines regular wooden rolling blinds with the venetian blind. In the *Journal of the Union of Engineers and Architects in Israel* 3 (1954) its inventor presented it as follows:

> A short time ago we invented a special fixture for rolling blinds, produced by the "Brisol" company according to a method that is protected by Israeli Patent no. 5874. This fixture enables any manufacturer of rolling blinds to assemble a blind whose rungs can turn on a horizontal axis.

② Cover of catalogue for prefabricated elements, Bidud ("Isolation") Company, 1950s. Ben Yosef Dov, Yitzhak Bachar.
③ Rambam Hospital, Haifa, 1968. Façade studies. Arieh Sharon, Eldar Sharon.
④ "Design perfection requires Trisol," advertisement in the journal *Engineering and Architecture*, 1960.
⑤ Trisol Company advertisement in the journal *Engineering and Architecture*, 1960.

> The action of the blind is quite simple. While it is being lifted or lowered by the regular cord, the rungs remain closed because they are hung on chains.[4]

The "Brisol," which heralded standardized carpentry while preserving the aura of the unique architectural detail, allowed for a large combination of different types of blinds, but its mechanism was somewhat awkward and precluded its mass integration in the Israeli housing project.

> Trisol:

The "Trisol" was developed in 1957 by inventor Ram Ben-Tal and was designed by the architect David Best for the IsrAsbest factory, which was looking for ways to integrate asbestos into construction. The innovation—a mechanism used to fold, slide, and shift the angles of asbestos blinds, which were already set in place—enabled the convenient closing of balconies and the extension of apartments with an additional living area, hidden from the sun and the neighbors, without blocking cross-ventilation. Marketed aggressively, within just a

④ ⑤

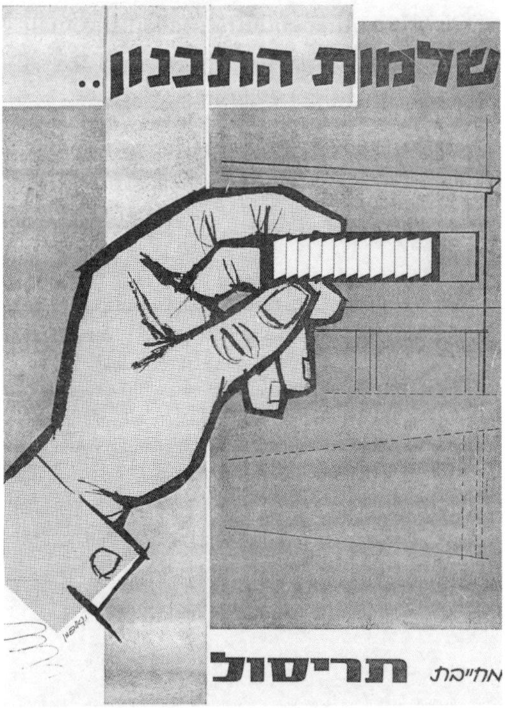


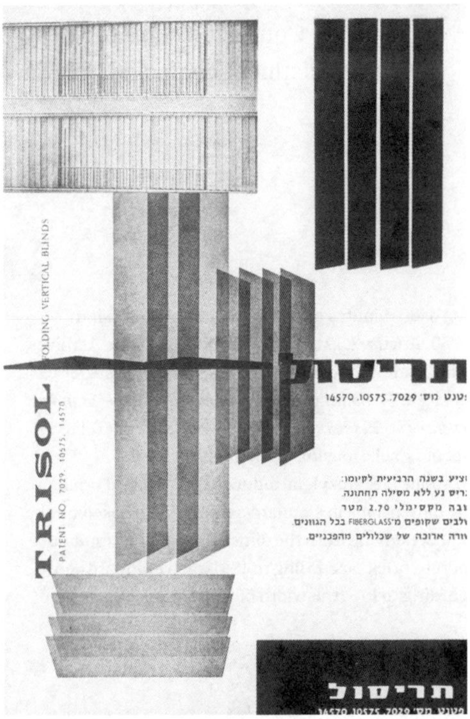

few years it had become a commonplace marker of the Israeli apartment building. The shortcomings of the "Trisol" were its weight, its fragility, and its delicate mechanism.

The popular use of the "Trisol" to enclose balconies invoked numerous appropriations by prominent architects, who managed to transform its vernacular quality into stylized elevations. A particularly elegant example is the apartment building designed by Avraham Yasky and Amnon Alexandroni on the corner of the Shmaryahu Levin and HaNevi'im streets in Tel Aviv, which lays the "Trisol" widthwise and alternates it with quasi-Oriental wooden lattices to create a flat screen-façade.

In 1961 the Trisol company invented a plastic blind with an aluminum frame, replacing the cumbersome asbestos blind. In 1964 the aluminum pocket window was developed; together with the plastic blind, it replaced the wooden windows and wooden blinds in popular construction. Due to its light weight, low technology, and cheap price, the plastic-aluminum Trisol became the most ubiquitous architectural gadget in Israel for decades.

The Trisol offered the prospect of enclosing balconies and extending apartments without sealing them; effortless and fairly exact control over the amount of light, air, and privacy indoors; and inexpensive, instantaneous, durable, "temporary" (hence requiring no permit), almost do-it-yourself installation. All of this proved particularly suitable to the local material and mental climate. From the late 1950s to the late 1970s and beyond, the Trisol was the philosopher's stone of Israeli domesticity, turning the austere housing block and the existentially minimal dwelling unit into makeshift platforms and transforming the dweller into an amateur architect-builder relentlessly inventing ways and means to frame, attach, adjust, expand, disguise, and interpret the urban bylaws in his own way.

Concerted efforts to export the "Trisol" to other countries failed: it remains a distinctively Israeli artifact. ■

1 Dov Yosef, minutes of Israeli Government Session #29/30, August 2, 1949 [in Hebrew] (Israel State Archives).

2 David Tenne, introduction to *Principles and Details for the Planning of Standard Construction Details; Part I: Standard Carpentry for Residential Buildings* [in Hebrew] (Tel Aviv: State of Israel, Housing Ministry, 1963), p. III.

3 Alexander Piekarczyk introduces the standard brick: "The dimensions in standard carpentry are based on the module, deriving from the dimensions of the standard concrete brick, according to IS [Israeli Standard] no. 5. According to IS 5, the width of the block is 40 cm. The construction seam between bricks is of a width of 1 cm. Brick plus seam of 41 cm = 1 cm + 40 cm, equaling two block-modules. [...] By this same Israeli Standard, the height of the block is 20 cm. Its height with the seam – 21 cm = 1 cm + 20 cm." Alexander Piekarczyk, "Principles of the Planning of Standard Carpentry," in *Principles and Details*, p. VII.

4 Shmuel Rosov, "A New Folding Blind," *Journal of the Union of Engineers and Architects in Israel* 3 [in Hebrew] (1954), p. 5.

⑥ People's culture house, Beersheba, 1955. Zeev Rechter, Moshe Zarhi, Yaacov Rechter.
⑦ Computer and Information Systems Center, Human Resources Corps, IDF, Ramat Gan, early 1960s. Aba Elhanani, Israel Lotan.
⑧ Computer and Information Systems Center, Human Resources Corps, IDF, Ramat Gan, early 1960s. Aba Elhanani, Israel Lotan.
⑨ Classroom corridor, Medical Research Institute, Givat Ram campus, Hebrew University, Jerusalem, 1955. David Anatol Brutzkus. Photographer: Alfred Bernheim. Hebrew University Photography Archive.
⑩ Beit Brodetsky immigrant hostel, Tel Aviv, 1956–1960. Robert Bennett. Photographer: Benny Bedarshi.

⑥

⑦

⑧

⑨

⑩

⑪

⑬

⑫

⑭

15

20

21

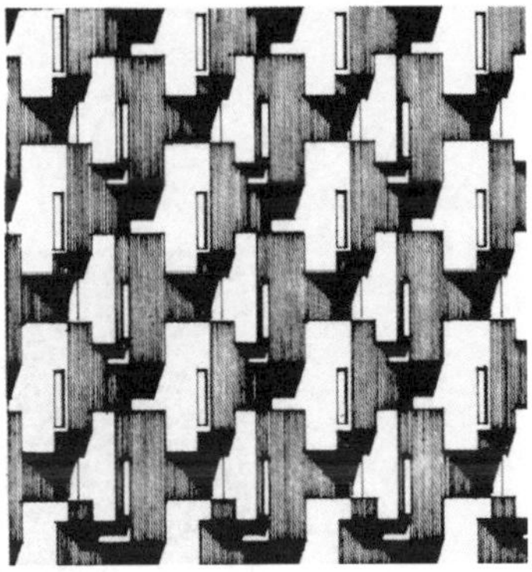

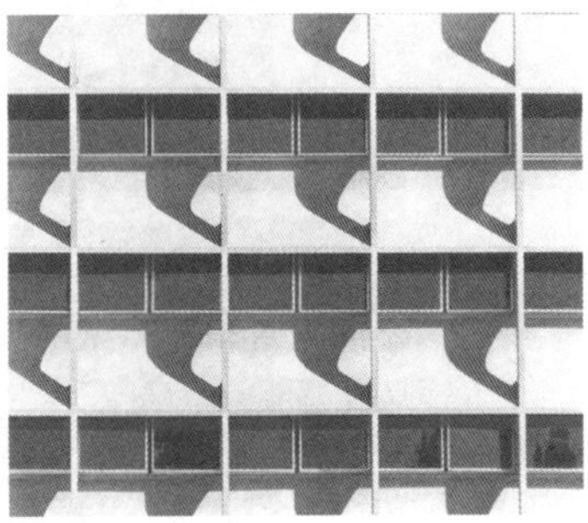

16 17 18 19

⑪–⑫ Apartment building, Tel Aviv, 1959. Avraham Yasky, Amnon Alexandroni.
⑬ Apartment building, Tel Aviv, 1961. Avraham Yasky, Amnon Alexandroni.
⑭ Apartment building, Tel Aviv, 1955. Avraham Yasky, Shimon Powsner.
⑮ Dan Hotel, Tel Aviv, 1960s. Heinz Fenchel. Photographer: Yitzhak Kalter.
⑯–⑱ Brise-soleil patterns of various hospital façades, early 1970s. Arieh Sharon, Eldar Sharon.
⑲ Israel-America House Tel Aviv, 1970–1973. Detail. Arieh Sharon, Eldar Sharon, M. Tintner.
⑳–㉑ Soroka Medical Center, Beersheba, 1954–1964. Ventilated corridor. Arieh Sharon, Benjamin Idelson, Micha Amitai, Ora Faradis.
㉒–㉓ Arieh Sharon family house, Tel Aviv, 1960. Arieh Sharon.

㉒

㉓

# Luxus

# Israeli Designers Still Seeking a Style

TEL AVIV—Twenty-four years after her birth, Israel's character—in architecture and design as well as other areas—is still developing.

"There is no Israeli style yet," says Rafi Blumenfeld, a leading designer. "If you find a good home it is not Israeli but acquired abroad.

"We have no original materials of beauty that can inspire style, no great traditions of design like the Dutch and the Danes, no special ways of life, like the Japanese.

"Our history was one of life in ghettos, and Jews looked upon culture as the culture of the Book. All other cultures were neglected. Our tradition produced scientists, musicians, doctors, but in building—we were not associated with it."

Mr. Blumenfeld maintains that the absence of a tradition makes Israelis good designers. "We have a complex about being backward," he says. "We are eager to know what is going on elsewhere, which American or Danish designers are not."

And in some areas, he says, Israelis already excel: "We have good painters, weavers, cabinetmakers. Our craftsmen and artists give a certain flair to simple, contemporary homes. Accessories will give an air of Israeli design, but this is a matter of decoration, not applied art."

Mr. Blumenfeld heads a 20-member staff with offices in Jerusalem and Tel Aviv. His firm is working on three hospitals, two universities, seven hotels, two city libraries, two department stores and ten homes.

Dora Gad, who designed the Israel Museum in Jerusalem, El Al Israel Airlines, Boeing 747 interiors, the Bezalal Art Academy in Jerusalem and the Hilton Tel Aviv, said, "Style develops slowly. It will take more than two or three generations."

In the interiors of El Al's jumbo jets Mrs. Gad used strong colors—white, magenta, orange, deep blues and silver.

Bright stripes run the length of the planes, giving "a feeling of space, strong horizontal direction." The colors, the designer said, "stress the fact of modern space and giving a feeling of flight."

They are also used for El Al's seating arrangements, uniforms of flight personnel and even such things as serving carts and blankets. Mrs. Gad also designed El Al's Zurich ticket office, in which she tried to suggest a Middle East mood. Tiles on the wall and floor, in white and brown tones, are designed to suggest the warmth and cold of Israel, she said, as is a wool rug in brown and blue that covers the ceiling. These warm tones are in striking contrast to the red and blue floor-to-ceiling columns.

Mrs. Gad, who is working on El Al's terminal at Kennedy Airport, says all the work she has done for the airline is coordinated and created to reflect the image of the company.

"It has to show that the company buys the latest equipment," she says, "and this gives the passenger a feeling of confidence. If everything is coordinated then the passenger feels it has been created for him."

Mrs. Gad said she does not like to design home interiors. "If you want to do a good job you must get very involved with the family. They become dependent on you and want you to do more. I am more concerned with how the home is lit, if it is done in warm or cold tones. I am more concerned with that than with choosing the furniture."

She agrees with Mr. Blumenfeld that Israel looks outward for her style of life.

"We have no neighbors, we live in a sort of vacuum. An Israeli, unable to go to Beirut, goes to New York, so we have to be more interested in the world at large than any other Middle Eastern country."

Mrs. Gad praised the craftsmen who came to Israel during the nineteen-thirties from Bulgaria, Germany and Poland, but said their skills are not being learned by their children. "In other, larger countries, where you can make thousands of pieces of one design," she said, "craftsmen were merged into industry, and the government assisted the development of the industry. We don't have the small craftsmen or the industry. We're riding two chairs, that's why we look to imports."

The problem has been eased for the consumer, though, since the Six-Day War of 1967, when former Egyptian and Jordanian territories were acquired. "Now Israelis can buy Bedouin rugs from Gaza or the Old City without spending much money," Mrs. Gad said. "Our market has been enriched by Arab crafts such as Hebron glass, Arab stools and wicker chairs. If you have good taste, this can enhance living space. You don't have to have Danish furniture."

Unlike interior designers in the United States, Israelis in the profession are trained architects. Both Mr. Blumenfeld and Mrs. Gad consider themselves architects first. When she works for El Al or Hilton, Mrs. Gad said, "I do the architecture and interior at the same time. You create everything at the same time. You don't just decorate. It grows from the very beginning, and you give it your heart and mind."

Mr. Blumenfeld, who came to Israel in 1933 from his native Germany, served with the Jewish Brigade in the British Army and was wounded during World War II in Holland. He received a Government grant to study architecture in London, and in 1952 opened his own office in "interior architecture."

Mr. Blumenfeld said it is easier for a European to fit into the Israeli interior-design profession than for an American.

"If we are designing a home," he explains, "90 per cent of the manufacturing is done by small workshops, so we have to prepare shop drawings for furniture, fittings, ceilings, doors. Everything has to be specified and then put out for bid.

"So we must know, besides decorating schemes, shop drawings, which are not required of American designers because of mass production and availability from catalogues. In America you get a specialist. Here you have to be more or less all-around."

Mr. Blumenfeld feels it will take time to produce an Israeli style. "To bring about a culture is a lengthy process. It comes with generations. We have to be taught beauty. . . . We need a certain peace of mind which can only come with time."

Yet, as more immigrants from the Western countries flow into Israel and more Israelis travel abroad, their impact is being felt. As more money is put into circulation for home furnishings, Israeli manufacturers are starting to devote time to design and quality, and their products are starting to win a share of the market.

The combination of new immigrants, industrial development and travel abroad "is creating a bigger demand for good design," Mr. Blumenfeld says, "but original Israeli design will have to take its course."

①

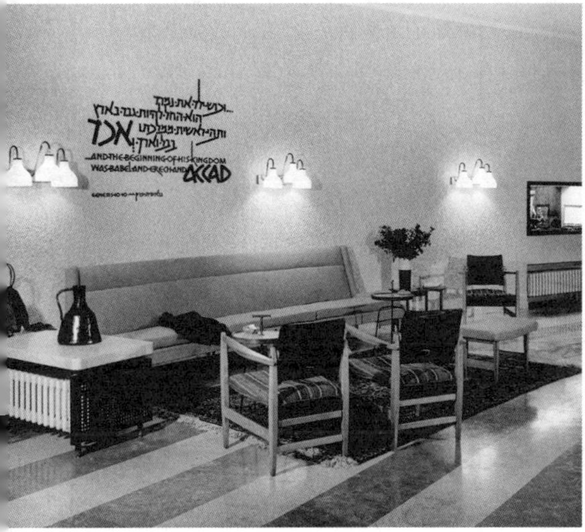


②

## Hotel Interiors

③

④

⑤

① Laurence J. Peit, "Designers in Israel Still Seeking a Style," *New York Times*, August 13, 1972.
② Dan Accadia Hotel, Herzliya Pituach, 1954–1955. Werner Joseph Wittkower. Interior design: Dora Gad, Yehezkel Gad.
③ Dan Hotel, Tel Aviv, 1950–1953. Interior design: Heinz Fenchel.
④ Dan Accadia Hotel, Herzliya Pituach, 1954–1955. Werner Joseph Wittkower. Interior design: Dora Gad, Yehezkel Gad.
⑤ Sharon Hotel, Herzliya Pituach, 1953–1957. Zeev Rechter. Interior design: Dora Gad, Yehezkel Gad.

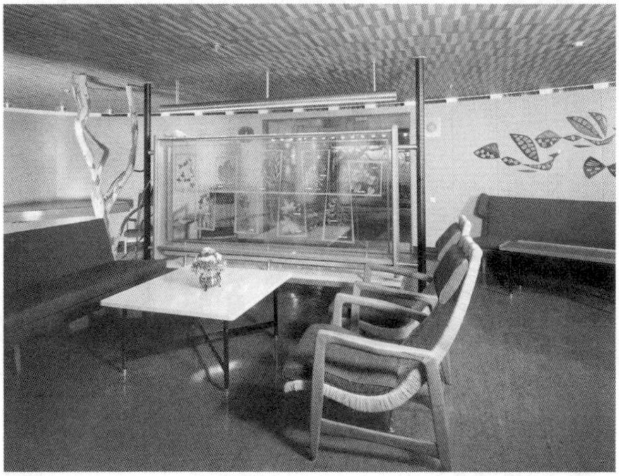

⑥

⑦

⑧

⑨

⑥ Interior of the ship *Israel*, 1954–1955. Munio Gitai Weinraub, Al Mansfeld, Dora Gad, Yehezkel Gad.
⑦ The reading room on the ship *Herzl*, ZIM shipping company, 1957–1958. Munio Gitai Weinraub, Al Mansfeld, Dora Gad, Yehezkel Gad.
⑧ Interior of the ship *Israel*, ZIM shipping company, 1955. Munio Gitai Weinraub, Al Mansfeld, Dora and Yehezkel Gad.
⑨ Interior of the ship *Shalom*, ZIM shipping company, 1964. Munio Gitai Weinraub, Al Mansfeld, Dora Gad, Yehezkel Gad.
⑩ Interior of the ship *Shalom*, ZIM shipping company, 1964. Munio Gitai Weinraub, Al Mansfeld, Dora Gad, Yehezkel Gad.
⑪ Interior of the ship *Shalom*, ZIM shipping company, 1964. Munio Gitai Weinraub, Al Mansfeld, Dora Gad, Yehezkel Gad.

⑩

⑪

⑫

⑬

⑭

⑮

⑯

⑰

⑱

⑫ Zilberg House, Savion, 1960. Mordechai Ben-Horin.
⑬ Wertheimer House, Ramat Gan, 1957. Israel Lotan.
⑭ Lipson House, Afeka, Tel Aviv, 1962. Avraham Yasky, Amnon Alexandroni.
⑮ Lipson House, Afeka, Tel Aviv, 1962. Avraham Yaky, Amnon Alexandroni.
⑯ Klir House, Savyon, 1964–1967. Ram Karmi.
⑰ Private house, Ramat Hasharon, 1951–1952. Moshe Zarhi.
⑱ Shavit House, Herzliya Pituach, 1960. Avraham Yasky, Amnon Alexandroni.

⑲

⑳

㉑

⑲ Kahane House, Ramat Gan, 1951–1952. Yaacov Rechter.
⑳ Eilyn House, Haifa, 1970. Al Mansfeld, Daniel Havkin.
㉑ Wiener House, Tivon, 1961. Perspective. Shimon Shapiro.
㉒ Weiss House, Tivon, 1958. Perspective. Shimon Shapiro.
㉓ Eisenberg House, Savyon, Tel Aviv, 1966–1967. Mordechai Ben-Horin.
㉔ Leshem House, Herzliya, 1972. Ziona Leshem.

㉒

㉓

㉔

# DOSSIER:
# DORA GAD’S DESIGNS

㉕

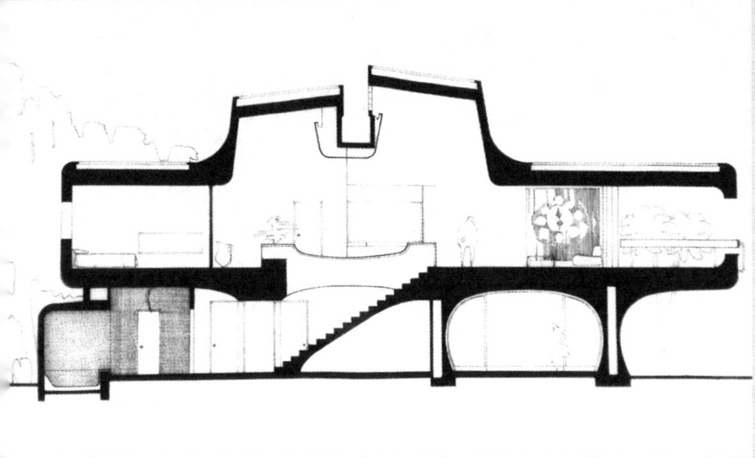

(26)

(25) Dora Gad, 1960s. Photographer: Peter Herzog.
(26) Dora Gad's house, Caesarea, 1974. Section. Dora Gad.

Dora Gad studied architecture at the Technische Hochschule in Vienna from 1930 to 1934 and immigrated to Tel Aviv in 1936. There, she initially worked for the architects Yehoshua Steinbock and Oskar Kaufmann (who designed the Volksbühne in Berlin and the Habima theater in Tel Aviv). By 1938 she and her husband, Yehezkel Goldberg, had begun to take on occasional small-scale projects, such as the design of the Elite Chocolate Shop and Café Landwer in Tel Aviv. Gad established herself as an interior designer.[1]

In the catalogue for a retrospective exhibition of her works at the Tel Aviv Museum of Art, she is introduced as no less than the national tastemaker:

> Some believed that along these shores one could have set up a relaxed version of Europe with top hats and white gloves, with a white parasol for the sunshine. She was never one of those. Quite the opposite: she loved the wildness and the primitiveness when she came to the country, and afterwards she was identified, more than any other architect, with "Israeliness," the representative of this country overseas.[2]

Architectural critic Esther Zandberg, in her essay "Panta Rei" for the exhibition catalogue, elaborates on the centrality of Dora Gad's work in the formation of a distinctive Israeli taste and look:

> Her creations, in my opinion, propose a basic premise that there should be a local hue and an Israeli taste, in contrast to the other basic premises that have reconciled themselves to international taste. [...] This premise is grounded, first of all, in the list of projects that Dora Gad has planned or has collaborated in designing. The list is not a random one, and even a hasty glance at a partial list will point to a common denominator: the home of Moshe Sharett [the second prime minister of Israel, from 1954 to 1955] in Ramat Gan; the Zim passenger liners and the company's offices in Israel and abroad; the first Boeings of El Al and the company's branches abroad; the Knesset [parliament] building and the Israel Museum [...]; and the Hilton hotels in Tel Aviv and Jerusalem.
>
> All these projects fit the definition of public, representative, even national projects. Dora Gad's interior design, then, is part of the marketing of the image of the Israeli, and of the definition of his culture and taste, in his own eyes as well as for export purposes. This perhaps is the place to ask [...]: was it Dora Gad who invented this "Israeliness," or has what she invented come to be perceived as Israeli? By the way, Gad was the first to introduce the philodendron pot-plants into private living rooms and public halls which took the country by storm during the sixties and seventies and became a kind of symbol of the beginnings of local bourgeoisification.[3] ■

1 See Ran Shechori, ed., *Dora Gad: The Israeli Presence in Interior Design* (Tel Aviv: Architecture of Israel, 1997), pp. 11–19.
2 Ibid., p. 9.
3 Esther Zandberg, "Panta Rei," in *Dora Gad: The Israeli Presence*, pp. 249–251.

㉗

㉘

㉙

㉗ El Al Agency, London, 1970s. Interior design: Dora Gad. Photographer: Edgar Hyman.
㉘ ZIM Agency, Paris, 1960s. Interior design: Dora Gad. Photographer: Edgar Hyman.
㉙ El Al Agency, Amsterdam, 1970s. Interior design: Dora Gad.
㉚ Winning entry for the Regulo D'oro competition, Italy, 1966. Prototype of a flower pavilion for the Bedouin Market. Dora Gad.
㉛ Winning entry for the Regulo D'oro competition, Italy, 1966. Prototype of a flower pavilion for the Bedouin Market. Dora Gad.
㉜ Dora Gad presenting her winning entry for the Regulo D'oro competition, 1966.

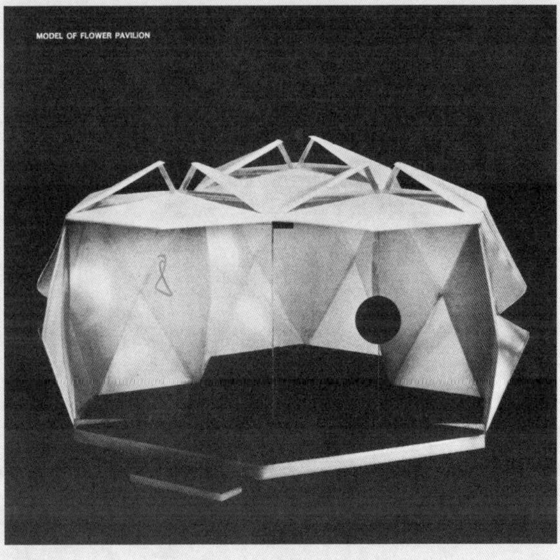


㉚ ㉛

㉜

㉝

㉞

㉟

(36)

(37)

(38)

(33) The Israel Museum, Jerusalem, 1963. Interior perspective. Dora Gad, Al Mansfeld.
(34) Archaeology Department of the Israel Museum, Jerusalem. Interior and display design: Dora Gad.
(35) Archaeology Department of the Israel Museum, Jerusalem. Interior and display design: Dora Gad.
(36) Knesset building, Jerusalem, 1966. Interior design: Dora Gad. Photographer: David Rubinger.
(37) Knesset building, Jerusalem, 1966. Interior design: Dora Gad. Painting: Marc Chagall. Photographer: Hillel Burger.
(38) Knesset building, Jerusalem, 1966. Interior design: Dora Gad. Painting: Marc Chagall. Photographer: Hillel Burger.

# Tropics

# Proxy Colonialism: The Export of Israeli Architecture to Africa and Asia

*"I work here," he added a moment later [...].*
*"At what, if I may ask?" inquired Friedrich.*
*The scientist's eyes grew dreamy as he replied, "At the opening up of Africa."*
*The visitors mistrusted their ears. Was the seeker after scientific truth a bit mad?*
*"Did you say, 'at the opening up of Africa'?" asked Kingscourt, suspicion gleaming in his eye.*
*"Yes, Mr. Kingscourt. That is to say, I hope to find the cure for malaria. We have overcome it here in Palestine thanks to the drainage of the swamps, canalization, and the eucalyptus forests. But conditions are different in Africa. The same measures cannot be taken there because the prerequisite—mass immigration—is not present. The white colonist goes under in Africa. That country can be opened up to civilization only after malaria has been subdued. Only then will enormous areas become available for the surplus populations of Europe. And only then will the proletarian masses find a healthy outlet. Understand?"*
*Kingscourt laughed. "You want to cart off the whites to the black continent, you wonder-worker!"*
*"Not only the whites!" replied Steineck, gravely. "The blacks as well. There is still one problem of racial misfortune unsolved. The depths of that problem, in all their horror, only a Jew can grasp. I mean the Negro problem. Don't laugh, Mr. Kingscourt. Think of the hair-raising horrors of the slave trade. Human beings, because their skins are black, are stolen, carried off, and sold. Their descendants grow up in alien surroundings despised and hated because their skin is differently pigmented. I am not ashamed to say, though I'll be thought ridiculous, now that I have lived to see the restoration of the Jews, I should like to pave the way for the restoration of the Negroes."*

Theodor Herzl,
*Old-New Land (Altneuland)*, 1902[1]

①

Africa is deeply rooted in the Zionist imagination. In *Old-New Land*, a second-rate utopian novel which is nonetheless commonly referred to as the clairvoyant founding text of political Zionism, Jews self-identify as both the ultimate exiles of the world (hence the compulsion to identify with the "Negro problem") and as modernity's migrant experts, the nomad agents of reform and progress. The scientist's lab in this text is an unequivocal metonymy of the Jewish colony. Its allusion could hardly be mistaken: if the Jews are to settle, it is in order to resolve the universal demographic and territorial conundrum. Literary Zion, here and in other seminal visionary texts of the time, is by and large an institute for colonial training, whereby agronomy, epidemiology, and *Arbeitswissenschaft* are rehearsed, and universal issues of immigration and redistribution of the means of production are debated.

Such is the genre of utopian fiction; it draws its textual pleasures precisely from the flow of slippages between the insatiable colonialist libido and the prudent reformist agenda. And as for the writer of the utopia, he is destined to eternal perplexity, as we may learn from the epilogue of *Old-New Land*: "I have meant to compose an instructive poem. Some will say it contains more poetry than instruction. That it has more instruction than poetry will be the verdict of others."[2]

②

A year after the publication of *Old-New Land*, at the Sixth Zionist Congress in 1903, Herzl announced his Uganda Plan for a provisional Jewish state in East Africa. The imaginary spilled over into the real. After negotiations with the British Colonial Secretary, Joseph Chamberlain, an "investigatory commission" was sent to examine the proposed territory, and the Jewish Territorialist Organization (JTO) was formed by supporters of the African interim plan. Between 1903 and 1905 expeditions were sent to locations in Mesopotamia, Cyrenaica (Libya), and Angola. Herzl died in 1904. The "Territorialists" (perhaps, ironically, the last non-territorial Zionists) proved to represent only a contested minority within the Jewish assembly. The poetry of "the opening up of Africa" would first become instructive fifty years later, with the work of emissary planners, engineers, and architects from the newly formed State of Israel.

The work of Israeli planners and architects in Africa and Asia—an activity remarkable in its relative scope and distribution for a small developing country—was a direct by-product of Israeli diplomacy in the "Third World" during the

① Members of the international seminar conference on housing and their Israeli hosts, Haifa, 1960.
② Architect Zalman Einav presenting a project in Addis Ababa to Emperor Haile Selassie, 1965.

③ Golda Meir with President Félix Houphouët-Boigny at Hôtel Ivoire Intercontinental, Ivory Coast, late 1960s. Wolfson-Color-Mayer Collection.
④ "Maon": An idea for a small new town designed by the Israeli Institute of Planning and Development, 1960s.

1950s and 1960s. The specter of political and economic isolation, which only increased following Israel's exclusion from the first Afro-Asian Conference in Bandung in 1955, impelled Israel to seek recognition and legitimacy and to establish networks of relationships with the new nations of the world. In the framework of such a diplomatic strategy, which often assumed a quasi-spiritual and missionary character, Israel turned to countries in Asia and Africa. These were chosen according to several criteria: first, they were in the early phases of independence at the time; second, they were seeking assistance to attain their goals of modernization; and third, they had not as yet taken a stance in the Arab-Israeli conflict.

Israel offered itself, and indeed was perceived, as an agent of modernity and progress. But more importantly, Israel was seen as a country that had itself recently been decolonized, attained independence, and garnered experience in the problems besetting developing countries. Moreover, Israel's relative political and economic weakness enabled the receiving countries to accept its aid without the risk of entering into the kind of dependency that came with sponsorship by the large powers at the height of the Cold War.

The export of architecture and planning, even if executed by private companies or individual consultants, was performed in the context of governmental aid and cooperation programs devised in 1952 by Golda Meir, foreign minister at the time, in the hopes of gaining political support at the United Nations Assembly in return. These aid programs began in Asia, specifically in Burma, and then spread to Africa. No fewer than twenty-three official Israeli institutions were involved in the programs, which were coordinated by the Agency for International Development Cooperation (Mashav) of the Israeli Ministry of Foreign Affairs.[3]

By 1957, Israel had established diplomatic relations with thirty-three African nations, including practically all of the black nations of sub-Saharan Africa, and had rapidly transformed into a major factor in the continent. To get a sense of its efforts, by 1964, the Israeli ratio of such exports to its total population was almost twice that of all the OECD countries combined. However, the so-called "honeymoon period" of the Israeli-African relationship soon came to an end. These relations were broken off in 1973 as a result of Arab pressure and the oil crisis.[4] In her autobiography, published just two years after the collapse of her African doctrine, Golda Meir wrote:

③

> We did what we did in Africa not because it was just a policy of enlightened self-interest—a matter of *quid pro quo*—but because it was a continuation of our own most valued traditions [...].
>
> [...] I am prouder of Israel's International Cooperation Programme and of the technical aid we gave to the people of Africa than I am of any other single project we have ever undertaken.[5]

In Africa, Israel chiefly proffered agricultural know-how, focusing specifically on introducing new technologies and crops; establishing agricultural farms and training centers; organizing rural institutions; and planning comprehensive regional and rural development projects.[6] But Israel was also engaged in other fields, such as medicine and public health, workers' unions and youth organizations, social work and community development, and certainly security and military training. In addition, African students arrived in Israel to receive training in various courses and seminars at the Afro-Asian Institute for Labor Studies and Cooperation, established by the Israeli Labor Federation.

④

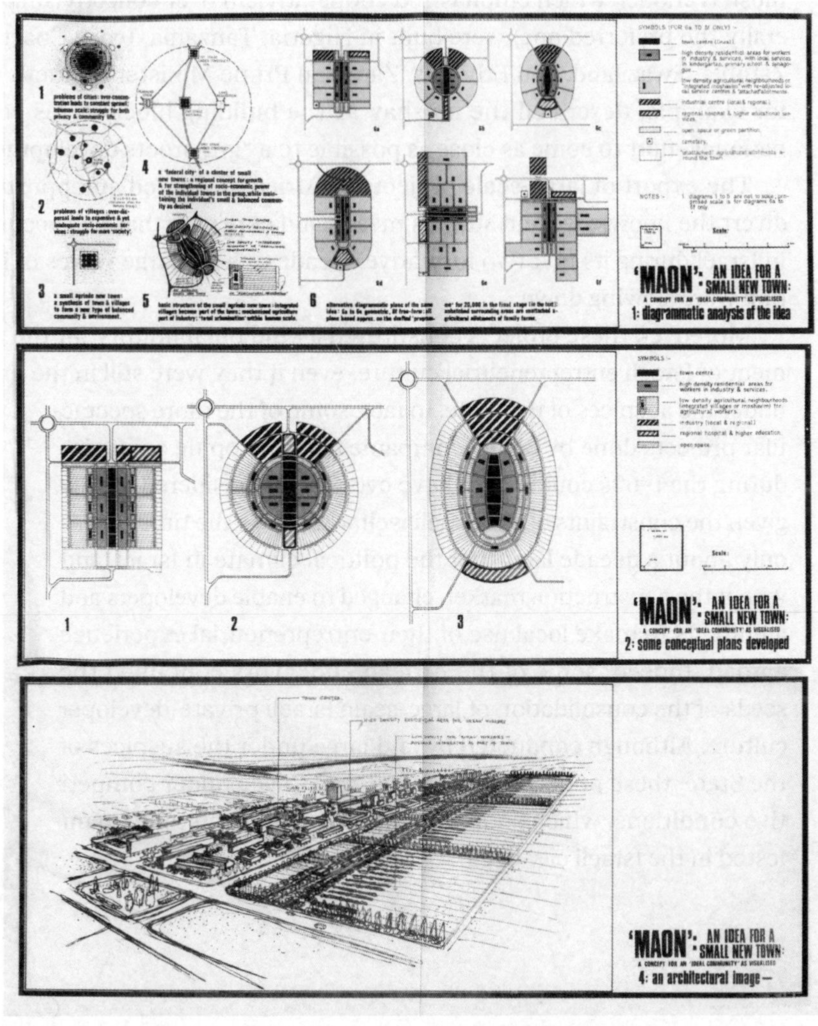

The Israeli ministries of foreign affairs and of housing, in collaboration with the Jewish Agency, established a planning institute especially to provide architectural and infrastructural services for developing countries. Called the Institute of Planning and Development (IPD), it supplied work for local planners and experts who had just completed the many national development missions and extensive public works of the 1950s in Israel. The IPD was headed by senior Israeli planners, and its commissions included regional plans for the nations of Chad (1963) and Sierra Leone (1965). These plans were attempts at the application or reinterpretation of Israel's master plan of 1950 (aka "the Sharon Plan") in Africa. By promulgating their local experience in managing the interrelations between urban centers and the agrarian hinterland, these experts functioned as conduits, transmitting modern regional theories, such as Walter Christaller's central-place theory, which were still intellectually fashionable during the 1960s.

The migration of doctrines, whether original or derivative, found its epitome in the proposed export of the Israeli collective-settlement prototypes, the kibbutz and the moshav, to African countries that were seeking models for developing peripheral areas and intensive agriculture. Such settlements (the moshav model, which emphasized cooperativism over collectivism, was generally the preferred one) were built in Nigeria, Tanzania, Ivory Coast, Kenya, Zambia, Swaziland, and Ethiopia. Zambian Prime Minister Kenneth Kaunda, for example, described the moshav as the building block in his country's national effort to come as close as possible to a "grassroots development."

The export of large-scale projects to Africa presented an opportunity to divert the knowledge and surplus means and expertise that had accumulated in Israel during its first two formative decades, as the large waves of immigration were slowing down.

Moreover, these projects constituted a kind of laboratory for the development of Israeli entrepreneurial culture, even if they were still in the name and under the auspices of the State. In fact, some of the more spectacular projects done by Israeli companies in developing countries during the 1960s could never have even been considered locally, given the constraints of the Israeli welfare state of the time. It was only about a decade later that the political climate in Israel, and with it the construction market, changed to enable developers and architects to make local use of their entrepreneurial experience abroad. Indeed, some of the African endeavors contained the seeds of the consolidation of large-scale Israeli private-developer culture. Although conducted by and large under the auspices of the State, these projects nonetheless took place under competitive conditions, which soon thereafter would begin to be manifested in the Israeli city itself.

⑤

⑤ A new hotel built by the Israeli-Nigerian "Niger-Sol" company, Ibadan, Nigeria, 1962.
⑥ Ife University (Obafemi Awolowo University), Ile-Ife, Osun, Nigeria, 1960s. Model. Arieh Sharon.

Infrastructure, such as roads, airports, and water and drainage systems, was built primarily by the Solel Boneh company, which established partnerships and opened up agencies in Africa, Asia, and Latin America. Solel Boneh was a public company that belonged to the Histadrut and was in effect controlled by the government, in order to achieve political objectives. Golda Meir aspired to turn Solel Boneh into a for-profit company, but not ostentatiously so: "I used Solel Boneh as a tool [for Zionist propaganda]; I don't want you to lose money over there, but for God's sake, no big profits."[7] Solel Boneh's strategy was to break into new markets through the establishment of joint companies which would be transferred to the host country after an initial start-up and mentoring period of five years. In this way, administrative and technical knowledge was transmitted, and the developing countries were able to carry out large projects that met international standards on their own, thus lessening their dependency on foreign companies. Such partnerships were established in Nigeria, Ghana, Sierra Leone, and Ivory Coast. After the nationalization of the daughter companies of Solel Boneh in Ghana, the corporation changed its "missionary" policy; in 1964 it began to work according to purely commercial considerations.[8] In many of Solel Boneh's international projects—in particular public structures, hotels, housing projects, and military facilities—the planning itself was also done by Israeli architects.

In his autobiography, *Kibbutz + Bauhaus: An Architect's Way in a New Land*, Arieh Sharon dedicated a chapter to the topic of planning in developing countries from 1960. This chapter contains in fact only a few schemes for hospitals and one fairly elaborate built project—Ife University in Nigeria—but it appears essential to the book, as though a biography of an Israeli architect of the period could not be considered complete without a portfolio of projects in developing

⑥
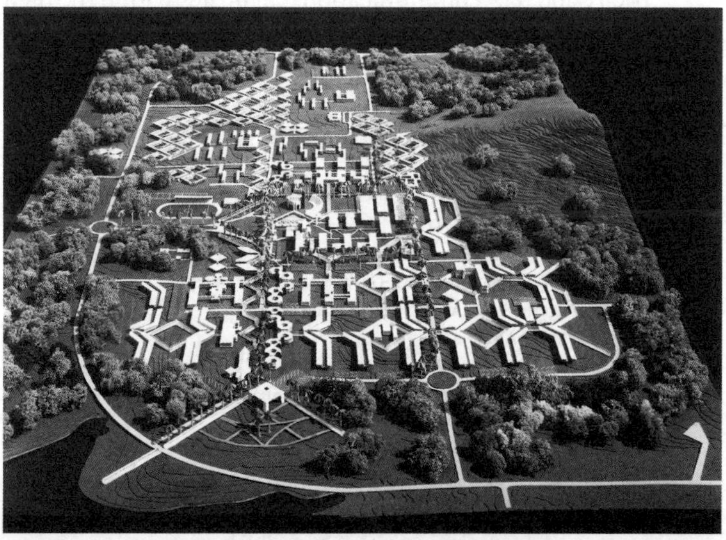

countries, some impressions of encounters with exotic cultures, and certain comments about tropical architecture. Before interpreting the contextual and pretextual circumstances of Israeli professional involvement in Africa on the whole, let us read Sharon's autobiographical chapter more closely. The prologue may sound both self-righteous and presumptuous to a foreign reader:

> Israelis have tried to contribute to the progress of new nations. The similarity of the problems makes the Israeli experience very useful to the countries concerned. Our planners and builders have applied their knowledge in the developing world.[9]

What allows Sharon to speak for Israelis in general and to introduce his own private work with such broad statements is the fact that after years as head of the Planning Department at the Labor and Construction Ministry and later at the Prime Minister's Office, he personifies the apparatus of national planning.

Sharon begins with a short description of a hospital scheme designed for developing countries, based on a flexible repetitive pavilion system with "a layout that may either be compact and dense for hot and dry countries, or loose and dispersed for hot and humid countries." Then he turns to recount his "most important challenge" in foreign territory, the building of Ife University in western ⑦
Nigeria, a project for which the work lasted almost two decades, from 1960 to 1978. What makes this story epic is Sharon's full engagement with the preliminary geographic, demographic, and infrastructural considerations of the Nigerian government. First commissioned to advise the government on the choice of site for the future university, he surveyed sixteen medium-sized towns and compiled data on their socio-economic structures and their services, amenities, and communication networks. In his report to the Nigerian government he indicates that:

> The town of Ife seemed to be the most appropriate site, considering the basic development factors and the existing services of water supply, elec- ⑧
> tricity and tele-communication. [...] Ife lies within the high-forest belt of the

⑦ Ife University (Obafemi Awolowo University), Faculty of Humanities. Ile-Ife, Osun, Nigeria, 1962. Arieh Sharon. Arieh Sharon Digital Archive.
⑧–⑨ Ife University (Obafemi Awolowo University), The Institute of Education. Ile-Ife, Osun, Nigeria, 1970. Arieh Sharon, Eldar Sharon. Arieh Sharon Digital Archive.
⑩ Ife University (Obafemi Awolowo University), The Library. Ile-Ife, Osun, Nigeria, 1966. Arieh Sharon, Eldar Sharon. Arieh Sharon Digital Archive.
⑪ Ife University (Obafemi Awolowo University), The Assembly Hall. Ile-Ife, Osun, Nigeria, 1970. Arieh Sharon, Eldar Sharon. Arieh Sharon Digital Archive.

⑨

⑩

⑪

⑫

⑬

⑭

⑫ Ife University (Obafemi Awolowo University), The Assembly Hall.. Ile-Ife, Osun, Nigeria, 1970. Arieh Sharon, Eldar Sharon. Arieh Sharon Digital Archive.
⑬ Ife University (Obafemi Awolowo University), The Secretariat. Ile-Ife, Osun, Nigeria, 1968. Arieh Sharon, Eldar Sharon.
⑭ Ife University (Obafemi Awolowo University), The Library. Ile-Ife, Osun, Nigeria, 1966. Arieh Sharon, Eldar Sharon.
⑮ Ife University (Obafemi Awolowo University), Postcard.

> region, 800 meters above sea level. Its climatic conditions of rainfall, temperature and humidity, can be regarded as favorable. […] The town is centrally located in the western region and favorably connected with other towns. […] Of special architectural interest is the Ife museum, exhibiting world-famous bronze heads. In Ife originated the fine terracotta sculptures, which had been evident only in the ancient Nok culture, and it is therefore regarded as the cradle of Yoruba culture.[10]

Following Sharon's report, the Nigerian government decided to send a delegation, consisting of "the ministers of culture and Labor, the leader of the Opposition, several professors of the future university and the advising architect and town planner,"[11] to study the plans of some British, American, and South American universities. The visit to the new university in Mexico City aroused a negative feeling of uncalled-for enormity. "Somehow each of us had in mind a smaller university, more human and intimate." But "the delegation was nevertheless strongly impressed by the great frescoes on the walls, painted by the famous Mexican artists Diego Rivera, Orozco and Siqueiros."[12] This is the moment when Sharon reveals his sources of inspiration and builds up his atavistic alibi:

> Later on, during the Ife construction, I was able to exploit these impressions by proposing sculptural Yoruba elements in the Ife University buildings. But the greatest lesson was given to us by the Aztecs' and the Mayans' old towns, the perfect architectural example of an urban ensemble, where the pyramidal temples, piazzas and sacred courtyards meet in such a convincing synthesis of order and space relations.[13]

⑮

INIVERSITY OF IFE, ILE-IFE, NIGERIA.
"Scenes From the most Beautiful Campus in Africa"

The delegation's next visit was to Brasília, where, "contrary to the sterile emptiness between the public buildings" designed by Niemeyer, "we saw the compactness of the residential super-blocks looking into one another."[14] The last visit was to Israel, where the campus of the Hebrew University in Givat Ram, Jerusalem, had just been completed. The delegation's impression was positive: "It was obviously the result of the simple character of the buildings, courtyards and gardens and the modest scale of teaching programs and goals."[15]

As Sharon relates, then, the Givat Ram Hebrew University campus, one of the most prolific modernist projects in Israel and a prime initiation site of the postwar generation of local architects, is the ur-form of the Ife University campus. Its *sachlich* rigor, small size, and efficient circulation—interwoven patios and gardens, covered walkways, and parallel north-south elevations—would be exported to the Nigerian wooded countryside. Interestingly enough, its very compactness was considered both practically desirable and culturally contextual. "We agreed with the professors that, in view of the local conditions and customs [...] the layout of the campus [...] should be as compact as possible," Sharon recalls.[16] Inbal Ben-Asher Gitler, in her thorough study of the architecture of the Ife University campus, observes that the compact yet flexible character of Sharon's scheme for the campus was inspired both by Sharon's earlier work and by the indigenous urban fabric:

> Adopting a variant of the loose grid scheme was, moreover, akin to the succession of courtyards of the traditional afin. In addition, the imposing campus entrance gate and sculptural secretariat gate connote, in their monumentality, the importance of the gate in both Yoruba palatial architecture and shrines. Thus, the choice of layout for the campus's main core closely followed modernist schemes, yet addressed local traditions of planning and architecture.[17]

Ben-Asher Gitler seems to be convinced that Sharon had a genuine interest in both traditional and modern Nigerian art, which he collected and readily used as a depository of images, motifs, and gestures. "The concrete façades of Oduduwa Hall were painted with white abstract and geometric form [...]. These abstract murals recall Yoruba wall paintings [...]. The circle-and-triangles pattern applied to the stage façade, as well as the abstract shapes of the piazza-facing one, translate abstract Yoruba forms and repetitive patterns into a modern idiom."[18] However, Ben-Asher Gitler points at the mechanisms of appropriation and reification of native art at work here and explicates the shortcomings of decontextualization: "The reduction of Yoruba formal vocabulary and its translation into clear geometric planes, that seem to 'float' on the wall in the Oduduwa Hall murals, clearly indicates a purely formal adaptation [...]." The appearance of local art "in a novel architectural building type created an entirely new

⑯ Architects Zalman Einav and Mikael Tedros stand in front of the Ethiopian Foreign Ministry Building, which they designed, 1965. *National Geographic.*
⑰–⑱ Imperial palace, Addis Ababa, Ethiopia, 1960s. Model. Zalman Einav, Michael Tedros.

discursive space, where local art no longer directly related to the cultural spaces and realities implicitly attached to it."[19]

Apparently, then, the Ife campus holds such a seminal place in Sharon's portfolio not because he regards it a derivative adaptation of Israeli modernism, but because he holds it to be a paradigm shift in his own oeuvre toward a more culturally inquisitive and environmentally sensitive architecture. And if his intellectual and emotional attraction to the native cultures of Africa is fairly subdued in his memoirs, his newfound fascination with functionalist methodology for adapting to climatic conditions brings him back to the conception of architecture his former teacher Hannes Meyer taught him at the Bauhaus in Dessau. The text introducing the project in Sharon's autobiography not only describes climatic parameters as the major determining factors in the design process, but also explicates his own creative contribution—the inverted pyramids—in relation to the body of work of Western, mainly British,[20] architects in Africa in the 1960s:

> One of the main planning considerations was to relate the building design to the climatic factors. Most of the public buildings in Nigeria are oriented from east to west, their main elevations facing north and south, thus being protected from heat and glare. This also ensures cross-ventilation by

⑰

⑯

⑱

⑲

prevailing breezes, coming mainly from the south. Many of these buildings erected by English or local architects use as sun protection either concrete canopies and frames around the windows, or louvers and pre-cast ornamental elements around the terraces. We proposed to make the buildings self-protecting against the monsoon rain and the intensive sun and glare by cantilevering the floors one over another. The humanities building was designed accordingly as a series of reverse pyramids along a climatic and functional utility principle. [...] This solution proved useful and efficient, because all the continuous openings [...] are protected and open to catch the breeze along the whole elevation line. [...] In subsequent buildings, we used a double pyramidal building system, also ventilated vertically by open interior courtyards. Most of the buildings are raised on pillars and interspersed by open terraces, to facilitate cross-ventilation. Thus the shaded, open spaces on the ground floor were connected directly to the surrounding garden areas.[21]

Indeed, photographs of the built campus, showing well-shaded and ventilated passages framed by the buildings' skeletons and shells, support Sharon's claims for structural rather than applicative approaches to climate-responsive architecture. His project certainly does not rely on climate-protection elements and fixtures, such as "concrete canopies and frames around the windows, or louvers and pre-cast ornamental elements around the terraces." In this sense, his tropical endeavor diverges from the doctrinaire Israeli architecture of the 1950s and 1960s, of which he himself was one of the main articulators. The contextual sensibilities, sculptural plasticity, and climatic ingenuity found in Africa would henceforth inform Sharon's projects at home; they spread over the entire architectural praxis of Israel in the late 1960s and the 1970s. Inverted pyramids became commonplace, as did the integration of art and folklore in both public and private buildings.

⑲ Parliament building of Sierra Leone, Freetown, Sierra Leone, 1956–1962. Dov Karmi, Zvi Meltzer, Ram Karmi.
⑳ Entrepreneur Moshe Meir presenting a model of the Abidjan Riviera, Ivory Coast, 1966. Thomas Leitersdorf.
㉑ Hotel Ivoire Intercontinental, Abidjan Riviera, Ivory Coast, late 1960s. Thomas Leitersdorf.
㉒ Kilimanjaro Hotel, Dar es Salaam, Tanzania, 1965–1968. Moshe Yarmitzki, Gabriel Margalit, Yaacov Marco.
㉓ Safari Hotel, Mikumi National Park, Tanzania, 1966–1968. Moshe Yarmitzki, Gabriel Margalit, Yaacov Marco.

⑳

㉑

㉒

㉓

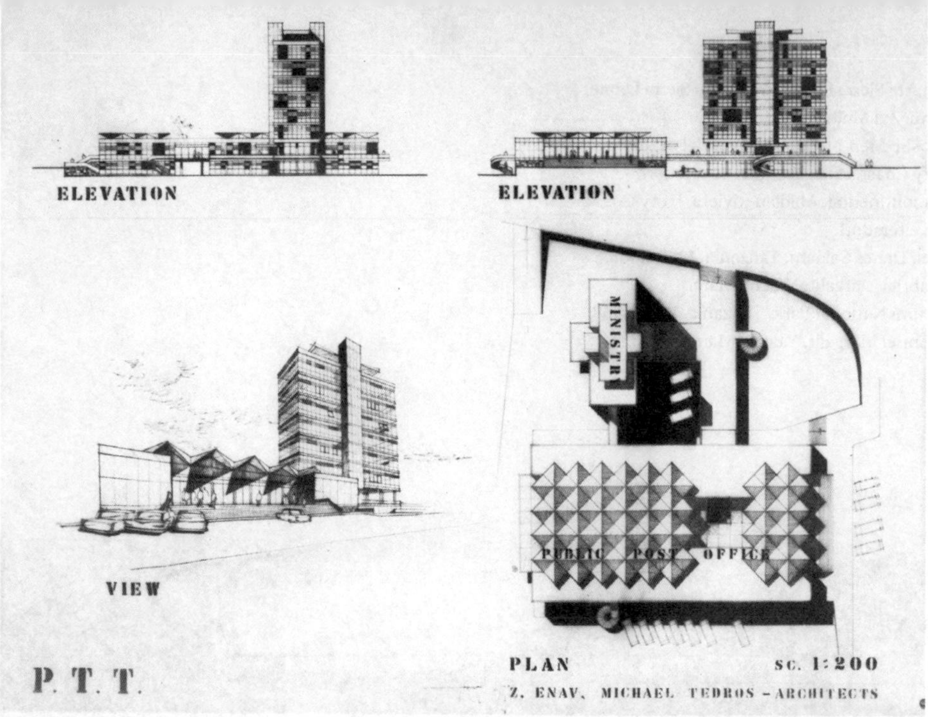


㉔

㉕

㉖

㉔ Commercial center and offices, Addis Ababa, Ethiopia, 1960s. Elevations, plan, and perspective. Zalman Einav, Michael Tedros.
㉕ American School, Ethiopia, late 1960s. Zalman Einav, Michael Tedros.
㉖ Low-cost standardized schools, Ethiopia, late 1960s. Zalman Einav, Michael Tedros.
㉗ Filwoha Thermal Baths, Addis Ababa, Ethiopia, 1959–1964. Plan. Zalman Einav, Michael Tedros.
㉘ Filwoha Thermal Baths, Addis Ababa, Ethiopia, 1959–1964. Zalman Einav, Michael Tedros.
㉙ Filwoha Thermal Baths, Addis Ababa, 1959–1964. Diagrams. Zalman Einav, Michael Tedros.

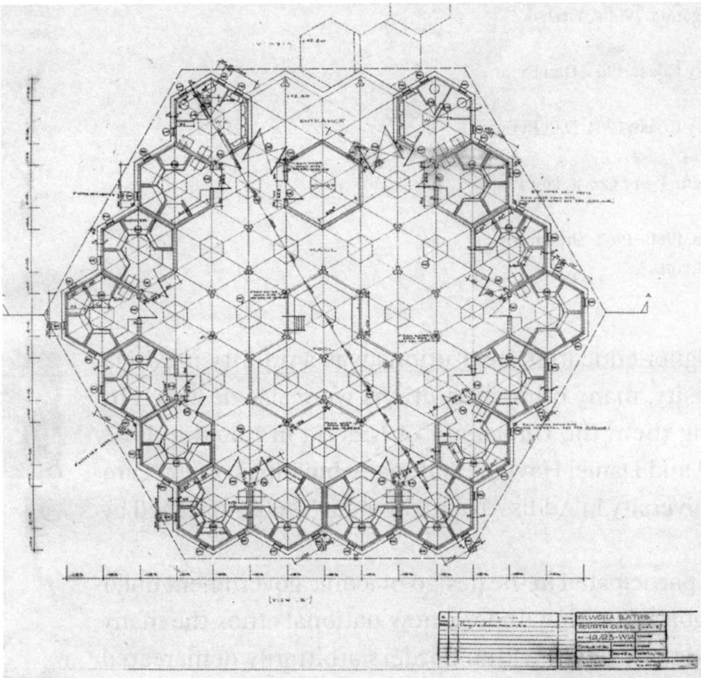
ENTRANCE
HALL
FILWOHA BATHS

27

28

29

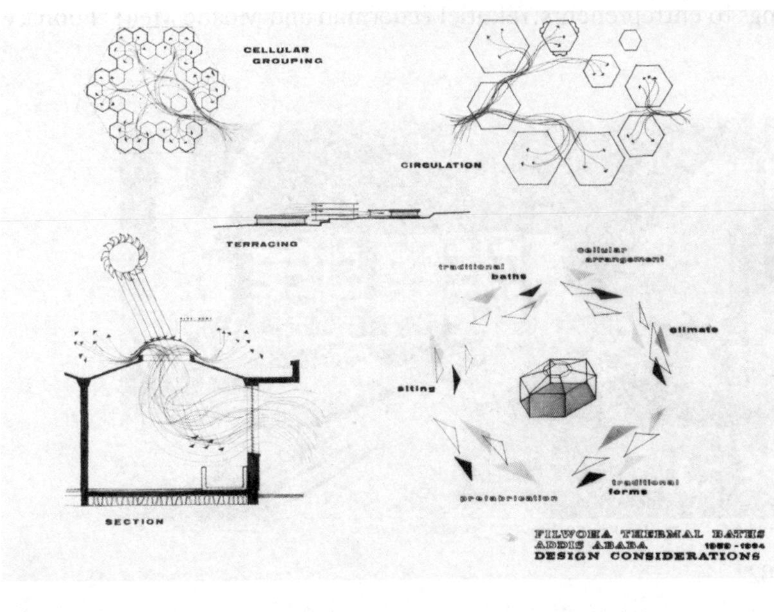
CELLULAR GROUPING
CIRCULATION
TERRACING
SECTION
traditional baths
cellular arrangement
climate
siting
prefabrication
traditional forms
FILWOHA THERMAL BATHS
ADDIS ABABA
DESIGN CONSIDERATIONS

㉚ Housing scheme, Kampala, Uganda, 1960s. Yitzhak Perlstein.
㉛ Housing project, Abidjan, Ivory Coast, 1964. Dan Eytan, Yitzhak Yashar.
㉜ Housing project, Abidjan, Ivory Coast, 1964. Dan Eytan, Yitzhak Yashar.
㉝ Housing project, Abidjan Riviera, Ivory Coast, late 1960s. Thomas Leitersdorf.
㉞ Housing project, Accra, Ghana, 1960–1962. Shulamit Nadler, Michael Nadler, Shmuel Bixon.

㉛

The establishment of higher education institutions was a priority in Africa. In addition to Ife University, many other institutions were also designed by Israeli architects, among them the University of Nigeria in Nsukka (1963, designed by Al Mansfeld and Daniel Havkin) and many buildings on the campus of Haile Selassie I University in Addis Ababa, Ethiopia (1960s, designed by Zalman Einav).

Israeli architects also participated in the design of iconic government buildings in Africa, with the goal of uniting under a new national ethos the many ethnic groups that found themselves within borders arbitrarily demarcated by the colonial powers. "Tropical modernism" was adopted as a "neutral" yet regional style, an alternative to favoring one ethnic culture over another. Dov Karmi and his team, for example, designed the parliament building of Sierra Leone in Freetown (1956–1962); its similarity to the Israeli Knesset building is not coincidental. Zalman Einav designed the palace of Haile Selassie, emperor of Ethiopia (1962), as well as the Ethiopian Foreign Ministry (1965). Engineer Shmaya Ben Avraham designed a complex structural folly for the summer palace of the Persian shah on the Caspian Sea (1970s), the construction of which was never completed.

Again, Africa was the first extensive site for private Israeli investment beyond the borders of the country—despite Foreign Minister Golda Meir's warnings to entrepreneurs Yekutiel Federman and Moshe Meir: "I don't want any

㉚

32

33

34

㉟ Proposal for urban development, Basra, Iraq, 1956–1957. Sketch. Zalman Einav.
㊱ Holiday resort, Abidjan Riviera, Ivory Coast, late 1960s. Model. Thomas Leitersdorf.
㊲ The Iranian shah's summer palace, Caspian coast, mid-1970s. Structural model. Shmaiah Ben Avraham.
㊳ Bandar Abbas Marina, Iran, mid-1970s. Model. Dan Eytan, Yitzhak Yashar.

speculation in Africa. You are going there to fulfill a national role."[22] The largest private project designed by Israeli architects in Africa was the Riviera in Abidjan, capital of Ivory Coast. At the beginning of the 1960s, the entrepreneur Moshe Meir initiated the expansion of the city along the natural coastal lagoon, to adapt it to 120,000 residents while turning it into an attractive tourist site. The Israeli architect Thomas Leitersdorf, whose own experience had been gained building on swampland in England, summoned Israeli foundations experts, who solved the problems of building on the lagoon. The ambitious project, which included an elevated train, was designed according to advanced models of urban planning and preservation of the local culture.[23] Leitersdorf also regarded climate management as a prerequisite in his African work, as he explained in a newspaper interview: "The [architectural] language is first and foremost derived from the climate. This is a place that has 98 percent humidity and you have to orient your buildings such that they catch the breeze. By contrast, my clientele was European, so I tried to blend the axial structure of the African village with the dimensions of the Western city."[24]

Many more hotels and resorts were built and designed by Israelis in Africa.[25] However, Israeli-exported architecture reached its most outlandish manifestation with the Hôtel Ivoire (late 1960s) on the Riviera of the Ivory Coast. The architecture of the hotel (also by Thomas Leitersdorf) corresponds to that of elegant Western retreats, but its interior design, by Heinz Fenchel (who designed the Dan Hotels in Tel Aviv), breaks astounding new ground in exotic opulence. An introductory essay in a catalogue of a retrospective exhibition of Fenchel's lifework refers to the Hôtel Ivoire's eccentricities and hints at Fenchel's training as a set designer:

> The Hôtel Ivoire and the adjacent commercial center, which were designed to draw investors and to place Abidjan on the international map, were designed in a Hollywoodesque style to include swimming pools, a casino, a conference hall, a movie theater, a supermarket, and an ice-skating rink. Every part of this monumental complex was meticulously planned, and its ceilings and walls were decorated with geometric patterns inspired by African culture. Here too, Fenchel introduced specially commissioned works by Israeli artists and craftsmen. The project was designed to give expression to the Ivory Coast's national aspirations, and to emphasize the development and progress that characterized Houphouet-Boigny's presidency.

35

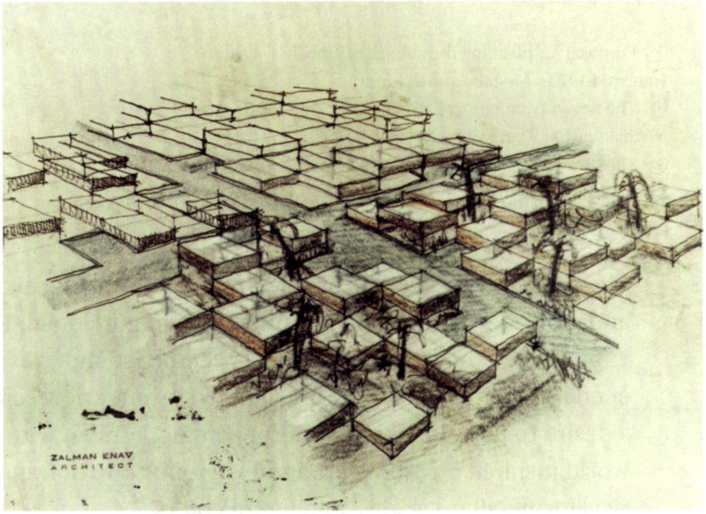


36

37

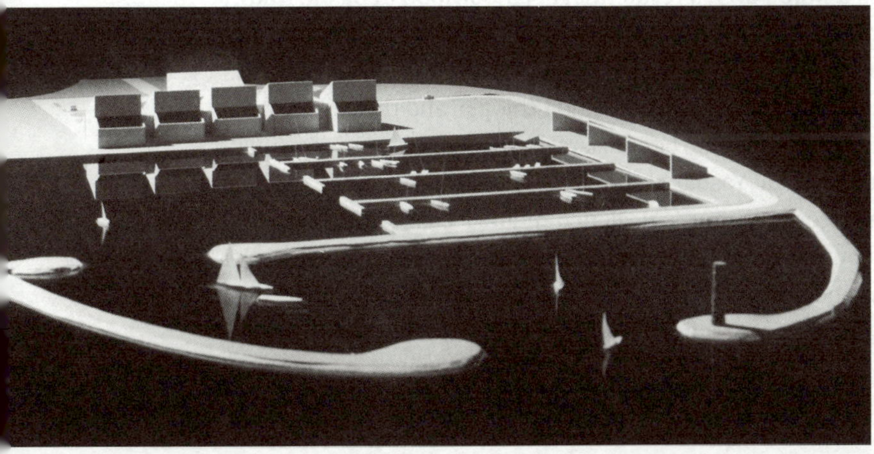

38

(39) Proposal for planning the suburb of Nobahar, Tehran, Iran, mid-1970s. Model. Zalman Einav.
(40) The new city of Bandar Bushehr, Iran, mid-1970s. Model. Yitzhak Yashar, Dan Eytan.
(41) The new city of Bandar Abbas, Bushehr, Iran, mid-1970s. Model. Yitzhak Yashar, Dan Eytan.

> The design of Hôtel Ivoire enabled Fenchel to enlarge his repertoire of forms and colors. As a European immigrant living in Israel, Fenchel constantly experienced the local dialectic between East and West. It seems that his encounter with African culture instilled in him a new sense of freedom, and a desire to fuse the world of European modernism with an abstract formal world inspired by ethnic art and by a repertoire of fragmented, a-symmetrical forms, sharp angles, and warm colors.[26]

Zalman Einav actually moved to Ethiopia after completing his studies at the Technion in Haifa and the Department of Tropical Architecture at the Architectural Association School of Architecture in London. He lived there for eight years, during which time he married a local woman, established a partnership with the local architect Michael Todros, initiated the establishment of an architecture school, and helped found the journal of the local architects' union. Aside from the prestigious projects on commission from the local government and aristocracy mentioned above, he designed a network of post offices, schools for the peripheral areas, military bases, and apartment houses in Ethiopia—all based on labor-intensive production technologies, with lightweight prefabricated building parts, suited to the economy of the underdeveloped areas.

Israel propagated its experience in the design of low-cost mass housing in seminars held in Israel by the Housing Ministry and the Jewish Agency's Afro-Asian Institute. Israeli architects designed housing projects in Africa that were quite similar to those being built in Israel in the same years, except for the fact that in Africa these constituted luxury housing projects for the ruling elite. In certain cases, Israeli architects were involved in the planning of entire cities and suburbs (in the 1970s Yitzhak Yashar and Dan Eytan, for example, planned the cities of Bandar Abbas and Bandar Bushehr in Iran; Einav planned a suburb of Tehran and, through a third party, a residential neighborhood in Basra, Iraq).

This architectural activity often complemented another Israeli export branch—that of military equipment and expertise in the training of local armies. Einav designed military bases in Uganda, Iran, and Ethiopia, and the experience he gained there was implemented years later in Israel, when new bases were built after the evacuation of the Sinai. Yashar and Eytan, who took part in the design of the Israeli nuclear reactor in Dimona, designed military bases in Uganda. In Iran they designed not only military and naval bases, but also a nuclear research city, a project that was shelved in the wake of Khomeini's revolution, marking the end of the Iranian chapter in Israeli involvement in the "Third World."

39

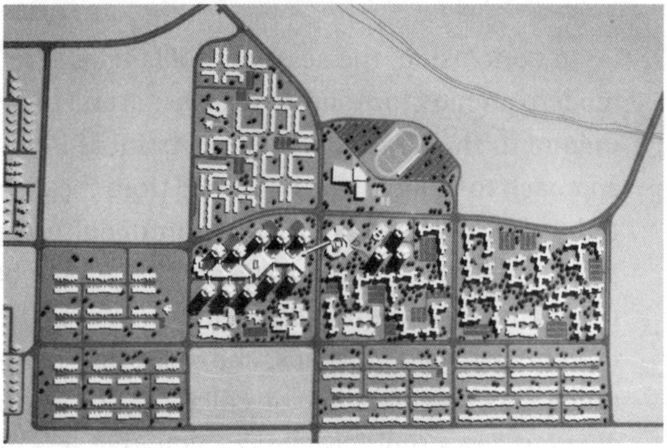

40

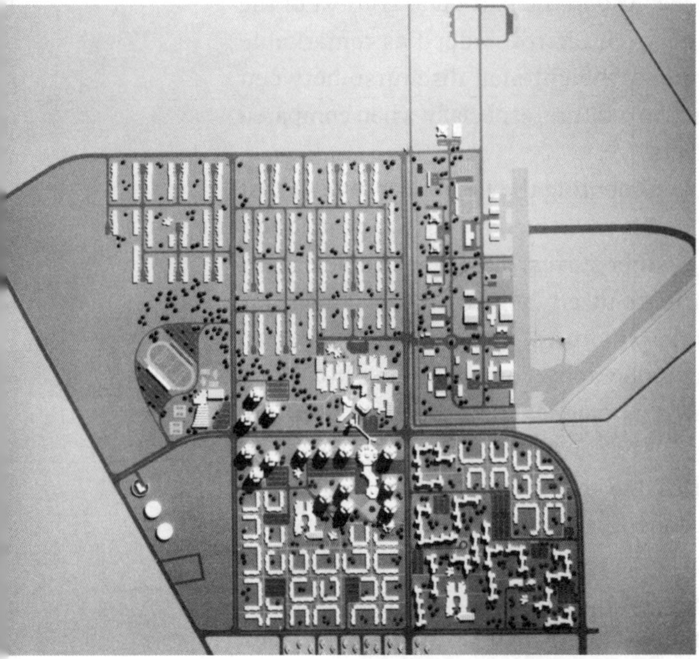

41

نو بهار
NOBAHAR
ENVIRONMENTAL DISTRICT
گروه شرکتهای ایرانل
GROUP OF COMPANIES

In conclusion, the search for a language that would accommodate both modern architecture and African visual and material heritage was certainly not unique to the Israeli architects. As Inbal Ben-Asher Gitler maintains, "this approach to Modernism developed from the discourse of Africanism and negritude, which were an important part of cultural production in Africa from the 1950s onwards."[27] In retrospect, it remains to be asked whether postcolonial tropicalism—with its often genuine interest and commitment to exploring native conditions, cultures, and identities; its soft rhetoric of "aid" and "assistance"; its participatory or collaborative operations—is indeed essentially different, less primitivist, less exploitative, less disempowering, than the earlier colonial modernism it sought to replace. And in the particular context of the Ife campus project, was the figure of Arieh Sharon indeed as remarkable as Ben-Asher Gitler claims in defining a "heightened discourse between modernism and its assimilation of a [native] culture, especially when compared to the work of other expatriate architects"?[28]

Another look at the photographs documenting the Ife project reveals that the former Bauhaus member finally found his own blend of geometric delirium and pagan Brutalism and concocted a rather surreal dialect of "tropical architecture." His atavistic fascination—hitherto utterly repressed—released a current of camouflage-like murals, gigantic sculptures, round openings, warped roofscapes, and overstated undulating topography, composing an astonishing setting that was promoted in postcards as "scenes from the most beautiful campus in Africa."

Even if this curious composition proved to be of no imperative consequence to modern African architecture, and constituted only a marginal footnote of neocolonial practices (in relation, for instance, to authoritative projects by Le Corbusier, Louis Kahn, or Doxiadis in developing countries), it nevertheless had an enchanting effect on Israeli architecture, which always fancied exotic transposition over indigenous intricacy. ■

1 Theodor Herzl, *Old-New Land*, trans. Lotta Levensohn (New York: Bloch Publishing, 1960). Originally published as *Altneuland* (Leipzig: Seemann, 1902).
2 Ibid.
3 See *The Role of the Israel Labor Movement in Establishing Relations with States in Africa and Asia: Documents* (Jerusalem: Hebrew University, 1989).
4 Although economic links continued and even intensified on more pragmatic terms. (For a fascinating account of the changing attitude of Africans toward Israel, see Barbet Schroeder's film *General Idi Amin Dada: Self Portrait*, 1974).
5 Golda Meir, *My Life*, 6th printing (London: Futura, 1978), p. 265.
6 See Mordechai Kreinin, *Israel and Africa: A Study in Technical Cooperation* (New York: Praeger, 1964). On the Israeli aid program and its priorities, see Joel Peters, *Israel and Africa: The Problematic Friendship* (London: British Academic Press, 1992); Abel Jacob, "Israel's Military Aid to Africa: 1960–1966," *The Journal of Modern African Studies* 9:2 (1971).
7 Hillel Dan, *On an Unpaved Road: The Legend of Solel Boneh* [in Hebrew] (Jerusalem and Tel Aviv: Schocken, 1963).
8 See Eliyahu Bieltzki, *Solel Boneh*, 1924–1972 [in Hebrew] (Tel Aviv: Am Oved, 1974), pp. 407–435.
9 Arieh Sharon, *Kibbutz + Bauhaus: An Architect's Way in a New Land* (Stuttgart and Tel Aviv: Karl Kramer Verlag and Massada, 1976), p. 125.
10 Ibid., p. 126.
11 Ibid.
12 Ibid.
13 Ibid., p. 127.
14 Ibid.
15 Ibid.
16 Ibid.
17 Inbal Ben-Asher Gitler, "Campus Architecture as Nation Building: Israeli Architect Arieh Sharon's Obafemi Awolowo University Campus, Ife-Ife, Nigeria," in *Third World Modernism: Architecture, Development and Identity*, ed. Duanfang Lu (New York: Routledge, 2010), p. 123.
18 Ibid., p. 129. Ben-Asher Gitler further mentions the sculptural elements on campus as deriving directly from African art. She quotes Harold Rubin, Sharon's project architect in situ: "As a native of South Africa I was aware of the sculptures which are mostly figurative but are executed in very abstract forms."
19 Ibid., p. 130.
20 Sharon was probably referring to Maxwell Fry's and Jane Drew's project for the University of Ibadan.
21 Sharon, *Kibbutz + Bauhaus*, p. 128.
22 According to Yekutiel Federman's son, Mickey, Meir said these things to his father as he departed for Africa. Mickey Federman, in a discussion with the author, 1999.
23 After the fact, Leitersdorf brought the urban ideas that he had experimented with in Africa back to Israel and implemented them in Ma'aleh Edumim, one of the largest Jewish settlements in the West Bank, which he designed.
24 In Noam Dvir, "Into—and Out Of—Africa," *Haaretz*, September 24, 2010, http://www.haaretz.com/weekend/week-s-end/into-and-out-of-africa-1.315438. The final clause in this citation is included only in the original Hebrew article, published in *Haaretz* on September 17, 2010.
25 Arie Rosov, who designed the Dan Carmel Hotel in Haifa for investor Yekutiel Federman (1959–1963), designed hotels in Ibadan (1962) and Port Harcourt in Nigeria. Zalman Einav designed hotels and thermal baths in Addis Ababa, Ethiopia (1963–1965). The office of Yarmitzky, Margalit, and Marco designed the Hilton hotels in Kenya and Madagascar (1967–1971), as well as a chain of safari hotels in Tanzania.
26 Arie Berkowitz, "'A Complex Puzzle': Heinz Fenchel, Architect and Designer," in *Chaim Heinz Fenchel: A Complex Puzzle*, exh. cat. (Tel Aviv: Rubin Museum, 2012), p. 286.
27 Ben-Asher Gitler, "Campus Architecture," p. 133.
28 Ibid., p. 133.

# DOSSIER: HEINZ FENCHEL'S EXTRAVAGANCE

(42) The decorative beamed ceiling of the casino at Hôtel Ivoire, Abidjan, Ivory Coast, 1978. Sketch. Heinz Fenchel. Courtesy of the Federman and Fenchel families.

Heinz Fenchel studied architecture in the late 1920s at Berlin's Hochschule für Bildende Künste in Charlottenburg, attending courses taught by Hans Poelzig as well as Cesar Klein's theater and stage-design class.[1] In 1928 he began working with the German film company Universum-Film AG (UFA) in Neubabelsberg, first as an assistant stage designer and later as art director. He worked at UFA for eight years, until his immigration to Palestine in late 1936, and was involved in the production of forty-five German and international films. In addition to his work as a set designer, he was also involved in several architecture and interior design projects for both private homes and commercial businesses.[2] In Palestine, Fenchel's career as a set designer came to an end, and a fifty-year oeuvre of architecture, interior design, and furniture design—in and of public buildings, homes, hotels, offices, stores, and cafés—began.[3] In a monograph published on the occasion of a retrospective exhibition of his lifework, his stylized décors are explicated in the context of Tel Aviv's 1930s émigré culture:

> Early on in his career, Fenchel became known for ascribing great importance to interior design and to the role of design in creating a specific lifestyle. He strived for uncompromising perfection, and his meticulously executed, European-style designs were perceived as a luxury—especially given the ideologically (as well as objectively) motivated cultural thrust to create a local melting pot and forge an "Israeli Style" in fashion, food, dance, music, and design. The Jewish immigrants who arrived from Germany during the 1930s, however, had difficulty accepting his emphasis on integration and assimilation. They perceived the local Jewish community's culture as "Eastern European," and sought to recreate the bourgeois, urban culture they had left behind in Germany.[4]

Later on, in the 1950s, as Fenchel's style became more modernist and internationalist, it paradoxically also became ever more Israeli. Arie Berkowitz, writing in the monograph, detected "a gradual shift away from his original neo-classical schemes, which created a 'respectable,' 'foreign' atmosphere; over time, and especially during the 1950s and 1960s, his work gradually took a modernist turn under the influence of local trends."[5]

During the 1960s and 1970s, Fenchel became one of the most prolific and imaginative Israeli architects operating in Africa. His major designs there were commissioned by the Israeli entrepreneur Moshe Mayer; among them were the Ducor Palace Hotel, "the first modern luxury hotel in Monrovia, Liberia,"[6] and the Hôtel Ivoire in Abidjan, Ivory Coast, "one of the world's most beautiful hotels,"[7] which has gradually grown into a "multi-purpose complex viewed as one of the most ambitious building projects in Africa."[8] In addition to his major built projects in Africa, Fenchel's archive documents numerous colorful sketches of proposals for villas, hotels, congress halls, cinemas, and playgrounds in Liberia and Ivory Coast. These constitute the most eccentric Israeli attempt at architectural Africanism ever. ■

1 See Ines Sonder, "Chaim Heinz Fenchel: His Life and Work in Germany," in *Chaim Heinz Fenchel: A Complex Puzzle,* exh. cat. (Tel Aviv: Rubin Museum, 2012), p. 305.

2 Ibid., pp. 301–302.

3 See Arie Berkowitz, "'A Complex Puzzle': Chaim Heinz Fenchel, Architect and Designer," in *Chaim Heinz Fenchel: A Complex Puzzle*, p. 296.

4 Ibid., p. 294.

5 Ibid., p. 291.

6 Ibid., p. 286.

7 Ibid.

8 Ibid.

43

44

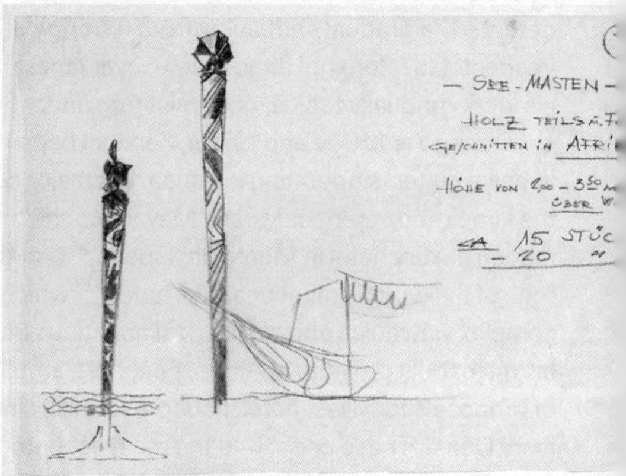
— SEE-MASTEN —
HOLZ
CA 15
– 20

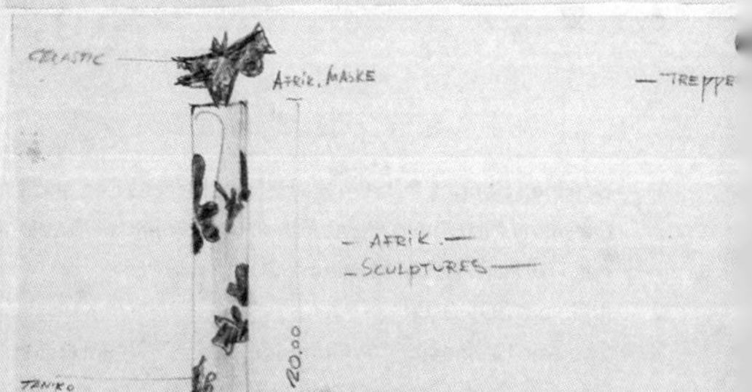
AFRIK. MASKE
— TREPPE
— AFRIK. —
— SCULPTURES —
ca 3,00 ∅

(43) Casino, Hôtel Ivoire Intercontinental, Abidjan, Ivory Coast, late 1960s. Heinz Fenchel. Courtesy of the Federman and Fenchel families.
(44) Casino, Hôtel Ivoire Intercontinental, Abidjan, Ivory Coast, late 1960s. Interior. Heinz Fenchel. Courtesy of the Federman and Fenchel families.
(45) Casino, Hôtel Ivoire Intercontinental, Abidjan, Ivory Coast, late 1960s. Preparatory sketches. Heinz Fenchel. Courtesy of the Federman and Fenchel families.

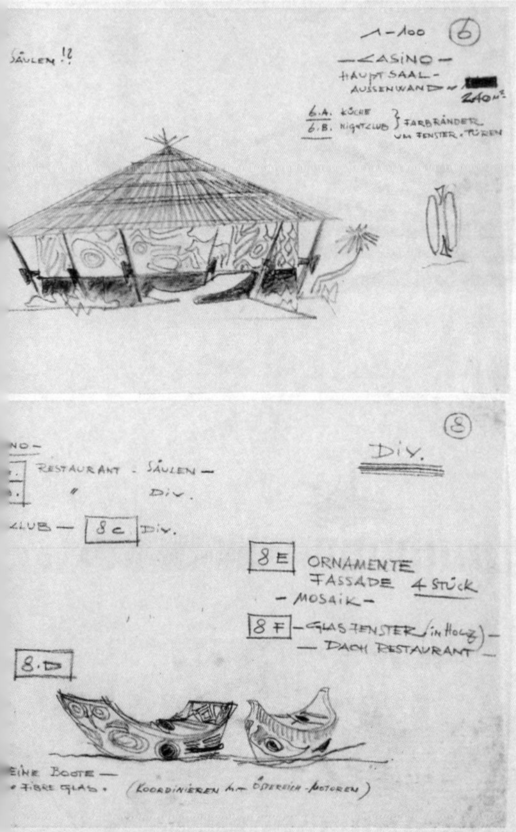


(45)

㊻

㊼

(48)

(49)

(46) Hôtel Ivoire Intercontinental, Abidjan, Ivory Coast, late 1960s. Thomas Leitersdorf and Heinz Fenchel. Courtesy of the Federman and Fenchel families.
(47) Congress hall, Hôtel Ivoire Intercontinental, Abidjan, Ivory Coast, 1978. Sketches. Heinz Fenchel. Courtesy of the Federman and Fenchel families.
(48) Proposal for houses, Abidjan, Ivory Coast, 1970s. Heinz Fenchel. Courtesy of the Federman and Fenchel families.
(49) Proposal for a house, Abidjan, Ivory Coast, 1970s. Heinz Fenchel. Courtesy of the Federman and Fenchel families.

# Commemoration

## Sites of Mourning and Melancholia

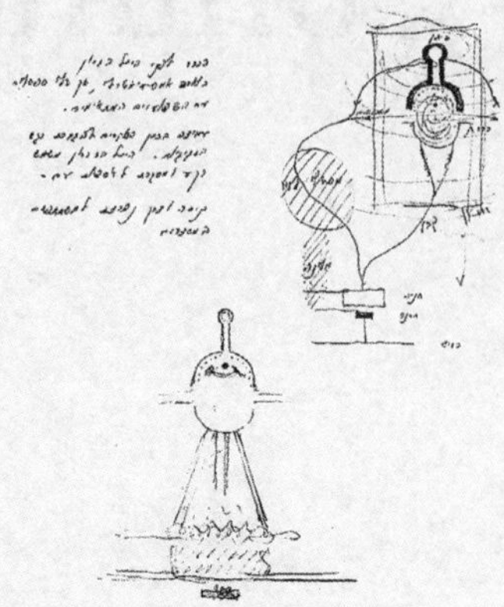

①

Due to the circumstances of its founding, a particular culture of mourning, commemoration, and forgetfulness developed in the State of Israel, devotedly memorializing the Holocaust of European Jewry and Israel's territorial wars, thoroughly manufacturing the oblivion of the Palestinian *Nakba*, consistently transforming the native landscape, and resourcefully devising new architectural typologies, artistic genres, theatrical formats, and musical habits.

The causal overlay of the Jewish Holocaust and the Israeli wars entangled the entire geography, citizenry, and culture of representation in a web of melancholic routines and memento mori. In addition to the official memorial days and related ceremonies that punctuated daily life; alongside the literature, art, and music of mourning that affected the national *Bildung* and public mood; on top of the (mostly, but not only, Brutalist) memorials, monuments, museums, military graveyards, education centers, and reenacted battlegrounds—established by the State, by Jewish organizations, by municipal authorities, by labor unions, by schools, and by cultural institutions—the terrain itself was ritualized as a surface redeemed by blood and tears. The "desolate" landscape was rehabilitated by nature reserves, national parks, and woodlands to create space for the national pastime of necrology. Most effective among the Israeli commemorative projects was the afforestation operation (see chapter "Forests"), which was executed with a special vigor by the Jewish National Fund after Statehood in order to simultaneously glorify and mask the traumatic birth of the nation. Cultural critic Sigal Barnir astutely contextualized this operation:

> [Afforestation] played a major role in the creation of a new identity for the place, the erasure and disappearance of the Palestinian fabric of life and landscape, and was a spatial expression of the slogan "a land without a people for a people without a land." While the forests covered up a natural landscape and left no trace of the villages that were erased, they turned into a space of collective Jewish commemoration. If you stroll today in any of these forests you will come upon hundreds of gravestone-like plaques, commemoration signs, memorial walls, to the point that sometimes it is hard to tell if this is a place of amusement and leisure, or one huge cemetery.[1]

According to the official Israeli body count, over 6,000 Jews—almost one percent of a population numbering 650,000 at the time—were killed in the "War of Independence" which lasted from November 1947 to the spring of 1948. One third of the fallen were civilians. The idea of building a central memorial site to this formative war and to wars to come was initially raised by Prime Minister Ben-Gurion; various political agencies and nongovernmental organizations then brought it up time and again. The plan never materialized, however, and commemoration, like any other building endeavor during the first years of Statehood, was decentralized and utilized as a dispersed landmark. Attempts to unify and serialize memorials were made, as can be gleaned from a letter sent on June 8, 1952, by Shimon Peres, then deputy director of the Ministry of Defense, to the head of the military unit for commemorating fallen soldiers: "The Minister of Defense [Ben-Gurion] would like to examine the possibility of erecting memorial pillars wherever a major incident occurred during the War of Independence. These pillars should not necessarily be linked specifically to the names of the fallen, but their main purpose should be to mark the sites of battle and to honor their memory."[2]

The serial pillars were not erected, and national commemoration was fragmented into more than nine hundred singular—indeed, sculptural—memorial sites, not including Holocaust monuments. This is the largest number per capita in the world, reflecting a ratio of about one memorial to every twenty-one fallen. (In Europe, by comparison, the ratio is one to ten thousand.) In addition, more than three hundred local-communal memorials were scattered in a new distinctive building type known as *Yad Labanim*—a memorial to the fallen sons which also functioned as an art museum or a theater. Moreover, commemorative walls and objects appeared in schools; in courtyards of community and cultural centers; in clubs, libraries, hospitals, and synagogues; in playgrounds and sports grounds; in gardens and parks; in office buildings; and in military camps. Ultimately, every organization, every community, every urban and rural settlement, every civic and military institution, every school and university in Israel had its own *pinat hantzaha* ("memorial corner"), commemorative plaque, or dedicatory artwork. Artists, artisans, designers, and architects developed an elegiac spectrum.[3] The protocols of the central competitions committee of the Union of Engineers and Architects in Israel between January 1949 and January 1951, for instance, deal almost exclusively with national competitions for commemoration sites, military cemeteries, and various battleground monuments. Most significant was the competition which determined the architectural and graphic etiquette of the generic Israeli military cemetery and the uniform gravestone for fallen soldiers. The winning entry, by architect Asher Hiram, was executed in nine military cemeteries and 160 military sectors in civilian cemeteries.

Jerusalem, the new capital, was central to the formation of national pathos. In the city's master plan, prepared in 1949 by a team headed by architect Heinz Rau, a hill on the western outskirts was designated for national commemoration. It soon became known as "Memorial Mountain" (Heb. *Har Hazikaron*) for

① Early proposal for Yad Vashem, memorial to Holocaust victims, Jerusalem, 1942(!) Sketch. Munio Gitai Weinraub, Al Mansfeld.
② Memorial to the fallen soldiers, Kiryat Haim, 1953. Munio Gitai Weinraub, Al Mansfeld.
③ Memorial to the fallen in the War of Independence, Kiryat Haim, 1948–1953. Munio Gitai Weinraub, Al Mansfeld.

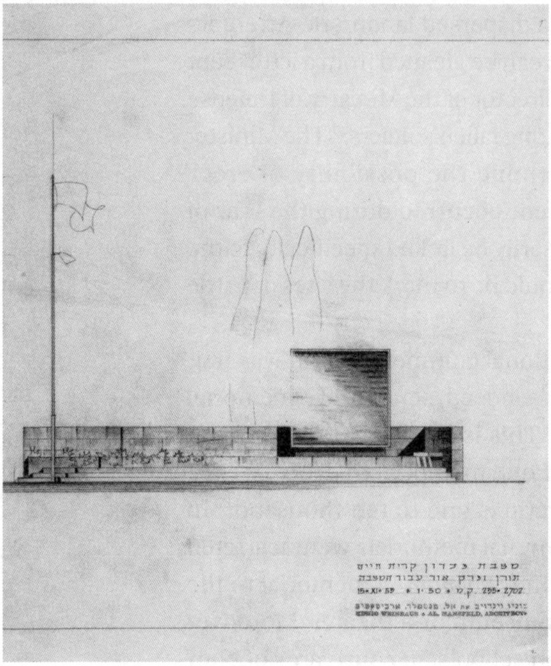

②

③

its ceremonial consolidation of Yad Veshem (the central Holocaust museum and archive), Theodor Herzl's tomb, a burial site for the nation's leaders, and a military cemetery. In a 1951 international competition for the design of Herzl's tomb, the winning entry by architect Yosef Klarwein proposed a flat-domed structure echoing the topography of the Judean hills. The final built version, however, was an open memorial with a black monolith tombstone.

In January 1951, Ben-Gurion established a civic commemoration committee. In its first meeting, he expressed his intuitive iconoclasm, arguing that the memory of fallen heroes should not be immortalized in stone monuments or memorial forests, but rather be inscribed in the emotions of generations to come through public ceremonies, composed requiems, and published anthologies of texts written by the fallen soldiers. The committee nevertheless established a policy of monument proliferation across the country and determined the character of the national memorial days.

It was decided that the memorial day for fallen soldiers (Heb. *Yom Hazikaron*) should fall on the day before Independence Day, serving as a moralizing prelude to it. Holocaust and Resistance Remembrance Day (Heb. *Yom Hashoah Ve'hagvura*) was dated just after Passover in order to highlight the Warsaw Ghetto Uprising, which took place during Passover in 1943. In 1959 this day was constitutionalized by the parliament as a national memorial day, opened by a countrywide siren announcing two minutes of silence and stillness (emphatically observed by Israelis). After 1967, with the government's decision to institute Jerusalem Day, a complete catastrophic schedule was set up, drawing a circuit of lament that begins with the mythical exodus from Egypt (Passover) and culminates in the alleged unification of Jerusalem. The enactment of the national memorial days according to the Hebrew calendar symbolically embedded the calamity of the Diaspora and the brutal becoming of the State of Israel in the abiding chronicles of Jewish martyrdom. ■

1 Sigal Barnir, "On Forests as Commemorative Sites," in *Borderline Disorder*, ed. Zvi Efrat, catalogue of the Israeli pavilion, 8th International Architecture Biennale in Venice, 2002, p. 133.

2 Cited in Ilana Shamir, *Commemoration and Memory* [in Hebrew] (Tel Aviv: Am Oved, 1996), p. 41.

3 The design of memory was considered a "public issue of great priority" and was discussed immediately after the war, in June 1949, in a survey of artists organized by Eugen Kolb (who would become director of the Tel Aviv Museum) which was published in the *Al Hamishmar* newspaper. Some of the artists participating in the survey, Dov Feigin and Nathan Rapoport among them, argued that the heroic formative period should be engraved in the "mold of the homeland" in a way that would be expressive of the State's dramatic foundation and would allow for mass ritual.
Eugen Kolb, "How Should the Monuments for Our Wars of Liberation Be Designed?," *Al Hamishmar*, June 2, 1949. Cited in Shamir, *Commemoration and Memory*, p. 41.

④ Proposed master plan for the Yad Vashem Holocaust memorial, Jerusalem, 1946. Perspective drawing. Munio Gitai Weinraub, Al Mansfeld.
⑤ Yizkor memorial tent, Yad Vashem, Jerusalem, 1957–1961. Perspective drawing. Arieh Elhanani, Arieh Sharon, Benjamin Idelson.
⑥ Hall of Remembrance, Yad Vashem Holocaust Memorial Museum, Jerusalem, 1957–1961. Arieh Elhanani, Arieh Sharon, Benjamin Idelson.

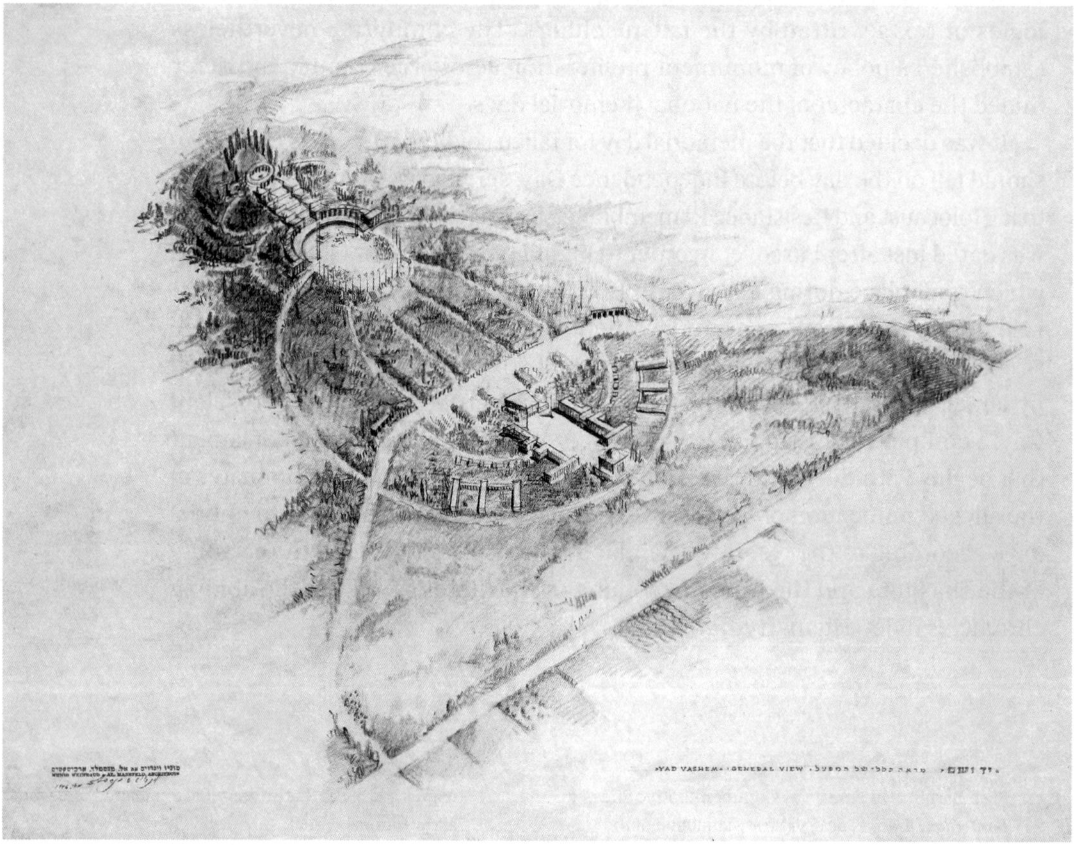


④

⑤

⑥

⑦

⑧

⑨

⑦ Competition entry for Theodor Herzl's tomb, Mount Herzl, Jerusalem, 1951. Sketch. Artist: Yitzhak Danziger.
⑧ Competition entry for Theodor Herzl's tomb, Mount Herzl, Jerusalem, 1951. Model. Artist: Yitzhak Danziger.
⑨ Winning competition entry for Theodore Herzl's tomb, Mount Herzl, Jerusalem, 1951. Model. Yosef Klarwein. Photographer: Alfred Bernheim.
⑩ "Public Competition for a Memorial to Those Who Broke Through to Jerusalem," *Engineering and Architecture*, August 1962.

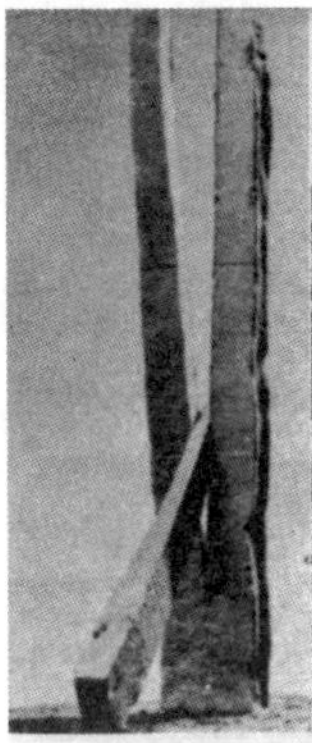

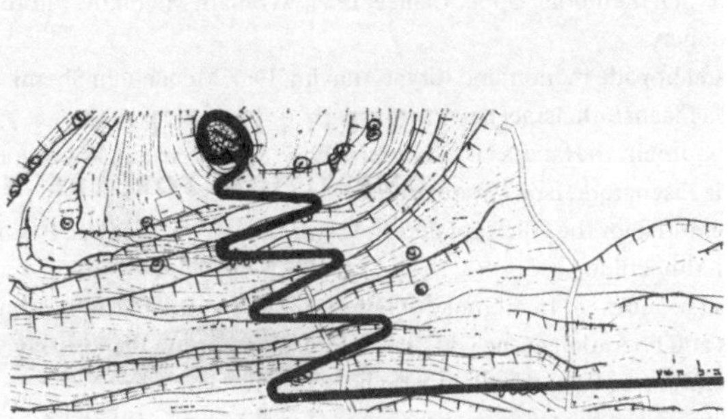

**פרס שלישי: ק. אלול**

THIRD PRIZE : K. ELLUL

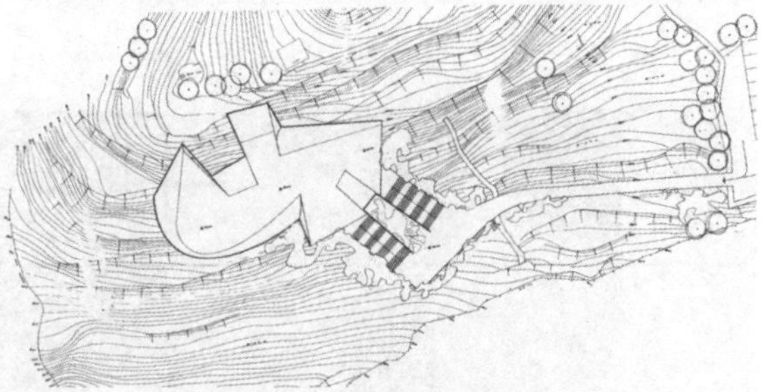

**פרס שלישי: א. קאופמן, מ. קדישמן, מ. שוורץ**

THIRD PRIZE : E. KAUFMANN, M. KADISHMANN, M. SCHWARTZ

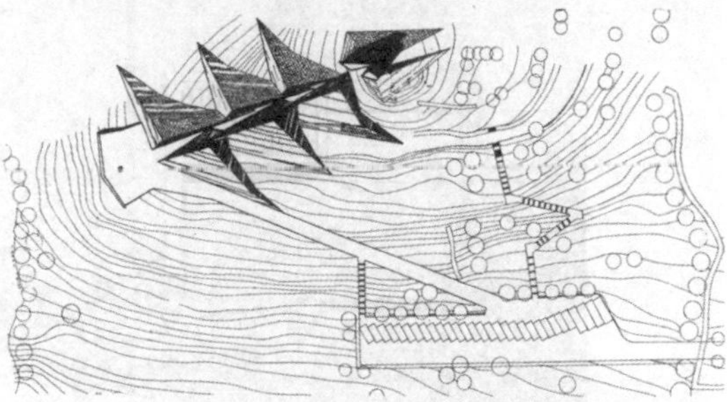

**פרס שלישי: ע. לוי, ב. ז'רום**

THIRD PRIZE : A. LEVY, B. JEROME

**קנייה: א. אל־חנני, ג'. בייל**

HON. MENTION : A. EL-HANANI, J. BYLE

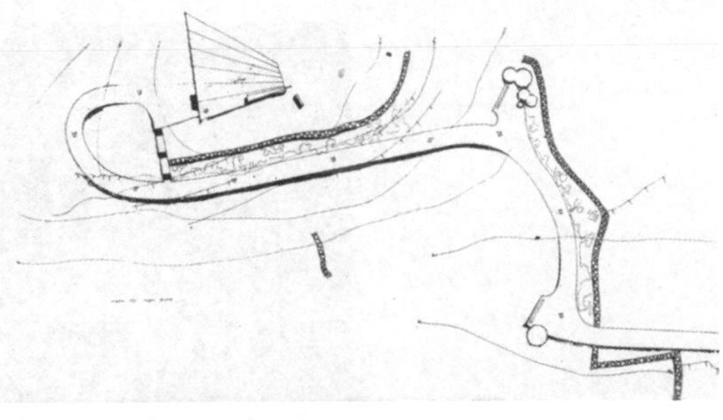

⑩

⑪ Tel Chai memorial, Upper Galilee, 1934. Avraham Melnikov. Photographer: Fritz Cohen.
⑫ Harel brigade monument, Kiryat Anavim, 1951. Menachem Shemi. Photographer: Yehuda Eisenstark. Israel State Archives.
⑬ Monument to Hadera city founders, 1965. M. Zilberman. Photographer: Yehuda Eisenstark. Israel State Archives.
⑭ Memorial for the fallen soldiers in Hayarden Valley, Tzemah, 1960s. Shemi Almoznino.
⑮ Bird monument in memory of fallen soldiers in the battle for the Mount of Olives and liberation of the Old City of Jerusalem during the Six-Day War, 1986. Yona and David Palombo. Photographer: Yaacov Saar.
⑯ Memorial to the fallen soldiers in the War of Independence. Kfar Saba, 1958. Leitersdorf and Belsizman.
⑰ Memorial to fallen soldiers, Beit She'an, 1960. Munio Gitai Weinraub, Al Mansfeld.

⑪

⑫

⑬

⑭

⑮

⑯

⑰

⑱

⑲ ⑳ ㉑

⑱ “Ammunition Hill” Memorial, Jerusalem, 1968–1975. Benjamin Idelson, Gershon Tzipor.
⑲ IDF parade on Independence Day, Jerusalem, 1968. Meyer A. Baskin Judaica Book Fund, Harvard Library.
⑳ IDF parade on Independence Day, Jerusalem, 1968. Meyer A. Baskin Judaica Book Fund, Harvard Library.
㉑ IDF parade on Independence Day, Jerusalem, 1968. Meyer A. Baskin Judaica Book Fund, Harvard Library.
㉒ The “Steel Division” monument, Yamit, 1977. Israel Goodovitch.

㉒

㉓

㉔

㉕

㉖

(27)

(28)

(29)

(30)

(23) Yad LeBanim Memorial to fallen soldiers, Tel Aviv, 1960–1963. Israel Lotan, Zvi Toren.
(24) Yad LeBanim Memorial to fallen soldiers, Tel Aviv, Interior. 1960–1963. Israel Lotan, Zvi Toren.
(25) Yad LeBanim Memorial, Herzliya Museum of Art, 1965–1975. Yaacov Rechter, Moshe Zarhi. Photographer: Moshe Gross, Keren Or Studio.
(26) Culture and Commemoration Center, Kibbutz Nitzanim, 1965–1967. Nahum Zolotov. Sculpture: Moshe Sternschuss.
(27) "Massua" Memorial and Amphitheater, Kibbutz Tel Yitzhak, mid-1960s. Kuba Gever.
(28) Yad Mordechai Holocaust Museum, Kibbutz Yad Mordechai, 1966–1968. Arieh Sharon, Eldar Sharon, Mordechai Dubrovsky.
(29) Yad Mordechai Holocaust Museum, Kibbutz Yad Mordechai, 1966–1968. Arieh Sharon, Eldar Sharon, Mordechai Dubrovsky.
(30) Buckminster Fuller at the Kibbutz Yad Mordechai Holocaust Museum, 1970.

31

32

33

34

㊱

㉟

㊲

㊳

㉛ Negev Brigade Monument, Beersheba, 1963–1968. Aerial view. Dani Karavan. Photographer: Moshe Milner. Government Press Office.
㉜ Negev Brigade Monument, Beersheba, 1982. Dani Karavan. Photographer: Herman Chanani. Government Press Office.
㉝ Negev Brigade Monument, Beersheba, 1963–1968. Dani Karavan. Photographer: Amiram Harlap.
㉞ Negev Brigade Monument, Beersheba, 1963–1968. Dani Karavan. Photographer: Yitzhak Amit. Harvard College Library.
㉟ Ted Kennedy and his wife, Joan, visit Yad Kennedy, John F. Kennedy memorial and peace forest, 1983. Harvard Library.
㊱ Yad Kennedy memorial, Aminadav, 1966. Aerial view. David Resnick. Photographer: Yitzhak Amit. Harvard College Library.
㊲ Yad Kennedy memorial, Aminadav, 1966. David Resnick. Photographer: Moshe Pridan. Government Press Office.
㊳ Ted Kennedy and his wife, Joan, visit Yad Kennedy, John F. Kennedy memorial and peace forest, 1983. Harvard Library.

# DOSSIER:
# THE GHETTO FIGHTERS' HOUSE

The official website of the Ghetto Fighters' House reads as follows:

> The Ghetto Fighters' House – Itzhak Katzenelson Holocaust and Jewish Resistance Heritage Museum—known as the "House"—is not only the first Holocaust museum in the world but also the first of its kind to be founded by Holocaust survivors.[1]

Established in 1949 and inaugurated in 1951, the museum was designed as the centerpiece of Kibbutz Lohamei HaGetaot. The survivors living in this commune chose not only to conduct their lives around the "House," but also to literally animate it with their own narration. For decades, the museum's exhibits had no titles or captions and could not be comprehended without the bodily presence, the voice, and the personal enactment of the survivors.

Architect Samuel Bickels, a member of another kibbutz and a prolific designer of communal landscapes and buildings, reacted to this incredible subject-object configuration with a barrage of sketches, drawings, and models which frantically construct and dismantle, embed and alienate, domesticate and monumentalize the haunting memories of the Ghetto Fighters' community. The built result is a severe quasi-classical edifice raised above a broad amphitheater for yearly gatherings. Inside, sensuous spaces are organized around a central void, and surfaces are softly lit by natural light. ■

1 "About the Ghetto Fighters' House," Ghetto Fighters' House Museum, accessed July 21, 2017, http://www.gfh.org.il/eng/?CategoryID=229.

40

41

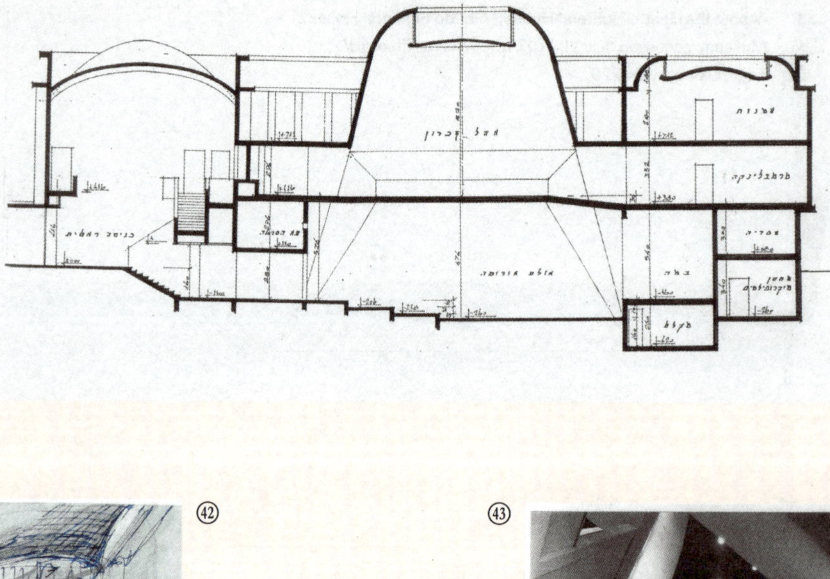

42

43

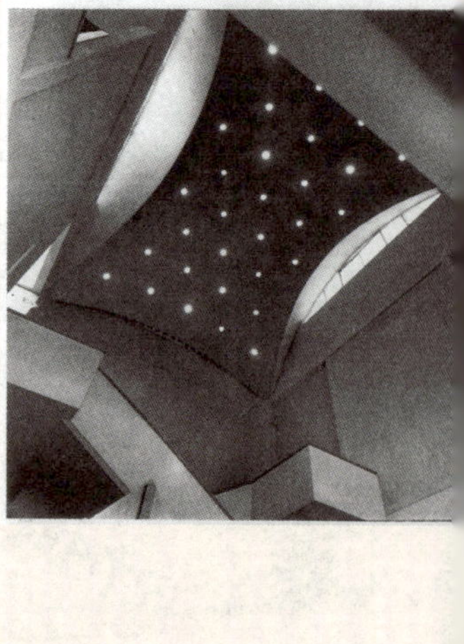

(39) The Ghetto Fighters' House, Kibbutz Lohamei HaGetaot, 1953. Perspective. Samuel Bickels. Bickels Archive, Mishkan Museum of Art, Ein Harod.
(40) The Ghetto Fighters' House, Kibbutz Lohamei HaGetaot, 1953. Sketch of memorial hall. Samuel Bickels. Bickels Archive, Mishkan Museum of Art, Ein Harod.
(41) The Ghetto Fighters' House, Kibbutz Lohamei HaGetaot, 1953. Section. Samuel Bickels. Bickels Archive, Mishkan Museum of Art, Ein Harod.
(42) The Ghetto Fighters' House, entrance hall, Kibbutz Lohamei HaGetaot, 1953. Sketch. Samuel Bickels. Bickels Archive, Mishkan Museum of Art, Ein Harod.
(43) The Ghetto Fighters' House, entrance hall, Kibbutz Lohamei HaGetaot, 1953–1959. Samuel Bickels.
(44) The Ghetto Fighters' House, Kibbutz Lohamei HaGetaot, 1953. Model. Samuel Bickels. Bickels Archive, Mishkan Museum of Art, Ein Harod.
(45) The Ghetto Fighters' House, view from the amphitheater, Kibbutz Lohamei HaGetaot, 1953–1959. Samuel Bickels.
(46) The Ghetto Fighters' House, Kibbutz Lohamei HaGetaot, 1953–1959. Samuel Bickels.

(44)

(45)

(46)

⑰

⑱

⑲

(47) Holocaust Remembrance Day ceremony at the Ghetto Fighters' House, Kibbutz Lohamei HaGetaot, 1960s.
(48) Holocaust Remembrance Day ceremony at the Ghetto Fighters' House, Kibbutz Lohamei HaGetaot, 1960s.
(49) Holocaust Remembrance Day ceremony at the Ghetto Fighters' House, Kibbutz Lohamei HaGetaot, 1960s.
(50) Model of concentration camp Treblinka, The Ghetto Fighters' House – Itzhak Katzenelson Holocaust and Jewish Resistance Heritage Museum and Study Center, Kibbutz Lohamei HaGetaot, 1960s.
(51) Yitzhak Tabenkin visiting the Ghetto Fighters' House – Itzhak Katzenelson Holocaust and Jewish Resistance Heritage Museum and Study Center, Kibbutz Lohamei HaGetaot.
(52) Model of the Warsaw ghetto, The Ghetto Fighters' House – Itzhak Katzenelson Holocaust and Jewish Resistance Heritage Museum and Study Center, Kibbutz Lohamei HaGetaot, 1960s.

(50)

(52)

(51)

# Privatization

①

②

③

## "Build Your Own Home"
## Photographs by Gilad Ophir

The "Build Your Own Home" campaign signaled the neoliberal turn of the Israeli welfare state. For some critics, this is rather tantamount to the postmodern turn of Israeli architecture. It was by and large a State-instigated crusade against State-sponsored public housing, against any urban theory whatsoever, and against both productivist and picturesque perceptions of the rural. This about-face of the "Israeli Project" began in the late 1960s and early 1970s in a few disparate projects launched by Labor administrations,[1] but it only became a nationwide policy and a pervasive catchphrase after the 1977 political turnabout which saw the right-wing Likud Party's rise to power and the socialist Labor Party's loss of hegemony.

Prime Minister Menachem Begin and Housing Minister David Levy effectively accelerated the system of releasing, parceling, marketing, and leasing State-owned land in order to stimulate the private building industry, propagate expansion-by-sprawl, turn rental residents of social housing into property owners, encourage "spontaneous" resourcefulness, and speed up programs of territorial ethnification of regions of "national priority." (Most blatant was a 1980 government campaign which was officially called "Jewification of the Galilee.") Gradually, from the late 1970s on, most government settlement and housing campaigns would be in the Occupied Territories of the West Bank—and, paradoxically, these were based to a large extent on the lure of the Hebrew notion of *tzmudei karka* (lit. "tied to the ground," referring to detached or semi-detached homes).

Residents of "second Israel," as the new-towners of the 1950s and 1960s were called, could now become landlords, with their own domestic identity and public face; protest the patronizing project of the Labor regime; and demand symbolic retribution for their effacement in generic housing blocks (Heb. *shikunim*). The State's top-down engineered landscapes were rapidly interspersed with "bottom-up" clusters or rings of architectural bric-a-brac. The modernist austerity, forced similitude, contrived solidarity, and inflated public-spaciousness of yesterday's garden cities became a liability of the old regime, dreary memorials to the days of Bolshevism.

In a curious turn of events, owning a villa became a patriotic act and residing in suburbia signified a national, as opposed to social, commonality. The placelessness and hollowness of the sprouting dormitory "communities" liberated a veritable grassroots nouveau riche citizenship that is presumably sociopathic, manifestly unsustainable, and hilariously anti-architectural, but certainly not apolitical. Indeed, such a frenzied vernacular could be interpreted as an impulsive dissident culture aiming at shattering the modernist ethos, enraging the tasteful connoisseurs, and tentatively establishing a crossbreed identity,

④

⑤

⑥

as persuasively claimed by architectural critic Eran Tamir-Tawil. According to him, the local "Build Your Own Home" campaign was an outburst of repressed antagonism of Mizrahi Jews (the immigrants from Arab countries who were the main residents of the new towns) toward local "modernism with its Brutalist shades and manners," mixed with their desire to adopt the Western cultural framework by appropriating "elements from pre-modern European traditions."[2]

Among Israeli artists, the most attentive recorder of the architectural vicissitudes of the "Build Your Own Home" episode is Gilad Ophir, whose work on this topic amounts to an uncanny photographic archive. In the essay called "Emptied Walls and Constructed Landscapes," researcher and curator Rona Sela expounds on Ophir's work and its political and cultural context:

> In the course of the past five years, Gilad Ophir has been obsessively preoccupied with the creation of an Israeli version of the contemporary "build your own home" ideal, manifested in the futuristic suburbia erected on the dunes of Holon, Rishon LeZion, Rehovot, Or Akiva, Giv'at Olga, as well as Shoham and Ma'ale Tivon. A photographic chronicle of a specific time and place. A documentation. This archive comprises two levels. The first one is concrete, visible; a storehouse of images in which the critical field—social, political, and aesthetic—is exposed. The second level is abstract and spiritual. Gideon Levi, in an article in the *Ha'aretz* newspaper, touches upon critical points similar to those expressed by Ophir: "At the end of the day, the shoes are as dusty as after a month of reserve duty in the desert. The road to one of the great Israeli dreams still passes through sand dunes and rocky soil. Of course, it's no longer a question of a pioneer enterprise—conquering the desert or draining the swamps. Not even a Zionist settlement project. Simply a house-and-garden, a duplex, penthouse, garden terrace, sun terrace [...] at a good location, preferably with a view of the sea, or at least of a prospective local country club which is bound to be built here, on a 'Dutch-style' tiled alley, ten minutes drive from Tel Aviv, eight from Kfar Saba, or five from the center of Rishon LeZion."[3]
>
> Ophir's unflattering Israeli archive reflects an outward-looking society which adopts building styles belonging to other cultural traditions (France, Switzerland, Spain) [that are] not always compatible with the local climate (such as sloping red tile roofs). These hybridized motifs of houses lacking proper architectural design are like an ironic fulfillment of the forgotten dream of the pioneer settlers—a contemporary cultural absurdity. The constructions in the photographs look like emptied and prettified tombs [...] or sanctuaries. These alienated constructions are replete with nouveau riche features—outsize dimensions, stylized fences, kitschy capitals. "Who buys them? You cannot define them as young couples, rather as people looking for better homes. People in the Dan region, say, who're a little better off, who already have two cars."[4] The "compressing" of the houses on a small

⑦

⑧

⑨

plot of land and the lack of space between them crush the urge of intimacy that lies behind the dream of a private house-and-garden, when that intimacy is imposed by walls, watchdogs, burglar alarms. The ridiculous billboards and pretentious names of the neighborhoods complement this surrealistic Israeli scenery, which attracts and repels Ophir at one and the same time.[5] ■

1 The first so-called "Build Your Own Home" neighborhoods were initiated by the Ministry of Housing in the desert new town of Arad in 1967 and in the Jerusalem suburb of Giv'at Ha'mivtar in 1968. Avraham Ofer, housing minister of the Labor party since 1974, extended the system to new neighborhoods in the towns of Yavne, Ashkelon, Bet She'an, and Ma'alot, among others.

2 Eran Tamir-Tawil, "Suburb, Villa, and Build Your Own Home: The Ethnic Perspective," *Arsitecture* [in Hebrew] (blog), 2010.

3 Gideon Levy, "Society Will Install Jacuzzis in the Cottage," *Haaretz* supplement, April 20, 1995, pp. 14–16.

4 Ibid.

5 Rona Sela, "Emptied Walls and Constructed Landscapes," in Gilad Ophir, *Cyclopean Walls* (Tel Aviv: Tel Aviv Museum of Art, 1995).

①–③ *Cyclopean Walls*: La Village, Kiryat Rishon, 1992. Gilad Ophir. Courtesy of the artist.

④ *Cyclopean Walls*, La Village, Kiryat Rishon #34, 1992. Gilad Ophir. Courtesy of the artist.

⑤ *Cyclopean Walls*, La Village, Kiryat Rishon #7, 1992. Gilad Ophir. Courtesy of the artist.

⑥ *Cyclopean Walls*, La Village, Kiryat Rishon. Child playing. Gilad Ophir. Courtesy of the artist.

⑦–⑧ *Cyclopean Walls*, La Village, Kiryat Rishon, 1992. Gilad Ophir. Courtesy of the artist.

⑨ *Cyclopean Walls*, Orot neighborhood, Or Akiva, 1993. Gilad Ophir. Courtesy of the artist.

⑩–⑪ *Cyclopean Walls*, Shoham, 1993. Gilad Ophir. Courtesy of the artist.

⑫ *Cyclopean Walls*, La Quartier, Rishon Lezion West, 1992. Gilad Ophir. Courtesy of the artist.

⑬ *Cyclopean Walls*, Baron Gardens, Kiryat Rishon, 1992. Gilad Ophir. Courtesy of the artist.

⑭ *Cyclopean Walls*, Kiryat Rishon #49, 1992. Gilad Ophir. Courtesy of the artist.

⑮ *Cyclopean Walls*, Kiryat Rishon, 1992. Gilad Ophir. Courtesy of the artist.

כאן נבנה בית מגורים
תכנון : אמיאור אדריכלים
BR

⑩

⑪

בונה כאן את
Le Quartier
לה קרטייה
שכונת קוטג'ים יוקרתיים
חדרים
ISCO
כאן
הקוטג' לדוגמא
ISCO

⑫

גני הברון
משרד מכירות בלעדי
אנגלו סכסון, רוטשילד 58
טל: 9677717
החברה המבצעת:

(13)

איטונג
שמואל אולפינר בונה
זר הורד
קוטגים - גן • קוטגים גג
מדורגים ומפוארים במיוחד
שכונת קוטגים יפיפיה
נאות דברת

(14)

(15)

# Speculation

① Kikar Hamedina (State's Square), Tel Aviv, 1964. Proposal. Oscar Niemeyer, Aba Elhanani, Israel Lotan.

# Net Israel—Upwards

By David Avidan[1]

Why are land (and apartment) prices in Tel Aviv and Jerusalem higher than in most big cities around the world, which have a lot more to offer (New York, London, Paris, and so on)? I'm not sure if I'm the first to pose this question, but I'm convinced that it's a good and intriguing and at the same time neglected and rare one. Despite the question's rarity, however, the answer is not complicated, in part because it's not an economic answer. Land in Israel is expensive for two reasons: A. Its blood rate (a result of the continuous war effort needed to keep hold of and defend it); B. The Jewish greed for land, after two thousand years of lack.

The second answer requires more elaboration than the first, self-evident one. Those parts of world Jewry that immigrated to Israel and became Israelis are a group of immigrants without a land-owning past for thousands of years. Only here, for the first time, were they given the chance to own pieces of land. The dormant psycho-territorial instinct quickly awakened, becoming within a few years (long before the founding of the State) a major Israeli characteristic.

There is perhaps no other country in the world today in which the attitude to buying an apartment (or a plot) is as dramatic and celebratory as in Israel, both in its urban centers and in the periphery. This characteristic has turned into such an obsessive fixation that the very Israeli takeover of any land has become a mystical-ecstatic experience, while the very need to give back land to others—even in the not so near future—strikes many, perhaps the large majority, as a national disaster. [...]

There is perhaps no people for whom the expression "the territorial imperative" is more fitting than the Israelis. The problem would not have been so terrible if it were possible to live in peace with, that is, if no one were disputing the territorial aspirations of most Israelis. The trouble is that it *is* terrible, and that it is impossible to live in peace with, and that there *is* someone who is disputing these territorial aspirations.

The Israeli territorial imperative is faced with a desperately defiant, stubborn, and generations-old Arab territorial imperative. The conflict between these two imperatives is not only absurd but truly demonic, precisely because of the great similarity between them. [...]

All the above is a description of the situation, as I see it with maximum objectivity, rather than an assertion of my position. Both sides suffer from an exaggerated and archaic territorial orientation, although the Arabs' relation to land and home is more natural and authentic than the Jewish conception, for which having a hold over the land is a new, thrilling, as-yet-undigested and preadolescent experience. By contrast, the Arabs—and even the Germans—have difficulty understanding the Israeli need for a multiply-reinforced psychological safety belt to prevent a new Shoah. Thus the region's interterritorial drama is perpetuated as each side threatens the other with the worst—the Arabs with the annihilation of Israel, and the Israelis with the indefinite occupation of Arab land.

The trouble is that this conflict, which periodically threatens world peace—or at least peace in the region—takes place in an age in which the national-territorial way of thinking, in its old sense, is making way for a more international, federal, and to a certain extent even trans-global conception. Protracted territorial struggles erode the vital energy and creative potential of all sides. [...]

This is where the observation ends and the vision starts. And the name of the vision is Net Israel—Upwards.

Gross Israel—with a million Arabs and their lands and a floundering economy—is, no doubt, an international military power for short ranges of combat. [...] And what's worse: it's a backward country, with an agrarian settling ideology. Artificially enlarged, but with low-built structures. One big flat village. Even Tel Aviv is essentially a dwarf city. And the ideal of living in Herzliya-Pituach and Savion still attracts the Israeli newly-rich.

But Net Israel—without a million Arabs and with a recovering economy after another peace agreement or two or more—will be even more powerful. I see a country in which all the building planning from now on is upwards, a country of skyscrapers everywhere, even in the moshavim and kibbutzim, a country that—as a single unit—will offer the same accumulation of powerful urban energy that we see in New York, for example. [...]

In other words: I see Israel as a whole turning from a village into a city, shrinking a little widthwise and soaring upwards, investing energy in itself rather than in surroundings held by force. An Israel that prepares itself for the year 2000 and that can play a major role in uniting the entire region, with its plentiful resources—one day, in the not too distant future—into one bloc such as in Western Europe. [...]

The first step is to wean ourselves off the territorial complex, a weaning off that would also effect changes among the Arabs. Although it was said that man is dust and to dust he will return, the Sages for their part proclaimed that when descending Israel will sink to dust, and when ascending it will rise up to the stars.

[David Avidan (1934–1995) was a poet, playwright, filmmaker, publicist, and artist.]

1 The article from which this excerpt was taken was published in Hebrew in the literary magazine *Moznaim* 59: 7–8 (January–March 1986), pp. 6–56. It is translated into English for the first time here. Translator: Michal Sapir.

## Farewell to the Welfare State: Speculation of Size

②

In contradistinction to the all-too-present notion of the massive national project, the ambition of the large object was initially lacking in the Zionist architectural imaginary. The first signs of interest in sizable buildings appeared only in the late 1950s, once the Israeli project had survived its first decade. The very first appearances of architectural largeness were not related to an authoritative representation of the State apparatus—in fact, the construction of such projects as the Knesset parliament building or the Binyenei Ha'Uma national convention center were postponed or prolonged precisely due to their monumentality. Nor were they related to ostentatious private or corporate investment, which would be perceived not merely as bad taste, but as a betrayal of the common good.

First to be amplified was the housing block, the proverbial "melting pot." In the late 1950s, several super-blocks were designed and built, in particular in the model-housing complexes in Beersheba and Haifa. The longest of these was the "quarter-kilometer block" in Beersheba (1959–1964), designed by Avraham Yasky and Amnon Alexandroni.[1] These early super-blocks are an indication neither of the streamlining of production and construction processes, nor of efficient use of land resources; they are only a sign of their own anomaly, their experimental colossality.

In the early 1960s, the super-blocks multiplied and grew in length, though mainly on paper, proliferating in design magazines and international competitions launched in Israel at the time. Examples are the competition for the planning of the Manshiya district on the Tel Aviv–Jaffa border, or the competition for the planning of the city center of Ashdod. In practice, horizontal enormity was not a real option, even under the particular conditions in Israel of (over 95 percent) nationalized land and an almost entirely State-sponsored housing industry. Its seductiveness was entirely reflexive—an architectural overdose by and for architects.

④

At the beginning of the 1960s in Tel Aviv, about a dozen "multiple-storey houses" equipped with elevators, dubbed "sky-scrapers," sprouted up. These eight- to twelve-storey harbingers of vertical magnitude were seen by the local public as revolutionary buildings—but even before the public could get used to these, there arose in the heart of "little Tel Aviv," amidst the two- to three-storey eclectic-style buildings of the 1910s and 1920s, an awesome structure that alone would dominate the Tel Aviv cityscape for the next thirty-five years: the Shalom Tower, an initiative of the Meir family, designed by the architects Yitzhak Perlstein and Gideon Ziv.

The product of a complex business deal that included private capital and government investment, at a fantastic cost (in those days) of 25 million dollars, the Shalom Tower was 140 meters in height and 35 storeys above ground level ("the tallest building of its kind between Milan and Tokyo"[2]), with 26 fast elevators and escalators. Its innovative building method used concrete beams laid like a bridge between two concrete towers, and it was constructed according to the strict California earthquake standards (Shmaya Ben Avraham, the building's engineer, said, "The safest place to be during an earthquake in Tel Aviv is the Shalom Tower."[3]) Its 100,000 square meters of public and commercial space (just like in New York's Chrysler Building) contained office floors filled with government offices, banks, lawyers, accountants, insurance companies, and the like; a commercial sublevel had three parking levels and room for some 1,000 cars. It was constructed with 400 tons of iron, 35 kilometers of water pipes, 500 kilometers of electrical and telephone wires, 100,000 electrical bulbs, and 37.5 tons of ceramic tiles. It boasted a sophisticated air-conditioning system (the first of its kind in Israel) and a no-less-advanced system of aluminum windows. Finally, a (civilian and military) lookout from the roof provided a panoramic view of the city; on a clear day you could see the entire width of Israel, from the sea to the West Bank mountain ridges.

③

The palpably visible success of the homegrown Shalom Tower project paradoxically aroused a passion for the charms of foreign professionals. Even before construction was completed, as the citizens of the city still gazed in wonderment at the vision of the "rising form," which daily added a new celestial threshold to the skyline, architects from around the world were invited—

② Supermarket and apartment building, Tel Aviv, Perspective. 1958. Nahum Zolotov.

③ View of the El Al Building from the north, ca. 1960. Dov Karmi, Zvi Meltzer, Ram Karmi. In the background, the Shalom Tower is under construction.

④ Shalom Tower under construction, Tel Aviv, ca. 1960. Yitzhak Perlstein, Gideon Ziv, Meir Levy.

whether privately, by big developers (and given the royal treatment, meeting with ministers, Labor Federation leaders, and military personnel), or via pretentious international competitions—to scribble their visions of grandeur. As for the Shalom Tower, it came to be viewed as a local experiment lacking in imagination and impetus, signifying at the very most a kind of foreplay to an as-yet-unleashed urban Eros.

As historical perspective comes into focus regarding the actual development of the Hebrew city, the revolutionary eccentricity of the Shalom Tower becomes clearer, and the premature tendency to marginalize its importance and substantiality is exposed. For instance, in a 1964 article surveying Tel Aviv's skyscraper fashion, the Shalom Tower, which already stood tall at the time, is "forgotten":

> In Tel Aviv the construction of tall buildings, of 12 to 30 storeys, preceded the arrival of [Oscar] Niemeyer, but these are for the most part awkward and clumsy buildings that are not distinguished, except in their height, from Tel Aviv's boring strip of stilt houses. With only a few exceptions (the earliest of these being [the] supermarket building [on Ben Yehuda Street]; the Neot Aviv building on the corner of Ibn Gabirol and Shaul HaMelekh [...]; and the commercial center on the property of the electric company [...]), which are built with charm and with a feeling of spaciousness, most of the high buildings designed by Israeli architects, rather than relieving the atmosphere in Tel Aviv, only weigh upon it. There was nothing unique about them to justify the demand from the clerks in charge of the construction regulations for a different attitude and approach.[4]

Although the Shalom Tower's existence is hinted at here ("30 storeys"), it is not even included in the list of "tall buildings" that have something "unique" about them. The writer chooses instead to enthrall the public with a description of the speculative plan for the Nordiya Compound (later the Dizengoff Center) proposed by the Brazilian architect Oscar Niemeyer, which allowed itself five times the "aerial rights" (i.e., floor area ratio) permitted in the city's zoning regulations. The very presence

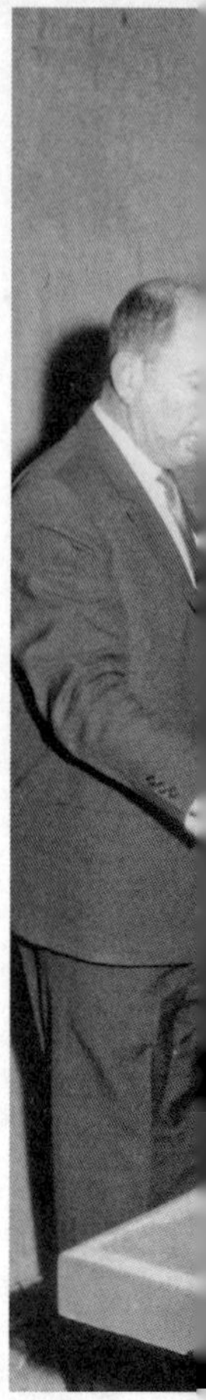

⑤

⑤ Yitzhak Rabin with a model of the Shalom Tower, 1960.
⑥ Shalom Tower under construction, Tel Aviv, early 1960s. Yitzhak Perlstein, Gideon Ziv, Meir Levy.

and activity of the famous international architect in Israel was seen as hastening the vertical salvation of the city:

> We needed the name and authority of a genius like Niemeyer in order to convince the executive echelon that vertical construction is, or can be, different from regular construction. [...] Even if Niemeyer's plan isn't the actual pioneer in vertical construction in Tel Aviv, it is certainly the most powerful innovative force for the proper conception of vertical construction. One should assume that the project in and of itself will encourage, and even inspire, Israeli architects to pick up this new trend. Niemeyer gave vertical construction the stamp of fashion. Now everyone will want to build skyward.[5]

Foreign experts added a vital cosmopolitan luster to the Israel of the early 1960s, which was still the "working man's Israel" but sought to alter its status and its (self-)image as a developing country through the trappings of a burgeoning entrepreneurial culture. Openness to the world was perceived as a prerequisite—purely symbolic, of course—to local development. When it comes to architecture (which requires no special knowledge or inspiration that could not be found locally), this phenomenon seems all the more ludicrous, unmasking a desire for the a priori positioning of Israeli capitalism, even before it had a real market, through a bricolage of exotic architects.

But why not emphasize the practical, strategic aspect of importing foreign architects? Beyond the excitement aroused by international trends and the premature aspiration to have one's own hyper-modernist object, like the Seagram Building in New York or the Pirelli Tower in Milan, business had a clear interest in using the mediatic distraction of foreign architects to cut through urban bylaws and zoning regulations, bureaucratic red tape, and residues of old ideologies and habits. In the 1960s there was the feeling that such a celebrity strategy could succeed in liberating the Israeli city from its structural pettiness. This pettiness, we should remember, was the consequence not of a slow historical evolution or of provinciality for its own sake, but rather of a systematic planning mode based on well-grounded environmental, social, and cultural arguments that often met under the generic title of "garden city." The overall sub-urban propensity dictated a fairly generous spreading out, a parcelization into small plots, and a far-reaching consideration for the pedestrian (as opposed to the driver)—but it left very few plots free for corporate initiatives. The scarcity of large plots in the hearts of cities fueled speculative projects in the few locations that became available and compelled both the authorities and private developers to reenvision the city. In Tel Aviv, in effect the only capitalist city in 1960s Israel, the imagination of the future focused on three major sites: the Nordiya Compound, Kikar Hamedina and the Manshiya Compound.

In her book *Dionysus at the Center*, cultural critic Tamar Berger investigates the Nordiya site, a 37-dunam plot in the heart of Tel Aviv that housed some 350 families in about 200 cabins, as a paradigm of the beginnings of speculative urbanism in Israel. The following passages from Berger's book situate the proposals of I. M. Pei—who came to Israel in 1960 at the invitation of the entrepreneur Moshe Meir and was the first of the foreign architects of largeness—and Oscar Niemeyer within the local narrative.

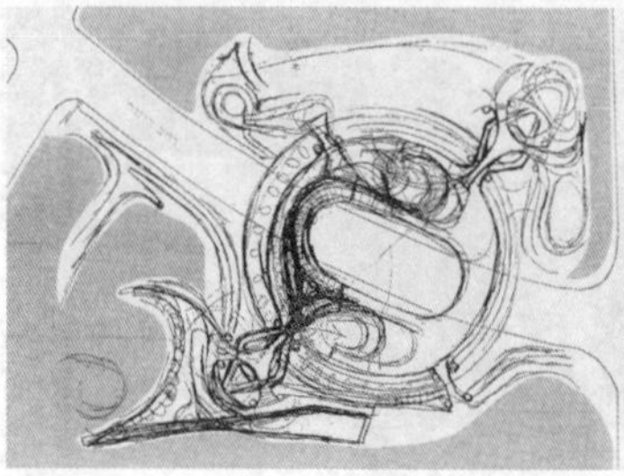

⑦

⑧

> In 1958 "Nordiya Homes" came along. This was, in effect, the first company to express any real interest in building on the neighborhood's land. It was made up of two parts: the Haifa contracting group of Tenenbaum, Mandelman, Katz, and Sayed, and the American National Engineering Company (Shulman). For the 37 dunam, the company paid the Israel Land Development Corporation 600,000 Israeli lira.
>
> Things were moving along. The municipal council rushed, even before an official decision was reached, to recommend that the authorized institutions make dispensations for the contractors. These were led to understand that the 300,000-lira loan was ensured and that the floor area ratio would be increased. Mayor Levanon announced to the press that he had no authority on this matter, but about a month later the workers' groups complained that the town-planning committee had approved the deviations. They weren't pleased with the generous credit, either. In February 1959 the municipal finance committee approved the contract with the contractors, and in early March the council approved the loan. In addition, the contractors were permitted to put up six-storey buildings to house the evacuees.
>
> In April, the groundbreaking ceremony for two seven-storey buildings was held. The municipality approved the master plan for the construction of the neighborhood,

which was to include skyscrapers, businesses, offices, a cinema, parking lots, and several residential units. The neighborhood numbered 1,300 souls and 207 shacks. Newspaper reports gave the clear impression that a solution was at hand.

A short time after the groundbreaking ceremony, the Hinawi plot made its way to the bank, sprawled out in the safe, and loitered there for many years, getting fatter. [...] In 1962, when a new master stepped in, it became clear just how much it had grown: it was now worth five million Israeli lira. Indeed, 1960 to 1962 witnessed rises of hundreds of percent in the value of "construction plots in a ripe environment," and such was the land of Dizengoff Center. The value of land increased at a much greater speed than money.

The new master was Yekutiel Federman, owner of the Dan Hotel chain, who came in when the Engineering Company backed out. He apparently paid 25 million Israeli lira, which conferred on him control of 73 percent of the company's shares.

Then, more or less, a veritable planning revolution happened on paper. Moshe Meir, whose family, like the Pilz family, had left a substantial mark on the city—he built the Shalom Tower in 1960—invited the American architect Ieoh-Ming Pei to plan a few large projects. [...]

Meir was not officially connected to the Nordiya project, but he was a kind of proxy for the landowners. This becomes clear from, among other things, letters sent by the original architects, Elhanani and Lotan, firmly clarifying to Pei: "we are the winners of the planning competition for Nordiya, and any invitation on the part of the construction company for you to plan it is null and void." Pei's plan for Nordiya included three towers, one cylindrical and the other two shorter and elliptical, and a long, narrow rectangular building behind the tall tower, enclosing the area of the site.

[...] Meir did end up becoming involved with the initiative, and the plan was shelved. But one goes and another comes. In 1964 the earth trembled with the arrival of

⑨

⑦ Nordiya, later known as Dizengoff Center, 1971–1972. Sketch for commercial center. Ram Karmi.
⑧ Nordiya, Tel Aviv, 1961. Proposal for office, residential, and commercial center. Model. I. M. Pei.
⑨ Nordiya, Tel Aviv, 1961. Proposal for office, residential and commercial center. Model. I. M. Pei.

Oscar Niemeyer, at the invitation of Federman from Nordiya Homes.[6]

Pei did not merely design large, highly profitable objects for his clients. He went to the trouble of offering the urban rhetoric that would prime the public for the transition from a centralized conception of sprawl to scattered initiatives of density: Size is a prerequisite for the city. Density is a condition for space. Compactness is a prerequisite for openness. These are the bottom lines that reached Israel with a delay of almost half a century. In the brochure accompanying his proposal for the Nordiya Compound, Pei wrote:

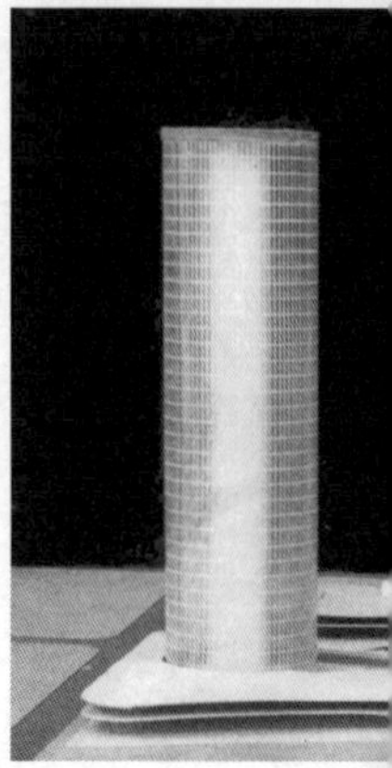

⑩

> Instead of being covered with another cluster of low buildings, the site will be boldly developed as a unified whole, with three high-rises on a wide and open base. They will connect harmoniously with one another and integrate organically into the surrounding city. [...] The plan, which prefers vertical construction on a limited area to low horizontal construction, enables the rest of the site—almost two thirds of the area—to function as a public and open meeting place in the heart of the city.[7]

Such demonstrative concern for the fate of the entire city and the welfare of all its citizens is a clear sign of detachment from the contiguous urban fabric, a disposition to ignore the specifics of the given site, and an intention to cut it off from its existing infrastructures. This was always the subtext of the discourse of bigness. The text, in varying words and sounds, has been much the same since the invention of the elevator:

> Today already, Tel Aviv suffers from too much sprawl and unreasonable distances—and still the area manages to be chaotic, horrifically choked and crowded, noisy and intolerably jammed up. The unrestrained sprawl of the city, homogeneous almost from end to end, accentuates the critics' complaints about its monotony and architectural paucity. [...] While most of the buildings—even groups of buildings—tend to obey the pattern dictated by its immediate surroundings, Nordiya must look towards the horizon and initiate a dialogue with the entire city.[8]

Let us remember that a similar, almost identical, language of architectural paucity served the preachers of dispersal, the knights of the small scale who actually turned the slogan "From the City to the Village" into flesh and blood in the 1950s: "The old cities in Israel and also in Europe [...] are built in a monotonous continuum of houses, streets, and residential neighborhoods which stretch out endlessly and make the lives of their inhabitants unbearable."[9]

Either way, Pei's Nordiya plan aimed much farther than the precedent of the Shalom Tower. It did not propose a tall building, a landmark, or a monument, but rather imagined a new city. The Shalom Tower was born out of an urban master plan (in force to this day) intended to create a linear CBD (central business district) that would form the backbone of the developing city. It envisioned itself, and the buildings of its kind that were meant to line up alongside it in the future, as adapting the city to itself. Its enduring loneliness—arrogant or melancholic—in the skies of Tel Aviv has (until recently) immortalized the futile attempts to engineer the market forces along absurd urban axes invented by planning teams in the municipality. Pei's proposal for Nordiya, on the other hand, neither realized nor conformed to some existing urban plan, but imagined a commercial compound that would defeat all the others by quantitative means: it was not merely a large prosthesis on a small body, but a "unified whole" that mocked and obviated the existing city.

When Oscar Niemeyer arrived in Israel in early 1964 at the invitation of the prominent entrepreneur Yekutiel Federman, the local debate about "future urban visions" was already in full swing. The public swooned at the ideas of the genius from Brazil; local newspapers rushed to publish the photogenic models he produced; investors were ready to translate his virtuoso sketches into buildings; the senior ranks of the establishment hastened to adopt his spectacular verticality and to give the go-ahead for his instant glass towers.

⑪

Niemeyer spent about half a year in Israel, while he was in political exile from Brazil. He arrived with a small team of assistants—a model-maker, an accountant, and a structural engineer—and was housed at the Tel Aviv Dan Hotel and the Haifa Dan-Carmel, both owned by Federman.[10] During his exile in Israel, he managed to plan a series of large projects including the Nordiya Compound and Kikar Hamedina in Tel Aviv; Haifa University and the Panorama Towers in Haifa; and a "vertical city" in the Negev Desert; as well as some side jobs, such as a mansion in Caesarea for his Israeli patron, Federman. His résumé for 1964, published in his 1968 book *Quase Memórias*, is dedicated almost entirely to projects in Israel.[11] As he accumulated commissions in Israel, the situation back in Brazil was deteriorating:

> My time in Israel was prolonged for many months, first due to invitations for new projects which came one after the other, and later because the friends from Brazil reported to me in their letters [...] that the new regime annulled my political rights, that the army was looking for me in Brasília, and that the police entered my office in Rio and conducted a search there. [...]
>
> For six months I resided at the Tel Aviv Dan Hotel as Federman's guest. I shut myself away on the mezzanine floor that was allocated for me as a work space and there I worked day and night like crazy. [...] After six months, we opened in the hotel an exhibition called *Six Months in Israel* which displayed the prepared projects. The exhibition aroused in the visitors—who were facing such a quantity of work achieved in such a short period—feelings of wonder and respect. In addition to the plans and models, the exhibition also included explanatory texts and schemes of reinforced concrete calculations, which prevented superfluous questions and provided solid proof of the feasibility of the plans presented. The Nordiya complex, Panorama, The Negev City, Haifa University [...] these projects demonstrated that the opinions of the clients or of the local technicians did not bother me at all. [...] I was compelled to work only out of loyalty to my own way in order to produce singular and diverse works that would satisfy me and justify my stay in Israel.[12]

⑫

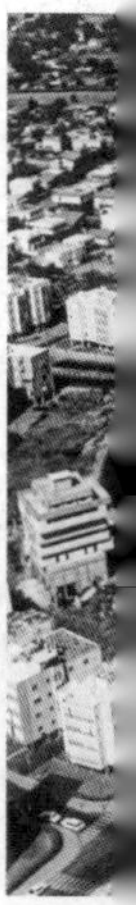

⑩ – ⑫ Nordiya, Tel Aviv, 1964. Proposal for office, residential, and commercial center. Model. Oscar Niemeyer, with Aba Elhanani, Israel Lotan, David Resnick, Chaim Tibbon.
⑬ Kikar Hamedina, Tel Aviv, 1960. The inner space of this roundabout is one of the most expensive lots in Tel Aviv and was subject to countless speculative projects. As of 2017, only the outer ring is built. The round square is still devoid of buildings.

Niemeyer was not asked to produce brochures with didactic explanations about urbanism, and even less to prepare precise plans detailing his ideas and defending their validity. A *Haaretz* writer reported:

> After two weeks in Israel, Mr. Niemeyer gave a lecture last night in front of dozens of architects and engineers at the Engineers' House in Tel Aviv, in which he outlined the principles of his plan for the rebuilding of the Nordiya neighborhood. [...] Of late, Mr. Niemeyer has gained world fame for the greatness of his works—the public buildings in the new capital of Brazil, Brasília, which began to be built in 1958 under the then president of Brazil, Juscelino Kubitschek. There are those who see Mr. Niemeyer as the greatest architect of our time. [...] His plans for the Nordiya neighborhood might well therefore "place" Tel Aviv on the map of world architecture.[13]

The fantastic quantitative standards set down by Pei on the Nordiya lot provided Niemeyer with programmatic development data. All that remained was to streamline and stylize the project. The clumsy buildings sprouting straight out of the ground, the generous plazas between them, and the covered streets connecting the various parts of the project—planned by Pei in such a way that almost two-thirds of the area of the site was wide open and would serve as a "public meeting place in the heart of the city"—were replaced, in Niemeyer's vision, by "concrete plateaus" including commercial floors and a free-form platform with three elegant round glass towers on it. The description by the *Haaretz* writer overlooks none of its fictional quality:

(13)

> The three spires will contain residential units, businesses, offices, and entertainment, and they will "grow" out of two concrete plateaus containing two storeys, each housing coffee shops, a cinema, a school, a medical center, and other services, which on most of the area will be covered with gardens. A ramp will descend from street level to the underground levels, which, among other things, will contain 3,000 parking spots, thereby easing the parking strain in the area of Dizengoff Square and the busy street.
>
> Mr. Niemeyer's plan had three incarnations, though the principle—three tall buildings—remained intact from the

> architect's first moment of inspiration, around the time of his arrival in Tel Aviv. Some say that he was impressed by the towers rising above Herzliya Square [the Shalom Tower], but that he was surprised to hear that these were just the elevator shafts, which would be concealed by the floors being built. And then it was as if the idea of three high spires was born, the tallest of which would tower over the hilltop where Dizengoff Street begins.[14]

(14)

The original construction cost of the Nordiya project was estimated at between 10 and 15 million Israeli lira. After Niemeyer's lecture at the Engineer's House, the talk was of 100 million Israeli lira. *Haaretz* also reported on a compromise with the original competition winners, the architects Aba Elhanani and Israel Lotan, who were added to the planning team along with the architect David Resnick, Niemeyer's former student. Tamar Berger sums up the Niemeyer affair at Nordiya as follows:

(15)

> The authorization process for the plan was sluggish. Federman complained about this, gently, to the mayor in October 1964: "My dear Yehoshua, I was sorry to hear that you are once again not feeling well," he wrote. "Prof. Niemeyer writes that he must prepare for the continuation of this project into 1965, but he has the impression that the plan has not received the proper treatment it would have received in another country."
>
> The plan was transferred to the local committee and in 1965 it was approved with a few changes. Now it included a three-storey underground parking lot, a fourth underground level with a modern commercial center, and above it another center, three glass apartment towers, the highest, of forty storeys. The entire area of the plan covered 37 dunam, among them 100,000 square meters of built-up area. The construction, it was estimated, would begin in a year.[15]

Like Pei before him, Niemeyer was also invited to propose a plan for Kikar Hamedina. Nordiya's 37 dunam were dwarfed in comparison with the 90 dunam handed over, this time by the municipality, to Niemeyer, in cooperation with architects Aba Elhanani and Israel Lotan.

(16)

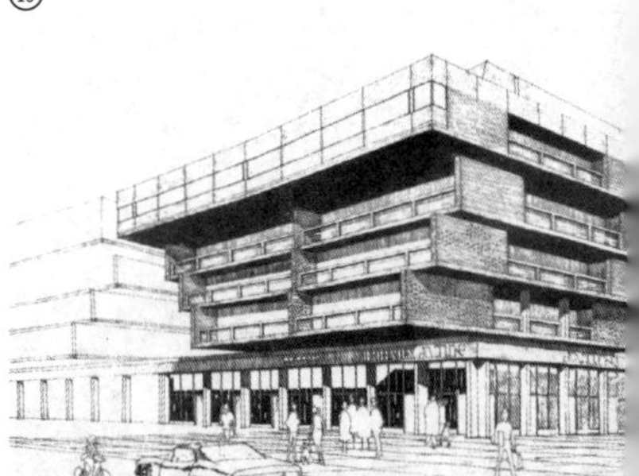

Kikar Hamedina's story is completely different from that of Nordiya. It is not an urban remnant whose distorted form documents the pains and passions of the site, but a perfect

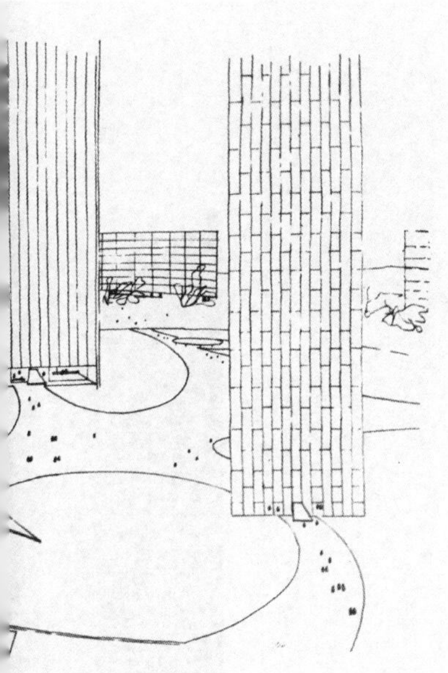

circle cut out of the map of the city, a deliberate "hole" left as an arena for speculative projects. Nordiya is loaded with historical and physical context. Its power as a literary topos stems from its being a living fabric. By contrast, Kikar Hamedina is empty; it is the city's only non-place. Here Niemeyer did not have to create an artificial base that would correct the flaws of the existing plot in order to carry his elegant towers. The circle's circumference promised complete protection from the idiosyncratic interference of the city and cleared the area for architectural composition.

In Kikar Hamedina as well, Niemeyer designed three towers that would eventually merge into one giant tower. But this time—paradoxically because of the tabula rasa, which ostensibly allowed the design process to be liberated from contextual stipulations—uncertainty grew regarding the cost of the project and the duration of its construction. A *Maariv* journalist reported that the deputy mayor of the city answered a question with: "We commissioned the project from Niemeyer—and we should assume that the project will be accepted." When reporters asked how much the project would cost, "Mr. Rabinovitz thought it over and then said: '200 million lira... if not a lot more than that.'"[16] Aba Elhanani, usually an articulate speaker, submitted a statement that was no less perplexing: "The project is not overly grandiose. Physically speaking, the construction can be completed within five years, but in terms of financing, the construction could stretch out for eighteen years. It is not an out-of-the-ordinary structure for Tel Aviv. Such structures already exist."[17]

After the ebbing of initial excitement at the great ideas of the foreign architects, voices began to be heard among the public and in the professional community about the impulsiveness of the big projects and the lack of coordination between them. Their necessity was even questioned. Shabtai Tevet's article about the hyperactivity in Tel Aviv, for example, sounds downright satirical:

⑭ Kikar Hamedina, Tel Aviv, 1960. Proposal for a residential and commercial project. I. M. Pei.
⑮ Kikar Hamedina, Tel Aviv, 1964. Proposal for a residential and commercial project. Oscar Niemeyer.
⑯ Kikar Hamedina, Tel Aviv, 1964. Proposal for residential and commercial buildings at the outer ring. Oscar Niemeyer, Aba Elhanani, Israel Lotan.

The clash between the Nordiya towers and the Manshiya project symbolizes a version writ large of the many smaller clashes that happen daily. As the dynamic development of Tel Aviv unfolds, it takes us ever further away from anything that might ever be a plan for the urban center of Tel Aviv. Today no fewer than fifteen projects are helping drag the future center to hell.

[...] The great fireworks-like diffusion first and foremost undermines all that is good and spacious about vertical construction, because the centers are surrounded by low residential construction and are, one way or the other, immersed in it. The main problem in such a situation is that there is no possibility of widening the streets and opening up areas to create open spaces.

[...] This fireworks-style construction is done according to hasty commercial impulses. Suddenly it seems worthwhile to build a large building on such-and-such a spot, and then suddenly something similar becomes worthwhile in a different place, but the overall question must be: How many new offices does Tel Aviv need, how many new businesses, how many commercial centers? [...] Where will we find all the factories and businesses [to fill] the numerous offices in the new construction projects, those that have begun, those that are completed, and those that are yet to be, whether in private projects or in the Manshiya project?[18]

⑰

⑱

A more professional and ethical critique was formulated by Michael Kuhn, the most profound of the architect-critics of the period, in *Engineering and Architecture: The Union of Engineers and Architects in Israel*, under the unequivocal title "Eradicate the Speculative Approach in Building":

⑲

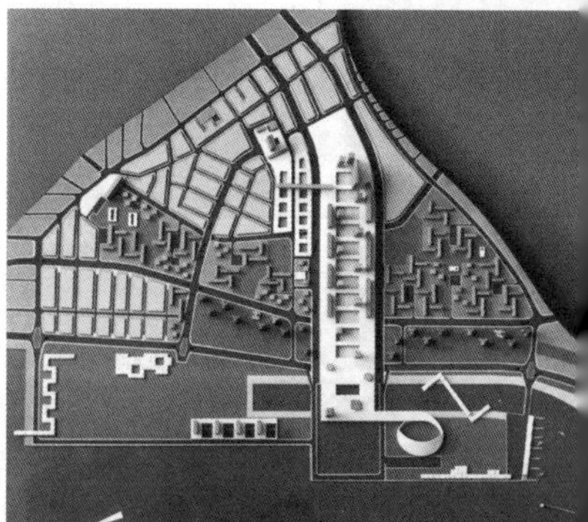

Today we are witnessing the waste of the once-in-a-lifetime opportunity to plan the city center: for example, the extensive Manshiya area, located in the geographic center of the city, between Tel Aviv and Jaffa, and bordering on the coast, has been handed over to private interests for fragmented planning that is completely disconnected from the overall planning of the city. A new player has arisen in the country in the field of urban planning, and it is: the Government Tourism Corporation (perhaps because the millionaires who visit the country come under the auspices of this esteemed company). The center of Tiberias and, rumor has it, also

other central places in the country, has been handed over to capitalists from abroad without planning and without bearing the best interests of the city in mind. If we add to this the planning of the area of the Herzliya Gymnasium, whose program was not determined by the municipality but by private interests—who, by the nature of things, are focused on the largest possible profits—then what we have before us is a rather horrifying picture. The architectural community must demand the reconsideration of these activities, which close the books on the serious planning of their cities.[19]

1964, Niemeyer's Israeli year, earned the title "mega-year" in the historiography of international architecture. Reyner Banham awarded 1964 a special status because during this year several major projects were carried out under the general title of "megastructure," and several publications laying out the theoretical groundwork and preliminary definitions for megastructures were issued, such as architect Fumihiko Maki's *Investigations in Collective Form*:

The megastructure is a large frame in which all the functions of a city or part of a city are housed. It has been made possible by present day technology. In a sense, it is a man-made feature of the landscape. [...] Inherent in the megastructure concept, along with a certain static nature, is the suggestion that many and diverse functions may beneficially be concentrated in one place. [...] Professor [Kenzo] Tange presents a proposal for a mass-human scale form which includes a megaform and discrete, rapidly changeable functional units which fit within the larger framework.[20]

(17) Entry for the international competition for planning the Manshiya district, Tel Aviv, 1963. Jan Lubiez-Mycz, Donald Reay.
(18) The jury of the international competition for planning the Manshiya district, Tel Aviv, 1963. Arieh Sharon, head of the jury, explains the projects to Prime Minister Levi Eshkol. Yael Aloni Photo Collection. Courtesy of the Azrieli Architectural Archive, Arieh Sharon Collection.
(19) Entry for the international competition for planning the Manshiya district, Tel Aviv, 1963. Or, Gwirtzman, Horman, Mertens, Chechik.
(20) Entry for the international competition for planning the Manshiya district, Tel Aviv, 1963. Or, Gvirtzman, Horman, Mertens, Chechik.

(20)

㉑

㉒

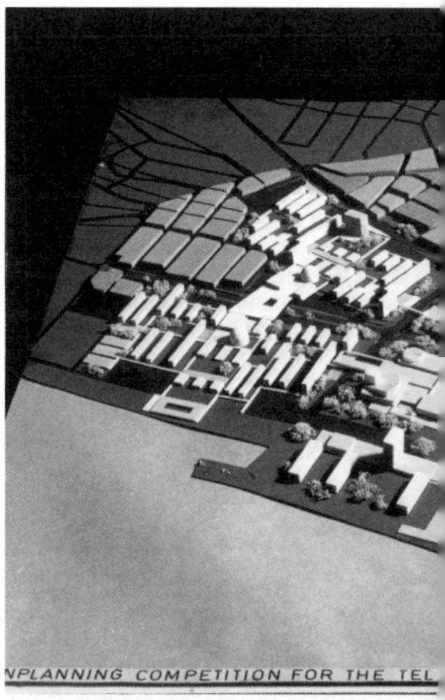


㉑ Entry for the international competition for planning the Manshiya district, Tel Aviv, 1963. Z. Polak, J. Skrzydczak, H. Frey, Z. Pawlowski. Yael Aloni Photo Collection. Courtesy of the Azrieli Architectural Archive, Arieh Sharon Collection.
㉒ The international competition for planning the Manshiya district, Tel Aviv, 1963. The jury with Prime Minister Levi Eshkol. Yael Aloni Photo Collection. Courtesy of the Azrieli Architectural Archive, Arieh Sharon Collection.
㉓ The international competition for planning the Manshiya district, Tel Aviv, 1963. The jury with Louis Kahn. Yael Aloni Photo Collection. Courtesy of the Azrieli Architectural Archive, Arieh Sharon Collection.

㉓

㉔

㉕

㉔ The international competition for planning the Manshiya district, Tel Aviv, 1963. The jury with Prime Minister Levi Eshkol. Yael Aloni Photo Collection. Courtesy of the Azrieli Architectural Archive, Arieh Sharon Collection.

㉕ Entry for the international competition for planning the Manshiya district, Tel Aviv, 1963. Or, Gwirtzman, Horman, Mertens, Chechik. Yael Aloni Photo Collection. Courtesy of the Azrieli Architectural Archive, Arieh Sharon Collection.

㉖

㉘

Maki's definition offers such insights as a "man-made feature of the landscape" and a "mass-human scale form" and adds new key terms to the professional jargon, such as "large frame" and "rapidly changeable functional units." All of this suggests the surfacing of a new conception of bigness (more complex, restless, and pretentious than its forebears), though it is still entirely unclear when a project or building transcends the cumbersomeness of big and engages the hyperactivity of mega. Reyner Banham, for his part, in a laconic summation, makes sure to leave the question open: "In their time, all megastructures were large buildings—but not all large buildings of the time were megastructures."[21]

There is no reason today to try to hone retrospective definitions—but for the sake of completing the account of Israeli architecture's preoccupation with size, one may add the observation that the size of the megastructure is indecipherable because it is never really defined. This is precisely its modus operandi. Its immensity is vague. Its ominous presence is an aftereffect of its minimizing strategy, a strategy that ostensibly relies on modular fragmentation, cellular dispersion, self-generative growth, clustering, flux, open-endedness, and so on. Its structures are always giant miniatures—super-temporal, super-local, elastic, formless—hypothetically adaptable to every situation and contingency on the ground.

In all that concerns architectural fashions, in particular the structuralist, megastructuralist, or mini-megastructuralist taste, the Israel of the early 1960s was considered entirely up-to-date. It was even discussed in international professional journals as one of the most experimental scenes of the period. Planning and design competitions, local and international, transformed the country into a laboratory for radical urban and architectural ideas. The ephemerality and flexibility attributed to the megastructures; the futuristic rusticity inscribed in their DNA; their mathematical neutrality; their lack of scale; their capacity of infill, sprawl, and self-replication on the territory; their ability to hover and hang in the air; their amphibious longings—all these invited ex-machina solutions to the local architectural narrative, which, after a formative decade of total commitment to the doctrinaire order of the welfare state, was exposed in all its political and cultural complexity.

Two international architectural competitions held in 1963, the first in Tel Aviv (the Manshiya complex) and the second in

(27)

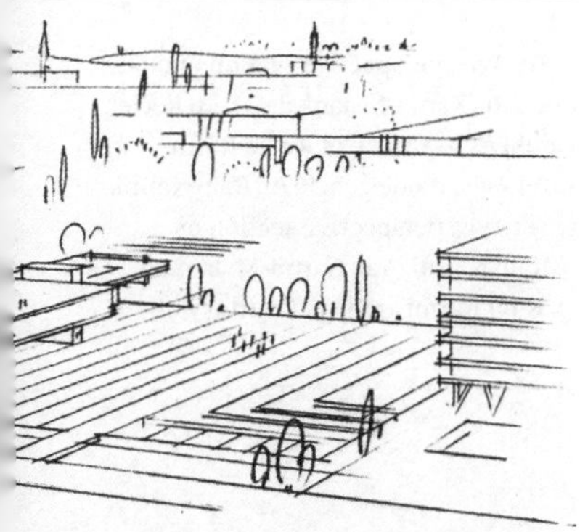

Jerusalem (the municipality building), thoroughly illustrate the two sides of the megastructuralist coin: a new contextual sensitivity that no longer settled for "characterless buildings," and an audacious detachment that invented tangled plug-in cities and animated cartoon structures.

In Tel Aviv, proposals included super-blocks stretching out for kilometers; multilayered roads "weaving" the entire city into a colossal urban machine; and vertical clusters emerging from artificial islands dotting the shoreline.

The competition for the Jerusalem municipality displayed oversized towers and flanking megastructures hovering above the city, refraining from touching its historic fabric. The winning entry, by architects Al Mansfeld and Daniel Havkin, proposed a tower commanding a view of the city (another proposal of theirs, more diffuse, earned second prize). Mayor Teddy Kollek opposed the proposed site of the competition (King George Street), and in 1972 the site of the Russian Compound, near the Old City, was chosen. This time Mansfeld and Havkin proposed a "flexible cumulative system" of floating blocks with hanging office floors at varying heights supplied by service towers. A collage prepared by the architects, in which the project is transplanted to the Jerusalem horizon, reveals a wild vision of gigantic pilotis and cantilevered "skyhooks" that would gradually replace the Old City.

In 1970s Israel, the appeal of the megastructure began to wane, in particular that of the more instrumental genre, which propagated images of sci-fi "urban" technology. The main reason for this was the sudden construction boom that began after 1967 and redirected architectural energies toward the actual construction of new towns and neighborhoods. The fantastic paper architecture of the 1960s liberated the sublimated architecture of the 1950s; the politics of post-1967 Greater Israel offered a new, more tangible, release for the local architecture of bigness through oversized projects which, although they may not have met all the criteria of megastructuralism, certainly

(26) Jerusalem City Hall competition, 1964. Photomontage. Second proposal by Al Mansfeld and Daniel Havkin.
(27) Jerusalem City Hall as an accumulative megastructure at the "Russian Compound" site, 1974. Model. Proposal by Al Mansfeld and Daniel Havkin, 1974.
(28) Jerusalem City Hall as a tower. Perspective. Jerusalem City Hall competition, 1964. Winning entry. Al Mansfeld, Danicl Havkin.

㉙

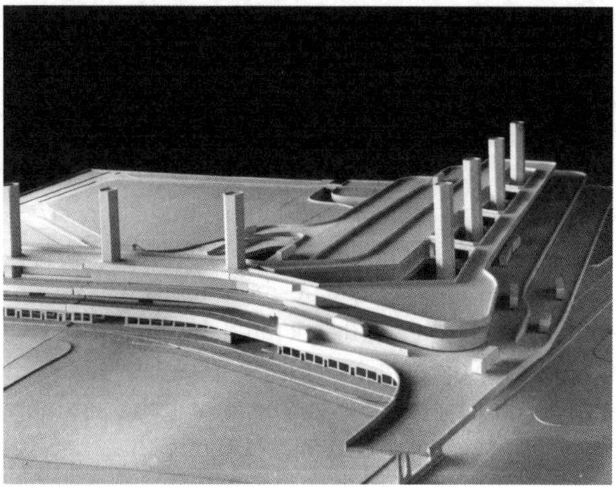

㉚

㉙ Central bus station, Tel Aviv, perspective section of final proposal, 1967. Ram Karmi, Ada Karmi-Melamede, Haim Ketzef, Ben Peleg. Ram Karmi archive. Courtesy of Rivka Karmi.
㉚ Central bus station, Tel Aviv, model, ca. 1970. Ram Karmi.
㉛ Central bus station, Tel Aviv, perspective section of primary proposal, 1966. Ram Karmi, Ada Karmi-Melamede, Haim Ketzef, Ben Peleg. Ram Karmi archive. Courtesy of Rivka Karmi.

31

internalized some of its main attributes. For instance, the Hebrew University campus on Mount Scopus—*the* architectural icon of post-1967 Israel (see dossier "The Hebrew University Campus" in chapter "State Architecture")—could not have taken its form without the quest for bigness, open-ended accumulative systems, and expansionist pseudo-urban structures. After all, what could better fit the new need to figuratively express a resolute occupation of territories and domination of landscapes?

(32)

Under unique geopolitical circumstances, and without any gradual evolutionary process, the (theoretical) architecture of lightness, impermanence, adaptability, mobility, and informality was exchanged for an official architecture—once again "stately," once again nationalist, but now openly so—of mass and weight, of stoned fortifications and ersatz Orientalism (misappropriated arches, domes, and casbah formations). The bohemian utopianism of the 1960s was replaced by the passive-aggressive patriotism of the 1970s and 1980s—particularly, but certainly not exclusively, in the Occupied Territories around Jerusalem.

(33)

The visions of vertical size in 1960s Israel were for the most part left unrealized. The precedent that is the Shalom Tower was before its time. The promise of a linear CBD in the heart of the city gave rise in the 1990s to a few random towers on Rothschild Boulevard. Niemeyer's Nordiya scheme of three office towers positioned on top of a shopping mall was incarnated, decades later, in the Azrieli Center, Tel Aviv's biggest and tallest architectural venture of the 1990s. The Nordiya plot itself was filled to the edges with the Dizengoff Center, a mega-mall and urban amoeba that in time sprouted an office and a residential tower. The interior circle of Kikar Hamedina remains to this day a vacant playground for real-estate and architectural speculations. Manshiya, meant to house a million square meters of business and residential space, never took off as the city's CBD; it became an enclave of bulky hotels and office buildings disjoining Tel Aviv and Jaffa.

In retrospect, it seems that the episodic import of foreign architects played a didactic role in the preparation of the local public for the momentous transition from the productivist pathos of a proletarian society and the egalitarian ethos of the welfare state to the praxes of a free consumerist society and the aesthetic of competitive profit. The foreign architects' proposals—which in hindsight may seem improbable,

reductionist, or merely iconic—helped overcome the psychological barrier of size and in certain cases set the floor-area-ratio bar astronomically high. It remains dubious, however, if they contributed sustainably to the build-up of a local architectural culture. A 1963 project by Ram Karmi—a tower and transportation infrastructure along the Ayalon ravine—was left on paper, but did presage the gradual migration of the urban business center of Tel Aviv to the east, away from the coastline and the fragile inner-city fabric. During the past few decades, the tremendous development of the linear "Ayalon City"[22] along the infrastructure of the intercity highway and railroad signaled the acceleration of the "spontaneous" blow-up of "air rights"—pragmatic, opportunistic, sui generis, instinctively utilitarian, entirely unurban, though vigorously architectural at random. The climax of metropolitan hubris is also its demise: no master plan, no urbanistic doctrine, and no municipal ideology. Vertical size locates itself where it is most effective and begins to consolidate the vertebrae of what could be expectantly hypothesized as the future megalopolis of the Israeli-Palestinian city-state. ■

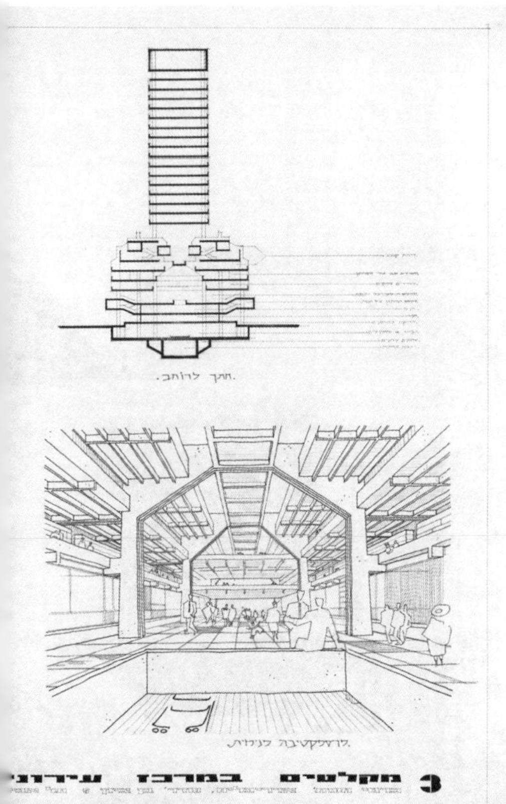


㉞

㉜ Office towers, commerce and infrastructure above Ayalon highway, Tel Aviv, model, 1963–1964. Ram Karmi. Ram Karmi archive. Courtesy of Rivka Karmi.
㉝ "Bomb shelters in the city center," proposal for mixed-use infrastructure and towers: cottage housing, offices, parking, six-lane highway and underground metro tunnel surrounding big public air-raid shelter, model, 1960s, Tel Aviv. Ram Karmi. Ram Karmi archive. Courtesy of Rivka Karmi.
㉞ "Bomb shelters in the city center," proposal for mixed-use infrastructure and towers: cottage housing, offices, parking, six-lane highway and underground metro tunnel surrounding big public air-raid shelter, section, 1960s, Tel Aviv. Ram Karmi. Ram Karmi archive. Courtesy of Rivka Karmi.

1 For the sake of comparison, this building is about 3 meters narrower and about two-thirds the height of its archetype —Le Corbusier's Unité d'Habitation in Marseille— although it is some 90 meters longer.
2 "Israel's Peripatetic Builder," *Fortune* (June 1966).
3 Shmaya Ben Avraham, in a discussion with the author, 1999.
4 Shabtai Tevet, "The Trend of Skyscrapers," *Haaretz* [in Hebrew], June 19, 1964.
5 Ibid.
6 Tamar Berger, *Dionysus at the Center* [in Hebrew] (Tel Aviv: Hakibbutz Hameuhad, 1998), pp. 182–185.
7 I. M. Pei and Partners, *Nordia, Tel Aviv* (New York: I. M. Pei and Associates, Architects and Planners, 1960).
8 Ibid.
9 Arieh Sharon, *Physical Planning in Israel* [in Hebrew with an English abstract] (Jerusalem: Government Printing Press and Survey of Israel Press, 1951), p. 8.
10 For further reading on Niemeyer's stay in Israel, see Zvi Elhayani, "Niemeyer in Israel," in Zvi Efrat, *The Israeli Project*, vol. 1 [in Hebrew] (Tel Aviv Museum of Art, 2004), pp. 280–281.
11 Oscar Niemeyer, *Quase Memórias: Viagens – Tempos de Entusiasmo e Revolta, 1961–1966* (Rio de Janeiro: Civilização Brasileira, 1968), pp. 30–48.
12 Ibid.
13 "Three Round Skyscrapers Instead of a Poor Neighborhood in Tel Aviv," *Haaretz* [in Hebrew], May 11, 1964.
14 Ibid.
15 Berger, *Dionysus*, p. 185.
16 Yehuda Svoray, "Israeli Building: Between Dream and Reality," *Maariv* [in Hebrew], November 29, 1964.
17 Aba Elhanani, cited in Yoram Perry, "Speaking Highly of Kikar Hamedina," *Davar* [in Hebrew], July 8, 1965.
18 Tevet, "Trend of Skyscrapers."
19 Michael Kuhn, "Eradicate the Speculative Approach in Building," *Engineering and Architecture: The Union of Engineers and Architects in Israel* 8 [in Hebrew] (1960).
20 Fumihiko Maki, *Investigations in Collective Form* (Saint Louis: Washington University Press, 1964), pp. 8–9.
21 Reyner Banham, *Megastructure: Urban Futures of the Recent Past* (New York: Harper and Row, 1976), p. 7.
22 The evocative title Ayalon City was first suggested by architect and writer Sharon Rotbard. See his "Ayalon City," on the website *Reading Machine, Babel* [in Hebrew], http://readingmachine.co.il/home/articles/article_009.

35

㊱

㊲

㊳

㉟ Hotels under construction at the Tel Aviv shore, 1970s. Photographer: Ami Erev. Shikun & Binui historical archive.
㊱ Dizengoff Center, 1999. Daniel Bauer. Built 1973–1974. Architects: Yitzhak Yashar, Aliza Toledo.
㊲ IBM Building, 1978. Avraham Yasky, Yaacov Gil, Yosef Sivan. Photographer: Ran Erde.
㊳ Israel-America House, Tel Aviv, 1970. Arieh Sharon, Eldar Sharon. Arieh Sharon digital archive.

# DOSSIER: OSCAR NIEMEYER'S EXILE

(39) Oscar Niemeyer and David Resnick visit the archaeological site of Ein Ovdat, Negev, 1964. Courtesy David Resnick.

By 1953 the Sharon era at the Planning Department had run its course. With the election of a new government, comprised of a different political coalition, the Planning Department was shifted to the Ministry of the Interior under a new minister, Israel Rokah. Formerly the mayor of Tel Aviv, Rokah was a liberal who, against the hegemonic socialist fiber, did not endorse planning as an ideological action, and instead insisted on pragmatic and procedural aspects. He appointed Ya'akov Dash, a technocrat and a direct disciple of Patrick Abercrombie, as the new head of the Planning Department. While the national master plan prepared by Sharon and his team was already in full operation in situ and nothing could halt or divert its momentum, a new skepticism regarding Zionism's romance with the rural began to emerge. During the late 1950s and early 1960s there were frequent debates within professional and administrative circles calling for the adjustment of planning policies, and particularly for rethinking the architecture of the Israeli new town.

(40)

Among numerous dissenting experiments, built and unbuilt, which proclaimed utter dismissal of the garden-city paradigm, two noteworthy and rather hyperbolic urban enterprises stand out: Ashdod, a rapidly growing port town south of Tel Aviv, conceived and designed as a capitalist city by Jewish-American developers (described in chapter "Hyper-Urbanism"); and the (unbuilt) City of the Negev, a vertical futurist casbah in the desert designed by the Brazilian communist expatriate Oscar Niemeyer and defined by him, strangely enough, as a "kibbutz city."[1]

In his *Quase Memórias*, Niemeyer relates that he was overwhelmed by the dramatic splendor of the Negev Desert and captivated by his visit to Sde-Boker, Ben-Gurion's kibbutz, "where I learned what a kibbutz is—a cooperative of a sort in which money is stripped of the vulgar meaning attributed to it by capitalism."[2] Ben-Gurion himself was no less overwhelmed by meeting the architect of Brasília. While discussing with Niemeyer the need to establish a new town in the south of Israel, he reportedly promised him he could build to the sky—momentarily renouncing his own territorial doctrine of horizontal dispersal and his architectural etiquette of low profile and minimum cost.

An article in a local magazine described the actual commissioning of the Negev City project:

> Oscar Niemeyer's plan for a city in the Negev was commissioned by the Housing Ministry: "We are all immersed in our everyday work and daily problems. So this time we have turned to someone from the outside, who sees things with different eyes," architect Shmuel Shaked, director of the physical planning branch of the Housing Ministry, explained to me. "We asked Niemeyer to propose his own solution for settling the Negev—not a detailed plan for some defined place, but a general conceptual plan. He proposed something clear

(40) Oscar Niemeyer, *Quase Memórias*, 1968. Book cover.
(41) Oscar Niemeyer, *Quase Memórias*, 1968. Page indicating 1964 as his year in Israel.
(42) Haifa University campus, 1964. Sketches. Oscar Niemeyer, from *Quase Memórias*.

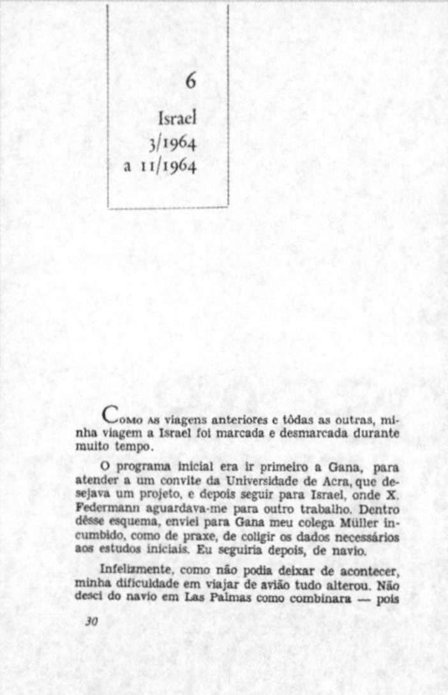

6

Israel
3/1964
a 11/1964

Como as viagens anteriores e tôdas as outras, minha viagem a Israel foi marcada e desmarcada durante muito tempo.

O programa inicial era ir primeiro a Gana, para atender a um convite da Universidade de Acra, que desejava um projeto, e depois seguir para Israel, onde X. Federmann aguardava-me para outro trabalho. Dentro dêsse esquema, enviei para Gana meu colega Müller incumbido, como de praxe, de coligir os dados necessários aos estudos iniciais. Eu seguiria depois, de navio.

Infelizmente, como não podia deixar de acontecer, minha dificuldade em viajar de avião tudo alterou. Não desci do navio em Las Palmas como combinara — pois

30

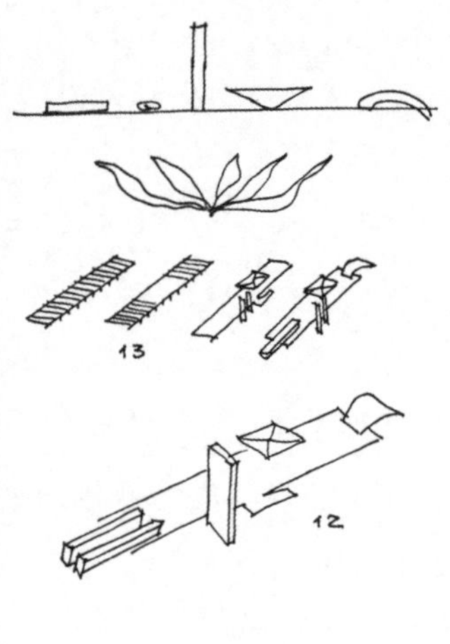


(41) (42)

and simple—a prototype for a city in the Negev with many virtues, which is both very modern and architecturally beautiful."[3]

The writer went on to describe and evaluate the project:

> The most revolutionary of Oscar Niemeyer's Israeli plans is, without a doubt, his proposal for a vertical city in the Negev, which he also defines as a "kibbutz city." According to the plan, the entirety of the city's forty thousand residents will live in thirty- to forty-storey skyscrapers. A few dozen such apartment buildings, towering hundreds of meters in the air, will be clustered around an elevated central square made entirely of cast concrete. The immense concrete plaza will house the municipality and other public buildings, as well as a well-shaded "Mediterranean market."[4]

The originality of the urban plan was complemented by a totally introverted dwelling scheme (indeed, a vertical commune):

> No less revolutionary than the general plan of the city are the plans of the apartments that Niemeyer plans to install in the skyscrapers. These will be two-storey apartments—about one hundred of them, placed alongside and one on top of another in fifteen or twenty layers, in each one of the skyscrapers. The most surprising feature of the apartments is the fact that they will have no outside windows; in order to protect the tenants from the Negev sun and sandstorms, Niemeyer places all of the windows facing the private "inner courtyard" adjacent to each apartment. This "courtyard" is nothing more than a large tunnel-like balcony which perforates the skyscraper diagonally.[5]

Niemeyer himself described his desert city as the ultimate antithesis to the horizontal new towns built thus far in Israel:

> The project we have planned will not be a repetition [...] of what has already been built in Israel, but something completely different; it may seem somewhat fanciful to less sensitive eyes, but it is nonetheless reasonable and respectable. In the project I have envisioned a solution for future problems, and the excellence of its planning will certainly only become more excellent in Israel—a country of culture and optimism that believes in advanced solutions, solutions that other countries, wealthier and more prosperous than it, tend still to reject out of hand.[6]

Yet the detailed description of his futuristic city sounds all too familiar:

> The city is cultivated just like a park, with no unnecessary asphalt streets, and with a network of wide, unpaved, picturesque, and green paths among which the residential blocks are placed. The commercial and leisure services are distributed throughout the small pedestrian streets, sometimes leading to modest rustic squares and sometimes to the lawns in front of the residential areas. All this is arranged meticulously according to the traffic principles that guide and regulate the project in its entirety. [...] The approach to vehicular traffic is one of the defining aspects of the Negev city, which is based on an absolute separation between vehicular and pedestrian traffic. [...] Indeed, had we planned low buildings of six, ten, or even fifteen storeys, we would not have been able to preserve the spirit of the original idea—of a city in which distances do not exceed 500 meters, in which people are not dependent on automobiles and instead can quietly

(43)

(44)

(43) Haifa University campus, 1964. Model. Oscar Niemeyer with Shlomo Gilead.
(44) Haifa University campus, 1964. Model. Oscar Niemeyer with Shlomo Gilead.
(45) Haifa University campus, 1964. Photomontage. Oscar Niemeyer with Shlomo Gilead.

(45)

> and tranquilly use the ground level. [...] This solution allows human beings to live in the heart of the menacing wilderness of the desert, which they wish to repair and to alleviate.[7]

Indeed, isn't the City of the Negev—with its pastoral setting, picturesque paths, strict zoning principles, separation of urban functions, and hygienic and homogeneous subtext (as well as its kibbutz fancy)—none other than a vertical garden city, just like Le Corbusier's Ville contemporaine, or most other vertical cities of tomorrow? ■



1 Cited in Joseph Levite, "The Future Landscape of Israel," *Bamahane: The Official IDF Magazine* [in Hebrew], February 23, 1965, p. 10.
2 Oscar Niemeyer, *Quase Memórias: Viagens – Tempos de Entusiasmo e Revolta, 1961–1966* (Rio de Janeiro: Civilização Brasileira, 1968), p. 47.
3 Levite, "Future Landscape of Israel," pp. 10–11.
4 Ibid.
5 Ibid.
6 Niemeyer, *Quase Memórias*, p. 37.
7 Ibid., p. 42.

(46)

(46) Panorama Hotel, Tel Aviv [sic], 1964. Model. Oscar Niemeyer, from *Quase Memórias*.
(47) Caesarea housing project, 1964. Sketches. Oscar Niemeyer.
(48) Caesarea housing project, 1964. Sketches. Oscar Niemeyer, from *Quase Memórias*.

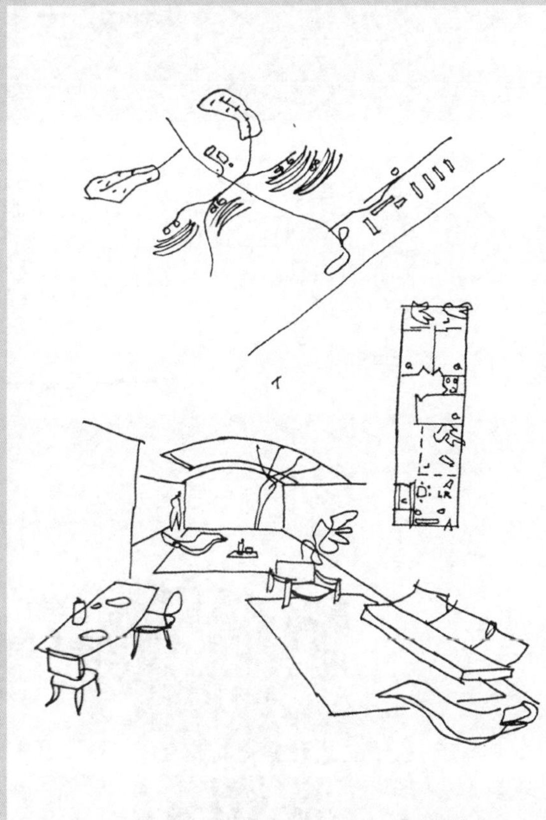

(48)

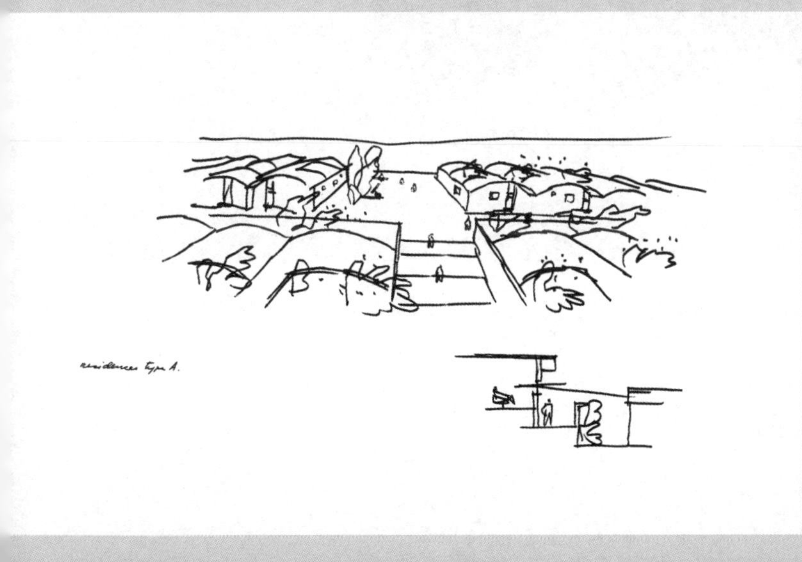


(47)

2

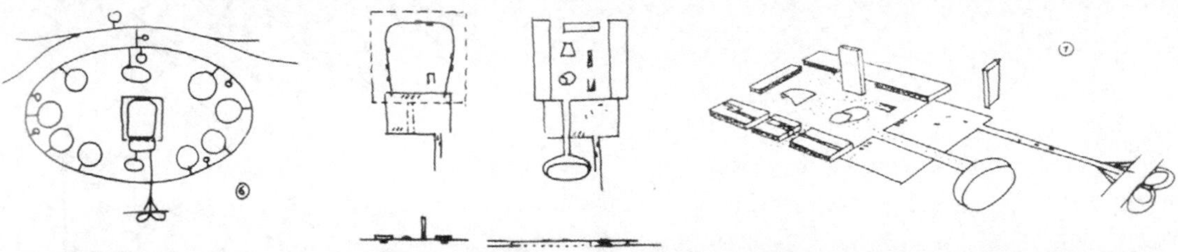


3

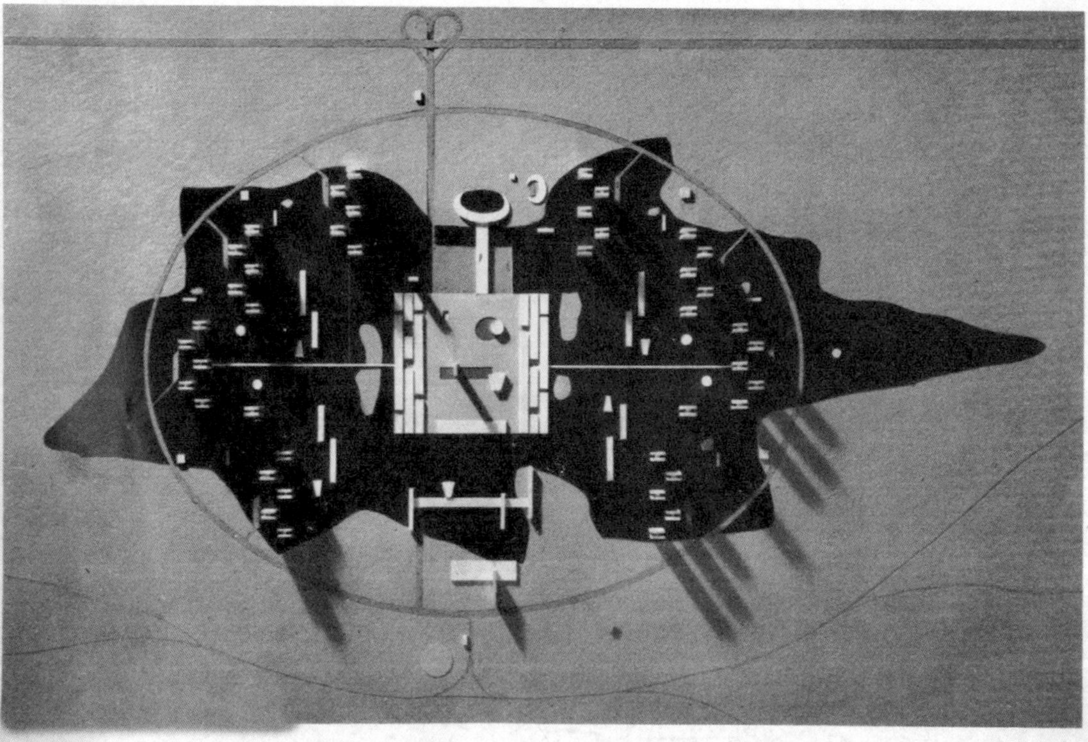

4

(49)

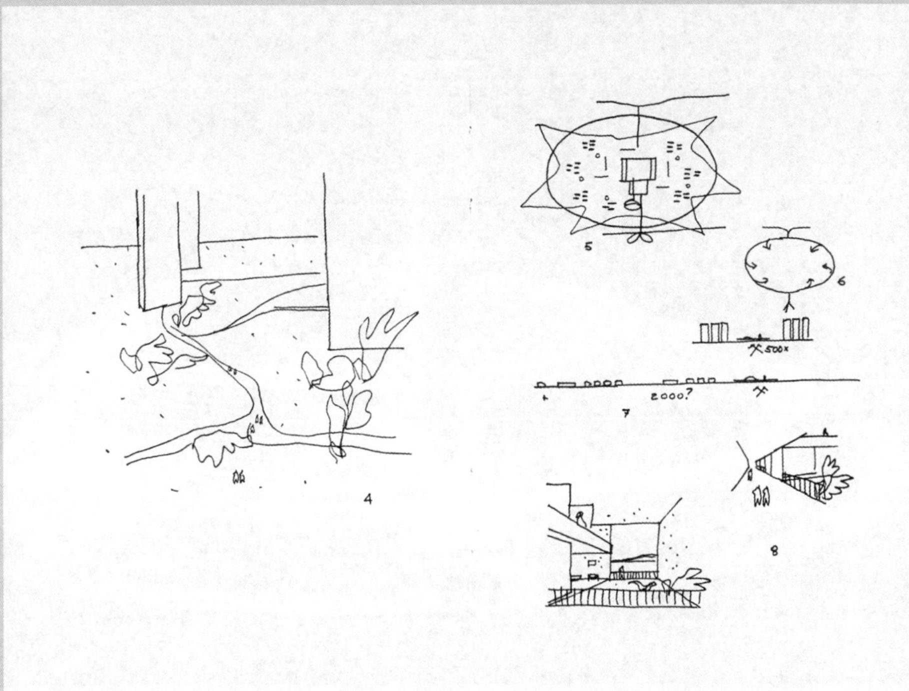


partimentos sanitários. O resto seria flexível, possibilitando tôdas as variações, inclusive construção interna por etapas, o que tornaria mais acessível para todos.

Estas, as características da solução adotada para a habitação no Negev, solução que a idéia urbanística exigia, cercada de parques e jardins, com escola primária, creche, jardim de infância, clube, mercado, etc., com o homem integrado na natureza hostil do deserto que deseja corrigir e amenizar. Solução que deliberamos adotar definitivamente, no dia em que a comparamos com outras usualmente aceitas, vendo pela comparação como ela é lógica e econômica. O desenho 7 (pág. 39) mostra como no Negev as distâncias teriam se ampliado com a utilização de prédios de menor porte, e o desenho 3 (pág. 36) o que aconteceria com Eilat se tivessem fixado um plano idêntico ao que agora elaboramos, eliminando ruas, centenas de edifícios, preservando o solo e a paisagem admirável.

5 — O centro comercial é o local onde se situa a municipalidade, o hotel, o comércio, os bancos, os escritórios comerciais, o teatro, cinemas, restaurantes, etc. (Des. 9.) É o local que reflete a vida da cidade, onde os homens se encontram e se aproximam para os assuntos de trabalho e diversão. Visando garantir êsse clima indispensável, evitamos o comércio local, isto é, junto às habitações, preferindo reduzi-lo a um pequeno mercado para as necessidades quotidianas mais imediatas. A zona comercial e recreativa tem o tráfego de serviço projetado em nível inferior, permitindo aos pedestres percorrê-la tranqüilamente sem as preocupações de trânsito que conhecemos. São ruas estreitas cheias de sombra e movimento, praças singelas e convidativas, umas como grandes salões abrigados dos ventos do deserto, outras abrindo para o centro cívico e zonas de esporte. (Des. 10.) E sugerimos a utilização nesse setor de uma unidade construtiva pré-fabricada, um módulo que, repetido, garante a unidade desejável nos elementos previstos: galerias, ruas, praças, etc. Módulo que poderia, inclusive, ser usado em duas alturas, como fizemos na *Praça da Sombra*, localizado no centro do

42

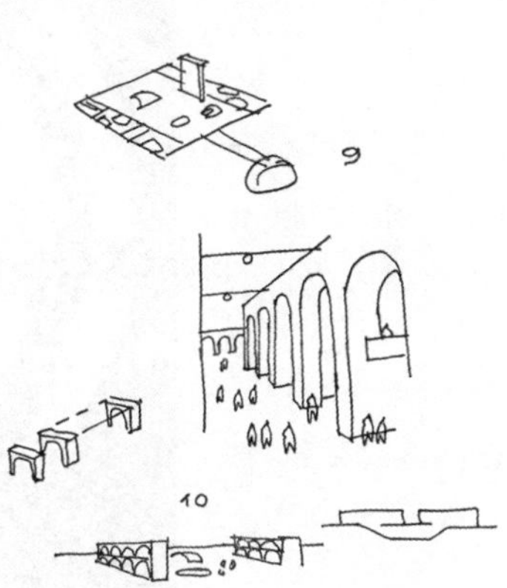


(50) (51)

(49) The Negev city. Model and sketches. 1964. Oscar Niemeyer, from *Quase Memórias*.
(50) The Negev city. Sketches. 1964. Oscar Niemeyer, from *Quase Memórias*.
(51) The Negev city. Sketches. 1964. Oscar Niemeyer, from *Quase Memórias*.

(52)

(53)

(52)–(53) Kikar Hamedina, Tel Aviv, 1964. First proposal for a residential and commercial project. Model. Oscar Niemeyer, with Aba Elhanani and Israel Lotan.
(54)–(55) Kikar Hamedina, Tel Aviv, 1964. Second proposal for a residential and commercial project. Plan. Oscar Niemeyer, with Aba Elhanani and Israel Lotan.
(56) Kikar Hamedina, Tel Aviv, 1964. Second proposal for a residential and commercial project. Elevation. Oscar Niemeyer, with Aba Elhanani and Israel Lotan.
(57) Kikar Hamedina, Tel Aviv, 1964. Second proposal for a residential and commercial project. Model. Oscar Niemeyer, with Aba Elhanani and Israel Lotan.
(58) Villa in Caesarea, 1964. Model and sketches. Oscar Niemeyer, from Quase Memórias.

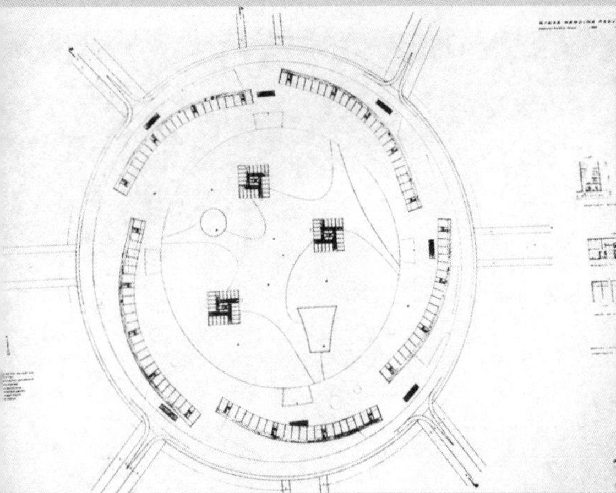

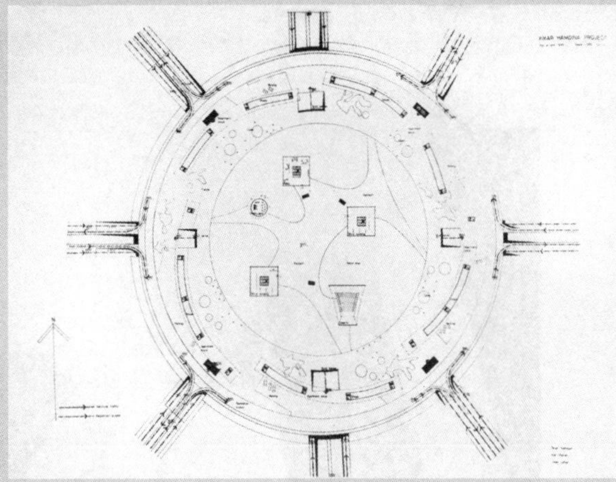

(54) (55)

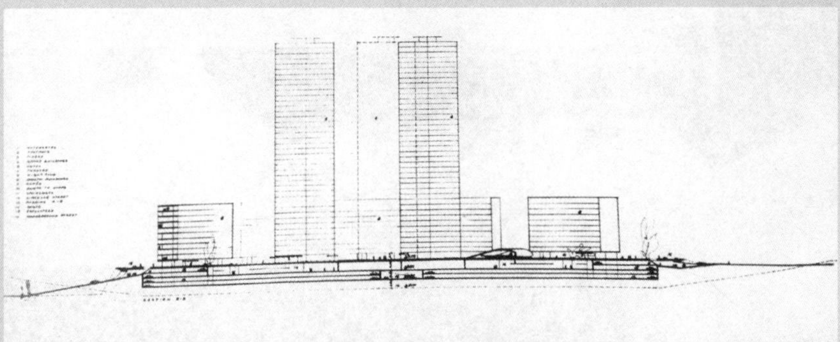

(56)

(57)

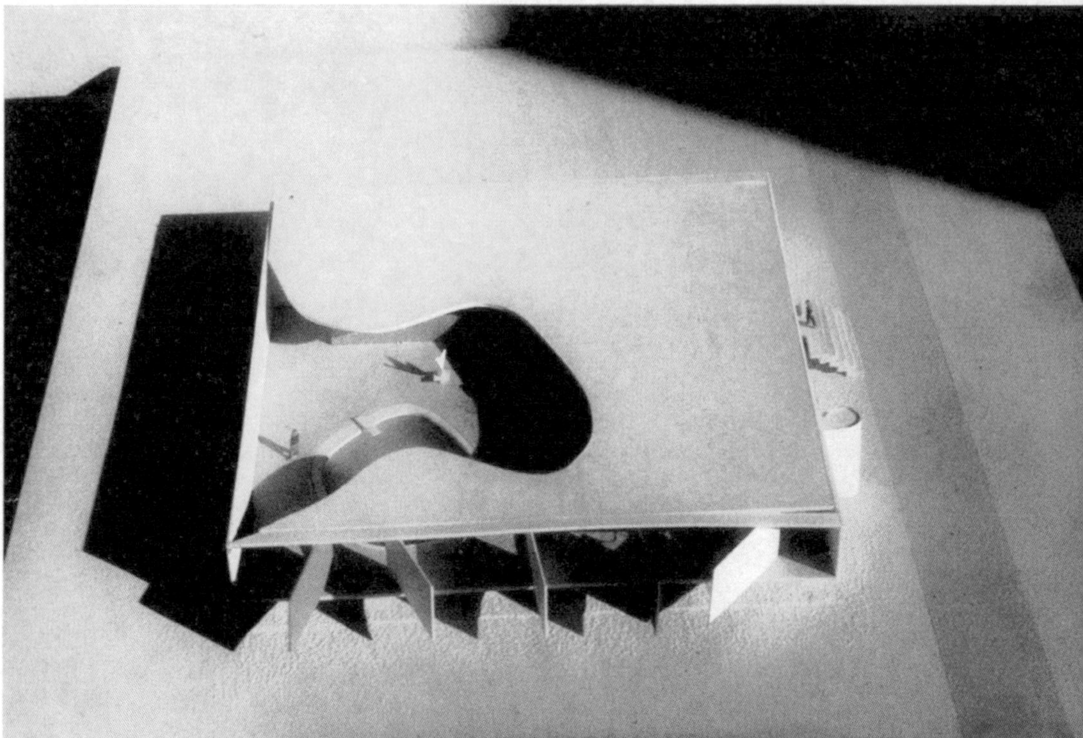

10

**10.** *Résidence à Césarée, maquette;* **11.** *Croquis d'étude de la maison.*

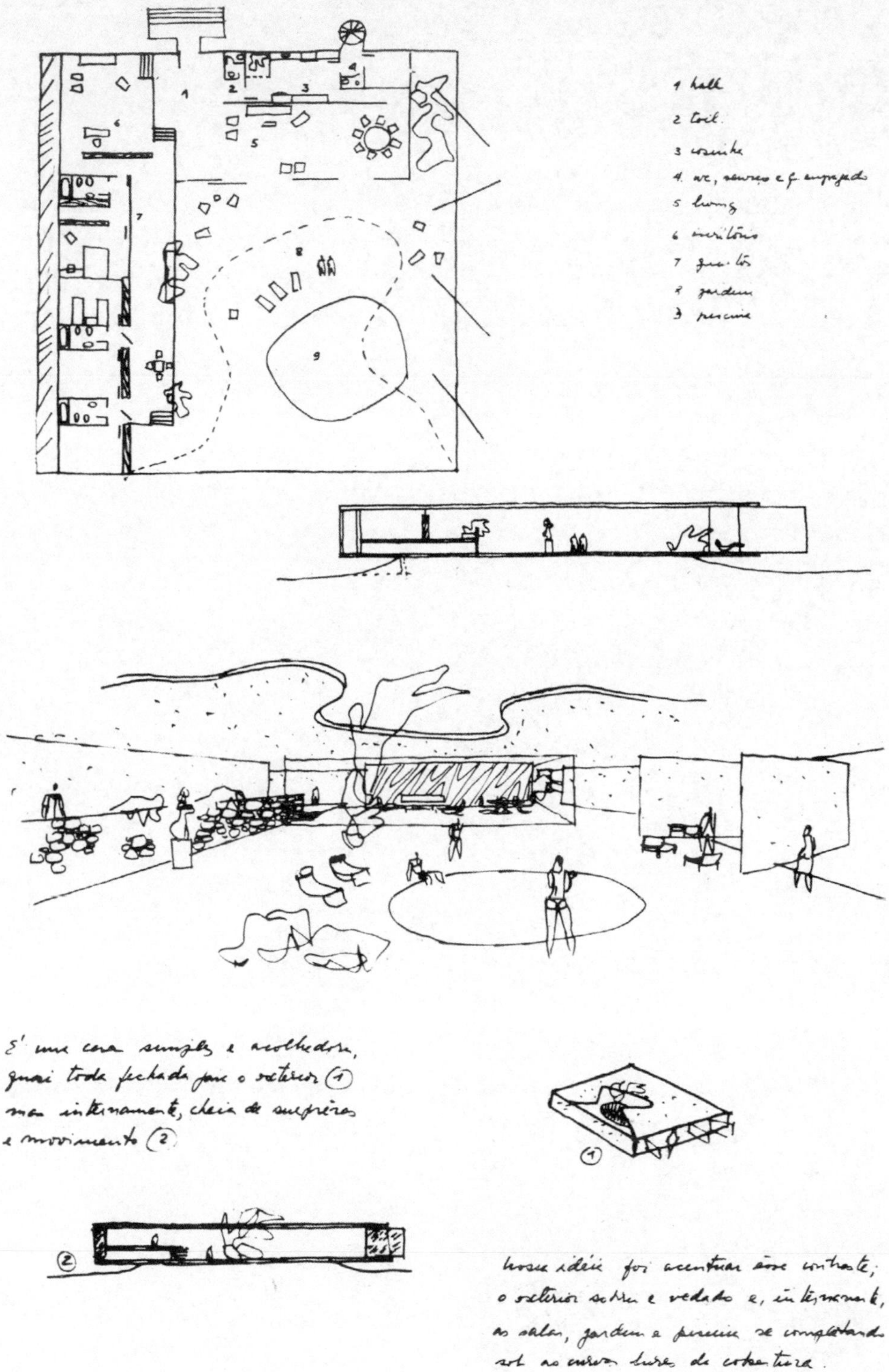
1 hall
2 toil.
3 cozinha
4. wc, serviço e q. empregada
5 living
6 escritório
7 quartos
8 jardim
9 piscina
É uma casa simples e acolhedora, quase toda fechada para o exterior (1) mas internamente, cheia de surprêsas e movimento (2)
Nossa idéia foi acentuar êsse contraste; o exterior sóbrio e vedado e, internamente, as salas, jardim e piscina se completando sob as curvas livres da cobertura.

81

11

(58)

# Appropriation

① Members of the Town-Planning Subcommittee of the Jerusalem Committee look at an aerial photo of the Old City of Jerusalem at the Van Leer Institute, 1970. Photographer: Yitzhak Amit. Judaica Collection, Harvard Library.

## Recasting Jerusalem

When the master plan for a unified Jerusalem under Israeli rule—nearly four years in the making—was released in 1968, only months after the momentous War of 1967, Mayor Teddy Kollek invited a select group of international scholars to visit the city and form an advisory committee on the new master plan.

Much like the "select group of intellectuals" on board the *Futuro*, Theodor Herzl's allegorical ship in *Old-New Land*, who were invited to be both the advising "oracles" and the "distinguished judges" of the Zionist colonization project,[1] the members of the so-called Jerusalem Committee—renowned architects, planners, historians, authors, diplomats, and clerics—were asked to review and debate the plan, and also to give their blessing to Israeli custody of the Old City of Jerusalem following the 1967 conquest of East Jerusalem, which included the addition of over 100 square kilometers to the municipal boundaries of the city.

Teddy Kollek, "the second King Herod," as Prime Minister Yitzhak Rabin called him in retrospect, was certainly the most ambitious builder of Jerusalem in modern times. During his twenty-eight years as mayor, the city of Jerusalem tripled in size, doubled its population, negotiated dozens of urban plans and architectural ventures, and was transformed "from a provincial backwater" into a vibrant political and cultural center. In his letter of invitation to the international experts, Kollek wrote:

> The physical beauty of Jerusalem embodies the universal spiritual truths basic to all faiths and people. To enhance the natural charm of Jerusalem is to make manifest a belief in the love of beauty and the desire for peace inherent in all mankind.[2]

It seems that in the name of "universal spiritual truths," Kollek hoped not merely for professional authorization and moral endorsement, but indeed for an international front to protect the city from its unruly appropriation by the Israeli cultural apparatus.

The first meeting of the committee, which included such figures as Christopher Alexander, Bruno Zevi, Lewis Mumford, Louis Kahn, Arne Jacobsen, Philip Johnson, Isamu Noguchi, Henry Moore, Jorge Luis Borges, and Isaiah Berlin, took place in July 1969. Participants were shown around the Old City and received a tour of the Archaeology Department in the Israel Museum, which had opened four years earlier. Lastly, they were given a presentation of the plan drafted for the Jerusalem Park: an area of 600 acres around the Old City walls which would create "a vibrant, unifying element, linking the Old City with the hills to the east and with the new Jerusalem quarters to the west."[3]

This seemingly benign proposal was presented to the committee by the commissioner of the National Parks Authority, a governmental body entrusted with both the preservation of historical heritage sites in the country and the development of recreational landscapes that would create a new bond between the people, the terrain, and the official narrative of [Jewish] homecoming (see chapter "Ruins of Time").

Despite the blatant politics of clearing the "Arab slums" for the sake of a green belt around the Old City, Kollek was able to focus the committee on issues of appearance by appealing to a sense of global responsibility. He assured them that the mission of Jerusalem's reconstruction belonged not only to the city's native residents or current occupants, but rather "in a sense, to the entire world, to all those people who are Jerusalemites in their hearts and minds."[4]

Indeed, the committee's initial neutrality was Kollek's temporary success. "We came here inspired by the profound significance that Jerusalem has for millions of

② Louis Kahn, Buckminster Fuller, Philip Johnson, Arieh Sharon, and other members of the Town-Planning Subcommittee of the Jerusalem Committee tour Jerusalem, December 1970. Photographer: Yitzhak Amit. Judaica Collection, Harvard Library.
③ Buckminster Fuller, Arieh Sharon, and other members of the Town-Planning Subcommittee of the Jerusalem Committee tour Jerusalem, December 1970. Photographer: Yitzhak Amit. Judaica Collection, Harvard Library.
④ Buckminster Fuller, Arieh Sharon, and Louis Kahn at the subcommittee's Jerusalem tour, December 1970. Photographer: Yitzhak Amit. Judaica Collection, Harvard Library.
⑤ Buckminster Fuller photographs the Old City from Mount Scopus, Jerusalem, December 1970. Photographer: Yitzhak Amit. Judaica Collection, Harvard Library.
⑥ Members of the Town-Planning Subcommittee of the Jerusalem Committee, with the wall of the Old City in the background, December 1970. Photographer: Yitzhak Amit. Judaica Collection, Harvard Library.
⑦ Philip Johnson, December 1970. Photographer: Yitzhak Amit. Judaica Collection, Harvard Library.

②

③

④

⑤

⑥

⑦

⑧ Buckminster Fuller views the Judean Desert, December 1970. Photographer: Yitzhak Amit. Judaica Collection, Harvard Library.
⑨ Members of the Town-Planning Subcommittee of the Jerusalem Committee, with the King David Hotel in the background, December 1970. Photographer: Yitzhak Amit. Judaica Collection, Harvard Library.
⑩ Mike Turner and Nikolaus Pevsner tour the Old City, Jerusalem, December 1970. Photographer: Yitzhak Amit. Judaica Collection, Harvard Library.
⑪ Buckminster Fuller and Teddy Kollek, mayor of Jerusalem, view the Temple Mount, December 1970. Photographer: Yitzhak Amit. Judaica Collection, Harvard Library.
⑫ Isamu Noguchi, Arieh Sharon, and other members of the Town-Planning Subcommittee of the Jerusalem Committee tour the Old City, December 1970. Photographer: Yitzhak Amit. Judaica Collection, Harvard Library.
⑬ Buckminster Fuller, Jerusalem, December 1970. Photographer: Yitzhak Amit. Judaica Collection, Harvard Library.

⑨

⑪

⑩

⑬

⑫

people throughout the world, its way of life and its spirit," reads the official statement of the committee, which emphasized the need to protect the city's beauty.[5] Aligning with the National Parks Authority's mission, they declared the archaeological digging an important aspect of the process of preservation: "in our opinion, this must be carried out with full consideration for archaeological excavations; for each new discovery helps relate the future form of the city to the past."[6] An essentialist correlation between reconstruction and preservation was thus established: the city's contemporary living organism would rise from its (selectively) excavated past. Keeping this in mind, mild approval was given to the Jerusalem Park proposal:

> We believe that we must not succumb to the temptation of using the extraordinary wealth of tangible remnants of the past to make the city a museum or a stage set. Jerusalem must be kept a living city. In keeping with this principle, the plan of the Jerusalem Park appears to us satisfactory [...] it would serve to reinforce the unity and vitality of Jerusalem.[7]

Encouraged by the Jerusalem Committee's initial fervor, the following year Kollek met in New York with a number of architects and artists, among them Buckminster Fuller, Louis Kahn, and Jacques Lipchitz, as well as several prominent leaders of the Christian and Jewish communities. A *New York Times* headline of June 3, 1970, read "Jerusalem Plan Backed by Fuller: Restore Biblical Dwelling as Bridge to the Past":

> R. Buckminster Fuller, the builder of the geodesic dome, called yesterday for the restoration of Biblical dwellings in Jerusalem to bridge the past to the present. "The world citizens of our time need a sense of continuity; it's psychologically very important." [...] Mr. Fuller [...] said a plan by Teddy Kollek [...], to restore some of the dwellings recently unearthed within the historic walls of the Old City, represented a "major contribution" in efforts to rebuild a sense of history alongside modern technology.[8]

Fuller also claimed that today's youngsters are eager to enrich their lives with notions of past traditions, as they wish to "experience the sense of mystery that comes with the restoration of history."[9] At the end of the New York meeting, Kollek "announced that an architecture conference of architects would be held in Jerusalem in December."[10] As announced, in December 1970 the committee reconvened to devise the Town-Planning Subcommittee of the Jerusalem Committee.

(14)

The Town-Planning Subcommittee discussed core issues such as housing schemes, transportation routes, pedestrian circulation, and commercial redevelopment. The composition of the committee was modified accordingly, as several clergymen, diplomats, artists, and authors were not included, while distinguished architects and architectural historians such as Buckminster Fuller, Nikolaus Pevsner, Richard Meier, and Moshe Safdie were added. With a total of thirty international members and forty local planners and government officials, the subcommittee examined four plans: "The Master Plan 1968 Interim Report," "A Plan for the Central Business District," "The Jerusalem Transportation Plan for 1985 (1970)," and "The Old City of Jerusalem and Its Environs, Outline Planning Scheme, 1970." They also toured, once again, the Jewish Quarter of the Old City, the new housing projects on its periphery, the Hebrew University on Mount Scopus, the Mount of Olives, the so-called Jerusalem National Park, and the city center.

"The challenge was exciting and awesome," recalled Arieh Sharon in his autobiography (see chapter "Project"). Sharon, along with his son Eldar and two other architects, was in charge of one of the four plans presented to the committee: "The Old City of Jerusalem and Its Environs, Outline Planning Scheme, 1970," which included an area of 2,500 acres of the Old City as well as its surrounding hills. Following previous observations by Fuller and others, who commented that the city should not be preserved as a frozen museum, Sharon stressed that Jerusalem should not be just a religious center, but also a lively contemporary city "full of people of various races and religions who live, study, work and spend their leisure hours within its walls."[11]

Keeping vehicles outside and paving walking routes within, Sharon hoped to create "a city of pedestrians moving freely and unimpeded from house to house, shop to shop, from home to school, to mosque, to church or synagogue, and from the gates and piazzas to the bazaars [...]."[12] In addition, the plan detailed the restoration phases of the destroyed Jewish Quarter and outlined new housing schemes for 85,000 inhabitants, both inside and outside the walls. Kollek was devising a plan to move the Arab population out of the Jewish Quarter: "There were only a few Arab families who had lived in the Quarter for a generation or two," he wrote in his autobiography of 1978, "and some of these were reluctant to leave. But with these exceptions, all the Arabs in the Jewish Quarter were only too happy to receive ample compensation and settle outside of the Old City."[13]

Regrettably for Kollek, the committee utterly rejected all plans presented to it by the Israeli planners and expressed its dismay regarding the modernist principles the plans embodied. To the international scholars, the plans were brutally modern and vigorously Zionist: they encapsulated prewar zoning paradigms and functionalist tendencies, which to the committee—a group of experts disenchanted with grandiose urban-renewal projects back in their home cities—seemed incredibly outdated.[14] The *Jerusalem Post* did not fail to pronounce "Planners Under Fire" in a headline: unlike the previous year, when Kollek and the planners were let off with a warning, this time, the "Foreign critics were not wielding a scalpel on the Masterplan, but a Guillotine."[15]

⑮

⑯

⑱

⑰

⑲

⑭ Buckminster Fuller, Jerusalem, December 1970.
⑮ Members of the Town-Planning Subcommittee of the Jerusalem Committee tour the Old City of Jerusalem with Teddy Kollek and Arieh Sharon, December 1970. Photographer: Yitzhak Amit. Judaica Collection, Harvard Library.
⑯ Isamu Noguchi, Louis Kahn, Buckminster Fuller, and Bruno Zevi, 1970. Photographer: Yitzhak Amit. Judaica Collection, Harvard Library.
⑰ – ⑳ Members of the Town-Planning Subcommittee of the Jerusalem Committee tour the Old City of Jerusalem, December 1970. Photographer: Yitzhak Amit. Judaica Collection, Harvard Library.

⑳

㉑

㉒

㉕

㉓

㉔

㉑ Members of the Town-Planning Subcommittee of the Jerusalem Committee at the Van Leer Institute, 1970. Photographer: Yitzhak Amit. Judaica Collection, Harvard Library.
㉒ Bruno Zevi, Buckminster Fuller, Teddy Kollek, and other members of the Town-Planning Subcommittee of the Jerusalem Committee. December 1970. Photographer: Yitzhak Amit. Judaica Collection, Harvard Library.
㉓ Buckminster Fuller and other members of the Town-Planning Subcommittee of the Jerusalem Committee tour the Old City of Jerusalem , December 1970. Photographer: Yitzhak Amit. Judaica Collection, Harvard Library.
㉔ Nikolaus Pevsner, Bruno Zevi, Buckminster Fuller, Louis Kahn, and other members of the Town-Planning Subcommittee of the Jerusalem Committee. December 1970. Photographer: Yitzhak Amit. Judaica Collection, Harvard Library.
㉕ Arieh Sharon presents the master plan of the Old City of Jerusalem to Members of the Town-Planning Subcommittee of the Jerusalem Committee at the Van Leer Institute, 1970. Photographer: Yitzhak Amit. Judaica Collection, Harvard Library.

The committee's underlying aspiration was that Jerusalem be neither contemporary nor functional; its horizon was to be spiritual, not civic, and it should not, under any circumstances, be treated as a *normal* city. The committee's final statement of December 1970 described the city's glories as the cause of the incredible complications involved in their task, saying that "these strong characteristics of the city magnify and complicate all the normal problems which beset the development of any city today." Their tone was not nearly as forgiving as in the previous gathering, and their final verdict could not have been clearer—it was time for the Israeli planners to hold back and reassess.

> We feel [...] that there are contradictions among the different plans which have yet to be resolved [...] other essential concepts have not perhaps been grasped. [...] In the spirit of mutual confidence which underlay our frank exchanges and with the desire that the best possible plan for Jerusalem should finally be formulated, we make the following suggestions and recommendations: The Masterplan should be restructured. The planning process ought to be reassessed.[16]

Kollek's plan had backfired. "What we want are competent opinions on town planning," he pleaded. But his competent guests responded skeptically to the Israeli visionary plans to "normalize the city." "Most of them have been enraged by what they have seen, some of them wept, others were nearly hysterical, and at least one was taken ill."[17] Local officials were bewildered: "It had apparently never occurred to them that anyone would take a town plan so to heart."[18]

"Jerusalem is the place where man first began to use his mind," declared Buckminster Fuller, following his previous appraisal of the plan for a park and preservation campaign. He now denounced any private ownership or state control whatsoever, arguing that it "belongs to all of us" and should therefore be owned by all, thus becoming a de-sovereign "'world-man-territory' of world citizens."[19]

While Fuller described Jerusalem as a pivotal epicenter of history, Lewis Mumford extended this notion in order to find the force that could unify the city "despite all present division and antagonism," which he believed could be found within the foundations of the city before its erection. The key for unity in a place of divisions, he claimed, could be found in "the structure of the city, its topography, its soil, its ancient walls, its historic sites." He asserted that "in Jerusalem not merely the fate of Israel, but the destiny of the world in the centuries to come may actually be at stake."[20]

Landscape architect Lawrence Halprin backed Mumford, preaching for an environmental perception "based on the harmonic principles of light, land and hills"—the physical fragments that preceded the city.[21] Alona Nitzan-Shiftan writes that the critic Wolf von Eckardt "stressed that Jerusalem required unique skills for translating 'poetic-subjective experiences such as sacredness, charm and mystery into architecture design terminology of stone, concrete and asphalt.'"[22]

The Jerusalem Committee's plea for a halt to rapid modernization was partially effective: a municipal report from 1973 specified that several plans for high-rise buildings would be canceled, that the highway system proposed earlier would be downsized, that fourteen areas should be designated for preservation, and that the plaza outside the Damascus Gate was to be left undeveloped.

> The latter served as a theoretical testing ground in 1979 when architects Peter and Alison Smithson arrived in Jerusalem to find an answer to a long-lost question, the "question of the planless brief for a city."[23]

The Smithsons wanted to provide the citizens of Jerusalem with "ideas that open the way to solutions without making these possibilities into constraints in the way an official plan does."[24] Their architectural intervention clears the site of urban debris and carves out a negative space for urban activity by exposing a fragment of the archaic terrain of the city:

> We proposed to clean out the head of the Tyropean valley to bedrock, to give back the original topography that the surroundings still indicate [...].[25]

The radical proposal (drawn by Alison Smithson and Lida Papadopoulou, 1979, 1981–1983) suggested an elongated hole, a cut through the city's historical layers, exposing, as it were, a place which "still remains as an underlying sense of the terrain that has been largely left from Byzantine times down the ages."[26] The so-called *hole* fascinated them. In hand-drawn sketches at first and in meticulous and detailed measured drawings later on, they traced the ancient routes and population flows around the *hole* and articulated its significance as a marketplace.

The plan outlined in detail how the *hole* could function in the city: the transfer of goods could be facilitated by different means of transportation; patterns of circulation for motorized vehicles and pedestrians would be scheduled according to various hours, days, and seasons in accordance with the varying times of prayer of the three religions of Judaism, Christianity, and Islam. The document is a strange combination of matter-of-fact solutions with imaginary fantasies: "the bedrock level allows the load-transfer depot, whose use overlaps with the lorry-for-hire park, to be slid below the level of the quay-side-like street of the Prophets [...]."[27] As for the future, Alison Smithson would not speculate beyond the image of the petrified city and instructs the reader "to found any new work on rock, so as to speak of belonging to a city built of stone." This brief reiterates the *Aberdeen Free Press* report that "the only 'new Jerusalem' is the old one: The gray, austere, ancient, rock-built Palestinian capital."[28]

"What has been is what will be," proclaimed the nihilist king of Jerusalem, "and what has been done is what will be done; there is nothing new under the sun."[29] ■

1 Theodor Herzl, *Old-New Land*, trans. Lotta Levensohn (New York: Bloch Publishing, 1960), p. 223. Originally published as *Altneuland* (Leipzig: Seemann, 1902).

2 First letter of invitation from Teddy Kollek to Lewis Mumford (March 26, 1969). Retrieved from the Lewis Mumford Papers, University of Pennsylvania, Philadelphia. Cited in Alona Nitzan-Shiftan, "Modernisms in Conflict: Architecture and Cultural Politics in Post-1967 Jerusalem," in *Modernism and the Middle East*, ed. Sandy Isenstadt and Kishwar Rizvi (Seattle: University of Washington Press, 2008), p. 181.
A comprehensive documentation of the Jerusalem Committee's proceedings and correspondence can also be found at the archives of the Isamu Noguchi Foundation and Garden Museum, New York.
Alona Nitzan-Shiftan's book *Seizing Jerusalem: The Architectures of Unilateral Unification* (Minneapolis: University of Minnesota Press, 2017) is a thorough account and analysis of the architectural "Israelization" of Jerusalem.

3 Arieh Sharon, *Kibbutz +Bauhaus: An Architect's Way in a New Land* (Stuttgart and Tel Aviv: Karl Kramer Verlag and Massada), p. 180.

4 "The Jerusalem Committee: Proceedings of the First Meeting," p. 13. Cited in Nitzan-Shiftan, "Modernisms in Conflict," p. 166.

5 Ibid.

6 Ibid.

7 "The Jerusalem Committee: A First Statement," July 4, 1969, Jerusalem. Retrieved from the Architectural Archives of the University of Pennsylvania, Philadelphia.

8 Henry Raymont, "Jerusalem Plan Backed by Fuller: Restore Biblical Dwelling as Bridge to the Past," *New York Times*, June 3, 1970.

9 Ibid.

10 Ibid.

11 Sharon, *Kibbutz + Bauhaus*, p. 168.

12 Ibid., p. 177.

13 Teddy Kollek, *For Jerusalem: A Life* (New York: Random House, 1978), pp. 227–228. Cited in Joost R. Hiltermann, "Teddy Kollek and the Native Question," *Middle East Report*, no. 281 (May–June 1993), pp. 24–27.

14 Nitzan-Shiftan, "Modernisms in Conflict," pp. 161–187.

15 Abraham Rabinovich, "Planners Under Fire," *The Jerusalem Post*, December 25, 1970, p. 20. Cited in Nitzan-Shiftan, "Modernisms in Conflict," p. 165.

16 "Final Statement of the Jerusalem Committee," 1970. Retrieved from the Architectural Archives of the University of Pennsylvania, Philadelphia.

17 Arthur Kutcher, *The New Jerusalem: Planning and Politics* (London: Thames and Hudson, 1973), p. 88. Cited in Nitzan-Shiftan, "Modernisms in Conflict," p. 165.

18 Ibid.

19 Susie Harries, "Pevsner in Jerusalem," *Nikolaus Pevsner – Bringer of Riches: Talking about Nikolaus Pevsner – The Man, His Life and His Work* (blog), June 3, 2010, accessed December 28, 2016, https://susieharries.wordpress.com/2010/03/06/pevsner-in-jerusalem/.
Fuller, quoted by Ari Avrahami in "Jerusalem's Not So Golden Plan." Cited in Nitzan-Shiftan, *Modernism in Conflict*, p. 166.

20 Lewis Mumford to Teddy Kollek, December 1970. Cited in Kutcher, *New Jerusalem*, p. 9. Cited in Alona Nitzan-Shiftan, "Frontier Jerusalem: The Holy Land as a Testing Ground for Urban Design," *Frankel Institute Annual*, vol. 2008, pp. 46–49. Available online (accessed August 3, 2017): https://www.bjpa.org/search-results/publication/19443.

21 Harries, "Pevsner in Jerusalem."

22 Nitzan-Shiftan, "Modernisms in Conflict," p. 170, citing Wolf von Eckardt, "Summing Up a Period," a postscript to David Kroyanker and Yael Guiladi, *Jerusalem, 1978: Between Two Decades; Planning and Development* [in Hebrew] (Jerusalem, 1978), p. 452.

23 Alison Margaret Smithson and Peter Smithson, *The Charged Void: Urbanism* (New York: Monacelli Press, 2005), p. 214.

24 Ibid.

25 Ibid., p. 216.

26 Ibid., p. 214.

27 Ibid., p. 219.

28 "Jerusalem Transformed," *Aberdeen Free Press*, December 24, 1920. Cited in Annabel Wharton, "Jerusalem Remade," in *Modernism and the Middle East*, p. 54.

29 Ecclesiastes 1:9. The book of Ecclesiastes is called *Koheleth* in Hebrew. King Solomon, son of King David, is said to be Koheleth, the author of Ecclesiastes.

㉖ Members of the Town-Planning Subcommittee of the Jerusalem Committee debate at the Van Leer Institute, 1970. Photographer: Yitzhak Amit. Judaica Collection, Harvard Library.

WORLD COMMITTEE FOR JERUSALEM

A FIRST STATEMENT

We were invited by the Mayor of Jerusalem to form an advisory committee to study the cultural, human and aesthetic needs of the City and its surroundings. We came here inspired by the profound meaning that Jerusalem has for millions of people all over the world.

We found the City already deeply engaged in rehabilitation and reconstruction work as well as in revealing archaeological exploration; with people of all ages from all over the world contributing their science and their energy to the task.

1. We consider that, at this special moment, great and urgent care is required to provide Jerusalem with a framework for the protection and enhancement of its beauty, its way of life and its spiritual meaning. It is our conviction that this task is an urgent duty for everyone and that it transcends all other considerations.

2. Our visit to Jerusalem convinced us that much of the work to be done is overdue. To delay any longer the rehabilitation of the walls, the clearance of slums, the protection of sites would create irreparable harm. The many and essential values involved require immediate study and prompt action. The preparatory work of the authorities is, in our opinion, both valid and far-sighted. This work must be carried on with a particular emphasis on archaeological excavations; for each new discovery helps relate the future form of the City to the past.

3. We believe that we must not succumb to the temptation of using the extraordinary wealth of tangeable remnants of the past to make the City a museum or a stage set. We must keep Jerusalem alive, intensely alive; a constantly evolving image.

4. In keeping with this principle, the project of a park appears to us satisfactory, in so far as it does not lead to a segregation between the walled city and its surroundings but that, on the contrary, it serves to reinforce the unity and vitality of Jerusalem.

/2.

(27) Documents of the Jerusalem Committee, 1969–1972. The Isamu Noguchi Foundation and Garden Museum, New York.

assist authorities in reviewing proposed projects prior to issuance of a building permit.



5. Where rebuilding is concerned within the walled City, we think that all authentic remnants of the past, both of artistic and historical value, should be rigorously preserved. As for new building, while the scale and skyline should harmonize with the historical townscape, freedom of expression should not only be allowed, but encouraged. We appeal to all creative minds of today to contribute and to bear witness to the truth that contemporary art is the best instrument by which we can respect the past.

6. We are well aware that the great variety of facts to be investigated and decided upon will compel us to consult technicians in many fields. But we must avoid the confusion and compromise which are the inevitable result of uncoordinated planning. Hence, we suggest that the Municipality of Jerusalem be empowered to create an office of coordination to reconcile the divergencies and implement whatever plans it adopts.

7. Now that Jerusalem is, at last, freely accessible to all, we call upon all cultural and spiritual groups active throughout the world to come here, as we did, and join in the challenging and great adventure of ensuring the universal character of the future Jerusalem.

Jerusalem is unique. Unique also is the invitation tendered by the local authorities to people from lands afar to come and advise them on the work to be done in the City for the protection of its beauty and of the meaning attached to it by the rest of the world.

We gratefully acknowledge that fact. We hope that, at some time, our Muslim brothers will join us in this great task which involves a deep respect for their way of life as for their most beautiful shrines and treasures.

Some of us came to Jerusalem from countries where lack of opportunities and motivation, confusion about ideals, depreciation of the highest values and even racial antagonism have created, among young and old, disorder and conflicts seemingly impossible to control. We found in Jerusalem a boundless devotion to work, a motivation and a common fervor which are the best cures for these evils. For this, too, we are grateful.

Jerusalem, July 4, 1969

THE JERUSALEM COMMITTEE
Townplanning Subcommittee
December 19-21, 1970

## FINAL STATEMENT

We were invited by the Mayor of Jerusalem as a townplanning subcommittee of the Jerusalem Committee, to review a number of plans for the future development of Jerusalem: "The Master Plan 1968, Interim Report"; "A Plan for the Central Business District"; "The Old City of Jerusalem and its Environs, Outline Townplanning Scheme, 1970"; "The Jerusalem Transportation Plan for 1985 (1970)".

We should like to begin by expressing our appreciation of what is much more than a generous invitation but, we hope, a valuable example of international cooperation beneficial to the development of a city with which a large part of the world is concerned. We hope very much that this cooperation will be continued.

We should also like to put on record our admiration for the scrupulous care which is being taken of the many works of art and historical monuments of all nationalities and religions, and of the effort made to incorporate these effectively in the plans.

The very glories of Jerusalem are so many that they make the problems of development unusually complicated. One has only to realise that:

- Jerusalem is a very great spiritual center, important to several great religions.
- Jerusalem is the capital of Israel.
- The inhabitants of Jerusalem form a unique mosaic of diverse peoples and the results are the exceptional appearance of the city, with its synagogues, mosques and churches and its many historic monuments.
- Jerusalem is a creative intellectual center, with its many institutions of religious and secular learning and of culture.
- Jerusalem landscape is again exceptional, not only in its beauty but for its essential significance in the history of three religions.

These strong characteristics of the city magnify and complicate all the normal problems which beset the development of any city today.

The interim plans presented the essential resources for our deliberations. We feel, however, that there are contradictions among the different plans which have yet to be resolved and that in each plan a number of concepts need further consideration. Other essential concepts have not perhaps been grasped.

We believe that some of the weaknesses in the plans which have been noted may be due to administrative difficulties at the center.

In the spirit of mutual confidence which underlay our frank exchanges and with the desire that the best possible plan for Jerusalem should finally be formulated, we make the following suggestions and recommendations:

The Master Plan should be restructured.

The planning process ought to be reassessed.

The collection of data provided in the submitted reports is valuable. We were impressed by the thoughtful and stimulating quality of the propositions put forth, by the wide range of concern. The earnestness which underlies the pursuit is clear to any dispassionate observer. The subcommittee feels, however, without exception, that there has not been sufficient consideration of alternatives, clarification of the basic ideas, nor the expositation of a unified theme. To guide the planners there is need of a set of broad principles of an overall coordination of policies, while the alternatives should be clearly set out.

The physical planners of the city have need above all of a comprehensive vision of it. We agree with those who formulated these plans that the special qualities of Jerusalem call for the most creative efforts from the planning profession; all that has been learned of methodology and the deepest insight into the related sciences have to be brought to bear. What the plan calls for are principles of physical order, a set of planning guidelines so firm that they will directly generate the plan of a great city as it evolves, and so well grounded in functional, social, economic, emotional and symbolic issues that agreement on them may gradually be reached.

In our judgement the first step to be taken in this exceptionally difficult task is to set up a mixed task force composed, on the one hand, of people well versed in the plans and, on the other, of those who can bring dispassionate perspective to bear.

This task force should report directly to the relevant government ministries and to the Mayor and should be given adequate guidelines by which it can review the plans and make recommendations and should be requested to complete this process within six months.

It should feel free to consult with this subcommittee who make themselves available and with any other groups of citizens and professionals which the task force deems necessary.

In specifying the course of action to be pursued in this six-month interval, we recognize the difficulty of formulating in advance and that a great deal of discretion must be left to the task force. We should like to suggest that the members of the present subcommittee submit to the Jerusalem Committee as soon as possible their proposed guidelines or broad areas in which such guidelines can be helpfully formulated.

We assume that since this city is complex and unique, every effort will be made at the national level to overcome the complications and facilitate the implementation of the final recommendations.

In view of the complexities of executing an ideal plan to meet the ambitious goals that the planning of Jerusalem deserves it is recognized that financial grants and aids of considerable magnitude must be forthcoming. It is our hope that the often expressed world concern with Jerusalem will be backed by concrete financial manifestations and generosities.

We believe that a continuous relationship between the subcommittee and the planners of Jerusalem is a useful and, if sometimes frustrating, a rich interchange. It stands ready to constitute itself in any form which is deemed desirable, as a committee of the whole or recognizing that specific tasks can best be handled by smaller numbers, as groups or individuals.

We are much heartened by the willingness of all parties concerned to reveal frankly their innermost concepts about the potentials of the great city, by the reservoirs of goodwill encountered and by a political leadership which is ready to encourage and accept the most advanced townplanning in order to meet the merging problems of the present and the future.

December 21, 1970

ועד ירושלים

THE JERUSALEM COMMITTEE

P.O.B. 557 JERUSALEM • TELEPHONE 25932

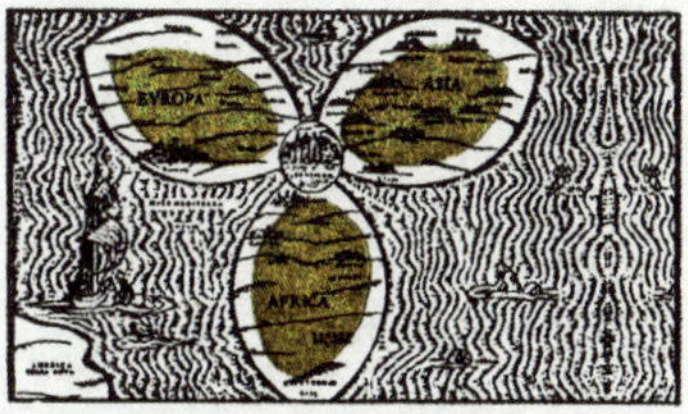

May 30, 1972

Comments By Professor Buckminster Fuller During His Visit, April, 1972

Almost a year and a half ago when I was here for the Jerusalem Committee Town Planning Sub-Committee Meeting, I went away quite dismayed about many things to do with the future of the city. During my present visit, I have met with the new Urban Planning Unit and, to my astonishment, feel that all the conditions which everybody had abhorred had been met, although they are not met forever because there are going to be pressures and pressures reoccur. But I feel the team is thoroughly aware of these pressures and have actually found solutions already met. Having come expecting to be dismayed, I was absolutely in a state of joy with surprise - and I feel that if the whole Committee knew what was happening, they too would agree that this was a great surprise. The Planning Team is low-key fundamentally and they are going for the right things.

We live in one tiny world and therefore Jerusalem more than ever really belongs to that world - there are no people on earth who do not have some kind of connection with Jerusalem and it is not just because it is a beautiful piece of archaeology and architecture - it is still has its open vista to eternity out there in the wilderness - a great mystery. And I think now that I have witnessed today that that will be kept under control and probably will be able to carry on.

Teddy said he was concerned with the human side - that people need housing so badly. The first thing the Planning Team talked to me about was the "human side" - they are concerned about it and are going to be involved in the problem. I think, and the team agrees, that more and more contact with the public is required. I propose that the team under Kollek and the engineers' auspices, undertake to acquire a large model of Jerusalem - total Jerusalem. This should be done by students - perhaps one part of Jerusalem done by students at the Technion and another by students at another university or school. I suggest you have some colour control so that you have some uniformity of modeling by the different groups. And then I would have the model used for television and I would have weekly or monthly shows about the planning of Jerusalem, getting all the people in the city to make comments and design suggestions.

.../2

Professor Buckminster Fuller Comments
Page Two

I recommend that you have a really large scale model of total Jerusalem - including the total surrounding, as yet unoccupied territory, done in relief and have within it the mountains and plateaux removable and you can change this plateau and change that one so that different solutions can be put there. By having it as a television model, your television camera can really come in like a helicopter over it, let them take the camera out in a real helicopter. I think that this can be by far the greatest tool you ever have.

I really came here with my heart quite heavy - I expected to find things much worse than when I left before, and I found it just exactly the other way and I think I can relieve many of the Committee and regain their enthusiastic support once more and get them backing this young team (Urban Planning Unit).

.Noguchi:--- May I bring up a matter which is very premature but I think it is a sort of suggestive of the kind of problems that lie ahead and that is in the development of the Jewish Quarter which seems to be the one thing that allows for imaginative approach to our entry into the Old City. It is the question of the Dung Gate. That gate, walled gate, annoys me the most because it is a kind of...it is an insult in a sense and was intended, I believe, as an insult to the Jewish people and I understand there was originally a small hole for a donkey for doing it and I personally, I understand that the road is going to be lowered because of archeological work and so on and that will raise the level of the gate and enlarge it somewhat, I personally

Prof Kahn --- I just want to make a few remarks which are inspired by what has been said by Mr. Sandberg and Bruno Zevi and the Mayor as one who has been also very much inspired by the general ambiance of Jerusalem. I see as the first two gentlemen who spoke, the emergence of new images which could be built around a composite order of stone and concrete and modern materials. I really do see that a more varied construction could come out of it. I cannot say that it should be entrusted to everybody to do, that is my apprehension because when I visualize a composite order, it is something which is not just patching together concrete and stone, but each one given its natural role which concrete alone cannot do, and what stone cannot do, be recognised, I see stone but I cant leave it out...concrete inner structures which make stone look ridiculous and in the same way using backup of concrete to immitate arches. That kind of construction being prevalent in the present work is most depressing would lead to chaos in construction.

But I do see great beauty that could emerge out of the circumstances of the Jerusalem loves you might say and the particular character which can be derived out of the mere being in the presence of everything around. I see a composite order then of concrete and stone right in the Jewish Quarter. I see a new scale in what has been circumstantially made by clearing the space in front of the Wall and while Mr. Zevi said the same thing as what I am going to say, only he didn't in his fluid way, but he did not condemn what was done really. What he said was now it must be given a new scale. He said that and I...that hit mà as being truly what should be done and I think it is just a different thing now than it was. And it can be equally as beautifully handled as it could have been at the extension of                and rather the loved saying of being confine- Now, it is something else. And even that scale is now saying something to the Jewish Quarter which is not keeping it in the same, we might say, scale as it now is indicated. It is no reason why the buildings cannot be taller, just so that general contour is not defiled. They can be taller, but they cannot be gigantly taller one taller one short, one taller one short, but something which is a new kind of level, which just respects the contour that is there, except that it is much more built up. This would give you a wonderful opportunity also for gardens, protected gardens, because they need height for protection, courts, gardens, buildings that can stand with a kind of authority near the wall, the Wall now being deepened I think will give the opportunity for a strength and a statement of determined purpose that I believe the previous associations of back-bending and taking-it-on-the-chin kind of attitude that probably the Wall had before. I see greatness out of the words that were said previously and I myself is inspired by those words and I think it is very possible to make a beautiful new scale in the Jewish Quarter of that sector.

# DOSSIER:
# LOUIS KAHN'S RUIN

㉘

Most illustrious of the post-1967 stone or paper ruins, and most astounding of the reoccupations within the Jewish Quarter of the Old City of Jerusalem, was Louis Kahn's Hurva (lit. "ruin") Synagogue.[1] The Hurva Synagogue had been built in the early eighteenth century and was destroyed by Muslims soon afterward. After standing in ruins for over 140 years (hence becoming known as "The Ruin"), it was rebuilt in 1864 and became the central synagogue for Ashkenazi Jews. The synagogue was demolished again by the Jordanian Legion after their takeover of the Jewish Quarter in the War of 1948.

Louis Kahn's proposal for the rebuilding of the Hurva had no iconographic affiliation whatsoever with the historic building—nor with any typological tradition of synagogue buildings, for that matter. His projected monolith invoked both an archaic Mesopotamian ceremonial ziggurat and a shapely Brutalist figure. The design was based on "pylons of Jerusalem stone on each side enclosing four huge central pillars of reinforced concrete, so that the pylons function as a container and the pillars as its content."[2] It was certainly an out-of-scale and out-of-time monument, dominating the skyline of Jerusalem and competing with the mosques on Temple Mount and the Church of the Holy Sepulchre.

Israeli architect Ram Karmi admiringly describes Kahn's Hurva as a paradigm shift from the all-too-instrumental and mundane architecture of Israel's formative decades to the brazenly symbolic representation of pathos, destiny, and grandeur:

> The Israeli architecture, whose role it had been to supply a shelter for hundreds of thousands of new immigrants quickly and cheaply, stood for pure functionalism. It did not succeed in expressing through artistic perfection the national experience of a people returning to its homeland [. . .]. It may be that the new society that was established in Israel lacked the necessary intensity of experience to create a structure like the *Hurva*. It had not yet found an architectural language whose strength was in expressing sentiments and destinies such as these, [. . .] and still had not created many buildings to answer to demands so complex and complicated. In all that may touch upon buildings of great symbolic and emotional value, we were left stuttering. It may be that the new building of the *Hurva* is an opportunity to try and fill this space.[3]

Teddy Kollek, then mayor of Jerusalem, was more skeptical about the overpowering size and historical ambition of Kahn's project: "Should we in the Jewish Quarter have a building of major importance which 'competes' with the Mosque and the Holy Sepulchre, and should we in general have any building which would compete in importance with the Western Wall of the Temple?"[4] Kahn's project was put aside, as was a later proposal by Denys Lasdun. Instead, an arch was eventually built on the Hurva site, commemorating the old synagogue and embalming the ruin as a national emblem. When the synagogue was finally rebuilt in 2010, the arch was integrated in the restored dome. ■

1 See "The Rehabilitation of the Hurva Symposium," in *The Rebuilding of the Hurva*, ed. David Cassuto [in Hebrew] (Jerusalem: Ministry of Education and Culture, 1970), pp. 33–34.

2 Luis Mariano Akerman, "The Evocative Character of Louis I. Kahn's Hurva Synagogue Project, 1967–1974," in *The Real and Ideal Jerusalem in Jewish, Christian and Islamic Art*, ed. Bianca Kühnel (Jerusalem: Center for Jewish Art of the Hebrew University, 1998), p. 247.

3 Ram Karmi, in *Rebuilding of the Hurva*, p. 25.

4 Letter from Teddy Kollek to Louis Kahn, August 29, 1968, in "Hurva Synagogue All Correspondence," Kahn Collection, file 030.II.A.39.1.

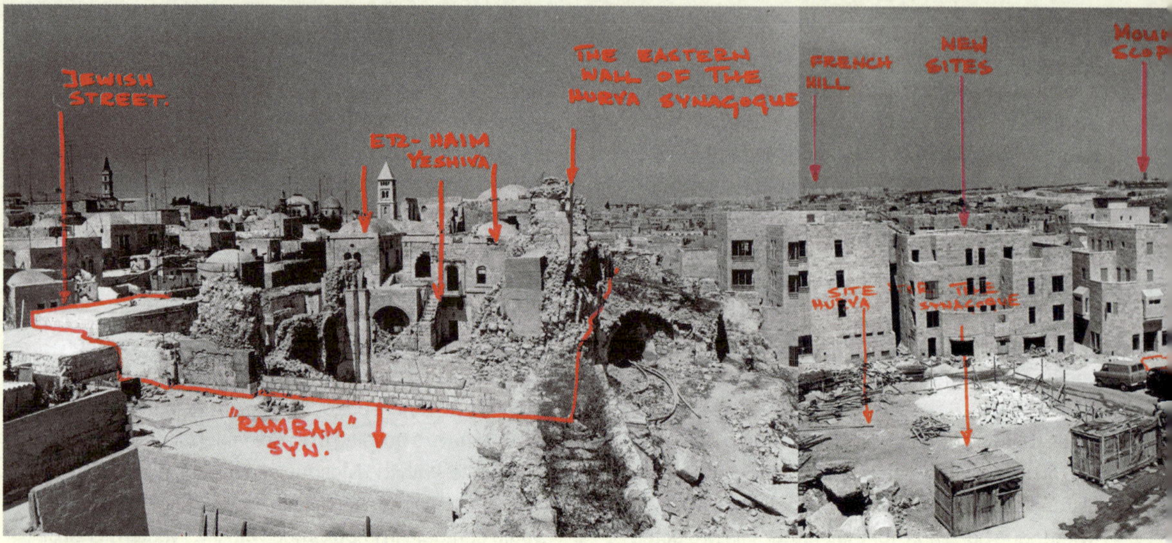
JEWISH STREET.
ETZ-HAIM YESHIVA
THE EASTERN WALL OF THE HURVA SYNAGOGUE
FRENCH HILL
NEW SITES
"RAMBAM" SYN.

30

31

(28) Hurva Synagogue: model of the Old City of Jerusalem with the proposed synagogue, 1968. Louis Kahn. The Louis I. Kahn Collection, University of Pennsylvania.
(29) The Jewish Quarter and the surroundings of the old Hurva Synagogue, 1968. The Louis I. Kahn Collection, University of Pennsylvania.
(30) The ruins of the old Hurva Synagogue, 1968.
(31) The old Hurva Synagogue after restoration of the ark, 1970s.
(32) Hurva Synagogue: model of the Old City of Jerusalem with the proposed synagogue, 1968. Louis Kahn. The Louis I. Kahn Collection, University of Pennsylvania.

(29)

(32)

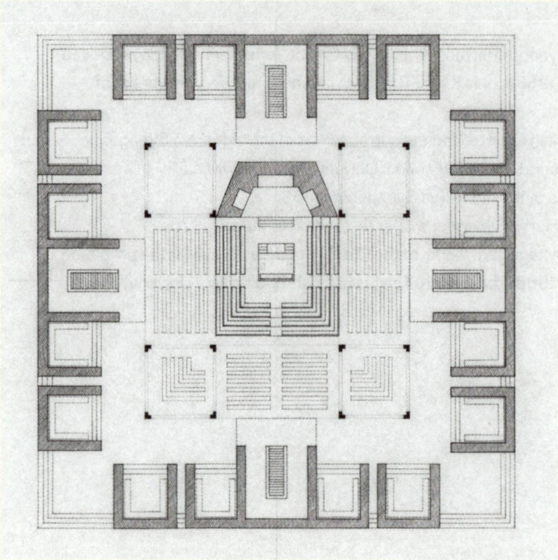

(33)

(33) Hurva Synagogue, floor plan, 1968. Louis Kahn. The Louis I. Kahn Collection, University of Pennsylvania.
(34) Hurva Synagogue, model, 1968. Louis Kahn. The Louis I. Kahn Collection, University of Pennsylvania.
(35) Hurva Synagogue, model, 1968. Louis Kahn. The Louis I. Kahn Collection, University of Pennsylvania.
(36) Hurva Synagogue, model, 1968. Louis Kahn. The Louis I. Kahn Collection, University of Pennsylvania.
(37) Section through the Old City of Jerusalem, showing the relationship between the Hurva, Temple Mount and Dome of the Rock, 1968. Louis Kahn. The Louis I. Kahn Collection, University of Pennsylvania.

(34)

(35)

(36)

(37)

# Occupation

① "Road 443 #1," 2001. Miki Kratsman.

② Panorama # 1, 2002. Daniel Bauer.

## Borderline Disorder

The rather vague diagnosis of "borderline disorder" may be the most concise definition of Israel's distinctive territorial mentality. After all, what other state has accumulated such a stockpile of political and military maps, border disputes, ownership claims, interim arrangements, definitions of sovereignty, zones of control, envelopes of aerial reconnaissance, covers of ground surveillance, bands of separation walls, and loops of surrounding fences, as well as a horrific catalogue of checkpoints, roadblocks, bypass roads, travel restrictions, and "safe passages"?[1] All of these exist in order to sustain an agenda of precarious formlessness, to relentlessly negotiate and postpone the moment of decisive political contours, and to perpetuate the defensive-offensive all-over-ness of the volatile frontier.

In her dissertation, "Talking Borders: The Construction of a Political Territory in Israel, 1949–1957,"[2] Adriana Kemp deals with the interplay between territorial borders and the formation of national identity in Israel. According to Kemp, Israel's borders were conceived simultaneously according to two different and often contradictory cultural languages: a colonialist-territorialist language that defines the border as a barrier dividing states from each other, while uniting the members of the nation inside the border; and a spatial language that presents the boundary as a frontier, challenges the Cartesian (linear) definition of borders, and, in so doing, blurs the distinctions between "internal" and "external." The first definition was aimed at domesticating the space and transforming it into a delineated sovereign territory, while the second, unique though not exclusive to the Israeli case, emptied the concept of border of its original political meaning by at once depoliticizing the outlines and politicizing the spaces beyond them. These spatial practices created new geopolitical maps based not on sustainable agreements, but on pioneering activities and the establishment of "facts on the ground." This portrayal of spatial nationalism renders ongoing and infinite the process of constructing the nation-state. The open-ended process in itself, rather than the finite cartography, is the Zionist apotheosis, since it generates the desired force of proactive patriotism.

From the end of the nineteenth century up to the establishment of the State, Jewish settlement in Palestine operated according to a frontier strategy of "points": literally striking a stake into the territory by establishing isolated settlements or clusters of settlements, with the eventual goal of joining them together into a territorial continuum. The frontier, unlike the border, not only defined the outer contours, but had the ability to expand into the interior of the country.

The image of a net—flexible enough to modify its shape according to circumstance, stronger than the sum of its gaping holes, lacking any center or hierarchy—can be aptly applied to the ideology and modus operandi of early Zionism. The soft, vague, amorphous, ostensibly compromising net is the rhetorical antithesis of the Zionist right-wing revisionist ideology of the "iron wall," which proffers the clear, maximalist, angular lines of the map of the "two banks of the Jordan."[3] It is interesting, however, to note the inversion of the stances of Left and Right that began after 1967. While the clear lines of the early Revisionists morphed into the left-wing slogan "*Yesh Gvul!*" (lit. "There is a border!"; fig. "That's enough!"), the original Labor Movement strategy of border-blurring and "striking a stake" was adopted by the right-wing settlers in the Occupied Territories, and was symbolically expressed in the title of the settler magazine *Nekuda* ("Point").

At the April 1948 meeting of the provisional People's Administration to discuss the Declaration of Independence, David Ben-Gurion registered his opposition to drafting and announcing the borders of the imminent State. This fundamental issue was thus not written into the Declaration, and any decision about the State's borders was postponed until the results of the war became clear. But toward the end of the fighting—as the Zionists debated among themselves about the missed opportunity to take control of the entire Land of Israel; as then commander of the southern front, Yigal Alon, stated that "one cannot

③ "Wall." *This Place*, Tel Aviv Museum of Art, 2011. Josef Koudelka.

imagine a stronger border than that of the Jordan [river]"; and as Menachem Begin came out against the "freezing of the artificial borders, the borders of segmentation"—Ben-Gurion adamantly insisted on the acceptance of the principle of partition, with the results of the war serving as status-quo borders.[4] Thus, in contrast to "natural" or "historical" conceptions of border, the first prime minister of Israel defined the border as an open-ended project—a diplomatic, military, and colonial enterprise subject to ongoing negotiations.

While Israeli representatives engaged in talks about a permanent settlement at the United Nations Reconciliation Conference in Lausanne in 1949, they balked in the end, fearing that such a settlement would exact a heavy price in the form of the return of hundreds of thousands of Palestinian refugees and the relinquishing of territories in the Negev and the Galilee. The temporary borders were perceived as a better option than permanent borders—in effect the borders of the Partition Plan. But the provisional nature of the borders was only expressed outwardly. To itself, Israel said that "until the final peace comes, the Armistice Lines will be borders for all intents and purposes. There will be no restrictions on the sovereignty that Israel enjoys within these borders. The only restriction placed upon it, in the demilitarized zones, is the prohibition of the army from entering into them."[5] The Arab countries also tolerated the temporary status of the borders, but from a different point of view; by their measure, the Armistice Lines, as mere cease-fire lines, did not delineate a territory that was under Israeli sovereignty.

The Armistice Agreements were signed in the first half of 1949, with the purpose of defining the (temporary) legality of the borders until the signing of binding peace accords.[6] The outside borders of the Armistice Agreements were almost identical to those of Mandatory Palestine, with the exception of the so-called Green Line, which was drawn in the West Bank and the Gaza Strip based on the positions of the rival armies at the time of the cease-fire.

The strategy of point-settlement was manifested graphically in the perforated borderline that appeared on the maps. On paper, such a graphic convention denotes temporary border markings. In practice, it is a penetrable boundary that invites infiltration. In order to overcome this, one must thicken it (from a "line" to a "strip," from a "border" to a "frontier area"). On the ground, the border was loosely marked by painted barrels, columns, signs, and occasional minefields—only rarely by a continuous fence. Meanwhile, the lines drawn on the maps were often translated, depending on the topographical circumstances, into strips with a width of 250 to 300 meters, which created territories of undefined sovereignty, a sure cause for border disputes.

The most problematic border was that between Israel and Jordan, the Green Line, along the West Bank: 360 kilometers, bending and twisting, with no natural boundaries. The Green Line was described in an Israeli police report from the beginning of the 1950s as an example of the way in which borders should never be drawn. [...] This border runs through and dissects lands belonging to a single owner; it passes just meters from vital transportation arteries; it separates inhabitants—farmers live on one side of it while lands that they cultivated for generations were annexed to the territory on the other side of the same border. And the main thing—it separates two Arab towns that are connected by family ties, and, even worse than that, it sometimes splits entire villages in two.[7]

At the Government Session of October 1949, Ben-Gurion requested a creative solution for the border. His proposal could be considered one of the first manifestos of Israeli defense landscaping:

> We have strange borders. We need barricades, but I have despaired of the possibility of making barricades. [...] We will plant trees; these plantings will be calculated to stave off the enemy. [...] The tree trunk will slow down the infiltrating enemy. At a certain size it can also stop a tank. This is just one advantage of forestation.[8]

Israeli statistics from the first years of Statehood indicate some 10,000 to 15,000 cases of infiltration per year—primarily of Palestinian refugees trying to return to their homes. This number gradually decreased, with about 4,500 infiltrations in 1955.[9] The official response to the phenomenon was the establishment of a ring of new settlements along the borders, with the goal of "stopping up the gaps" against individual infiltrators and foiling more general Arab claims for territorial concessions. The frontier was perceived at the time as a strip of land adjacent to the international border or the cease-fire line. It varied in width from one place to the next according to topographical conditions, vulnerability, settlement needs, and settlement density. The route of the temporary borders created Israel's proverbial "narrow waistline," which rendered the entire center a frontier—stretching, in effect, from the eastern boundary to the sea. The "internal frontier," on the other hand, gradually lost the meaning that it had in the days of the Tower and Stockade settlements, following the expulsion and flight of the Arabs from their cities and villages during the war and their replacement with the Jewish population that was arriving in massive waves of immigration.

The State encouraged settlement on the new frontier and portrayed settling the periphery as a crucible for the formation of the "State pioneer." Ongoing security problems, however, led families and sometimes entire communities to abandon these settlements. To counter this flight, the Land Settlement Department of the Jewish Agency conducted an intensive propaganda operation and occasionally even summoned military and police forces to block the exits from the settlements. Proposals were raised to pass legislation that would authorize the State to determine where people would live, or quite literally to turn citizens into "border stones." At the Government Session of October 1953, where the situation in the army and other security issues were discussed, Ben-Gurion said:

> I will now move on to nonmilitary issues, though these are security issues of utmost importance: the new settlements arouse incomparably grave concern. In the War of Independence, settlement played a decisive role, in my opinion—not during the war itself, because in the midst of the war, when we fought against the Arab army, the settlements no longer played a security role. [...] Their decisive role was prior to that, because they gave the public faith and confidence in our forces. The fact that five and a half months after the outbreak of the war, up to two days before the declaration of the State, not a single settlement fell—Gush Etzion fell in the last two days—this gave the people confidence. The question of confidence is central. [...] Right now we have some 400 new settlements. Some of them are adequate, in my opinion, but there are many settlements—in the current situation, should a war break out—whose inhabitants will surely flee, and I do not fear for the fate of those settlements but for the fate of Israel. If such a thing happens and they flee, panic will seize the entire country. When they see refugees running away from their settlements, the panic will spread first of all among the new immigrants, who are the majority. It will also spread among the veteran population. I see in this as grave a danger as ever. [...] We must resolve this problem.[10]

The disadvantages of the method, it seems, were clear. Fixing it would happen by inversion: if one could not rely on civilian settlers to function as soldiers, then one must buttress the frontier with soldiers, who would establish quasi-civilian settlements. The solution came in the form of the settlements of the Israel Defense Forces' Nahal ("Fighting Pioneering Youth"), whose original purpose was to forge a connection between Israeli-born youth and new immigrants at the fringe of the national territory. Between 1950 and 1956, no fewer than twenty-six such Nahal outposts were established in the frontier areas. In the two years following, nine additional Nahal settlements were built.[11]

By the mid-1950s it was clear that a long, narrow strip of frontier settlements was not enough to guarantee full territorial security. The goal at that stage was to thicken the frontier and to build an adequate home front. The idea of development areas—which had been raised in professional circles even before the establishment of the State and which proposed a comprehensive civilian settlement framework based on a system of rural settlements and district towns—gained legitimacy. In planning terms, this meant the marriage of two conceptions: that which guided the early stages of frontier settlement (linear, defensive, fortress-like); and that which guided the policy of population dispersal and construction of regional new towns, as laid out in the 1950 national master plan (see chapter "Project"). The deployment of settlements in the development areas did not have a particularly defensive or strategic structure; taken on its own, it was meant to create a critical mass of stable settlement on the home-front side of the border. Over the course of a decade and a half, nine development areas were established in the frontier zone: Korazim, Ta'anakh, Modi'im, the Jerusalem corridor, Adullam, Lachish, Adorayim, Besor, and the Arava. The total territory of the development areas came to 2,285 square kilometers, about 10 percent of the territory of Israel. When added to the area of the frontier strip proper, an additional 10 percent or so, the official "frontier" of Israel covered about a quarter of the territory of the State.

According to Kemp, Israel's struggle against infiltration and its aspiration to seal its borders yielded a "dialectic between isolation and penetration"; Israeli military breaches of the border became a method of sealing off that same border. Calculated actions—patrols, ambushes, field training, and confrontations, all beyond the border—became "State ritual": symbolic and educational practices that etched the meaning of the border into the national consciousness and expressed a view of reality in which it was accepted not only that the border must be fortified from the inside, but that securing it would be achieved by its trespassing.

Thus the border became a dynamic action, one marking a territory that is not finite, but open-ended and mobile.[12] Deterritorialized territorialization, the quintessence of the military conception of space, became the guideline of official Israeli policy and served as a complementary principle to the regional planners' conception of centralized decentralization. Jointly, these attitudes dictated the relentless shaping of a vigilant civilian periphery and the continual expansion and undulation of the "national frontier" for decades to come. ■

④ "Erez #3," 2003. Miki Kratsman.

1 The architecture of Israeli occupation was first argued and astutely decoded in Rafi Segal's and Eyal Weizman's *A Civilian Occupation: The Politics of Israeli Architecture* (Tel Aviv and London: Babel and Verso, 2003). Its comprehensive theorization was laid out in Eyal Weizman's *Hollow Land: Israel's Architecture of Occupation* (London: Verso, 2007).

2 Adriana Kemp, "Talking Borders: The Construction of a Political Territory in Israel, 1949–1957" (PhD diss., Tel Aviv University, 1997).

3 Revisionist Zionism refers to the ideological and political movements stemming from the World Union of Zionist Revisionists, founded in 1925 by Ze'ev Jabotinsky (1880–1940). Jabotinsky strongly opposed any partition of Palestine, rejected the romantic view of the East, and believed in the cultural superiority of Western civilization. The East, in his view, represented psychological passivity, social and cultural stagnation, and political despotism. Geostrategically, therefore, Zionism was to be permanently allied with European colonialism against the Arabs. Jabotinsky's worldview is condensed in two articles published in 1923 under the title "The Iron Wall." See Avi Shlaim, *The Iron Wall: Israel and the Arab World* (London: Allen Lane, 2000).

4 See Mordechai Bar-On, "The Struggle over the Achievements of 1948: Israel's Defense Policy," in *The First Decade, 1948–1958*, ed. Zvi Zameret and Hanna Yablonka [in Hebrew] (Jerusalem: Yad Izhak Ben-Zvi, 1997).

5 Ibid.

6 Upon the signing of the Armistice Agreements in 1949, Israel's borders measured 985 km in length. The sovereign territory of the State of Israel within these borders was 20,770 $km^2$. Including the Mediterranean coastline, the total length of the borders came to 1,251 km. Israel's shared border with Jordan was close to 650 km (which included 360 km in the West Bank, along the Green Line), with Egypt 250 km, and with Syria and Lebanon about 70 km each. The territories conquered in 1967 added 65,580 $km^2$ to Israel's territory, over three times its sovereign territory up until then, but its borders with Syria and Jordan were simultaneously shortened by 200 km. See Elisha Efrat, "Patterns of Fringe Settlement in Israel," *Studies in the Geography of Israel* 11 [in Hebrew] (Jerusalem: Hebrew University Department of Geography, 1981), pp. 87–100.

7 Israel National Police, Counter Infiltration Section, "Infiltration: Annual Survey, 1.1.1952–31.12.1952," cited in Benny Morris, *Israel's Border Wars, 1949–1956* [in Hebrew] (Tel Aviv: Am Oved, Sifriyat Ofakim, 1996), p. 16. Published in English as *Israel's Border Wars, 1949–1956: Arab Infiltration, Israeli Retaliation, and the Countdown to the Suez War* (Oxford: Clarendon Press, 1993).

8 Minutes of Israeli Government Session #2, October 4, 1949 (Israel State Archives).

9 See Benny Morris, *Israel's Border Wars, 1949–1956*.

10 Minutes of Israeli Government Session #8, October 20, 1953 (Israel State Archives).

11 According to Elisha Efrat, after June 1967, the Nahal settlements were reenergized as a tool for defining the boundaries in the Occupied Territories, at first in the formerly demilitarized zones or next to the new border lines (the Jordan Valley, the Rafah Salient, the Golan Slopes). But following the overturn in the 1977 elections, the Nahal's activities were redirected from the border zones into the heart of the conquered territory, and the frontier once again became an internal one, as in the days of Tower and Stockade. In 1967 Israel had 134 frontier settlements, which created a contiguous narrow settlement strip along the Lebanese and Syrian borders; along the Green Line with Judea and Samaria in the West Bank; and within Jerusalem, a divided frontier city. This contiguity was suspended in the South Hebron Hills, thinned out in the Arava Valley, and almost nonexistent along most of the border with the Sinai Desert, becoming dense once again along the Gaza Strip.

12 Kemp, "Talking Borders."

⑤ "Abu Dis," 2003. Miki Kratsman.

⑥ Gilo neighborhood, first stage, Jerusalem, early 1970s. Avraham Yasky, Yaacov Gil, Yosef Sivan. Aerial photo: Ran Erde.
⑦ Gilo neighborhood, Jerusalem, model, early 1970s. Avraham Yasky, Yaacov Gil, Yosef Sivan.
⑧ Kiryat Arba, early 1970s. Photo: Ran Erde.
⑨ Gilo Dalet, Jerusalem, mid-1970s. Israel Levitt. Photo: Ran Erde.
⑩ French Hill, Jerusalem, early 1970s. Shmuel Shaked, Gideon Ziv. Photo: Ran Erde.
⑪ Shikun & Pituach team working on Ma'alot Dafna project, Jerusalem. Still from a film by the Ministry of Housing, mid-1970s. Standing on the right: Ilan Efrat.
⑫ Satellite image of Gilo neighborhood, Jerusalem, mid-1970s.
⑬ Ma'alot Dafna, Jerusalem, mid-1970s. Yehuda Drexler, Shikun & Pituach team.
⑭ Ramot Aleph, Jerusalem, early 1970s. Yehuda Drexler. Photo: Ran Erde.
⑮ East Talpiot, Jerusalem, early 1970s. David Best, Adam Eyal. Photo: Ran Erde.
⑯ IBA building (Israel Broadcasting Authority), Jerusalem, model, 1968. Ariel Mayslits, Shlomo Peled.
⑰ Mount Scopus Campus, Hebrew University, Jerusalem, model, 1971. Ram Karmi, David Reznik, Shmuel Shaked, Haim Ketzef.
⑱ Housing project in East Talpiot, Jerusalem, early 1970s. Yaakov Rechter. Photo: Ran Erde.

⑥

⑦

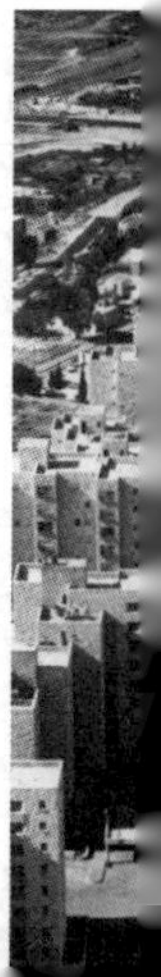

⑧

⑫

⑨

⑩

⑪

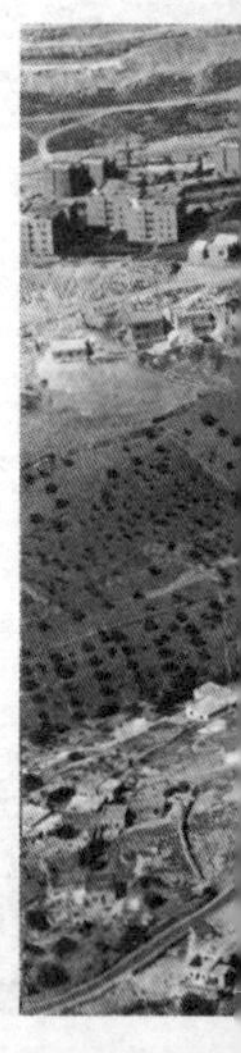

14

13

15

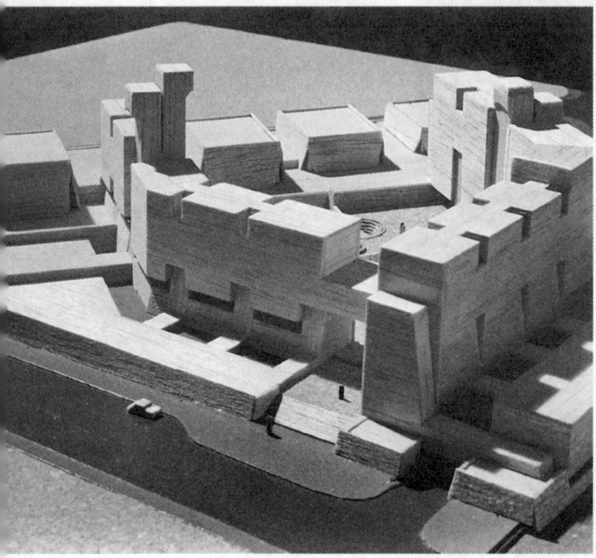

⑯

⑰

⑱

⑲

⑳

(21)

(22)

(23)

24

⑲ Police Central Command Headquarters (Metzudat Kfir), Neve Yaakov, Jerusalem, 1969-71. Ariel Mayslits, Shlomo Peled.
⑳ Neve Yaakov, Jerusalem, early 1970s. Yaakov Hertz.
㉑ Harry S. Truman Institute, Hebrew University, Mt. Scopus, late 1960s. Gershon Anekstein.
㉒ Housing cluster, Gilo, Jerusalem, mid-1970s. Salo Hershman.
㉓ Unidentified project, model, post-1967.
㉔ Commercial center of Gilo, Jerusalem, early 1970s. Avraham Yasky, Yaakov Gil, Yosef Sivan.

# DOSSIER: Excerpts from B'TSELEM'S REPORT: BY HOOK AND BY CROOK: ISRAELI SETTLEMENT POLICY IN THE WEST

㉕ "Erez #1," 2003. Miki Kratsman.

The following excerpts are from a 2010 report researched and written by Eyal Hareuveni, edited by Yael Stein, translated by Zvi Shulman, and published by B'Tselem, an Israeli nongovernmental organization which monitors human rights violations in the Occupied Territories.[1]

Some half a million Israelis are now living over the Green Line: more than 300,000 in 121 settlements and about one hundred outposts, which control 42 percent of the land area of the West Bank, and the rest in twelve neighborhoods that Israel established on land it annexed to the Jerusalem Municipality. [...]

The settlement enterprise has been characterized, since its inception, by an instrumental, cynical, and even criminal approach to international law, local legislation, Israeli military orders, and Israeli law, which has enabled the continuous pilfering of land from Palestinians in the West Bank.

The principal means Israel used for this purpose was declaration of "state land," a mechanism that resulted in the seizure of more than 900,000 dunams of land (sixteen percent of the West Bank), with most of the declarations being made in 1979–1992. [...]

In addition, the settlements seized control of private Palestinian land. [...]

To encourage Israelis to move to the settlements, Israel created a mechanism for providing benefits and incentives to settlements and settlers [...]. Most of the settlements in the West Bank hold the status of National Priority Area A, which entitles them to a number of benefits: in housing, by enabling settlers to purchase quality, inexpensive apartments, with an automatic grant of a subsidized mortgage; wide-ranging benefits in education [...]; for industry and agriculture, by grants and subsidies [...]; in taxation, by imposing taxes significantly lower than in communities inside the Green Line [...].

***

[...] The settlements, constructed in blatant breach of international humanitarian law, lead to the ongoing violation of many human rights of the Palestinian residents of the area, including the right to property, the right to equality, the right to an adequate standard of living, the right to freedom of movement, and the right to self-determination. [...]

***

In the West Bank, there are now more than 200 settlements that are connected to one another, and to Israel, by an elaborate network of roads. This network cuts across the areas that were handed over to Palestinian control, creating territorial islands of Areas A, which are under full Palestinian control, and Areas B, whose civil affairs are under Palestinian control.

The settlements were established along three strips running north to south, and around the Jerusalem metropolitan area.

The *Eastern Strip* includes the Jordan Valley, the shores of the Dead Sea up to the Green Line, and the eastern slopes of the mountain ridge that splits the West Bank lengthwise. The first settlements, built in the late 1960s, were established in this strip, which includes the largest land reserves in the West Bank. [...] The water resources in this strip have enabled the settlements there to develop agriculture that requires intensive irrigation.

The *Mountain Strip*, which is also called the watershed line, spans the peaks of the ridge that cuts the West Bank [and adjacent areas] lengthwise [...]. Situated along the strip are the six largest and most populated Palestinian towns in the West Bank—Jenin, Nablus, Ramallah, East Jerusalem, Bethlehem, and Hebron. One chain of settlements in the strip is spread out along Route 60, which is the main north-south traffic artery in the West Bank. These were built to ensure Israeli control of this traffic artery and to prevent Palestinian construction that would create contiguous Palestinian built-up areas on both sides of the road. Most of the road is in Area C, which is under complete Israeli control. [...]

The *Western Hills Strip* includes the area west of the mountain ridge through to the Green Line. The width of this strip varies from 10 to 20 kilometers, and the settlements in it run east to west alongside the latitudinal roads that connect to Route 60. The boundaries of these settlements lie close to one another, creating contiguous, or almost contiguous, urban expanses. Many of these settlements lie west of the Separation Barrier route. [...]

***

Throughout the years of Israel's occupation of the West Bank, the settlement enterprise has been promoted under every government. Its main objective is to gain control of as much land as possible in the West Bank for the purpose of establishing and expanding settlements. The settlement enterprise has divided and separated the areas under Palestinian control, turning them into disconnected enclaves and blurring the border between Israel and the West Bank.

While developing the settlement enterprise, Israel also established and institutionalized two separate legal systems in the West Bank: one for settlers, which de facto annexes the settlements and grants their residents all the rights accorded to citizens of a democratic country; and the other, a military judicial system that systematically violates the rights of Palestinians and denies them any real power in shaping the policies that influence their lives [...]

***

Given the illegality of the settlements from the outset, and in light of the ensuing violations of human rights, B'Tselem again demands that the government of Israel remove all the settlements. This must be done in a manner that respects the settlers' human rights, including payment of compensation.

Until then, several interim measures can be taken immediately to reduce the infringement of human rights. Among other steps, the government of Israel must cease all new construction in the settlements, cancel existing building plans, and freeze procedures for seizing additional land. The government must also cancel all the benefits and incentives given to encourage Israeli citizens to move to the settlements. °

1 Eyal Hareuveni, *By Hook and by Crook: Israeli Settlement Policy in the West Bank*, trans. Zvi Shulman (Jerusalem: B'Tselem, July 2010), accessed May 26, 2017, http://www.btselem.org/download/201007_by_hook_and_by_crook_eng.pdf.

㉖ – ㉘ The first trailers marking an outpost of a new Jewish mountain settlement in the West Bank, 2000. Daniel Bauer.

㉖

㉗

㉘

Note:
The names of the architects responsible for the master-plans of the settlements presented here were not publicly known prior to the research done for this publication by architect Alon Sarig.

㉙ Shavei Shomron, 2016. Google Earth. Founded: 1977. Master plan: Moshe Ravid, 1998.

㉚ Kochav Hashahar, 2010. Founded: 1977. Master plan: Aharon Erlich, 1995.

㉛ Gilo, Jerusalem, 2016. Google Earth. Founded: 1971. Master plan: Avraham Yasky, Yaacov Gil, Yosef Sivan.

㉜ Yakir, 2013. Google Earth. Founded: 1981. Master plan: Yossi Naim, 1986.

㉝ Har Bracha, 2016. Google Earth. Founded: 1983. Master plan: Avraham Gibbor, 2008.

㉞ Otniel, 2016. Google Earth. Founded: 1983. Master Plan: Ali Forty, 1997.

㉟ Elon More, 2016. Google Earth. Founded: 1979. Master plan: Moshe Ravid, 1997.

㊱ Yakir, 1983. Photo: Nati Harnik.

㊲ Karney Shomron, 2012. Founded: 1978. Master plan: Simha Schwartz, 1994.

㊳ Beitar Illit, 2016. Google Earth. Founded: 1985. Master plan: Yaacov Yaar, 1988.

㊴ Beit Yatir. Google Earth. Founded: 1983. Master plan: Elza Kaplan, 1989.

㊵ Ma'aleh Adumim, 2016. Google Earth. Founded: 1975. Master plan: Thomas Leitersdorf, Racel Valdan, 1979.

(41) Alon, 2016. Google Earth. Founded: 1990.

(42) Maale Efrayim, 2012. Founded: 1978. Master plan: Israel Levitt, 1983.

(43) Mitzpe Yericho, 2016. Google Earth. Founded: 1978. Master plan: World Zionist Organization, Settlement Department, 1987.

(44) Kfar Adumim, 2016. Google Earth. Founded: 1979.

⑮ Hermesh, 2016. Google Earth. Founded: 1982. Master plan: Shahar Yehoshua, 1996.

⑱ Na'ale, 2013. Google Earth. Founded: 1984. Master plan: Shmuel Shaked, 1984.

⑯ Hinanit, 2016. Google Earth. Founded: 1981. Master Plan: World Zionist Organization, Settlement Department, 1988.

⑰ Alfei Menashe, 2013. Google Earth. Founded: 1983. Master plan: Yasky and partners, 1985.

㊾ Ariel, 2016. Google Earth. Founded: 1978. Master plan: Ministry of Housing 1988.

㊿ Ma'aleh Adumim, 2016. Photo: Moshe Milner. Founded: 1975. Master plan: Thomas Leitersdorf, Racel Valdan.

(51) Ofarim, 2016. Google Earth. Founded: 1981. Master plan: Ze'ev Baran, 1991.

(52) Har Bracha, 2000. Photo: Moshe Pridan.

(53) Etz Efraim, 2014. Google Earth. Founded: 1985. Master plan: Ilan Maromi, 2002.

(54) Beit Arye, 2016. Google Earth. Founded: 1981. Master plan: Elza Kaplan, Avraham Gibbor, Rachel Valdan, 1990.

(55) Shvut Rachel, 2016. Google Earth. Founded: 1991. Master plan: Shahar Yehoshua, 2015.

㊱ Eli, 2015. Google Earth. Founded: 1984.

㊲ Tkoa, 2016. Google Earth. Founded: 1977. Master plan: Yaacov Molcho, 1997.

㊳ Har Homa, Jerusalem, 2010, Getty Images. Founded: 1991. Master plan: Kolker, Kolker, Epstein, 1995.

# Appendix

# BIBLIOGRAPHY



## A


Abdelqader, Senan. "Architecture of Dependency." *The Israeli Presentation, 7th São Paulo International Biennial of Architecture* [in Hebrew]. Tel Aviv: Israeli Council of Culture and Art, 2007.

Abu-Lughod, Ibrahim, Roger Heacock, and Khaled Nashef, eds. *The Landscape of Palestine: Equivocal Poetry*. Birzeit: Birzeit University Publications, 1999.

Adler, Gerald M. "The Israeli-Palestinian Conflict, 1860–2006: Legal Aspects in a Historical and Political Context." Unpublished paper, 2008.

Adler, Leo. "Why (Is Israeli Architecture Based on Western Patterns)? Thoughts of a New Immigrant." *Habinyan Bamisrah Hakarov*, no. 1 [in Hebrew] (1934), p. 11.

Albright, William Foxwell. *Palestine: A Study of Jewish, Arab and British Policies, Volume 1*. New Haven: Yale University Press, 1947.

Aleksandrowicz, Or. "Civilian Demolition: The Premeditated Destruction of Jaffa's Manshiya Neighborhood, 1948–1949" [in Hebrew], *Iyunim Bitkumat Israel (Studies in Israeli and Modern Jewish Society)* 23, 2013.

Amir, Tula. *Nahum Zolotov: Architect and Planner* [in Hebrew]. Tel Aviv: Ama, 2011.

Anderson, Benedict. *Imagined Communities: Reflections on the Origin and Spread of Nationalism*. London: Verso, 2006.

Angel, Shlomo. "Preparing for the Coming Urban Expansion in Developing Countries." Unpublished paper, 2008.

Anis, Ruth, and Yosef Ben Arev. *Gardens and Landscape in the Kibbutz: 60 Years of Development* [in Hebrew]. Tel Aviv: Ministry of Defense, 1994.

Avermaete, Tom, Serhat Karakayali, and Marion von Osten, eds. *Colonial Modern: Aesthetics of the Past, Rebellions for the Future*. London: Black Dog Publishing, 2010.

Avruch, Kevin. "Kibbutz and Moshav." In *Israel: A Country Study*. Washington, DC: Federal Research Division, 1990.

Azoulay, Ariella. *Act of State: A Photographed History of the Occupation, 1967–2007* [in Hebrew]. Tel Aviv: Etgar, 2008.

Azoulay, Ariella. *Constituent Violence, 1947–1950: A Genealogy of the Regime and "A Catastrophe from Their Point of View"* [in Hebrew]. Tel Aviv: Resling, 2009.

Azoulay, Ariella. "Hunger in Palestine: The Event That Never Was." In *Territories: Islands, Camps and Other States of Utopia*, edited by Anselm Franke, Eyal Weizman, and Rafi Segal. Cologne: Walther König, 2003.


## B


Banham, Reyner. *Megastructure: Urban Future of the Recent Past*. New York: Harper and Row, 1976.

Barnir, Sigal. "On Forests as Commemorative Sites." In *Borderline Disorder*, edited by Zvi Efrat. Catalogue of the Israeli pavilion at the, 8th International Architecture Biennale in Venice. Israel: Israeli Council of Culture and Art, 2002.

Bar-On, Mordechai. "The Struggle over the Achievements of 1948: Israel's Defense Policy." In *The First Decade, 1948–1958* [in Hebrew], edited by Zvi Zameret and Hanna Yablonka. Jerusalem: Yad Izhak Ben-Zvi, 1997.

Bar Or, Galia. "The Initial Phases: A Test Case." In *Kibbutz: Architecture without Precedents*, edited by Galia Bar Or and Yuval Yasky. Catalogue of the Israeli pavilion at the 12th International Architecture Biennale in Venice. Israel: Israeli Council of Culture and Art, 2010.

Bar Or, Galia, and Yuval Yasky, eds. *Kibbutz: Architecture without Precedents*. Catalogue of the Israeli pavilion at the 12th International Architecture Biennale in Venice. Israel: Israeli Council of Culture and Art, 2010.

Barthes, Roland. *The Fashion System*. Berkeley and Los Angeles: University of California Press, 1990.

Be'eri, Shabtai. "The Planning of Construction in the Commune in Socialist Thought" (1952). In *Kibbutz: Architecture without Precedents*, edited by Galia Bar Or and Yuval Yasky. Catalogue of the Israeli pavilion at the 12th International Architecture Biennale in Venice. Israel: Israeli Council of Culture and Art, 2010.

Bein, Alex. *Immigration and Settlement in the State of Israel* [in Hebrew]. Tel Aviv: Am Oved, Hasifriya HaZiyonit, 1982.

Ben Arev, Yosef. *Gardens and Landscape in Israel* [in Hebrew]. Tel Aviv: Hakibbutz Hameuhad, 1980.

Ben-Gurion, David. "Daroma." In *Vision and Path* [in Hebrew]. Tel Aviv: Workers' Party of the Land of Israel, 1957.

Ben-Gurion, David. *Rebirth and Destiny of Israel*. London: Thomas Yoseloff, 1959.

Ben-Gurion, David. "The Imperatives of the Jewish Revolution" (1944). In *The Zionist Idea*, edited by Arthur Hertzberg. Philadelphia: Jewish Publication Society, 1997.

Ben-Gurion, David. *The War Diary: The War of Independence, 1948–1949*, vol. 3 [in Hebrew], edited by Gershon Rivlin and Elhanan Oren. Tel Aviv: Ministry of Defense, 1982.

Ben-Gurion, David. "Zionist Players and Their Role at This Time." In *On Settlement: Collected Writings, 1915–1965* [in Hebrew], edited by Menachem Dorman. Tel Aviv: Hakibbutz Hameuhad, 1986.

Ben-Meir, Dov. *The Histadrut Lexicon* [in Hebrew]. Tel Aviv: Am Oved – Culture and Education Series, 1980.

Ben-Sira, Yaakov. "Prof. C. H. Holuday: In Memoriam." *Engineering and Architecture: The Union of Engineers and Architects in Israel* 19, booklet 3 [in Hebrew] (1961), p. 94.

Ben-Sira, Yaakov. "Sir Patrick Abercrombie: An Appreciation." *Journal of the Union of Engineers and Architects in Israel* 15, booklet 3 [in Hebrew] (1957), pp. 12–13.

Benvenisti, Meron. "In the Light of the Morning After." In *A Civilian Occupation: The Politics of Israeli Architecture*, edited by Rafi Segal and Eyal Weizman. Tel Aviv and London: Babel and Verso, 2003.

Benvenisti, Meron. *Intimate Enemies: Jews and Arabs in a Shared Land*. Berkeley: University of California Press, 1995.

Benvenisti, Meron. *Sacred Landscape: The Buried History of the Holy Land since 1948*. Berkeley: University of California Press, 2000.

Benvenisti, Meron. *The Dream of the White Sabra* [in Hebrew]. Jerusalem: Keter, 2012.

Berger, Tamar. *Dionysus at the Center* [in Hebrew]. Tel Aviv: Hakibbutz Hameuhad, 1998.

Berger, Tamar. "I Want One Too: Towards a Definition of Neoliberal Visibility." In *The Urburb: Patterns of Contemporary*

*Living*, edited by Roy Brand and Ori Scialom. Catalogue of the Israeli pavilion at the 14th International Architecture Biennale in Venice. Montreal: Sternthal, 2014.

Berkowitz, Arie. "'A Complex Puzzle': Heinz Fenchel, Architect and Designer." In *Chaim Heinz Fenchel: A Complex Puzzle*. Exhibition catalogue. Tel Aviv: Rubin Museum, 2012.

Berler, Alexander, and Shmuel Shaked. *25 Development Towns in Israel*. Jerusalem: Ministry of Housing, 1966.

Bieltzki, Eliyahu. *Solel Boneh, 1924–1972* [in Hebrew]. Tel Aviv: Am Oved, 1974.

Biger, Gideon. *Crown Colony or National Homeland* [in Hebrew]. Jerusalem: Yad Izhak Ben-Zvi, 1983.

Biger, Gideon. *The Role of the British Administration in Changing the Geography of Palestine, 1918–1929*. London: Department of Geography, University College, London, 1979.

Biger, Gideon, and Nili Liphschitz. *Green Dress for a Country: Afforestation in Eretz Israel; The First Hundred Years, 1850–1950* [in Hebrew]. Jerusalem: Ariel, 2004.

Bishara, Azmi. "Entre lieu et espace." In *Preoccupations d'espace: Jerusalem au pluriel*, edited by Corinne Diserens. Marseille: Image en Manoeuvres and Carta Blanca Editions, 2001.

Bogner, Dieter. *Friedrich Kiesler: Architekt, Maler, Bildhauer, 1890–1965*. Vienna: Löcker, 1988.

Boness, Stefan. *Tel Aviv: The White City*. Berlin: Jovis, 2012.

Borochov, Ber. *Nationalism and Class Struggle: Selected Writings*. New York: Poale Zion-Zeire Zion of America, 1937.

Boyarin, Jonathan. *Storm from Paradise: The Politics of Jewish Memory*. Minneapolis: University of Minnesota Press, 1992.

Brutzkus, Eliezer. "Ashdod: An Idea and Its Materialization." *Bulletin of the Environmental Planners' Union* 10 [in Hebrew] (1969).

Brutzkus, Eliezer. *Problems of Geographical Distribution of Population*. Jerusalem: Government Printing Press, 1956.

Brutzkus, Eliezer. "The New Towns in the Framework of the National and Regional Plan." *Journal of the Union of Engineers and Architects in Israel* 14, no. 2 [in Hebrew] (1956), p. 7.

Brutzkus, Eliezer. "The Rural Settlement and the Urban Settlement in the State of Israel: Which is Preferable?" *Journal of Environmental Planning* 33 [in Hebrew] (September 1985).

Brutzkus, Eliezer. "Transformations in the Network of Urban Centers in Israel." *Engineering and Architecture: The Union of Engineers and Architects in Israel* 3 [in Hebrew] (1964).

Buber, Martin. *Paths in Utopia*. Translated by R. F. C. Hull. London: Routledge and Kegan Paul, 1949.

Burt, Michael. "An Experiment in Polyhyparic Structures." *Alef Alef* (August 1973), pp. 15–17.

# C

Chinski, Sara. *Kingdom of the Meek: The Social Grammar of the Israeli Art Field* [in Hebrew]. Bnei Brak: Hakibbutz Hameuhad, 2015.

Chyutin, Michael, and Bracha Chyutin. *Architecture and Utopia: Kibbutz and Moshav* [in Hebrew]. Jerusalem: Magnes, 2010.

Cohen, Erik. "The City in the Zionist Ideology." *Jerusalem Urban Studies 1*. Jerusalem: Institute of Urban and Regional Studies, Hebrew University, 1970.

Cohen, Jean-Louis. *Architecture in Uniform: Designing and Building for the Second World War*. New Haven and London: Yale University Press, 2011.

Cohen, Mitchell. *Zion and State: Nation, Class and the Shaping of Modern Israel*. New York: Columbia University Press, 1992.

Colomina, Beatriz. *Domesticity at War*. Cambridge, MA: MIT Press, 2007.

# D

Dan, Hillel. *On an Unpaved Road: The Legend of Solel Boneh* [in Hebrew]. Jerusalem and Tel Aviv: Schocken, 1963.

Danforth, Loring M. *The Macedonian Conflict: Ethnic Nationalism in a Transnational World*. Princeton, NJ: Princeton University Press, 1995.

Davidi, Sigal. *The Feminine Presence in Israeli Architecture* [in Hebrew]. Tel Aviv: United Architects' Association, 2009.

Deleuze, Gilles, and Félix Guattari. *Anti-Oedipus: Capitalism and Schizophrenia*. New York: Viking Press, 1977.

Darin-Drabkin, Haim. *Housing and Absorption in Israel* [in Hebrew]. Tel Aviv: Gadish, 1955.

Drexler, Yehuda. "Architects Are Not Active in the Shaping of the State." *Alef Alef* 3 (1974), pp. 4–5.

# E

Efrat, Elisha. *Settlement Geography in Israel* [in Hebrew]. Tel Aviv: Ahiasaf, 1981.

Efrat, Zvi. "Model State." In *Territories: Islands, Camps and Other States of Utopia*, edited by Anselm Franke, Eyal Weizman, and Rafi Segal. Cologne: Walther König, 2003.

Efrat, Zvi. "The Haunt of the Rural: Zionist Colonization and Space Planning." In *Collectivize!* Vol. 1 of *Essays on the Political Economy of Urban Form*. Berlin: Ruby Press, 2013.

Efrat, Zvi. "The Israeli Project: Pictogram." In *Space, Land, Home* [in Hebrew], edited by Yehouda Shenhav. Jerusalem: Van Leer Jerusalem Institute, 2003.

Efrat, Zvi. "The Plan." In *Space, Land, Home* [in Hebrew], edited by Yehouda Shenhav. Jerusalem: Van Leer Jerusalem Institute, 2003.

Efrat, Zvi. "The Politics of New Towns in Israel." In *The Urburb: Patterns of Contemporary Living*, edited by Roy Brand and Ori Scialom. Catalogue of the Israeli pavilion at the 14th International Architecture Biennale in Venice. Montreal: Sternthal, 2014.

Ehrlich, Avraham. "Leopold Krakauer." *Tvai* 13–14 [in Hebrew] (1974), pp. 92–98.

Ehrlich, Avraham. "On Landscape and Architecture." *Tvai* 1 [in Hebrew] (1961), pp. 35–38.

Elhanani, Aba. "Our Israeli Architects' Contribution to Modern Architecture." *Engineering and Architecture: The Union of Engineers and Architects in Israel* 5–6 [in Hebrew] (1961), pp. 133–136.

Elhanani, Aba. "Richard Kauffmann." *Tvai* 11 [in Hebrew] (1972), pp. 3–11.

Elhanani, Aba. "The Shaping of a Style." *Tvai* 9 [in Hebrew] (1965), pp. 3–7.

Elhanani, Aba. *The Struggle for Independence: Israeli Architecture in the Twentieth Century* [in Hebrew]. Tel Aviv: Ministry of Defense, 1998.

Elhyani, Zvi. "Horizontal Ideology, Vertical Vision: Oscar Niemeyer and Israel's Height Dilemma." In *Constructing a Sense of Place: Architecture and the Zionist Discourse*, edited by Haim Yacobi. Burlington: Ashgate, 2004.

Elhyani, Zvi, and Michael Jacobson. *The Architecture of Nadler-Nadler-Bixon-Gil, 1946–2010*. Tel Aviv: A. R. Printing, 2016.

Eliav, Y. "Proposal for Houses in the Arava." *Journal of the Union of Engineers and Architects in Israel* 12, booklet 3 [in Hebrew] (1954), p. 26.

Engel, David. *Zionism*. Harlow: Pearson Education Limited, 2009.

Epstein-Pliouchtch, Marina, and Michael Levin. *Richard Kauffmann and the Zionist Project* [in Hebrew]. Tel Aviv: Hakibbutz Hameuhad, 2016.

Even-Zohar, Itamar. "The Emergence of a Native Hebrew Culture in Palestine: 1882–1948." In *Studies in Zionism*, no. 4 (1981).

# F

Fausch, Deborah, Paulette Singley, Rodolphe El-Khoury, and Zvi Efrat, eds. *Architecture: In Fashion*. New York: Princeton Architectural Press, 1994.

Fehl, Gerhard. "The Nazi Garden City." In *The Garden City: Past, Present and Future*. London: E & FN Spon, 1992.

Fiedler, Jeannine. *Social Utopias of the Twenties: Bauhaus, Kibbutz, and the Dream of the New Man*. Wuppertal: Müller und Busmann, 1995.

Finkelstein, Israel, and Neil Asher Silberman. *The Bible Unearthed: Archaeology's New Vision of Ancient Israel and the Origin of Its Sacred Texts*. New York: Free Press, 2000.

Flapan, Simha. *Zionism and the Palestinians*. New York: Barnes and Noble, 1979.

Franke, Anselm, Eyal Weizman, and Rafi Segal, eds. *Territories: Islands, Camps and Other States of Utopia*. Cologne: Walther König, 2003.

Friedman, Yona. *L'Architecture mobile: Vers une cité conçue par ses habitants*. Paris: Casterman, 1970.

Friedman, Yona. *Structures Serving the Unpredictable*. Rotterdam: NAi Publishers, 1999.

Foucault, Michel. *The Order of Things*. New York: Vintage Books, 1971.

# G

Gad, Dora. "The Ceiling in Modern Architecture." *Tvai* 1 [in Hebrew] (1966), pp. 19–49.

Gelvin, James L. *The Israel-Palestine Conflict: One Hundred Years of War*. New York: Cambridge University Press, 2005.

Gitzin-Adiram, Milana, Erez Ella, and Dan Handel, eds. *Aircraft Carrier: American Ideas and Israeli Architectures after 1973*. Ostfildern: Hatje Cantz, 2012.

Glikson, Artur. "Architecture as the Humanization of Environment." *Adrikhalut* 4 [in Hebrew] (1966), pp. 2–3.

Glikson, Artur. "Geddes as Planner." *Journal of the Union of Engineers and Architects in Israel* 12, booklet 5 [in Hebrew] (1954), pp. 17–18 and 37.

Goodovitch, I. M. *Architecturology: An Interim Report*. Tel Aviv: AD Publishing Co., 1967.

Gordon, Aharon David. "Our Tasks Ahead." In *The Zionist Idea*, edited by Arthur Hertzberg. Philadelphia: Jewish Publication Society, 1997.

Gordon, Aharon David. "People and Labor." In *The Zionist Idea*, edited by Arthur Hertzberg. Philadelphia: Jewish Publication Society, 1997.

Greenberg, Itzhak. "The Reforms on the Member's Company Following the Great Immigration." In *Between Immigrants and Veterans* [in Hebrew], edited by Dalia Ofer. Jerusalem: Yad Izhak Ben-Zvi, 1996.

Grossman, David. *Sleeping on a Wire: Conversations with Palestinians in Israel*. New York: Farrar, Straus, and Giroux, 1993.

Grossman, David. *The Yellow Wind*. New York: Farrar, Straus, and Giroux, 1988.

# H

Hacohen, Dvora. *Immigrants in a Storm* [in Hebrew]. Jerusalem: Yad Izhak Ben-Zvi, 1994.

Hailey, Charlie. *Camps: A Guide to 21st-Century Space*. Cambridge, MA: MIT Press, 2009.

Hanin-Rabinowitz, Ruth. *Cooperative Settlements as Models for the Zionist Garden Colony and a School Farm* [in Hebrew]. Haifa: Pardes Publishers, 2006.

Harlap, Amiram. *New Israeli Architecture*. Rutherford, NJ: Fairleigh Dickinson University Press, 1982.

Harpaz, Nathan. *Zionist Architecture and Town Planning: The Building of Tel Aviv (1919–1929)*. West Lafayette, IN: Purdue University Press, 2013.

Hashimshoni, Aviya. "Architecture." In *Israeli Art* [in Hebrew], edited by Binyamin Tamuz. Tel Aviv: Massada, 1963.

Hatuka, Tali. *Revisionist Moments: Political Violence, Architecture and Urban Space in Tel Aviv* [in Hebrew]. Tel Aviv: Resling, 2008.

Hatuka, Tali. *State-Neighborhood* [in Hebrew]. Tel Aviv: Resling, 2012.

Hays, Michael K. *Modernism and the Posthuman Subject: The Architecture of Hannes Meyer and Ludwig Hilberseimer*. Cambridge, MA: MIT Press, 1992.

Hecker, Zvi. "Polyhedra." *Mosag* 12 (1976), pp. 46–50.

Hecker, Zvi. "Polyhydric Architecture." *Tziyur VePisul* 8 (1974), pp. 38–44.

Heilbronner, Oded, and Michael Levin. *Israeli Modernism or Modernism in Israel* [in Hebrew]. Tel Aviv: Resling, 2010.

Heinze-Mühleib, Ita. *Erich Mendelsohn: Bauten und Projekte in Palästina (1934–1941)*. Munich: Scaneg, 1986.

Helphand, Kenneth. *Dreaming Gardens: Landscape Architecture and the Making of Modern Israel*. Santa Fe, NM: Center for American Places, 2002.

Herbert, Gilbert, and Ita Heinze-Greenberg. *The Beginnings of Modern Architecture in Israel: The First Power Stations, 1921–1932* [in Hebrew]. Haifa: Israel Electric Co., Division of Communication and Public Affairs, 1997.

Herbert, Gilbert, and Silvina Sosnovsky. *Bauhaus on the Carmel and the Crossroads of Empire*. Jerusalem: Yad Izhak Ben-Zvi, 1993.

Hermann, Tamar S. *The Israeli Peace Movement: A Shattered Dream*. Cambridge, MA: Cambridge University Press, 2009.

Herzl, Theodor. *Old-New Land*. Translated by Lotta Levensohn. New York: Bloch Publishing, 1960.

Herzl, Theodor. *The Jewish State*. Translated by Harry Zohn. New York: Herzl Press, 1970.

Hess, Moses. *Rome and Jerusalem: A Study in Jewish Nationalism*. New York: Bloch Publishing, 1918.

Hoffman, Milo. "Why Shade the Windows?" *The Israeli Centre for Building Quarterly* 23 (1976), pp. 161–166.

## I

Ingersoll, Richard. *Munio Gitai Weinraub: Bauhaus Architect in Eretz Israel*. Milan: Electa, 1994.

*Israel Builds: New Trends in Planning of Housing*. Jerusalem: Ministry of Housing, 1968.

*Israel Builds, 1970: Interdisciplinary Planning*. Jerusalem: Ministry of Housing, 1970.

## J

Jacob, Abel. "Israel's Military Aid to Africa: 1960–1966." *The Journal of Modern African Studies* 9:2 (1971).

Jacobson, Michael. *The Architect Who Designed the City Hall: Menachem Cohen; Projects* [in Hebrew]. Israel, 2014.

Jones, Clive, and Emma Murphy. *Israel: Challenges to Identity, Democracy and the State*. London and New York: Routledge, 2002.

## K

Kahana, Freddy. *Neither Town nor Village: The Architecture of the Kibbutz, 1910–1990* [in Hebrew]. Ramat Efa'al: Yad Tabenkin, 2011.

Kahn, Louis. *Trenton Jewish Community Centre*. New York: Princeton Architectural Press, 2000.

Kallus, Rachel. "The Political Construct of the 'Everyday': The Role of Housing in Making Place and Identity." In *Constructing a Sense of Place: Architecture and the Zionist Discourse*, edited by Haim Yacobi. Burlington: Ashgate, 2004.

Kallus, Rachel, and Hubert Lu-Yon. "The National House and the Personal House: The Place of Governmental Housing in Designing the Space." In *Space, Land, Home* [in Hebrew], edited by Yehouda Shenhav. Jerusalem: Van Leer Jerusalem Institute, 2003.

Kallus, Rachel, and Tali Hatuka. *Architectural Culture: Place, Representation, Body* [in Hebrew]. Tel Aviv: Resling, 2005.

Karmi, Ram. "Louis Kahn: In Memoriam." *Alef Alef* 4 (1974), pp. 3–4.

Karmi, Ram. *Lyric Architecture* [in Hebrew]. Tel Aviv: Ministry of Defense, 2001.

Karmi, Ram. "The Architecture of Shadow (The Town Centre of Beer Sheva)." *Adrikhalut* 3 [in Hebrew] (1966), pp. 28–29.

Karmi-Melamede, Ada, and Dan Price. *Architecture in Palestine during the British Mandate, 1917–1948* [in Hebrew]. Jerusalem: Israel Museum, 2014.

Kaufman, Y. "The Eilath House." *Journal of the Union of Engineers and Architects in Israel* 6, booklet 3 [in Hebrew] (1953), pp. 11–14.

Kemp, Adriana. "The Border as the Face of Janus: Space and National Consciousness in Israel." In *Space, Land, Home* [in Hebrew], edited by Yehouda Shenhav. Jerusalem: Van Leer Jerusalem Institute, 2003.

Kerstein, Itzhak. "The Conflict between National and International Ideas in the Kibbutz Movement." PhD diss., University of Ottawa, 1967.

Khalidi, Walid. *All That Remains: The Palestinian Villages Occupied and Depopulated by Israel in 1948*. Washington, DC: Institute for Palestine Studies, 1992.

Kimmerling, Baruch, ed. *The Israeli State and Society: Boundaries and Frontiers*. Albany: State University of New York Press, 1989.

Kimmerling, Baruch. *Immigrants, Settlers, Natives: The Israeli State and Society between Cultural Pluralism and Cultural War* [in Hebrew]. Tel Aviv: Am Oved, 2004.

Klein, Alexander. "Climate Influences on the Organic Design of Floor Plan and Façade." *Journal of the Union of Engineers and Architects in Israel* 5 [in Hebrew] (1942), pp. 2–4.

Klein, Yossi. *The Beginning of Tel Aviv's Americanization: The Demolition of the Tel Aviv Hebrew Gymnasium Building and Its Replacement by the First Israeli Skyscraper "Shalom Mayer Tower" (1959–1966)* [in Hebrew]. Jerusalem: Carmel, 2011.

Kohn, Wendy, ed. *Moshe Safdie*. London: Academy Editions, 1996.

Kozlovsky, Roy. "Temporal States of Architecture: Mass Immigration and Provisional Housing in Israel." In *Modernism and the Middle East: Architecture and Politics in the Twentieth Century*, edited by Kishwar Rizvi and Sandy Isenstadt, pp. 140–161. Seattle: University of Washington Press, 2008.

Kreinin, Mordechai. *Israel and Africa: A Study in Technical Cooperation*. New York: Praeger, 1964.

Kroyanker, David. *Architecture in Jerusalem – Periods and Styles: Modern Buildings 1948–1990* [in Hebrew]. Jerusalem: Keter, 1991.

Kroyanker, David. *The Architecture of Hecker-Yellin, 1920–1945* [in Hebrew]. Jerusalem: Keter, 2006.

Kroyanker, David, and Yael Guiladi. *Jerusalem, 1978: Between Two Decades; Planning and Development* [in Hebrew]. Jerusalem, 1978.

Kutcher, Arthur. *The New Jerusalem: Planning and Politics*. London: Thames and Hudson, 1973.

## L

Lavon, Selig. "Scope and Limitations on High Buildings." *Tvai* 2 (1966), pp. 78–79.

Le Corbusier. *Modulor 2, 1955 (let the user speak next)*. London: Faber, 1958.

Le Corbusier. *The Decorative Art of Today*. Cambridge, MA: MIT Press, 1987.

Le Corbusier. *Vers une architecture*. London: Architectural Press, 1970.

Levin, Michael. *Modern Architecture in Israel*. Milan: Skira, 2005.

Levin, Michael. *The Transformation of Villa Savoye into the National Library: Le Corbusier's Influence on Two Generations of Architects in Israel*. Chicago: Spertus College of Judaica Press, 1977.

LeVine, Mark. *Overthrowing Geography: Jaffa, Tel Aviv, and the Struggle for Palestine, 1880–1948*. Berkeley: University of California Press, 2005.

LeVine, Mark. "Planning to Conquer: Modernity and Its Antinomies in the New-Old Jaffa." In *Constructing a Sense of Place: Architecture and the Zionist Discourse*, edited by Haim Yacobi. Burlington: Ashgate, 2004.

Lichfield, Nathaniel. *Israel's New Towns: A Development Strategy*. Jerusalem: Ministry of Housing, 1972.

Lin, Nimrod. *Deconstructing Jaffa*. Tel Aviv, 2011.

Lisak, Moshe. *The Extensive Immigration of the 1950s: The Failure of the Melting

*Pot* [in Hebrew]. Jerusalem: Bialik Institute, 1999.

Lissovsky, Nurit, and Diana Dolev. *The Gardens of Lipa Yahalom and Dan Zur* [in Hebrew]. Tel Aviv: Babel, 2012.

Livnae, Ami. "The Architect as Resident and the Government." *Tvai* 12 (1972), pp. 70–71.

Lockman, Zachary. *Comrades and Enemies: Arab and Jewish Workers in Palestine, 1906–1948*. Berkeley: University of California Press, 1996.

## M

Mansfeld, Al. "A Structuralist Approach to the Design of Town and Building: Designing for Growth, Change, Uncertainty." *Adrikhalut* [in Hebrew] (1978), pp. 14–17.

Mansfeld, Al. *Designing for Growth and Change with Open-Ended Cumulative Systems: Buildings and Projects in Israel*. Haifa: Faculty of Architecture and Town Planning, Technion, 1976.

Mansfeld, Al. "On Building without Plaster." *Journal of the Union of Engineers and Architects in Israel* 10, booklet 2 [in Hebrew] (1952), pp. 14–17.

Marcuse, Herbert. *Eros and Civilization: A Philosophical Inquiry into Freud*. London: Routledge and Kegan Paul, 1956.

Medoff, Rafael, and Chaim I. Waxman. *The A to Z of Zionism*. Lanham: Scarecrow Press, 2008.

Meir, Golda. *My Life*. London: Futura, 1978.

Meiri-Dann, Naomi, and Shmuel Meiri. "Between Victory and Destruction: The Changing Narrative of the Division of Steel Memorial." *The Journal of Israeli History* 28, no. 2 (September 2009), pp. 213–230.

Meishar, Naama. "Fragile Guardians: Nature Reserves and Forests Facing Arab Villages." In *Constructing a Sense of Place: Architecture and the Zionist Discourse*, edited by Haim Yacobi. Burlington: Ashgate, 2004.

Metzger-Szmuk, Nitza. *Dwelling on the Dunes, Tel Aviv: Modern Movement and Bauhaus Ideals*. Paris: Editions de l'éclat, 2004.

Metzger-Szmuk, Nitza. *Houses in the Sand: International Style Architecture in Tel Aviv, 1931–1948* [in Hebrew]. Tel Aviv: Tel Aviv Fund for Development and Ministry of Defense, 1994.

Minta, Anna. *Israel bauen: Architektur, Städtebau und Denkmalpolitik nach der Staatsgründung 1948*. Berlin: Reimer, 2004.

Misselwitz, Philipp, and Eyal Weizman. "Military Operations as Urban Planning." In *Territories: Islands, Camps and Other States of Utopia*, edited by Anselm Franke, Eyal Weizman, and Rafi Segal. Cologne: Walther König, 2003.

Misselwitz, Philipp, and Tim Rieniets. *City of Collision: Jerusalem and the Principles of Conflict Urbanism*. Basel: Birkhäuser, 2006.

Model House Research Group, ed. *Transcultural Modernisms*. Vienna: Sternberg, 2013.

Moholy-Nagy, Sibyl. *Matrix of Man: An Illustrated History of Urban Environment*. New York: Praeger, 1968.

Monk, Daniel Bertrand. *An Aesthetic Occupation: The Immediacy of Architecture and the Palestine Conflict*. Durham, NC: Duke University Press, 2002.

Morris, Benny. *Israel's Border Wars, 1949–1956: Arab Infiltration, Israeli Retaliation, and the Countdown to the Suez War*. Oxford: Clarendon Press, 1993.

Morris, Benny. *The Birth of the Palestinian Refugee Problem, 1947–1949* [in Hebrew]. Tel Aviv: Am Oved, Sifriyat Ofakim, 1991.

Mort, Jo-Ann, and Gary Brenner. *Our Hearts Invented a Place: Can Kibbutzim Survive in Today's Israel?* Ithaca: Cornell University Press, 2003.

Mozingo, Louise. *Pastoral Capitalism: A History of Suburban Corporate Landscapes*. Cambridge, MA: MIT Press, 2011.

## N

Naor, Mordechai, ed. *Immigrants and Transit Camps, 1948–1952* [in Hebrew]. Jerusalem: Yad Izhak Ben-Zvi, 1986.

Near, Henry. *Origins and Growth, 1909–1939*. Vol. 1 of *The Kibbutz Movement: A History*. Oxford: Oxford University Press, 1991.

Neufeld, Yosef. "On Organic Building." *Habinyan Bamisrah Hakarov* 1 [in Hebrew] (1934), p. 43.

Neufeld, Yosef. "Richard Kaufmann: Fifty Years Old." *Habinyan* [in Hebrew] (1937).

Neuman, Eran. *David Yannay: Architecture and Genetics* [in Hebrew]. Tel Aviv: Tel Aviv Museum of Art, 2014.

Neumann, Alfred. *L'Humanisation de l'espace: Le système mφ*. Collection Espace. Boulogne-sur-Seine: Editions Architecture d'Aujourd'hui, 1956.

Neumann, Alfred. "Morphologic Architecture." *RAIC Journal* 40 (May 1963). Later republished in *Zodiac* 16 (1966).

Neumann, Alfred. "On Planning." *Journal of the Union of Engineers and Architects in Israel* 10, booklet 3 [in Hebrew] (1953), pp. 17–18.

Niemeyer, Oscar. *Quase Memórias: Viagens – Tempos de Entusiasmo e Revolta, 1961–1966*. Rio de Janeiro: Civilização Brasileira, 1968.

Nitzan-Shiftan, Alona. "Bleached Houses." In *Space, Land, Home* [in Hebrew], edited by Yehouda Shenhav. Jerusalem: Van Leer Jerusalem Institute, 2003.

Nitzan-Shiftan, Alona. *Seizing Jerusalem: The Architectures of Unilateral Unification*. Minneapolis: University of Minnesota Press, 2017.

## O

Ophir, Adi, ed. *50 to 48: Critical Moments in the History of the State of Israel—Essays and Chronicle* [in Hebrew]. Jerusalem and Tel Aviv: Van Leer Jerusalem Institute and Hakibbutz Hameuhad, 1999.

Oppenheimer, Franz. *Merchavia: A Jewish Co-operative Settlement in Palestine*. Cologne and New York: Co-operative Society for Erez-Israel and Jewish National Fund, 1914.

Oren, Amiram. *Drafted Territories: The Creation of Israeli Army Hegemony over the State's Land and Its Expanses during Its Early Years (1948–1956)* [in Hebrew]. Tel Aviv: Madaf, 2009.

## P

Peled, Yoav. *Class and Ethnicity in the Pale: The Political Economy of Jewish Workers' Nationalism in Late Imperial Russia*. London: St. Martin's Press, 1989.

Penslar, Derek J. *Zionism and Technocracy: The Engineering of Jewish Settlement in Palestine, 1870–1918*. Bloomington: Indiana University Press, 1991.

Peters, Joel. *Israel and Africa: The Problematic Friendship*. London: British Academic Press, 1992.
Potash, Ilan. "Settlements and Borders." In *A Civilian Occupation: The Politics of Israeli Architecture*, edited by Rafi Segal and Eyal Weizman. Tel Aviv and London: Babel and Verso, 2003.

## R

Rabinovich, Dani. "The Forgotten Option: The Communal Urban Housing." In *Space, Land, Home* [in Hebrew], edited by Yehouda Shenhav. Jerusalem: Van Leer Jerusalem Institute, 2003.
Ratner, Yohanan. "The Influence of the Bill of Ordinance on Architecture in Israel." *Habinyan Bamisrah Hakarov* 8 [in Hebrew] (1936), pp. 3–4.
Ratner, Yohanan. "Will Israel Have a National Style of Architecture?" *The Technion Yearbook*. Haifa: Technion, 1950.
Rechter, Osnat. *Yaacov Rechter, Architect* [in Hebrew]. Bnei Brak: Hakibbutz Hameuhad, 2003.
Reiffer, Rephael. "Is Indigenous Jewish Style Possible in Architecture?" *Tziyur VePisul* 11 [in Hebrew] (1976), pp. 40–41.
Rolef, Susan Hattis. "The Knesset Building at Givat Ram—Planning and Construction." *Cathedra for the History of Eretz Yisrael and Its Yishuv* 96 [in Hebrew] (July 2000).
Rosenhek, Zeev. *Housing Policy toward the Arabs in Israel in the 1950s–1970s* [in Hebrew]. Jerusalem: Floersheimer Institute for Policy Studies, 1996.
Rotbard, Sharon. *Avraham Yasky: Concrete Architecture* [in Hebrew]. Tel Aviv: Babel, 2007.
Rotbard, Sharon. "Wall and Tower." In *A Civilian Occupation: The Politics of Israeli Architecture*, edited by Rafi Segal and Eyal Weizman. Tel Aviv and London: Babel and Verso, 2003.
Rotbard, Sharon. *White City, Black City: Architecture and War in Tel Aviv and Jaffa*. Cambridge, MA: MIT Press, 2015.
Rubin, Carmela. *Chaim Heinz Fenchel: A Complex Puzzle* [in Hebrew]. Tel Aviv, 2010.

## S

Safdie, Moshe. *Beyond Habitat*. Cambridge, MA: MIT Press, 1970.
Safdie, Moshe. *For Everyone a Garden*. Cambridge, MA: MIT Press, 1974.
Salama-Ortar, Ilana. "Elementerre – Elementaire." In *Preoccupations d'espace: Jerusalem au pluriel*, edited by Corinne Diserens. Marseille: Image en Manoeuvres and Carta Blanca Editions, 2001.
Saleh, Abdul Jawad, and Mustafa Walid. *Palestine: The Collective Destruction of Palestinian Villages*. Amman and London: Jerusalem Center for Development, 1967.
Salim, Tamari. *Jerusalem 1948: The Arab Neighbourhoods and Their Fate in the War*. Jerusalem: Institute of Jerusalem Studies and Badil Resource Center, 1999.
Schlon, Rachel. "Concrete." In *The Hebrew Encyclopedia* [in Hebrew]. Jerusalem: Massada, 1958.
Schlon, Rachel. "Progress of Building Research in Israel – Bibliography." *Engineering and Architecture: The Union of Engineers and Architects in Israel* 16, booklets 5 and 6 [in Hebrew] (1958), pp. 166–170.
Scialom, Ori. "Urburb, Neither City nor Suburb: A Look at the Israeli Constructed Environment." In *The Urburb: Patterns of Contemporary Living*, edited by Roy Brand and Scialom. Catalogue of the Israeli pavilion at the 14th International Architecture Biennale in Venice. Montreal: Sternthal, 2014.
Segal, Rafi. "Conflicts and Negotiations as Spatial Practices: A Conversation with Ron Pundak." In *Territories: Islands, Camps and Other States of Utopia*, edited by Anselm Franke, Eyal Weizman, and Rafi Segal. Cologne: Walther König, 2003.
Segal, Rafi, and Eyal Weizman, eds. *A Civilian Occupation: The Politics of Israeli Architecture*. Tel Aviv and London: Babel and Verso, 2003.
Segal, Rafi, and Eyal Weizman. "The Battle for the Hilltops." In *A Civilian Occupation: The Politics of Israeli Architecture*, edited by Segal and Weizman. Tel Aviv and London: Babel and Verso, 2003.
Segal, Rafi, and Eyal Weizman. "The Mountain." In *A Civilian Occupation: The Politics of Israeli Architecture*, edited by Segal and Weizman. Tel Aviv and London: Babel and Verso, 2003.
Sfard, Michael. *The Wall and the Gate: Israel, Palestine, and the Legal Battle for Human Rights*. New York, St. Martin's Press, 2018.
Shadar, Hadas. *Beer Sheva: Brutalist and Neo-Brutalist Architecture* [in Hebrew]. Tel Aviv: Bauhaus Center, 2014.
Shadar, Hadas. *Sunstroke: Brutalist Construction in Be'er Sheva: Re-examination of National Architecture* [in Hebrew]. Jerusalem: Yad Izhak Ben-Zvi, 2016.
Shafir, Gershon. *Land, Labor and the Origins of the Israeli-Palestinian Conflict, 1882–1914*. Berkeley: University of California Press, 1996.
Sharon, Arieh. *Hospitals in Israel and the Developing Countries*. Tel Aviv: Emanograph, early 1970s.
Sharon, Arieh. *Kibbutz + Bauhaus: An Architect's Way in a New Land*. Stuttgart and Tel Aviv: Karl Kramer Verlag and Massada, 1976.
Sharon, Arieh. *Physical Planning in Israel* [in Hebrew]. Jerusalem: Government Printing Press and Survey of Israel Press, 1951.
Sharon, Arieh. *Planning Jerusalem*. Jerusalem: Wiedenfeld and Nicolson, 1973.
Shechori, Ran, ed. *Dora Gad: The Israeli Presence in Interior Design*. Tel Aviv: Architecture of Israel, 1997.
Sheikh, Fazal and Weizman, Eyal. *The Conflict Shoreline: Colonization As Climate Change in the Negev Desert*. Steidl Books, 2015.
Shenhav, Yehouda. "The Politics of Space in Israel." In *Space, Land, Home* [in Hebrew], edited by Shenhav. Jerusalem: Van Leer Jerusalem Institute, 2003.
Shiloni, Zvi. *Jewish National Fund and Settlement in Eretz-Israel: 1903–1914* [in Hebrew]. Jerusalem: Yad Izhak Ben-Zvi, 1990.
Shlaim, Avi. *The Iron Wall: Israel and the Arab World*. New York: W. W. Norton and Company, 2001.
Shoshani, Mordechai. "On Function and Image." *Adrikhalut* [in Hebrew] (1978), p. 48.
Slymovics, Susan. "Discourses on the Pre-1948 Palestinian Village: The Case of Ein-Hod / Ein-Houd." *Traditional*

*Dwellings and Settlements Review* 4, no. 2 (1993), pp. 27–37.

Slyomovics, Susan. *The Object of Memory: Arab and Jew Narrate the Palestinian Village*. Philadelphia: University of Pennsylvania Press, 1998.

Smithson, Alison, ed. *Team 10 Primer*. Cambridge, MA: MIT Press, 1968.

Solomon, Susan G. *Secular and Spiritual Humanism: Louis I. Kahn's Work for the Jewish Community in the 1950s and 1960s*. Ann Arbor, MI: UMI, 2001.

Sonder, Ines. *Lotte Cohn: Baumeisterin des Landes Israel; Eine Biographie*. Frankfurt: Jüdischer Verlag im Suhrkamp, 2010.

Sonder, Ines. *Lotte Cohn, Pioneer Woman Architect in Israel: Catalogue of Buildings and Projects*. Tel Aviv: Bauhaus Center, 2009.

Spiegel, Erika. *New Towns in Israel: Urban and Regional Planning and Development*. New York: Praeger, 1967.

Sternhell, Zeev. *The Founding Myths of Israel: Nationalism, Socialism and the Making of the Jewish State*. Translated by David Maisel. Princeton: Princeton University Press, 1998.

## T

Tabenkin, Yitzhak. "On the Problems of Kibbutz Building" (1921). In *Kibbutz: Architecture without Precedents*, edited by Galia Bar Or and Yuval Yasky. Catalogue of the Israeli pavilion at the 12th International Architecture Biennale in Venice. Israel: Israeli Council of Culture and Art, 2010.

Tal, Emanuel. *The Structure Image of the Early Kibbutz* [in Hebrew]. Tel Aviv, 1991.

Talmor, Daniella, and Michael Burt. *Conceptual Architecture* [in Hebrew]. Haifa: Haifa Museum, Museum of Art, 1998.

Talmor, N. "Government Building Construction." *Engineering and Architecture: The Union of Engineers and Architects in Israel* 25, booklet 2 [in Hebrew] (1967), pp. 23–24.

Teut, Anna. *Al Mansfeld: Architekt in Israel / Al Mansfeld: An Architect in Israel*. Berlin: Ernst und Sohn, 1999.

Trezib, Joachim Nicolas. *Die Theorie der zentralen Orte in Israel und Deutschland: Zur Rezeption Walter Christallers im Kontext von Sharonplan und "Generalplan Ost."* Berlin: De Gruyter Oldenburg, 2014.

Troen, S. Ilan. *Imagining Zion: Dreams, Designs, and Realities in a Century of Jewish Settlement*. New Haven: Yale University Press, 2003.

Tumarkin, Igael. "Integration between Art and Architecture." *Adrikhalut* [in Hebrew] (1966), pp. 62–65.

Tuvia, Miriam, and Michael Boneh. *Binyan Ha'aretz: Public Housing in the 1950s* [in Hebrew]. Tel Aviv: Hakibbutz Hameuhad, 1999.

*Twenty Years of Building* [in Hebrew]. Tel Aviv: General Federation of Jewish Labor in Palestine, Engineers Architects and Surveyors Union, 1940.

Tzur, Moki, and Yuval Daniaeli. *A Home, a Place: From the Files of Architect Chilik Arad* [in Hebrew]. Giva'at Haviva: Yad Ya'ari, 2013.

Tzur, Moki, and Yuval Daniaeli. *Mestechkin Builds Israel: Architecture in the Kibbutz* [in Hebrew]. Bnei Brak: Hakibbutz Hameuhad, 2008.

## V

Vanstiphout, Wouter. "The Source Code: Modes for a Perfect Society." In *Common Ground: A Critical Reader*, edited by David Chipperfield, Kieran Long, and Shumi Bose. Catalogue of the 13th International Architecture Biennale in Venice. Venice: Marsilio, 2012.

Virilio, Paul. *Bunker Archaeology*. New York: Princeton University Press, 1994.

## W

Ward, Alex. *Shimon Shapiro: Making Architecture*. Jerusalem: Israel Museum, 2006.

Weizman, Eyal. *Forensic Architecture: Violence at the Threshold of Detectability*. Zone Books, MIT Press, 2017.

Weizman, Eyal. *Hollow Land: Israel's Architecture of Occupation*. London: Verso, 2007.

Weizman, Eyal and Sheikh, Fazal. *The Conflict Shoreline: Colonization As Climate Change in the Negev Desert*. Steidl Books, 2015.

Weizman, Eyal. "The Politics of Verticality: The West Bank as an Architectural Construction." In *Territories: Islands, Camps and Other States of Utopia*, edited by Anselm Franke, Eyal Weizman, and Rafi Segal. Cologne: Walther König, 2003.

Weyl, Martin. "The Creation of The Israel Museum." In *The Israel Museum*. New York: Vendome Press, 1995.

Wigley, Mark. *White Walls, Designer Dresses: The Fashioning of Modern Architecture*. Cambridge, MA: MIT Press, 1995.

Williams Goldhagen, Sarah, and Rejean Legault. *Anxious Modernisms: Experimentation in Postwar Architectural Culture*. Montreal and Cambridge, MA: CCA and MIT Press, 2000.

## Y

Yacobi, Haim, ed. *Constructing a Sense of Place: Architecture and the Zionist Discourse*. Burlington: Ashgate, 2004.

Yacobi, Haim. *Israel and Africa: A Genealogy of Moral Geography*. New York: Routledge, 2016.

Yacobi, Haim. *This Is No Africa: Boundaries, Territory, Identity* [in Hebrew]. Jerusalem and Bnei Brak: Van Leer Jerusalem Institute and Hakibbutz Hameuhad, 2015.

Yacobi, Haim, and Shelly Cohen. *The Politics of Space in Israel* [in Hebrew]. Tel Aviv: Hargol, 2007.

Yacobi, Haim, and Tovi Fenster. *Remembering, Forgetting and the Construction of Space* [in Hebrew]. Jerusalem: Van Leer Jerusalem Institute, 2011.

Yadin, Yigael. *Masada* [in Hebrew]. Tel Aviv: Maariv Library and Shikmona, 1962.

Yagid-Haimovici, Meira. *Dov Karmi: Architect-Engineer Public Domestica* [in Hebrew]. Tel Aviv: Tel Aviv Museum of Art, Helena Rubinstein Pavilion for Contemporary Art, 2011.

Yasky, Yuval. "Neither City, Nor Village – A Kibbutz." In *Kibbutz: Architecture without Precedents*, edited by Galia Bar Or and Yuval Yasky. Catalogue of the Israeli pavilion at the 12th International Architecture Biennale in Venice. Israel: Israeli Council of Culture and Art, 2010.

Yatziv, Gadi. *The Sectorial Society* [in Hebrew]. Jerusalem: Bialik Institute, 1999.

Yavin, Shmuel. *Absorption Centers and Hostels* [in Hebrew]. Tel Aviv: Institute for Building and Technical Research, 1969.

Yavin, Shmuel. *Bauhaus in Jaffa: Modern Architecture in an Ancient City* [in

Hebrew]. Tel Aviv: Bauhaus Center, 2006.

Yiftachel, Oren. *"Ethnocracy" and "Glocality": New Perspectives on Society and Space in Israel* [in Hebrew]. Beersheba: Ben-Gurion University of the Negev, Negev Center for Regional Development, 1999.

Yiftachel, Oren. "Settlements as Reflex Action." In *A Civilian Occupation: The Politics of Israeli Architecture*, edited by Rafi Segal and Eyal Weizman. Tel Aviv and London: Babel and Verso, 2003.

Yiftachel, Oren, and Alexander Kader. "On Power and Land: Land Policy in Israel." In *Space, Land, Home* [in Hebrew], edited by Yehouda Shenhav. Jerusalem: Van Leer Jerusalem Institute, 2003.

## Z

Zameret, Zvi, and Hanna Yablonka, eds. *The First Decade, 1948–1958* [in Hebrew]. Jerusalem: Yad Izhak Ben-Zvi, 1997.

Zandberg, Esther. *Land City: Local Essays* [in Hebrew]. Tel Aviv: Babel, 2010.

Zaslavsky, David. *Immigrant Housing in Israel: Construction, Planning, and Development, 1950–1953* [in Hebrew]. Tel Aviv: Am Oved, 1954.

Zertal, Idith. *Days and Deeds: A Life of Moshe Soroka* [in Hebrew]. Tel Aviv: Hotsa'at Maḥbarot le-sifrut, 1975.

Zertal, Idith, and Akiva Eldar. *Lords of the Land: The Settlers and the State of Israel, 1967–2004* [in Hebrew]. Or Yehuda: Kinnert, Zmora-Bitan, Dvir, 2004.

Ziv, Neta, and Hanan Shamir. "Bnaei Baetha: Big Politics and Small Politics in the Struggle against Land Discrimination." In *Space, Land, Home* [in Hebrew], edited by Yehouda Shenhav. Jerusalem: Van Leer Jerusalem Institute, 2003.

Zubida, Hani and Raanan Lipshitz, eds. *Stop! No Border in Front of You! About Borders and the Lack of Them in Israel 2017*. Israel: Yedioth Ahronoth Books and Chemed Books, 2017.

# LIST OF ARCHIVES

## Israel

Archives Department, National Library of Israel
Arieh Sharon digital archive
Azrieli Architecture Archive
Beit Hatfutsot – The Museum of the Jewish People
Ben-Gurion Archive, Ben-Gurion House, Tel Aviv
Ben-Gurion Archives, Ben-Gurion University of the Negev
Bezalel Archive, Bezalel Academy of Arts and Design
Bickels Archive, Mishkan Museum of Art, Ein Harod
B'Tselem Archive
Center for the Built Heritage, Architecture Faculty, Technion
Central Zionist Archives
The David Tuviyahu Archives of the Negev
Dora Gad Collection, College of Management, Rishon LeZion
Ein Harod Ehud archive
Ein Harod Meuhad archive
Ghetto Fighters' House Archives, Kibbutz Lohamei HaGetaot
Government Press Office (GPO)
Haifa City Archives
Hebrew University Central Archive
Hebrew University Photography Archive
Information Centre for Israeli Art, The Israel Museum
Israel Antiquities Authority Archives
Israel Architecture Archive
The Israel Defense Forces (IDF) Archives
Israel Electric Company archives
Israel Museum Archives
Israel State Archives
Israeli Film Archive, Jerusalem Cinematheque
Jerusalem City Archive
Jewish National Fund Archive
KKL-JNF Photo Archive
The Lavon Institute for Labor Movement Research Archives
Mekorot [national water company] archive
Netivei Israel – National Transport Infrastructure Company Ltd.
Public Works Department archive
Rechter Archive
Shikun & Binui historical archive and Solel Boneh archive
The Shoahan and Asher Halevy Yad Izhak Ben-Zvi Photographic Archives
Steven Spielberg Jewish Film Archive
Technion Historical Archive
Tel Aviv Municipal Archives
Tel Aviv University Archives
Yad Tabenkin Archives, Ramat Efal
Yad Yaari, Hashomer Hatzair Institute for Research and Documentation, Givat HaViva

## International

Austrian Frederick and Lillian Kiesler Private Foundation, Vienna
Bakema and Van den Broek collection, State Archive for Dutch Architecture and Urban Planning, Rotterdam
Constantinos A. Doxiadis Archives, Benaki Museum, Athens
The Isamu Noguchi Foundation and Garden Museum, New York
The Judaica Collection, Harvard Library, Harvard University, Cambridge, MA
Louis I. Kahn Collection, Architectural Archives, University of Pennsylvania
Matson (G. Eric and Edith) Photograph Collection, The Library of Congress, Washington, DC
The New York Public Library digital collections, New York
Patrick Abercrombie collection, University of Liverpool
Philip Johnson collection, Avery Drawings & Archives, Avery Architectural and Fine Arts Library, Columbia University, New York
The R. Buckminster Fuller Collection, Stanford University, California

# INDEX

# IMPRINT

Zvi Efrat: The Object of Zionism
The Architecture of Israel

Concept: Zvi Efrat, Matthias Görlich, Rebekka Kiesewetter
Graphic design: Studio Matthias Görlich, Darmstadt
(Matthias Görlich, Pawel Wolowitsch, Anna Kraus, Charalampos Lazos)
Lithography: Scancolor GmbH, Leipzig
Translation of texts by Julius Posner and Hannes Meyer: Jan Caspers
Copyediting: Rita Fobes
Proofreading: Michael Pilewski, Elias Quijada Link
Printing and Binding: optimal media GmbH
Published by
Spector Books
Harkortstraße 10
04107 Leipzig
www.spectorbooks.com

Distribution
Germany, Austria: GVA, Gemeinsame Verlagsauslieferung Göttingen GmbH&Co. KG, www.gva-verlage.de
Switzerland: AVA Verlagsauslieferung AG, www.ava.ch
France, Belgium: Interart Paris, www.interart.fr
UK: Central Books Ltd, www.centralbooks.com
USA, Canada, Central and South America, Africa, and Asia: ARTBOOK|D.A.P., www.artbook.com
Australia, New Zealand: Perimeter Distribution, www.perimeterdistributione.com

© 2018 for the text: the auther and Spector Books, Leipzig
© 2018 for the all illustrations: the individual authers of the images and their assignees

1. Auflage/First edition
Printed in Germany
ISBN: 978-3-95905-133-0

Typeface: Eliza by Pawel Wolowitsch and Camelot Typefaces
Gerstner Programm by Karl Gerstner and Stephan Müller, published by Lineto

This publication is made possible in part from the Barr Ferree Foundation Fund for Publications, Department of Art and Archaeology, Princeton University.
With kind support by The Israeli Foundation for the Advancement of Man and Keimfarben GmbH.